Business Law:
Principles and Practices

Business Law:
Principles and Practices

EIGHTH EDITION

ARNOLD J. GOLDMAN
Law Firm of Goldman & Goldman

WILLIAM D. SIGISMOND
Monroe Community College

SOUTH-WESTERN
CENGAGE Learning

Australia • Brazil • Japan • Korea • Mexico • Singapore • Spain • United Kingdom • United States

SOUTH-WESTERN
CENGAGE Learning

Business Law: Principles and Practices, 8th edition
Arnold J. Goldman
William D. Sigismond

Vice President of Editorial, Business: Jack W. Calhoun

Editor-in-Chief: Rob Dewey

Acquisitions Editor: Vicky True

Developmental Editor: Jan Lamar

Marketing Manager: Jennifer Garamy

Marketing Communications Manager: Sarah Greber

Assoc. Content Project Manager: Jana Lewis

Media Editor: Kristen Meere

Manufacturing Buyer: Kevin Kluck

Production Service: MPS Limited, A Macmillan Company

Sr. Art Director: Michelle Kunkler

Photography Manager: Deanna Ettinger

Text Permissions: Katie Huha

Internal Designer: Juli Cook/Plan-It-Publishing, Inc.

Cover Designer: Rose Alcorn

For product information and technology assistance, contact us at
Cengage Learning Customer & Sales Support, 1-800-354-9706

For permission to use material from this text or product, submit all requests online at **www.cengage.com/permissions**
Further permissions questions can be emailed to
permissionrequest@cengage.com

Exam*View*® is a registered trademark of eInstruction Corp. Windows is a registered trademark of the Microsoft Corporation used herein under license. Macintosh and Power Macintosh are registered trademarks of Apple Computer, Inc. used herein under license.

© 2008 Cengage Learning. All Rights Reserved.

Library of Congress Control Number: 2009943790

Student Edition:
ISBN-13: 978-1-4390-7922-5

ISBN-10: 1-4390-7922-6

South-Western Cengage Learning

5191 Natorp Boulevard

Mason, OH 45040

USA

Cengage Learning products are represented in Canada by Nelson Education, Ltd.

For your course and learning solutions, visit **www.cengage.com**

Purchase any of our products at your local college store or at our preferred online store **www.ichapters.com**

Printed in the United States
1 2 3 4 5 6 7 13 12 11 10 09

Brief Contents

PART 7   Real and Personal Property, Bailments, and Wills and Estate Planning

PART 8   Consumer and Creditor Protection

PART 9   Insurance

Contents

PART 2   Contents

PART 3   Purchase, Sale, and Lease of Goods Under the UCC

PART 4   Negotiable Instruments

PART 5   Agency, Employment, and Labor Law

PART 6   Business Organization and Regulation

CHAPTER 26

CHAPTER 27

PART 8   Consumer and Creditor Protection

PART 9 Insurance

Preface

The American colonists found law a vital force in their lives. It was a way to avoid chaos and preserve liberty. We are now well into the twenty-first century, and belief in the rule of law is more than ever center stage in our lives. Time has given legitimacy to our laws and legal institutions even though this legitimacy has been challenged along the way. There was a period of time in the 1970s when people showed downright disrespect for law and legal institutions. Recently, there have been attempts by government to circumvent the rule of law in order to deal with individuals attempting to subvert the American way of life. Nevertheless, people have continued to show faith in the rule of law by relying on the courts to solve many of their problems. Going to court is almost a ritual. A common phrase is, "See you in court." This is as common as saying to someone, "Have a good day." People are involved in court trials in many ways, either as plaintiffs in lawsuits as viewers watching a fictional trial on TV or in the movies, as spectators attending an actual court trial, or by reading a newspaper article involving a high-profile criminal case. Whatever way they deal with the rule of law, law is constantly on their "radar screen." The trend is clear: Law will continue to be written and will govern our lives because it is not only a necessity as a tool for protecting individual liberty, but also because people have a great respect for the rule of law. The authors believe that this respect goes beyond the boundaries of the United States. This having been said, learning about the law continues to be a priority.

To the Instructor

Business Law: Principles and Practices, 8th edition, like prior additions, will give your students an overview of general legal principles to apply wherever the need for their application exists, and hopefully through your daily instruction, enriched by your many experiences, students will learn that no person or institution is above the law. Your authors, with respect for your position as instructors, also hope that what has been stated in the opening paragraph of this Preface about law, will become embedded in the minds of your students. Finally, thank you for using our textbook.

To the Student

We hope that our approach to presenting the information contained in this new edition and that the instruction you receive in your business law class will encourage you to get excited about the material and do further research on the topics that interest you. You will discover as you study the chapters in this book what legal problems are "out there" and that there are different ways to solve these problems, either through court action, arbitration, mediation, or negotiation. Who knows, this college law course may pique your interest and stimulate your thinking about a career in the legal profession. Good luck in whatever career you finally choose and may you retain the knowledge you've learned in these pages for future reference.

New and Updated Coverage in the Eighth Edition

All chapters in the eighth edition of *Business Law: Principles and Practices* reflect changes in the law and legal procedures that have occurred since the publication of the seventh edition. Some text material in the chapters has been reorganized, expanded, and rewritten for clarity and comprehension. Several chapters have been extensively revised to accommodate new laws or to incorporate new material. Some new cases appear in many of the chapters. Whether you have used prior editions of this text or are a new user, you will find that the authors have written in a clear conversational writing style, using nontechnical language to ensure that students in various levels of reading skill will be motivated to read the material.

The highlights to content changes and updates that were made in the eighth edition are as follows:

Part I. Understanding the Law

The biggest change in Chapter 1 deals with the impact of unethical behavior in the workplace. Chapter 2 gives you a complete picture of the small claims court process. Material on the court system in the United States has been revised. In Chapter 3, some of the material relating to crimes under the section "Selected Personal and Business Crimes" has been rewritten. Chapter 4 has been somewhat restructured and some chapter problems replaced.

Part II Contracts

In Chapter 7 material on revocation of an offer has been rewritten. A new section on facsimile transaction has been added and some material dealing with online contracts has been moved to Chapter 15 and expanded. Chapter 12 has been restructured and a new figure added to clarify the written material on delegation of duties. In Chapter 13, a new chart has been added, indicating the ways that contracts may be discharged. A new section dealing with performance to the satisfaction of another has been added.

Part III Purchase, Sale, and Lease of Goods

In Chapter 15, the material on formation of e-sales contracts has been rewritten and upgraded. In Chapter 16, changes to the UCC under the 2003 amendments have been incorporated into this chapter. Chapter 18 has been substantially revised and updated.

Part IV. Negotiable Instruments

Chapters 19 through 22 reflect new changes to the negotiable instruments law under the UCC and the banking laws. The significant changes deal with new rules and new strategies for bank customers, new ways that banks deal with customers, and new laws that govern the way banks and customers deal with each other. A new federal law, the Check Clearing for the 21st Century Act, or simply Check 21 Act is discussed in detail.

Part V. Agency: Employment and Labor Law

The section updates regulations affecting employer-employee relations including employees' rights to privacy and insurance protection.

Part VI. Business Organization and Regulation

Increased attention is given to security regulation and insider trading.

Part VII. Real and Personal Property, Bailments, and Wills and Estate Planning

This section gives increased attention to estate tax law changes and contains a new section covering supplemental needs trusts.

Part VIII. Consumer and Creditor Protection

Information on new bankruptcy rules, liability of airlines for death or injuries on international flights, effectiveness of the UCC filing statements and new application of Article 9 of the UCC, defenses to a suit by a surety, new laws guaranteeing rights of credit card holders, passage of the Do Not Call Registry rules, new rules for airline liability for loss of or damage to baggage is included.

Pedagogical Devices to Assist Students

Listed here are some of the features of the text to help students master the material.

Chapter Highlights

These give students an overview of what is covered in each chapter.

In-text Examples

These examples throughout the chapters help students master the legal concepts presented by association with real-life situations.

Chapter Summaries

Each chapter summary presents a brief review of the salient points discussed in the chapter. Reading the summary of each chapter is an excellent way to review the material prior to a quiz or test. Summaries can also be used in conjunction with the Key Points listed in each chapter of the Study Guide.

Important Legal Terms

In the margins of each chapter are key terms found in the chapter.

Questions and Problems to Discuss; Cases for Review

Most chapters end with questions, minicases, and actual cases taken from court files to help students apply legal concepts learned in the chapters.

Suppose You're the Judge

These end-of-chapter cases present trial scenarios, arguments at trial, and follow-up activities that ask students to play the role of the judge.

Ethical Emphasis

An ethics case is at the end of each part in the text. Ethics cases also appear in the Instructor's Resource Manual at the end of each chapter. Suggested answers can be found in the Instructor's Resource Manual.

Illustrations

Some chapters include illustrations and/or tables to bring out and expand upon key points in the chapter.

Appendices

Several appendices are provided in the text:
Appendix A Understanding Statutes and Court Decisions
Appendix B Doing Legal Research on the Internet
Appendix C Comparison Between Contract Law Under the Common Law and Sales Law
        Under the UCC
Appendix D The Constitution of the United States

Supplemental Materials

Instructor's Resource CD-ROM (IRCD)

The Instructor's Resource CD-ROM includes the following text supplements: Instructor's Resource Manual, Test Bank, ExamView, and PowerPoint slides.

Instructor's Resource Manual

Instructors have access to a comprehensive electronic Instructor's Resource Manual (IRM) that has been prepared by the text authors. It is available both on the text's companion Web site and on the IRCD. The IRM includes the following features: an extensive preface offering challenges to the instructor; selected learning strategies and pedagogical principles; and useful Web sites and teaching notes for each chapter that include chapter highlights, teaching points, teaching tips, problem areas to anticipate, solutions to chapter questions and case problems, and additional activities.

Test Bank

The Test Bank, which has been prepared by the text authors, includes true/false, multiple-choice, fill-in-the-blank, and short answer questions for each chapter in the text. It is available on the IRCD and the companion Web site.

ExamView™

ExamView™ is a computerized testing software program containing answers to all of the questions in the test bank. This program is an easy-to-use test creation software package compatible with Microsoft Windows. Instructors can add or edit questions and provide customized instructions. It is available on the IRCD.

PowerPoint Slides

PowerPoint slides provide outlines of the topics covered in each chapter. They can be used for lecture or review. Instructors can access the PowerPoint slides on the companion Web site. They are also available on the IRCD.

Study Guide

To help students learn the legal concepts covered in the text, a print Study Guide that has been prepared by the authors is available for purchase. The study guide includes key points in the chapter, true/false questions, multiple-choice questions, matching questions, case problems, and/or completion questions.

Textbook Companion Web Site

Available at www.cengage.com/blaw/goldman, the companion Web site offers an array of teaching and learning resources, including interactive quizzes to help students study the material covered in the text, key terms and flashcards, instructor supplements (for instructors only), and a link to the online case updates.

Business Law Digital Video Library

Cengage Learning's Business Law Digital Video Library offers five kinds of videos for classroom or student review. Over 70 online video clips bring business law alive, particularly for the visual learner, to help bridge common experiences to legal ideas, spark student discussion, and tutor core concepts. Access is available as an optional package with each new text at no additional cost. If Business Law Digital Video Library access did not come packaged with the textbook, it can be purchased online at www.cengage.com/blaw/dvl.

Global Economic Watch

Make the current global economic downturn a teachable moment with Cengage Learning's Global Economic Watch—a powerful online portal that brings these pivotal current events into the classroom. The Watch includes

- **A content-rich blog** of breaking news, expert analysis and commentary—updated multiple times daily—plus links to many other blogs
- **A powerful real-time database** of hundreds of relevant and vetted journal, newspaper, and periodical articles, videos, and podcasts—updated four times every day
- **A thorough overview and timeline of events** leading up to the global economic crisis
- **Discussion and testing content,** PowerPoint® slides on key topics, sample syllabi, and other teaching resources

For more information on how you can access this resource, please visit www.cengage.com/thewatch.

Acknowledgments

Even though *Business Law: Principles and Practices* is in its eighth edition and not a new text, the authors still had to work on many fronts before the package was completed. Due to substantial changes to the law over the last few years, the chapters have been extensively revised. Our sole aim is to convey these updates clearly for the understanding and learning of our students. When the final product goes to press and copies are distributed to instructors and students, we hope that our effort paid off and our readers find value and knowledge throughout the entire *Business Law* package.

In addition, we would like to thank the Cengage Learning team that was heavily involved in the development and production of this edition—Vicky True, Jennifer Garamy, Michelle Kunkler, and especially Jan Lamar, our Developmental Editor and Jana Lewis our Associate Content Project Manager. We cannot thank both of them enough for the extraordinary support that they gave us as we progressed through changes to the seventh edition. Their professionalism and patience certainly showed up during our contacts by phone or email as we worked to update our chapters. We also discovered that Cengage Learning is a top notch organization, and we are proud to be affiliated with the company.

Arnold J. Goldman
William D. Sigismond

PART 1

Understanding the Law

After studying Part I, you should be able to:

1. explain the term *law*.
2. demonstrate a knowledge of the need for a legal system.
3. trace the development of U.S. law from Roman law and the English common law.
4. demonstrate a knowledge of the primary sources of law in the United States.
5. discuss the differences between civil law and criminal law.
6. determine what is appropriate ethical behavior in a business environment.
7. outline the structure of the federal and state court systems in the United States.
8. distinguish between a private wrong and a public wrong.
9. demonstrate a knowledge of legal wrongs, both criminal and civil.
10. compare the procedures in a civil action and a criminal action.
11. recall the steps taken in a lawsuit from start to finish.
12. evaluate alternative ways to settle disputes between two or more parties other than by litigation (a lawsuit).

CHAPTER 1

Foundations of Law and the Role of Ethics in Business

CHAPTER PREVIEW

Chapter Highlights

This opening chapter focuses on law and ethics. It describes what law is, why it is needed, where it came from, and what functions it serves. This chapter also points out that although the modern emphasis in the United States is on statutory law, Americans also rely heavily on case law and rules of administrative agencies to protect a right or to correct a wrong. Civil law, which protects individuals from harm by other individuals, is discussed in contrast to criminal law, which protects society from harmful acts of individuals. The chapter ends by pointing out the need for business firms to operate within ethical guidelines as well as the legal boundaries demanded by society or suffer some very severe consequences and how companies are dealing with ethical challenges in the ordinary course of their work.

WHY LAWS ARE IMPORTANT

History provides us with reasons why laws are important. Throughout history violence by individuals and groups has been used as a way to resolve disputes. People's individual feelings or biases have caused them to take action which has resulted in terror, loss of life, and destruction of property. Clearly, then, we must have laws to regulate human behavior. Otherwise, anything goes. The law provides a guarantee that justice will be carried out according to rules established by federal and state courts and the judiciary and not as the result of individuals' feelings or biases. Those who obey the law will be protected and those who do not will be punished. The following instances of violent crimes demonstrate that violence by individuals and groups has indeed been used as a way to resolve disputes.

Joseph Smith, founder of the Mormon religion, was murdered in June 1844 by a mob in Carthage, Illinois, because of his unconventional religious beliefs that put him at odds with those more traditional believers. In July 1994, Megan Kanka, a seven-year-old girl living in New Jersey, was raped and murdered by a twice-convicted sex offender who lived across the street from her home. Dr. Barnett Slepian was murdered in his home near Buffalo, New York, in October 1998 by a sniper because he performed abortions. James Brady, press secretary to former President Ronald Reagan, was seriously injured in an assassination attempt on the president in March 1981. These instances of violent crimes serve as reminders that, throughout history, violence by individuals and groups has been used as a way to resolve disputes.

It has therefore become obvious that the only alternative to violence is some system of rules of order (laws) for society's members. The federal government responded by passing legislation such as Megan's Laws and the Brady Law. Megan's Laws require local law enforcement agencies and the public to be notified when known sex offenders move into their communities. The Brady Law establishes a five-day waiting period and a criminal background check on individuals who purchase handguns from firearms dealers. Thus, without these laws and other protective laws, living in a modern society would parallel living in a primitive society where lawlessness prevailed.

THE NATURE OF LAW

law enforceable set of rules of conduct

Law can be defined as rules established and enforceable by a government—federal, state, or local—to regulate the conduct of individuals and groups in a society. Just as there are rules for playing a game, so there are rules for living with other people in society, whether that society is a neighborhood, a town, a city, a state, a nation, or the entire world. The rules that make up law are actually legal duties that are imposed on people and that require them to act in a certain way. When people do not follow these rules, they violate the law. Through the courts, individuals injured by those who violate the law are provided with legal remedies, such as requiring the wrongdoer either to pay money damages, go to prison, or in some cases both. Keep in mind that the object of any legal rule is justice, or fairness. Can we therefore say that when a court provides a remedy to an injured party because someone violated his or her rights this decision is fair? Theoretically, yes; in our practical world, however, the word *fair* is often challenged based on people's perception of fairness. Take the O.J. Simpson murder trial. As you may recall, Simpson, a national football hero, was acquitted by a jury of murdering his ex-wife and her friend in June 1994. However, poll after poll taken after the trial revealed people's disagreement with this jury verdict. They said it was unfair. Although the legal process was followed in determining Simpson's not-guilty status, people's perception that the not-guilty verdict was unfair may have had merit. Thus, the saying "justice always prevails" may mean to many only that the process of bringing a court case to conclusion was followed, not that the outcome was necessarily fair. Although absolute justice is therefore unattainable, the legal process is the best rule that could be devised under the circumstances.

THE LEGITIMATE FUNCTIONS OF LAW

We did conclude that if people are to live together peacefully, law must be an important part of their lives. Be aware, however, that this need for law presents a dilemma. Every time a law is created, a person's freedom to act is in some way restricted; at the same

FIGURE 1.1
Purposes of a Legal
System

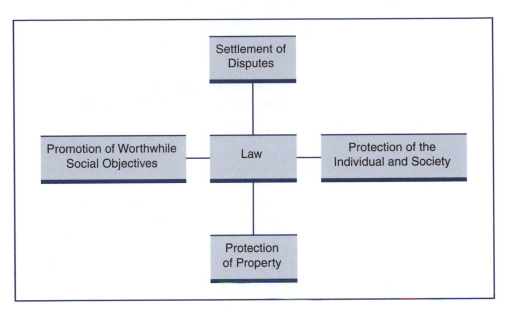

time, trying to settle disputes without resorting to law will produce chaos. Given this dilemma, what functions can law legitimately serve without unduly restricting a person's freedom? There are four, as illustrated in Figure 1.1:

- Settlement of disputes
- Protection of the individual and society
- Protection of property
- Promotion of worthwhile social objectives

Settlement of Disputes

People in a society do not all behave in the same manner, and sometimes it is hard to tell where one person's rights end and another's begin. There needs to be a peaceful way to settle disputes between individuals. Suppose that you start playing your stereo too loudly, or have an all-night party on your patio with guests making a lot of noise, and these acts are disturbing to your neighbor. You feel that you have a right to do these things. Your neighbor doesn't feel the same way. The result could be that you fight it out with words or fists, or even guns. Your neighbor instead, could call the police and file a complaint against you for disturbing the peace. According to law, as you may know, this is allowed since you violated the neighbor's right to peace and quiet. While calling the police may be distasteful to you, the police officer who arrives on the scene may settle the dispute between your neighbor and you and if by his presence and discussion you insist that you were within your rights, the officer could exercise his right under the law to either arrest you or order you to appear in court at a later date.

Law thus serves to protect the rights of each individual and to regulate conduct between persons in a society. Law provides stability, allowing people to develop their own interests without infringing on the rights of others.

Protection of the Individual and Society

One of the major reasons for the development of law was to protect the individual. Freedom to live without fear—fear that someone who commits a crime against you, such as stealing from you, or killing a family member—is so important that a perpetrator of these crimes will be punished and may also be sued by their victims for money damages.

Many laws that are designed to protect the individual also protect society by keeping our cities and towns safe places to live and work. For example, society needs protection from thieves, muggers, murderers, vandals, and others who violate all individuals' rights when they commit harmful acts. As another example, without orderly plans for the development of land, it would be possible for shopping malls, condominiums, parking lots, or hotels to crop up in the middle of residential areas.

Protection of Property

Law protects property as well as people. Our society places much value on the importance of property and the need to protect it. Our laws protect property in many ways. Those who destroy or damage property may be punished or may have to compensate the injured party. The government may not take private property for public use without just compensation. Governments may tax property but only if the tax is fair and reasonable. Those who own property may, upon dying, pass it on to other persons, subject only to reasonable rules.

Promotion of Worthwhile Social Objectives

Law is not limited to regulating conduct between individuals or between individuals and their society. Law may also be used as a positive force to promote worthwhile social objectives. The Social Security system is a good example. The system was established by the Congress of the United States to aid the aged, the poor, and the disabled. Through a system of contributions and salary deductions required by law, the government helps those who need some form of public assistance.

Promoting good health and educational opportunities is another example of the use of law to promote worthwhile objectives. Congress has enacted many laws establishing and financing medical centers and research facilities. Grants are given each year for extensive medical research, treatment programs, and immunization. Both federal and state governments assist education through legislation. Tax dollars help support many colleges, and many students receive government scholarships to study in the United States and in other countries. Many states help pay for the high cost of education by giving tax deductions for educational expenses.

Promoting commerce is also an important goal. Our society believes that law should not be limited to regulating competition in promoting trade. It should also be used to assist in other ways. One example is the use of tax dollars for research to improve trade and develop new products. Another example is the use of public funds to finance businesses and business expansion. By providing direct loans or insuring private loans, government enables many small businesses to get started and to expand as the need arises.

DEVELOPMENT OF LAW

Although many societies and nations have contributed to the development of law, Roman law and English common law were the most important influences on law as we know it today.

Roman Law

Prior to the Romans, most law was oral. Decisions were made by judges or juries, but a written record of those decisions was not kept. Instead, the decisions were passed on by word of mouth from generation to generation. The Romans developed the concept of written codes that everyone could know and understand. These codes, or laws, were to be so complete that they would guide almost every aspect of life. During the reign of the

Emperor Justinian (A.D. 527–565), a great body of law was developed and written. It eventually became known as the Justinian Code. When this code was revised by Napoleon I of France in 1804, it became known as the Napoleonic Code. The Napoleonic Code is the basis of much of the law of Europe today as well as China, Japan, some South American countries, Mexico, and the state of Louisiana. Louisiana state law is based on the Roman law because the state was settled primarily by people of French descent.

Common Law

common law unwritten law based on local English customs

The second great influence on the development of law was the English system of law. Developed in England following the Norman conquest of A.D. 1066, the English system of law is called common law. **Common law** refers to the body of legal decisions made by English court judges, under the authority of the king, over a period of many years. Unlike the written Roman law, the common law in its early stages was oral. English judges traveled to various communities in their locality to hold court and try cases. They made legally binding decisions based on local customs and traditions but did not write those decisions down. As a result, common law is often referred to as the "unwritten law." Each case produced a new oral law that served as a **precedent**, an example or standard for deciding subsequent cases involving the same or similar facts. This practice of judges following the precedents established by previously decided cases evolved into a doctrine called **stare decisis**, which means "to stand by a decision which was previously decided." The doctrine generally demands that a prior decision be followed, but it can be overturned and a new rule established if there is a good reason to do so. For example, societal changes can determine that a precedent is no longer applicable, or a court may decide that a precedent is simply incorrect.

precedent example or standard for deciding subsequent cases involving the same or similar facts

stare decisis practice by which judges follow precedents in previously decided cases

When Henry II became king in 1154, he institutionalized common law by creating a unified body of common law. He did this by incorporating and elevating local customs to the national level, thereby ending local enforcement of the unwritten customs dealing with criminal and civil matters. Laws were put in writing, arbitrary remedies (e.g., trial by having the accused snatch a stone from a hot fire) were eliminated, and the jury system was sworn on oath to decide criminal and civil cases rather than using an informal group of community members. One of the first printed books containing important decisions of English court judges was *Blackstone's Commentaries,* published in several volumes from 1765 to 1769. The English common law system became the model for the legal system of the United States after the attainment of independence from England.

SOURCES OF LAW IN THE UNITED STATES

Although much of our law originated in English common law, we also rely on other sources of law to meet the changing needs of our society. Our primary sources of law in the United States are constitutions, statutes, administrative regulations, and court decisions (Figure 1.2).

Constitutions

A constitution is the fundamental written law of a state (e.g., the state in which you live) or nation (e.g., the United States). It defines the individual's rights and duties and describes the government's structure and functions, its powers and limitations, and the relationship between the government and individual citizens.

constitutional law law derived from the U.S. Constitution and the constitution of the individual states

There are fifty-one constitutions in the United States: the federal or U.S. Constitution and one for each of the fifty states. **Constitutional law** is the law stated in these

FIGURE 1.2
Sources of Law in the
United States

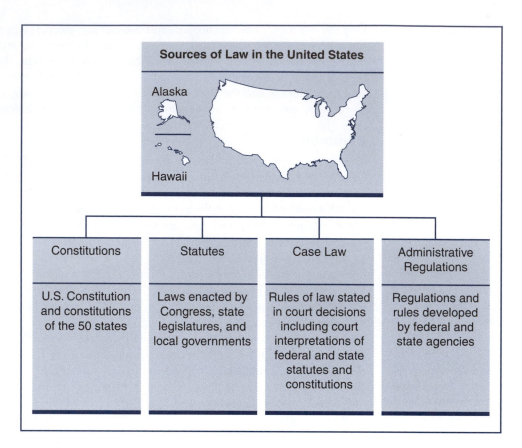

constitutions. Most state constitutions are modeled after the U.S. Constitution. The U.S. Constitution, the supreme law of the land, takes precedence over all state constitutions. No law, whether enacted by Congress or by a state legislature, may conflict with the basic principles of the U.S. Constitution. If it does, a court may declare the law invalid or "unconstitutional" and thus unenforceable. Each state has its own constitution, which is the supreme law within its boundaries. If a state or local government passes a law that conflicts with the state constitution, that law may also be declared invalid by a court of law.

Constitutional law evolves primarily from judicial interpretation of the meaning of the Constitution as issues arise. Because the Constitution is written in broad, general terms, interpretations are necessary to allow for unanticipated circumstances. For example, the Fourth Amendment to the Constitution protects people from unreasonable searches; the term *reasonable search,* however, is not spelled out. In a landmark case, the U.S. Supreme Court interpreted this amendment. The interpretation stated that if a lawful custodial arrest has taken place, a full search of the person is permitted and is considered a "reasonable" search under the amendment (*United States* v. *Robinson,* 414 U.S. 218).

statutes laws passed by
legislative bodies rather
than by the courts

acts laws passed by
Congress

Statutes

Statutes, also called legislation, are laws that have already been formally passed by legislative bodies rather than by the courts. Legislative bodies exist at all levels of government. At the federal level, legislation passed by Congress is called **acts**. At the state level, this same legislation passed by the legislatures of the fifty states is referred to as *statutes.*

ordinances laws passed by local governments such as cities, towns, and villages

Legislation passed by local governments (cities, towns, and villages) is called **ordinances**, (**zoning laws** for example). In contrast to common law court cases, which are written as opinions of judges explaining court decisions and are called *holdings,* statutes are written in textbook form. Statute law is frequently referred to as the *written law.*

The modern emphasis is on statutory law and especially on its more specialized sub-fields, such as bankruptcy laws, workers' compensation laws, consumer protection laws, marriage and divorce laws, security regulations, and laws dealing with the sale of goods. One reason that statutory law is emphasized is that legislatures usually take the initiative in identifying and acting on issues that result from the numerous technological, social, and economic innovations in our society. The laws legislatures make can be sweeping and comprehensive and, if necessary, can be enacted rapidly. In contrast, the courts deal only with issues that arise in actual cases brought before them by individuals and businesses. The journey of a case through the courts is often slow, and the issues the case focuses on are generally narrow in scope. Changes in the law that result from such cases are usually small and are limited to a specific situation.

Congress has the power to pass laws that have national importance. Such areas as national defense, commerce between the states, and postal regulations are all within the power of Congress to regulate. As stated earlier, these federal laws take precedence over any state laws. State and local governments may pass laws involving matters over which Congress does not exercise control. For example, state and local governments have enacted laws and regulations covering such matters as marriage and divorce, zoning, vehicle and traffic control, and taxation for local purposes. Just as state laws may not conflict with federal law, local laws may not conflict with state or federal law.

Court Decisions

case law law arrived at through court decisions

Although the modern emphasis is on statutory law, still a substantial portion of U.S. law is created through decisions that judges and juries hand down in court cases. This law is known as **case law**, a modern version of the common law of England. Consequently, common law doctrine and principles are still an important part of the United States legal system. In some court cases, no statute may exist governing the dispute. Or if a statute does exist, it could be interpreted in different ways because of the language used by our lawmakers. In such cases, federal and state courts must decide what the law is. The meaning is left in question until it becomes the subject of litigation. Then a court will decide the matter and set forth in a written opinion the rule or principle on which its decision was based.

These court decisions produce precedents that have the force of law. Other courts will follow these precedents when they decide similar cases in the future. The advantage of the stare decisis concept (the practice of following previous decisions) is predictability; it enables people to act in a certain way, knowing that they can rely on established law. Judges very seldom overrule previous precedents because the risks of a new opinion being overturned by a higher court are substantially increased. Sometimes there is no existing precedent, as with emerging cases dealing with disputes in cyberspace (the Internet). Under these circumstances, a judge's written opinion, which ultimately becomes the decision in a case, must contain a solid legal argument justifying the decision. This decision may in turn become a standard precedent for judges to use in deciding later cases.

You can see that although legislatures are primarily responsible for passing laws, courts in effect pass laws by interpreting or modifying existing laws or by making decisions that create new precedents. These precedents are as effective as laws passed by the U.S. Congress or by state legislatures.

A classic example of case law is *Robinson* v. *California,* decided by the Supreme Court in 1962 (370 U.S. 660). Robinson's conviction by the Municipal Court of Los Angeles as a narcotic addict was based on a California statute making it a criminal offense (punishable by a jail sentence) for a person to "use, or be under the influence, or be addicted to the use of narcotics." A higher state court affirmed the lower court's decision. Upon appeal to the U.S. Supreme Court, the decision was reversed on the theory that being "addicted to the use of narcotics" was an illness. The court reasoned that a statute (law) that made a criminal offense (punishable by a jail sentence) of that or any other illness—such as insanity, leprosy, or venereal disease—is unconstitutional, because it would be an infliction of cruel and unusual punishment and would thus violate the Eighth and Fourteenth Amendments to the Constitution. The significance of *Robinson* v. *California* is that it is now a precedent case: The high court's decision—namely, that narcotics addiction is no longer punishable as a crime—represents case law in the United States.

Administrative Regulations

administrative regulations rules made by administrative agencies that have the same force and effect as statutes and court decisions

It is impossible for legislatures to make all the necessary rules or for courts to handle all of the cases. Consequently, a great deal of the regulation of individuals and businesses in the United States today is done by administrative agencies at the federal, state, and local levels. These agencies have been delegated the power to make rules called **administrative regulations**, which have the same force and effect as statutes and court decisions. In addition to making laws, these agencies can also take legal action against violators of their rules in much the same way that courts do. Agencies often begin their legal action after first conducting an investigation of individual's or organization's records and other documents either through a subpoena or by going on site by first obtaining a search warrant.

The federal agencies are created by Congress. The Federal Trade Commission is an agency created by Congress to regulate commercial activities and prevent unfair trade practices. The Federal Communications Commission regulates various forms of communication, including radio and television. Protecting the environment from abuse is the task assigned to the Environmental Protection Agency.

State administrative agencies are created by state legislatures. The Bureau of Motor Vehicles, one such agency, develops rules and regulations for the operation of motor vehicles within each state.

Local administrative agencies are created by city councils or by town or village boards. A zoning board, one example of a local agency, regulates the height, size, uses, and suitability for particular purposes of residential and commercial land and buildings.

Although administrative regulations have the same force and effect as statutes and court decisions, these rules can be challenged in the courts. A business or an individual may challenge them on the basis that they are unconstitutional, vague, or beyond the power granted to the agency.

Over the years, administrative agencies have grown rapidly. A major reason for this growth is that many laws needed to deal with social and economic issues in the United States today—such issues as unsafe automobiles, pollution of the environment, unfair competition, and employee discrimination—cannot be addressed by legislatures in the traditional manner of passing laws. Legislatures have neither the technical expertise possessed by the staff of a particular administrative agency nor the necessary time to devote to the specialized problems that continually emerge in certain fields such as space exploration, atomic energy, and air and water pollution and often require new or changed legislation. Furthermore, the courts are already overburdened. Given these conditions, an administrative agency's ability to make rules and regulations that have the same force and effect as statutes and court decisions offers a viable alternative for individuals and businesses that wish to recover a right or correct a wrong.

CIVIL LAW VERSUS CRIMINAL LAW

Miller was driving home from shopping on a winter afternoon when he saw a snowball coming toward his car. The snowball, which contained a rock, hit the hood of his car with a thump. Miller stopped the car, got out, and discovered a large dent in his hood caused by the snowball. When Miller spotted Blackman hiding behind a nearby parked car and confronted him, Blackman admitted to throwing the snowball.

In this case, Miller has two causes of action against Blackman resulting from the snowball-throwing incident; a civil action and a criminal action. However, before discussing this case, let us make a distinction between civil law and criminal law. The distinction between the two is a very important concept in our legal system.

In the United States, all law can be divided into two broad categories: civil law and criminal law. All law other than criminal law is known as civil law. The differences between these two categories of law are significant because in our legal system, civil cases are completely separate from criminal cases. Separate laws govern each type of case, and each seeks a different remedy.

civil law law dealing with the relationships between individuals

Civil law establishes rules that protect the rights and property of individuals from harmful acts by other individuals. The person who is harmed because another person violated civil law may initiate a civil action (lawsuit) against that person seeking compensation (money damages) for the harm caused. An example of a case title indicating a civil action is *Roberts* v. *Radcliff*. Civil actions may be brought, for example, for child support, contract violations, injuries or damage caused by automobile accidents, divorce, libel, invasion of privacy, and violations of property rights. Violations of civil law are discussed in detail in Chapter 4.

criminal law laws that deal with the relationships between individuals and society and that maintain order

Criminal law establishes rules to protect society from acts of individuals that are considered so dangerous, or potentially so, that they threaten peace and order within a society. A person accused of committing a crime is subject to arrest and, if convicted, punishment. It is for this reason that in criminal cases the government (state or federal) brings the proceeding against the accused individual. An example of a case title indicating a criminal action by the state is *State of Ohio* v. *Albertson* an example of a case title indicating a crime against the federal government is *United States* v. *Blackman*. Crimes include such acts as stealing, murder, home invasion, forging a person's signature on a check, and violating some traffic laws.

Although a person may be the subject of a criminal prosecution for the commission of a crime, he or she may, in certain cases, be the subject of a civil lawsuit brought by the victim of the crime. A comparison of civil and criminal law is made in Table 1.1. In the Miller case, Miller could bring a civil suit against Blackman for intentionally destroying property. When Blackman threw the snowball containing a rock, he damaged Miller's car, and Miller is entitled to money damages. The state could bring a criminal action against Blackman for intentionally destroying property. Blackman's act of throwing the snowball was not only an act against Miller, it was also an act against society, and Blackman should be punished for his wrongdoing.

equity nonmonetary relief granted by courts when money damages are inadequate

As noted earlier, in a civil lawsuit, courts generally are confined just to awarding money damages as relief to the injured party. Money damages, though, are not always suitable or adequate for certain violations of rights. In such cases, our legal system recognizes the principle of **equity**, or nonmonetary relief. This remedy dates back to medieval England. Equity grants relief in accordance with principles considered fair and just. For

TABLE 1.1   A COMPARISON OF CIVIL AND CRIMINAL LAW

	CIVIL LAW	CRIMINAL LAW
Protects	An individual's rights and property from the harmful acts of other individuals, such as slander or trespass, or from a person's breach of contract.	Society from the harmful acts of individuals, such as theft, murder, or driving while intoxicated.
Provides	Money damages (compensation) or equitable relief to a person who is harmed by the wrongful conduct or breach of contract of another person. Equitable relief consists of ordering a person to perform a certain act (specific performance) or to cease carrying on certain conduct (injunction).	Punishment in the form of capital punishment, imprisonment, or fines imposed on a person who is found guilty of violating the law.
Requires	A civil lawsuit by the person harmed (plaintiff) so as to recover.	Prosecution (criminal action) by government (federal or state) acting for society (plaintiff) against the accused person.
Type of wrong addressed	Private (individual versus individual). An example of a case title indicating a civil action is *Ramirez* v. *Ames.*	Public (society versus individual). Examples of case titles indicating a criminal action are *United States* v. *Moll* (federal) and *State of Nevada* v. *Martin* (state).
Required to win	Preponderance of the evidence (one party presenting more convincing evidence to the jury than the other party).	Determination of guilt beyond a reasonable doubt (jury entirely convinced of guilt).

TABLE 1.2   DIFFERENCES BETWEEN LAW AND EQUITY

	LAW	EQUITY
Begin a proceeding	Initiate a lawsuit	File a petition
Parties	Plaintiff and defendant	Petitioner and respondent
Remedy sought by the injured party	Sum of money for damages to compensate for the loss sustained	Enforcement of a right (specific performance) or the prevention of further violation of a right (injunction)
Reason remedy is sought	Money adequately repays the injured party for a loss.	Damages are difficult to measure in money terms; therefore, an award of money to an injured party would be unfair.
Decision on the remedy is made	By a judge or jury	Solely by a judge (with an advisory jury in some states)
Legal name for the decision	Judgment/Order	Decree/Order
Remedy enforced	Execution of a judgment initiated by the plaintiff	Contempt proceedings initiated by the plaintiff if the defendant fails to perform

example, if a lawsuit arises and money damages are an unsuitable remedy, a court of equity may allow the injured party to seek specific performance (carrying out a contractual agreement according to its original terms) or an injunction (order the other party to refrain from certain conduct).

Although judges hear equity cases today, virtually no states have special equity courts (often called *chancery courts*). A judge hears the case of a person seeking a remedy in equity in the same court where other cases are also tried. (For centuries, common law and equity were administered in England by two separate sets of courts.) Some basic distinctions between law and equity are described in Table 1.2.

UNIFORM LAWS

Much of our laws of business developed from the early merchants and traders in England who administered these laws through merchant courts that were separate from the regular courts. These laws were known as the *law merchant.* The law merchant became a part of English common law. As the United States developed, each state passed its own statutes to govern most commercial transactions. As interstate business increased in the United States, there was felt the need for greater uniformity of law on particular subjects. Consequently, the National Conference of Commissioners on Uniform State Laws made up of lawyers chosen by the states was formed upon the recommendation of the American Bar Association to oversee the preparation of uniform laws. "Uniform" means that laws on a particular subject will be the same throughout the country. States are encouraged to adopt these uniform laws, but it is not mandatory. The commissioners have approved several uniform laws and various states have adopted one or more of them. For example, the Uniform Commercial Code (UCC), one such uniform law, has been adopted in all fifty states (Louisiana has adopted only portions of it), the District of Columbia and the Virgin Islands. The UCC, which plays a major role in the area of commercial law, will be discussed in some detail in Parts III and IV of the text.

THE IMPACT OF UNETHICAL BEHAVIOR IN THE WORKPLACE

This section focuses on business ethics and the impact of unethical behavior in the workplace. There is a discussion of the role of ethics in a business setting, ethical challenges in the workplace, and what businesses should do to establish a strong ethical foundation. Unfortunately, some businesses, especially large corporations, have steered away from properly implementing strong ethical practices within their organization, and as a result, their managers and directors have made unethical decisions that have led to their day in court dealing with a serious civil or criminal matter. The Enron Corporation debacle is a good case study in unethical behavior by upper-level management interested in making a quick profit. Their selfish and irresponsible behavior toppled Enron, resulting in one of the largest bankruptcies in U.S. history. The result was that millions of stockholders (many of them employees of the company) lost billions of dollars. Employees of the company who were stockholders were prompted by top management to buy more stock in Enron while top managers were selling their shares. The value of the stock dropped to almost nothing. Employees lost their money and their jobs.

Unethical behavior in business is not new. It actually dates back to the very beginning of business and commerce. Today, however, ethical challenges seem pervasive and more challenging. Consequently, ethics is playing an even greater role in reshaping today's business world and businesses are being asked to comply with ethical standards as never before. Corporate scandals involving ethical violations that have evolved in recent years (e. g. the Enron ease) have especially outraged public investors who, as the result of deceptive, unfair, and manipulative practices by large corporations, lacked good solid information when buying and selling securities (e.g., stocks). In response, Congress passed the Sarbanes-Oxley Act of 2002. A key provision imposes stricter disclosure requirements to the Securities and Exchange Commission by corporate CEOs and CFOs and also imposes harsh penalties for failure to do so. Corporate officers must personally certify that the information reported accurately represents the financial condition of the business.

The idea is to stop deceptive accounting practices like those that caused stockholders of the Enron Corporation to lose billions of dollars.

Business Ethics

Ethics is the inquiry into the moral judgment people make in deciding what is right or good as they live each day. People are moved to deal with others because of their own ideas of what is right and wrong. Often their conscience is their guide, and they act based on human experiences, religious upbringing, and family customs and traditions.

Business ethics is the branch of ethics that focuses on what is right, just, and fair in the world of business based on the decisions businesspersons make in their daily activities in the workplace.

Jacobs was the CEO of a large Wall Street firm. The chief financial officer informed Jacobs that even though the firm was profitable, no bonuses could be paid to the top executives at the end of their fiscal year because the funds were needed to cover the firm's physical plant expansion program. Jacobs made the decision, with board of directors' approval, to lay off 100 lower-level personnel to cover the cost of the bonuses.

In this example, while Jacobs did nothing illegal, what he did may be consideredunethical.

Historically, businesspersons needed to consider only the law in making decisions. The proposition that what is legal is also ethical prevailed. Profit maximization for the benefit of its owners was a major goal in most business organizations. Ethical considerations did not factor into decision making. In other words, a business's social and moral obligations to its customers, its creditors, its employees, and its competitors were not of utmost importance. Further, there was a bias by state legislatures and the courts in favor of profitable business practices and a reluctance to stifle business decisions made by business owners and managers on the theory that outsiders should not second-guess the business judgment of people who were presumed to know what they were doing. This profit mentality still exists today.

The following case is a good example of an unreasonably dangerous product (the gas tank of a car could explode, causing death to the person or persons in the car if and when an accident occurred) placed on the market based on management's belief that there was a responsibility to ensure that the company made a profit, regardless of safety factors. Nevertheless, what the company did was perfectly legal.

The Johnson Motor Company ordered the production of a new-model car knowing that the fuel tank designed to be located behind the rear axle could explode in an accident. Nevertheless, the president of the company, faced with serious competition from overseas firms in the manufacture of a similar make and model and with the potential for increased costs to modify the location of the fuel tank, ordered production of this model as quickly as possible. His decision to begin production was further influenced by the result of four crash tests—one was successful, with no explosion occurring—plus the finding of the federal agency overseeing safety standards that the location of the fuel tank met its minimum standards.

In another case, a company reduced its employee costs so as to position itself to remain profitable without regard for the welfare of the employees.

The board of directors of Cutler's, a large corporation that manufactures electric window wiper motors for certain makes and models of cars, was confronted with a decreasing market share and consequently declining sales. The board voted to cut the highest-paid employees with the most seniority from the workforce and retain the less experienced employees on the lower end of the salary scale.

Cutler's board of directors asserted that the board's responsibility was to ensure that the corporation made a profit for the firm's shareholders and that this obligation overrode any ethical responsibility to the discharged employees regardless of their status in the company. The shareholders in the corporation, like those of any large corporation that was no longer profitable, would most likely welcome the board's move if they were assured that the corporation could maintain its same level of productivity with the lower-paid workers and still make a profit. The point here is that, although the board's decision was legally correct (as long as it did not violate the union contract), it was unethical because it showed little concern for the discharged employees, who were "punished" for their seniority.

There are many disturbing examples of unethical practices in business: unfair hiring and termination policies on the part of employers, employers lying in communication with employees about company business policies, employer violations of contract obligations with employees, and executives of a company secretly getting rich at the expense of employees. Other examples are customers who buy merchandise only to discover that the manufacturer produced an unsafe product that could easily cause an injury through normal use, customers who were cheated by an unscrupulous salesperson into purchasing inferior merchandise, and customers who "fell for" a product because of deceptive advertising. In addition is the dishonesty of business executives in their dealings with a company's creditors. Executives may lie about the financial health of the business when attempting to borrow money to pay for inventory or to meet the company payroll. These few but powerful examples point out what avenues businesspeople will sometimes take to maximize profit.

From all the publicity that has occurred over the last few years, it would seem that violations of business ethics occur only in large corporations; keep in mind, however, that ethical violations may occur in other forms of business enterprises, especially partnerships. Often, one or more partners violate their duty of good faith and loyalty to the other partners and act in their own best interests. This could occur, for example, when in the course of business a partner fails to account to the other partners for profits derived from a transaction or transactions conducted on behalf of the partnership. Take the case of a managing partner in a real estate business who collects fees from property leased to several individuals and deliberately does not report the entire amount collected to the partners. This action by the partner is unethical and, of course, illegal.

The Role of Ethics in a Business Setting

Nobody will argue that the primary responsibility of business owners of small companies as well as boards of directors of large corporations is to ensure that the business remains profitable, and nobody will argue that profit does enable the business to survive. On the other hand, it can be argued that concentrating on profit maximization often leads to conflict with ethical issues that arise within the concept of business practices. While it may be difficult for business owners and managers to minimize moral dilemmas in their role as decision makers, they cannot afford to do so. A lack of solutions to ethical issues could be a pathway to disaster. An extreme but realistic repercussion might be that a business is forced to shut down even though it is making a profit. Less severe but serious consequences may be that owners and managers are constantly challenged to do the right thing by employees, consumers, suppliers, and the general public. Studies show, for example, that consumers have few qualms about avenging what they believe is a breach of corporate trust. If a company fails to respond quickly to an ethical crisis, it will likely experience the wrath of court challenges, government intervention, consumer boycotts of a company's products, their defection to other brands, and their initiation of strongly worded letters to top management officials. This public distrust and negative publicity are especially true in sensitive areas such as employee relationships (e.g., wrongfully discharging employees and dishonestly carrying out contractual obligations); consumer rights issues (e.g., product safety and deceptive advertising); finance-related issues, notably those related to Wall Street (e.g., insider trading) and large corporations (e.g., corporate takeovers); and what constitutes a livable environment (e.g., controlling pollution and offshore drilling for natural resources).

> Price was a director in the Langley Corporation, which produced gaming equipment for casinos. Langley's stock was much in demand because its value and dividend distributions were on the rise, the company was well respected on Wall Street, and the stock was reasonably priced. The board of directors of Langley decided to order a stock split in a ratio of 2:1—that is, two shares for every one share held by a stockholder as of a certain future date. In advance of any public notice, Price telephoned several of his friends who were not stockholders and suggested that they purchase shares of Langley stock so as to gain the benefit of the stock split. As a result of Price's notification, some of his friends did so and benefited from the increased number of shares that were distributed to stockholders (at a lower price) through the stock split.

In this example, not considering that Price subjected himself to an illegal transaction called insider trading, it could be argued that this kind of activity is unethical because it precludes equal access to the new market information possessed by an insider to all public investors. As a director of the Langley Corporation and an insider, Price had a tremendous informational advantage. Any outsider not a friend of Price who wished to invest could not legally acquire access to what Price knew until that information became public. The consequences for the Langley Corporation if Price's actions are revealed to the public may be negative publicity, a loss of customers (especially those concerned with ethical issues), and ultimately, a loss of profits from the sale of stock followed by a drop in the stock's price. As a practical matter, then, business owners and managers need to consider both the ethical and legal aspects of a situation when making decisions. The answer to the question "Is it ethical?" is as important as the answers to the questions "Is it profitable?" and "Is it legal?"

ETHICAL CHALLENGES IN THE WORKPLACE

Role of Managers

Managers serve at all levels of an organization. High-level managers make key decisions about policy and strategy. At this higher level, a manager's attitude toward creating an ethical environment within his or her organization is crucial. Just as managers need to make good economic decisions resulting in profitability of the business, they must also make good decisions to prevent ethical misconduct that could be costly to the company. Managers show total commitment to an ethical work environment by personally acting ethically on a daily basis. For example, if employees see their manager lying on his or her time sheet about the use of vacation or personal time or cheating on business miles traveled, it will encourage employees to "follow the leader."

Ethical Issues Faced by Managers

Business owners and managers face many ethical issues in the ordinary course of their work. Ethical issues in business are often tied to those issues most often taken up by the courts, written about in the newspapers, argued over in Congress and state legislatures, and complained about by the general public. Some issues of major concern involve the following:

1. *Invasion of privacy.* The supervisory role now entails monitoring the work of employees such as eavesdropping on their telephone conversations, viewing the input and output that appear on their computer terminals, maintaining hidden cameras to spy on them during the workday, and requiring psychological testing in areas measuring other than job-related abilities such as testing to determine trouble-making potential and dishonesty.

2. *Restrictions placed on employees while under an employment contract.* A restriction is often placed on an employee who invents and patents a product while employed. Many companies require its employees to sign an agreement to turn over this and all other patent rights to the employer even though the invention is beyond the scope of the company business and even though the patent was developed on the employee's own time.

3. *Sexual harassment on the job.* Improper sexual conduct in the workplace is not uncommon. Male supervisors may deny employment or promotions to a woman subordinate unless she grants him sexual favors, or he may make her uncomfortable in her work environment unless she succumbs to his sexual advances.

4. *Sphere of influence.* It is true that a firm has a legitimate interest in employee behavior if this behavior significantly influences work performance. This sphere of influence could apply to off-the-job activities in some cases. However, what constitutes a significant influence is not always clear. Sometimes employers cross the line and attempt to fire an employee for what he or she is doing off the job that fails to meet the sphere of influence test. For example, Mary, a manager of a popular department store who receives excellent performance evaluations from her supervisor, was being watched by store security for the after-hours company she kept and was fired because her supervisor didn't like her friends. Her behavior did not significantly influence her work performance. Firing Mary is only inviting legal problems for the manager and the department store. On the other hand, Mark, an excellent customer service supervisor who is fired after being arrested and given probation for making several obscene phone calls to various women from his home in the evening or on weekends, might lose in court. Mark must prove that his behavior had no significant effect on his future work performance.

5. *Management style.* The manager of a company or a public entity who uses his or her position to determine what is right or wrong when it comes to workplace issues including ethical issues that arise on the job often creates bad working conditions. The employee either goes along with it and is miserable or quits. The very bright police lieutenant who cannot make captain after coming in first on the promotion test because she won't play the political games promoted by the police chief doesn't have much of a choice. Think of what you would do if you were in this position with a family to support, two children in college, and the possibility of obtaining another comparable position elsewhere slim. Unethical behavior also arises when a company gives raises to those employees who help make the company profitable by using unethical tactics. An example would be the chief financial officer of a company requires you, as the person in the accounting department filling out the papers to secure a company loan, to exaggerate the value of the company's assets.

Unethical issues such as those described here have no place in any business organization that wishes to foster ethical conduct. The next section discusses the first and perhaps the only program that some companies implement to deal with unethical conduct.

Building Sound Ethical Practices

Ethics in the workplace is a compelling force today. A company that maintains strong ethical practices will definitely experience positive growth in all aspects of its business operations including sales, profits from sales, customer satisfaction, employee fulfillment and retention, and of course the company's reputation in the community. A large corporation's positive growth can be felt nationwide and even worldwide. To build a strong business ethic within a company means to incorporate ethical concepts into daily business decision making. This is not necessarily an easy task. It is one thing to acknowledge the importance of the task, but to actually incorporate the ethical concepts first requires preplanning and then implementation. Implementation will include a business code of ethics with a built-in rewards system. Employees will be more apt to respond to a code of ethics with a reward system for good ethical behavior.

The following steps comprise one of many plans that could be used to build sound ethical practices within a company.

- Develop an ethical vision for the company. What ethical issues does the company feel are important to the overall heath of the company—employees, shareholders, customers, and the community in general? What this is leading to is the development of a code of ethics stating a company's ethical priorities that can be distributed to each employee. Fundamental issues to be reviewed for incorporation into this code include employee satisfaction (personal and workplace), community issues, honesty, integrity, fairness, customer respect, environmental concerns that cause harm to others, and loyalty. One outcome of a code will point out to all employees, including company officers and managers, that the profit motive is not the sole objective of the company. More will be said about codes of ethics later in the chapter.
- Determine how the company's vision matches that of the employees. You can do this through an employee survey and a series of small-group focus meetings. You can also survey customers to determine their feelings about the company's services and/or products.
- Reconcile the company's ethical vision to that of the employees. When there is conflict as to ethical goals, consider a compromise, or if management feels strongly about a particular ethical goal, then this goal must be declared paramount under the circumstances. Imposition of an ethical goal, of course, is not the best choice. The parties may escape from this dilemma by compromise, thus arriving at an alternative plan that is acceptable to both parties. Keep in mind that there are no easy solutions to ethical dilemmas in which fundamental values conflict as, for example, trading off honesty between employer and employee for fairness (not acting arbitrarily). If, however, the parties are sincerely determined to resolve the dilemma, a compromise will result.
- Implement the code of ethics that was developed in the company's decision making. From this point on there needs to be an honest commitment by both management (employer) and employees to carry out the ethical vision that evolved from all the hard work devoted to the development process. A commitment to business ethics and the willingness to invest in communicating it internally and externally should lead to some very positive results. For example, employees may act more responsibly and honestly and become more loyal to the company. In turn, the company may show more fairness in dealing with employees and encourage more professional development which, in turn could increase opportunities for employee growth within the company. As a result, the company's business may grow its customer base.

Development of Business Codes of Ethics

There has been a dramatic increase in the development of business codes of ethics over the last several years because ethical conflict arises in business that strains relations between management and employees or between the business and its external contacts. This conflict sometimes leads to court trials that impose legal liability on businesses based on these ethical issues.

code of ethics document outlining the type of ethical behavior expected of an employee on the job

A **code of ethics** consists of rules or standards that establish a framework for professional behavior and responsibilities within a company setting. Many businesses have developed a program that includes ethical training programs and the distribution of a code of ethics to each employee. A code will not solve all ethical problems, but its development and implementation will raise the ethical sensitivity of staff so that they at least know when a decision they face involves an ethical choice about what is acceptable business practice and what is not, and also why ethics and integrity are important to their organization. Once the code is in place, management should develop a plan to monitor the extent to which the company is living up to its ethical values. Tools to do this might include surveys and the establishment of performance indicators for each section of the code of ethics.

The overreaching theme in a business code of ethics may be summed up as follows: As a representative of a company, you must act with honesty and integrity in all matters within the company and outside the company wherever business is conducted. Typical inclusions in a business code of ethics are

- Employees are expressly forbidden from revealing or communicating to any third party confidential information entrusted to them.
- Employees must avoid involvement in outside activities that could conflict with the employee's loyalty.
- Employees must avoid situations where personal interests conflict with those of the company.
- Company assets such as time at work, work products, vehicles computers, and software are not meant for personal use.
- Employees are not to accept lavish gifts from suppliers.
- Employees are not to disclose nonpublic information to anyone outside the company unless disclosure is required for business purposes.

The Role of the Legal System in Ethical Disputes

Some behavior is considered purely unethical; other behavior, although unethical, may also be serious enough to be considered criminal in nature and therefore subject a violator to a fine or even incarceration, or it may be considered a civil matter and therefore subject the violator to litigation (a lawsuit), resulting in the payment of money damages. In the example on page 14 in which the Johnson Motor Company placed an unreasonably dangerous product on the market, a person injured while driving this car because the gas tank exploded would have the legal right to bring a civil lawsuit against the company. If this person can prove in court that the Johnson Motor Company deliberately placed this unsafe car on the market, damages awarded to him or her could include reimbursement for injuries suffered as well as damages imposed as a punishment (called *punitive damages*).

Ethical violations, and especially those that amount to civil and criminal wrongs, may not always be evident to employees of a company; alternatively, employees may simply be unconcerned with their behavior. Therefore, a code of ethics that clearly defines the type of behavior expected of employees and that makes reference to what can be considered legal and ethical violations becomes a very important document for minimizing unacceptable behavior in a company. Even though a code is well written, employees may draw a conclusion that what is not mentioned in the code is allowed. In addition, the document should be updated frequently to allow for changing conditions in the company. To protect a company from civil lawsuits and the pursuit of criminal actions against its employees by outsiders, it is advantageous to hire a code enforcement officer to deal with violations internally before they become major issues. The code enforcement officer should also hold information sessions with employees to help them become thoroughly familiar with the company's code of ethics.

Summary

Clearly, we must have laws to regulate human behavior. Otherwise, anything goes. History has provided the reasons why. Those who obey the law will be protected and those who do not will be punished.

Law has many legitimate functions. Four of them are settlement of disputes, protection of the individual and society, protection of property, and promotion of worthwhile social objectives.

The most important influences on the U.S. legal system were Roman law and English common law. Roman law is the basis of much of the law of Europe today, whereas English common law and equity became the model for the legal system of the United States.

The primary sources of law in the United States are constitutions, statutes, court decisions, and administrative regulations. Although the modern emphasis is on statutory law, including the regulations of administrative agencies, a substantial portion of the law in the United States is created through court decisions.

One way to classify law is as civil law and criminal law. Civil law protects the rights and property of individuals from harm by other individuals. Criminal law protects society from the harmful acts of individuals.

States have adopted uniform laws ensuring that the laws governing commercial transactions will be the same throughout the country. One such law is the Uniform Commercial Code (UCC), which has now been adopted in all fifty states, the District of Columbia, and the Virgin Islands.

Business ethics focuses on ethical behavior (what is right and wrong in business settings). Today, business firms must operate within ethical guidelines as well as legal boundaries. Failure to respond to an ethical crisis leaves a firm vulnerable to court challenges, government intervention, consumer boycotts, public distrust, and negative publicity. An unethical business decision can sometimes end up in court as a civil or criminalmatter.

Important Legal terms

acts
administrative regulations
business ethics
case law
civil law
code of ethics

common law
constitutional law
criminal law
equity
ethics
law

ordinances
precedent
stare decisis
statutes

Questions and Problems for Discussion

1. Ludwig was the director of human resources for the Krantz Technology Company. He played in a business-related golf tournament and won. Several people participated in this tournament. The prize was a ten-day all-expense trip to Bermuda. Ludwig accepted the prize and notified the vice president of human resources, his supervisor, for approval, which was granted. Was the decision to accept the price ethically correct?

2. Discuss the truth or falsity of this statement: "In the United States, judges rely solely on statute law to arrive at decisions while trying a case in court."

3. Why are administrative agencies important?

4. Abbott shot and wounded three men who were attempting to rob him in the subway of a large city. He had been robbed before in the same area and under the same circumstances. If convicted, do you think Abbott should be punished if he believed that what he did was ethically correct?

5. Jerome had acupuncture performed on his knee as the result of a football injury. The treatment by the licensed acupuncturist resulted in his getting a severe infection that required medical treatment at a hospital and then several visits to his doctor for additional treatment. Jerome, who had a part-time job, lost several days at work and lost several hundred dollars in pay. He then decided to bring a legal action against the acupuncturist for his lost pay. Would his court action be a civil or criminal matter?

6. Clay stole a car from Mooney's driveway. While driving the car down Main Street at an excessive rate of speed, Clay ran into Page's store window, causing extensive damage. Can Mooney and Page bring a civil action against Clay? Can the state take action against Clay? Explain. What functions does the law serve in this case?

7. What is the difference between statute law and case law? Is one more important than the other in the U.S. legal system?

8. What are the effects on a company that fails to build a strong ethical base into its everyday decision making?

9. Do you think it is unethical for a company to test current employees for illegal substances?

10. The Vanity Corporation spent several million dollars advertising its mouthwash as having the ability to cure colds and sore throats. After several years of advertising, the Federal Trade Commission (FTC) declared that Vanity's claim about the mouthwash constituted false advertising. The FTC determined that the original formula had not changed since 1900, when Vanity first started manufacturing the mouthwash, and that no such claim of the mouthwash curing colds and sore throats had been made in the company's early days. Did the Vanity Corporation act ethically in making claims for its mouthwash even though no physical harm could come to consumers who used the product?

11. Sentinel, a national automotive chain with auto centers throughout the United States, mailed coupons to consumers advertising discounts on brake jobs. Actually, this advertising was a bait-and-switch scheme to get consumers into Sentinel's auto centers and convince them that additional repairs were needed. Sentinel had also established quotas for repair services that employees were required to meet. The company made millions of dollars on this scheme. Once the scheme was discovered, Sentinel's auto repair license was revoked and lawsuits were initiated against the company. Sentinel settled the lawsuits out of court, and as part of the settlement, it offered various types of auto repairs free of charge. Did Sentinel act ethically in this case? Why do you think Sentinel settled its claims out of court?

12. The Kaiser Company manufactured a device women could use to prevent pregnancy. This device was sold to more than 3 million women. Thousands of women filed lawsuits against the company because the device was found to be defective, causing problems of infection and health defects in children born to them. The company aggressively fought these lawsuits in court, although there was overwhelming evidence that the device was truly defective. Was it unethical for the Kaiser Company to contest lawsuits filed against it knowing that it was responsible for the injury?

CHAPTER 2

The Legal System in the United States and Its Constitutional Foundation

CHAPTER PREVIEW

Chapter Highlights

This chapter presents an overview of the legal system in the United States, names the personnel who play primary roles in helping the courts function smoothly, points out the different names given to the courts, and describes the types of cases that courts have the authority to decide. (It may surprise you that the U.S. Supreme Court will not hear every case that is presented for consideration.) Finally, the chapter briefly outlines the constitutional principles that have a significant effect on the U.S. legal system and that set it apart from legal systems in other countries.

THE ROLE OF THE JUDICIARY IN THE UNITED STATES

In Chapter 1 it was pointed out that nonpeaceful means of settling disputes are not only unlawful but could also create more trouble. Of course, two people engaged in a dispute could simply forget what happened and get on with their lives. Sometimes that is what happens. In other cases, what does a person do? One answer is to take the case to court. Remember, however, before a person can bring a lawsuit, the case to be presented must have merit, that is, (1) the case must be brought in good faith and (2) the party bringing the case must have a factual basis for winning in court. Frivolous cases (cases with no merit) tie up an already overburdened legal system. Judges refer to frivolous cases as absurd. Take the case of the prison inmate who claimed his rights were violated because his cell mirror was too high to use while he shaved. Under federal law, frivolous litigation has consequences. One example is that the losing party must pay the prevailing party money for any damages suffered. Another federal law, aimed at attorneys, fines them for using frivolous arguments during any hearing or trial.

Under the system of government in the United States, the courts represent the judicial branch of the United States government. They have been assigned the responsibility of settling disputes by interpreting and enforcing law. The courts carry out their responsibility by deciding cases that are brought before them. To decide a case means to listen to a dispute and then render a decision. Whatever the issue—civil or criminal liability of a wrongdoer, enforceability of a contract, or the resolution of a constitutional question—when the case is decided, the court will enforce the law by imposing punishment for a criminal violation, or in the case of a civil violation, by awarding damages to the injured party or granting relief in equity. Keep in mind that while U.S. courts are interpreting law, they are in many cases setting policy. They have, for example, decided important cases brought by special interest groups in such controversial areas as discrimination, abortion, and the environment.

Structure of the U.S. Judiciary

The United States has two separate and distinct court systems: (1) the federal (national) court system established by the U.S. Constitution and the U.S. Congress and (2) the state and local court system established in each state under state law. With courts located throughout the country, principally in the larger cities, the federal court system uniformly follows the same rules and procedures. In contrast, each state has its own court system with courts located in virtually every town and county. State courts handle over 95 percent of all cases such as traffic offenses, divorces, wills and estates, and buying and selling property because all these areas are governed primarily by state laws. Consequently, these are the courts with which citizens have the most contact. If there were no state or local courts, many cases could not be heard at all because the U.S. Constitution limits the cases that can be brought in federal courts. If you recall, O.J. Simpson's civil and criminal trials were both heard in California state courts. Although rules and procedures vary somewhat among the states, there are similarities between the two systems. Both systems have three levels of courts with different types of jurisdiction:

- trial courts, where cases start (lower courts)
- intermediate courts called "courts of appeals" that review judicial decisions and jury verdicts in the trial courts
- courts of last resort, which hear further appeals and generally have final authority in the cases they hear

Jurisdiction

jurisdiction power to hear and decide a case

standing to sue a person has legitimate issues giving him or her the legal right to bring a lawsuit

appellate courts courts that hear appeals of lower court decisions

Jurisdiction is the authority to hear and decide a case. Trial courts have *original jurisdiction* because they try cases for the first time. Keep in mind that to bring a lawsuit, a party must have **standing to sue**. This means that the plaintiff (person bringing the suit) must have a good reason to do so (i.e., a personal interest in the outcome of the lawsuit such as suffering harm from an assault or robbery).

The next level of courts above the trial courts is the **appellate courts**. These courts have *appellate jurisdiction,* or the authority to review cases that have already been tried in the lower courts and to make decisions about these cases without holding a new trial. Appellate judges determine only whether errors of law are made during a trial. They reach decisions by listening to the oral arguments presented by the attorneys for the parties to the appeal, reading the written information (briefs) presented by these attorneys, and reviewing the record of the trial court proceedings. No new information such as additional facts or proof is permitted. Appellate court judges may affirm the trial court decision, reverse it, or order a new trial. Further appeals in both federal and state courts are taken to the next level, identified in the previous section as courts of last resort.

At both the federal and state levels, there are civil and criminal courts. Civil courts handle cases involving disputes between individuals, between a person and a business, or between businesses. Disputes are usually settled by an award of money damages or a relief in equity to the "winning party." Criminal courts hear cases between a governmental unit—such as the state or federal government (acting for society)—and a person or business accused of a crime. Criminal courts determine whether a crime has been committed and also set punishment for those who are found guilty of committing a crime (most criminal cases take place in state courts). Finally, a few special courts at both the federal and state levels deal only with certain types of cases.

Subject Matter Jurisdiction

No court can decide every kind of case. A case can be properly brought in a certain court only if the court has jurisdiction over the person and over the subject matter of the dispute. "Jurisdiction over the subject matter" means that the court can hear and decide only certain types of cases. Some courts have **general** (or unlimited) **jurisdiction**, the power to hear and decide almost any type of case brought before them; other courts have **limited jurisdiction**, the power to hear only certain cases limited by type (such as civil *or* criminal), by the amount of money involved, and by the geographic area. Some courts, for example, can handle cases involving civil money damage claims but only up to a certain amount and only within city or county limits. Other courts can handle cases involving civil money damage claims of any amount within a wide geographic area. Still others deal only with specific disputes, such as those relating to juveniles.

general jurisdiction
power of a court to hear almost any case brought before it

limited jurisdiction
power of a court to hear only certain kinds of cases

> Otero wished to sue Clawson for $100,000, claiming that a permanent injury resulted from a car accident due to Clawson's carelessness. Both parties reside in New York State, County of Monroe, Rochester, New York. This case lies within the jurisdiction of the New York Supreme Court Monroe County, which is a trial court in that state.

In this example, if Otero goes to the wrong court, proper jurisdiction will not exist, and she will not be able to obtain a valid hearing. Moreover, if the case is heard in a court without proper jurisdiction, the decision handed down will be unenforceable.

Personal Jurisdiction

"Jurisdiction over the person" means that a court can hear and decide a case because it has authority over the *parties* in the case, generally in a certain geographic area. The party who brings the case into court automatically comes under the court's jurisdiction. The defending party is brought under the court's jurisdiction through a legal process that describes the nature of the complaint and names the person or legal authority requesting that the case be brought to court. For example, the issuance of a summons (described in Chapter 5) in a civil lawsuit brings the defending party under the jurisdiction of the court. Personal jurisdiction includes a person domiciled in a particular state and, according to the U.S. Supreme Court, a nonresident temporarily present, if the summons is served in that state.

Lloyd sued Schnell to recover a sum of money for a financial loss he suffered when Schnell backed out of a legal contract. Both parties live in the state of Nevada. Lloyd should file a lawsuit in the appropriate Nevada court and then issue a summons to Schnell so as to bring Schnell within the jurisdiction of that court.

In a criminal case, an arrest (described in Chapter 3) made by means of an arrest warrant issued by a judge brings a person accused of a crime (the defending party) into court.

Jurisdiction in Cyberspace

The term *jurisdiction* as described on pages 24 and 25 is a preelectronic age definition and generally refers to a court's power to hear a case and settle a dispute involving persons or property located within state boundaries but generally not beyond. This fundamental principle was established in 1877 by *Pennoyer* v. *Neff,* 95 U.S. 714. Since then, several cases have extended jurisdiction outside the boundaries of a particular state by enacting long-arm statutes based on political and commercial reality. There was pressure to provide citizens and businesses of a particular state with the ability to sue nonresidents in local course. For example, in 1945, the case of *Washington* v. *International Shoe Co.* 326 U.S. 310 established the "minimum contact" rule. In this case, the court held that a state may sue a nonresident corporation provided the corporation has regular and systematic contacts within the state bringing the lawsuit and provided the exercise of jurisdiction does not violate the rules of due process and fair play. Several cases since *International Shoe* have invoked the minimum contact rule and allowed lawsuits involving people and businesses in other states. So the question arises: Does cyberspace require the formal creating of a separate jurisdiction? The answer is probably no because it has become clear from decided cases that a defendant does not have to be physically present in a particular locale for a person or business in one state to do business with a person or business in another state. However, for those situations in which U.S. laws are impossible to apply to the Internet without creating substantial limitations on the technology, cybercommunities have been formed. Similar to an association of people, the cybercommunities or organizations create and define laws applicable to their community and work with other communities to resolve issues when there are differences through a process called computer-mediated communications.

THE STATE COURT SYSTEM

As noted earlier, each state, as well as the District of Columbia, has its own court system established by legislation and also a state's constitution. It is important to recognize that the names of the individual courts handling the same types of cases vary from state to state. Nevertheless, it is possible to make some general observations about the organization of state courts. Each state court system includes (a) trial courts of limited jurisdiction, (2) trial courts of general jurisdiction, (3) intermediate appellate courts (but not in all states), and (4) an appellate court of final resort, which is often called the supreme court. The supreme court is analogous to the United States Supreme Court. Figure 2.1 shows a typical state court system. State courts have authority to decide nearly every type of case, subject only to the limitations of the U.S. Constitution, their own state constitutions, and state law. A state court decision generally is not binding on the courts of other states.

Trial Courts of Limited Jurisdiction

Trial courts of limited jurisdiction generally try traffic cases, as well as minor civil and criminal cases. These courts have such names as justice court, magistrate's court, and municipal (city) court.

FIGURE 2.1 The Federal and State Court Systems

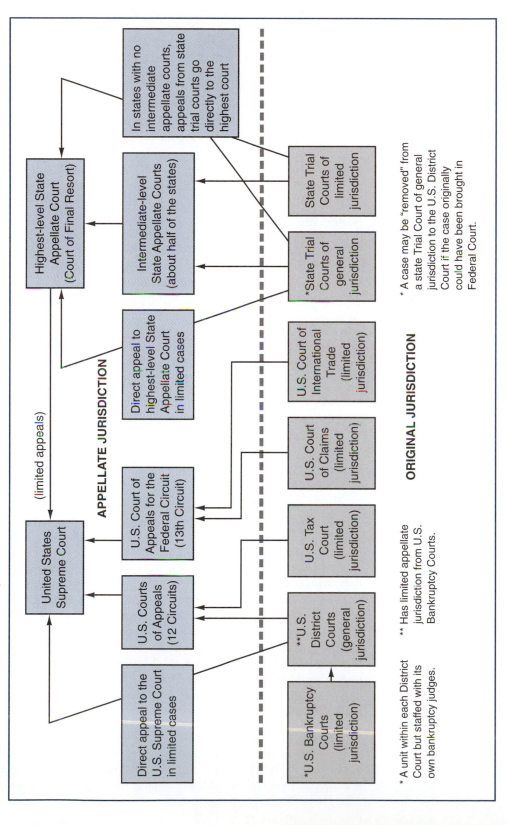

Small Claims Court

A court of limited jurisdiction that is of special interest is the **small claims court**, sometimes called magistrate court or justice of the peace court. This is a local court established to provide a fast, informal, and inexpensive forum for resolving certain types of small disputes on civil matters. A criminal case cannot be settled in a small claims court. Small claims courts exist in all states and commonly hear cases involving violation of contract rights (e.g., loan repayment), negligence, nuisance, minor personal injuries (e.g., automobile accident), landlord–tenant disputes, breach of warranty, and property loss or damage claims. Keep in mind that, while small claims court proceedings are informal, the judge will be applying the same laws to your case as if your case were being tried in a more formal court. Only an individual eighteen years of age or older can sue another person or a corporation in small claims court. If you are younger than eighteen, your parent or guardian may sue on your behalf. Court procedures are established by state law and there are differences in the operating rules of small claims courts from state to state including the maximum amount for which you can sue. The one aspect that appears to be the most variable from state to state is where to sue. It could be in the county where you live or in the county where the defendant (person being sued) resides or works or has a place of business; or you can bring suit where the disputed activity took place (e.g., where a contract was signed or in a case arising from a personal injury where the accident happened), or where a corporation does business. Nevertheless, how to prepare and present a case properly is similar in all states. The average case is heard within thirty to ninety days after the complaint is filed. The actual hearing generally lasts one hour or less (sometimes only fifteen minutes) and there is no jury. A typical small claims court case might be a suit by a tenant against a landlord who for no good reason refuses to return the tenant's security deposit.

> Levin, a tenant, rented an apartment from Hale, the landlord, for one year. Levin gave Hale a security deposit amounting to one month's rent. At the end of the one-year lease, Levin move out, but Hale refused to return the security deposit, claiming tenant damage beyond normal wear and tear. Although Levin proved she had not caused the damage to the apartment, Hale still refused to return the security deposit. Levin sued Hale in small claims court to secure the return of the security deposit.

Although the tenant in this example had a valid claim, she might have been discouraged from pursuing it in another court where legal fees and court costs might have exceeded the amount of the security deposit. Small claims court was a convenient, inexpensive way to recover her legitimate claim.

Advantages of Filing a Small Claims Court Claim   Although the rules vary from state to state and although the court's jurisdiction is limited in both subject matter and dollar amount, there are three distinct advantages to taking a case to small claims court. First, technical rules of evidence and procedure normally followed in a court trial are not strictly applicable. Second, the parties may proceed without attorneys, although most states do not bar attorneys from small claims court. (It has been noted by the National Center for State Courts that people who represent themselves in small claims court win just as often without them.) Finally, a dispute that can be resolved only by court action remains economically feasible because such action does not involve attorneys' fees.

Limitation on Amount of Your Law Suit   The maximum amount for which a person may sue in small claims court varies by state. The range in many states falls between $2,000 and $7,000. The upper limit for which suits can be brought in small claims court is continually on the rise with some states running as high as $15,000.

If you are seeking an amount that exceeds the small claims court limit for your state, you may still bring your case to small claims court, but if you win your case you will be unable to claim any amount over the jurisdictional limit.

> You signed an agreement with a contractor to add a room to your house that you intended to use as a workout room. The cost was $40,000 which you paid upon completion of the room. One month later, you discovered deficiencies amounting to $5,000. The contractor refused to correct these deficiencies and so you hired another contractor to do the work and sued the original contractor in small claims court for the money. The jurisdictional limit in your state for bringing a small claims action is $2,000. Consequently, if you win your case, you will be "out" $3,000 and you will not be able to return to court again and demand this amount. You need to decide before you take action whether it is more important to collect what you can in small claims court or sue in a higher court on the chance that you will recover the total $5,000, but only after deducting attorney's fees and higher court costs.

Filing a Complaint   A small claim is fairly easy to file. The injured party (the claimant or plaintiff) simply goes to the small claims court clerk's office, fills out a complaint form stating the amount of money in dispute and the reasons for suing. (In many jurisdictions a complaint form is available online and in some states you are even allowed to submit the form online.) You will be asked by the court clerk to pay a modest fee. After the claim is filed, the court notifies the defendant (the person against whom the action is being brought) usually by certified mail within thirty days. The claims notice tells the defendant the date, time, and place where the case will be heard, a brief statement of the reasons the plaintiff is suing, and the amount of money involved. Keep in mind that you file a claim only if you have decided that you have a good case. Ask yourself, "Did I suffer real monetary damage and did the person I plan to sue cause that loss?" Don't worry that you cannot define the legal theory on which to bring your claim. The judge will do that. Just be able to state the facts clearly. To illustrate, consider the following example:

> You took your $1,500 tailor-made JOSEPH suit to Martin's Laundry and Dry Cleaning. The suit, only three months old, was returned with holes in the jacket and pants. In your complaint you might start off by saying: "I took one tailor-made suit to Martin's Laundry and Dry Cleaning and it was returned in a severely damaged condition (holes in front of jacket and on left pant leg—photos attached). JOSEPH placed cost of repairing the damaged material at $350.

Keep in mind that the purpose of your complaint form is not to present evidence (this you will do at the trial or hearing) but simply to inform the defendant that he or she is being sued.

Court Procedures   A trial (hearing) date is usually set within four to six weeks of filing. At the trial, the plaintiff (claimant) and defendant each have a chance to tell their story to the judge (without a jury) and to present evidence and/or witnesses. Keep in mind that while small claims court proceedings are informal, the judge will be applying the same laws to your case as if your dispute were being tried in a more formal court Consequently, you are not going to get just a Yes you won, or No you lost decision. If you are the plaintiff, you will present your case first. Be prepared with appropriate evidence on your behalf and be brief and to the point. The judge usually has a crowded calendar and other people may be waiting to have their case heard after your trial is over. In the dry cleaning case, you could present either the suit or a photograph (most likely approach) of the damage, a cancelled check for the purchase of the suit, and the bill from Martin's Laundry and Dry Cleaning indicating that you paid to have the suit dry-cleaned.

If it is an accident case, you may ask an eyewitness to appear on your behalf, or if the case involved a breach of contract, you would bring a copy of the written contract unless the contract was oral; in the latter case, a witness to the contract would be helpful to you. If an eyewitness cannot attend or does not wish to appear on your behalf at the hearing, he or she may prepare a letter containing the relevant information (some small claims courts will not accept letters or written statements from witnesses). After hearing both sides of the argument, the judge considers the evidence and renders a decision. The decision will usually be mailed to the parties within a few days of the hearing. It would be rare for the judge to announce his or her decision immediately after the trial. Once the judge's decision is reached, it is entered in the court record and becomes officially known as a judgment and the loser, who now owes money, becomes a judgment debtor.

Appeal   The rules governing appeals vary greatly from state to state so check your state laws to determine if you do have the right of appeal. A few states allow no appeal; a few other states allow either party to appeal. The common approach (most states) allows only the loser to appeal. If you defaulted (didn't show up for the hearing), you cannot appeal. In many states, appeals can only be based on a legal error or mistake (i.e., the judge incorrectly applied the law). For example, a defendant appealed claiming that, according to the laws of her state, she was entitled to a larger amount of damages than she was granted in a decision by the small claims court judge. The appeals court would hear this case based on mistake. A few states allow an appeal on the facts in the case, that is, that the judge came to the wrong conclusion in deciding who won the case. An appeal must be filed promptly, usually from ten to thirty days after the decision was made by the judge hearing the original case.

Collecting Your Small Claims Award   The judgment you win (if you do) simply means that you have the right to collect the amount of money you were seeking from the defendant. Don't think, however, that you can just demand the money and you will receive a check in the mail from the defendant. You may receive that check, but most likely you will need to take legal action to collect what is owed to you because the defendant stated that he or she cannot pay or won't pay. Also, if the defendant has appealed, you will need to wait for the outcome of the appeal. If there was no appeal, you may then begin the collection process immediately. I say "you" because the judge will not participate in the collection process. Collecting the money is in your hands. Keep in mind that your judgment is valid for many years (in most states between ten and twenty years). You could start by sending a polite letter asking for payment. (Don't in any way attempt to harass the defendant into paying in the letter or go to his or her residence and verbally threaten him or her. If you do, you could find yourself being sued.) If you get no response, then there are legal options available to you. Here are some possibilities: You might be able to get an order from the sheriff or marshal directing the defendant's employer to take the money owed to you out of his or her wages (called garnishment). Or, if you discover that the defendant has a bank account, you might be able to get an order from the sheriff or marshal directing the bank to pay the amount from that account. Or at great expense (probably up to 50 percent), hire a collection agency to seek payment for you, or secure a lien on the defendant's real property hoping to eventually to get paid when the defendant either sells or refinances this property. Keep in the mind that these and other possibilities will take up your time, cost you money, and then you may discover that the defendant is "judgment proof"—that is, the defendant has no money and is unlikely to acquire any in the foreseeable future. In the long run you might simply say forget it and get on with your life.

In a few states—for example, New York—where corporations and partnerships are not allowed to sue in small claims court, there is a **commercial claims court** in which businesses may sue debtors up to a certain limit (in New York the amount is currently $3,000). This court is especially convenient for small businesses, which can take customers, subcontractors, and other businesses to court, typically to receive payment for their bills. Commercial claims court offers businesses the same low-cost, represent-yourself alternative that small claims court offers to individuals. For example, a veterinarian who runs an animal hospital under the corporate name of "Caring for Animals" may take the owner of a dog treated at the hospital to court for not paying the bill.

commercial claims court special lower court, similar to small claims court, that allows businesses to sue debtors up to a certain limit.

Other Trial Courts of Limited Jurisdiction

There are other trial courts that have a greater amount of limited jurisdiction to try cases. These courts have the authority to hear civil matters involving large sums of money (e.g., $25,000) and/or major criminal cases involving felonies. These courts may also have appellate jurisdiction to hear cases from the lowest courts of limited jurisdiction. There are also specialized courts with limited jurisdiction. Examples of these courts include the probate (or surrogate's) court, which handles wills, the administration of estates, and the guardianship of minors and incompetents, and domestic relations (or family or juvenile) court, which deals with family difficulties and juvenile delinquency cases.

Trial Courts of General Jurisdiction

Trial courts of general jurisdiction may hear cases involving any question (civil or criminal), any amount of money, or any degree of crime. They generally handle all serious disputes. A civil injury case involving a large sum of money or a major crime could be handled by such a court. Pursuing petty claims in this court is discouraged if the case can be settled in one of the local courts of limited jurisdiction, like city or justice court. In some states, a trial court of general jurisdiction is called the superior court; in others, it is called the court of common pleas, the circuit court, or the district court. In at least one state, New York, it is called the supreme court.

Intermediate Appellate Courts and the Court of Final Resort

At a higher level of the state court system are the appellate (review) courts. As mentioned previously, these courts review cases decided in the trial courts of both general and limited jurisdiction and determine whether a mistake of law was made during the trial. A mistake of law may consist, for example, of a trial judge allowing attorneys to ask witnesses improper questions. In about three-quarters of the states, intermediate courts of appeal exist to review these cases. Arguments in appellate courts are presented in the form of written briefs, or judges may hear oral arguments when they fixed it appropriate. In the remaining states, the court of final resort is the only appellate court. Where intermediate courts do exist, they usually decide a majority of cases, which relieves the burden of cases on the court of final resort. With a few exceptions, they are called supreme courts. As in the appellate courts, arguments in the court of last resort are made in written briefs submitted to the court and sometimes in oral arguments.

The state's court of final resort may be called by various names: the court of appeals, the supreme court of appeals, the supreme court, or the supreme judicial court. This court will hear a case that has come from a lower court through an intermediate appellate court only when permission is given to the appealing party by the intermediate appellate court. If an appeal is denied, the intermediate appellate court's ruling stands.

In limited cases, appeals may be taken directly to the state's court of final resort from the trial court, as when the question involves the constitutionality of a state or federal statute or the death penalty. There is no appeal from the decisions of this court to a federal court unless a federal law or question of constitutionality is involved.

There is a common misconception that anyone can appeal a case. Actually, the opportunities for successful appeal are limited. The appealing party must show that he or she would have won the case if the error of law had not been made during the trial. Another factor that limits the appeals process is its cost. One major expense is attorney's fees. Another major expense is the cost of reducing to writing the entire record of the court trial (word for word). A copy of this record of the trial must be presented to each appellate court judge so that he or she can study it in great detail.

Drug Courts

drug courts courts that handle drug-related crimes

Innovative courts called **drug courts** have proliferated across the United States to handle drug-related crimes such as possessing or purchasing drugs and drug peddling with the ultimate goal of stopping the abuse of alcohol and other drugs and related criminal activity by offenders. There are currently more than 1,500 drug courts operating in all fifty states. Drug courts are intended to substitute mandatory treatment for incarceration. More than 1 million arrests are made each year for drug crimes, and efforts in regular courts to deal effectively with these crimes have failed. Diversion programs that placed defendants into drug rehabilitation programs did not work in many cases because oversight of such programs by drug treatment personnel was too loose. Defendants often dropped out, and the system often didn't catch up with them for months or years or until they were arrested for another crime.

Drug courts are generally designed to fit the needs of a particular community, with input from local drug court judges, prosecutors, public defenders, police, drug treatment center personnel, and community leaders. For example, many drug courts target first-time offenders, whereas others target habitual offenders. These drug courts have established a system of accountability on the part of a defendant, immediate consequences with teeth for failure to comply, and a reward system for completion of the program. Generally, defendants aren't required initially to plead guilty to their crimes. Instead, they agree to enter a drug treatment program with the understanding that if they fail, they will be prosecuted on the original charges and end up in jail; if they are successful, however, the crime is often erased from their record. Typically, program participants are monitored for progress. They must have regular drug tests, return to court periodically (e.g., once a month) for a review of their progress, undergo counseling, participate in a job-training program, and if necessary, work toward a high school diploma. Of course, a drug court program is not for everyone. A defendant with a history of violent crime, a drug-trafficking arrest, or more than a designated number of previous nondrug felony convictions will most likely not qualify for the program. Although it may be difficult at this time to measure success, some research findings show that defendants referred for treatment through a drug court stay in treatment until completion to avoid a jail sentence. Those in a position to make judgments are taking a wait-and-see attitude about the future of drug courts.

Mental Health Courts

Mental health courts have been created in numerous jurisdictions across the United States. Congress approved legislation for these courts in the autumn of 2000 to target a problem facing many American cities: how to deal with people who are mentally ill and become involved in the criminal justice system and end up incarcerated. Treating defendants with mental illnesses who had been sentenced to prisons and jails is costly, and it is considered nearly impossible to provide humane and just treatment under these conditions. In a mental health court, the defendant (person accused of committing a crime), if found guilty, is "sentenced" to treatment rather than jail. Treatment involves regular sessions with a psychiatrist, a caseworker, and a probation officer. When the defendant is initially brought to court, the prosecutor and defense counsel work as a team to determine what is best for the defendant, now called the "client." In determining what an appropriate sentence should be, the judge acts as much like a social worker on the bench as a jurist, considering the client as someone who may need treatment in a hospital or a community treatment center. The treatment plan employed is one recommended by a court clinician after interviewing the client. Supporters say that this approach is good because inmates with mental illness are more expensive to house in jail than in treatment centers. Their mental illness often delays their release. On the other hand, there is a public safety issue: Some clients arrested for violent misdemeanors or drunken driving may have been given probation and assigned to check in at a local clinic for treatment but failed to report. Some prosecutors say that just because a person has a mental illness does not mean that he or she should not be held accountable for his or her actions. Consequently, one county participating in the mental health court project has reserved the option of sending offenders to jail if they violate the terms of their probation. Appearance in a mental health court is strictly voluntary. Every client must agree to transfer the case from the court in which they would normally be tried.

THE FEDERAL COURT SYSTEM

Article III (Section 1) of the U.S. Constitution created the Supreme Court and gave Congress the power to create inferior federal courts and to determine their jurisdiction. Federal courts decide cases that involve the Constitution, federal laws enacted by Congress or the U.S. government, including cases dealing with the relation of the United States and other nations and their representatives or their citizens. They also deal with cases where state court jurisdiction is inappropriate. The Constitution provides that federal judges and justices of the Supreme Court be appointed for life terms (for good behavior). Appointments are made by the president and are confirmed by the U.S. Senate.

The Federal Court Structure

The U.S. Supreme Court is the highest court in the federal judiciary. Congress has established two levels of federal courts under the Supreme Court: the trial courts and the appellate courts. In addition, there are specialized courts with limited jurisdiction, including U.S. Bankruptcy Courts, which handle the cases of financially troubled debtors; the U.S. Court of International Trade, which settles controversies over matters involving international trade and customs issues; the U.S. Tax Court, which has jurisdiction over matters involving controversies between taxpayers and the Internal Revenue Service; and the U.S. Court of Federal Claims, which has jurisdiction over most claims for money damages against the United States, disputes over federal contracts, unlawful "taking" of private property by the federal government, and a variety of other claims against the United States. The decisions in these specialized courts may be directly reviewed in the U.S. Courts of Appeals. Figure 2.1 illustrates the organization of the federal court system.

Federal Trial Courts

The federal district courts (referred to as the U.S. District Courts) are the trial courts of the federal court system. Within limits set by Congress and the Constitution, the district courts have both general and original jurisdiction to hear nearly all categories of federal cases, including both civil and criminal matters. The United States is divided into judicial districts. The number of districts is determined by Congress and varies over time, primarily because of population changes. Each state has at least one district court, and the more populous states—such as California, New York, and Texas—have several. U.S. District Courts are also located in the District of Columbia, Puerto Rico, and the territories of Guam, the Virgin Islands, and the Northern Mariana Islands. Currently, there are ninety-four federal judicial districts. Each district includes a U.S. Bankruptcy Court as a separate unit of the district court. (Bankruptcy cases cannot be filed in state court.) District courts hear cases that fall into two categories: federal issues and diversity of citizenship.

Federal issues are those that pertain to federal statutes (federal law) passed by Congress. They include crimes such as counterfeiting, mail theft, narcotics sales, bank robbery, violation of the federal income tax laws, and treason committed against the federal government; injury cases in which citizens suffer damages caused by federal employees; environmental pollution cases; problems with copyrights and patents; and broken contracts. Also included under the umbrella of federal issues are those that pertain to the U.S. Constitution—such as a violation of a person's rights under the Constitution—and problems concerning treaties of the United States.

Diversity-of-citizenship cases apply to citizens of different states who are involved in a lawsuit based on state laws. Such cases can be tried in a U.S. District Court. The amount of the claim, however, must exceed $75,000. A major reason for allowing this type of suit is to prevent the court of one state from showing partiality for its citizen over the citizen of the other state during any court procedure stemming from the lawsuit. If the parties agree, however, their case may be tried in state court.

> Marta Rollands, a citizen of Ohio, was walking along a sidewalk on a busy street in Athens, Ohio, one day when a large drum containing cleaning fluid rolled off a passing truck traveling at high speed. She suffered severe injuries and incurred a great deal of pain and suffering. As a result, she could not work for one year. Rollands now wishes to sue the trucking company for $200,000 to cover her injuries, pain and suffering, and loss of work over and above what her insurance will cover. The trucking company does business in Ohio but has its headquarters in Indiana. Because the amount of the claim exceeds $75,000, Rollands could bring her lawsuit in federal court on the basis of diversity of citizenship.

In this example, Rollands could, if she wished, sue not in federal court but instead bring the lawsuit either in Ohio (because the trucking company did business there) or in Indiana (because the trucking company was headquartered in that state). For the reasons stated earlier, however, it would be wiser for Rollands to bring the lawsuit in federal court.

Finally, as units of the U.S. District Courts, bankruptcy courts hear requests from individuals and businesses seeking relief because they can no longer pay their creditors and wish to either liquidate assets to pay their debts or create a repayment plan. (More will be said about bankruptcy in Chapter 36.)

Intermediate Courts of Appeal

The United States, including the District of Columbia, is divided into twelve circuits (regions), each with a court of appeals. Each circuit court hears appeals from all the district courts located within its circuit. A circuit includes three or more states. The District of Columbia, however, is a separate circuit and has its own court of appeals. A thirteenth federal circuit court of appeals is authorized to hear appeals from federal courts of any district (nationwide jurisdiction) if the case relates to certain copyright, trademark, or patent issues. It may also hear appeals from the U.S. Court of Claims and the U.S. Court of International Trade. Decisions of this court are binding throughout the United States. The thirteen federal circuits, including the D.C. circuit and the federal circuit, are shown in Figure 2.2.

Neither the federal appeal courts nor the U.S. District Courts has jurisdiction to review decisions of the highest state courts.

The U.S. Supreme Court

The Supreme Court of the United States, located in Washington, D.C., is the highest court in the federal court system and the highest court in the land (see Figure 2.1). It is the only court created by the Constitution. When the Supreme Court rules on constitutional issues, that judgment is virtually final. A party seeking review will file a petition asking the court to issue a **writ of certiorari**. This writ grants permission for the court to hear this case. Once the court renders a decision, this decision can rarely be altered. Further, all other courts in the United States are required to follow that decision in similar cases. This consistency helps guarantee equal justice for all Americans. The vast majority of its work is appellate. The Supreme Court does, however, have limited original jurisdiction in some instances—for example, in cases involving foreign ambassadors—but the Court rarely exercises this power.

writ of certiorari grants permission for a case to be heard by the U.S. Supreme Court

Each year thousands of civil and criminal cases are tried in state and federal courts, and each year the Supreme Court receives thousands of petitions from these courts requesting certiorari. However, it only hears on average between 150 to 200 cases that deal with the most important legal questions in the nation. In those civil cases that the Supreme Court dismisses, the preceding judgment by a federal court of appeals or a state's highest court stands as the final decision in the case. If certiorari is sought from a decision in a criminal case and denied, the criminal defendant who originally took the case to the Supreme Court, may request a *writ of habeas corpus*, which is a demand to have the case reviewed.

The justices of the Supreme Court meet to decide which appeals they will hear. By tradition, most appeals will be heard only with the consent of at least four justices.

The Supreme Court, which has national jurisdiction, hears appeals from the thirteen U.S. Courts of Appeals and from the highest state courts when a question about a constitutional issue or some other federal question is involved. It usually only hears cases that involve matters of great national importance and not cases that affect only the parties actually involved in the lawsuit. Ordinarily, a case must first be tried in one or more of the state or lower federal courts before it will be heard in the Supreme Court. Sometimes decisions rendered in the U.S. District Courts, special federal courts, and the highest state courts may be appealed directly to the Supreme Court (Figure 2.3).

The statement "I'll take my case all the way to the Supreme Court" is more an expression of a person's frustration or dissatisfaction with a lower court ruling than a reality. Those who direct an appeal to the Supreme Court cannot demand, as a matter of right, that the Court hear their case, even if a federal question is involved. In other words, there is no absolute right of appeal to the U.S. Supreme Court. Actually, very few cases go all the way to the Supreme Court; only the nine justices who comprise the Court (eight associate justices and the chief justice) and hear the cases decide which ones they will take. There is good reason for this practice. Each year, thousands of civil and criminal cases are tried in state and federal courts.

FIGURE 2.2 The Thirteen Federal Judicial Circuits

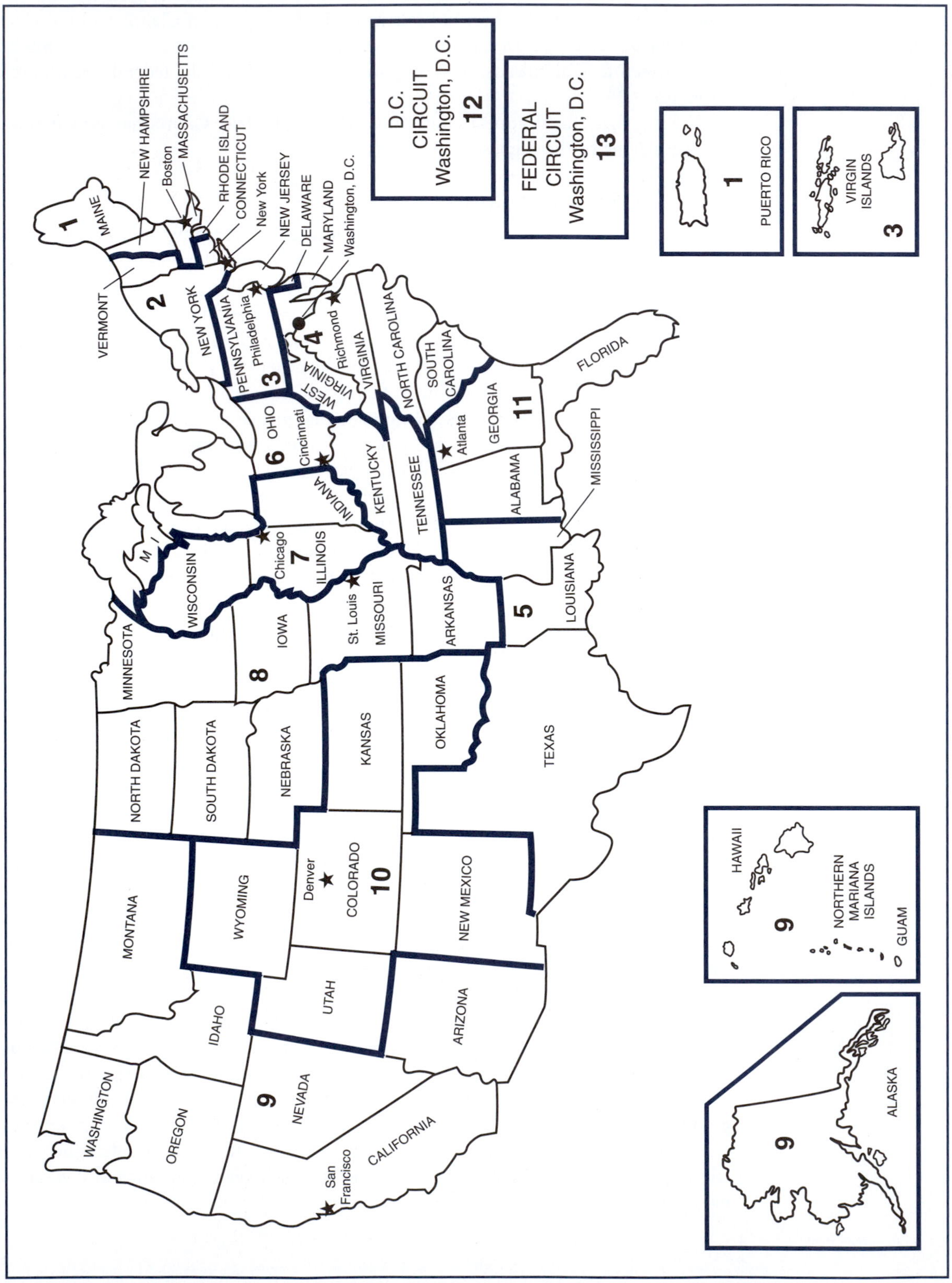

FIGURE 2.3 The Road to the Supreme Court

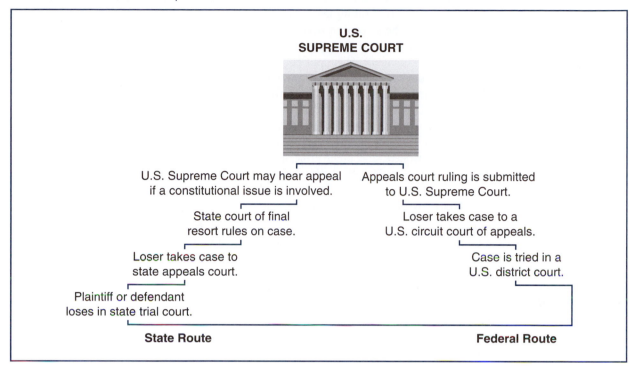

PARTICIPANTS IN THE LEGAL SYSTEM

The federal and state courts require the assistance of many people. Some of the personnel who play primary roles in helping the courts function smoothly are the attorney, the judge, and the jury.

The Role of the Attorney

An attorney is professionally trained and licensed to practice law and perform various roles in the justice system. During a court trial and in prior court proceedings, your attorney must zealously advocate for you. Keep in mind that your attorney, in addition to his or her relationship with you before and after trial, must interact with the court, opposing counsel, and other parties. These relations, however, are strictly regulated by law as well as by a Code of Professional Responsibility and rules of ethics.

Attorneys also conduct other business such as drafting wills and settling a domestic or marital dispute. In serving clients, the attorney must provide the best possible advice and must represent you with skill and integrity. In preparing to meet with you, the client, to help resolve a legal matter or to defend you in court on a civil or criminal matter, the attorney must spend large blocks of time outside the office preparing.

It is important to know when to consult an attorney. Sometimes it is absolutely essential. An arrest or an indictment for a crime (discussed in Chapter 3) is an example of a situation in which legal counsel is essential. The risks of being treated unfairly or improperly, of being held without bail, or of being found guilty and being sentenced improperly are too great to bypass legal advice. If you have been accused of a crime and you cannot afford an attorney, the court will appoint an attorney to represent you.

You should also consult an attorney before executing certain legal documents. For example, contracts are binding legal documents that may have serious, long-term effects. An attorney may be helpful in negotiating the terms of a contract.

At other times, the services of an attorney are advisable, but not essential. Planning for the development of real estate or for the start of a business is often helped by the advice of a knowledgeable attorney. Seeking and obtaining financing for the purchase of a home or the expansion of a business are also occasions when the assistance of an attorney is helpful.

There are many ways to find a reliable attorney. The bar association in your community is a good source of information. Other sources are friends, relatives, employers, accountants, bankers, and other professionals. In addition, many attorneys today advertise and provide information about their areas of specialization.

The Role of the Judge and the Jury

A trial judge is the person who presides over a trial, listens to attorneys argue their clients' cases to ensure that the evidence presented during the trial on behalf of the parties is relevant, and determines that the rules of trial procedure are not violated. The judge rules on points of law that arise during the trial, and at the conclusion of the trial, he or she instructs jurors regarding the law of the case before they retire to the jury room. If there is no jury, the judge alone decides the outcome of the case. In criminal cases, it is the judge who sentences those who are found guilty. In felony cases, the defendant has a constitutional right to a jury trial but may waive this right. If the defendant waives this right, the case will be decided by the judge.

The jury is a body of citizens randomly chosen from a cross section of the community in which the trial is to be held. Juries are used in both civil and criminal cases. You are entitled to a jury of your peers. A right to trial of your peers, however, doesn't mean that you have the right to a jury of people just like yourself. For example, a female defendant can't request an all-women jury. Rather, a jury of your peers means a representative selection of members of the community. Trial by jury in serious criminal cases is guaranteed in the Sixth Amendment and in the constitutions of many states. Supreme Court decisions interpreting the due process clause of the Fourteenth Amendment have applied the Sixth Amendment guarantee to state criminal cases, *Duncan* v. *Louisiana,* 391 U.S. 145 (1968). It is interesting to note that nearly a million Americans serve on juries each year.

During a trial, it is the jury that decides what really happened. Its role is to listen to the facts presented during a civil or criminal trial, weigh the testimony, determine which of the facts presented are true, and then decide on money damages, equitable relief, or punishment. In both civil and criminal cases, the juror is expected to be impartial and to decide the facts based on the evidence presented at trial and not based on any fixed personal view. The number of jurors will vary depending on whether the trial is civil or criminal and according to the particular state where the jurors reside.

More information about the roles of the attorney, the judge, and the jury is given in Chapters 3 and 5.

THE CONSTITUTIONAL FRAMEWORK OF THE U.S. LEGAL SYSTEM

The legal system of the United States is unique. Although other countries have legal systems that resemble ours, the U.S. system combines elements almost unknown in other countries. The following sections discuss briefly the constitutional principles on which this system is based.

Separation of Powers

separation of powers concept of independent branches of government

The U.S. system of government and law is based on a concept known as **separation of powers**, which is set out in the U.S. Constitution. This concept establishes three distinct and independent branches of the federal government: the legislative branch, Congress, which makes laws; the executive branch, the president, which enforces laws; and the judicial branch, the Supreme Court and lower courts, which interprets the laws. Each branch is independent of the others, and each has its own predominant power. This organization of the federal government was established when the Constitution was originally drafted. It was meant to prevent any one branch from obtaining more power than another branch and from gaining absolute control of the government.

As a practical matter, the concept of separation of powers is not always followed. Courts often "make law" by interpreting existing law. That interpretation may change a law in the same manner that a legislature might change it. Courts also make decisions that are often political in nature, such as deciding whether a certain political party may appear on an election ballot. These acts are incidental, however; for the most part, our judicial system concentrates on interpreting laws.

A distinctive characteristic of our legal system is that it combines statute laws (laws enacted by legislatures) and decisions made by courts. In contrast, most other civil law systems rely almost completely on statutes.

Another important principle of our legal system is that of "constitutionality." The U.S. Constitution is the supreme law of the land. Each state also has a constitution that is the supreme law in that state. Statutes, governmental actions, and court decisions may be declared invalid if they violate the principles of either the state or the federal constitution.

Judicial Review

judicial review power of a court to review the decisions of a lower court

The concept of **judicial review**, while not mentioned in the U.S. Constitution, is an important part of our legal system. It gives higher courts the power to review decisions of a lower court and rule on their constitutionality. Federal courts review acts of the U.S. Congress and state legislatures, and the U.S. Supreme Court reviews decisions of the highest state courts. This review process allows decisions and laws to be reversed or changed if they are not in harmony with existing laws and constitutions. The Supreme Court case of *Marbury* v. *Madison,* 5 U.S. 137; 2 L. Ed. 60, established the basis for the concept of judicial review by declaring an act of Congress unconstitutional. In a more recent decision, *Roe* v. *Wade,* 410 U.S. 113; 93 S. Ct. 705; 35 L. Ed. 2d 147, the Court struck down a Texas statute that made performing an abortion a crime.

Judicial review is a cornerstone of our Constitution. In the United States, our courts serve as the supreme protector of the rights of the individual. In no other country do so many citizens look to the courts to advance the interests of both individual citizens and society in general. In other countries, those who believe that their rights are being violated seek help from the legislature or from the administration. In this country, it is more likely that these matters will be brought to the courts.

Accommodation of Interests

accommodation of interests acknowledgment of the equitable consideration of parties involved in a dispute

Another principle of our legal system is that of **accommodation of interests**. As it is practiced in the United States, law is not simply a matter of right versus wrong. Law is more a matter of acknowledging the equitable considerations of the parties involved in a dispute. A tenant, for example, may be evicted for nonpayment of rent. A court, however, will often give the tenant time to raise the money needed to pay the rent, even though the law doesn't provide for this. This action helps the tenant and may prevent the tenant from becoming a burden on society.

Litigation

Our legal system operates almost exclusively within the framework of **litigation**—that is, a lawsuit or legal action. The Constitution does not give the courts the power to offer advisory opinions or to answer hypothetical questions. Courts may provide answers only to the questions brought before them in the form of lawsuits. This framework ensures that the courts will not interfere with the rights and duties of the legislative and executive branches of government.

Judicial decisions that are based on litigation depend on *adversarial system*, a development of the common law. Opposing parties enter our courts for a trial before a judge or a judge and jury and in the presence of an audience, the public. They are represented by attorneys who are adversaries (opponents) of each other. The system provides each side with the opportunity to present its case (and to point out the weaknesses in its opponent's case) to a neutral judge. The lawyers on each side follow the same statutes, case law, and rules of procedure. Each attorney attempts to ensure that her or his point of view should prevail and that the opposing attorney's point of view should lose. They do so by producing evidence in their client's favor and by attempting to disprove the evidence presented by the opposing party. The underlying thought is that this process will bring out all important evidence and that the result will be the truth. In reality, however, one party to a lawsuit may have advantages that are powerful enough to affect the outcome of a trial. The ability to hire a team of attorneys, or a single attorney with a high degree of expertise, experience, and skill, or the ability to pay expert witnesses and jury consultants can help win cases that might otherwise have been decided in favor of the opposing party.

All this having been said, you should be aware that formal adversarial trials are not always necessary. In fact, the majority of civil and criminal cases are resolved without a trial. The defendant in a criminal action will either plead guilty or negotiate a plea bargain asking to plead guilty to a lesser charge. Similarly, many civil cases are settled before trial through pretrial conferences.

The Bill of Rights

The First Amendment is considered the most important amendment in the **Bill of Rights** because without the freedoms in this amendment, it would not be possible for Americans to assert any other rights they have. It guarantees freedom of expression, which includes the five freedoms of religion, speech, press, assembly, and petition. Speech can take many forms. The spoken and written word, artistic media, and even symbolic action such as burning a flag as a political protest have all been held to be protected speech. There is a strong desire to protect speech as a fundamental right no matter how offensive it may be. As the result of the Supreme Court case *Reno v. American Civil Liberties Union* (117 S. Ct. 2329, 138 L. Ed. 2d 874), protected speech now includes electronic speech (the Internet). This includes traditional forms of speech displayed as words or images on a computer, as well as Internet addresses (e,g., a person's speech on a Web site or bulletin board) or domain names and some aspects of software programs. In setting the stage for electronic speech to be included among those areas of speech to be protected, the Supreme Court recognized that in a democracy there is a free flow of information around the world, much of which constitutes free expression. Placing electronic speech under the umbrella of speech protected by the First Amendment has caused some problems. For example, there has been a strong movement in the United

States toward "hate speech" and using the Web and chat rooms to carry on these activities. While "hate speech" is protected to a point, danger arises in the difficulty of determining at what point the effect of this speech incites others to perform illegal acts. Another example is the difficulty in determining the appropriate limitations to place on speech before limiting access by children to material on the Internet. Attempts by Congress to write laws protecting minors (children under eighteen years of age) were declared unconstitutional because the wording was too broad and too vague and was still likely to be an unconstitutional infringement on free speech. The result of the back-and-forth attempts by Congress and the courts to agree what should go into a law protecting minors from the abundance of pornographic and adult material available on the Web was to criminalize only the use of an interactive computer system to transmit indecent communication to any person under eighteen years of age. Other forms of speech protected by the First Amendment are *commercial speech* and *corporate political speech*. Substantial protection is given to both. Commercial speech generally takes the form of advertising by businesses. In the interest of protecting consumers from advertising deemed false, or, under certain circumstances improper, a state may restrict certain types of advertising. In regard to corporate political speech, corporations are, like individuals, free to express themselves on controversial issues as, for example, supporting certain candidates campaigning for political office.

The Fourth Amendment protects the individual's right to privacy by prohibiting unreasonable search and seizure by the government. If an unreasonable search and seizure should occur, the evidence obtained cannot be used in a trial. The Fifth and Sixth Amendments guarantee a number of rights that fall under the heading of "due process of law." One such right is the right against self-incrimination. Another is the right to a public trial before an impartial jury. To guard against the use of torture to extract confessions, the founders of our nation declared that individuals could not be compelled to be witnesses against themselves. It is up to government to prove guilt, not up to the individual to prove innocence. In addition, a person may not be tried twice for the same offense, and private property may not be seized for public use without just compensation for the property owner.

With a few exceptions, the Fourteenth Amendment applies the Bill of Rights to the states. In addition, it guarantees the equal protection of the law to all persons. Equal protection means that the state and federal governments cannot treat one person differently from another unless there is a legitimate reason for doing so.

Summary

Sometimes people involved in disputes with others have issues serious enough to bring to a court of law. This alternative may be the only way to protect each party's legal rights. Under our system of government, the courts have been assigned the responsibilities of protecting our legal rights by interpreting and enforcing law. (In Chapter 1, we learned that law consists of rules of conduct that require people to act in a certain way.) The courts carry out their responsibility by deciding cases that are brought before them.

The court system of the United States is made up of state and federal courts. Both court systems have various levels of courts with different types of jurisdiction—general, limited, original, and appellate. Jurisdiction covers both civil and criminal cases. In both systems, there are lower-level courts called trial courts, where cases are first tried. These courts have original jurisdiction. Higher-level courts have appellate jurisdiction, the authority to review lower-court cases. In both systems, a highest court has the last say in a case. A state's highest court may be called by various names.

There are some courts of special interest in the various states. One is a small claims court designed to expedite cases by doing away with technical rules of evidence. There are also drug courts, which handle the large volume of drug-related crimes. Mental health courts have been created in several jurisdictions across the United States. In a mental health court, the defendant, if found guilty, is sentenced to treatment rather than jail.

In the federal system, the highest court is called the Supreme Court. The Supreme Court is the highest court in the land and has national jurisdiction. Very few cases reach this Court because it hears only the toughest cases involving the most important legal questions. The Supreme Court, which has mainly appellate jurisdiction, will hear a case from the thirteen U.S. Courts of Appeals and from the highest state courts only if a constitutional issue or a federal question is involved.

The attorney, the judge, and the jury all play a key role in helping the courts to function smoothly.

Several constitutional principles significantly influence the U.S. legal system. One important principle is separation of powers—the independence of the legislative, executive, and judicial branches of government. A second important principle is judicial review, the power of higher-level courts—especially the U.S. Supreme Court— to review decisions of lower courts and to reverse or change laws that are not in harmony with existing laws, state constitutions, and the U.S. Constitution. A third important principle that makes our legal system unique is accommodation of interests, where equitable considerations of the parties involved in a dispute are acknowledged. A fourth principle, litigation, gives courts the power to provide answers to questions brought before them in the form of lawsuits. Finally, the underlying principles of the Bill of Rights (the first ten amendments to the U.S. Constitution) have a substantial impact on court decisions when it comes time to determine the boundaries of individual rights of citizens.

Important Legal Terms

accommodation of interests
appellate courts
Bill of Rights
commercial claims court
drug courts

general jurisdiction
judicial review
jurisdiction
limited jurisdiction
litigation

separation of powers
small claims court
standing to sue
writ of certiorari

Questions and Problems for Discussion

1. a. What is the difference between a trial court and an appellate court?
    b. What are the roles of attorneys, judges, and juries during a trial?
2. What constitutional principles significantly influence the U.S. legal system?
3. Would the U.S. Supreme Court hear the following cases? Explain why or why not.
    a. A Fourth Amendment search and seizure case is appealed from the highest state court of Pennsylvania. Three justices of the U.S. Supreme Court vote to hear the case. The remaining six justices believe the issue has already been decided in a similar case heard by the Court a year prior to the case currently being considered. Those six vote not to hear the Pennsylvania court appeal.
    b. A female college student is fined $150 for speeding on a major street in a large city. She claims she wasn't speeding and vows to take her case directly to the Supreme Court.
    c. A state has made it a crime to criticize state government. Nichols, the publisher of a small-town newspaper, sued in the appropriate state courts to declare this law unconstitutional (in violation of the First Amendment right of free speech) but lost.
4. What are some strong reasons for taking your case to a small claims court?
5. What is the significance of the minimum contact rule as it relates to the power of a court to hear a case and settle a dispute?
6. You are a resident of New Jersey. While at a mall, you were assaulted by a gang. You were severely injured and blinded in one eye. May you sue the gang for monetary damages even though the gang was arrested and convicted for the assault upon you?

7. Vira, who lived in Virginia, was owed $80,000 by Caldwell, who also lived in Virginia. Vira sued in a state court to collect the amount due and won. Caldwell was unhappy with the decision and appealed to the highest state court, where she also lost the case. Caldwell then thought about appealing to a federal court, hoping for better treatment. Does a federal court have jurisdiction to hear her case?

8. A high school teacher not on tenure was dismissed for writing a letter to the school board questioning the methods used by the school board and superintendent to raise money for athletic programs. In her letter, she also criticized the superintendent for attempting to keep teachers in the school district from expressing their opinions about an upcoming bond issue proposal. As a result of her letter, she was dismissed from her position as a math teacher. She sued the school board and the superintendent for violation of her right of free speech. Does a teacher have the right to speak against the superintendent and the school board?

CHAPTER 3

Personal, Business, and Cyber Crimes and Criminal Procedure

CHAPTER PREVIEW

Prologue

Nature of Criminal Law
Classification of Crimes

State and Federal Criminal Laws

Selected Personal and Business Crimes
Assault
Robbery
Arson
Burglary
Theft
Identity Theft
Driving While Intoxicated
Dram Shop Act

Cyber crime
Significant Legislation Affecting Cyber crimes

RICO: Racketeer Influenced and Corrupt Organizations Act

Common Defenses to Crimes
Infancy
Insanity
Involuntary Intoxication
Duress
Justification
Entrapment
Mistake Based on Wrong DNA Evidence

The Criminal Justice System
Police
Courts
Corrections

Chapter Highlights

This chapter deals with criminal law, including personal, business, and cyber crimes and the primary steps in the criminal justice system to deal with those who commit these crimes. Initially, the chapter describes the two major classifications of crimes. It then lists and describes the crimes most often handled by criminal justice agencies at various levels of government. A brief discussion follows of a federal law, the Racketeer Influenced and Corrupt Organizations Act (RICO), designed originally to prevent criminal infiltration of legitimate businesses but later expanded to include many other civil wrongs flowing from criminal activity. The chapter also deals with some common defenses, or excuses offered by accused persons for committing a crime, and the primary steps in the criminal justice system that are followed when a person actually commits a crime or is suspected of committing a crime.

PROLOGUE

Recall from Chapter 1 that civil law and criminal law are distinguished from one another. Civil law establishes rules that protect the rights and property of individuals from harmful acts by other individuals, a business, or a government. An individual who suffers personal harm or property damage may initiate a civil lawsuit seeking money damages. The defendant in such a lawsuit may be a person, the state, a business, or a government agency. This lawsuit would take the form *Named Plaintiff* v. *Named Defendant* (e.g., *Bennington* v. *Maraboli*). Similarly, a business, the state, or a government may bring a civil action against an individual. In contrast to the criminal law, however, no civil action can be undertaken that is not initiated by the injured party. In essence, civil law deals with private wrongs. A good example of a private wrong is a tort. Chapter 4 will deal with this area of the law. Criminal law, in contrast to civil law, has to do with crimes. Criminal law is the subject of this chapter.

NATURE OF CRIMINAL LAW

Criminal law, also called penal law, establishes rules to protect society from acts of individuals that are considered so dangerous, or potentially so, that they threaten peace and order within a society. It is primarily statutory law, whereas at one time it was primarily common law. All states have enacted penal codes (statutes) defining various crimes. What were at one time considered common law crimes are now included in a state's penal code. The Model Penal Code (MPC) published by the American Law Institute serves as a model for many states in developing and revising their statutory codes. The MPC is not law but, as the name implies, simply a model that is offered to states as a way to bring standardization to American criminal law. When an individual violates a criminal law established by a state or federal statute, he or she has committed a **crime** and is subject to arrest and, if convicted, punishment. For this reason, in criminal cases, the government (state or federal) brings the proceeding against the accused individual. A criminal action would take the form of the state as the plaintiff and the accused as the defendant. Depending on the seriousness of the crime, punishment may consist of a prison or jail sentence, a fine, or even death for harm done to society. Persons found guilty of criminal acts have permanent criminal records.

crime wrongful act against society defined by law and made punishable by law

Classification of Crimes

Crimes are classified according to their degree of seriousness (Figure 3.1). A **felony** is a crime of a serious nature for which the punishment may be death or imprisonment for more than one year, usually in a state or federal prison. A **misdemeanor** is a crime that is less serious than a felony and is punishable by imprisonment for no more than one year, usually in a local institution such as a county jail.

felony serious crime punishable by death or imprisonment for more than one year

misdemeanor less serious crime punishable by a jail sentence of less than one year

FIGURE 3.1
Classification of Crimes According to Degree of Seriousness

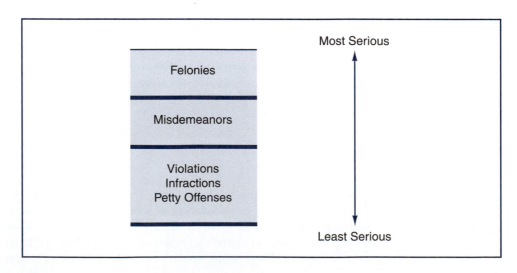

A few states have another classification of wrongs less serious than misdemeanors; these wrongs are variously termed *violations, infractions,* or *petty offenses.* Although the punishment for these wrongs may be confinement in a local jail, the acts are not considered criminal acts. The offender therefore has no permanent criminal record. Violations of town, city, or county ordinances, public disturbances, and minor traffic violations are included in this category of wrongs.

STATE AND FEDERAL CRIMINAL LAWS

The U.S. Congress has passed federal criminal laws (statutes) making certain crimes federal offenses. State legislatures in each of the fifty states have also passed laws (statutes) making certain offenses crimes against the state.

Criminal statutes vary from one state to another. Consequently, an act that is a crime in one state may not be a crime in another. Similarly, a violation of a criminal statute may be a felony in one state but a misdemeanor in another.

Some crimes, such as bank robbery and the possession and sale of narcotics, violate both federal and state criminal laws. Offenders can therefore be tried in either state or federal court.

SELECTED PERSONAL AND BUSINESS CRIMES

The federal government and each of the states have their own body of criminal law and determine by statute what types of conduct constitute felonies or misdemeanors. As mentioned earlier, crimes are public wrongs. To be charged with a crime means to be formally accused of that crime. The formality of charging a person with a crime will be covered later in this chapter. This section presents the basic features for a number of crimes often handled by criminal justice agencies at the various levels of government. Some crimes may take place in a business setting and therefore may be referred to as business crimes. Crimes considered to be **cyber crimes**—those committed with or through the use of computers or computer technology—will be given brief treatment later in the chapter.

cyber crimes crimes committed with or through the use of computers or computer technology

Assault

assault crime of unlawfully causing physical injury to another; tort of threatening another with bodily harm

The crime of **assault** occurs when one person unlawfully causes physical injury to another person—for example, by striking, beating, kicking, choking, or some other means. The injury does not have to be severe or cause great physical pain to be considered an assault, but merely the unlawful application of physical force on the victim.

> Three teenage boys torched a homeless man outside a church where he had bedded down for the night on a cardboard box. Each teen set his pant legs on fire. When the homeless man stood up, the flames spread across his body, severely burning his face, chest, and stomach. Two passerbys immediately extinguished the flames and called an ambulance. Hospital personnel determined that while the homeless man would survive, he would be severely disfigured. These teens could be charged with the crime of assault.

Some state codes may have several categories of assault, such as assault in the first and second degree. In these cases, the severity of the physical injury will be greater and require serious physical injury, disfigurement, or the use of a deadly weapon or dangerous instrument. Assault with a deadly weapon or dangerous instrument (one that is capable of causing death), such as a knife that causes serious physical injury or disfigurement, would most likely be a felony. In the past, the crime of assault referred only to the *threat* of physical injury; the crime of *battery* referred to the actual physical contact. Modern criminal statutes have abolished assault and battery as separate crimes and use the term *assault* to cover both acts.

Robbery

robbery forcible taking of money or personal property from another

Robbery is the act of unlawfully taking another person's money or personal (movable) property against his or her will by means of force or the threatened use of force. The money or property may be on the victim's person or simply in the victim's presence. (If the use or threat of force is absent—for example, picking pockets and purse snatching—no robbery has taken place; rather, another crime, such as larceny, which is discussed later, has occurred.) Pushing, jostling, or striking with a fist are sufficient to substantiate the force element in robbery. Robbery is generally regarded as a felony. Most states have degrees of robbery that bring a more severe penalty when the robbery is committed with a deadly weapon.

> Gale, a convenience store owner, was attacked and beaten by a man who demanded all the money in the cash drawer. Upon taking the money, he fled. The man has committed a robbery.

States with a first-degree robbery statute may require that the robbery take place inside a residence.

Arson

arson intentional, illegal burning of a home, building, or personal property

The knowing and malicious burning of any dwelling, house, other buildings (e.g., storage buildings or manufacturing facilities), or motor vehicle by fire or by means of explosives is called **arson** and is a felony. In most states, arson includes the property of the arsonist if there is an attempt to defraud the insurance company. Two frequent motives for arson are revenge and a desire to collect on fire insurance policies. Arson also includes the burning of personal property.

> Manny set fire to and destroyed a federal court building because one of his children had been arrested by federal authorities for the sale of dangerous drugs. Manny was guilty of arson.

Burglary

burglary unlawfully entering another's home or building with the intent to commit a crime

In most states, **burglary** is the crime of unlawfully entering (not breaking and entering) another person's dwelling house (home), apartment, boat used for regular residence, or a building such as a store or barn, or even a locked automobile at any time of the day or night without permission and with the intent to commit any type of felony. An offender who successfully carries out a burglary may be charged with both burglary and the other crime. Burglary is a felony. Even if the person does not commit a crime inside the building, the *intent* to commit the crime is enough to classify the act of entering as burglary. Most burglaries occur during daylight hours because of the work and social patterns of individuals in today's society.

> Marcus entered the penthouse apartment of a famous actress through the unlocked front door about 3 A.M. The security alarm was off and her bodyguard was off duty. He rummaged around the den, a spare bedroom, and a room used as an office but never tried to get into the bedroom where it appeared the actress was sleeping. Marcus left with valuable jewelry through the unlocked front door. Marcus could be charged with burglary and larceny (stealing). If he had left without stealing anything, he could still be charged with burglary.

Theft

theft unlawful taking of a person's property without the use of force and with the intent of permanently depriving the person of the property

Recall that robbery is the act of taking another person's personal (movable) property through force or the threat of force. **Theft** is a broader term, and it describes offenses relating to the unlawful taking of another person's property *without the use of force or violence* and with the intent to deprive the person of the property permanently. Note that theft does not include land since land cannot be taken away. The most common forms of theft are listed here.

larceny intentional theft of the money or personal property of another

Larceny   In most states, **larceny** is known as the intentional stealing (taking and carrying away) of money or the personal (movable) property of another person with the intent to steal. Although most larceny arrests involve the stealing of tangible property such as computer software, many states broaden the definition of larceny to include intangibles such as electricity (called theft of services), intellectual property (e.g., copyrights), and other intangibles to which an owner has a contractual or legal right such as claims to money. The law classifies larceny as either *grand larceny* (generally a felony) or *petit larceny* (generally a misdemeanor). The classification depends on the value of the property stolen and the state in which the crime was committed. For example, stealing an item worth $1,000 or less in New York State would be petit larceny.

> Ralph sees a new Corvette parked on a residential street with the doors unlocked and the key in the ignition. He gets behind the wheel, looks around to check that no one sees him, and drives away. Because he needs money, he finds a garage mechanic willing to buy the car for $8,000. Ralph sells the car and keeps the money. If the owner reports the car as missing and Ralph is apprehended by the police, he will most likely be tried in criminal court for grand larceny.

shoplifting taking merchandise from a store without paying for it

Shoplifting is a form of larceny. **Shoplifting** is the crime of taking merchandise from a store without paying for it. It is a serious problem for retail businesses. Merchants' rights in shoplifting incidents are mentioned in Chapter 4 in the discussion of the tort of false arrest.

embezzlement unlawful use or stealing of property by one who has been legally entrusted with the property

Embezzlement   The crime of **embezzlement** is the unlawful and fraudulent conversion of money or personal property by a person to whom it has been entrusted (e.g., an employee) by or for its rightful owner. The essence of embezzlement is unlawful conversion (unauthorized use) after taking legal possession.

> Samson, an administrator for a law firm, was charged with stealing more than $300,000 from her firm. She would pay the firm's bills and make deposits into the firm's bank accounts. Underreporting the amount of money she deposited into the firm's bank account and recording the lower amount onto the firm's ledger allowed her to steal the difference but balance the account. Samson was guilty of embezzlement since the funds were originally entrusted to her.

forgery making a false written instrument or the material alteration of an existing genuine written instrument with the intent to deceive

Forgery   **Forgery** is the making of a false written instrument or the material alteration of an existing genuine written instrument with the intent to deceive. Changing the date on a check that has been issued to you, for example, generally would not be forgery because changing the date does not constitute a material alteration. However, changing the amount on the check or writing a check on someone else's account and forging that person's signature would constitute forgery.

> Fetzner, who was ill, gave Thompson, a friend, written authorization to pick up a $1,000 paycheck from the health club where Fetzner worked. Instead of turning the check over to Fetzner, Thompson signed Fetzner's name and attempted to cash the

check at Fetzner's bank. The bank teller became suspicious when Thompson said that he had left all his identification cards at home and called her supervisor, who in turn immediately called the police. Thompson was taken into custody and charged with the crime of forgery.

false pretense
unlawfully obtaining, through deception or trickery, possession of another individual's lawful property

False Pretenses   The crime of obtaining money by **false pretenses** (also referred to as criminal fraud or deceit) occurs when one or more individuals knowingly and unlawfully obtain title to and possession of the lawful property of another individual by deception or trickery. Victims of false pretenses could be ordinary consumers or businesspeople. There are many Internet scams involving con artists who entice people to turn money over to them under false pretenses.

Jardine needed money to pay some heavy debts that he had run up through gambling. To raise funds to pay these debts, he induced some of his friends to invest in a telecommunications company he claimed he was starting. He gave his friends a brochure that contained pertinent information about his company and assured investors that it had good earning potential. Leslie, one friend who had already invested several thousand dollars, discovered through an investigation that the brochure produced by Jardine was false and that no such company existed. Leslie attempted to recover her money, but it was too late. Jardine used the funds to pay his debts and then disappeared. If found, Jardine could be charged with false pretenses.

blackmail crime in which a person illegally obtains money or other property by making threats; also called extortion

Blackmail   The crime committed by a person who threatens to reveal damaging or embarrassing information (which is true) in order to extract money or goods from the victim is called **blackmail** or extortion. The blackmailer most likely will have physical proof such as photographs or letters on which she or he bases the threat. Instead of a threat to expose a victim's secrets, the blackmailer may rely on a threat to do physical harm or to destroy property. In commercial blackmail, a business is the victim. The blackmailer, for example, threatens an action which would be devastating to the company's reputation. States differ as to whether the money or goods must be received in order to complete the crime.

The leader of a street gang in a large city threatened to burn several small businesses in a certain section of the city unless the owners paid a weekly "protection fee." The gang leader is guilty of blackmail.

receiving stolen property possession of property acquired as the result of some wrongful or dishonest act of taking

Receiving Stolen Property   **Receiving stolen property** occurs when an individual receives property knowing that it was stolen with the intent of depriving the true owner of the property. In most states, this crime requires that the person receiving the property knows the property was stolen. Paying an unreasonable price for stolen property may be considered knowledge. In a few states, it is sufficient to show that a person should have been aware that there is a likelihood that the property was stolen.

Wilkins is offered a cell phone for $15 from a person who says he got it and several others from the phone company during a special inventory sale. That cell phones are usually rather expensive should prompt Wilkins to contact the phone company and ask about that special sale. Otherwise, Wilkins may be prosecuted for possession of stolen property.

Insider Trading   An individual sometimes receives advance inside information about the stock of a publicly held corporation, which the general public or the current shareholders

insider trading
receiving and profiting from advance inside information about the stock of a publicly held corporation

are not yet aware of, and uses the information to his or her advantage to make a profit or to prevent a loss. This individual is guilty of **insider trading**, which is a violation of Section 10(b), Rule 10b-5 of the Securities and Exchange Act of 1934. The rule makes it clear that if you do possess inside information about certain stock, you are not to disclose it nor are you to conduct transactions around this stock until the information is made available to the general public. A recent example of insider trading involved Sam Waksal, former CEO of ImClone, who was convicted of insider trading and is currently serving a sentence at a federal prison. He had sold his stock in the company on advanced news that the Food and Drug Administration (FDA) was going to reject ImClone's application for its new cancer drug called Erbitux. As a result of the information he received, he rushed to sell the stock before it dropped in value. On the other hand, Martha Stewart, owner of Martha Stewart Living Omnimedia Inc., carried on a suspicious stock transaction involving stocks she owned in ImClone (as an outside party) that led to a full-fledged investigation by the Securities and Exchange Commission. She was accused of insider trading because she sold her stock in ImClone based on information given to her by her stockbroker, which logic would define as entirely routine and lawful (that ImClone was trading heavily and that the Waksal family was selling). The federal government could not make the charge of insider trading stick because the U.S. laws defining insider trading are so obscure that even the most skilled traders could wind up being accused of illegal trades. Thus, decisions to charge a person with insider trading are made on a case-by-case basis. Since Waksal was CEO of the company and was proven to have received inside information, he was convicted. However, because Stewart was merely a stockholder presumably receiving information from her stockbroker, the federal government did not charge her with this crime based on lack of sufficient evidence; in the words of the court: "lack of proof beyond a reasonable doubt" (U.S. District Court, New York, 305 F. Supp. 2d 368).

bribery unlawful payment used to secure new business, obtain proprietary information, or manage some personal gain

Bribery   **Bribery** is considered an unlawful payment (called a kickback or payoff) offered by one person (briber) to another person, encouraging the person being bribed to use his or her influence to obtain a favor for the briber. Bribery includes bribery of public officials and commercial bribery. Commercially, people make bribes to secure new business or to obtain proprietary information. Bribes are made to public officials for basically the same reasons. Bribery, generally a felony, occurs for the briber when the bribe is offered. Accepting the bribe is a separate crime. Thus, even if the person being bribed rejects the bribe, the briber can still be found guilty of bribery.

> Russell, a private contractor, is interested in obtaining the final bids on the construction of a new town hall for the town of Hampton. He asks his friend who works at the town hall to obtain a list of bids for him. The rule in the town is that the lowest bid must be accepted. Russell will then rework his bid if necessary. As an incentive to obtain the necessary information, Russell promises his friend 15 percent of the bid price if he wins the contract. The friend accepts the bribe and obtains the list of bids. Both parties are guilty of bribery.

Identity Theft

identity theft unlawfully obtaining and using personal identifying information of another person

A person is guilty of **identity theft** when he or she intentionally obtains personal identification information of another person without authorization and uses this information to commit fraud or other crimes. Personal identification information includes a Social Security number, a credit card number, a savings account number, or a motor vehicle operator license number. This information can be obtained by going through a person's trash, by stealing someone's mail, or by hacking into a computer system to gain access to a person's

Internet transactions. A common form of identity theft is to take over an existing credit card account and make unauthorized charges to it. The identity thief can prevent being discovered by contacting the card issuer and changing the billing address on the account. In an extreme case of identity theft, the thief may completely assume a person's identity and then open a bank account and obtain multiple credit cards. If a business gets careless about the way it conducts business, a person with criminal intent is easily capable of perpetrating the crime of identity theft using stolen personal information.

> Charter Bank, in an attempt to be customer friendly, advertised that a customer could obtain a bank loan over the Internet in one minute or less. Johnson, an ex-convict, applied and was extended a loan only on a name and Social Security number he furnished. This information was verified by the bank to be a real person by the name of Roberts; the bank, however, was unaware that Johnson had stolen Robert's identity. Because of the one-minute promise, the bank failed to verify other important information for Johnson, such as address, telephone number, and date of birth. The failure of the bank to verify credentials more thoroughly resulted in its becoming the victim of identity theft by approving this bank loan.

Identity theft is serious. Some victims spend hundreds of dollars and many days repairing damage to their good name and credit record. Some victims may even lose out on job opportunities or be denied loans for education or housing because of negative information on their credit record reports.

Although taking the identity of another person is a relatively new crime, most states now have statutes that deal specifically with this offense, and most classify it as a felony. The federal Identity Theft Act, signed into law in 1998, applies to thefts of $50,000 or more. Under this law, a person convicted of identity theft can receive a prison sentence of up to fifteen years and a possible fine and forfeiture of any personal property used to commit the crime.

Driving While Intoxicated

driving while intoxicated (DWI)
having consumed sufficient alcohol that the ability to properly operate a motor vehicle is affected

If you operate a motor vehicle (car, truck, motorcycle, or a commercial vehicle) while intoxicated, you are subject to criminal penalties. The courts have defined **driving while intoxicated (DWI)** (or in some states, driving under the influence—DUI) to mean that a person has knowingly and voluntarily consumed alcohol to such an extent as to substantially affect his or her ability to properly operate a motor vehicle. Without guidelines, this definition would be difficult for a court to apply to a DWI case. Accordingly, states have set a standard to determine legal intoxication, and they use either chemical tests of a person's blood, breath, urine, or saliva, which is .08 percent in all states (meaning 0.08 of 1 percent by weight of alcohol is in a person's blood) or a field sobriety test. A field sobriety test usually involves a police officer's assessment of the physical or cognitive ability (e.g., erratic driving, slurred speech, unsteady gait, bloodshot eyes) at the point where the driver was stopped. A driver with a blood-alcohol content (BAC) at or above .08 percent is "per se intoxicated" in the eyes of the law. This means that no additional proof of driving impairment is necessary. As the BAC rises, a person becomes increasingly intoxicated. Penalties following conviction vary sharply by state, but in all cases, they are highest for accidents involving injury or death and for repeat offenders. Some states have statutes requiring mandatory jail time for drunk-driving convictions involving a death or an injury. Generally, for drivers who are arrested in accidents in which there were no injuries or major damage, the penalties may involve a fine, imprisonment, a loss of driving privileges, or a combination of these punishments. Jail terms for first offenders are more common than they used to be. In some cases, judges may sentence offenders to do community service in such places as hospital emergency rooms and morgues.

The results of a field sobriety test conducted by the officer at the scene of the stop can provide legal grounds for an arrest and for conducting a full-scale blood alcohol content test either at the scene of the stop (with a mobile DWI processing unit) or at the police station. In most states, you can refuse to take the breath test, but by so refusing, the officer can still arrest you (on common law grounds) if there is probable cause that you are drunk. Probable cause can include the result of a field sobriety test (e.g., walking heel to toe in a straight line) or observing slurred speech, bloodshot eyes, or clumsiness. Merely smelling alcohol on your breath alone would not be enough to warrant an arrest. A full-scale test at the scene or at the police station determines the presence and quantity of consumable alcohol in a person's blood. A Breathalyzer machine is often used for this purpose. If however, you are involved in an accident in which someone is injured or killed, the Supreme Court allows the police officer to demand a blood test. Such tests are more scientifically solid than breath tests and will stand up better in court. (A field sobriety test is rebuttable through proof on the part of the driver). The actual blood test, however, must be performed by medical personnel. Although every state has "implied consent" laws stating that people who have driver's licenses automatically agree to submit to a breath, blood, or urine test to determine whether they are sober, they may still refuse to take these tests; they would then, however, be subject to having the license revoked immediately after a summary hearing. If convicted on other evidence, people who refused would then be subject to higher fines or jail terms.

A conviction for drunk driving usually carries with it some stiff penalties. Although these penalties vary from state to state, they will generally entail the loss of a driver's license for a specified amount of time, a fine, and possibly jail or prison time. Other penalties may include probation, community service, driver rehabilitation school, and substance abuse counseling. In addition to drunk-driving penalties, a driver involved in a fatal accident could face criminal charges of homicide or assault. There may also be civil penalties. These rules may seem harsh, but they exist for good reason. Impaired driving is the most frequently committed violent crime in America. According to statistics, intoxicated drivers are twenty-five times more likely to have accidents than are drivers who are not intoxicated.

Dram Shop Act

dram shop act law imposing liability on bars and taverns selling alcoholic beverages to intoxicated persons

Throughout the country, public awareness of the drunk-driver problem has revived a century-old law called the dram shop act. The **dram shop act** imposes liability on bars or taverns selling alcoholic beverages to an intoxicated person or to any person under the influence of an alcoholic beverage (some states include the sale to minors). Two Rochester, New York, restaurants together paid $2 million to a person injured in a DWI-related crash. The injured person was struck by an intoxicated driver who had been drinking earlier at the two restaurants. Some state courts have extended civil liability under the dram shop laws to include liquor stores and grocery stores that sell to intoxicated persons and minors and have also extended liability to persons who host private parties.

CYBER CRIME

computer crime using a computer for fraudulent purposes

A **computer crime** is a crime committed with or through the use of computers. Many of these crimes are existing traditional crimes committed in cyberspace and are therefore referred to as *cyber crimes*. Very often, traditional law with some modification (issues of personal jurisdiction) is applied to crimes committed in cyberspace. In addition, governments have enacted new laws that relate directly to wrongs committed in cyberspace. Cyber crimes are very much in the news today. They range from simple pranks by kids who enjoy the intellectual challenge of criminal activity (as if the computer were a video game) to extracting information from a nation's governmental computers for espionage purposes by a highly skilled technician. The motivation behind this type of criminal activity is a result of the much more prevalent role of computers in the lives of individuals and families, in the business world, and at the federal and state government levels. Unfortunately, the growth of computers and computer applications has opened up a new frontier of crime.

The fact that computers are used to commit crimes does not necessarily make those crimes computer crimes. A person such as a drug dealer who uses a computer to keep computerized records of drug deals is not a computer criminal. In addition, individuals who steal computers or computer equipment or use computer facilities to commit traditional crimes such as theft or blackmail would not generally qualify as computer criminals. These crimes could be prosecuted under traditional law.

Computer criminals are those that primarily employ computer technology to commit their crimes; some traditional laws, however, may also be violated. Using the Internet to sell fake driver's licenses and pocketing the money or running an illegal raffle on the Internet that solicited $20 chances to win an expensive automobile are examples of what it would take to be considered a computer criminal. The person carrying on these illicit activities can be classified as a computer hacker. Some other examples of cyber crimes include altering a computer program that enables you to steal money; harrassment and stalking in cyberspace; creating a destructive computer virus that shuts down computers at your place of business; infiltrating the computerized files at your college and making unauthorized grade changes; distributing child pornography on the Internet; as a department head in a business, placing a fictitious person on a computerized payroll and then taking the money for personal use; as a bank employee, gaining access to a customer list to steal bank account numbers; and finally, as a citizen of a foreign country, breaking into a U.S. Department of Defense computer network, extracting information, and then selling the information to another foreign country (cyberterrorism). Intent determines the severity of the crime. Where no criminal intent beyond mischief or curiosity exists, such as that of a young child getting the urge to explore on a computer, the crime may be handled by the police as a minor offense. However, where there is a serious intent to interfere with another person's legitimate access to computers, prosecution will in most states generally be for improper access plus some other crime such as theft or fraud.

Significant Legislation Affecting Cyber crimes

Virtually every state has passed computer crime legislation. Some have enacted new comprehensive computer crimes statutes, and others have simply modified existing criminal statutes to fit computer crimes. Every state prohibits unauthorized access to another's computer, and most states prohibit the alteration, deletion, or modification of another's computer data without authorization. Most state laws specify stiff fines and prison terms for those who tamper with or illegally gain access to data in computers. The Computer Fraud and Abuse Act (CFAA) and the Electronic Communications Privacy Act (ECPA) are federal statutes that have made it easier for prosecutors to file charges against individuals for computer-related crimes without having to make existing laws "fit" these particular offenses. The CFAA prohibits unauthorized access to federal computers (to obtain classified or restricted government information), to the computers of a financial institution (to obtain financial records), or to the computers of a credit reporting agency and a credit card issuer (to obtain credit card information). Liability for unauthorized access to other computers depends on whether there was an intent to defraud or cause damage. You may recall that a Cornell graduate student was convicted of violating the CFAA for creating an Internet "worm" that was transformed into a virus that infected thousands of computers at military sites, medical research facilities, and other universities all in a matter of hours. The ECPA prohibits the unauthorized interception and disclosure of the content of electronic communications of another person, including voice mail and electronic mail, and to unlawfully use the information obtained. For example, gaining access to another person's e-mail without permission constitutes a crime under the ECPA.

In many investigations of computer-related crimes, federal agencies assist local investigators. (One of the duties assigned to the Secret Service is the investigation of computer fraud.) Even if the case results in a local prosecution, federal agencies may assist as long as the crime violates federal law.

RICO: RACKETEER INFLUENCED AND CORRUPT ORGANIZATIONS ACT

RICO Racketeer Influenced and Corrupt Organizations Act

The Racketeer Influenced and Corrupt Organizations Act (**RICO**) was enacted in 1970. To put it bluntly, RICO was intended to destroy the Mafia. As a result, a long string of mob bosses once considered untouchable were convicted and incarcerated for extortion, bribery, kidnapping, arson, robbery, loan sharking, murder, prostitution, illegal drug sales, the infiltration of legitimate businesses (investing income obtained from illegal activities), interstate transportation of stolen property, embezzlement of union funds, and wire and mail fraud. In the 1980s, however, civil lawyers discovered that a certain section of the RICO act applies not only to a wide variety of federal and state criminal acts, but, in addition, to civil violations (related to criminal activity) whether by members of organized crime or by lawful businesses. Better yet, any person who succeeded in establishing a civil RICO claim would automatically receive judgment in the amount of three times the actual damages. As a result, creative attorneys began to depict just about any civil wrong flowing from criminal activity as allowing them to file a civil RICO action. Civil wrongs involving common law fraud, product defect, and breach of contract as well as those civil wrongs flowing from the crimes of mail and wire fraud are common examples prompting attorneys to initiate a law suit. Congress made the act relatively easy to enforce by lowering the standards of proof required to seize assets, allowing for substantial amounts of money to be forfeited. In one drug-smuggling case, nearly $50 million in airplanes, vehicles, real estate, and cash were seized, whereas in another drug case, the federal government seized an entire shopping center and several homes. However, during the 1990s, the federal courts, guided by the United States Supreme Court, "slowed down" the number of civil lawsuits allowed under RICO. Consequently, today it is not easy to bring a civil action under the RICO statute, and the statute is very seldom brought against Mafia bosses and their underlings. Rather, it is applied in almost any context to individuals, businesses, political protest groups, and terrorist organizations. In a recent case, Eastman Kodak Company brought a suit against three individuals alleged to have been involved in a kickback and bribery plot that illegally deflated the value of Kodak property in Rochester, New York. While the three individuals faced criminal charges, none of the charges involved racketeering.

defense reason an accused offers to excuse his or her guilt in a criminal action; also, reason offered by defendant in a lawsuit for being relieved of responsibility

COMMON DEFENSES TO CRIMES

Sometimes individuals are not criminally responsible for their acts due to certain defenses. Figure 3.2 depicts these defenses. A **defense** is an argument that a defendant (the accused in a criminal action) brings out at trial to legally excuse his or her guilt to a crime and therefore win an acquittal. Some common defenses to criminal liability are

FIGURE 3.2
Defenses to Crimes

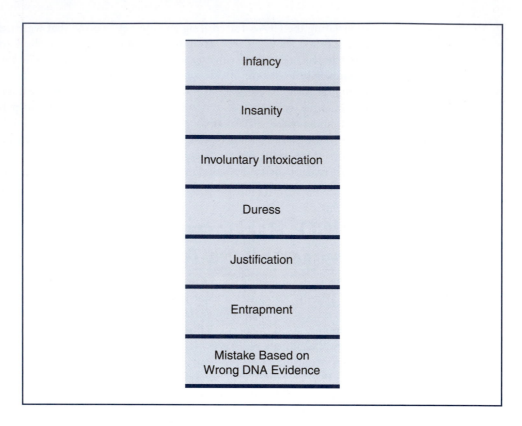

infancy, insanity, involuntary intoxication, duress, justification, entrapment, and mistake based on wrong DNA evidence.

Infancy

Most states today do not impose full criminal liability on children under the age of eighteen; a number of states set the age of responsibility at sixteen, and some set it at seventeen. These children are referred to as juvenile offenders rather than as criminals and are subject to juvenile court jurisdiction rather than the jurisdiction of adult criminal courts. The decision of how to handle a juvenile is based on the seriousness of the crime; the manner in which the offense was committed; the juvenile's prior record; and the cooperation, attitude, and behavior of the juvenile and parents involved. The juvenile may be placed on probation and under the supervision of a probation officer or in a rehabilitation facility, such as a group home. Juveniles who commit serious offenses and whose behavior poses a threat to society are placed in a secured juvenile detention facility.

When juveniles above a certain age commit serious crimes, they may be tried as adults. In most states, children below the age of seven cannot be charged even with juvenile offenses, no matter how serious their actions may appear to others.

Insanity

Whether an accused was insane (of unsound mind) at the time he or she committed a criminal act is generally decided by a court after hearing all the evidence in the case. Psychiatrists for the defense usually produce evidence that the accused had a mental disease or defect and, consequently, did not know right from wrong. Psychiatrists for the prosecution often testify in court that the accused did indeed know what he or she was doing. The court weighs the conflicting testimony before rendering its decision. A few jurisdictions recognize that an accused can be partially insane with respect to the circumstances surrounding the commission of a crime but sane as to other matters. In practice, the defense of insanity is seldom used.

Involuntary Intoxication

Like insanity, involuntary intoxication resulting from ingestion of alcohol or other drugs is a defense to a criminal act because the intent (the desire) to commit a crime is lacking. A person with a drugged mind cannot distinguish right from wrong. Intoxication is involuntary when the accused can show that he or she was forced to take the intoxicating substance or to consume the alcohol without knowing what it was. Involuntary intoxication may result from secretly spiked punch or drug-laced foods.

Duress

duress crime committed by a person who was forced to act against his or her own free will

An accused who has committed a crime under **duress**—forced to act against his or her own free will—may have no criminal liability for the unlawful act. An example of duress is a mother forced to rob a bank by someone holding her children hostage. There is no criminal intent on the part of the mother, and therefore, the mother has committed no crime. The mother must, however, show that there was a threat of death or serious bodily harm, either to her or to another person, such as a family member (in this case, her children). The mother must also show that there was fear that the threat would be carried out and that there was no reasonable opportunity to escape the threatened harm. Duress will excuse a person from liability from any crime except one in which the accused is compelled to take someone else's life.

Justification

Justification excuses a person for the commission of an act that otherwise constitutes a crime. The act is generally committed to avoid harm to one's person or property, as in self-defense. Justification might be used as a possible defense when a burglar enters a house to commit a robbery and is killed by the homeowner, who shoots to protect his life or property. In this case, reasonable cause existed to take another's life, and the homeowner may have no criminal liability.

A person acting in self-defense can use enough force that is reasonable to prevent harm. For example, a person you are arguing with at a party gives you a slight push. You then pull a knife out of your pocket and cut his face. Your action is unreasonable. A slight push does not justify a cut on the face with a knife. A higher degree of force called deadly force could be considered reasonable to counter an immediate threat of death or great bodily harm. Further, once a threat has passed and you have successfully defended yourself, it would be improper for you to continue using force.

Entrapment

entrapment a law enforcement officer persuading or forcing a person to commit a crime

Entrapment applies when a law enforcement officer persuades a law-abiding person to commit a crime. The key to the entrapment defense is that the accused had no intention of committing the crime and in fact would not have committed it until persuaded to do so by the officer. Why would a law enforcement officer "set up" a person to commit a crime and then make an arrest? An officer might use this strategy to trap a known criminal who has committed crimes and has been arrested but, for lack of evidence or through legal technicalities, has not been convicted. Entrapment is not a defense if a person has already made up his or her mind to commit a crime and then does so with assistance from a law enforcement officer.

A police officer suspects that Miles is a drug dealer. His suspicion is based on information provided by a reliable informant. The officer, wearing a concealed video recorder, attempts to buy cocaine, an illegal drug, from Miles, indicating that he needs it to treat a medical condition. Miles claims that he himself knows nothing about drugs but is aware of someone who might be able to procure cocaine. The officer agrees to meet Miles two hours later. When Miles returns two hours later and offers to sell the drugs to the officer, the officer arrests him.

In this case, Miles's attorney could offer entrapment as a defense if Miles is charged with of selling illegal drugs, claiming that he was induced to commit a crime he would not otherwise have committed.

Mistake Based on Wrong DNA Evidence

DNA evidence has altered what criminal investigations can achieve at a crime scene. It has exonerated individuals wrongfully arrested and who might otherwise have been wrongfully convicted and imprisoned and even awaiting execution on death row. DNA evidence can be obtained from fluids and other substances produced by the body such as blood, semen, urine, saliva, perspiration, hair, and skin. It can be matched to the suspect as evidence that he or she was present at the crime scene. A person's fingerprints were at first considered the way to associate a suspect with a crime. However, DNA has rapidly become the method of choice when it comes to linking suspects with crime scenes because investigators have a much better chance of finding DNA evidence than of locating a good fingerprint. Furthermore, though each person's fingerprints are distinctive, a person's DNA is more distinctive. Every cell in the human body contains DNA, and DNA molecules contain the genetic code. The probability against the DNA of one individual matching another is in the hundreds of millions or even billions. Does DNA evidence found at a crime scene conclusively establish guilt? The answer is no; however, once DNA is matched to a suspect, a prosecutor or defense attorney would have much stronger evidence of guilt.

THE CRIMINAL JUSTICE SYSTEM

The United States has two distinct criminal justice systems: federal and state. Each system is composed of three elements: the police, courts, and corrections. A person who has committed a crime or is suspected of having committed a crime is handled through one of these two systems. Figure 3.3, which displays the primary steps in the criminal justice system at the state and local levels, outlines the process that takes place when a felony is committed. The steps broadly parallel the federal system. A person accused of a crime is protected by many guarantees found in the Constitution, particularly the Fourth, Fifth, Sixth, and Eighth Amendments in the Bill of Rights. This means that officials involved in the criminal justice process must respect the rights of accused individuals throughout the entire process. These guarantees apply to federal crimes and, through the Fourteenth Amendment, to crimes covered by state laws.

Police

arrest to take into police custody

The first step in the criminal justice process is the arrest by a police officer of a person who has actually committed or is suspected of committing a crime. The term **arrest** means that a person is taken into custody for the purpose of charging him or her with a crime. An arrest occurs whether a person submits to authority or is seized by force. An arrest is complete when the suspect is no longer free to walk away from the arresting

FIGURE 3.3
Primary Steps in a
Felony Criminal Case

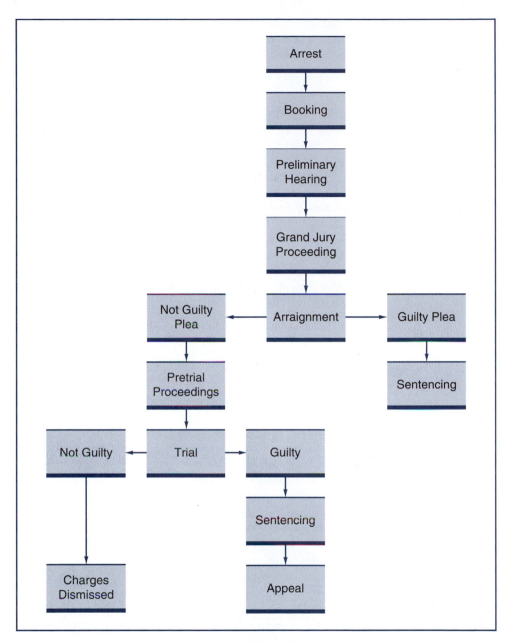

officer. If the criminal act was not committed in the police officer's presence, the arrest must be made on **probable cause**, a reasonable belief that a crime has been committed and that this person is likely the one who committed it, or the officer has knowledge that a crime has been committed and there is probable cause to believe that the crime was committed by a particular suspect. It should be emphasized that probable cause is more than suspicion. Reasonable suspicion is the standard that a police officer uses to stop a person briefly and ask questions but not take that person into custody. In other words, the person stopped for questioning would be free to go at any time.

Early one evening Greene, a police officer, received a call on his police radio that a person passing in front of the Niagara National Bank (which was closed) reported a male loitering on the bank's property in a manner to suggest that he might be "casing" the

probable cause
reasonable belief that a
crime has been
committed or certain
facts exist

bank for a break-in. Greene proceeded to the scene. Upon arrival, he immediately drove around behind the bank and spotted the person in question with burglar tools at the back entrance to the bank. Greene then took the person into custody.

In this example, the arrest was legal since Greene had probable cause to believe that the suspect was about to attempt an unauthorized entry into the bank.

After a police officer arrests a person, the Fourth Amendment gives the police officer the legal right to conduct a reasonable search of that person and the area immediately around him or her for evidence and for hidden weapons. (This is true even if the officer and the arrestee are of different sexes.) If the arrested person is driving a car, it may also be searched. As the result of expanded U.S. Supreme Court rulings (*United States* v. *Ross,* 456 U.S. 798; *New York* v. *Beltron,* 453 U.S. 454), the police, with probable cause, may search every part of a vehicle and the contents that may conceal the object of the search. Examples are the glove compartment, the trunk, and any sealed container, package, or bag found in these places. While most cases involve the glove compartment and the trunk, a search may be conducted under the car as well as under the hood or behind the rear seat. Since there is a greater expectation of privacy in the trunk of a car because the contents of the trunk are shielded from public view, a greater justification is required for police officers to get into the trunk (*Gill* v. *State of Texas,* 625 SW 2d 307, 310–312). A good example is *Irvin,* 210 S.W. 3d. 360 (MO. Ct. App) in which the finding of a small quantity of marijuana in the passenger compartment permitted the officer to search the trunk for more. The vehicle may be searched even if the police officer doesn't get around to conducting this search until after the person arrested has left the vehicle as, for example, when he or she is handcuffed and in the backseat of the police car. (A review of *New York* v. *Belton* referred to previously allowed this interpretation.) (The Supreme Court has recently ruled that police officers who have probable cause to stop drivers suspected of wrongdoing may also search the personal belongings of passengers simply because of the passengers' presence in the car.)

Following an arrest, the suspect is usually taken to a police station and "booked." Booking is the official police processing of the arrest, meaning that a record is made of the arrest. It consists of entering in the police log the suspect's name, the time of arrest, and the offense. The suspect is then fingerprinted and photographed and may be required to participate in a lineup. A lineup is a procedure in which a suspect is placed in a group for the purpose of being viewed by a witness. All suspects in custody (arrested) who are interrogated (questioned) must, according to the Fifth and Sixth Amendments, first be warned that they have the right to remain silent, that anything they say may be used against them in a court of law, and that they have the right to an attorney.

Miranda warnings
rights read to a suspect upon arrest

These rights, which are read to a suspect, are commonly called the **Miranda warnings**, based on the famous *Miranda* v. *Arizona* case (384 U.S. 436), decided in 1966 (although the *Miranda* decision was challenged, the Supreme Court, nevertheless, in 2000, held that the Miranda rights were constitutionally based). The opportunity to exercise these rights must be afforded to the suspect throughout the interrogation. If a police officer questions a suspect immediately after the arrest without giving the suspect the Miranda warnings, nothing the suspect says can be offered into evidence against the suspect at trial. Figure 3.4 shows an official document listing these rights. An accused who voluntarily decides to answer any questions may also stop and refuse to answer further questions at any time, as long as the suspect unequivocally and assertively requests to exercise this right. A statement such as "maybe I should talk to a lawyer" is not enough.

Jonas is arrested for obtaining money fraudulently. He is booked at the police station and read the Miranda warnings. The police question him over a long period of time without food or water or sleep. Jonas finally agrees to talk to the police and confesses to the crime.

FIGURE 3.4
Rights Read to a Suspect
Who Is Interrogated
After Arrest

MIAMI POLICE DEPARTMENT
NOTIFICATION AND WAIVER

Mr.
Mrs. . . . .,I am now advising you that you have
Miss
a right to remain silent and that you do not have to answer any questions if you
do not wish to; also, that anything you do say to me can be used against you
in a court of law; also, that you have a right to consult with an attorney before
answering any questions and to have the attorney present with you during the
questioning by me if you so desire; also, that if you cannot afford an attorney,
then one will be provided for you. If you do consent and agree to discuss this
matter with me without an attorney present, you can terminate the discussion at
any time.

Do you understand what I have just told you?   RESPONSE: . . . .

Do you agree to waive these rights and do
you consent to discuss this matter with me?   RESPONSE: . . . .

Officer: Complete reverse side of this card.

THE UNDERSIGNED POLICE OFFICER READ THE NOTIFICATION ON
THE REVERSE OF THIS CARD TO THE INDIVIDUAL NAMED AND RE-
CEIVED THE RESPONSES INDICATED AT THE TIME AND DATE NOTED
BELOW.

DATE . . . . TIME . . . . .M.

PLACE . . . .

PERSON INTERVIEWED . . . .

OFFICER(S) INTERVIEWING . . . .

. . . .

. . . .

. . . .

. . . .

This Waiver/Notification, properly completed, will become a part of the Case File.

In this case, Jonas did not freely and voluntarily waive his Miranda rights. The actions of the police during the interrogation amounted to coercion.

In most cases, an arrested person can be released on bail at any stage in a criminal proceeding. **Bail** is the security given to the court to release a person from jail and to ensure the person's appearance at a hearing or trial. Bail usually consists of cash or other property. The amount of bail depends on the seriousness of the crime and the probability that the accused may flee. If the accused shows up in court when required, the bail is returned; if not, the bail is forfeited. A defendant who fails to make bail is confined in jail until the required court appearance. Instead of bail, the court may release the person "on recognizance"—a promise to appear in court when required—when the accused has strong community and family ties and steady employment. Suspects charged with very serious crimes will usually be held in jail until trial.

bail money or property
given to a court to
obtain the release of a
person from jail

Courts

Within a reasonable time (usually forty-eight hours) after arrest, the accused must be brought before a judge for a procedure called the **initial appearance**. At this appearance, the suspect will be informed of the charge for which he or she is being held, given the

initial appearance
person's first
appearance before a
judge after being
arrested

Miranda warnings, and told of the right to post bail (if this was not determined at the arrest phase). It is quite possible that at this point the judge may determine that there is not sufficient evidence to hold the suspect for further criminal proceedings and will dismiss the case.

After the accused has been arrested and booked and has made an initial appearance before a judge, the next step in some states (generally the states that do not use grand juries) is a rather formal hearing called a **preliminary hearing**, held to further evaluate whether sufficient evidence exists to proceed to trial with the accused's case. The preliminary hearing (conducted in the manner of a minitrial) has many of the characteristics of a criminal trial but is not nearly as elaborate. Both the prosecutor and the defense counsel are usually present at this hearing. Prosecutors rarely call witnesses, saving them for the actual trial. If a judge believes that the chance of a conviction is slight, the charge against the accused is dismissed.

Whether a preliminary hearing takes place, the next step in the criminal justice process is to formally accuse the arrested person. One method for accomplishing this is the indictment by a grand jury. An **indictment** (sometimes called a *presentment*) is a formal, written accusation of a crime by a grand jury against an individual (Figure 3.5). A grand jury consists of a group of people (generally about twenty-three) from the community (the term *grand* refers to the relatively large number of jurors called to serve). It does not try cases—that is, it does not determine guilt or innocence—but formally (by majority vote) determines whether the accused should go to trial for a crime or have the charges against him or her dismissed for lack of evidence. Generally, the grand jury used in almost all states hears only the prosecutor's side of the case and therefore is likely to find probable cause. The prosecutor—usually the district attorney (D.A.)—represents "the people." The prosecutor often presents witnesses to testify against the accused (the defendant). Instead of an indictment by a grand jury, some states bring formal charges by means of an *information*. This document serves the same purpose as an indictment. The information, however, is filed by the prosecutor based on the evidence obtained at the preliminary hearing.

A person who has been formally accused of a crime, by either an indictment or an information, must then be arraigned. An **arraignment** occurs when the defendant is brought before a judge, formally notified of the charges in the indictment, and asked for a plea to the charges of either guilty or not guilty to all elements of the crime. If a guilty plea is entered, the judge must determine if the defendant understands the consequences of such a plea. If the judge is satisfied, no trial is necessary and the defendant is scheduled for sentencing. Prior to the sentencing, the court orders a presentence report. This report gives detailed background information about the defendant's education, family, employment, and previous criminal record, as well as personal, social, and emotional histories.

If the defendant pleads not guilty, the next stage will be the *pretrial proceedings*. These proceedings consist of hearings on behalf of the accused (by his or her attorney) asking that the charges be dismissed because of lack of evidence or because of other defenses, such as insanity. At this time, plea negotiations may also take place: The accused may enter a guilty plea in return for the prosecutor's assurance that he or she will ask the judge to reduce the charge or sentence. If the pretrial proceedings do not bring results, the case will be scheduled for trial. In felony cases, the defendant has a constitutional right to a jury trial but may waive this right. If the defendant waives this right, the case will be decided by a judge. During the trial, both the prosecutor and the defendant's lawyer may present evidence. Acting for the state, the prosecutor must present evidence to substantiate the charge against the defendant. The defense attorney may challenge the validity of the prosecutor's evidence and may also present additional evidence.

preliminary hearing
hearing immediately following an arrest to determine if probable cause for the arrest existed and whether continued restraint of the accused was warranted

indictment formal, written accusation by a grand jury that one has committed a crime

arraignment charging a person with a crime and asking for that person's plea

FIGURE 3.5
A Grand Jury Indictment

STATE OF NEW YORK
COUNTY COURT
COUNTY OF MONROE

THE PEOPLE OF THE STATE OF NEW YORK

VS.

LINDA SUZANNE GORDON

THE GRAND JURY OF THE COUNTY OF MONROE, by this indictment, accuse the defendant, LINDA SUZANNE GORDON, of the crime of Burglary in the First Degree, in violation of Section 140.30, subdivision 2, of the Penal Law of the State of New York, committed as follows:

The defendant, on or about August 12, 2008, in the County of Monroe, State of New York, did enter the dwelling house of another, to wit, James Mason, with the intent to commit a crime therein, and while in the dwelling, caused physical injury to James Mason by shooting him in the neck.

Ronald A Vats

RONALD A. VATS
DISTRICT ATTORNEY
OF MONROE COUNTY

Although in many respects the trial itself resembles a civil trial (discussed in Chapter 5), several significant points apply only to a criminal trial:

- The defendant is presumed innocent until proven guilty.
- The defendant must be proven guilty beyond a reasonable doubt. Although the Supreme Court has not defined "reasonable doubt," the proof must be so conclusive and complete that all reasonable doubts no longer exist in the mind of the ordinary person. Some judges would say that the jury would need to be 90 percent certain.
- Evidence obtained in an illegal manner must be excluded from the trial.
- The defendant does not have to testify, and no unfavorable conclusions may be drawn from this failure to testify.
- The defendant has the right to be present to hear all the evidence presented.

- The defendant has a constitutional guarantee of a speedy trial.
- In criminal cases, twelve jurors (in most states) as well as alternates are required.
- The verdict is required to be unanimous. (Less than unanimous verdicts, however, have been held constitutionally permissible in state trials).

If the verdict is not guilty, the charges are dismissed, and the defendant is released from the criminal process. After either a conviction or a plea of guilty, the defendant is brought before the judge for sentencing. Sentencing is the last stage of a criminal trial. The judge, who has studied the presentence report, tries to make the sentence appropriate for the defendant and yet remain within the guidelines set down by the law. Options open to judges include incarceration with the possibility of parole, fine, probation, community-based programs, home confinement, shock incarceration, boot camp (for youthful offenders), or a combination of these. In states that allow it, the death penalty is also an option in some murder cases.

After conviction, however, the defendant can appeal to the next-higher court, asking for a review of the case. In most jurisdictions, this right of appeal is automatic. The appeals court, based on its review, may uphold the conviction reached in the lower (trial) court. If the appeals court decides to reverse the conviction, the defendant is discharged. Also, if an error of law—such as improper introduction of evidence—is found in the procedures used in the case, the appeals court may reverse the decision of the lower court and order a new trial. It should be noted that there is no absolute right on the part of a criminal defendant to appeal a criminal conviction to the U.S. Supreme Court. (Chapter 2 discussed ways in which cases reach the U.S. Supreme Court.)

Although the defendant can appeal a conviction to the next-higher court, a prosecutor normally cannot appeal the case if the defendant is found not guilty.

Corrections

After a convicted offender is sentenced, the responsibility of carrying out the sentence moves to the state or to the federal government if the conviction is for a federal crime. Offenders sentenced to prison serve their time as inmates in a maximum-, medium-, or minimum-security institution. If prison personnel believe that the inmate is ready to live in the community, the inmate may be paroled from prison after serving only part of the sentence. **Parole** is a reward allowing early release for felons who have done well in prison and seem to be a good risk for successful return to the community. The inmate is then required to participate in a community-based correction program under the supervision of a parole officer. Community-based correction programs include a variety of activities and programs within the community; for example, the paroled inmate may be required to attend personal- and job-counseling seminars and behavior modification sessions or to live in a nonsecured halfway house, departing daily to attend work or school and returning after work to participate in group therapy sessions. Parolees are subject to strict rules that guide their behavior and limit their activities. Any parolee who violates these rules can be returned to the institution to serve the remainder of the sentence.

parole conditional release from prison allowing a person to serve the rest of a prison sentence outside prison

Instead of receiving a prison sentence, an offender may have the sentence suspended and be given probation. **Probation** (conditional discharge) allows a person convicted of an offense to avoid prison and remain free in the community subject to certain rules and conditions, usually under the supervision of a probation officer. If the rules are violated, probation may be revoked and the offender sent to prison under the terms of the original sentence. Rules imposed upon a probationer will depend on the offense committed. For example, a child molester can be forbidden to associate with young children, and a tax violator can be required to submit his or her tax return to the probation officer periodically for review. In many cases, the probationer is required to pay restitution to the victim of his or her crime.

probation allowing a person convicted of an offense to avoid prison and be free on good behavior, usually under the supervision of a probation officer

Summary

Civil law has to do with civil (private) matters. It establishes rules that protect the rights and property of individuals from harmful acts by other individuals or a business or government. An individual harmed by others may initiate a lawsuit and seek compensation in the form of money damages. Criminal law, on the other hand, has to do with crimes (public wrongs). It establishes rules to protect society from acts of individuals who are dangerous and threaten peace and order against society as a whole. A person who commits a crime is subject to arrest by the government and, if found guilty, is punished by confinement, a fine, or in certain cases, death for harm done to society. Serious crimes called felonies are punishable by death or by imprisonment for more than one year. Misdemeanors, less serious than felonies, are punishable by confinement for up to one year. Wrongs less serious than misdemeanors—variously called violations, infractions, or petty offenses—are not crimes but could bring a short sentence in a local jail.

There is no uniform law of crimes. The federal government and each state define and punish crimes according to their own guidelines. Even among states, criminal statutes vary. An act that is a crime in one state may not be a crime in another state.

The selected crimes discussed in this chapter were assault, robbery, arson, burglary, many forms of theft, insider trading, bribery, identity theft, driving while intoxicated, and computer crimes. RICO, a federal law originally passed to prevent criminal infiltration of legitimate businesses, also reaches white-collar crimes whether by criminal organizations or by otherwise lawful businesses. Cyber crime is committed with or through the use of computers. Significant legislation has been passed at both the state and federal levels to deal with cyber crimes. Two important federal laws dealing with computer crimes are the Computer Fraud and Abuse Act and the Electronic Communications Privacy Act. The most common defenses—reasons that accused individuals offer to excuse guilt for criminal acts—raised in the chapter are infancy, insanity, involuntary intoxication, duress, justification, entrapment, and mistake based on wrong DNA evidence.

People who commit crimes are handled through either the federal or state criminal justice system, which consists of the police, the courts, and corrections. The first step is the arrest of the individual suspected of committing a crime. This arrest is usually based on probable cause, a reasonable belief that a crime has been committed and that the arrested person is probably the one who committed it. When arrested for a felony, the accused is "booked," interrogated, and at an initial appearance before a judge, formally notified of the crime he or she is suspected of committing. A preliminary hearing may then be held to further evaluate whether sufficient evidence exists to proceed to trial. If the charge is not dismissed at this point, a grand jury is convened. This body generally is composed of twenty-three people who examine evidence presented by the prosecutor; they may issue an indictment, formally accusing the defendant of the crime. (Sometimes the formal accusation is made by means of an information filed by the prosecutor.)

At the arraignment, which is the next step, the accused is formally notified of the charges in the indictment and asked to plead guilty or not guilty. If the defendant pleads not guilty, the next stage will usually be pretrial proceedings. If these proceedings produce no results, a trial will be scheduled. At the trial, the prosecutor, acting for the state, must prove beyond a reasonable doubt that the defendant has committed the crime of which he or she is accused. Only upon conviction can the defendant be sentenced. If there is no appeal or if the appeals court upholds the conviction rendered in the lower court, the sentence will be carried out.

From arrest to conviction, the defendant is entitled to numerous constitutional guarantees, including the right to Miranda warnings and the right to bail.

Important Legal Terms

arraignment	blackmail (extortion)	cyber crimes
arrest	bribery	defense
arson	burglary	dram shop act
assault	computer crime	driving while intoxicated (DWI)
bail	crime	duress

embezzlement	initial appearance	probable cause
entrapment	insider trading	probation
false pretense	larceny	receiving stolen property
felony	Miranda warnings	RICO
forgery	misdemeanor	robbery
identity theft	parole	shoplifting
indictment	preliminary hearing	theft

Questions and Problems for Discussion

1. Milmur, at age seventeen, wrote a computer program creating a worm that took over thousands of computers. A computer security analyst called it "the most advanced worm yet." It disrupted commerce and people's lives. Milmur agreed to plead guilty to a federal charge of unauthorized access to a computer to further a fraud since he used the program to steal credit card information and defraud people nationwide. Friends and family urged the judge to be lenient in his sentencing, claiming he was a brilliant computer programmer who had the skills to help the country defend itself against the growing threat of cyberterrorism. If you were the judge would you exercise leniency in your sentencing?

2. Rines was a married man with three young children. Carter, an acquaintance of Rines, had seen Kim, a young college professor, and Rines together on several occasions at various social functions. One evening, Carter followed them to a hotel and discovered that they had checked into the same room. Under the pretext of being a bellhop with a message, Carter went to the room and photographed the couple, partially dressed. Carter then sent the photo to Rines at his place of business with a note threatening to also send a picture to Rines's wife unless he was paid $10,000 in cash. Rines was to place the money in an envelope and leave the envelope in Carter's PO box at the main post office within one week. Rines notified the police and then followed Carter's instructions. Carter picked up the money at the post office and was immediately arrested. With what crime will Carter be charged?

3. The Best Cab Company was hired by the county's Department of Social Services to take many of its Medicaid clients to various locations in a large city. Social Services was then billed for all the transportation costs. Following an audit of Social Services records, the cab company was indicted by a grand jury on the following charges: inflating mileage, overstating fares and charging higher individual rates for group rides, charging two-way fares for one-way trips, and charging different rates for identical trips. What crime (or crimes) did the cab company commit?

4. Police officer Ron Schmurtz pulled a car over to the side of the road for making an illegal U-turn. When he approached the car, he discovered five teenage boys. The officer looked the vehicle over but had no reason to be suspicious about any criminal activity taking place in or around the vehicle. However, because the driver and his passengers were teenagers, he felt that they used drugs. Consequently, he ordered them all out of the car, searched the car's interior, and discovered some illegal drugs. Schmurtz then placed all the teenagers under arrest. Was the search that Schmurtz conducted legal?

5. How can a police officer determine whether a driver is "under the influence"?

6. Furman was driving her truck down Main Street in her hometown without wearing a seatbelt. A police officer observed the seatbelt violation, pulled Furman over, placed her in his squad car, and drove her to the local police station, where she was made to remove her shoes and jewelry and empty her pockets. Officers took her mug shot and placed her alone in a jail cell for about an hour, after which she was taken before a judge and released on bond. She was charged with violating the seatbelt law, a misdemeanor. She pleaded no contest to the seatbelt misdemeanor and paid a $100 fine. Furman then filed suit, alleging that the actions of the town, the judge, and the police violated her Fourth Amendment right to be free from unreasonable seizure. She contended that rules forbade police officers to make

warrantless misdemeanor arrests except in cases of breach of the peace tending toward violence. Is Furman correct?

7. Walkman, a student at Banes College, stole several new football helmets from the college sports locker room. He sold the helmets for a very low price to Favor, the owner of a local sporting goods store. After reading an article in the newspaper about the theft, the owner of the store was quite sure the helmets he purchased from Walkman were the ones that had been stolen. Nevertheless, he did not notify either the police or the appropriate college personnel that he had bought the helmets. Instead, he marked them for sale at a special price and placed them on a shelf with other football gear. Although he paid Walkman for the football helmets, is Favor liable for the commission of any crime? Is Walkman? Explain.

8. Furenya was employed as the manager of a state-controlled betting parlor, the Off Track Betting Corporation. One of her responsibilities was to deposit the daily receipts of money in a local bank. Because she was heavily in debt, Furenya devised a way to take $300 from each deposit to pay her personal creditors. She continued this practice for over a year until the state auditors made a surprise check of the betting parlor's accounting records. When a shortage was discovered and traced to Furenya, she was arrested. With what crime could she be charged?

9. Evans, an unlicensed financial planner, met with Ann Gilmore, a prospective investor, to review her investment portfolio and to recommend a placement for the $100,000 that Gilmore recently inherited. He recommended that she invest $100,000 in certain mutual funds. She agreed and made out a check to Evans as he requested. In turn, he agreed to invest the money in the mutual fund company and send the company the $100,000. Evans never intended to invest the money. Instead, he used the money personally to pay bills and to purchase a new car. What crime has Evans committed? Explain.

10. A police officer on routine patrol in her police car at about 3 A.M. received a call over the police radio describing a burglary in progress at a pizza parlor in her patrol zone. When she arrived at the pizza parlor, a short distance from where she received the call, she spotted a person who was getting into a car parked next to the pizza parlor. If the police officer wished to make an arrest in the belief that this person had committed the robbery, what would be the basis for the arrest?

Cases for Review

1. Police officers arrived at Grant's home to investigate a tip that Grant's residence was being used to sell drugs. At the time, Grant was not at home, but he did arrive home in his car while police were questioning a man and woman parked in front of the house about possession of drug paraphernalia. He parked at the end of the driveway, got out of his car, and shut the door. One of the police officers, who was some 30 feet away, called to Grant, who responded by going to the patrol car. The police officer immediately arrested Grant, handcuffed him, and locked him in the back seat of the police car. The police officer then went back and searched Grant's car which, of course, was 30 feet away. The search revealed a gun and a bag of cocaine in the pocket of a jacket on the backseat. Grant was charged with possession of a narcotic drug for sale and paraphernalia (i.e., the plastic bag in which the cocaine was found). Grant moved to suppress the evidence seized in the car on the grounds that the warrantless search violated his Fourth Amendment rights—more specifically that the police had no right to search the car since it was not within reaching distance at the time of his arrest. Was Grant correct? (Electronic Citation: 2001 FED App. 0067P 6th Cir)

2. As part of an investigation into illegal narcotics activity, police officers went to the home of Cindy Lou Cates and interviewed her about her involvement in buying and selling narcotics. Cates had realized that the officers wanted to interview her and therefore asked a friend to arrange the meeting, stating her desire to cooperate with the investigation. The officers drove an unmarked car, were not in uniform, and did not draw their weapons at any time during the interview. The interview took place on the porch

of her house, and Cates was free to leave when she so desired. The officers stressed to Cates that whether or not she submitted to the interview was a choice that had to be of her own free will. Cates never indicated a desire not to talk. At different times, she got up from her chair and entered the house, unescorted. The interview lasted several hours. During the interview, Cates recounted her activities buying and selling narcotics, including that she purchased narcotics from a number of individuals and resold to others. Two months after the interview, Cates was indicted by a grand jury. During her trial, her attorney moved to dismiss any statements she had made to the officers during her interview with them and later in the trial asked the court to declare a mistrial. The attorney argued that these statements were made during custodial interrogation and without the benefit of Miranda warnings. The attorney claimed that Miranda warnings must be given whenever law enforcement officers interrogate a suspect who has been arrested or whenever under any other circumstances the suspect is deprived of his or her freedom of action in any significant way. The judge in the lower court ruled that no mistrial was warranted in this case, and Cates was convicted. She appealed her case. Should the appeals court uphold Cates's conviction? (*United States* v. *Cates,* U.S. 8th Circuit Court of Nebraska)

3. Marlowe received money from her husband's life insurance policy following his accidental death in a swimming accident. A friend of a friend named Walton who worked for the U.S. State Department convinced her to invest some of the proceeds in gold that he could purchase for her in Brazil. Walton stated to Marlowe that she could then resell this gold in the United States and triple her money. Marlowe turned over $25,000 to Walton who, instead of investing the money, opened a bank account using a false name (Roberts) and then later withdrew the money in cash. Name and discuss the crime for which Walton could be found guilty. (*State of Utah* v. *Roberts,* 711 P. 2d 235)

4. Russello was a member of an arson ring consisting of arsonists, insurance adjusters, and property owners. A group member would buy a building, the arsonists would burn it, and the insurance adjusters would help the owner recover inflated insurance awards. The group members would then share in the proceeds. During one period of time, the group burned several buildings. Russello, who owned a professional building in Tampa, Florida, arranged for his building to be burned and then settled with the insurance company, receiving $350,000, the highest amount possible. Russello in turn invested the money in legitimate enterprises. The federal government brought criminal RICO charges against Russello. A U.S. District Court found Russello guilty and ordered forfeiture of the insurance proceeds. A U.S. Court of Appeals affirmed the lower court judgment. Russello appealed to the U.S. Supreme Court. Are the insurance proceeds obtained by Russello subject to forfeiture under the criminal RICO statute? (*Russello* v. *United States,* 464 U.S. 104)

5. Two police officers were patrolling an area where drug trafficking had been reported. They spotted an automobile driven by Johnson circling in the area and observed that the car had a broken taillight. The officers pulled the vehicle over and advised Johnson that he was being stopped for the broken taillight, which violated a state statute. The officer then discovered that Johnson was driving with a suspended driver's license. He was placed under arrest and given a pat-down search. This search revealed crack cocaine in the defendant's pocket; a search of the trunk revealed that marijuana was present. Johnson asked the court for a motion to suppress the evidence on the grounds that the police officers had no right to stop and search his vehicle for a broken taillight. Was Johnson correct? (*United States* v. *Johnson* 324 F. 2d 263)

6. Bower was encouraged by an acquaintance, who was actually an informer, to sell cocaine to a government undercover agent. The agent then arrested Bower for the possession and sale of a drug. Bower claimed entrapment as a defense. During the trial, evidence was introduced to show conclusively that Bower was in the business of selling cocaine and that the sale to the undercover agent was not really induced by the agent but was actually just another opportunity that presented itself to Bower. Is the defense of entrapment valid in this case? (*United States* v. *Bower,* 575 F.2d 499 U.S. Court of Appeals)

7. Ward, a former employee of ISD, a computer company, was employed by UCC, a competing computer service company. Ward was charged

with obtaining trade secrets illegally through the use of a computer terminal. Using a UCC data telephone, Ward dialed a secret number and gained access on his terminal to an ISD program without authority to do so. He then got a printout of the ISD program. The ISD program gave ISD an advantage over its competitors, including UCC. When charged with theft, Ward claimed he stole nothing tangible and therefore that no crime had been committed. He contended that he only caused impulses to be transmitted over the phone and onto a screen and that, once he did that, getting a printout was not theft. Does making a printout of secret information taken from another's computer constitute computer theft? (*Ward* v. *Superior Court, Alameda County Cal* 3 Computer Law Service Rptr., 206 Cal. Super. Ct.)

8. Arthur Dixon, executive director, and James Hinton, housing coordinator for United Neighborhoods Inc. (UNI), were in charge of administering federal funds received from the Department of Housing and Urban Development (HUD) for the city of Peoria, Illinois. They had the authority to enter into contracts with suppliers and tradespeople to provide the necessary materials to rehabilitate houses in the city of Peoria. While contracting with the suppliers and tradespeople, they used their positions to extract a 10 percent payment back on all contracts they awarded. What crime have Dixon and Hinton committed? (*Dixon and Hinton* v. *United States,* 465 U.S. 482)

9. Simons, a government employee, was provided with a computer with Internet access in a private office. There was an office policy which mandated the use of computers for only work-related activities and prohibited their use for accessing unlawful materials. The policy further stated that from time to time electronic audits would be conducted to ensure compliance with this policy. One audit revealed that Simons accessed Web sites relating to "sex." Simon's employer, by means of a search warrant, thereafter undertook a number of searches to verify what the audit revealed. It was determined that Simons had downloaded over 1,000 files that were related to child pornography. The hard drive on Simon's computer was immediately removed from his office as evidence. Simons went to court and requested that the evidence obtained by these searches of his computer and office be suppressed on the grounds that such searches violated his Fourth Amendment rights. Was he correct? *United States* v. *Simons* 3d (2000 WL 223332, 4th Cir.)

CHAPTER 4

Tort Law: Traditional Torts and Cyber torts

CHAPTER PREVIEW

An Overview of Tort Law

Classification of Torts

Intentional Torts
  Assault and Battery
  False Imprisonment
  Infliction of Emotional Distress
  Defamation
  Invasion of Privacy
  Wrongful Death
  Malicious Prosecution
  Fraud
  Interference with Contractual Relations
  Trespass
  Conversion

  Nuisance
  Theft of Trade Secrets

Defenses to Intentional Torts

Torts Resulting from Negligence

Defenses to Negligence

Strict Liability in Tort

Cyber Torts
  Online Defamation
  Online Privacy

Remedies for Torts

Tort Litigation Reform

Chapter Highlights

This chapter deals with the wrongful acts, called *torts*, that harm others and with the legal rights that victims have. Intentional (deliberate) torts are discussed first. Negligence, an unintentional tort, is then discussed. The third and final category of torts discussed is strict liability, or "liability without fault." A person being sued for a tort may offer certain defenses, or reasons to either reduce or eliminate his or her liability for a tort. The chapter discusses these defenses. Early in the chapter, the point is made that tort law is changing to meet both the social changes in the United States and the changing relationships between and among individuals. The chapter concludes with a brief discussion of possible reforms being considered in state legislatures to reduce the number of lawsuits in this country. New ways to commit a tort are growing, especially those committed on the Internet called cyber torts. Cyber torts will be discussed briefly in the chapter.

AN OVERVIEW OF TORT LAW

tort wrongful act causing injury to another person or damage to another's property

A sixteen-month-old child choked on a peanut butter sandwich and suffered brain damage. Rubin, who was having breakfast at a local diner, was severely scalded when a waitress carelessly spilled burning hot coffee on her arm and leg. Are these situations unusual? Unfortunately, injuries occur every day where someone else is responsible. Yet people have a duty not to cause harm to others. If they violate that duty and someone suffers a loss, the victim may sue the wrongdoer in tort. A **tort** occurs when a person sustains either physical or emotional injury to his or her person or property damage as the result of some other person's deliberate wrongful act or that other person's carelessness (failure to act reasonably).

tort law law dealing with private wrongs and affecting individuals rather than society as a whole

Tort law, which deals with a body of "private wrongs," is primarily case law (common law) including past and present (more modern) decisions. It was developed to protect people from the wrongful conduct of others in areas that are not covered by criminal law, which deals with "public wrongs" as pointed out in past chapters. New ways to commit a tort are growing, especially those committed on the Internet. These are called cyber torts.

The person committing a tort is subject to a civil lawsuit and will be required to pay the victim compensation, called money damages, on the theory that society places demands on all citizens not to harm others or their possessions. Many wrongful acts are both torts and crimes because they harm both society and the individual. In such cases, the wrongdoer could be brought to court as the defendant (person against whom a legal action is brought) in separate civil and criminal trials. The two separate suits will not be barred by the rule against double jeopardy.

> Harder, eighteen years old, was charged with intoxication manslaughter as the result of killing Kelley with her automobile while "stoned out of her mind" on marijuana. Harder had also taken some prescription medication. The jury found that Harder was driving erratically, weaving in and out of traffic. Kelley's death occurred when Harder jumped the median on a major highway and hit Kelley, who was coming toward her (Harder) from the opposite direction. Harder was traveling at an excessive rate of speed. In addition to this conviction, Harder could be sued in a civil tort action by Kelley's next of kin for wrongful death.

It is interesting to note that criminal law is primarily statutory, but even in this age of legislation, tort law still has strong ties to the common law and has evolved primarily from particular cases. As social conditions change, relationships between individuals also change. New technologies, different moral values, and different fundamental beliefs have led to new torts being recognized, others being abolished, and present torts being applied to new situations. In recent years, for example, there has been increased recognition of a person's right to be protected against intrusions on peace of mind. This increased recognition has given rise to a tort called *mental distress* (discussed later in the chapter). This tort has been used successfully against those who harass others, such as against collection agents who use unorthodox tactics to secure payment of a debt and in the process cause the victim to suffer severe mental stress. Another response to social change has occurred in the area of the tort of defamation (libel and slander). The case of *New York Times Co.* v. *Sullivan* (376 U.S. 254), decided by the Supreme Court in 1964, laid the groundwork for the rejection of the concept that all defamatory speech is subject to a lawsuit. More is said about this case and its effect on the law of defamation later in the chapter.

CLASSIFICATION OF TORTS

Under the law, torts are classified as intentional torts, torts resulting from negligence, and torts based on the concept of strict liability. In intentional and negligent torts, the law imposes liability because of one person's "fault" in causing another person's harm. On the other hand, in strict liability torts, a person is held liable in the absence of either intent or negligence; that is, the person is liable without fault. Keep in mind that some of the torts discussed can occur not only on a personal basis, but also in a business environment.

All persons, including minors (those who have not reached legal age), are legally responsible for their torts, which is especially true of the so-called intentional torts such as assault and battery. A minor's age is material, and a minor can escape liability when she or he is sued for negligence. (Intentional and negligent torts are discussed next.)

INTENTIONAL TORTS

intentional tort when one person deliberately inflicts injury to another person or damages that person's property

An **intentional tort** occurs when one deliberately inflicts injury on another or deliberately does damage to his or her property. The person committing the act wishes to harm you.

Intentional torts include (1) assault and battery, (2) false imprisonment, (3) inflection of emotional distress, (4) defamation, (5) invasion of privacy, (6) wrongful death, (7) malicious prosecution, (8) fraud, (9) interference with contractual relations, (10) trespass, (11) conversion, (12) nuisance, and (13) theft of trade secrets.

Assault and Battery

assault unlawfully threatening another person

Under civil law, an **assault** is a threatening act by one person that leads another person to believe that he or she is about to suffer bodily harm. The victim, as a reasonable person, must believe that the threat is real—that something is going to happen here and now—even though the person making the threat may not actually intend to carry it out. Pointing an unloaded gun at someone and threatening to shoot, for example, is an assault as long as the person being threatened believes that the gun is loaded. A person who threatens to shoot but has no gun, however, will generally not be considered to have committed a tort.

In addition, a threat to carry out an unlawful act cannot be considered an assault if it does not seem reasonable that the threat can be carried out.

> Gorgen, an unemployed laborer, was behind in his monthly payments on a personal loan from the Best Finance Company. The finance company's attempts to collect the installments due were unsuccessful. One evening, a collector, a burly, 6-foot-tall man from the finance company, appeared at Gorgen's house, pounded on the door, and said: "I am a bill collector. If you don't pay up what you owe to the Best Finance Company, I am going to take it out of your hide!" Gorgen became frightened and refused to unlock and open the door. He now brings a legal action against the collector for assault, claiming that the collector's words placed him in fear. Since it does not seem reasonable that the bill collector could carry out his threat at that time, the bill collector's conduct generally will not be considered an assault.

battery unlawfully striking another person

The tort of **battery** consists of the intentional and wrongful physical contact with a person without consent. The physical contact may be harmful and cause injury—as in kicking, shoving, throwing an object that strikes a person, or disfiguring a person. Merely touching a person offensively—for example, by displaying affection without permission—also constitutes a battery. A battery may also involve contact with anything attached to the body, such as when a display of affection consists of kissing the sleeve of a person's blouse. Battery very often includes an assault because the wrongdoers will generally threaten to commit the battery (assault) before actually doing it, and when the threat is carried out, a battery occurs.

> Cambisi, a waitress in a coffee shop, got angry with a customer and threatened to throw a cup of coffee in the customer's face unless he left the restaurant. The customer refused to leave, so the waitress carried out her threat and threw coffee in his face. Cambisi committed both assault (the customer saw the coffee coming at him) and battery (the customer got the coffee in his face).

The courts have held that a battery occurs even if there is no physical contact, such as when a prankster pulls a chair out from under a person who then sits down and is injured when he or she "hits" the floor. Although there is no physical contact between the prankster and the person sitting down, the prankster has committed a battery because the intended consequences of removing the chair is that the victim falls to the floor. As far as the law is concerned, it is the same as pushing the victim to the floor. On the other hand, if the removal of the chair had been unintended, there is no battery.

Injuries inflicted during contact sports such as boxing, football, and wrestling are generally not considered the result of a battery as long as the contact is within the rules of the game.

False Imprisonment

false imprisonment
unlawfully restricting a person's freedom of movement

False imprisonment occurs when a person is unlawfully and intentionally forced by another person to remain in a certain place—a room, an automobile, a boat, a building, an office, a hotel lobby, or some spot on the open street—so that his or her freedom of movement is restricted and no reasonable escape route is available.

At the beginning of his psychology class, Professor Hicks asked Sullivan to remain after class to discuss her poor attendance record. At the end of the class, Sullivan refused to stay because of another commitment. Professor Hicks then blocked the entrance to the door so that Sullivan was not able to leave as she wished to do. Sullivan may claim false imprisonment.

In this case, if the classroom had another exit (that would not lead to injury) and Sullivan could easily have left through that exit, she would have no claim for false imprisonment. To be falsely imprisoned, the confinement must be total.

false arrest
unauthorized detainment by an officer of the law

When a person is unlawfully detained by an authorized official, such as a police officer, a security guard, or a loss prevention officer in a store, the term **false arrest** is used.

Kessler, a taxi driver parked at a cab stand, was suddenly approached by several police officers. They ordered him out of his cab at gunpoint, frisked and handcuffed him, and put him in the back seat of a squad car. He was driven to the police precinct station and charged with breaking into a house, assaulting the homeowner, and stealing her money and jewelry. Kessler's arrest was based on the victim's identification of him from a photo that had been "doctored" by the police investigators to resemble the description of the man believed to have attacked her. Police suspected that a cab driver was involved, but at first, the victim could not identify Kessler from the group of photographs presented to her. When the real assailant was arrested a few hours later, Kessler was officially freed from all blame. Police action in this case constituted false arrest.

One of the most common and most litigated false arrest situations is that of the retail merchant who detains a customer suspected of shoplifting (the crime of theft). In most states, a merchant has no legal liability for the detention if he or she can prove that reasonable grounds existed to believe the customer had shoplifted. In a lawsuit, the test of reasonableness will be left to the jury. The jury will weigh this question after taking into consideration what the average, cautious, intelligent person would have done in similar circumstances, given the facts in the case. Even if the test of reasonableness is met, however, the merchant could still be liable if the customer is detained for an unreasonable length of time or in an unreasonable manner.

One way for the retailer to avoid liability in a false arrest suit is to prove that the customer consented to being detained, perhaps by freely accompanying a security guard to the detention area after being stopped as a suspected shoplifter. Whether the customer went freely may again be a question decided by a jury.

While vacationing, Phoenix, a seventy-year-old man, went shopping in the men's department of a large clothing store. While trying on a suit, he changed his clothes in the dressing room and placed his expensive belt in his overcoat pocket, with the gold buckle hanging out. Phoenix purchased the suit but left it for alterations. As he stepped out of the door to leave the store (forgetting to place the belt back on his pants), a security guard standing at the door spotted the belt. He firmly grasped Phoenix's arm and told him that he had better come to the security office and explain to the manager where he got the belt. In the meantime, another security guard stepped in front of Phoenix to prevent him from leaving. Under these circumstances, Phoenix agreed to return to the store. As he returned, he suffered a heart attack and subsequently was hospitalized for several weeks. A jury in this case would probably determine that Phoenix was illegally detained and would award him damages.

In this case, the jury would reason that the conduct of the security guards was not reasonable under the circumstances and that Phoenix, with one security guard firmly grasping his arm and the other standing in front of him, had no choice but to return to the store.

Some courts have dismissed shoplifting cases because a customer was stopped inside the store and had not passed the checkout counter. Customers accused of shoplifting defended on the grounds that, although it may have appeared to the security guard that the items in question were being concealed, they intended to pay for the items when they reached the checkout counter. In these cases, a reasonable doubt as to the intention of the customers existed in the minds of the jurors.

Infliction of Emotional Distress

infliction of emotional distress when one person's extreme conduct causes severe mental suffering in another; also called outrage

The tort of **infliction of emotional distress** (also called *outrage*) occurs when one person's extreme and outrageous conduct causes severe emotional suffering in another as a result of public humiliation, shame, anxiety, fright, or grief. Courts today allow a person to recover damages for the infliction of emotional distress, regardless of whether this distress is associated with physical injury.

To prevent people from flooding the courts with trivial lawsuits for the normal emotional stresses of day-to-day living—such as insults, obscene or abusive language, discourtesies, and profanity—courts have ruled that the person suing must prove that his or her emotional stress was beyond the bounds of decency and was severe and atrocious. The stress must be more than a reasonable person would expect to endure, for example, if a person is high-strung, the standard for outrageousness is lower than for a person of average temperament. Based on this ruling, the element of outrageous conduct is rigorous and difficult to prove. Consequently, some courts may require the victim to produce evidence of a physical or emotional illness established by a medical professional such as a physician or psychiatrist.

> Pogue, a practical joker, amused himself late one evening by phoning his friend's wife and telling her an untrue story. He said that her husband, while on the way home from the business meeting he was attending, had been in a serious accident and had been taken to a local hospital, where he was listed in critical condition. Pogue's friend's wife became hysterical, requiring sedation and weeks of hospitalization. The shock produced serious and permanent physical consequences. As a result, the wife could legally sue Pogue for intentionally inflicting emotional distress on her.

Today, lawsuits for the infliction of emotional distress are often brought against collection agencies for the unreasonably humiliating tactics they use to force debtors to pay bills. A review of court cases indicates that representatives of collection agencies have harassed debtors by making threatening remarks ("you will lose your job if you don't pay") and calling them names ("deadbeat"). The conduct of these representatives in some cases caused their victims to require hospitalization for severe emotional stress, and the victims brought lawsuits against them.

Defamation

defamation oral or written false statements that injure a person's reputation

slander oral false statements that injure a person's reputation

libel written false statements that injure a person's reputation

Oral or written false statements that injure a person's reputation are called **defamation**. A person's reputation is injured when he or she is held up to hatred, contempt, or ridicule, causing others to lose respect for or avoid that person as a result. Oral defamation is called **slander**, whereas written defamation is called **libel**. Libel is considered more harmful than slander because the printed word is more permanent than the spoken word and therefore can be circulated more widely. Because slander is considered less harmful, those suing for this tort must show that they suffered a financial loss. (The law does not presume that the communication of the statements caused the person suing any damage.) Only rarely do those suing for libel have to prove monetary loss. (The law presumes that some damage will flow from the communication of the written statements, such as the loss of reputation and respect in the community.)

To sue for either slander or libel under the states' laws, a private citizen must prove that the false (untrue) statements were "published"—that is, communicated to at least one other person.

> Mario had been jilted by his fifty-year-old girlfriend Tina after three years of going together. In fact, they were about to become engaged. Mario was so despondent and so angry over his breakup with Tina that he wrote a sixty-page manuscript called "The Tina Chronicles," where he falsely said she had HIV and bipolar disorder. He then sent copies of the manuscript to Orchard Middle School, where Tina taught sixth grade; to the Midcliff Central School District Middle School, where Tina had previously taught; to Tina's mother; and to Tina's adult children. Tina's attorney produced medical test results showing neither Tina nor Mario had HIV. The bipolar claim was unsupported. Since Marios' manuscript was a book of lies which he had distributed to Tina's coworkers and family (this distribution constituted publication) and since Mario deliberately distributed copies of the manuscript to injure Tina's reputation, Tina could bring a tort action against Mario for libel.

Sometimes determining whether an oral or written statement is defamatory becomes a question of law for a court to decide. In such cases, the court must review the phraseology used and decide whether it is reasonable to assume that the offending words are defamatory in the context in which they were said or written. If something is false but does not damage reputation, there is no claim. Courts are guided by the First Amendment's guarantee of free speech, keeping in mind that the amendment does not establish an absolute freedom for citizens to speak or publish. Courts have to balance the reputation of one person with the free speech rights of the other person. This amendment does protect a person's right to state an opinion (make a personal comment) about someone else. For example, ridiculing (making fun of) a person, calling him or her names, or making an insulting remark about the person's ancestry generally cannot become the basis of an action for defamation, no matter how offensive the remarks might be. On the other hand, the First Amendment does not protect a person whose expressions incite a riot.

The defamatory statement communicated to a third person may be made either intentionally (deliberately) or negligently (carelessly).

> Judge Crance was at a party when she told another judge that he was incompetent and should not run in the next election. Others at the party overheard Crance's statements. Her remark amounts to slander.

In this case, the publication element would be satisfied even though Crance intended her remark only for the judge. She was negligent in her communication. Crance, however, would have had no liability if only the judge had heard her remark. Derogatory remarks made directly to a person in a face-to-face conversation that others do not hear do not constitute publication, even though these remarks are false. Similarly, sending a letter containing derogatory remarks directly to the victim, with the intention that no one else read it, does not amount to publication. Persons who repeat or republish defamation can also be held liable by a plaintiff (person suing). The plaintiff can sue the first person to speak or write a libelous comment as well as those who repeat the defamation.

True statements are not defamatory, no matter how much hurt a person suffers. However, the evidence to prove the truth may just not be readily available. For example, if you tell people that your family attorney has a long history of mental instability, you should be ready with substantial evidence such as health records, sworn statements of other clients, or written documentation of your relationships with your attorney to show that he does have this history. Only then can you be free of a lawsuit for defamation. But keep in mind that your "positive" feeling and all your accumulated evidence about the truth of the information you collected is one thing; proving it in court is another.

In 1964, the U.S. Supreme Court swept aside states' laws on defamation as they applied to certain people who were involved in matters of public concern. Until the 1964 ruling, state law allowed any person to succeed in a lawsuit for defamation simply by proving that statements made about him or her were false and defamatory. The Supreme Court's 1964 decision in *New York Times Co.* v. *Sullivan* changed that. Balancing the right of states to protect the good names of their citizens against the right of free expression, the Court stated that from now on, a public official must prove that published statements about his or her public—not private—life were not only false and defamatory but also that the person or persons who published them did so with actual malice. Without proof of actual malice, the public official would have great difficulty winning a defamation case, especially against the media. This decision by the Supreme Court, really aimed at the media, gave reporters the right to publish in areas of public concern without regard to the public official's interest in his or her reputation. Actual malice is defined as either a deliberate lie or reckless indifference to truth (the person publishing the statements doesn't care whether they are true or false). In this *New York Times* decision, the Court held that people in public life must both expect and accept a harsher degree of criticism about their conduct and motives than must private citizens. The Court reasoned that public persons have access to the media and thus can rebut criticisms about their life; also, public persons place themselves in the limelight and therefore leave themselves open to discussion by the public. Public officials have been broadly defined as holders of major offices (having substantial administrative or policymaking responsibilities) in the executive, legislative, and judicial branches of the government; also included in this definition are low- and middle-level public employees, such as police officers, public school teachers and college professors, incumbents in public office, and candidates running for public office.

> In a newspaper editorial, Alent, the governor of a large midwestern state, was called "corrupt and a graft collector and not worthy of being elected to another term." Alent, claiming that these statements were untrue, initiated a lawsuit against the newspaper for libel. Because Alent can be considered a public figure, she would have a more difficult time proving her case.

In other leading cases since 1964, the Supreme Court extended the actual malice requirement to public figures, further reasoning that information about their public life also deserves constitutional protection. As defined by the Court, public figures fall into two categories: those who are famous or widely known, giving the public a legitimate interest in all phases of their lives, and those private citizens who voluntarily attract public attention. Famous and widely known public figures include sports figures, movie stars, well-known entertainers, inventors, and former presidents. An example of a private citizen who voluntarily attracted public attention is a college football coach who came into public prominence by being accused of fixing a college football game. A retired general (no longer a public official) who made a speech on a college campus to influence public opinion and caused students to protest is another example of those who become public figures by thrusting themselves into public controversy.

In view of the foregoing discussion, it can be said that the law of defamation has been significantly affected by the *New York Times* rule. Whereas suits against private citizens are governed by state laws, suits against public officials and public figures are now governed by the stricter federal constitutional standard (requiring proof of actual malice) as set down in *New York Times Co.* v. *Sullivan*. Comparing the state standard with the federal constitutional standard, you will discover that it is easier for a private person to recover for defamation than a public figure.

Invasion of Privacy

Invasion of privacy evolved as a common law right and was later supplemented in some instances by state statutes and as a federal constitutional right derived through Supreme Court decisions which ruled that there were "zones of privacy" implicit in the Bill of Rights. The right to privacy, however, is not expressly mentioned in the Bill of Rights. Federal privacy rights not only prevent governmental or state action, they can also govern private companies, such as a law passed by Congress (the Fair Credit Reporting Act of 1970) requiring credit bureaus to implement procedures to prevent the reporting of obsolete or inaccurate information about an individual.

invasion of privacy
violating one's right to
be left alone

The essence of the right of privacy is that a person has the right to be left alone or to be free from unauthorized publicity and from wrongful intrusion into his or her private life by another person or the government. A violation of these rights is called **invasion of privacy**. Under common law and state statutes, invasions of privacy generally occur in one of the following forms:

1. Using a person's name or picture for an advertisement or other commercial purpose without consent.

Parratto, a professional photographer, photographed Antonina, a statewide beauty contestant, without express or implied permission and exhibited her image in a public art and photography show in a large metropolitan city gallery where she lived. The show attracted art and photography enthusiasts from around the city. Several visitors to the gallery purchased her photograph. Parratto received a commission for these sales. Antonina could sue Parratto for damages for violating her statutory right to privacy and for using her image for commercial purposes.

A statement called a *release* (generally in writing), giving another permission to use a picture for the purpose covered in the release, waives any right of privacy that might be infringed upon as a result of the publication of the photograph.

2.   Intruding upon a person's right to be left alone. Examples include peeping in windows; compulsory blood testing; illegally searching someone's suitcase; entering, without permission or legal authority, into a person's house or office; or tapping a person's telephone and then listening to the person's private conversations when such tapping is prohibited by federal and/or state law. In this context, there is increasing concern about the amount of information on individuals that is stored in databases (computer data files). Computers have made it possible to collect and store a vast amount of private information concerning people's income, phone calls, credit purchases, and other personal data. Many people fear that these data files threaten our right to privacy. Since the early 1970s, the federal government has passed several laws to limit the use of and access to computer data banks.

3. Wrongfully disclosing true but offensive and embarrassing information about another person's private life that the public does not have the right to know.

> Fanton, a high school principal, unknown to his district superintendent or to anyone else in the district, was under the care of Dr. Ralph Moresee, a psychiatrist, for mental problems that in no way interfered with his job. At a school district social function, Dr. Moresee discussed Fanton's psychotherapy sessions with some of Fanton's colleagues, including the superintendent of schools and two board members. Fanton was in no way dangerous, and there was no need for Dr. Moresee to warn others about him. As a result of Dr. Moresee's revelation about Fanton's condition to the superintendent and board members, Fanton lost his job as principal.

In this case, Dr. Moresee had no legitimate reasons to discuss Fanton's psychotherapy sessions with Fanton's superiors and colleagues even though the information was true. The information was not noteworthy. It dealt with a person's private life and was not of the nature that the public had a right to know about. Consequently, the discussion by Dr. Moresee amounted to an invasion of privacy. On the other hand, if Fanton were a public official such as a member of Congress representing people's interests in government, his mental state would be of concern to the public, and therefore, invasion of privacy would not be an issue. The right to privacy of a public official or a public figure is given less protection than that of private citizens who become involved in matters of public interest and whose personal and/or family background is exposed to public view (as in the preceding case). The courts permit an invasion of a person's privacy in these cases because there is a legitimate public interest in newsworthy events.

4. Publicizing information that creates a false picture of a person. The information must be untrue, highly offensive, and place the other person in a false light. An example of such information is an article written in a law journal implying that a certain attorney was unethical and dishonest, when in fact she or he was not. Publishing such a story would also involve the tort of defamation. A person might be more inclined to bring suit for being placed in a false light, however, because the law allows more time to bring that type of suit than it does for defamation.

Wrongful Death

wrongful death
wrongful act that causes the death of another

A person who commits a wrongful act that intentionally causes the death of another can be sued for damages for **wrongful death**. Intentionally killing a bank teller during the course of a bank robbery is an example of a situation in which the family of the deceased person (usually the spouse, children, or parents) could sue.

A wrongful death action can also be pursued if the victim was killed accidentally (e.g., by a person driving in an intoxicated condition or high on drugs) or died as a result of the negligent (careless) act of another, as in the following example.

> A high school allowed students to leave the building or eat in the cafeteria, but those who chose to stay were required to leave the building after eating and remain there until the bell rang to announce the resumption of classes. John, a fifteen-year-old freshman at the school, ate his lunch quickly and then went outside to play football with his friends. During the game, a fight broke out and one of the boys, who was high on cocaine, pulled out a gun and accidentally shot John who was not one of the students involved in the fight. John's parents could sue the boy (and maybe the boy's parents) for wrongful death.

The measure of damages is the loss of income (e.g., as a wage earner), companionship (enjoyment of a close relationship), and services (as a mother, wife, husband, etc.) that the surviving relatives would have received from the deceased had she or he not been killed. Damages are sometimes hard to determine, especially when juries must measure the impact of the death of a very young person as in the preceding case problem or other factors such as the value of companionship. Courts nevertheless instruct juries in these cases to "fix" an award based on what they think is appropriate, keeping in mind that every life has some pecuniary value.

Malicious Prosecution

malicious prosecution wrongfully initiating a lawsuit against one who has done no wrong

The tort of **malicious prosecution** arises when one individual, without a legitimate reason and solely to harass another individual, initiates either a criminal or a civil action against that other individual. To sue for this tort, a person must show among other things that (1) there were no real grounds for the criminal or civil action (i.e., the instigator of the action did not honestly believe that the accused did anything wrong), (2) there was an intent to injure, and (3) the action was not successful.

> Wentis gave Bright, his fiancée, a diamond bracelet as an engagement gift. When Bright broke off the engagement, Wentis became very angry and promised to "get even with her." He then sued Bright for conversion, claiming that he had lent her the bracelet to wear to a formal party and that she had then refused to return it to him. During the trial, Bright introduced testimony from the jeweler to prove that she was with Wentis when he purchased the bracelet and that Wentis had told the jeweler that it was an engagement present. Wentis lost the case. Bright could then sue Wentis for malicious prosecution.

Fraud

fraud deliberate false statement or concealment of a material fact.

The tort of **fraud** occurs when false statements of fact are deliberately made to deceive, resulting in injury or loss to another. Facts that are deliberately hidden may also constitute fraud. Fraud is discussed in greater detail in connection with the law of contracts in Chapter 14.

> Because of an economic downturn, the Zilo Computer Company, in an attempt to make its financial statements look better, falsely boosted sales figures by reporting sales as being made before the merchandise was actually sold. This maneuver made it appear that the company was making a profit when in reality it was losing money. The practice of falsely reporting sales amounted to accounting fraud.

Interference with Contractual Relations

interference with contractual relations intentional procuring of breach of a valid contract

A person who intentionally and without proper justification persuades one party to breach his or her legally enforceable contract with another party has committed the tort known as **interference with contractual relations**. The rationale for such a tort is that to allow a third person to interfere with a contract to the point where one of the parties breaches it would weaken the value of contracts.

> Petrosino, a well-known computer consultant, was in the second year of a three-year contract with the Rex Corporation. Convinced that Petrosino was the only person who could solve their computer problems, the chief executive officer of Computer International lured Petrosino into breaking his contract with Rex and coming to work for Computer International at a substantially higher salary. Petrosino did break his contract, and as a result, Rex suffered a huge monetary loss on a new project Petrosino was working on. Rex has

a cause of action against Computer International for intentional interference with a contract, as long as Computer International was aware that a contract existed between Rex and Petrosino and that its offer to Petrosino would interfere with that contract.

Trespass

trespass illegally entering or remaining on the property of another

Trespass is an unlawful interference with someone else's possession of his or her real or personal property. Real property is land and anything permanently attached to the land, such as a building, whereas personal property consists of something tangible and movable. Walking on or driving over another person's land without permission or refusing to leave a building after the owner has withdrawn permission to remain are examples of a trespass to real property. Posting "No Trespassing" signs conspicuously around the real property is always a good idea. Then a person caught on the landowners property without permission can more easily be established as a trespasser. Vandalizing a car by breaking a window and destroying a person's car phone is an example of a trespass to personal property.

A group of college students held a picnic on McDowell's beachfront property without permission while McDowell was on vacation. These students committed a trespass.

A person who owns real property generally owns a reasonable amount of the air space above the land. Therefore, a person may be liable as a trespasser by allowing the branches of a tree growing on his or her property to hang over onto a neighbor's property, thus violating this neighbor's air space.

A person also commits a trespass by wrongfully throwing or placing an object on another's property, such as by dumping garbage on another person's land.

Conversion

conversion wrongfully exercising control or ownership over another's personal property

The tort of **conversion** occurs when one person wrongfully takes control of the personal property (a car, an item of clothing or jewelry, etc.) of another and exercises the right of ownership, thus depriving the owner of the use of the property.

One evening, in front of a neighborhood grocery store, Cooper spotted a car with its motor running. He drove away in the car and left the state for several weeks to visit a friend. On the way back to his home state, he was stopped for speeding. When he could not produce evidence to show that the car was registered in his name, he was taken into custody. Cooper admitted the car was stolen. The owner of the car could bring an action against Cooper for conversion.

Conversion also occurs when someone purchases stolen property and then, after a proper demand is made, refuses to return it to its rightful owner. Still another example of conversion is taking building materials from a neighbor's garage for personal use and with no intent of returning them.

A person who commits the tort of conversion may also be found guilty of the crime of theft (stealing).

Nuisance

nuisance use of one's property to annoy or disturb others

A **nuisance** arises when a person uses her or his property unreasonably or unlawfully or when her or his conduct is unreasonable, causing discomfort or inconvenience to others. There are two types of nuisances: public and private. A public nuisance is an act that affects the general public. Communities, for example, may enact a public nuisance law that subjects individuals in a neighborhood who conduct illegal drug sales, prostitution, or disorderly conduct to civil penalties. A public nuisance that occurs in many older neighborhoods is abandoned rundown houses with property maintenance issues such as falling gutters, sinking roofs, boarded-up windows, and unmowed lawns. A private nuisance is an act affecting a limited number of individuals—often just one person or one household—for example, excessive noise, smoke, pollution, or fire hazard.

> Schultz operated a small music shop in his garage that was open in the evening between the hours of 7 P.M. and 11 P.M. The loud noises from people trying out various musical instruments disturbed the next-door neighbors. Such noise may be a nuisance, and the next-door neighbors may be able to stop Schultz from running his shop out of his garage. Also, there may be a zoning ordinance prohibiting a for-profit business in a residential area.

There are no hard-and-fast rules to determine when a certain act is considered a private nuisance. The courts tend to consider the effect of the act on the average person and the commonsense realities of the situation. For example, a college student races the motor on his or her cycle several nights a week at midnight, causing a neighbor to lose sleep from the loud noise. This act may be considered a nuisance. If done during the day, however, this same act would probably not be considered a nuisance.

It is often more important to end a nuisance than to sue and recover money. To end a nuisance, the injured party would ask the court to issue an **injunction**, a court order restraining a person from doing or continuing some act.

injunction court order forbidding a person from doing a certain act

theft of trade secrets unlawfully acquiring information vital to a business

Theft of Trade Secrets

Theft of trade secrets occurs when one person or business unlawfully acquires and uses the trade secrets of another person or business. A trade secret consists of any information (e.g., financial, scientific, technical), technique, or process that is used in a business and that gives this business an advantage over a competitor that does not know about it. It may be a secret formula (e.g., Coca-Cola), a chemical compound, a marketing technique, a process of manufacturing, a customer list, or anything else that would have value to a competitor.

A trade secret may be acquired by industrial espionage (e.g., electronic surveillance, spying), bribery, fraud, or interception of communications. A competitor who wrongfully obtains a trade secret or a trusted employee who wrongfully discloses such information commits a tort.

DEFENSES TO INTENTIONAL TORTS

Earlier in this chapter, some defenses were discussed under the various categories of torts, such as truth as a defense to the tort of defamation. The following defenses can also reduce or eliminate liability for the tort:

1. ***Consent.*** A person may consent to a tort by words or may imply consent by conduct. For example, a professional football player implicitly consents to the physical contact associated with that sport by agreeing to participate. Therefore, an injured player usually cannot sue for battery. The person giving consent must have the ability to do so. A person who is mentally incompetent, for example, generally cannot give consent if unaware of the consequences of his or her consent.

2. ***Privilege.*** The privilege to say or do something, even if another is injured, is allowed by law under certain circumstances. For example, a witness at a criminal trial is allowed to make statements that might constitute slander outside the courtroom. The

statements are privileged as long as they relate to the issues in the trial. Self-defense is a privileged action available to a person who is in danger of being physically harmed and who cannot seek police protection in time to prevent bodily injury.

   3. *Necessity.* In an emergency, a person may need to act to protect himself or herself from harm or the threat of imminent harm but in the process may commit an intentional tort. If the emergency is sufficiently great and the person acts reasonably, the law may excuse the tort, recognizing that what the person did constituted a necessity. Many of the decided cases involve threats of harm from forces of nature, such as fires, floods, and storms. Consider the case of a person who docks his or her small boat on private property during a severe storm and then finds shelter on the property. This person is not a trespasser in the sense that he or she can be expelled from the land. Nevertheless, this person may be required to compensate the owner of the land for any damages done to the property by the boat.

TORTS RESULTING FROM NEGLIGENCE

In addition to the intentional torts, there is the tort of negligence. Negligence is an unintentional tort. In negligence cases, the defendant (person being sued) never set out (intended) to commit the act (e.g., injury to another person) he or she is accused of committing. Rather, the act of **negligence** stems from careless or thoughtless conduct on the part of the defendant. The result of this carelessness proximately (directly) causes injuries to another person or damages to another person's property. Torts are one of the largest areas of litigation, and the charge of negligence is the source of a large percentage of these lawsuits.

   A person bringing a lawsuit for negligence must prove certain elements. Generally, the courts decide whether the proof is adequate or not. The elements are the same whether the plaintiff was injured by a careless driver, exposure to asbestos, or a surgeon who performed an incorrect operation. Each of these elements is now discussed.

   1. *The defendant had a legal duty to act carefully*. A duty of care arises whenever a person should reasonably anticipate (foresee) that harm or injury is likely to result if he or she acts or fails to act in a certain way. This "foreseeability" test implies that the defendant should have known better and, consequently, should have behaved differently.

> Anglin was late for work. As he approached a busy intersection in his car, he began to speed up because the caution light was showing and was about to change to red. The light changed before he got to the intersection but, because of his lateness, Anglin decided to "chance it" and go through the red light. As he did, he injured a pedestrian who had the right of way and was crossing the street at the crosswalk.

   A court in this case would probably decide in favor of the pedestrian, reasoning that Anglin had a legal duty to stop at the red light (as motor vehicle laws require) and that he should have "foreseen" that "chancing it" by going through a red light created the risk of injury, property damage, or both. In contrast, take the case of a patient's death after a successful operation because careless orderlies dropped the patient down a flight of stairs. In this case, a court would probably rule that the doctor who performed the operation is not liable for negligence because the patient's death was not "foreseeable" by the doctor.

   2. *The defendant breached the duty to act carefully*. Once it is determined that a duty exists, the person suing for negligence must show the court that the defendant breached that duty by failing to act carefully. In making its decision, the court will apply the hypothetical "reasonable person" standard, which constitutes society's judgment on how a person should behave in certain circumstances. The court will compare the conduct of the defendant with the conduct of the "reasonable person," defined as a normal, average

negligence breach of a legal duty to act carefully, resulting in injury to another or damage to another's property

individual. In deciding what is normal, the court will consider the person's age, intelligence, experience, and physical condition; for example, is he or she blind or deaf? It is not enough that the defendant believed in good faith that he or she was being careful. The real issue is how the "reasonable person" would have acted. Because of this issue, a minor child, for example, may not be held to the same standard for a negligent act as an adult.

3. The defendant's failure to act carefully proximately caused the plaintiff's (person suing) injury. After proving that the defendant had a legal duty and that there was a breach of that duty (i.e., the defendant failed to act carefully), the plaintiff in a negligence action must demonstrate that the breach proximately caused the plaintiff's injuries. *Proximately* means that the damages or injury has directly resulted from the negligence. In an example of the patient who died because of being dropped down a flight of stairs after a successful operation, the doctor's operation was not the proximate cause of the patient's death. The direct cause of the patient's death was the carelessness of the orderlies.

4. The defendant's negligence caused the plaintiff to suffer physical injury or damage. As the final element of a negligence action, the plaintiff must prove that he or she suffered a physical injury or damage. In most states, a defendant may also be liable if, in addition to physical injury (e.g., the loss of an arm or leg), the defendant caused emotional distress (e.g., mental harm such as shock or fright).

malpractice
professional's improper or immoral conduct in performing duties done intentionally or through carelessness or ignorance

A number of lawsuits for negligence center on malpractice. **Malpractice** is negligence committed by a professional that causes the recipient of his or her services to suffer an injury, loss, or damage.

The term *professional* is usually applied to a doctor, nurse, dentist, hospital worker, attorney, accountant, public official, or any person who is considered to be a member of a profession.

> Lynch was scheduled for surgery to repair a hernia. During the operation, doctors also confirmed bladder cancer, a condition that had been suspected but had gone untreated for months despite an MRI and other continuing signs that this condition existed. A review of the case by Lynch's attorney revealed that doctors failed to act on her cancer symptoms which ultimately caused her death shortly after the hernia operation. Lynch's doctors are subject to a malpractice lawsuit by Lynch's next of kin.

In this case, malpractice was probably easily determined. Suppose, however, that you had open heart surgery and complications set in that caused severe pain and suffering requiring extended hospitalization. Then, because you became immobile, home care was required for several months. To win a malpractice case against the doctor, you would first have to determine if the doctor's actions violated the standards of good medical practice. In court, the jury would rely on expert witness testimony (at least one other competent heart surgeon considered a specialist) to determine what he or she would have done under the same circumstances.

DEFENSES TO NEGLIGENCE

People who are sued for negligence may present defenses for their actions that can reduce or even eliminate their liability for this tort. One such defense is contributory negligence. **Contributory negligence** refers to any negligence on the part of the injured person that led (contributed) to the injury. If contributory negligence can be proved, the injured party may be denied damages, even if the negligence was slight.

contributory negligence defense that injured party's negligence led to injury

> You were hit by Arnold, who was speeding at the time of the accident. You sued Arnold for negligence. At the trial, Arnold's attorney proved that you did not cross

Chapter 4: Tort Law: Traditional Torts and Cyber torts   85

the street at the crosswalk, nor did you look to the right and left before stepping off the sidewalk into the street. Because your own negligence contributed to the accident, you could lose your case.

comparative negligence comparing the negligence of the injured party and the one being sued

In almost all states, the harsh rules of contributory negligence have been replaced by the doctrine of comparative negligence, which is considered fairer because in most accidents no one person is 100 percent at fault. With **comparative negligence**, the negligence of the injured party who is suing (plaintiff) and that of the person being sued (defendants) are compared. Consequently, if the injured party is partially at fault, he or she can still collect, but the award of damages would be reduced by the percentage of fault on his or her part.

A jury awarded Minster $100,000 in damages for injuries for a car accident caused by Lovenhim; however, Minster was 25 percent at fault.

Under the rule of comparative negligence, Minster would be entitled to only $75,000 ($100,000 minus 25 percent). Furthermore, Minster could have had an adjustment to his damage award until he was 50 percent at fault. If he had been found to be more than 50 percent at fault (e.g., 51 percent), in most states he would be unable to collect any amount of damages.

assumption of risk defense against people who voluntarily expose themselves to a risk of harm, suffer an injury, and then sue

Another defense is assumption of risk. People who voluntarily expose themselves to a risk of harm, suffer an injury, and then sue may be met in court with the defense known as **assumption of risk**. This defense can be raised by defendants (the persons being sued) who present evidence that they have been freed of responsibility for any wrong. A prime example involving assumption of risk is the fan who buys a ticket to attend a baseball game and then, while sitting in the spectator section in the ballpark, is injured by a stray baseball hit by a player. In this case, the fan may not have grounds to sue. Spectators who purchase a ticket assume the risk and accept the harm that may result (i.e., when they enter a ballpark to watch a game, a stray ball hit by a player may end up in the spectator section, hit someone, and cause an injury).

Keep in mind that negligence involves carelessness and that an unavoidable accident is not carelessness but rather an accident that occurs no matter how careful you are. A person who suffers a heart attack behind the wheel of a car and causes an accident is not liable for damages unless she or he was on heart medication and decided to drive in spite of having sharp pains in the chest indicative of a heart attack. Further, there is no liability when a child darts out in front of your car from behind a parked car in a strictly residential area if you are driving slowly and carefully and strike the child.

STRICT LIABILITY IN TORT

strict liability legal responsibility for harm done to another even when there is no proof of fault on the part of the party that caused the harm

The third and final area of tort liability is **strict liability**. Under this concept, the law imposes liability on people for reasons other than fault. Thus, strict liability is referred to as "liability without fault." The courts and legislatures responding to society have concluded that, regardless of how careful a person is, certain activities and certain products on the market present high risks of harm. Those who carry on these activities or sell these products should therefore be liable for any harm caused to innocent victims. For example, people who keep on their property trained or domesticated animals (e.g., wolves and lions) considered naturally dangerous to humans are strictly liable for harm caused by the animals if they escape, no matter how careful the owners were in handling these animals. Strict liability is most often imposed on merchants, such as manufacturers of consumer products, who sell these products in an unreasonably dangerous and defective condition because they have the responsibility of assuring that their product is safe when used as directed. More is said about the sale of defective products to the public in Chapter 18 under the topic of product liability.

> Genae underwent LASIK surgery at Holbrook Eye Associates. During the surgery, a surgical blade broke in Genae's eye and erratically cut her cornea. Genae suffered severe pain for several months following the surgery and now has hazed vision and needs a corneal transplant. She sued Holbrook Eye Associates under the theory of strict liability for a defective blade produced by the Merchant's Manufacturing Company that turned out to be unreasonably dangerous.

CYBER TORTS

cyber torts wrongful acts causing personal injury or damage committed on the Internet

Some torts are committed in cyberspace. They are called **cyber torts**. They arise from communications on the Internet such as e-mail, blogs, Web site postings, or use of software. Like traditional torts, recovery from damages for a cyber tort is a civil matter. Unlike traditional torts committed in the "real world" often resulting in physical injuries, damages resulting from cyber torts are primarily reputational or economic.

Online Defamation

Messages that Internet users send through cyberspace are not immune from lawsuits if one of the users can prove damage to his or her reputation. Defamation laws are enforceable in the virtual world just as they are in the real world. Consequently, users are responsible for making sure the information they distribute is not defamatory. Existing laws relating to defamation, however, do not totally address defamatory statements made in cyberspace (online). Decisions in some major cyberspace libel cases have become legal precedent and are currently being followed in deciding online defamation cases. Owners or operators of a network of computers who write and publish on the network or provide a service to third parties as publishers and have editorial or censorial control are liable for defamatory material that appears on their servers. A publisher could be the editor of an electronic newsletter, the operator of a bulletin board with monitoring capabilities where users are permitted to post messages that can be read by other users, or a discussion leader who sends messages to other members of a discussion group consisting of members from around the country or even around the world. If an Internet service provider is found to be a distributor, the Internet service provider will not be considered liable for materials that appear on its servers. A distributor is viewed much the same way as companies are legally viewed. Just as telephone companies attempt no control over what information is communicated across their wires and are not legally liable for the content of such communications, the service provider supplies the means for the user to send any message completely unedited or uncensored. Compare servers as distributors to newsstands and bookstores under traditional law. They generally are not liable for anything they sell.

> Savin, a full-time journalist also had a side business in which he published an electronic newsletter called the Cyber Express. He was sued by Michael Elray, owner of the Elray Corporation, for an article published by Savin in the Cyber Express. The article questioned Michael's marketing practices and at one point called the marketing practices scams. The article further stated that the attorney general's office had officially identified the marketing practices as scams. Michael's lawsuit was for libel. Michael Elray would win if he could prove that Savin's article was false and that his reputation was damaged.

Online Privacy

The power of the computer is increasingly recognized as a threat to privacy. Web site owners have the ability to gather personal information about you as you surf the Web, and they can then use this information as they see fit. Often, a Web site owner or manager will sell information such as your address, age, income, place of business, and a variety of other details about your life to a third party at a profit. Thus, your very personal information that you most likely do not wish to share with anyone becomes a valuable commodity. Some online guidelines developed through online privacy groups recommend that businesses post a notice on their Web sites stating how personal information will be used and to whom it will be disclosed. Further, these guidelines give Web site users an opportunity either to remove personal information or to demand that the information provided be kept private.

Another area dealing with privacy is the right of employers to tap into employees' e-mail. Employers contend that employees have no reasonable expectation of privacy with respect to information found in computers connected to a company-sponsored network. No warning, however, is displayed. While no law may have been violated, both employers and employees should agree on what their expectations are concerning messages and information that appear on the network. Employees should at least insist that a warning be displayed prominently in the work-place areas.

Another serious invasion of privacy is the ability of individuals to eavesdrop on cell phone conversations. Congress has made it a crime to listen in on cell phone conversations as part of the Electronic Communications Privacy Act of 1986. However, this type of activity is a very popular pastime in spite of the law. A person tapping into cell phone conversations can pick up credit card numbers with expiration dates, listen to a spouse making plans to cheat on his or her mate and hear just plain old gossip that might be used as a blackmail scheme.

REMEDIES FOR TORTS

damages money paid by a defendant to a successful plaintiff in civil cases to compensate the plaintiff for his or her injuries

The usual remedy available to the injured party for a tort is to sue in a court of law and recover money damages from the person who committed the wrong. Contrary to what many people think, however, **damages** are not automatically awarded every time a tort is committed and a lawsuit filed in court. Similarly, if the person being sued in tort is insured through an insurance company, it will not result in automatic damages. An important requirement must be met before a person injured by a tort has a cause of action: He or she must prove damages. Generally, the purpose of damages is to restore the injured party to the position he or she was in before the tort was committed (status quo).

The amount of damages a person can recover depends on the harm caused and the kind of tort committed. Million-dollar awards are not uncommon in the areas of medical malpractice and product liability, especially if the victims have suffered a seriously disabling injury. In the case of a deliberate tort, both compensatory damages and punitive damages may be awarded. **Compensatory damages** are actual, measurable damages suffered—such as hospital bills, doctor's bills, pharmacy bills, and wages lost while a person's injuries prevent him or her from working—as well as those damages not so easy to measure, which courts call "pain and suffering." Pain and suffering refer to both the actual physical pain and the mental anguish that result from the tort. Examples of pain and suffering include the pain suffered from a back injury or the loss of an arm or leg and the emotional trauma of a permanent disfigurement caused by an automobile accident. Because there is no fixed rule by which to calculate pain and suffering, there is

compensatory damages actual measurable damages

punitive damages
damages imposed
upon a wrongdoer as
punishment for inten-
tionally committing a
wrongful act

wide latitude for the amount that can be awarded. **Punitive damages** (also called *exemplary damages*), often referred to as "vindictive damages" or "smart money," are imposed on the wrongdoer by the court as punishment for an intentional tort, mostly in cases involving gross negligence, that is, where the activity that led to harm is extreme and the law believes there is a need to present a strong civil law deterrent. Although juries have broad discretion to award punitive damages in personal injury cases, in recent years the U.S. Supreme Court has expressed its unease with the size of punitive damages (see *Browning-Ferris Indus., Inc.* v. *Kelco Disposal, Inc.*, 492 U.S. 257; *Pacific Mut. Life Ins. Co.* v. *Haslip*, 499 U.S. 1; and *TXO Prod. Corp.* v. *Alliance Resources Corp.*, 113 S. Ct. 2711) and has said that punitive damage awards should be "reasonable and proportionate to the amount of harm." Many states have followed suit with legislation placing a cap on punitive damages.

> Ritz hired a certified, personal trainer to guide him through a series of exercises. When a severe pain occurred in his lower back, the trainer told Ritz to ignore it, that the pain would go away. The intensity of the pain increased as Ritz continued his exercising. When he couldn't stand the pain any more, he went to a doctor only to discover that he had a herineated disk caused by doing improper exercises. Ritz could sue the trainer for the tort of negligence.

If successful in his lawsuit, Ritz would most likely be awarded compensatory damages. The amount awarded would depend on the actual amount spent for medical bills and the pain and suffering he endured.

Sometimes money damages will not provide the kind of relief needed. Remedies in equity (as discussed on page 11) protect parties when monetary damages are not adequate. If, for example, someone is disturbing you by creating a nuisance, what you may really want the court to do is to stop the nuisance rather than award you money damages. You can do so by seeking an injunction, which is a remedy in equity (see nuisance, page 81).

TORT LITIGATION REFORM

"Jury awards $15 million in punitive damages to Lung Cancer Victim." A headline like this was common a few years ago. Today, in state after state, however, the tide has turned. Easy money in injury lawsuits is gone. Businesses once thought to be gravy train expresses are really going in reverse. Companies, such as cigarette and pharmaceutical companies, that were vulnerable to large verdicts have turned it around and actually won their cases at trial or had the trial verdict reversed by the highest court in the state. Steps have even been taken in many states to scale back on how much people bringing lawsuits can recover. California, Georgia, and Texas have placed a cap of $250,000 on punitive damages unless the defendant acted with a specific intent to harm. At least a half dozen states have passed laws restricting the kinds of asbestos suits that can be filed, while still several other states have statutes saying you can't sue and make yourself a fat cat on money damages awarded to a defendant who suffered from a hot coffee spill such as occurred in a lawsuit against McDonalds. Michigan has virtually wiped out all lawsuits against drugmakers in the state. It is really a tough time to be a plaintiff's attorney customed to making large sums in attorneys' fees based on the damages won at trial, especially now that states have a cap on punitive damages. These changes have not come all at once, but in waves starting in the late nineties and reaching a high point around 2003.

Summary

A tort, known as a private wrong, is an intentional harmful act or simply a failure to act carefully (negligence). In either case, physical or mental injury to a person or damage to a person's property results. Torts committed on the Internet are called cyber torts. The violator of a private wrong is subject to a civil lawsuit and will be required to pay money damages. Generally, all persons, including minors, are legally responsible for their torts. Torts are classified as either intentional, negligent, or strict liability.

Intentional torts, those deliberately committed, include assault and battery, false imprisonment, infliction of emotional distress, defamation, invasion of privacy, wrongful death, malicious prosecution, fraud, interference with contractual relations, trespass, conversion, nuisance, and theft of trade secrets. A defendant (person being sued) in a civil lawsuit may avoid liability for these torts by proving defenses such as consent, privilege, and necessity.

Negligent torts arise because someone was careless. Negligence may be defined as the failure to act carefully when there is a foreseeable risk of harm to others. When a lawsuit is based on negligence, the courts will apply the hypothetical "reasonable person" standard. A reasonable person is a normal, average individual. A number of lawsuits for negligence center on malpractice, which amounts to negligence committed by a professional person. Three defenses are available to a defendant in a lawsuit for negligence: contributory negligence, comparative negligence, and assumption of risk. Comparative negligence is the rule in almost all states because it is considered fairer than the other two defenses.

The third and final area of tort liability is strict liability, often referred to as "liability without fault."

In strict liability lawsuits, defendants may be held liable even though they acted carefully (without negligence) and had no intention of harming others or their property. Society, however, acting through the courts, requires those who carry on high-risk activities or who sell products that could be unreasonably dangerous to the public to assume responsibility for their actions.

The usual remedy available to an injured party for a tort is to sue in court and to recover money damages. The amount of damages that can be recovered depends on the harm caused and the kind of tort committed. Damages generally are classified as compensatory or punitive (also called *exemplary damages*). In the case of an intentional tort, the injured party is entitled to both categories of damages. Compensatory damages refer to an award of money that repays the injured party for losses actually suffered, such as hospital and doctor's bills, and for "pain and suffering" resulting from any physical injury. Punitive damages are above and beyond compensatory damages and are imposed by a court as punishment on the wrongdoer.

Equitable remedies, such as an injunction, protect parties when monetary damages are not adequate.

Tort reform has changed the landscape for determining the type of lawsuits people can file and how much they can recover. Many states have brought an end to exceptionally large awards for personal injury lawsuits, especially in the area of punitive damages, by establishing a cap of $250,000 unless the defendant acted with a specific intent to harm. It appears that the tide has turned and that the days of easy money in injury lawsuits are over.

Important Legal Terms

assault
assumption of risk
battery
comparative negligence
compensatory damages
contributory negligence
conversion
cyber torts
damages
defamation
false arrest

false imprisonment
fraud
infliction of emotional distress
injunction
intentional tort
interference with contractual
    relations
invasion of privacy
libel
malicious prosecution
malpractice

negligence
nuisance
punitive damages
slander
strict liability
theft of trade secrets
tort
tort law
trespass
wrongful death

Questions and Problems for Discussion

1. Jasetti, a jockey, fell from a horse while riding in a race. The accident left him a paraplegic. It occurred when Fell, the jockey riding next to him in the race, cut in front of his horse, causing Jasetti to fall. Jasetti sued Fell for negligence, claiming he broke racing rules by cutting in front of another horse before he was clear. Should Jasetti recover damages?

2. Courtney, a twenty-two-year-old call girl, became involved with a married politician who paid her several thousand dollars for an ongoing relationship. Once Courtney's identity became known and her relationship with this politician discovered, newspapers and Web sites splashed photos of Courtney in suggestive poses along with write-ups on the front and inside pages. The photos distributed to the media actually came from MySpace pages. Her attorney lashed out at the media for thrusting the twenty-two-year-old woman into the public light without her consent. The attorney, further contending that she was not a public figure, indicated that he was taking steps to bring a lawsuit for defamation against the various media outlets that published her image and wrote about her. A spokeperson for the media lashed back and stated that the photos that appeared on MySpace were found to be noteworthy since the politician was in a high-ranking position. The spokesperson also made the point that the photos distributed were relevant to the story about Courtney's relationship with the politician. Do you think that Courtney's attorney has a case?

3. Daniels, age seventy, who was experiencing severe chest pains, was immediately admitted to South View Memorial Hospital. Dr. Rose, an internist and Daniels's personal physician for many years, did a thorough examination including an angiogram and concluded that there was a blockage in two arteries leading to the heart. Her diagnosis was that Daniels was having a heart attack. With Daniels's consent, surgery was immediately performed, but the severe chest pains did not subside. Consequently, Daniels's wife requested that Dr. Andrews, another well-known internist, take over the case. Dr. Andrews upon examination determined that the severe chest pains were actually the result of a kidney

stone attack. He told Daniels's wife that such an attack often produced severe chest pains similar to the pains experienced by a person having a heart attack. Daniels, within a few weeks and with his consent, then underwent a procedure for dissolving the several kidney stones. As a result of this procedure, the chest pains subsided. Does Daniels have a case against Dr. Rose?

4. Lacey Myers, seventy-six years of age, claims that she has suffered severe emotional distress over a situation concerning her dead husband who was buried by mistake in a section of the cemetery that isn't really a cemetery. Cemetery officials concede that the mistake was theirs and insist that the body will need to be moved to an appropriate part of the cemetery at no charge to Myers. She has been given an ultimatum to reach an agreement within a certain period of time, like one day, or her husband's remains will automatically be moved. The struggle between Myers and cemetery officials has been going on for months through their attorneys. In her own words, Myers claims "that where a person is buried, that's where they should stay. It's a sacred trust." Where her husband is buried there is plenty of open space and she claims that her husband loved open space. A cemetery official noted, however, that where her husband is buried will never become part of the cemetery. Under these circumstances, would Myers have an action in tort for severe emotional distress?

5. When his wife died of Alzheimer's disease in an Ohio hospital, Gomez instructed the attending physician to have her brain preserved for research purposes to help determine causes of the disease. The brain was placed in chemicals and sent to the National Research Lab for study. The package containing the brain, however, was lost when it arrived at the lab; it was never found. The husband, who said he would "never be able to totally bury" his wife because of the loss, suffered severe mental shock and was treated for several years by a well-known psychiatrist. For which tort or torts, if any, can the husband sue the National Research Lab?

6. Corey, a high school student, while in an electronics store noticed a sign on the wall that read: "Free—Take One." Below the sign was a table

with a box of pocket calculators mistakenly left there by a stock clerk. Corey put one of the calculators in his pocket and walked out of the store. Renwall, the store manager who saw Corey take the calculator, rushed out of the store after him shouting: "Stop you thief." Corey, unaware that Renwall was talking to him, disappeared into the large crowd on the street. Later that day, James, a customer who resembled Corey, went into the same electronics store and headed for the restroom. Renwall spotted the boy and, thinking it was Corey, locked the restroom door and called the police. James had no means of escape since there were no windows in the bathroom. When it was discovered that James was not the one who was in the store earlier, the police released James. Does James have a cause of action against Renwall and the electronics store?

7. What effect did the Supreme Court decision in *New York Times Co.* v. *Sullivan* have on the laws of defamation as they existed in the various states?

8. Dr. Huggins, a dentist, was staying at the Ritz Hotel in Nashville, Tennessee, where he had a suite. When he went into the bathroom to shave, he flipped the light switch on the wall. When he did, he received a tremendous jolt that threw him into the door frame, causing permanent injury to his right shoulder. He sued the hotel for negligence for failure to maintain electrical fixtures in a reasonably safe condition. The essence of his claim was that he could no longer work at his profession. Can Dr. Huggins legally recover damages from the hotel?

9. Coleman, a salesperson for a security company, wanted to get even with Cloos, the superintendent of the West Ridge School District, for not purchasing burglar alarms for the school district from Coleman's company. Coleman wrote a letter to the board of education falsely accusing Cloos of having been arrested in a neighboring community for possession of drugs. She also wrote that Cloos paid the local politicians to keep the incident off the police records. On what grounds could Cloos sue Coleman?

10. Marks was meeting her sister and a friend for dinner at a swanky restaurant. It was a warm summer evening, and because she was early, Marks decided to wait outside. She stood in front of the restaurant until her sister and friend arrived. Within a few minutes, a police car drove up and a police officer got out and forced Marks into the car, accusing her of being a prostitute. She was taken to the police precinct station, where she was questioned and released without being charged. She had no previous convictions and was employed as a full-time account executive at a local securities investment firm. Can Marks sue the police department for false arrest?

11. Popovici, an untenured college English teacher, was being considered for a permanent appointment. When the president of the college discovered that she was separated from her husband and seeking a divorce, he brought this information to a board of trustees meeting and recommended that she not be rehired at the end of the term. The board of trustees agreed, and Popovici was not granted tenure. She was then requested to leave her teaching position as soon as the current school year ended. The president's request to the board that Popovici not be rehired was based strictly on his fear that her divorce would harm the college's "image." Popovici was otherwise considered an "excellent teacher" and had been recommended for tenure by her department chairperson. Did the president's recommendation to deny Popovici's tenure appointment, based on her marital situation, constitute a wrongful intrusion into her private life?

Cases for Review

1. A man with a developmental disability and the mental capacity of a five-year-old made several visits to a retail store. Each time he was there, he caused a disturbance and was asked to leave. On one occasion when he was asked to leave, he threatened to kill the store owner. At this time, the police were called and they arrested the man at the request of the store owner. He was charged with trespassing. The incident caught the eye of a local television station, which did a TV story on the man's trial and identified the retail store involved. The television station's version of the incidents that occurred in the store left out key facts about the man's threatened violence on

several occasions while in the store and his admission of the threat he made to kill the store owner. As a result of the poor publicity, the store received several complaints about what was perceived as mistreatment of a person with a mental disability. The store owner sued the television station for defamation, contending that the TV version of what took place in the store damaged his reputation. Does the store owner have a case against the TV station? (*Mohr.* v. *Grant*, 68 P.3d 1159, Ct. App. Wash.)

2. LeDoux, an EMT, provided emergency medical attention to Julie Pachowitz at her residence. Because she was unresponsive and had poor vital signs, Pachowitz was taken to a hospital for treatment. When LeDoux came in contact with Slocomb, a good friend of Pachowitz who worked at another hospital, LeDoux told Slocomb that Pachowitz had taken a drug overdose. LeDoux was thinking that as a friend Slocomb could help Pachowitz with her drug problem. When Pachowitz learned that LeDoux had disclosed her drug problem to Slocomb, she sued LeDoux for invasion of privacy for publicizing private facts about her private life that was none of Slocomb's business. Does Pachowitz have a cause of action for invasion of privacy? (*Pachowitz* v. *LeDoux*, N.W. 2d, Ct. App., Wisc.)

3. Cinquanta needed repairs to a neon sign hanging in front of his restaurant. He asked Burdett to do the repairs. Upon completion, a disagreement occurred over payment of the cost of the repairs. Cinquanta claimed that the insurance company would pay, but Burdett wanted his money immediately, which did not happen. One evening Burdett and some of his friends went to the restaurant and ordered expensive meals but refused to pay the bill. Cinquanta insisted on payment and would not accept Burdett's request to substitute the cost of the meals as payment for the repairs. Burdett, in front of his friends and other patrons in the restaurant, called Cinquanta a "crook" and a "dead beat," claiming that the insurance company had not paid the bill for the repairs. Cinquanta sued Burdett for slander, claiming injury to his reputation as a business owner. Was Burdett's statement grounds for slander? (*Cinauanta* v. *Burdett* 154 Colo 37, 388 P2d 779)

4. Fischer was a guest at the Red Lion Inn, where he was attending a seminar. He went for a swim at the end of the first day of the seminar and then, still in his wet bathing suit, went directly to the vending machine to purchase a bottle of pop. When he inserted the money into the vending machine, he received an electrical shock because of defective wiring. The electric shock was so severe that it left him impotent, as confirmed by a doctor. Fischer sued Pepsi Cola Bottling Company, owner of the vending machines at the inn, for negligence. He claimed that Pepsi, although aware of the electrical problems that made the use of the machines dangerous, did not "pull" routine maintenance to correct these problems. Should Fischer be successful in his lawsuit? (*Fischer* v. *Pepsi Cola Bottling Company*, 972 F.2d 906)

5. Kimberly Dickerson entered a Wal-Mart Store in Jefferson Parish in Louisiana with some friends. Kimberly left her friends and went to the area of the store that sold stamp albums. She purchased the stamp album and a pack of gum, which the store clerk placed in a bag. Kimberly then went to another area in the store where one of her friends was waiting. This area was in a secluded part of the store. She proceeded to place her hand in the Wal-Mart bag to retrieve the gum she had just purchased. At that moment, Mrs. Neal, a customer service manager, came along and saw what Kimberly was doing. Since Kimberly's moves seemed suspicious, she snatched Kimberly's bag, searched the bag, discovered a receipt, and then sent them to the area where they claimed their other friends were shopping. This whole incident lasted about one minute. Kimberly was never told that she was being detained and that they could not leave the store. Kimberly and her parents sued Wal-Mart for false imprisonment. Does she have a legitimate cause of action? Keep in mind that Louisiana law gives quasi-police powers to merchants to protect against shoplifting and gives them immunity from liability from malicious prosecution when the merchant has reasonable cause to believe that a theft of goods has occurred on their premises. (*Vaughn* v. *Wal-Mart Stores*, 734 So.2d 156, Ct. App. Louisiana, Fifth Circuit)

6. Gonzalez was injured while a passenger in Garcia's car. Garcia, who had been drinking heavily, lost control of the car and caused it to roll over, landing on its side. Gonzalez sued for damages for negligence. Garcia claimed comparative

negligence as a defense. Testimony in court revealed that Gonzalez knew Garcia was intoxicated. The court concluded that Gonzalez could have taken a cab or called his wife for a ride. Instead, he took a dangerous route and rode with Garcia. Does Gonzalez's decision to ride with Garcia amount to negligence that makes him partially liable for the accident? (*Gonzalez* v. *Garcia*, 142 Cal. Rptr. 503)

7. This case deals with medical malpractice in which both the plaintiff and the defendant were doctors. The suit was brought by Dr. David Axelrad, a psychiatrist, the patient, against Dr. Richard Jackson, an internist, the attending physician. After months of intermittent abdominal cramps and diarrhea, Dr. Axelrad sought treatment from Dr. Jackson because the pains became more acute. Dr. Jackson prescribed a laxative and an enema for fecal impaction. Returning home, Axelrad followed his doctor's orders and immediately felt severe abdominal pain with nausea and chills. His wife took him to an emergency room, and he was hospitalized for further testing. Based on those tests, another doctor operated two days later for what was thought to be appendicitis but turned out to be diverticulitis and a perforated colon. A portion of the colon was removed and a temporary colostomy constructed. Axelrad subsequently had further surgery to reconnect the colon, which became complicated by a severe drug reaction. During the court trial, several facts came up that made it sound as if both doctor and patient were at fault. While conceding a patient with diverticulitis should not be treated with enemas, Dr. Jackson testified he did not suspect diverticulitis as it is normally associated with fever, constipation, and pain in the left lower quadrant, while Axelrad had reported no fever, diarrhea, or pain throughout his abdomen. During the trial, accusations of negligence went back and forth between the two doctors who asserted how each had been negligent. It was hard for the jury not to believe both since each could legally be considered an expert. A critical fact that came before the jury at the original trial was that both the plaintiff and defendant, as doctors, failed to reveal information that was significant to the medical malpractice case brought by Dr. Axelrad,

How do you think the case was decided? (*Jackson* v. *Axelrad*, 142 S.W. 3d. 418 421 (Tex App-Houston).

8. Gielskie was left totally paralyzed from the chest down as a result of an injection of tetanus antitoxin serum. The serum was provided by the New York State Department of Health, which included instructions on how to give the injections. The instructions stated that there were a number of methods of giving injections of this serum. Evidence indicated that doctors differed on which method to use. Gielskie sued the state of New York, claiming malpractice. Should Gielskie succeed? (*Gielskie* v. *State*, 9 N.Y.2d 834)

9. Berger, a firefighter, responded to a chemical boilover at Lipson's chemical manufacturing plant, the boilover having been caused by Lipson's negligence. When Berger arrived on the scene, he asked whether any toxic chemicals were involved and was told there were none. Actually, toxic chemicals were involved, and Berger was injured when he attempted to control the boilover. In response to Berger's suit for damages, Lipson argued that a person, such as a firefighter, who engages in a hazardous activity in the normal course of duty, assumes the risk of danger and should be barred from recovery for injuries. Should the court accept this line of reasoning? (*Lipson* v. *Superior Court*, 644 P.2d 822)

10. Hairston purchased and took delivery of a new car from Haygood Lincoln-Mercury. As he drove home from the Lincoln-Mercury dealership, the left rear wheel came off the car. Because there was no shoulder on the road, he stopped the car in the far right lane. A passing motorist who stopped to help parked his van 20 feet behind Hairston's car. A flatbed truck, driven by Alexander and owned by the Alexander Tank and Equipment Co., came along and struck the van, knocking it into the rear of Hairston's automobile. Hairston, who had been standing between his car and the van, was killed. There was conclusive evidence that Alexander was negligent in failing to keep his truck under proper control. Hairston's wife, Bettye, sued both Haygood and the Alexander Tank and Equipment Co. for damages, alleging that their negligence had caused her husband's death. Should Hairston's wife succeed in her lawsuits? (*Hairston* v. *Alexander Tank and Equipment Co.*, 311 S.E.2d 559)

CHAPTER 5

Litigation and Alternatives for Settling Civil Disputes

CHAPTER PREVIEW

Chapter Highlights

The first part of this chapter outlines the general procedures one may go through when a decision is made to bring a civil lawsuit. The remainder of the chapter explores several alternatives for settling legal disputes outside the courtroom.

PROLOGUE

Litigation has become a way of life in this country. "See you in court" used to be a real threat. Now it is as common as "Have a nice day." Many Americans are now demanding their day in court. They are suing one another with unprecedented frequency. Some are just greedy, whereas others are egged on by attorneys excited at the prospect of huge financial windfalls. Thousands of civil cases are filed in federal and state courts every year. Juries are often sympathetic to victims bringing suits, especially when the defendants have "deep pockets," and frequently award large sums of money to victims of torts (especially negligence) and to those suffering losses from breach of contract, inappropriate real estate transactions, matrimonial problems, illegal or unconscionable consumer transactions, antitrust violations, patent infringements, and other causes. Many of today's cases would have been laughed out of court a few years ago. When something goes wrong, people use the occasion to try to make money, especially when a large corporation is involved. For example, an $8 an hour worker ordered a hamburger at a fast food restaurant. She was instead given a cheeseburger by mistake. Not knowing of the error until she had practically eaten the entire cheeseburger (according to the worker), she suffered a severe allergy attack from the cheeseburger. She sued the company for $10 mllion even though the company offered to pay all her medical expenses.

As discussed later in this chapter, there are ways to settle a disagreement between two or more parties other than by *litigation* (a lawsuit). It goes without saying that if you become involved in a legal controversy, you should try to settle out of court. (It has been estimated that upward of 90 percent of all civil cases are settled before they get to trial.) There are advantages to an out-of-court settlement.

A major reason for finding alternatives to a lawsuit is that the person you are thinking of suing may be *judgment proof*—that is, unable to pay even if you win the case. Also, because of the backlog of court cases, delays of up to three years (and sometimes even longer) before a case can be heard are not unusual. During such delays, witnesses may die or move away, and evidence may be lost or forgotten. Furthermore, if the losing party appeals the trial court's decision to a higher court, settlement could be delayed as long as ten years. Also consider that lengthy legal proceedings can be an emotionally draining experience. The prospects of a prolonged courtroom battle may require you, and possibly other members of your family, to face hostile attorneys involved in the trial as well as in pretrial hearings. And although all the signs of winning may be in your favor, you still run the risk of losing. Finally, you must ask yourself whether a successful court battle is worth its cost to you in court and attorneys' fees.

The first step in deciding whether to sue is to discuss your legal problem with an attorney. After you have this discussion and fully understand your options, you may discover that the case cannot be settled in any way other than by litigation.

To help you better understand what litigation is all about, the next several pages of this chapter discuss the steps in a lawsuit from beginning to end. (Remember, however, that each court has its own rules and regulations governing the procedures for bringing a lawsuit.) Although procedures vary from court to court and from state to state, certain procedures or stages are basic to all suits. Figure 5.1 illustrates these steps. The following scenario traces one person's experiences in the litigation process. The general steps followed in criminal and civil cases are compared in Table 5.1.

EXPLORING A PERSONAL INJURY LAWSUIT

Bill Allen (age thirty-five), an executive for a large advertising firm, had a wife, Martha (age thirty), and a daughter, Karen (age five). His job was secure and paid him a salary of $100,000 a year; he had a good future with the firm. He and his wife shared an excellent relationship. They enjoyed doing things together, such as playing tennis; going to concerts, plays, and movies; and gardening and landscaping around their new house. Above all, they were both devoted parents who took an active interest in bringing up their young daughter.

One evening, Bill Allen was driving home from work, and as he traveled (within the speed limit) on an open stretch of road, his car was struck by a tractor-trailer belonging to the Laiden Trucking Company. The driver of the truck, who was traveling in the opposite direction at a high rate of speed and in an intoxicated condition, had crossed the center line, driving head on into the Allen car. Allen, trapped inside the car, had to be removed by a special crew called to the accident scene. Witnesses verified Allen's version of the accident, and police called to the scene verified that the driver of the truck had been drinking.

After several months in the hospital, where he was recovering from serious internal injuries and undergoing painful therapy, Allen's doctors determined that he would be paralyzed from the waist down and would have to spend the rest of his life in a wheelchair. He also would face many years of pain and the possibility of additional medical treatment. It was also determined that he was suffering emotionally. He was upset that he could no longer work to support his family or do the things his wife and he had done together and with their daughter. Allen had some savings, but because his wife was not

FIGURE 5.1 The Primary Steps in a Civil Lawsuit

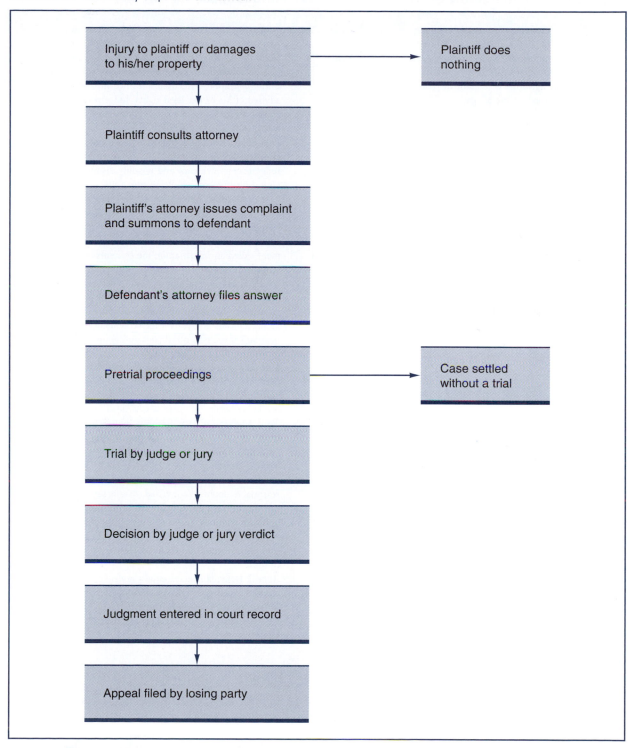

TABLE 5.1   COMPARISON OF CIVIL AND CRIMINAL PROCEDURES

CIVIL	CRIMINAL*
1. *Complaint.* Paper prepared by injured party's (plaintiff's) attorney informing defendant of the reasons for legal action. Complaint accompanied by a summons officially announcing to the defendant the commencement of a lawsuit based on the allegations (claims) made in the complaint.	1. *Arrest.* Accused person taken into custody, "booked" (record of arrest entered in police records), fingerprinted, and photographed, interrogated, released on bail, or confined.
2. *Answer.* Defendant forwards to plaintiff's attorney a response to the charges made in the complaint. Defendant will be in default for failure to respond to complaint.	2. *Initial appearance.* Accused informed of the charges and advised of his or her legal rights. Judge reviews case and possibly dismisses charges; or accused is released on bail (if not already released) or confined.
3. *Pretrial proceedings.* Consists of filing motions, discovery, and pretrial conference.	3. *Preliminary hearing.* (Some states) Formal hearing with attorneys present to evaluate evidence against accused. Judge reviews evidence and possibly dismisses charges.
4. *Trial.* Selection of jury. Presentation of evidence by attorneys to the jury (or a judge if a nonjury trial). To win a successful verdict, an attorney must prove his or her case by a preponderance of evidence (evidence more convincing than that of opposing counsel). In some states, verdict of jury need not be unanimous.	4. *Grand jury proceeding.* Prosecutor (D.A.) presents evidence to the grand jury, which then brings formal charges against the accused (an indictment) or dismisses the charges for lack of evidence. (Formal charges in some states are made by the D.A. through issuance of a document called an information, the contents of which are based on evidence obtained from the preliminary hearing.)
5. *Judgment.* The official decision of the jury is entered in the court record. Case is now said to be adjudicated.	5. *Arraignment.* Formal notification to accused of charges against him or her made in the indictment or information. Accused is then asked for a plea of guilty or not guilty. If accused pleads guilty, date for sentencing is set. (There is no trial.) If accused pleads not guilty, pretrial hearings are scheduled. Bail may be reexamined.
6. *Appeal.* The party who loses the lawsuit has the option to appeal the decision of the trial court to a higher court.	6. *Pretrial proceedings.* Hearings on behalf of accused asking that charges be dismissed for various reasons. Plea negotiations may also take place. If these hearings do not bring results, the case is scheduled for trial.
7. *Constitutional guarantees.* Basically none for either the plaintiff or the defendant.	7. *Trial.* Selection of jury. Presentation of evidence by the prosecutor (D.A.) for the state and by the accused (generally by accused's attorney) to the jury (or to a judge alone if a nonjury trial). Guilty verdict by jury must be unanimous (in most states) and must be proven beyond a reasonable doubt. If convicted, date is set for sentencing.
	8. *Sentence.* Presentence report made detailing defendant's previous criminal record and his or her personal, social, and emotional background. Sentence may be prison, fine, probation, community-based programs, or a combination of these.
	9. *Appeal.* Defendant may request review of case by higher court if found guilty in lower court. If defendant is found not guilty, the prosecutor cannot appeal the case.
	10. *Constitutional guarantees.* Lie with the defendant, not the victim.

*Based on the proceedings in a felony case.

working, the money would not be enough for the family to maintain the same standard of living they were used to before the accident occurred. The Allens also would have to pay thousands of dollars in medical bills not covered by his health insurance. Allen decided to seek the advice of an attorney, but not having had any legal problems, he had no idea which attorney could best handle his case. His friends recommended attorneys whom they had retained in the past. One friend also suggested that he contact the local bar association for the names of attorneys.

Investigation

Allen contacted Jan Heisman, an attorney for a large law firm with a good reputation for settling negligence cases similar to his. At this meeting, Allen described in detail all the facts relating to the accident and provided the names of the witnesses. Heisman indicated to Allen that before she took the case, she would first conduct a preliminary investigation to determine the validity and practicability of bringing a claim. She further explained to Allen that he should decide as soon as possible if she was going to be the attorney handling his case so that she could begin her preliminary investigation. Heisman told Allen that timing is critical if accurate information is to be obtained because memories fade, people move, and records can be misplaced. Heisman obtained a medical release from Allen so that she could examine the hospital and medical records relating to his case. She also interviewed and received statements from the witnesses to the accident. The preliminary investigation completed, Heisman then requested another meeting with Allen to present her evaluation of his case in terms of the course of action she would recommend.

Heisman concluded that Allen indeed had a case (or cause of action) based on negligence, that if the case came to trial he stood a good chance of achieving a favorable verdict, and that the amount of the award would be considerable because of his high medical bills and because his earning capacity had been destroyed by his inability to return to work as a result of the "pain and suffering" (physical pain and emotional stress) inflicted in the accident. Heisman discussed with Allen the possibility of settling out of court, noting, however, that the amount of the settlement would be considerably less. Heisman made the point that the trucking company's attorney, knowing that Allen would probably receive a large award of money, might use shrewd legal tactics to delay the start of the lawsuit in an attempt to find damaging information about him to use in court. In turn, Allen, out of desperation and frustration might decide to settle out of court for less money in order to pay bills or simply get on with his life. It is Allen's call on when to settle and not Heisman's. Keep in mind that it would be unethical for Heisman not to inform Allen of any offers to settle by the insurance company. (Remember Heisman's fee comes from the settlement fee.) Allen, nevertheless, should listen to Heisman's advice before accepting any offer from the insurance company. If the insurance company in its behind-the-scenes investigation or during the course of the trial discovered damaging evidence about Allen, a settlement figure may be offered, which of course, would be considerably less than Heisman and Allen consider to be a fair figure. What happens next then becomes a test of endurance between plaintiff and defendant. Knowing that Allen still has a good case, the insurance company may wait as long as possible to settle out of court. This settlement could occur at any stage of the trial up until the time that a jury verdict is rendered. The big advantage to the insurance company is that it has held on to the settlement money (probably drawing interest in an investment account) for as long as possible.

Decision to Sue and Establishment of Attorney's Fees

Given all these facts, Allen evaluated them carefully, including Heisman's advice to go to trial. He decided to proceed to trial and to retain Heisman as his attorney. Heisman discussed with Allen the expenses of litigation, including the matter of attorneys' fees. Heisman explained that there were at least three bases for attorneys' fees: an hourly rate, a flat rate, and a contingency fee. She further explained that in personal injury lawsuits, the attorneys were often paid a *contingency fee,* in Allen's case, a percentage (the standard fee is 33 percent) of the money damages collected from the trucking company if the case was decided in Allen's favor; if Allen lost the case, there would be no fee. (If the case settled prior to a trial, the fee would be around 25 percent.) Heisman then drew up a client-attorney contract and indicated in the contract that payment was to be based on a contingency fee. Heisman was officially retained to represent Allen, and preparation for the trial began.

ANATOMY OF A LAWSUIT

This section provides a detailed chronology of the steps taken in a lawsuit from start to finish.

How a Lawsuit Begins: Summons, Complaint, Answer

Bill Allen's lawsuit begins when Heisman, as an officer of the court, prepares and delivers a complaint and summons to the appropriate representative of the Laiden Trucking Company. A **complaint** (Figure 5.2) states the names of the parties to the lawsuit, in this case, Bill Allen and the Laiden Trucking Company. The complaint also sets out the *cause of action,* the facts and circumstances that Bill Allen, on whose behalf the suit is brought, believes are the basis for the legal action and states the remedy being sought. In this case, Allen is seeking $3 million for medical expenses, "pain and suffering," and court costs. A **summons** (Figure 5.3) is a written notice to the party being sued (in this case, the Laiden Trucking Company) indicating that a lawsuit has been filed and ordering an authorized representative of the company to appear in court or to answer in writing within a designated period of time (such as twenty days).

Now that the lawsuit is officially under way, Bill Allen legally becomes known as the **plaintiff** because he is bringing the lawsuit. The Laiden Trucking Company becomes known as the **defendant** because it is the party against whom the lawsuit is brought. (In a criminal action, the plaintiff is the state or federal government acting for the people—society—and the defendant is the person accused of committing a crime.) A person called a *process server* usually delivers a copy of the summons and complaint to the defendant, wherever that person can be found. In some cases, the "papers" may be left with a responsible individual at the home of the defendant or may be sent by certified mail.

After the representative of the Laiden Trucking Company has been served with the complaint and summons, he or she should contact the company's lawyer, who will then draw up an **answer** (Figure 5.4) to the complaint. The complaint and the answer taken together are called the **pleadings.** The answer is a written response to the *allegations* (claims) made by the plaintiff. The answer may deny all charges and give legally sound reasons in defense of these charges, or it may deny some charges while admitting others. An actual appearance in court by the defendant to deliver the answer is not necessary. In this case, the Laiden Trucking Company's attorney would simply deliver a *notice of appearance* to Bill Allen's attorney. This notice acknowledges that the defendant has received the summons. A failure to acknowledge gives the plaintiff the right to a *judgment by default,* which means that Bill Allen could then proceed to prove his case in the court having jurisdiction and, if successful, could receive money damages. The judge of the court would make a decision based only on the evidence presented by Allen's attorney. In a judgment by default, the attorney for the Laiden Trucking Company would not be permitted to present evidence on behalf of the company.

Pretrial Proceedings

Before a lawsuit is brought to trial, both parties to the suit have a chance to develop their cases and prepare for trial. Pretrial proceedings usually consist of *motions, discovery,* and a *pretrial conference.*

A **motion,** which may be filed by either party, is a written or oral request to a judge to take some specific action. For example, after studying the complaint, the attorney for

---

complaint document listing the details of a lawsuit being filed and the relief sought

summons written notification to the defendant that a lawsuit has been filed

plaintiff one who begins a legal action

defendant party against whom criminal charges or a lawsuit is brought

answer formal written statement by a defendant responding to a civil complaint and setting forth the grounds for defense

pleadings complaint and answers taken together

motion request to a judge for a ruling on a point of law

summary judgment
motion for immediate judgment filed by either plaintiff or defendant, based on the information in the complaint and the answer

the Laiden Trucking Company may choose to file a motion to dismiss the lawsuit, claiming that the facts stated in the complaint are not adequate and do not entitle Bill Allen the relief he is seeking ($3 million). If the judge grants a motion to dismiss, the case is dismissed, effectively ending the lawsuit. Or if Heisman, Bill Allen's attorney, thinks the Laiden Trucking Company lacks a sufficient defense to win the suit, she may, for example, make a motion for immediate judgment (called a **summary judgment**). By this motion, Heisman asks the court to decide the issue based on the statements in the

FIGURE 5.2 Complaint

STATE OF NEW YORK
SUPREME COURT
COUNTY OF MONROE

BILL ALLEN

                         Plaintiff,   COMPLAINT

                             VS.

LAIDEN TRUCKING COMPANY

                          Defendant

    The Plaintiff, BILL ALLEN, complaining of the Defendant, LAIDEN TRUCKING COMPANY, and through his attorney, Jan Heisman, Esq., alleges and respectfully shows the Court as follows:

  1. That at all the times hereinafter mentioned, the Plaintiff, BILL ALLEN, was a resident of the City of Rochester, County of Monroe, State of New York.

  2. That at all the times hereinafter mentioned, the Plaintiff, BILL ALLEN, was the owner and operator of a 2003 Chevrolet automobile bearing New York State license plate number: NY 689-42.

  3. Upon information and belief, and at all the times hereinafter mentioned, the Defendant, LAIDEN TRUCKING COMPANY, was a domestic corporation organized and existing under and by virtue of the laws of the State of New York, and had its principal place of business located in the City of Rochester, County of Monroe, State of New York.

  4. Upon information and belief, and at all the times hereinafter mentioned, the Defendant, LAIDEN TRUCKING COMPANY, owned a 2005 International Tractor-Trailer bearing New York State license plate number: NY 138JJ.

  5. Upon information and belief, and at all the times hereinafter mentioned, and more particularly, on the *3rd day of July, 2007*, employee of the Defendant, LAIDEN TRUCKING COMPANY, was operating the tractor-trailer owned by the Defendant with its permission, knowledge and consent, and within the scope of its business interests.

  6. That Route 390 is a public road running in a general northerly and southerly direction in and through the City of Rochester, County of Monroe, State of New York.

  7. That on or about the *3rd day of July, 2004*, between the hours of 6 and 7 o'clock in the evening of said day, the Plaintiff, BILL

FIGURE 5.2 Complaint (continued)

```
        BILL ALLEN    Plaintiff,              Complaint        page 2
                       VS.
        LAIDEN TRUCKING COMPANY    Defendant
       _____

        ALLEN, was operating his motor vehicle in a general northerly
        direction on Route 390 at a point approximately one-quarter of a
        mile south of Exit 29.
          8. That at the same time and place, the tractor-trailer owned by
        the Defendant, LAIDEN TRUCKING COMPANY, was traveling in a general
        southerly direction on Route 390 and crossed into the northbound
        lanes of traffic striking the automobile of the Plaintiff, BILL
        ALLEN, causing the Plaintiff, BILL ALLEN, to sustain serious permanent
        personal injuries as will be hereinafter more particularly set
        forth.
          9. That the Defendant, LAIDEN TRUCKING COMPANY, was careless and
        negligent, in that its employee was operating Defendant's tractor-
        trailer at a high and excessive rate of speed in view of the
        conditions then and there prevailing; that he failed to sound,
        signal, or give any notice or warning of his approach; that he
        failed to keep the tractor-trailer in the southbound lanes of
        traffic and crossed into the northbound lanes of traffic; that said
        employee was further careless and negligent, in that he was
        operating said tractor-trailer when his ability to do so was
        impaired by alcohol, or additionally, when he was driving while
        intoxicated.
          10. That as a result of the carelessness and negligence of the
        Defendant, LAIDEN TRUCKING COMPANY, as has hereinbefore been set
        forth, the Plaintiff, BILL ALLEN, was made sick, sore, lame, and
        disabled; that he suffered and will in the future continue to suffer
        great pain and physical as well as mental anguish; and that the
        Plaintiff, BILL ALLEN, is informed and believes that he has sustained
        permanent injuries, and that he will never fully recover from the
        effects of same.
          11. Due to the carelessness and negligence of the Defendant,
        LAIDEN TRUCKING COMPANY, as aforesaid and the injuries resulting
        therefrom, the Plaintiff, BILL ALLEN, has been, and will in the
        future be, incapacitated and prevented from performing the duties
        incident to his usual occupation in life, and that he lost, and
        will in the future lose, the wages therefrom.
          12. That no fault or negligence on the part of the Plaintiff, BILL
        ALLEN, herein contributed to or caused said accident herein and the
        injuries resulting therefrom, but that the same were caused wholly
        and solely by reason of the carelessness and negligence of the
        Defendant, LAIDEN TRUCKING COMPANY, herein.
```

complaint and in the answer. In either case, if the judge grants the motion, further proceedings, including a trial, are avoided. Other pretrial motions might include a motion by defense counsel to strike some allegation(s) from the complaint or to dismiss the entire complaint.

discovery pretrial steps taken to learn the details of the case

Discovery refers to the pretrial steps taken by the plaintiff and the defendant to learn in detail the nature of the other's claim or defense. In today's court systems, every effort

FIGURE 5.2 Complaint (continued)

BILL ALLEN   Plaintiff,   Complaint   page 3
               VS.
LAIDEN TRUCKING COMPANY   Defendant

---

13. Due to the carelessness and negligence of the Defendant, LAIDEN TRUCKING COMPANY herein, the Plaintiff, BILL ALLEN, sustained among other things, serious internal injuries and paralysis from the waist down, which will be permanent in nature, and he has been out of work for a year, all in compliance with Section 5102 of the New York State Insurance Law.

14. That as a result of the carelessness and negligence of the Defendant, LAIDEN TRUCKING COMPANY herein, and the injuries sustained by the Plaintiff, BILL ALLEN, the Plaintiff, BILL ALLEN, has been damaged in the sum of $3,000,000.00.

WHEREFORE, the Plaintiff, BILL ALLEN, demands judgment against the Defendant, LAIDEN TRUCKING COMPANY, in the sum of $3,000,000.00, together with the costs and disbursements of this action.

Dated: August 15, 2008

                                        Jan Heisman, Esq.
                                        Attorney for Plaintiff
                                        350 Main Street
                                        Rochester, NY 14606
                                        (585) 555-9201

TO: HILL AND DALE
    Attorneys for Defendant
    2700 Bleek Tower
    Rochester, NY 14732
    (585) 555-9348

---

interrogatories series of written questions directed to the adversary in a civil trial who must answer by written replies made under oath

deposition a witness's sworn statement in writing containing out-of-court testimony

is made to encourage discovery so that both parties will be fully prepared for trial and surprises will be avoided. Consequently, discovery is a vital step in any litigation. The process ensures that all potential testimony and other evidence are made available to both sides. Discovery techniques include a series of written questions called **interrogatories** that are sent to the opposing party in the lawsuit, who must truthfully answer them under oath (an attorney usually helps with the preparation of the answers); **depositions**—which are sworn statements from witnesses taken outside the courtroom who, for good cause, may not be able to be present at the trial; compulsory physical and mental examinations by doctors chosen by the other party in personal injury cases in which a person's condition is a

FIGURE 5.3 Summons

STATE OF NEW YORK
SUPREME COURT
COUNTY OF MONROE

BILL ALLEN
301 Blaine Street
Rochester, New York 14839

                Plaintiff   SUMMONS
                VS.

LAIDEN TRUCKING COMPANY
383 Ipswich Avenue
Rochester, New York 14631

                Defendant
_____

To the above named Defendant
    YOU ARE HEREBY SUMMONED to answer the complaint in this action
and to serve a copy of your answer, or, if the complaint is not
served with this summons, to serve a notice of appearance, on the
Plaintiff's Attorney(s) within *20* days after the service of this
summons, exclusive of the day of service (or within 30 days after
the service is complete if this summons is not personally delivered
to you within the State of New York); and in case of your failure to
appear or answer, judgment will be taken against you by default for
the relief demanded in the complaint.
    Upon your failure to appear or answer, judgment will be taken
against you by default for the sum of $3,000,000.00 together with
the costs and disbursements of this action.

Dated: August 15, 2008

Notice: The object of this action is to recover for injuries
sustained in a motor vehicle accident caused by defendant's
negligence. The relief sought is monetary damages in the sum of
$3,000,000.00 for medical expenses, pain and suffering, and court
costs.

                        Jan Heisman, Esq.
                        Attorney for Plaintiff
                        350 Main Street
                        Rochester, NY 14606
                        (585) 555-9201

matter of controversy; and the request for production of documents or other things in the possession of the other party for inspection. At this time, Heisman will introduce the records of the hospital, statements from the doctors who examined Bill Allen, and the statements of the witnesses to the accident. The attorney for the Laiden Trucking Company may require Allen to submit to a physical examination by an independent doctor. Discovery techniques, which generally take place after the motions have been filed and dealt with, sometimes result in the compromise and settlement of a claim at this stage.

FIGURE 5.4 Answer

STATE OF NEW YORK
SUPREME COURT
COUNTY OF MONROE

BILL ALLEN
301 Blaine Street
Rochester, New York 14839

                              Plaintiff   ANSWER
                         VS.

LAIDEN TRUCKING COMPANY
383 Ipswich Avenue
Rochester, New York 14631

                         Defendant
───

  1. Defendant, LAIDEN TRUCKING COMPANY, admits the allegations in
paragraphs 3, 4, and 6 of the complaint.
  2. Defendant, LAIDEN TRUCKING COMPANY, states that it lacks
knowledge or information sufficient to form a belief as to the truth
of the allegations in paragraphs 1 and 2 of the complaint.
  3. Defendant, LAIDEN TRUCKING COMPANY, denies each and every other
allegation of the complaint.

                         AFFIRMATIVE DEFENSE
     That any injuries or damages which the plaintiff may have
sustained, if any, at the time and place mentioned in the complaint
herein were caused for the most part by the carelessness and
negligence of the plaintiff himself and that if any carelessness,
negligence, or want of care upon the part of defendant caused or
contributed to such injuries and damages of the plaintiff it bore
only a slight proportion to the entire negligence attributable to
both plaintiff and defendant in causing such injuries and damages.
        WHEREFORE, defendant LAIDEN TRUCKING COMPANY, demands judg-
ment against plaintiff dismissing the complaint, plus costs and
disbursements.

Dated: August 30, 2008

                                   HILL AND DALE
                                   Attorneys for Defendant
                                   2700 Bleek Tower
                                   Rochester, NY 14732

Jan Heisman, Esq.
Attorney for Plaintiff
350 Main Street
Rochester, NY 14606

pretrial conference
hearing before a trial in
which parties discuss
the facts; may lead to
settlement of the case

After a lawsuit is placed on the court's trial calendar, awaiting its turn to be heard, a **pretrial conference** may be held to see whether the suit can be settled without a trial. The pretrial conference includes a judge, the opposing attorneys, and often, the parties to the suit. At this conference, the judge and the two opposing attorneys discuss, evaluate, and narrow down the issues in the case (taken from the complaint and the answer), and they review the results of the discovery process with a view to working out a settlement if possible. A *settlement* is an agreement between the parties to resolve the lawsuit without a trial. Many suits are settled at the pretrial conference stage after the judge has made recommendations for settlement. When a settlement is reached, the parties agree to dismiss the lawsuit. If no settlement can be reached, the judge and the attorneys then discuss the details of the trial.

The Trial

Unless Bill Allen reaches a satisfactory settlement agreement with the Laiden Trucking Company during the pretrial proceedings, the case will be placed on the calendar (sometimes called the docket), which lists the cases to be heard over a certain period of time. Bill Allen's case will come to trial as *Bill Allen* v. (versus) *Laiden Trucking Company.* If Allen and the Laiden Trucking Company do not demand a jury trial (both must agree), the case will come to trial before a judge (called a bench trial). If either party demands a jury trial, the case will be set for trial and a jury will be selected (impaneled). (Assume for the remainder of this discussion that the parties have requested a jury trial.)

The first step of the trial is to select jurors—called **petit jurors**—from a panel of prospective jurors summoned to the courthouse for jury duty. They are chosen at random from many lists such as voter registration lists, driver's license lists, social services lists, and state income tax lists. (Traditionally, the number of jurors has been twelve, but many states have reduced that number to eight or even fewer in civil actions.) Those selected must be citizens of the United States and within a certain age group. Some states, like New York State, are loosening the age requirement and now allow citizens of any age beyond adulthood to serve as jurors if they wish to do so. Many states have eliminated automatic exemptions for various professionals such as doctors, lawyers, judges, police officers, and teachers, making it virtually impossible to get out of jury duty now no matter what your profession is.

Jurors are subject to examination before serving. This examination to determine potential jurors' qualifications and suitability to serve is called the **voir dire** examination. In the typical procedure, jurors take their seats in the jury box in the courtroom where the case will be heard. The judge and the attorneys then question potential jurors to determine whether they are impartial and will decide the case fairly. A prospective juror who is biased, is related to someone involved in the case, or has an interest in the outcome of the case will be dismissed. This process is called **removal for cause.** Each attorney may also question jurors to determine which ones will be most favorable to his or her client's case. Each attorney has a limited number of **peremptory challenges,** which means they can dismiss a limited number of potential jurors without giving any reason. During voir dire, potential jurors may be dismissed because they have already formed opinions. Such dismissals are especially common in high-profile civil and criminal cases.

When the jury has been selected or impaneled, the opposing attorneys make *opening statements.* These statements give the judge and jury an overall picture of the facts and issues in the case and an idea of what each attorney intends to prove.

After the opening statements, the plaintiff presents his or her case. In our case, Heisman will therefore be first to present **evidence**—legal proof—to support Bill Allen's claims. She will do so by questioning witnesses for Allen through **direct examination.** (If witnesses do not voluntarily appear to testify, they can be ordered to do so by means of a court order called a **subpoena.**) Heisman may also present further evidence in the form of documents or charts, such as Allen's hospital record and other medical records attesting to his serious internal injuries, the painful therapy, and the paralysis for the rest of his life. The attorney for Laiden Trucking Company as the opposing attorney may then cross-examine Allen's witnesses. The purpose of **cross-examination** is to enable the opposing attorney to discover and bring to the attention of the jury any false or

petit jurors jurors for civil or criminal trial

voir dire (meaning "to speak the truth") questioning of potential jurors by the judge and opposing attorneys to determine prior knowledge of the facts of the case and a willingness to decide the case only on the evidence presented in court

removal for cause dismissal of a prospective juror during the selection process because of the juror's inability to be impartial

peremptory challenge right of each attorney in a court case to dismiss a prospective juror arbitrarily

evidence information submitted in testimony that is used to persuade a judge and/or jury to decide the case for one side or the other

direct examination questioning a witness by the attorney who called the witness

subpoena court order requiring testimony in a case

cross-examination questioning a witness by the attorney who did not produce the witness

inconsistent statements that Allen's witnesses have made in their direct testimony. When all Allen's witnesses have been questioned, the trucking company's attorney calls his or her witnesses for direct examination. Allen's attorney will then have a chance to cross-examine these witnesses.

After all the evidence has been presented, the attorneys make their *closing arguments,* summarizing for the jury the testimony supporting their clients and arguing that they should win the case because they have proved their cases by a *preponderance of evidence,* that their evidence is more convincing than that presented by the opposing side by even the slightest bit. The judge then instructs or *charges the jury,* which means that he or she advises the jurors of the rules of law that must be applied to the facts presented during the trial. In this case, because Allen is suing for negligence, part of the judge's instructions to the jury will state the elements that must exist to constitute negligence. Following the instructions, the jurors retire to the jury room to discuss the facts in the case. When they reach a **verdict**—a decision—the jurors return to the courtroom. (In some states, the verdict does not have to be unanimous in a civil case.) After the verdict is announced in open court, a judgment is entered. A **judgment** is the official decision of the jury entered into the court record. If a jury verdict awards Allen $3 million, for example, the court clerk at the request of the judge will enter the amount in the court records as a judgment against Laiden Trucking Company. After the judgment is entered in the records, the case is then said to be decided or **adjudicated.**

verdict decision of a jury

judgment official decision by a judge in a lawsuit tried without a jury

adjudicated judgment in a lawsuit

Posttrial Proceedings

The party who loses the lawsuit has options. One option is to appeal the decision of the trial court to a higher court. Each party to a lawsuit is generally entitled to one appeal. The appeal is held in an appellate court. (The appeals procedure was discussed in Chapter 2.) If the Laiden Trucking Company loses to Bill Allen and has to pay him $3 million, the company, through its attorney, may request a higher court to review the case. The attorney may ask that the trial court's decision be reversed or at least modified—reducing the amount of damages—or may request a new trial. Such a request is unlikely to happen, however, unless the trial court judge made a critical legal error during the trial. For example, in this case, the attorney for Laiden Trucking may show that the judge disallowed certain evidence that the attorney wanted to introduce and that was favorable to the company, which may have changed the outcome of the jury's decision.

As noted in Chapter 2, the appeals procedure is not simple. It requires a lot of preparation on the part of the attorneys and consequently is quite expensive. (In an appeal, attorney's fees could run as high as 45 percent of the amount collected as money damages, instead of the usual 33 percent.)

ALTERNATIVES FOR SETTLING DISPUTES

Not all legal disputes need end up in a courtroom. Before charging headlong into the court clerk's office to file a lawsuit, it is important to realize that litigation is expensive, time consuming, stressful, and aggravating. Increasing numbers of individuals and businesses in the United States are now voluntarily giving up their day in court and agreeing to participate in other faster, less formal, less emotional, and less expensive ways of settling their disputes. Some of these alternative dispute resolution (ADR) programs are arbitration, mediation, the minitrial, the summary jury trial, the private trial, and informal settlement between the parties. Keep in mind that these programs take place outside the courtroom. These ADR programs, especially arbitration and mediation, have now greatly expanded over the last several years and are the trend in resolving disputes that arise especially in business and industry. By some estimates, more than 90 percent of all civil cases are settled before trial. If you consider how the number of disputes between corporate employers and their employees involving wrongful termination, sexual harassment, discrimination, and breach of an employee contract has increased over the years as well as the expense of litigating such suits, and that the growth of federal and state laws has expanded aggrieved employees' rights to jury trials, you will understand why. Businesses have responded by including in their labor contracts with employees and in their employee handbooks a clause that requires the parties to submit their disputes to arbitration or mediation and, in some cases, a minitrial. Countless other disputes are now settled through informal proceedings, including consumer complaints against businesses, insurance claims, international commercial disputes, and labor-management disputes (e.g., wrongful termination, sexual harassment, and discrimination). One big advantage of out-of-court proceedings is that disputes can be dealt with while they are "live," rather than having the parties reconstruct facts at great cost years later before judges or juries. An important point to keep in mind is that these alternatives for settling disputes may be employed even if the parties are already involved in litigation. Very often, the parties find their involvement in the lawsuit so overwhelming (e.g., time, lawyer fees, evidence gathering) that they become more interested in settling. Thus, they resort to one of the alternative ways to settle. This is possible up until the moment the jury returns with the verdict.

Arbitration

Arbitration is a complete substitute for a trial by a judge or jury. It is a more suitable alternative where the parties have already tried to work together and cannot come to a mutually agreeable resolution. In **arbitration,** parties submit their dispute to one or more impartial persons, called arbitrators, to render a binding decision after hearing arguments from the parties and their witnesses and reviewing evidence. The decision of the arbitrator(s), called an **award,** is final and binding on the parties unless they agree to nonbinding arbitration. In this case, the parties retain the right to go to court; however, going to court is done on a limited basis. An award, generally confirmed as a court judgment, is then used to collect payment from the losing party through judicial enforcement. Arbitration may be consensual (most common) or compulsory (i.e., required by state statute in certain cases, e.g., disputes involving public employees such as police officers).

The arbitrator may be an attorney or a person skilled in the area that is the subject of the dispute. A list of arbitrators is available through such organizations as the American Arbitration Association (AAA), a nonprofit organization that offers dispute resolution services to businesses, individuals, consumers, unions, and others. Services are available through AAA headquarters in New York City and through offices located in many other cities throughout the United States. ADR services are now available online through AAA and in some cases through for-profit firms around the country. Arbitration cases are scheduled for hearings quite rapidly, and the normal rules of evidence are often waived. It is usually not necessary for a party to be represented by an attorney at an arbitration hearing. The parties agree in advance to be bound by the decision of the arbitrator and not to appeal the case to a formal court unless either party can show that a gross error or fraud took place in the proceedings or that the award was illegal. Unless specifically required to by the agreement, the arbitrator need not provide the reasons for rendering the decision. Many cases brought to AAA settle in thirty to sixty days and even in less time if the parties wish to settle sooner.

arbitration nonjudicial determination of a dispute by a third party rather than by a judge or jury

award binding decision in an arbitration

Business owners who don't want the delays, legal fees, the specter of uncontrolled punitive damages, the potential of "runaway" jury awards, and public exposure that accompany lawsuits have turned to arbitration. Binding arbitration clauses such as the following are often added to business contracts:

> If a dispute arises out of or relates to this contract, or breach thereof, and if the dispute cannot be settled through negotiation, the parties agree first to try in good faith to settle the dispute by arbitration administered by the American Arbitration Association under its Commercial Arbitration Rules before resorting to litigation, or some other dispute resolution procedure.

Binding arbitration provisions are now a common feature of banking, insurance, health care, the securities industry, and communication service contracts as well as contracts for the sale or lease of consumer goods. In some communities, referral to arbitration is mandatory for civil cases involving a certain sum of money.

Mediation

mediation intervention by a third person to settle a dispute between two parties

Another method of resolving disputes outside court is mediation. **Mediation** requires disputing parties to meet with an impartial (neutral) third person, called a mediator, who assists them in reaching a compromise solution. The mediator, usually a person with expertise in the disputed area, such as an attorney, an engineer, or a health professional, is not authorized to render a decision or to force the parties to accept settlement as is an arbitrator. Rather, a mediator helps the parties reach their own agreement by encouraging the exchange of information and ideas between them and at times recommending and persuading. Thus, the parties have the power to determine their own outcome by reaching a mutually acceptable resolution of their dispute.

Virtually every other dispute resolution process (e.g., arbitration) cedes all or part of the power to determine outcomes to a third party. Parties have the option of trying mediation first without giving up any right to proceed to arbitration or litigation. In fact, previously standardized arbitration clauses are now being preceded by a requirement that the parties retain the services of a mediator and negotiate in good faith before the initiation of any adversarial proceeding (litigation). The consensus among mediators is that almost all disputes are mediatable. Recent successes in areas such as civil fraud, where previously mediation was thought inappropriate, are testimony to the flexibility of the process. Yet mediators are willing to concede that litigation is generally required to resolve pure legal questions or matters of public policy. Mediation is particularly useful in settling labor disputes to achieve better working conditions and wages, in resolving insurance claim disputes, in family conflicts such as disagreements over visitation rights between separated and divorced parents, in settling disputes between landlord and tenant, in customer/store owner disputes, in disputes between business partners, and in conflicts between neighbors. Unlike arbitration, where there is a winner and a loser, both parties at a mediation leave the session feeling that they have "won" what they wanted on the issues that had to be decided.

Several small claims courts now encourage parties to first take their cases to mediation. In fact, it is mandatory in a few small claims courts. If the parties are unsuccessful at mediation, they can still go to court. Experience shows, however, that when parties agree to mediation, the majority of cases are settled.

Minitrials

The minitrial has also been used successfully by large corporations in cases involving complex litigation. Lawyers for both sides present their case to a neutral adviser (usually a retired judge), and the plaintiff and defendant (generally officers of the corporation with decision-making powers) are both present. These presentations may last a few days and will include an exchange of information; opposing lawyers will point out the strengths and weaknesses of their respective positions. To support their positions, the attorneys may produce witnesses and documents.

At the end of the presentations, with some questioning in both directions, the plaintiff and defendant will retire, without their lawyers, to consider what they've heard and to try privately to negotiate an agreement. If this first stage of the minitrial does not produce a settlement, the minitrial adviser then renders a nonbinding decision based on how he or she thinks the case would be decided in court. The plaintiff and defendant take this additional information and try to work out a solution. This process, which requires intensive, direct communication between plaintiff and defendant, helps each side reach a better understanding of the other's position and thus enhances the chance for a settlement that will be less costly than going to court. Because of the complex nature of a minitrial, it is often resorted to if a dispute cannot be resolved by a voluntary exchange of information or by mediation.

The Summary Jury Trial

The summary jury trial is used for cases that would normally be heard by a jury. It occurs after a lawsuit has been initiated but before the trial. The opposing lawyers present a summary of their cases to a "sample" jury of five or six people. The lawyers then converse with jury members and ask such questions as "Why did you reach that decision?" The jury's decision, although it has no binding effect, gives the lawyers some idea of how a jury might decide in an actual trial. When the lawyers see the reaction of the sample jury, they may temper their positions and negotiate a settlement. If no settlement is reached, the parties involved then have the right to take their case to court for a regular trial.

Private Trial

The private trial is an approach based on the "rent-a-judge" concept. The disputing parties hire a retired judge with the power to enter a legally binding judgment. A number of states have passed legislation giving these judges the power to try cases and to make decisions relative to these cases. The judges are paid an hourly rate plus administrative costs. This approach to settling disputes has led to the creation of firms that employ retired judges of many ranks for hire to those in need of their services.

Negotiation

Another form of ADR is negotiation in which parties privately discuss the facts, questions, and demands under dispute and attempt to find a mutually satisfactory solution. Sometimes more can be gained by simply sitting down and talking with the other party to the dispute. Most people dislike trouble, and many fear engaging in any kind of legal "warfare." A private meeting may lay the legal matter to rest quickly, make you feel better personally, and allow you to divert the funds that you would otherwise spend to more worthwhile endeavors.

If informal compromise and settlement do not work, don't leap to litigation. Try the other alternatives to litigation discussed in this chapter. If you look at ways to resolve a conflict on a continuum, it is negotiation, mediation, arbitration, and then all-out war through litigation. Remember that litigation should be your last resort. It may be necessary to go this route only because the complexity of the issues can better be handled by courts, where the formal procedures employed are better safeguards for the parties. For example, if you have been libeled and wish to publicly clear your name, litigation should be considered first.

ONLINE DISPUTE RESOLUTION

Online dispute resolution (ODR) provides the opportunities to employ the processes of arbitration, mediation, and negotiation in the online environment. It is actually designed to settle disputes over the Internet when litigation (litigants meet face-to-face in court) is too time consuming or too expensive, especially if the parties are at a distance (e.g., different states). The area of dispute resolution is just one of many traditional processes that are moving from the offline physical environment to the online virtual environment because it is more flexible, efficient, and economical. This would be especially true in the field of commerce, where there has been an extraordinarily rapid growth of online transactions requiring the resolution of disputes using a similar vehicle. Of course, the parties to a dispute may attempt to resolve a problem on their own informally through e-mails or online chats (a faster version of e-mails), choosing from among several dispute methodologies, including arbitration, mediation, or negotiation.

No one will argue that multi-issues, especially those that are complex, could not easily be resolved over the Internet. In these multi-issue disputes, nothing could really replace the interactive and flexible communication process of a face-to-face meeting. ODR nevertheless does have a place in the offline processes involving one of the ADR programs. It could be used, for example, to locate information helpful to the parties that may be obtained through no other sources than the Internet (information can be obtained anyplace that it is located) or to frame and reframe information provided to each party. Also, it can cut down on face-to-face meetings before, during, or after arbitration, mediation, or negotiation.

Online dispute resolution may work best if the dispute involves a single issue, such as a dispute in a contract involving money. Yet, it is possible to work online even if there are multiple issues by engaging a dispute resolution company that specializes in ODR and that will take a more structured approach toward resolution of the dispute. In this case, the parties would sign a contract with the company, which would then put in place a step process first trying, for example, mediation and moving to arbitration if necessary. The company would provide the dispute resolution professionals and the "tools" necessary to complete the process from the initial dispute to resolution. Where speed is necessary, the dispute resolution company may even be able to complete the process agreed to by the parties in a matter of days.

Although there are challenges to the online dispute resolution process, including the ethical standards that need to be addressed, it has an important future in the way disputes are settled.

ELECTRONIC FILING

Courts around the country are getting in on e-commerce. And why not? With the vast majority of lawyers online, it is only natural for courts to accept e-filed documents and to respond to them online. Already, court clerks, judges, and attorneys in some courts are accessing the full text of pleadings (complaint and answer taken together in a civil lawsuit) over the Internet. Some bankruptcy courts in New York and California have a substantial number of their case files wholly filed electronically. Some courts are moving cautiously and are simply allowing summons, complaints, and answers to be e-filed. The explosion of noncourt e-filing has also smoothed the way. It follows a cultural shift because millions of consumers and businesses pay their bills online, make plane reservations online, do their banking online, and so on. So why not do court business online? Jurisdictions that have not as yet "picked up" on e-filing will soon be added to the list of those that have. E-filing will play a major role in streamlining the litigation process in the courts and will potentially be a cost savings in most cases to law firms, the courts, and clients.

Another way courts have adapted to the online world is to establish Web sites. What is placed on a court Web sites will be decided by the court. Some of the information you might find is the names and phone numbers of judges and other court personnel with a listing of their job titles, decided cases by the court with the court's opinion, useful legal forms, information about pending trials, and your status as a juror on call.

Summary

If legal disputes cannot be resolved informally by the parties themselves through agreement and compromise, they may end up in court. Settlement by litigation—a lawsuit—is expensive, time consuming, and emotionally draining, and the outcome of the court trial is uncertain. Besides, the person being sued may be judgment proof.

People who, after discussing their options with an attorney, decide that their case cannot be settled in any other way generally end up in court. Before a court trial takes place, however, the plaintiff's attorney prepares and delivers to the defendant a complaint (the basis for the legal action) and a summons (a written notice to appear in court). Through an attorney, the defendant then issues a response called an answer. Once the issues in the case are known (taken from the complaint and the answer), pretrial proceedings follow. Pretrial proceedings usually consist of motions, discovery, and a pretrial conference. If no settlement is reached at these proceedings, the case will come to trial.

If the plaintiff and defendant do not demand a jury trial, the evidence in the case will be presented to a judge alone (bench trial). If either party demands a jury trial, the first step before the trial begins is to select, or impanel, a jury. Once the jury is impaneled, each attorney—the attorney for the plaintiff and the attorney for the defendant—presents evidence to this jury to support his or her client's case. After all the evidence has been presented, the judge instructs the jury as to the law that must be applied in the case. The jury then deliberates and reaches a verdict. After the verdict is announced in the courtroom, it is officially placed in the record as a judgment against the losing party. The party who loses the lawsuit may appeal the case to a higher court.

Increasing numbers of people are turning to quicker, less expensive ways to settle their legal problems—for example, arbitration, mediation, minitrials, the summary jury trial, private trials, and negotiation.

Online dispute resolution has an important future in resolving differences among individuals and businesses that employ arbitration, mediation, and negotiation.

Important Legal terms

adjudicated
answer
arbitration
award
complaint
cross-examination
defendant
deposition
discovery

evidence
interrogatories
judgment
mediation
motion
peremptory challenges
petit jurors
plaintiff
pleadings

pretrial conference
removal for cause
subpoena
summary judgment
summons
verdict
voir dire

Questions and Problems for Discussion

1. A Native American tribe entered into a construction contract with C & L Enterprises (C & L) to install a roof on a tribe-owned commercial building in Oklahoma. The property lies outside the tribe's reservation. The contract contained three key positions: (1) all disputes arising from the contract would be settled by arbitration; (2) the award rendered by the arbitrator would be final; and (3) judgment must be entered in any federal or state court having jurisdiction. After the execution of the contract, but before C & L commenced performance, the tribe changed the roofing material in the contract and hired another company to install the roof. C & L, claiming breach of contract, requested arbitration. The tribe claimed sovereign immunity and declined to participate in any arbitration proceeding. The arbitrator received evidence and rendered an award in favor of C & L. The contractor then filed suit to enforce the award in the district court of Oklahoma County. Again the tribe claimed immunity. The district court denied the motion and affirmed the award set by the arbitrator. Is the tribe liable for breach of contract? (*C & L Enterprises, Inc.* v. *Citizen Band Potawatomi Indian Tribe of Oklahoma 532 U.S. 411*)

2. Reynolds recently purchased the Strand Movie Theatre in Chicago. He sued the United Picture Corporation contending that United and several Chicago movie theater owners illegally attempted to keep him from showing first-run movies in violation of federal antitrust law. Before the lawsuit was brought to trial, the attorneys for United provided Reynolds with a series of questions to which he was requested to respond under oath. The questions focused on matters related to the trial. Must Reynolds answer these questions?

3. Two competing companies that manufactured pool tables and swimming pools had a disagreement over whether one of them had engaged in false and deceptive advertising. They both agreed to bring the case to binding arbitration using only one arbitrator. Following the arbitration hearing, the losing party claimed that the award confirmed as a court judgment was not binding because there was no trial by jury. Is the losing party correct?

4. Schultz is a bus driver for the Total View Bus Company. While on her night run in a large city, she rear ended a car. Two passengers on the bus who were injured sued Schultz and the Total View Bus Company, alleging negligence for allowing Schultz to drive with very impaired vision. As part of the pretrial procedure, the attorney for the plaintiff (passengers) petitioned the court to require Schultz to undergo a complete eye examination by a specialist (ophthalmologist). The court complied with the request. Schultz objected to the examination. Can she be ordered to take the eye exam?

5. Compare petit jury with grand jury as mentioned in Chapter 3. How are they similar? How do they differ?

6. Rearrange the following list in the order in which they occur in point of time: verdict, closing arguments, summons and complaint, voir dire, summary judgment, direct examination, judgment, cross-examination, charge to jury, answer.

7. a. A witness is willing to testify concerning certain facts in a case, but she lives in another state. How can her testimony be secured for evidence in the trial?

   b. How does discovery, a pretrial procedure, contribute to the efficiency of a court?

8. Gruhn was fraudulently induced to make a large stock purchase from a broker who was a member of the New York Stock Exchange. The stock was actually of little value. Claiming damages of $75,000, Gruhn agreed to arbitrate her case under the New York Stock Exchange rules. Without explanation, the arbitrator awarded her $500. Can Gruhn appeal her case to a court of law?

9. Compare the burden of proof required in a civil case mentioned in this chapter with the burden of proof required in a criminal case as mentioned in Chapter 3. Why do you think a higher burden of proof is required in a criminal case?

10. This chapter described a lawsuit involving Bill Allen, a thirty-five-year-old advertising executive, and the Laiden Trucking Company. Allen sued Laiden for $3 million. Based on the facts in this case, do you think a jury would consider this amount excessive? Why or why not?

11. In conducting the voir dire examination for the trial of *Bill Allen* v. *Laiden Trucking Company,* Allen's attorney, Jan Heisman, got the following response from a prospective juror:
Heisman: "Have you been reading the newspaper accounts or listened to any news reports about the accident in question?"
Juror: "Yes. After reading and listening to the reports, I felt that Allen should assume much of the responsibility for the accident."

    What step should Heisman take at this time to protect Allen from this prospective juror?

12. Can Heisman, as attorney for Bill Allen, request that a juror be dismissed simply because Heisman has the feeling that this juror will be detrimental to Allen's case?

THE CASE OF THE POLITICALLY INCORRECT SIGN

Disturbed by the number and variety of signs that individuals were putting up within its borders, a city council passed a law prohibiting all signs on private property except for advertising purposes in commercial areas. Houston, a homeowner, pasted a sign on the front door of his house containing an American flag with these words underneath the flag: "Down with City Council—Our rights are being violated." Houston was arrested for violating the law.

The Trial

During the trial, a city representative described how many signs had appeared on homes and on lawns, ruining the appearance of the city. He explained that many other cities and villages had experienced the same problems and that the ordinance was reasonable and the only way to solve the problem. Houston testified that the sign he had put up was a small one and that other city residents had raised flags on national holidays and put up signs showing their patriotism; none of those persons had been arrested.

The Arguments at Trial

The city's attorney argued that a city had the authority to regulate signs within its borders to protect the appearance and value of properties. She argued further that the law did not unduly restrict free speech as there were other ways for residents to express their views: radio, television, and the newspapers. Houston's attorney argued that the regulation violated the freedom of speech provisions of state and federal constitutions, was too broad, too vague, and was unreasonable. He argued that the city could have limited the law by restricting signs over a certain size and in certain locations. He further argued that it was unreasonable to restrict the expression of opinions except for use of the media.

Questions to Discussion

1. Who has the stronger arguments, the city or Houston? Why?
2. Do you need any additional information to determine the facts?
3. If you were the judge or jury hearing this case, for whom would you decide? Why?
4. What type of legislation, if any, do you think should be enacted to limit signs in neighborhoods to protect their appearance?

The Argonaut Corporation's major stockholders adopted a resolution to financially support socially beneficial programs in the large city where they were located and to join in the Annual Giving to a local college. The board resolution stated that these commitments were "in the best interests of the company." Several minority stockholders questioned the propriety of this resolution, claiming that it involved an activity that was outside the powers of the corporation. The resolution did make it clear, however, that contributions to identified socially beneficial programs and to the local college would not draw from funds necessary to pay dividends to its stockholders.

Question to Discuss

Can a corporation ethically make charitable contributions from corporate funds without the board of directors being challenged successfully by the minority stockholders on the grounds that this resolution is an abuse of power that would constitute a breach of good faith, which they are bound to exercise toward the stockholders?

Contracts

After studying Part II, you should be able to:

1. recognize the requirements of a valid contract.

2. classify contracts as valid, void, voidable, or unenforceable.

3. explain the requirements of a valid offer and acceptance, the first important elements in a binding contract.

4. summarize the various forms of consideration, when consideration is necessary to form a binding contract, and the exceptions to the rule requiring the presence of consideration in a contract.

5. determine what makes parties competent to contract and the effects of various incapacities.

6. distinguish between a legal and an illegal agreement and the consequences of entering into an illegal agreement.

7. demonstrate a knowledge of the six types of contracts that are frequently required to be in writing to be enforceable and point out the effects of failure to comply with the writing requirement.

8. point out the circumstances in which parties to a contract may transfer their rights and obligations after the contract has been made.

9. summarize ways in which contracts may be ended and the various remedies available to the parties for breach of the contract.

10. be able to apply the online rules that have evolved from traditional contract situations.

CHAPTER 6

Contract Law: A Beginning

CHAPTER PREVIEW

What a Contract Is	**Formal and Informal Contracts**
	Express and Implied Contracts
The Elements of a Valid Contract	**Executory and Executed Contracts**
Contract Terminology	
Bilateral and Unilateral Contracts	**Contracts Governed by Precedent**
Valid, Void, Voidable, and Unenforceable Contracts	**or Statute**

Chapter Highlights

Written and unwritten (oral) contracts form the basis of many of our personal and business transactions. There are two sets of contract rules to learn. The next nine chapters devoted to contract law deal with common law contracts, the first set of contract rules. In general, they deal with contracts that do not involve the sale of goods. The second set is the contract rules contained in Article 2 of the Uniform Commercial Code (UCC). Contract law under Article 2 governs transactions involving the sale of goods (i.e., tangible personal property). You will find that many of the laws governing contracts under the two sets are the same, but you will also find that the UCC relaxes the rules of the common law and takes a slightly different approach. Contracts under the UCC will be discussed in Chapters 15 through 18. This chapter defines what a contract is, identifies the essential elements necessary to form a contract, and then briefly discusses each element. The remainder of the chapter is devoted to terminology associated with contract law. A sample contract is presented to show what a typical written contract looks like. The chapter concludes with an explanation of a contract governed by precedent and one governed by statute.

WHAT A CONTRACT IS

contract legally binding agreement between two or more competent persons

A **contract** is any voluntary legally binding agreement between two or more people or businesses that sets forth what the parties will or will not do. Whether you realize it or not, you enter into contracts on many occasions: when you take your car to a garage for repairs, enroll in a college, rent an apartment, purchase a DVD, buy something at a garage sale, take your clothes to the cleaners, use your credit card, or join a health club. Each person, or "party," obtains certain rights and assumes certain obligations that will be enforced in a court of law.

> You promise in writing to buy your friend's used motorcycle. Under the terms of the contract, you have the right to the motorcycle and an obligation to pay your friend the agreed-upon price. Your friend has the right to collect the price you agreed to pay and an obligation to deliver the motorcycle to you.

Contracts are often simple and easy to understand, such as when you buy clothing in a store or order food in a restaurant. Other contracts, such as buying a car or a house, are more complicated. In some cases, you do not sign your name to a formal document, but that does not make the contract any less significant because an informal written contract—or even an oral contract—may be binding. Often, people fail to realize that a contract has been made and therefore also fail to live up to the agreement. If the contract is trivial, no one really suffers if it is broken. If the contract is important, however, it causes a hardship if the parties fail to live up to its terms.

People form many agreements that at first glance appear to be contracts but are not real contracts because no legally binding obligations between the parties are created. Such agreements will not be enforced by the courts. A strictly social agreement—generally considered to be one that does not create legally binding economic obligations for the parties or one in which the failure by one party to carry out his or her part of the agreement would not cause the other party to suffer damage recognizable by courts—is an example of an agreement that a court will not enforce.

> Marlo, president of a small-town bank, agreed to drive you, a large depositor at the bank, to the golf course. Marlo forgets and you have to take a taxi.

> Cohen, a close friend, agreed to sell her 2000 car for $2,000, and you agreed to buy it.

The courts would hold that the first example, the invitation to drive you to the golf course, is admittedly an agreement, but it is a social agreement and therefore legally un-enforceable. Marlo will not be required to pay your taxi fare. The second example, the sale of the used car, created binding economic obligations on both sides and is enforceable in court. Therefore, Cohen must sell you the car and you must buy it.

THE ELEMENTS OF A VALID CONTRACT

Four essential elements must be present for an agreement to have the status of a contract: agreement, consideration, competent parties, and legal purpose (Figure 6.1). These elements are introduced briefly here, but each element is covered in detail in Chapters 7 through 10.

Agreement is the initial step toward forming a contract. It is accomplished by a process called *offer* and *acceptance*. The person who makes the offer is called the *offeror*. The person to whom the offer is made is called the *offeree*. When the offeree accepts an offer, the first requirement of a valid contract has been satisfied.

> Hudek (the offeror) offered to sell Hopkins (the offeree) some camera equipment for $300. Hopkins accepted the offer. This was offer and acceptance, one of the elements of a binding contract.

Consideration is something of value exchanged by each party to bind the agreement. Consideration may be money or it may be property, such as a watch or a car.

Consideration may also consist of doing something you are not legally bound to do, refraining from doing something you have a legal right to do, or promising to do or not do something.

> At a garage sale, O'Grady agreed to buy a set of used encyclopedias from Moran for $100. The $100 and the set of encyclopedias are the consideration for this contract.

> A seriously ill uncle offered Ling, a pharmacy student at a local college, $10,000 to leave school and run the uncle's business. Ling agreed. Because Ling had a legal right to continue in pharmacy school, this act of refraining (not continuing in pharmacy school) was consideration for the uncle's promise to pay Ling $10,000.

Capacity means having the legal and mental ability to enter into binding contracts. In the eyes of the law, however, some parties lack the ability to enter into contracts freely. These people may legally avoid (cancel) contracts made with others and demand the return of the consideration paid. Among those not considered competent are minors

FIGURE 6.1
The Elements of a Valid
Contract

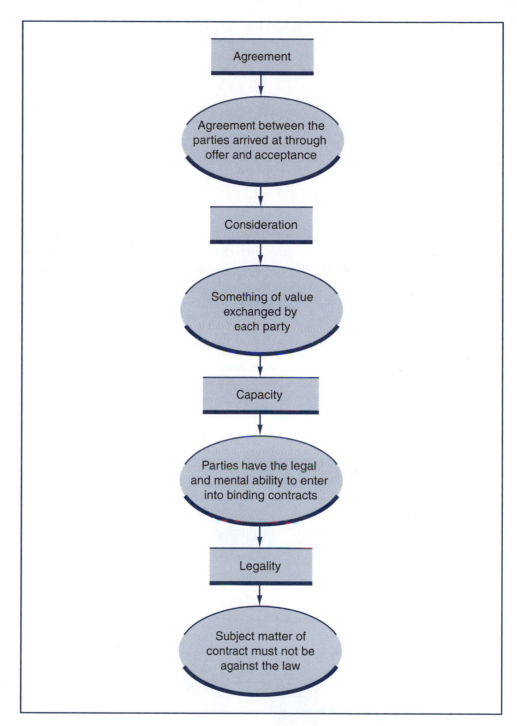

(in most states, persons under the age of eighteen), persons under the influence of alcohol and other drugs, and people who are mentally ill.

Harris, age sixteen, lives in a state where the legal age for making contracts is eighteen. She entered into a contract with Michaels, an adult, to buy software for her computer but then changed her mind. Because Harris is a minor, she can legally avoid the contract.

legality the point that a contract must not be against the law

Legality means that the contract must not be against the law. The courts will not enforce a contract if the parties knowingly enter into an illegal agreement and then demand performance. This is true even if all the other elements of a contract are present. A contract that interferes with the proper administration of justice is one example of an illegal contract.

You were an eyewitness to an automobile accident caused by a negligent driver. The driver who caused the accident promised you $1,000 if you would not testify at the upcoming trial. You agreed not to testify. Because this contract interferes with the proper administration of justice, it is illegal and would not be enforced by a court.

If offer and acceptance, considerations, competent parties, and legality are present, a contract has been created. If any one element is missing, a contract does not exist, and the agreement will not be enforced against either party by a court of law. If one of the parties does not carry out her or his part of the contract, that person may be sued for breach of contract. **Breach of contract** is the failure to carry out one's part of the agreement. Breach of contract is discussed in detail in Chapter 14.

breach of contract failure to perform the obligations required by a contract

For certain types of contracts, there is another requirement: the agreement must be in writing. This requirement is discussed in Chapter 11.

CONTRACT TERMINOLOGY

All contracts may be classified in the following ways: (1) bilateral or unilateral; (2) valid, void, voidable, or unenforceable; (3) formal or informal; (4) express or implied; and (5) executory or executed. These classifications are not mutually exclusive and may apply to the same contract. Consequently, a contract could be express, valid, bilateral, and informal.

Bilateral and Unilateral Contracts

bilateral contract contract in which one party makes a promise in return for a promise made by another party

A contract is either bilateral or unilateral (Figure 6.2). An offer for a **bilateral contract** (the most common type) is one in which a promise (offer) is made by one party in return for a promise made by another party. In other words, both the offeror and the offeree make promises, and these promises form the basis of the contract.

FIGURE 6.2 Ways in Which Parties Reach Agreement

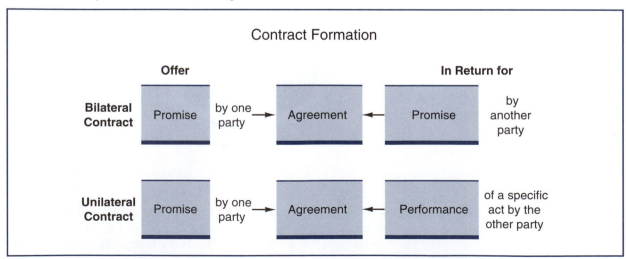

Oliver promised to pay Douglas $500 if Douglas promised to drive Oliver's car from Los Angeles to Boston. As soon as Douglas promises to perform the act required, a bilateral contract will be formed (a promise for a promise).

unilateral contract contract in which one party makes a promise in return for the performance of an act by another party

An offer for a **unilateral contract** is one in which a promise (offer) is made by one party in return for the performance of a specific act by the other party. In other words, the contract does not become effective until the act is performed.

Archie promised to pay Milligan $100 to repair Archie's garage door. The contract is not effective until Milligan actually performs the act of repairing Archie's garage door (a promise for an act).

Sometimes the offeror's promise is ambiguous as to whether a bilateral or unilateral contract is intended. If there is ambiguity as to which it is, it is presumed to be a bilateral contract.

Valid, Void, Voidable, and Unenforceable Contracts

valid contract contract containing all the essential elements

Contracts may be classified in terms of their enforceability. A **valid contract** is one that contains all the essential elements of a contract: offer and acceptance, consideration, competent parties, and legal purpose. It is legally binding on all parties to the agreement.

Colt, a competent party, offered to sell some fence posts to Craft, also a competent party, for $100. Craft accepted. This agreement is a valid contract because it has all the essential elements of a contract.

void contract contract that has no legal effect and cannot be enforced

Technically, a void contract is not a contract at all. A **void contract** has no legal effect, and neither party can enforce the contract against the other in a court of law. A void contract usually is an agreement that lacks any one of the essential elements of a contract or that has a subject matter that, unknown to the parties, does not exist at the time the agreement is made, thus making performance impossible.

You purchased a CD player that you knew was stolen. Because selling stolen property is illegal, the essential element of legal purpose is missing. The contract is void and therefore unenforceable by either party to the agreement.

voidable contract contract enforceable against all parties until the party legally entitled to avoid the contract decides to do so

A **voidable contract** is a contract that is completely valid and enforceable against all parties unless and until a party legally entitled to avoid the contract decides to do so by claiming some defect in the creation of the agreement. A minor, for example, may avoid some contracts.

Miller, a minor, purchased some sports equipment for $200 from Darby, an adult who owned Darby Sporting Goods. Two days later, Miller returned the merchandise and asked for a refund, claiming the equipment was no longer needed. Because he is a minor, Miller has the right to avoid the contract and get his money back. Until it is canceled, however, the contract is enforceable against both parties.

unenforceable contract contract that is legal but fails to meet some requirement of the law

An **unenforceable contract** is one that is legal in all respects but fails to meet some requirement of the law. As a result, a court will not enforce the contract against either party. For example, the law requires that some contracts, such as contracts for the sale of land, be in writing. If they are not, the contracts are unenforceable, even though they are legal in all other respects.

Formal and Informal Contracts

formal contract written
contract prepared with
certain formalities,
including a seal

A **formal contract** is a written contract prepared with certain formalities. A check is one example of a formal contract because it must use a particular form or style of language. In early common law times, a formal contract was one that was under seal—that is, closed with wax and imprinted with one's insignia or special mark. Most jurisdictions today have abolished the use of the seal as a means of validating a contract.

informal contract
contract prepared
without formalities

An **informal contract** does not require any particular formalities. The parties are free to use any style of language they wish. Informal contracts may be oral or implied; they do not have to be written unless required by statute. Although the language used in an informal written contract may be as elaborate or as sketchy as the parties desire, it should include the date, the name and address of each party, the consideration of one party, the consideration of the other party, and the signature of each party to the agreement. These elements are shown in the example of an informal written contract in Figure 6.3.

Express and Implied Contracts

express contract
contract in which the
agreement is
specifically stated

An **express contract** is one in which the agreement is specifically stated. An example of an express contract is an insurance policy, in which all the terms of the contract are written as part of the policy. Express contracts may be either oral or written.

Many contracts are made orally. When you buy gasoline for your car, groceries for your dinner, or film for your camera, you make an oral contract. As simple as these transactions seem, all the necessary elements of a contract are present. Oral contracts should be limited to simple transactions that can be carried out quickly.

Written contracts should be used whenever important matters are involved or the agreement is complicated. Written terms cannot be easily changed. If a misunderstanding arises later, it is easy to establish the terms actually agreed upon. For example, you orally agree with Innes, a friend, to buy her used bicycle for $300. If Innes changes her mind, you could sue her for breach of contract, but you might lose the suit because you lack proof. A written contract of Innes's original intention to sell you the bicycle would make it easier for you to win in court.

A word of caution. Even though an agreement is put in writing, that does not make it legal and/or binding. For example, a written contract regarding a bet on a sporting event such as a baseball game would generally be illegal and thus nonenforceable regardless of any writing.

It may be harder to prove the existence of oral contracts, but from a practical standpoint, if all contracts had to be in writing, our daily lives would be very complicated.

implied contract
contract formed from
actions of the parties

An **implied contract** (a contract implied in fact) is one in which the parties form a contract from their actions rather than from a specific oral or written agreement.

You wanted to visit a friend who lives across town. The bus fare was $1.25. You got on the bus and dropped $1.25 into the coin box. The resulting contract is implied because neither you nor the bus driver agreed either orally or in writing to form a contract. Rather, your actions and those of the bus driver created the contract.

In some instances, a contract may be partially express and partially implied.

Johnson was enrolled in the auto technology program at a local college. A classmate asked her to make some repairs to his car but did not mention paying Johnson for the work. Johnson agreed to do the work, expecting to be paid. When the job is completed, the classmate has a legal obligation to pay the "going price" (the price generally charged by mechanics in business for doing the same work). Although the agreement between Johnson and her classmate to make the repairs was express, the agreement by the classmate to pay the going price was implied.

FIGURE 6.3 Informal Written Contract

CONTRACT

THE COLONIAL HOME IMPROVEMENT COMPANY
18 Brickstone Drive
Washington, D.C. 22182

April 22, 2008

The Colonial Home Improvement Company agrees for the sum of eight thousand dollars ($8,000) to construct a deck at the rear of the premises at 12 Harris Street, Washington, D.C., owned by Ruth Boyd. Said porch shall be constructed of redwood and shall be seven (7) feet in width and ten (10) feet in length, and shall stand five (5) feet off the ground. The expected date of completion is May 13, 2005.

TERMS:

Consideration from Ruth Boyd shall be the sum of one thousand dollars ($1,000) as down payment immediately upon signing the contract. The balance of seven thousand dollars ($7,000) shall be paid as follows:

One thousand dollars ($1,000) upon commencement of construction

Six thousand dollars ($6,000) upon completion of construction

Upon commencement of construction, any payment two days in default shall render the entire balance due and owing.

The Colonial Home Improvement Company agrees to furnish quality building materials, experienced workers, and top-quality service. Any dispute arising from the terms of this contract including an interpretation of the terms "quality" and "experienced" shall be settled by arbitration consisting of two (2) arbitrators, one of whom must be a member of the Building Trades Association.

This writing constitutes the full agreement and understanding of the parties signed herein.

Mark Peterson

The Colonial Home
Improvement Company

Ruth Boyd

Customer/Homeowner

---

quasi contract
contract implied in law
to prevent one from
benefiting at another's
expense

In certain cases, the courts create a fictional contract, called a *quasi contract*, despite the wishes and intentions of the parties so as to promote justice. A **quasi contract** (a contract implied in law) means "as if there were a contract." Actually, no real promises have been made by the parties, and none of the other elements of a true contract is present. The courts create the quasi contract so that one party will not be *unjustly enriched* (i.e., receive a benefit) at the expense of the other party. An implied-law contract is just as legally binding as an express contract. For example, Dr. Restov comes upon the scene of an accident and renders the necessary medical aid to Claire, who is injured and unconscious. Restov has a claim in quasi contract against Claire for the reasonable value of services rendered. The explanation for allowing Restov to collect is that Claire, if able, would have promised to pay for the services rendered, and therefore, the court will impose that promise on Claire.

Executory and Executed Contracts

executory contract
contract that has not been fully performed by one or all parties

executed contract
contract that has been completely carried out

With regard to performance, a contract is either executory or executed. An **executory contract** is one that has not been fully performed by one or all of the parties. An **executed contract** refers to a contract in which all parties have completely carried out their parts of the contract.

> You hire a friend to install a stereo system in your new car. At this time, the contract is executory because neither party has performed. When your friend completes the job satisfactorily and presents the bill to you, the contract is still executory because you have not yet paid for the work. When you pay your friend, the contract will be executed because it has been completely performed by both parties.

CONTRACTS GOVERNED BY PRECEDENT OR STATUTE

One source of contract law is the common law—that is, court decisions that have been rendered by judges since earlier times. Obviously, judges from different states will render different decisions based on customs and traditions. The results of their decisions, called precedents (described in Chapter 1), therefore vary from state to state.

Some areas of contract law are governed by modern statutes that uniformly apply in all states. These uniform laws make it much easier for people from different states to carry on business with one another. A good example of modern statute law is the Uniform Commercial Code (UCC) that, as stated earlier in the chapter, deals with the sale of goods. Common law will continue to govern those contracts that have not been modified or replaced by statutory law such as the UCC.

Summary

This introductory chapter about contracts lays the foundation for the study of common law contracts (i.e., contracts not dealing with the sale of goods). A contract, as defined in this chapter, is any voluntary legally binding agreement between two or more people or businesses that sets forth what the parties will or will not do. Some agreements appear to be contracts but are only social in nature and are therefore legally unenforceable in the courts.

A valid contract must fulfill the following four requirements: (1) agreement, reached through a process called offer and acceptance; (2) consideration, something of value given up by each party; (3) capacity means having the legal and mental ability to enter into binding contracts; and (4) legality, an agreement not against the law.

Contracts may be classified as bilateral and unilateral; valid, void, voidable, and unenforceable; formal and informal; express and implied; and executory and executed. These classifications are not mutually exclusive and in fact may apply to the same contract.

In certain cases, the law considers it unjust that a person should receive a benefit (called unjust enrichment) at the expense of another person. Under these circumstances, a court-created contract (called a quasi contract) allows the person who conferred the benefit to recover its value from the benefited person, even though there is no contract between the two parties requiring any payment.

Some contracts are governed by common law precedents, whereas others are ruled by modern statutes, one of which is the Uniform Commercial Code (UCC).

Important Legal terms

bilateral contract

breach of contract

contract

executed contract

executory contract

express contract

formal contract

implied contract

informal contract

legality

quasi contract

unenforceable contract

unilateral contract

valid contract

voidable contract

void contract

Questions and Problems for Discussion

1. The Radiant Heating and Air Conditioning Company installed a central air-conditioning unit in Randy's house. At the time of signing the contract with Radiant Heating, Randy made a down payment, but she has not as yet paid the balance due. Is her contract with Radiant Heating executory or executed?

2. Stack agreed to sell Haag a set of used encyclopedias if she paid him $150. Haag paid Stack the $150. Is this contract
   a. valid, voidable, or void?
   b. express or implied?
   c. unilateral or bilateral?

3. Yates, a vice president of the Washington Irving Bank, met with Morrow. They reached an agreement whereby the bank promised to loan Morrow money at 7½ percent interest per year for ten years if Morrow would bring all his personal and corporate banking business to Washington Irving Bank. The bank made loans to Morrow at this rate for five years until Yates resigned from the bank. Morrow was then notified by the bank that because of economic conditions it would need to charge a higher rate of interest on any new loans that were made. Morrow sued the bank for breach of contract, claiming that the bank had to continue the 7½ percent rate of interest because of the agreement. Should Morrow win this case?

4. Jane Ives lived in Linwood, New Jersey, with her three school-age children. All three students went to Cosgrove High School, which covered grades 9 through 12. By law, the school district had to furnish transportation for her children because they lived more than 2 miles from school. They were, however, wrongfully refused transportation by the district. Consequently, Jane drove the three children to school every day for a year. At the end of the school year, she asked the school district to reimburse her for the expense incurred in using her car to drive the children to school. The school district refused to pay her, and so she brought suit to recover the money. Does she have a case?

5. Tamara agrees to purchase a house through a real estate agent. When asked if anything serious is wrong with the house, the agent replied that there was nothing wrong (although he was aware of termite infestation). Once the contract was signed and Tamara moved in, she discovered the termite problem. Assuming that all elements of a contract were met, what was the status of the contract once Tamara had discovered the termite problem?

6. Dante offered to pay Heckter $5,000 to burn down Dante's restaurant so that he could collect money from the insurance company on a fire insurance policy he had acquired when he first opened the restaurant. Since opening the business, Dante had been losing money and now needed funds to pay longstanding obligations. Heckter burned down the restaurant as requested. Is Heckter entitled to the $5,000?

7. Tankel started a lawn-cutting service business. He randomly selected names from the phone book and sent notices to these individuals stating that he agreed to cut their lawns based on lawn size plus a 15 percent profit. He sent such a letter to Gibbs. Has a contract been formed between Tankel and Gibbs?

8. Compare and contrast a contract implied in fact and a contract implied in law.

9. Griffin went away for the weekend to a resort. While he was gone, a lawn service seeded his

lawn and landscaped his backyard by mistake. The lawn service had actually contracted with Griffin's neighbor. Nevertheless, the lawn service billed Griffin for $750. Griffin refused to pay, claiming he had not contracted with them to have lawn work done. Is Griffin liable for the payment?

10. Carver took his car to Dorschel Motors to have work done on the engine. He specifically told the head mechanic to repair, not replace, the engine. Instead of repairing the engine, the head mechanic instructed the mechanic who worked on the car to replace the engine with a rebuilt motor. Carver did not know of this work until he was handed the bill. When Carver asked why his instructions were not followed, the head mechanic stated that replacing the engine was the most economical thing to do. Was Carver liable for the bill, which included the cost of the engine and labor?

Cases for Review

1. Michelle and Lee Marvin, who lived together from October 1964 through May 1970 without marrying, entered into an oral agreement stating that while they lived together they would share their earnings and all property acquired and would hold themselves out to the general public as husband and wife. Michelle even took Lee's last name. She agreed to give up her career as an entertainer and singer to devote herself full time to Lee as a companion, homemaker, housekeeper, and cook. In return, Lee agreed to provide her with financial support for the rest of her life. In May 1970, Lee asked Michelle to leave and refused to provide further support for her. She then sued him for one-half of the money and property acquired during the time they lived together. Lee defended on the grounds that Michelle was not entitled to anything. He claimed that their agreement was illegal, having been based on an immoral and illicit relationship in which Michelle was to perform sexual favors for him. Michelle claimed that although part of their relationship was sexual, the agreement to live together with Lee was not tied to their engaging in sexual relations but rather to sharing their earnings and property rights. Is Michelle entitled to her claim? (*Marvin* v. *Marvin*, 557 P.2d 106 Cal.)

2. Dobos was admitted to a hospital with a serious condition that required around-the-clock nursing care. The hospital, on orders from Dobos's doctor, requested Nursing Care Services, Inc., to care for Dobos while she was in the hospital and for a two-week period while she was at home. When Nursing Care Services sent a bill, Dobos claimed she was not liable because she had not signed a written contract or personally made an oral agreement for their services, although she was well aware of what her doctor had requested and had readily accepted the care provided. Under what theory can Nursing Care Services collect? (*Nursing Care Services, Inc.* v. *Dobos*, 380 So.2d 516)

3. Sonnenburg and Hartnett were patients at an Indiana state mental hospital. Even though they were patients, they helped out with various duties at the institution, such as mowing the lawn, washing dishes, preparing meals, and performing office duties. They performed these duties on an ongoing basis even though they were repeatedly told by hospital personnel that they would not be paid for their services. Later, Sonnenburg and Hartnett changed their mind and decided to sue for services performed, claiming unjust enrichment on the part of the state. They claimed that it was only fair that they received compensation for their work. Should Sonnenburg and Hartnett be successful in a lawsuit based on unjust enrichment? (*Bayh* v. *Sonnenburg*, 573 N.E. 398)

4. Landsberg wrote a manual for winning at Scrabble. He then contacted the owners of the Scrabble game asking for permission to sell this manual under the Scrabble trademark. Instead, owners of the Scrabble game requested a copy of the manual. Later, the owners published their own strategy manual. Since no express contract was entered into between Landsberg and the Scrabble owners, Landsberg received no compensation for his manual. Landsberg sued the Scrabble owners, contending that the disclosure of his manual was confidential and for the limited purpose of obtaining permission for the use of the Scrabble trademark. Landsberg further contended that if

the Scrabble owners intended to use his manual commercially, although there was no formal contract to do so, he should by implication have received adequate payment after some sort of negotiation. The Scrabble owners should not have assumed that the manual was given to them by Landsberg for free. Was Landsberg correct? (*Landsberg* v. *Scrabble Crossword Game Players, Inc.*, 802 F.2d 1193)

5. Swetman and others were college teachers whose contracts expired at the end of the school year. They had been teaching for a number of years, and all had tenure (permanent status), but they had no specific contract for the coming year. They applied for unemployment compensation for the summer months. Compensation was denied because the teachers had tenure, and both the teachers and the college expected that the teachers would be teaching next year. Was it implied that the teachers would have a teaching job for another year? (*Swetman* v. *Gerace*, Fla., 349 So.2d 977)

6. Brown entered a 7-Eleven store (in the state of California) to purchase a lottery ticket on a giveaway of over $7 million. He handed the salesperson a list of numbers he wished to play but was informed that the terminal had malfunctioned and could only give out tickets with terminal-generated numbers. Brown refused and then sued the state of California and the 7-Eleven for breach of a unilateral contract. He argued that the state's advertising of the lottery constituted an offer and that he had accepted by tendering his own numbers to play and the appropriate amount of money but was refused the opportunity to play on this basis. He further argued that had the salesperson at the 7-Eleven allowed him to buy the lottery tickets using his own numbers, he would have won. Did a unilateral contract exist between Brown, the state of California (which ran the lottery), and the 7-Eleven store (which was unable to sell him the tickets) based on Brown's arguments? (*Brown* v. *California State Lottery Commission*, 284 Cal. Rptr. 108)

CHAPTER 7

Agreement: Offer and Acceptance

CHAPTER PREVIEW

Chapter Highlights

This chapter discusses the first and foremost element of any contract: agreement, reached through a process called offer and acceptance. Offer and acceptance are defined first. Then a discussion of the offer follows: what is required to make it valid and how it ends. The chapter presents a discussion of the acceptance: who can accept, what makes an acceptance legally binding, and whether a person who has been made an offer assents to it by remaining silent. A concluding section briefly discusses entering into a contract online (electronically). This topic will be fully discussed in part III, "purchase, sale, and lease of goods."

HOW AGREEMENT IS REACHED

The first and most important requirement of a legally enforceable contract is that the parties must agree on the subject of the contract. After that, a contract may be made in any manner sufficient to show agreement. **Offer and acceptance**, often called mutual assent or a "meeting of the minds," is the process by which the parties to a contract agree to its terms. These terms may be made orally, in writing, or by conduct of the parties that recognizes the existence of a contract. Once there has been a valid offer and acceptance, the parties are well on their way to having a legally binding contract because few problems occur with consideration, competency of the parties, and legality. An **offer** is a *promise* by one person to do something if the other person either *performs* an act or *promises* to do or not do something. An **acceptance** takes place when the person to whom the offer was made agrees to do what was requested in the offer. The **offeror** (promisor) is the person who makes the offer (promise), and the **offeree** (promisee) is the person to whom the offer (promise) is made.

> Crumb (the offeror) said to Spring, "I'll sell [meaning I promise to sell] you my drum set for $300." If Spring (the offeree) says, "I'll buy the set at that price," she has accepted Crumb's offer (promise to sell). If the other elements are present, a contract is formed.

offer and acceptance process by which parties to a contract agree to its terms

offer promise made by one person to do something if another person either performs an act or promises to do or not do something

acceptance agreement by offeree to do what offeror requests in offer; agreement by seller of real property to buyer's purchase offer

offeror one who makes an offer

offeree one to whom an offer is made

THE OFFER

The first step toward making a contract is for the offeror to make an offer (a promise) to the offeree. It is essential that the offer be seriously intended, definite, and communicated to the offeree by the offeror.

Offer Must Be Seriously Intended

The offeror must clearly and seriously intend to make an offer to the offeree. If no offer is intended, acceptance by the offeree cannot result in a legally binding agreement. An offer obviously made in jest, anger, or under great excitement is not binding on the offeree.

> Your expensive new lawn mower has been giving you a lot of trouble. After it stopped running several times while you were mowing the lawn, you yelled to your neighbor, "For five bucks, I'll sell you this lemon!" Your neighbor said, "You've got a deal." Your neighbor then came over to you and held out $5. As you were obviously angry at the time you made the statement, you did not make a valid offer and do not have to sell the lawn mower.

Objective Theory of Contracts   To determine whether an offer has been made, the courts will ignore the subjective intention (secret or inner feeling) of the offeror and look to his or her words and conduct as understood by a reasonable person (in this case, the offeree). In other words, intent is determined by the *objective theory of contracts*. The theory is that a party's intention to enter into a contract is judged by objective facts such as what the party said while making the offer, how he or she said it, and how it could be interpreted by a reasonable (average) person. If the offeree, as a reasonable person, interprets a statement by the offeror who appears to be in a serious frame of mind, as an offeree it can be accepted regardless of what the offeror actually intended or meant. For example, as a joke, you offer to sell a friend an expensive painting worth $1,000 for $100. Your friend, who knows nothing about paintings, accepts the offer. If your friend is honestly unaware of your secret intent (that you were joking), a binding agreement will result.

Offer Must Be Definite

An offer that is indefinite—terms such as price, subject matter, and quantity are omitted or other material terms are vague or ambiguous—cannot be accepted. A court will not enforce contracts with unclear terms because the court will be unable to determine whether both parties intended to contract.

> Bennett says to Haas, "I can sell you two antique chairs from my collection at $2,000 per chair." Haas replied, "I'll take them."

preliminary negotiations in contract law, discussions between parties that usually lead one party to make an offer

In this case, the law would not view Bennett's statement as a bona fide offer because it was too indefinite. Bennett's statement was simply one of intention to sell the antique chairs at some time in the future. To rise to the level of a bona fide offer, Bennett would have had to make a statement such as, "I offer to sell you two antique chairs from my collection at $2,000 per chair." Actually, the type of statement Bennett made to Haas may be the start of what is called **preliminary negotiations**, whereby the potential offeror "sounds out" the potential offeree's intention to enter into a contract. The parties will talk back and forth until one party eventually makes a genuine offer that can be accepted.

If the court after hearing all the evidence determines that the parties do wish to contract, it will explore ways to do so. Missing terms may be supplied by what the parties have done in prior dealings with each other, according to usage in the trade, or by implication. For example, you asked a plumber to come to your house immediately to repair a broken pipe that was flooding your cellar. Although you did not discuss the cost of the repairs ahead of time, a court would decide that a reasonable fee (what other plumbers would charge) had been implied because of your request (offer) to enter into a contract for the plumber's services. A reasonable fee would be determined by what other plumbers in the area receive for performing the same service. The omission of minor terms will generally have no effect on the formation of a contract as long as the parties intended to enter into a contract.

Offer Must Be Communicated

The offeree must know that an offer has been made and must know the terms of the offer. If not, there can be no legal acceptance by the offeree. The offer may be communicated orally, as by telephone or face to face, or in written form, as by letter or telegram. In either case, the offer must be communicated directly from the offeror, or the offer is not valid.

> You mailed a letter to Hughes offering to sell Hughes a used cell phone for $100. The letter was lost in the mail. Because the letter was never delivered, no offer was communicated to Hughes.

An offer may also be implied from the conduct of the offeror. An implied offer results, for example, when you deposit the proper coins in the fare box on a bus. Although you do not state your offer in words, the driver understands that when you deposit the coins, you are making an offer.

Invitations to Make Offers

Businesses frequently offer their goods and services to the public at large through advertising. Newspapers, magazines, mail-order catalogs, circulars, radio and television, displays in store windows, price tags on merchandise, and even price quotations that companies send to customers are ordinarily in this category. Most courts however consider these forms of advertising to be preliminary negotiations that only invite a potential customer to make an offer to the advertiser to purchase. Because of this interpretation, an advertiser may legally reject what members of the general public may perceive as offers for legitimate reasons. Most states have advertising statutes that impose civil or criminal liability upon unethical businesspersons who refuse to sell goods or services in conformity with the terms of their advertisements.

> An advertisement for the Hartman Floor Company appeared in the local newspaper, offering floor tiles at 15¢ per tile. The correct price was actually 50¢ per tile. Barnhart entered the store and ordered 200 tiles at 15¢ each. The salesperson refused to sell the tiles at that price, claiming there was an error in the advertisement. Because the newspaper advertisement was only an invitation to make an offer, the store was not obligated to sell the tiles to Barnhart at 15¢ each.

If the language used is directed specifically to a particular individual or group of individuals and not the general public, an advertisement can constitute an offer. The following advertisement is worded in a way that the courts would probably hold to be an offer: "On Friday, December 6, we will sell one brand-new Arco washer/dryer for $300 to the first customer who buys $300 worth of cash merchandise." A vendor who wishes to avoid any legal entanglements with a member of the general public over an advertisement being a legal offer should provide a conspicuously displayed disclaimer stating that the advertisement is only an invitation to make an offer to buy.

bid offer made at an auction

At auction sales, an auctioneer invites members of the audience to make offers. At an ordinary auction, called an auction "with reserve," the bidder makes the offer in the form of a **bid**. Acceptance of a bid takes place when the auctioneer either says "Sold" or lets the gavel fall. The auctioneer does not have to accept a bid, even from the highest bidder. Typically, an auctioneer will reject a bid below the price that the seller is willing to accept. Until acceptance takes place, an article may be withdrawn from the sale by the auctioneer. Likewise, a bidder may withdraw a bid before it is accepted by the auctioneer. All auctions are held "with reserve" unless otherwise announced.

If an auction is announced or advertised to be "without reserve," the auctioneer may not withdraw the article from sale once a bid has been made and must sell it to the highest bidder. The bidder, however, may withdraw a bid at any time before the auctioneer accepts it. Withdrawal of the bid does not automatically restore a prior bid.

Another type of bid is that made by a contractor, for example, in response to an invitation from a large company to build a new building for the company or to add on to the current structure. Again, the invitation to submit a bid is not an offer, and the contractor does not bind the company by submitting one. The bid rises to the status of an offer once the company has accepted the bid.

How an Offer Ends

An offer ends when it is accepted by the offeree. An offer may also end by lapse of time, rejection, counteroffer, revocation, death or insanity of the offeror or offeree, illegality, or impossibility.

Lapse of Time   If the offer contains a fixed time limit, the offer ends at that time. When no fixed time is stated, the offer ends at the end of a reasonable time. What is a "reasonable" time depends on the circumstances in each case. Among the factors considered in determining reasonable time are whether the price of the article (e.g., shares of stock) changes rapidly, whether the article is perishable, or whether the offeror has a chance to sell the article to a third party.

> On April 2, Isaac wrote to Leary and offered to sell several household items for $400. Isaac did not state how long the offer would remain open. On November 10, Leary contacted Isaac and accepted the offer. Isaac, however, refused to sell the items to Leary, claiming that a reasonable time had passed and the offer had ended.

rejection refusal of offer by offeree

Rejection   An offer is ended by **rejection** when the offeree refused the offer made by the offeror. The offeree cannot later decide to accept the offer. The offer does not end, however, until the offeror actually receives a communication of the rejection from the offeree either directly or indirectly.

> Marlo sent Benson a letter offering to sell Benson a vacation home for $200,000. Benson sent a return letter to Marlo stating that she was not interested but thanked Marlo for thinking of her. Two weeks later, Benson changed her mind and sent Marlo a letter accepting the offer. This second offer was not valid because Benson had initially rejected Marlo's offer.

To terminate the offer indirectly, the offeree's language or conduct must be analyzed carefully to determine where the offeror, as a reasonable person, could assume that a rejection has been made.

> Frank offers to sell Matthew a used treadmill for $450. Matthew replies, "The price is a little high, but I'll think about it."

In this example, Matthew has not rejected Frank's offer. A reasonable person would conclude that Matthew had not rejected the offer but had simply inquired about the firmness of the offer. Matthew can still accept and bind Frank to the sale of the treadmill (assuming that all other elements of a contract are present).

Counteroffer   A **counteroffer** is an offer made by the offeree to the offeror, changing the terms of the original offer. The counteroffer, which must actually be received by the offeree, ends the original offer (a type of rejection) and replaces it with a new offer. The two parties now switch roles, and the offeree becomes the offeror. If the original offeror (now the offeree) accepts the counteroffer, a legally binding agreement results.

> Darwood says to Megel, "I'll sell you my golden retriever for $350 if you will also buy her puppy for $150." Megel says, "I'll buy the dog, but I really do not want the puppy." This statement amounts to a counteroffer by Megel. If Darwood accepts Megel's counteroffer, agreement has been reached.

A counteroffer may be worded by the offeree in a way that clearly indicates the original offer has not yet been rejected and is still being considered. The offeree may simply wish to find out whether other terms would be acceptable. Under modern law, this inquiry will not prevent the formation of a contract.

> Bean offered to sell Rand six CDs for $8 each. Rand replied, "I'm considering your offer, but I think the price is high. Would you take $6 a CD?"

In this example, Rand's response to Bean's offer does not end the original offer. Rand was simply asking about the possibility of getting the CDs at a lower price. He was not indicating an unwillingness to accept the original offer. If Bean states that she will not take anything less than $8 a CD and if Rand agrees to pay this amount, a legally binding contract will result.

Revocation   The offeror has the legal right to withdraw an offer at any time before it is accepted. Withdrawing an offer is known as **revocation**. Revocation becomes effective when it is actually communicated to (received by) the offeree. For example, a letter of revocation mailed January 1 and delivered to the offeree's home or place of business on January 5 becomes effective on January 5. (*Note*: A rejection must also be received to be effective.) Usually the offeror notifies the offeree directly about the revocation ("I am withdrawing my offer of May 1"). The offer also ends, however, if the offeree indirectly hears about the revocation from another person or if the offeror does something that indicates revocation, such as selling the subject of the offer to another person.

> Thompson offered to sell a dining room set to Corey for $500. However, before Corey accepted the offer, he learned from Moss, a friend, that Thompson had in the meantime sold the set to Kay. Because Corey had not yet accepted the offer, the revocation was legal and ended the offer.

This example also brings out the point that a revocation is possible even though the offeror (in this case Thompson) promises to hold the offer open. The offeror may not, however, be able to revoke the offer, if an option exists. An **option** is actually a contract in which the offeror agrees to keep the offer open for a certain period of time or until a certain date. (The offeror loses the power to revoke the offer for the time mentioned in the option.) What makes the option contract irrevocable is that the offeree gives the offeror consideration (generally money) to keep the offer open. In the preceding example, if Corey

counteroffer offer made by offeree to offeror, changing the terms of the original offer

revocation withdrawal of an offer

option agreement to keep an offer open and irrevocable for a certain time

had given Thompson $50 as a down payment, an option contract would have been created. Without the $50, no option existed, allowing Thompson to withdraw the offer as she did.

The money given to create an option becomes part of the contract price. In the preceding case, if Corey had created an option by giving Thompson a $50 down payment and decided to take the set, the final payment to Thompson for the dining room set would have been $450. Keep in mind that the offeree is under no obligation to exercise the option. If Corey outright rejected the option contract agreement, she would have lost her $50 and Thompson would have been free to sell the dining room set to someone else.

In some states, a written promise by the offeror to keep an offer open for an agreed time cannot be revoked even though no consideration is paid by the offeree.

In a unilateral contract, if an offeree has clearly begun to perform the act requested in the offer before the offer is withdrawn and the offeror knows that performance has begun, some courts will not allow the offeror to revoke the offer. This approach is based on the equitable principle of fair play.

> You offer your neighbor $250 to repair the damage to your storage shed. In response to your offer and with your knowledge, the neighbor begins the work. At this point, you may not be able to revoke your offer.

An offer that has been properly accepted can no longer be revoked.

> On November 25, Crombach sent a telegram to Mayer offering to sell a camper for $1,500. Mayer sent a telegram to Crombach at 11 A.M. on November 26 accepting the offer. Late in the afternoon of November 26, Crombach telephoned Mayer and indicated that he was withdrawing the offer. The withdrawal of the offer was ineffective because Mayer had already properly accepted the offer.

A reward offer made to the general public may be revoked in the same manner that was used to tell people of the offer. If the announcement of a reward, for example, is placed in a local newspaper, it may be revoked by running another notice in the same paper. Even a member of the general public who performs the act requested without knowing that the offer has been revoked cannot ask to have the offer enforced. It is impossible to give personal notice to all the people who had learned of the offer.

Death or Insanity   If the offeror dies or becomes insane before the offer is accepted by the offeree, the offer ends even though the offeree does not know of the offeror's death or insanity. An offeror declared insane by the courts is incompetent and therefore not able to understand the offer made or the consequences of making the offer.

> Chan offered to sell you a set of golf clubs for $175. You accepted the offer a week later, unaware that Chan had just died in a hunting accident. Your acceptance was not effective because Chan's death ended the offer.

The death or insanity of the offeree also terminates an offer. Agreement cannot be reached if the offeree is not alive to accept the offer. Although death ends an offer, it does not terminate a contract already formed before the death of one of the parties (except one for personal services). In the previous example, if you had accepted Chan's offer before he died, a legally binding contract would have been made. The person in charge of Chan's estate would be obligated to sell you the golf clubs.

Illegality   An offer ends if the offer itself becomes illegal before it is accepted by the offeree because a law has been passed making the offer illegal.

> Kelvin offered Spicer, a contractor, $25,000 to build an addition on her house, which she planned to use as a dental office. Before Spicer accepted the offer, the city passed

an ordinance making it illegal to operate such a business in Kelvin's neighborhood. Because the city made it illegal for Kelvin to operate the dental office, the offer ended.

Impossibility An offer ends if the offer becomes impossible to carry out before the offeree accepts it.

> You offered to sell a motorboat to a friend for $900. Before your friend could accept the offer, the boat was destroyed in a fire at the marina where it was docked. Because the boat was destroyed, the offer ended.

THE ACCEPTANCE

A legally binding agreement is reached when the offeree accepts the offer made by the offeror. Acceptance is the offeree's approval of the proposal made by the offeror. For the acceptance to be valid, it must meet certain requirements. The acceptance must be accepted only by the offeree, agree with the offer, and be communicated to the offeror by the offeree. Keep in mind that acceptance is the usual manner in which an offer is terminated.

Acceptance Only by Offeree

Because the offer is directed only to the offeree, only the offeree can accept it. If a person other than the offeree accepts the offer, the acceptance does not result in a legally binding agreement.

> You offered to sell Hickman a camera for $75. Hickman refused but told Agnew, a friend, about the offer. Agnew then accepted your offer. Because the offer was intended only for Hickman, Agnew could not legally accept it.

An offer of a reward made to the general public may be accepted by any person who knows of it. This offer is accepted by performing the act requested.

> The Tri-State Transit Company placed an ad in a local newspaper offering a $1,000 reward to anyone who furnished information leading to the arrest and conviction of the person or persons who had damaged several Tri-State buses. Holmes, who knew Watson was responsible for the damage, learned of the reward and notified the police. Based on Holmes's information, Watson was arrested and convicted. Holmes acted in response to the reward offer, and the information given to the police led to Watson's arrest and conviction; Tri-State was therefore legally obligated to pay Holmes $1,000.

Most states have concluded that the offeree is not entitled to the reward without prior knowledge of the offer. Some states, however, have ruled that a person may collect a reward with or without prior knowledge of the offer. If there has been partial performance before learning of the offer or reward, modern law generally permits the offeree to accept by completing the requested act.

Acceptance Must Agree with the Offer

Under common law rules, the acceptance must be a "mirror image" of the offer. In other words, the acceptance must match, term by term, what was requested in the offer (this is the mirror image rule). Any material change in, or addition to, the terms of the original offer automatically terminates that offer. The acceptance then becomes a counteroffer that need not be accepted. The original offeror can, however, accept the terms of the counteroffer and create a valid contract. Counteroffers were discussed on page 135.

In a *unilateral contract* (a promise for an act), acceptance is the doing of the act requested. For example, you say to Fields, "I promise to give you $20 if you rake my yard and trim the bushes." Acceptance of your offer takes place when Fields completes the yard work. This agreement is a unilateral contract because Fields accepted by performance (completing the yard work), not by a promise (that he would complete the yard work).

In a *bilateral contract* (a promise for a promise), the offeree's promise is the acceptance. For example, you say to Fields, "I promise to give you $20 if you promise to rake my yard and trim the bushes." Acceptance of your offer takes place when Fields promises to do the work requested. This agreement is a bilateral contract because Fields accepted by a promise (to complete the yard work), not by performance (completing the yard work).

Often, the offeror may not be dealing face to face, or does not care how the offeree accepts, or it may not be clear from the offer whether acceptance is to be by a promise or by the performance of an act. In either case, modern law permits the offeree to accept the offer either by promising to perform the act requested (creating a bilateral contract) or by actually performing the act (creating a unilateral contract). This is especially true if a sale of goods under the Uniform Commercial Code (UCC) is involved (UCC2–206 (1)(b)).

In very important transactions, it is common for both parties to sign a written document. If the offeree is required to accept by signing the written document, which has already been signed by the offeror, agreement is reached when the document has been signed by the offeree and delivered to the offeror.

Acceptance Must Be Communicated to the Offeror

An acceptance is not effective until it has been communicated to the offeror. Furthermore, the offeror is in control of the offer. As such, the offeror has the power to determine both the manner (performance or promise) and medium (mail, telegram, fax, etc.) of acceptance. If the offeror asks for performance (a unilateral contract), the offeree can accept only by doing the act requested. If the offeror specifically seeks a promise (a bilateral contract), the offeree can accept only by making a promise. In a unilateral contract, once the offeree completes the act requested in the offer, no further communication to the offeror is required. Acceptance is evidenced by performance. Of course notice may be required by the offeror or by law, or the right to enforce the contract is lost. As a practical matter, however, the offeror must know about the completed act before the promise made to the offeree can be carried out. Because of the problems that can arise from disputes concerning acceptances of unilateral contracts, courts are hostile to this category of contract. The Uniform Commercial Code eliminates many of the common law distinctions between bilateral and unilateral contracts.

> You stored your motorcycle at a local motorcycle center for the winter. You agreed to pay a mechanic $100 to make necessary repairs to it. Acceptance took place when the repairs were completed. If, however, the mechanic wants the $100 before the winter is over, you must be notified that the repairs have been completed.

In a bilateral contract, the offeree's acceptance must be properly communicated directly to the offeror. When the parties are negotiating orally—face to face or by telephone— acceptance is properly communicated when the offeror clearly hears and understands the offeree's acceptance. Problems could arise, however, if the parties involved are not dealing face to face. Thus, certain rules have been laid down to determine when the acceptance takes place.

mailbox rule a common law rule used in contracts stating that an acceptance made in response to an offer is binding when placed in the mailbox, properly addressed

If the offeror specifies that a certain means of communication be used—for example, traditional mail services, a telegram, fax, or FedEx—acceptance takes effect (even though the means used to accept the offer does not reach the offeror) and a contract results as soon as it is properly communicated by the offeree using the mode specified by the offeror. This rule is often referred to as the **mailbox rule**, also called the deposited acceptance rule, because once an acceptance has been deposited with the proper means of communication, it is no longer in the offeree's possession. A letter properly communicates acceptance when it is dropped (stamped and addressed) into a mailbox or given to an authorized person in the post office to mail. A telegram properly communicates acceptance at the time it is given to the telegraph company to be sent. A majority of courts uphold the mailbox rules.

> Tay, a resident of New York City, wrote to Morasse, of Buffalo, New York, offering to sell a two-volume set of law books at a reduced price. Morasse, realizing that the offer was a "good deal," immediately sent a telegram agreeing to buy the books at the stated price. Morasse's telegram was lost and never reached Tay. An agreement resulted, however, because Morasse's acceptance was valid as soon as he gave the telegram to the telegraph company to send.

Ordinarily, the offeror will not insist on a specific means of communicating the acceptance. Nevertheless, modern court decisions allow acceptance of an offer to be effective when sent by (1) the same medium the offeror used to send the offer or a faster means; (2) mail, if the parties are at a distance; or (3) any medium that is reasonable under the circumstances. The definition of "reasonable" may be a question for a court to decide. Generally, however, the medium of communication chosen by the offeree is considered reasonable if it falls into one of the following categories:

- It was the same one used by the offeror, or a faster means.
- It was one that the parties customarily used in prior dealings with each other.
- It was customarily used within the trade or business in which the parties are engaged.
- It appeared to be appropriate as determined by the language of the offer. (For example, the offeror sends an offer by fax but indicates that the offeree need not respond immediately; an acceptance by letter would probably be considered reasonable under these circumstances.)

There are two exceptions to the rule that a contract is formed when an acceptance is sent by authorized means. First, if the offeree uses a medium other than that requested by the offeror (e.g., FedEx overnight delivery is requested by the offeror but instead the offeree uses first-class mail, which may take up to five days to deliver), acceptance in most states is not effective until the offeror actually receives the communication (assuming that the offer is still open). If the offer has expired, the offeree's acceptance becomes a counter offer, leaving it to the offeror to decide whether to accept. If, however, the acceptance is actually received by the offeror in a timely manner despite the means by which it was transmitted by the offeree, it is considered to have been effective when sent. If the first-class letter reached the offeror the next day (i.e., at the same time FedEx was due to arrive), the court would consider this acceptance as valid. The second exception occurs if the offeree first sends a rejection but later changes her mind and later sends an acceptance. The first communication received by the offeror governs. Thus, if the rejection arrives first, there is no contract.

The offeror may place conditions on the acceptance. The offeror may, for example, state that the acceptance must be received by a certain date. If the offeror's conditions are not met, the acceptance is not legally binding.

TABLE 7.1   COMMUNICATION OF OFFER AND ACCEPTANCE

SITUATION	MADE BY	COMMUNICATED	EFFECTIVE
Offer	Offeror	Directly	When received by offeree
Revocation	Offeror	Directly or indirectly	When received by offeree
Rejection	Offeree	Directly or indirectly	When received by offeror
Acceptance	Offeree	Directly (bilateral agreement)	When sent, if the means of communication requested by offeror is used or any reasonable means is used (when none is specified by the offeror)
			When received, if the offeree uses a means other than that requested by the offerer
			When received, if the offeror specifies that acceptance will not be effective until actually received
Acceptance	Offeree	By beginning to perform act requested (unilateral agreement)	When act requested is completely performed

Sanford sent a letter to Zebart offering to sell a computer for $3,500. In his letter, Sanford stated, "Acceptance of this offer is not binding unless it is received by me in my office by 5 P.M. on May 1." Zebart's acceptance would take place only if Sanford receives the acceptance by 5 P.M. on May 1.

The mailbox rule applies only to acceptances. Revocations and rejections do not become legally binding when they are sent but take effect only when they are received by the offeree and offeror, respectively.

The rules relating to the communication and acceptance of an offer are summarized in Table 7.1.

Facsimile Transaction

The transmittal of a document by fax is simultaneous. Consequently, the offer is accepted as soon as it is sent. If the document being faxed is to serve as an original (e.g., a contract), have it signed and notarized before sending it. To be extra sure include a statement on the document indicating that the faxed document and the faxed signature serve as originals. If the document you are faxing is intended as a contract, include language defining the document as the final written agreement between the parties.

Silence as Acceptance

As a general rule, the offeree's silence or in action is not regarded as acceptance, even if the offeror states that it is. An offeree has no legal obligation to reply even if an offer says, "Failure to reply will amount to acceptance."

Huff wrote to Walden offering her $300 for her pedigree show dog. In the offer, Huff stated, "If I do not hear from you within ten days, I shall consider my offer accepted." Walden, the offeree, has no legal obligation to reply to the offer, and her silence cannot be regarded as acceptance. She does not have to sell the dog to Huff.

In some cases, acceptance may be implied by an act of the offeree. For example, when the offeree silently accepts benefits, knowing that they are not made as a gift, an implied acceptance arises. In such a case, the offeree is equally bound unless he or she speaks out and rejects the offer.

Martin, the owner of a fruit and vegetable stand at the farmer's market, buys regularly from Bart, a local farmer. Bart arrived at the farmer's market early one morning and left a load of assorted fruits and vegetables at Martin's stand. Because Martin had not yet arrived, Bart left a note that included the price. Bart had left fruits and vegetables at Martin's stand in this manner on four other occasions; each time, Martin had accepted and paid for the items. This time, when he arrived at the stand, Martin read the note and tore it up. He left the fruits and vegetables to spoil without notifying Bart that he did not want them. Martin is liable for the price of the fruits and vegetables.

In this example, Martin's silence amounted to an implied acceptance. Because he had accepted fruits and vegetables in this manner on four previous occasions, Martin led Bart to believe that Martin would continue to accept fruits and vegetables unless notification to the contrary was sent to Bart.

If both the offeror and offeree agree, silence may be considered acceptance. For example, you say to a friend who has offered to sell you a set of law books for $250, "If you don't hear from me by Friday, you may assume that I accept your offer."

FORMING CONTRACTS ONLINE

Courts to some extent continue to apply common law principles and existing statutory law to the formation of contracts online. Keep in mind, however, online contracts have created legal issues not adequately addressed by the common law and existing statutory law. Consequently, new laws have been drafted to address contract issues peculiar to the online world. Since a large percentage of online contracts involve business-to-business or business-to-consumer sale of goods and services, the substance of these new online laws will be discussed in Part III, "Purchase, Sale, and Lease of Goods," that deals with the Uniform Commercial Code (UCC) which provides the framework of rules that deal with business transactions.

Summary

Agreement, the first and most important requirement of a legally enforceable contract, is reached through offer and acceptance. An offer made by one person, the offeror, is a promise to do something if the other person performs an act or promises to do or not do something. An acceptance is an agreement by that other person, the offeree, to do what was requested in the offer.

To be legally effective, the offer must be made with serious intent, be definite (clearly stated), and be communicated to the offeree. Intention is determined by words and conduct and not by the secret intention of the offeror. This is called the objective theory of contracts. Advertisements are too indefinite to be offers. Rather, the law interprets them as invitations for potential customers to make offers to the advertisers. If the language used in an advertisement is specific enough, the advertisement can constitute an offer. At an ordinary auction (called an auction "with reserve"), the offer made by the bidder is accepted when the auctioneer (the offeree) says "Sold" or lets the gavel fall.

Some offers are not accepted. An offer can be ended in seven ways: lapse of time, rejection, counteroffer, revocation, death or insanity of the offeror, illegality, and impossibility. Neither a rejection nor a revocation is effective until it is received by the other party (either directly or indirectly). A counteroffer terminates the original offer and, in effect, is a rejection of that offer unless the wording clearly indicates that the original offer is still also being considered. Unless an option exists, the offeror can revoke an offer even though he or she has promised to hold it open for a stated period. An option is a contract in which the offerer agrees not to revoke the offer for a certain period of time in return for some consideration, usually money, from the offeree.

Only the offeree can accept the offer. Offers of reward made to the general public are legal. Most states, however, require that offers of reward must be communicated to the offeree for a valid acceptance to occur. Under common law rules, the acceptance must be a "mirror image" of the offer, which means that the acceptance must match, term by term, what was requested in the offer. Any changes or additions to the terms of the original offer would amount to a counteroffer. In bilateral contracts, communication of the acceptance usually is necessary, but that is not true for unilateral contracts. In unilateral contracts, the offeree accepts simply by completing the act requested in the offer. As a practical matter, however, the offeror must know about the completed act before the promise made to the offeree can be carried out.

Although a rejection and a revocation must be received by the other party to be effective, an acceptance to an offer may be effective when properly sent if an offeree uses a means of communication requested by the offeror or uses any reasonable means when none is specified. If an unauthorized means is used (one other than that requested by the offeror or one not considered reasonable), however, acceptance is generally not effective until the offeror actually receives the communication (assuming the offer is still open). As a general rule, the offeree's silence does not constitute acceptance.

The traditional manner of forming contracts in the business world (especially those contracts governed by the UCC) have been replaced by the formation of contracts electronically. Since online contracts have created legal issues not adequately addressed by common law and existing statutory law, new laws have been drafted under the UCC. Those laws will be discussed in Part III, "Purchase, Sales, and Lease of Goods."

Important Legal terms

acceptance	offer	option
bid	offer and acceptance	preliminary negotiations
counteroffer	offeree	rejection
mailbox rule	offeror	revocation

Questions and Problems for Discussion

1. a. What is the legal ramification that arises when one party makes an offer to another party?

   b. When making a statement with the idea that an offer is being made, the offeror must distinguish his statement from what other types of statements?

2. O'Mally offers to sell her townhouse to Doctor for $200,000. Doctor asks her if she would be willing to accept $175,000. Is Doctor's offer considered a counteroffer?

3. Park used her digital recorder to record an offer she wished to make to Reape by mail. Her secretary typed the offer and placed it on Park's desk for Park to review. Before the offer had been sent to Reape, Park called Reape, told her what she was doing, and stated that she would mail her the official offer to which Reape could respond. Instead of waiting for the offer to come in the mail, Reape immediately mailed an acceptance to Park. Was this acceptance valid?

4. Redfern, who recently opened a retail lighting fixture business, advertised on a local television station and in a local newspaper, quoting grand opening sale prices on many items he had in stock. The grand opening sale was to last for one week. He did not realize how successful the sale would be. After the second day, he ran out of the sale items but financially could not afford to offer rain checks. There were several unfilled orders. Several customers threatened to sue Redfern in small claims court. Do these customers have a legal right to the merchandise that they ordered?

5. Carpinski, in response to a letter by the Marion School District board of education, submitted a bid on May 1, offering to perform custodial services at Marion High School for a two-year

period at a salary of $30,000 per year. At a board of education meeting held on May 13, the board passed a resolution offering Carpinski a salary of $25,000 per year. On May 15, Carpinski received a copy of this board resolution in the mail. Does a contract exist between Carpinski and the board of education?

6. On May 12, Leonard offered to sell Ginrich, an acquaintance, a used washer-dryer for $400. Leonard told Ginrich that he had until May 17 to accept this offer. On May 13, Leonard received an offer to purchase the washer-dryer for $450 from Bolton, a friend. Leonard immediately accepted Bolton's offer. On May 14, Bolton saw Ginrich and mentioned that he (Bolton) had just purchased a washer-dryer from Leonard. On May 15, however, Ginrich notified Leonard that he accepted the offer to buy the washer-dryer for $400. Was Ginrich's acceptance valid?

7. Floyd, who lived in New York City, wrote a letter to Okcum in New Mexico offering to buy a piece of real property that was for sale. On receipt of the letter, Okcum mailed an answer accepting the offer. After the letter was sent, Okcum changed his mind and sent a telegram rejecting the offer. The telegram and the letter reached Floyd at the same time. Did a contract result?

8. On June 1, Essler mailed an offer to Weinberg to sell some household furniture at a special price of $500, stating, "Your acceptance must be received by me no later than June 12." Weinberg then mailed an acceptance on June 7 but, due to a postal delay, the acceptance did not reach Essler until June 15. Was Weinberg's acceptance binding on Essler?

9. Masters, an antique dealer, promised Shatraw, an international dealer in rare antiques, that if Shatraw could obtain some rare vases from India within three weeks, he would pay Shatraw's airfare to India to obtain them and in addition to

the cost of the vases would give him a bonus of $1,000. Shatraw did obtain the vases within the three-week period and delivered them to Masters. However, when Shatraw requested his money, Masters claimed that there was no contract because of lack of consideration for the promise he made and would not pay Shatraw. Is Masters correct?

10. Dalton Jewelers in Chicago engaged in lengthy negotiations with Repp Realty Company in New York City for the purchase of a new building. The price of the building kept the parties from concluding an immediate agreement. Repp's written offer to sell was $500,000. The representative for Dalton Jewelers finally replied by telegram offering $400,000, saying, "Take it or leave it." Repp Realty filed the telegram for future reference but did not respond. Dalton then sent a letter stating that Repp should disregard its prior communication offering $400,000 and that it accepted the offer of $500,000. Repp Realty wrote back stating, "The price is now $600,000. Take it or leave it." Dalton promptly sent a telegram to Repp Realty saying that it held Repp to its original offer of $500,000. Is Repp legally bound to sell the building to Dalton Jewelers for $500,000?

11. On February 8, Leggett sent a telegram offering to sell Picarro a personal computer. Picarro received the telegram the same day (February 8). Picarro mailed a letter of acceptance on February 9 at 11 A.M., which reached Leggett on the afternoon of February 12. At 1:30 P.M. on February 9, Picarro received a telegram from Leggett revoking the offer. Was the revocation effective?

12. On April 13, Afton offered by mail to sell his lawn care business to Baird for $175,000. On April 19, Baird telegrammed his acceptance, which was delayed and did not reach Afton's office until April 21. On April 20, Afton died. Was there a legally binding agreement?

Cases for Review

1. Turilli, owner of the Jessie James Museum in Stanton, Missouri, stated that the person shot to death and buried in 1882 as the notorious Jessie James was an imposter and that the real Jessie James lived for many years after he supposedly was shot to death under the alias of Frank Dalton. This statement brought a lot of attention to

Turilli's museum. To prove his point, Turilli went on television nationwide and offered a reward of $10,000 to anyone who could prove that his statement was not true. After hearing the offer, a proven relative of Jessie James came forward with substantial evidence that James truly had been killed and buried in 1882, as alleged in the history books. Despite this evidence, Turilli refused to pay the reward. James's relative sued to recover the $10,000. Turilli claimed that his television statement was not a real offer. Had Turilli made a true offer? (*James* v. *Turilli,* 473 S.W.2d 757)

2. Monk and Jenkins leased a building they owned to Tuneup Masters for five years. The lease contained a provision to extend the lease an additional five years by sending a certified or registered letter at least six months prior to the expiration of the lease. Within that five-year period, the vice president of Tuneup Masters exercised the renewal option by delivering a letter to the U.S. Postal Service and having it certified. This letter to the landlords was lost in the mail. Not having received the letter, the landlords refused to renew the lease. Tuneup Masters claimed that the renewal was valid even though the certified letter was lost. Is Tuneup correct? (*Jenkins* v. *Tuneup Masters,* 190 Cal. App. 3d 1, 235 Cal. Rptr. 214)

3. Spanos was three years behind in property tax payments on a building he owned. He listed the property for sale with a real estate agent and was made an offer of $230,000 in writing from D'Agostino. Spanos drew a line through the $230,000 figure and wrote in $235,000, initialed the price change, signed the offer, and returned it to D'Agostino. D'Agostino would not accept the offer as changed. Spanos orally informed D'Agostino that he would restore the price to the original $230,000. D'Agostino drew a line through the $235,000 figure that Spanos had inserted in the offer, wrote in $230,000, initialed the change, and returned the offer to Spanos. Spanos, however, never initialed the document after D'Agostino changed the written price back to $230,000. Spanos and D'Agostino never did arrive at a mutually acceptable price. Spanos instead sold the property to another buyer. D'Agostino, upon hearing of this sale, brought an action against Spanos requiring him to sell the property to him. Should D'Agostino win his case? (*D'Agostino* v. *Bank of Ravenswood,* 563 N.E.2d 886)

4. The Mitchells owned a small secondhand store. They attended an auction at a place where they often purchased merchandise for their store. One of the items for sale at the auction was an old safe that had a locked compartment but no key. The

safe was part of an estate and sold at the auction for $50. After the auction, the Mitchells took the safe to a locksmith to have the compartment opened. When opened, the compartment contained over $30,000 in cash. The locksmith called the City of Everett police where the Mitchells lived and where the auction took place. The police then temporarily impounded the money until the rightful owner could be identified. Both the Mitchells and the estate that initially owned the safe laid claim to the money. Who was the rightful owner of the money? (*City of Everett, Washington* v. *Mitchell,* 631 P.2d 366)

5. Calan Imports ran an add in the *Chicago Tribune* to sell an older model Volvo station wagon. The newspaper was instructed to advertise the price of the automobile at $1,795, but through an error on the part of the newspaper, it was advertised at $1,095. O'Brien saw the advertisement, went to Calan Imports to see the car, and stated that he wished to purchase it at the advertised price. When Calan Imports discovered the error in the advertised price, it refused to sell the car to O'Brien. O'Brien sued for breach of contract. Should he win his case? (*Calan Imports, Inc.* 262 N.E.2d.758)

6. Steinberg applied to the Chicago Medical School, paying the required $15 application fee. He was later notified that his application was rejected. He sued the school for breach of contract, claiming that the school did not evaluate his application according to the academic entrance criteria printed in the college's informational brochure. He claimed that the medical school instead made its decisions on criteria that were not listed in the brochure, such as the ability to pledge large sums of money to the school. Was there a contract formed between the college and Steinberg to review his application based on the criteria in the informational brochure? (*Steinberg* v. *Chicago Medical School,* 41 Ill. App.2d 804,354 N.E.2d 58)

7. Zehmer and his wife owned a 471-acre farm. In a restaurant one night, Lucy said to Zehmer that he bet Zehmer wouldn't take $50,000 cash for the farm. When Zehmer replied he didn't think Lucy had the cash, Lucy said he would get it if Zehmer would put it in writing that he would sell him the farm. Zehmer then wrote on a piece of paper, "I agree to sell the…farm to W.O. Lucy for $50,000 cash." Zehmer said in an undertone at the time that he thought it was a joke. When Zehmer later

refused to sell the farm to Lucy, Lucy brought an action to enforce the contract. Is Lucy entitled to purchase the farm? (*Lucy* v. *Zehmer,* 196 Va. 493, 84 S.E.2d 516)

8. Ledbetter, sheriff of Dallas County, posted a reward of $500 for the capture of an escaped murderer. Broadnax, not knowing of the reward, captured and returned the prisoner to the sheriff. After he returned the prisoner, Broadnax learned of the reward and claimed it. The sheriff would not pay. Was Broadnax legally entitled to the reward? (*Broadnax* v. *Ledbetter,* Tex. 99 S.W. 1111)

9. Morrison prepared a contract in Florida to purchase some Florida land owned by Thoelke. Morrison then mailed the contract to Thoelke, who was in Texas. Immediately after receiving the contract, Thoelke signed it and placed it in the mail, addressed to Morrison's attorney in Florida. Before the contract was received by Morrison's attorney, Thoelke called the attorney and canceled the contract. Morrison, however, recorded the contract. Thoelke filed a lawsuit to have the contract declared void, claiming that canceling the contract prior to its receipt by Morrison was a valid cancellation. Is Thoelke correct? (*Morrison* v. *Thoelke,* Fla.155 So.2d 889)

10. MacDonald Group is the managing general partner of Fresno Fashion Square, a shopping mall in Fresno, California. The regional mall has several major tenants as well as smaller stores such as Edmond's of Fresno, a jeweler. Edmond's signed lease with MacDonald stated that not more than two jewelry stores could be located in the mall. Nevertheless, MacDonald, after expanding the mall, gave notice to Edmond that it intended to rent space to other jewelry stores. The lease, however, did not state anything about additional jewelry stores being allowed in the new part of the mall. Edmond's sued MacDonald, claiming that the lease also applied to mall additions. Was Edmond's correct? (*Edmond's of Fresno* v. *MacDonald Group, Ltd.,* 171 Cal. App.3d 598)

CHAPTER 8

Consideration

CHAPTER PREVIEW

Chapter Highlights

This chapter deals with consideration, the second element required in a contract. It opens with a discussion, supported by examples, pointing out that if an agreement lacks consideration, neither party can enforce the agreement unless it has already been carried out. The chapter then describes what consideration consists of and how much consideration is necessary to make a deal. There is a brief discussion of the terms *moral consideration* and *past consideration*. The remainder of the chapter is devoted to special problems relating to consideration and some exceptional situations in which agreements without consideration can be enforced.

THE REQUIREMENT OF CONSIDERATION

Chapter 7 discussed agreement, the first element of a contract. Another requirement of a legally enforceable contract is consideration. Even though there has been an offer and acceptance, an agreement may not ripen into a contract without the presence of consideration. Together, offer, acceptance, and consideration are the three most important elements in the formation of a contract. Once established, the intention to create a legal relationship would be present. If no consideration is present, the contract may not be enforceable even if it contains a clause stating that is should be enforceable. **Consideration** is something of legal value that each party gives to the contract to bind the agreement. Suppose, for example, that your friend (the **promisor**, or person making a promise) promised to give you (the **promisee**, or person to whom the promisor make the promise) $200 if you repair his computer. You repaired the computer, and your friend paid you $200. The consideration your friend gave to the contract was $200. The consideration you gave to the contract was repairing the computer. Keep in mind that the parties must exchange something of value, but not necessarily of equal value, nor does consideration necessarily need to be monetary. (The next section will further explain this issue.) What the exchange does require, however, is that the value exchanged by each party induced the other to enter into the agreement.

Johnson sold his son real estate valued at $500,000 for $1.00. A court most likely would not recognize this transaction as a valid contract since Johnson's relationship with his son is what induced him (Johnson) to enter into the contract, not the price.

consideration something of value given by each party to bind an agreement

promisor one who makes a promise

promisee person to whom a promise is made

gift voluntary transfer of property without consideration

Under the common law, the parties to a contract are not bound unless both give consideration; consequently, a promise to make a gift is unenforceable. A **gift** is a voluntary transfer of property without consideration. If you promise to give a friend an electronic thesaurus as a birthday gift, your promise is not legally binding even if your friend accepts. You, the offeror, have received nothing of value (consideration) in return from your friend, the offeree.

You will discover later in this chapter that there are exceptions to this rule regarding the exchange of consideration. You will also discover later in the text that there are exceptions under the UCC.

The presence or absence of consideration is unimportant once an agreement has been executed (carried out). For example, you and a friend agree to exchange graduation gifts. You give your friend a digital recorder as a graduation gift, but she does not give you anything. A court will not cancel the agreement and return the recorder to you because your friend gave no consideration.

Generally, both written and oral promises require consideration. Some states have laws providing that certain written contracts are valid without consideration.

THE NATURE OF CONSIDERATION

The consideration demanded by the promissor (offeror) and given by the promisee (offeree) may be a benefit to the offeror, such as money, a computer, jewelry, or a cell phone. Often, however, the consideration does not have a monetary value and does not benefit the offeror. Instead, the consideration may consist of a sacrifice by the offeree. This sacrifice is called **legal detriment**. Legal detriment is consideration when the offeree, at the request of the offeror:

legal detriment consideration that is a sacrifice by the offeree

1. Does something (an act) or promises to do something he or she is not legally bound to do. Wadsworth, a multimillionaire industrialist, told a group of sixth-grade students in a speech at their commencement exercises that if they stayed in school and graduated from high school, he would pay each successful high school graduate's tuition to any four-year college in the United States. Each current sixth-grade student's completion of high school (an act that the student was not legally bound to do) was consideration for Wadsworth's promise to pay his or her college tuition.

2. Refrains (from an act) or promises to refrain from doing something she or he has a legal right to do. This refraining is called **forbearance**.

forbearance refraining from doing something one has a legal right to do

A famous entertainer with a gross annual income of over $5 million promised his young friend full support for life, a $10,000 monthly salary, and a one-half interest in all the entertainer's real estate if the friend would refrain from pursuing his planned career in education and become the entertainer's bodyguard, chauffeur, and secretary for life. The friend had a legal right to pursue a career in education; therefore, refraining from this act was consideration for the entertainer's promise to do the things he promised for his young friend.

ADEQUACY OF CONSIDERATION

As stated earlier in the chapter, the presence of consideration in an agreement is essential. In the past, however, courts have not questioned whether the consideration received by each party was sufficient or fair in light of the consideration the other party gave. The parties have been free to enter into an agreement on terms they can agree upon, even though one party may obtain a "better deal."

> Cullen owned a racehorse worth $25,000 that had not made a good showing in the last six races. He decided to sell this horse at any cost just to get rid of it. Farnsworth, his friend, seriously offered him $200, and Cullen seriously accepted the offer. The horse then went on to win the next three races at the track, bringing the owner a substantial amount of money. Cullen had second thoughts and demanded a return of the horse, claiming that the consideration he received was too small. Because a serious offer was made by Farnsworth and was seriously accepted by Cullen, who received the consideration he requested, Cullen was bound by the agreement even though the horse was worth $25,000.

Modern courts and legislative bodies have changed the historical view of consideration. They now protect individuals from contracts that are so one-sided as to be unconscionable (unfair). Unconscionable contracts are discussed in Chapter 10.

The courts will question the adequacy of the consideration if the contract calls for the exchange of different quantities of things that are identical in nature or have a fixed value, such as money. A promise to pay a friend $200 in return for the friend's promise to immediately pay you $20 (money promised for money) is not enforceable. Yet a promise to pay $200 in return for a promise to deliver a book worth $20 is binding. Because the items exchanged are not identical in nature, the adequacy of the consideration is unimportant to the validity of the contract. It is difficult to compare the worth of different items, so adequacy of consideration must be judged by the parties to the contract.

In extreme cases, the courts will also question the adequacy of the consideration. In such cases, inadequate consideration can indicate fraud, duress, or undue influence (discussed in Chapter 14). For example, at the time Fleming purchased a used motorcycle, the salesperson deliberately misrepresented the condition of the motorcycle and charged him more money than it was worth. Under these circumstances, the courts will permit Fleming to avoid the agreement because he relied on the salesperson's statements.

nominal consideration
dollar or other small sum of money used to bind a contract

Often, a written contract states that the consideration given for a promise is $1 or some other small amount. This small sum of money is called **nominal consideration**. Courts will enforce contracts with such small consideration if the amount was actually paid and if the offeror intended that amount to be the price for the promise. If, however, the $1 amount was stated in the contract only to make it appear that the contract contained consideration, but the $1 was not actually paid, the courts will not enforce the contract.

In most states, seals placed on contracts are not substitutes for consideration. Article 2 of the UCC has abolished the effect of a seal with regard to the sale of goods.

MORAL CONSIDERATION

Sometimes an offeror makes a promise because he or she feels it is the right thing to do. In other words, this person (the offeror) feels a moral commitment to make such a promise. In most states, courts adhere strictly to the requirements of consideration concerning moral obligations and would say that a moral promise is no more enforceable than any other promise unsupported by consideration. At best, a court would conclude that the offeror intends to make a gift. Consider the following example:

> Speedy, who had a great deal of affection for her aunt, promised to pay the rent on her apartment while the aunt was in the hospital and unable to work. Because Speedy received no consideration from her aunt for Speedy's moral promise to pay, the promise Speedy made is not legally binding.

A minority of courts would take a different position and hold that a moral obligation is sufficient to enforce a promise even without return consideration, especially if the promise of the offeror involved a humanitarian gesture. In these few states, a promise such as the one Speedy made in the example might very well be enforceable.

Past Consideration

past consideration
promise made for an act that has already taken place

Past consideration is a promise made for an act that has already taken place. This doctrine has the same status with the courts as moral consideration. Because consideration is something of value given by the offeree at the time of the promise made by the offeror, past consideration is therefore legally no consideration at all in most states. In other words, for the consideration to be valid, the offeror's promise must induce the offeree to act.

> A friend helped you study for a final exam in your business law course. After the exam, you promised to give your friend $25 for the help. Because it was a promise to pay for help that had already been given, you are not obligated to pay the $25.

The offeree must give the consideration *after* the offeror makes the request. If before the exam you had promised your friend $25 to help you study for the final exam and your friend had agreed, the promise would be binding. In that case, your promise induced or motivated your friend to help you.

In some states, a written promise to pay for an act already performed (past consideration) is binding.

Sometimes a court will incorporate a past benefit into a contract and thereby deem that the contract has sufficient consideration to be enforceable. This, of course, presumes that all the other requirements of a valid contract are present.

> Marcum lived in an apartment owned by Summers. Summers asked Marcum to make certain repairs which Marcum did, knowing that he would be paid for his work. Upon completion of the repairs, Marcum submitted a bill for his services, which Summers paid.

In this example, the agreement is enforceable. Although the repairs Marcum completed were a past benefit, he completed the work at the request of Summers. It wasn't as if Marcum did the work and then brought it to the attention of Summers. This latter situation is a straightforward case of past consideration.

Special Problems Relating to Consideration

Many problems involving consideration (or the lack of it) arise during the performance of a contract. Courts often deal with these problems on an individual basis. Although many such problems occur, one common problem involves the preexisting legal obligation.

Preexisting Contractual Agreement

Sometimes the offeree, after beginning performance under the terms of an already existing agreement, will not continue to perform unless the offeror makes a new promise to pay more money. A new promise by the offeror to pay more money is not legally binding. The offeree has furnished no additional consideration for the new promise because there is a preexisting legal duty to perform.

> Pierre-Philippe, a building contractor, prepared a bid in writing to build a small shed behind Medford's house for $2,000. After beginning work, Pierre-Philippe discovered

that he required more materials than originally planned. Pierre-Philippe informed Medford that he would not continue the job until Medford agreed to pay an additional $500 for the extra necessary materials. Medford orally promised to pay. Pierre-Philippe was already legally obligated to complete the work for $2,000. He furnished no additional consideration for Medford's promise to pay him $500 more. Medford is therefore not legally required to pay the additional $500.

By doing or agreeing to do something extra—something not covered by the existing agreement—the offeree *would* be providing the additional consideration required in return for the offeror's promise to pay more money. If, in the example, Pierre-Philippe had agreed to make the shed larger than originally agreed, he would have provided consideration in return for Medford's new promise to pay an additional $500, and Medford would be required to pay the additional money.

In the interest of fairness and equity, the courts sometimes allow exceptions to the preexisting rule for circumstances not anticipated by the parties when the contract was made. Thus, in the preceding case, the courts might allow Pierre-Philippe to collect the extra compensation agreed upon ($500) if he had honestly run into some unforeseeable circumstance that caused him to lose money. A hurricane (considered an act of God) that destroys part of the shed during the construction period is one example of an unforeseen circumstance. These courts believe that as long as a person in Pierre-Philippe's position is not in any way negligent or dishonest, he or she should be entitled to collect.

In some states, a written agreement that changes an existing agreement and that is signed by the promisor needs no additional consideration.

Preexisting Duty to Pay a Debt

Some promises are not legally enforceable because one of the parties (the debtor) has a preexisting duty to pay a debt to the other party (the creditor). For example, the creditor may agree (promise) to accept part payment (a smaller sum of money) from the debtor in full payment of the debt. Nevertheless, if there is no dispute about the existence of the debt or its amount, the debt is called a **liquidated claim** and the promise is not legally enforceable. The debtor has given no consideration for the creditor's promise to accept less money; the debtor is already legally obligated to pay the full amount. Even if the creditor accepts the smaller amount, the creditor may still collect the remainder of the debt.

liquidated claim debt, amount of which is not in dispute

> Sellers owed you $500. On the due date, Sellers told you that she could not pay the full $500. You orally agreed to accept $400 in full settlement of the debt. Sellers agreed and paid you the $400. Because Sellers gave you no consideration for your promise to accept less than the full amount owed ($500), you may recover the balance due of $100.

If a creditor accepts less money plus additional consideration from the debtor, the debt will be canceled. If, in this example, you agreed to accept $400 plus three DVDs worth $50, the entire $500 debt would be canceled because you have agreed to the additional consideration. The additional consideration may take any form; the value of the consideration is unimportant as long as it is an *additional* consideration.

In some states, if a creditor accepts part payment of a debt and gives the debtor a written release from the remainder of the debt, the release cancels the entire debt without additional consideration.

unliquidated claim debt, amount of which is subject to an honest dispute

Part payment of a debt can cancel a debt if there is an honest dispute over the correct amount of the debt—called an **unliquidated claim**—and the parties agree to a compromise. Instead of going to court to settle the dispute, the debtor and creditor each give up this legal right. They agree instead to settle out of court on an amount somewhere between the amount the debtor claims is owed and the amount the creditor claims is correct. This compromise is legally binding and represents full settlement of the entire debt. One legal argument in support of this rule is that the consideration in the compromise agreement is each party's refraining, or promising to refrain, from contesting the amount in court.

> Dodge hired Finzer to construct a human performance lab in an existing room of her home. When Finzer completed the job, he sent her a bill for $10,000. Dodge disputed the bill, claiming that a fair price was $8,500. She claimed that this figure was based on the exact same job performed for several of her friends and neighbors by other contractors. Finzer responded by saying that his work was quality work and was worth $10,000 but that in view of her report of what friends and neighbors paid, he would accept $9,000 in full settlement of the disputed bill. Dodge agreed and paid the $9,000. The $9,000 paid by Dodge cancels the $10,000 debt.

Part payment of a disputed debt may also cancel that debt if the creditor accepts and cashes a check marked on its face "payment in full." Courts in most states reason that if any part of the debt is in dispute, the entire debt is unliquidated. A payment that is made by the debtor and accepted by the creditor as payment in full is binding.

> Crandall, who owned a landscaping service, orally gave Drake an estimate of $475 for cutting down two trees on Drake's property. Crandall then cut down the trees, claiming that Drake orally agreed to the work. Drake insisted, however, that she had authorized only an estimate. In an effort to settle the dispute, Drake mailed Crandall a check for $325 with the notation on the check "paid in full." Crandall cashed the check and then sued Drake for the additional $150.

In this example, Crandall could not collect the $150 ($475–$325). Drake's check for $325 was an offer to settle the dispute. When Crandall cashed the check, he accepted this offer to settle. The result would be the same even if before cashing the check, Crandall had crossed out the "paid in full" notation. If Crandall wishes to protect his rights fully, he should, in addition to not cashing the check, return it to Drake with a note stating that he is not agreeing to accept the tendered amount as full payment of the debt.

Not all states would consider that part payment of a disputed debt by a check marked "paid in full" would cancel the debt. Some, like New York State, hold that a creditor may collect the balance of the debt if he or she endorses the check with the statement, "This check is cashed under protest." Courts in these states argue that the amount of money a debtor claims he or she owes is liquidated and that there is a preexisting duty to pay it. Actually paying this debt therefore cannot be consideration for the creditor's implied promise (cashing of the check) to release the debtor from the unpaid balance.

If a person owes money to several people, part payment of the debt owed to each of the creditors may cancel the entire debt if all the creditors agree. A **composition of creditors** is an arrangement in which all creditors agree to accept a certain percentage of the total amount owed by the debtor in full settlement of a debt. Creditors who agree to the composition actually receive no additional consideration from the debtor in return for their promise to accept less money. Courts, nevertheless, will enforce such an agreement because no one creditor receives the full amount of the debt owed. Creditors generally agree to this type of arrangement only when they believe they will never be able to collect the full amount owed to them by the debtor.

composition of creditors agreement among creditors to accept a percentage of total owed by debtor in full settlement of debt

> Werner owed $4,000 to Vienna and $2,000 to Hobbs, for a total of $6,000. The two creditors agreed to accept 50 percent of their claims in full settlement of the debt.

Under this arrangement, Vienna received $2,000 (50 percent of $4,000) and Hobbs received $1,000 (50 percent of $2,000). Because Vienna and Hobbs agreed to take less money in full payment of the total debt owed by Werner, the remainder of the debt is canceled.

A creditor's promise to extend the due date of a debt is not enforceable unless the debtor gives additional consideration. If no additional consideration is given by the debtor for the creditor's promise to extend the time for payment, the creditor may legally demand repayment before the end of the extension.

Graves owed McHale $400. When the debt was due, Graves did not have the money and asked McHale for a three-month extension. McHale orally agreed. Before the three months were up, McHale changed his mind and sued Graves for the money. Because Graves gave no consideration for McHale's promise to extend the time of payment by three months, McHale's promise is not legally enforceable.

A debtor may legally obtain an extension of the due date if the creditor agrees to the extension and receives additional consideration. Suppose, in the example, McHale agreed to extend the due date and accepted a part payment of the debt from Graves before the original due date. The part payment by Graves would be the additional consideration needed in return for McHale's promise to extend the due date by three months.

In some states, a creditor's written promise to extend the due date of a debt is enforceable without additional consideration.

Preexisting Duty to Perform a Legal Obligation

A person who performs or promises to perform his or her legal obligation gives no consideration for an offeror's promise to pay money. Into this category fall police officers, judges, legislators, and other public officials. A promise, for example, to pay a police officer a reward for the arrest of a person who burglarized your home is not legally enforceable. The arrest of criminals, and in this particular case, a burglar, is part of a police officer's legal obligations. He or she cannot gain privately from this obligation.

AGREEMENTS ENFORCEABLE WITHOUT CONSIDERATION

Up to this point, the emphasis has been on situations in which consideration was required for promises to be enforceable. There are exceptional situations, however, in which promises can be enforced without consideration. In an effort to avoid injustice, courts base their decisions to enforce such promises on principles of equity. If ordinary contract law instead of equity were the basis, these same promises would not need to be enforced because consideration is lacking.

Promises to Charitable Organizations

pledge promise to make a gift to a charitable, religious, educational, or scientific institution; bailment created when personal property is deposited as security for repayment of a debt

A promise to make a gift to a charitable, religious, educational, or scientific organization or to some other institution such as a library, museum, or hospital that depends on voluntary contributions is usually enforceable without consideration. This promise is called a **pledge** or subscription. The pledge can be oral (e.g., a donation called in to a television station during a charity telethon), but it is usually in writing. Before your pledge is binding, you must acknowledge it. In states where a pledge is required in writing, the donor is often asked to sign a pledge card (Figure 8.1). There are different theories for enforcing such a promise.

FIGURE 8.1 Pledge Card

Yes, my gift to the Highland Hospital Foundation will help provide new and expanded services for Highland's patients and will directly support the high quality of personalized patient care to which Highland is committed.
My tax deductible check is enclosed for $__________.

Through this gift, I/we will be considered a:

☐ *Contributor* ($5–24)

•☐ *Member* ($25–99)
Receives "Highland Highlites" four times a year.
Recognition in hospital publication.

•☐ *Fellow* ($100–499)
Receives all of the above plus free personalized Emergency Medical Card. Invitation to annual reception.

•☐ *Patron* ($500–999)
Receives all of the above plus invitation to annual recognition dinner.

•☐ *Founder* ($1000 or more)
Receives all of the above plus recognition in hospital lobby as leading contributor. Invitation to special Founder's event. Free tickets to hospital functions.

Please make check payable to:
Highland Hospital Foundation, Inc.
Every gift large or small is important to Highland.

•Second Century Associate

Thank You

PLEASE PRINT

Name (circle) Miss Ms. Dr. Mr. Mrs. __________
Please specify the way you wish your name to appear in the annual report of gifts. •

Address __________

City ______ State ______ Zip ______

Telephone ( ) __________

Please designate my (our) gift:
☐ A regular donation; †☐ In honor of; †☐ In memory of; †☐ In appreciation of:

Name ______ Occasion ______

• Donors' names are acknowledged in our hospital publication unless you instruct us otherwise.

†Acknowledgement of gift is sent immediately and no amount is mentioned.

Send acknowledgement of gift to:

Name __________

Address __________

__________ Zip ______

Relationship to person honored __________

☐ This gift will be matched by my (spouse's) employer. Enclosed is the Matching Gift Form supplied by my (spouse's) employer.

☐ Please send me more information in regard to estate tax and income tax savings from a charitable gift to Highland.

One theory is that the organization, even before payment of the pledges, will rely on the total amount of pledged money and enter into various contracts or make other expenditures. Under the circumstances, it would be unfair to the organization to permit any person to withdraw a pledge.

The Preservation of Animals in Tennessee, Inc., an educational and scientific not-for-profit corporation organized for the purpose of protecting wild animals, establishes and maintains refuge areas for wild animals within Tennessee. To build more refuge areas and maintain present ones, the corporation depends on voluntary contributions from the public. Montgomery, who had a real love of animals, responded to a request by the corporation to contribute and, like many other people, signed the following pledge on June 8, 2005: "In consideration of my interest in animals and in consideration of the pledges of others, I hereby agree to pay to the order of the treasurer of The Preservation of Animals in Tennessee, Inc., the sum of two thousand dollars ($2,000). (signed) Gloria M. Montgomery." Based on this pledge and the pledges of others, several more refuge areas for wild animals were built in certain areas of the state between June 8, 2005, and November 1, 2005, at a cost of $300,000. Montgomery refused to pay her pledge as agreed, claiming that she now desired to use the $2,000 for a trip to Europe during the winter holidays. The corporation notified her that she was legally liable for payment of the $2,000 and that it would take action through legal channels to collect the money if she did not pay. In a return letter to the corporation, she insisted she was not liable because her pledge was merely a promise to make a gift and that she had received no consideration from the corporation for this promise. Because the corporation built several new refuge areas for wild animals relying on the pledges, Montgomery is legally obligated to pay the $2,000 regardless of the lack of consideration, as she claimed.

Another theory is that the promise to pay is made in consideration of the promises of others to also give. The promise of each promisor is supported by the promises of others.

Generally, a pledge may be withdrawn at any time before the institution takes steps to begin construction. Some courts, however, hold that once made, a pledge may not be withdrawn.

Promissory Estoppel

promissory estoppel
equitable doctrine applied by the courts to enforce a promise unsupported by consideration

Courts in some states occasionally apply the equity doctrine of **promissory estoppel** to enforce a promise unsupported by consideration on the part of the offeree if it would be grossly unfair not to enforce the promise since the result could lead to harsh result. In short, the offeror is prevented by law (stopped) from claiming a defense (no consideration for his or her promise) that would normally be available.

> Martin was an employee of Case for twenty-five years but had not received any benefits. Nevertheless, Case promised to pay Martin a pension of $1,300 a month for life whenever Martin decided to take retirement. Case made it quite clear to Martin, however, that he was not asking her to retire, nor did he wish her to retire. Martin retired two years later, making no plans to work anywhere else. Instead, she simply relied on the monthly income Case agreed to provide; in fact, she would not have retired without it. After a few years, Case discontinued the pension. Martin was then too advanced in age to look for another job and sued Case to continue payment of the pension. Case claimed that his promise to pay the pension in the first place was never supported by consideration on Martin's part.

The court in this example would probably rule in Martin's favor based on the equity doctrine of promissory estoppel because the purpose of this doctrine is to enforce a promise even though consideration is lacking. Case made a promise of a monthly income for life, and Martin relied on this promise. Case however, reneged on this agreement. It would obviously be grossly unfair if she were not able to continue to collect the pension. An injustice could be avoided only by enforcing Case's promise.

Promises Involving the Statute of Limitations

Each state has a statute of limitations legally preventing a creditor from collecting a debt after a certain period of time. The time varies from state to state but generally runs from three to six years, with six years being very common. After this period passes, the creditor can no longer initiate a lawsuit against the debtor. At times, however, a debtor with a guilty conscience wishes to repay the money that he or she owes even though the time limit for collection has passed. Because the debtor actually has no legal obligation to pay, however, the promise cannot serve as consideration. The debtor's promise amounts at best to a moral obligation to pay, and a moral obligation is not consideration. In most states, however, if the debtor offers to repay the debt in writing, the courts will make an exception to the past consideration rules governing consideration and enforce the debtor's promise. This new promise is binding according to the terms contained in the new agreement for another statutory period.

Summary

As a general rule, the parties to a contract are not bound unless consideration is given by both of them, even though there has been an offer by one party and an acceptance by another party. Consideration consists of a promise on the part of the offeror in return for some tangible benefit, such as money or a computer, given by the offeree. Or as is often the case, consideration on the part of the offeree may consist of legal detriment. Legal detriment is a sacrifice by the offeree—the doing of an act or refraining (forbearance) from doing an act or merely a promise to do or to refrain. An example of legal detriment is when, in exchange for a promise of $5,000 by the offeror, the offeree agrees (promises) to stop smoking.

Although the presence of consideration in an agreement is essential, courts do not usually question whether the consideration received by each party is sufficient or even fair. The courts may raise this question if there is evidence of fraud, duress, or undue influence or if the contract is unconscionable (grossly unfair) because the parties who entered into the contract had unequal bargaining powers.

In most states, a moral promise is no more enforceable than any other promise unsupported by consideration. A minority of courts, however, hold that if the promise of the offeror involved a humanitarian gesture, a moral obligation is sufficient to enforce a promise even without return consideration. Past consideration is also not consideration because the offeror's promise did not induce the offeree to act. Instead, the offeree acted first and then was promised something by the offeror.

The performance of a preexisting contractual obligation by the offeree (other than the payment of debts) is not consideration for an offeror's promise because the offeree is not required to do more than was originally agreed to. By doing or agreeing to do something not covered by the existing agreement, however, the offeree would be providing the additional consideration required in return for the offeror's promise to pay more money. Some states have modified these rules when unforeseeable circumstances are involved.

Applying the preexisting rule to the payment of debts, a distinction is made between liquidated and unliquidated debts. If a creditor agrees (promises) to accept part payment from a debtor in full payment of a liquidated claim (no dispute exists about the existence or amount of the debt), the promise is not enforceable. The debtor is already legally obligated to pay the full amount. If, however, a debt is unliquidated (an honest dispute does exist over the amount of the debt), the acceptance by the creditor of a part payment of that debt cancels the remainder. The debtor and creditor each gave up the legal right to go to court to settle the dispute. Part payment of a disputed claim also cancels the remainder of the debt if the creditor accepts and cashes a check marked "paid in full." Regardless of this majority view, some states still hold that a creditor may collect the balance of the claim. A person such as a public official who is already legally obligated to perform a duty under the law gives no consideration for his or her promise to pay money. This public official cannot gain privately from the duty to perform a legal obligation.

In exceptional situations, courts will enforce promises made without consideration. Often, these situations involve promises (pledges) to make gifts to charitable, religious, educational, or scientific organizations under the doctrine of promissory estoppel or as the result of a promise made after a debt expires under a state's statute of limitations.

Some of the rules of consideration will change when the UCC is studied in future chapters.

Important Legal terms

composition of creditors
consideration
forbearance
gift
legal detriment

liquidated claim
nominal consideration
past consideration
pledge
promisee

promisor
promissory estoppel
unliquidated claim

Questions and Problems for Discussion

1. Jenetta agreed to work as an administrative assistant for Di Brin, owner of the BuildWell Construction Company for $2,500 a month. After six months on the job, Jenetta claimed that because her wages were inadequate, her current contract was terminated. Is she correct?

2. Discuss the differences among adequate consideration, moral consideration, and past consideration.

3. Martins joined an amateur football team. Before he officially started playing in league games, he, like the other players, signed a contract with Holland Park, the owner of the football field where the games were to be played. As part of the contract, Martins acknowledged that football was a dangerous activity and agreed to personally assume all risks in case he is injured. During the football season, Martins was injured at a scheduled game. He then sued Holland Park, claiming that maintenance of the football field was inadequate for the sport being played and that this lack of maintenance caused his injury. When presented in court with the contract containing the release from injury clause, Martins claimed that the clause was not valid because of lack of consideration. Is Martins correct?

4. Visca, while visiting a friend's house, was injured when some heavy ceiling tiles in the bathroom came loose, fell, and hit her squarely on the head. She suffered a slight concussion. Her friend gave her money to see a doctor and to pay for the prescriptions ordered by the doctor. In turn, Visca agreed orally not to sue her friend for the injury she received. Several weeks later, because Visca complained of severe headaches and had to make several more visits to a doctor and continue with medication, she decided to sue her friend for additional expenses and pain and suffering. Can Visca recover the additional money?

5. Graves was struck by a car driven by Koons. They then had a dispute as to whether or not the accident was Koons's fault and as to the extent of Graves's injuries. They finally agreed that Koons would pay Graves $1,500 (and he did) in return for Graves's promise to release Koons of all liability. In the event that Graves's actual damages later turn out to be in excess of $1,500, is Graves still bound by his promise of release?

6. When Glocker received her bill from Lawnmark, a lawn care company, she became very angry about the amount that the company claimed she owed. She immediately wrote a letter to the company's general manager, giving her version of the amount owed and including a check for that amount. She marked on the face of the check "paid in full settlement of the claim by the Lawnmark Company." The general manager cashed the check and immediately sued Glocker to recover the remaining balance. Can the general manager legally collect?

7. Delacruz, a nuclear reactor specialist, while employed at the Municipal Gas and Electric (MGE) nuclear power plant was offered a job with the U.S. Government Nuclear Regulatory Commission at a much higher salary. She was to begin work with the commission immediately. Since her contract with Municipal Gas and Electric had not yet expired, MGE offered to increase her salary if she would complete her present employment contract with them. Delacruz agreed and stayed on until her contract with MGE expired. MGE then refused to pay the promised increase in salary. Is Delacruz legally entitled to the salary increase for staying on with MGE?

8. The City of Newland through its financial director entered into a contract with Armae, a waste management contractor, to haul away all the city's waste products for a certain price. After the contract was made, several new rental units were built in the city, and Armae, based on his higher costs, asked the city for an additional $20,000 dollars a year. At a public meeting all city council members voluntarily voted to authorize the mayor to pay Armae the additional amount. Several community citizens who attended the meeting then sued the city, claiming that the additional compensation should have been denied. They based their claim on the theory that a contract was already in place and that there was no consideration for the payment of the increased compensation. Were the contract modification and additional $20,000 per year to Armae valid?

9. The board of directors of Hill Haven, a home for the elderly, was accepting donations to build an

additional dormitory at the home. Hogan promised in writing to donate $3,000 for the proposed addition. Relying on this and other pledges, the directors contracted for the construction of the dormitory. Is Hogan bound by the promise to donate $3,000?

10. Davies was employed in the data-processing division of a bank. Desmond and Zwick, owners of a firm that manufactured athletic equipment, orally promised Davies a position as office manager if she would quit the bank job and work for them. Davies quit her job at the bank, but Desmond and Zwick did not keep their promise to hire her. Can Davies legally enforce the promise made by Desmond and Zwick to hire her?

Cases for Review

1. Apfel, a company that sold computer systems, sold a computerized system for trading securities on the market to Prudential-Bache Securities, an investment bank. Before the purchase was made, Prudential-Bache thoroughly reviewed Apfel's system, which had been made known only to them, and deemed that the system fit its business needs. This review was followed by a sales contract in which Prudential-Bache agreed to make periodic payments for employing this system. Prudential-Bache encouraged its customers to use the system and for at least two years was the only company to offer these services. During this time, they handled millions of transactions, which of course produced income for the company. After a few years, Prudential-Bache had a change in personnel. The contract with Apfel was reviewed, and the new management decided to cancel and not make further payments. The new management claimed that the contract with Apfel had no value to them and that therefore there was no consideration to bind the parties. Their "no value" claim stated that the computerized system was not as secret as had been conveyed to them and that other investment companies were also using the system. Was Prudential-Bache in a position to claim that no consideration was present because of its claim that it had no value to the company? (*Apfel* v. *Prudential-Bache Securities, Inc.,* 600 N.Y.S.2d 433)

2. After working for the company for several years, Love and Morris, employees of Airco, Inc., were asked to sign employment contracts containing a noncompete clause. Airco stated that employees were asked to sign so as to prevent future competition from former employees who decided to leave the company. Although Airco never formally made any promises, both employees believed that signing the agreement would either make their jobs more secure or give them a better chance for promotion. About a year and a half after signing the agreement, Love and Morris left Airco and went to work for a competitor. Airco then petitioned the court to enforce the noncompete provisions of the two men's employment contracts. Love and Morris contended that they received no consideration for signing the noncompete covenant in their contract. Were they correct? (*Milner Airco, Inc.* v. *Morris,* 433 S.E.2d 811)

3. Elvis Presley, a well-known singer and entertainer, was a wealthy person. When engaged to Ginger Alden, he promised Alden's mother, Jo Laverne Allen, to pay off the remaining mortgage debt on the Alden home. However, Presley died before he had the chance to pay off the mortgage. The legal representative of Presley's estate refused to follow through on the promise to pay the mortgage debt amounting to around $40,000. Jo Laverne Alden sued the Presley estate to enforce Presley's promise. Was Presley's promise to pay the mortgage enforceable against the estate? (*Alden* v. *Presley,* 637 S.W.2d 862)

4. Ralston was injured when she fell down a church stairway. Matthew, agent for the company that insured the church, promised Ralston that the insurance company would pay her hospital and medical expenses if she did not sue the church. Ralston agreed, but the insurance company refused to pay her expenses, claiming that charitable and religious organizations in the state of Kansas were not liable for negligence. The company stated that Ralston had no valid claim and that her promise not to sue was not consideration. Did Ralston have a valid claim? (*Ralston* v. *Matthew,* 173 Kan. 550)

5. Williamson was about to lose a house that she owned but was mortgaged. She agreed to sell the house to Matthews for an amount she thought would pay off the mortgage and leave enough money for her to purchase a mobile home. After making the sale, Williamson went to her attorney and said that she wished to back out of the house sale because the selling price was inadequate. She claimed that she had not charged Matthews enough to pay off her mortgage and then be able to purchase a mobile home. Could the sale of the house to Matthews be voided for lack of consideration? (*Williamson* v. *Matthews*, 379 So2d 1245 Ala)

CHAPTER 9

Capacity

CHAPTER PREVIEW

Capacity to Contract	**Persons Under the Influence of Alcohol or Other Drugs**
Minors	
Minors' Liability on Ordinary Contracts	**Persons with Mental Illness**
Misrepresentation of Age by a Minor	Court Declared Incompetence
Ratification by a Minor	Mental Incompetence Not Adjudged by a Court
Minors' Liability for Necessaries	
Parents' Liability for Minors' Contracts	
Minors' Liability for Torts	

Chapter Highlights

This chapter explores the third required element of a legally enforceable contract, namely, the capacity to contract. The opening section first defines competent parties and then lists the categories of individuals (minors, intoxicated persons, and those with mental illness), who are considered incompetent and therefore have a limited capacity to enter into contracts. The remainder of the chapter outlines in some detail the liabilities of these incompetent individuals on ordinary contracts and for the goods and services that the law considers necessary to life and health. The discussion of incompetent persons' contracting capacity occurs under the following categories: minors, persons under the influence of alcohol or other drugs, and persons who are mentally ill. It will be interesting to learn how far the law goes to protect minors, and even to refer to them as "infants" in many of their court decisions.

CAPACITY TO CONTRACT

capacity to contract legal and mental ability to understand the nature of an enforceable agreement

In addition to the requirements of agreement and consideration, a third requirement of a valid contract is that the parties have the **capacity to contract** or contractual capacity. Contractual capacity is the legal and mental ability of a person to understand that he or she is entering into an agreement that is enforceable by law. It is a defense available to an otherwise valid contract. Each party to an agreement is considered to have contractual capacity until proof is presented otherwise. The proof must come from the person alleged to lack the capacity to contract.

By law, some persons are considered incompetent and have a limited capacity to enter into contracts. This category includes minors, persons under the influence of alcohol and other drugs, and some persons who are mentally ill. These individuals are given substantial protection by law. Their contracts are voidable. They may make agreements, but they have the legal right to set aside—or refuse to carry out—these agreements. This right of an incompetent to set aside an agreement is called **disaffirmance**. Persons who are mentally ill and have been declared insane by a court are completely incompetent and do not have the legal capacity even to contract. Their contracts are void. Competent parties generally deal with incompetent parties, especially minors, at their own risk.

disaffirmance refusal of incompetent party to carry out the terms of an agreement

161

MINORS

In virtually all states, a person (male and female) is considered a minor until age eighteen. At age eighteen a person is then legally an adult (i.e., as having reached the age of majority) for the purpose of making a contract for goods and services that are not necessary. (More will be said about necessaries later in the chapter.) The age of majority may still be twenty-one for other purposes as, for example, the purchase of alcohol. By law, a person reaches majority at 12:01 A.M. on the day before his or her birthday of the age of majority. For example, if your birthday is November 4 and you live in Texas, you legally become eighteen at 12:01 A.M. on November 3.

An agreement between a minor and an adult is voidable only by the minor. Unless and until the minor decides to set aside or disaffirm, however, the agreement legally binds both parties.

> Maranti, a minor, signed an agreement with a business school to take a fifteen-week accounting course. One week later and before starting classes, she changed her mind and notified the school that she would not be taking the course. The school, nevertheless, demanded that Maranti fulfill the terms of the agreement or else pay for the cost of the course. As a minor, Maranti had the right to avoid this agreement.

The law in all states grants minors the right to avoid or disaffirm agreements, and it does so for their protection. The law presumes that minors are immature and therefore lack judgment and experience.

There are many situations in which a minor may have as much ability to make an agreement as an adult. It is difficult, however, for courts to analyze each agreement made by a minor to determine competence. As a result, the law grants the right of disaffirmance to all minors, regardless of whether the agreement is fair or unfair to the minor, whether it does or does not benefit the minor, or whether the minor is ten or seventeen years old.

The courts, however, will not allow a minor to use the right to disaffirm agreements as a "sword" to injure adults. The law permitting disaffirmance was intended only to protect the minor.

> Hanna, a minor, purchased an airline ticket from New York City to Los Angeles so that he could visit some relatives. The airline was running a special fare of $350 round trip. When Hanna returned from his trip, he went to the airline office in New York City and demanded his $350 back, claiming that as a minor he could disaffirm his agreement with the airline. Because it appears that Hanna was trying to use his minority to take advantage of the airline, a court may not let him disaffirm the agreement.

Adults can avoid suffering losses by refusing to enter into agreements with minors. If an adult does deal with a minor, the adult may ask that a parent, guardian, or other adult sign the agreement along with the minor. A **guardian** is an adult appointed by the court to have custody and care of a minor in place of his or her own parents until the minor reaches the age of majority. The parent, guardian, or other adult is legally bound on the contract even though the minor disaffirms it.

guardian court-appointed adult who has custody and care of an incompetent party

Minors' Liability on Ordinary Contracts

A minor may disaffirm (avoid, "pull out of") an agreement with an adult at any time, from the time the agreement is made until the time the minor reaches the age of majority and for a reasonable time after reaching majority. What is reasonable will be determined on a case-by-case basis. Some states, however, have passed laws establishing a maximum period.

> Nathan, five days away from his eighteenth birthday, purchased a Gavern GPS Unit for $189.99 from Office Rex and secured it to the dashboard. Office Rex was aware that Nathan was a minor. Two days after reaching his eighteenth birthday, he returned the GPS, stating that he was dissatisfied with the performance of this particular unit, and he demanded his money back. Office Rex refused, claiming that Nathan was now an adult and therefore could no longer disaffirm the contract. However, since Nathan disaffirmed the agreement within a reasonable time after reaching majority (two days) and returned the GPS, he is entitled to a return of his $189.99.

The minor may disaffirm by informing the adult orally, in writing, through a formal lawsuit, or by any conduct that shows an unwillingness to be bound by the agreement. If the agreement is completely executory (if it has not been completely enforced), the agreement ends and the minor has no further obligation.

If the agreement between the minor and the adult is fully or partially executed, and the minor has transferred consideration—money, property, or other valuables to the competent party—the minor may still disaffirm and recover from the adult any consideration given. If the consideration has been sold or has depreciated in value, the adult must pay the minor the cash equivalent. As a general rule, the minor must also return whatever consideration was received from the adult. In most states (majority view), however, the minor may disaffirm the agreement even though the consideration received by the minor cannot be returned because it has been lost, damaged, or destroyed, even though the minor might have been negligent; has deteriorated from lack of care; or has depreciated in value. If, for example, the minor disaffirms the purchase of a car after the car has been damaged in an accident, she or he need only return the damaged car. The courts reason that if immaturity leads a minor to make an unwise contract, this immaturity will also cause the minor to be careless in caring for the property.

An increasing number of states, feeling that the majority view frequently results in a severe financial loss to the nonminor, no longer permit disaffirmance unless the minor returns the consideration (or its equivalent) or at least pays for any damage to or depreciation in the value of the consideration. In these states, if a minor, for example, buys and pays $500 for a pair of skis but decides six months later to return the skis (which now are worth only $200), the minor can recover only $200, not the $500 originally paid.

A minor may not recover personal property sold to an adult who in turn sells it to a third party. The Uniform Commercial Code provides that a person who obtains a voidable title—for example, the adult who buys property from a minor—has the power to transfer a valid title to a good faith purchaser.

> Nichols, a minor, sold gym equipment consisting of a stair-master, and a punching bag to Cox, an adult, for $800. Cox in return resold the equipment to Bernstein, a good faith purchaser. Cox, with a voidable title, transferred a valid title to Bernstein. Nichols could disaffirm this agreement only if Cox still had possession of the gym equipment.

If two minors enter into an agreement, either or both may disaffirm and recover any consideration. The minor, if no longer in possession of the consideration, has no obligation to return it.

There are some exceptions to the general rule that gives a minor the right to avoid an agreement. Until reaching majority, a minor cannot disaffirm an agreement for the sale of real estate to an adult. The minor may, however, legally retake possession of the property and use it or rent it to other people until he or she reaches the age of majority. In some states, a minor who does not take possession of the real estate until reaching majority may recover rent or any other profit that the adult acquired from the property while it was in the adult's possession.

Laws in many states prevent minors from disaffirming certain agreements. In these states, for example, a minor may not disaffirm a life or accident insurance contract, an education loan, a contract for transportation with a common carrier (e.g., an airline ticket), a contract with a college, a sale of stock, a bank account transaction, a contract involving the minor's business such as one to perform services as an actor or musician, a court-sanctioned agreement, enlistment in the armed forces, and marriage.

Misrepresentation of Age by a Minor

Occasionally, minors deliberately misrepresent themselves as being over the age of majority so as to induce the other party to contract with them. Under the common law, a minor would still have the right to disaffirm the contract and recover any consideration given. Most states, however, have changed this rule because of the law's unfairness to adults. As a result, there is a lack of uniformity among states as to the liability of the minor in such cases. In several states, when the contract is executory, a minor who misrepresents his or her age is prohibited from disaffirming the contract. If the contract is fully performed (executed), some states will not allow minors to disaffirm unless they can return the consideration received. In other states, courts allow a minor who misrepresented his or her age to disaffirm but then hold the minor liable in damages for the tort of fraud. Given this lack of uniformity in this matter, the laws of individual jurisdictions should be checked.

Ratification by a Minor

ratify to approve something

A minor may ratify a contract after reaching the age of majority. To **ratify** means to approve, in this case a previously voidable contract. Upon reaching the age of majority, the minor obtains complete legal capacity to act. Once ratified, agreements become legally binding, and the minor's privilege to disaffirm them ends. The minor must ratify the agreement within a reasonable time after reaching majority. What is "reasonable" will depend on the circumstances in each case.

Ratification by the minor may be oral or written. Ratification may also be implied from the minor's conduct, which clearly indicates an intention to be bound by the agreement. For instance, a minor may ratify an agreement after reaching majority by accepting and cashing a dividend check on stock purchased as a minor. Ratification also takes place if after reaching majority, the minor pays for the property he or she purchased while a minor or sells the property to someone else. If the minor fails to disaffirm an executed agreement within a reasonable period of time after reaching majority, ratification occurs and the right to disaffirm the contract has been lost.

> Three weeks before reaching majority, Angora bought a car and agreed in writing to pay for it in monthly installments. One week after reaching majority, she made the first monthly payment. Two days later, Angora damaged the bumper and the fender in an accident. She then returned the car to the dealer and asked for a refund. By making the first payment and by using the car after reaching the age of majority, Angora ratified the agreement made as a minor and could no longer disaffirm. She will be held to the terms of the installment contract.

Ordinarily, if an agreement is completely executory, the minor's failure to act after reaching majority is considered disaffirmance.

Three days before reaching majority, Bannister agreed to purchase a car from a used-car dealer. Some mechanical work had to be done, and delivery and payment were postponed for one week. When notified that the car was ready for delivery, Bannister did nothing about it. Because she did not act, she disaffirmed the executory agreement, and the car dealer cannot require her to buy the car.

A minor cannot ratify part of an agreement and disaffirm another part. The *entire* agreement must be either ratified or disaffirmed.

The week before Apter reached majority, he purchased a tuxedo and its accessories from Varden's Tuxedo Shop to attend a formal dance. A few days after reaching majority, Apter returned the accessories and demanded the return of the purchase price for these items. Because he purchased the items together, Apter must either keep the tuxedo and accessories or return the whole outfit for a refund of the entire purchase price.

Minors' Liability for Necessaries

Minors are generally responsible for payment for necessaries purchased from adults. If that were not the case, adults would be unwilling to supply minors with those things necessary for their existence. Therefore, this rule is for the protection of the adult.

necessaries things a person needs to live, such as food, clothing, and shelter

Necessaries are those things a person actually needs to maintain the minor's standard of living. Traditionally, necessaries are food, clothing, and shelter. The concept of necessaries, however, has been expanded by court decisions to include medicine and medical services, the services of an attorney in tort and criminal cases, a basic public school education, an education to learn a trade, the tools necessary for that trade, and services reasonably necessary to enable the minor to earn money required to provide the necessities of life (e.g., paying an employment agency for securing a job).

Genevese, age sixteen, decided to leave high school to seek employment to support herself. She contracted with the Manpower Employment Agency for a fee to locate a job for her. Manpower did find a job, but Genevese refused to pay the fee, claiming that she was a minor and therefore had no liability to the agency. In an action against Genevese, Manpower will most likely win because Genevese is liable for necessaries, including payment to an employment agency for securing a job.

Luxury items (items used for pleasure) such as CD players, boats, television sets, jewelry, cameras, and sporting goods are generally not considered necessaries. Automobiles and trucks have caused considerable controversy, but many courts hold that such vehicles are considered necessaries when used by the minor for business purposes (e.g., going to and from work).

station in life person's economic and social status in a community

Courts usually consider changing community standards and hold that the decision about whether an item is a necessary actually depends on the minor's station in life. A minor's **station in life** refers to the minor's social and economic status in the community. It takes into consideration such things as the minor's financial condition and marital status, whether the minor already has a supply of necessaries, whether the parents or guardians are presently furnishing the necessaries, and whether the minor is emancipated. An **emancipated minor** is one who is self-supporting and is no longer subject to parental control and authority. A significant implication for parents is that they lose the right to the child and earnings. Emancipation is not presumed but must be proved in most cases. The burden of proof is on the one asserting emancipation. The usual ways in which a minor becomes emancipated are through marriage, by engaging in full-time employment, by court order, by consent of the parent, by establishing a residence

emancipated minor minor who is no longer under the control and authority of his or her parents

independent from the custodial parent, or upon the death of the parent otherwise providing support. In addition, entering the armed forces is one other circumstance that generally constitutes emancipation. A minor may request a court's permission to be considered an adult to start up a business. The emancipated minor exercises general control over his or her life. Some courts even consider minors who live at home emancipated if they pay living expenses to parents and use the remainder of their earnings as they see fit. Emancipation, however, must be proved, and the burden of proof is on the person claiming emancipation.

> Scott, an emancipated minor living away from home, was injured in a skiing accident. A physician called to the scene of the accident set Scott's broken leg. Later, the physician sent a bill for his services. Scott refused to pay, claiming that as a minor she was not responsible for the bill. Because Scott was a self-supporting minor, she was responsible for paying the physician's services, as necessary.

Applying the station-in-life rule sometimes makes it difficult to determine whether an item is or is not a necessary. When a minor and an adult disagree about whether an item is a necessary, the outcome may have to be decided in a court of law.

A minor must pay only for necessaries actually furnished, not for necessaries to be furnished in the future.

> To learn a trade, Goodman, an emancipated minor, contracted with a correspondence school to take a twenty-week course in computer programming. After five weeks, Goodman lost interest and dropped out of the course. He did, however, pay the school for five weeks of instruction. The correspondence school claimed that Goodman was liable for the remaining fifteen weeks of instruction according to the agreement. Goodman may avoid the original contract made with the school and pay only for the five weeks of instruction he actually received.

The minor's obligation to pay for necessaries is based on a quasi contract (a contract implied in law). The minor is required to pay only the reasonable value of the item or service received, not the price stated in the agreement. Thus, although an adult is protected when selling necessaries to a minor, there may be a disagreement about the price, which may have to be settled in a court of law.

> Kelly, an emancipated minor, obtained a job as a mechanic with a large car agency. Under the terms of the employment agreement, she was to complete a three-month training program with the company at her own expense. At the end of the training period, she would purchase from the company the tools she needed for the job. Kelly discovered that whereas she had paid $900, several of her friends taking the same training program had paid only $600. Kelly is entitled to a return of $300.

Parents' Liability for Minors' Contracts

Unless parents agree to become liable, they generally have no legal liability for contracts made by their minor children acting on their own. For this reason, businesspeople often require parents to sign any contract made with a minor. The parents then become personally liable even if the minor backs out of the contract. Parents do, however, have the legal duty to support their minor children until they reach the age of majority or if they are emancipated prior to age eighteen. So whether they have signed a contract or not, parents who neglect a minor child are liable for the reasonable value of any necessaries furnished to him or her. Consequently, if a minor child needs clothing that isn't being provided by the parents, the child may purchase the needed items, and the parents can be held liable for payment. This obligation to support generally continues until minors are emancipated. Normally there is no obligation on the part of parents to pay for a college education, but when parents separate, provisions may be included in a seperation agreement by which parents voluntarily undertake this obligation.

Minors' Liability for Torts

Minors can disaffirm most contracts they make, but they are generally liable for their torts. (Refer to Chapter 4 for a discussion of torts.) A minor's age is important in determining the minor's tort liability. In the case of deliberate torts, a minor is generally liable regardless of age. For torts of negligence, the age varies from state to state. In many states, minors under the age of fourteen are considered incapable of committing an act of negligence. In those states, minors over the age of fourteen who commit negligent acts are treated as adults.

> While driving through town, Marks, age seventeen and a minor, threw an empty soft drink can from the car window. Rossini was crossing the street and the can hit her in the eye, causing injury. Although Marks is a minor, she is liable for her tort of negligence.

Parents are not usually responsible for the torts of their children. They may, however, be held responsible if they tell a child to commit a tort or if they fail to take action to prevent a tort from being committed—for example, if they fail to take action to stop a child from repeating acts that the child has been warned about in the past. Parents are also liable if they place a dangerous instrument in the hands of a child, as would be the case if they gave their child a pellet gun and the child injured someone. The parents are held liable because, in the case of a lawsuit, the victim has a better chance of recovering damages from the parents than from the child.

> Neighbors warned the Bakers that their son Todd had thrown rocks at other children on several occasions. The Bakers could be held liable for injuries caused by Todd to other children.

In many states, parents are automatically liable for the intentional damage caused by children under a certain age. These state laws were passed with the idea that parents who knew they were liable for their children's intentional acts would exercise more control over their children's behavior. State statutes vary in strictness and in the maximum parental liability.

Persons Under the Influence of Alcohol or Other Drugs

Another category of incompetency applies to persons who are so intoxicated by alcohol or other drugs that they do not realize what they are doing when they enter into agreements. Slight intoxication is not enough to destroy a person's ability to make contracts. Nevertheless, it is not necessary that a person be so intoxicated that she or he is completely helpless. The person must be so affected that she or he does not understand the seriousness or the consequences of the agreement. Obviously, then, if the person understood the legal consequences, the agreement is enforceable despite the person's intoxication.

Courts have little sympathy for individuals who want to disaffirm their contracts because of intoxication on the theory that intoxication is a voluntary act. Therefore, avoidance due to intoxication is rather uncommon. As a result, a person who enters into a contract while intoxicated may avoid it on becoming sober only if the other party purposely caused the person to become drunk or had reason to know that the person was drunk and unable to understand the consequences of the transaction.

If the intoxicated person has the legal right to disaffirm, she or he must do so within a reasonable time after becoming sober. Otherwise, the person loses that right to disaffirm, and the agreement is considered ratified. Most courts will not permit disaffirmance unless the intoxicated person returns any consideration received from the other party.

> While intoxicated, Babitz sold a valuable coin collection worth several hundred dollars to Lyness for $50. Lyness knew that Babitz was intoxicated and unable to understand the consequences of the deal. When Babitz became sober and discovered her mistake, she immediately offered to return the $5 to Lyness in exchange for the coin collection. Lyness refused, claiming that an agreement had been formed.

In this example, a court would probably determine that because Lyness knew that Babitz was intoxicated and unable to understand what she was doing, Babitz may disaffirm the agreement.

Like minors, intoxicated persons are liable in quasi contract for the reasonable value of necessaries actually furnished to them.

PERSONS WITH MENTAL ILLNESS

Persons with mental illness are considered incompetent because, unlike normal persons, they are unable to comprehend either that they are making a contract or the effect of the contract on them. Their ability to comprehend their intended purpose when dealing with others has been lost, and their mind becomes clouded or confused. A distinction must be made, however, between a person with mental illness who has been judged incompetent by a court and one who has not been so judged.

Court Declared Incompetence

If a person with mental illness has been determined incompetent by a court, the person is considered legally insane. Such a determination is usually made only after legal hearings and examinations by psychologists or psychiatrists. After the formal declaration of insanity, any agreement made by the person declared insane is void even though the other party to the contract was unaware of the court order. The court will usually appoint a guardian to take care of the business affairs of the person declared insane and, if necessary, to enter into agreements on her or his behalf. The appointment of a guardian serves as public notice that the person declared insane (called a *ward*) cannot make contracts. If the person declared insane does make a contract, the guardian may disaffirm it. The guardian must first return any consideration that the ward received, unless it has been damaged or destroyed or has deteriorated. A party dealing with an individual under guardianship may recover the fair value of any necessaries provided to the person declared insane. The money for these necessaries usually comes from the savings or other property of the person declared insane. When guardianship ends, the person declared insane regains the capacity to make a contract.

Mental Incompetence Not Adjudged by a Court

The contracts of persons with mental illness not judged incompetent by a court are voidable. These persons may be suffering from an illness, such as serious depression, split personality, loss of a sense of reality brought on by a traumatic experience (e.g., a war experience), or from brain damage. During these periods, they may be incompetent to enter into any contract. There may be other times, however, when they can enter into contracts just as any other person could. The burden of proof is on the person claiming the incompetency. A person with mental illness who can prove mental illness at the time of the contract may, during a period of normalcy, disaffirm or ratify the contract. Once the contract is ratified, it can no longer be disaffirmed. Innocent parties who are unaware of the other person's mental illness and who could not reasonably be expected to know about it are protected when they deal with these individuals. To disaffirm a contract under these circumstances, the person with mental illness must be able to return the consideration (or its equivalent in money) received under the contract to the innocent party.

> Garrison suffered brain damage in an automobile accident and had periods of confusion. During one of his confused periods, he sold a set of used golf clubs to Atkinson for $40. Atkinson was unaware of Garrison's mental illness. Garrison then wished to get his clubs back but was unable to return the $40 because he had spent the money foolishly. Because Garrison could not return the money and Atkinson was unaware of Garrison's condition, the courts generally would not permit Garrison to disaffirm the contract.

Like minors, this class of persons with mental illness is liable in quasi contract for the fair value of necessaries actually furnished to them.

In cases involving intoxication and mental illness (except those cases involving people judged incompetent by a court), incapacity of the individual is not the only basis used by the courts to make a decision. The fairness of the agreement to the parties involved is very important. Thus, if the contract seems fair and reasonable, and the other party with whom the incompetent is dealing has no reason to suspect that anything is wrong, the court most likely will declare that the party is competent and not allow a disaffirmance.

Summary

Some persons, such as minors, persons under the influence of alcohol and other drugs, and mentally ill persons not declared insane, have only a limited capacity to contract. Incompetent persons with a limited capacity to contract may back out of their contracts. This legal right to back out is called disaffirmance. Others are so completely incompetent that they have no legal capacity at all to contract. Persons with mental illness declared insane by a court are in this category. Competent parties generally deal with incompetent parties, especially minors, at their own risk.

Minors may usually disaffirm (avoid) ordinary contracts they make any time before reaching majority and for a reasonable time thereafter. Adults who make contracts with minors, however, do not have this right to disaffirm and are bound by agreements they make. A minor cannot disaffirm an agreement for the sale of real estate (real property) to an adult until the minor reaches his or her majority. Moreover, statutes in many states prevent minors at varying ages from disaffirming certain agreements such as those relating to life

insurance, a loan of money, a sale of stock, and a contract involving the minor's business. When a minor lies to an adult about his or her age, the various state courts handle the matter differently, using fairness to the adult as a guide. In several states, when the contract is executory, a minor who misrepresents his or her age is prohibited from disaffirming the contract. If the contract is executed, the minor in some states may disaffirm but must return the consideration received. Other states allow the minor to disaffirm but then hold the minor liable for fraud. Minors may ratify (approve) agreements they make with adults only after reaching the age of majority. Once ratified, these agreements become legally binding, and the privilege to disaffirm ends. Minors, however, cannot ratify only a part of an agreement and disaffirm another part. The entire agreement must be either ratified or disaffirmed. Minors have a quasi-contractual liability for the reasonable value of necessaries (items a person needs to live) actually received. A minor's station in life determines whether an item is a necessary. Parents generally have no legal liability for contracts made by their minor children unless they agree to become liable. Parents do, however, have the legal duty to support their minor children until the minors are emancipated.

Some agreements made by persons under the influence of alcohol or other drugs are voidable. Upon becoming sober, these persons may disaffirm an agreement made while intoxicated only if the other party purposely caused the person to become drunk or knew that the person was drunk and unable to understand the consequences of the transaction. An intoxicated person who has the right to disaffirm must do so within a reasonable time after becoming sober or lose that right. He or she is, however, liable for the reasonable value of necessaries actually furnished to him or her.

Agreements made by persons with mental illness who have been declared legally insane by a court are void. Agreements made by persons with mental illness not declared insane by a court are voidable if these persons can prove their disability. When they understand what they did, they may disaffirm or ratify the contract, provided they return the consideration received under the contract to the innocent party. All persons with mental illness (whether legally declared insane or not) are liable for the reasonable value of necessaries furnished to them.

Contractual capacity is the legal and mental ability of a person to understand that he or she is entering into an agreement that is enforceable at law.

Important Legal Terms

capacity to contract
disaffirmance
emancipated minor

guardian
necessaries

ratify
station in life

Questions and Problems for Discussion

Unless otherwise stated, assume that the age of majority is eighteen in all problems in this section.

1. Necessities under the common law were limited to those items absolutely necessary for survival, namely, food, clothing, and shelter. Over time, this definition has expanded due to the evolutionary nature of law. What significant changes have been made?

2. How does the right of a minor to rescind a contract differ from the right of an intoxicated person to rescind?

3. Reno entered into a contract with his seventeen-year-old son by which the son agreed to support the father in consideration of the father's transfer of certain property to the son immediately. The son supported the father under the agreement for ten years and then quit. The father then sued for breach of contract. The son challenged the father's lawsuit on the ground that he was a minor when the contract was made. Is the son correct?

4. Mance, one week before his eighteenth birthday, purchased a DVD player from the Computer Outlet store and paid $150 cash for the item. A

week after his birthday, he purchased a hand-held police scanner for $95 from Radio Shack and also paid cash. A week after he purchased the police scanner, Mance wished to disaffirm both contracts and recover $150 from the Computer Outlet store and $95 from Radio Shack. Will Mance be allowed to disaffirm one, both, or neither of these contracts assuming that both purchases were within the guidelines of selling to minors?

5. Kimble, a seventeen-year-old minor, sold his new iPod to Taymes, an adult, for $150 because he needed money. Taymes, in turn sold the iPod to Dressler, also an adult, for $175. A month after the sale of the iPod to Taymes, Kimble demanded to re-buy it from Taymes. Having learned of the sale to Dressler, Kimble then demanded the return of the iPod from him (Dressler), offering to pay $175. Is Dressler obligated to sell the iPod back to Kimble?

6. Schaber, a minor, paid $950 for a used motorcycle. Two months later, while driving around town, she ran into a fire hydrant and wrecked the motorcycle. Schaber, still a minor, returned the

wrecked motorcycle to the dealer and demanded the return of her $950. Is she entitled to recover the entire $950?

7. Week, a band leader, hired Taylor on a one-year contract to work as a soloist, not knowing that she was only seventeen years old. Taylor had said nothing about her age. When Week discovered that Taylor was only seventeen, he discharged her. Did Week have a legal right to break the contract?

8. Moses, a self-supporting minor, purchased a van to carry on his business activities and to commute from his home to the college he attended part time. Before reaching majority, he tried to disaffirm the purchase of the van, but the dealer refused to accept return of the van or to refund the purchase price. Can Moses require the dealer to take back the van and return the purchase price?

9. Connor, age seventeen, moved away from home. She rented a room in a nearby town and orally agreed to pay the landlady $160 a month for six months. Connor paid rent for three months and then moved out without paying the remaining three months' rent. The landlady claims that Connor is liable on her agreement to pay rent for the remaining three months even though she moved out. Is the landlady correct?

10. Attilio, a wealthy seventeen year old who had inherited money from her grandparents, was planning to become a professional violinist. She agreed with a local music establishment to purchase a Lagetto violin worth $3,000, advancing the store a $1,000 deposit toward the purchase price. Attilio then wished to rescind the contract with the music store. The music store contended that this expensive violin was a necessity because of her career plans to become a professional violinist. Attilio contended that since she already owned one other violin, a Storiani worth $3,000, which technically was suitable for her needs, this second violin was not a necessity. Her only reason for the second purchase was the fact that it was once owned by a nationally acclaimed violinist. Is she correct?

Cases for Review

1. Jesset, who had been committed to a mental institution, was later released as having shown signs of increased mental stability. When her husband died several years later, Jesset's son had her re-committed because he felt that the shock of her husband's death caused a relapse into mental instability. Prior to her re-admittance, she had signed a contract with the undertaker for her husband's funeral expenses but failed to pay. The undertaker sued, but Jesset, through her son, claimed that she was not liable because of her mental incompetency. Court records show that Jesset was never legally declared insane. Further, while dealing with the undertaker, there was no reason for him (the undertaker) to believe that Jesset was incompetent in any way, and the son made no mention of her illness. Is Jesset legally bound to pay the funeral expenses? (*Melbourne* v. *Jesset*, 110 Ohio App 502, 163 NE 2d 773)

2. Williamson, an alcoholic who was threatened with foreclosure on her house, entered into a contract to sell it for $17,000. Smith, an attorney who had read about the foreclosure in the newspaper and who knew about Williamson's drinking problem, contacted Williamson and assured her that he could resolve her problem. Smith did have the sale of the house overturned. The court found that Williamson was intoxicated at the time of the sale and was paid only $1,700, thinking she had received $17,000. To ensure payment of the legal fees, Williamson again signed a mortgage contract, giving Smith temporary ownership of her house. Because Williamson refused to pay the mortgage, Smith had to bring a foreclosure action (sell the property to get his money) on the mortgage. Williamson objected to the foreclosure proceedings on the grounds that she was severely intoxicated (and that she had a history of alcoholism) and that she did not understand what she was signing. She claimed that this lack of understanding made the mortgage she gave to Smith void. Was Williamson's intoxication sufficient to void the mortgage? (*Smith* v. *Williamson*, 429 So.2d 598)

3. Marshall, age seventeen, was ejected from his parents' home shortly after his graduation from high school. He then rented an apartment with

Fletcher, a girlfriend. They signed a lease together, and Marshall paid part of the security deposit and the rent. One month after they moved into the apartment, Marshall turned eighteen (age of majority) and continued to pay the rent for about one and one-half months. Then, because he and Fletcher were not getting along, he moved out and discontinued paying his share of the rent. Fletcher continued to make rental payments but sued Marshall for his share because his name was also on the lease. Marshall claimed that because he signed the lease while a minor he was not responsible for any rental payments after he moved out. Is he correct? (*Fletcher* v. *Marshall*, 632 N.E.2d 1105)

4. Power, age seventeen, purchased an automobile insurance policy from Allstate Insurance Company but rejected the underinsured motorist clause. Shortly after the policy was issued, Power, now an adult, was injured in an automobile accident. He then sought to reinstate the underinsured clause that he had initially rejected as a minor and claim money for his injuries under this clause in the contract. Allstate refused to permit Power to collect under this clause. Was Allstate correct? (*Power* v. *Allstate Insurance Co.*, 440 S.E.2d 406)

5. Husband, who was suffering from schizophrenia and manic depression, had been in and out of a mental hospital, but at no time had he been declared insane by a court. In fact, he continued to work at his job as a design engineer during the day, returning to the hospital at night. His wife initiated a separation agreement because of the husband's mental condition, although her husband did not really want a separation. At a time when he was depressed and did not fully understand the impact of the agreement, he did sign it. The agreement was signed by both parties in the presence of the wife's attorney, although the husband did not receive any legal advice from an attorney and did not really know the exact contents of the agreement. Later, when the husband realized what he had done, he requested that the separation agreement be canceled. The wife refused. Is the husband entitled to have this agreement canceled? (*G.A.S.* v. *S.I.S.*, 407 A.2d 253, Del. Fam. Ct.)

6. Goldberg, a minor, hired an attorney to sue Perlmuter for personal injuries. When the case was settled, the attorney asked for his fee. Goldberg, however, asked the court to hold that the contract with the lawyer was void because Goldberg was a minor when the contract was made. Is this request valid? (*Goldberg* v. *Perlmutter*, 308 Ill. App. 84)

7. Bethea, a minor who needed a car for her work, purchased one and financed it through Bancredit. Bethea could not make the payments, and Bancredit sued for the balance due on the car. Bethea claimed she was not liable because she was a minor when she signed the contract. Is Bethea liable for the balance due? (*Bancredit, Inc.* v. *Bethea*, 65 N.J. Super. Ct. 538, 168 A.2d 250)

8. Watters was nineteen when he entered into a contract to buy a car. He stated that he was twenty-one (the age of majority in his state) and that he was in business. A short time later, the car was destroyed in an accident. Watters then sued the seller to recover his payments on the grounds that he was a minor. Will he succeed? (*Watters* v. *Arrington*, 39 Ga. App. 275)

9. Dwaine Ebsen, a minor, lived with his mother, Violet, who was a widow. For personal and life-style reasons, they could not get along, so Dwaine decided to move out. From the time he moved, he did not receive any monetary support from his mother. While living away from home, he was shot and taken to a hospital. Dwaine remained in the hospital for two weeks and "ran up" a considerable hospital bill, which was sent to his mother for payment. When Violet refused to pay, the bill was turned over to a collection agency for payment. Is Violet liable for payment? (*Accent Service Company* v. *Ebsen*, 306 N.W.2d 575)

Legality

CHAPTER PREVIEW

Chapter Highlights

This chapter examines the last requirement of a valid contract: legality. Initially, the chapter discusses the nature and general effect of illegal agreements, the circumstances under which agreements are deemed illegal, and the exceptions to the rule that courts will not enforce illegal agreements. The remainder of the chapter lists and describes the agreements that are generally recognized as being illegal in most states. The final section points out the effect of an agreement that is partially legal and partially illegal.

THE NATURE AND GENERAL EFFECT OF ILLEGAL AGREEMENTS

The fourth and last requirement of a valid contract is that it must be made for a legal purpose. As discussed in Chapters 7 through 9, to rise to the level of a contract, an agreement must contain an offer and an acceptance, both parties must receive consideration, and both parties must be competent. Even if these requirements are fulfilled, however, the agreement will still not be recognized as a contract in a court of law if the purpose of the agreement is illegal. The general rule is that illegal contracts are void (never existed) and thus unenforceable. The courts in this case leave the parties to such agreements where they are in the bargaining process.

Some agreements, such as agreements to commit crimes, are entirely illegal; others contain only clauses that are illegal. In the event of a lawsuit, a court will simply refuse to hear a case involving an illegal agreement if both parties know the agreement is illegal; in such a case, both parties are **in pari delicto** (equally at fault). Neither party can successfully sue the other to seek enforcement of the agreement, to recover for breach of contract, to regain any consideration given, or for unjust enrichment. The court will sometimes hear a case involving an agreement that contains one or more illegal clauses

in pari delicto persons equally at fault or equally guilty

if the agreement is legal in every other respect. If the court hears the case, it will simply not enforce the illegal clauses.

An agreement (or a clause in an agreement) is illegal if its purpose, or the manner in which it is carried out, is forbidden by state statute or opposed to a state's public policy. Courts in each state have their own interpretation of the term *public policy*, what is right and wrong. Generally, however, agreements opposed to public policy contain terms that are immoral or unethical or that interfere with the health, safety, or general welfare of the public. Courts often refuse to enforce such agreements even though they have not been expressly declared illegal.

Exceptions to Effect of Illegality

Despite the general rule that an illegal contract is void and unenforceable and that the court leaves the parties where they were in the bargaining process, there are exceptions to the rule that courts will not enforce illegal agreements. These exceptions are intended to prevent the injustice that can result from a rigid application of the general rule. One exception occurs when the two parties are not equally at fault (not in pari delicto). A court may rule in favor of the more innocent party if recovery serves the public interest in some way. For example, when one individual unknowingly deals with a person who is not licensed as required by state law, a court will permit the innocent party to recover any money paid to the unlicensed person for services performed. The focus here is on the conduct of the less guilty party rather than on the illegality of the subject matter of the contract, which is considered incidental to the bargain. Another exception is ignorance of the facts as to the illegality of an agreement. Although the courts will not enforce such an agreement, they will allow a person who has fully performed his or her part of the agreement unaware of the illegality to recover any fees due. If, for example, you were hired by a manufacturer to transport illegal merchandise from California to New York, you could still collect your fee as long as you were not aware that you were transporting illegal merchandise. Still another exception relates to gambling. Statutes in some states permit a person who suffers gambling losses over a certain amount at such forms of gambling as cards and dice to recover these losses from the winner. These statutes apply only to gambling that is held at places other than legalized gambling casinos. Under such a statute, for example, a person may recover losses over a certain amount that occurred at a "friendly" poker game at a house party. The purpose of these statutes is not to protect those who lose money. Their purpose is to discourage gambling by putting people on notice that they may have to return their winnings to the loser.

Types of Illegal Contracts

There are two reasons a contract may be illegal. The contract is in violation of state statutes or the contract is opposed to public policy. The illegal agreements discussed in this chapter are generally recognized as illegal in most states. Keep in mind that while illegal contracts have civil penalties, one or both parties may also be subject to criminal penalties if the act to be performed according to the agreement is a crime.

AGREEMENTS FORBIDDEN BY STATE STATUTES

First we discuss agreements that violate state statutes. State legislatures have passed laws declaring certain types of agreements illegal and void because they cannot be performed without violating the state's civil and criminal statutes, licensing statutes, gambling statutes, usury statutes, or Sunday statutes. Keep in mind that a contract or a clause in a contract may be illegal even though there is no specific state statute prohibiting what is to be performed under the terms of the contract.

Agreements That Violate Civil and Criminal Statutes

Agreements are illegal if they require one party to commit a tort or a crime. Examples of common torts are assault and battery, slander, libel, fraud, and the infliction of emotional distress on another. Arson, murder, burglary, larceny, robbery, selling illegal drugs, and buying stolen property are examples of acts that are considered crimes. Agreements to commit any one of these torts or crimes could not be enforced by either party. They would be absolutely void. To allow people to go to court to obtain enforcement of these types of agreements, which are so obviously contrary to law, would be ridiculous.

> Johnson entered into an agreement to sell illegal drugs to Morgan for $1,500. The court most likely would rule this agreement to be void and unenforceable.

In this example, even if Morgan paid the $1,500 in advance, a lawsuit to get the money back will most likely not be successful because the transaction was illegal (selling illegal drugs) in the first place.

Agreements to protect one party from the consequences of his or her tort or crime are also illegal.

> The mayor induced one of her campaign workers to break into the home of an opponent in the upcoming election and to remove papers that would be helpful in the mayor's reelection campaign. The mayor agreed to pay the worker a large sum of money and to protect the campaign worker from criminal charges if caught. The agreement was illegal. The mayor and the campaign worker were both criminally liable for their illegal acts.

Agreements That Violate Licensing Statutes

licensing statutes laws requiring persons to be licensed to practice their occupation

All states have **licensing statutes**, laws that require some individuals to have a license or permit to practice their occupations. These laws are designed to protect people from dealing with unqualified individuals. In most states, doctors, dentists, nurses, lawyers, pharmacists, public accountants, surveyors, architects, real estate brokers, insurance agents, funeral directors, barbers, veterinarians, beauticians, electricians, plumbers, and contractors must be licensed. When state statutes require a person to have a license to perform services for the general public, an agreement made with an unlicensed person is illegal.

Because the agreement is illegal, an unlicensed person cannot legally collect for the services performed. In some states, a person who performs services without the required license is guilty of a crime punishable by a fine, imprisonment, or both.

> Weinstein completed graduate school and graduated with a degree in veterinary medicine. He had not, however, passed the state boards qualifying him for a license to treat animals. When a family, aware that Weinstein had graduated as a vet but unaware that he had not passed the state boards, asked him to treat their family dog for a serious hip problem, he did so and then sent them a bill. Later, the family discovered that he was not yet licensed and refused to pay. Because Weinstein was practicing veterinary medicine illegally (without a license), he could not collect the fee for his services. Weinstein may also be criminally liable for practicing medicine without a license.

If a person *unknowingly* deals with an unlicensed individual, the courts will allow that person to recover any money paid.

Some licensing statutes are merely intended to obtain revenue for the state or local government. Any person paying the fee can obtain a license without showing competence in a particular trade or profession. Because the purpose of such revenue-raising licensing statutes is not the protection of the public, agreements made with unlicensed persons are legally binding. The unlicensed person, however, is still subject to a criminal penalty for violating the licensing statute. In assessing the penalty, courts will take into consideration such factors as harm resulting from failure to obtain the license and the extent of knowledge of the persons involved.

> For $250, Arden hired Gammons, an auctioneer, to sell Arden's household goods at a public auction. The state's only requirement for an auctioneer's license, which Gammons did not obtain, was the payment of a $100 fee. After the auction, Arden learned that Gammons was not licensed and, as a result, refused to pay Gammons the $250. Because the statute was for revenue purposes only, Arden must pay Gammons the $250. Gammons, however, is guilty of violating the licensing law and may face action from the state.

Agreements That Violate Gambling Statutes

Gaming in the United States has undergone a great boom, from Native American casinos and other regulated commercial casinos, to gaming online (Internet gaming). Each state is free to regulate or prohibit it. If you count state-run lotteries, almost every state allows some form of gaming. At this point we should distinguish between gaming and gambling. Both refer to agreements in which one party wins and another party loses purely by chance even though skill (in most cases) is involved. **Gaming**, however is an activity that has been legalized, and consequently, those who participate are not subject to criminal prosecution, even if they make a profit while engaged in the activity. **Gambling**, on the other hand, is an illegal activity simply because the law does not sanction it. For example, going to a casino and winning money is legal and would be considered gaming; however, organizing a poker game at your home and arranging to make a profit for yourself on each hand would be considered gambling. A simple poker game in which all players are on an equal footing (no one earns anything from the game other than as a mere player) would be gaming as long as social games are allowed in the state where the game takes place. It would be referred to as social gambling. Some states do not allow social gambling and may even consider participation in such an activity a misdemeanor. States that do allow social gambling may place a limit on what a player may win or lose. Bingo is considered gaming, but it could become gambling if a bingo party is arranged without getting a license in states where a license is required.

Legal gaming activities in many states include state lotteries; casino betting; parimutuel betting on horses at race tracks; bingo games; Monte Carlo nights; and raffles conducted by charitable, religious, and educational organizations; slot machines; keno; video blackjack machines; and video poker games. The most popular forms of illegal games are "numbers," which is actually a lottery, and betting with bookies, typically sports betting (e.g., a football pool or a bet on a prize fight). There are also homespun illegal games such as playing cards for money in your own home or at club meetings. Games such as those used by stores for promotional purposes are legal as long as they do not require participants to buy some article or ticket. States look at gaming in economic terms. In return for legalizing certain forms of gaming, a state collects a percentage of the gaming profits.

gaming legal form of playing for stakes, such as in a lottery

gambling illegal agreement in which one party wins and another loses purely by chance

Internet (online) gambling that originates primarily from offshore sites, while illegal in the United States, has been popular. All a person has to do to commence gambling is to open an account, deposit funds in this account, and start betting. These offshore sites, however, compete with state lotteries (which are legal) for business. Congress passed the Unlawful Internet Gambling Act of 2006. This act made it more difficult to place bets online by restricting (actually outlawing) certain financial transactions, such as using credit cards and checks in placing bets, with Internet gambling sites worldwide. As a result, many offshore gambling and gaming providers reacted by shutting down their services for U.S. customers.

Those who gamble illegally may be classified as casual gamblers or professional gamblers. **Casual gamblers** participate in a gaming event socially and for pleasure. **Professional gamblers** engage in gambling activities as a business or profession, hoping to make a profit. Their involvement with gaming is generally considered a crime. Casual gamblers are not ordinarily subject to a criminal penalty (police seldom bother them), but they may not generally enforce their gambling agreements in court; as gamblers, they are performing an illegal act.

casual gambler one who gambles for pleasure

professional gambler one who gambles as a profession or business

> Martin and Spicer lived in a state in which casual gaming was illegal but not criminally wrong. They made a $100 bet on a heavyweight boxing match. When Martin won the bet, Spicer refused to pay the $100. Because the bet was illegal, Martin could not collect from Spicer even if Martin decided to sue in small claims court. Because they were casual gamblers, neither party was criminally liable.

Agreements That Violate Usury Statutes

interest fee paid by borrower to lender for the use of money; also, legal right to use of or claim on real property

usury charging a higher rate of interest than allowed by law

Many states have laws that limit the interest a lender can charge. **Interest** is the compensation or fee that a borrower pays to a lender for the use of money. If the interest rate charged by the lender exceeds the legal rate allowed by state law, the lender has committed **usury**. Interest rates are simple, not compound, interest unless otherwise stated. Usurious agreements are illegal. You might also say the usury is a complicated area of law and sometimes confusing because many types of loans are exempt from the usury laws of a particular state and each state handles the legal ramifications of the law differently. To determine what interest rates are considered usurious and the penalties imposed, you would need to visit each state's usury law statute books or contact the state agency that regulates banking and commerce.

> Madison wished to buy a used car to drive to a local college where she was enrolled and to her part-time job. She did not have good credit so banks in the community where she lived turned her down for a car loan. She saw an ad in the local paper in which an individual was offering to sell a used older-model car for $5,000. When Madison contacted this individual, this individual was willing to sell her the car but would charge interest at the rate of 20 percent per year until the car loan was paid off. If you lived in a state where 14 percent was the maximum allowed by statute, Madison's agreement with the lender would generally be considered illegal.

Usury laws were passed to protect certain borrowers from paying excessively high interest rates. Since the loan to Madison would be considered usurious and the lender was an individual and not a bank or a finance company, she could file a complaint in the small claims court in her town, village, or city and present legal proof that the rate of interest for the loan was above that allowed by the statute in her state. She would most likely win her case. The civil penalty for usury varies among states. In many states, the lender will be denied the right to collect any interest. In some states, the lender forfeits the excess interest received over the rate allowed. In a few states, the court is given permission by statute to set the amount of damages, which could end up being double the usurious rate.

A person familiar with the usury law of his or her state might say, "I am paying much more than that (referring to the usury law of her state) on my car loan at my bank." That is correct! Banks, licensed pawnbrokers, credit unions, and finance companies have separate rules thanks to a series of Supreme Court decisions which changed things to facilitate business deals. If the usury rate in a particular state is 24 percent, a bank or small loan company in that state may legally be charging 30 percent or more. Or, a so-called payday loan or tax refund loan may have a legal rate over 300 percent. National banks, as the result of the Supreme Court ruling in *Marquette National Bank* v. *First of Omaha Corp.*, are able to charge their customers (no matter where the customers are located) the rate of the state where the bank has its main offices. In this Supreme Court case, even though the customers in Marquette lived in Minnesota, the fact that the bank had its main offices in Nebraska allowed it to charge its Minnesota customers the higher Nebraska interest rate. Following the passage of this law, a deluge of national banks moved their main offices to states that either repealed their usury statutes or had no interest rate cap. The result is that outer space has become the limit for consumer-loan rates. It has been stated that some of the rates being charged by lending institutions may embarrass loan sharks.

Usury statutes apply only to loans of money, not to sales of merchandise on credit, even if the seller charges a higher interest rate than is permitted. Although credit sales are not governed by state usury laws, they are regulated by other state statutes and by the federal Truth in Lending Law. Usury laws and the Truth in Lending Law will be further discussed in Chapter 36.

Agreements That Violate Sunday Statutes

Sunday laws laws governing types of transactions that can be performed on Sunday

Sunday laws, or blue laws as they are sometimes called, govern the types of transactions that can be performed on Sundays. People's attitudes have changed since Sunday laws were first passed during the colonial period. As a result, laws restricting business and other activities on Sundays have been changed by modifying state statutes, by passing local ordinances, or by court decisions. Most states have either repealed or modified their Sunday statutes. Sunday laws that remain are often not enforced with the exception of those related to the sale of alcoholic beverages. In the few remaining states that have such statutes, the types of contracts that are illegal vary from state to state. The most common statute declares an agreement illegal and void if it is made on a Sunday or is to be performed on a Sunday. A court will not aid either party if there is a violation of a Sunday law.

Some courts hold that parties to an agreement made on a Sunday may ratify it on a regular business day. Complete performance by both parties or partial performance by one party also acts as a ratification of the agreement. After ratification, the courts consider the agreement remade on the weekday and enforce it as such.

In most states, repayment of money due on a Sunday or legal holiday can be postponed until the first business day after the Sunday or holiday.

Murphy, who borrowed $250 from McGrath, agreed to repay the loan in sixty days. The due date of the loan fell on a Sunday. Murphy would not be obligated to repay the loan until Monday, the next business day.

Sunday laws do not apply to agreements made to protect life, health, or property or made on behalf of religious or charitable organizations. In some states, Sunday laws do not apply to persons who observe the Sabbath on some other day.

AGREEMENTS OPPOSED TO PUBLIC POLICY

An agreement, or a clause in an agreement opposed to public policy may be illegal even though there is no specific state statute prohibiting its performance under the terms of the agreement. Such agreements are considered illegal and void in most states, however, because they are opposed to public policy and would negatively impact society. While public policy may be viewed as a "catchall," it most often applies to contracts that are injurious to peace, health, good order, or established morals of society (a public sense of what is right and wrong). Agreements in this category include those that disclaim liability for negligence, interfere with the administration of justice, interfere with the performance of a public duty, harm marriage, unreasonably restrain competition and trade, create a monopoly or limit competition, or are unconscionable.

Agreements That Disclaim Liability for Negligence

exculpatory clause
contract clause excusing a party from liability for negligence

Businesspeople and others often place **exculpatory clauses** in agreements, excusing themselves in advance (or at least limiting their liability) from any payment for injury or damages caused by their acts. An exculpatory clause is viewed with disfavor by the courts because it may enable a person to escape paying damages for wrongful conduct. Courts tend to judge the legality of such clauses on a case-by-case basis. An exculpatory clause is generally held to be contrary to public policy and therefore void and unenforceable against an injured party. Although recognizing the importance of freedom of contract, the courts also wish to protect members of the general public who are not always alert to the consequences of signing a contract containing a clause that relieves businesspeople from liability. Such clauses are especially likely to be held unenforceable if one party is required to sign the agreement on a take-it-or-leave-it basis because the other party is in a superior bargaining position. A contract written exclusively by one party considered to be in a superior bargaining position and containing unfavorable clauses is called a **contract of adhesion.** Examples of those in superior bargaining position include apartment owners, banks, leasing companies, and car dealers.

contract of adhesion
contract containing clauses with unfavorable terms supporting a party seen as holding a superior bargaining position

> The Randy White automobile dealership agrees to repair the transmission of a car brought into the dealership by Seager, one of its regular customers. The dealership, however, placed a clause on the work order (contract) in fine print that the dealer "will not be liable for any mistakes it may make during the repairs." This clause is unenforceable especially because the dealership is in a superior bargaining position. However, it will be liable if, because of negligence on the part of the mechanic doing the repairs, the transmission is not properly repaired.

> Karen leased an apartment from Todd in a rundown neighborhood. Shortly after signing the lease and moving in, Karen fell down a flight of stairs in an unlit stairwell when an unrepaired step collapsed. She was severely injured. When Karen brought a suit for injuries suffered, Todd's lawyer introduced into evidence a clause in fine print in Karen's lease that stated: "The tenant agrees to hold the owner of the premises harmless from any claims for injuries no matter how caused." Despite this clause, Todd is still liable because the exculpatory clause in the lease is unenforceable: It is a violation of public policy.

Not all exculpatory clauses are against public policy. This is especially true when the party seeking enforcement is not considered to be in a superior bargaining position because of the nature of the service it provides. Health clubs and amusement parks are good examples of businesses in this category. They often use exculpatory clauses to limit their liability for injuries to those who accept their services. Even so, the clauses inserted in any agreement cannot be too broad.

> When Benz became a member of the Supercare Health Spa, he was required to complete and sign an application that included a release, on which was written in bold print, "relieving the spa owners and operators from all risks of injury that a member suffers while participating in club activities." One evening, as Benz was leaving the shower at the spa, he slipped on the wet tile floor, fell, and was injured. It was determined that the injury resulted from the spa's negligence in maintaining the shower room. The spa claimed that regardless of this fact, the release form that Benz signed relieved the owners from liability. The spa would probably lose this case.

In this example, a court would probably rule that the exculpatory clause contained in the application was against public policy and void. The clause as written was too broad: It relieved the club of liability *for all injuries* sustained by a member while participating in club activities (i.e., regardless of how the injury occurred). If the spa wished to include in its application a clause that could be upheld in court (and that would therefore be binding on those who signed), the clause should have been worded so that the spa was relieved of liability *for negligence only* (negligence of spa employees or negligence in maintaining spa equipment). Wording that narrowed the grounds for relieving the spa of liability would have increased the chances of the court's ruling in favor of the spa if a lawsuit arose.

Exculpatory clauses that relieve a party from liability for injury or damage beyond its control will usually be upheld in court.

In most cases, courts will not enforce exculpatory clauses that attempt to relieve a contracting party from his or her own criminal conduct, from intentional injury or damages, or from gross negligence. To uphold such clauses would place the rights and safety of the party or parties signing such agreements in jeopardy.

In some states, exculpatory clauses in certain types of contracts, such as leases, have been declared illegal by statute.

Agreements That Interfere with the Administration of Justice

Agreements that tend to interfere with the proper administration of justice—that prevent the law from being applied fairly—are illegal. Examples of agreements that tend to obstruct justice include an agreement to pay a witness to give false testimony or to conceal evidence during a court trial, an agreement to pay a juror to vote a certain way in a trial, and an agreement not to prosecute a person who has committed a crime in return for a sum of money.

> Russ was the receiver of taxes for the town of Millan. Because she was heavily in debt due to gambling, she embezzled $5,000 from the tax fund to pay off her debt through an accounting manipulation of the tax records. The town supervisor discovered what Russ had done and promised not to report the matter to the police if she agreed to pay him $1,000. Russ agreed but then changed her mind and refused to pay this money to the supervisor. The supervisor could not enforce this illegal agreement in a court of law.

Furthermore, because these agreements may also require the commission of a crime, the parties may be subject to criminal penalties.

Agreements That Interfere with the Performance of a Public Duty

People have the right to expect that elected and appointed officials will perform their duties properly and honestly. Agreements that tend to prevent the proper performance of duties by public officials are opposed to public policy and therefore illegal. An agreement to bribe a judge, a police officer, or the district attorney in return for a favor is illegal. Likewise, an agreement is illegal if a public official agrees to accept money for performing a legal duty, for promising *not* to perform a legal duty, or for promising to use personal influence to affect the passage of a law.

lobbying trying to influence lawmakers to vote for or against legislation

Lobbying is the practice of trying to influence the members of a legislative body to pass or defeat certain bills. As a rule, lobbying is not illegal. You can make an agreement to pay an attorney or an expert in a particular field to present your case to the lawmaker, leaving it up to the lawmaker to decide on the issue. An agreement to influence a legislator's decision by using bribery, threats, or other improper means, however, is illegal.

> An influential state senator agreed to accept $10,000 from Taber in return for influencing other legislators to pass a law permitting a certain expensive drug to be removed from the prescription list and made an over-the-counter drug. The senator succeeded in getting the law passed, but Taber refused to pay. Because this agreement was illegal, the senator could not seek payment from Taber in a court of law.

Because these agreements, like many other agreements mentioned in this chapter, often involve the commission of a crime, the parties to an agreement that interferes with the performance of a public duty may be subject to criminal penalties.

Agreements That Harm Marriage

Our society favors and encourages marriage and family life. Therefore, agreements that place unreasonable restraints or tend to discourage marriage completely are generally illegal. For example, agreements are illegal if one party promises never to marry, promises not to marry for an unreasonable amount of time, or promises not to marry a certain person.

> Siegel, fearing his only daughter would leave him, promised to give her $15,000 if she would never marry. The daughter agreed and accepted the $15,000. Two years later, she married. Siegel sued to recover the $15,000. The agreement is illegal, and he is not entitled to recover the money.

On the other hand, an agreement that places a reasonable restriction on marriage is legally binding. For example, the courts have held that an agreement to postpone marriage until reaching the age of majority is legal. This postponement is considered legal detriment.

Because the law seeks to preserve marriage, an agreement between a husband and wife to obtain a divorce for consideration is illegal and will not be enforced.

> Jason promised to give his wife $50,000 and a trip around the world if she would divorce him. His wife obtained a divorce, but Jason refused to carry out his part of the agreement. Because this agreement was illegal, Jason was not legally bound.

Agreements That Unreasonably Restrain Competition and Trade

covenant a promise not to compete

Agreements with clauses called covenants that unreasonably restrain or restrict competition and trade are illegal. A **covenant** is a promise not to compete for a specified time in a certain geographic area. This promise may be contained in a separate contract standing by itself or it can be a clause added to a contract. Covenants not to compete are often found in contracts for the sale of an ongoing business, or included in employment contracts. Illegality is determined by the degree of restrictiveness sought by the party preparing the agreement. Covenants that are too restrictive are illegal, void, and therefore, unenforceable.

When a person buys a business such as a recording studio, a tool and dye business, or a computer sales and service center, that person is also buying the seller's goodwill, the continued patronage of old and loyal customers. No one would want a business if the seller could open a similar business nearby and draw away the old customers. The purchaser needs some assurance that customers will continue to trade at the old store. Consequently, it is customary to include in the purchase agreement a clause that prevents the seller from competing in the same business within a certain territory for a certain period of time. This clause is referred to as a covenant not to compete (also known as a noncompete agreement). A covenant is legal and enforceable if the territory and time restrictions are reasonable enough to protect the interests of the purchaser. If the restrictions are unreasonable, the clause is illegal and void because the effect is to curtail competition and restrain trade, which violates the antitrust laws. A very unique business may require a longer noncompete time than a business in a more conventional area.

A territory restriction should not go beyond the trade area of the business. The trade area for a small card and gift business might be a mile or two. If a business is citywide, such as a laundromat with stores in various neighborhoods, a clause restricting competition anywhere in the city might be reasonable. Similarly, if the business is statewide or national, such as a well-known chain of motels, a restriction not to compete anywhere in the state or nation may be upheld as reasonable.

A time restriction should not be longer than is reasonably necessary for the purchaser to obtain the goodwill of previous customers and attract new customers. In the sale of a popular fine dining local restaurant, twenty-five years would be unreasonable, two or three years may be reasonable, while a restriction of one year or less is pretty safe.

> Santos operated a computer sales and service center in a town of about 35,000 people. He sold his business to Murdock. The written sales agreement included a clause preventing Santos from opening a computer sales and service center in the town for a period of six months. Because both the time and territory restrictions were reasonable for a town of 35,000 people, the clause in the sales agreement would most likely be enforced in a court of law.

Territory and time restrictions imposed by the purchaser of a business may also be imposed by an employer upon an employee who leaves his or her present job to work for a competing business. Should an employee sign? There is no right answer. However, you should know that noncompete agreements have become more common, and they are not going away. As loyalty between businesses (especially corporations) and their employees hits an all-time low, employers claim that more employees are defecting to competitors and divulging company secrets, keeping their companies, employers say, from maintaining their competitive position. They can't risk having competitors obtain trade secrets, which can be anything the employer deems sensitive or privileged: information about new software, hardware, telecommunications, customers, or whatever. To protect themselves, employers are increasingly asking all workers—not just the executives—to sign noncompete agreements preventing these workers from either setting up a similar business or working for a competitor who provides the same services as the old employer. Even employees forced out of their job may be required to sign a noncompete agreement. Noncompete clauses are common in industries ranging from pharmaceuticals, high-tech, and telecommunications to fast-food, sales, and consumer products. Generally speaking, agreements with noncompete clauses are interpreted according to the rule of reason, which means that they must be reasonable in terms of time period, geography, and what the person can and cannot do. Today's noncompete clauses generally bar someone from working for a rival for six months to five years. A five-year noncompete clause may run into trouble in some states as being too restrictive. According to the rule of reason, an employee skilled in two fields can be restricted in one field but not both.

> When Detailman was hired at Tangles, a local hair salon, he was required to sign an employment contract that included a noncompete clause agreeing not to work for another salon within the 79904 ZIP code area for eighteen months after leaving the current salon. He did leave Tangles after three months and was immediately hired by a salon in the same ZIP code area. The new salon, however, specialized in ethnic hair care. Detailman had to be completely retrained in this area of expertise. All the training received at Tangles was actually of no use to him. Detailman did not provide his new employer with a customer list from Tangles. His former employer at Tangles sued Detailman, claiming that he (Detailman) was in violation of his noncompete clause.

In this example, assuming that Detailman was not violating any technical requirements under the law, a court most likely would rule that he was not in violation of his noncompete agreement and could not be stopped from competing. The new salon was providing completely different services than Tangles. In addition, Detailman did not provide his new employer a customer list of his clients from Tangles, which most likely would have been considered insignificant after only three months of employment at this salon.

Frequently, a partnership agreement between professional people contains a clause stating that upon retiring or leaving the partnership, the partner will not start a competing business. These clauses are also enforceable if the restrictions on territory and time are reasonably necessary to protect the remaining partners.

Court Treatment of Unreasonable Noncompete Clauses   Courts generally do not favor noncompetition agreements because they prevent a person from working and earning a living. Consequently, many states either prohibit or heavily regulate these clauses. Noncompete agreements have been invalidated when an employee was fired without cause (did not do anything wrong) or was not reasonably compensated in exchange for signing the noncompete agreement. These states have taken this approach because so many noncompete clauses are deemed too restrictive. When noncompete clauses are found to be unreasonable, courts in different states generally will follow one of these guidelines:

1. Throw out the clause entirely, leaving the remainder of the agreement to be enforceable.
2. Apply the blue pencil doctrine, which holds that the court has the power to rewrite the covenant so that it is less restrictive.

Applying the blue pencil doctrine is not what the courts wish to do. Most courts instead will follow the first procedure. Most important, if you are asked to sign a noncompete agreement that can substantially affect your livelihood, contact an attorney first.

Agreements That Create a Monopoly or Limit Competition

A monopoly occurs when one person or business controls all or nearly all the trade or supply of a particular item within an area to the exclusion of all competition. An agreement to create or maintain a monopoly is not only opposed to public policy but is also a violation of federal and state laws. These laws, called *antitrust laws*, are discussed in more detail in Chapter 28.

Four trash-hauling companies in a certain city attempted to avoid a "trash war" by agreeing not to solicit each other's accounts through agreements containing covenants not to compete. During the seven years that this agreement lasted, the companies brought in more than $20 million in total revenue. Because the trash-hauling companies tended to create a monopoly, their agreements were illegal and therefore unenforceable. What the trash haulers did might also be considered a criminal conspiracy. If convicted, the penalty could be a fine, imprisonment, or both.

Not all monopolies are illegal, however. Companies such as utilities companies are given the exclusive right by government to provide a product or service within a certain area. Only when a business deliberately and unreasonably seeks to eliminate competition is it illegal. Microsoft Corporation is a good example. It started as a partnership in 1975, but due to the ingenuity of the two original partners, it has become a giant corporation and has developed into the worldwide leader in services and Internet technologies for personal and business computing. The U.S. Department of Justice brought a lawsuit claiming that Microsoft used its power to target competitive companies and should be broken up to weaken its monopoly power and increase competition, even though it appears that Microsoft became a dominant force as a result of the skill and innovative practices of its original founder. The business has developed into what might be considered a natural monopoly with no evil intent, but simply a focus on developing technology for the next-generation Internet. Microsoft is working to enable businesses to be collaborative and offers an unprecedented range of integrated and customized solutions that enable their customers to act on information wherever and whenever they need it.

An agreement that limits competition by controlling or fixing prices, dividing up trade territory, or limiting production is also considered illegal and violates both federal and state antitrust laws.

Agreements That Are Unconscionable

unconscionable agreement contract so unfair or one-sided that it will not be enforced

Unconscionable agreements violate public policy. An **unconscionable agreement** is one that is entered into under the following circumstances: (1) A party lacks the knowledge and/or understanding of the terms of the agreement or (2) the agreement is too grossly unfair or harsh. With regard to the first reason, some contracts are written in a very legal form using "lawyer language" that one party to the agreement does not understand. Or the agreement may contain terms in very small print limiting the liability of one of the parties or include hidden clauses in fine print that the party obligated to sign the agreement missed. With regard to the second reason, there are no limits to the types of contracts a court will find unfair or harsh. Among modern court decisions, including decisions governing the sale of goods under the UCC, unconscionability has been applied to contracts involving questionable sales tactics, unequal bargaining power of the parties, the basic illiteracy of one party, and grossly excessive price terms. Unconscionability has been applied to standard contracts that favor one party over another, such as a lease that favors the landlord or an insurance policy that favors the company and must be accepted on a take-it-or-leave-it basis, contracts with clauses disclaiming liability, and contracts with provisions requiring a buyer to waive certain legal rights.

Belmede, a migrant from a foreign country with an inability to speak English well, signed a car loan to purchase a van through a dealership that supposedly charged her 15 percent interest. The salesperson told Belmede that as an immigrant with little credit history, 15 percent was the best she could expect. She was unaware that other local dealers were charging as low as 4 percent. Belmede, a single mother of four who was working two jobs, felt she had no other choice. She signed the original paper work agreeing to pay what she thought was 15 percent interest and made a down payment of $2,500. A week later the dealership called her back to sign additional paperwork, saying that the van would be repossessed if she didn't sign. Belmede signed without reading anything. A friend encouraged her to check with another dealership offering vans at a lower interest rate. This new dealership reviewed her paperwork with the original dealership and discovered that she was actually paying 29 percent interest. Her $9,000 van was going to cost her more than $16,000 over the life of the loan, despite her having paid $2,500 as a down payment. Belmede attempted to get out of her loan agreement with the original car dealer but was turned down. When she refused to continue payments as agreed, the original car dealer sued.

Because this contract seemed unfair (unconscionable), a court most likely would refuse to rule in favor of the original car dealership that had made what would be considered a predatory car loan.

PARTIALLY ILLEGAL AGREEMENTS

An agreement may be partially legal and partially illegal. The legal part of the agreement may be enforced if it can be separated from the illegal part. If the agreement is so complicated that it is not possible to separate the illegal part, the entire agreement is void and unenforceable.

McGrail was studying to become a licensed electrician. It was illegal in his state to perform services for the public without a license. Nevertheless, he purchased and then installed some light fixtures for a neighbor. Even though McGrail could not collect for the cost of his labor in installing the light fixtures because he was not properly licensed, he could collect for the cost of the light fixtures.

Summary

In addition to offer and acceptance, consideration, and competent parties, the law imposes a requirement that the purpose of the agreement be legal. Agreements that are completely illegal are usually void and unenforceable. Some agreements are entirely illegal; others may only contain illegal clauses. There are exceptions to the rule that courts will not enforce illegal agreements. One exception occurs when both parties are not equally at fault. A court may in this case come to the aid of the party who was unaware of the facts that made the agreement illegal. For example, an individual who unknowingly deals with an unlicensed person may be permitted to recover any money paid to this person for services performed. Another exception is ignorance of the facts as to the illegality of an agreement. Although the courts will not enforce such an agreement, they will allow a person who has fully performed his or her part of the agreement not aware of the illegality to recover any fees due.

An agreement may be illegal either because it is forbidden by state statute or because it is opposed to a state's public policy. Agreements that have been made illegal by most state legislatures are those that violate civil and criminal statutes, licensing statutes, gambling statutes, usury statutes (those in which a lender charges a higher rate of interest than that allowed by law), or Sunday statutes. Internet (online) gambling in the United States is now illegal due to the passage of the Unlawful Internet Gambling Act of 2006. One main reason for the passage of this law was that this form of gambling was competing for business with some gaming (legal) activities in the various states. Agreements that are illegal in most states because they are opposed to public policy (based on a public sense of what is right and wrong) include agreements that contain clauses (called exculpatory clauses) that disclaim liability for negligence, interfere with the administration of justice, interfere with the performance of a public duty, are harmful to marriage, unreasonably restrain competition and trade, create a monopoly or limit competition, or are unconscionable (grossly unfair).

An agreement may be partially legal and partially illegal. If it can be separated from the part that is illegal, the legal part of the agreement may be enforced.

Important Legal Terms

casual gambler	gaming	professional gambler
contract of adhesion	in pari delicto	Sunday laws
covenant	Interest	unconscionable agreement
exculpatory clause	licensing statutes	usury
gambling	lobbying	

Questions and Problems for Discussion

1. Which of the following answers is correct? Contracts in restraint of trade are
   a. always void.
   b. always valid.
   c. sometimes valid.
   d. always unenforceable.

2. What is an "unconscionable" agreement?

3. What are covenants not to compete? What is the standard used to judge their legality?

4. Manix paid the local district attorney $1,500 a month for a year not to prosecute him for operating an illegal gambling establishment. Manix then decided to quit the business. He now seeks to recover the money paid to the district attorney on the grounds that his payment over the year amounted to a bribe and was therefore illegal. Can Manix recover the money?

5. Karns leases his small private plane to others interested in recreational flying. One Sunday morning, Ashbery rented the plane for the day. Karns was unaware that Ashbery rented the plane to haul illegal drugs from one location to another, which is in violation of both state and federal law. Can Ashbery refuse to pay Karns the rental fee claiming that the agreement was illegal?

6. Moran owned a woodcarving business situated in a plaza in Valley Forge, Pennsylvania. He carved unique items such as toys, picture frames, and miniature model cars that would sell quickly. His products were very popular, and people would come to his plaza store to make purchases. Moran also traveled to various parts of Pennsylvania selling his items at various town events. Because his items were unique, he had no competition. Ritz, a person who worked for Moran and possessed the same talents, offered to buy the business if Moran would sign the following statement as part of the contract of sale: "I agree not to reenter my current business in Valley Forge, Pennsylvania, or to travel anywhere in the state of Pennsylvania to sell the items that I currently make and sell or to compete in any manner; I further agree to refer all business contacts that call me, to Ritz. This clause is valid for ten years." In violation of this agreement, Moran opened a similar business in competition with Ritz and in violation of the noncompete agreement. Is the covenant not to compete valid and enforceable in this case?

7. Madison took his Porsche to the Downtown Repair Shop for some major repairs that would take three days. The repair order form prepared by the repair shop that he signed contained the following statement: "Not responsible for loss or damage to cars or articles left in cars in case of fire, theft, or any other cause beyond our control." While at the repair shop and under its control, Madison's car was stolen. Madison sued Downtown Repair Shop for failing to redeliver the car to him. Is Downtown Repair Shop liable?

8. You and Higgins made a $50 bet on the outcome of the Super Bowl. After your team won, Higgins refused to pay you the $50. Could you legally sue Higgins for the $50?

9. Rene, who came from a wealthy family, was a teacher in what was considered a rural school district. She and her friend Curtis, an attorney,

lived together although they were not married. Rene got pregnant. She got frightened that a nonmarital pregnancy would prevent her from getting tenure (a permanent appointment) on her job. She and Curtis agreed to get married and stay married until after she had the baby and received tenure on her job, both of which would occur in approximately one year. For doing this, Rene promised to give Curtis $35,000. They wrote up an agreement specifying the conditions under which they would marry and then divorce. Rene had her child and also got a permanent appointment at her school. The conditions having been fulfilled, they then divorced, but Rene refused to pay Curtis the $35,000. Can Curtis legally collect this money?

10. Lando, chairwoman of an environmental group, was interested in the passage of a bill that banned smoking in all public places. For $2,000, she hired an attorney to draft the bill and argue for its passage before a senator interested in environmental matters. This senator was convinced of the value of the bill and urged other senators to vote in favor of its passage. The bill was passed by the legislature and became law. The attorney then demanded payment. Can Lando refuse payment on the grounds that what the attorney did was illegal?

Cases for Review

1. Jorge Arrospide Sr. gave his son, Jorge Arrospide Jr., power of attorney to act on his behalf. To pay his father's medical bills, Jorge Jr. borrowed $4,000 on behalf of his father from Carboni, giving Carboni a secured note. There was no other source of funding available. Carboni said, "Take it or leave it." Carboni added on interest at the rate of 200 percent per year. (This loan was exempt from the usury laws in California because Carboni was a licensed real estate broker.) The 200 percent interest rate was ten times the interest rate then prevailing in the credit market for similar loans. Carboni also advanced additional funds to Jorge Sr. When Jorge, Sr., failed to make any payments on the note after demand, Carboni sought to foreclose on Jorge Sr.'s real property. By this time, the amount of the debt with interest was 100 times the original debt. Jorge Sr. argued that the loan agreement was unconscionable and that the original debt should be re-formed to reflect a lower rate of interest. Carboni argued that the loan was legitimate and that Jorge Sr., should not have borrowed the money if he could not pay. What do you think the outcome should be? (*Carboni* v. *Arrospide*, 2 Cal. Rptr. 2d 845)

2. Eelbode, who applied for a job at the Travelers Inn, was required to take a preemployment physical exam. He was sent to the Chec Medical Center. As part of his physical, he met with Grothe, a physical therapist who put him through certain tests involving bending exercises in which he had to use his back and his knees.

Prior to the physical, he was required to sign a document releasing the Chec Medical Center and the Washington Readicare Medical Group and its physicians from all liability arising from injury to him while participating in the exam. During the exam, he did suffer an injury to his back and his right leg. Eelbode filed a suit against Chec and Grothe, claiming that he was injured because of a strength test that was improperly administered. Grothe and Chec filed a motion of summary judgment asking that the case be settled in their favor because of the statement that Eelbode signed. Should Eelbode be successful in his lawsuit? (*Eelbode* v. *Chec Medical Centers, Inc.*, 984 P.2d 436)

3. Singletary, as owner of a multistory building, leased the first floor to Topp Copy Products. A toilet in an apartment above Topp Copy Products developed a leak and did substantial damage to Topp Copy's inventory in the leased space. Topp Copy sued Singletary for water damages based on negligence. Singletary claimed that his defense was an exculpatory clause in the lease agreement that stated that he was released from any and all liability for damages that "may result from the bursting, stoppage, and leakage of any water pipe . . . and from any damage caused by the water . . . and contents of said water pipes." Topp Copy disagreed with Singletary, stating that an exculpatory clause did not relieve Singletary from negligence caused by his or her own negligence. Is Topp Copy correct? (*Topp Copy Products, Inc.* v. *Singletary* 626 A.2d 98)

4. In the state of Hawaii, a person must meet certain educational requirements and pass a written exam to be granted a license to practice architecture. Once the initial license is received, an annual license fee is required to maintain the license. Wilson was granted an architecture license and paid the first annual fee. One year he failed to pay this fee. During this time, he contracted with clients for approximately $34,000 of architectural services. The defendants refused to pay the bill because Wilson had not renewed his license. Wilson sued for his fees. Could he collect even though he had not renewed his license? (*Wilson v. Kealakekua Ranch, Ltd., and Gentry Hawaii,* 551 P.2D 525)

5. Berner and a number of other investors purchased stock from a San Francisco—based stock brokerage firm known as Bateman Eichler by getting an inside tip from one of the brokers employed by the firm (an illegal practice called *trading on insider information*). Based on the tip, the stock would rise in value, and the investors would make a large profit. When the tip turned out to be false, Berner and the other investors sued the stock brokerage firm for its losses because the market price of the stock fell far below the prices they paid for it. The trial court dismissed the complaint, concluding that the agreement to purchase the stock was illegal because the parties to the lawsuit were in pari delicto. Consequently, the plaintiffs were absolutely barred from recovery. An appeals court reversed the lower court's ruling and claimed that, regardless of the in pari delicto ruling by the lower court, Berner and the investors could still collect. Bateman Eichler appealed this decision to the U.S. Supreme Court. Should the Supreme Court decide in favor of Bateman Eichler, the stock brokerage firm? (*Bateman Eichler, Hill Richards Inc.* v. *Berner,* 472 U.S. 299, 310)

6. The University of California Medical Center admitted Tunkl as a patient. While under sedation and unable to read, Tunkl was required, as a condition for admission, to sign a document containing a clause releasing the hospital from any and all liability for the negligent or wrongful acts of its employees. Alleging personal injuries from the negligence of two physicians at the Medical Center, Tunkl sued the hospital for damages. Can the hospital excuse itself from any and all liability from the wrongful acts? (*Tunkl* v. *Regents of University of California,* 383 P.2d 441)

7. Beaver participated in the annual Elkhart Grand Prix go-kart races in Elkhart, Indiana. She signed an exculpatory agreement containing the release of the race organizers from all liability associated with the races unless a claim at issue involved willful misconduct. During the event in which she drove, a piece of polyurethane foam padding used as a course barrier was torn from its base and it ended up on the track. One portion of the packing struck Beaver in the head, and another portion was thrown into oncoming traffic, causing a multikart collision during which Beaver sustained severe injuries. Beaver filed an action against the race organization, claiming that the foam padding used on the course was defective. She further claimed that because of the defects in the padding that the exculpatory agreement was illegal and void. The race organizers contended that the exculpatory agreement released her from any liability. Who is correct? (U.S. Court of Appeals, 7th Circuit, 246 F. 3d 905)

CHAPTER 11

Formal Requirements—Statute of Frauds/E-Signatures

CHAPTER PREVIEW

Chapter Highlights

This chapter identifies the relatively few contracts that are required by the law of each state (called a statute of frauds) to be in writing to be enforceable in court. The chapter also summarizes the essential information that the writing must contain so as to satisfy the law. A brief opening discussion points out the advantages that written contracts have over those that are made orally. This is followed by a discussion of parol evidence, a rule determining whether oral testimony external to a written contract that changes the terms of this written contract may be introduced at a court trial. The concluding pages of the chapter introduce the electronic signature (e-signature) as a way to sign records.

THE STATUS OF ORAL AND WRITTEN CONTRACTS

In most circumstances, oral contracts are just as enforceable as written contracts if they contain all the elements necessary to make a contract legally binding (those discussed in Chapters 7 through 10) and if the terms of the oral contracts can be proved in a court of law. In fact, most contracts are *not* in writing. Nevertheless, many lawsuits based on breach of valid oral contracts have been dismissed by courts because the parties who brought them could not sufficiently establish their terms.

Written contracts have advantages over oral contracts. A written contract needs no witnesses to establish its existence and its terms. The writing is taken as proof of the parties' intent to actually contract and to include certain specifications of terms within the scope of the contract. If there are no witnesses to an oral contract, one of the parties might deny that the contract ever existed or might disagree on the exact terms of the contract. Even if there are witnesses to an oral contract, they may disagree about the contract's exact terms. To avoid misunderstandings and disagreements and to reduce the possibility of perjury (lying under oath) by one party or the other, you should ensure that all important contracts are in writing. Keep in mind that putting a contract in writing does not guarantee that at the time of performance the contract terms will not be questioned or become a "battleground" for a major dispute based on an interpretation of terms by the parties. The courts still need to decide what the disputed terms mean.

Relatively few contracts are required by law to be in writing; they are discussed in the pages that follow. Re-creating the intentions of the parties can be difficult in the absence of a written agreement.

CONTRACTS REQUIRED TO BE IN WRITING

statute of frauds law
requiring that certain
types of contracts be in
writing

Every state has a law requiring that to be enforceable in court, certain kinds of contracts must be in writing. This law, called the **statute of frauds** (based on the English Statute of Frauds passed in 1677), does not pertain to all contracts but only to six specific types. These six contracts, said to be "within the statute," are believed to be historically important enough to put into written form. The statute of frauds does not eliminate the other essential elements of a valid contract (offer and acceptance, consideration, competent parties, and legal purpose). It simply adds the requirement of written evidence that a contract existed.

Virtually all statutes of fraud require the following types of contracts to be in writing to be enforceable:

1. A contract to personally pay the debt of another person.
2. A contract by an executor or administrator to personally pay the debts of a deceased person.
3. A contract involving the sale of an interest in real property
4. A contract made in consideration of marriage
5. A contract that by its terms cannot be performed within one year from the date the agreement was formed.
6. A contract for the sale of goods or merchandise for the price of $5,000 or more. (Under the 2003 amendments to Section 2-201 of the Uniform Commercial Code. It may be some time before the states actually adopt this figure. The amount was $500. The new figure reflects over fifty years of inflation.) This particular type of contract will be discussed in Chapter 15.

In addition to these contracts, some states require other types of contracts to be in writing. These contracts may include a contract appointing an agent to sell real estate, a promise to pay a debt discharged in bankruptcy, or a promise to be released from an ordinary debt, as well as various types of consumer transactions such as a loan of money. If a state statute does not require that a contract be in writing, an oral contract is enforceable.

The statute of frauds applies only to executory contracts, that is, contracts that have not been fully performed. If, however, two parties fully perform an oral contract that should have been in writing, the agreement would not be void, but unforceable. The contract is valid for all other purposes. If both parties elect to go through with their oral agreement they may, and no third party may complain that the contract is oral. Only the original parties to the contract may raise this issue.

Randazzo sold Merkel 2 acres of land in the town of Wallworth for $100,000 to build a bed and breakfast. The contract had been made orally. Shortly thereafter, Randazzo changed his mind and backed out of the deal. He returned the purchase price to Merkel and asked for the return of the document of ownership for the land. Merkel refused. Randazzo then asked the court to void the contract because it was not in writing as required by the statute of frauds for a sale of land. The court refused, ruling that because the agreement had been fully performed, the statute of frauds did not apply.

A Contract to Personally Pay the Debt of Another Person

A contract one person (the guarantor) makes with a creditor to pay a third person's debt (called a contractual or secondary promise) must be in writing to be enforceable. Under this type of agreement, called a *guaranty*, the guarantor's promise to pay is secondary to the promise of the person who owes the money (the debtor). That is, the debtor is still responsible for paying the debt; the guarantor is responsible *only* if the debtor fails to pay. (This type of contract may be a bit unusual because we generally assume that a person does not normally take on another person's debt. Therefore, the statute of frauds requires written evidence of this unusual arrangement.) If necessary, the creditor would first be required to sue the debtor and obtain a judgment. A judgment in this case is a court order directing the debtor to pay the debt owed to the creditor. If the debtor refuses, the creditor could then proceed against the guarantor.

> Julian, who recently graduated from college, was hired by a large firm as an account executive. Because he needed a car to get to work, he went to a car dealer in the large city where he lived and put in a bid on a new car. Because Julian did not have a credit history, the dealer was unwilling to sell him the car unless a responsible person with good credit would guarantee payment. His uncle, a well-known businessperson in the same city, agreed in writing to become responsible for any payments his nephew failed to make. Because the uncle's promise to pay was secondary (agreed to pay only if the nephew did not) and since the guarantee to pay was in writing, the uncle becomes responsible for any of the payments his nephew fails to make.

An agreement does not come within the statute of frauds if you make yourself primarily responsible for the payment of a debt. An oral agreement in this case would be enforceable.

> Forman said to his friend, the owner of Miles Furniture Mart: "It is my daughter's birthday and she wants the dining room set she saw at your store. Go ahead and sell it to her, but send me the bill."

In this example, Forman did not promise to pay if the daughter did not pay. Instead, Forman assumed primary responsibility for the amount of the daughter's purchase. Because the debt became Forman's alone, the owner of Miles Furniture Mart would look only to Forman for payment.

A Contract by an Executor or Administrator to Personally Pay the Debt of a Deceased Person

An *executor* or *administrator* is one who handles the property (or estate) of a deceased person. The executor or administrator gathers the assets of the deceased, pays all debts, and distributes the remaining property according to the terms of a will or state law. The executor is not personally responsible for the debts of the deceased; the debts are paid out of the deceased person's estate. If, however, there is not enough money to pay all the debts, an executor or administrator may promise to pay the debts from her or his own personal funds (such promises are relatively unusual). Such an agreement, which is actually an agreement to become responsible for the debts of another, must be in writing to be enforceable.

> When he died, Morten had an estate worth $100,000 but owed creditors $120,000. Morten's daughter, the executor of the estate, wanted to clear her father's name. She made an oral agreement with the creditors to pay the additional $20,000 owed by her father out of her own pocket. This oral agreement by Morten's daughter was not legally enforceable by the creditors.

A Contract Involving the Sale of an Interest in Real Property

A contract for the sale of real property or any interest in real property must be in writing to be enforceable. **Real property** is land or anything permanently attached to the land such as a building. The contract of sale, sometimes called a purchase offer, consists of an offer by the buyer and an acceptance by the seller. The purchase offer must also contain the other essential elements of a contract.

real property land, rights to land, and anything permanently attached to the land

> Newman placed a sign on her front lawn advertising her house for sale. Julian saw the sign, stopped, inspected the house, and orally offered Newman the $140,000 asking price. Newman accepted. After Newman had taken down the sign and worked out the details of the sale, Julian refused to go through with the purchase of the property. Because the statute of frauds requires that all contracts for the sale of real property be in writing, Julian was not bound by the oral contract.

It is not uncommon for people to enter into oral contracts involving real property. If, in the example, Julian made a deposit on the house, the oral contract for the sale of the house would still not be enforceable. In the eyes of the law, the deposit could be returned without injury to Julian. On the other hand, Newman may have immediately transferred possession of the house to Julian, with the deed of ownership to be given later. In this case, if Julian made improvements to the house, such as painting and making certain repairs, the law most likely would not permit Newman to cancel the sale and retake possession of the house because the agreement was not in writing.

A contract for a temporary transfer of an interest in real property must also be in writing. An *interest* in this sense is a legal right to the use of or a claim on real property. Examples of interests include mortgages, easements, and leases. A *lease* is an agreement by which an owner of real property rents that property to another party. In most states, an oral lease for a term of one year or less is valid.

> Clinton orally agreed to rent a house from Jeffers for one year. This oral agreement does not have to be in writing to be enforceable because it is only for one year.

A Contract Made in Consideration of Marriage

The writing requirement for a contract in consideration of marriage applies only if a promise to marry is made in consideration for some promise other than a mutual promise to marry. Mutual promises to marry are valid contractual promises, and are enforceable even if there is no written evidence. For example, if Martina and Brown each orally promise and agree to marry each other, their agreement is binding. If, however, Martina agrees to marry Brown only if Brown will turn over certain property to him, this agreement will not be enforceable in court unless it is in writing. The rationale for requiring a writing in this type of marriage arrangement is that it is rather uncommon today, and the courts therefore want evidence to show that the parties actually reached such an agreement.

The people who plan to marry for the first time may agree to give up rights or take on obligations that are not an implied obligation of the marriage itself. They may do so through a **prenuptial agreement**. Prenuptial (also called antenuptial) agreements, however, are not enforceable unless they are in writing. Further, they do not take effect until the parties marry. Prenuptial agreements are especially useful for couples who, having been married before and having accumulated property, plan to marry again but wish to regulate inheritance rights.

prenuptial agreement agreement by a couple planning to marry regarding the rights and obligations of each person

> Whitney and Banks decide to marry. It is a second marriage for both. They sign a prenuptial agreement whereby each promises to waive any inheritance rights to the other's money and/or property accumulated up to the point of their second marriage.

Each wishes the children of his or her prior marriage to be the sole heirs (those entitled to inherit) of the money or property.

In this example, a court will hold the agreement enforceable as long as Whitney and Banks understood the legal consequences of what they agreed to do and knew the full extent of each other's property. Courts are increasingly upholding prenuptial agreements, provided they are fair and reasonable and were entered into freely (i.e., made without threats).

A Contract That by Its Terms Cannot Be Performed Within One Year from the Date the Agreement Was Formed

A contract must be in writing if its terms cannot be carried out exactly within one year of the date of the agreement. If it can be carried out in exactly one year, or even less time, an oral contract is valid. The one year period starts to run the day after the contract is formed. This is referred to as the "One Year Rule." For example, a nationally and internationally known singer enters into a contract on August 10, 2008, to perform in a large city in September 2010. This contract must be in writing because it cannot be performed prior to September 2010. That was an easy case. It could get a little more complicated than that because the year legally begins when the contract is made, not when performance is to start.

Sullivan, a wealthy cattle rancher, planned to take a year off and travel with his family. On March 13, he orally agreed to hire Elridge for that one year to take charge of his property and his business interests. Elridge was to work from May 1 of that year to April 30 of the next year. Because the contract cannot be completed within one year of the date of the agreement (March 13), it must be in writing to be enforceable. The date of May 1 is not significant in determining whether or not the contract has to be in writing.

The key for determining whether an oral contract is enforceable under the one-year rule is the *possibility of performance*, not the actual performance. The statute of frauds does not apply if it is possible to carry out the terms of the contract exactly within one year. For example, Redman orally promises "to work for Dykes as a personal security guard for Dykes's lifetime" in exchange for Dykes's promise to pay him a monthly salary of $10,000. Courts, however, interpret such language to mean that because it is possible—although not probable—that Dykes might die within a year, an oral contract is enforceable even though it may not be completed for several years.

Sometimes the court's interpretation of what is possible is a bit far-fetched, but nevertheless will still stick to the rule that if performance is possible exactly within one year, an oral contract is enforceable. Consider the following example:

A magazine subscription company promised the senior class of Redwood High School, with whom the magazine company has an oral contract, that any student who sells $10 million of magazine subscriptions during the coming senior class magazine drive (lasting one month) will earn an all-expense paid trip to Europe for his or her entire family.

In this example, the relevant question is: Can it happen? The answer, of course, is yes! It is possible that a student will sell that many dollars worth of magazines in one month simply because some rich relative will buy them. Is that likely to happen? Probably not. Because it is possible that the contract can be fulfilled, the oral contract would be binding.

Some courts will apply the equitable doctrine of promissory estoppel (discussed in Chapter 8) to allow recovery by a person who could not otherwise enforce a contract in this situation because of the statute of frauds requirement.

THE SUFFICIENCY OF THE WRITTEN RECORD

memorandum informal written evidence of an agreement required by the statute of frauds

In most states, the written evidence of a prior oral agreement required by the statute of frauds is an informal **memorandum** (record). A formal written contract signed by both parties is not necessary but may be used if desired. It is not necessary that the writing be made at the time of the contract. An oral agreement is enforceable even if it is within the statute of frauds as long as there is some writing that refers to the agreement and its terms. Some courts have held that a tape or video recording may even satisfy the writing requirement.

Generally, the memorandum should contain at least the following information:

- The names of the parties.
- The subject matter of the agreement (real property, a debt, employment, etc.).
- The consideration.
- All material terms with reasonable certainty.
- The signature of the party against whom enforcement is sought—that is, the party being sued, normally the buyer. (The party seeking enforcement need not have signed the memorandum.)

FIGURE 11.1 Informal Memorandum

Phoenix, Arizona
January 17, 2009

AYERS MANUFACTURING COMPANY AND DONOVAN JENKINS JR. hereby agree as follows:

 AYERS MANUFACTURING COMPANY agrees to hire **DONOVAN JENKINS JR.** as sales manager at a guaranteed salary of $5,000.00 per month for the duration of the contract. The employment period to begin February 3, 2009, is to continue for five (5) years, until February 3, 2014.

AYERS MANUFACTURING COMPANY

By _Roy Ayers_____
President

Donovan Jenkins Jr.

The signature of the party being held responsible may be handwritten, printed, typed, stamped, or may even be in electronic form and may appear anywhere in the memorandum. An example of an informal memorandum is shown in Figure 11.1.

> While visiting Stein at her cottage on the lake, Wayne convinced Stein to sell the cottage to him. Wayne wrote out a memorandum of the agreement, signed it, and sent it to Stein. Stein did not sign the memorandum. When Stein changed her mind about selling the cottage, Wayne brought an action in court to force her to sell. Because Stein, the party being sued, had not signed the memorandum, there was no valid evidence of an agreement. The court would not require her to sell the cottage to Wayne.

The memorandum may consist of a single document or multiple pieces of paper (letters, telegrams, sales slips, invoices, faxes, or e-mails). If the memorandum consists of several documents physically attached, at least one of them must contain the signature of the party who will be held responsible. The other unsigned documents in the series must show that their content is related to the signed document.

ELECTRONIC SIGNATURES (E-SIGNATURES)

The handwritten signature alone as a way to sign documents has not been necessary for some time. Typed or printed signatures are also allowed, especially in signing a negotiable instrument (see Chapter 19). Now comes the electronic signature, or e-signature, "invented" to accommodate electronic commerce. The e-signature is a generic term that refers to all the methods by which one can sign an electronic record. A very common method by which a person can sign electronically is the digital signature. It is an electronic substitute for a manual signature that serves the same function as a manual signature. A digital signature created by a computer signifies an intent to sign. This new method of signing documents, especially contracts, has not been without problems, however. One problem is whether agreements made in a purely online environment using e-signatures are legally binding. After all, prior to e-signatures, a person used a pen and signed the contract in his or her own unique handwriting. The question of legality was not generally questioned because the contract was most likely signed in the presence of some official person. Another problem involves the states. Most states have laws governing e-signatures; however, these state laws are not uniform. Thanks to federal legislation signed into law on October 1, 2000, the legality issue has been resolved. The law, known as the Electronic Signatures in Global and International Commerce Act (E-SIGN Act), removes the uncertainty as to the legality of electronic contracts and different forms of electronic signatures that have been developed. Such contracts and signatures are now considered just as legal and enforceable as traditional paper contracts that have been signed in ink. The law states, among other things, that no contract, record, or signature may be denied "legal effect" solely because it is in electronic form. Documents not covered by the E-SIGN Act include prenuptial agreements, court papers, divorce decrees, wills, evictions, foreclosures, and health insurance terminations.

There is a downside to using an e-signature: It offers little security. Your signature could be intercepted online by thieves and used for fraudulent purposes. You are actually placed in the same position as if your credit card were stolen. Consequently, you should consider carefully whether you wish to sign anything online. Despite these limitations, the E-SIGN Act provides increased opportunities for contracting online. Online contracts eliminate time and costs associated with exchanging paper documents requiring signatures created off-line, as when opening a bank account or obtaining a loan or a mortgage. Keep in mind that contracting parties must both agree to use electronic signatures; otherwise, the electronic signature is not valid.

Parol Evidence Rule

parol evidence rule
rule stating that terms
of a written contract
cannot be changed by
prior oral or written
agreements

Once a contract has been put in writing as the final expression of agreement between the parties, it is protected by the parol evidence rule from a claim by either party that what is in the contract is not their real intention. The **parol evidence rule** states that when a contract has been put in writing as the final and complete statement of agreement between the parties, parol evidence—evidence of an agreement, oral or written, made prior to, or at the time of, signing the written agreement—cannot be presented in court to change, alter, modify, or add to the terms of this written agreement. In other words, neither party can say that he or she agreed to do something other than what was included in the written contract. A court will not allow parol evidence because the court presumes that the written contract contained all the terms and provisions intended by the parties. Any term not included is, by law, considered intentionally omitted by the parties. In short, "What you see is what you get."

> "Now and Then," a band, entered into a written contract with Tiffany Community College to play at the spring fling for $1,200. Shortly before the contract was signed, the band leader asked the student activities director to reimburse the band for hiring four persons to help set up and tear down the band's equipment. The student activities director orally agreed to pay this expense. After the spring fling, the student activities director paid the band leader $1,200 but refused to pay the additional $150 for the extra workers. The band sued the college to recover the $150. Because the written contract did not contain a provision to pay for the set-up people, a court will not permit the band leader to introduce evidence that the student activities director orally agreed to pay this additional sum. The band is bound by the terms of the signed, written contract.

Parol evidence may be introduced, however, when the evidence does not change the terms of the written contract. For instance, parol evidence may be introduced to explain certain terms or words that are vague or confusing. Parol evidence may also be introduced to prove that the written contract lacked certain terms originally agreed upon but accidentally left out of or typed incorrectly in the written contract. Parol evidence may also be presented to show that the written contract was illegal, that one party was persuaded to make the contract by the fraud (deceit) of the other party, or that one person was mentally incompetent.

> Campo, on an application for a job as manager of a large store, lied when he said that he had never been arrested and convicted of a major crime. He had actually been arrested, convicted, and sentenced to prison for robbery. Campo was hired and signed a three-year contract. Six months later, the store owner discovered the lie and fired Campo, who sued for breach of contract. The owner could introduce parol evidence to show that, because he relied on Campo's statement of having no arrest record, he was persuaded through fraud to make the contract with Campo.

The parol evidence rule applies only to agreements made prior to or at the time of signing the written agreement. As a result, oral proof of any changes to the writing after the written contract was made can be presented in court. The party presenting the proof, however, must show that the later agreement contained consideration.

> Carlson, a person knowledgeable in electronics, agreed in writing to repair your CD system for $200. After beginning work, she discovered that more things were wrong than she had previously thought. Carlson informed you that she would not continue the work until you agreed to pay her an additional $50. You orally promised to pay, and Carlson agreed to continue. When the work was completed, you refused to pay

the additional $50. Carlson sued in small claims court and offered as proof your oral agreement to pay her the $50. This oral agreement could legally be introduced in court, but Carlson would still lose the case. Carlson, already legally obligated to complete the repairs for $200, furnished no consideration for your promise to pay the additional $50.

In the final analysis, the key in determining whether parol evidence will be allowed is whether the contract put in writing is intended to be the final and complete agreement between the parties. If it is so intended, then it is considered as an integrated contract, and any outside evidence will be excluded.

A written contract may be changed by a subsequent oral agreement if the written contract was not required to be in writing under the statute of frauds. If the contract being modified must be in writing, the modification must also be in writing.

Summary

Although a written contract has an advantage over an oral contract in that it needs no witness to establish its existence or its terms, most contracts are made orally. Oral contracts are just as legal as written contracts if they contain offer and acceptance, consideration, competent parties, and legal purpose and if the terms of these oral contracts can be proven in a court of law. Every state, however, has a law called the statute of frauds, which requires certain contracts to be in writing to be enforceable. The most common of these are (1) a contract to personally pay the debt of another person; (2) a contract by an executor or administrator to pay the debt of a deceased person; (3) a contract involving the sale of an interest in real property; (4) a contract made in consideration of marriage; and (5) a contract that by its terms cannot be performed within one year from the date the agreement was formed.

The written evidence required by the statute of frauds may be an informal memorandum. It must, however, contain all the essential terms of the agreement, including the names of the parties, the subject matter of the agreement, the consideration, and any material terms. It must be signed at least by the party who will be held responsible. Contracts and other important documents can now be signed electronically if all parties agree to use e-signatures.

The courts assume that a written contract contains all the agreed-upon terms of an agreement. Therefore, in the event of a lawsuit, the courts will not allow the introduction of parol evidence to change or add to the terms of a written contract. Parol evidence, however, may be admitted in court to explain vague or confusing terms in a written contract; to show that agreed-upon terms were accidentally omitted or incorrectly typed; or to prove that the written contract was unenforceable because of illegality, fraud, or mental incompetence. Oral changes to a written agreement made subsequent to the writing are allowable. Oral changes are not allowable, however, if the written agreement was required by the statute of frauds to be in writing. If the contract being modified must be in writing, the modification must also be in writing.

Important Legal terms

memorandum
parol evidence rule

prenuptial agreement
real property

statute of frauds

Questions and Problems for Discussion

1. As you read through the chapter, what are four key points that were made about the statute of frauds?

2. What test is used to apply the statute of frauds to contracts that take more than a year to perform?

3. What are three important points that were made in the chapter about the parol evidence rule?

4. Thompson, the owner of a successful floral shop, orally promised Franks, an experienced floral arranger, a bonus of $10,000 and a monthly salary if Franks would work for Thompson for two years. The bonus was to be paid at the end of the two-year period. Franks actually did work for the full term of the oral agreement. Will the statute of frauds prevent Franks from collecting the bonus?

5. The Roc Co. entered into an oral contract to pay Willis and Associates, a certified public accounting firm, $35,000 to perform a complete audit of its accounting records. The report was to cover a period of ten months but due fourteen months from now. Willis agreed orally to perform the audit and to begin within three months. Regardless of the delay in beginning the audit, Willis agreed to meet the fourteen-month deadline for completion. Does the contract fall within the statute of frauds?

6. Marlan's son was arrested for driving while intoxicated and had to hire an attorney to defend him in court. The attorney requested to be paid $1,500, one-half in advance and the remainder at the conclusion of the court hearing. Because the son did not have the funds, Marlan, in the presence of several other attorneys in the law office, told his son's attorney that he would pay the fee out of his own pocket following the court hearing. Because Marlan was a well-to-do businessperson in the community, the attorney agreed to these terms. Following the court hearing in which the son was convicted, Marlan refused to pay as agreed, claiming that the attorney had done a poor job representing his son. The attorney sued, but Marlan defended, claiming that his agreement to pay was not legally binding on him because it was made orally. Can the attorney collect her fee?

7. Lopez orally leased Payne's house for one year at $450 a month. After moving in and paying the rent for one month, Lopez moved out. When Payne sued to recover the rent for the eleven months remaining on the lease, Lopez claimed that, because the lease was not in writing, she was not liable. Is Lopez correct?

8. Lisi, vice president of the National Football Association, made arrangements to hold the association's annual convention at the Marvel Hotel and Convention Center. He met with Brock, the hotel manager, one year before the scheduled event. They orally came to terms on several important points, including room rates, meal prices, and exhibit space charges. Brock was then replaced by a new manager, Talbot. Lisi met with Talbot to review the oral agreement he had made with Brock, intending to draw up a written contract to cover these points. Talbot had no record of this agreement and refused to honor any prior arrangements, claiming instead that because of inflation, prices should be raised 20 percent. Can Lisi legally require Talbot to abide by the original oral agreement he had with Brock?

9. McLean orally agreed to manage several of Orcini's aerobics studios in Los Angeles for three years at a salary of $35,000 a year. After six months, McLean decided to quit her job and move to the East Coast. Orcini had to hire a new manager at a salary of $38,000 a year. Orcini claimed that McLean was liable for damages of $3,000 a year for breach of contract until McLean's original contract expired. Is Orcini correct in his claim?

10. Bain lived in Bristol Harbor, a resort area along the Atlantic coast. She entered into a written agreement to sell her daily catch of fresh lobster at an agreed price to a local restaurant owner during the tourist season. At the end of the tourist season, Bain sued the restaurant owner for an additional $2,000. At the trial, she claimed that shortly before signing the contract, the restaurant owner orally agreed to pay her a $2,000 bonus. Can Bain introduce the oral agreement as evidence and collect the $2,000 bonus?

Cases for Review

1. A landlord entered into a lease (contract) with a tenant. A clause in the lease stated that the tenant would use the premises only for a gasoline station, car wash, and related activities. The landlord sued to terminate the lease, claiming that the tenant had violated an oral agreement, which was made at the time the lease was drawn up, not to add a convenience store to the gas station. Was this oral agreement binding on the tenant? (*Snow* v. *Win*, 607 P.2d 678)

2. Whitman Heffernan Rhein & Co., a financial advisory company, sued the Griffin Company to recover compensation for services rendered in negotiating the purchase of a business (Resorts International) from Donald Trump. The agreement between Whitman and Griffin had been made orally, but it should have been in writing under the New York statute of frauds. The trial court decided for Griffin, but Whitman appealed. Should the appeals court decide for Whitman? (*Whitman Heffernan Rhein & Co. Inc.* v. *The Griffin Co.,* 557 N.Y.S.2d 342)

3. Jones (appellee) signed a printed contract form agreeing to purchase a house from Long. Long also signed the form. At the time of signing, Jones also made a down payment as evidence of her good faith to go through with the contract. The down payment was to be applied to the purchase price upon completion of the sale of the house. Jones later refused to go through with the contract and ended up suing Long for the return of the down payment. At trial, Jones introduced parol evidence that an understanding existed between Long's agent and her that she could not buy the house unless she sold her house first, and that her house was not sold. Jones won her case at the trial level. Long appealed on the grounds that it was improper for the trial court judge to rule for Jones based on the parol evidence rule regarding the agreement between Long's agent and Jones. Long claims that the contract for the sale of the house had been reduced to writing as the final and complete agreement and parol evidence could not be introduced to alter that agreement in any way. How would you rule in this case? (Court of Appeals of Kentucky, 319 S.W.2d 292)

4. Bratman, an attorney, had a client who was injured in an automobile accident and was being treated by Dr. Healy. Bratman orally promised to pay Healy his medical fees out of the proceeds of any award made to his client as the result of a lawsuit based on the accident if the client did not pay the fees. When the client was awarded $15,000 for his injuries, Bratman refused to pay Healy, invoking the statute of frauds. Can Healy legally hold Bratman liable for his oral promise to pay? (*Healy* v. *Bratman*, 409 N.Y.S.2d 72)

5. Malo, an architect, signed a contract with Gilman to design an office building. Nothing was said in the contract about the size, style, or maximum cost of the building, only an estimated cost. When the bids for the building came in, they were so much more than the estimated cost that Gilman decided not to build the building. He also refused to pay Malo for his services. In court, Gilman tried to introduce evidence that there had been conversations about maximum costs. Malo claimed that this was not possible under the parol evidence rule. Is Malo correct? (*Malo* v. *Gilman*, Ind. 379 N.E.2d 554)

CHAPTER 12

Transfer of Contract Rights and Duties

CHAPTER PREVIEW

Transfer of Rights and Duties
  Assignment—Transfer of Rights
  Delegation—Transfer of Duties
  Rights and Duties That Cannot Be Transferred

Notice of Assignment

Formalities Required for Assignments

Assignment by Law

Rights of the Assignee

Legal Effect of a General Assignment

Chapter Highlights

This chapter focuses on a discussion of the transfer of contract rights and obligations, at some point in time after the contract has been drawn up, to people not originally connected to the contract. You will discover that certain rights and obligations can be transferred freely from one person to another, whereas others can be transferred only with the permission of all parties involved. The chapter points out the responsibilities of those individuals to whom rights and obligations have been transferred. The chapter also points out that some rights may not be transferred if prohibited either by statute or public policy, by the contract itself, or by the courts. You will also learn that in some cases, the transfer is accomplished automatically by law.

TRANSFER OF RIGHTS AND DUTIES

Once two parties enter into a legally enforceable contract, they acquire certain rights and assume certain duties (obligations) under the terms of their contract. Take the following example. Richardson obtained a $5,000 loan from her millionaire uncle, to cover tuition and books the first year of college. She agreed to repay the loan in monthly installments of $200 over the next thirty months. The uncle's right under the contract is to receive the payment from Richardson; his duty under the loan agreement is to deliver $5,000 to Richardson. Richardson's right under the contract is to receive the loan money from her uncle and her duty is to pay back the loan.

The common law of contracts and Article 2 of the UCC dealing with the sale of goods allows the parties to an original contract (e.g., Richardson and her millionaire uncle Albert) to transfer their rights and obligations in that contract to other people through an assignment or a delegation. The sections that follow discuss how an assignment and delegation legally occur.

Assignment—Transfer of Rights

assignment   transfer of contract rights from one person to another

assignor   one who transfers a contract right to another

assignee   one to whom a contract right is transferred

obligor   one obligated to pay money or complete an act for another under a contract

A party to a contract may legally transfer her or his rights under the contract by an **assignment**. The person transferring the rights is called the **assignor**. The person to whom the rights are transferred is called the **assignee**. The assignee is a third person who is not a party to the original contract. In the previous example, suppose that Albert owed Clayton $6,000 and that Albert transferred to Clayton the right to receive the monthly payments of $200 from Richardson. This transaction would be called an assignment. After receiving notice of the assignment, Richardson would be required to make the monthly payments directly to Clayton as noted in Figure 12.1. In this agreement, Richardson's status is that of obligor, whereas Albert would be the assignor, and Clayton the assignee. An **obligor** is a party to a contract who is required to perform for another by paying money or by completing an act.

As a general rule, rights may be freely transferred without the permission of the other party to the contract. Therefore, in the example, Albert does not need Richardson's permission to transfer to Clayton the right to receive Richardson's monthly payments. Rights to the payment of money (e.g., wages, accounts receivable, or royalties on books) and rights to the delivery of goods are the most common types of rights that may be unconditionally assigned without permission of the other party to the contract. After the assignment, the assignor (in this case, Albert) in the example no longer has an interest in the right that was assigned ($10,800 in monthly payments of $200). His contractual right has been *extinguished*. This right now belongs exclusively to the assignee (Clayton). The obligor (the other party to the original contract) now must perform for the assignee (Clayton).

Lending institutions such as banks very often assign (sell) their right to receive monthly loan payments from customers to whom they have lent money to other banks or companies that buy these rights. If you obtain a loan from your bank to purchase household furniture, you may receive notice stating that your bank has assigned its rights to receive payment on the loan to another bank or business and that, when the time comes to make your monthly payments, you must make the payments to that other institution. Why would a bank sell these rights? One reason is because they need liquidity (cash) to help pay off their current expenses. Of course, lending institutions that sell their rights to receive loan money do not receive back all that is owed to them. The receiving institution will only buy these rights if it can make money on the deal.

FIGURE 12.1
An Assignment of Rights

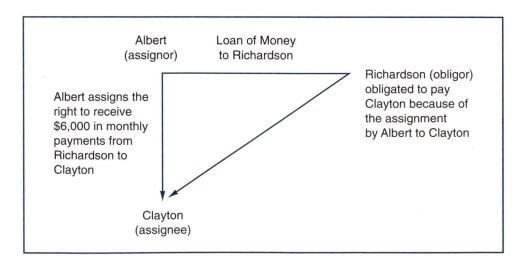

You owed Citizens Bank $20,000, agreeing to make monthly payments to them of $500. You made five monthly payments totaling $2,500 and then received notice that your account has been assigned (sold) to Morgan Central Bank, a much larger bank. Morgan might have offered Citizens Bank $10,000 for the $17,500 you still owed to Citizens, and Citizens accepted the offer because it needed the cash.

Delegation—Transfer of Duties

delegation transfer of performance of one's duty under a contract to another

Although rights under a contract can be assigned, obligations cannot. Obligations under a contract are legally transferred by **delegation**. Unless a clause in the contract prohibits delegation, a party to a contract may ordinarily *delegate* (called the *delegator*) or appoint another person to perform the obligation in her or his place even over the objections of the other party to the contract. The person appointed to perform this obligation (called the delegatee) is, like an assignee, a third person who was not a party to the original contract. Even though the performance of an obligation may be delegated, the *responsibility* for making sure that the obligation is carried out *cannot* be delegated. The delegating party (delegator) continues to be liable for breach of contract if the terms of the contract are not properly carried out or not carried out at all. The delegator is also liable for performance of the contractual duty.

The accounting firm of Anthony, Farrell, and Wise occupied four floors of a large office building. It contracted with Ron's Janitorial Services to clean the offices five evenings a week for the next two years. After the first year, Ron decided to take the summer off and take his family to a resort area. In his absence, he delegated the janitorial services he was performing for the firm and his other customers to a friend who owned Clean Bright Janitorial Services.

obligee person to whom a contractual duty is owed

This example constitutes a delegation of duties, not an assignment. Referring to Figure 12.2, Ron's Janitorial Services is the delegator, and Clean Bright Janitorial Services is the delegatee. The accounting firm is the **obligee**, or the person to whom a contractual duty is owed. Ron is not relieved of his cleaning responsibilities to his customers, including the accounting firm. Should Clean Bright not perform the janitorial duties properly, Ron's firm will be liable as well as Clean Bright.

FIGURE 12.2

An Assignment of Rights

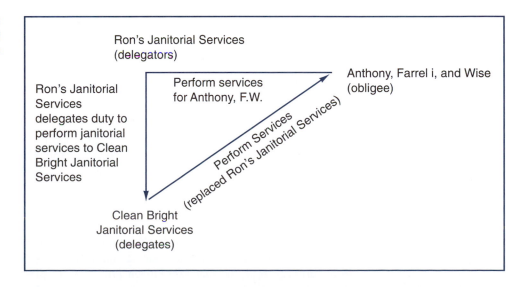

Ron's Janitorial Services (delegators)

Ron's Janitorial Services delegates duty to perform janitorial services to Clean Bright Janitorial Services

Perform services for Anthony, F.W.

Anthony, Farrel i, and Wise (obligee)

Perform Services (replaced Ron's Janitorial Services)

Clean Bright Janitorial Services (delegates)

novation a substitution
of parties within a
contract

The delegator may wish to be completely discharged of his or her duty to perform to an obligee. This may be accomplished through a **novation**, which is a substitution of parties. It would occur if the delegator obtained consent from the obligee to substitute the delegatee in the delegator's place. In the previous example, Ron (delegator) would need to receive consent of the accounting firm (obligee) to substitute Clean Bright (delegatee) in its place. Of course, Clean Bright would also need to consent.

Only obligations that are nonpersonal may be delegated. An obligation is nonpersonal if its performance is standardized and does not depend on a unique skill, knowledge, or talent or is one in which no personal trust or confidence is involved. For example, a building contractor often hires plumbers, electricians, and carpenters and delegates to them the duties of completing certain portions of a building. In these cases, the law presumes that the jobs these people perform are mechanical in nature and can be performed by any qualified person.

Consideration for a delegation is not necessary. If no consideration is given, the delegation is considered a gift from the delegatee to the delegator.

It should be noted that assignments and delegations may take place concurrently.

Rights and Duties That Cannot Be Transferred

Not all contract rights and obligations may be legally transferred. The right to receive a person's services cannot be assigned without the consent of that person. Because a personal relationship may have led to a contract in the first place, it would be unfair to force one party to perform personal services for someone who may be a stranger or may not be agreeable to the obligor. The right to work for someone, for example, is so personal that it cannot be assigned without permission.

You were hired as a swimming instructor at a private club for one year. Six months after you started work, Jason, the owner of the club and your employer, sold the club to Culkins. Jason assigned the remaining six months of your contract to Culkins. Because you signed a contract to work for Jason, Culkins could not require you to work for her without your permission.

In this example, the personal relationship you enjoyed with Jason was affected by the change of employers from Jason (the assignor) to Culkins (the assignee). You are free to choose whether to work for Culkins or to seek employment elsewhere.

Contract obligations that require a special skill or knowledge or that involve personal trust and confidence may not be delegated without permission. The special qualities of a person are often the reason a contract is made. If you make a contract with another person based on your trust and confidence in that person's ability, you are entitled to receive performance from that person and no one else, unless you agree to a substitution.

Members of a profession, such as doctors and lawyers, as well as other individuals such as musicians, artists, athletes, singers, and public speakers, are recognized as having special skills and talents. Individuals in trades, such as plumbers, bricklayers, and carpenters, are not included because the law recognizes that their work can be performed by any other person having the same skills. The skilled person who delegates an obligation under a contract to another person without permission is subject to a lawsuit for breach of contract.

As student senate president at Benton Community College, you signed a contract with The Leftovers, a band, to play for a fundraising concert at the college. The band was chosen because of its national fame and its ability to draw large audiences. One week before the concert, the band leader called and said that because the band was going on a European tour, another well-known group would play at the college. You not only could refuse to accept the services of this other band but could also sue the original band for breach of contract for not performing according to the contract.

Other situations in which rights may not be transferred are if the parties include a strongly worded statement in their contract prohibiting an assignment without consent ("any attempt to assign this contract is absolutely void") or if the assignment is against public policy (e.g., assigning to someone else your right to sue) or is otherwise illegal. Some courts have refused to honor an assignment if the obligor can prove to a court that an assignment would materially alter his or her obligation. For example, you assign an insurance policy on your home to a friend who also owns a home. The policy covers fire, theft, vandalism, and other disasters. Your assignment is void because the condition on which you were issued a policy is based on the risk involved on your home. The risk on your friend's home may not be the same. It may be greater and therefore will materially alter the insurance company's obligation to your friend if he or she files a claim under the terms of the insurance policy originally drawn up on your home. A clause in a contract making it clear that a right is not assignable is usually honored, but some exceptions do occur. For example, a contract cannot prevent an assignment of the right to receive money. The purpose of this exception is to encourage the free flow of money as part of today's modern business practices. State statutes also place some restrictions on assignments. Most states, for example, have laws controlling the assignment of wages to creditors in an effort to protect the wage earner. Another example is a state statute that prohibits the assignment of workers' compensation benefits by a person who has earned these benefits from a job injury.

NOTICE OF ASSIGNMENT

Once a valid assignment of rights has been made, it becomes effective immediately. Legally, giving notice is not required; however, it is advisable to give notice. If no notice is given, the obligor would not know that an assignment had been made and would perform the obligation for the assignee. This lack of notice has some consequences:

1. Full performance before being notified of an assignment releases the obligor from any legal obligation to the assignee.

   Rowley owed $300 to a dermatologist for treatment of a skin problem. The dermatologist, who owed $300 to a local bank, assigned to the bank his right to collect the money from Rowley. Before receiving a notice from the bank, however, Rowley paid the dermatologist in full. The bank cannot legally collect the $300 from Rowley. It must collect from the dermatologist.

2. Part performance before receiving notice of an assignment reduces the obligor's responsibility to the assignee. If, in the preceding example, Rowley had paid the dermatologist $100 before receiving a notice from the bank, the bank could collect only $200 from Rowley. It would have to collect the other $100 from the dermatologist.

After a notice of assignment is received, the obligor must pay or perform for the assignee. Payment or performance to the assignor would not relieve the obligor of the obligation to the assignee. Of course, acceptance of pay or performance by the assignor under these circumstances is a wrongful act. The assignor would be bound to return any benefits received under the assignment to the obligor.

An assignor may either mistakenly or fraudulently assign the same right to two different people. The question arises as to which assignee has better rights. There are several rules used by the courts to resolve the problem. A popular rule most often observed in the United States is the *New York rule,* which allows the first assignee to receive the assignment to receive all the rights. Some states, however, follow the *English rule*, which provides that the first assignee to give notice to the obligor prevails.

A notice of assignment may be oral or written. (A written assignment is preferred because it is more difficult to prove that on oral assignment was made.) If, however, the original contract was in writing as required under a state's statute of frauds, the notice of the assignment must also be in writing. After receiving a notice of assignment, the obligor should contact the assignor to make sure that the assignment was actually made. This step is especially important if the obligor does not know the assignee.

FORMALITIES REQUIRED FOR ASSIGNMENTS

An assignment needs no special format. Any oral or written words that clearly indicate a person's intent to make an assignment are sufficient. It is always best to put an assignment in writing. This writing may be made on a separate paper or on the back of a written contract containing the rights to be assigned. An example of an informal written assignment is shown in Figure 12.3.

Sometimes a written assignment is required by the terms of the contract or by a state statute (as is the case with wage assignments). If the *original contract* was required to be in writing under a state's statute of frauds, the assignment must also be in writing. An example of a formal written assignment is shown in Figure 12.4.

Consideration is not required to have a valid assignment. If the assignee gives up consideration in exchange for the contract right, the legal relationship between the assignor and assignee is based on contract. If the assignee gives no consideration, the assignment is based on a gift. A gift assignment occurs, for example, when a parent assigns money from a stock fund to a child as a holiday gift.

ASSIGNMENT BY LAW

Most assignments are made voluntarily. When a person dies, however, his or her nonpersonal rights and obligations are transferred automatically by law to an executor or administrator (an individual who handles a deceased person's property).

> Marlowe owed Jordan $250. Jordan died before Marlowe could repay the loan. The right to collect the $250 from Marlowe was assigned by law to Jordan's executor or administrator.

If a person owes money when he or she dies, the responsibility for paying that debt is also assigned to the person's executor or administrator.

Nonpersonal rights and obligations are assigned or delegated automatically by law to a trustee when a person becomes bankrupt. Bankruptcy (discussed in Chapter 41) legally excuses the borrower from paying certain debts. Rights the borrower has against others, however, are first collected by the trustee to help pay off the outstanding debts.

RIGHTS OF THE ASSIGNEE

When rights under a contract are assigned, the assignee receives exactly the same rights that the assignor had before the assignment took place. It is said that the assignee "steps into the shoes of the assignor." This saying means that if the obligor has a valid excuse for not performing for the assignor under the original contract, the same excuse is also good against the assignee.

FIGURE 12.3

Informal Assignment of
a Contract Right

FDIC
Federal Deposit Insurance Corporation   New York Region

August 5, 2009

Dear Mortgage Holder:

On August 1, 2009, the rights of your mortgage loan were
transferred from Monroe Savings Bank, Buffalo, New York, to
Manufacturers and Traders Trust Company (M & T Bank), Buffalo,
New York. This transfer does not affect or alter the original
terms of your mortgage loan in any way.

All future mortgage payments should be made payable to
M & T Bank and mailed to the following address:

M & T Bank
PO Box 92814
Buffalo, NY 14692-8914

If you should have any questions about this transfer, please
call M & T Bank, Loan Operations, at (716) 555-3250.

Sincerely,

R Peter Morrow

R. Peter Morrow
Manager
M & T Branch Bank

You purchased your college ring for $250 on thirty days' credit from a local jewelry store selected to sell the rings for your college. The jeweler persuaded you to buy a particular ring because she said that it was 18-karat gold. Actually, the jeweler knew that the ring was only 10-karat gold. A few days after the sale, the jeweler assigned her claim against you for the $250 to a creditor. You discovered that the jeweler had lied about the quality of the ring and refused to pay. As you refused to pay the jeweler because of her deliberate misstatement (fraud), you can also legally refuse to pay the assignee.

The assignor does not guarantee that the obligor will perform after the assignment is made. The assignor does, however, guarantee that the right exists and that it is a legally enforceable claim against the obligor. If the obligor has a valid legal excuse for not

Know all Men by these Presents:

That, *on this*   Tenth   *day of*   May   ,20–

I, JANET JONES of 1419 Scott Street, Tempe, Arizona,

party of the first part;

for and in consideration of the sum of - - - ONE ($1.00) - - - - - - - - - *Dollar*

and other good and valuable considerations, the receipt whereof is hereby acknowledged, have sold,
and by these presents do sell, grant, assign, convey, transfer, set over and deliver unto

JASON HUNTER of 3640 Grandin Road, Tempe, Arizona, party of the
second part, all my right, title, and interest to moneys due me
from Roger Sing of 125 Mt. Vernon Street, Tempe, Arizona, for his
purchase of my camping and hiking equipment on April 12, 20--,
and for which he agreed to pay two hundred dollars ($200.00) on
or before June 1, 20--.

In Witness Whereof, the said party of the first part ha s hereunto set her
hand and seal the day and year first above written.

Signed, Sealed and Delivered   ......Janet Jones................... (L.S.)
    in presence of   ......Lee Mason................... (L.S.)
                                ......John H. Hunter................... (L.S.)

performing, the assignee must go back to the assignor to collect on the original claim. In
the previous example, the creditor cannot collect the $250 from you and must therefore
recover the $250 from the jeweler.

If the assignment was made as security for a debt (when, for example, the assignor
owes the assignee money) and the claim is not collectible, the assignor still has the obligation to pay the money to the assignee.

Curry owed McIntyre $500. McIntyre, who owed Ramsey $500, assigned his claim
against Curry to Ramsey. Curry, who was notified of the assignment by Ramsey, was
unable to pay because he was unemployed and was short of funds. Ramsey (the assignee) can collect from McIntyre (the assignor) because Ramsey took the assignment
as security for a debt.

LEGAL EFFECT OF A GENERAL ASSIGNMENT

When a contract is transferred to a third party but contains only language of assignment, the modern view held by the courts is that this wording creates both an assignment of rights and a delegation of duties unless the language or the circumstances indicates the contrary. The UCC fully supports this view. For example, "I John Denver assign my contract (or 'all rights under my contract') with Steve Wilder to Roger Deveny." These statements imply that Deveny, the assignee, receives all the rights under the terms of the contract that Denver had, but also that Deveny would be responsible for performing the duties that were required to be performed by Denver, the assignor. Denver also remains liable if Deveny fails to perform the duties required under the original contract between Denver and Wilder.

Summary

Parties to a contract may transfer their rights and obligations to other people through an assignment or delegation. An assignment involves the transfer of contract rights. A delegation involves the appointment of another to perform one's duties under a contract.

When an assignment is made, the assignee receives exactly the same rights that the assignor had before the assignment took place. Thus, if the obligor has a valid excuse for not performing for the assignor under the original contract, the same excuse is also good against the assignee. Nonpersonal rights under a contract can be legally assigned without the obligor's permission, whereas rights to receive personal services may not be assigned without the consent of the person who is to perform the services. Rights also may not be transferred if the parties include a provision in their contract prohibiting an assignment, if the assignment is against public policy or otherwise illegal, if the assignment would violate a statute, or if a court disallowed the transfer.

In a delegation, only the performance of an obligation is transferred; the delegating party is still responsible for its proper performance. Duties that require a special skill, knowledge, or talent may not be delegated without permission of the person who is to receive the services.

An assignment may be oral or written, unless a written assignment is required by the terms of the contract or by state statute. Until notice of an assignment is received, the obligor can legally perform for the assignor. Once a proper notice of assignment is received, however, the obligor must pay or perform for the assignee. A notice of assignment may be oral or written, unless a state's statute of frauds requires that it be in writing. When a contract is transferred to a third party but contains only language of assignment, the modern view held by the courts is that this wording creates both an assignment of rights and a delegation of duties.

Important Legal terms

assignee	delegation	obligor
assignment	novation	
assignor	obligee	

Questions and Problems for Discussion

1. Mr. Long executed the following legal document: "In consideration for goods sold to me on account by George Northman, I hereby transfer to George Northman all claims I may have against H. Hall arising from his debt of $1,500 to me."

   (signed) Thomas Long
   March 21, 2004

a. Who is the assignor?

b. Who is the assignee?

c. Why is Mr. Northman a party to this document?

d. Why is H. Hall a party to this document?

2. On August 1, Sodus Fisheries contracted in writing to deliver to Boston Markets 2,000 pounds of lobsters at $5 a pound. The lobsters were to be delivered on October 1, with payment to follow on November 1. On August 7, Sodus Fisheries entered into a contract with the Maine Lobster Company under the following conditions: "Sodus Fisheries assigns all rights under its contract with Boston Markets dated August 1 to the Maine Lobster Company." Would this agreement also create a delegation of duties?

3. Majors owes Johnson $1,000. Johnson transfers to another city because of her job. Majors is unable to pay Johnson before she (Johnson) leaves so Johnson gives Anderson a note stating, "I hereby give you the right to collect and retain $1,000 owed to me by Majors. (signed) Johnson." Anderson presents the note to Majors and requests payment of the $1,000. Majors refuses to pay on the ground that this note cannot be used as a notice of assignment, claiming that it is too informal. Majors insists on a letter that is sworn to before a notary public. Can Majors refuse to pay because the note is too informal?

4. Nichols paid a bribe of $50,000 to Galvin, the mayor of a large city, to "look the other way" while Nichols brought drugs from out of the country by airplane into the city's airport for transport to other cities. The mayor accepted the bribe and gave an order for police not to intervene in the project. Once the bribe was paid, Galvin turned the money and the plan over to the FBI and had Nichols arrested. Nichols was tried and convicted of a felony (bribery) and sentenced to prison. Shortly after his conviction, Nichols assigned the money in writing to Barber, a close friend. Barber attempted to collect the money from the FBI on the basis of the assignment to him but was refused payment. The FBI claimed that regardless of his status as an assignee, Barber was not legally entitled to the money. Do you agree with the FBI?

5. On June 2, Sibley Co. assigned to the HMCK Bank for $70,000 its entire interest in a $75,000 account receivable due in sixty days from Farmer. On June 4, HMCK Bank notified Farmer of the assignment. On June 7, Farmer informed HMCK that Sibley Co. had committed fraud in the transaction out of which the account receivable arose and that payment would not be made to HMCK. Should HMCK begin an action against Farmer? If Farmer is able to prove Sibley Co. acted in a fraudulent manner, can he successfully assert fraud as a defense?

6. The Marco Roofing Company entered into a written contract to put a new roof on Beldon's house. The contract stated that "an assignment of the contract would render the contract void." After completing the roofing job but before any payment was made by Beldon, the Marco Roofing Company, despite the written clause prohibiting an assignment, assigned its right to payment from Beldon to the First National Bank. Can the First National Bank enforce payment of the contract against Beldon?

7. LeBaron was a CPA (certified public accountant) hired by Rochester Copier, a small retail business that sold office equipment, to examine its financial records and make recommendations to the owners. LeBaron discovered that due to several other commitments, the examination could not be completed for several months. Therefore, without consulting Rochester, LeBaron sent Yancy, an equally competent CPA, to examine Rochester's records. Must Rochester accept the services of Yancy?

8. Cancho assigned to Plonski the right to collect $500 from Pitt. Pitt, who was not notified of the assignment, paid the $500 to Cancho. Can Plonski collect the $500 from Pitt?

9. Forman, a star player for a major league baseball team, was engaged to speak at a sports banquet sponsored by a veterans' organization in a large city. One week before the banquet, Forman learned that he was scheduled to make a television appearance on a major network on the same night as the banquet. Forman offered to send an equally well-known player from his team. The veterans' club refused to permit this substitution and canceled the sports banquet. Could the organization legally cancel the banquet and sue Forman for breach of contract?

10. Egan owed Terry, a pilot, $500 for flying lessons. Terry assigned his claim against Egan to Ross. Before Ross had notified Egan of the assignment, Egan paid Terry $250 on account. May Ross still recover the $500 from Egan?

Cases for Review

1. Mack, a dealer, sold Hudgens a used car on credit. At the time of the sale, Mack fraudulently informed Hudgens that the car was in good condition; in fact, the car needed extensive repairs. When Hudgens attempted to return the car to Mack within the thirty-day guarantee period, Mack refused to take the car back. In the meantime, Mack had assigned Hudgens's contract to Universal CIT Credit Corp. When Hudgens refused to pay on the contract, Universal CIT sued him. Hudgens's defense was that he had the right to set aside the contract based on fraud. Was Hudgens correct? (*Universal CIT Credit Corporation* v. *Hudgens*, 356 S.W.2d 658)

2. Siler agreed to complete a project for Mountain Bell. To finance the project, Siler borrowed money from First National. As security for the loan, Siler assigned to First National his right to collect from Mountain Bell upon completion of the project. First National never notified Mountain Bell of the assignment. Consequently, Mountain Bell did not pay First National when the money was due but instead paid Siler. First National then sued Mountain Bell for that same payment. Is Mountain Bell obligated to pay First National after it has already paid Siler? (*First National Bank of Rio Arriba* v. *Mountain States Telephone & Telegraph Co.*, 571 P.2d 118)

3. Smith owned several condominiums which he offered for sale. Each purchaser was required under the terms of Smith's contract to assume the responsibility to pay, among other things, taxes. Smith assigned (sold) his interest in these condominiums to Roberts, who failed to pay the taxes on the units according to the terms of the contract. Roberts claims that in purchasing Smith's interest she was acquiring only the right to collect payments from individual purchasers, but not the duty to pay taxes. The contract of sale, however, expressly stated that the provisions would bind the "successors and assigns," and Roberts was aware of these provisions, including the payment of taxes. Roberts was sued by her purchasers of these condominiums compelling her to pay the taxes. The question is whether the court should require Roberts to assume the duty to pay these taxes as part of the assignment made to her by Smith. What do you think? (6 Utah, 2d 314, 313 P2d 465)

4. Greer purchased property from Lancaster. Greer made a cash payment and entered into a credit contract with Lancaster for the remainder of the purchase price. Greer assigned this contract to someone else, and Lancaster sued to have the assignment invalidated. Was the contract assignable? (*Lancaster* v. *Greer*, Tex. 572 S.W.2d 787)

5. Mr. and Mrs. Ehrens separated. According to their separation agreement, Mr. Ehrens was to pay his wife support payments of $600 per month. Mrs. Ehrens assigned the right to receive the money to Elkin. Mr. Ehrens stopped making the support payments, claiming that the right to receive the money could not be assigned. Elkin sued. Was Elkin legally entitled to the money? (*Elkin* v. *Ehrens*, 43 Misc. 2d 493, 251, N.Y.S.2d 560)

6. Basic Construction Co. signed a contract to build some buildings for the State University of New York. Basic hired Stone as supervising architect. One of Stone's duties was to personally arbitrate disputes that might arise between Basic Construction Company and the state of New York. A subcontractor sued both Basic and Stone on a dispute that had been arbitrated by someone other than Stone. Stone claimed that he could not be held liable because the decision had been made by a person to whom Stone had delegated his duties as arbitrator. Is Stone liable? (*John W. Johnson, Inc.* v. *Basic Construction Co.*, 292 F.Supp.300)

7. National Commercial Bank issued a credit card to Mr. and Mrs. Eldridge. Mrs. Eldridge used the credit card to make a purchase at Malik's store and by mistake left the card at the store. Before Mrs. Eldridge could return for the card, it disappeared from Malik's possession and was used to make unauthorized purchases of over $3,000. Mr. and Mrs. Eldridge then assigned to the National Commercial Bank all claims that they had against Malik for negligence on the part of Malik in letting the card fall into someone else's hands. Malik claimed that because the Eldridges could be held liable for only $50 for unauthorized use of the credit card, the bank as assignee could also be held liable for only $50. Is Malik correct? (*National Commercial Bank and Trust Co.* v. *Malik*, N.Y. 72 Misc. 2d 865)

CHAPTER 13

The Termination of Contracts: Discharge

CHAPTER PREVIEW

How Contracts End	Novation
	Accord and Satisfaction
Discharge by Performance	
Degrees of Performance	**Discharge by Operation of Law**
Performance to the Personal Satisfaction of Another	Impossibility or Impracticability
	Bankruptcy
Discharge by Agreement of the Parties	Statute of Limitations
Rescission	Material Alteration of a Written Contract

Chapter Highlights

Contracts end (terminate) in either of two ways: discharge or breach of contract. Termination by breach is the subject of Chapter 14. This chapter discusses the most important ways in which contracts are discharged, naming full performance as the most common way. Prior to a full discharge of their contract, however, the parties may be in one of many positions. The parties may be in a position where, by law, they must accept slightly less than they agreed to under the terms of the contract. Or by choice or circumstances, they may decide to discharge their original contract and enter into a new agreement with different terms. If the parties wish, they may simply call off the contract because they want to since the contract is impossible to perform or because one of the parties was dishonest.

How Contracts End

Eventually, a valid enforceable contract comes to an end, and the rights and duties that existed under the contract are no longer in effect. A contract ends (terminates) either because one or both parties are discharged from any further obligation under the contract or because one of the parties breached the contract and thus incurred liability to the other party in damages or some form of equitable relief. Discharge by breach of contract is discussed in Chapter 14. Discharge of contracts by performance is the subject of this chapter. The various methods of discharge are shown in Figure 13.1

Discharge by Performance

A contract is usually discharged by performance; that is, the parties have fulfilled their duties under the terms of the contract as promised. Performance must take place at the time and place stated in the contract. If no time is stated, the contract by law must be completed within a reasonable time. As is often the case, the definition of "reasonable" is sometimes left to the courts to decide.

FIGURE 13.1 Contracts Discharged

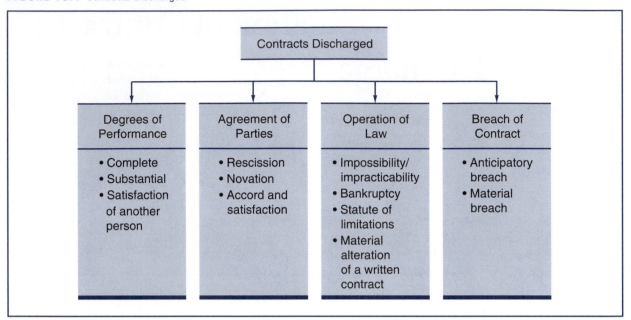

Performance may be the doing of an act such as ending construction of a condominium complex, or the paying of money. The offer by one party—who is ready, willing, and able to perform—to another party to perform an obligation to the terms of the contract is called a **tender of performance**. If the other party refuses to allow the tendering party to perform the act required, the contract is generally discharged and that other party becomes liable for breach of contract.

tender of performance
offer to perform obligations of a contract

The Charisma Remodeling Company signed a contract to remodel MacLean's kitchen. The first day that the company employees appeared on the job to begin work, MacLean refused to let them begin work because he had changed his mind about doing any remodeling. This refusal by MacLean discharged the contract and Charisma was no longer obligated to perform. In addition to not being required to perform, Charisma has a legal claim against MacLean for breach of contract.

When the tendering party (the debtor) is required to pay a sum of money and the other party refuses the debtor's offer to pay, the refusal does not discharge the contract. The refusal does, however, excuse the debtor from paying any interest charges or court costs in the event of a lawsuit. The debtor, however, must be ready to pay the money at any time.

Degrees of Performance

Full performance is the most common method by which contracts are discharged. A contract is discharged by **full performance** when both parties do all that they agreed to do under the terms of the contract.

full performance when both parties do all they agreed to do under a contract

You hired Quigley to rebuild the motor in your car for $350. Quigley satisfactorily completed the job and you paid him $350. Because both Quigley and you fully performed, the contract was discharged.

substantial performance performance in good faith of all but the minor details of a contract

The law does not always require full (complete) performance of a contract; it will allow minor deviations. This type of performance, called **substantial performance**, is slightly less than full performance. (Courts sometimes say 95 percent or better performance.) A person who substantially performs has, in good faith, fulfilled all the major requirements of the contract, leaving only minor details incomplete. One standard often applied to building contracts is that substantial performance means the building should be usable for the purpose intended. Consequently, the courts will permit the party who performed to recover the contract price less the amount needed to correct any defects in the performance. Recovery is permitted because it would be unfair to deny all payment when the performance is essentially complete. Recovery under the common law doctrine of substantial performance is more often applied to construction contracts than to sales contracts.

> A building contractor agreed in writing to build Stern a house for $150,000. When the house was completed, Stern discovered that the front and back doors were not hung properly and that the bookcase in the family room was not flush against the wall. The contractor was not deliberately negligent but was behind schedule and failed to correct the defects. Stern hired a carpenter to make the changes at a cost of $1,000. Because the house was substantially completed and the defects were minor, the contractor can collect $150,000 less the $1,000 paid to the carpenter.

It might also happen that one party made minor deviations contrary to the terms of the contract. If, in the preceding example, the contractor used less expensive light fixtures and different designs than those called for in the building contract because the required fixtures were not immediately available, Stern would still be required to pay the contractor the $150,000 and could not subtract the cost paid to install the correct fixtures.

Substantial performance, however, does not apply to contracts calling for the payment of money. If you borrow $1,000 with interest for ninety days, you cannot repay $995 plus the interest. You must repay the full $1,000 plus interest.

Performance to the Personal Satisfaction of Another

The contract you enter may require, as a condition, that your performance personally satisfy the other party to the contract. Normally, satisfaction means performing to the expectations of a reasonable person (at least substantial performance). If a personal satisfaction clause is inserted in a contract by the parties, or the court in a particular state requires personal satisfaction (meaning complete in every detail to the party's liking), the party making the personal judgement must act in good faith, and may not object to performance simply to avoid carrying out his or her part of the bargain.

> Colts, CEO of a large manufacturing company, made a special trip to New York City to order three made-to-order suits from a world-renowned tailor at a cost of $3,000 per suit. The specifications were dark blue, medium grey, and brown; imported wool; four buttons; narrow lapels; one-half inch cuff on pants; tight fit; no break in the pant (fitted to the top of the shoe); silver buttons on the blue and grey suits and gold on the brown suit. The agreement with the tailor stated that the suits, when completed, must be to the full satisfaction of the customer. Colts, according to the agreement, would make the final decision as to whether the suits were acceptable.

DISCHARGE BY AGREEMENT OF THE PARTIES

At the time they are made, some contracts state exactly when they will end. Such a contract would be discharged by mutual agreement on the specified date. In other contracts, the parties mutually agree to release each other on the happening of a certain event, even though the intended performance by one or both parties has not been completed. If the contract is completely executory, the release of one party is the consideration for the release of the other party.

Brody agreed in writing to act as a chauffeur for Eastman for two years. Both parties changed their minds before Brody started work and mutually agreed to cancel the contract. This executory contract was thus discharged.

Another way that a contract ends through agreement is that the parties may make a new agreement that will discharge or modify the obligations of one or both parties under the original agreement. The new agreement could take the form of a rescission, a novation, or an accord and satisfaction.

Rescission

rescind to cancel a contract and return parties to the position that existed prior to the making of the contract

The parties may mutually agree to call off the contract before either party has performed and revert back to the position they were in prior to forming their agreement. To call it off legally means to **rescind** the contract. In plain English, it means forget it. The mutual rescission is binding as long as each party agrees to give up the consideration received, which is the promised performance of the other party. If one party has already performed his or her part of the agreement, a request by the other party to cancel would not be enforceable because the performing party has received no consideration for the request to call off the original contract. Additional consideration would need to be offered by the party attempting to end the contract.

You entered into a contract with Flannigan, owner of Kitchen's Unlimited, to completely remodel your kitchen for $20,000 and made a down payment of $2,000. Before starting the project, Flannigan asked to be relieved from the contract. Since you were able to hire another contractor, you agreed to release Flannigan from his obligation to work for you, and Flannigan agreed to return your $2,000. This was a case of mutual rescission and the original contract between Flannigan and you was discharged.

Novation

novation substitution of a new party for one of the original parties to a contract

After entering into a contract, the parties may agree to release one party from the obligation to perform. A new, third party would be substituted who would then assume this obligation by means of a novation. In a **novation**, the original contract is actually terminated and a new contract formed between the remaining party to the original contract and the new party. The other terms of the new contract generally remain the same as those in the original contract. This substitution requires the consent of both original parties and the new, third party.

Just before completing law school, Vincent purchased a set of law books from the Laramie Law Book Company. Vincent signed a contract to make monthly payments over a two-year period. Six months later, Vincent discovered that he could not keep up the monthly payments. Washington, Vincent's college roommate, agreed to assume responsibility for the payments. The Laramie Law Book Company agreed to cancel its contract with Vincent and enter into a new contract with Washington. This substitution of parties is a novation.

Accord and Satisfaction

accord agreement to accept performance different from that in original contract

An **accord** is an agreement by one party in an original contract to accept from the other party performance that is different from the performance agreed on in the original contract. Actually, the old contract is breached by one of the parties, and they make a new

satisfaction performance of the terms of a new agreement resulting from an accord

substitute contract new contract entered into to replace a contract before a breach occurs

contract. **Satisfaction** is the actual performance of the accord. An accord alone is not enough to discharge the original contract. There must be both an accord and a completed satisfaction to discharge the original contract. If the new agreement is made before the original contract is breached, this new agreement is called a **substitute contract**.

> You borrowed $300 from Santos for your college fees. When you were unable to repay the loan when it was due, Santos agreed to accept your stereo set in place of the $300 (the accord). The original agreement was discharged only after Santos received and accepted the stereo set (the satisfaction).

An accord and satisfaction are often used to settle an honest disagreement about the amount of money that a debtor owes to a creditor.

DISCHARGE BY OPERATION OF LAW

Up to this point in the chapter, only the discharge of contracts resulting from the action of one or both parties to the contract has been considered. This section examines how contractual obligations may be discharged by operation of law.

Impossibility or Impracticability

Once a contract has been made, performance may become impossible. Impossibility refers to an unforeseen event that prevents a party from performing a contract as promised. Objective and subjective impossibility, however, must be distinguished. **Objective impossibility** excuses parties from their contractual duties as long as there is proof that the contract absolutely could no longer be performed by either party or by anyone else. In other words, nonperformance is unavoidable. The following situations generally qualify under the common law as objective impossibility to legally discharge contractual obligations:

objective impossibility performance becomes absolutely impossible and therefore unavoidable because of some extreme difficulty

1. Destruction of the subject matter of the contract
2. Death, serious illness, or other incapacity in a personal services contract
3. Change in the law

Destruction of the Subject Matter   If the subject matter that is essential to the performance of the contract is destroyed through no fault of either party, the contract is discharged because there is no way for the contract to be fulfilled. Such a situation is considered an objective impossibility. If the contract had been partly performed before the impossibility arose, the courts usually permit recovery for work performed up to the time of the impossibility.

> The Detrex Company contracted to paint the exterior of Lunt's house for $900. After Detrex had applied one coat of paint, the house was destroyed by fire. The contract was discharged. Detrex could, however, recover for labor and paint used before the fire occurred.

Death or Serious Illness   A personal services contract (a contract involving a person who has special skills and talents, e.g., a rock star) is discharged if the person obligated to perform that personal service dies or becomes seriously ill or disabled.

> Hind, a country music star, was rushed to Rock Memorial Hospital after collapsing from severe stomach pains in his hotel room two hours before his scheduled concert at Arlan College. Hind's serious illness discharged this personal services contract.

Change in the Law   Sometimes a law is passed after a legally constituted contract is made that makes performance illegal. In this case, the contract is discharged. This law could be a local ordinance, a state statute, a court decision, or a government regulation.

> Ibsen contracted to sell Hilton ten cases of fireworks for use at a July 4 celebration. Because of the increasing number of accidents resulting from the use of fireworks, the state passed a law making the sale of fireworks illegal. Because performance of this contract was made impossible by the passage of the state law, the contract was discharged.

Sometimes unforeseen circumstances, such as strikes, fires, insolvency, shortages of materials, riots, droughts, and price increases, arise after the contract has been formed, making performance by one of the parties unreasonably (extremely) difficult but not impossible to perform. In such cases, even though the contract can be performed, the individual required to perform says, "I am unable to fulfill the obligations required in the contract." This situation, referred to as *subjective impossibility*, will not discharge a contract unless there is a contingency clause in the contract.

> Morna, who was to be married in a few months, made arrangements for her wedding reception at Planters' Party House. Planters' was a chain that had Party Houses in several locations. Morna picked one of Planters' three locations in the city in which she lived. Five days before the wedding was scheduled, Morna was notified by the manager of all the Planters' Party Houses in her city that the Party House that she had selected for her wedding had accidentally burned down and that Planters' could no longer accommodate her.

In this example, it was not impossible for Planters' to perform. It could have scheduled the wedding at one of its other city locations, assuming there was room. This case is one of subjective impossibility; consequently, Planters' is not discharged because there was a reasonable opportunity to provide a substitute location. Planters' could have guarded against the risk of fire by including a contingency clause in the contract stating that the contract is discharged and performance excused for circumstances beyond its control.

commercial impracticability
doctrine recognizing those unanticipated events in which performance, while still possible, creates a hardship for the party obligated to perform and as a result discharges the contract

Because of the harshness of the common law rule, modern case law supported by UCC Section 2-615 allows a discharge under the doctrine of **commercial impracticability**, which is a less rigid doctrine than impossibility. This doctrine recognizes those unanticipated events in which performance (while still possible) would be extremely burdensome and would create a hardship for the party obligated to perform. Consequently, performance is excused and the contract is discharged. Although modern law deliberately refrains from listing all possible unanticipated occurrences, the doctrine has been cautiously applied to events that radically alter the original performance in certain cases—for example, those involving severe shortages of raw materials due to an act of God, a war, an embargo, a local crop failure, or an unforeseen shutdown of major sources of supply or that must not have been within the cognizance of the parties when the contract was made. These factors must either have caused a marked increase in price quite disproportionate to what would reasonably have been contemplated (e.g., ten times more than an original estimate) or have precluded the seller totally from obtaining the supplies necessary for his or her performance.

> Alco Oil Co. agreed to supply 3,000 barrels of jet fuel to Monsoon Airlines. Alco's supply of crude oil (the source of jet fuel) from Alaska, however, was cut off because the destruction of equipment used to obtain the oil resulted in a severe shortage. The destruction was caused by a sudden series of earth tremors (act of God). To fulfill

the terms of the contract with Monsoon Airlines, Alco would have to obtain oil from other sources at a price at least ten times the original cost. In these circumstances, Alco may be excused from performance.

Relief on grounds of impracticability is unavailable if a party seeking to be discharged did not employ all due measures to ensure that his or her source would not fail, that he or she willfully did something to cause the event to occur, failed to foresee at the time the contract was made that the event could happen (negligence), or agreed in the contract to assume an obligation to perform despite impracticability. The common law rule is opposed to the concept of commercial impracticability, claiming that it weakens the stability of a contract.

Bankruptcy

A person who is hopelessly in debt may resort to bankruptcy to be relieved of many, but not all, of those contract debts. Bankruptcy technically does not discharge a debt. It simply prevents a creditor from suing to collect the money from a person who has more contract debts than money to pay them. Bankruptcy is discussed in Chapter 36.

Statute of Limitations

statute of limitations
law fixing a time limit within which lawsuits must be started

All states have a **statute of limitations**, which fixes a time limit within which a lawsuit must be filed after a contract has been breached. This time limit varies greatly from state to state (Table 13.1). After the time limit has passed, any action for breach of contract is outlawed, or barred, by statute. The contract is not discharged, but the legal means to enforce the contract is lost. What this generally means is that a valid claim filed after the statute has expired is usually denied. The person responsible for the breach may, after the right of action is outlawed, choose to fulfill the contract but is not legally obligated to do so. Many states permit the debt to be revived if a new promise is made in writing or there is evidence of partial performance. The following examples bring out these points.

It is important to determine when the contract is legally breached. In the case of money owed, the time of the breach is figured from the due date of the debt.

Your doctor charged you $150 for a physical examination made on March 3, 2004. She requested full payment within thirty days (by April 2, 2004). The doctor tried to collect from you and then, on July 1, 2010, finally sued you to recover the money. The statute of limitations in your state was six years. Because the doctor had only until April 1, 2010, to collect from you, she is barred from suing you after that date.

Collection agencies sometimes aggressively try to collect by threatening to sue even after the statute of limitations has expired. If an agency follows this practice, it has probably violated the federal Fair Debt Collection Practices Act (FDCPA).

If the borrower makes a voluntary part payment after the due date, the time limit under the statute starts all over again from the date of this part payment.

Maytag borrowed $500 from Ziegler on September 4, 2000, and promised in writing to repay the loan in full one year later (by September 4, 2001). Maytag, who was unemployed, failed to repay the loan on the due date. He did, however, make a part payment of $300 to Ziegler on September 4, 2002. Because of the part payment, Ziegler has until September 4, 2008, to file a lawsuit to collect the $200.

If the borrower makes a part payment on a debt or promises in writing to repay a debt barred by the statute of limitations, the creditor's right to collect this debt is legally

TABLE 13.1   LIMITATIONS FOR CIVIL ACTIONS FOR BREACH OF ORDINARY CONTRACT[A]

STATE	TIME LIMIT (YEARS) WRITTEN	TIME LIMIT (YEARS) ORAL	STATE	TIME LIMIT (YEARS) WRITTEN	TIME LIMIT (YEARS) ORAL
Alabama	6	6	Montana	8	5
Alaska	3	3	Nebraska	5	4
Arizona	6	3	Nevada	6	4
Arkansas	5	3	New Hampshire	3	3
California	4	2	New Jersey	6	6
Colorado	6	6	New Mexico	6	4
Connecticut	6	3	New York	6	6
Delaware	3	3	North Carolina	3	3
District of Columbia	3	3	North Dakota	6	6
Florida	5	4	Ohio	15	6
Georgia	6	4	Oklahoma	5	3
Hawaii	6	6	Oregon	6	6
Idaho	5	4	Pennsylvania	4	4
Illinois	10	5	Rhode Island	10	10
Indiana	10[b]	6	South Carolina	3	3
Iowa	10	5	South Dakota	6	6
Kansas	5	3	Tennessee	6	6
Kentucky	15	5	Texas	4	4
Louisiana	10	10	Utah	6	4
Maine	6	6	Vermont	6	6
Maryland	3	3	Virginia	5	3
Massachusetts	6	6	Washington	6	3
Michigan	6	6	West Virginia	10	5
Minnesota	6	6	Wisconsin	6	6
Mississippi	3	3	Wyoming	10	8
Missouri	10	5			

[a]Does not include sales contracts under UCC Section 2-725.
[b]Six years if contract is for payment of money.

reinstated. In this case, the statute starts over again as of the date of the part payment or written promise.

On September 8, 1992, one of your debts for $200 was outlawed by the six-year statute of limitations in your state. You paid the creditor $50 on December 31, 1992, and promised to pay the remainder of the debt ($150) in three weeks. When you failed to pay the balance as promised, the creditor sued. The $50 payment on December 31, 1992, reinstated the right of the creditor to collect the balance of $150 until December 31, 1998.

If the party to be sued leaves the state (e.g., by entering the armed forces or transferring to a new job) or is under a disability (e.g., by being confined to a prison or mental institution), the time spent away from the state or under the disability is not counted in determining whether the debt is outlawed by a statute of limitations. The statute begins to run again when and if the debtor returns to the state or is no longer under the disability. Extending the statute in this way is called *tolling*.

Galvin retained an attorney to represent him in a lawsuit. The lawyer submitted her bill for $500 on April 1, 1990, payable immediately. Galvin paid the attorney $75. On April 10, 1990, Galvin moved out of the state to begin a new job. When the attorney later discovered that Galvin had returned to the state on May 8, 1997, she brought an action to collect the balance of $425. Galvin refused to pay, claiming that the debt had been outlawed. Because the time between April 10, 1990, and May 8, 1997, did not count, the debt was still legally collectible. (The time runs from May 8, 1997.)

The statute of limitations is sometimes unfair to creditors. Borrowers legally owe the money, and creditors are entitled to be paid. On the other hand, an unreasonable delay in bringing legal action makes it more difficult for a borrower to prove the facts. Evidence may be lost or destroyed, and witnesses may have relocated to another state or may have died.

The Uniform Commercial Code, Section 2-725, provides a four-year statute of limitations for contracts involving the sale of goods. (This topic is discussed in Chapter 15.) In 2003, UCC 2-725 was amended by adding a provision extending the limitation period up to one additional year.

Material Alteration of a Written Contract

If one party to a contract deliberately makes a material change in its terms without the permission of the other party, the contract is discharged. This change in the terms of the contract is called **alteration**. An alteration is material if the rights or duties of the parties are changed.

alteration deliberate material change in a contract by one party without consent

> You signed a contract with Element K to take a desktop publishing course at a cost of $2,000. The person who interviewed you at Element K did not give you, nor did you ask for, a copy of the contract. Because the interviewer received a commission for each signed contract, she changed the cost on your contract to $2,500. When you discovered the alteration, you had the legal right to terminate the contract and could not be sued for breach of contract.

Summary

Contracts come to an end (terminate) in either of two ways: discharge or breach of contract. When a contract terminates, the rights and duties that existed under the contract are no longer in effect. This chapter concentrated on a termination of contracts by discharge.

Contracts may be discharged by performance, by agreement of the parties, and by operation of law. Performance may be either full or substantial. Substantial performance is slightly less than full performance. (Some courts demand 95 percent or better.) If the parties agree to a discharge at a certain time, the time will generally be stated in the contract, or the parties may instead agree to a discharge through release (at a stated time or upon the happening of a certain event), rescission, novation, or accord and satisfaction. The law excuses the parties from their performance under a contract because of objective impossibility. Unforeseen and unpredictable hardships that occur after the contract is made and simply make performance more difficult do not meet the definition of objective impossibility. A contingency clause would have to be placed in a contract to discharge it for such hardships. The law recognizes only the following situations as reasons to discharge a contract because of objective impossibility: destruction of the subject matter; death, serious illness, or other incapacity in a personal services contract; and change in the law. Because of the harshness of the common law rule, modern case law allows a discharge under the doctrine of commercial impracticability. The statute of limitations or a proceeding in bankruptcy may become the reason for discharging a contract if the debtor cannot afford to pay. In these cases, creditors are prohibited from bringing court action against the borrower to enforce the contract and pay what is owed. Under the rules of bankruptcy, some money is recoverable as part of the discharge. Bankruptcy will be discussed in detail in Chapter 36. Finally, if a court finds evidence that a contract has deliberately been changed in any material way by one party without the consent of the other party, it will excuse performance by the nonconsenting party based on the legal concept of alteration.

Important Legal terms

accord

alteration

commercial impracticability

full performance

novation

objective impossibility

rescind

satisfaction

statute of limitations

substantial performance

substitute contract

tender of performance

Questions and Problems for Discussion

1. How does commercial impracticability change the way that contracts are discharged because they are too difficult to perform? Is commercial impracticability a common law or statutory doctrine?

2. Generally, in an action for beach of contract involving the payment of money, the statute of limitations time period would be computed from the date the
   a. contract is signed.
   b. contract is negotiated.
   c. contract is breached.
   d. parties agree on date.

3. Martinson purchased some real estate from the American Realty Company. He paid 25 percent down and signed papers giving American a twenty-year mortgage on the property. After five years, Martinson defaulted (couldn't pay). Martinson's friend Bloomingdale became interested in the property and agreed to assume Martinson's obligation under the terms of the mortgage as it was written, which was acceptable to American Realty. Bloomingdale then paid off the past due mortgage payments plus some other fees, and in turn, American Realty accepted him as the new owner and the person who would continue to make the mortgage payments. American Realty then discharged Martinson from the mortgage contract. What was the legal doctrine used to discharge Martinson from his obligation under the terms of the mortgage?

4. Vance, a peanut grower, entered into an agreement to provide 2,000 pounds of peanuts to Timmons, a peanut processor. Severe rains, however, caused flooding and destroyed the peanut crop to be supplied by Vance. Vance argued that his contract with Timmons was discharged. He claimed that because the subject matter of the contract (the peanuts) was destroyed, he could not deliver the product as initially promised. Do you agree that the contract was discharged?

5. Brite hired Flannigan to re-create a lighthouse scene and its surroundings based on an actual lighthouse that existed in a small town close to a large body of water. The contract was conditioned on her (Brite's) personal satisfaction that the painting represented the actual scene. Upon completion of the painting, Brite admitted that the painting was perfect but rejected it because she was out of money. Can Flannigan sue for breach of contract?

6. LaChase Construction Company contracted to build a house for Archie. When 25 percent of the house was completed, Archie fired LaChase for not following the building plans and because there were several defects in the construction to date. Archie hired another contractor to complete the construction of the house and to correct the defects. LaChase sued Archie for breach of contract, claiming that it had substantially performed the contract at that point in time when it was discharged. Was LaChase correct?

7. Maybe borrowed $10,000 from Quimby and gave Quimby a promissory note for that amount. The due date of the note was September 30. On September 10, Maybe offered and Quimby accepted $8,000 in full satisfaction of the note. On October 7, Quimby demanded that Maybe pay the $2,000 balance on the note. Maybe refused claiming that the $8,000 payment satisfied his obligation to Quimby. Do you agree?

8. Margaret had a large debt that became outlawed under the statute of limitations. Margaret, after inheriting several thousand dollars, e-mailed the creditor and promised to repay the debt. Two

months later, the creditor, who had not yet received any payment, sued Margaret for collection. Is the creditor entitled to payment because of Margaret's promise?

9. In August, The Cooper Manufacturing Co. contracted with Millard Oil Company for the delivery of 75,000 gallons of heating oil at the price of $2.20 per gallon at regularly specified intervals during the upcoming winter season. Due to an unseasonably warm winter, Cooper took delivery on only 65,000 gallons. When Millard sued Cooper for breach of contract, Cooper claimed that it was impossible to complete the contract because of the unseasonably warm weather. Is Cooper liable for breach of contract?

10. Josten, a contractor, agreed in writing to build a warehouse for Blanda according to specific plans. Josten deliberately and without Blanda's consent deviated substantially from the plans. As a result, Blanda refused to pay Josten any money due under the terms of the contract. Josten, claiming substantial performance, contended that he was entitled to the contract price less the amount needed to correct any defects in the performance. Was Josten correct?

Cases for Review

1. Grevas entered into a contract with the Surety Development Corporation to have a prefabricated house built for $16,385. A completion date was set, but according to Grevas, the house was not ready for occupancy on that date. As a result, Grevas refused to pay the balance due. Surety Development then sued for the money, claiming substantial performance. According to testimony at the trial, the house was actually far from finished on the morning of the date it was to be completed. Surety Development Corporation, however, initiated a crash program, with workers all over the place doing whatever was necessary to complete the house by the end of that day. In fact, by day's end, the house was finished and ready for occupancy, with only minor details to be completed. Grevas, who had taken a tour of the premises early in the morning of the completion date set in the contract, remarked that the house could not possibly be completely finished and ready for occupancy by the end of the day. Consequently, he never returned later that day to inspect the premises. Was the Surety Development Corporation entitled to the balance due on the house? (*Surety Development Corp.* v. *Grevas*, 192 N.E.2d 145)

2. Deive signed a contract for membership in a physical fitness program. The contract provided that he was obligated to make payments whether he participated in the program or not. Deive had a lung ailment when he signed the contract but never mentioned it to the operators of the program. After he had signed the contract, Deive's doctor told him that participation in the program would be dangerous to his health. Deive tried to cancel the contract and refused to pay his fees. The plaintiff sued for breach of contract. Can Deive cancel the contract based on impossibility of performance? (*Trans-State Investments, Inc.* v. *Deive*, 262 A.2d 119)

3. The LaCumbre Golf and Country Club contracted to extend membership privileges, including use of its golf course, to guests of the Santa Barbara Hotel for $300 per month. When the hotel was totally destroyed by fire and no longer able to take in guests, it stopped making monthly payments on a contract it had with the country club. LaCumbre then sued the hotel to recover the balance owed on the contract. During a court trial, the hotel contended that the destruction of its building excused further performance of its responsibilities under the contract. Is the hotel correct? (*LaCumbre Golf and Country Club* v. *Santa Barbara Hotel Co.*, Cal. 271 P. 476)

4. Sugarhouse sued Anderson for nonpayment of a promissory note and obtained a judgment against him for $2,423.86. For two years, Anderson had financial difficulties and couldn't pay the judgment. When he learned that he could get a loan to help him pay a portion of the judgment, he reached an agreement with Sugarhouse to pay $2,200 in full settlement of the judgment. Anderson then gave Sugarhouse a check for $2,200. Before the check was cashed, however, Sugarhouse found out that Anderson had some property that he was about to sell. Sugarhouse then refused to go through with the settlement. Anderson asked the court to enforce the settlement agreement he had made with Sugarhouse. Will

Anderson succeed? (*Sugarhouse Finance Co.* v. *Anderson*, Utah 610 P.2d 1369)

5. Bergman, a contractor, sued Parker, a builder, for breach of their contract to construct an apartment building. Parker contended that the contract was terminated by impossibility because he was unable to obtain a building permit. He refused to go ahead with the construction. At the trial, however, Bergman introduced evidence to show that Parker could have obtained a building permit by making modifications, which were acceptable to Bergman, to his building plans. Should Bergman's suit be successful? (*Bergman* v. *Parker*, D.C. 216 A.2d, 581)

6. Joseph Goldberg, Inc., a builder, contracted to build a theater for Fisher. The U.S. Fidelity and Guaranty Company guaranteed completion. After work had been started on the building, it was stopped by order of the commissioner of buildings because of a local ordinance that prohibited the construction of a theater within 200 feet of a church. Fisher then sued U.S. Fidelity as guarantor for breach of contract. U.S. Fidelity contended that the contract was terminated because

of an impossibility to perform. Is U.S. Fidelity correct under the common law rule? (*Fisher* v. *United States Fidelity and Guaranty Company*, 212 Ill. App. 66, 39 N.E.2d 67)

7. L and E Facto rented a banquet hall owned by Pantagis Enterprises for a wedding reception at a cost of $10,578, paid in advance. A clause in the contract excused Pantagis from performing due to an act of God, or other unforeseen events. A power failure occurred in the area around the banquet hall soon after the reception got under way. As a result, the lights and air conditioning went off, which caused problems for the band and the videographer taking pictures. Heat caused the guests to be unbearably warm and uncomfortable, and it led to a fight between an employee and a guest. The police were called and they evacuated the hall. The Factos sued for breach of contract to include a return of their prepayment and money to cover the money paid to the band and the videographer. Are they entitled to money damages for breach of contract as requested? (*Facto* v. *Pantagis*, 390 NJ Super. 227 915 A.2d 59)

CHAPTER 14

The Termination of Contracts: Breach of Contract

CHAPTER PREVIEW

Breach of Contract	Fraud
	Duress
Remedies for Breach of Contract	Undue Influence
Legal Remedies	Mistake
Equitable Remedies	
	Remedies for Fraud, Duress, and Undue Influence
Defenses for a Breach of Contract Suit	

Chapter Highlights

The first part of this chapter discusses termination of contracts by breach, the second way in which a contract ends. The discussion includes a definition of *breach*, the types of breach that may occur, and the various remedies available to an injured party who is the victim of a breach of contract. Sometimes parties breach their contracts and offer one of many defenses for not performing. The second part of this chapter deals with some of these defenses. You will learn that a party who raises one of these defenses successfully is released from blame or responsibility in a breach of contract suit.

BREACH OF CONTRACT

actual breach when one party fails to perform the obligations required by a contract

anticipatory breach breach of contract occurring before stated time of performance

Another way in which a contract ends is by breach. An **actual breach** occurs when one party without excuse fails to perform some or all of the obligations required by a contract. Contracts are usually breached after the performance date. Sometimes, however, a contract is breached before the performance date. This failure to perform is called an **anticipatory breach**. Before the time for performance stated in the contract, one party says, "I'm not going to perform." When that happens, the injured party may immediately declare the contract ended and sue for any damages caused by this breach. Legally, the injured party does not have to wait until the performance date has passed to sue but may choose to do so, hoping that the breaching party will undergo a change of mind and perform the contract on schedule. The breaching party does have the right to back out of the decision to breach the contract and continue his or her obligation by giving proper notice. This may occur, however, as long as the nonbreaching party has not made arrangements to enter into a similar contract with another party. For any breach, the injured party has certain remedies.

REMEDIES FOR BREACH OF CONTRACT

remedy course of action an injured party may take to get satisfaction for breach of contract

A **remedy** is a course of action available to the nonbreaching party (the party hurt by the breach) to obtain satisfaction, in court if necessary, for an injury caused by breach of contract. A remedy may be either legal or equitable. In a legal remedy, the injured party is awarded money damages. When money alone does not provide satisfaction to the injured party, courts will provide an equitable remedy (discussed later in this chapter). Money damages are the most frequently granted remedy for breach of contract in a court of law.

If the breach is material, the injured party may treat the contract as ended and thereby be relieved from her or his duty to perform. The injured party may also sue for money damages for this breach. A **material breach** is an unexcusable failure to perform substantially the obligations required by a contract.

material breach
violation of contract so substantial that it destroys the value of the contract and therefore excuses further performance by the injured party

> Metzinger signed a contract to work for a marketing research company beginning June 1. On June 1, the company refused to allow Metzinger to begin work. By preventing Metzinger from beginning work, the company created a material breach. The contract was discharged. In addition, Metzinger may sue the company for money damages for breach of contract.

Since there are no clear-cut rules, a court will often decide whether a material breach has occurred. Most breaches of contract, however, are minor breaches. If a breach is minor, the contract is not ended. Both parties must still perform, but the injured party may sue for damages.

> Munson, a mechanic, agreed to replace parts on Tracy's motorcycle by June 10. Completion of the work, however, was delayed until June 20. Because the delay amounted to a minor breach, the contract remains in force, but Tracy may sue for any damages incurred because of the later completion date.

waiver voluntary surrender of a given right

The injured party may waive his or her rights when the other party breaches the contract. A **waiver** is the voluntary surrender of a given right. As a result of this waiver, the contract is canceled. To be on the safe side, the breaching party should ask for a written release. The written release, however, must be supported by consideration, except in those states where an agreement in writing needs no consideration.

Legal Remedies

Once a contract has been breached, the injured party has the right to sue for money damages. Damages, determined either by the parties to a contract or by a court, are awarded to compensate the injured party financially for her or his loss; therefore, they must be established with reasonable certainty. Sometimes the injured party attempts to make a profit from the breach of contract, which is unfair. The money damages awarded should, by law, place the injured party in the position she or he would have been in if the contract had been carried out. Damages may be:

1. Compensatory (to cover direct losses)
2. Consequential (to cover indirect losses that are foreseeable)
3. Punitive (to punish and deter similar future conduct)
4. Nominal (a small amount to recognize a breach occurred, but no actual damages suffered)
5. Liquidated (an amount specified in the contract)

You may remember that compensatory and punitive damages were covered in Chapter 4 in relationship to tort law. In this chapter, these same damages as well as nominal and consequential damages will be discussed again, but in relationship to contract law.

Compensatory Damages   Damages awarded to the injured party as compensation for a direct (actual) loss or injury caused by the breach of contract are called *compensatory damages*. The right to recover compensatory monetary damages for breach of contract, which can be determined by the courts with reasonable certainty, is always available to the injured party.

mitigate the damages
to try to hold damages down once a breach of contract occurs

As soon as the breach occurs, the injured party has a duty to **mitigate the damages**. That is, the injured party must make a reasonable effort to minimize the amount of damages and prevent them from increasing. Mitigation is required to assure that the damages awarded do not exceed the amount necessary to compensate the injured party.

> On June 1, you hired a roofer for $6,000 to replace a twenty-five-year-old roof that was beginning to cause water problems on the inside of your house. You signed a contract for the roofer to begin the job on June 20. He agreed. The roofer, however, never came to complete the job. You took your time finding another roofer. In the meantime, heavy rains caused damage to the interior of your house. Finally, on August 1, you hired another roofer to complete the job but at a cost of $7,000, which was $1,000 more than the contract price of the original roofer that you hired. You then sued the original roofer for the damages done to the interior of your house.

In this example, you would be entitled to damages of $1,000, the difference between the price specified in the contract with the original roofer and the price charged by the second roofer that you hired. It is not likely that you could recover for the rain damage unless you could show that it was not reasonably possible to procure any other roofer to complete your roof. In the absence of such proof (you took your time finding another roofer), the duty to mitigate damages would keep you from collecting more than $1,000.

In addition to damages, the losing party also pays court costs (e.g., witness fees and filing fees). Each party pays her or his own attorney's fees.

Consequential damages indirect damages awarded for breach of contract because they were or should have been forseeable by the breaching party

Consequential damages are indirect damages based on whether the breaching party to a contract knew or should have known that a loss would result from the breach. This is called the forseeability test. If, for example, a car dealer delivers a used car purchased under contract to a buyer with defective brakes and injuries result, the buyer may be able to collect consequential damages as part of their award for compensatory damages.

liquidated damages
damages set in advance by the parties and stated in the contract

Liquidated Damages   The amount of damages awarded to an injured party in case of a breach may be agreed to by the parties in advance (fixed amount) and stated in the contract. This amount is called **liquidated damages**.

> Kerry signed a lease renting an apartment for one year from Snider. A clause in the lease stated that the security deposit of $250 would be forfeited as liquidated damages if Kerry gave up the apartment before the end of the lease.

A liquidated damages clause will be enforced if the court determines that the amount is a reasonable forecast (the best approximation and not a guess) of the loss that may result or does result from the breach. In the example, $250 is the amount needed by Snider to prepare the apartment for new tenants.

A court will not enforce a liquidated damages clause if the amount appears to be a penalty to deter a breach of contract. The court will ignore it and instead award whatever compensatory (actual) damages could be proven.

> Westside Health Group contracted with Comnetix Computer Systems to maintain Westside Health Group's computer system. Westside's staff depends on the proper operation of its computer system at all times. A liquidated damages clause in the contract provided that Comnetix pay $1,000 for each day that Comnetix was late responding to a service call, regardless of the time of day or night. On March 3, Comnetix was notified that Westside's computer system failed, but Comnetix did not respond until March 6. Westside Health Group sued Comnetix under the liquidated damage provision of the contract.

In this example, if as a result of the lawsuit by Westside it was determined by the court that the liquidated damage clause was inserted in the contract only to deter a breach of contract (as opposed to a good faith effort to estimate probable damages), that clause will be deemed a penalty and will be declared void.

The theory behind a liquidated damages clause is to save the cost of litigating the case—that is, going to court and having the parties to the lawsuit appear, along with their witnesses, and convening a jury to hear testimony.

nominal damages
damages awarded for breach of contract when no real loss or injury occurs

Nominal Damages   The court awards **nominal damages**, usually a very small amount such as $1, when an injured party establishes that a contract has been breached but fails to prove that he or she has suffered actual damages.

> Samuels, owner of the Uptown Automotive Station, made a contract to buy twenty cases of motor oil from the Apex Wholesale Company at $25 per case. When Apex breached the contract and did not deliver the motor oil, Samuels purchased the same number of cases at $21 per case from another wholesaler. Because Samuels suffered no actual loss, only nominal damages would be awarded in a suit against Apex.

Nominal damages may also be awarded to an injured party who has sued to establish a court decision (precedent) concerning her or his rights in a legal dispute that may occur in the future.

Punitive Damages   Money damages awarded to the injured party in the contract (in addition to compensatory damages) to punish the breaching party for wrongful conduct and to deter similar future conduct by that party are called *punitive damages* (or *exemplary damages*). Punitive damages are generally not awarded in breach of contract suits. The modern trend, however, is for state statutes to allow punitive damages when evidence shows that the breaching party also committed a tort by maliciously, fraudulently, or willfully causing the breach. One example is an insurance company that without cause denies a legitimate insurance claim.

Equitable Remedies

As noted earlier in the chapter, equitable remedies are allowed by courts when money damages will not adequately compensate the injured party for her or his loss or are not available or determinable. Equitable remedies include:

1. rescission (call the contract off).
2. specific performance (force the breaching party to go through with the contract).
3. injunction (the breaching party to the contract is ordered to refrain from carrying out his or her part of the agreement).

rescission voluntary mutual surrender and discharge of each party's contractual rights under a contract

Rescission   When a breach occurs, the parties may choose to call off their contract and end further performance. This step is called rescission. **Rescission** consists of a voluntary mutual surrender and discharge of each party's contractual rights under a contract. If a contract is rescinded, both parties must return any consideration received under the contract. Once rescission has occurred, the original contract no longer exists. Both parties are restored to the original position that they occupied prior to the formation of the contract. Rescission is often used as a remedy when the breaching party induced the injured party to enter into the contract by fraud, duress, or undue influence; when the breaching party wished to exercise his or her right as a minor to rescind; or when the parties voluntarily agree to call off the contract for whatever reason (as discussed on page 216 of Chapter 13). Rescission must be accomplished promptly so that both parties can be restored as nearly as possible to their original positions (status quo).

Rescission is the easiest when the contract is executory. For example, Ralph and Hopkins mutually agree to call off their contract to have Ralph build a pool for Hopkins before the pool is started. Problems often occur if the parties attempt to rescind a bilateral contract where one party fully performed his or her duties under the contract.

Specific Performance   When money damages are not adequate and do not fairly compensate for a loss and rescission is not the proper remedy, the injured party may sue for specific performance. **Specific performance** is a court order forcing the breaching party to carry out the contract according to its original terms. Specific performance is generally granted only if the subject matter of the contract is rare or unique and an identical item cannot be purchased elsewhere. For example, a contract for the sale of real property will generally be enforced because each piece of land is considered unique and unlike any other piece. Consequently, money damages will not compensate the buyer. Specific performance will also be granted in contracts for the sale of such personal property as rare paintings and books, antiques, relics, and heirlooms. It is difficult to put a value on a priceless work of art or an heirloom.

> Mansfield contracted to sell Downing a castlelike home located on a mountain overlooking a large body of water. Mansfield changed his mind and refused to close the sale.

In this example, land is considered unique and not interchangeable. Therefore, the court could require Mansfield to sell the property to Downing as promised. Downing could accept compensatory damages or could simply rescind the contract. He may not, however, be satisfied with these remedies because he has his mind set on this unique home, and to him, nothing else is comparable.

The courts will not order specific performance in a personal services contract (one involving a person who has special skills and talents). It is in no one's best interests to force one party to work for someone else. For example, a musician who has played with a band and who refuses to continue with that band cannot be forced to remain even though under contract. The musician, however, could be sued for damages for breach of contract.

Injunction   In special cases where damages, rescission, and specific performance will not adequately compensate for a breach of contract, the court may grant an injunction to the injured party. As you recall from page 82, an injunction is a court order that forbids a person from doing a certain act.

> Rivera was the heavyweight boxing champion. He agreed with Liberty Arena to fight the winner of the Schultz–Freeling match for the title of heavyweight champion of the world. To keep Rivera in top shape and to prevent his being injured before the title fight, his contract with Liberty Arena prevented him from fighting anyone else prior to that bout. In violation of this agreement, Rivera, having been promised a large sum of money by a sports management group, agreed to fight another heavyweight boxer before the title bout at Liberty Arena. When Liberty Arena found out about his plan, it brought suit against Rivera and asked the court for an injunction to prohibit Rivera from fighting prior to the title match.

In this example, the court most likely would have granted the injunction, as it was the fairest remedy. Liberty Arena, which held Rivera's contract for the championship fight, did not want money damages or a rescission of the contract; it wanted Rivera to fight. There was a lot of money at stake in the title fight, and it would have been unreasonably difficult determining and proving how extensive Liberty Arena's damages would have been.

specific performance
court order requiring a party to carry out a contract according to its original terms

DEFENSES FOR A BREACH OF CONTRACT SUIT

When a breach of contract occurs, the injured party has a right to sue the party who broke the contract. The breaching party (the defendant in the lawsuit) may offer one of many defenses for not performing on the contract. As you recall, *defenses* are reasons offered by a defendant (the party being sued) that are meant to release her or him from blame or responsibility. In a breach of contract suit, the defenses offered are intended to excuse the breaching party from further liability under the contract. You have already learned of some actions that affect the performance of the terms of a contract (lack of competency, impossibility, illegal purpose, and lack of proper form). These actions may be used as defenses. Other defenses are fraud, duress, undue influence, and mistake. In these cases the breaching party claimed that he or she actually did not agree to the terms.

Fraud

A person who persuades another to enter into a contract by making a false statement about a material fact or by concealing a material fact is guilty of fraud. In simple terms, **fraud** consists of deception. Such a contract is voidable by the victim of the fraud. That is, the victim may refuse to go through with the contract and may use fraud as a defense if sued for breach of contract. The following elements all are necessary to establish fraud:

1. A false statement or concealment of a material fact must be made.
2. The false statement or concealment must be intentional.
3. The victim actually relied on the false statement or concealment.
4. The victim must offer proof of damages.

False Statement or Concealment of a Material Fact   The false statement, oral or written, must be about a material fact. A material fact is one that is important enough to influence another's decision. A mere statement of opinion or a prediction is not fraud. For example, a salesperson's statement that "this TV set is the best you can buy for the money" is an opinion (called sales puffing), not a fact. A statement such as "with this mower you can cut an acre of lawn on less than a gallon of gasoline," however, is a statement of fact that can be tested.

A person who conceals a material fact is also guilty of fraud. The concealment must prevent the victim from discovering the truth about material facts.

> Rommel and Associates, CPAs, audited the financial statements of the McGill Company. The financial statements contained misstatements that resulted in a material overstatement of McGill's net worth. The lead CPA was aware of these misstatements but, nevertheless, at McGill's request, expressed in writing an unqualified opinion that the net worth as stated on the books was correct. McGill had requested this falsification so as to obtain a bank loan. Based on this report, McGill was temporarily approved for a $1 million loan by Charter Bank and was given a $200,000 advance as part of the agreement pending the bank's pre-loan investigation. During Charter's investigation of McGill, it discovered the falsification. Charter canceled the remaining amount promised to McGill as a loan and demanded the return of the $200,000. McGill refused. Charter successfully sued McGill, claiming fraud. Both Rommel and Associates and McGill would also be subject to criminal liability.

Generally, silence is not fraud. A person does not have to volunteer all the details to the other party. Although in a sense this is concealment, the law allows it as part of the bargaining process. Today, however, many jurisdictions insist on non-concealment and

fraud entering into a contract intentionally making a false statement about a material fact or concealing a material fact.

honesty in business transactions so if a person's silence creates a false impression about certain facts, that person has a duty to speak out. Buying a house is a good example of how silence could amount to fraud, especially if the buyer's questions relating to defects in the house are not answered properly.

Intentional Misstatement or Concealment   The speaker must know that what is said or done is false and must deliberately intend to mislead the victim. (This aspect of fraud is the most difficult to prove.)

> Arden, an automobile tire dealer, sold four new tires to Limrick. To make the sale, Arden told Limrick that the tires were guaranteed for 50,000 miles. Actually, Arden knew that the average life of that brand was only 20,000 miles. When Limrick discovered the truth, he would not go through with the purchase and tried to return the tires. Arden refused to accept them and sued Limrick. Because Arden had deliberately lied about the tires, Limrick can use fraud as his defense.

Fraud also occurs when a person who should have known the facts of a situation carelessly makes a statement without really knowing whether it is true or not (reckless use of the truth).

> Kotch, a door-to-door salesperson for the Home Utility Company, sold Arnold an expensive set of kitchen utensils. Arnold made the purchase because Kotch told her that the utensils were solid copper. As it turned out, the utensils were only copper plated. The salesperson did not know that the utensils were only copper plated and never checked with the company to find out. Because Kotch should have checked with the company, Arnold may claim fraud as a defense in a breach of contract suit.

Reliance on False Statement or Concealment   The victim of fraud must actually rely on the false statement or concealment and suffer a loss or injury. There is no fraud if the victim is not deceived because he or she makes an independent investigation but enters into the contract anyway. There has been no reliance on the false statement or concealment.

> Delmar, an automobile dealer, received in trade a car that had been damaged in an accident. He explained to Tinker that the car had been thoroughly repaired and that many parts had been replaced. When Tinker took the car for a trial run, she had it examined by a mechanic. The mechanic told Tinker that the frame had been badly bent and that the repair job had not completely straightened it. Nevertheless, because of its low price, Tinker bought the car. Because Tinker did not rely on Delmar's statement, she cannot claim fraud if she later tries to get out of the contract.

Victim Must Offer Proof of Damages   The victim of fraud is entitled to bring a lawsuit. Unless the victim has suffered actual legal damages (compensatory damages) as a result of the fraud and can offer proof of these damages, however, a court would award only nominal damages.

Duress

duress forcing one to enter into a contract by using violence or threats of violence

Valid contracts are made by persons who enter into them of their own free will. **Duress** occurs when one person compels another to enter into a contract through physical force (e.g., pointing a gun at a person or taking a person's hand and making the person sign a written contract) or by other improper threats so extreme that a victim loses all ability to assent voluntarily. Because it involves the use of physical force or improper threats, duress destroys a person's free will to decide whether or not to enter into a contract. This type of duress is rather uncommon, but it renders the agreement voidable by the victim. Under modern law, threats include economic pressure if it is wrongful.

> Duff, owner of an apartment complex, wrongfully threatened to terminate Romano's present lease and to initiate eviction proceedings against her if she refused to sign a new three-year lease at a much higher rent. Duff did so knowing that Romano was physically handicapped and bedridden. Because Duff's actions amounted to duress, Romano, who signed the lease, can cancel if she wishes.

The threat by one person to bring a lawsuit against another person to enforce a legal claim is not duress. Assume, for example, that a friend owed you money but refused to pay. If you threatened to sue your friend in small claims court unless payment was made, your friend could not refuse to pay claiming duress. You have a right to use whatever legal means are available to collect the debt.

Undue Influence

undue influence power or dominance used to make persons enter into a contract against their will

Undue influence is the power or dominance that one person has—and uses for personal advantage—over another person. No force or threats are used, as in duress, but the stronger-minded person can exercise so much influence that the victim ends up doing whatever the other person wishes. A contract entered into because of undue influence is voidable by the victim.

Undue influence is often difficult to determine. Mere persuasion is not undue influence. The victim must be incapable of using her or his own free will. Undue influence may arise when the parties have a close confidential or personal relationship. Examples of such relationships are those between lawyer and client, doctor or nurse and patient, parent and child, and husband and wife.

> Paton, an elderly woman, lived with her son, who was Paton's only child and sole support. The son persuaded Paton to sell him some land worth $150,000 for $50,000. Shortly before the transfer of title, Paton discovered that her son was going to resell the property to Vestel for $175,000 for construction of an apartment complex. The mother refused to go through with the sale. In the breach of contract suit that followed, the court found that the son had taken advantage of his mother's trust in him to persuade her to sell the land. Paton could avoid the contract.

Mistake

unilateral mistake error about certain facts made by only one party to a contract

mutual mistake error about certain facts made by both parties to a contract

People often attempt to back out of a contract because they claim that they made a mistake (misunderstood, misinterpreted, or drew a wrong conclusion) about certain facts in a contract. Not all mistakes, however, will allow people to avoid the contracts they made. A mistake made by one party is called a **unilateral mistake**. A mistake by both parties about the facts is called a **mutual mistake**. Most mistakes are unilateral. A unilateral mistake may be caused by ignorance, forgetfulness, poor judgment, or carelessness. As a general rule, if only one party has made the mistake (a unilateral mistake), the contract remains in force. The contract would be voidable, however, if the nonmistaken party knows or reasonably should have known of the mistake (because the mistake was substantial) or if the mistake was caused by the fault of the nonmistaken party. In addition, some courts allow rescission when the effect of the unilateral mistake makes enforcement of the contract unconscionable.

> By mail, Farley offered to sell Sprinkler, a medical student, a set of medical encyclopedias for $195. Sprinkler immediately mailed a letter of acceptance. When she

received the acceptance, Farley discovered that she had typed $195 instead of $295, as she had intended. Farley refused to mail the books to Sprinkler, who sued. Because this mistake by Farley was due to her carelessness, it had no effect on the contract. Sprinkler most likely could enforce the contract for $195.

Jason Corporation, a building contractor, offered to sell Marcus, another contractor, some used construction equipment. When preparing the written offer, Jason's secretary typed the price as $15,600 instead of $156,000. Marcus received this offer in the mail and quickly accepted it. When Jason received the acceptance from Marcus, however, he noticed the error and refused to sell the equipment to Jason at the $15,600 price. Marcus sued for breach of contract.

In these examples, the price set forth in the offer was substantially less than the equipment's fair market value. In the second example, there was an extremely large math error. A court would argue that Marcus, being a contractor himself, should have known that; therefore, the court would not allow the sale at $15,600. To honor the contract at the lower amount would, in the eyes of the court, permit Marcus to take unfair advantage of Jason.

Certain types of mutual mistakes can serve as defenses in breach of contract suits because they show there has been no meeting of the minds. They are mutual mistakes about the existence of the subject matter and mutual mistakes about the identity of the subject matter.

Mutual Mistake About the Existence of the Subject Matter

The subject matter must exist at the time the contract is made. If it does not, there can be no contract. The offeror cannot offer to sell something that doesn't exist. Likewise, the offeree cannot accept an offer for something that no longer exists.

You made a contract to sell a friend your motorboat, which was stored at a marina near your summer home. Unknown to both of you, the marina and the boat were destroyed by fire two days earlier. Nonetheless, your friend, who had spent a lot of money building a boathouse, sued for damages. Because the boat had been destroyed, you can claim mutual mistake as a defense.

Mutual Mistake About the Identity of the Subject Matter

If both parties are mistaken about the subject matter that is the basis of the contract, there can be no meeting of the minds and therefore no contract.

Rapp owned two racehorses, one younger than the other but both named Pogas Song. Rapp offered to sell her racehorse to Peters. In making the offer, Rapp had the older horse in mind. Peters accepted, thinking that he was buying the younger horse. Learning of the error, Peters sued to force Rapp to sell him the younger horse. Rapp, because of the mutual mistake about the identity, cannot be forced to sell Peters the younger horse.

If one or both persons make a mistake (unilateral or mutual) about the value or quality of the subject matter, this mistake in judgment will not excuse either party from carrying out the contract.

You sold your friend an old ring for $10; neither of you knew its true value. Later, you discovered that the ring was considered a piece of antique jewelry worth $500. You demanded the return of the ring. Your friend is entitled to keep the ring.

REMEDIES FOR FRAUD, DURESS, AND UNDUE INFLUENCE

Fraud, duress, and undue influence make a contract voidable. The victim of one of these acts also has remedies. The victim may either rescind or ratify the contract.

If the contract is rescinded, the victim must return any consideration received and is entitled to recover anything given as consideration, by a lawsuit if necessary. The victim may also sue for damages.

If the victim chooses to ratify, the contract is as valid as if no fraud, duress, or undue influence had occurred. As with rescission, the victim may sue for damages for actual loss or injury suffered.

> You were induced to purchase a used car through fraud. Before you purchased the car, the dealer stated that the engine had recently been rebuilt. Actually, it had not. After you bought the car, you had engine troubles and the car stopped running.

In this example, if you wanted to keep the car, you could choose to ratify the contract and sue the dealer for damages. In this case, damages would be the cost of repairing the engine.

Summary

In addition to discharge, another way in which a contract ends is by an actual breach. This type of breach occurs when one party fails to perform an obligation according to the terms of the contract. Although breaches of contract usually occur after the date for performance, some take place before the performance date. This type of breach is called an anticipatory breach.

For any breach, the injured party has a course of action called a *remedy*. Remedies available to the injured party are either legal or equitable. In a legal remedy, the injured party is awarded money damages. Money damages, the most common remedy for breach of contract, are awarded to compensate the injured party financially for her or his loss. Money damages may be compensatory, liquidated, nominal, or punitive. Equitable remedies are provided by a court when money does not adequately compensate the injured party for his or her loss. Equitable remedies include rescission, specific performance, and injunction.

A material breach—that is, one that is substantial— usually ends a contract, and the injured party no longer needs to perform. In addition, the injured party can sue for damages. A minor breach does not end a contract. Both parties must still perform, but the injured party may sue for damages. As soon as a breach occurs, the nonbreaching party has a duty to mitigate the damages—that is, to make a reasonable effort to hold down the amount of damages. Instead of suing, the injured party may elect to waive his or her rights (not sue) when the other party breaches the contract.

The defendant in a breach of contract suit may claim such defenses as fraud, duress, undue influence, and mutual mistake. These four acts make a contract voidable by the victim. In some cases, they make the contract void and excuse the victim from further liability under the contract.

A victim of fraud, duress, or undue influence may either rescind the contract and recover any consideration given or ratify the contract and sue for actual damages suffered.

Important Legal terms

actual breach
anticipatory breach
consequential damages
duress
fraud
liquidated damages

material breach
mitigate the damages
mutual mistake
nominal damages
remedy
rescission

specific performance
undue influence
unilateral mistake
waiver

Questions and Problems for Discussion

1. Connors and Ferris entered into a contract in which Connors was obligated to deliver certain goods to Ferris by March 8. On March 1, Connors told Ferris that he would not deliver the goods called for in the contract. The reason for refusing to deliver the goods was simply a change of mind at this time. Connors told Ferris that he would think more about it and possibly deliver the goods sometime in the future. Can Ferris successfully sue Connors immediately or must he wait to see what Connors decides to do?

2. What kind of restriction is placed on a person who is entitled to compensatory damages?

3. Christa Construction Co. entered into a contract with Milkin to sell a movie complex housing ten theaters for $1,000,000. The contract required Milkin to pay the entire amount at closing. Christa, just prior to the closing, refused to complete the sale of the theater complex. Is Milkin entitled to any relief?

4. Mercer agreed to buy a set of law books from his instructor, who said that without them Mercer would not be able to pass the course. The instructor was the agent for the book company in the area and made a large profit from each sale he made. May Mercer refuse to buy the books from his instructor?

5. Tina Townsend, age twenty-five, a well-known comic, signed a contract for $20,000 with Stillman to perform at Stillman's Country Dinner Theater for five nights. Because Townsend had a drinking problem, a clause in the contract stipulated that she should not take a drink for the five nights she was to perform. Another clause stated that if Townsend were to drink and appear for her performances in an intoxicated condition, 10 percent of her salary would be withheld as

liquidated damages. After having several drinks, Townsend made her opening night appearance. Reviewers in the local newspapers described her as "a very stumbling but entertaining alcoholic." Despite the reviews, Townsend's performances filled the theater to capacity each night of her five-night engagement. Stillman, however, still withheld $2,000 of Townsend's salary, although she had appeared in an intoxicated state only on opening night. Townsend brought an action against Stillman to recover the $2,000 withheld from her salary. Should she recover the money?

6. In purchasing a new automobile, Blacklaw ordered it with no extra equipment except power steering. She did not read the contract presented to her before signing it. She learned later that the car included power steering, radio, air conditioning, and tinted glass. What effect, if any, did Blacklaw's mistake have on the contract?

7. Flynn, who received a ring from his uncle's estate through a properly executed will, sold it to a jeweler for $400. At the time of purchase, the jeweler in good faith indicated to Flynn that he (jeweler) was unaware of the value of the ring. Several weeks later, Flynn discovered that the ring was worth at least $3,000 and now asks to recover possession from the jeweler. Should Flynn be entitled to recover the ring?

8. Dunes called the Sauna Resort Hotel and made a reservation for his family of four for July 6–12. A letter of confirmation signed by the hotel manager stated: "This is to confirm your reservation for the period July 6 to July 12 inclusive. The rate for the Fernwood Cottage No. 10 Accommodation (American Plan) you requested is $600. A $100 deposit is required in advance to guarantee this accommodation. Please sign the original of

this confirmation letter and return it to this office with the required deposit. Keep the other copy for your files." Dunes immediately signed and returned the letter along with a certified check for $100. In settling Dunes's account at checkout time, the manager discovered that a typing error had been made in the quoted price of the accommodation listed in the confirmation letter. The quoted price should have been $700, not $600. Dunes refused to pay the additional $100 when requested to do so by the hotel manager. Can the Sauna Resort Hotel require Dunes to pay this additional amount based on the hotel's error?

9. Deveney, who had been hired by Rollins Community College as a marketing instructor, was asked to provide the college with a copy of his M.B.A. (master of business administration) degree, which he did. Six months after Deveney began teaching, the director of personnel discovered that Deveney had no M.B.A. of his own as required by the college. Deveney had instead "borrowed" a retired person's M.B.A. diploma and had cleverly removed the retired person's name and inserted his own. What action can the college take?

10. The seniors at Washington College booked their Graduation Ball at the Washington Plaza Hotel for June 1. The student activities director signed the contract and sent a deposit of $500 to the hotel as required to guarantee the booking. Two weeks before the ball, the seniors decided instead to hold the affair at the new convention center just down the street from the Washington Plaza Hotel. The student activities director went along with the change and signed another contract with the manager of the convention center. The student activities director then called the Washington Plaza Hotel and canceled. What action, if any, can the hotel take?

11. Cooper Manufacturing Co. contracted with Bright Computers to maintain Cooper's computer system. Cooper's manufacturing process depends heavily on its computer system operating properly at all times. A liquidated damages clause in the contract provided that Bright Computers pay $1,000 to Cooper for each day that Bright was late responding to a service request. On December 8, Bright was notified that Cooper's computer system was "down." But Bright did not respond to Cooper's service call until December 11. If Cooper sues Bright under the liquidated damage provision of the contract, what should the result be?

12. Strouse bought a used motorcycle from Biker's World and agreed to pay for it in monthly installments. When Strouse asked about mileage, the salesperson stated that the motorcycle had been driven only 4,000 miles, had never been raced, and needed no major engine repairs. In fact, the motorcycle had been driven over 6,000 miles, had been entered in several racing contests, and needed major engine repairs. Strouse soon discovered the salesperson's misrepresentations, returned the motorcycle, and refused to make any more payments. In a breach of contract suit, can Strouse claim fraud as a defense?

13. Johnson interviewed for a position with an automobile agency and was offered the job, which he accepted. The contract called for Johnson to begin work on June 1, 2008. On June 1 when he reported for work, he was told that his job offer had been revoked but that he could re-apply at a later time. Does Johnson have a legal action against the automobile agency?

14. Benson, a homeowner, made a contract with a roofer to repair her roof, which had begun to leak slightly. Several months after the contract was made, the roofer still had not come to do the job, nor had Benson contacted him to ask when he was coming. In the meantime, the condition of the roof deteriorated to the point where heavy rains severely damaged the interior of Benson's house. Benson then sued the roofer for breach of contract, claiming that since he did not show up to repair the roof, he should be liable for the interior damage caused by the heavy rains. Is Benson correct?

Cases for Review

1. Robert and Sandra Bell hired McCann to build a house for them at a contract price of $45,000. McCann then changed his mind and refused to build, claiming that he would make no profit. The Bells then advertised for bids from other contractors. The lowest bid was $54,500, which

the Bells accepted. They then brought suit against McCann for the difference between the original contract price and the market price ($54,500 – $45,000), less the extras of $4,562 that were discussed but had not been included in the contract. Thus, the Bells were awarded $4,938 in damages by the trial court. McCann appealed, claiming that the trial court applied an improper measure of damages. Do you agree with McCann? (*Bell* v. *McCann*, 535 P.2d 233)

2. Watts Construction Co. was awarded a construction contract with Cullman County to complete a County Water Works Improvement Project. One section of the contract provided that it would not become effective unless and until approved by a certain federal agency, namely, the Farmers Home Administration, U.S. Department of Agriculture. The agency's approval was delayed, which in turn delayed the initiation of the project. In response to this delay, Watts Construction Co. requested a 5 percent increase in the contract price due to seasonal and inflational price increases. In his letter to Cullman County, Watts stated, "If this is not agreeable with you, please consider this letter a withdrawal of our bid." Cullman County refused to pay the additional 5 percent and hired another company to take on the project. Watts then informed the county that he was willing to perform the contract at the original price (without the 5 percent price increase) but with certain modifications. The county refused and Watts sued for breach of contract. Should he be successful? (*Watts Construction Co.* v. *Cullman County*, 382 So.2d 520)

3. Wolf was a popular sportscaster for ABC. He breached his contract and signed on with CBS where he was going to be paid a much higher salary. Wolf's ABC contract required him to negotiate a renewal contract in good faith with ABC during the last ninety days of his contract. The ninety-day period ended and in fact his entire contract expired with ABC, but with no good faith renewal negotiations on Wolf's part. Wolf then signed on with CBS. ABC now seeks an injunction against Wolf to prevent his leaving ABC and working for CBS. Should ABC be successful in obtaining an injunction? (*American Broadcasting Companies, Inc.* v. *Wolf, Court of Appeals, NY*, 420 N.E. 2d 363)

4. Knutton, owner of a music company, entered into a contract with Cofield, a restaurant owner, in which a jukebox was to be installed in Cofield's restaurant, with the parties sharing the receipts. The contract provided that if Cofield discontinued using the jukebox before the expiration of the contract, Cofield would pay Knutton a sum of money for the unexpired term of the contract based on the average of the amount paid from the time the jukebox had been installed. Prior to the expiration of the contract, Cofield disconnected the jukebox and installed one belonging to another company. Knutton sued for damages for breach of contract. Cofield, however, claimed that the damages being sought were a penalty and not liquidated damages. Was Cofield correct? (*Knutton* v. *Cofield*, 273 N.C. 355)

5. Burns and his wife bought a new car from a dealer and financed it through the Manhattan Credit Co. The finance company assured Burns that it would take care of the insurance but in fact did not arrange for enough coverage. A few months after the car was purchased, the car was damaged beyond repair, and the insurance wasn't enough to cover the damage. Burns and his wife sued to cancel the contract of sale because of the false statements made by the finance company regarding the insurance coverage. Can the sale be legally canceled? (*Manhattan Credit Co.* v. *Burns*, 230 Ark. 418, 323 S.W.2d 206)

6. Palmer was a retail florist. He sold his business to Flower Haven and agreed not to engage in the retail florist business in his city for five years. Before the end of the five years, Palmer went back into the business, and Flower Haven sued for an injunction. Can Palmer be stopped from going into the flower business again before the end of five years? (Assume that five years is reasonable.) (*Flower Haven, Inc.* v. *Palmer*, Colo. 502 P.2d 424)

7. Kennedy gave a promissory note (a promise to pay money) for $20,000 to Ragsdale, the president of Onslow Livestock Corp., to purchase shares of stock in the corporation. Ragsdale had told Kennedy that the corporation was a "going concern." In reality, the company was losing money, had many debts, and generally was "going under." Ragsdale attempted to obtain a judgment against Kennedy when Kennedy failed to pay the promissory note. Does Kennedy have a defense for not paying the promissory note? (*Ragsdale* v. *Kennedy*, 286 N.C. 130)

THE CASE OF THE OFFER TOO GOOD TO BE TRUE

Jason, by mistake, opened up a letter intended for his neighbor. The letter, from a major automobile manufacturer, read as follows: "We offer to sell you one of our deluxe convertibles for $100.00* Use the enclosed card to indicate your acceptance and return it to us together with your check in the amount of $100." The asterisk was printed on the reverse of the letter next to the following language: "provided you are the winner in a drawing to be held in one month."

Jason never saw this language. He returned the acceptance card together with his check and never received the convertible. He sued the car manufacturer for breach of contract.

The Trial

During the trial, the manufacturer's representative explained that this type of advertising had been used for many years by many different types of companies and that everyone knew that this type of offer was limited and usually dependent on a person being selected in a drawing. He explained that the offer had been sent out to a limited number of people, chosen because of their prior ownership of the manufacturer's vehicles. He introduced in evidence a copy of the letter, showing that all the details of the offer had been printed in large-size type. Jason explained that even though the letter was not meant for him, there was no name at the top of the letter, and he assumed the offer was meant for the general public. He stated further that he never looked at the reverse of the letter because he thought the offer was clear.

The Arguments at Trial

The manufacturer's attorneys argued that an offer was never made to Jason, only to his neighbor, and thus Jason could not have accepted the offer. Also, the offer was not made to the general public but only to a limited group, and thus the offer could only be accepted by a member of that group. They argued further that the offer and qualifying statement were in clear language and printed in large-size type so that a potential buyer would understand the nature of the offer. Jason's attorney argued that because a name did not appear at the top of the offer, the offer should be considered as having been made to the general public, and therefore Jason had a right to accept the offer. She further argued that the qualifying statement should have been printed on the front of the letter and not on the reverse side where it might not be read. She claimed that a valid offer had been made and that the offer had been accepted properly by Jason.

Questions to Discuss

1. Who do you feel has the stronger argument, the car manufacturer or Jason?
2. If you were the judge or jury deciding this case, for whom would you decide? Why?
3. Based on the facts, do you believe there was a mistake of fact or an incomplete contract?
4. Would your answers to any of these questions be different if the neighbor's name and address had been printed at the top of the letter or if the qualifying statement had been printed at the bottom of the first page of the letter?

Maurino, seeking employment as the general manager of a ski resort owned by Giles, was hired and promised that he could stay on at least until Giles reached the age of 65. One reason for this was that Giles, during a background investigation, discovered that Maurino was an extremely hard worker and was very capable as a manager. At the time, Giles was 55 years of age. Satisfied with this arrangement, Maurino quit his job at another resort and went to work for Giles. However, no written employment contract existed between the parties. At age 58, Giles died suddenly of a heart attack, and Giles's son, who inherited the ski resort, fired Maurino. Maurino told the son that he had worked long hours at the resort and never took a vacation from the time he was hired until Giles's death. He also told the son the promise of employment made to him by his father. However, since no written contract existed, Maurino's hard work was not taken into consideration and the promise made by Giles was completely ignored. Giles's son said that the firing still stood. Maurino then sued for breach of contract. Because the contract was made in a state that had a statute requiring contracts for longer than one year to be in writing, the court ruled in favor of the son.

Question for Discussion

If you were Giles's son, would you have handled the case this way or would you have decided that working hard is a normal requirement of any job?

PART **3**

Purchase, Sale, and Lease of Goods Under the UCC

After studying Part III, you should be able to:

1. summarize the ways in which the Uniform Commercial Code (UCC) has changed the common law rules of contracts, especially as they relate to offer and acceptance, consideration, and the writing requirements for contracts under the statute of frauds.

2. apply the provisions of Articles 2 and 2A of the UCC to sales and lease contracts, respectively.

3. determine the point at which risk of loss (and in some cases, title) passes from buyer to seller in the various types of sales and lease contracts.

4. discuss the duties of the buyer and seller in a contract for the sale and lease of goods.

5. summarize and analyze remedies available to the buyer and the seller for breach of the sales and lease contract.

6. explain product liability and three well-recognized theories of product liability available to injured parties as the bases for personal injury lawsuits.

CHAPTER 15

Formation of Sales and Lease Contracts

CHAPTER PREVIEW

Chapter Highlights

This chapter is the first in a unit of four chapters (Chapters 15 through 18) dealing with the laws governing sales and lease contracts under Articles 2 and 2A of the Uniform Commercial Code (UCC). The UCC, also commonly referred to as the Code, is a group of laws governing commercial (business) transactions throughout the United States. You will discover that the study of the law of sales is a continuation of the study of the common law principles of contracts except in those cases modified by the Code. This introductory chapter discusses many of the key modifications that Article 2 of the Code has made in the common law principles of contracts to accommodate the needs of people dealing with one another in a modern business world. Some of the greatest modifications have been made to the rules of offer, acceptance, and consideration. This chapter introduces and defines several terms that you will encounter when dealing with sales and lease contracts and discusses the formation of e-sales contracts. There is some discussion of Article 2A, which covers any transaction that creates a lease of goods. You will discover that the laws governing lease contracts are essentially the same as those governing sales contracts under Article 2 of the UCC. Article 6, Bulk Transfers, will be discussed minimally.

THE LEGAL SETTING FOR A SALE OF GOODS

The most common and most important business transactions deal with the sale of goods: clothing, computers, building materials, auto parts, food, boats, cars, office equipment, raw materials, and so forth. This unit of four chapters examines contracts for the sale of goods. At first, sales transactions were governed strictly by common law principles, which varied considerably from state to state. Then came The Uniform Sales Act drafted by the National Conference of Commissioners on Uniform State Law (NCCUSL) as an attempt to bring some uniformity to sales transactions. A large number of states did adopt this act; however, more reform was needed. Sales law remained rigid, formalistic, technical, complex, and unclear. It was not keeping pace with changes in society. Definitely outdated, its application seems almost foolish by today's standards. The NCCUSL recognized the need to have sales laws that reflected modern commercial reality with built-in flexibility when difficulties arise between parties engaged in business transactions and went to work and developed a stronger group of uniform laws called the **Uniform Commercial Code (UCC)**. The UCC, consisting of nine operative articles, emerged as a very important comprehensive body of statute law—simple, clear, modern, uniform, and flexible. It is consistently updated and amended. The latest 2003 amendments to Article 2 (Sales) and Article 2A (Leases), for example, were written to accommodate electronic commerce. While it is national in scope (i.e., applicable throughout the country) having been adopted in whole or in part by all fifty states (Lousiana has not adopted Articles 2, 2A, and 6) plus the District of Columbia and the Virgin Islands, some states have departed from the recommended provisions and adopted statutes with variations or modifications that would apply more to the business laws of their state. Federal courts also use principles in Article 2 for sales of goods. The provisions of the UCC are not mandatory. That is, freedom of contract is a basic principle of the Code. In fact, the effect of provisions of this act may be varied by agreement except as otherwise provided in the act.

This unit will deal mainly with two of the nine articles, namely, Article 2 (Sales) and Article 2A (Leases). Article 6, Bulk Transfers, will be discussed, but minimally. We will study the changes to the common law principles of contracts discussed in previous chapters. Where the common law has not been modified by the UCC, you will find references throughout the text indicating that it (common law) has also been liberalized by borrowing from principles found in the UCC.

Uniform Commercial Code (UCC) uniform laws governing commercial transactions

THE SCOPE OF ARTICLE 2 OF THE UCC

Article 2 of the UCC governs contracts for the sale of goods for any dollar amount. A **sale**, according to Section (UCC 2-201), is a contract that transfers title to (ownership of) goods from the seller (vendor) to the buyer (vendee, also known as the purchaser) for a consideration (price). The price can be money, other goods, services, or real estate. **Goods** may be defined as items of property that are tangible and moveable (UCC 2-103). *Tangible property* is physically in existence—it can be touched. *Movable property* means that the item can be carried from place to place and therefore is considered personal property. Excluded from the definition of movable would be *real property* such as land and things attached to land. The 2003 amendments expressly includes growing crops and timber to be cut as goods.

Also defined as goods are minerals (including gas and oil), and structures such as a shed if severance (separation) is to be made by the seller. If the buyer is to sever the minerals or structures from the land, these items are not goods, but real property, and any sale would be governed by real property law, not the UCC. Other "things attached" to realty but capable of severance without substantial harm to the land are considered goods regardless of who severs them. For example, a portable heater attached to a wall only by means of bolts could be considered goods, whereas a bathtub would be considered a part of the real property because its removal would do substantial damage to the walls and floor. Also defined as goods are money that is bought and sold as a commodity

sale contract that transfers title in goods from seller to buyer for a price

goods tangible personal property

(e.g., Confederate dollar bills), the unborn young of animals, and items specially manufactured for a buyer (special orders).

The term *goods* does not include intangible (not physical) personal property (e.g., shares of stock or *rights* to real property that has only conceptual existence). An example of intangible property would be your right to the income from a trust fund that had been set up to provide money for you to go to college. The 2003 amendments exclude "information" as goods if sold separately, as for example architectural plans placed on a computer disk. However, the sale of "smart goods," such as an automobile which contains many computer programs, is considered a transaction in goods.

Even though a sale of services may also supply goods (considered a mixed sale), a sale of services such as medical services and legal services is not covered by Article 2. Article 2 applies to a mixed sale only when the sale of goods is the primary purpose of the transaction. The UCC provides no direction for deciding cases based on mixed sales. The courts therefore decide this issue on a case-by-case basis.

> Johnson entered the Henry Hudson Memorial Hospital for the purpose of having a pacemaker installed. The pacemaker was defective, causing injury to Johnson. Johnson sued the hospital under Article 2 of the UCC for breach of warranty. She claimed that the hospital was a supplier of a good subject to Article 2 of the UCC.

In this case, a court would most likely rule against Johnson. The primary function of a hospital is to provide medical services. It does not routinely stock pacemakers or sell them to the general public. Implanting the pacemaker was part of the professional service provided to Johnson. Therefore, the hospital was not liable for breach of warranty under the UCC because the UCC did not apply.

The UCC, Article 2, applies to all sellers and buyers of goods, whether they are merchants or nonmerchants. In a few limited provisions of Article 2, however, some special rules apply solely to sales contracts between merchants (i.e., transactions in which both the seller and buyer are merchants because of a merchant's expertise in commercial transactions). Two such areas of importance are firm offers and contract modifications. A **merchant** is a person who either deals regularly in the sale of goods involved in the sales contract (e.g., a retailer, a wholesaler, or a manufacturer) or professes by occupation to have specialized knowledge of these goods (e.g., a purchasing agent for a large corporation). In short, the merchant is a professional, a commercial expert so to speak, compared with the **nonmerchant**, who is an occasional or casual seller.

merchant one dealing regularly in the sale of goods or having specialized knowledge of goods

nonmerchant casual or occasional seller

> Joseph A. Bank, owner of a large retail clothing store, purchased 150 suits from Jeness Clothing Manufacturers. Bank and Jeness are both merchants because, as a retailer (Bank) and a manufacturer (Jeness), they both deal regularly in the sale of goods.

> North sold a used DVD recorder to a close friend. In this case, North is a nonmerchant or occasional seller.

The provisions of the UCC are not mandatory. That is, freedom of contract is a basic principle of the Code as stated in Section 1-102: "The effect of provisions of this Act may be varied by agreement except as otherwise provided in this Act."

FORMATION OF THE SALES CONTRACT

A sales contract must contain the same essential elements as other contracts: offer and acceptance, consideration, competent parties, and legal purpose. In general, the rules that apply to basic contract law also apply to sales contracts; in some areas, however, the

UCC modifies those rules as they relate to sales of goods. The individuals who developed the UCC believed that the "old law" no longer met the needs of modern business practices.

In effect, the Uniform Commercial Code has relaxed the rules relating to sales transactions by removing many of the technical requirements found in common law contracts. Under the UCC, it is now far easier to form a binding sales contract. For example, the "mirror-image" rule discussed on page 137 in Chapter 7 no longer applies under the Code. The mirror-image rule, under basic contract law, states that the acceptance of an offer cannot legally add, alter, omit, or change any terms in the offer. This rule, which tended to obstruct the formation of a contract, has been replaced by a rule that is more practical and reduces delay in forming a contract. This change alone is better suited to the special needs of merchants who are in the daily business of trading in goods. More important, however, is that the Code allows a contract to be enforced as long as the parties really intended to make the contract, even in cases in which essential terms—such as those specifying price, quantity, place and time for delivery, and terms of payment—are for some reason missing. The Code states that the contracting parties can add these terms at a later time. If the parties do not add the necessary terms, other provisions of the Code will determine a fair price or the proper place for delivery and payment. The UCC rules are so practical that, as mentioned earlier, many courts have even applied some of these modern principles to nonsales transactions under the common law.

To offset these relaxed rules, the Code insists on two conditions that the parties cannot waive or disclaim. First, the parties to the contract must perform their obligations in good faith (honestly), without manipulating contract terms to take advantage of another party, especially when misunderstandings arise or when unforeseen events occur. Second, if the parties to the contract are of unequal bargaining power—such as in a contract between a merchant (a professional) and a consumer (a nonprofessional or inexperienced person, who may know very little about the goods being purchased)—the dominant party must avoid being unfair in dealings with the other party. In other words, the UCC holds merchants to a higher standard than ordinary persons, insisting on honesty and reasonable commercial standards of fair dealing in the trade. If unfairness occurs, a court could refuse to enforce the contract because it is unconscionable. Unconscionable contracts were discussed in Chapter 10.

The sections that follow and the remaining chapters in Part III point out in more detail the important areas in which the UCC has modified common law contracts.

Offer

Under common law, the terms of a contract must be definite (i.e., able to ascertain its essential terms), but under the UCC, a sales contract will not fail for indefiniteness even if some of the terms (e.g., price or quantity) are left open (UCC 2-204, 2A-204). These terms could be negotiated later if both parties were comfortable with the arrangement. The key to this rule, however, is that the contract must be definite enough for the court to identify the agreement and conclude that the parties at least *intended* to make a contract. Without such an identification, the court could neither enforce the contract nor make an appropriate award for damages (with reasonable certainty) if the contract is breached. If necessary, the courts will fill in the missing terms by applying the various rules found in the Code (UCC 2-305–UCC 2-311). Note that under the common law, an agreement with vague or missing terms would have been thrown out by the courts.

Sands, the owner of a winery, signed an agreement with the Pensack Corp. to purchase some new machinery for her business. Before she could take delivery, the machinery first needed some modifications to fit it into a specific location at the winery.

The modification would take approximately two weeks. Some of the details relating to delivery and payment were left blank, to be filled in prior to delivery. When the equipment was ready, Sands received a call from the manager at Pensack informing her that the equipment was ready for delivery. Sands said, "Never mind. I have gone elsewhere to purchase the equipment at a lower price." Pensack, who sued Sands for the expense of preparing the equipment for delivery, should be successful in spite of the fact that some of the details of the contract were missing. The court will likely reason that the conduct of both the parties showed an intent to contract.

For ordinary contracts, an offeree must pay the offeror consideration to keep an offer open, unless as in some states, the offer is in writing (discussed in Chapter 7). Otherwise, an offer can be revoked at any time before it is accepted. The Uniform Commercial Code modifies these rules and distinguishes between merchants and nonmerchants. The UCC provides that if an offer by a merchant to buy or sell goods in a signed record that gives assurance to keep an offer open, the offer is firm. (*Note:* It is necessary that the offer be both written and signed. The signature under the 2003 amendments is broad enough to include an e-signature or any mark used as a person's signature.) In other words, the offer cannot be revoked during the time stated, even if no consideration is paid by the offeree. If consideration is paid by the offeree, then an option contract arises and not a merchant's firm offer. The time stated in such an offer, however, may not exceed three months. If no time is stated, the offer remains open for a reasonable time but for no longer than three months (UCC 2-205). (*Note:* Only the offeror need be a merchant under this rule.)

> On July 1, Johnson of Listwood Motors offers to sell a Porsche to Schwartz for $50,000. Johnson signs a written assurance to keep the offer open until August 1. On July 20, Johnson sells the Porsche to another interested buyer for $55,000. On July 31, Schwartz tenders the $50,000 for the car. Johnson would be liable to Schwartz for the breach of contract because Johnson cannot furnish the car as agreed in his firm offer.

If the written firm offer is actually a form contract supplied by the offeree, the offeror must also sign a separate firm offer assurance. This procedure ensures that the offeror knows about the offer. It might be that a firm offer is "buried" some place in the offeree's form contract, and the offeror may not see it and sign unaware that it contains a firm offer.

Acceptance

In many cases, both parties to the contract are merchants, and they are carrying on business over a long distance. Therefore, acceptance by the offeree may be communicated by any means reasonable under the circumstances, unless the offeror specifies the method by which acceptance must be made. (This same rule exists under the common law.) The acceptance is effective when properly sent (UCC 2-206–2A-206).

> On February 8, the Barrons and Lippson Corporation sent a letter offering to sell Bundy, owner of Bundy's Clothing Fashion Barn, a new line of men's sport shirts at a considerably reduced introductory price. The letter stated that the offer would be good until February 20. When Bundy received the letter on February 10, he immediately sent a telegram of acceptance. Because an employee of the telegraph company failed to send the telegram, however, the telegram never reached the Barrons and Lippson Corporation's home office. Since Bundy used a commercially reasonable means of acceptance, a valid contract was formed on February 10 when he sent the

telegram. If Bundy wished (provided he had proof that the telegram was sent), he could legally demand that Barrons and Lippson send the merchandise according to their offer.

The Code even permits acceptance of an offer by performing rather than by communicating. The UCC states, for example, that an offer to buy goods (the buyer initiates the offer) can be treated as though a unilateral contract offer has been made. The seller can accept such an offer either by shipping the goods to the buyer or by treating the offer as a bilateral contract offer and promptly communicating to the offeror a promise to ship the goods (UCC 2-206). This section of the Code resolves the problem caused by an ambiguous offer in which the offeree was unable to determine whether the offeror wanted a return promise or an act. The Code says that the offeree can use either method of acceptance.

The Code goes one step farther and states that the seller, if he or she chooses, may promise to ship or actually ship *conforming* (meets the standards set down by the contract) or *nonconforming* (substitute) goods (UCC 2-206). A shipment of nonconforming goods is simultaneously regarded both as an acceptance (and therefore results in a contract) and as a breach of contract for which the buyer may pursue appropriate remedies. The seller, however, may, within a reasonable amount of time, clearly notify the buyer that the shipment is nonconforming and that it is offered only as an accommodation or as a favor to the buyer. In this case, the shipment constitutes only a counteroffer, and the buyer is free to accept or reject the goods. If the buyer decides to use the nonconforming goods, there is a contract.

> Wiggins, the owner of Lasting Treasures, a craft store, ordered one hundred 36-inch grapevine wreaths from Star Vineyards. Star Vineyards shipped one hundred 40-inch wreaths, the only size in stock, knowing that Wiggins needed wreaths immediately for an upcoming craft show. Star then notified Wiggins that the 40-inch wreaths were sent as an accommodation. This shipment of 40-inch wreaths is not an acceptance but a counteroffer. A contract will result only if Wiggins accepts the 40-inch wreaths.

In this example, if Star Vineyards ships one hundred 40-inch wreaths instead of one hundred 36-inch wreaths and fails to notify Wiggins that a substitute was made as an accommodation, Star Vineyard's shipment acts as both an acceptance of Wiggins's offer and a breach of contract. Wiggins now has the right to sue Star Vineyards for an appropriate amount of money damages.

Under the common law, an offeree who is required to accept by completing the act requested (unilateral request) must notify the offeror of performance only if the offeror would not otherwise know the act is being completed. In this context, the UCC applies a stricter rule, stating that if the beginning of a requested performance (e.g., beginning to manufacture and/or ship the goods) is a reasonable method of acceptance, the offeree must notify the offeror of such beginning within a reasonable time. An offeror who is not reasonably notified of acceptance may treat the offer as having lapsed before acceptance (UCC 2-206).

> Anderson, in New York City, placed an order for parts for his car with the Zee-Bart Co. in Boston. Three months went by, but Anderson did not hear from Zee-Bart. Anderson then bought the parts elsewhere. Finally, after the fourth month, the parts arrived from Zee-Bart. At this point, Anderson would have the right to reject the parts Zee-Bart sent; four months generally would be considered an unreasonable length of time.

As mentioned on page 246, the UCC eliminates the mirror-image rule and replaces it with a rule that is more practical because of the way merchants do business today.

Because of this concept, however, there is no longer the single-document structured contract. A purchase order containing very unusual terms could be construed as part of the contract if a vendor does not carefully review all the fine print on the order. Agreements are made by exchanges of written forms: The offeror spells out his or her needs in a purchase order, and the offeree accepts the order and promises delivery with a confirmatory memorandum. Each business drafts its own standard form containing terms that serve its own best interests. The terms on the separate forms, however, often do not agree. Hence, the question arises: Is performance measured by the offeror's terms or the offeree's terms (which include modifications)? This situation is referred to as the "battle of the forms." To resolve this battle, the Code provides a solution under Section 2-207. When both parties are merchants, new or additional terms will not destroy acceptance, as would be the case under the common law's mirror-image rule but will automatically become part of the contract without further consent of the offeror unless (1) the offerror expressly gives notice to the offeree limiting acceptance to the terms of the offer, (2) the offeror gives notice to the offeree within a reasonable time rejecting the new terms, or (3) the new terms materially alter the contract (e.g., a big change in price or some other unreasonable element of surprise). There is no contract if the additional terms so materially alter the terms of the original offer that the parties cannot agree on the contract (UCC 2-207).

> The Merkle Company, a wholesaler of hardware supplies, using its own purchase order offered to sell Benson, buying coordinator for a retail hardware outlet in a different city, a variety of tools at a special price. Benson immediately returned an acceptance in the form of a confirming memo. In the memo was a request that the Merkle Company pay the freight charges, which were determined to be reasonable. No objection was made to Benson's request by the Merkle Company. Because both parties were merchants, and because none of the UCC exceptions applied, the freight charges would automatically be paid for by the Merkle Company as part of the original contract.

If one or both parties are nonmerchants, the courts will not automatically uphold the new terms. When requested by a nonmerchant, any additional terms are simply offers for inclusion in the contract. The offeror (party receiving the writing with the proposals) can then choose to accept these proposals (offers) or reject them. Whether these provisions are accepted would be governed by the usual rules of offer and acceptance. So if the offeror accepts the proposals, they are part of the contract; if not, the contract is formed according to the terms of the original offer submitted by the original offeror (UCC 2-207).

Consideration

Under common law rule a change in an existing contract must be based on consideration. This rule applies to both sales and lease contracts. Under the UCC, the parties must still exchange consideration; however, an agreement modifying a contract for the sale of goods needs no consideration to be binding (UCC 2-209; 2A-208). The Code treats the change in the contract as a matter of good faith rather than a matter of consideration; that is, the court considers what is fair to the parties involved. If, however, the statute of frauds requires the contract to be in writing or the contract itself prevents changes to the contract that are not in writing, any modifications without consideration made to that contract must also be in writing to be enforceable (UCC 2-209–2A-208).

Statute of Limitations

Under ordinary contract law, an action for breach of contract must be brought within six years of the time of the breach. Under the UCC, however, an action for breach of a sales contract must be started within four years of the breach. The 2003 amendments to UCC 2-275 containing the four-year limitation period extended the limitation period for up to one additional year to allow for a discovery of a breach beyond the four-year period, but no longer than five years after the right of action accrued. The parties to a sales contract may agree to reduce this four-year period to as little as one year but may not agree to extend it beyond four years (UCC 2-725).

Statute of Frauds

A contract for the sale of goods may be oral or written. The statute of frauds provision of the UCC, however, states that sales contracts for goods priced at $500 or more ($5,000 under the 2003 ammendments), and lease contracts requiring total payments of $1,000 or more must be in writing to be legally enforceable in a court of law (UCC 2-201–2A-201). The party who is liable for performance of the contract must sign it, although it is a good idea for both parties to sign.

> Bray signed an order for a stove and refrigerator for $600 from Modern Kitchens Appliance Store, to be delivered the next day. When the stove was delivered, Bray refused to accept it, claiming he had changed his mind. Because the agreement was in writing as required and was signed by Bray, Bray is legally obligated to accept and pay for the stove.

The UCC has greatly relaxed the statute of frauds requirement of the written memorandum as evidence of a sale. One important element is intent to form a contract. Then there is the requirement of "some writing"—a check, a letter, an invoice, an order blank, and so on—as evidence that a contract for the sale of goods has taken place. Another essential term of the sale—the *quantity*—must be in the writing. The contract is not enforceable beyond the quantity shown in the writing. In case of a lawsuit, other essential terms of the transaction (e.g., price or the time and place of payment or delivery) that are in dispute but that are not included in the writing can be proved by oral testimony.

Enforceable Oral Sales Contracts

The UCC allows some exceptions to the written requirements of the Statute of Frauds (UCC 2-201; 2A-201). Oral contracts for the sale of goods for $500 ($5,000 under the 2003 amendments) or more will, if proved, be enforced under the situations described in the following sections.

Buyer Receives and Accepts the Goods   An oral contract for the sale or lease of goods will be enforced if the buyer or lessee both receives and accepts all the goods. "Receipt of goods" means that the buyer physically takes possession of them. "Acceptance of goods" means that the buyer indicates, by words or actions, an intention to become the owner.

> Johnson made an oral contract with a dealer to buy a used tractor for $1,500. The tractor was to be delivered on a Monday, and Johnson was to pay for it on Thursday. The tractor was delivered on Monday as agreed, and Johnson accepted it but then refused to pay for it on Thursday, claiming he was not bound by the oral contract. Because Johnson received and accepted the goods, he is liable.

An oral contract will also be enforced if the buyer or lessee receives and accepts part of the goods. The oral contract will be enforced only for the portion of the goods actually received and accepted by the buyer or lessee. If the goods cannot be separated, the entire contract is unenforceable.

Baylor read in the newspaper that Rudnick Furniture Store was having a summer furniture sale. She telephoned the store and ordered a patio table and chairs for $800 and two family room chairs for $350 each, for a total of $1,500. She had looked at these items in the store a few days earlier. Rudnick agreed to deliver the items. When the items arrived, Baylor decided to accept and pay for only the patio table and chairs. Baylor is legally obligated to pay for only the patio table and chairs.

Buyer Makes Full Payment

The entire oral contract is enforceable if the buyer or lessee makes full payment for the goods under the terms of the sales contract.

Cobb orally agreed to purchase a used snowmobile from the Arctic Cat Snowmobile Company and paid $700 cash. When the snowmobile was delivered the next day, Cobb refused to accept it and demanded the return of her $700. She claimed that because the agreement was not in writing, she was not bound to accept the snowmobile. Cobb was liable, however, because she had paid for the snowmobile in full.

Buyer Makes a Part Payment on the Goods

An oral contract is binding if the buyer or leasee makes a part payment on the goods. The contract is enforceable, however, only for those goods covered by the part payment. If the goods cannot be separated, the oral contract cannot be enforced against the buyer.

Bono made an oral contract to purchase a stereo system from Sound-Com for $600. The system included a receiver, $280; a turntable, $130; and speakers, $190. She made a part payment of $280, the cost of the receiver. The turntable and speakers were temporarily out of stock, but Bono did take the receiver at the time of the sale. Bono later changed her mind and decided to use her old turntable and speakers and keep only the receiver that was already paid for. Sound-Com insisted that Bono was obligated to take the entire stereo system. Because the contract was oral, Bono was liable only for the receiver that she had already paid for. She was not liable for the price of either the turntable or the speakers.

The courts have ruled that an oral contract for the sale of goods consisting of a single item is binding when the buyer makes a down payment (*Lockwood* v. *Smigel*, 96 Cal. Rptr. 289).

Sacco offered to sell her used Rolls-Royce to Ruff for $20,000. Ruff accepted the offer and paid Sacco $1,000 as a down payment. The balance was to be paid upon delivery of the car. Sacco never delivered the car but instead sold it to someone else. Ruff sued for damages for breach of an oral contract. Sacco would be liable.

Specially Manufactured Goods

An oral contract for goods to be specially manufactured for the buyer or obtained for a particular lessee is enforceable. The contract is enforceable, however, only if (1) the goods to be manufactured are not suitable for resale or lease to others in the regular course of the seller's or lessor's business and (2) the seller or lessor before receiving notice that the buyer did not want them, made a substantial beginning on the manufacture of the goods or made commitments for the manufacture of the goods. This rule protects the seller or lessor who would have to absorb the loss if the buyer did not take the goods. Goods made to a buyer's or lessor's specifications or imprinted with the buyer's or lessor's name generally cannot be resold to others.

The Realty Door Company, a manufacturer of custom exterior doors, orally contracted with Spoleta Contractors to design and build custom $3,000 outside doors for a new house that Spoleta was building. After Realty had completed substantial work on the doors, Spoleta advised Realty to cancel the contract. Realty, however, finished the doors and shipped them to Spoleta. Spoleta refused to accept delivery, claiming that the contract cannot be enforced because it was not in writing as required by the statute of frauds. Nevertheless, Spoleta is liable; the doors were custom made for him, they were not suitable for sale to others in the ordinary course of the seller's (Realty Door Company) business, and Realty had made a substantial beginning of their manufacture before receiving a notice of repudiation from Spoleta.

An oral contract is not enforceable if the contract is completely executory—that is, if the terms of the contract have not been carried out—when notice of repudiation is received from the buyer. If Spoleta had canceled the order before Realty Door Company had started to manufacture the doors, the oral contract would not be enforceable.

Admission in Court of an Oral Contract

If a person being sued admits in court (on the witness stand) that an oral contract for the sale or lease of goods was in fact made, the contract will be enforced. Under the 2003 amendments, the exception to admission in court has been broadened to include out-of-court admissioned "under oath." Enforceability, however, is limited to the quantity of goods admitted.

> You orally agreed to buy a set of encyclopedias for $800 from the Educational Book Company. Delivery of the books by the company and payment by you were to take place on a certain date. On that date, the books were delivered but you refused to accept them. The company could not win in a suit against you unless you admitted in open court that the oral contract for the encyclopedias was actually made.

Written Confirmation Between Merchants

The written confirmation between merchants rule is one of the few special rules within Article 2 of the UCC that applies only to the sale of goods and only between merchants. The rule states that if two merchants make an oral agreement, the statute of frauds requirement is satisfied if one of them sends a written confirmation of the oral agreement to the other merchant. The merchant receiving the confirmation must give written notice of objection to this confirmation within ten days after receiving it. If the receiving merchant does not give written notice within that time, the contract will be enforceable, even though the receiving merchant has not signed anything.

> Cavanna, a North Carolina merchant who sells women's apparel, placed a telephone order for ten dozen hats from PSI, a wholesaler in New York City. PSI sent Cavanna a signed invoice for the hat order (written confirmation), giving details of their oral agreement. If Cavanna does not send PSI a written objection to the contents of this invoice within ten days of receipt of the invoice, the oral (telephone) contract will be enforceable.

UNCONSCIONABILITY

The doctrine of unconscionability was discussed in Chapter 10. This doctrine, which has been around for centuries, has become significantly more important under the UCC 2-302. Because of changes in the way people do business in the modern world, the ethical behavior of merchants can now be controlled more directly by courts. Under basic contract law (common law principles), the parties to a contract were considered equals; if the contract turned out to be unfair to one party (generally, the consumer), this consumer had no recourse at law. He or she had agreed to the terms, and that was that. Courts of equity very often refused to grant relief of a contract that was unfair (unconscionable). A party who signed an unfair contract had to find other ways to get relief. A common device was to have the contract declared void on the grounds that it was against public policy. Now, under the Code, courts, using normal legal processes, can deal directly with such problems and can exercise discretion that traditionally belonged to equity courts. Under the UCC, courts have expanded powers to deal with unfairness and to ensure that all contracts seem perfectly ethical. They may evaluate a contract or any clause (referred to as "term" under the 2003 amendments). If the contract or any part of it is deemed unconscionable at the time it was made, the court can (1) refuse to enforce the contract, (2) enforce the contract minus the unconscionable clause or clauses, or (3) limit the application of any unconscionable clauses to avoid an unconscionable result. In the latter case, an example would be an unconscionable contract, in which it was determined that a contract entered into by a consumer involved an inflated price for an item thus rendering the contract unconscionable, could be re-formed to eliminate some of the monthly payments to allow for the inflated price (UCC 2-302).

Nevertheless, only contracts that are so extremely unfair to one of the parties as to "shock the conscience" of the court have been found unconscionable. Typically, the courts have held unconscionable contracts that involve uneducated consumers who are placed in a position of having unequal bargaining power, contracts in which the seller is in a position to impose his or her will on a consumer who would not have contracted if he or she had known all the facts. Too often, this consumer is a person who speaks little English and cannot read, let alone understand the language of a standard form contract. This person often pays an excessive price (two or three times greater than the average retail price elsewhere) or agrees to waive certain basic rights such as the right to sue in the event of dissatisfaction with a product.

THE PAROL EVIDENCE RULE

course of dealing
conduct between parties that took place prior to a specific dispute

course of performance
way in which a particular transaction has been carried out

usage of trade
standard custom or widely accepted practice in a particular occupation that can be applied to a dispute

Recall the parol evidence rule that was discussed in Chapter 11. According to this rule, when a contract has been put in writing as the final expression of agreement between the parties, parol evidence—evidence of an oral agreement made prior to or at the time of signing the written agreement—cannot be presented in court to change or add to the terms of this written agreement. Parol evidence can be presented in court to give meaning or add clarity to unclear language. The UCC reaffirms this basic contract-law rule, along with the exceptions noted in Chapter 11, but the Code goes beyond these exceptions. For example, the court will not allow evidence of contradictory terms. It further states that when a written sales contract made in today's modern business world is in dispute, the contract should be interpreted in light of surrounding circumstances. Evidence is allowed from three sources: course of dealing, course of performance, and usages of trade (UCC 2-202; 2A-202). A **course of dealing** refers to any conduct that took place between the parties prior to the present dispute (e.g., a series of agreements showing a pattern of dealings between the parties) and that can be followed to interpret their wording in the present disputed agreement (UCC 1-205). A **course of performance** refers to the way in which a particular transaction has been carried out (UCC 2-208). Repeated acts—such as the acceptance without objection of several deliveries of goods that do not technically meet the requirements of the disputed contract—may be sufficient to help a court decide what the parties actually intended. A **usage of trade** refers to a standard custom or a widely accepted practice in a particular occupation that can be applied to the disputed contract (UCC 1-205). For example, customary practice in the farm produce business may be to state in the sales contract a reasonable estimate rather than an exact number of each fruit and vegetable to be purchased.

FORMATION OF THE LEASE CONTRACT

lease rental agreement for real or personal property

lessor landlord; owner of goods

lessee tenant; renter of goods

Some people and companies prefer to lease rather than buy. The parties to a lease contract are governed by Article 2A of the UCC, which governs all leases (e.g., automobiles, furniture, hand tools, or industrial equipment). Many of the Article 2 rules governing sales law carry over to Article 2A, lease law, with some variation in these rules because of the difference between a sale (a transfer of ownership) and a lease (a transfer of possession). Like Article 2, Article 2A was amended in 2003 and these amendments have been recommended to the states for adoption. Article 2A defines a **lease** as a transfer of possession and use of goods (tangible personal property) for a certain period of time by a **lessor** (owner) to a **lessee** (renter) based on a consideration with the expectation that the goods will be returned to the owner at the end of the lease term. Article 2A recognizes two types of leases: *consumer leases* and *finance leases.* A consumer lease is made by a lessor who regularly engages in the business of making leases and is made to a lessee for personal, family, or household usage (e.g., renting an automobile, furniture or hand tools). Under the 2003 amendments, Article 2A does not include a dollar amount on a consumer lease contract. The amendment allows states, if they wish, to place a dollar amount on the total leases. A finance lease is a special type of lease generally involving three parties instead of two. The lessor's primary function in a finance lease is to provide financing to the lessee for a lease of goods provided by the supplier. For example, under a finance lease arrangement, a manufacturer supplies goods pursuant to the lessee's instructions or specifications. The lessor will then either purchase those goods from the supplier or act as the lessee in leasing them from the supplier. In turn, the lessor will lease or sublease the goods to the lessee. A business leasing heavy equipment is an example of a finance lease. Parties to a lease, like the parties to a sale, are classified as merchants or nonmerchants. Leases may also be subject to the rules providing for firm offers. Protections are provided for a lessee in the ordinary course of business through warranties similar to those given under Article 2. If a court finds that a lease or a clause in a lease was unconscionable at the time it was made, a court may refuse to enforce the lease or clause that is unconscionable. One difference that does exist is that the statute of frauds requires that leases having total payments (excluding options for renewal or options to purchase the goods) of $1,000 or more be in writing. Some leases, like consumer leases, have special rules.

FORMATION OF E-SALES CONTRACTS

The fundamentals of contract law as expressed in the Uniform Commercial Code (UCC) provide a strong basis for transacting business online and for handling many of the issues raised by the application of traditional principles of law to online contracts. This online concept is strongly supported by both the federal and state governments. The Uniform Commercial Code, as passed, has relaxed the rules of traditional contract law, making it easier to apply the Code to online transactions. In addition, the Uniform Electronic Transactions Act and the Federal Electronic Signatures and National Commerce Act provide that electronic contracts and signatures are not to be denied legal enforceability simply because they are in electronic form. This places them on par with paper agreements. Further, new laws have been created to apply to situations in which existing laws do not adequately address contract issues peculiar to the online world.

Why was all this action necessary on the part of the federal and state governments? Simply because more and more businesses and individual consumers are making legally binding and enforceable contracts on the Internet. Contracts are formed daily by businesses doing business with their vendors and with consumers who shop online for computers, treadmills, clothing, jewelry, compact discs, books, and many other types of goods. Both businesses and consumers bank online, while many travelers purchase their airline tickets directly from the airlines and make hotel reservations directly with the hotel rather than process their request through a travel agency.

Online Offers and Acceptances

Contracts can arise online in numerous ways as long as the parties have the intent to form a contract. Offers and acceptances may be exchanged by e-mail; Web site (goods advertised online); electronic data interchange (EDI) where computers "talk to each other"; or by a combination of electronic communication with traditional faxes, human involvement (oral discussion by phone), or written communication. Many contracts involve e-mails between the offeror and the offeree or a click-on agreement in which the offeree clicks "Yes" or "Agree to Terms" (or some similar phrase) on the computer screen to an e-mail offer made by the offeror. For example, you send a person an e-mail that reads, "I will sell you my computer hard drive and printer for $1,500," and that person responds with an e-mail stating that she will buy the items at the offered price. The electronically transmitted offer and acceptance resulted in a contract by extending the principles of law learned earlier in this chapter and in the chapter on offer and acceptance (Chapter 7). A principle of contract law learned was that a contract including an offer and acceptance may be formed in any manner sufficient to show agreement. Such agreements can be made orally, in writing, or by conduct of the parties that recognizes the existence of a contract. The courts will say that there is no reason an electronically transmitted offer such as an e-mail should not meet this requirment. Another principle of contract law learned was that an offer may be accepted by any reasonable method of communication. The courts' interpretation of this principle is that acceptance by e-mail as well as any other form of electronic message or by conduct such as "clicking" a button fits the definition of any reasonable method of communication. Both of these principles are an influence of the UCC being applied to traditional common law contract situations. Under the UCC, these same principles apply to such cases. For example, Marvin's Stationary Outlet, a retail store, purchased paper supplies (goods) for his business from Gateway Stationary Wholesale House through an online ordering system. After placing his order online, including entering the amount of the transaction, he clicked the box stating, "Agree to the conditions in this offer." The click amounted to an acceptance.

Like the mirror-image rule, the mailbox rule has given way to technology. Recall the mailbox rule from Chapter 7 indicating that acceptance of an offer results as soon as it is deposited with the communicating agency by the offeree. With the advent of contracts being formed online, the need for the mailbox rule becomes obsolete since online acceptances when sent are now communicated instantly to the offeror.

Disputes have surfaced regarding the formation of contracts online in spite of the preceding statement that electronic contracts have the same enforceability as paper transactions. For example, it is sometimes unclear in an online agreement whether the offeree voluntarily assented to the terms contained in the offer. Under these circumstances, it is best for an offeror as master of the offer to be specific about how he or she wishes the offeree to accept and when the acceptance becomes effective. Of course, the first rule should be that the seller's Web site display the full contract to make the potential offeree aware of the terms of the contract that he or she is going to accept. Another suggestion would be for the offeror to be sure to give the offeree a clear choice between accepting and rejecting the offer and what constitutes an acceptance or a rejection. Still another choice would be for the offeree to require a re-formation of the offer by the offeror asking for more clarity and having the offeror re-send it to the offeree. Sometimes, back-and-forth requests for clarity on the Internet cause more confusion as to what was offered and whether or not there was an acceptance that would lead to a legal contract.

Writing Requirement

Electronic communications using a tangible medium are acceptable as a writing requirement. The courts will accept telegraphed messages, telexes, Western Union Mailgrams, and faxes, but not such mediums as communications on chat lines or electronic bulletin boards (unless printed out) or even e-mails kept in a computer log.

Signature Requirement

A key issue facing the parties who are forming a contract online is the verification of e-signatures in order to reduce the risk of fraud and claims of unauthorized use of an e-signature. The digital signature method described in Chapter 11 is a common method employed by the parties to a contract, especially a seller and a buyer. Another common form is a "smart card," which stores digital information about the signer and may be used to verify a person's identity. Companies having a concern about fraud can purchase the services of a security firm to verify e-signatures.

Mistakes in Electronic Communications

Mistakes in electronic transmission can and do occur. Two common reasons are human error, such as keyboarding in the wrong information, or a programming error, such as a flaw in a computer program. Both errors result in the recipient receiving information that is different from what was sent. How mistakes are handled will depend on (1) whether the party receiving the wrong information would be harmed if the contract was declared void, (2) whether it would be harmful to hold the person receiving the wrong information accountable, or (3) what stage the contract is at when the mistake was discovered.

Summary

Laws relating to the sale of goods (sales law) have their origin in the common law principles of contracts. Article 2 of the Uniform Commercial Code (UCC), however, which governs sales law, has made changes that meet the needs of merchants and consumers who deal with one another contractually in a modern business world. In effect, the UCC has relaxed the rules relating to sales transactions by removing many of the technical requirements relating to contracts under the common law. Under the UCC, it is now far easier to form a binding sales contract. In fact, a sales contract may be made in any manner sufficient to show that the parties intended to be bound, even though essential terms such as price, quantity, place and time for delivery, and terms of payment are missing. These missing terms can be added later by the parties or supplied under other provisions of the Code. To offset these relaxed rules, however, the Code does insist that the parties perform in good faith (honestly) and that the dominant party deals fairly with the other party to the sales transaction.

The UCC defines a sale as a contract that transfers ownership of goods from the seller (vendor) to the buyer for a price. Under the UCC, goods are defined as tangible personal property—that is, something movable. The term *goods* includes items such as software, growing crops and timber to be cut, minerals (including gas and oil), and structures, if severance is to be made by the seller; money bought and sold as a commodity; the unborn young of animals; items specially manufactured for a buyer; and items that are attached to real property and can easily be removed without doing material harm. The term *goods* does not include intangible (not physical) personal property, such as shares of stock.

Article 2 generally applies to all sellers and buyers, whether they are merchants or nonmerchants. In a few limited provisions of Article 2, some special rules apply only to sales contracts between merchants. A merchant is a professional. He or she either sells goods of the type involved in the sales contract (e.g., a retailer) or has specialized knowledge of these goods by virtue of his or her profession (e.g., a purchasing agent for a big company). A nonmerchant is a casual seller.

Article 2 of the UCC has made substantial modifications to contracts under the common law in the areas of offer and acceptance and consideration. Moreover, an action for breach of contract under the Code must be brought within four years of the breach. The 2003 amendments to UCC 2-75 extended the limitation period for up to one additional year under certain circumstances. Under the UCC statute of frauds, most contracts for the sale of goods costing $500 or more must be in writing to be enforceable. In some cases, however, oral contracts for more than $500 ($5,000 under the 2003 amendments) are enforceable. Under the Code, courts can now deal directly with unconscionable contracts—that is, contracts that are unfair in a court of law. Before the Code, the unethical behavior of merchants, which is the basis of unconscionability, was handled in an indirect way in equity court.

The Code reaffirms the parol evidence rule and its exceptions. This rule states that after a contract has been reduced to writing as the final expression of agreement between the parties, oral or written evidence cannot change or add to the terms of the written contract. The exceptions to the parol rule permit evidence that will clarify the written document but not change its terms. The Code broadens the type of evidence that may be introduced to help interpret (but not change) disputed contracts. It allows evidence based on widely accepted practices in a particular occupation and on dealings between the parties at various times either before or after the disputed contract was made.

Some people and companies prefer to lease goods rather than purchase them. If so, the parties to the lease will be governed by Article 2A of the UCC. Leasing involves a transfer of possession, whereas a sale involves a transfer of ownership (title) under Article 2 of the UCC.

The Uniform Electronic Transaction Act and the Federal Electronics Signatures and National Commerce Act have placed e-contracts on a par with paper agreements by stating that electronic contracts and signatures are not to be denied legal enforceability simply because they are in electronic form. Electronic communications using a tangible medium such as telegraphs, telexes, Western Union Mailgrams, and faxes are acceptable as a writing requirement. If a signature becomes necessary to satisfy the statute of frauds, the merchant seller and the consumer buyer should work out the method by which an electronic signature may be substituted for a manual signature.

Because disputes have surfaced regarding the formation of contracts online, certain precautions should be taken to ensure that offerors and offerees create offers and acceptances that clearly protect themselves against these disputes.

Important Legal terms

course of dealing	lessee	sale
course of performance	lessor	Uniform Commercial Code (UCC)
goods	merchant	usage of trade
lease	nonmerchant	

Questions and Problems for Discussion

1. Under the UCC, Article 2, Sales, a firm offer will be created under which of the following circumstances?
   a. Offeree is a merchant.
   b. Offeree provides consideration.
   c. Offer is made by a merchant in a signed writing.
   d. Offeror is a nonmerchant.

2. Under the UCC, Article 2, Sales, which of the following statements is correct?
   a. All contracts must be in writing.
   b. Merchants and nonmerchants are treated the same.
   c. The parties to the contract must perform their obligations in good faith.
   d. The contract cannot involve a sale of goods of more than $500.

3. Which of the following would not be considered under the UCC's definition of goods?
   a. unborn young of animals
   b. growing crops
   c. a cell phone
   d. shares of stock

4. Assume that seller A sends B, the buyer, a form offering to sell certain goods. B returns a form accepting the offer. The two forms do not agree on every point. Do A and B have a contract under Article 2? Why or why not?

5. Bell, purchasing agent for the Hiram Paint Company, mailed a purchase order to the ABC Can Company requesting 50,000 new paint cans. The order form contained, among others things, a condition stating, "The buyer may reject any defective goods within twenty days of delivery." The ABC Can Company sent a return letter confirming the order. The letter contained a condition stating, "An objection to goods shipped must be made in writing within five days of receipt of the goods." On the eighth day after receipt of the shipment of cans, Bell filed an objection to 5,000 cans he stated were defective. Is this objection legally valid?

6. The R & R Door Co. (R&R), a manufacturer of custom interior and exterior doors, orally contracted with Rolland to design and build custom interior doors for Rolland's new house at a price of $1,500 per door or a total cost of $6,000 for four doors. After R&R had competed substantial work on the doors, Rolland changed his mind and decided against custom doors because of the price. He so advised R&R of his decision and stated that he would not take delivery of the custom built doors. Nevertheless, R&R finished the small amount of work that had to be done and delivered the doors to Rolland. Rolland claimed that he was not legally bound to take the doors since the contract was not in writing as required by the statute of frauds. Is Rolland correct?

7. On May 2, Mavrick orally contracted with the Target Appliance Center to buy for $475 a TV for his new apartment. Mavrick and the Target salesperson both agreed that delivery would be made on July 2. On May 10, Mavrick phoned Target and requested that the delivery date be moved to June 2. The Target salesperson agreed with this request. On June 2, Target failed to deliver the TV to Mavrick's apartment because of a shortage in the warehouse. The Target salesperson then informed Mavrick that it would now deliver the TV on July 2 as originally agreed. Mavrick insists that Target has breached its contract with him. Target contends that its agreement to deliver on June 2 was not binding. Is Target's contention correct?

8. On May 2, BenFonte Hardware sent Cooper Industries a signed purchase order that stated, in part, the following: "Ship for May 8 delivery 300 Model B-W socket wrenches at current dealer price. Terms 2/10/30." Cooper received BenFonte's purchase order on May 4. On May 5, Cooper discovered that it had only 200 Model B-W socket wrenches and 100 model B-Z socket wrenches in stock. Cooper shipped the Model B-W and Model B-Z wrenches to BenFonte without any explanation concerning the shipment. The wrenches were received by BenFonte on May 8. Is Cooper's shipment an acceptance of BenFonte's offer or a counteroffer?

9. Cole, a retail auto parts dealer, needed some parts quickly. He sent a telegram to Veterans Wholesale Auto Parts, requesting that the necessary parts be sent immediately. Two days later, Cole followed up with a telephone call to Veterans. Five weeks later, the parts arrived, but Cole rejected them, claiming that they arrived too late. Cole had made other arrangements. Veterans sued Cole for breach of contract. Was Cole liable for breach of contract?

10. Colonial, a manufacturer of custom exterior doors and windows, verbally contracted with Crista Contractors to design and build a custom door for a house that Crista had built in a very exclusive tract. After Colonial had completed substantial work on the door, Crista informed Colonial that the house had been destroyed by fire and that Crista was canceling the contract. Nevertheless, Colonial finished the door and shipped it to Crista, who refused to take delivery. Crista contends that the contract cannot be enforced because it violated the statute of frauds for not being in writing. Is Crista's contention correct?

Cases for Review

1. Ralston Purina contracted to buy soybeans from McNabb. Poor weather damaged most of the soybeans, making it impossible for McNabb to deliver his crop by the deadline date. Ralston Purina agreed to modify the contract, without additional consideration, to allow delivery at a later date. When McNabb still could not deliver by the new deadline date, Ralston Purina sued for breach of contract based on the new deadline date. McNabb admitted damages but claimed that Ralston Purina, an experienced purchaser of soybeans, was not acting in good faith when it modified the contract, knowing that the price would rise as the result of the crop failure. McNabb therefore contended that the modification was not good and that the measure of damages claimed by Ralston Purina should be based not on the price as of the new deadline date but on the price of soybeans as of the date McNabb originally agreed to furnish the soybeans but failed to do so. Do you agree? (*Ralston Purina Co.* v. *McNabb*, 381 F. Supp. 181)

2. Auburn Plastics sent a letter to CBS offering to manufacture molds that CBS used to make parts for toys. The letter offer stated that CBS had fifteen days to accept or the option would lapse and that if CBS did accept the offer and required delivery of the molds, there would be a 30 percent charge for services. CBS waited four months to respond to the offer. It sent a purchase order for the molds but included a condition that CBS had the right to demand delivery of the molds from Auburn Plastics at any time without payment of the service charge. Auburn accepted the offer through an acknowledgment form but stated that the service charge would apply. When CBS demanded immediate delivery of its order, Auburn refused to deliver the molds unless CBS paid the 30 percent charge for services. CBS then obtained an order directing the sheriff to seize the molds. Did CBS have the right to do that? (*CBS, Inc.* v. *Auburn Plastics, Inc.*, 413 N.Y.S.2d 50)

3. Hemphill, a football player at Southern Illinois State University, was furnished with a uniform and helmet. While playing a game, he was injured and claimed that his defective helmet furnished by the college caused the injury. Hemphill sued the school, its athletic director, and the head coach under Article 2 of the UCC dealing with merchants and the liability of merchants. Was Hemphill correct in bringing a lawsuit under Article 2? (*Hemphill* v. *Sayers*, 552 Supp. 685)

4. St. Charles Cable TV, which was building a new cable television system, contacted Eagle Comtronics, Inc., by phone and agreed to buy several thousand descrambler units for its cable system. The descramblers were shipped to St. Charles along with a sales acknowledgment form containing terms and conditions of the sale. St. Charles made partial payment for the descramblers before discovering that some of the units were defective. Eagle accepted a return of the defective units. St. Charles then attempted to return all the units, asking that they be replaced by a newer model. When Eagle refused to replace all the old descramblers, St. Charles stopped paying Eagle. Eagle sued for breach of contract, but St. Charles claimed that no valid contract existed between the parties. Was St. Charles correct? (*St. Charles Cable TV* v. *Eagle Comtronics, Inc.*, 687 F. Supp 820)

5. Barron owned and operated a sod farm. Edwards orally agreed to purchase Barron's entire sod crop for $300. Before the sod was removed, Barron notified Edwards that he had changed his mind and further stated that because the sod was part of the real estate, the oral agreement was invalid under the statute of frauds. Edwards sued for breach of contract, stating that the sod was personal property (goods) because it could easily be removed without doing damage and that the oral contract was valid. Was Edwards correct? (*Barron* v. *Edwards,* 45 Mich. App. 210)

6. Lewis orally agreed to sell Hughes a house trailer for $5,000 cash. Shortly after the oral agreement was made, Hughes informed Lewis that he would not pay the full $5,000 in cash. He wanted to pay it over a period of time or to pay Lewis $3,500

immediately in full settlement. Lewis sued for breach of the oral contract. Hughes contended that an oral contract for a sale of goods of $500 or more was not binding under the statute of frauds unless it was in writing. During the trial, however, Hughes repeatedly testified that he had informed Lewis that he would purchase the mobile home for $5,000 cash. In these circumstances, should Lewis be awarded damages suffered as a result of the breach of the oral contract? (*Lewis* v. *Hughes,* 276 Md. 247, 346 A.2d 231)

CHAPTER 16

The Sales Contract: Transfer of Title and Risk of Loss

CHAPTER PREVIEW

Relevance of Title and Risk of Loss in Sales Law	**Bulk Sales**
Present Sale Versus Contract to Sell	**Sales or Leases by Nonowners**
Risk of Loss in Absence of a Breach	Seller Had a Void Title
Delivery Without Movement of the Goods	Seller Had a Voidable Title
Delivery with Movement of the Goods—Carrier Cases	Merchant Was Given Temporary Possession
	Risk of Loss Where There Is a Breach of Contract
Sales on Approval or Return	

Chapter Highlights

This chapter concentrates primarily on the rules that determine when risk of loss (financial responsibility) passes from seller to buyer after the contract is made and the goods have been damaged, destroyed, or lost while being delivered. The chapter also spells out the rights of third parties, who may acquire goods from the buyer under various circumstances. You will learn that although title, or legal ownership, of goods is a very important concept, it is not as important under the Uniform Commercial Code (UCC) as it was in the past. Early in the chapter, some very important terms are defined. A knowledge of these terms will give you a better understanding of the concepts and principles discussed in the chapter.

RELEVANCE OF TITLE AND RISK OF LOSS IN SALES LAW

A significant aspect of Article 2 of the UCC is to downplay what has been considered the main point under the common law relating to the sale of goods for over one hundred years—the location of title to the goods that formed the basis of the sale to the buyer. Important issues relating to the sale of goods, such as who bears the risk of loss, when the seller can initiate an action for the price, and when the buyer has the right to take possession of the goods, was then arbitrarily assigned to the party who held the title. The UCC Article 2, thanks to the drafters of the Code, recognized the unfairness of this doctrine based on cases decided over the many years that this doctrine existed. These cases brought to light that it was often difficult to predict when the title passed or better yet, when title was even established. While the drafters of the Code did de-emphasize title and dissociated it with determining who bears the risk of loss if goods are damaged, destroyed, or lost, it is important in other contexts. Title, for example, prevents the seller's unpaid creditors from claiming goods when the title to those goods has passed to the buyer. Title also determines whether goods are the subject of a present sale or simply a contract to sell.

The parties to a contract determine when the title, or ownership, of goods passes from seller to buyer. The parties also determine when the risk of loss—financial responsibility for lost, damaged, or destroyed goods—passes from the seller to the buyer. Typically, however, most lawsuits involve situations in which (1) goods are damaged, destroyed, or lost after the contract is made and (2) both the seller and the buyer claim they are not a fault. If the contract does not specify when title and risk of loss pass from buyer to seller, the courts will use the rules set out in Article 2 of the Uniform Commercial Code to determine liability. The Code provides some definite rules for special situations.

The UCC provisions relating to when title passes do not apply to leasing contracts since title to goods is retained by the owner (lessor) of the goods. However the information in this chapter relating to risk of loss and when goods are identified apply to both sales and lease contracts.

The primary emphasis in this chapter is on the UCC rules for shifting risk of loss rather than on the rules that determine when title passes. The reason for this emphasis was stated previously, namely, that the UCC rules for shifting loss are more important than the rules for passing title.

You should note that, under UCC rules, the decision about who will suffer risk of loss depends on whether the sales contract had been breached at the time the loss occurred. If either party has committed a breach of contract, the risk of loss usually falls totally or in part on the party who committed the breach (UCC 2-510). Such cases are discussed briefly in this chapter; examined in more detail are those situations in which no breach of contract has taken place and both parties to the sales contract are silent as to who bears the risk of loss. Generally, the concepts in this chapter (except that of title) also apply to lease contracts.

PRESENT SALE VERSUS CONTRACT TO SELL

present sale sale in which title to goods passes from seller to buyer at the time parties make the contract

A contract for the sale of goods involves either a *present sale* or a *contract to sell*. When a **present sale** of goods is made, title passes from the seller to the buyer at the time the parties make the contract. As consumers, most of what we purchase in our daily lives is covered by present sale contracts. Title passes immediately because the goods are physically in existence and identified as the specific goods designated in the contract. A cash sale is a present sale, as is a credit sale of identified goods.

identified goods exact goods being sold that have been decided on by seller and buyer

Goods become **identified goods** (told they are yours) when the seller and the buyer decide on (single out) the exact goods to be sold. This can happen before or after the formation of the contract. The important thing is that the identified goods to be sold are now distinguishable. Identification (although far less than complete ownership) has legal consequences for the buyer. Section 2-501 of the UCC gives the buyer a "special interest" in the goods and gives the buyer the right (1) to inspect the identified goods and (2) to recover damages from any third party who interferes with this property. These rights, however, do not exist absent identification. Thus, when you select a *particular pair* of skis at a sporting goods store, the goods become identified. Keep in mind that risk of loss and title cannot pass to the buyer from the seller unless the goods are identified to the contract (UCC 2-105).

contract to sell sale in which title to goods passes from seller to buyer at a future time

future goods goods not yet in existence and not yet identified

Identification also gives the parties the right to enter into a **contract to sell**. In a contract to sell, the seller promises to sell future goods and to transfer title at a later time. **Future goods** are goods not yet in existence and not yet identified.

You placed a special order for a new car with a car dealer. The car was to be manufactured to your specifications. This sale was a contract to sell. Title will not pass to you until the car is in existence and has been identified as the car you ordered.

fungible goods a unit is the equivalent of any other unit

If the goods are **fungible** (one unit is the equivalent of any other unit), identification takes place when the contract is made. For example, if a gasoline station chain agrees to purchase 500,000 gallons of gasoline, identification occurs immediately when the contract is formed.

The seller and the buyer may not always agree on the exact time at which identification took place unless they placed a notation in their contract. Identifying the skis for purchase in the sporting goods store noted in the earlier example was relatively easy. Very often, however, identification will take place between merchants after the contract has been made. At the time the contract is made, the merchant seller simply agrees to furnish a specified number of items from his or her general inventory. Then, at a later time, the merchant seller will separate the specific items specified in the contract. At this point, a disagreement may arise. In such cases, the Code contains detailed provisions to establish when identification takes place (UCC 2-501). There could not, of course, be a present identification of future goods.

RISK OF LOSS IN ABSENCE OF A BREACH

Article 2 of the UCC takes a very practical view of who should bear the risk of loss in the event that goods are destroyed, damaged, or lost. The rules under the UCC are discussed in the following sections and illustrated in Table 16.1. Keep in mind that, as indicated earlier in the chapter, these rules apply only if the seller and the buyer, for whatever reason, have failed to state in their agreement who will bear the risk of loss.

The Code places the loss on the party who is most likely to insure the goods as they move to their destination point or on the party who seems to be better able to prevent a loss of these goods. If the seller legally must bear the risk of loss, he or she cannot recover the price of the goods from the buyer; if the buyer has already paid the price, the seller is obligated to return it. If the buyer legally must bear the risk of loss, he or she is liable for the price of the goods, even if the price has been paid, but the goods have not been received.

Delivery Without Movement of the Goods

Frequently, the buyer is to pick up the goods from the seller (merchant or nonmerchant) as, for example, at the seller's place of business or home (no shipment or delivery required). In this case, risk of loss passes upon the buyer's receipt of the goods. Receipt requires taking the physical possession of the goods. (UCC 2-509). Until then, it is the seller who suffers any loss. This rule applies even if the buyer has made full payment. The UCC, in this

TABLE 16.1   RULES FOR PASSAGE OF RISK OF LOSS FROM SELLER TO BUYER UNDER THE UCC

CONTRACT TERMS	RISK OF LOSS PASSES TO BUYER
Sale by a merchant requiring	
• Delivery Without movement of goods	On receipt (physical possession) of goods by the buyer
• Delivery with movement of goods	
• Delivery to carrier only	When goods are properly delivered to an independent (for-hire) carrier at the shipping point
• Delivery to destination points	When goods are properly tendered (offered) to the buyer after reaching the destination point
Sale on approval	When the buyer accepts goods in his or her possession by approval, whether by words or by conduct
Sale or return	At the time of the sale

case, protects the buyer who has no control over the goods (until they are picked up) and it is unlikely that he will carry insurance on goods not yet in his possession.

> Welcome Motors, a car dealer, sold a new car to Merrin. The car was left at the dealership for two days after the sale was made for prepping and to remove some minor scratches. While the car was at the dealership, a fire resulting from defective wiring destroyed part of the dealership, along with Merrin's car. Under the UCC, Welcome Motors, a merchant, bears the risk of loss because it had possession of the car.

Delivery with Movement of the Goods—Carrier Cases

Shipping terms such as FOB (free on board, a delivery term) may be used in a sales contract that requires or authorizes shipment of the goods to a particular destination. Since these terms relate to which party will bear the costs of delivery, and unless otherwise agreed, they also determine who bears the risk of loss, and the parties must agree on their meaning. If they are used without having been defined, then the UCC states that the terms be interpreted according to how they are used in the "trade or profession" of the parties to the contract.

If the contract requires or authorizes the seller to ship the goods by carrier, the following rules apply.

Shipment Contracts If the seller and the buyer agreed on FOB terms requiring the seller only to ship the goods by carrier (but not to a particular destination), risk of loss passes to the buyer when the conforming goods are properly delivered to the independent carrier at the shipping point (**shipment contract**). A truck owned by a department store that delivers goods is not an independent carrier under the UCC because the goods are not taken out of the possession of the seller. A proper delivery occurs when the seller places the goods in the possession of the carrier, makes a contract for their transportation, and promptly notifies the buyer of the shipment (UCC 2-209, 2A-219). The seller has performed his or her part of the contract. From the shipping point on, the buyer is responsible for any loss. If the seller and buyer agree, the shipping terms would be FOB shipping point. The specific shipping point may be mentioned, such as FOB New York.

> The Modern Appliance Company of Albany, New York, ordered twenty-five microwave ovens from Arlen Stove Manufacturers in Detroit, Michigan, terms FOB Detroit (the shipping point). These terms indicated that the merchandise was to be "free on board" until Detroit. After that, Arlen would no longer be responsible for any loss. Thus, if the ovens were lost or damaged after leaving Detroit, Modern Appliance Company would have to bear the loss.

Destination Contracts If the seller and the buyer agreed on FOB terms requiring the seller to deliver the goods to a particular destination, such as the buyer's store or warehouse (**destination contract**), risk of loss passes from seller to buyer only after the goods have reached their destination point and then only after the goods have been properly tendered (offered) to the buyer—that is, after the buyer is properly notified of the arrival of the goods and is given a reasonable time thereafter to pick them up (UCC 2-509; 2A-219). Upon proper tender, the risk of loss passes to the buyer whether or not the buyer takes actual delivery of the goods. If the seller and buyer agree, the shipping term would be FOB destination.

> Vardi, a food merchant of Salem, Massachusetts, purchased 2,500 pounds of spaghetti from the Caro Food Company of Buffalo, New York, terms FOB Salem (destination). Several cartons of spaghetti were lost before reaching Salem. Caro would bear the loss because the terms indicated that Caro was responsible until the goods arrived in Salem. Of course, the carrier would be liable to Caro for any loss caused by its negligence.

shipment contract
terms indicate that seller has risk until goods are given to the carrier for shipment to buyer

destination contract
indicates that seller has risk until goods are actually delivered to buyer's location

SALES ON APPROVAL OR RETURN

A "sale on approval" and a "sale or return" both presuppose under UCC 2-326 that a contract for sale is contemplated by the parties, but the rules governing how this happens stand apart from the ordinary rules when title and risk of loss pass. This is because of the peculiar nature of the transactions. In both cases, the buyer, if not satisfied with the goods, can return them even if they conform to the contract (UCC 2-326).

sale on approval transaction in which goods are delivered to buyer for trial purposes

In a **sale on approval** sometimes called a "sale on trial," goods are delivered to the prospective buyer, an ultimate consumer, by a merchant (merchant seller to consumer buyer) for a stated period of time with the understanding that the goods may be returned if the consumer buyer is not satisfied after examining and even testing the goods before making the purchase. The goods, however, remain the property of the merchant seller, who also retains title and risk of loss, until the consumer buyer accepts them. If no time is specified, the buyer may keep the goods for a reasonable time. There is no sale until the buyer accepts these goods. Consequently, risk of loss (from causes beyond the buyer's control), as mentioned previously, remain with the seller until acceptance takes place. Upon acceptance, the buyer becomes liable to the seller for the purchase price that was originally agreed to when the sale on trial was initially authorized.

The buyer is considered to have accepted the goods if one of the following occurs (1) The buyer signifies acceptance by saying 'yes' or performing some act such as making payment, (2) the buyer keeps the goods beyond the specified time or beyond a reasonable time, or (3) the buyer subjects the goods to unreasonable usage inconsistent with the purpose of trial. Notice this type of sale arises if the delivered goods are primarily for use (i.e, delivery is to an ultimate consumer). If the buyer decides not to give approval but instead returns the goods, the seller pays the expenses connected with the return and bears the risk of loss.

Adams "purchases" a complete tool set from Lowman's Home Depot with a guarantee that he can return the set after a thirty-day free home trial. Fifteen days of carefully using several of the tools to his satisfaction, he returned to Lowman's and charged the cost of the set on his credit card. The act of charging the tool set amounted to acceptance by Adams. Consequently, Adams is liable for payment. If he had returned the set within the fifteen day period because he was dissatisfied, Adams would have no obligation to make payment even though he had used some of the tools.

sale or return present sale under which buyer may return goods after a set or reasonable time

A **sale or return** is considered a present sale of goods; consequently, the buyer accepts title ownership and risk of loss immediately at the time of the sale. This type of sale under the UCC is made if the buyer purchases goods primarily for resale—that is, as a merchant buying from another merchant who then will resell to an ultimate consumer. The merchant buyer may, however, cancel the sale of goods after a specified or reasonable time if the goods fail to be resold to an ultimate consumer and to return these goods to the merchant seller. The merchant buyer must pay any expenses connected with the return of the goods to the merchant seller, such as shipping expenses (UCC2-327). In the meantime, since the merchant buyer still owns the goods, creditors may lay claim to them.

Martinson, a clothing retailer and owner of Martinson's Retail Men's Shop, purchased twenty dozen assorted sport shirts from Green's Wholesalers for a Father's Day sale. Martinson was told that he could return any unsold shirts that were in good condition after the sale. Immediately after the sale, Martinson returned five dozen shirts that were not sold.

This case is an example of a sale or return since it involves two merchants. If the shirts were in poor condition, Martinson could not return them since ownership and risk of loss already passed to him immediately at the time of the sale. For those he did return in good condition, he could claim a refund or receive credit on future purchases. Note that Martinson could not claim credit for any shirts taken by shoplifters since he still owned the goods at the time they were stolen.

BULK SALES

bulk sale sale of all or a major part of a merchant's stock of goods, fixtures, and equipment at one time

A **bulk sale** occurs when a merchant sells all or a major part of the business's assets—materials, supplies, merchandise (goods available for resale to customers), or other inventory (e.g., equipment)—at one time, and this sale does not occur in the ordinary course of the merchant's business (UCC 6-102). Although the term *major part* (of the inventory) is not defined, most courts have interpreted the term to mean greater than 50 percent of the total value of the inventory. Bulk transfers are covered under Article 6 of the UCC. The rules in Section 6-102 were designed to protect creditors from fraud when there is a bulk transfer of goods, which usually occurs upon the sale of an entire business. Occasionally, a merchant will sell his or her business without notifying or paying creditors and will then pocket the money and disappear.

The bulk transfer law under Article 6 of the UCC gives creditors the right to void a bulk sale (within a six-month period) if the buyer or the seller does not notify them at least ten days before the sale takes place—that is, ten days before the buyer takes possession of the property transferred in bulk or makes payment for it, whichever happens first. By voiding the sale, creditors can disregard the sale, seize the goods as if the merchant still owned them, and have the goods sold to satisfy claims of money owed to them.

> Karpinski sold her entire computer software business—merchandise, office furniture, and equipment—to Harvey. DeLuth, a creditor to whom Karpinski owed $5,000, sought to have the sale declared void on the grounds that neither Karpinski nor Harvey provided notice of the sale. DeLuth was legally entitled to have the sale set aside.

Today, the majority of states have repealed Article 6 on the grounds that modern business methods and changing laws, as well as improved communications, make it difficult for merchants to sell the assets of their business and abscond with the cash they received. For example, credit-reporting technology now enables creditors to determine the debtor's credit history and discover liens against the debtor's assets quickly. Some states that still desire continued bulk sales regulation follow the original version of Article 6 or have adopted a Revised Article 6. This revision offers improved creditor protection while reducing the obstacles to good faith sales. Under Revised Article 6, noncompliance does not render the sale void, nor does it otherwise alter the buyer's rights in or title to the inventory. Rather, a noncomplying buyer is simply liable for money damages to any creditor who is injured as a result of the buyer's failure to comply. Also, a noncomplying buyer may escape liability completely by proving that he or she made a good faith effort to comply with Article 6 or in good faith believed that Article 6 did not apply to the sale. Revised Article 6 applies to sellers whose equity in the business is at least $10,000, but not more than $25,000,000 (UCC 6-103).

SALES OR LEASES BY NONOWNERS

A person may be in possession of goods that he or she neither owns (lacks title) nor has authority to sell. What happens if this person, who by virtue of having possession, decides to sell the goods? Does the buyer get a good title (ownership) to these goods? It depends.

Seller Had a Void Title

UCC 2-403 states that a purchaser obtains only such title to goods as the seller had. A person with no title cannot pass a legal title to someone else. The following example brings out this point.

> Baker stole a CD player from Lennert's car and sold it to Wood for $200. Wood did not receive title to the CD player because, as a thief, Baker received only possession, but not title, from Lennert. Under these circumstances, Lennert has the right to demand the return of the compact disc player from Wood and does not have to pay Wood $200, even though Wood had no knowledge of the theft.

The same result would occur if the goods were only leased.

Before making a purchase, the buyer can require the seller to produce evidence of ownership of the goods. A **bill of sale** is written proof of such ownership. It is written evidence that title to personal property has been transferred from a seller to a buyer. If the bill of sale has been stolen or forged, the buyer obtains no title.

bill of sale written proof of ownership of goods

The bill of sale may be an informal written document, such as a sales slip from a department store, or it may be a more formal document, which is sometimes used for large purchases. A formal bill of sale describes the item, gives the name of the buyer, states the price of the item, and contains the signature of the seller. In an informal bill of sale, usually only the price and the item are given (Figure 16.1).

> Morrison purchased a portable television set from the Amart Department Store and received a bill of sale signed by the manager of the store. Six months later, Morrison decided to get a floor-model TV and advertised the portable set for sale in the newspaper. Arons offered to buy the portable TV but wanted proof that the set legally belonged to Morrison. Morrison produced the bill of sale from Amart. Arons can request a new bill of sale showing the transfer from Morrison to Arons.

The general rule that a purchaser obtains only such title to goods as the seller had is subject to at least two exceptions: (1) when the seller had a voidable title or (2) when a merchant was given temporary possession of goods and unlawfully sells them to a good faith purchaser for value (UCC 2-403).

Seller Had a Voidable Title

A buyer with a voidable title can transfer a valid (good) title to a third party who obtained the goods for value and in good faith. Under the UCC, value is any consideration that will support a simple contract. A good faith purchaser is a person who is not aware that anything is wrong with the transaction. The rationale here is to encourage and make safe good faith purchases in the business world.

> Riley purchased a used station wagon from a used-car dealer. The car dealer accepted Riley's older car as part of the purchase price. Riley said the car had been driven only 50,000 miles. A check of the odometer confirmed this statement. A short time later, however, a mechanic who was preparing the car for resale for the used-car dealer discovered that the car had actually been driven more than 100,000 miles.

In this example, Riley had a voidable title to the station wagon because it was obtained from the dealer through fraud. The dealer in this case could rescind the contract and recover the station wagon. If, however, Riley sold it to Bacon, a third party who was unaware of the fraud, Bacon would receive a valid (good) title and could keep the station wagon. The seller's only recourse would be to sue Riley to recover damages for fraud. The same rule would apply if the transaction were a lease rather than a sale.

FIGURE 16.1
Informal Bill of Sale

BILL OF SALE: VEHICLE

Description of Vehicle

Make _____ Model _____ Year _____

Body Type _____ License Number _____

Identification Number _____

For the sum of _____ Dollars ($_____) and/or other

valuable consideration in the amount of $_____, the receipt of

which is hereby acknowledged, I/we did sell, transfer and deliver to

_____
Buyer   City

_____
State   Zip Code

on the _____ day of _____ 20____ my/our right,

title, and interest in and to the above-described vehicle.

    I/We certify under the penalty of perjury that: (1) I am/We are
the lawful owner(s) of the vehicle, and (2) I/We have the right to
sell it, and (3) I/We guarantee and will defend the title to the
vehicle against claims and demands of any and all persons
arising prior to this date, and (4) the vehicle is free of all liens
and encumbrances.

Signature of seller _____ Date _____

_____
City   State   Zip Code

Merchant Was Given Temporary Possession

Often, people give a merchant temporary possession of goods they own to be picked up at a later time, such as when the goods need to be repaired. The merchant might, without the permission of the owner, sell these goods to a buyer in the ordinary course of business. A **buyer in the ordinary course of business** is one who purchases goods in good faith from a seller who normally deals in the goods requested by the buyer. In this case, the buyer has no knowledge that the goods do not really belong to the merchant and legally becomes the owner of the goods. In this case, the buyer receives a valid

buyer in the ordinary course of business one who purchases goods in good faith from a seller who normally deals in the goods

title. The original owner would have the right, however, to sue the merchant for the tort of conversion to recover money damages resulting from the loss of ownership of the goods.

> Gifford left her computer to be repaired by a merchant who both sells and repairs computers. The merchant sold the computer to Jarvis. Jarvis received a valid title to the computer because he purchased it without knowledge that the computer belonged to Gifford. Gifford can hold the merchant liable for the value of her computer.

In this example, Jarvis did receive a valid title because Gifford owned the computer. Suppose, however, that Gifford had stolen the computer from a person named Roberts and then left it for repairs. Further suppose that the computer repairperson then sold the computer to Jarvis. Jarvis would, under these circumstances, have obtained a good title against Gifford, who entrusted the computer to the merchant, but not against Roberts, the real owner. A similar rule under Article 2A applies to leased goods.

RISK OF LOSS WHERE THERE IS A BREACH OF CONTRACT

As mentioned at the beginning of the chapter, when one party breaches a sales contract, the Code places the risk of loss on the party responsible for the breach. That is also true of a lease contract. The rules of transfer, however, are different depending on whether the seller or the buyer is responsible for the breach.

If the seller breaches the contract by delivering nonconforming goods (goods that do not meet the description in the contract), risk of loss remains with the seller until either the seller cures (corrects) the defect or the buyer accepts the goods in spite of the defects. The nonconformity, however, must be serious enough to allow the buyer to legally reject the tender (offer) of delivery.

> The Image Watch Company, a retailer, ordered several name-brand, U.S.-made watches that were in high demand from the Mirsaidi Watch Manufacturers on terms FOB shipping point. In an attempt to deplete its inventory, Mirsaidi instead sent a cheaper watch that had a low consumer demand, thinking that Image would accept the watches as a special holiday offering. The truck with the shipment of watches was in an accident en route to the Image Watch Company, and the watches were destroyed. The risk of loss falls on Mirsaidi Watch Manufacturers because of the breach of contract (sending nonconforming watches).

In this example, had Mirsaidi shipped the correct watches, the risk of loss would have fallen on the Image Watch Company because the goods had been sent FOB shipping point.

Sometimes the buyer will accept a shipment of goods (along with the risk of loss) and then discover that the goods are nonconforming. This situation may occur with large shipments of goods that cannot reasonably be inspected thoroughly within moments of delivery. In this case, the buyer can revoke the acceptance but must assume responsibility for any loss up to the buyer's insurance coverage. Any additional loss falls on the seller.

It might be the buyer who breaches the contract by rejecting the goods once they have been identified but before taking delivery. Actually, the risk of loss is still with the seller, but because the buyer is in breach, any loss beyond the seller's insurance coverage lies with the buyer. Keep in mind, however, that the buyer bears the risk of loss for only a commercially reasonable time (what is reasonable in the trade) after the seller learns of the breach.

Summary

The parties to a sales contract do not always specify in the contract when title and risk of loss are to pass from seller to buyer. In such cases, rules set down under Article 2 of the UCC apply.

Under the Code, the rules for shifting risk of loss are more important than the rules for deciding when title passes. Although significant in many respects, title has lost some of its importance. Deciding who suffers risk of loss depends on whether a sales contract has been breached at the time of the loss. This chapter dealt with risk of loss mostly in situations in which no breach of contract had taken place.

In a sale of goods by a merchant, if delivery to the buyer does not require movement of the goods (e.g., pickup is made at the seller's place of business), risk of loss passes to the buyer when the buyer takes physical possession of the goods.

If the seller is only to ship the goods, risk of loss passes from seller to buyer on proper delivery to an independent (for-hire) carrier. If the seller is to deliver the goods to their destination, risk of loss passes a reasonable time after the buyer has been given notice that the goods are available for pickup at the destination point.

In a sale on approval, risk of loss and ownership remain with the seller until the buyer accepts the goods by approval. This type of sale is made by a merchant to an ultimate consumer. A sale or return is a present sale in which the buyer accepts risk of loss and ownership of the goods at the time of the sale; both the risk and title will revert to the seller if the buyer returns the goods. This type of sale is made by a merchant buying goods primarily for resale, such as a merchant selling to a merchant.

When one party breaches a sales or lease contract, the Code places the risk of loss on the party responsible for the breach. The rules of transfer, however, differ depending on whether the seller or the buyer is responsible for the breach.

Bulk sales are covered under Article 6 of the UCC. A sale of goods in bulk (bulk sale) is the sale of all or a major part of the stock of merchandise, materials, supplies, or other inventory at one time. This sale does not occur in the ordinary course of business. It generally includes the sale of the entire business. The bulk-sales law protects creditors by giving them the right to void a bulk sale (within a six-month period) if the bulk sale buyer does not notify them at least ten days before the sale takes place. A majority of states have repealed Article 6. States still desiring to continue bulk-sales regulation follow the original version of Article 6 or have adopted a Revised Article 6, which provides creditors with better protection.

As a general rule, a buyer obtains only such title to goods that the seller had. A person who has no title cannot pass a title on. Thus, a thief cannot pass legal title on to a purchaser. The UCC, however, allows at least two exceptions to this general rule: (1) A buyer with a voidable title can legally transfer a valid title to a third party who obtained the goods for value and in good faith and (2) any merchant who is given temporary possession of goods can legally transfer a valid title to those goods to a buyer in the ordinary course of business.

If the seller breaches the contract by delivering non-conforming goods, risk of loss remains with the seller until either the seller cures the defect or the buyer accepts the goods in spite of the defects.

Important Legal terms

bill of sale
bulk sale
buyer in the ordinary course
    of business
contract to sell

destination contract
fungible goods
future goods
identified goods
present sale

sale on approval
sale or return
shipment contract

Questions and Problems for Discussion

1. When goods are shipped by common carrier, the UCC treats the contract as which of the following?
   a. sale on trial
   b. a destination contract
   c. a shipment contract unless a destination contract is specified
   d. a destination contract unless a shipment contract is specified

2. If the terms of a contract create doubt about whether a transaction is a "sale on approval" or a "sale or return," the question will be resolved as a sale or return if the buyer took
   a. the goods for use
   b. the goods for resale
   c. delivery of the goods
   d. both b and c

3. Article 2 of the UCC
   a. eliminates the concept of title
   b. considerably enhances the importance of title
   c. considerably reduces the importance of title
   d. eliminates any reference to title

4. A dispute has arisen between two merchants over the question of who has the risk of loss in a given sales transaction. The contract does not specifically address the point. The goods were shipped to the buyer who rightfully rejected them because they were not conforming. What factor will be most important in resolving this dispute?

5. Johnson purchased a television set on thirty days' credit from Martinson & Kelly TV Sales and Service Center. While filling out the credit application, Johnson made false statements about his credit rating. Shortly after the purchase was made, Johnson moved to another city without paying for the TV set. Before moving, however, he sold the TV set to Carvel, who knew nothing of the fraudulent transaction. Martinson & Kelly traced the sale of the TV to Carvel and demanded the return of the set. May Martinson & Kelly legally recover the TV set from Carvel?

6. The Corey Corporation entered into a contract to sell machine parts to G&H Wholesalers. Corey shipped machine parts different from those specified in the contract, and G&H rejected them. Corey made no mention of the nonconformity, nor did Corey make any attempt to re-send conforming goods. One day after G&H informed Corey that the parts were rejected, they were destroyed by fire in G&H's warehouse. Corey attempted to recover that cost of the machine parts in spite of the fire loss, claiming that the risk of loss rested with G&H. Is the Corey Corporation correct?

7. Doser sold a radar detector to Erdle. Doser had stolen the detector from a local electronics store, but Erdle did not know this. May the owner of the store recover the radar detector from Erdle?

8. Carbide Corp. agreed to purchase 200 computers from Pulsefeeder Suppliers. Pulsefeeder is a wholesaler of office equipment, and Carbide is an office equipment retailer. The contract required Pulsefeeder to ship the computers to Carbide by common carrier, "FOB Pulsefeeder Suppliers, Loading Dock." Which of the parties bears the risk of loss during shipment?

9. Newman Funding Co., located in New York City, sells rare coins by mail throughout the United States. Preston, a resident of Sturgis, South Dakota, ordered and received several shipments of coins from Newman through the mail in response to Newman's newspaper advertisement. The shipments were always sent "on approval" for fifteen days. Preston would keep and pay for several coins and then return to Newman fully insured those coins that he did not wish to keep. On the latest shipment of coins worth over $50,000 and sent on a fifteen-day approval period, Preston returned all the coins via certified mail and insured them for the maximum allowed of $500. Newman never received the coins. Who bears the risk of loss for these coins, Newman or Preston?

10. Harkness purchased a calculator from BBL Calculator Company on a sale or return basis on February 1. No time for return was specified. On August 5, Harkness returned the calculator, claiming that he had changed his mind. BBL refused to take the calculator back, however, claiming that Harkness had kept it beyond a reasonable time. Was BBL correct?

Cases for Review

1. Clark, a merchant, sold a boat to Chatham, a consumer buyer, for cash. The sale took place at the Parkside Marina, Clark's place of business. Chatham, however, was about to go on a business trip and asked Clark to keep the boat at the marina until his return. A severe storm struck soon thereafter. When he returned, Chatham could not take delivery of the boat because it had sunk as the result of the storm. Nevertheless, Clark refused to refund the cash price to Chatham, claiming that, because a present sale had been made, risk of loss passed to Chatham, thereby making Chatham liable to absorb the cost of the boat. Is Clark correct? (*Chatham* v. *Clark's Food Fair, Inc.,* 127 S.E.2d 868)

2. Hughes purchased a new Lincoln Continental from Al Green Motors for $30,490 and made a down payment of $2,490. The balance due was financed through a local bank. Hughes took immediate possession, but it was agreed that she would return the car to the dealership for normal newcar preparations. On the way home, Hughes was in a car accident that, through no fault of hers, caused extensive damage to the car. Regardless of the damage, the car dealer issued a certificate of title (ownership) to her after receiving a check from the bank through which she financed the car. Hughes now claims that Al Green Motors had no right to issue her a certificate of title because the car, having been damaged, was not the car she bargained for, an undamaged Lincoln Continental. Al Green Motors claimed it had every right to issue the title because it was not responsible for the damage to the car. Is Al Green Motors correct? (*Hughes* v. *Al Green, Inc.,* 418 N.E.2d 1355)

3. Harrison, the owner and operator of a men's clothing store in Westport, Connecticut, ordered a variety of clothing items from Ninth Street East, a clothing manufacturer in Los Angeles. Harrison was notified that the terms of the sale were FOB Los Angeles. When the truck carrying the goods arrived at Harrison's store, Harrison's wife insisted that the goods be placed inside the door, but the carrier refused. The dispute was not resolved, and the carrier kept the merchandise and left the store premises. The merchandise was subsequently lost by the carrier. Harrison notified Ninth Street East of the nondelivery of the goods. Many attempts were made to locate the merchandise, but without success. Ninth Street East then sued Harrison for the purchase price of the goods. Harrison refused to pay. Is Ninth Street East entitled to payment? (*Ninth Street East, Ltd.* v. *Harrison,* Conn. 259 A.2d 772)

4. While he was a soldier in the U.S. Army during World War II, Lieber found some of Adolf Hitler's personal effects. Twenty-two years later, while Lieber was living in Louisiana, his chauffeur stole the collection and sold it to a dealer, who then sold it to Mohawk. Mohawk had no knowledge of the background of the collection and bought it in good faith. When Lieber learned that Mohawk had the collection, he demanded its return. Must Mohawk return the collection to Lieber? (*Lieber* v. *Mohawk Arms, Inc.,* 64 Misc. 2d 206, N.Y.S.2d 510)

5. On November 7, 1960, Crosby purchased a tractor and plow for $3,000 from Lane Farm Supply, Inc., on an approval basis. The length of time of the trial period was not definitely stated. After the purchase, when questioned about payment, Crosby indicated that he would pay for the equipment after a big deal had been completed. Crosby used the tractor and plow until the tractor was burned in his barn on January 1, 1961. Lane Farm Supply insisted that because Crosby owned the equipment, he was responsible for the loss. Was Lane Farm Supply correct? (*Lane Farm Supply, Inc.* v. *Crosby,* 243 N.Y.2d 725)

6. B&B Parts Sales, Inc., delivered merchandise to a store owned by Collier. The bill that accompanied the merchandise had the words "Sold to" printed on it, followed by Collier's name and address. The agreement was that any equipment not sold would be picked up in ninety days by B&B Parts. While the merchandise was in Collier's store and before the ninety days were up, the store was burglarized and most of the merchandise was stolen. Collier claimed that the risk of loss was on B&B Parts. B&B Parts claimed that the sale was on a sale-or-return basis. Was B&B correct? (*Collier* v. *B&B Parts Sales, Inc.,* Tex. 471 S.W.2d 151)

7. Medico Leasing Company gave possession of a car to Smith, a merchant engaged in the used-car

business. It was agreed that Smith would sell the car for Medico. Smith sold the car to Wessell Buick Co. but kept the money. Medico sued Smith. Because Smith had no money, Medico then tried to recover the car from Wessell Buick. Wessell Buick claimed that it had purchased the car from Smith, a merchant, in good faith and had every right to keep the car. Was Wessell Buick entitled to keep the car? (*Medico Leasing Company* v. *Smith,* 457 Okla. 2d 548)

8. Crump bought a TV antenna and tower from Lair for $900, payable in monthly installments of $7.50. The set was installed and Lair agreed to maintain it, but the contract was silent about insurance or repairs. Nine months later, the set was struck by lightning and badly damaged. Who was responsible for the loss? (*Lair Distributing Co.* v. *Crump,* 48 Ala. App. 72, 261 S.2d 904)

9. Draper, the plaintiff, contracted with Meiners, a dealer in farm equipment, to buy a Minneapolis-Moline tractor and a new plow after trading in an old tractor and an old plow plus a cash payment of $5,300. The contract also required the dealer to install a cab and a radio on the tractor before delivery. The defendant, who was the manufacturer of farm equipment, delivered the tractor to the dealer in January, but not the cab because it was not in stock. In the meantime, the dealer showed Draper the tractor and he was told it was his. The tractor was even identified as his by giving it a customer number (804). In February, the completion of a routine audit disclosed the dealer to be greatly in arrears for substantial sums of money owed to Minneapolis-Moline (the defendant). The defendant then repossessed all its products on the dealer's premises, including the tractor that had been set aside for Draper. Draper never did receive the tractor. He had to use his old tractor for spring plowing and incurred unexpected expenses of $400, which would not have happened with the new tractor. Consequently, Draper sued the defendant (Minneapolis-Moline) for this amount. The defendant claimed that the tractor did not belong to Draper and therefore was not responsible to pay the $400. Is the defendant (Minneapolis-Moline) correct? (100 Ill. App. 2d 324, 241 N.E.2d 342)

CHAPTER 17

The Sales Contract: Performance, Breach, and Remedies for Breach

CHAPTER PREVIEW

Performance of the Sales Contract
Performance by the Seller
Perfect Tender Rule
Exceptions to the Perfect Tender Rule
Performance by the Buyer

Breach of the Sales Contract

Remedies for Breach Available to the Buyer
Sue for Breach of Warranty
Cancel the Contract and Cover

Cancel the Contract and Sue for Damages
Seek Specific Performance or Replevin

Remedies for Breach Available to the Seller
Cancel the Contract
Resell the Goods and Sue for Damages
Sue to Recover the Purchase Price
Sue to Recover Damages for Nonacceptance
Withhold Delivery of the Goods
Reclaim the Goods from the Buyer

Chapter Highlights

The first part of this chapter focuses on performance of the sales contract: what is legally expected of the seller and the buyer for them to discharge their obligations under the contract. The second part details options (remedies) available to the buyer and the seller if one or the other breaches (fails to perform) the contract. The discussion covers first the remedies available to the buyer and then those available to the seller. As you study the rules in the chapter relating to performance and breach, remember that they apply only to cases in which the seller and buyer have failed to specify in the sales contract how they will fulfill their obligations. Keep in mind that the principles discussed in this chapter also apply to lease contracts.

PERFORMANCE OF THE SALES CONTRACT

Performance refers to the process whereby the seller and the buyer carry out their obligations according to the terms of the contract. The seller generally is the first party to perform a sales contract by tendering (making available) the goods called for in the tendered contract. The buyer then performs by accepting and paying for these tendered goods according to the terms of the contract (UCC 2-301). All the obligations of the seller and the buyer associated with performance are contained in the sales contract. If disputes arise because the contract is unclear, either the Uniform Commercial Code (UCC) or customs of the trade fill in the gaps. Both parties are required under the Code to perform their contractual obligations in good faith (honesty) and to act in a commercially reasonable manner of fair dealing [UCC 2-103]. Neither party should, for example, attempt to manipulate the contract terms or to delay performance for an unreasonable period of time. A final overriding obligation is for the parties to maintain the highest level of cooperation in carrying out their respective duties. Any failure to coop-erate can be treated as a breach of contract.

Performance by the Seller

conforming goods
goods that meet requirements of a contract

The seller's first obligation is to tender (offer) **conforming goods**—that is, goods that exactly meet the description of the goods in the contract. Secondly, the seller must prop-erly notify the buyer that the goods are ready for delivery and lastly, the seller must make the goods available to the buyer. How delivery is accomplished will depend on the arrangements to which the seller and buyer agreed. If the parties do not agree, or if they fail to consider how delivery is to be made, the rules in the Code will govern (UCC 2-503). Often, the goods are made available to the buyer at the seller's place of business or, if there is no place of business, at the seller's residence. Delivery under these circum-stances does not require the seller to move the goods to the buyer's place of business or residence; it simply means making the goods available to the buyer.

> Isaac Heating Inc., manufacturer of residential furnaces, entered into a contract to sell Barton's Home Heating Equipment Company three name brand furnaces with com-ponents. Both are merchants in the same large city. Delivery is to be at Isaac's place of business. Barton is notified that he may pick up the exact equipment he ordered at his convenience.

In this example, Isaac made a proper tender by offering goods that conform to the contract and properly notified Barton that the goods were ready for pick up. Isaac also made the goods available at a specific location. In essence, Isaac has performed his part of the contract obligations under the sales contract.

If the goods are in a place different from the seller's place of business or residence (e.g., in a warehouse), that is the place for delivery. If the seller is required to ship the goods, a proper delivery occurs when the seller places the goods in the possession of an independent (for-hire) carrier and notifies the buyer that the goods have been shipped. If the contract requires the seller to deliver the goods to a particular destination, a proper tender of delivery occurs when the goods are delivered to the destination point and the buyer is notified of their arrival. If the seller does not notify the buyer and an unreason-able delay or loss results, the buyer may reject the shipment.

In all cases, tender must be at a reasonable time. If no definite time for delivery is set, the seller must give the buyer a reasonable time to accept delivery. If, for example, goods are immediately ready for delivery, a reasonable time would be very short.

Perfect Tender Rule

perfect tender rule
obligates the seller to tender goods that exactly match the terms of the contract

The UCC imposes the **perfect tender rule** on the seller. This common law rule has been preserved by the UCC. This rule obligates the seller to tender goods that exactly meet the requirements of the contract. If the goods or the tender of delivery fail to conform to the contract exactly, the buyer may (1) reject all the goods ordered, (2) accept all the goods, or (3) accept part of the goods and reject the rest (UCC 2-601).

> Riverside Corporation enters into a sales contract to ship 200 boxes of sport shirts to Best Buy, a clothing retailer. Upon inspection of the delivered goods, Best Buy discovers that 150 boxes of sport shirts conform to the contract, and 50 boxes do not conform. Because Riverside has failed to make a perfect tender of 200 boxes of shirts, Best Buy may reject the entire shipment and bring action against Riverside for breach of contract.

Because this rule is harsh, the Code has allowed various exceptions that may limit its effect. These exceptions apply to both the seller and the lessor.

Exceptions to the Perfect Tender Rule

Agreement of the Parties   The Code allows the parties to agree to some adjustment that will avoid rejection. For example, the seller and buyer may decide in their original contract that the exclusive remedy for defective goods is to return them to the seller for repair, adjustment, or replacement and that this step precludes rejection (UCC 2-601).

Good Faith   The clause in the Code alluding to good faith actually applies to every contract that comes within the rules of the UCC. Good faith, as stated previously, describes honest and fair dealings between seller and buyer (UCC 1-201;2-103). For example, a buyer with the right to reject goods he or she contracted to buy should not back out on some nonmaterial technicality when the real reason was a discovery that the deal was no longer profitable.

Cure   The seller does have the right to correct the defect (repair, adjust, or replace) of any nonconforming goods that the buyer rejects so as to avoid being held in breach. This right to **cure**—that is, the seller's right to correct a defect in goods sold to the buyer—substantially restricts the right of the buyer to reject goods. The seller will definitely be able to cure if the defect is simple. For example, a seller delivers a color television to the buyer. When the buyer turned on the set, it did not function properly, the picture having a reddish tinge. The buyer rejected the set, demanding the return of the purchase price. The seller believed that the set was acceptable and had no reason to know, at the time of delivery, that the set was defective. When the seller offered to correct the defect, which was relatively simple, the buyer refused and sued for the return of her money. In this case, the seller most likely would be able to correct the defect since the adjustment was minor. If the cure is complicated, or if the defect is so serious that a cure will not give a buyer substantially what was bargained for, the seller has no right to cure and the buyer is entitled to reject the goods (UCC 2-601).

cure seller's right to correct a defect in nonconforming goods

This right of correction or cure is permitted if the seller notifies the buyer of the intention to correct the defect. The seller must then deliver conforming goods (which the buyer must accept) before the time for performance expires (UCC 2-508; 2A-513). This right of cure prevents a buyer from rejecting goods merely because he or she wished to back out of a deal that was not profitable. Once the time for performance under the contract has expired, the seller or lessor can still exercise the right to cure if he or she had reasonable grounds (e.g., a price allowance) to believe that the nonconforming tender would be acceptable to the buyer or lessee (UCC 2-508). If, for example, a buyer has in the past accepted a substitute brand of goods, the seller has reasonable grounds to believe that the buyer will again accept a substitute or the seller cannot exercise the right of cure because he discovered a hidden defect and does not disclose this defect to the buyer but later asserts this defect as a defense in a lawsuit. In such a case, the seller can cure within a reasonable time even though delivery of the conforming goods will take place after the time limit for performance stated in the contract.

If the buyer rejects the goods, he or she must do so within a reasonable time and must reasonably notify the seller of this intention. Rejection allows the buyer to treat the contract as ended (canceled), make other arrangements to purchase the goods, recover the purchase price from the seller if it has already been paid, and collect any damages suffered.

A buyer who rightfully rejects a delivery after taking possession of the goods must hold the goods with reasonable care for a time sufficient to allow the seller to remove them but has no further obligation concerning them. If the seller fails to give instructions after notification of rejection, the buyer (merchant or nonmerchant) may (1) place the rejected goods in storage; (2) ship them back to the seller; or (3) resell them, with the proceeds going to the seller. In all cases, the buyer is entitled to reimbursement for expenses (UCC 2-602; UCC 2-604).

Performance by the Buyer

The buyer's duties arise only after the seller's duties are completed and the buyer has had the opportunity to inspect the goods. The buyer is obligated to accept the goods if they conform to the contract and to pay for them in accordance with the contract. Acceptance refers to the buyer's willingness to become the owner of the goods tendered. If problems arise over "in accordance with the contract" usage of trade, the course of dealing and performance and general circumstances must be given consideration to help determine the meaning of these words (UCC 2-302).

Inspect the Goods   The buyer has the right but not the duty to inspect the goods (at any reasonable place and at any reasonable time, and in any reasonable manner) before accepting delivery to determine if they conform to the contract (UCC 2-513). Failure to inspect operates as a waiver. Further, a poor inspection has the same effect as a complete inspection. If the seller is required to ship the goods to the buyer, inspection may be made at the place of arrival. The goods are usually inspected before the buyer pays for them, but if they are sent COD (collect on delivery) or if the contract requires it, the buyer must pay for the goods before inspecting them. Payment in these circumstances, however, does not constitute acceptance of the goods. The expenses of inspection must be borne by the buyer but can be recovered from the seller if the goods do not conform and are rejected (UCC 2-513). The buyer may lose the right to revoke or reject goods that are nonconforming by failing to inspect them in a timely manner.

Acceptance and Payment   If there has been a proper tender of delivery and if an inspection reveals that the goods conform to the contract, the buyer as mentioned has a duty to accept the goods and pay for them according to the terms of the contract (UCC 2-607). A buyer or lessee who takes any of the following actions after a reasonable opportunity to inspect the delivered goods will have shown his or her desire to accept the goods: (1) signifies to the seller or lessor in words or by conduct that the goods are conforming or that the goods will be taken despite their nonconformity; (2) fails to reject the goods within a reasonable time after their delivery or tender by the seller or lessor; or (3) acts inconsistently with the seller's ownership rights in the delivered goods, such as reselling the goods. If either the goods or the delivery fails to conform to the contract, there is no duty on the part of the buyer to accept or pay (the buyer may accept any part and reject the rest) (UCC 2-601).

BREACH OF THE SALES CONTRACT

Most sales transactions are concluded without problems. The sales agreement is made, the seller transfers the goods to the buyer, and the buyer either pays cash or asks for credit. Sometimes, however, a situation occurs that causes the seller, the buyer, or both to refuse to carry out his or her part of the sales agreement.

As with other types of contracts that are breached, the wronged party may take action against the other party to obtain justice. In a sales contract, the seller and buyer may, in the sales agreement, provide for remedies in the event of a breach of the contract by one party or the other. If they do not, the remedies provided in the UCC will apply (UCC 2-703; UCC 2-711; UCC 2-714). The UCC provides a range of remedies designed to provide balance in rights between the seller and buyer and to bring about a successful

TABLE 17.1 REMEDIES FOR BREACH OF SALES CONTRACT	
REMEDIES OF BUYER	**REMEDIES OF SELLER**
Sue for breach of warranty.	Cancel the contract.
Cancel the contract and cover.	Resell the goods and sue for damages.
Cancel the contract and sue for damages.	Sue to recover the purchase price.
Seek specific performance or replevin.	Sue to recover damages for nonacceptance.
	Withhold delivery of the goods.
	Reclaim the goods from the buyer.

conclusion to a sales transaction with the overriding purpose of the UCC remedies being to return the injured party to status quo, or the same position he or she would have been in if the other party had not breached the contract. Therefore, the Code insists on the following:

1. The remedies for breach be cumulative; the selection of one remedy does not bar the injured party from pursuing another remedy.
2. The remedies be liberally administered. For example, mathematical precision in calculating damages is not necessary—simply base damages on the definiteness and accuracy that the facts reveal, and nothing more.
3. Either party to a sales contract under Article 2 of the UCC may demand adequate assurance of performance once the contract is made, but before performance is due, when reasonable grounds for insecurity exists with respect to the performance of the other party. Refusal to give written assurance will release the other party from all obligations from the sales contract (UCC 2-609).

Keep in mind that certain remedies will be available at some times and other remedies at other times. The facts of each case determine the remedy that is available and whether more than one remedy is available to the injured party. (Table 17.1 summarizes these remedies.)

REMEDIES FOR BREACH AVAILABLE TO THE BUYER

The buyer's remedies arise when the seller breaches the sales contract by failing or refusing to deliver or tender the goods, or by sending nonconforming goods. In these cases, the buyer may (1) sue for breach of warranty, (2) cancel the contract and cover, (3) cancel the contract and sue for damages, or (4) seek specific performance or replevin.

Sue for Breach of Warranty

A buyer who receives nonconforming goods may accept them anyway and then recover damages from the seller for breach of warranty. A warranty (discussed in greater detail in Chapter 18) is a guarantee by the seller that the goods are not defective and that they are suitable for the use for which they are intended. An action for breach of warranty usually occurs when the nonconformity could not be discovered on inspection and, because the goods have been accepted, rejection is no longer possible. The buyer may sue for breach of warranty only after notifying the seller that the goods do not conform to the contract.

Marcus, owner of J & S Engine Performance Center, ordered three dozen batteries from a sample presented to him by a salesperson for the Excel Battery & Tire Company. When the batteries arrived, Marcus accepted them and paid $600, the amount due. One week later, a customer who had purchased one of the batteries returned it to Marcus because it had gone dead. By testing the batteries still in his possession, Marcus discovered that they were of inferior quality and did not conform to the sample. Marcus notified Excel of his findings. Because the batteries were not as warranted, Marcus is entitled to sue Excel for breach of warranty.

If a breach of warranty is proved, the buyer may recover damages from the seller. Damages are generally the difference between the value of the goods accepted and their value had they conformed to the warranty. Damages also include expenses incurred by the buyer because of the breach of warranty. In addition, damages may include money for any bodily injury or property damage that resulted from use of the nonconforming goods.

You purchased a used car from the Quansit Used Car Agency for $2,000. During a conversation with a salesperson, you asked if the car had good brakes. The salesperson replied, "They're brand new." The day after you purchased the car, the brakes gave out and you were injured when the car ran into the side of a building. Damages for breach of warranty would be the difference between $2,000, the price you paid for the car, and the amount the car was actually worth. In this case, damages would also include money for hospital and medical bills, as well as for pain and suffering.

Cancel the Contract and Cover

cover buyer's right to purchase substitute goods if seller does not deliver the goods required or sends nonconforming goods

A buyer who rightfully rejects nonconforming goods (thereby causing a breach of contract by the seller) may cancel the contract, obtain any part of the purchase price already paid, and then cover the purchase. To **cover** means to buy substitute goods elsewhere to replace those originally due from the seller. This remedy permits the buyer to obtain without delay (cannot wait for a damage award to be made) the goods needed for use or for resale. The buyer who exercises the right to cover and suffers a loss is permitted to recover the difference between the cost of cover and the contract price of the original goods, plus any expenses, such as transportation expenses, necessary to obtain the substitute goods. A buyer who chooses cover does not have to obtain the goods at the cheapest price available. All that he or she has to do is act reasonably and in good faith. The right to cover applies both to merchants who buy from manufacturers and wholesalers and to consumers who purchase from merchants.

Mandrin Drug Store contracted with the Superior Pen Company to purchase 1,000 ballpoint pens to be sold at a special back-to-school promotion. The pens, which cost $1 each ($1,000 total), were to be delivered within one month. One week before the delivery date, Superior refused to deliver the pens, which other companies were then selling for $1.10 each. Because the pens were needed for the special promotion, Mandrin could purchase them from another company at $1.10 each ($1,100 total) and then sue to recover damages from Superior in the amount of $100 ($1,100−$1,000). Mandrin could also recover from Superior the amount of any expenses required to get the pens from another company.

The option to cover is also available to a buyer when the seller repudiates the contract or fails to deliver the goods.

Cancel the Contract and Sue for Damages

The buyer has no duty to cover if the seller breaches the contract by sending nonconforming goods. The buyer may instead cancel the contract, obtain any part of the purchase price paid, and sue for damages for nondelivery. If a seller repudiates the sales contract or fails to deliver the goods, the buyer can also sue for damages. In either case,

market price price at which goods are currently bought and sold

damages would be the difference between the contract price and the market price at the time the buyer learns of the breach, plus any expenses. **Market price** is the price at which goods are currently bought and sold in the business world. In a period of inflation, market prices may change fairly quickly.

> Joplin, owner of a jewelry store, purchased fifty electronic watches from the LCD Precision Watch Company, paying one-fourth of the total price as a down payment. When the wrong watches were sent, Joplin refused to accept them and demanded the return of her down payment. Because the wrong watches were sent, Joplin had the right to have her down payment returned and to sue LCD for damages.

If the buyer does not suffer actual (or real) damages, he or she is entitled to nominal damages, such as a dollar, for a technical breach of contract. The buyer's purpose in bringing a lawsuit under these circumstances would be to show in the court records that a cause of action existed and that he or she was successful.

Seek Specific Performance or Replevin

In some circumstances, if the seller breaches the contract, the buyer may demand that the seller deliver the goods described in the sales agreement (UCC 2-716). This action, you may recall, is called *specific performance*. To obtain specific performance, the buyer must be unable to find substitute goods (to cover) because the goods contracted for are unique (e.g., works of art, antiques, custom-made products, or goods considered to be one of a kind) or because there are no suppliers of equal quality. This remedy is very rarely exercised under the Code. In today's world, the market for goods is highly developed and sophisticated, and substitute goods are not that difficult to find. Under the UCC, the term *unique* as it relates to specific performance has been broadened and goes beyond what was considered unique in Chapter 14. Examples of unique goods under the UCC include goods that cannot be obtained elsewhere because there are spot shortages or because sellers have discontinued offering them as being unprofitable.

> The United Metals Corporation made a contract to deliver several units that fit into the interior of blast furnaces owned by the Kostic Blast Furnace Company. The units, made of nickel, were hard to obtain on the open market because of a temporary shortage of nickel. Knowing this fact, United Metals refused to deliver the units unless Kostic Blast Furnace paid more money. Because these units could not be obtained elsewhere, Kostic would be forced to shut down its operations. In these circumstances, Kostic could be granted specific performance by the courts.

replevin action by the buyer to recover through court order goods originally ordered but wrongfully detained by the seller

Another remedy exists for the buyer of goods that are not unique (i.e., not ordinary goods) and that are originally identified and ordered but wrongfully detained by the seller. If the buyer, after a reasonable effort, cannot buy these goods elsewhere (cover), the buyer can exercise the right of **replevin** to obtain the goods (UCC 2-716). To exercise the right of replevin, a buyer must obtain a court order that orders the seller to deliver the goods to the buyer.

> Riggins, who designs and makes furniture, entered into a contract with Arnold, the owner of a local sawmill, to purchase twenty oak logs. Riggins personally selected the logs and made arrangements with Arnold for a delivery date. Before the delivery date, however, the market price of oak rose considerably. As a result, Arnold refused to deliver the logs to Riggins at the contract price. Because the logs had been identified in the contract and because he could not cover after making a reasonable effort to do so, Riggins could exercise his right to replevy the logs under the UCC (after first obtaining a court order).

REMEDIES FOR BREACH AVAILABLE TO THE SELLER

The UCC also provides remedies for the seller if the buyer breaches the sales contract. A buyer generally breaches the contract by refusing to go through with the contract, by wrongfully refusing to accept or keep the goods, or by failing to pay for the goods. If the buyer breaches the contract, the seller may (1) cancel the contract, (2) resell the goods and sue for damages, (3) sue the buyer for the purchase price, (4) sue the buyer for damages for nonacceptance, (5) withhold delivery of the goods, or (6) reclaim the goods from the buyer.

Cancel the Contract

A seller who is notified that the buyer will not go through with the contract may simply cancel (rescind) all performance due the buyer under the contract. If the seller cancels the contract, he or she may then, in addition, choose any of the other remedies that the UCC makes available to the seller for breach of contract. These remedies are discussed below.

> The Clover Pool Company ordered seven above-ground pools from the Waterlaken Manufacturing Company for a total of $35,000. Clover agreed to pay $5,000 as a down payment before delivery of the pools and the balance over a five-month period. Clover did not make the down payment as agreed. The Waterlaken Company could cancel all performance due the Clover Pool Company under the contract and sue for an additional remedy.

Resell the Goods and Sue for Damages

The seller who has possession of goods, either because delivery was withheld or because the buyer refused to accept them, may resell the goods if there is a market for them and may then sue the buyer for damages. The amount of damages would be the difference between the resale price and the original contract price, plus any expenses necessary to resell the goods. The resale may be at either a public auction or a private sale.

> On November 15, Blevins, who owned a retail clothing store, placed a special order for ten dozen shirts of assorted colors and sizes from Smith-Gormly Wholesalers. Because Blevins had planned to have a pre-Christmas sale, she asked Smith-Gormly to rush the shipment. Smith-Gormly notified Blevins that the merchandise would be shipped on November 28. On November 27, Blevins notified Smith-Gormly that she had changed her mind, no longer wanted the merchandise, and would not accept the shipment. In these circumstances, Smith-Gormly could resell the goods to someone else and sue Blevins for damages.

Sue to Recover the Purchase Price

A seller who still has possession of the goods but is unable to resell the identified goods elsewhere may choose to hold the goods for the buyer and sue for the purchase price. This remedy is the parallel to the buyer's remedy for specific performance. Here the seller desires exactly what has been bargained for, the price that was agreed to by both parties (UCC 2-703; 2-709). It could, however, prove to be a burden because it requires the seller to hold the goods for the buyer until the goods are paid for. The seller must then deliver the goods to the buyer.

A department store received a special order from a local hotel for draperies of a special size and design for the entire hotel. The hotel owner later refused to accept the draperies or to pay the purchase price of $15,000. Because the draperies were made specifically for the hotel and would therefore be difficult to resell in the normal course of business, the department store may sue to collect the purchase price from the hotel and then turn the draperies over to them.

This remedy of suing for the purchase price is also a postacceptance remedy, meaning that the seller can sue once the buyer has accepted the goods but refuses to pay for them. Suing for the purchase price under these circumstances may not be a good remedy. The buyer is probably not paying because he or she is insolvent.

Sue to Recover Damages for Nonacceptance

If the buyer refuses to accept the goods, the seller may choose to sue the buyer for damages for not accepting the goods. This remedy is usually selected if the seller is unable to sell the goods or prefers not to sell them. Damages in this case are the difference between the market price of the goods at the time and place they were to be delivered to the buyer and the unpaid contract price, plus any expenses caused by the buyer's breach of contract.

A novelty shop ordered several boxes of novelties from the Ruoff Novelty Corporation totaling $1,500 but then wrongfully rejected the shipment. If the market price at the time the novelties were rejected by the buyer was $1,200, Ruoff could sue for damages of $300, plus any other expenses caused by the breach.

Withhold Delivery of the Goods

insolvent unable to pay debts as they fall due

unpaid seller's lien right of unpaid seller to retain goods sold to insolvent buyer until goods are paid for in cash

The seller may legally withhold delivery of the goods purchased on credit if the seller discovers before delivery that the buyer is **insolvent** (unable to pay debts that are due) or has failed to make a requested payment before the date set for delivery. The seller may withhold delivery even though ownership (title) of the goods has passed to the buyer. By exercising an **unpaid seller's lien**, the seller may retain these goods until the buyer pays the purchase price in cash. If the purchase price is not paid within a reasonable time, the seller may cancel the contract and either resell the goods or cancel and sue for money damages for nonacceptance. The lien is lost, however, if the seller delivers possession of the goods to the buyer.

stoppage in transit right of unpaid seller to notify carrier or warehouse operator not to deliver goods to insolvent buyer

The seller may discover that the buyer is insolvent only after the goods have been delivered to a carrier for shipment to the buyer or after the goods have arrived at their destination and are being stored in a warehouse until the buyer picks them up. In either case, the seller should notify the carrier or the warehouse operator not to deliver the goods to the buyer. If the seller is successful in preventing delivery of the goods—referred to as **stoppage in transit**—the seller's right to withhold the goods until paid for continues. The UCC also permits an unpaid seller to stop goods in transit when the buyer is guilty of fraud in making the contract.

On March 9, Rusk, owner of Skate Town, a popular roller skating rink, ordered fifteen dozen pairs of roller skates from the Ball Bearing Company. Ball Bearing was to ship the skates on March 11, and Rusk was to pay for them on March 13. The Ball Bearing Company shipped the skates on schedule, but Rusk failed to pay as agreed. Ball Bearing immediately checked on Rusk's credit and found that he was a poor credit risk. Ball Bearing then notified the carrier not to deliver the skates. Because Rusk was unable to pay, Ball Bearing had the right to stop delivery.

Reclaim the Goods from the Buyer

The seller who sold the goods on credit may not discover the buyer's insolvency until after the buyer has received the goods. At that point, it would obviously be too late to withhold the goods or to stop them in transit. The UCC, however, permits a seller who loses possession of goods to reclaim them upon discovering a buyer's insolvency if a demand is made within ten days after the buyer has received the goods (UCC 2-702). If the buyer has resold the goods to a good faith purchaser (a person not aware that anything is wrong), the seller may not reclaim the goods but may sue the buyer for damages. In the case of perishable goods, the seller will usually not choose to reclaim the goods.

> Five days after selling and delivering fifteen microwave ovens to Johnson, Rubin Wholesalers discovered that Johnson was insolvent. If Rubin acts before ten days have expired, it can demand that Johnson return the microwave ovens.

The ten-day limitation on recovering goods from an insolvent buyer does not apply if the buyer has made false statements in writing about her or his solvency within three months of the delivery. The three-month period starts with the date on which the false statement was given to the seller.

Summary

The seller performs the sales contract by delivering conforming goods; the buyer performs by accepting and paying for these goods, assuming, of course, that there has been a proper delivery by the seller and an inspection reveals that the goods do conform to the contract. If goods are delivered COD, the buyer must pay for them before an inspection can be made. The perfect tender rule under the UCC requires the seller to tender goods that exactly meet the requirements of the contract. Because the perfect tender rule is a harsh rule, the Code has allowed some exceptions (a major exception being to *cure,* or correct). The UCC governs performance unless the seller and the buyer make other arrangements in the sales contract. If either the goods or the delivery does not conform to the contract, the seller has the right to cure the defect under certain circumstances. If the seller does not cure, or is not allowed to, the buyer may reject the goods, in effect canceling the contract. If after a reasonable inspection the buyer accepts nonconforming goods, however, he or she may no longer reject them.

Most sales contracts are concluded without problems; that is, both seller and buyer meet their obligations as required. In case of a breach by one party or the other, however, there are remedies provided by the UCC or in the sales agreement. Remedies available to the buyer for breach of the sales contract by the seller include (1) suing for breach of warranty, (2) canceling the contract and cover, (3) canceling the contract and suing for damages, and (4) seeking specific performance or replevin. The buyer may exercise more than one of these remedies depending on the individual case. Remedies available to the seller if the buyer breaches the sales contract include (1) canceling the contract, (2) reselling the goods and suing for damages, (3) suing the buyer to recover the purchase price, (4) suing the buyer to recover damages for nonacceptance, (5) withholding delivery of the goods, and (6) reclaiming the goods from the buyer.

Important Legal terms

conforming goods	insolvent	replevin
cover	market price	stoppage in transit
cure	perfect tender rule	unpaid seller's lien

Questions and Problems for Discussion

1. Under Article 2 of the UCC dealing with the Sale of Goods (and when no agreement exists between buyer and seller), the seller's obligation to the buyer is to
   a. deliver the goods to the buyer's place of business.
   b. set aside conforming goods for inspection by the buyer before delivery.
   c. provide conforming goods, give the buyer reasonable notification that the goods are ready for delivery, and inform the buyer how delivery is to be accomplished.
   d. deliver all goods that are a part of the contract to a common carrier.

2. Flanagan Inc. of Ohio, a manufacturer of custom-made kitchen cabinets, contracted in writing with Bright Home Builders in Rochester, New York, to design and build custom kitchen cabinets for five large new homes being built by Bright in the Rochester area. The price to Bright was $60,000 and the cabinets were to be ready for delivery by May 15. The arrangements for shipping were FOB Ohio. Flanagan would deliver the cabinets to a trucking company by May 15 for shipment to Bright. On May 14, Flanagan did deliver the cabinets to the trucking company and notified Bright. On May 16, while en route to Rochester, the truck was involved in a five-car crash and the entire shipment of cabinets was completely destroyed. Is Bright entitled to specific performance because of the unique nature of the goods?

3. If some part of a shipment of goods does not conform to the contract,
   a. the seller generally must be given an opportunity to cure the defect
   b. the buyer can immediately reject the entire shipment and cancel the contract
   c. the buyer cannot accept the part of the shipment that is conforming
   d. the buyer must accept the shipment at a reduced price

4. On January 8, 2002, O'Grady purchased a new Buick from Hoselton Motors. O'Grady gave Hoselton a down payment on the car and financed the rest of the purchase price through her bank. She picked up the new car on January 10 and drove it a few places, including a local mall and to a doctor's appointment. On January 11, the car broke down and had to be towed back to Hoselton Motors for necessary repairs. She once again picked up the car on January 13, but again, it broke down and had to be towed back to Hoselton. This pattern of malfunctioning went on for several months (well into April). Each time, the car was returned to Hoselton for repairs. Finally, O'Grady wrote a letter to Hoselton's revoking the sale. She followed up by returning the car and requesting a return of her down payment. Hoselton claimed that O'Grady's request to void the contract is not a valid option because Hoselton did not have a chance to cure the defects. Is Hoselton correct?

5. On November 15, the Bon Ton Corporation entered into a contract to purchase 100 leather chairs from Rudnick Manufacturing Company. Both companies are in the same city. Bon Ton prepaid 50 percent of the purchase price but then became insolvent on November 21. Rudnick learned of this insolvency on November 22 and on that same day made a formal demand on Bon Ton to return the chairs. Can the Rudnick Company recover the chairs, even though they had already been delivered to Bon Ton?

6. Saxby Corporation sold goods to Scotsman. Scotsman arbitrarily refused to pay the purchase price. Under what circumstances will Saxby not be able to recover the price if it seeks this remedy instead of other possible remedies?

7. McDonald, owner of Sports Craft, a sporting goods store, contracted to purchase 200 footballs for $2,000 from the Pro Manufacturing Co. With no explanation, Pro Manufacturing shipped 100 footballs instead of the 200 called for in the contract. McDonald had already prepaid $1,000 on the purchase. What sales remedy or remedies could McDonald pursue?

8. Berry, a merchant and owner of a fabric store, ordered fabric from Lanny, a wholesaler. Lanny sent the goods specifically ordered by Berry. When the rolls of fabric arrived, Berry did not take time to inspect them. She simply signed the order, which included a statement certifying that the goods were acceptable; paid the transportation

company the amount due for the goods; and returned a copy of the signed order to Lanny. Later, Berry discovered several imperfections in the material. What rights, if any, does Berry have under these circumstances?

9. Projansky, owner of a retail leather goods store, entered into a contract to purchase luggage from the Likely Manufacturing Company for $2,000. Likely later refused to deliver the luggage at that price, claiming that inflation had caused the price of luggage to rise 15 percent since the contract with Projansky was made. Projansky then purchased the luggage from another company for $2,400 and sued Likely for $400. Should Projansky recover?

10. Salim entered into a contract to build a custom-made sailboat for McGregor for $8,000. On the delivery date, McGregor told Salim that he had changed his mind and no longer wanted the sail-boat. Salim tried to sell the boat elsewhere but couldn't because of its special features. Salim then sued McGregor for the purchase price. Should Salim recover damages from McGregor?

Cases for Review

1. Scampoli, a merchant, sold and delivered a new TV set to Wilson. When Wilson discovered that the set did not work properly, he asked Scampoli to correct the problem. Scampoli's repairperson, however, could not fix the set at Wilson's house and stated that the TV set would have to be taken back to the store and dismantled to determine the cause of the problem. Wilson refused to let the set go; instead, he demanded that Scampoli deliver a new TV or else refund his money. Scampoli said no to the refund and insisted that he be given the opportunity to correct the problem with the TV before returning the purchase price. Does Scampoli have the right to attempt to cure the problem? (*Wilson* v. *Scampoli*, 228 A.2d 848)

2. Supronics Corp., a manufacturer of ordinary types of lipsticks and nail polish, agreed to sell Hillmor Sales a small quantity of nail polish and lipsticks at close-out prices. Supronics then "pulled" the order so as to combine it with a larger shipment to another larger retailer. Hillmore demanded that Supronics go through with the contract and deliver the goods requested based on the remedy of specific performance— that the merchandise was unique and purchased at close-out prices. Was specific performance a proper remedy? (Part 1, *NY Law Journal*, 6 UCC Rept. Serv. 325)

3. Dr. Sedmak and his wife collected Chevrolet Corvettes. They learned about a limited-edition Corvette designed to commemorate the official pace car of the Indianapolis 500 and became interested in purchasing one. (Chevrolet manufactured only 6,000 of these pace cars.) The Sedmaks went to a local Chevrolet dealer and discovered that the dealership had received only one of these cars. The sales manager agreed to sell this car to them. When the Sedmaks went to pick up the car and pay for it, they were told that because of the great demand for this limited edition, the dealership had decided to auction it off to the highest bidder. The Sedmaks sued the dealership for specific performance. Must the dealership deliver the car to them? (*Sedmak* v. *Charlie's Chevrolet, Inc.,* 622 S.W.2d 694)

4. Neff purchased from the Hanna Lumber Company prefabricated wooden trusses, which were manufactured according to preengineered specifications. Although the truss system was represented as structurally sound, it collapsed the day after its installation. The collapse occurred when a weak and defective truss broke, causing the remaining truss system to collapse. An inspection of the system following its delivery to Neff would not have revealed the flaw in design or material that caused the collapse. Neff sued for breach of warranty, asking for damages caused by failure of the truss system. Can Neff recover? (*Neff* v. *Hanna Lumber Company,* 579 S.W.2d 95)

5. Flavorland Industries, Inc., entered into a contract to sell Schnoll a load of goose necks (bottom round cuts of beef) at a stated price with delivery to be completed on October 6 or October 7. Flavorland, unable to make the delivery, notified Schnoll before the delivery date and tried to make a further agreement on delivery. After advising Flavorland that it could not accept a different delivery date, Schnoll purchased other beef to cover the original order. The cost was $2,438.61

higher than the original contract price. Can Schnoll recover from Flavorland the amount of its cover? (*Schnoll Packing Corporation* v. *Flavorland Industries, Inc.,* 167 N.Y.Super. 376)

6. Downing purchased a TV set from Wood Radio and TV Service and put $100 down on the purchase price. He agreed to pay the balance and take the set when his new home was finished. When Downing went to pay the balance and accept delivery of the TV set, he was informed that the set had been sold to a third party. Can Downing purchase another TV set elsewhere and sue Wood Radio and TV Service to recover his down payment and any difference in cost of the TV set? (*Downing* v. *Arnold Wood Radio and TV Service,* 243 Ark. 137)

CHAPTER 18

Product Liability Law

CHAPTER PREVIEW

Product Liability Law: An Overview

Product Liability: A Comprehensive Definition

Development of Product Liability Law

Negligence

Warranty Liability
  Express Warranties
  Implied Warranties
  Warranty of Title

Exclusion of Warranties
Breach of Warranty
Magnuson-Moss Warranty Act

Strict Liability

Misuse of Product by Injured Party

Damages Recoverable in a Product Liability Case

Chapter Highlights

This chapter focuses on product liability: the liability that manufacturers and other sellers have to immediate purchasers, users, and consumers of products, or to affected bystanders, for physical injury and property damage caused by defective products they place on the market. The chapter opens with an overview of product liability followed by a discussion outlining the significant shift in the law surrounding the protection of the public from harmful products placed on the market. The remainder of the chapter is devoted to three well-recognized theories of liability—negligence, breach of warranty, and strict liability—that a buyer may use as the basis for recovery if he or she is injured by a defective product. Similarities and differences among these theories are noted. Some discussion in the chapter revolves around the Magnuson-Moss Warranty Act, a federal law that Congress passed to help prevent deceptive practices in the field of warranties (guarantees) made by sellers of products. The chapter ends with a brief discussion of damages recoverable in a product liability case.

PRODUCT LIABILITY LAW: AN OVERVIEW

The following summary is based on a real case, the circumstances of which formed the basis for a product liability law suit based on a defective product.

> The night of November 24, 2004, was a night of horror for the Ricter family. As father, mother, and three of their four children slept in their beds, the Mohawk Energy Company sent a dangerous surge of electrical power into the Ricter house, causing a fire and several small explosions that consumed the entire house and killed all the occupants. The surge of power passed through a defective transformer secured to a pole situated immediately outside the Ricter home. The Mohawk Energy Company had recently replaced an older transformer with this new defective one.

If the remaining son in this case were to sue for the death of his parents and his siblings, he would likely bring his claim against the manufacturer of the transformer for injuries due to the defect in the transformer. This case would come under what the law terms *product liability*, which is what this chapter is all about.

Lawsuits resulting in big monetary awards, often in the millions of dollars, involving product liability have become very common because each year many Americans are injured and often left permanently disabled while others die in consumer-product-related accidents. Consequently, product liability issues have become increasingly important to manufacturers and others who sell products to the general public due to the spread of the doctrine of strict liability (which will be discussed later in this chapter) and the enactment in many states of comprehensive protection statutes providing for specific remedies for a variety of product defects.

Much of the law surrounding product liability is found at the state level and is based on common law (judge-made law that developed gradually over time because of the principle of stare decisis as discussed in Chapter 1). The common law has been codified and put into Restatements, the most current being Restatement of the Law of Torts, Third: Product Liability. These Restatements are authored by the American Law Institute made up of law professors, practicing attorneys, and judges. Although Restatements are not binding authority in and of themselves and courts are under no obligation to adopt Restatements as law, courts often do however, because they accurately restate in an orderly form the already established law in a particular jurisdiction. Furthermore, because Restatements are a codification of common law principles, it is easier for lawyers and judges to refer to a Restatement rather than search through a string of old common law cases in order to reach a principle of law about a case before the courts.

PRODUCT LIABILITY: A COMPREHENSIVE DEFINITION

product liability liability of manufacturers and sellers of products to persons harmed by defects in the products

Picking up on the discussion in the opening paragraph, it is time to define product liability so as to clear up any confusion as to what it encompasses. **Product liability** refers to the liability that manufacturers or other sellers in the chain of sale (e.g., wholesalers and retailers) have not only to immediate purchasers, but also to the general public (e.g., someone to whom the product was loaned, given, etc.; a consumer, a bystander) for physical injury or property damage caused by defective products they place on the market or for the failure of these products to perform adequately once they are purchased. The cornerstone of a plaintiff's case is the product's defect. There are three types of defects that incur liability:

1. *Manufacturing defects* occur during the construction or production of the item and usually involve poor-quality materials or shoddy workmanship that cause the product to depart from its intended design even if all possible care is exercised.
2. *Design defects* exist before the product is manufactured and occur where the product design is inherently unsafe or useless due to poor engineering and poor choice of materials no matter how carefully manufactured; harm could have been reduced by adoption of an alternative design, which if used, would have reduced the chance of foreseeable injury.
3. *Marketing defects* deal with poor or improper instructions as well as failure to warn consumers of hidden dangers or foreseeable risks posed by the product that could have been avoided or reduced had the information been known.

DEVELOPMENT OF PRODUCT LIABILITY LAW

caveat venditor "let the seller beware"

There has been a significant shift in the law over the years. This shift has increased protection for the public by expanding the liability of manufacturers and sellers. The rule of **caveat venditor**, or "let the seller beware," now prevails. This rule reflects the view that the seller should bear the burden of determining that goods conform to certain standards.

caveat emptor "let the buyer beware"

The rule of **caveat emptor**, or "let the buyer beware," has practically been abandoned by the courts and has little application today. This strict rule had its heyday in the nineteenth and early twentieth centuries when buyers were expected to examine goods they were buying and to rely on their own judgment about whether these goods were of suitable quality and free from defects. This rule assumed that both seller and buyer were in an equal position to bargain. In today's society, however, the seller has more product knowledge, and the consumer possesses far less bargaining power than the seller. Besides, we live in an era of just prices and fair dealing in transactions. As noted in Chapter 15, the UCC insists upon these principles.

The trend today, as reflected in modern court cases, is to allow anyone who is harmed by a product to sue whoever is in any way responsible. This was not always the case. At one time the doctrine of privity prevailed. This doctrine stated that an injured person (the ultimate consumer) was limited to suing only the immediate seller with whom she or he had a contract. This meant that the manufacturer who actually produced the defective product and then sold this product to the retailer, who in turn sold it to the ultimate consumer, had no liability. Consequently, this left the ultimate consumer without a remedy since it was the manufacturer, and not the retailer, whose negligence caused the harm. Fortunately for the consumer, the doctrine of privity has in most cases been abandoned. We will talk briefly about this rule again when we discuss warranties later on in the chapter. The landmark case of *MacPherson* v. *BuickMotor Co.* (111 N.E. 1050), a famous New York State Court of Appeals case, established beyond question that the manufacturer or any other seller in the chain of distribution (e.g., a wholesaler or retailer) responsible for placing the defective product on the market is liable. This case further established that the initial buyer, that person's family members, any bystanders, and users as well as persons who lease the product or hold it for the purchaser may sue.

In most jurisdictions, a person suing because of an injury from a defective product may sue (as the plaintiff) under one of three theories of liability: negligence, breach of warranty, or strict liability (see Table 18.1); however, since most product liability cases are determined at the state level and since each state requires different elements to be

TABLE 18.1   THEORIES ON WHICH PRODUCT LIABILITY CASES ARE BASED

THEORY OF LIABILITY	BASIS FOR LEGAL ACTION	DEGREE OF PROOF REQUIRED	WHO CAN SUE	WHO CAN BE SUED
Negligence	Tort	Defective product. Negligent conduct (fault) must be established. Product defect caused buyer's injury.	Anyone harmed.	All parties in chain of distribution.
Breach of warranty	Contract	Existence and breach of warranty. Breach caused buyer's injury.	Under the UCC in most states: the buyer, members of the buyer's family, household guests.	Immediate seller.
		Notice of breach given to seller.	According to modern case law, anyone harmed.	All parties in chain of distribution.
Strict liability	Tort	Product was unreasonably dangerous when it left the manufacturer's or other seller's control, and the buyer suffered an injury without reference to negligence.	Anyone harmed.	All parties in chain of distribution.

proved to win a case, it would be best for anyone bringing a law suit for a defective product to consult with an attorney as to which theory is most appropriate for his or her situation. The theories presented here will reflect general principles upon which the plaintiff can base his or her case under each theory of liability. Also keep in mind that a plaintiff cannot bring a civil action based on one of the defects discussed earlier, since these defects are not of themselves legal claims. Instead, a particular defect would be offered as the central theme of a lawsuit based on one of the three theories of liability.

In view of the seller's increased liability, there has been a great proliferation of product warnings.

NEGLIGENCE

Negligence, as a tort, was discussed in Chapter 4, and basically the same principles will apply to product liability cases. While the Restatement, Third, has made some changes, and as mentioned previously many courts now cite the Restatement, it still does not supersede many of the long-standing rules of negligence.

According to the Restatement, Third, negligence is the failure of a person to exercise reasonable care at all times and under all circumstances, taking into consideration the safety of individuals and their property. The Restatement did not alter the definition of negligence (the duty to exercise reasonable care under all circumstance); it simply expanded upon this definition. Furthermore, one of the elements of proof required in a negligence action (as discussed in Chapter 4) is that "the defendant's failure to act carefully, proximately caused the plaintiff's (person suing) injury." The Restatement, Third states that harm caused by the plaintiff's failure to act carefully must be "within the scope of the defendant's liability" which in the past has been referred to as proximate cause.

In order to sue under the negligence theory, you, as the plaintiff bringing the lawsuit, must first show that the manufacturer or other seller had a duty to sell a safe product; that the product you purchased was not safe, but defective; that the seller knew or should have known that the product was defective but breached that duty; and finally, that you suffered an injury (damage) caused by the carelessness (negligence) of the seller and not as the result of some unrelated illness or accident. It won't be enough to show that the defect in the product you purchased might hurt someone. Proving that the seller had a duty to sell you a safe product should be no problem since the laws of each state require all sellers to guarantee the safety of their products.

An ultimate consumer who purchases a defective product and is injured, dies, or suffers property damage most likely will initiate a lawsuit. (In case of death, the person's estate would bring the suit.)

The driver for a local soft drink company delivered several cases of its soft drink to a restaurant. When a waitress was placing glass bottles of the drink in a large refrigerator in the restaurant's kitchen, a bottle exploded in her hand. The bottle broke into two jagged pieces and inflicted a deep cut, severing blood vessels, nerves, and muscles in the palm of her hand and thumb. The waitress could sue the soft drink company for negligence.

Negligent conduct very often relates to a manufacturer's improper design of the product, a failure to inspect the product properly for defects after it leaves the assembly line, a failure to test the product adequately, or a failure to warn of a known danger related to the product.

Suing under the negligence theory of product liability is often an unsatisfactory remedy for the injured plaintiff to pursue because proving specific acts of negligence on the part of the defendant is difficult. For example, it may be hard to prove that the manufacturer was careless in designing the product or failed to test the product after it came off the assembly line. Determining negligence in this case may involve a visit to the manufacturer's plant to examine the facilities and processes used to produce and test a product. Acquiring information in this fashion could be costly and futile.

WARRANTY LIABILITY

warranty guarantee by seller that goods are not defective and that they are suitable for intended use

The story of warranty begins with a contract for the sale of goods. In that contract, as an inducement to buyers, sellers guarantee that the products they sell will conform to certain qualities, characteristics, or conditions; that they are suitable for the use for which they are intended; and that the goods are free of defects. This guarantee by a seller is called a **warranty**. If a warranty is false, the seller has committed a breach. If the buyer suffers harm as a result of the breach, he or she may bring an action for damages. When suing for breach of warranty, you have to prove that the seller (e.g., the manufacturer) broke a written or implied promise that the goods are free from defects. No negligence or fault need be shown. You also, of course, must show that the breach caused your injury.

Breach of warranty-based product liability claims is concerned with both express and implied warranties that can arise in a sale or lease contract.

Express Warranties

express warranty seller's statement of fact, promise, description, or model that buyer relies upon when purchasing goods

An **express warranty** is an oral or written guarantee given by manufacturers and sellers (e.g., retailers). Exactly what they promise in their express warranties is entirely up to them. A manufacturer's express warranty is generally in writing, either on a separate card or as part of the instructions packed with the product. As indicated, express warranties may be oral or written. Accepting an oral warranty is not a good idea because the buyer may have a problem establishing its existence if the seller should deny having given such a warranty. Under the UCC, a seller's express warranty may arise in several ways (UCC 2-313). The seller may make a factual statement or a promise, orally or in writing, about the product. The seller may also describe the goods to the buyer or show the buyer a sample of the item being sold. To constitute an express warranty, the statement, description, or sample must be part of the basis of the sale; (UCC 2-313) that is, it must be one of the reasons that the buyer purchased the goods. Under the Code, the burden is on the seller to disprove the existence of an express warranty. Consequently, if an express warranty is not intended, the seller should be cautious about any promise made to the buyer.

Statement of Fact or Promise Any oral or written statement of fact or any promise made to the buyer by the seller relating to the goods creates an express warranty.

> You went to a used car dealer to purchase a used car with a V-8 engine and saw a model you liked; because of your lack of knowledge about cars, however, you could not tell whether it had a V-8 or a V-6 engine. When you asked the salesperson, she said: "This car absolutely has a V-8 engine." Based on this response and your desire for the car, you made the purchase. A few days later, not satisfied with the performance of the engine, you took the car to a garage for an evaluation, only to discover that the engine was a V-6.

In this example, the salesperson's statement is an express warranty. You bought the car not only because you liked the color and that it was in excellent condition but also because of the salesperson's guarantee, "This car absolutely has a V-8 engine." The salesperson did not actually use the word *warranty* or *guarantee*, but that is not necessary. Under the UCC, her statement would be taken to mean, "I guarantee [promise] that this car has a V-8 engine." The salesperson could argue in court that she did not intend to give a warranty, but a court of law would follow the UCC and would probably say she did. It is not necessary that a seller intend to make a warranty. If what is said or done induces the person to buy the product, under the Code an express warranty is created. Further, a seller may make a false statement about a product unknowingly, but in good faith. This false statement, nevertheless, could constitute a breach of express warranty. For example, a college student purchased a shoulder bag after being told by the shop owner that "this shoulder bag will hold up to twenty-five pounds." After one week of carrying textbooks and notebooks weighing twenty-five pounds in the bag back and forth to class, she was on her way to class one day from her dorm when the straps broke and the bag fell from her shoulders. In an attempt to keep from falling she twisted her back and required medical attention from a chiropractor for several months. The shop owner is liable for breach of an express warranty.

A seller's written statement or promise may be expressed in the written contract of sale or in a separate document. Manufacturers and sellers can even create warranties through their advertisements in newspapers, brochures, and TV commercials. For example, because a TV commercial by the manufacturer said it was safe to drive on mountainous terrain at high rates of speed, you purchased a pickup truck with four-wheel drive. Courts have ruled that if you are injured while trying to do what the ad said the truck could do, a breach of an express warranty has occurred for which you may file an action for damages.

Sellers often make a variety of statements about their products. As a buyer in the marketplace, the law holds you responsible for determining which of these statements are warranties and which are simply puffing. **Puffing**, or statements by salespersons expressing their opinions about the goods they sell, does not form an express warranty (a statement of fact). The statement, "This car has the best used-car value in town," made to you by a salesperson as an inducement to purchase the car is not an express warranty. It is merely the salesperson's opinion. On the other hand, a statement of opinion made to a layperson by a seller who works as an expert is generally considered to be a warranty.

The Code does not distinguish between representations of fact and opinion. Courts, however, have held that the more specific the statement, the less likely it will be treated as opinion or puffing as a matter of law.

Because an express warranty is considered part of the sales contract, part of the purchase price is consideration for the warranty. If there is a breach of warranty by the seller, the buyer may recover damages, but the sales contract remains in force.

Under the UCC, it is not essential that a warranty be given by the seller at the time of the sale. A warranty, oral or written, given by the seller following the transaction becomes a part of the original sales contract without additional consideration (UCC 2-209). An oral warranty is enforceable even though the original sales contract was in writing. As a practical matter, however, the buyer must be able to prove the existence of an oral warranty, or it will not be enforced by the courts.

Harkness purchased a guitar from the House of Music without any warranty. About a week after Harkness made the purchase, she expressed some concern about a guarantee and talked to the owner of House of Music about it. The owner said, "I guarantee all musical instruments I sell against all defects for one year." This oral warranty, although made after the sale of the guitar, was binding.

puffing salespersons' statements expressing opinions about goods they sell; type of advertising that exaggerates the quality of merchandise

Description of the Goods If the buyer purchases goods after they are described by the seller, either orally or in writing (including drawings), there is an express warranty that the goods obtained by the buyer will conform to the description. If you purchase goods after reading a description in a catalog or on the label of a can or box, an express warranty of description is also created.

> You purchased a can of Quick-Sun at a drugstore because the words on the label stated that the contents, when applied, would give you a deep tan within fifteen minutes. This description on the can is an express warranty.

Sample of the Goods Sometimes the buyer purchases goods after inspecting a sample or model of these goods. In this case, there is an express warranty that the goods delivered to the buyer will conform to the sample or model.

> The local jeweler was taking orders for class rings. Before you ordered a ring, the jeweler showed you a sample of the ring you intended to buy. The jeweler, by showing you the sample, made an express warranty that the ring delivered to you would be like the sample.

Implied Warranties

implied warranty obligation imposed upon seller by law

An **implied warranty** is an obligation the law imposes on a seller. An implied warranty is not in writing and is not part of the sales contract. When a sale of goods is made, however, certain warranties become part of the sale even though the seller may not have intended to create them. These implied warranties protect the buyer when there is little or no opportunity to inspect the goods or the seller does not expressly warrant the goods. Breach of the implied warranty is grounds for a suit for money damages if injury or damage results from use of the product. In some cases, disaffirmance of the contract is also grounds for a lawsuit for breach of warranty. The UCC has established two types of implied warranties: the implied warranty of merchantability and the implied warranty of fitness for a particular purpose (UCC 2-314; UCC 2-315). The question sometimes comes up about how long an implied warranty lasts. In most states, an implied warranty lasts forever. In a few states, however, the implied warranty lasts only as long as an expressed warranty that comes with the product. In these states, if there is no express warranty, the implied warranty lasts forever.

merchantable goods goods fit for the purposes for which they would ordinarily be used

Merchantability If a sale of new or used goods is made by the merchant who ordinarily deals in these goods, there is always an implied warranty that the goods are merchantable. **Merchantable goods** are goods that are fit for the ordinary purposes for which they are manufactured and sold and also are of average quality. Merchants have been held liable for breaching this warranty for many reasons as for example because of a dead mouse found in a soft-drink container or a worm found in a can of peas. Section 2-314 of the Code outlines the minimum requirements of merchantability. In addition to what was stated, also included under the Code are the requirements that goods (1) be adequately contained, packaged, and labeled and (2) pass without objection in the trade under the contract description. If you purchase a pocket calculator, you have the right to expect that it will perform the functions (e.g., addition and subtraction) indicated on the calculator and that you will not unexpectedly be harmed because of improper manufacturing or labeling.

> You purchased an electric razor from Grigsby's Department Store. The first time you used the razor, a defect caused the motor to burn out. Because the razor was not

merchantable, Grigsby's Department Store was liable for breach of the implied warranty of merchantability.

The implied warranty of merchantability is a very broad warranty. It also applies to the sale of food or drink that is consumed on the premises (as in a restaurant) or elsewhere (e.g., food purchased from a store and eaten at home) (UCC 2-314). In this case, merchantability means that the food is fit for human consumption.

The test of merchantability in the case of foods is generally based on what a reasonable person can expect to find in the food. For example, a person eating a doughnut would not expect to find a human fingernail embedded in the doughnut whereas a person can reasonably expect or anticipate finding a small fish bone in his or her fish chowder soup that he or she ordered in a restaurant. A classic case on the reasonable expectation test is *Webster* v. *Blue Ship Tea Room* (347 Mass. 421 N.E.2d 309). The case involved a Mrs. Webster who ordered fish chowder soup in the Blue Ship Tea Room. After three or four spoonfuls of the chowder she became aware that a fish bone had lodged in her throat. She was taken to the hospital where the bone was removed. She sued the Blue Ship Tea Room alleging breach of the warranty of merchantability. The court denied her claim. In reaching its conclusion, the court said: "We should be prepared to cope with the hazards of fish bones, the occasional presence of which . . . do not impair their fitness or merchantability." This opinion illustrates one approach a court might take. Consequently, each case brought to court involving a merchantability-of-food case will need to be decided based on the facts of the case.

An implied warranty of merchantability exists whether a merchant is selling to another merchant or to an ultimate consumer. No implied warranty of merchantability, however, exists in a sale of goods by a nonmerchant. For example, if you sell two snow tires at a garage sale, there is no implied warranty of merchantability.

Fitness for a Particular Purpose   An implied warranty that goods will be fit for a particular purpose arises if at the time the contract is made, the seller knows or has reason to know the buyer's purpose and the buyer relies on the seller's skill or judgment to select something suitable (UCC 2-315). (This warranty cannot be applied when the buyer and seller have equal skill and knowledge.) This warranty applies to both merchants and nonmerchants.

> Preston told Hunter, the owner of a retail paint store, that he wanted to paint the exterior of his brick house. Hunter recommended Clean Gloss Shingle and Shake paint and told Preston how to apply the paint. Preston followed the instructions carefully and applied 6 gallons. Three months later, most of the paint had peeled, flaked, or blistered. Hunter is liable for breach of an implied warranty of fitness for a particular purpose.

Goods recommended by the seller under their trade name continue to give the buyer protection under the implied warranty of fitness for a particular purpose as long as there was actual reliance on the seller's judgment.

> Carp went to Auto Finishers and asked for a cleaner that would remove spots from the cloth upholstery in her new car. The seller recommended Easy Clean, the trade name of a new product on the market. When applied, however, the cleaner discolored Carp's upholstery. When Carp discovered that several other people had the same experience with Easy Clean, she had the cleaner professionally tested at a laboratory. The lab report indicated that the chemicals in the cleaner were too strong. The store was liable for breach of the implied warranty of fitness.

If the buyer does not rely on the seller's judgment but personally selects the goods, including brand-name items, or describes to the seller the type of goods he or she needs, the implied warranty of fitness for a particular purpose does not apply.

Warranty of Title

In every sale of goods under the UCC, there is an implied warranty of title by the seller, both merchant and nonmerchant (UCC 2-312). In other words, the seller automatically guarantees that he or she owns the goods (has good title) free of any encumbrances and liens and has the right to sell them.

> Heinz sold a police scanner, which she had stolen, to Vance. Vance was unaware that it had been stolen. McAllister, the true owner, identified the police scanner to the police by the serial number, and it was returned to him. Vance can sue Heinz for breach of the implied warranty of title.

The warranty of title is an implied warranty. To distinguish it from those implied warranties that may be excluded from a sales contract, however, it is not designated as such under the UCC.

Exclusion of Warranties

disclaimer of warranty
statement in a contract that excludes a warranty

Under the UCC, the seller may exclude certain express and implied warranties (UCC 2-316). A statement in a contract that excludes a warranty is called a **disclaimer of warranty**. If a disclaimer is used, the seller must use specific language set forth in the UCC to eliminate these warranties.

Express Warranties   The seller may exclude an express warranty as part of a sales contract by being careful not to induce a person to buy the goods by making factual statements or promises, by describing the goods, or by producing a sample or model of the goods. The seller may also exclude an express warranty by using clear, specific language. For instance, the following warranty is legal and binding: "The goods sold under this agreement are warranted from defects in workmanship and materials for ninety days. No other express warranty is given and no affirmation by the seller, by words or actions, shall constitute a warranty."

Sometimes a sales contract includes an express warranty by the seller and also includes a statement that no express or implied warranties exist. In this case, the sentence eliminating the warranties is not binding. Take, for example, the following statements made by a seller in a sales contract: "Your Super Permanex trash container is made of thick-wall, high-molecular-weight, high-density plastic. Its rugged handles can lift up to 250 pounds. The seller makes no express warranties of this product." The sentence stating that there are no express warranties has no effect. The statements made about the trash container amount to an express warranty even though the word *warranty* or *guarantee* was not used.

Any oral warranties made by the seller, before or at the time of the sale, that are contrary to the terms of the written warranty given with the goods are not binding. Where a written warranty exists, only the terms stated in that written warranty are enforceable.

> Marcus purchased a refrigerator from a local appliance dealer and, at the time of the sale, received a written manufacturer's warranty stating in part that, "For 90 days from date of delivery, Roncone Refrigeration [manufacturer] will remedy any defect or replace any part or parts found to be defective." The salesperson told Marcus that "Roncone will remedy any defects free of charge for 120 days even though the written

warranty says 90 days." Because the salesperson's oral warranty is contrary to the written warranty, the oral warranty is not binding.

Implied Warranties   If, before entering into the sales contract, the buyer has examined a sample or model of the goods or has refused to examine them after being given the opportunity to do so by the seller, there is no implied warranty as to defects that were or should have been obvious. This rule of caveat emptor, as noted on page 291, has practically been abandoned by the courts. It applies as long as there is no fraud on the part of the seller, such as concealing obvious defects.

You purchased a used car from the A-1 Car Company. At the time of purchase, you inspected the car but failed to notice that the two front tires were bald. Any attempt by you to cancel the contract with A-1 should fail. Bald tires constitute an obvious defect. You should have discovered this defect when you inspected the car.

The expressions "as is" and "with all faults" make it clear that no implied warranties exist and that the buyer takes the risk as to the quality of the goods.

Lloyd purchased a blender for cash from Cole's Department Store, which was running a special sale. A large sign at the counter next to the blenders read: "Prices as marked and all merchandise purchased 'as is.'" Later, when Lloyd attempted to use the blender, she found that it did not work properly. The store was not liable under an implied warranty of merchantability because the sign identified the sale of the blender as an "as is" sale.

The expressions "as is" and "with all faults," or similar expressions, will not exclude an implied warranty of title. The warranty of title is excluded only if the seller specifically states that no warranty of title is given or when the circumstances of the sale indicate that the seller does not have a clear title to the goods being sold.

The student government of Geneva University took charge of lost and found articles. To raise money for underprivileged children, the student government officers had a Christmas sale of the lost and found articles in their possession. Given the circumstances of the sale, it should be clear to any buyer that the student government does not have clear title to the goods being sold.

The implied warranty of merchantability may be excluded either orally or in writing, but the word *merchantability* must be used. If the exclusion is in writing, the clause excluding merchantability must be conspicuous. According to the UCC, a term or clause is conspicuous when it is written so that a reasonable person would notice it. The following clause, written in large, bold print, excludes the warranty of merchantability: **SELLER MAKES NO WARRANTY OF MERCHANTABILITY WITH RESPECT TO THE GOODS SOLD UNDER THE TERMS OF THIS AGREEMENT.**

The implied warranty of fitness for a particular purpose can be excluded only in writing. Although the writing must be conspicuous, no specific language need be used. The language used in the following example is sufficient: **WE MAKE NO OTHER WARRANTIES, EXPRESS OR IMPLIED, BEYOND THE WARRANTY EXPRESSED IN THIS AGREEMENT.**

Breach of Warranty

Breach of a seller's warranty ordinarily entitles a buyer to recover damages. It is a second basis for suing under the theory of product liability. The greatest asset to the individual suing lies in the fact that it is not necessary for the plaintiff (injured party) to prove that the defendant was in any way negligent. The right to damages may be lost, however, unless the plaintiff proves that (1) a warranty existed, (2) there has been a breach of the warranty, (3) the breach of warranty caused a loss or injury, and (4) notice of the breach was given to the seller. The buyer must give notice of the breach within a reasonable time after he or she has discovered or should have discovered that the goods were not as warranted. If the buyer fails to notify the seller of any breach within a reasonable time after it was discovered or should have been discovered, he or she is barred from any remedy against the seller (UCC 2-607). As the injured party, the buyer would then have to seek another remedy. Recall also that sellers, as they are entitled to do under UCC 2-316, may and often do disclaim express and implied warranties. If a seller does give an express warranty, it often contains restrictions and limitations. Another drawback relates to an inspection of the goods. If the buyer inspects the goods but fails to discover "noticeable" defects or for some reason refuses to inspect the goods, he or she waives any benefits from implied warranties against defects that an inspection reasonably should have detected.

Originally, because a warranty was part of a sales contract, a lawsuit for breach of an express or implied warranty was based on whether the buyer had entered into a contract of sale for a product with the seller. Parties who have contracted with each other are said **privity of contract** to be in **privity of contract**. When privity of contract is required, only the buyer can sue contractual for breach of warranty and can sue only the immediate seller.
relationship

> Atkinson purchased from the Ace Drugstore two bottles of Sun-Pro lotion, which was guaranteed by the manufacturer, the Altra Corporation, to protect a person's skin from sunburn. Atkinson gave a bottle to his sister to use. After they applied some of this lotion, their skin was severely sunburned.

Under the privity of contract rule, only Atkinson could sue, and he could sue only the Ace Drugstore, with whom the contract for the purchase of Sun-Pro was made. To recover for any damages, the sister would have to sue Atkinson, her brother.

The privity requirement as to who can sue for breach of warranty has been eliminated under the UCC and in the courts (the decision in the *MacPherson* case cited on page 291 was a landmark decision in the abolition of the privity requirement), thus allowing people other than the buyer to sue. Three alternatives (A, B, and C) are allowed under the Code (UCC 2-318). All three alternatives have eliminated the privity requirement. States may, if they wish, select from among these three. Most states have eliminated the privity concept and adopted one of the alternatives. Alternative A, which has been most widely adopted, extends the seller's warranty to any member of the buyer's family or household or a guest in the buyer's home who suffers personal injury while using or consuming the product. Alternative B has been adopted in some states. It extends alternative A to anyone who suffers personal injury while using or consuming the product, (even a passing stranger would be covered under this alternative). Alternative C not only extends coverage to anyone while using or consuming the product, but it covers any injury, not simply personal injury, but also property damage. This third alternative follows the trend of modern court decisions by extending the rule beyond injuries to the person. Applying alternative A, the most popular alternative to the previous example, Atkinson's sister may also sue the immediate seller.

The UCC is neutral on relaxing the privity requirement that deals with the issue of who can be sued for breach of warranty. Under the UCC, the immediate seller remains as the person against whom a lawsuit may be directed. It is left to the courts to decide on a case-by-case basis if anyone beyond the immediate seller can be sued. Consequently, modern courts, with the impetus of the landmark case *Henningsen* v. *Bloomfield Motors, Inc.* (32 N.J. 358), have also dropped the privity requirement and now permit all individuals harmed by a product to sue not only the immediate seller but also all parties in the chain of distribution. This chain may include not only the retailer but also the manufacturer and the wholesaler. Again referring to the example given earlier, both Atkinson and his sister could, under case law, sue the manufacturer for their injuries.

Magnuson-Moss Warranty Act

Magnuson-Moss Warranty Act law preventing deceptive warranties and requiring terms and conditions to be clear and understandable

The federal **Magnuson-Moss Warranty Act** of 1975 was passed by Congress to protect purchasers of consumer goods (those goods used for personal, family, or household purposes). The act applies only to written warranties. The purpose of the act is to make available to consumer purchasers adequate and understandable information about written warranties. Up to 1975, most warranties were not understandable and were unfair; furthermore in some instances, those giving the warranties did not live up to the promises made in the warranties. This act has not replaced UCC warranty law, but in certain cases, it imposes additional standards and remedies.

Under this act, the terms of any warranty must be disclosed in simple and readily understood language and must be accessible to the consumer, as by attaching the warranty to the package or placing it in a binder with signs posted informing consumers of its availability. The law does not require manufacturers and sellers to give written warranties. If they choose to give a warranty and that warranty is written, and if the warranted goods cost more than $10, however, the warranty must be prominently labeled as either a "full" warranty or a "limited" warranty. In addition, if the cost of the goods is more than $15, the Federal Trade Commission requires that certain additional information in the nature of disclosures be made fully and conspicuously in "readily understood language." Such disclosures include, but are not limited to, the parts that are covered by the warranty, the length of the warranty period (e.g., "full ten-year warranty"), a step-by-step explanation of the procedure the consumer should follow to obtain performance of any warranty obligation, and whether the enforceability of the written warranty is limited to the original buyer or is extended to every buyer who has owned the goods during the term of the warranty period. Furthermore, if a written warranty is given, the implied warranties of merchantability and fitness for a particular purpose cannot be eliminated by the manufacturer or seller.

A *full warranty* gives the buyer much more protection than a limited warranty. For example, a full warranty many times does not have a time limit. Further, it requires a defective product to be repaired within a reasonable time at no cost to the owner. If it cannot be repaired, the "lemon clause" of the act requires the manufacturer or seller to refund the buyer's money or to replace the product. *Limited warranties* have more restrictions than full warranties. Limited means be cautious, something is missing. For example, a limited warranty may cover only parts, not labor; allow only a prorated refund or credit (smaller refunds or credit depending on how long you've had the product); require you to return a heavy product to the store for service; cover only the first purchaser; charges for handling. A product can carry more than one written warranty. For example, it can have a full warranty on part of the product and a limited warranty on the rest. Very importantly, the seller can limit the time the goods are covered by any implied warranties, but it has to respond to the duration of the express warranty. Also, with a limited warranty, the buyer is not guaranteed a refund or a replacement if the product cannot be fixed. Most limited warranties cover parts, but not labor. When only a limited warranty is given, this fact must be conspicuously designated. An example of a limited warranty is shown in Figure 18.1. It deals with a paper shredder.

To help consumers make better informed decisions, warranty information about a product must be readily available in the store for customer inspection. Provisions in the

FIGURE 18.1
Limited Express
Warranty

LIMITED WARRANTY

General Binding Corporation ("GBC") warrants to the original purchaser the cutting blades on this product to be free from defects in workmanship and material under normal use and service for a period of five (5) years after purchase. GBC warrants to the original purchaser that all other parts of this product to be free from defects in workmanship and material under normal use and service for a period of one (1) year after purchase. GBC's obligation under this warranty is limited to replacement or repair at GBC's option completely without charge for material or labor of any warranted part found defective by GBC.

THIS WARRANTY IS IN LIEU OF ALL OTHER EXPRESSED WARRANTIES. REPRESENTATIONS OR PROMISES INCONSISTENT WITH, OR IN ADDITION TO, THIS WARRANTY ARE UNAUTHORIZED AND SHALL NOT BE BINDING UPON GBC. IN NO EVENT SHALL GBC BE LIABLE FOR ANY SPECIAL, INCIDENTAL OR CONSEQUENTIAL DAMAGES, WHETHER OR NOT FORESEEABLE. SOME STATES DO NOT ALLOW THE EXCLUSION OR LIMITATION OF SPECIAL, INCIDENTAL, OR CONSEQUENTIAL DAMAGES, SO THE ABOVE EXCLUSION OR LIMITATION MAY NOT APPLY TO YOU.

ANY IMPLIED WARRANTIES ARE LIMITED IN DURATION TO THE DURATION OF THIS WARRANTY. SOME STATES DO NOT ALLOW LIMITATIONS ON HOW LONG AN IMPLIED WARRANTY LASTS, SO THE ABOVE LIMITATION MAY NOT APPLY TO YOU.

This warranty shall be void if the product has been subjected to misuse or damaged by negligence or accident, or altered by anyone other than authorized agents of GBC.

This limited warranty gives you specific legal rights, and you may also have other rights which vary from state to state.

act provide formal and informal procedures for settling claims for breach of warranty. One significant feature allows consumers to recover attorney's fees if a lawyer is needed to enforce a warranty.

STRICT LIABILITY

Along with negligence and breach of warranty, the third major area of product liability that a buyer may choose as the basis for recovery if he or she is injured by a defective product is strict liability. This theory, based on tort law, is now the dominant product liability theory used as a basis for recovery for lawsuit in nearly every state. Section 402a of the Restatement, Third, of Torts imposes strict liability in tort on merchant sellers for both personal injuries and property damage. The injured party suing as the plaintiff simply needs to show that the product was unreasonably dangerous at the time it left the manufacturer's or other seller's control and that he or she suffered an injury. These issues are ordinarily questions of fact for a jury to decide. "Unreasonably dangerous" means that the product poses a risk of substantial harm due to a product defect beyond the comprehension of the consumer who purchases the product. The injured party does not have to prove that the defect causing the injury resulted from negligence (fault) nor does the injured party need to depend on the existence of a warranty. Strict liability focuses on the product itself and not on the conduct of the manufacturer or others in the chain of sale. Courts in strict liability cases are interested that a product defect arose but not how it arose. Consequently, even an innocent manufacturer—one that has not even been negligent—may be liable if the injured party can show a link between the defective product and the injury. Without proving to the court that this link exists, the injured party may not prevail under the strict liability theory.

> Viscount underwent LASIK surgery at Dell Eye Associates. The blade used for the surgery broke in her eye during the surgical procedure and cut her cornea. Viscount now has hazed vision and, according to her doctor, she will need a corneal transplant. Since the failed eye procedure, Viscount has suffered severe and painful injury. Roberts and Thiel Inc., the company that manufactured the blade, admitted the blade was defective. Viscount sued Roberts and Thiel for strict liability and most likely will be successful.

Strict liability cases often hinge on testimony by expert witnesses establishing or denying a link between an alleged defect and an injury. If you are injured by a product, you should consult an experienced attorney who can advise you about the potential success of your case and how the manufacturer and other defendants are likely to try to avoid liability. It is essential to the success of your case that you keep adequate records surrounding the circumstances in which the injury occurred, as for example taking photographs of the site where the injury occurred and of the product that caused the injury, repair records, and receipts showing your purchase of the product. These and other similar records are vital to building a successful case.

The average consumer can presume that the product is not unreasonably dangerous and harmful if, for example, there are no warnings in the instructions that come with the product and if there are no other references to danger on the product label. The manufacturer or other sellers cannot claim as a defense that reasonable care was used to discover defects in the manufacture of the product, that reasonable care was used to prepare and sell the product, or that there was no privity of contract.

The effect of the strict liability theory in most states is therefore to make the manufacturer, seller, or whoever is in any way responsible for the harm (e.g., the designer of the product) liable without question for the safety of the product. It allows not only the buyer to sue, but also other persons who used the goods and suffered injury or damage because of the defect.

> While driving his new car within the speed limit down the main street of his hometown, Arnet struck a parked car and was seriously injured. The accident resulted because the newly designed steering column on this model of car broke, causing Arnet to lose control of the car. Arnet successfully sued the car manufacturer and recovered damages under the doctrine of strict liability.

In this case, although the car manufacturer proved that it was not negligent because it had used all possible care in manufacturing the car, the court nevertheless concluded that the design of this new model met the criteria for being unreasonably dangerous because the defective steering column was not a danger that a reasonably prudent person would be subjected to in a new car.

The effect of the strict liability theory has wide implications. American importers of goods from foreign countries generally become the subject of lawsuits for damages involving defective and/or dangerous goods passed on to suppliers in the chain of distribution in the United States. While not involved in the actual manufacturing of these goods, importers, nevertheless, have the opportunity to inspect the goods for defects. If sued by retailers or ultimate consumers, however, they find it virtually impossible to recover from the foreign governments with whom they deal for the amount of damages they paid out. Retailers often protect themselves by requiring importers to provide proof of product liability insurance. Thus, importers assume most of the risk from the products purchased in foreign markets.

Misuse of Product by Injured Party

Consumer who clearly misuses a product cannot recover if an injury results. In many product liability lawsuits, manufacturers and sellers raise the improper conduct of the buyer as a defense to lawsuits by injured buyers. They claim that the buyer used their product either knowing that it was defective or in a manner not foreseeable by the seller, such as in the case of a teenager who mounts the motor from a lawn mower onto a bicycle and is then thrown from the bike while riding because the motor stalls and "dies out." If a use is foreseeable, then the seller must take measures to guard against it. Although manufacturers and sellers may generally have good cases, courts still offer some protection to the buyer by applying the comparative negligence doctrine (see page 85) or limiting a seller's defense by requiring that the buyer's misuse of a product not be foreseeable by the seller. Subsequent alteration of the product by the user or consumer would also be an obstacle to recovery. Section 402A of the Restatement, Third, of Torts indicates that liability exists (on the part of manufacturers) only if the product reaches the user or consumer without substantial change in the condition in which it was sold.

There are instances when a defect might not be inherent in a product, but an injury could result if a consumer ignores common-sense hazards related to the product. For example, the person who uses an electric appliance while taking a shower and suffers an injury might attempt a lawsuit against the manufacturer for product liability. Of course, the lawsuit would, in most cases, not be successful based on the contention of the manufacturer that the consumer is or should be just as knowledgeable about the product as the company selling it. Nevertheless, manufacturers, for added protection against such a consumer-initiated lawsuit, often print labels on their products, warning against common-sense hazards because it is not always predictable how courts in a particular jurisdiction might rule.

Damages Recoverable in a Product Liability Case

If you are the plaintiff in a lawsuit (person bringing the action) for a defective product and you have a successful case, you are entitled to damages resulting from this product. Chapter 4 relating to torts and Chapter 5 pertaining to lawsuits should have given you a good idea of the type of damages to expect in a civil lawsuit. However, we will briefly review the types of damages to which you may be entitled. First, there are compensatory damages that include medical bills such as payments to your doctor and to the hospital, lost earnings from being out of work, and expenses connected to any property damaged as a result of the defective product. A major component of compensatory damages is "pain and suffering," which refer both to physical pain and mental anguish that result from your injury. If you are married and the injury has affected the relationship with your spouse, you may be entitled to loss of consortium damages. (Your wife may also be entitled to these damages.) Finally, you may under very strict circumstances be entitled to punitive damages if the court feels that the conduct of the defendant (the manufacturer or other seller) was so awful that he or she should be punished and deterred from doing anything like this again.

Tort reform seems to be on everybody's mind, but especially businesses when it comes to tort reform related to product liability. Businesses have sought relief from Congress and state legislatures, contending that they are vulnerable to even the most suspect cases. Because of the decision in an Alabama case (*BMW* v. *Gore*, 517 U.S. 559 116 S. Ct. 1589, 134 L. Ed. 2d 609) awarding compensatory damages of $4,000, but punitive damages of $2,000,000, the Supreme Court drew up some guidelines to assist trial judges in determining whether a jury's punitive damages award is excessive: (1) the degree of blame placed on the defendant; (2) the degree of difference between the harm suffered by the plaintiff and the amount of punitive damages to be awarded; (3) the difference between the punitive damages to be awarded in the current case and the civil and criminal penalties paid in comparable cases. The Supreme Court's rationale for proposing these guidelines was that there are limits under the Constitution to the amount of punitive damages that can be imposed. As mentioned in Chapter 4, many states have placed a cap on punitive damages at varying amounts.

It is important in a strict product liability case that, if you have been injured by a product, this product be kept and not altered in any way. Keep your proof of purchase and the warranty information (including the instruction booklet) that came with the product. Also obtain and write down the name of the person who sold you the product and the name or names of any witnesses to the event causing your injury. These records can be vital to building a successful case. Consult your attorney as soon as possible to first determine that you have a case and second, if you do have a case, that under her or his guidance, you gather the evidence for future hearings or a trial.

Summary

A buyer injured by a defective product may sue (as the plaintiff) a manufacturer and other sellers in the chain of distribution (as defendant or defendants) under the umbrella of product liability based on one of three well-recognized theories of liability: negligence, breach of warranty, or strict liability. (A summary of theories on which product liability cases are based and the implication of each appears in Table 18.1.) The trend in modern court cases is to allow not only the buyer of the defective product but also anyone who is harmed by this defective product to sue, and to sue whoever is in any way responsible.

The buyer who sues for negligence must prove that the defendant's negligence caused a defective product to be placed on the market and that this defective product caused the buyer to suffer personal injury or property damage. Negligence, however, is often an unsatisfactory remedy because it is hard to prove. If the buyer instead chooses to sue for breach of warranty, he or she must establish the existence and the breach of a warranty, an injury resulting from the breach, and that notice of the breach was given to the seller. It is not necessary to prove that the defendant was negligent. There are disadvantages to suing for breach of warranty, most notably that the buyer will have no basis for a lawsuit if the seller exercised his or her right under the Code to disclaim express and certain implied warranties. The most popular theory of liability under which to sue is strict liability. This theory, like negligence, is based on tort law. Unlike negligence, however, the buyer does not have to prove that anyone was negligent. In other words, it is a no-fault approach. The buyer must only show that at the time it left the manufacturer or another seller in the chain of the sale, the product was unreasonably dangerous due to a defect in design manufacturing, or marketing, and caused injury or damage as a result. Nearly every state has now accepted the concept of strict liability, which is outlined in Section 402A of the Restatement, Third, of Torts.

If you are the plaintiff in a lawsuit for a defective product and you win your case, you are entitled to damages resulting from this product.

Congress passed the federal Magnuson-Moss Warranty Act to help prevent deceptive warranty practices. This act has not replaced warranty law but rather imposes additional standards and remedies.

In many product liability lawsuits, manufacturers and sellers offer as a defense to lawsuits by injured buyers the improper conduct of the buyer (e.g., using the product in an unauthorized way).

Article 2 of the UCC provides for two types of warranties made by sellers: express warranties and implied warranties. Express warranties arise in several ways. The seller may make a factual statement or a promise about the product, may describe the goods to the buyer, or may show the buyer a sample of the item being sold. To constitute an express warranty, the statement, description, or sample must be part of the basis of the sale. Implied warranties are imposed on a seller by law. The two types of implied warranties are the implied warranty of merchantability and the implied warranty of fitness for a particular purpose. Another type of implied warranty exists under the Code but is not designated as such: the implied warranty of title. Express warranties can be excluded from sales contracts by using clear, specific language that meets the requirements of the UCC or simply by refraining from using language, descriptions, or samples that induce people to purchase the goods. The expressions "as is" and "with all faults" exclude all implied warranties except the implied warranty of title. The implied warranty of title is excluded only if the seller specifically states that no warranty of title is given or if the buyer realizes or should realize that the seller does not own the goods. If the buyer examines the goods, sample, or model or has refused to do so after a demand by the seller, there is no implied warranty as to the defects that were or should have been obvious.

Important Legal terms

caveat emptor
caveat venditor
disclaimer of warranty
express warranty

implied warranty
Magnuson-Moss Warranty Act
Merchantable goods
privity of contract

product liability
puffing
warranty

Questions and Problems for Discussion

1. Under the UCC, goods sold by merchants are generally covered by a warranty both express and implied. An example of an express warranty would be a warranty of
   a. fitness for a particular purpose
   b. merchantability
   c. conformity of goods to sample or description
   d. strict liability
2. Under the UCC, when there has been a sale of goods, which of the following statements is correct regarding the warranty of merchantability?
   a. The warranty cannot be disclaimed.
   b. The warranty arises as a matter of law.
   c. The warranty arises when the buyer relies on the seller's skill and judgment in selecting the goods purchased.
   d. The warranty must be in writing.
3. To establish the basis of a lawsuit for strict liability for personal injuries that result from the use of a defective product, the injured party (the consumer) must prove that
   a. the product sold was unreasonably dangerous due to a defect
   b. the seller was negligent
   c. the seller breached the contract with the consumer
   d. there was privity of contract
4. Thompson purchased a used car from Van Bortal Sales for $450. A clause in the written contract in boldface type provided that the car was being sold "as is." Another clause provided that the contract was intended as the final expression of the parties' agreement. After driving the car for one week, Thompson realized that the engine

was burning oil. Thompson telephoned Van Bortal and requested a refund. Van Bortal refused based on the original agreement but orally gave Thompson a warranty on the engine for six months. The engine exploded three weeks later. Can Thompson collect based on the oral warranty given to him by Van Bortal?

5. Ayrault was driving her car to the family doctor for an appointment. When she stopped for a red light, the car behind her "rear-ended" her car. Upon impact, Ayrault's car caught fire and was totally destroyed. Ayrault was rushed to the hospital with several burns. She did survive but was permanently scared. An investigation by the insurance company revealed that the gasoline tank was designed with weak walls such that any impact could rupture the tank and cause the car to catch fire, even when the tank was correctly assembled and installed. Could Ayrault sue the car manufacturer?

6. The B&L Food Company prepared, packed, and sold quality food products to wholesalers and retailers. Marvin, while grocery shopping at Gregg's Red & White retail store, purchased several cans of "Ma's Fancy Baked Beans." At dinner one evening, Eva, Marvin's sister, bit into a spoonful of the beans and cut her mouth on small pieces of glass that were embedded in the serving of beans on her plate. Can Eva, a third party, bring an action against either Gregg's Red & White or the B&L Food Company?

7. The county of Ontario, New York, ordered twenty-three cell doors for the new wing of the Ontario County Jail. The vice president of the company that was to manufacture the doors told the jail superintendent that he knew exactly how the cells should be constructed; the jail superintendent relied on the vice president's statement. When the cell doors were delivered, the bars were so far apart that prisoners could wriggle through them. Instead of the standard 5 inches, the bars were 5¾ inches apart. What warranty has been breached? What is the basis for this breach of warranty?

8. Bertram purchased a reconditioned paper shredder from Alliance Paper Co. for use in her business. Before putting the shredder into use, she made some modifications that she felt would improve the efficiency of the shredder. The manufacturer of the paper shredder originally was Cohen Office Furniture and Office Equipment Co. While shredding some important office documents, an employee of Bertram was injured because the shaft holding the shredder blade came loose and severed his finger. Based on a claim of strict liability, the employee sued Cohen Office Furniture for his injuries. Legally, does the employee have a claim?

9. Dayton purchased a rug from Max Floor Covering because the owner stated that the rug was "a genuine Oriental rug." Could this statement be considered an express warranty?

10. Jason and several members of her college soccer team purchased team jackets after seeing a sample shown to them by a salesperson from the Champion Sportswear Company. When the jackets arrived and Jason found that hers was quite different from the sample, she returned the jacket to the company. The company refused to take it back. Did Jason have the right to return the jacket? (Assume that Jason is an adult.)

Cases for Review

1. Walker owned several pizza parlors that operated under the name of El Fredo Pizza, Inc. He planned to open a new parlor and to purchase a new oven. When a friend suggested that Walker purchase an oven from the Roto-Flex Oven Co., Walker contacted an agent from that company and negotiated the purchase of a new oven. Walker made clear the particular purpose for which he was buying the oven—to cook pizza— and that he was relying on the agent's skill and judgment in selecting a suitable oven. Based on the agent's suggestion, Walker contracted to purchase a custom-built, Roto-Flex "Pizza Oven Special." Once the oven was installed, Walker had nothing but trouble—uneven heating—which caused the pizza to be improperly cooked when it came out of the oven. Roto-Flex attempted to fix the oven but could not. El Fredo brought action against Roto-Flex for breach of the implied warranty of fitness for a particular purpose. Should El Fredo be successful? (*El Fredo Pizza, Inc.* v. *Roto-Flex Oven Co.*, 291 N.W.2d 358)

2. McDonald's, a leading fast-food chain of restaurants in the United States, was sued by Arnold

Pellman and other teenagers, all New York residents who frequently ate at McDonald's outlets, contending that they suffered adverse health effects, including becoming overweight as the result of eating McDonald's food containing high levels of cholesterol, fat, salt, and sugar. They further contended that McDonald's failed to warn the public of the high quantities of unhealthy ingredients in their products. McDonald's produced evidence that they made their nutritional information available online and that such information was also available upon request. The plaintiffs (Pellman and others) failed to show a direct relationship between their eating McDonald's fast food and the adverse effects on their health. Should Pellman and the other teenagers be successful in their lawsuit against McDonalds?

3. Balch purchased a dog for $800 from Newberry, who operated a kennel. Before the sale, Balch informed Newberry that he wanted a male dog for breeding purposes. Newberry stated that the dog had the ability to produce pups of pedigree quality. Balch relied on this fact when he purchased the dog. After the purchase, Balch discovered that the dog was sterile and therefore of no value to Balch for breeding pups. Could Balch demand the return of his $800 after returning the dog? (*Balch* v. *Newberry*, Okla. 253 P.2d 153)

4. Hook sold two milk trucks, together with two milk routes, to Janssen. At the time of the sale, Hook told Janssen that the trucks were in good condition. Janssen, however, had inspected the trucks before purchasing them. He was aware that the trucks needed repairs and were in generally poor condition. After purchasing the trucks, Janssen spent a considerable amount of money for work done on the trucks. He then brought a lawsuit against Hook for the amount spent, claiming that the statement by Hook that the trucks were in good condition amounted to a breach of an express warranty. Is Janssen correct? (*Janssen* v. *Hook*, 272 N.E.2d 386)

5. Henningsen purchased a brand-new Plymouth automobile from Bloomfield Motors and gave it to his wife as a gift. While driving the new car, Henningsen's wife crashed into a brick wall and was injured because a defect in the steering wheel caused her to lose control of the car. She sued Bloomfield Motors for her injuries under the breach of the implied warranty of merchantability. Bloomfield Motors claimed that there was no privity of contract between them and Mrs. Henningsen and that she could not recover. Can Mrs. Henningsen recover from Bloomfield Motors? (*Henningsen* v. *Bloomfield Motors*, N.J. 161 A.2d 69)

6. While Lovitz was shooting at clay targets at the McCaun Gun Club, his Remington Model 1100 shotgun manufactured by the Remington Arms Co. exploded in his hands. Lovitz, who suffered injuries to his left hand and thumb, sued Remington, claiming that a manufacturing defect in the shotgun made the company strictly liable for his injuries. Remington contended that prior to shipment the gun was field tested, but the test did not reveal any defects. An expert witness stated at trial that each time the gun was fired, tiny particles of manganese sulfide escaped into the steel barrel causing it to crack and that the cracks continued to expand, causing the gun to explode. Can Lovitz sue Remington for injuries based on product liability? (*Lovitz* v. *Remington Arms Co. Inc.*, 532 N.E.2d 1091)

7. Husted purchased a used car from Reed Motors and obtained a loan through the First National Bank. The car broke down and could no longer be used. Husted refused to pay the balance due on the car. At the time the car was purchased, the contract signed by Husted contained a conspicuous clause stating that the buyer accepted the car in its present condition. The contract also contained other language indicating that the car was sold "as is." Was Husted responsible for paying the balance due on the car? (*First National Bank of Elgin* v. *Husted*, Ill. 205 N.E.2d 780)

8. Maritime entered into a contract to purchase a helicopter from Fairchild. Among the relevant provisions typed into the agreement in normal size, lowercase print on a regular printed form was a clause stating that the sale was to be made "as is" and that the seller gave no express or implied warranties except the warranty of title. Maritime had problems with the helicopter and sued Fairchild for an implied warranty, claiming that the helicopter was not merchantable. Fairchild defended, saying that the clause in the contract, which stated that no warranties were given with the sale of the helicopter, acted as a disclaimer of the implied warranty of merchantability. Is Fairchild correct? (*Fairchild Industries* v. *Maritime Air Services, Ltd.*, 333 A.2d 313)

THE CASE OF THE FAULTY AIR-CONDITIONING SYSTEM

The Ridgeway Theater purchased a large airconditioning system from Blair Manufacturing Co. The system was purchased and installed in May, prior to the start of the summer season. The sales contract contained a statement that the system would provide sufficient cooling for 1,500 people to a maximum temperature of 72°. The statement further said, "The seller makes no express warranties for this product." At the beginning of June, it became apparent to Ridgeway that the system did not work properly; it provided cool air, but not enough to enable patrons to be fully comfortable. Ridgeway complained to Blair about the air-conditioning system and withheld payment but continued to use the machine during the summer months because there was not enough time to order another system; without any air conditioning at all, the theater would have had to close down. All efforts to repair the system failed, and at the end of the summer, Ridgeway demanded that Blair take the machine back. Blair refused to accept the machine and brought suit against Ridgeway for the purchase price.

The Trial

Ridgeway testified that the temperatures during the summer in the area where the theater was located were extremely warm and that air conditioning was absolutely essential to enable customers to feel comfortable during the showing of movies. The theater stated that it relied on the wording in the sales contract that the system would produce sufficient cooling. It further stated that it could not return the air-conditioning system immediately after delivery because the theater would have had to close down and lose its costumers for the entire summer. The theater also stated that returning a large system involved a great deal of effort and expense and that it did not want to return the system until it had obtained significant use from it.

The Arguments at Trial

Blair's attorneys argued that the specific wording in the sales contract disclaiming any express warranties prevented Ridgeway from claiming that the system was defective. They further argued that the theater should have returned the system immediately when it discovered that the system was faulty. They also argued that when the theater used the system for three months and received many benefits from it, it automatically gave up its right to rescind the contract and return the system.

Ridgeway's attorneys argued that because of the size and weight of the system and the costs involved in returning it, Ridgeway had a legal right to use the system for a reasonable amount of time and then return it. They further argued that the statement in the sales contract that the system would produce sufficient cooling outweighed the importance of the statement that there were no express warranties. The theater also argued that by keeping the machine and getting some benefit from it, it was able to mitigate its damages. Otherwise, the theater could have held the manufacturer responsible for the loss of profits.

Questions to Decide

1. Who has the stronger arguments, Ridgeway or Blair? Why?
2. If you were the judge or jury hearing the case, for whom would you decide on the question of the warranty? Why?
3. If you were the judge or jury hearing the case, for whom would you decide on the question of the right to rescind the contract? Why?
4. What do you think the law should be with regard to a problem of this nature involving something that is not easily returnable?

Rogers went to a local restaurant in her hometown, where she purchased a chicken sandwich. As she ate the sandwich, she felt something stuck in her throat. She began to choke and turn blue. The manager immediately called the rescue squad, and it arrived in a matter of a few minutes. She was taken to the hospital, where the doctor on duty in the emergency room removed a rather large chicken bone from her throat. Rogers remained in the hospital overnight and was released the next day but remained home from work that day because her throat was very sore. She also was emotionally upset, and upon diagnosis, her doctor urged her to remain home for several days. Even though she did return to work after several days had elapsed, she had to remain under a doctor's care until she worked through this period of emotional instability. Rogers consulted with an attorney and, as a result, decided to sue the restaurant for the implied warranty of merchantability on the grounds that the chicken sandwich she purchased was not fit for human consumption. The state where she lived had not yet passed a law dealing with food cases like the Rogers case. The state legislators were dealing with two possible approaches: that injury from eating food had to meet the foreignnatural test or the reasonable expectations test to be considered a breach of the implied warranty of merchantability. In this case, the bone was a chicken bone natural to chicken (and not a foreign object) and therefore, should this theory be applied, Rogers would lose her case.With the reasonable expectations test, the jury would decide who should win based on the facts in the case.

Question for Discussion

If Rogers decided not to take her case to court but to let an arbitrator decide, and you were that arbitrator, what ethical reasons might you give for deciding the case for either party?

PART 4
Negotiable Instruments

After studying Part IV, you should be able to:

1. relate the various types of negotiable instruments and distinguish among the various parties involved.

2. distinguish between the two basic classes of negotiable instruments: promises to pay money and orders to pay money.

3. describe the two major functions of negotiable instruments.

4. describe the requirements necessary to make negotiable instruments negotiable.

5. explain the process of negotiation—that is, how negotiable instruments are transferred from one party to another.

6. explain the meaning of the term *endorsement* and name five types of endorsements.

7. restate the holder in due course (HIDC) concept and explain the significance of one's having the status of an HIDC.

8. explain the liabilities of the primary and secondary parties for payment of negotiable instruments.

9. describe the legal effect of personal and real defenses on a holder in due course.

10. summarize the rights and responsibilities that banks and their customers have to each other.

11. trace the path of a check through the check-collection and payment channels.

12. describe the impact of electronic banking on bank–customer relations.

13. chart a new plan for conducting your business transactions in the twenty-first century.

CHAPTER 19

Nature and Types of Negotiable Instruments

CHAPTER PREVIEW

Negotiable Instruments—An Introduction

Negotiable Instruments—Uses and Types
Promissory Notes and Certificates of Deposit: Promises to Pay
Drafts and Checks: Orders to Pay

Requirements for Negotiability
Written Form
Signature
Unconditional Promise or Order to Pay

Fixed Amount of Money
Payable on Demand or at a Definite Time
Payable to Order or Bearer

Contain No Understanding or Instruction Beyond the Promise or Order to Pay
Drawee Named with Reasonable Certainty

Added Language and Omissions Not Affecting Negotiability

Chapter Highlights

The purpose of this chapter is to introduce you to negotiable instruments: written documents that may be used either as a substitute for money (e.g., checks) or as a way to extend credit (e.g., promissory notes). Negotiable instruments as governed by Revised Article 3 of the Uniform Commercial Code (UCC) are the subject of this and the next three chapters. This chapter identifies the types of negotiable instruments available in the business community and describes the basic features of each type. Specimen documents that appear in the chapter help you better understand these basic features. The chapter also introduces the concept of negotiability (transferability), a key feature of negotiable instruments, and examines the language that must be used to make negotiable instruments transferable without worry of being uncollectable.

NEGOTIABLE INSTRUMENTS—AN INTRODUCTION

Negotiable instruments may be new to you, but learn as much as you can about them because they play an important role in your life. You will use these instruments to conduct your business either on a personal level or perhaps as a person in business once you complete your college education and enter your planned career field. These next four chapters deal with negotiable instruments and how they can be used as a substitute for money when conducting everyday business transactions. Modern technology has made dealings with financial institutions much easier and quicker. In essence, it has made life in the fast lane better. The information in these chapters is just a tip of the iceberg of what you need to know about electronic commerce and how quickly business transactions are conducted in the business world, but you will quickly learn one thing: Modern business cannot be carried on without the use of negotiable instruments.

Article 3 of the Uniform Commercial Code (UCC) is the statutory law that governs negotiable instruments. The revision of this Article occurred in 2002 to accommodate the changing conditions in the business world. For example, today check processing is done electronically. You can write a check in the morning, and the amount can be deducted from your account by the end of the day. In the past you could count on at least a few days before it was cleared by your bank. This was called the "float" period. (Wow! Are banks going to make money from bounced checks now.)

NEGOTIABLE INSTRUMENTS—USES AND TYPES

negotiable instrument written document that can be used as a substitute for money or as a credit device

A **negotiable instrument** (also referred to simply as an instrument) is a signed writing that orders or promises payment of a fixed amount of money with or without interest. It can be used either as a substitute for money or as a credit device (a means of extending credit). When a person pays a bill by check, the check substitutes for money. When a person buys a used automobile and gives the dealer a promissory note agreeing to pay for the car in ninety days, the note is a credit device. The seller has actually extended ninety days of credit to the buyer. Each instrument serves a different purpose. Keep in mind that as a substitute for money, a negotiable instrument becomes a very powerful piece of paper because it can be passed on like money without fear that it is not collectable. In Chapters 20 and 21, you will learn more about this special aspect of a negotiable instrument.

There are four types of negotiable instruments: drafts, checks, notes, and certificates of deposit. (Actually, under revised Article 3, a certificate of deposit is treated as a note.) Drafts and checks constitute *orders* to pay, while promissory notes and certificates of deposit involve *promises* to pay. Negotiable instruments may also be classified as either *demand instruments* or *time instruments*. A demand instrument is payable on demand—that is, payable immediately after it is issued and thereafter for a reasonable period of time. Checks are demand instruments because they are payable on demand. A time instrument is payable at a future date.

Promissory Notes and Certificates of Deposit: Promises to Pay

promissory note instrument by which one person promises to pay a sum of money to another

maker one who makes out and signs a promissory note

payee one who receives payment on a check, draft, or promissory note

A **promissory note** is a written promise by one party, the **maker**, to pay a certain amount of money to another party, usually the **payee** (two parties are involved). The money may be payable either on demand or at a specified time. A promissory note is used to obtain goods and services on credit or to borrow money. For example, Figure 19.1 shows that Arnold Liteman borrowed $3000 at 4 percent interest from Werner Klemp for ninety days.

FIGURE 19.1
Promissory Note

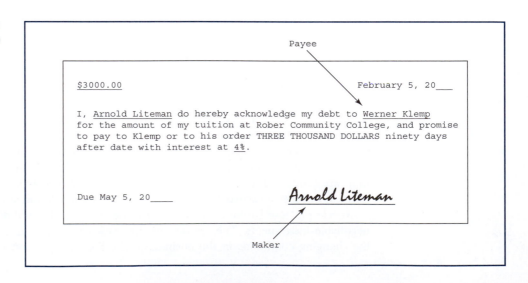

Payee

$3000.00   February 5, 20____

I, Arnold Liteman do hereby acknowledge my debt to Werner Klemp for the amount of my tuition at Rober Community College, and promise to pay to Klemp or to his order THREE THOUSAND DOLLARS ninety days after date with interest at 4%.

Due May 5, 20____   *Arnold Liteman*

Maker

FIGURE 19.2 Certificate of Deposit

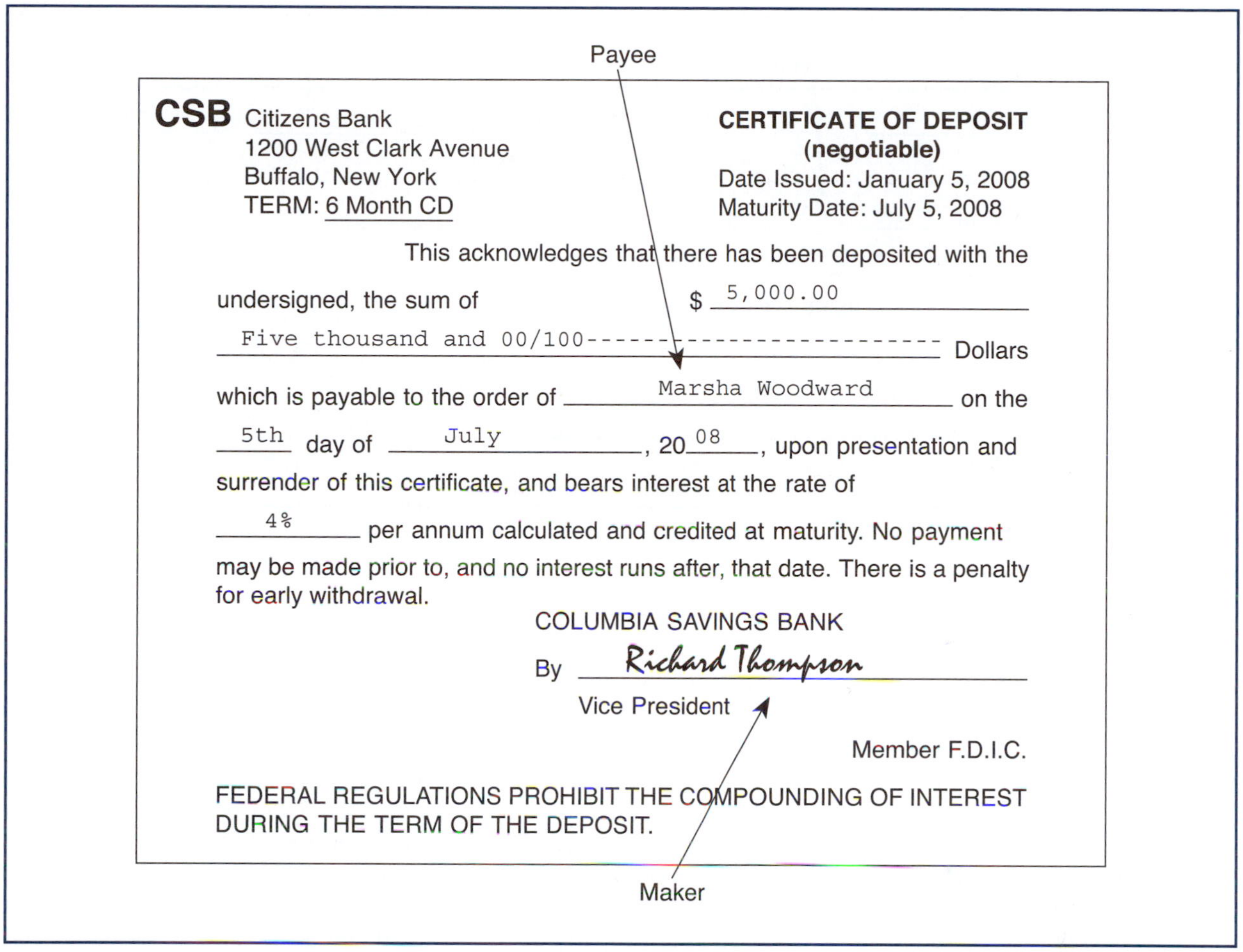

Payee

CSB Citizens Bank
1200 West Clark Avenue
Buffalo, New York
TERM: 6 Month CD

CERTIFICATE OF DEPOSIT
(negotiable)
Date Issued: January 5, 2008
Maturity Date: July 5, 2008

This acknowledges that there has been deposited with the undersigned, the sum of $ 5,000.00

Five thousand and 00/100------------------------ Dollars

which is payable to the order of ___Marsha Woodward___ on the 5th day of ___July___, 20_08_, upon presentation and surrender of this certificate, and bears interest at the rate of ___4%___ per annum calculated and credited at maturity. No payment may be made prior to, and no interest runs after, that date. There is a penalty for early withdrawal.

COLUMBIA SAVINGS BANK

By ___Richard Thompson___

Vice President

Member F.D.I.C.

FEDERAL REGULATIONS PROHIBIT THE COMPOUNDING OF INTEREST DURING THE TERM OF THE DEPOSIT.

Maker

certificate of deposit
bank's promise to repay an amount left on deposit for a certain time

draft instrument in which drawer orders drawee to pay a certain sum to payee

drawer one who signs a check or draft ordering drawee to pay the payee

drawee party to a check or draft who is ordered to pay the payee

A **certificate of deposit** (commonly called a CD) is an instrument containing an acknowledgement that a sum of money has been received by a bank, and a promise by the bank to repay the sum of money to a depositor. A certificate of deposit is a note of the bank. The bank promises to repay the money to the depositor with interest after a certain period of time. The certificate of deposit shown in Figure 19.2 is an acknowledgment by the Citizens Bank (the maker) that it received $5,000 from Marsha Woodward (the depositor-payee) on January 5 (date of issuance) and that the $5,000 will be repaid with interest at the rate of 4 percent per year on July 5 (date of maturity).

Drafts and Checks: Orders to Pay

A **draft** generally involves three parties. It is a written order by one party, the **drawer**, to a second party, the **drawee**, to pay a sum of money to a third party, the payee, on demand or at a definite future time. Thus, the drawer "draws" the draft on the drawee. The drawee is ordinarily a person. (A note has two parties: One party promises to pay another.) The draft has many uses. For instance, suppose that Catherine Karshick owes William McKinney $500 and Claire Arden owes Karshick $500 and Karshick is transferring her right to receive $500 from Arden to McKinney. Assume also that McKinney and Arden live in the same city and Karshick lives in another city. It

FIGURE 19.3 Draft

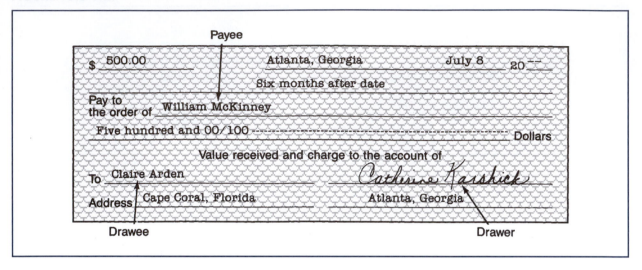

> would be possible for Karshick to draw a draft for $500 naming Arden as the drawee and McKinney as the payee. Karshick could send the draft to McKinney, who would then present it for payment to Arden. Figure 19.3 represents the draft Karshick would send to McKinney in this situation. For the drawee (Arden) to be obligated to honor the order, the drawee must be obligated to the drawer (Karshick) either by agreement or through a debtor-creditor relationship. Drafts may be payable "at sight" (i.e., on demand, meaning immediately upon presentation to the drawee for payment), or they may be "time drafts" (i.e., payable at a future date). A draft can be both a time and a sight draft—that is, payable at a stated time after sight. A form of time draft known as a **trade acceptance** is often used by a seller of goods as a credit device. It is drawn by the seller on the buyer. The seller (drawer) will send to the buyer (drawee) a draft that names the seller or some third party as the payee. If the buyer accepts, he or she has agreed to pay the seller or any holder who makes proper presentment (demand) a sum of money at a specified future date.

trade acceptance form of draft used by seller as a credit device

A **check**, the most common form of negotiable instrument, is a specialized type of draft drawn on a bank and payable on demand. While checks are negotiable instruments, they are mainly covered by Article 4 of the Uniform Commercial Code (Banking Law). The drawee is always a bank, and the drawer is the depositor. The payee is the person to whom the check is made payable. A check is the most common way of making payments. In Figure 19.4, Carol Masters, who has money in a checking account at First Federal Bank, made out a $500 check payable to John Miles. First Federal would be required to pay the $500 when the check was presented for payment at the bank by John Miles. Of course, Carol Masters would need at least $500 on deposit at the First Federal Bank.

check type of draft in which the drawee is always a bank

A check can also be drawn by a bank on another bank. This instrument is known as a *bank draft*. (Article 3 of the UCC defines a bank draft as a teller's check.) Checks are discussed in more detail in Chapter 22.

There is another type of check that came into existence because of the passage of the Check Clearing for the 21st Century Act (also referred to as The Check 21 Act passed in 2004). This act creates a new type of negotiable instrument called a *substitute check*. A substitute check is a legal copy of your original check. Consequently, you can use it the same way you would use the original check. This type of check and its purpose will be discussed in Chapter 22.

FIGURE 19.4 Check

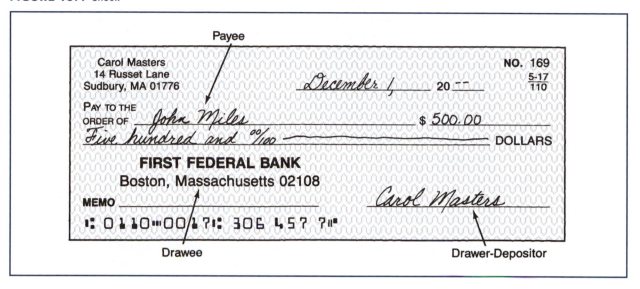

TABLE 19.1   TYPES OF NEGOTIABLE INSTRUMENTS

TYPE OF INSTRUMENT	DISTINGUISHING TRAITS	PARTIES
	Two Parties	
Promissory Note	A written promise by one party (maker) to pay money to another party, usually the payee (or to bearer)	Maker—the party who promises to pay Payee—the party to whom the promise is made
Certificate of Deposit (CD)	A note (special promise) issued by a bank to a depositor acknowledging that money was placed on deposit	Maker—the party who promises to pay Payee—the party to whom the promise is made
	Three Parties	
Draft	A written order by one party to another to pay a third party (or to bearer)	Drawer—the party who initiates and signs the order to pay Drawee—the party who is ordered to pay Payee—the party to whom the drawee is ordered to pay
Ordinary Check	A draft drawn on a bank and payable on demand	Drawer—the party who initiates and signs the order to pay (depositor) Drawee—the party who is ordered to pay (always a bank) Payee—the party to whom the check is made payable

Table 19.1 summarizes briefly the four types of negotiable instruments: notes, certificates of deposit, drafts, and checks that were discussed on the previous pages.

REQUIREMENTS FOR NEGOTIABILITY

negotiable legally transferable from one person to another

To be **negotiable** (legally transferable) and be governed by Revised Article 3 in determining the rights and liabilities of the parties, an instrument must meet each and every requirement of negotiability. In the law of negotiable instruments these requirements are critical. Negotiability gives each person who receives the instrument a special privilege that is discussed in Chapter 21. Any missing element removes the instrument from Article 3, makes it nonnegotiable, and places it under the coverage of common law contracts (assignments) with, of course, loss of its special privilege.

To qualify as a negotiable instrument under Article 3, Section 3-104, the instrument must (1) be in writing; (2) be signed by the maker or drawer; (3) contain a promise or order that is unconditional; (4) be payable in a fixed amount of money with or without interest; (5) be payable either on demand, or at a definite time; (6) be payable to order or bearer; (7) contain no understanding or instruction beyond the promise or order to pay; and (8) designate a drawee (in case of a draft) with reasonable certainty.

Written Form

To promote certainty and prevent fraud, negotiable instruments must be in writing (UCC 3-103). There is no such thing as an oral note or check. Printing, typewriting, and handwriting are examples of the types of permanent materials that are necessary to satisfy the requirement. If handwritten, pen or pencil may be used, although ink is preferable to prevent someone from altering the written paper. A negotiable instrument written on a piece of tree bark or a coconut would not satisfy the requirement because they lack permanence. The instrument must also meet the requirement that the instrument is freely transferable. For example, you write on the side of a shed, "I promise to pay $1,000 to the order of Franklin." Although technically this writing meets the requirement of a negotiable instrument, a shed would not be acceptable as an instrument for transfer in the ordinary course of business and thus would be nonnegotiable. The best thing is to place the instrument on traditional paper, which ensures that the permanency and transferability requirements are met and that people will readily accept the instrument.

Signature

The signature on the instrument must be signed by the maker (for a promissory note or a certificate of deposit) or drawer (for a draft or a check) or their authorized agents. The signature, which may appear in the body of the instrument (e.g., "I, Merle Hanley, promise to pay . . ."), generally appears in the lower right corner. According to the UCC, a signature may include any symbol executed or adopted by a party with the intention to adopt or accept a writing (UCC 1-201). The signature may be made manually or by machine and could consist of a trade or assumed name, initials, an X (if witnessed), a rubber stamp, or even a thumbprint (UCC 3-401). In some cases (e.g., rubber stamp or thumbprint), proof of the signature may be required. Parol (oral) evidence, however, is admissible to identify the signer. Although the Code is lenient on what is acceptable as a signature, one should be careful about accepting an instrument that is signed in an unordinary way, as people have a tendency to question an unusual type of signature.

> The Atlas Company paid its employees by check each week. Because the company issued a large number of checks, it mechanically stamped the signature of its treasurer on each check rather than having the treasurer sign each check personally. This mechanically stamped signature in no way affects the negotiability of the checks.

Unconditional Promise or Order to Pay

A promissory note or certificate of deposit must contain words on the face of the instrument indicating a promise to pay. The words "I promise to pay" in Figure 19.1 clearly indicate that a promise has been made. With a certificate of deposit, no express promise is required because the bank's acknowledgment of the deposit and the other terms of the instrument clearly indicates a promise by the bank to repay the sum of money (UCC

3-104). A phrase such as *IOU, Joan Hartman, $50.00* merely acknowledges that a debt exists; it does not contain a promise to pay and therefore is not negotiable.

To be negotiable, a draft or check must order the drawee to pay. For example, the word *pay* that is printed on a draft or check (see Figures 19.3 and 19.4) constitutes this order. It is a demand, not a request, on the drawee by the drawer to pay a third party, the payee.

The promise or order to pay must be payable without any conditions attached (it must be unconditional). Otherwise, the instrument is nonnegotiable (UCC 3-104) and (UCC 3-106). The Code specifically states that a promise or order is unconditional unless it is made conditional because it states (1) there is an express condition to payment, (2) the promise or order is governed by another writing, or (3) rights or obligations in regard to the promise or order are stated in another record (UCC 3-106).

> Mary (the maker) gave Britton (the payee) a promissory note for $500. The note contained a statement that it was "payable only if Pogas (a racehorse) won a race at Winton Downs (a racetrack) on July 1." Because the note was payable only upon the happening of a certain event (if Pogas won a race at Winton Downs on July 1), which may not occur, it was nonnegotiable.

In this example, the condition is obvious because it is stated on the instrument ("payable only if Pogas won a race at Winton Downs on July 1"). Because the note is nonnegotiable as a result of the condition, its utility as a substitute for money or as a credit device is almost nonexistent. No one could safely purchase this note from Britton without first checking to see if the condition has been met, in this case, that the racehorse Pogas won the race at Winton Downs on July 1. In fact, no one would probably accept such an instrument. Thus, this requirement of an unconditional promise or order to pay is a practical one. After all, people do not want to spend time and money investigating whether or not the condition stated on a negotiable instrument will be met.

There were situations under the original Article 3 that made it difficult to determine whether the instrument was payable unconditionally. Revised Article 3 has taken great pains to clarify the meaning of the term *unconditional.* There is a presumption that every promise or order is unconditional unless a condition is evident from reading the instrument.

> Belter delivered a promissory note to Gather promising to pay him $10,000 for building a shed on her farm. Belter, however, made an oral statement placing a condition on payment by stating that the money would be paid only if Gather met all contractual specifications.

In this example, the promissory note is still negotiable because negotiability is determined by what is written on the face of the instrument; it would not be affected by any statements made beyond the instrument itself.

Revised Article 3 eliminates as conditional a statement on an instrument that says "payment is to be made only out of a particular fund." Such a statement no longer destroys negotiability even though payment depends on the existence of such a fund (UCC 3-106). For example, suppose the terms in a note include the statement that payment will be made out of the marketing research fund. This statement will no longer make the note nonnegotiable. This change, like others, emphasizes how the revised article aims to remove as many conditions imparing negotiability of an instrument as possible.

A promise or order is conditional if the rights or obligations associated with the promise or order are to be found in another writing; however, a mere reference to another writing does not make the promise or order conditional (UCC 3-106). For example, if an instrument contains a statement such as, "the debt from this instrument arises from the sale of a car as per our written contract," it does not render an instrument nonnegotiable.

Fixed Amount of Money

The requirement that the instrument be payable in a fixed sum of money (UCC 3-104) is designed to make it easy for the taker of the instrument to know the exact amount that will be received. The taker must be able to compute this amount from the face of the instrument without reference to any external data. A note or check payable in merchandise or anything other than money, such as services, is not negotiable. Furthermore, "money" does not require payment in U.S. currency. A note or check payable in a foreign currency that is the legal currency of that foreign country is fully negotiable. Thus, a sum payable in German marks, French francs, Japanese yen, or Italian lira would not hinder negotiability. Unless specified otherwise in the instrument, if the instrument is payable in foreign currency, Section 3-107 of the UCC provides that payment may be made in the equivalent amount of U.S. dollars, calculated at the place of payment on the day on which the instrument is paid.

> Albert, of Pittsburgh, Pennsylvania, gave Hanson, who lived in the same city, a note promising to pay "one ounce of platinum." Because platinum is not legal currency in the United States, Albert's note is not negotiable.

Article 3 applies the fixed-amount requirement only to the principal. Thus, a $500 note payable with 8 percent interest is still negotiable. Moreover, if the instrument does not state a rate of interest, it is payable without interest. Article 3, as revised, also allows for the payment of interest that cannot be definitely ascertained from the instrument itself. An example is a statement included on the instrument indicating that the interest is payable at "the prime rate" or a statement indicating that interest is payable at a fixed or variable rate. The results of these statements are still consistent with the rule that the fixed-amount requirement applies only to the principal. Under the old Article 3, both principal and interest had to be determined from the face of the instrument. Other fees, like interest, that do not affect the fixed-amount requirement are collection fees and attorney's fees. A sum payable is a fixed amount even though it is payable in installments. If the person who is required to pay the instrument has an option of paying something in addition to money or paying something other than money, the instrument is not negotiable.

> Rickets gave Bellini a promissory note that read, in part, "I (Rickets) promise to pay Bellini two hundred dollars ($200) or one used stereo set." This note is not negotiable.

Under the UCC, if there is a discrepancy between the amount written in words and the amount indicated in figures on an instrument, the amount written in words would be paid. If the words are not clear, however, the figures will control (UCC 3-114). For example, if the words on a check are "One hundred dollars" and the figures are "$1,000," the check would be for $100, but if the words read "Seven fifty-five dollars" and the figures are "$7.55," the check would be for $7.55.

Payable on Demand or at a Definite Time

To be negotiable, an instrument must be payable either on demand or at a definite time (UCC 3-104). "Payable on demand" means payable at the time when the payee presents the instrument for payment to the person obligated to pay it (upon request). Also qualifying as payment on demand would be statements such as "payable at sight" or "payable on presentment." It is not necessary that the obligated party know ahead of time when the demand will be made (see Figure 19.4).

An instrument can also be payable at a definite time. An instrument is payable at a definite time if it states that it is payable (1) on a specified date such as "payable on or before January 13, 2002" (because the maker has the option of paying before the scheduled due date, this factor did not make the time of payment uncertain); (2) within a definite period of time such as "payable sixty days after sight" (but an instrument "payable ten days after my death" is not negotiable because, although death is certain, the time when death will actually occur is not certain); or (3) on a date or time readily ascertainable at the time the promise or order is issued, such as is "payable on the day of the next presidential election," an event that is certain to happen. If nothing is said about the due date, the instrument is payable on demand. A check is a good example of an instrument payable on demand because no time of payment is stated on the instrument.

A time instrument may contain an acceleration clause, which requires the debtor to pay off the amount owed on a loan sooner than the stated due date. For example, if the debtor is paying in monthly installments and then fails to make a monthly payment, the payee or other holder of this time instrument may demand payment of the entire amount due immediately after the missed payment instead of waiting until the actual date. Nevertheless, the instrument is negotiable because it would still be payable on a definite date if there was no acceleration clause. It is this date that governs negotiability under the UCC (UCC 3-108).

If there is a clause calling for an extension and the extension is at the option of the holder, even without a time limit, negotiability is not affected since the holder is given a right that he or she would have without the clause. If, however, the extension is to be at the option of the maker or acceptor, or is to be automatic, an extension to a further definite time must be stated or the time of payment remains uncertain and the order to promise is not a negotiable instrument (UCC 3-108).

The importance of the requirement that a negotiable instrument be payable on demand or at a definite time is that the holder of the instrument must know when the note must be presented for collection and whether it is current or overdue. If an instrument were payable upon the happening of an event in the future, the holder might not know when that event occurred and therefore would not know when to present the note for payment. That situation would destroy the whole reason behind negotiability: easy transfer of negotiable instruments.

Payable to Order or Bearer

To be negotiable, an instrument must contain words of negotiability. The words *order* and *bearer* are words of negotiability (UCC 3-104); by using these words in the instrument, the maker or drawer states that the instrument is payable to the original payee or to someone else designated by the payee. An instrument is **payable to bearer** if it is to be paid to anyone who has possession of it. For example, the phrase *Pay to Henry Ling or bearer* means that the instrument is payable to Henry Ling or to anyone else who bears (possesses) it. An instrument containing any of the following terms also make it payable to bearer: "Pay to the order of cash;" "Payable to bearer: Pay to the order of cash;" "Payable to the order of bearer." An instrument is **payable to order** if it is to be paid to a specific identified person or to anyone that person designates. For example, the phrase *Payable to the order of Martha Mandry* means that the instrument is payable to Martha Mandry or to whomever Martha Mandry orders the paper to be paid. In this way, the instrument remains transferable. An instrument made payable to bearer, "Cash," "To the order of cash," "Myself," "To the order of bearer," or to a fictitious person such as

payable to bearer words directing an instrument to be paid to person holding it

payable to order words directing an instrument to be paid to named payee or to whomever payee orders the paper to be paid "payable to Superman," is considered payable to the bearer. Without either the word *order* or the word *bearer,* payment of the instrument would be restricted to the original payee. Some courts hold an instrument nonnegotiable if these magic words are missing even if the instrument states on its face "This instrument is negotiable."

> Bendix borrowed $2,000 from his friend Burr and gave Burr a promissory note that read: "One year after date, I promise to pay Adam Burr two thousand dollars ($2,000) with interest at 8% (Signed) William Bendix." Because this note does not contain either of the words of negotiability ("pay to the order" or "pay to the *bearer*"), the instrument is not negotiable. Adam Burr cannot legally transfer this promissory note to another person.

Revised Article 3 provides that a check meeting all the requirements of being a negotiable instrument except for including the words *to the order of* is nevertheless a negotiable instrument (UCC 3-104). Thus, a check "payable to Arnold Eckert" is a negotiable check. This revised rule does not apply to instruments other than checks.

Contain No Understanding or Instruction Beyond the Promise or Order to Pay

A negotiable instrument must be straightforward and very specific. If the instrument contains an order or promise to do anything else in addition to or in lieu of the payment of money, it will be nonnegotiable. For example, a promise to pay $500 and a set of chef's knives would not be negotiable.

Drawee Named with Reasonable Certainty

In the case of a draft or a check, the drawee must be named in the instrument with reasonable certainty. This rule permits the payee, or any individual who receives the instrument from the payee, to know the person who is responsible for payment.

Added Language and Omissions Not Affecting Negotiability

The UCC does not prevent instruments from being negotiable because information is lacking or because certain information is added. The date of issue on a note or check may be important, but it does not affect negotiability if it is omitted. An undated instrument such as a check is considered to be dated as of the date it is delivered. That date may be filled in by the person who receives the instrument. A postdated check (a check dated after its actual date of issue) is also fully negotiable. It is like a note payable in the future (a time draft) and will be paid on or after the date appearing on its face. An antedated check (one that is dated before the time it was written) also has no effect on negotiability. Negotiability is also not affected because it designates a particular kind of currency or money in which payment is to be made.

For notes, it is common to insert information regarding the place of payment of the instrument, such as "Payable at First Federal Bank of Boston, Massachusetts." The words *Value received* are often inserted on the face of the note, meaning that consideration was given for the instrument. This information does not affect payment and, if omitted, does not make an instrument nonnegotiable. The sum in figures, which is generally included, has no effect on negotiability if not included as part of the instrument or is a different amount from what is written in words. If a party adds handwritten or typewritten language that is inconsistent with the preprinted language on the instrument (note or draft), the handwriting takes precedence over both the typewritten and preprinted language. Typewritten language takes precedence over preprinted language.

As noted above, Article 3 provides that a check is nevertheless negotiable even though it does not contain the words *to the order of.*

Summary

A negotiable instrument is a signed writing (record) that can be used either as a substitute for money or as a means of extending credit. There are two classifications of negotiable instruments: promises to pay and orders to pay. Within these two classifications, the UCC specifies four types of instruments: drafts and checks, which are orders to pay, and promissory notes and certificates of deposit, which are promises to pay. Notes and certificates of deposit have two parties. The maker is the person making the promise to pay, and the payee is the person to whom the note and certificate of deposit are made payable. Drafts and checks have three parties. The person issuing the draft or check is the drawer, the person ordered to pay is the drawee, and the person to whom the draft or check is payable is the payee. A check is a type of draft in which the drawee is always a bank and the drawer is the depositor. Instruments may be either negotiable or nonnegotiable depending on the language used in the instrument.

To be negotiable, an instrument must meet the following requirements: It must (1) be in writing; (2) be signed by the maker or drawer; (3) contain an unconditional promise or order to pay; (4) state a fixed amount of money; (5) be payable on demand (or at sight) or at a definite time; (6) be payable to order or to bearer; (7) contain no understanding or instruction beyond the promise or order to pay; and (8) designate a drawee (in the case of a draft) with reasonable certainty.

Certain language that is added, such as the place where the instrument is payable and the words *Value received,* has no effect on negotiability. Certain information that is lacking, such as the date of issue of the instrument, the place of payment, and the sum in figures, likewise has no effect on the negotiability of the instrument; neither does the practice of postdating or antedating a check. Negotiability is also not affected because it designates a particular kind of currency or money in which payment is to be made. If a party adds handwritten or typewritten language that is inconsistent with the preprinted language on the instrument (note or draft), the handwriting takes precedence over both the typewritten and preprinted language. Typewritten language takes precedence over preprinted language. Finally, under Revised Article 3, a check lacking the words *to the order of* is still negotiable.

Important Legal terms

certificate of deposit
check
draft
drawee
drawer

maker
negotiable
negotiable instrument
payable to bearer
payable to order

payee
promissory note
trade acceptance

Questions and Problems for Discussion

1. Which of the following statements regarding negotiable instruments is not correct?
   a. A certificate is a type of note.
   b. A check is a type of draft.
   c. A promissory note is a type of draft.
   d. A certificate of deposit is issued by a bank.

2. Under Article 3 of the UCC, which of the following documents would be considered an order to pay?
   a. only a draft
   b. only a certificate of deposit
   c. both a draft and a certificate of deposit
   d. neither a draft nor a certificate of deposit

3. Which of the following statements is correct regarding the requirements for an instrument to be negotiable?
   I. The instrument must be in writing, be signed by both the drawer and the drawee, and contain an unconditional promise or order to pay.
   II. The instrument must state a fixed amount of money, be payable on demand or at a definite time, and be payable to order or to bearer.
   a. I only
   b. II only
   c. both I and II
   d. neither I nor II

4. Which of the following circumstances would prevent a promissory note from being negotiable?
   a. an acceleration clause that allows the holder to move up the maturity date of the note in the event of default
   b. a clause that allows the maker to satisfy the note by the performance of services or the payment of money
   c. the signature that appears in the body of the instrument
   d. if the instrument is to be paid in German marks

5. An order instrument involves three parties. The three parties are:
   a. drawer, drawee, maker
   b. maker, payee, drawee
   c. drawer, drawee, payee
   d. drawee, payee, payor

6. May a maker or acceptor have an option to extend payment without destroying negotiability?

7. Study the check in Figure 19.5 and then answer the following questions:
   a. Who is the drawer? The drawee?
   b. Who is the payee?
   c. Is this check payable on demand or at a future time?

8. What kind of writing is required for a negotiable instrument?

9. Why does the promissory note in Figure 19.6 fail to meet the requirements of negotiability?

10. Would the promissory note in Figure 19.7 be negotiable in the following circumstances (state a reason for your answer):
    a. If the words *Value received* had been omitted?
    b. If the date July 1, 2002, was omitted?
    c. If Ronald Brown had written the note in his own handwriting as follows: "I Ronald Brown promise to pay to the order of Alexis Smith five hundred and 00/100 dollars or one used car"?

FIGURE 19.5

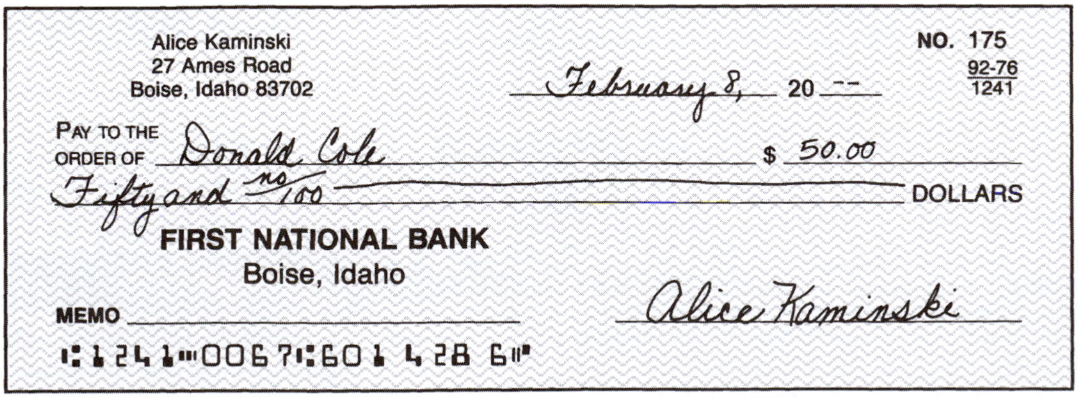

Alice Kaminski
27 Ames Road
Boise, Idaho 83702

NO. 175
92-76
1241

February 8, 20 --

PAY TO THE ORDER OF *Donald Cole* $ *50.00*

Fifty and no/100   DOLLARS

FIRST NATIONAL BANK
Boise, Idaho

MEMO _____

Alice Kaminski

⑆1241⑈0067⑆601 428 6⑈

FIGURE 19.6

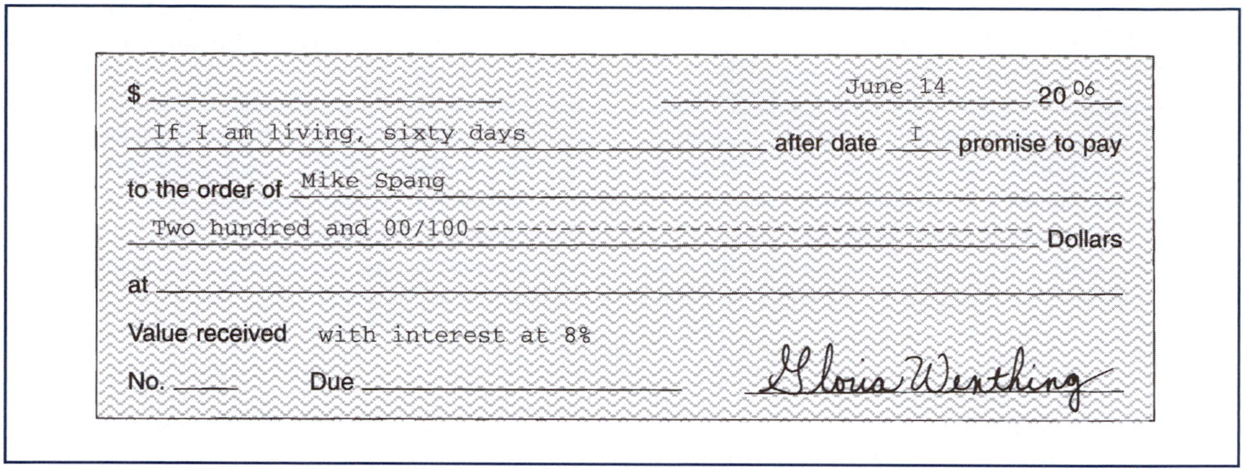

$ _____   June 14   20 06

If I am living, sixty days   after date   I   promise to pay

to the order of   Mike Spang _____

Two hundred and 00/100 ------------------------------   Dollars

at _____

Value received   with interest at 8%

No. _____   Due _____   *Gloria Wenthing*

FIGURE 19.7

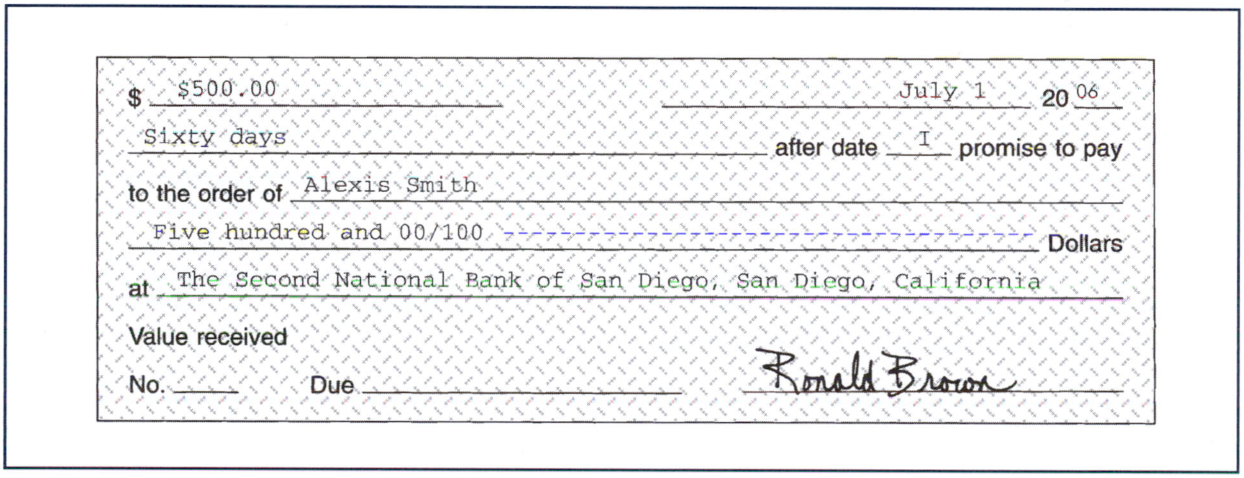

$ $500.00 _____   July 1   20 06

Sixty days   after date   I   promise to pay

to the order of   Alexis Smith _____

Five hundred and 00/100 ------------------------   Dollars

at   The Second National Bank of San Diego, San Diego, California

Value received

No. _____   Due _____   *Ronald Brown*

Cases for Review

1. Horne made out a note for $100,000 payable to Clark and written on the note was a restriction that the note could not be transferred or pledged without Horne's consent. Horne did, however, sign a letter authorizing Clark to use the note as collateral for a loan. Clark pledged the note as collateral for a $50,000 loan from First State Bank of Gallup. After making several payments, Clark defaulted on the loan. First State Bank tried to collect, but Horne refused to pay claiming that the note was not a negotiable instrument and therefore invalid in the hands of the bank. Did the restriction noted on Horne's promissory note prevent the note from being negotiable in spite of the letter of authorization? (*First State Bank of Gallup* v. *Clark & Horne*, 570 P.2d 1144)

2. Lindsay signed a note to Clements that stated, "On or about five years from date, I promise to pay Bonnie M. Clements $25,000 without interest." When Lindsay failed to pay the note, Clements sued. Lindsay claimed that the note was invalid because it did not contain any fixed

or determined future time for payment. Will Clements recover on the note? (*Clements* v. *Lindsay,* La. 320 So. 2d 608)

3. Mr. and Mrs. Hinphy borrowed money from DeRouin and signed a document stating, "I have this day borrowed $12,000 from David DeRouin to be paid on demand. (Signed) Mrs. W. Hinphy and W. Hinphy." More than three years later, DeRouin sued the Hinphys for failing to pay the amount due. The Hinphys claimed that the document was not a note but was only an acknowledgment of indebtedness that was no longer valid because of a three-year statute of limitations. Are the Hinphys correct? (*DeRouin* v. *Hinphy,* La. 209 So. 2d 352)

4. Dr. W. H. Bailey drew up a promissory note payable to California Dreamstreet, an investment firm. The note read as follows: "Dr. William H. Bailey promises to pay to the order of California Dreamstreet the sum of $329,800." Dreamstreet then negotiated the note to Cooperative Centrale Raiffeisen–Boerenleenbank B.A., a foreign bank. Bailey defaulted and Cooperative Centrale filed suit against him to recover on the note. Is the note executed by Bailey a negotiable instrument? (*Cooperative Centrale Raiffeisen–Boerenleenbank B.A.* v. *Bailey,* 9 UCC Rep. Serv.2d 145)

5. Fabacher gave a promissory note to Hoss. At the top of the note, the date was given as well as the figure $6,002.19. The body of the note read, "Pay to the order of." The name of the payee was never inserted, nor was any amount. Was the note enforceable? (*Hoss* v. *Fabacher,* Tex. 578 S.W.2d 454)

6. Andersen gave the following undated, handwritten promissory note to the Great Lakes Nursery Corporation for the purchase of 65,000 trees: "Robert Andersen promises to pay to Great Lakes Nursery Corporation at Waukesha, Wisconsin, six thousand four hundred twelve dollars with interest at 7% per annum." Great Lakes Nursery, in payment of a debt, transferred the note to the First Investment Co., which questioned its negotiability. Is this note negotiable? (*First Investment Co.* v. *Andersen,* Utah 621 P.2d 683)

7. Robinson had purchased a certificate of deposit (CD) from a bank and had the instrument made payable to him. On its face, the instrument stipulated that if Robinson was deceased at the time the instrument was to be paid, that payment should be made to his stepdaughter, Wygant (payee). Before the note was due, Robinson remarried and changed the name of the payee from Wygant to that of his new wife. When Robinson died, Wygant claimed the proceeds from the CD. Her contention was that the CD was a negotiable instrument that required her to sign it before it could be transferred to Robinson's new wife. Was Wygant correct? (*West Grely National Bank* v. *Wygant and Robinson,* 650 P.2d 1339)

CHAPTER 20

Issue, Transfer, Indorsement, and Discharge of Negotiable Instruments

CHAPTER PREVIEW

The Issue and Transfer of Negotiable Instruments	Payment
Transfer by Assignment	Alteration
Transfer by Negotiation	Statute of Limitations
	Bankruptcy
Indorsements	Cancellation
Discharge of Negotiable Instruments	

Chapter Highlights

This chapter deals with the negotiation (transfer) and discharge of a negotiable instrument. The first section discusses the concept of negotiation—how promissory notes, certificates of deposit, checks, and drafts are transferred to third parties by the payee—and the rights these third parties acquire after negotiation. One issue that is crucial in determining the rights that third parties have after the negotiation of a negotiable instrument is whether the transferred instrument is an order instrument (one payable "to the order" of a named person) or a bearer instrument (one payable to anyone who possesses it). The chapter points out the differences between order instruments and bearer instruments. Two other topics covered are the various ways in which people sign their name (called an indorsement) to an instrument they wish to negotiate and the effect an indorsement has on the instrument being negotiated. The remainder of the chapter examines ways in which a negotiable instrument can be discharged—that is, the circumstances that will take away the liability a person has on the instrument.

THE ISSUE AND TRANSFER OF NEGOTIABLE INSTRUMENTS

The circulation of negotiable instruments begins when either the maker or the drawer creates an instrument (e.g., a note or check) and delivers this instrument to the payee. This first delivery to the payee (usually for value) is called an **issue**. Once issued, a negotiable instrument can be transferred by *assignment* or by *negotiation*.

issue original transfer of commercial paper by maker or drawer to payee

Transfer by Assignment

If you recall from Chapter 12, an assignment is a transfer of rights under a contract from the assignor to the assignee, and this transfer by assignment gives an assignee only those rights that the assignor possessed. Consequently, any defenses that can be raised against the assignor can normally be raised against the assignee. This same principle applies to an

327

instrument issued to the payee but which fails to qualify as a negotiable instrument because of the failure to meet the requirements of negotiability as outlined in Chapter 19. The transfer becomes an assignment in which the transferee (person receiving the instrument from the payee) simply becomes an assignee possessing only the rights held by the assignor (payee). Additionally, the assignee is subject to the same claims and defenses against the assignor.

Transfer by Negotiation

negotiation transfer of commercial paper in such a way that transferee becomes a holder

holder one in possession of commercial paper

Negotiation is the transfer of possession of an instrument voluntarily or involuntarily to another person who as the result of this transfer becomes a **holder** (UCC 3-201). Consequently, if the transfer by the payee, the first holder, to a third party is by negotiation, the third party, like the payee, also becomes a holder. From this point on, any person who receives this instrument by negotiation also becomes a holder. According to the rules of negotiable instruments, becoming a holder is significant because he or she will acquire more rights than a person who receives the instrument under the rules of assignment previously discussed. Under the UCC, each holder has the same rights as the previous holder (UCC 3-203). Keep in mind that an instrument may be negotiated many times before it is finally presented for payment. How an instrument is negotiated depends on whether it is an order instrument or a bearer instrument.

Negotiation of Order Instruments   An order instrument is one payable *to the order of* a named payee. It may be negotiated only by indorsement (a signature) and delivery (a transfer of possession) of the instrument as seen in Figure 20.1 (UCC 3-201). For example, an employer issues a payroll check (e.g., *pay to the order of George Gooding*). While out shopping, George Gooding purchases an item of clothing at Joseph Banks, Clothier. He pays by using his payroll check. He would sign his name on the back of the check (indorsement), give it to the salesperson at Joseph Banks (delivery), and receive cash back after paying for the clothing. Gooding has *negotiated* the check to Joseph Banks by indorsement and delivery.

A check is shown in Figure 20.2. The first negotiation of this check occurs when Walter Archer (the payee) indorses it (signs it) and then delivers it to the third party. After receiving the instrument by negotiation from Walter Archer, the third party, now a holder, may again negotiate the instrument, once more indorsing it and delivering it to another person. This other person also becomes a holder and could in turn negotiate the instrument (the check) by indorsement and delivery. This process continues until the holder in possession of the check decides to present the instrument to the party responsible for payment. (The question of who is responsible for payment is discussed in Chapter 21.)

For an instrument to be properly negotiated, the entire amount must be transferred. You as payee cannot negotiate part of the amount.

Negotiation of Bearer Instruments   An instrument payable to bearer is negotiated by delivery (transfer of possession) alone (UCC 3-201). A check payable to *Cash* is an example of a bearer instrument. An indorsement (signature) is not necessary. After

FIGURE 20.1
Negotiation of Order Instrument Requires Indorsement and Delivery

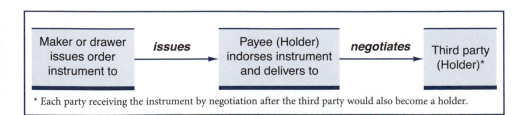

Maker or drawer issues order instrument to → *issues* → Payee (Holder) indorses instrument and delivers to → *negotiates* → Third party (Holder)*

* Each party receiving the instrument by negotiation after the third party would also become a holder.

FIGURE 20.2
Indorsed Check

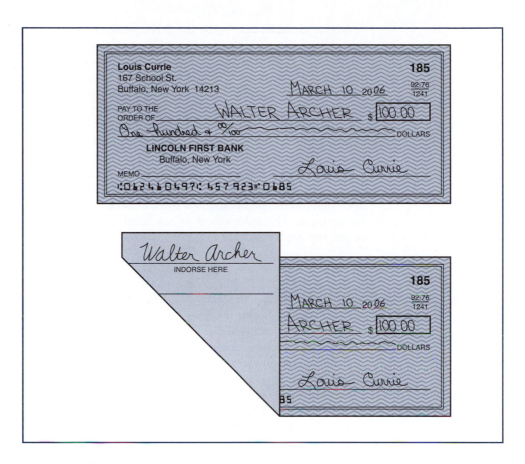

FIGURE 20.3
Negotiation of Bearer
Instrument Requires
Delivery Only

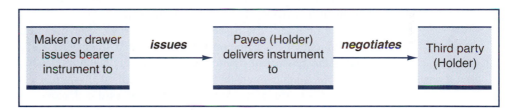

negotiation, the transferee (person receiving the instrument) becomes a holder. This procedure is outlined in Figure 20.3.

O'Leary owed Jenkins $100 and gave him a check payable to "Cash" (bearer) in the amount of $100. Jenkins wanted to buy some parts for his car and gave the owner of the parts store the same check (without an indorsement). The check was negotiated to the parts store owner by delivery.

Because a bearer instrument is payable to whomever is in possession of it, a thief or finder would become a holder by negotiation, even though this transfer was involuntary (UCC 3-201).

Noriko writes (issues) a check payable to "Cash" and hands it over to Montrois, who puts the check in her handbag. The check is later stolen from her by Karns.

In this example, despite the involuntary transfer of possession to Karns, this transfer brought about two results: (1) Karns became a holder and (2) Karns received the check by negotiation. At this point, however, Karns himself has no rights in the check. Now, let's take this example one step further. Karns, who as a holder has the power to negotiate the instrument, delivers (transfers) the check to Beldonis (who knew nothing about the theft) for a consideration. Beldonis has also received this check by negotiation and becomes a holder. Beldonis acquires all rights to the check, and Montrois will lose all rights to recover the proceeds of the check from that person. Montrois, however, can recover the money from the thief if the thief can be found.

Although bearer paper can be negotiated by a transfer of possession alone, in practice banks normally require the bearer to indorse the instrument so as to impose the liability of an indorser. A good example is when a check payable to "Cash" is presented to a bank for payment. The indorsement is not required by the UCC. (Indorser liability is discussed in Chapter 21.)

INDORSEMENTS

indorsement writing one's name on the back of a negotiable instrument to transfer ownership

An **indorsement** is a signature other than that of a signer as maker, drawer, or acceptor made on an instrument for the purpose of (1) negotiating the instrument, (2) restricting payment of the instrument, or (3) incurring indorser's liability on the instrument (UCC 3-204). The Code is liberal on what constitutes a signature. It can be handwritten, typed, or printed. A person can even make his or her mark or provide a thumbprint (UCC l-201). The signature customarily appears on the back of the instrument (blue or black ink is generally used). It may also appear on a sheet of paper called an **allonge**, when there is no more room on the instrument itself. The allonge must be firmly affixed to the instrument so as to become part of it (UCC 3-204). Using a paper clip would not suffice, but a staple most likely would be acceptable. The person indorsing (signing) is called the **indorser**. The person to whom the instrument is indorsed and delivered is the **indorsee**. One purpose of indorsing the indorsement as indicated in the above definition is to negotiate the instrument (if it is classified as an order instrument).

allonge attachment to a negotiable instrument on which indorsements are placed

indorser one who negotiates an order instrument by indorsement and delivery

indorsee the person to whom an order instrument is negotiated.

The indorser—the payee—should write his or her name exactly as it appears on the instrument. If the name on the instrument is misspelled, the person indorsing can sign using the misspelled name, the correct name, or both. Generally, you indorse using the name as it appears on the instrument, followed by the correct name. According to the Code, a signature may include a trade or assumed name, a symbol, or virtually any mark that will authenticate a writing. There are four basic types of indorsements: blank, special, restrictive, and qualified. Each type has a special purpose.

blank indorsement indorsement consisting solely of indorser's signature

A **blank indorsement**, shown in Figure 20.4, consists only of the signature of the indorser (the first indorser is the payee) on the reverse side of the instrument (UCC 3-205). A blank indorsement makes the instrument payable to the bearer and is similar

FIGURE 20.4
Blank Indorsement

to cash; it may then be transferred by delivery alone without further indorsement. An instrument with this type of indorsement should not be sent through the mail. As noted earlier in this chapter, anyone in possession of a bearer instrument, including a thief or finder, can negotiate it.

special indorsement

indorsement directing payment to a specified person

A **special indorsement** specifies the person to whom the indorser intends to make the instrument payable—that is, the name of the indorsee (UCC 3-205). This type of indorsement consists of a statement that the instrument is being transferred to a particular (named) person, followed by the signature of the indorser (Figure 20.5). Such phrases as *Pay to the order of Roberta Fisk (signed) R. Folger* or simply *Pay to Roberta Fisk (signed) R. Folger* are acceptable forms of a special indorsement. It is not necessary to use the word *order* or *bearer* in the indorsement. The instrument is still negotiable and may be further negotiated. This type of indorsement, often referred to as a 'full' indorsement, is used to prevent an instrument such as a check from being cashed by an unauthorized person. Unlike a check with a blank indorsement, a check with a special indorsement may not be transferred by delivery alone. Further negotiation requires the signature of the person to whom the instrument was transferred. For protection, it is legal for a person who has a negotiable instrument containing a blank indorsement to change this indorsement into a special indorsement by writing above the blank indorsement words such as *pay to the order of* and then the name of a specific person (UCC 3-205).

restrictive indorsement

indorsement limiting what transferee may do with instrument

A **restrictive indorsement** requires the indorsee to comply with instructions stated in the indorsement regarding what is to be done with the money stated on the face of the instrument. A person receiving a check, for example, might wish to make sure that the check is deposited in her or his account. A restrictive indorsement, such as the "for deposit only" shown in Figure 20.6, would accomplish this requirement. The bank (indorsee) receiving the check must obey the indorsement and deposit the funds in the account

FIGURE 20.5
Special Indorsement

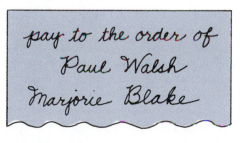

pay to the order of
Paul Walsh
Marjorie Blake

FIGURE 20.6
Restrictive Indorsement

for deposit only
Marjorie Blake

of the indorser. (This form of restrictive indorsement is the most frequently used.) People often use a restrictive indorsement to safeguard a check mailed to a bank because a thief or finder of the check cannot then cash it because the indorsement says "for deposit only." Sometimes a person paying for services with a check might want to make sure that the work was done properly before payment was made. That person could write a restrictive indorsement such as "Pay to the order of Dan Mooney upon satisfactory completion of the construction of my garage." A restrictive indorsement does not destroy the negotiability of an instrument (UCC 3-206); however, as long as the instrument is negotiable on its face, the restriction on the indorsement with respect to parties other than the indorser and indorsee is ineffective in preventing further transfer or negotiation. Accordingly, if a payee indorses "Pay Tripp Only," Tripp may negotiate the instrument to subsequent holders who may ignore the restriction on the indorsement just as if the instrument read "Pay to Tripp." Further, an indorsement such as "for deposit only" allows only a bank to acquire the rights of a holder following this indorsement and also gives the bank the right to specially indorse the instrument to a person who is not a bank. If, however, conditional language appears on the face of the instrument, the instrument is not negotiable because it does not meet the requirement that it contain an unconditional promise to pay.

qualified indorsement
indorsement limiting indorser's liability

An indorser who uses a **qualified indorsement** like the one illustrated in Figure 20.7 has chosen to transfer the instrument but to disclaim any liability if the instrument is dishonored. The other indorsements we discussed are considered *unqualified indorsements*. Those individuals who use an unqualified indorsement implicitly promise to pay the holder or any subsequent indorser the amount of the instrument in the event that the maker or drawer defaults on the payment (UCC 3-415). To illustrate a qualified indorsement, suppose that Anthony Maynard wishes to negotiate a check made payable to him to Nori Strut but does not wish to assume any liability of the drawer or subsequent indorsers won't pay. He would indorse the check by writing "Pay to Nori Strut, without recourse. (Signed) Anthony Maynard." *Without recourse* means not liable as an indorser.

Regardless of the limiting feature of a qualified indorsement, an instrument with this indorsement can still be negotiated because it can be combined with any other type of indorsement such as a blank or special indorsement. These other indorsements will actually determine how the instrument is further negotiated. For example, the indorsement in Figure 20.7 tells us that originally an instrument was made payable to Marjorie Blake and that Blake negotiated the instrument with a special indorsement ("Pay to") to Paul Walsh. Blake also qualified the indorsement ("Without recourse"). Figure 20.7, then, is an example of a special qualified indorsement. For Walsh to negotiate the instrument to another holder, say, Mike Harrington, he would have to first indorse it and then deliver it to Harrington (indorsement plus delivery) since it is an order instrument. Other combinations involving the qualified indorsement are "Without recourse, (signed) R. Michaels"

FIGURE 20.7
Qualified Indorsement

> Pay to Paul Walsh
> without recourse
> Marjorie Blake

(a blank qualified indorsement); "For deposit only, without recourse, (signed) B. Bertrum" (restrictive, qualified, and blank indorsement); "Pay to Johnson if she completes work today, without recourse, (signed) R. Megan" (restrictive, qualified, and special).

DISCHARGE OF NEGOTIABLE INSTRUMENTS

A negotiable instrument may be discharged in several ways, including payment, material alteration, the statute of limitations, bankruptcy, and cancellation. The effect of a discharge is that the parties to the instrument are released from liability.

Payment

When the party who is primarily liable for payment pays the amount of the instrument in full to the holder, this payment will normally discharge all parties to the negotiable instrument (UCC 3-602; UCC 3-603). This process is the usual way of discharging liability on a negotiable instrument. If payment is made by any other party, however—for example, by an indorser (a secondary party)—only this indorser and subsequent parties on the instrument will be discharged. The party making this payment (in this case, the indorser) has the right to recover on the instrument from any prior parties. If a party pays to a bad faith holder (e.g., a holder who acquired the instrument by theft), that party is not discharged (UCC 3-602). Although payment is generally in money, the party to whom payment must be made may agree to accept a different consideration of equal value, such as merchandise or personal property.

Alteration

If the holder of a negotiable instrument alters it in any significant and fraudulent manner, that alteration will discharge the obligation of any party whose liability is changed by the alteration. This rule is to protect innocent parties who take the instrument without knowing that it has been altered. What constitutes a significant and fraudulent alteration depends on the facts in each case. An alteration may consist of an addition, a substitution, a deletion, or an unauthorized completion of an incomplete instrument. For example, a change in the written amount and the amount in figures on a negotiable instrument from $1,000 to $10,000 with an intent to deceive is both significant and fraudulent.

Statute of Limitations

If a negotiable instrument is not paid on time, a state's statute of limitations begins to run from the due date of the instrument. If a suit is not brought within the statutory period (usually six years), the instrument is discharged.

> Kraig gave a promissory note to Melvin on March 8, 1996, payable in ninety days. Kraig did not pay the note when due. Seven years later, Melvin brought suit against Kraig to collect on the note. Melvin would not succeed because the note was discharged by the statute of limitations on June 6, 2002, six years from the due date.

Bankruptcy

If a party to a negotiable instrument becomes bankrupt and a debt for which the instrument has been given is discharged, the instrument is also discharged.

Cancellation

Cancellation of an instrument will discharge the liability of all parties (UCC 3-604). It consists of any act that indicates that the underlying obligation is ended. Cancellation by the holder may be accomplished by deliberately destroying or defacing the negotiable instrument or by marking it "paid," "void," or "canceled." Delivery of the note back to the maker will also cancel it.

Wyler wrote a promissory note payable to Richards, who was a close friend, in return for a $100 loan. When the note became due, Wyler was unable to repay the loan. Richards then canceled the note by tearing it up and telling Wyler to forget about making the $100 payment.

Summary

The circulation of negotiable instruments begins when the maker or the drawer issues an instrument to the payee. The payee is then entitled to collect payment on the instrument or to pass it on to a third party. One way to pass it on is by negotiation. This is possible as long as the instrument meets the requirements of negotiability. The third party who takes possession of the instrument by negotiation becomes, like the original payee, a holder. How a negotiable instrument may be negotiated depends on whether the instrument is an order instrument or a bearer instrument. Order instruments are negotiated by indorsement and a transfer of possession (delivery). Bearer instruments are negotiated by a transfer of possession (delivery) alone. Indorsement is not required. There are four basic indorsements: blank, special, restrictive, and qualified. A blank indorsement, which consists only of the signature of the indorser, makes an instrument payable to the bearer. A special indorsement names the person who will receive the instrument and includes the signature of the indorser. A restrictive indorsement requires the indorsee to comply with instructions stated in the indorsement. For example, a check presented to a bank with the indorsement "for deposit only" requires the bank to deposit the funds in the account of the indorser. An instrument negotiable on its face, however, cannot be rendered nonnegotiable by using a restrictive indorsement. Thus, after the directions are carried out, the instrument may be further negotiated. A qualified indorsement ("without recourse") frees the indorser from liability if the negotiable instrument is not paid by the maker or drawee when due. In addition to the four basic indorsements, an accommodation indorsement can be used to guarantee payment of an instrument. A negotiable instrument can be discharged by five means: payment, alteration, the statute of limitations, bankruptcy of a party, and cancellation.

Important Legal terms

allonge	indorsement	qualified indorsement
blank indorsement	indorser	restrictive indorsement
holder	issue	special indorsement
indorsee	negotiation	

Questions and Problems for Discussion

1. What is the significance of an instrument qualifying as a negotiable instrument when it comes to the transferability of the instrument?
2. A note is made payable to the order of Ann White on the front. On the back, Ann White signs it in blank and delivers it to Jerry Fine. Fine puts "Pay to Jerry Fine" above White's indorsement. Which of the following statements is false concerning this note?

a. After Fine wrote "Pay to Jerry Fine," the note became order paper.

b. After White indorsed the note but before Fine wrote on it, the note was bearer paper.

c. Fine needs to indorse this note to negotiate it further, even though he personally wrote "Pay to Jerry Fine" on the back.

d. The note is not negotiable because Fine wrote "Pay to Jerry Fine" instead of "Pay to the order of Jerry Fine."

3. You are examining some negotiable instruments for a client. Which of the following indorsements can be classified as a special restrictive indorsement?

   a. Pay to Roman Kubica if he completes the contracted work within 20 days (signed) Ann Carmody.

   b. Pay to Roman Kubica without recourse (signed) Ann Carmody

   c. For deposit only, (signed) Ann Carmody

   d. Pay to Roman Kubica, (signed) Ann Carmody

4. Armond wrote a check payable to Gaston. Gaston negotiated this check to Wright using a blank indorsement. Fearing that she would lose the check before she got to the bank, Wright converted the blank indorsement into a special indorsement by writing the words "Pay to the order of Wilma Wright" over Gaston's signature. Was that legal?

5. What are the requirements for a person to become a holder?

6. Berra made out and signed a promissory note payable to the order of Streb. Streb placed a blank indorsement on the note and gave it to Harder. Harder in turn transferred the note by delivery alone (no indorsement) to Bell. Does Bell become a holder?

7. Kagel, who owed money to Ryan, offered Ryan a check signed by Shepherd as the drawer and payable to "Bearer." Ryan asked Kagel to add his signature as indorser, claiming that otherwise ownership of the instrument would not pass to her. Was Ryan correct?

8. Under the UCC, Article 3, which of the following statements best describes the effect of indorsing a check "without recourse"?

   a. The person who signed the check has no liability.

   b. The person makes no promise or guarantee of payment on dishonor.

   c. The person converts the check into order paper.

   d. Both b and c.

9. Anchor was the maker of a $500 promissory note payable to Carter. Carter transferred the note to Petty using a qualified indorsement. What advantage did Carter gain by using a qualified indorsement?

10. What type of indorsement should be used by a person who wishes to mail a check to his bank for deposit into his account?

    a. blank

    b. restrictive

    c. qualified restrictive

    d. special

Cases for Review

1. Taylor owed Citizen's National Bank over $40,000 and wrote three promissory notes payable to the bank at 15 percent interest (on each note). Because the notes were past due, the bank increased the rate of interest to 22½ percent. To reflect the change in the interest rate, a bank official simply crossed out the 15 percent figure on the face of the instrument and wrote in 22½ percent. The bank claimed that this was normal business procedure. Once the change was made, Taylor was notified by the bank of the change in interest rates. When the bank sued Taylor to recover on the three notes, Taylor claimed that he had been discharged because the bank had fraudulently altered the interest rate on the notes. The bank official testified at trial that after the bank notified Taylor of the change in rates, Taylor went to the bank, consented to the increase, and signed an extension of time to pay the notes. Taylor's only comment was that the new rate was "awfully high." At trial, the court ruled in favor of the bank. What do you think the court's rationale was for its decision? (*Citizen's National Bank of Wilmar* v. *Taylor*, 368 N.W.2d 913)

2. Wilson, office manager of P & R Dental Supply Company was confronted with a discrepancy in her company's inventory by an auditor reviewing

the company's books. She had cashed several checks and kept the money for her own personal use, when actually the checks should have been deposited to P & R Dental Supply Company. The company president had given Mrs. Wilson the authority to indorse checks on the company's behalf and then deposit them into the company account at the bank. Mrs. Wilson did use a rubber stamp with the company name on it, but the stamp was actually a blank indorsement rather than a restrictive indorsement containing the words "For Deposit Only." P & R Dental claimed that the bank should not have given Wilson the cash from the checks since she used a company stamp. Was the bank acting illegally by giving Wilson the money? (*Palmer & Ray Dental Supply of Abilene* v. *First National Bank*, 477 S.W.2d 954—a Texas Case)

3. Hargrove sold cars that were financed by loans to his customers from the First National Bank. Three customers signed promissory notes payable to the bank, and Hargrove wrote his own name on the reverse side of the notes. When the customers failed to pay the notes, the bank sued Hargrove, claiming that he had indorsed the notes. Was Hargrove's signature an indorsement? (*First National Bank of Atlanta* v. *Hargrove*, Tex. 503 S.W.2d 856)

4. Barnes was the payee of a $5,088.70 check drawn by Portland Cement Association. Barnes indorsed the check "J.Y. Barnes, for deposit only" and placed the check for mailing in a cooperative mailing rack in the lobby of a building in Denver. The envelope containing the check was stolen by Woodward, who passed himself off as Barnes and opened a checking account in Cherry Creek National Bank in the name of Jack Y. Barnes. Woodward deposited the check into the account, and the check was paid by Cherry Creek. Barnes then sued Cherry Creek to recover the money, claiming that the check had been restrictively indorsed and could be paid only to the real Jack Barnes. Will Barnes succeed? (*Barnes* v. *Cherry Creek National Bank of Denver*, Colo. 432 P.2d 471)

5. Gold signed a promissory note payable to her step-father as evidence of a loan from him and from her mother. When she did not pay the amount due on the note and her stepfather sued her for the balance due, Gold claimed that her mother had canceled the obligation. There was proof that her mother had in fact orally canceled the note. Must Gold pay the balance due? (*Community National Bank & Trust Company, Executor of Michel Thorgevski* v. *Mary J. Gold*, N.Y. 45 A.D.2d 947)

Rights and Duties of Parties

Chapter Highlights

This is a very important chapter in the study of negotiable instruments because of the introduction of the holder in due course (HIDC) concept. First, however, the chapter discusses the parties who have liability for payment of a negotiable instrument, the extent of this liability, and what the holder of a negotiable instrument must do to hold these parties liable for payment. Then comes a discussion of what the heart of Article 3 of the UCC is all about, that is, to determine how a holder becomes a holder in due course (HIDC) and the unique status the law gives to a HIDC. The concluding pages of the chapter explain how, in certain transactions, a ruling of the Federal Trade Commission deprives holders from acquiring holder in due course status. These pages also briefly outline the liability of accommodation parties, those who sign instruments for the purpose of lending their names and credit to other people.

LIABILITY OF PARTIES TO A NEGOTIABLE INSTRUMENT

To hold a person contractually liable on a negotiable instrument, his or her signature or that of an agent must appear on the instrument (UCC 3-401). (Chapter 20 describes what is acceptable as a signature under the Uniform Commercial Code.) Of course, this liability does not apply to a bearer instrument because no indorsement is needed. Parties to a negotiable instrument who have liability for payment of the instrument are classified as either primary parties or secondary parties. **Primary parties** are those who are first obligated to pay the instrument. Examples of primary parties are makers of promissory notes and drawees (acceptors) who agree to pay drafts at the request of drawers.

By accepting a draft, the drawee becomes primarily liable for payment to the payee or to any other holder of the draft. After accepting the draft, the drawee is known as the **acceptor**. Acceptance, which must be in writing, usually consists of the word *Accepted* stamped or written on the face of the instrument, the signature of the drawee, and the date it was accepted. The refusal of the drawee to accept the draft amounts to a dishonor

primary parties parties who are first responsible for paying a negotiable instrument

acceptor drawee who agrees to pay a draft

of the instrument. This is not the case with checks. A bank can refuse to become the acceptor, but this refusal does not amount to a dishonor. Here is the explanation. When accepted by the bank, checks are considered to be *certified*. Certification means that the bank is now primarily liable for payment when the check is subsequently presented for payment by any holder (UCC 3-409). The bank, however, has no obligation to certify the check and become the acceptor. By law the bank is simply required to pay the amount of the check if funds are available in the drawer's account.

The liability of primary parties is unconditional, meaning that they are obligated to pay according to the terms of the instrument without the holder having to resort first to another party. The maker or acceptor agrees to pay the instrument according to its terms whenever it is presented for payment, even if it is presented for payment many months or even years after the due date. The only exception to this liability is for an instrument that is not presented for payment before the statute of limitations runs out.

> Melrose (payee), who held Carpinski's $300, three-month promissory note dated October 15, presented it to Carpinski on January 25 and demanded payment. Carpinski refused to pay it, claiming that presentment had not been made on the proper date. Because Carpinski is primarily liable for payment, Melrose can still legally collect the $300 even though the due date (January 15) had passed when the request for payment was made.

secondary parties
parties responsible for payment of a negotiable instrument only if the primary party fails to pay

Secondary parties are those who are legally obligated to pay the holder only after the primary party who is expected to pay fails to do so. Their liability is therefore said to be conditional. Examples of secondary parties are drawers of checks (or drafts) and unqualified indorsers of any negotiable instrument.

> Agor writes a check on her checking account with Charter One Bank payable to the order of Gloria Montgomery. Charter One refuses to pay the noncertified check when Montgomery presents it to the bank for payment due to insufficient funds in Agor's account. Agor, therefore, as the drawer will be liable to Montgomery.

In this example, if Charter One Bank had certified the check, it would have become the acceptor and consequently liable for payment to Montgomery.

Let's take this example a step further. Suppose that Montgomery indorses the check on the back of the instrument using a blank indorsement and passes it on to Roberts, who now becomes a holder. Roberts presents the check for payment to the bank, but the bank refuses because of insufficient funds in Agor's account. Roberts can then present the check for payment to Montgomery based on the fact that as an indorser she has secondary liability. Secondary parties would be liable only if the holder of the paper takes the following steps: (1) presenting the instrument for payment to the primary party in a proper and timely manner, (2) having the primary party dishonor the instrument (refuse or be unable to make payment), and (3) giving timely notice of dishonor to the secondary party. An indorser may limit his or her secondary liability by using a qualified indorsement, using such words as *without recourse*. If that is done, the indorser is not liable for nonpayment of the instrument by the primary party even if the conditions of presentment, dishonor, and notice of dishonor are met.

The secondary liability of drawers differs from that of unqualified indorsers. Perhaps an example will help clarify this difference. In the example, we will use a check, where the drawee is always a bank.

Assume that McCall has an account at Midtown Bank. McCall (the drawer) writes a check on that account and makes it payable to Wright (the payee). Wright indorses and gives the check to Feinstein, who becomes the holder. Assume also that Midtown Bank

FIGURE 21.1
Liability of Parties

Maker (Note)	Acceptor* (Draft)	Drawer (Drafts/Checks)	Indorser (All Instruments)
Primary	**Primary**	**Secondary**	**Secondary**

*A drawee who accepted responsibility for payment of a draft. Until accepted, he or she has no liability on the instrument.

refuses to pay the check when Feinstein presents it at the bank because it was more than six months old (UCC 4-402).

Because of the UCC rule, Feinstein cannot complain to Midtown Bank. The burden of paying Feinstein is then placed on McCall, the drawer, who is the secondary party. Moreover, McCall must pay even if the conditions of presentment, dishonor, and notice have not been met. If Feinstein wanted to collect from Wright, the indorser, he would be required to meet the conditions set forth earlier. In other words, Feinstein would have to present the check to Midtown Bank for payment, have Midtown dishonor the instrument, and then give notice to Wright that Midtown had dishonored the check. Only then would Wright be liable for payment and only if Wright had not used a qualified indorsement.

The primary and secondary liability of the parties to a negotiable instrument discussed on the previous pages is outlined in Figure 21.1.

Presentment for Payment

presentment demand for payment of commercial paper made by holder; also, indictment

Presentment is a demand for payment of a negotiable instrument to a primary party. It is made by a person entitled to enforce the instrument, generally the holder. Presentment must be made (1) to the proper person, (2) in a proper manner, and (3) at the proper time (UCC 3-414; 3-415; 3-501). The proper person to whom presentment must be made depends on the type of instrument involved. If the instrument is a note or a certificate of deposit (CD), it must be presented to the maker for payment. Presentment of a draft is made to the drawee for acceptance, payment, or both. A check is presented to the drawee (bank) for payment (UCC 3-501; 3-502).

Presentment can be properly made by any commercially reasonable means, including oral, written, or electronic communication, (e.g., fax or e-mail), but it is not effective until the demand for payment is received by the person to whom presentment is made (UCC 3-501). A proper presentment can also be made at the place specified in the instrument. If the person who is to receive it is not there (at the proper time), presentment is excused.

Presentment at the proper time depends on whether the instrument is a time instrument or a demand instrument. When an instrument is due on a certain date (e.g., a promissory note), presentment must be made on or before that date. Demand instruments have different rules. They must be presented within a reasonable period of time after date or issue or after the secondary party becomes liable on the instrument. A domestic uncertified check must be presented within thirty days of its date to hold the drawer secondarily liable and within thirty days after an indorsement to hold the indorser secondarily liable (UCC 3-414;3-415). The determination of what is "reasonable" depends on the type of instrument, the requirements of the Code, and the customs of a particular bank or business.

In all cases, presentment must be made at a reasonable time of day—that is, during normal working hours. Persons to whom presentment is made can require proof of identity of the person making presentment and can demand that the instrument be surrendered when payment in full is made.

The demand for payment by the holder is very important because demand must be shown before a dishonor (see the following definition) can take place. Further, only if dishonor takes place may the holder bring suit. Finally, if no dishonor can be shown, the liability of the secondary parties to an instrument may be discharged.

Dishonor of Instrument

dishonor refusal of a party to pay or accept an instrument

Dishonor of an instrument is the refusal of the primary party to pay an instrument when it is properly and timely presented for payment. An instrument is also dishonored when presentment is excused (e.g., death of the primary party) and the instrument is not properly accepted or paid (UCC 3-502, 3-504).

A refusal of the primary to pay sometimes does amount to dishonor, as for example, when a holder such as the payee of a check without proper identification presents the check for payment to the teller of the drawer's bank but is refused payment. Payment can rightfully be postponed until proper identification is made. The initial refusal of payment by the bank does not amount to a dishonor.

Notice of Dishonor

notice of dishonor notice given to the secondary party orally or in writing that the primary party has refused to pay instrument

If a primary party dishonors an instrument, **notice of dishonor** must be given to the secondary party by the holder to hold the secondary party liable for payment. If notice is not given, or is given improperly, the secondary party may be released from any obligation to pay. Notice of dishonor may be given by any commercially reasonable means, including an oral, written, or electronic communication and is sufficient if it reasonably identifies the instrument and indicates that the instrument has been dishonored or has not been paid or accepted (UCC 3-503). To be effective, notice by any party (other than a bank) must be given within thirty days following the day on which the person receives notice of dishonor, or within thirty days following the day on which dishonor occurs (UCC 3-503).

> Carey was the maker of a sixty-day promissory note for $250 due on July 8. When Phillips, a holder, presented the note to Carey on July 8, Carey dishonored it. On September 1, Phillips gave Marvel, an indorser, notice of the dishonor and requested payment of the note. Marvel is not liable for payment of the instrument, however, because notice of dishonor was not given within thirty days after Carey dishonored the note.

Indorsers of negotiable instruments are generally liable in the order in which they indorse the instrument. An indorser who is required to pay can recover from a prior indorser, provided that the prior indorser has been notified.

> Martin issued a promissory note payable to the order of Perkins. Perkins indorsed the note to Armish, Armish indorsed it to Bello, and Bello indorsed it to Harter. When Harter, the last holder, promptly and properly presented the note to Martin for payment, Martin refused to pay. Harter then notified Bello and collected the amount due. To collect, Bello must notify Armish. If Armish wishes to collect, she must notify Perkins.

A delay in both presentment and notice of dishonor may be excused in certain circumstances. For example, if a holder cannot present a note for payment because a snowstorm has made travel impossible, the holder would be excused until a reasonable time after the storm, when travel is again possible.

Presentment and notice of dishonor may also be waived by the parties. Many lenders provide for such waivers in their loan agreements and loan documents because it speeds up the process of collection of negotiable instruments.

If a bank incorrectly or wrongfully dishonors an instrument, it can be held liable to the wronged party. The bank is liable for all damages actually resulting from its actions. For example, a bank's refusal to honor a check could result in a loss of business or a bad credit rating for the drawer.

Unauthorized Signatures

No person is generally liable on an instrument unless the person signs the instrument (UCC 3-401). What constitutes a signature was discussed in Chapter 19. What happens if the signature on the negotiable instrument is unauthorized, as for example, when the signature is forged, or made by one exceeding his or her authority? The effect is that the unauthorized signature is not binding. There are, however, exceptions that will allow the signature to become valid as far as its effect as a signature is concerned; nevertheless, the person who signed the instrument in an unauthorized way is not relieved of any criminal liability (UCC 3-403). One exception that will allow an unauthorized signature to be effective is when the person whose signature is forged accepts the result of the transaction involving his or her signature. This amounts to a ratification of the transaction. The forged signature imposes full liability of the instrument on the party whose name was forged in the capacity on which the forger signed and transfers any rights that a signer may gain in the instrument. The transaction that results is limited to parties who take or pay the instrument in good faith. A party who takes the instrument knowing that the signature has been forged cannot recover from the signer whose name appears on the instrument (UCC 3-403).

> You steal a check from your father's checkbook, make the check out to yourself for $500, sign your father's name as the drawer of the check, and then cash the check. Your father has two choices: accept what you did or turn the matter over to the police and have you arrested for forgery.

THE TRANSITION FROM HOLDER TO HOLDER IN DUE COURSE

Attention to this point has focused on understanding what it takes to achieve the status of a holder. We know that a payee to whom an instrument has been issued may, as noted in Chapter 20, transfer the instrument to a third party. One important way is by negotiation. Under these circumstances, the third party also becomes a holder, and each succeeding party who receives the instrument by negotiation also becomes a holder. It is desirable to attain the status of holder for two reasons. The first reason is that you would have an advantage in litigation if the right of payment should arise. A holder does not need to prove anything (with a few exceptions) other than it has not been paid according to its terms. Questionable circumstances surrounding the instrument will not be dealt with in court in your quest to recover on the instrument. This kind of proof is tantamount to winning the litigation. The second and biggest reason is that only a holder is eligible to attain the unique status of a holder in due course (HIDC). With this second point, keep in mind that all holders in due course must first be holders, but not all holders are holders in due course. A **holder in due course** is a holder who gains a special

holder in due course
one who holds an instrument subject only to real defenses.

privilege, the privilege of enforcing payment of the negotiable instrument even though certain reasons for not paying, called personal (limited) defenses, are introduced in court by the party obligated to pay. All these defenses are cut off by having holder in due course status. Personal (limited) defenses are discussed later in the chapter. The reason for establishing the holder in due course rule is to give a negotiable instrument a high degree of marketability—that is, to encourage people to use a negotiable instrument like money by giving them some assurance that the instrument will be paid when presented to the proper person. Mainly attracted by instruments held by people with holder in due course status are professional risk buyers who are in the business of buying up commercial paper.

If an instrument is not negotiable and therefore does not meet the requirements of negotiation, the transfer by the payee is considered an assignment, as noted in Chapter 20. Consequently, the person receiving the instrument under these circumstances becomes an **ordinary holder** and has the legal rights of an assignee of a simple contract. Unlike a holder in due course, an ordinary holder does not gain the privilege of enforcing payment of the instrument when personal defenses are raised by the party obligated to pay.

Holder in due course (HIDC) status is not presumed, which means that a holder must *prove* he or she is a holder in due course. To qualify as a holder in due course, the holder must take the instrument (1) for value, (2) in good faith, (3) without knowledge of defects, that the instrument is overdue, that it has been dishonored, or that there are any claims or defenses to it (UCC 3-302).

ordinary holder one who does not qualify as holder in due course and is subject to both real and personal defenses

For Value

To qualify as a holder in due course (HIDC), a holder must give value for the instrument (UCC 3-302; 3-303). Value, however, is not equivalent to the concept of consideration required under an ordinary contract (UCC 3-303). What is the difference? Consideration includes executory promises, but value does not. "I promise to sell you a computer in return for your promise to pay." Your promise to pay is consideration for my promise to sell, and vice versa. But it is not value. More than a mere unexecuted promise is necessary to change the status of a holder to that of holder in due course. A person takes an instrument for value by performance—that is, completing the act for which the instrument was given, such as delivering the goods for which a check is sent in payment; by taking the instrument in payment of, or as security for, a prior debt; or when the take makes an irrevocable commitment to a third person, as by providing a letter of credit (UCC 3-303). Thus, a holder is not yet considered a holder in due course if he or she arranges to pay for the instrument at a later time or plans to perform services agreed to at some future date. The reason is that the holder has not as yet given value. A person who receives a negotiable instrument as a gift cannot be a holder in due course because he or she has given nothing in payment. The usual consideration for an instrument is money, although the amount need not be equal to the amount written on the face of the instrument.

> Your uncle indorsed and delivered to you as a gift for your birthday a promissory note made by Salvatore. The note, payable to the order of your uncle as payee, was originally obtained from Salvatore for a debt owed to your uncle.

In this example, your uncle becomes a holder in due course because he took the instrument in payment of a prior debt. Even though you received the note by negotiation (indorsement plus delivery), however, it was a gift to you. Therefore, because you gave no value for it, you are an ordinary holder but did not become a holder in due course.

In Good Faith

The second requirement to qualify as an HIDC is that the holder take the instrument in good faith (UCC 3-302). Article 3 defines good faith as "honesty in fact and the observance of reasonable commercial standards of fair dealing" (UCC 3-103). It requires the holder to act honestly while in the process of acquiring the instrument. This means Revising all the information about the instrument that is available. It entails the absence of bad faith, and bad faith is dishonesty. It is not bad faith if the holder merely does not have knowledge of a defect in an instrument. But it is bad faith and dishonest if a holder deliberately chooses to ignore certain facts about an instrument, such as the instrument is defective when she received it or did not make any effort to examine an instrument that might possibly excite the suspicions of a reasonable person. Actually, most holders are holders in good faith simply because, in most cases, they are so far removed from the transaction they are involved in that no word of any possible trouble ever reaches them.

This requirement of good faith applies only to the holder. Whether or not the person transferring the instrument acted in good faith is not relevant. Consequently, a holder could purchase the instrument from a thief and still become a HIDC as long as the purchase was in good faith.

> Carl bought a promissory note with a face value of $10,000 from Richie for a payment of $100. The disparity in the price versus the face value should have alerted Carl to investigate how Richie came into possession of the note. It could have been stolen by Richie. In this case, Carl most likely would not qualify as a holder in due course.

Without Knowledge That the Instrument Is Defective

The third requirement to qualify as an HIDC is that the person who accepts a negotiable instrument have no notice that it is defective in one of the following ways (UCC 3-302): (1) It is overdue or has been dishonored, (2) there is a claim or defense against the instrument by another person, and (3) the instrument is so irregular or incomplete as to call into question its authenticity. A person is put on notice if he or she has actual knowledge, has received notification of a defect, or from all the known facts and circumstances surrounding the instrument, a reasonable person of average intelligence can conclude that something may be wrong with the instrument.

> A promissory note due and payable on January 20 (a business day) was negotiated to you on February 1. Although you obtained the overdue note by negotiation, you are an ordinary holder, not a holder in due course. That the instrument has not been paid when due should convey the suspicion that something is wrong.

> You accept a check marked NSF (not sufficient funds). This marking on the check constitutes notice of dishonor. Therefore, you cannot became a holder in due course.

If there is evidence on the face of the instrument that the signature has been forged or that the paper itself has been altered in some way or the instrument is incomplete in some material respect (e.g., an element of negotiability is lacking), a person accepting that instrument cannot become a holder in due course. A reasonable person would have questioned whether the instrument was valid.

> Gerard made out a promissory note, written in ink, for $1,000. The note was payable to Monroe Business School. The owner of the business school, who needed money to keep the school going, erased the $1,000, inserted the figure of $5,000, and negotiated the note to the bank, a creditor of the school.

In this case, the bank was not a holder in due course. Evidence of the alteration (e.g., rough spots on the paper where the erasure was made) should have alerted the bank to a possible alteration. Because the note had been altered, Gerard would not have to pay the $5,000 when the bank presented the note for payment. Gerard would, however, be liable for $1,000, the original amount of the note.

HOLDER THROUGH A HOLDER IN DUE COURSE: THE SHELTER PRINCIPLE

shelter principle transferees of negotiable instruments get all the rights of the transferor

It is possible for a person to gain the rights and privileges of a holder in due course without actually being a holder in due course. This rule is referred to as the **shelter principle** and is based on UCC 3-203, which states that a transferee of a negotiable instrument gets all the rights of the transferor. The following example will bring out this point.

> Gennier made out a note for $10,000 and issued this note to Grant. As the payee and a bona fide holder, Grant transferred the note to Masterson. Because Masterson took the note in good faith, for value, and without notice of any claims or defenses, he became a holder in due course. When the note came due, Masterson presented it for payment to Gennier who simply refused. Masterson became angry and sold the note (which was now overdue) at a large discount to the Rumble Collection Agency. When the Rumble Agency demanded payment from Gennier, he again refused, this time speaking out and claiming to have been defrauded by Grant, the payee, and asserted fraud in the inducement a personal defense.

In this example, the Rumble Collection Agency was by no means a holder in due course because the note was overdue, making it ineligible to become an HIDC. However, it did take the instrument from Masterson who was an HIDC. Therefore, because of the shelter principle, the Rumble Agency as transferee of the note took whatever rights its transferor (Masterson) had. Since Masterson was an HIDC, the Rumble Agency also obtains the rights of an HIDC. The Rumble Agency was thus entitled to payment from Gennier. (If you recall, fraud in the inducement claimed by Gennier is a personal defense not valid against a holder in due course.)

DEFENSES

personal (limited) defenses defenses arising after an instrument is executed that cannot be used against holder in due course

universal (real) defenses defenses valid against all holders of negotiable instruments

In relationship to negotiable instruments, there are two categories of defenses—*personal defenses (limited)* and *universal (real) defenses*. The Code does not attempt to detail all defenses. A *defense* is a legal reason offered by a primary or secondary party for avoiding payment to a holder for the amount due on the instrument. **Personal (limited) defenses** are not valid against holders in due course but are valid against ordinary holders. This means that a holder in due course may collect on the instrument despite any personal (limited) defenses offered by a party obligated to pay. **Universal (real) defenses** on the other hand, are valid against all holders, including holders in due course. A party claiming a real defense against a holder of a negotiable instrument is not liable for payment of that instrument. State law generally determines whether defenses are real or personal.

Personal (Limited) Defenses

Personal (limited) defenses, which may arise either before or after an instrument has been negotiated, include (1) fraud in the inducement, (2) lack of consideration, (3) payment at or before maturity, (4) lack of delivery, (5) unauthorized completion of an incomplete instrument, (6) slight duress, and (7) breach of warranty. It is important at this point to understand that the UCC does not specifically deal with personal defenses. The Code simply states that a holder in due course takes the instrument free and clear of all claims and defenses, except those listed as real defenses. Real defenses challenge the validity of the instrument itself. All other defenses referred to here as personal defenses are similar to those that may be raised in an action for breach of contract (a negotiable instrument is a contract). Consequently, the validity of the instrument itself is not being questioned. What is being questioned are the circumstances surrounding the contractual agreement. The following personal defenses are the most common examples, but others exist.

Fraud in the Inducement   The defense of fraud in the inducement (ordinary fraud) arises when a person is persuaded to sign an instrument because of false statements by another person. The person is fully aware that he or she is signing a negotiable instrument but is not aware that the other party has misrepresented a material fact concerning the transaction so as to persuade this person to sign the paper.

> You wished to buy a used car from Whalen, who was very eager to sell the car. Whalen told you that she had recently had the motor overhauled. You relied on this statement and agreed to buy the car, signing a promissory note for $2,000 to pay for the car. Shortly thereafter, you discovered that Whalen had lied about having the motor overhauled.

In this example, you could refuse to pay the note because as one of the immediate parties, you have a good defense against the instrument: fraud in the inducement. If Whalen had negotiated the note to another person who would be a holder in due course, however, you would be liable for payment to that person. The defense of fraud in the inducement is not good against holders in due course. You could, of course, sue Whalen for damages suffered from the tort of fraud.

Lack of Consideration   As in any contract, consideration makes a promise to give a negotiable instrument binding. Lack of consideration is a defense between the immediate parties to an instrument, but it is not a defense against a holder in due course.

> Jenkins purchased a laptop computer from Raven. When Raven told Jenkins that the computer would be delivered in a few days, Jenkins made out a promissory note to Raven and delivered the note to her. The laptop computer was never delivered to Jenkins. In the meantime, Raven negotiated the note to Harris as payment for a debt. Harris became a holder in due course.

In this example, the lack of consideration was a personal defense that Jenkins could raise against Raven. Because Raven negotiated the note to Harris, a holder in due course, however, the defense of lack of consideration is not valid against Harris. Harris could collect on the note from Jenkins, who could then sue Raven.

Payment at or Before Maturity   A person who pays the amount due on a negotiable instrument should take actual possession of the instrument. The same is true for an instrument that is canceled before the due date by mutual agreement. If this paid-up or canceled instrument is not retrieved, it may either deliberately or accidentally fall into the hands of a third party through negotiation. That party would be a holder in due course.

> You borrowed $500 from Heinz to make a down payment on some ski equipment. You gave Heinz a thirty-day promissory note. At the end of fifteen days, you paid off the note but did not ask Heinz for its return.

In this example, if Heinz negotiated the note before its maturity date to a person who becomes a holder in due course, you must pay the note again on the due date.

Lack of Delivery   An instrument may unintentionally be transferred (delivered) from one person to another, for example, through loss or theft. Even in these circumstances, lack of delivery is not a valid defense against a holder in due course. It is, however, a valid defense between the two immediate parties to the instrument. Lack of delivery may involve either a complete or an incomplete instrument.

A *complete instrument* is one on which all important blanks have been filled in, including the signature of the maker or drawer.

> You made out a check payable to "Cash" and left it on a table in your family room. A burglar who entered your house stole the check and negotiated it to a holder in due course. The holder in due course could collect the amount of the check from you, but the burglar could not.

An *incomplete instrument* is one lacking information because all the blanks have not been filled in by the maker or drawer. If, through carelessness or theft, the instrument is negotiated to a holder in due course, the maker or drawer does not have a valid defense against that person.

> Jerome made out a promissory note and signed it, but he did not write in the name of the payee. Jerome lost the note. Adler found the note, filled in his own name as payee, and negotiated it to Black, a holder in due course. Although Adler could not collect from Jerome, Black could.

Unauthorized Completion   In certain circumstances, a signed instrument may be transferred to another person with some of the blanks not filled in. The maker may authorize this person to complete the instrument according to the maker's instructions. If the blanks are completed in an unauthorized manner, however, the maker does not have a valid defense against a holder in due course.

> Raleigh, who was in the specialty food import business, gave his agent a blank check and authorized the agent to fill it in for the correct amount of a purchase he was asked to make. The agent instead filled it in for a larger amount and then cashed the check. Raleigh would have to pay the full amount of the check to a holder in due course. Raleigh would not, however, have to pay the agent the larger amount.

Slight Duress   "Slight duress" refers to threats that prevent a person from exercising her or his own free will. A person forced to give a negotiable instrument under slight duress will not be liable on the instrument to the person who actually committed the duress. The defense of slight duress, however, cannot be used against a holder in due course. If the person who acquired the instrument through duress has already collected, the maker can recover damages if he or she finds the guilty person.

> Barnes was a professor at Valley Forge Community College. Fisher, another professor at the college, was in desperate need of money and threatened to tell the personnel office that Barnes had a criminal record unless Barnes gave him $1,000. Barnes did not have the cash, but Fisher agreed to take a check payable to him. He indorsed the check and cashed it at a local grocery store. As a holder in due course, the owner of the grocery store could collect the amount of the check from Barnes.

Breach of Warranty   If a negotiable instrument such as a promissory note or a check is issued for a sale of goods with a warranty attached and there is a breach of that warranty, a holder in due course who comes into possession of the instrument is not affected by this breach of warranty liability that exists between the original parties to the contract.

> Marcan enters into a contract to purchase several pair of pliers for his hardware store. The cost is $1,000. Payment by Imperial is requested prior to shipment. Marcan sends a check to Imperial. Imperial in turn indorses the check and passes it on to the manufacturer of the pliers from whom Imperial made its purchase. When Marcan receives the pliers, they are found to be defective because they will not open and close properly. Marcan can claim breach of the implied warranty of merchantability as a defense to payment of his $1,000 bill to Imperial. However, because Imperial negotiated the check to the manufacturer and assuming the manufacturer to be a holder in due course, Marcan cannot avoid payment of the check.

Universal (Real) Defenses

Universal (real) defenses challenge the validity of the instrument itself. In other words, they make a negotiable instrument void from the time of its creation and stop even a holder in due course from collecting on the instrument. The theory is that the one holding the instrument is really not a holder, and therefore, no one who receives the instrument could be a holder in due course. Real defenses arise only rarely. These defenses include (1) fraud in the execution, (2) forgery, (3) minority, (4) material alteration, (5) illegality, and (6) serious duress.

Fraud in the Execution   Fraud in the execution of an instrument occurs when one person obtains a negotiable instrument from another person through fraud or trickery. In other words, a person never intends to create a negotiable instrument. The maker in this case could avoid payment to all parties, including a holder in due course, because there was never an intent to create the instrument.

> Lutz, who was selling magazine subscriptions in an apartment building, told a customer that besides being a salesperson, he also was a handwriting analyst. He told the customer to sign her name on a piece of paper, which he handed to her. After leaving the apartment building, Lutz wrote a promissory note above the signature and then indorsed the "note" to Gimbel, a holder in due course. Gimbel could not legally collect on this instrument. The magazine customer could raise the real defense of fraud in the execution because she never intended to create a note.

Forgery   A person whose name is forged to an instrument has a universal (real) defense against all holders. Even a holder in due course cannot collect from the maker or drawer.

> Karlan, a holder in due course, presented a promissory note for payment to Cato, whose name appeared as the maker. Cato proved that her signature had been forged. Karlan cannot collect from Cato.

Minority   Minors can avoid liability on negotiable instruments in the same manner that they can avoid liability on simple contracts. Chapter 7 pointed out that all states strongly protect minors from adults who are often in the position to take advantage of them through contractual dealings. Even holders in due course cannot collect on an instrument signed by a minor as a maker, drawer, or indorser (except for necessaries).

> As payment for a CD player, Langdon, a minor, wrote a ninety-day promissory note for $600 to Arnold, the payee. The note was negotiated to Marvin, a holder in due course, who demanded payment from Langdon. As a minor, Langdon may refuse to pay Marvin.

Material Alteration   A material alteration made in a fraudulent manner is a universal (real) defense that is valid against all holders. An alteration is material when the rights and obligations of the parties are changed, such as when the amount of the instrument is increased or the due date is changed. The defense of material alteration is good against a holder in due course only for the changes made in the instrument. That is, a holder in due course can enforce the instrument for the amount before the alteration.

> Carson, the payee of a check, changed the amount of the check from $500 to $5,000 and then negotiated it to Spicer, a holder in due course. Spicer could legally demand that Carson pay $500.

Illegality   Illegality is most frequently associated with gambling or usury. Whether illegality may be used as a universal (real) defense or a personal (limited) defense against a holder in due course depends on state statute. If the transaction for which a negotiable instrument is given is illegal or void by state statute, illegality is a universal (real) defense that is good against even a holder in due course. If, however, the transaction for which a negotiable instrument is given is not void by state statute, but voidable illegality is a personal (limited) defense and is not good against a holder in due course.

> Perkins gave Engle a note in payment of a gambling debt. Engle negotiated the note to Heller, a holder in due course. Perkins refused to pay Heller the amount of the note when it was properly presented to her. In Perkins's state, gambling was illegal. Therefore, the note Perkins gave Engle was void, and Heller, even as a holder in due course, could not collect.

Serious Duress   Serious forms of duress, such as a threat of force or violence, forcing a person to sign an instrument, or threatening a person at gunpoint, are considered universal (real) defenses and are good against all holders, including a holder in due course.

> Comfort was physically forced by LaGrange, a known organized-crime figure, to sign a promissory note for $1,000. LaGrange negotiated this note to O'Hara, a holder in due course. O'Hara could not legally collect from Comfort, even as a holder in due course.

Figure 21.2 summarizes the types of personal (limited) and universal (real) defenses.

THE FEDERAL TRADE COMMISSION HIDC RULE

In 1976, to protect consumers, the Federal Trade Commission (FTC), which has the authority to prohibit unfair business practices, ruled that the holder in due course concept cannot be used against ultimate consumers when they buy goods or services on credit from a merchant-seller. (This federal law, which in effect abolishes the HIDC doctrine as it applies to consumer transactions, overrules the UCC provisions.) The FTC declared that if a consumer gives a seller a negotiable instrument (e.g., a promissory note) and the

FIGURE 21.2
Defenses Against
Holders of Negotiable
Instruments

Classification of Defenses	Types of Defenses
Personal (limited) defenses Good against ordinary holders but not against holders in due course	1. Fraud in the inducement 2. Lack of consideration 3. Payment at or before maturity 4. Lack of delivery 5. Unauthorized completion 6. Slight duress 7. Breach of warranty
Universal (real) defenses Good against all holders, including holders in due course	1. Fraud in the execution 2. Forgery 3. Minority 4. Material alteration 5. Illegality 6. Serious duress

seller negotiates the instrument, the party taking the instrument (e.g., a bank or a finance company) cannot become a holder in due course. Rather, this party is placed in the position of an assignee and takes the instrument subject to all claims and defenses that the buyer could assert against the seller.

Sanders purchased a $600 microwave from Kitchens Unlimited and gave Kitchens Unlimited a negotiable instrument for that amount. A salesperson for Kitchens Unlimited had made false statements about the appliance (fraud in the inducement) to induce Sanders to make the purchase. The appliance turned out to be defective. In the meantime, Kitchens Unlimited negotiated the instrument to the First National Bank, which presented the note to Sanders for payment.

Under the ordinary rule, fraud in the inducement is a personal defense that is not good against a holder in due course. Thus, in the example, even though Kitchens Unlimited lied and even though the appliance turned out to be defective, the First National Bank, not being a party to the fraud, could still collect from Sanders. Sanders's only recourse would be to try to collect from Kitchens Unlimited. In such cases, recovery is difficult and frequently impossible.

Under the FTC ruling, however, the First National Bank was not considered to be a holder in due course. Sanders could assert the defense of fraud in the inducement against the bank and withhold payment of the instrument until the seller corrects any deficiencies.

The FTC rule applies to consumer credit transactions in which (1) a consumer signs a sales contract that includes a promissory note, (2) the consumer signs an installment sales contract with a waiver of defense clause, and (3) the seller arranges consumer financing with a third-party lender. The FTC rule, however, does not apply when a consumer purchases goods or services and pays by check because that is not a credit transaction. The party to whom a check has been negotiated may qualify as a holder in due course.

The FTC rule requires each consumer credit transaction to contain the following clause in at least 10-point, boldface type. The type as shown here is 10-point boldface:

NOTICE

ANY HOLDER OF THIS CONSUMER CREDIT CONTRACT IS SUBJECT TO ALL CLAIMS AND DEFENSES WHICH THE DEBTOR COULD ASSERT AGAINST THE SELLER OF GOODS OR SERVICES OBTAINED PURSUANT HERETO OR WITH THE PROCEEDS HEREOF. RECOVERY HEREUNDER BY THE DEBTOR SHALL NOT EXCEED AMOUNTS PAID BY THE DEBTOR HEREUNDER.

ACCOMMODATION PARTIES

accommodation parties third parties who lend their name (signatures) on an instrument as security against nonpayment by a person obligated to pay

Accommodation parties are third parties who lend their name (signature) on an instrument as security against nonpayment by a person obligated to pay (UCC 3-419). It might be that a person's credit rating is doubtful or has not yet been established. Consequently, the person cannot borrow money from a lending institution.

Accommodation parties may sign in one of two ways: as a *comaker* or as an *indorser*. One who signs as a comaker has primary liability and is called an accommodation maker, while one who signs as an indorser on behalf of the payee has secondary liability and is called an accommodation indorser. The distinction is important.

Martin wished to borrow $15,000 from a bank but did not have a sufficient income or a strong credit history. The bank agreed to lend Martin the money on a promissory note but only if he found a credit-worthy comaker. Miles, his friend, agreed to become an accommodation maker.

In this example, Miles has become a maker with a maker's liability (i.e., primary liability). Miles is totally and fully obligated on the note even though she signed as a favor to her friend Martin. The bank is not required to first try to collect from Martin and then, if unable to do so, turn to Miles. The bank, upon default in payment by Martin, may go directly to Miles first. There is absolutely no difference between an ordinary comaker and an accommodation party who signs as a comaker. However, if Miles ends up paying the bank, she has the right of reimbursement from Martin (the maker) (UCC 3-419).

The person who signs as an accommodation indorser is likely to make the instrument more marketable. His or her status as an indorser is like any other indorser with secondary liability on the instrument. The only difference between an accommodation indorser and a "regular indorser" is that if the accommodation party pays the instrument, he or she may collect from the party accommodated (UCC 3-419).

Barton wishes to borrow $10,000 from Able. Able, however, requires Barton to obtain Carrier's signature on the instrument as an accommodation indorser before the loan will be made. Carrier agrees to sign. Carrier now becomes liable to Able as an indorser of the instrument. If Barton later refuses to repay the loan, Able can proceed against Carrier, the accommodation indorser.

Summary

Parties liable for payment on negotiable instruments are classified as either primary parties or secondary parties. Makers of notes and drawees (acceptors) of drafts are examples of primary parties. Drawers of checks (or drafts), the payee, and indorsers of any negotiable instrument are examples of secondary parties. A primary party has unconditional liability for payment of the instrument according to its terms, whereas the liability of secondary parties is conditional. To hold a secondary party liable, the holder of the paper must (1) present the instrument for payment to the primary party in a proper and timely manner, (2) have the primary party dishonor the instrument, and (3) give timely notice of dishonor to the secondary party. Generally, the drawer as a secondary party has to pay even if the conditions of presentment, dishonor, and notice are not met.

Keep in mind that a person first becomes a holder starting with the payee to whom an instrument has been issued by either the maker (note) or drawer (draft or check). The payee who decides to transfer the instrument on may do so by assignment or negotiation. Negotiation is the preferred way. When an instrument is negotiated, each successive person who takes the instrument also becomes a holder. As a holder, that person is eligible to obtain the unique status of a holder in due course. To qualify as a holder in due course, a holder must take the instrument for value, in good faith, and without knowledge that the instrument is defective. A holder who does not qualify as a holder in due course is considered an ordinary holder and is in the same legal position as an assignee of a contract. It is possible for a person to gain the rights and privileges of a holder in due course without actually being a holder in due course. This rule is referred to as the shelter principle. Defenses against holders of negotiable instruments are classified as personal (limited) defenses and universal (real) defenses. Personal (limited)

defenses are good against ordinary holders, assignees, and the immediate parties to commercial paper, but they are not good against holders in due course. Universal (real) defenses are good against assignees and all holders, including holders in due course. Personal (limited) defenses include (1) fraud in the inducement, (2) lack of consideration, (3) payment at or before maturity, (4) lack of delivery of a complete instrument, (5) unauthorized completion of an incomplete instrument, and (6) slight duress. Universal (real) defenses consist of (1) fraud in the execution, (2) forgery, (3) minority, (4) material alteration, (5) illegality, (6) serious duress, and (7) breach of warranty.

Under the Federal Trade Commission HIDC rule, if a consumer who buys on credit gives a seller a negotiable instrument and the seller negotiates the instrument, the person taking the instrument cannot become a holder in due course. The FTC rule, however, does not apply when a consumer purchases goods or services and pays by check. The party to whom a check has been negotiated may qualify as a holder in due course.

Sometimes, as a favor or for some consideration, people lend their names and credit to other people whose credit rating is doubtful as an accommodation. Some accommodation parties sign instruments as comakers, others as indorsers. The liabilities of comakers and indorsers differ. One who signs as a comaker has primary liability while one who signs as an indorsers has secondary liability.

Important Legal Terms

acceptor
accommodation parties
dishonor
holder in due course

notice of dishonor
ordinary holder
personal (limited) defenses
presentment

primary parties
secondary parties
shelter principle
universal (real) defenses

Questions and Problems for Discussion

1. A maker of a note will have a real defense against a holder in due course as a result of any of the following conditions except
   a. material alteration
   b. forgery
   c. Fraud in the execution
   d. lack of consideration

2. Which of the following parties has (have) primary liability on a negotiable instrument?
   a. drawer of a check and the drawee of a time draft before acceptance
   b. drawee of a time draft before acceptance
   c. drawer of a check and the maker of a promissory note
   d. maker of a promissory note

3. Why is the shelter principle an important legal concept as it relates to negotiable instruments?

4. A holder in due course will take free of which of the following defenses?
   a. serious duress
   b. fraud in the execution
   c. a wrongfully filled-in amount payable that was omitted from the instrument
   d. an instrument with a forged indorsement

5. Sampson's name appeared as a maker of a $500 note. On the due date, Robbins, a holder in due course, presented the note to Sampson for payment. Sampson proved the signature to be a forgery and refused to pay. Can Robbins legally collect from Sampson?

6. Which of the following defenses is good against a holder in due course if pleaded by the maker or drawer of a negotiable instrument?
   a. lack of consideration
   b. fraud in the inducement
   c. forgery
   d. nondelivery of a completed instrument
   e. incapacity of parties

7. If there are no defenses to a negotiable instrument, do you have to be a holder in due course to collect on the instrument?

8. What is the significance of being an ordinary holder as compared to a holder in due course?

9. Sagamore borrowed $200 from Copp, to whom she gave a promissory note due and payable on January 15. One week before the note was due, Sagamore met Copp at a local bank and paid him the $200. Copp promised to mail the note to Sagamore the next day. Instead, Copp made a gift of the note to his nephew. Could the nephew collect the amount of the note from Sagamore?

10. Martin made out a promissory note payable for $5,000 and issued the note to Pask. Pask transferred the note to Grimes, who became a holder in due course because he purchased it in good faith not knowing of any defects in the instrument. When the instrument became due, Grimes, without an explanation, refused to pay. Grimes, instead of representing the note to Martin again for payment, then decided to sell the note which was now overdue to Tiller at a discount price simply because Grimes needed the money. Tiller, because of the discount price, still purchased the note knowing it was overdue. Tiller then demanded payment from Martin, who now claimed fraud in the inducement on the part of Pask. Does Tiller have the right to collect on the note from Martin, the maker, even though Martin claimed fraud?

Cases for Review

1. Carl and Beulah Humphrey signed as maker and comaker of a note for a line of credit of $50,000 from the Grand Island Production Credit Association to purchase cattle. When the Humphreys failed to pay the outstanding balance on the line of credit, Grand Island sued Mr. and Mrs. Humphrey to recover the unpaid balance of $13,936. Mrs. Humphrey contended that Carl alone was liable for payment, even though she had signed the note, because she has since divorced Carl. Did Beulah Humphrey have primary liability on the loan along with her ex-husband or should she be excused from payment? (*Grand Island Production Credit Association* v. *Humphrey*, 388 N.E. 807)

2. Betty Ellis and her husband, W. G. Ellis, issued a promissory note to the Standard Finance Co. in the amount of $2,800. After receiving the note, Standard issued a check to the couple for $2,800. Both Betty and her husband indorsed the check and then cashed it. Shortly after this, the Ellises were divorced and her ex-husband went into bankruptcy. In the meantime, Standard Finance Co. sold the note to Wayne National Bank, which was aware of the circumstances surrounding the note. When the note became due, Wayne sued Betty Ellis as a holder in due course for the amount of the note. Betty, however, refused to pay it, claiming that Wayne could not be a holder in due course because she never saw or used the money—that it all went to her ex-husband. Consequently, she never gave value for the note. Is Betty correct? (*Standard Finance Company Ltd.* v. *Ellis*, 657 P.2d 1056)

3. Barnes received a promissory note from Park Place in the amount of $34,400, payable on or before January 1, 1973. Three officers of the corporation indorsed the note as individuals.

Barnes apparently believed that he was not going to be paid and wrote each indorser on December 7, 1972, to say that he would sue if the note was not paid. The note was not paid on January 1, 1973, and Barnes presented the note for payment on March 20, 1973. Nine days later, Barnes sent out a notice of dishonor to each indorser. If Barnes sues the indorsers on the note, can he succeed? (*Barnes* v. *Park Place Homes, Inc.,* La. 289 So.2d 859)

4. Locke gave a promissory note to Consumer Foods, Inc. The note read, in part, "Buyer agrees to pay to Seller." Consumer Foods assigned the note to Aetna Acceptance Corporation. When the note wasn't paid and Aetna brought an action against Locke, Locke's defense was that the note was not negotiable because it was not payable to order or to bearer. As a result, Aetna was not a holder in due course and was subject to personal defenses that Locke had. Is Locke correct? (*Locke* v. *Aetna Acceptance Corp.,* Fla. 309 So.2d 43)

5. Middle Georgia Livestock Sales bought cattle at an auction, paying by check. A couple of days later, Middle Georgia discovered that it had purchased stolen cattle and put through a stop-payment order on the check. Commercial Bank, however, cashed the check without knowledge of the stop-payment order. When the drawee bank refused payment, Commercial Bank sued the maker of the check. In this state, a transaction involving stolen goods is illegal and void. Can Commercial Bank collect from the maker? (*Middle Georgia Livestock Sales* v. *Commercial B & T Co.,* Ga. 182 S.E.2d 533)

6. The Paddocks hired Harper Realty to sell their hotel. The Paddocks agreed that if Harper sold the hotel, they would pay Harper a commission of $15,000, with $3,000 down and the balance in monthly installments. The Paddocks gave Harper a note for the $12,000. Harper negotiated the note to McLean, a holder in due course. When the payments were not made, McLean sued the Paddocks. The Paddocks' defense was that they were induced to sign the note because of a false representation by Harper that the note was required, when in fact it was not. Is this defense valid against the claim? (*McLean* v. *Paddock,* N.M. 430 P.2d 392)

CHAPTER 22

Checks and the Banking System in the Twenty-First Century

CHAPTER PREVIEW

Checks—An Introduction

The Bank-Customer Relationship

Duty of a Bank to Honor Checks
Postdated Checks
Stop-Payment Order

Obligations of a Depositor

Special Types of Checks
Certified Checks
Cashier's Checks
Traveler's Checks

Bank's Liability for Wrongful Payment of a Check
Alteration of a Check

Forgery of a Drawer's Signature
Forgery of an Indorsement
Missing Indorsement
Death of the Depositor

Availability of Funds from Deposited Checks

Check Processing—Pre-Twenty-First Century

Check Processing—Twenty-First Century

Electronic Funds Transfer

Online Banking

E-Money

Chapter Highlights

This chapter is significant in that it deals with new rules and new strategies for bank customers, new ways that banks deal with customers, and new laws that govern the way banks and customers deal with each other. Technological innovation in the twenty-first century has fostered the development of new business practices and brought into focus terms such as electronic commerce. A new federal law, the Check Clearing for the 21st Century Act, or simply the Check 21 Act, has been enacted. This act has created a whole new way of doing business with a bank if you write a check while still supporting the concept that checks are still very important in today's society. It allows banks to handle more checks electronically, which should make check processing faster and more efficient. The chapter begins with a discussion of the legal characteristics of checks. We then examine the legal responsibilities of banks and their customers once a check is issued, and from there move on to the special types of checks that are used in the business world. Continuing on in the chapter, the check collection process as modified by the Check 21 Act will be explained. In the final pages of the chapter we will review the various ways that funds may be transferred electronically as a way of paying for goods and services.

CHECKS—AN INTRODUCTION

Debit cards are now favored over personal checks for making retail payments; nevertheless, checks, and especially commercial checks, remain an integral part of the business world and are important enough for a federal law called the Check Clearing for the 21st Century Act (the Check 21 Act) to be passed in 2004. This act will be covered in more detail later in this chapter. You will discover how check processing (between the time a check is written and transferred to the payee and when it is returned to the checkwriter [drawer] as a receipt) has been brought into the twenty-first century given modern methods and technology. Overall, checks are governed by Article 3 and Article 4 of the UCC. Article 3 establishes the basic requirements of all negotiable instruments, while Article 4 deals with bank-customer relations, and bank-to-bank relations. Recall from Chapter 19 that a check is a specialized type of draft drawn on a bank (called the drawee). According to the Uniform Commercial Code (UCC), a depositor (drawer) of the bank orders this bank to pay a fixed sum of money on demand to someone else, called the payee (who then becomes a holder) (UCC 3-104). If you write a check from money on deposit in your checking account to pay for a used sports car that you purchased, you are the drawer, your bank is the drawee, and the car dealer from whom you purchased the car is the payee. Checks are much safer than currency. If someone steals a check and some cash from you, the thief can spend all the cash for whatever he or she wants. On the other hand, you can notify your bank to stop payment on your checks. You generally pay a bill through the mail by writing a check because sending cash through the mail is unsafe. Other known facts about checks are that not everyone will accept a check in payment for a transaction and that a check payment is not final until the check clears the bank.

THE BANK-CUSTOMER RELATIONSHIP

The bank-customer relationship begins when a depositor opens a checking account at a bank and deposits money into this account. Banks include savings banks, savings and loan associations, credit unions, and trust companies. From this point on, each time the depositor writes a check and the check is received by the bank, the bank charges the account to "cover" the amount of the check. Of course, the money used to cover the check comes from the funds on deposit in the customer's account.

The bank and the customer have established a relationship that is contractual in nature. Certain rights and duties result from this contract. The rights and duties not established by contract will be found in Article 4 of the UCC. Banks generally send their customers a monthly statement detailing the various transactions (e.g., checks written, direct deposits made, bank interest accrued, and perhaps canceled checks or photocopies of checks) in their checking accounts for the period of one month. Although not required to return them, banks must at least provide the depositor with check number, amount, and date of payment for each check written and received by the bank between the dates covered on the monthly statement. If the bank retains the canceled checks, it must keep the checks for a period of seven years (UCC 4-406). The depositor may, generally for a fee, obtain a canceled check (or an electronic copy of the original check) during this period. The customer has a duty to examine his or her monthly statement promptly and to report any suspected or known alterations or forged signatures and forged indorsements (UCC 4-406). A failure on the part of the depositor to perform this duty excuses the bank from liability under certain circumstances for any loss that the bank suffers (UCC 4-406). Bank-depositor liability is discussed later in the chapter.

Another relationship that is created when a depositor opens a checking account at a bank is a debtor-creditor relationship. As long as the depositor has money deposited in a bank, the bank is a debtor of the depositor for the amount deposited, and the customer becomes the creditor.

In certain cases, the reverse relationship may exist. If a bank lends money to a depositor, allowing the depositor to draw checks against that amount, the depositor is then a debtor of the bank. Although not obligated to do so, some banks may even permit some

overdraft check written without sufficient funds that will be paid by the bank

customers to write checks for more than the amount of money on deposit. Such checks are known as **overdrafts**. In effect, the bank lends the overdrawn amount to the depositor and thus becomes the depositor's creditor. The bank pays the overdraft on the strength of the customer's exemplary credit rating and the deposits he or she has in other accounts at the bank (e.g., certificates of deposit, CDs).

In addition to the debtor-creditor relationship, a principal-agent relationship may also exist. If a depositor receives a check drawn on another bank and deposits that check in her or his own bank, the depositor's bank becomes the agent to collect the amount of the check from the bank on which it was drawn. The agent is a person authorized to act on behalf of another, called the principal. Similarly, when the customer writes a check on his or her account, the customer in effect is ordering the bank as agent to pay the amount specified on the check to the holder when the holder presents the check to the bank for payment. To transfer checkbook funds between and among different banks, each bank acts as the agent of collection for its customer (UCC 4-201).

DUTY OF A BANK TO HONOR CHECKS

Keep in mind that a check is a special form of a draft. A check is always drawn on a bank, and the bank is always obligated to pay on demand (to honor) all checks written by the drawer-depositor, if there are sufficient funds to cover them.

When the bank receives a check, it pays the amount on the face of the check to the holder and then deducts that amount from the depositor's account. When two or more checks are presented for payment at the same time and the depositor's account is insufficient to pay them all, the bank may pay the checks in any order until funds in the depositor's account run out. A bank may, but need not, pay a **stale check**, a check that is more than six months old (figured from the date of the check) and that has not been certified (UCC 4-404). Such a check does not automatically become void after six months. If a bank pays in good faith without consulting the customer, it has the right to charge the customer's account for the amount of the check. As a practical matter, most banks do not pay stale checks until they have first contacted the depositor to be sure the depositor still wishes it to be paid.

stale check uncertified check more than six months old

If the depositor's bank dishonors (refuses to pay) a check for no good reason, the bank is liable for actual damages that result from injury to the depositor's reputation resulting from a bad credit rating or from being arrested and prosecuted (UCC 4-402). A depositor, however, has the responsibility of proving the wrongfulness of the dishonor and that the dishonor was the cause of the injury (UCC 4-402). The usual reason for a bank to dishonor a depositor's check is that there are insufficient funds in the account to cover the check. In this case, the bank notifies the drawer of the dishonor and returns the check to the holder marked "insufficient funds." The holder, in many cases, resubmits the check to the bank, hoping that the drawer in the meantime has deposited enough money into the account so that it will now clear. If the check still does not clear and insufficient funds remain, the bank may (e.g., for a good customer) pay the check and charge the customer's account and then collect the difference from the next deposit or from another account (e.g., a savings account). If the bank thinks that there are insufficient funds in a depositor's checking account but is in error, the bank is liable.

Nichols made out a check payable to Lark for $750 for a used motorcycle. Lincoln National Bank, the bank on which the check was written, refused to pay Lark, stating that there were insufficient funds in Nichols's account. Actually, the bank's records were incorrect because of an error in bookkeeping. Lincoln National Bank would be liable for actual damages suffered by Nichols.

A bank may also legally refuse to honor a depositor's check without liability for reasons other than insufficient funds or the check is stale or is questionable, such as when the check contains a material omission (e.g., lack of an amount in words), the bank is suspicious of either the check or the holder, or in the situations noted in the next sections dealing with postdated checks and a stop-payment order. If you deposit a questionable check, explain the details of the transaction. Until you know the check is good, don't withdrawal the money from your account.

A bank that dishonors a check has no liability to the payee or another holder even though the bank's refusal to pay was improper. A holder who wishes to recover under these circumstances must proceed against the drawer and other secondary parties in a civil lawsuit. The holder, however, must first notify these parties of the dishonor.

Postdated Checks

The UCC defines a check as a draft drawn on a bank and payable on demand (UCC 3-104). A check that is dated after its actual date of issue is called a **postdated check**. A postdated check, because it is not payable on demand, does not satisfy the UCC definition. Consequently, it has generally been held by most states that the giving of a postdated check does not constitute a present fraud nor is it within the scope of the bad check laws. A postdated check is perfectly valid and is often used in the same way as a promissory note: to pay for something in the future. Postdating a check has no effect on negotiability. A person who takes a postdated check therefore may become a holder in due course.

postdated check check dated after its actual date of issue

A bank has no obligation to pay a postdated check until its due date. It may, however, pay early without liability unless the drawer notifies the bank not to pay until the date on the check. If the drawer notifies the bank not to pay the check until the date on the postdated check but the bank ignores the request and charges the customer's account before this date, the bank may be liable for any damages incurred by the customer. This situation might occur if other checks prepared by the same drawer are dishonored because of insufficient funds resulting from premature payment of a postdated check (UCC 4-401). In some states, a bank is not liable for the premature payment of a postdated check unless the drawer notifies the bank that the check is postdated.

> You wanted to give your parents an anniversary gift at a party to be held in their honor. The party, however, was going to be held on June 21, one week before you got your next paycheck. A friend of yours who owned the Swiss Clock Shop agreed to take a check dated June 28 (seven days later) in payment of an unusual clock you wanted to buy for your parents. That check is a postdated check.

Stop-Payment Order

The drawer of a check may wish to prevent the check from being deposited or cashed. For example, you might want to stop payment if a check you wrote has been lost or if merchandise you purchased turned out to be defective and you were trying to get the payee to do something about this merchandise before you made payment. If you discovered fraud in a transaction, you might also wish to revoke the transaction by stopping payment on the check. Payment on a check is stopped through a **stop-payment order** (UCC 4-403). This order is an instruction by a depositor to the bank to refuse payment on a particular check when it is presented for payment. The bank is bound by this stop-payment order unless it arrives at the bank too late for the bank to act on it. If the bank pays the check over a valid stop-payment order, it is liable to the depositor and must credit the depositor's account but only for the actual loss suffered. The bank, however, must receive the order in the proper way and in a timely and reasonable manner.

stop-payment order order to a bank to refuse payment of a check

Halstead Company, manufacturer of pool tables, agreed on June 15 to sell twenty of these tables to the Porter and Bean retail outlet store for $500 each. Porter and Bean paid in advance for the tables with a check for $10,000. On June 16, Halstead notified Porter and Bean that it would not be able to deliver the pool tables as agreed. Porter and Bean immediately notified the bank to stop payment on the check. A few days later, the bank inadvertently paid the check to Halstead over the valid stop-payment order. The bank would be liable to Porter and Bean for $10,000. If, however, Halstead delivered fifteen pool tables at a cost of $7,500, and Porter and Bean agreed to this change in the agreement, then the bank would now only be liable to Porter and Bean for $2,500 for paying the check over the stop-payment order.

The bank customer (drawer) should be careful not to wrongfully stop payment on a check. A customer who does stop payment with no legal justification is liable (in the form of a lawsuit) to the holder for the amount of the check as well as for damages resulting from the consequences of the stop-payment order (consequential damages). If, however, the holder happens to be a holder in due course, personal defenses that the customer (drawer) might have to a lawsuit will not be valid.

A stop-payment order may be either oral or written. The UCC provides that an oral (usually by phone) stop-payment order is binding on the bank for only fourteen calendar days after the request is made unless the order is confirmed in writing. A written stop-payment order or an oral order confirmed in writing is effective for six months, at which time it must be renewed in writing (UCC 4-403). Renewals can continue to be made indefinitely. To avoid the possibility of the check being presented after the lapse of a stop-payment order, the customer could simply close the account. Most states have adopted the UCC rule permitting oral stop-payment orders. In some states, only a written stop-payment order is binding, but the bank may honor an oral stop-payment order if it wishes to do so. The most important requirement is that the order be given to a bank as soon as possible after the need for it arises.

You made out a check payable to "Cash" and put the check in your wallet. While shopping, you lost your wallet. You could request your bank to stop payment on the check. The bank is obligated to do so if you notify it promptly.

OBLIGATIONS OF A DEPOSITOR

If you have a checking account with a bank, the UCC imposes certain obligations on you as a bank customer (UCC 4-406). First, as a depositor, you have the obligation to act carefully and reasonably, whether writing a check or examining your monthly statement. One good example is your duty to keep enough money in your checking account to cover the checks you write. Another example is the obligation to examine the monthly statement of bank transactions and to advise the bank promptly of any mistakes. Finally, a third example is the duty to promptly report evidence of your signature being forged or your check having been altered in any way (UCC 4-406). Writing checks without enough money in an account could lead to accusations of writing bad checks. A **bad check** is one written by a drawer who knows there is not enough money in the checking account to cover it. The drawer knows that the drawee bank will refuse payment.

bad check check written by a drawer when there is not enough money to cover the check

Writing a bad check is a criminal act that could lead to the arrest of the drawer. Before starting criminal proceedings for passing a bad check, however, the bank generally must notify the drawer to place funds in the account to cover any bad checks. Under the statutes of many states, the law presumes that if the drawer does not deposit these funds within a specified time, that is evidence of an intent to defraud the holder. A drawer who writes a check that a bank dishonors for lack of funds remains liable to the payee or the holder in a civil suit.

SPECIAL TYPES OF CHECKS

There are special types of checks that perform different functions. These include certified checks, cashier's checks, and traveler's checks.

Certified Checks

certified check
personal check whose payment is guaranteed by a bank

Payment of a regular check depends on the availability of funds on deposit in the drawer's account. A **certified check** is a personal check that a bank guarantees to pay (UCC 3-409). In effect, the bank guarantees that there is enough money in the drawer's account to cover the check and promises to pay (honor) the check any time after it is issued (Figure 22.1). In essence, certification prevents the bank from denying liability. A certified check is considered as dependable as cash. Certification is accomplished by the drawer, the payee, or a subsequent holder taking the personal check to the bank on which the check is drawn. If the drawer's account has sufficient funds to cover payment, those funds are set aside by the bank and placed in its own certified check account for payment of the check, and the check is then marked "Certified." As mentioned in Chapter 21, a bank is not obligated to certify a check, and the bank's refusal to do so is not a dishonor of the check (UCC 3-409).

> Bak (payee) received a check for $100 from Abba (drawer) that was certified by Abba's bank. A few days later, Bak presented the check for payment at Abba's bank. The bank, however, would not cash it, claiming that Abba had closed her account. Because the check had been certified, Abba's bank was obligated to honor it.

A certified check is commonly used in important commercial and personal transactions, such as a down payment on the purchase of a business or a home. In these cases, large sums of money are involved, and the seller wants to be certain that the buyer's check is good.

If a drawer has a check certified, the drawer is still secondarily liable for payment of the check if for some reason the certifying bank cannot or does not honor the check when it is presented for payment. If the payee or a subsequent holder has the check certified, the bank becomes the only party liable for payment, and the drawer and any indorsers prior to certification are completely discharged (released from liability). Liability by the bank includes the amount of the checks, expenses, loss of interest, and consequential damages (UCC 3-411).

FIGURE 22.1
Certified Check

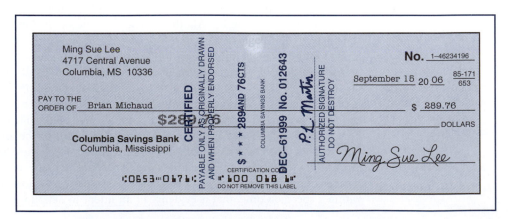

Payment of a certified check cannot be stopped. A certified check becomes a promise to pay by the bank and not by the depositor. The drawer of a certified check has no legal right to force a bank to stop payment on a certified check.

Cashier's Checks

cashier's check check drawn by a bank on its own funds

A **cashier's check** (sometimes called a bank check) is a check that a bank draws on its own funds payable to a specific payee (Figure 22.2) (UCC 3-104). You can purchase a cashier's check from a bank by paying the bank the amount of the check plus a fee for issuing the check. You do not need to have a checking account at the bank. The bank becomes both the drawer and the drawee, and the holder becomes the payee. Once issued, the cashier's check cannot be canceled and cannot become stale. The bank, which has been paid for the check, guarantees its payment. A bank that wrongfully refuses to pay a cashier's check becomes liable to the holder for all expenses incurred, loss of interest, and consequential damages (UCC 3-411).

A cashier's check is used when a person either does not have a checking account or does not want to go through the procedure of having a check certified. A cashier's check is considered safer than a personal check. At one time this type of check was readily acceptable in the business world. However, because this special check is also being counterfeited, banks now require one or more types of identification. No longer will the bank accept one without question.

Traveler's Checks

traveler's check check used primarily by travelers in which main feature is security against loss or theft

A **traveler's check** is a popular type of cashier's check issued primarily by private companies, such as American Express and the American Automobile Association (Figure 22.3). They may be purchased through a bank, but most major banks purchase and then issue them on behalf of these private companies. It is used primarily by tourists who want a safe method of carrying funds while traveling. A traveler's check differs from a cashier's check in two ways: It may be purchased in many denominations, such as $20, $50, and $100, and it is issued with the name of the payee omitted.

Purchasing traveler's checks is a simple matter. The buyer (drawer) pays for the checks in the requested denominations and pays a service charge to the issuing bank or company (drawee). The checks have two signature blanks. When the checks are issued, the traveler signs his or her name on each check in the presence of the person issuing the check. When a check is used to pay for goods or services, the traveler signs the check a second time, this time in the presence of the person receiving the check (UCC 3-104). At this point, the check becomes either bearer paper or order paper (by inserting the name of a payee).

FIGURE 22.2
Cashier's Check

FIGURE 22.3
Traveler's Check

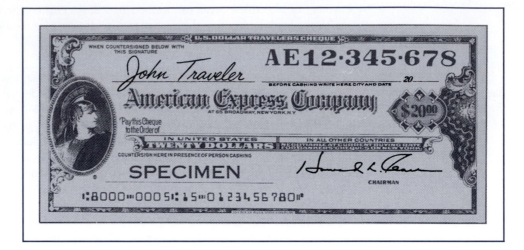

Traveler's checks have two primary advantages. They are readily accepted all over the world. In addition, the traveler can recover the value of the checks quickly if they are lost or stolen, provided notice of the theft or loss is given to the issuing company as soon as possible. Whether checks are lost or stolen, the traveler is protected even if her or his signature is forged and the checks are cashed.

BANK'S LIABILITY FOR WRONGFUL PAYMENT OF A CHECK

A bank's liability to the drawer is affected by the following circumstances: (1) alteration of a check, (2) forgery of the drawer's signature, (3) forgery of an indorsement, (4) missing indorsement, and (5) death of the depositor (drawer).

Alteration of a Check

The bank has an implied duty to examine checks presented for payment by its depositors (drawers) and to use ordinary care (standards applied in the banking business) when doing so (UCC 4-406). If a bank pays a check that has been materially altered, the bank is liable to the drawer for the amount of the alteration because the depositor's instruction to the bank is to pay the exact amount on the face of the check. A material alteration usually involves raising the amount—both the figures and the words—on the face of the check. A bank is held responsible for failing to detect the alteration because it has both the opportunity and the expertise to examine the check before honoring it. The bank, however, may charge the drawer's account for the original amount of the check. In addition, the bank may sue the person to whom the amount on the altered check was paid because the presenter of the check for payment and each prior transferor warrant that the check has not been altered. If a cashier's check is involved, however, the bank, as the drawer, cannot recover on this ground from the presenting party if the party is a holder in due course acting in good faith (UCC 3-417; UCC 4-208). The reason is that an instrument's drawer is in a better position than a holder in due course to know whether the instrument has been altered. Under these circumstances, the ultimate loser is the party who first paid the altered check. Because altering a check is criminal in nature, the forger can be prosecuted and made to pay the amount of the alteration. Such prosecution may not be easy because there is a good chance that this forger is judgment proof or cannot be located.

FIGURE 22.4
A Check That Has Not
Been Filled Out Properly

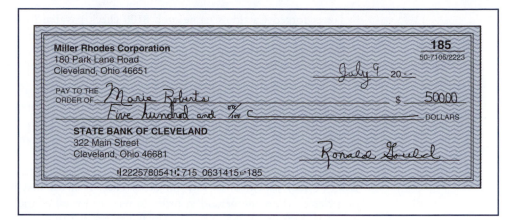

Given made out a check payable to Davis for $42. Davis raised the amount to $420 and cashed the check at a neighborhood grocery store. The store presented the check for payment at the local bank on which it was drawn. The bank paid the check and charged the $420 to Given's account. Given can recover $378, the amount of the alteration, from the bank. The bank is liable for this $378 difference but can recover the amount from the grocery store based on breach of warranty. The grocery store can seek recovery of the $378 from Davis if she can be located or is not judgment proof.

There are some exceptions to the rule regarding a bank's responsibility for an altered check. A drawer whose negligence contributes to the alteration may not be able to hold the bank responsible. Good examples are when a person writes a check and carelessly leaves too much space around the numbers and words (this practice allows a dishonest person to add additional numbers and words, as in Figure 22.4), or the person simply signs a check and allows a person like the payee to fill in the dollar amount (UCC 4-401). A bank may be relieved from liability if the bank takes reasonable precautions to examine checks before honoring them. Another exception is a failure by the drawer to notify a bank of alterations promptly (within a reasonable time) from the time the altered, canceled check is returned to the depositor. Failure to give prompt notice may relieve a bank from liability for paying an altered check, even though the bank was negligent (UCC 4-406).

Forgery of a Drawer's Signature

forged check check on which drawer's signature is made without authorization

A bank is generally liable to a drawer-depositor if it pays a **forged check**, one in which the drawer's signature is made without authorization. The bank must return to the drawer's account any money paid out as the result of the forgery. The bank has a duty to pay out funds according to the drawer's order. A check with a forged signature is not prepared and paid according to that order; therefore, a forged signature on a check has no legal effect as the signature of a drawer (UCC 3-403). The drawer must report the forgery promptly (within thirty calendar days of the receipt or availability of the bank statement and canceled checks or substitutes, if they are normally included) so as to hold the bank liable even if the drawer can show that he or she took reasonable care to prevent forgeries (UCC 4-406). It makes no difference whether the bank was or was not negligent. A bank has the drawer's signature on file (the bank requires a signature card from each person who opens a checking account) and assumes the burden of knowing that signature. Since verifying the signature on every check would amount to a high cost of doing business, banks keep this cost down by only verifying the signatures of checks that are written for large denominations (e.g., $1,000, $5,000, etc.).

Lester forged Cataldo's name on a $100 check payable to herself. She then indorsed the check for value to Matties, who was unaware of the forgery. Matties presented the check to Cataldo's bank and received payment. Cataldo discovered the forgery when he received his next bank statement and immediately notified his bank.

In this example, the bank must restore the $100 to Cataldo's account. The bank, however, cannot collect from Matties, who took the check in good faith and for value. By paying the check, the bank admits the genuineness of the drawer's signature. The bank is considered to have greater knowledge and experience than an indorser in detecting forgeries and is therefore liable for the loss.

Since it is possible these days to have more than one forgery by the same person, the UCC (4-406) provides for such an occurrence. It states that if there are a number of forgeries by the same person in order to recover for all of the forgeries, you must have reported the first forged check within the thirty-day time frame mentioned previously. Failure to notify the bank within the required time period discharges the bank's liability for all forged checks that it pays out prior to notification.

As with the alteration of a check, a drawer whose negligence substantially contributes to a forgery may not be able to require the bank to recredit his or her account for the amount of the check (UCC 3-406). The depositor's liability, however, may be reduced by the amount of loss caused by negligence on the part of the bank or person paying the instrument if the negligence substantially contributed to the loss (UCC 3-406). An example of such negligence is a drawer who signs checks in different ways from that shown on the bank's signature card. Such practices make it much harder for a bank to detect a forgery. Another example of negligence is the failure of a business owner to keep a signature stamp in a safe place so that unauthorized people have access to it. Still another example is the depositor's failure to examine his or her monthly statement of account and canceled checks (if returned by the bank) to discover if any entries on the statement seem out of line or if any of the signatures on the checks are forgeries.

Forgery of an Indorsement

The payee or subsequent holder may discover that his or her indorsement on the back of the check has been forged. Neither, however, would have any liability for the forgery. Furthermore, if the payor bank previously charged the depositor's (drawer's) account, it must recredit the amount charged.

Based on a warranty that all signatures on the check are authentic and authorized, a payor bank that pays a check with a forged indorsement can recover from the prior transferor, who in turn can collect from his or her transferor. The ultimate loss falls on the first party that took the check with a forged indorsement. (Keep in mind that a forged indorsement does not transfer title; therefore, any party who takes an instrument with a forged indorsement cannot become a holder.) Any further recovery must be from the forger if he or she can be located or is not judgment proof.

Marvin drew a check on M and G Bank made payable to the order of Rossiter, who took the check. Donovan stole the check from Rossiter, forged Rossiter's indorsement, and cashed it at a local farm market. The farm market presented the check to its bank, Charter Two, for collection, and Charter Two presented it to M and G Bank for payment. M and G paid the check. Marvin and Rossiter have no liability for the check. Based on breach of warranty, however, M and G Bank can collect from Charter Two; Charter Two can recover from the farm market, which can recover from Donovan, the person who stole the check.

A forged indorsement is treated differently from the forgery of a drawer's (depositor's) signature. A depositor has three years from the time the canceled check with the forged indorsement is returned to him or her to report the forgery. If not reported within this time frame, the bank is relieved of liability (UCC 4-111).

A forged indorsement on bearer paper has no effect on the validity of the paper. Bearer paper is negotiable by delivery alone, and an indorsement is not required.

If the name of a fictitious payee is put on a check and that name is then indorsed, the bank is not liable. In this situation, it is presumed that the drawer has been negligent. Thus, the drawee bank will not be responsible as long as it used reasonable care in accepting and cashing the check.

> At a Chamber of Commerce dinner, Savage introduced herself to Rickles as "Dr. Vera Ralston," a noted authority on cancer. She claimed to be raising money for the Cancer Foundation. Rickles donated $1,000 by writing a check payable to the order of "Dr. Ralston." Savage indorsed the check as "Dr. Ralston" and cashed it at the Taylor National Bank. The bank is not liable to Rickles.

Missing Indorsement

A bank may be liable for any loss that results from its cashing a check that lacks an indorsement. Failure to indorse a check is considered improper presentment, and the person presenting the check is not a holder.

> Genovese, a teacher, lost his paycheck. A finder presented the check for payment to the bank on which the check was drawn. A new teller at the bank cashed the check without an indorsement. The bank is liable for improperly paying the check.

Death of the Depositor

A depositor (drawer) may deposit checks in or draw checks on his or her account shortly before death. A check is an order to pay, and death revokes that order. A bank, however, may not be notified immediately of the drawer's death. Section 4-405 of the Code protects banks in this situation by providing that a bank may pay or certify a check that has been issued or whose collection has been undertaken, until it has knowledge of the drawer's death and has had reasonable time to act. Even with knowledge of the death, the bank may continue to pay or certify checks drawn against the account on or before the date of death for a period of ten days after the date of the drawer's death unless a person claiming an interest in that account (e.g., an heir) orders the bank to stop payment (UCC 4-405). This rule allows holders of checks issued shortly before death to cash them without having to file a claim against the deceased drawer's estate. Filing a claim, which in effect is a mere formality, could be burdensome on the bank. Without this provision, banks would constantly be required to check and see if their depositors are still living.

> On August 8, Marin gave Sikes a personal check for $500 drawn on the Midland Bank. Marin was killed in an accident on August 9. On August 10, Midland Bank cashed the check for Sikes, not knowing of Marin's death. Even though the bank was unaware of Marin's death, it had the authority to honor the check.

AVAILABILITY OF FUNDS FROM DEPOSITED CHECKS

The Expedited Funds Availability (EFA) Act of 1987 was passed to improve check processing procedures. The Federal Reserve Board then issued Regulation CC to implement this act. Regulation CC sets out the availability schedule for checks deposited with a depository bank (the first bank to receive funds such as cash or checks). One purpose of the EFA Act and Regulation CC was to reduce the "float period," the period between the time that a customer deposits a check and the time that the bank makes available to the depositor the funds represented by the check. Until this law was passed, consumer groups charged that Americans were losing millions of dollars annually because banks were freezing funds for undue amounts of time. They were making customers wait until the check had been honored by the payor bank. This delay sometimes took two weeks, even though 99 percent of the time the banks were getting credit for the money within two days.

The Expedited Funds Availability Act and Regulation CC now limit the number of days banks can place holds on checks that customers (a consumer or business entity) deposit in their accounts. Consequently, because of this law and because of the way banks do business (as will be outlined under the section Electronic Funds Transfer), the float time between the writing of a check and its deduction from a customer's account is considerably reduced. It also requires banks to disclose to depositors their policy as to when funds deposited are available for their use. Individual banks may set their own float time as long as they stay within the guidelines set by the federal laws referred to earlier. The law requires that any local check deposited must be available for withdrawal by check or cash within one business day following the banking day on which the deposit was made. A check is *local* if the first bank (depository bank) in which the check is deposited (and payment is to be made from this bank) and the bank on which the check is drawn (written) are located within the same Federal Reserve check processing region. (The Federal Reserve Board designates the locations of check processing regions.) Deposits include cash deposits and deposits by an electronic payment, government checks, cashier's checks, certified checks, the first $100 of a day's check deposits and checks for which the banks receiving and paying the checks are branches of the same institution. A banking day is any day or any part of a day that a bank is open to carry on substantially all of its banking activities.

In addition, the act requires that the first $100 of any deposit be available for cash withdrawal on the opening of the next business day after deposit. If a local check is deposited, the next $400 is to be available for withdrawal by no later than 5:00 P.M. on the next business day. For nonlocal checks, the funds must be available for withdrawal within not more than five business days. A nonlocal check is one deposited in a bank located in a different Federal Reserve check processing region than the payor-drawee bank.

CHECK PROCESSING—PRE-TWENTY-FIRST CENTURY

The check collection process begins when a person deposits a check into his or her personal checking account. The customer's local bank of choice is called a **depository bank** since it is the first bank to receive the check for payment. At this time, the bank credits the amount of the check to the customer's account, but this is only conditional credit because the check must go through a clearing process. After the amount of the check has been collected from the **payor bank** (the bank on which the check is drawn, namely, the drawee's bank), the conditional credit becomes final credit. The customer's depository bank will follow the rules described in the previous section when it comes to making the funds available from the check to the customer. This clearing process (actually the bank collection process) is governed by Article 4 of the UCC and the new Check Clearing in the 21st Century Act of 2003 (the Check 21 Act), which went into effect in 2004. *This new act will cause the check collection process to speed up some from what is described in this section as more banks implement this new act.*

depository bank the first bank to receive a check for payment

payor bank the bank on which a check is drawn

Let's follow the check in Figure 22.5 through the check collection process—that is, from the time it was issued until it was finally paid. To begin, Calvin Turner of Rochester, New York, issues a check to P.C. Innovations (the payee-holder) of Cleveland, Ohio, in payment for a computer he purchased while visiting a friend in Cleveland. At this point, P.C. Innovations in Cleveland, Ohio, if it wished, could collect on the check by presenting it directly to Central Trust Bank of Rochester, New York (Turner's bank), for payment. This step is not only an impractical one but also unnecessary, costly, and time consuming since the check is easily transferable. As a holder of the check, P.C. Innovations can negotiate it. What typically happens is that P.C. Innovations will deposit the check in its own bank (in this case, First Niagara of Cleveland, Ohio) and let this bank, as agent for P.C. Innovations, collect the amount of the check.

First Niagara, the depository bank, will conditionally (temporarily) credit the account of the payee (P.C. Innovations). First Niagara will then forward Turner's check to a series of **collecting (intermediate)** banks, usually one of the twelve Federal Banks, that collect checks for other banks. Each intermediate bank conditionally credits the account of the prior bank. As a collecting bank—a sub agent—it must forward the check to the next bank no later than midnight of the banking day following the day of receipt (UCC 4-202). The check will eventually reach Central Trust, Turner's bank, the payor bank.

collecting bank
collects checks for other banks, usually a Federal Reserve Bank

FIGURE 22.5
How a Check Is Processed for Payment

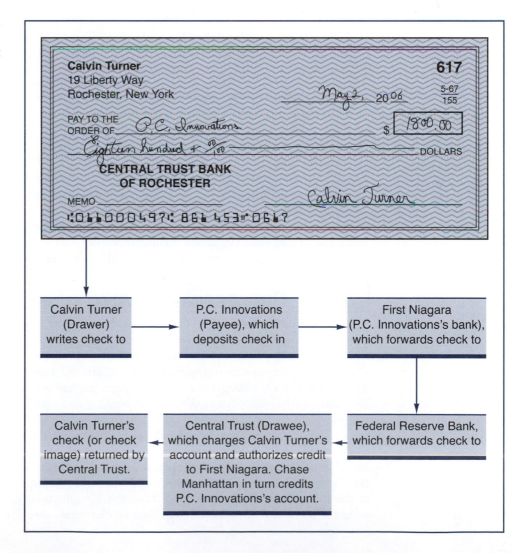

When Turner's check reaches Central Trust, upon which it was drawn, the bank debits (charges) Turner's (the drawer's) account (provided there is enough money to cover the check). Central Trust then authorizes a Federal Reserve Bank to credit the amount of the check to First Niagara's account in Cleveland, Ohio, which in turn credits P.C. Innovations's account. When the check is paid (honored), that is the end of the transaction. If the check is not paid (dishonored, in this case by Central Trust), each bank in the collection process revokes the provisional credit it gave, and the unpaid check is returned to the depositor (in this case, P.C. Innovations).

The collection process just described deals with check collections between customers of different banks. When both customers use the same bank, the check collection process is much simpler.

> Benton and Cateer both have their checking account at the Countrywide Bank. When the bank opened on Wednesday morning, Benton deposited into his checking account a $500 check made out to his order (the payee) by Cateer (the drawer). Countrywide issued Benton a conditional credit for $500.

In this example, Countrywide is both the depository bank and the payor bank. Under UCC 4-215, if the bank does not dishonor the check by the opening of the bank's second banking day, following its receipt, the check is considered paid. Thus, when the bank opens Friday morning, if Cateer's check was not dishonored, Benton's conditional credit becomes final.

Keep in mind that today, because of advanced technology, checks are processed in a different manner. At one time, an employee of each bank in the check collection process would manually handle each check that passed through the bank for payment or collection. Now, instead of checks being physically passed on from the depository bank, they may be transferred and processed electronically by each receiving bank. Your bank, as the final resting place for the check you wrote on that bank (payor bank), may have received only an image (picture) from banks involved in the check collection process. You in turn will also receive a check image for your records (UCC 4-110). These check images are valid as legal proof of payment according to the Internal Revenue Service, local and state governments, courts of law, and merchants.

Each bank has an obligation to use ordinary care in performing its collection operations. Ordinary care involves forwarding checks and sending out required notices correctly and within the time period mentioned earlier. Failure of a bank to use ordinary care in a collection process may subject it to liability for any losses suffered.

CHECK PROCESSING—TWENTY-FIRST CENTURY

The Check Clearing for the 21st Century Act, a federal act also known as the Check 21 Law, is in full swing. It has replaced much of the law of check processing that you have already read in the section of this chapter entitled "Check Processing—Pre-Twenty-First Century." Some points in the section, however, are still valid. This new law passed in 2004 has drastically changed the way that banks process over 70 billion checks a year. It is designed to move checks through the banking and clearing systems more quickly and more efficiently. Traditionally, banks have physically moved original paper checks from the bank where the checks are deposited to the bank that pays them, usually by truck or by air. Now they are moved back and forth electronically. This means less "float" time that gave you a few extra days to deposit money in your account. (Float time is the time between when a check is written and when it is presented for payment at the drawer's financial institution.) Your check might even clear the same day you write the check and be deducted from your account that same day, so be sure you have enough money in your checking account at the time you write a check. For banks this is good news because they are likely to be collecting a lot more money in bounced check fees, but of course this would not be good for the bank's customers.

substitute check legal copy of an original check

Substitute Check   When you write a check, you may never see that check again. That is because the Check 21 law creates a new kind of negotiable instrument called a **substitute check** which is a paper copy of an original check. It is specifically formatted so that it can be processed as if it is an original check. The front of a substitute check states: "This is a legal copy of your check." Since it is the legal equivalent of the original paper, parties cannot refuse to accept the substitute check for proof-of-payment purposes. You could also use the substitute check as part of your own recordkeeping file. A substitute check must be printed according to strict standards so that the substitute check can be used in the same way as the original check.

> Aaron from the state of Washington is visiting in New York City. He purchases some expensive jewelry for $8,000 and writes a check on his bank in Washington. The jewelry store presents the check to its bank in New York City for payment.

In this example, the check could clear quickly. The New York bank will send the information from the original check across the country electronically, have its branch or other partner print out a paper substitute check, and present it to Aaron's bank. Aaron's bank is required to accept the substitute check.

Prior to the Check 21 law, Aaron's check was physically moved from the New York Bank by truck or air back to his bank in the state of Washington. However, the route was not always a direct route. At a minimum, the check would first be processed through a Federal Reserve Bank. When the check reached Aaron's bank, it would be "cleared," meaning the funds would be taken out of Aaron's account and transferred into the jewelry store's account with the New York bank. This process could take a few days, but certainly not, say, one day.

Other Points About the Check 21 Law

- Your original check is kept by the bank that first receives it. It may be kept on file or destroyed. The receiving bank makes this decision.
- Some banks do not return checks at all. If you need a canceled check to prove a payment you made, you will need to make a request to your bank. Some banks charge a fee for these copies. Banks that return canceled checks may send you a mix of original checks and substitute checks.
- Under state and federal law you are protected against errors in your account, whether you receive original canceled checks or substitute checks, or both, with your account statement.
- The loss of "float time" of a few days between the time you write a check and the time the check clears is a serious enough disadvantage of the Check 21 law to alert you to be sure you have money in your account before you write a check.
- Instead of providing substitute checks, some banks may provide customers with image statements showing multiple pictures of canceled checks on a page.

electronic fund transfer (EFT) system allowing depositors to transfer money from their accounts to accounts of creditors and stores

ELECTRONIC FUNDS TRANSFER

An **electronic fund transfer (EFT)** is any transfer of funds over communication networks such as an electronic terminal, a telephone, a computer, or a magnetic tape. The advantages of electronic transfers can be summed up in one sentence: No physical transfers of cash or paper instruments are involved. EFT is practically instantaneous. Money can be transferred electronically from your bank account to that of a creditor or as a customer into the account of a store where you made a purchase. Think of EFT as an electronic marketplace, or a virtual shopping mall. Electronic processing is very common today and may be even more common in the future. Some advantages of EFT are

1. EFT payments are safer than checks; consequently less worries about forged, counterfeit, and altered checks.
2. EFT eliminates lost or stolen checks.
3. EFT makes payments easy and convenient.
4. EFT payments facilitate online banking at your financial institution.

You can even buy groceries via EFTs. You stop at a grocery store and buy groceries costing $100. You hand the cashier a plastic card (called a debit card) with a secret code number. The cashier inserts the card into a device linked to your bank's computer. The computer is then given instructions to immediately deduct the amount of your purchases from your bank account and to add that amount to the store's bank account. Because the transaction took place at the *point of sale,* it is referred to as a POS transaction. With such a system, no money or checks change hands. POS systems offer the following advantages: Consumers can carry less cash; checkout time is quicker, especially when compared with the time it takes to have a check approved; and the float time is eliminated.

Banks now have the equipment to handle some other electronic transactions. At *ATMs*, people can instantly receive cash from their checking or savings account by inserting a plastic identification card into an electronic terminal and entering a personal identification number (PIN). People can also deposit to an account, transfer funds between savings and checking accounts, pay credit card charges and utility bills, and even make mortgage payments. These ATMs are conveniently located on the bank's main premises and at its branches as well as in key locations such as shopping centers, supermarkets, airports, and apartment buildings. *Pay-by-Internet*—another type of electronic transaction—permits customers to access their bank's computer system using the Internet to direct the bank to transfer funds between their accounts (e.g., from checking to savings, or vice versa) or to transfer money from either a savings or checking account to a designated third party, such as a department store or a utility company.

Yet another type of electronic transaction allows a *direct deposit* to be made to a customer's account through an electronic terminal if the customer authorizes such a deposit in advance. Examples of this type of transaction include an employer making payroll payments directly into an employee's account and the federal government directly depositing Social Security payments into an eligible person's checking or savings account. A customer may also authorize a financial institution to automatically deduct the amount needed to pay, for example, utility bills or installment loans, at recurrent intervals and make payments to the required third party.

An electronic fund transfer relating to consumers is governed by the Electronic Fund Transfer Act (EFTA) of 1978. This act outlines the basic rights, duties, and liabilities of users of electronic fund transfer systems. In addition, the Federal Reserve Board, which has been empowered to issue regulations to help implement and interpret the act, has done so through Regulation E. The Electronic Fund Transfer Act and Regulation E have established certain consumer rights. For example:

1. If a customer notifies the issuer bank within two days of learning that his or her debit card, a plastic card that allows the bearer to transfer funds to a merchant's account, has been lost or stolen, the customer is liable for only $50 for unauthorized use. If a customer does not notify the bank within this two-day period, the customer's liability is $500. If the customer fails to notify the bank within sixty

days after an unauthorized use appears on the customer's bank statement, the customer can be held liable for more than $500. (Federal law allows states to reduce the liability on customers for lost or stolen debit cards.)

2. A bank must provide a customer with a record of a transaction made through a computer terminal.

3. A customer has sixty days from the receipt of a bank statement to notify the bank (orally or in writing) of any error that appears on a bank statement. The bank has ten days to investigate.

4. A bank can send an unsolicited EFT debit card to a customer only if the card is not yet validated (ready for use). An unsolicited card can be validated upon request of the consumer.

5. A bank must provide a monthly statement to an EFT customer at the end of the month that the customer conducts a transaction. Otherwise, a quarterly statement must be provided to the customer.

A bank is liable for wrongful dishonor if it fails to pay an electronic fund transfer when there are sufficient funds in the customer's account.

ONLINE BANKING

Online banking, which has been with us for some time, eliminates the need to make trips to the bank or to an ATM machine. Thousands of banks throughout the United States (and the world) offer online banking services. In fact several banks operate exclusively on the Internet. Many banks believe that they must offer online services; if not, they will lose customer base to banks that do offer these services. On the upside, online banking is less expensive for banks because they need fewer employees to maintain automated systems. In addition, online banking is profitable because banks charge fees for their online services.

Customers use computers to take advantage of the online services that a bank offers, such as paying bills, transferring funds among accounts, and initiating the process of applying for a loan. As yet, there is no way to deposit or withdraw funds online; no doubt, however, we will be able to transfer and otherwise move funds around electronically on the Internet in the not-too-distant future.

E-MONEY

Instead of using credit cards, for example, to pay bills or buy goods and services, why can't we use physical money to pay bills over the Internet? Major banks and technology companies are investigating ways to replace physical cash with virtual cash in the form of electronic impulses. These plans use *digital cash*, which is nothing more than a way of representing money (dollar bills and coins) in a digital form on an electronic medium. The physical dollars and coins through an electronic medium could be downloaded over a bank's telephone lines, stored on a computer, and transmitted to, for example, a pizza parlor to pay for the pizza that you ordered for home delivery. In other words, instead of using a credit card, you pay cash for what you buy over the Internet. Or you could pay a friend online the $50 you owe her. The main advantage of digital cash over a credit card is that you can use digital cash on a person-to-person basis, whereas a credit card payment can be made only to a seller that has registered with a credit card company. The use of digital cash when fully developed will change the way we use money.

Summary

A check is a substitute for money. While debt cards are favored over personal checks, checks, and especially commercial checks, remain an integral part of the business world. Their use is governed by the UCC. A debtor-creditor relationship exists between a bank and its depositor. After a depositor puts money in a bank, the bank owes that sum to the depositor and promises to pay the money either to the depositor or to someone else at the depositor's order. The bank is always obligated to honor the depositor's checks if there are sufficient funds to cover them and if the check is not stale—that is, more than six months old—or if the bank is suspicious of either the check or the holder. If a bank wrongfully dishonors a check, it is liable in damages to the depositor. A drawer may stop payment on his or her check by giving the bank a stop-payment order either orally or in writing. If the bank disobeys a stop-payment order and pays the instrument, it is liable to the drawer for any loss resulting from its failure to observe the order. Of course, a customer who stops payment without legal justification also has liability. His or her liability is to the holder for the amount of the check plus damages. Depositors have obligations to keep enough money in their checking accounts to cover checks written; to examine the monthly bank statement they receive and promptly advise the bank of any mistakes; to report check forgeries and alterations to the bank; and above all, not to write a bad check—that is, one written when there is an insufficient amount of money in the checking account to cover it.

There are special types of checks that perform different functions. These checks include certified checks, cashier's checks, and traveler's checks.

The bank may not charge the depositor's account when there is an alteration, a forgery, or a missing indorsement, assuming, of course, that the drawer was not negligent in the transaction. A bank may pay a check after the death of a drawer until it receives notice of the death or for ten days after the drawer's death.

Congress passed the Expedited Funds Availability Act in 1987 to improve check processing procedures. It then issued Regulation CC to implement this act. Regulation CC sets out the availability schedule for checks deposited with a depository bank. One purpose of the act was to reduce the "float period" between the time a customer deposits a check and the time the bank makes the funds represented by the check available to the depositor. Until this law was passed, banks were freezing checking account funds for undue amounts of time.

The check collection process in the twenty-first century has been modified with the passage of the Check 21 Act. It allows banks to handle more checks electronically. This makes check processing faster and more efficient. Prior to the Check 21 Act, checks were physically moved through the processing system. This meant more "float time" for checks. Now, a check written on a certain day may even "clear" and be charged to your account by the end of that day.

The electronic funds transfer (EFT) system allows money to be transferred electronically as a direct deposit into a customer's account or to the accounts of creditors or stores where the depositors have made purchases. The EFT system also provides customers with instant cash from their checking or savings account at ATM machines. Many banks also have the capability of providing online bank services to customers. An electronic fund transfer relating to consumers is governed by the Electronic Fund Transfer Act (EFTA) of 1978. In addition, the Federal Reserve Board, which has been empowered to enforce the provisions of the act, has adopted Regulation E to further interpret it.

A bank is liable for wrongful dishonor if it fails to pay an electronic fund transfer when there are sufficient funds in the customer's account. The use of digital cash (e-money), which would replace physical cash with virtual cash, is now being investigated by major banks and technology companies.

Important Legal terms

bad check	electronic fund transfer (EFT)	stale check
cashier's check	forged check	stop-payment order
certified check	overdrafts	substitute check
collecting banks	payor bank	traveler's check
depository bank	postdated check	

Questions and Problems for Discussion

1. A check written on December 3 is postdated to December 20 of the same year. Which of the following statements is correct?
   a. The check ceases to be demand paper and is payable on December 20.
   b. A postdated check destroys negotiability.
   c. A bank that pays a postdated check early is automatically liable to the drawer for damages.
   d. A person who takes a postdated check may not become a holder in due course.

2. Saxon died April 12. His sister-in-law immediately filed a claim against Saxon's estate for $500, the amount of a check issued to her on August 18 (eight months earlier) by Saxon for her services as an accountant. Liability was denied by the person in charge of Saxon's estate, who claimed that, because the check was more than six months old, it was void. Does a check become void because the payee failed to cash it within a six-month period?

3. A merchant would probably prefer that customers use which of the following types of payment?
   a. checks
   b. credit cards
   c. point-of-sale (POS) transfers
   d. automated teller machines (ATMs)

4. Perkins, a customer of Select Bank, had his checkbook containing several checks stolen. The thief wrote a check each week for $100 and forged Perkins's name on each check beginning in April 2005. The thief had no trouble cashing each check, and Select Bank charged each check to Perkins's account. Perkins, however, did not discover the forgeries until he reconciled the four monthly bank statements for May, June, July, and August all at one time in August 2005. At that time, he discovered sixteen forged checks, each written for $100. Perkins then notified the bank immediately of the forgeries and demanded that Select Bank credit his account for the full $1,600. The bank refused to do so. Is Perkins entitled to recover from Select Bank on these forgeries?

5. A burglar entered Bowie's house and stole, among other things, some blank checks from a checkbook. Bowie did not realize that the checks were missing. When Bowie received her bank statement, she found a canceled check for $50 on which her signature had been forged. She immediately notified her bank. Will the bank be liable to Bowie?

6. Haines died on March 8. Five days prior to her death, Haines had issued a check to Marcum in payment of a personal debt owed. Cherokee National Bank on which the check was drawn paid it to Marcum on March 9. The bank, however, had no knowledge of the death of Haines. Was payment by the bank proper in this case?

7. Marcus purchased a one-week package deal to a summer resort area through a travel agency. Because the price had to be paid in advance, Marcus sent the travel agency a certified check for $900 drawn on the Citizens National Bank. The next day he decided to cancel his trip and requested the bank to stop payment on the check. Could Marcus order the bank to stop payment on the certified check?

8. At a book fair on August 15, Lee, an encyclopedia salesperson, talked Tanaka into purchasing a set of encyclopedias for $450. Tanaka gave Lee a check for $450. Later in the day, Tanaka changed her mind about purchasing the books and issued an oral stop-payment order to her bank. On September 1, Tanaka went to the bank and signed a written stop-payment order, but the bank had already honored the check on August 31. Tanaka demanded that the bank return the money to her account. Must the bank comply with Tanaka's demand?

9. Martin paid a $100 debt to Adler with a personal check drawn on her account at the Arvac National Bank. Before properly negotiating the check to Chives, Adler raised the amount of the check to $1,100. Chives then cashed the check at the Arvac National Bank, obtaining $1,100. When Martin received her canceled checks and discovered the alteration, she asked the bank to

return the $1,000 to her account. If Martin was not negligent, must the bank comply with her request?

10. Randolph received a check drawn on Sagamore Bank by Michaels. It was dated May 1. On December 23, Randolph appeared at the Sagamore Bank to cash Michaels's check. If the Sagamore Bank refuses on the basis that the check was stale, then

a. the Sagamore Bank is liable to Randolph
b. the Sagamore Bank is not liable to any person
c. the Sagamore Bank is liable to Michaels
d. Randolph will take the loss since the check is stale

Cases for Review

1. Begg made out a check payable to the order of Newwall, a subcontractor, for $32,000 in November to cover work in progress. In January, Begg issued another check to Newwall to cover the entire amount owed to Newwall, including the original $32,000. At the same time, Begg issued a stop-payment order to the drawee bank for the original $32,000. In spite of the stop-payment order, the bank nevertheless honored the check when presented for payment by Newwall. When Begg examined his statement several months later, he discovered that the original check had been paid and therefore requested that the bank recredit his account for $32,000. The bank refused, claiming that Begg did not examine his statement in a timely manner and that, if he had done so, he would have seen that the $32,000 had been paid and therefore not issued the second check for the full amount of the cost of the work. Must the bank recredit Begg's account with $32,000? (*J. W. Reynolds Lumber Co.* v. *Smackover State Bank,* 836 S.W.2d 853)

2. Tally's personal secretary, who managed his Washington, D.C., law office, swindled him out of $52,825. In seven instances, she had signed his name on bank withdrawals from the American Security Bank. As custodian of Tally's bank records, the secretary had avoided detection for over four years. Tally brought action against the American Security Bank to recover the $52,825. Is the bank liable to Tally? (*Tally* v. *American Security Bank,* 355 UCCRS 215, U.S. District Court, D.C.)

3. Jerman bought several cashier's checks, payable to named payees, from a bank. The checks were cashed with forged indorsements, and Jerman lost her money. She sued the bank that issued and paid the checks. Is the bank liable? (*Jerman* v. *Bank of America National Trust & Savings Assn.,* 87 Cal. Rptr. 88)

4. Stewart received a check as a payee drawn on the Citizens' Bank. The bank refused to pay the check even though there were sufficient funds in the drawer's account. Stewart sued the bank on the check. Is Stewart entitled to collect from the Citizens' Bank? (*Stewart* v. *Citizens' and Southern National Bank,* Ga. 138 Ga. App. 209)

5. A certified check for $16 payable to Sam Goody was altered (after it had been certified) to $1,600. The check was then used to pay for merchandise costing $1,600 that had been ordered from Goody. The drawee bank refused to honor the check because of the alteration. Is the bank liable to Goody for the $1,600? (*Sam Goody, Inc.* v. *Franklin National Bank of Long Island,* N.Y. 57 Misc.2d 193)

6. Bank of America in error transmitted money to Sanati in a wire transfer. The bank immediately discovered its error and promptly attempted to recover this money from Sanati. Sanati refused to return the funds claiming that, because the bank was negligent when it transferred the money, the money need not be returned to the bank. Is Sanati correct? (*Bank of America* v. *Sanati,* 14 Cal. Rptr. 2d 615)

7. Siniscalchi wrote a check on his account in the Valley Bank of New York and then negotiated the check on to a holder. He placed a stop-payment order on the check with his bank two days after the holder had cashed the check. Siniscalchi, however, was unaware that the check had been cashed. Upon checking its transactions,

the Valley Bank discovered that Siniscalchi's check had been cashed and charged his account. Siniscalchi sued the bank, claiming that Valley Bank ignored his stop-payment order. Is the bank liable in damages to Siniscalchi for violating the stop-payment order? (*Siniscalchi* v. *Valley Bank of New York,* 359 N.Y.S.2d 173)

8. Kendall Yacht Corporation was running into financial problems. Its owners, Lawrence and Linda Kendall, obtained permission from its bank, United California, with which it had corporate accounts, to write overdrafts from this account temporarily. Because the account became so badly overdrawn, the bank dishonored a number of their checks. The Kendalls then brought suit, charging that the bank's wrongful dishonor of the checks damaged their reputation. They offered proof that several civil and criminal proceedings had been brought against them for writing checks against insufficient funds. Do the Kendalls have a legitimate cause of action against United California Bank? (*Kendall Yacht Corporation* v. *United California Bank,* 50 Cal. App. 3d 949)

THE CASE OF THE DISHONORED CHECK

Brogan had an option to purchase a valuable piece of land for $500,000, provided he exercised the option by a certain date by mailing a deposit check for $50,000. He drew a check for that amount on his account at Third American Bank and mailed it to the landowner. At the time he drew the check, he had $60,000 in his account but owed the bank $30,000 for a loan that was overdue. The bank refused to honor the check, Brogan's option became void, and the landowner sold the land to someone else, resulting in a severe loss to Brogan. Brogan sued the bank for damages.

The Trial

At trial, Brogan's attorneys proved the value of the land, Brogan's losses, and the fact that Brogan had always paid the bank on time, except for the most recent payment that was overdue. The bank's attorneys proved that Brogan was over sixty days late on his last loan payment and that it was their practice not to notify customers that there might be insufficient funds in their accounts to cover all checks written, as doing so would place an undue burden on the banking system.

The Arguments at Trial

Brogan's attorneys argued that a bank has no right to dishonor a check except for the normal reasons permitted by law, such as a suspected forgery, an improper indorsement, and so forth. They further argued that the bank, based on its relationship with Brogan, should have contacted him before dishonoring the check so that he could have taken other action to prevent his loss. The bank's attorneys argued that Brogan's being overdue on his last loan payment indicated he was in financial trouble, that they had a right to seize Brogan's account to cover the overdue payment, and that instead they simply refused to honor checks on Brogan's account until the overdue loan was paid. They further argued that based on banking industry customs, it is the responsibility of the customer and not the bank to make sure there are sufficient funds to cover checks written.

Questions to Discuss

1. Who do you feel has the better argument, Brogan or the bank?
2. Whom do you think the judge or jury will favor, Brogan or the bank?
3. Do you feel that Brogan should prevail because the bank can afford the loss more than Brogan?
4. Under what circumstances, if any, should a bank be able to offset a loan to a customer against that customer's bank account?

Actors, Inc., a union that represents 25,000 stage hands, hired Lund as their new comptroller. No attempt was made to verify his background or prior employment history. Actors, Inc., maintained its checking account with a New York City bank. Within the first three months, Lund forged the signature of the appropriate company officer on four Actors, Inc., checks totaling $200,000. The checks were made payable to a person named Regal. The forged signatures seemed quite authentic and did not cause any problem when presented to the bank for payment. The bank paid them without question. Lund then hastily resigned from his job. An audit of the books by the new comptroller revealed the forgeries. It was also revealed that Lund and Regal were one in the same person, that the information on his resume was not correct, and that he had a criminal record.

Question for Discussion

Should Actors, Inc., ethically be able to recover the money from the bank even though they felt honestly that the bank should pay?

PART 5

Agency, Employment, and Labor Law

After studying Part V, you should be able to:

1. name the federal and state laws that guarantee rights and benefits to employees and state what these rights and benefits are.

2. point out the distinguishing features between the employer-employee and principal-agent and indepedent contractor relationships.

3. describe the ways in which employer-employee and principal-agent relationships may be created.

4. list the duties of an employer or principal and an employee or agent within the relationship.

5. explain the liability of the employer or principal and the employee or agent within the relationship.

6. name the ways in which employer-employee and principal-agent relationships may be terminated.

CHAPTER 23

Employer-Employee Relationship

CHAPTER PREVIEW

Chapter Highlights

The employer-employee relationship is one of the most common legal relationships. This chapter begins with a description of how the relationship is created and how it is affected by labor-management relations when there is a labor union present. As parties to an employment agreement, employers and employees both have certain rights and obligations. The chapter discusses the duties that each has to the other and what each may expect from the other. The liability of an employer for the torts of an employee is also described. There is a great deal of legislation, on both the state and federal levels, that affects relations between employers and employees. The chapter describes and discusses some of the more important federal and state statutes, including those dealing with wages and hours, discrimination in employment, safety and health, and provision for the retirement and disability compensation of employees. The chapter includes a discussion of the change in the way the courts have treated the termination of the employer-employee relationship. It describes the many circumstances under which courts have been changing the traditional rule that an employer may terminate the employment of an employee at any time and regardless of cause. The chapter ends with a discussion of the hiring of aliens.

THE EMPLOYMENT PROCESS

employee one hired to work

employer one who hires another to work for him or her

An employer-employee relationship exists when one person, the **employee**, is hired to work, usually under the direction and control of another person called the **employer**.

The employment process generally begins with the completion of an employment application form. Most application forms ask for such basic information as your name, address, Social Security number, previous employment history, education, school activities, and salary or wages expected. Most forms also ask for personal references or for the names of people who can provide background data on you.

The Civil Rights Act, which was passed in 1964, prohibits hiring practices that discriminate against applicants because of sex, race, religion, or nationality. Questions relating to these factors may not be asked on the application form. Obviously, because these questions cannot be asked, an employer cannot take these factors into consideration when hiring you. For example, if a French restaurant is hiring a chef, a woman applying for the job may not be turned down simply because the employer feels that chefs are traditionally male or because the employer considers female chefs less qualified than male chefs. Of course, if the employer can show that a specific female applicant is not as well qualified as a male applicant, it is not a violation of the Civil Rights Act to hire the man.

Because of exceptions to the rule regarding discriminatory hiring practices, some questions cannot be asked on an application form or during an interview. Such exceptions relate to defenses to discrimination suits, discussed on pages 391–397.

CREATION OF THE EMPLOYER-EMPLOYEE RELATIONSHIP

The employer-employee relationship is most often created by contract, either orally or in writing. If the contract is to last for more than one year from the date it is made, however, it must be in writing to satisfy a state's statute of frauds.

> Brandon, an accountant, entered into a contract to work for Computer Net for a period of two years. This two-year contract between Computer Net and Brandon must be in writing to be enforceable.

The employer and the employee can include any terms they desire in the contract as long as the terms are not unlawful. Employment contracts for top-level positions, such as a president of a company, generally are in writing. These contracts include such terms as the length of time the contract will run, the amount of pay, fringe benefits, and a brief description of the position. Terms that are not discussed or not included as part of a written contract are implied or assumed to exist because of state and federal regulations applying to the employer-employee relationship.

Employee/Independent Contractor

The distinction between an employee and an independent contractor is often very important. The liability of an employer differs from that of a person who retains the services of an independent contractor, including the obligation to pay for payroll taxes, workers' compensation, disability insurance, and health insurance. Courts and the Internal Revenue Service look at the following factors in determining whether a person is an employee or an independent contractor: (1) the degree of control an employer exerts over an employee's work (the more the control, the more likely the person is an employee); (2) how the person is paid (payment by the job indicates the person is an independent contractor); (3) the term of employment (the longer the term, the more likely a court will consider the person an employee); (4) whether the worker is provided tools and materials (this is a sign of an employer-employee relationship); (5) whether the worker can work for more than one company at a time (this indicates an independent contractor relationship); and (6) whether the worker is trained by the person who hired him (this is sign of an employer-employee relationship).

RIGHTS OF EMPLOYERS

Employers and employees have certain expectations of each other in their working relationship. Some of these expectations are determined by the contract of employment and some are implied by law, but most are imposed by federal and state statutes.

Employers have the right to expect that employees who have stated that they have certain skills actually have those skills. Employers also have the right to expect certain performance levels from their employees. That is, employees are expected to achieve a reasonable amount of work. In addition, employers have the legal right to tell employees not only what tasks to perform but also how to perform those tasks.

An employee owes an employer the obligation not to reveal trade secrets or confidential information learned on the job. Whether a discovery or invention of the employee belongs to the employee or the employer depends on the nature of the invention, the terms of any agreement between them relating to inventions, and whether the employee was hired to work on certain processes leading to inventions.

You were employed in the personnel office of the Alliance Printing Company. A friend who owned a competing printing business asked you to obtain a list of Alliance's customers. Your friend intended to use this list to try to take customers away from Alliance. If you gave the list to your friend and your employer discovered what you had done, you could not only be fired but could also be held liable for any damages caused by your disloyal act.

Employees have an implied agreement to work exclusively for the employer during the hours of employment. They cannot, for example, do personal tasks or carry on the activities of a private business venture on company time. Employees are expected to follow reasonable instructions and to abide by company rules. An employee who fails to follow instructions can be fired.

You were hired as a stock clerk in the warehouse of a large department store. Your supervisor called you into her office and reminded you that you had been coming in late for work every day. You also took more time away from your job than the normal fifteen-minute breaks allowed each morning and afternoon. If you refuse to arrive at work on time and continue taking long breaks, you could be fired.

RIGHTS OF EMPLOYEES

The rights of an employee are regulated to a great extent by legislation, discussed in detail later in this chapter. An employer, however, has certain obligations to employees in common law that still exist today, although many of them have been enacted into statute law.

Employees hired by a company must be paid for the work that they do. If the employee belongs to a union, wages may be controlled by a collective bargaining agreement with workers who are in the same classification and who have the same skills and receive similar

fringe benefits
nonwage advantages received by an employee from an employer

wages. Most companies offer varying levels of **fringe benefits**—that is, nonwage extras that are paid for by the company. Examples of fringe benefits include life insurance, a pension plan or retirement plan, health and dental insurance, and paid sick days and vacations. Employees have the right to receive the same fringe benefits as others in their job classification.

An employee has the right to expect a reasonably safe workplace and safe tools and appliances. What is considered "reasonably safe" depends on the type of industry, the type of job performed, and other similar factors. An employer may be held liable to an employee for failure to exercise care if that failure causes injury to the employee.

Whenever hazardous work is involved, an employee has the right to expect that the employer will provide a sufficient number of skilled workers to perform the job. This right includes a duty on the part of the employer to provide sufficient explanations to prevent injury resulting from lack of instruction.

Access to Personnel Records

Employers keep many records regarding their employees. Some—such as payroll records, tax information, pension records, and information regarding illness and injury—are required by law. Others—such as reference and credit checks, job performance reports, and disciplinary action records—are kept for internal purposes.

All these records are important from the point of view of both employers and employees. An employer who fails to keep required information may be penalized for that failure. An employer who keeps information that is inaccurate or harmful to an employee may face legal action by the employee because an employee's right to privacy and to present and future employment may be seriously affected by incomplete, inaccurate, or harmful information in his or her personnel record.

Four basic questions govern an employee's right to privacy:

1. What information may an employer maintain about an employee?
2. When does an employee have the right to examine his or her personnel records?
3. In addition to the employee, who else may examine an employee's personnel records?
4. When is an employer required to correct inaccurate information or delete harmful information?

In general, in addition to information that must be maintained by law, an employer should keep only the information about an employee that relates to his or her ability to perform a job or to actual job performance.

Most states have laws covering an employee's right to inspect his or her personnel records and the procedures to be followed in such cases. Except for reference letters (the disclosure of which might violate the privacy of the writer) and information related to a criminal investigation, an employee may examine all other information in a personnel file.

Most state laws regulate procedures to be followed in examining a personnel file. These laws cover the method of making a discovery request, the place and time of the examination, and the persons who may or must be present when the examination occurs.

In most cases, access to personnel records by someone other than the employee is determined by the employer and not by state law. Because of potential lawsuits for invasion of privacy, libel, or slander, most employers severely restrict access to personnel records and maintain strict security in keeping such records confidential. Access to medical records is specifically and severely restricted by the Americans with Disabilities Act, which regulates how medical records must be maintained and who has access to them.

More than ten states have laws permitting an employee to request the removal or correction of inaccurate information from a personnel file or the insertion in the file of an explanation by the employee of any disagreement with the data. In other states, correction or removal of inaccurate data is at the employer's discretion.

Labor-Management Relations

labor union organization of employees formed to promote welfare of members in relation to their working conditions

collective bargaining discussions between union leaders and employer representatives

collective bargaining agreement contract negotiated between union leaders and company representatives

For many employees, the employer-employee relationship is affected by a **labor union**, an organization of employees formed to promote the welfare of its members. Union members generally select leaders to negotiate a contract with the company for which the members work. The contract between the employer and the union is arrived at through a series of discussions known as **collective bargaining**. The resulting contract is called a **collective bargaining agreement**.

In the collective bargaining process, union leaders, usually led by a chief negotiator, meet and discuss issues with representatives of the employer. Issues that may be discussed include working conditions, wages, hours to be worked, fringe benefits, retirement benefits, job security, promotion and layoff procedures, a grievance procedure for what are considered violations of the contract, and any other concerns management and union members may have. When agreement is reached by both sides, the union leaders must get approval of the contract from the union members they represent. If the members vote to approve the contract, a written contract is prepared, incorporating all the points on which both sides have agreed. Both the employer and the union are governed by this contract for the term of the contract.

If the union members do not approve the contract, the union leaders and company representatives must go through the collective bargaining process again in another attempt to reach an agreement the union members will accept.

Sweeney was hired as a machinist for the R&R Tool Company. All employees of the company were covered by a union contract, which outlined specific duties for each job classification in the company. One day Sweeney's immediate supervisor ordered him to help unload some heavy crates from a truck. He refused because this work was not in his job classification. The supervisor attempted to fire Sweeney, but because Sweeney was not required to perform tasks not included in his job classification (as outlined in the collective bargaining agreement), he could not legally be fired.

TERMINATING THE EMPLOYER-EMPLOYEE RELATIONSHIP

If an employment contract states a specific term for employment, the contract is terminated either at the end of the term or upon the occurrence of a specific event, such as improper conduct. If the employment contract (oral or written) does not state how long the agreement is to last, however, the traditional view is that in such circumstances, employment is at will. **Employment at will** means that in the absence of a contract or collective bargaining agreement, the employer or employee may terminate the relationship at any time for any reason whatsoever.

employment at will employment that either the employee or employer may terminate at any time for any reason

You were hired, on an oral agreement, by the manager of a supermarket at the minimum hourly wage. After three months, the manager discharged you from your job because the owner ordered a cutback in personnel. The owner has the legal right to discharge you and not be liable for damages.

The termination of an employment contract at will by an employer has occasionally resulted in injustice and hardship. Consequently, the at-will doctrine is gradually being eroded and modified in most states. The courts and state legislatures are doing so by laws and decisions providing exceptions to the at-will rule, indicating a growing acceptance of the requirement that an employee's discharge must be justifiable. Many believe that in the future, no one will be fired without just cause.

Some of the best-recognized exceptions to the at-will rule are (1) discharges in violation of law, (2) any discharge of an employee that goes against some well-defined public policy, (3) a discharge of an employee when there is an implied contract for a period of time, (4) discharges that violate stated employee policies and practices, (5) termination if not done in good faith, and (6) termination prohibited because of wrongful employer acts.

Termination in Violation of Law

Certain laws prohibit discharging an employee even if the employment is considered at will. The Civil Rights Act of 1964, Title VII (see page 388), prohibits discharge of an employee because of race, color, gender, age, religion, marital status, national origin, and disability. Under the Occupational Safety and Health Act (see page 392), an employee may not be discharged for complaining that an employer has violated the health and safety requirements of the act. The Fair Labor Standards Act prohibits discharging an employee who complains that an employer has violated the wage and hour provisions of the act. It also regulates the duration of work days an employer must provide, as well as salary and overtime requirements. It applies to workers forty years of age and older and to workplaces with twenty or more employees.

Termination That Goes Against a Well-Defined Public Policy

whistle-blower laws
legislation prohibiting an employer from firing an employee because the employee reports that the employer had violated certain laws

Many state legislatures have enacted **whistle-blower laws**, which prevent an employer from firing an employee if the sole reason for termination was that the employee filed a worker's compensation claim or reported a labor-law violation by the employer. Some of the statutes also prohibit firing an employee solely because the employee reports violations that may endanger the welfare of the employees or the public. A number of courts have approved of exceptions to the at-will rule even in the absence of specific statutes.

Most states prohibit an employer from firing an employee who refuses to perform an act that is illegal or violates public policy, such as committing perjury.

Termination Prohibited Based on an Implied Contract Term

Many courts have attempted to find an implied duration of an employment term even though such a term is not specifically stated in an employment contract. Rather than looking at any one fact to conclude that the contract was for a specific time, the courts will examine many factors. One of these is the circumstances in which a person was hired, such as that the employee always served for a specific period of time in prior jobs. Another is the type of work performed by the employee; the more executive the position, the more a court is inclined to imply a specific duration for the employment. One court has even held that employment for several years implies that the employee may not be fired without just cause.

The factor most often considered by the courts in determining whether the duration of an employment term may be implied is whether the employee's pay is stated in terms of a specific time period. Although the majority of courts do not follow the rule, a minority of courts have held that an employment contract that states the employee's compensation in terms of a specific period of time creates a presumption that the employee was hired for a specific period of time. Under this rule, the statement that an employee's salary is $10 per hour would not create any such presumption. A statement that the employee's salary is $20,800.00 per year (based on $10 per hour for a forty-hour week), however, would create such a presumption in those states in which the courts follow the minority view.

Discharge Affected by Employee Policies and Practices

Although many employees have neither written nor oral contracts, the companies for which they work often have employee policies and practices that are distributed to them in written form. Many of these practices and policies outline the steps that management must take before firing an employee.

In attempting to soften the results of the employment-at-will doctrine, courts in a number of states are holding that the right of an employer to fire an employee at will is restricted because of the existence of company employment policies outlining the procedures that must be followed before an employee can be fired. The basis for this reasoning is that such policies imply a contract between the employer and the employee regarding termination, even though there was no specific agreement to this effect. Of course, courts must still consider such factors as whether the policies were in existence when the employee was hired, whether the employee knew of these policies, and whether the employer had the right to change the policies at any time.

> Lerner was hired to run a riveting machine by Acme Company on an hourly basis. Two months after she was hired, Acme distributed a book to all employees containing the company's personnel practices, one of which dealt with firing procedures. Lerner is entitled to the benefit of these procedures if she is fired.

Regardless of whether the employment-at-will doctrine applies in a specific state, there is no doubt that an employer who can show good cause can discharge an employee and not be liable for breach of contract.

> Thornton signed a two-year contract to be a history professor at a university, claiming that he had taught previously at two major universities. Shortly after Thornton signed the contract, university officials discovered he had lied about his prior teaching experience. In this case, even though Thornton had a written contract for two years, university officials could discharge him immediately.

An employee has similar rights and may quit before the time stated in the contract if he or she has good reason. An example of good reason is an employer's failure to pay the employee the salary agreed upon in the contract. In this case, the employee could also recover damages for breach of contract by the employer.

Termination Prohibited Because of Wrongful Employer Acts (Torts)

A few courts have declared exceptions to the termination-at-will doctrine based on wrongful acts by employers. If an employee is fired using procedures deemed abusive, the employee may have a valid suit charging wrongful termination. In like manner, an employee who can show that he or she took the job under false pretenses may have a valid suit against an employer. For example, an employee who accepts a position as a financial officer but is then given a job as a salesperson may be able to sue the employer for fraud.

Termination Prohibited if Not Done in Good Faith

Some courts have found a termination invalid because of a lack of good faith on the part of the employer. One example would be when an employer convinces an executive at another company to leave and accept a job offer with all sorts of benefits and then fires the executive after a few months. Another example would be when an employee performs well over a period of years and the employer tells the employee that the job is permanent, but the employee is then fired without a good reason.

LEGISLATION AFFECTING EMPLOYER-EMPLOYEE RELATIONS

There are three areas of federal and state regulation of employer-employee relations: (1) labor-management, (2) employment discrimination, (3) sexual harassment.

Labor-Management

In 1932, Congress passed the Norris-LaGuardia Act, which provided federal protection to unions to organize and bargain collectively. It prohibited employers from attempting to coerce employees to not join a union. The collective bargaining process is governed by rules established under the National Labor Relations Act (Wagner Act) of 1935 and amended by the Labor Management Relations Act of 1947 (often called the Taft-Hartley Act). The National Labor Relations Act protects union growth and activities from unfair interference by employers. For example, employers may not prevent employees from organizing a union, nor may employers fire or discriminate against employees who do join a union.

It is also sometimes necessary to protect employees from unfair activities by a union. The Taft-Hartley Act prohibited a number of unfair union practices, including attempting to coerce employees to join a union, refusing to bargain in good faith, and secondary picketing—a union strategy to picket an employer with which it has no dispute to aid another union that does have a dispute with the employer.

closed shop company requiring union membership as a condition of employment

open shop business where employees are not required to join a union

union shop arrangement whereby new employees must join a union within a certain period of time after being hired

The Taft-Hartley Act prohibits a **closed shop**, a situation in which a company requires union membership as a prerequisite to employment. Also, under the Taft-Hartley Act and the Landrum-Griffin Act of 1959 (also an amendment to the National Labor Relations Act), when a union and an employer have an **open shop** arrangement, an employee cannot be forced to join a union as a condition of being hired or of keeping a job. Nor can the union force an employer to discriminate against an employee who is not a union member. An employer may, however, agree to have a **union shop**. Under this arrangement, employees need not be members of a union when they are hired, but they must join the union within a certain period of time, usually thirty days. Union shops are not permitted in states that have laws known as "right to work" laws. The Landrum-Griffin Act enacted to prevent union corruption also protects employees by regulating union elections, business procedures, and use of funds.

Employment Discrimination

Legislation, regulations, and judicial decisions now protect employees and unions, reversing the previous situation in which employers and unions were free to establish any conditions of employment they desired. With few exceptions, these laws apply to companies with fifteen or more employees.

Civil Rights Act (Title VII)   The Civil Rights Act of 1964, as amended by the Equal Employment Act of 1972, prohibits discrimination by employers on the basis of race, national origin, color, gender, or religion in the hiring, discharge, compensation, promotion, or training of employees. The Equal Employment Opportunity Commission (EEOC) was established to deal with employment discrimination cases. The EEOC has the power to stop unfair practices by seeking a court injunction if necessary or, as a final resort, by suing in court for damages.

The EEOC requires those employers that contract to provide products or services to the federal government to file an affirmative action plan with the government. **Affirmative action** is an effort by employers to recruit women and members of minority groups for the higher positions within their organizations that have traditionally been occupied by white men. Employers must first provide statistics relating to the breakdown of their employees into categories of race, religion, color, gender, and national origin. They must also study the surrounding area from which they intend to recruit employees, paying regard to the same categories. Employers must then submit a plan designed to increase the numbers of female and minority-group employees. The federal government has the right to cancel a contract with an employer that fails to comply with a plan submitted.

affirmative action duty of employers to recruit women and minorities for positions usually held by white men

Civil Rights Act of 1991

The Civil Rights Act of 1991 expanded protection against discrimination and in particular enables women and persons who have disabilities to obtain more damages as a result of discriminatory practices than were available under prior laws. Those bringing suit under this law can, if successful, receive punitive damages in addition to compensatory damages and expert witness fees.

Formerly, it was the employee claiming that a particular employment practice was discriminatory who had the burden of proving that it was unnecessary for the competent performance of the employee's job. Under the Civil Rights Act of 1991, it is now the employer that has the burden of proving that the particular practice complained of is in fact necessary for competent performance.

> Sally applied for a job on an oil well drilling team. The company refused to hire her, claiming that a woman would not have sufficient strength to perform the job properly. Under the Civil Rights Act of 1991, the employer would have the burden of proving that a certain degree of strength was necessary for the proper performance of this job and that Sally did not have that strength.

Age Discrimination in Employment Act

Congress passed the Age Discrimination in Employment Act in 1967 (amended in 1978) to encourage the employment of persons between the ages of forty and sixty-five. Employers of twenty or more employees cannot discriminate against people in this age group when they are interviewing and hiring applicants for a job. Neither may employers discriminate against them in promotions on the job or in any other way modify or change their conditions of employment. There are necessary exemptions. For example, a sports team could limit its players to those under a certain age. It does not prevent an employer from favoring older employees over younger employees.

There are many different forms of discrimination; some are obvious, some subtle. The various civil rights acts and regulations prohibit many types of discrimination, including the following:

1. Disparate treatment. This treatment occurs when an employer treats an individual differently from other employees without good reason, such as, when a woman is paid less than an equally qualified man who performs the same job. To prove this type of discrimination, a plaintiff must show that he or she (a) is a member of a protected group (because of race, gender, etc.); (b) is being treated differently from other employees who do the same or similar work; and (c) is being treated differently solely because of race, gender, religion, and so forth.

2. *Disparate impact.* This effect occurs when a company policy or rule, nondiscriminatory on its face, works to the detriment of a protected group. The defense to this type of discrimination is that there was a valid reason for it.

Ajax Motor Company had a rule limiting employment of car salespersons to those over 5′10″ tall. This rule would exclude most women and would be considered discriminatory, as there could be no valid business reason for it. A professional basketball team having the same requirement, however, would not be found to be discriminatory.

3. *Perpetuating discrimination.* This discrimination occurs when an employer actively discontinues a discriminatory practice but continues it in subtle ways through conduct.

The Otis Company had a rule restricting employment to white persons. It then rescinded the rule but adopted a policy that all new employees must be related to existing employees. This seemingly neutral policy would discriminate against African Americans and would be prohibited.

Sexual Harassment

Like other forms of discrimination, sex discrimination is prohibited by federal and state civil rights laws. Recently, sexual harassment has become the most widely publicized and discussed form of sex discrimination.

There are obvious types of sexual harassment, such as unwelcome advances or conduct indicating that submission to such advances is a condition of continued employment or promotion. The courts have had little difficulty with this type of case, provided adequate proof of such harassment is shown. Where such harassment is proved, a court may award damages, back pay, reinstatement, or a combination of such remedies.

The most difficult cases in which sexual harassment is charged involve a more subtle form of harassment: the creation of a "hostile working environment" that unreasonably interferes with the employee's job performance. A coworker or supervisor who makes unwanted physical contact, tells offensive jokes and stories, or makes comments about an employee's physical appearance would be guilty of creating such an environment. It is often difficult to prove this type of harassment, however; not every physical contact is considered sexual, and a joke may be offensive to one person but not to another. The courts have generally adopted the following tests to determine whether the conduct complained of can be deemed sufficiently severe to have created a "hostile working environment":

1. The harassing conduct must be part of an ongoing general practice, not just an isolated incident.
2. The harassing conduct must interfere with the performance of the employee's job when seen from the point of view of a reasonable employee in the plaintiff's position.
3. When the conduct complained of is that of a supervisor or coworker, it must be proven that the employer knew of the offensive conduct, or should have known of it, and yet failed to take prompt and sufficient measures to prevent it.

Blair complained that her supervisor was making unwanted sexual advances toward her and offered proof of it. Her employer said that he would investigate the matter within sixty days and send a letter to the supervisor requesting an end to this type of conduct. This remedy would be deemed insufficient action, and Blair's employer could be held liable for damages for sexual harassment.

Title VII of the Civil Rights Act of 1964 and other laws also protect job applicants and employees from discrimination because of their sexual orientation. These laws provide protection for bisexuals and homosexuals.

Equal Pay Act   The Equal Pay Act of 1963 (amended in 1972) makes it unlawful for employers to discriminate in the payment of wages because of gender. When performance on the job requires equal skill and responsibility, men and women must be given equal pay. For example, a female soccer coach must be paid the same wages as a male soccer coach if both coaches perform the same duties under similar working conditions. An employer has certain defenses to a suit brought under the act (and has the burden of proving those defenses), including the fact that pay was based on merit or the quantity of goods produced or services provided.

Americans with Disabilities Act (ADA)   The ADA, passed in 1990, prohibits discrimination in employment because of a potential employee's disabilities. It covers employers with more than fifteen employees. It also protects employees after they have been hired. The term *disability* is broadly defined; it covers both physical impairment (including AIDS), mental impairment (including learning disabilities), and pregnancy. The law does not obligate an employer to hire a person because of a disability. The law is a nondiscrimination law and is designed to prohibit discrimination against a potential or actual employee solely because of the disability, including even asking about an employee's disability at any time; the employer has the burden of proving that the disability prevents the potential employee from performing the job properly.

> Jones, a deaf person, could not be denied employment as a television repair person solely because of her disability. Jones, however, could be denied employment as a piano tuner because that job can be performed properly only by a person with excellent hearing.

The Americans with Disabilities Act covers more than discrimination in employment. It prohibits discrimination on the basis of disability by private entities in places of public accommodation. It also requires that both existing and new buildings and other facilities be modified and designed to make them easily accessible to and usable by disabled persons. Examples are adding Braille control panels in elevators, making store aisles wide enough to accommodate wheelchairs, and installing entrance ramps in front of buildings. Employers and others can receive tax benefits if they make the changes required by law.

Remedies   Not all the antidiscrimination laws that have been discussed provide the same remedies for violations, but the remedies available under them all are (1) job reinstatement, (2) payment of back pay, (3) injunction against future violations, (4) damages, and (5) legal fees.

Defenses

Employers have certain defenses in discrimination suits even though the practices complained of appear discriminatory. The available defenses depend on the law involved and on whether the alleged discrimination is direct or indirect. Direct discrimination involves obvious discrimination, such as giving male employees a longer work break than that given to female employees. Indirect discrimination involves practices that have an unintended discriminatory effect, such as giving employment interviews and tests only on a day when certain groups might be unable to participate because of religious requirements.

The basic defenses are as follows:

1. *Seniority.* Awarding promotions based on an existing, fair seniority program is a valid defense to a suit claiming discrimination.

2. *Business necessity.* If a company can show that it has a sound business reason for a certain practice that appears discriminatory, that reason will be a sufficient defense to a discrimination suit. The ability to read would be a valid requirement for a position as a book reviewer, for example; it would not be a valid requirement for a job as a refuse collector.

3. *Bona fide occupational qualifications (BFOQ).* The BFOQ defense is available to an employer who can show that a job requires specific traits or characteristics. The courts tend to limit this defense to cases of alleged gender discrimination. An airplane manufacturer could not refuse to hire a woman as a test pilot solely because of her gender, for example. Gender would be a good defense, however, for a play producer who refused to hire a woman for the role of Hamlet in Shakespeare's play.

Note that many states have enacted laws that supplement and often offer greater protection than federal legislation. In addition, Congress and the states have enacted many laws protecting employees' health and privacy in general and persons who are disabled, retired, and unemployed in particular.

LEGISLATION AFFECTING EMPLOYEES' HEALTH AND PRIVACY

Health and Safety

Occupational Safety and Health Act   The Occupational Safety and Health Act, a federal statute passed in 1970, requires most employers to meet certain health and safety standards issued by the Department of Labor. Employers are required to provide employees with safe working conditions in the buildings in which they work. Employers must also ensure that the machinery and equipment that employees use for their work are safe and that employees have the proper training necessary to operate machinery and equipment safely. In addition, the employee has the right to choose not to perform his or her assigned task because of a reasonable fear of death or serious injury. The employer may not discharge an employee because of this fear. The employee also has the right to inform the Occupational Safety and Health Administration (OSHA), a division of the Department of Labor, of any workplace condition that is immediately threatening and dangerous and to request that OSHA inspect that condition. An employer may be fined up to $1,000 for each violation reported by an employee or discovered during an OSHA inspection. An employer is also subject to a fine of up to $1,000 per day for each day that a serious violation is not corrected. In certain cases, criminal penalties may be imposed. Employees who report violations to OSHA are protected in the event that employers attempt to fire them. OSHA inspections of the workplace must be announced in advance in keeping with the Constitution's protection against unreasonable searches.

> Radcliff was employed by a company that processed and bottled baby food. While Radcliff was working at a conveyor belt, the feeder failed to operate because of a short circuit in the primary electrical unit that operated the system. Radcliff notified her employer, who failed to correct the situation. A short time later, the conveyor belt stopped again. Radcliff pushed a switch in the emergency electrical unit to get the conveyor started and was nearly electrocuted.

The company just described violated the Occupational Safety and Health Act by not providing safe working conditions for its employees. In addition, because of the company's failure to correct the situation, a fine and possible criminal penalty could be imposed if Radcliff reports the employer to an OSHA inspector or if the inspector discovers the electrical defect on an inspection of the plant.

Privacy

Legislation has been enacted and constitutional provisions have been evoked to prevent harassment of employees and invasion of their privacy.

Many employers require their employees to take lie detector tests as a condition of recruitment or continued employment. Because the admissibility of these tests in evidence is usually prohibited, the imposition of such a test is considered harassment and an invasion of privacy. Many states have polygraph laws that protect an employee's privacy, particularly in prohibiting the requirement that a job applicant must take a lie detector test. In 1988, Congress enacted the Employee Polygraph Protection Act. With certain exceptions (e.g., government employers), employers are prohibited from requiring such tests, using the results, or penalizing an employee either for refusing to take one or because of its results. In certain situations, such as when a theft or embezzlement has occurred, tests are permitted. Even in those cases, an employer cannot use the test results unless there is proof that reasonable grounds exist to believe that the employee was involved.

Employers often monitor the actions and performance of employees by electronic means. This may involve video cameras, eavesdropping on telephone lines, and monitoring computer use. Other than federal and state laws that limit or prohibit eavesdropping on employees' conversations, there are few laws or regulations limiting an employer's monitoring of an employee's activities.

Whether or not an employer can search an employee's desk or locker depends on whether an employee has what courts have called a "legitimate expectation of privacy." This refers to how reasonable your belief is that your belongings would be safe from intrusion. For example, if you have a key or lock to your desk or locker and you don't use it, you can't complain if a search is made. Also, if an employer has a well-publicized policy of searching employees' desks or lockers, you can't complain if searches are made. An employer must also have a reasonable excuse to search an employee's private areas. Searching because of security problems or because you work for the government in a sensitive position might be deemed reasonable.

Because the use of illegal drugs and alcohol can affect job performance and may contribute to workplace injuries, many employers want to test their employees for such substances periodically. Such testing, however, is an invasion of privacy because it may reveal other medical conditions that the person being tested does not want known or indicate drug usage that does not affect job performance. Both federal and state constitutions and regulations have been invoked either to permit or prohibit drug and alcohol testing of employees. So far, the courts have tended to decide each case on its own merits rather than adopting broad rules. If an employee's work involves national security or potential injury to the employee or to others, drug and alcohol testing are usually permitted. In general, such testing will be permitted if it is found to be accurate and is being used to detect current or recent drug use rather than past use.

Note that the Americans with Disabilities Act includes the former use of drugs and rehabilitation as a protected disability but specifically excludes the current use of illegal drugs as a disability.

Employee Protection: The Disabled, Retired, and Unemployed

**workers'
compensation** state
laws providing benefits
to employees who are
injured or become
seriously ill on the job

Workers' Compensation Laws   All states have **workers' compensation** laws (there are no federal workers' compensation laws). These laws provide benefits to employees who are injured or who become seriously ill on the job as a result of their work conditions, regardless of whether the employer or the employee was at fault. Some states cover employees who acquire what is known as an occupational disease, such as an illness contracted by a nurse as a result of exposure to a patient. The cost of workers' compensation is borne by the employer alone.

Employees who are covered by workers' compensation are entitled to receive (1) medical treatment, (2) a certain percentage of their regular wages if they will be away from their jobs recovering from injuries or illness, and (3) periodic payments for a permanent disability (e.g., the loss of an arm or a leg). Benefits are also paid to dependents of deceased employees. In those states in which employees are not covered by state laws, employers may provide workers' compensation benefits through private companies.

> Velasquez was employed in a factory that manufactured small tools. One day he was injured when a toolbox full of tools slipped from his hands and fell on his foot. He was unable to work for several weeks and incurred costly medical bills for treatment of the injury.

In this example, Velasquez would not be personally responsible for the medical bills; they would be covered under workers' compensation. In addition, Velasquez, while unable to work, would be entitled to some income in place of the wages he normally received as an employee.

Workers' compensation entitles an employee to recover for work-related injuries regardless of whether the injuries were caused by the employee's ordinary or gross negligence. Most workers' compensation laws, however, deny benefits to employees if they were injured while acting outside the scope of their employment, injured themselves intentionally, or were injured or died as a result of using alcohol or illegal drugs.

Social Security Act   The Social Security Act of 1935 and its amendments provide a continuing (but limited) income to those employees whose earnings are covered by the act. The Social Security system is actually a social insurance program. It provides benefits to employees or families whose earnings stop because of retirement or death or are reduced because of illness or any other physical disability.

Almost all persons in the United States are covered by Social Security. In fact, nine of every ten workers in the United States are covered, including self-employed persons. Federal government employees, who are covered by a separate plan, are the largest single group of people not covered by Social Security. Employees of state and local governments and religious and nonprofit organizations may choose to be covered. Special eligibility rules apply to farm workers, students, and those who work outside the United States.

The costs of the Social Security program are financed by contributions from both employees and employers. Employers must automatically deduct a certain amount from their employees' paychecks, contribute an equal amount and send both contributions to the Internal Revenue Service. The amount of the employee's contribution is fixed by Congress and is stated as a certain percentage of annual wages. For example, for the year 2009, both employers and employees have to contribute 6.2 percent on all wages up to $106,800 plus 1.45 percent of total wages for Medicare-family-employer plans. The contribution is 15.3 percent of a business's net earnings from self-employment.

The major types of insurance provided under Social Security are old age, survivors', and disability insurance; Medicare; and unemployment insurance. *Old age insurance* provides benefits to qualified workers who retire after age sixty-five. *Survivors' insurance* provides payments to the dependents of a wage earner who dies. *Disability insurance* provides a monthly income to a wage earner who is under sixty-five and unable to work because of sickness or injury.

The *Medicare* program offers health insurance to people age sixty-five and older, as well as to persons younger than sixty-five who have been disabled for two years. Part A, Hospital Insurance, which is premium-free, provides coverage for a limited time for inpatient hospital care, inpatient care in a skilled nursing facility following a hospital stay, and home health care. Part B, Medical Insurance, which requires premium payments by the insured, covers doctors' services, outpatient hospital care, diagnostic tests, medical equipment, and ambulance services.

Part D is a prescription drug benefit plan for the elderly and the disabled. Benefits started on January 1, 2006. The drug benefit is offered through private insurance plans to those who apply for it. The private plans are reimbursed by the Centers for Medicare & Medicaid Services (CMS). Enrollment for most beneficiaries is voluntary. Some costs must be borne by the beneficiaries of the plans.

The federal *unemployment insurance* system provides temporary compensation to persons who lose their jobs through no fault of their own. It is a substitute for a portion of the wages lost. The unemployment insurance program is financed by taxes paid by employers only. As a rule, benefits paid are a percentage of the worker's previous weekly earnings. There is, however, a minimum and maximum amount payable and a maximum length of time for which an unemployed person may receive benefits.

Cranshaw worked as a clerk in a steel warehouse 1 mile from her home. Her employer went out of business, and Cranshaw applied for unemployment insurance benefits. Cranshaw was told that a similar job was available in the area, but she refused to take it because it was 5 miles from her home. Cranshaw's refusal to take a similar, available job would prevent her from receiving any unemployment benefits.

Pension Protection

Many employers have established pension plans for their employees. Occasionally, employers failed to fund these plans properly, mismanaged the funds, or failed to pay benefits to employees who were fired or who quit voluntarily to work for someone else. To protect employees who depend on pension benefits for their retirement, Congress enacted the Employee Retirement Income Security Act (ERISA) in 1974. ERISA controls the length of time an employee must work before becoming **vested**—that is, before becoming entitled to pension benefits that cannot be taken away, the management of pension funds, and reporting requirements for employers.

vested when an employee becomes entitled to pension benefits

Health Insurance Protection

In 1985, Congress enacted the Consolidated Omnibus Budget Reconciliation Act (known popularly as COBRA) to protect an employee's health insurance protection. COBRA covers employers who maintain a health insurance plan and who employ twenty or more employees. It prohibits eliminating an employee's health insurance coverage upon termination of employment, whether termination is voluntary or involuntary. When an employee wishes to continue coverage after termination, the employer must continue coverage for up to eighteen months or up to twenty-nine months if the employee is disabled. The employee, however, is usually required to pay the insurance premiums to continue coverage.

Wages, Hours, and Minors

Fair Labor Standards Act   The federal Fair Labor Standards Act, also known as the Wage and Hour Law, requires certain employers to pay their employees a legal, minimum hourly wage, plus at least one and a half times their regular hourly wage for all hours worked over forty hours in a week. The minimum hourly wage is determined by Congress and is periodically revised. The Wage and Hour Law also contains provisions dealing with the employment of minors. It regulates the minimum age for employment, the hours minors are allowed to work, and occupations for which minors may and may not be hired. Some employees are exempt, such as executives, professionals, and outside salespersons.

Family and Medical Leave

Many employees must often decide whether to quit work to care for a newborn child or sick relative or to remain on the job. To enable employees to avoid having to make that choice, Congress enacted the Family and Medical Leave Act, effective in August 1993. The law requires employers with fifty or more workers to give their employees up to twelve weeks of unpaid leave during any twelve-month period (1) to care for a newborn child, (2) to care for a spouse or other close relative who has a serious medical problem, (3) to handle an adoption or the placement of a foster child, or (4) to assist an employee who has such a serious medical condition that it is impossible for that person to perform normal job activities.

In addition to medical and family leave, the law guarantees that when the employee returns to work, the employee will have his or her job back or an equivalent job, with no loss of job benefits or seniority rights. Health benefits continue while the employee is on leave. To be eligible for coverage under the law, the employee must have worked for the employer at least twelve months before requesting leave and at least 1,250 hours during that twelve-month period. Failure by the employer to comply with the law may result in lawsuits by the employee and the U.S. Department of Labor.

Although the law applies to businesses engaging in interstate commerce, thirty-five states and the District of Columbia had previously enacted similar laws, and many companies have for years been offering similar benefits voluntarily.

Health Insurance Portability and Accountability Act (HIPAA)

In 1996, Congress enacted the Health Insurance Portability and Accountability Act (HIPAA). It provides important insurance protection for working Americans and their families. For those employees who have either group health or individual health insurance policies, the act lowers an employee's chance of losing existing coverage, makes it easier for an employee to change health plans, and helps an employee buy insurance coverage upon the loss of employer-sponsored coverage. The act also ensures the privacy of health-related information.

VETERAN'S BENEFITS

In 1994, Congress enacted the Uniformed Services Employment and Reemployment Rights Act (USERRA), updated in 1996 and 1998. USERRA provides reemployment protection and other benefits for veterans and employees who perform military service, whether voluntary (enlistment) or involuntary (call up of reserves or National Guard).

Under the act, if a military member leaves a civilian job for service in the armed forces, he or she is entitled to return to the job with accrued seniority, provided certain eligibility criteria are met. These include that the job was a civilian one, the employer was informed in timely manner of leaving the job for military service, and that the release from service must have been under "honorable conditions."

THE HIRING OF ALIENS

Certain aliens are prohibited from accepting employment in the United States. The U.S. Immigration and Nationality Act of 1903, as amended by the Immigration Reform and Control Act of 1986, prohibits the recruitment or employment of aliens known to be unauthorized to accept employment. Immigrants, those aliens lawfully admitted for permanent residence in the United States, may be employed. Nonimmigrants, aliens who have been granted temporary admission for a specific purpose such as tourism or business, may not be employed.

A prospective employer must question a prospective employee and examine certain documents to determine his or her eligibility for employment before hiring the person. An employer who fails to comply and who hires an ineligible alien is subject to both civil and criminal penalties.

Summary

The employer-employee relationship is usually created by a contract, either oral or written. For many employees, the relationship is affected by a collective bargaining agreement, a contract between a labor union and management covering the terms of employment for employees who are union members.

The general rule has been that either an employer or an employee may end an oral or written contract at will if the contract fails to specify the length of the employment period. Recent court decisions, however, have watered down this rule by recognizing certain exceptions to the general rule, including discharges in violation of law, discharges that go against public policy, discharges that constitute a breach of an implied contract, and discharges that violate stated employee policies and practices.

Many federal and state statutes govern employer-employee relations. Some federal laws that affect this relationship are the Fair Labor Standards Act (wages, hours, and minors), the Civil Rights Act (prohibiting discrimination on the basis of race, color, gender, religion, or disability in the hiring, discharge, compensation, promotion, or training of employees), the Occupational Safety and Health Act (providing healthy and safe conditions on the job), and the Social Security Act (old age, survivors', and disability insurance; Medicare; and unemployment insurance). Three other federal laws protecting employees are the Employment Retirement Income Security Act (pension plan protection), the Americans with Disabilities Act (discrimination because of disability), and the Family and Medical Leave Act (unpaid leave for personal reasons).

Most states also have laws that protect employees who are either ill or are injured on the job as a result of work conditions. These laws include workers' compensation laws and disability benefits laws.

Important Legal terms

affirmative action
closed shop
collective bargaining
collective bargaining agreement
employee

employer
employment at will
fringe benefits
labor union
open shop

union shop
vested
whistle-blower laws
workers' compensation

Questions and Problems for Discussion

1. What is the trend in the law with regard to the employer's right to fire employees at will?

2. What are the rights and obligations of employers? What are the rights and obligations of employees?

3. Explain how a closed shop, a union shop, and an open shop are different from one another.

4. Does an employee have the right to refuse to take a lie detector test as a condition of employment?

5. What employment records does an employee have the right to examine?

6. What defenses might an employer have to charges of discrimination?

7. Blaine, an experienced commercial pilot, applied for a job at Eureka Airlines as a pilot. She was turned down because it had been the practice of the airlines for over thirty years to hire male pilots only. Is this a legitimate defense?

8. A store owner selling clothes for women between the ages of seventeen to twenty-five refuses to hire any salesperson over the age of twenty-five. Is this age discrimination?

9. Ferguson complained to a state agency that his employer was paying less than the minimum wage to certain employees. May the employer fire him because of this?

10. Shelly, one of three employees at a retail store, became pregnant and asked for maternity leave with pay. She was denied this and she brought suit against her employer. Will she succeed?

11. Brown, an employee of a tool and die company, asked for medical leave when his brother-in-law fell ill and required Brown's help. Is Brown entitled to unpaid leave under the Family and Medical Leave Act?

12. Blaine told an off-color joke in the presence of Brothers, a female employee. Under what circumstances may Brothers claim sexual harassment?

13. Curtis was being considered for a promotion in his company. He learned that his file contained an uncomplimentary reference letter that would hurt his chances for the promotion. He asks to see the letter. Is his employer required to show him the letter?

14. Butler was employed by Reed's TV Repair Service to pick up and deliver appliances in need of repair. While removing a television set from the company truck at Marsh's house, Butler dropped the set and completely destroyed it. Could Marsh hold Reed's liable?

15. Kraft, a nurse, was hired by Genesee Hospital at a beginning salary of $15,000 per year and was assigned to the surgical ward. A short time later, Timmons, also a nurse, was hired and assigned to the surgical ward to perform the same duties as Kraft. His salary, however, was only $12,000. When Timmons discovered the difference in pay, he complained to the administrator who had hired him. The administrator claimed that nursing was traditionally a job for women, that women performed better on the job and therefore should be paid more. Can Timmons force the hospital to pay him the same salary as Kraft?

16. You were hired under an oral agreement by the Metro Repair Shop as a mechanic. Soon after you were hired, you were involved in a car accident, lost the use of your right hand, and therefore could not perform your job properly at the repair shop. Could you legally be discharged from the job?

Cases for Review

1. Peterson stayed overnight at a rooming house while on business for his employer. He died from suffocation when his head became caught between two metal slats in the bed's headboard. His spouse brought a claim for workers' compensation, but the claim was denied on the grounds that his death did not arise out of and in the course of employment. Should the claim be denied? (*Peterson* v. *Industrial Commission*, Ariz. 490 P.2d)

2. Wieder, an associate with Skala's law firm, insisted that the activities of a fellow associate be reported to the Disciplinary Committee of the Bar Association. He was terminated from employment because of this and brought suit claiming his activities constituted whistle-

blowing, an exception to the employment-at-will doctrine. Should he succeed in his suit? (*Weider* v. *Skala*, N.Y., 144 Misc.2d 346)

3. Boxer Mike Tyson hired Rooney as his trainer, the term of the contract being "for as long as [Tyson] fought professionally." Tyson fired Rooney while Tyson was still boxing, and Rooney sued for breach of contract. Tyson claimed that the term of the contract was so indefinite that it was an "at-will" contract so that he could fire Rooney at any time. Who is correct? (*Rooney* v. *Tyson*, 91 N.Y.2d 685)

4. White, a truck driver employed by Inter-City, was driving a tractor-trailer along a highway when he got into a disagreement with Kuehn while attempting to pass his car. When both drivers pulled off the road to talk, White hit Kuehn on the head with a metal pipe, injuring him. White was convicted of assault. Kuehn sued both White and Inter-City for damages for his injuries. Is Inter-City responsible for White's actions? (*Kuehn* v. *White & Inter-City Auto Freight, Inc.*, Wash. 600 P.2d 679)

5. Nathan, a twenty-two-year-old nurse, worked in the surgical ward of Presbyterian Hospital in New York City. She was exposed for a period of about twelve days to a patient who had tuberculosis. As a result, she contracted tuberculosis in her right lung and had to leave work until she was cured. Was Nathan covered for payment under workers' compensation? (*Nathan* v. *Presbyterian Hospital in the City of New York*, 411 N.Y.S.2d 419)

6. Rhodes sold equipment for Gulberson Oil Tools. He was fired at age fifty-six, when his employer claimed that it was downsizing to cut costs. Six weeks later, Gulberson hired a person age forty-six to do the same job. Rhodes sued, claiming age discrimination. At trial, Rhodes offered proof of his abilities and experience. Gulberson claimed that Rhodes performed poorly but offered no proof. Should Rhodes's lawsuit succeed? (*Rhodes* v. *Gulberson Oil Tools*, 75 E.2d 989)

7. A company required a high school diploma or passing scores on intelligence tests as a condition of employment or of transfer to different jobs. It was shown that these conditions had nothing to do with measuring ability to learn to perform a specific job or category of jobs. Some African American employees sued the company, complaining this was racially motivated and a violation of the Civil Rights Act. Are they correct? (*Griggs* v. *Duke Power Co.*, 401 U.S. 424)

8. A school board rule required a pregnant school teacher to take unpaid maternity leave five months before the expected childbirth and to give notice six months before the expected birth. Such a teacher was not eligible to return to work until the next regular semester after the child was three months old. A pregnant school teacher sued the school district for violating the Due Process Clause of the Fourteenth Amendment to the U.S. Constitution. Was this claim correct? (*Cleveland Board of Education et. al.* v. *Lafleur*, 414 U.S. 632)

9. A county transportation agency adopted an affirmative action plan to promote women in jobs that were traditionally not open to women. The plan provided that sex of a qualified employee was one factor that could be considered in determining promotions. When a vacancy arose in one job position, the agency passed over a male applicant and instead selected a female applicant, both being equally qualified. The male applicant sued, claiming sex discrimination in violation of the Civil Rights Act. Was he correct? (*Johnson* v. *Transportation Agency*, 480 U.S. 616)

CHAPTER 24

Principal-Agent Relationship

CHAPTER PREVIEW

Chapter Highlights

A principal-agent relationship is an extremely common one that is used for both personal and business transactions. This chapter begins with a discussion of the concept of agency and the nature of the principal-agent relationship. An agency may be created in many ways, and there are many different types of agents. The chapter examines the different ways in which an agency may be created and the difference between general agents and special agents. The principal-agent relationship involves a great deal of trust, and each party has obligations and duties toward the other. The chapter discusses the obligations of the agent to the principal, including such implied duties as obedience and loyalty. Because of their relationship, the principal also has obligations to the agent, including compensation and reimbursement, as discussed in this chapter. Like the employer-employee relationship, the principal-agent relationship may be terminated in many ways. The chapter describes the different ways in which a principal-agent relationship may be terminated, including fulfillment of purpose, mutual agreement, and operation of law. Because the principal-agent relationship involves dealings with third parties, the question arises as to what notice must be given to third parties when an agency is terminated. The chapter ends with a discussion of the requirements for notifying third parties of the termination of the agency and the results if such notice is not given.

THE AGENCY CONCEPT

principal one who authorizes another to act for him or her in business transactions

A principal-agent relationship is created when one person, called the **principal**, grants authority to another person, called the **agent**, to act in place of and bind the principal in dealing with third parties. The relationship is outlined in Figure 24.1.

agent one who represents another in making business transactions

Although the principal-agent relationship may be used for personal purposes, its primary use is for business transactions. Many businesses can operate effectively only through the use of agents, which is particularly true for businesses organized as partnerships and corporations. In a partnership, each partner is an agent of the partnership and as such has the authority to bind the partnership in transactions related to the partnership business. A corporation, as an entity separate from its owners, can do business in its own name. Thus, it must depend on natural persons, such as the officers and employees, to act as agents for the corporation. Partnerships and corporations are discussed in greater detail in Chapters 26 and 27.

authority power to act for someone else

A principal who appoints an agent gives the agent **authority**, the power to perform acts on behalf of the principal and for the principal's benefit. Generally, whatever a person may do personally, he or she may do through an agent. An agent, however, may not do anything that would be harmful to the principal or that would be illegal. An agent cannot perform acts that are too personal to be performed by an agent, such as voting, serving on a jury, or making a will for the principal.

> Flynn appointed a friend to act as his agent to handle his finances. Flynn's agent does not have authority to make a gift of his money to Flynn's other friends.

CLASSIFICATION OF AGENTS

General Agents

general agent agent with authority to perform acts relating to all business matters of principal.

There are two types of agents: general and special. A **general agent** has the authority to perform acts that relate to all business matters of the principal. The general agent is considered to be in complete charge of the principal's business affairs.

> You appointed Gray, an attorney, to represent you in all matters relating to your business affairs. Gray is a general agent.

> Gray can do all the things you would do if you were personally taking care of your business affairs. For example, if you owned apartment buildings, Gray could collect the

FIGURE 24.1 The Principal-Agent Relationship

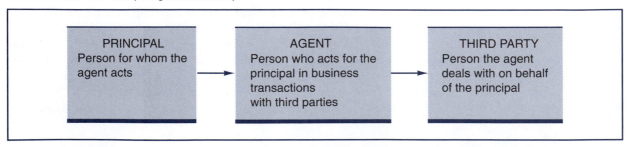

| PRINCIPAL
Person for whom the agent acts | → | AGENT
Person who acts for the principal in business transactions with third parties | → | THIRD PARTY
Person the agent deals with on behalf of the principal |

rents from tenants and authorize all repairs to the apartments. Gray could also draw money out of your bank account to pay your bills. Gray could even sell your company car if there was a good reason to do so.

Special Agents

A **special agent**, in contrast with a general agent, has the authority to perform one type of act or a limited number of acts relating to the principal's business.

> A friend gave you written authorization to sell her computer. You are considered a special agent for that transaction, and your authority is limited to selling the computer.

One type of special agent is a **broker**. A broker is an agent whose job is to bring a willing seller and a willing buyer together to form a contract. A real estate broker is a good example. Another type of special agent is a **factor**. A factor is a special agent who gets possession of the principal's property for the purpose of selling it. Factors collect the purchase price, deduct their fee or commission, and send the balance to the principal.

Gratuitous Agents

Agents do not always receive pay for the services they perform. Agents who do not receive compensation are called **gratuitous agents**.

> A friend handed you $80 and asked you to purchase two tickets for her to an upcoming rock concert at Holander Stadium. Your friend is the principal, you are a gratuitous agent, and the person who sells you the tickets is the third party with whom you deal on behalf of your friend.

A gratuitous agent who agrees to act for the principal has the same power to bind the principal as an agent who is paid. Because no consideration is given to the gratuitous agent in return for a promise to perform for the principal, however, the gratuitous agent cannot be forced to carry out an action for the principal.

WHO MAY SERVE AS PRINCIPAL AND AGENT

Principals who appoint agents must first be legally competent to act for themselves. In most states, minors may appoint agents. This move is not advisable from the agent's point of view, however, because the contract appointing the agent is voidable by the minor principal. Moreover, any contracts made by the agent for the minor are voidable unless the contracts are for necessaries.

> Robert, a minor, hired Vogue, an adult friend, as an agent to sell his motorcycle. Vogue sold the motorcycle to Hernandez, but Robert changed his mind and refused to deliver the bike to Hernandez. Because Robert, the principal, was a minor, he had the legal right to cancel the contract.

Because agents act not for themselves but for their principals, anyone can legally be appointed an agent. Thus, minors and other incompetents who lack the legal capacity to act for themselves may nonetheless act as agents. As agents, they may bind their principals to such business transactions as contracts. In some states, a person who has legally been declared insane may not be appointed an agent.

> Sandburg, an adult, hired Noble, a minor, as the general manager of her service station. Noble entered into a contract to purchase supplies for the station from the Seneca

Supply Company. When Sandburg discovered that Noble had purchased too many supplies because he overestimated the amount needed, she refused to be bound on the contract, claiming that Noble was a minor. Nevertheless, because Noble made the contract as Sandburg's agent, Sandburg was bound to pay Seneca for the supplies, even though Noble was a minor.

Both principals and agents may be either individuals, partnerships, or corporations.

RELATIONSHIPS SIMILAR TO AGENCIES

There are other relationships that are similar to the principal-agent relationship but that can be distinguished from it. Two of these are the employer-employee relationship and the independent contractor relationship.

Employer-Employee

The major difference between the principal-agent relationship and the employer-employee relationship is the degree of control exercised. An employee is not authorized to act in place of the employer. An employee is hired primarily to work under the employer's direction and is subject to the employer's control. The employer controls not only what the employee does but also how it is done.

An agent is authorized to act on behalf of the principal; although an agent is told what tasks to perform, he or she is not told how to carry out the tasks.

A person may act as both an employee and an agent. For instance, as an employee, the vice president in charge of the loan department of a bank must follow bank procedures determined by the bank president and perhaps the bank's board of directors in deciding who is or is not eligible for a loan. The vice president also enters into contracts with the bank's customers when granting them loans. In this second capacity, the vice president is an agent acting on behalf of the bank's president and board of directors, the principals.

Independent Contractor

independent contractor one hired to perform a task but not under hirer's direction or control

A person or business may be hired to perform services not as an agent, but as an independent contractor. An **independent contractor** is generally hired to perform a specific task and has complete control over the manner in which the work will be conducted. An independent contractor does not represent the hirer in dealings with third parties. Masons, plumbers, electricians, television repairpersons, and physicians are often independent contractors. For a more detailed discussion of independent contractors, see Chapter 23, page 382.

CREATION OF THE PRINCIPAL-AGENT RELATIONSHIP

A principal-agent relationship may be created by a contract, by appearance, by ratification, or by necessity.

By Contract

A principal may legally appoint an agent by means of an oral or written contract.

Frey was leaving for a winter vacation in Florida. She orally engaged Austin to act as her agent to handle all matters relating to an apartment building that she owned and rented to several tenants. This oral appointment of Austin was legal.

To prevent any misunderstandings between the principal and the agent (or between the agent and third parties) regarding the agent's authority, an agent should be given written authority. Written evidence of authority to act could be an informal instrument, such as a letter written by the principal to the agent containing all the essential elements of a contract. It could also be a formal written document such as the **power of attorney** shown in Figure 24.2. A power of attorney may be general or special. A general power of attorney gives the agent the authority of a general agent—that is, the power to do every act that can be lawfully performed by the principal. A special power of attorney gives the agent very restricted authority—the authority of a special agent.

In some cases, the statute of frauds must be satisfied. If the contract between the principal and the agent is for more than one year, the contract creating the agent's authority

power of attorney
formal written document giving agent authority to act

FIGURE 24.2 Power of Attorney

POWER OF ATTORNEY

KNOW ALL PERSONS BY THESE PRESENTS, that I, WILLIAM P. TEDESCI, 638 Fernwood Avenue, Topeka, Kansas, have made, constituted, and appointed, and by These Presents do make, constitute, and appoint KARA HIGGINS, my true and lawful attorney for me and in my name, place, and stead, to enter into any contract or contracts for the sale of premises owned by KARA HIGGINS and me in Newton, Missouri, on such terms as she shall in her discretion elect, and to execute in my behalf any deed or other conveyance of said premises, and to receive and deliver to me my share of the proceeds of any such sale, also giving and granting unto my said attorney full power and authority to do and perform all and every act or thing whatsoever requisite and necessary to be done in and about the premises, including obtaining of financing with regard to said premises, as fully to all intents and purposes as I might or could do if personally present, with full power of substitution and revocation, hereby ratifying and confirming all that my said attorney, or her substitute, shall lawfully do or cause to be done by virtue thereof.

IN WITNESS WHEREOF, I have hereunto set my hand and seal the 5th day of January, 2009.

William P. Tedesci

STATE OF KANSAS   )
COUNTY OF SHAWNEE) SS:

On this 5th day of January, 2009, before me, the subscriber, personally appeared WILLIAM P. TEDESCI, to me personally known to be the same person described in and who executed the foregoing instrument, and he acknowledged to me that he executed the same.

Luella M. Wolff

must be in writing. Likewise, if an agent is given the authority to sell real estate, the agent's authority must be in writing because a contract for the sale of real estate is required to be in writing.

By Appearance

agency by estoppel
situation in which one
party creates the
appearance that
another has the
authority to act as an
agent

If third parties are led to believe that a person is an agent because an appearance of a principal-agent relationship exists, an **agency by estoppel** is created. In this case, the so-called principal is *estopped* (prevented) by law from denying the relationship. Otherwise, the third parties would unjustly suffer damages or loss.

Southworth, a friend who owned a service station, asked Habbab to watch the station while Southworth went to lunch. He told her not to deal with any customers but simply to inform them that he would return in one hour. While Southworth was gone, a customer requested some automotive parts. Habbab sold the parts but guessed at the prices because no price list was available. When Southworth returned from lunch and discovered that Habbab had under-charged by $20, he called the customer to ask for the additional money. He explained that Habbab was not employed at the station and consequently had no knowledge of what prices to charge. The customer refused to pay the additional $20, claiming that she thought Habbab worked at the station and sold the parts at the correct price.

By leaving Habbab alone at the station, Southworth created the impression in the customer's mind that Habbab had the authority to deal with customers. The law now prevents Southworth from claiming that Habbab had no right to charge the prices she did. Because he allowed her to watch the station, Southworth must suffer the consequences of Habbab's act and cannot legally collect the additional $20. To allow otherwise would be unfair to the customer, who might not have purchased the parts had she known their true price.

By Ratification

If one person attempts to act as an agent for another and this other person approves the unauthorized act of the assumed agent, a principal-agent relationship arises by ratification (approval). Approval of the unauthorized act by the so-called principal has the effect of authorizing the agency.

Kowal, owner of a music store, learned that you had a violin for sale. Without your permission, Kowal, representing himself as your agent, sold the violin to Chambers for $10,000. Chambers gave Kowal a $1,000 deposit for the violin. When Kowal gave you the deposit and explained that he had sold the violin to Chambers, you accepted the money. By accepting the money, you ratified Kowal's act of selling the violin and created a principal-agent relationship. You cannot now legally change your mind and refuse to sell the violin to Chambers.

By Necessity

An emergency situation may require a person to act as an agent and thus may create a principal-agent relationship by necessity.

A tour group missed a flight to its home base, and the tour director arranged to house the group at a nearby hotel. Although not generally authorized to act as agent for the tour operator (the principal), the tour director had authority by necessity in this case because of the emergency.

If time permits and the principal is available, the agent must consult with the principal about a possible solution to the emergency. Furthermore, the agent receives no greater authority than that necessary to resolve the problem.

When a man and woman marry, the marriage relationship does not automatically give each person the authority to act as an agent of the other. The authority to act for each other develops naturally over a long period of time, such as when the wife as the wage earner willingly pays her husband's bills. Under these circumstances, the husband has the authority to continue to buy items and charge them to his wife's account.

On the other hand, under the domestic relations laws of most states, a husband and wife are responsible for furnishing each other and their minor children with the necessaries of life. If either fails to do so, the other may then purchase these necessaries and charge them to the other spouse's account (agency by necessity). For nonnecessaries, each spouse is liable only if an agency relationship can be established.

OBLIGATIONS OF THE AGENT TO THE PRINCIPAL

The duties of an agent to a principal are usually spelled out in the agency contract. In addition to the duties expressly mentioned, certain other duties are implied by law, based on the special relationship of trust and confidence. The usual implied duties are obedience, loyalty, reasonable skill, and accurate accounting. The agent also has a duty to communicate all pertinent information to the principal. A failure to live up to these obligations gives the principal the right to fire the agent. The principal may also recover damages for any loss suffered, which includes the right not to compensate the agent.

Obedience

The agent must follow all lawful instructions given by the principal. Failure to obey these instructions is grounds for dismissal and makes the agent liable in damages for any loss that results. Of course, if an emergency arises and the principal cannot be contacted, the agent is permitted to change the instructions as required by the situation and to use her or his own judgment. Any material change in the agent's original duties may amount to a breach of the agency contract.

> Atlas owned an automobile agency and instructed her salespeople not to sell cars to customers at prices below those set by the company. Reed, a salesperson who worked on commission, sold a car at a price 10 percent below the company's listed price. Reed would be liable to Atlas for any loss as the result of disobeying instructions. Reed could also be denied any commission due.

Loyalty

An agent is always expected to be loyal and to act in the best interests of the principal, and not in the agent's own interest or in the interest of another. In fact, the relationship is a **fiduciary** relationship, a relationship of trust and confidence. This includes the agent keeping confidential information learned about the principal's business during the course of the agency relationship. An example of a breach of loyalty by an agent is failing to turn over all money received for the principal while acting as an agent, including all secret profits such as gifts, bonuses, or commissions. The principal is entitled to this money and may demand it from the agent upon discovering that it was paid to the agent. Personally benefiting from a business deal or getting involved in conflict-of-interest situations (e.g., working for two principals or owning a competing business unknown to the principal) are also examples of breach of loyalty.

fiduciary one who acts for another in a position of trust

Banks was employed as a full-time salesperson for AGD Television Sales. Banks was also employed as a part-time salesperson for a competing firm, Acme Television Sales. Neither company was aware that Banks worked for the other.

In this case, Banks violated the duty of loyalty and is not entitled to collect compensation from either company. It is difficult, if not impossible, for an agent to work for two competing principals and to act in the best interests of both. This arrangement would be permissible, however, if Banks received the consent of both companies to work full time for one and part time for the other.

When not doing business for a principal, an agent is free to engage in any business as long as it is not a competing one.

Reasonable Skill

An agent is usually hired because he or she possesses some special knowledge or skill. In performing required tasks for the principal, the agent is expected to exercise the degree of skill he or she claims to possess. Of course, the agent must exercise at least reasonable skill. Reasonable skill is the degree of skill that average individuals would use in performing the same tasks for themselves. An agent who does not exercise the required skill is liable to the principal for any loss that results.

Nash, who recently inherited $25,000 from an aunt, hired Walker as an agent to invest this money in stocks to produce a stable income. Walker studied the stock market for several weeks and consulted several investors before buying stocks for Nash. Nevertheless, shortly after Walker invested the $25,000, the stocks went down in value because of a world crisis that affected the entire stock market. Walker could not be held liable for Nash's loss because at least reasonable skill was used in the purchase of the stocks.

Accurate Accounting

The agent must keep accurate, up-to-date records of all business transactions affecting the principal-agent relationship. Money collected on behalf of the principal should be turned over to the principal as soon as possible or, if the principal desires, placed in a bank account. The bank account should be opened in the principal's name, not the agent's. If money belonging to the principal is placed in the agent's account and it cannot be determined what amount belongs to the agent and what amount to the principal, the entire amount may be claimed by the principal.

Poore agreed to represent Frost, the owner of a small retail clothing store, by collecting payments due from Frost's credit customers. Poore placed the money in a personal bank account. Because Poore kept inaccurate records, there was no way of knowing what part of the money belonged to Frost. Poore could legally be required to turn over all the money in the bank account to Frost.

Communication

By law, a principal is understood to know any information the agent obtained from third parties while acting in the scope of authority, even if the principal does not actually receive this information. Because the agent represents the principal, what the agent knows, the principal knows. Therefore, the agent has a duty to communicate to the principal all matters coming to the agent's attention that would affect the principal's relationship with third parties.

Able offered to sell Corbett some electrical equipment through her agent, Melville, and gave Corbett three days to decide. Corbett accepted the offer within one day by informing Melville, but Melville did not tell Able of Corbett's acceptance until after the three days had expired. Able would be liable on the contract even though Melville did not inform her of Corbett's acceptance.

OBLIGATIONS OF THE PRINCIPAL TO THE AGENT

Principals likewise have certain fiduciary obligations to their agents. These obligations, imposed by contract or implied by law, are compensation, reimbursement, indemnification, safe working conditions, and cooperation.

Compensation

An agent who is not a gratuitous agent is entitled to compensation for work done according to the terms agreed on in the contract. If the agent's fee is not provided for by contract, the agent can expect to be paid a reasonable sum for the services performed. The principal must compensate the agent even when the principal-agent relationship arose because the principal ratified an unauthorized act. Sometimes compensation is on a contingency basis, such as when the agent earns a commission only after the sale of a product is concluded. In this case, the agent cannot collect the compensation from the principal until the contingency has occurred, which here is the completion of the sales transaction.

Reimbursement

The principal must reimburse (repay) an agent, even a gratuitous agent, for all necessary expenses the agent incurred in carrying out the principal's business. Usually, the agent pays the expenses connected with the agency from personal funds and then submits a bill to the principal. Reimbursable expenses include meals, lodging, airfare (or car mileage), entertainment expenses, and some incidental expenses such as telephone calls.

> Gerold, manager of Copy King Printing Company, attended a three-day business conference at a resort hotel to learn about new methods and techniques in the printing field. Gerold submitted an expense statement for airfare, $350; hotel room, $600; meals, $150; telephone calls to the company, $15; and cab fares, $75.

These expenses would probably be paid by Copy King because Gerold incurred them while on company business. An agent is not entitled to be reimbursed for expenses that are personal in nature or that were incurred as the result of the agent's misconduct or negligence, such as a speeding ticket.

> Blanchard, a traveling salesperson, spent a week in Florida on a business trip for the Ruston Restaurant Supply Company. After completing the business, Blanchard stayed three additional days at a neighboring resort hotel for a personal vacation. Blanchard could not ask for reimbursement from Ruston for these three days.

Business expenses that are unreasonable in view of what the agent was asked to accomplish for the principal are also not reimbursable.

Indemnification

The principal must indemnify the agent (protect the agent by making payment) for any personal loss incurred by the agent when the agent becomes liable to third parties while following the principal's lawful instructions. If the loss was incurred because of negligence or the agent's own misconduct, the principal is not bound to indemnify the agent.

> Chen was hired by the Beauty Mark Company to sell beauty products house to house in a certain town. Unknown to either Chen or Beauty Mark, an ordinance required all salespersons to register at the local town hall before selling any products in town. Chen, who was arrested and required to pay a $100 fine for failing to register, should legally be able to recover the money from Beauty Mark.

Safe Working Conditions

Just as an employer has a duty to provide an employee with reasonably safe working conditions, so too does a principal have an obligation to exercise the same degree of care for an agent. Failure to do so may make the principal liable to the agent for any injuries that the agent suffers. This obligation has been increased by statutes and regulations.

Cooperation

A principal has a duty to assist the agent in every way possible and to cooperate with the agent in the performance of the agent's duties. A principal may not, for example, bypass an agent and deal directly with a third party in an attempt to avoid paying a commission to an agent.

TERMINATION OF THE PRINCIPAL-AGENT RELATIONSHIP

A principal-agent relationship may be terminated by (1) fulfillment of purpose, (2) mutual agreement, (3) revocation of authority, (4) renunciation by the agent, (5) operation of law, or (6) subsequent destruction or illegality.

Fulfillment of Purpose or Lapse of Time

If the agent has authority to accomplish a specific act, the agency ends as soon as that act has been accomplished. For example, the authority of a real estate agent hired to sell your house ends when the house is sold. If an agent is hired for a specific period of time, such as six months or one year, the agency ends when this time period expires.

Mutual Agreement

The principal and the agent may mutually agree to end their relationship at any time.

Revocation of Authority

A principal may generally revoke an agent's authority and thus terminate the principal-agent relationship with or without cause at any time. Actually, the principal discharges the agent. If the discharge is for a good reason, such as a failure to follow instructions, the agent may not recover damages for breach of contract. Instead, the agent may have to pay money damages to the principal for causing the breach.

> Bush, a scout with authority to hire for a professional baseball team, was told not to sign contracts with any more players because the team was already overstaffed. Nevertheless, Bush signed a pitcher he thought would be an asset to the team. Bush could be discharged and made to pay damages for any loss caused by his act.

If an agent has been wrongfully discharged, the agent can collect unpaid compensation up to the time of discharge and, in addition, recover damages for the wrongful discharge.

> Volpe, a civil engineer, signed a two-year contract to design and oversee the construction of an office complex for Reed at a fee of $75,000 per year. Reed was pleased with Volpe's work, but when a personality conflict developed between the two at the end of the first year, Reed fired Volpe.

In this example, Volpe could recover damages because of the wrongful discharge before the expiration of the two-year contract. Volpe, however, is not entitled to the full $75,000 fee for the second year. The law generally requires the wrongfully discharged agent to seek other employment and to deduct any income for such work from the damages sought. Thus, Volpe would be entitled to $75,000 less any income from another job.

The authority of an agent may not be revoked unilaterally by the principal when the agent has an interest in the subject matter of the agency in addition to his or her compensation. In this case, the agency is said to be an **agency coupled with an interest**, and the agent must consent to the termination. This type of principal-agent relationship is not terminated even by events that normally end agencies by operation of law, such as the death or bankruptcy of the principal.

agency coupled with an interest agency in which agent has a personal interest in subject matter of the agency

> Drake left the United States to work with a firm in Europe. Before he left, he gave McIntyre permission to sell his car. McIntyre advanced Drake $1,000 with the understanding that McIntyre would be reimbursed out of the proceeds of the sale of the car. Before McIntyre had a chance to sell the car, Drake decided to revoke McIntyre's authority.

In this example, because McIntyre was to get the $1,000 lent to Drake back from the proceeds of the sale of the car, he had an agency coupled with an interest. Drake could not terminate the agency unless McIntyre consented to the termination. McIntyre could sell the car despite Drake's attempted revocation.

Renunciation by the Agent

An agent may refuse to continue to work for the principal. Of course, an agent who quits without just cause breaches the agency contract. The agent could be held liable for any loss suffered by the principal.

> Partridge had a contract with the Rundall Tool and Die Company to act as an agent to negotiate a new contract for the company with its employees. Halfway through the negotiation process, Partridge became dissatisfied with the way the negotiations were proceeding and quit. Rundall hired a substitute at a higher salary to complete the negotiations with the employees. Because Partridge breached her contract by wrongfully quitting the job, she was liable to Rundall for the additional salary paid to her substitute.

Operation of Law

By operation of law, certain situations will terminate a principal-agent relationship immediately. Among these situations are the death or insanity of either the principal or the agent, bankruptcy of the principal, and in some cases, bankruptcy of the agent.

> Goode was employed by Carey, owner of Talent Unlimited, to book bands to play at high school proms and other school dances. Goode booked a band to play at a local high school, unaware that Carey had died earlier in the day.

In this example, the principal-agent relationship terminated with Carey's death. Consequently, the contract Goode made with the school was void. An agent cannot make a contract for a deceased principal.

A bankruptcy petition filed by the principal to liquidate the business usually terminates the principal-agent relationship. The filing of a bankruptcy petition by the agent generally will not terminate the principal-agent relationship unless the purpose of the agency was affected. For example, if you are acting as a financial adviser to clients of your principal, who is a stockbroker, your filing of the bankruptcy petition would terminate the relationship because your credibility as a financial adviser would be destroyed.

A principal-agent relationship also terminates by operation of law when the subject matter of the agency is destroyed or when the performance of the agent's duties becomes impossible.

> Clemens was hired under a two-year contract to manage a Houston, Texas, branch of Prep Tax, a nationwide chain that prepared individual income tax forms. Six months later, the state of Texas passed a law requiring all income tax preparers to pass a licensing examination. If Clemens fails to pass the test, it would be illegal for him to continue as manager. The principal-agent relationship would be terminated by impossibility.

Subsequent Destruction or Illegality

A principal-agency relationship established for a specific purpose will end if the purpose becomes illegal, or prohibited by law, making the agency meaningless.

> You appointed Bergen as your agent to operate a gas station for you. If the zoning law changes and prohibits operation of a gas station in that area, the agency relationship will end.

A principal-agency relationship established to deal with specific property will end if the property is destroyed, also making the agency meaningless.

> Crane appointed Bellow as her agent to sell her home, with Bellow to receive a commission based on a percentage of the purchase price. If the home burns down before it is sold, the agency will terminate.

NOTIFYING THIRD PARTIES OF THE TERMINATION

The agent's actual authority ends when the principal tells the agent that authority has been revoked. Third parties with whom the agent deals may not always know this. Consequently, there is a general rule that third parties, unless otherwise notified by the principal, may presume that a principal-agent relationship continues to exist. Thus, the principal will continue to be bound by the agent's acts until third parties have been notified.

Third parties who have dealt regularly with the agent must be notified by the principal of the termination of the agent's authority, either personally or in writing. For all other third parties, a public notice, such as in a newspaper circulated in the area in which the agent has been operating, is sufficient even though a third party may not actually read the notice.

> Cooley was the manager of Racquet, a sporting goods store. As manager, Cooley purchased merchandise for the store on credit. The merchandise would then be paid for by Syms, the owner of the store. Syms sold the store to Cooley, who continued to buy merchandise from the same creditors. When Cooley did not pay the bills, one creditor sued Syms.

In this example, Syms failed to give creditors actual notice, personally or in writing, that Cooley was no longer an agent for the store, and Cooley therefore still had apparent authority to purchase merchandise in Syms's name. The creditor had a legal right to recover from Syms even for merchandise purchased by Cooley as the new owner of the store. Of course, Syms could then sue and recover damages from Cooley.

When a principal-agent relationship is terminated not by the principal but rather by operation of law (e.g., by death, insanity, or bankruptcy), notice to third parties is not necessary. Third parties generally become aware of the termination through publicity officially given these matters in newspapers, official records, or by other means.

Ordinarily, notice is not required to revoke the authority of a special agent because most people do not deal with such agents on a continual basis. If, however, the principal has led third parties to believe that the special agent has unusual authority—such as authority granted under a special power of attorney—actual notice of termination is required.

Summary

A principal-agent relationship is created when an agent is asked to enter into transactions, usually business transactions, with third parties and to act in place of and at the request of the principal. Agents make independent decisions and exercise judgment as if they were making the transactions themselves. Their authority may be very broad, in which case they are called general agents, or it may be very narrow, in which case they are called special agents. Agents who do not receive compensation for their services are called gratuitous agents.

A person may be hired as an employee rather than as an agent. The difference is that an employee acts under the direct control and supervision of the employer, but an agent makes independent decisions. A person may also be hired as an independent contractor rather than as an employee or an agent. The independent contractor also makes independent decisions and exercises judgment but does not deal with third persons on behalf of the hirer.

Principals who appoint agents must be legally competent. In most states, minors may appoint agents. Because agents act not for themselves but for their principals, agents are not required to be legally competent.

Minors and incompetents who are not prohibited by state law may act as agents.

A principal-agent relationship may be created by an oral or written contract, but it may also be created by appearance, by ratification, or by necessity.

An agent owes the principal certain duties based upon their special relationship of trust and confidence, including the duties of obedience, loyalty, reasonable skill, accurate accounting, and communication. The principal owes the agent the obligations of compensation, reimbursement, indemnification, safe working conditions, and cooperation.

A principal-agent relationship may be terminated by fulfillment of the purpose of the agency or lapse of time, by mutual agreement, by revocation of the agent's authority, by renunciation by the agent, by operation of law, or by subsequent destruction of the subject matter or illegality of the purpose.

As a general rule, third parties, unless otherwise notified by the principal, may presume that a principal-agent relationship continues to exist. The principal will continue to be bound by any acts that the agent performs in the apparent scope of authority until the principal gives notice of termination of the agency.

Important Legal terms

agency by estoppel
agency coupled with an interest
agent
authority
broker

factor
fiduciary
general agent
gratuitous agent
independent contractor

power of attorney
principal
special agent

Questions and Problems for Discussion

1. Describe the different ways an agency may be created.

2. Why is the agency concept so important to the conduct of business transactions?

3. What third parties should be notified when a principal-agent relationship is terminated? How should these third parties be notified?

4. Describe the six ways a principal-agency relationship may be terminated.

5. Margolis gave Frey a power of attorney as follows: "I, William R. Margolis, appoint Amanda Frey to represent me in my business, Eddy Meat Packing Company, and in my name to write checks and other such instruments, and do all such matters in reference to the business as may be required to lawfully conduct this business."
   a. Who is the principal?
   b. Who is the agent?
   c. What type of agency has been created: general or special?

6. Curry asked Gray to act as his agent in selling his car. Gray agreed to act without any consideration. When Gray sold the car, Curry declined to go through with the sale, claiming that Gray had no authority to bind him because he was not being paid for his services as agent. Was Curry correct?

7. Explain the difference between an agent and an independent contractor.

8. Describe the six ways a principal-agency relationship may be terminated.

9. Craig was hired as an agent to sell advertising on a commission basis. The advertising agency suffered a financial loss and declared bankruptcy. Does the act of filing for bankruptcy terminate the agency relationship?

10. Berman was an agent selling real estate for Eastern Realtors, Inc. While showing a home to a client one day, Berman discovered that water was leaking into the basement. He called a plumber to fix the leak, and when the plumber sent a bill to Eastern, they refused to pay on the grounds that Berman had no authority to call a plumber without their consent. Is Eastern correct?

11. Frey, an agent for Thomas, was asked to make a delivery as soon as possible to a customer, even if it meant exceeding the speed limit. Frey was stopped for speeding and fined $100. Is Thomas obligated to reimburse Frey for the fine he paid?

12. Frost, an appliance dealer, hired Jones, a minor, as an agent to sell real estate. Jones sold a home to Fallon, but Frost, unhappy with the transaction, tried to break the contract with Fallon, claiming that Jones was a minor and legally incompetent to enter into the contract. Is Frost correct?

13. Russ was hired by the Atrium Car Agency as a new-car salesperson on a commission basis. She was told by Atrium, her principal, that the sale of any new car must be approved by the owner of the agency. Russ did not follow these instructions and approved the sale of a new car on her own. The sale price was not acceptable to the principal. Russ tried to collect her commission on the sale, but the principal refused to pay. Could the principal deny Russ her commission?

14. Warren, a real estate broker, agreed to sell five buildings owned by Kraft, with a commission of 10 percent of the sales price. Prior to the sale of any buildings, Kraft revoked the agreement. Was Warren's authority to sell irrevocable as a power coupled with an interest?

15. Fyfe was an agent for Argus Corporation, a business that sold computers. Fyfe learned of a laundry that was for sale at a bargain price and bought it without disclosing this fact to the officers of Argus. Was this a breach of loyalty on Fyfe's part?

16. Oswald, an agent selling real estate for Manning, assaulted a spectator at a sports event. Is Manning liable for Oswald's crime?

17. Berg authorized Stillman to sell his guitar for $450. Stillman sold the guitar for $500 and kept the additional $50 for himself, claiming he was entitled to it as a commission. May Berg recover the $50?

Cases for Review

1. Leno joined a scuba diving class at the YMCA. The class was taught by an instructor who contributed his services to the YMCA and was not remunerated for them. The course was advertised by the YMCA, and Leno paid the YMCA for the course. Leno died as a result of an accident, and a suit was brought against the YMCA, claiming the instructor was an agent of the YMCA. Is this claim correct? (*Leno v. Young Men's Christian Association of San Francisco,* 17 Cal. App. 651)

2. Fields, a landowner, gave permission to the Clayton County Water Authority to construct a sewer line across his property. The authority in turn sub-contracted the work to the B&B Pipeline Company. The authority exercised no control over the method, manner, or means of construction. During construction, B&B damaged some trees on Fields's property. Fields sued the authority, claiming that as principal, the authority was responsible for the damage. Is the authority liable in this case? (*Fields v. B&B Pipeline Company, Inc.,* 147 Ga. App. 875)

3. Agrest had a power of attorney from a principal. He gave his principal's property to his own wife, who then proceeded to sell the property to a third party. The power of attorney was silent about the right to donate the principal's property. The principal sued Agrest, claiming that Agrest had breached his fiduciary duty. Will the principal succeed? (*Matter of Agrest,* 279 A.D.2d 471)

4. A nonprofit corporation had a checking account at Fleet Bank. An officer of the corporation borrowed money from the bank by falsely representing that he was acting as an agent on behalf of the corporation. The corporation had never done anything to indicate that the officer had authority to borrow money. Is the nonprofit corporation entitled to recover from the bank the money paid to the officer? (*Fleet Bank v. Consola, Ricciletti,* 703 N.Y.S.2d 182)

5. Vision Corp. was a sales agent for Production Products Company. Its sales agreement provided that either party could terminate the agreement at any time at the end of a month by giving sixty-day's advance notice. Production terminated the agreement after giving proper notice. Vision, however, claimed that regardless of the wording in the contract, there was an implied obligation of good faith, and therefore, the agreement could not be canceled at will but only for good cause. Is this claim correct? (*Production Products Company v. Vision Corp.,* 706 N.Y.S.2d 789)

6. A number of businesses purchased ads in a yellow pages publication published by Bell Atlantic and Nynex. The ads were solicited by an agent, R. H. Donnelley, Inc. After a problem arose, the businesses sued both telephone companies and Donnelley for breach of contract. Donnelley claimed that it was not liable because it was an agent of a disclosed principal. Will Donnelley succeed? (*Cruz v. Nynex Information Resources,* 703 N.Y.S.2d 103)

CHAPTER **25**

Principal-Agent, Employer-Employee, and Third-Party Relationships

CHAPTER PREVIEW

Liability of Principal and Employer to Third Parties

    Contract Liability of Principal

    Tort Liability of Principal and Employer

Liability of Agent and Employee to Third Parties

    Contract Liability of Agent

    Tort Liability of Agent and Employee

Criminal Liability of Principal, Agent, Employer, and Employee

Chapter Highlights

Chapter 24 covered the obligations that a principal owes to an agent and that an agent owes to a principal. This chapter discusses the liability of the principal and the agent and the employer and the employee to third parties with whom the agent and employee deal. It describes the liability of a principal to third parties when the agent enters into contracts with them on behalf of the principal. It also describes in detail the effect of the different types of authority that an agent may have. The chapter examines the liability of the principal and employer for torts committed by the agent or employee while acting within the scope of the purposes of the agency or the scope of employment. It then discusses the circumstances in which a principal and employer can be held liable toward a third person. Like the principal or employer, the agent and employee may also be liable to third parties. The chapter continues by focusing on the liability of an agent to third parties for contracts that the agent makes without obtaining authority from the principal or without disclosing the existence of a principal. The agent's and employee's liability to third persons for torts he or she commits is also discussed. The chapter concludes with a brief discussion of the liability of both principal and agent and employer and employee for criminal acts committed by an agent or employee.

LIABILITY OF PRINCIPAL AND EMPLOYER TO THIRD PARTIES

The principal is legally liable to third parties for contracts an agent makes as long as the agent operates within the authority given to her or him. A principal may choose to be bound by ratifying (approving) an unauthorized contract. The principal would then be liable on the contract as if it had been authorized in the first place.

In addition to contract liability, the principal may be liable to third parties who are injured as the result of torts committed by an agent who was legally acting for the principal.

Contract Liability of Principal

An agent has the authority to enter into contracts with third parties on behalf of the principal. Generally, the principal is bound by these contracts if the agent acts within the scope of authority. **Scope of authority** refers to the extent of the agent's authority and generally includes express, implied, and apparent authority.

Express authority is the authority the principal actually gives the agent either orally or in writing. A power of attorney is an example of express authority.

Implied authority describes the authority of an agent to perform duties not expressly given by the principal but understood by custom or as necessary to carry out the purpose of the agency. The principal does not usually list in writing every duty expected of the agent. If, for example, you are a professional manager and are hired to run a ski shop, the principal will probably not discuss with you every detail of running the shop. It is understood that you will do such things as pay utility bills, order proper merchandise, and keep an account of what you have sold. In many cases, the agent's authority is governed by customs in the particular trade or business.

Another type of implied authority is known as **emergency authority**, the authority that an agent has to act in the event of an emergency if the agent is unable to contact the principal for express authority to act. In such circumstances, the principal will be bound by the act of the agent.

> Bowles appointed Gerber as her agent to sell her condominium. While visiting a prospective buyer one day, Gerber saw that the person with whom she was talking had become extremely ill and required medical attention immediately. Gerber would have implied authority to call an ambulance for the ill person, even though Gerber has no express authority to do so.

Apparent authority is the authority that an agent has because a principal leads third parties to believe that the agent possesses such authority when in fact the agent does not. If a third party reasonably believes, from the principal's words or conduct, that the agent has such authority, the principal will be bound. The agent, however, will be liable to the principal for disobedience in making an unauthorized contract for which the principal is liable.

> Gibbons, a salesperson for Monumental Used Cars, was told not to sell cars on credit in the future but to sell for cash only. Nevertheless, he sold a used car to Tucker on credit so that he would not lose the commission on the sale. Tucker had purchased used cars from Gibbons on credit in the past and knew of other customers who had purchased cars from Monumental on credit. Because Gibbons had the apparent authority to sell cars on credit, a binding contract resulted between Monumental, the principal, and Tucker, the third party. Of course, Gibbons disobeyed instructions and would be liable in damages to his principal if Tucker failed to pay for the car.

Sometimes an agent performs an act that is outside the scope of her or his authority. As mentioned earlier, if the principal ratifies (approves) the agent's unauthorized act, the principal is as liable as if the act had been authorized in the first place. Ratification of an unauthorized act may be either express or implied. *Express ratification* occurs when the principal approves of the transaction either in writing or orally. *Implied ratification* occurs when a principal knows that an unauthorized act has taken place but decides to accept it and keep its benefits. In both cases, the principal must have been aware of all the facts and circumstances of the business transaction; otherwise, no ratification will have taken place.

scope of authority
extent of agent's authority to carry out principal's business

express authority
authority specifically given to agent by principal

implied authority
authority agent is understood to have to carry out purpose of the agency

emergency authority
authority an agent has to act in event agent cannot consult principal for express authority to act

apparent authority
authority principal leads third parties to believe agent has because of principal's words or conduct

Tort Liability of Principal and Employer

vicarious liability
person's liability for
someone else's acts

respondeat superior
doctrine that a princi-
pal is liable in certain
cases for the wrongful
acts of an agent

scope of the agency
extent of agent's duties
to carry out principal's
business

Both a principal and an employer may be held liable for torts committed by an agent or an employee. They may both be liable although they were personally not at fault, a theory known as **vicarious liability**; in the case of an employer, this liability is more specifically called **respondeat superior**. The rules governing the vicarious liability of a principal and employer for the wrongful acts of an agent and an employee are the same.

It would be unfair to hold a principal or employer liable for every wrongful act of an agent or employee. The law is that a principal is generally liable to third parties for torts committed by an agent only when the agent is carrying on the principal's business, known as the **scope of the agency**. The same holds true for an employer's liability to a third party: Liability exists only when the employee acts within the *scope of employment* as if the principal authorizes its agent to perform the act.

It is often difficult to determine whether an agent was acting within the scope of authority, or whether an employee was acting within the scope of employment, when a tort occurred. In general, if an act is committed in furtherance of the principal's or employer's business, it will be considered within the scope of the agency or employment.

If an agent or employee commits a tort while pursuing his or her own interests, the tort is not within the scope of the agency or employment, and neither the principal nor the employer would be liable.

> Buff, an employee of Ace Trucking, drove the company truck to a baseball game one night. While driving too fast for existing road conditions, his truck struck Blaine and injured him. Ace would not be liable for Buff's negligence because at the time of the accident, Buff was pursuing his own interests and was not on company business.

If an agent or employee maliciously commits an intentional tort (e.g., assault and battery) on a third party, the courts have interpreted such an act as a turning away from the principal's business or the employer's business and have held neither the principal nor the employer responsible. They could be held liable, however, if the agent or employee who committed the intentional tort did so in the belief that the intentional act would further the business of the agent or principal.

LIABILITY OF AGENT AND EMPLOYEE TO THIRD PARTIES

As long as an agent has the authority to act, the agent has no personal liability on a contract. The law does not recognize the agent who acts within her or his authority as a party to a contract. When an agent who has no authority to do so makes a contract, however, he or she is bound by the contract, but the principal is not.

Contract Liability of Agent

The agent is liable to third parties if (1) the agent enters into a contract without authority, (2) the agent does not disclose the principal's identity to third parties, (3) the agent is careless in signing a contract, (4) the agent voluntarily agrees to become liable on a contract, or (5) a person pretends to be an agent.

Agent Acts Without Authority   When a third party deals with an agent, the third party is in fact dealing with the principal. As a result, the law does not recognize the agent as a party to the contract when he or she acts within the scope of authority. Sometimes, however, an agent attempts to enter into a contract with a third person on behalf of the principal but lacks the authority to do so. If the principal does not ratify the transaction, the agent becomes personally liable to this third person. The agent's liability is based on an implied warranty that the agent has the authority to act as an agent on the principal's behalf.

> Sullivan, an insurance agent, authorized Black, whose home had been damaged by fire, to have repairs made to the house. Sullivan had no authority to permit such repairs without authorization from his insurance company. Because Sullivan exceeded his authority, he would be personally liable to Black if the insurance company did not approve his unauthorized act.

Agent Acts for Undisclosed Principal   An agent sometimes enters into a contract in the agent's name without disclosing the name of the principal. Individuals and businesses sometimes prefer to keep secret from third parties their connection with a particular transaction, and they ask an agent to contract in the agent's own name. When third parties dealing with an agent in such circumstances are unaware of the existence of a principal, the principal is known as an **undisclosed principal**. An agent who contracts for an undisclosed principal is as liable on the contract as if the agent were the principal.

undisclosed principal
principal whose identity is not known to third parties with whom agent makes contracts

> Manger purchased office buildings as investments. To maintain secrecy, he hired Rupp as an agent to purchase several office buildings in Rupp's name from Troy, owner of the buildings. Rupp is personally liable on this contract with Troy even though Rupp was authorized to enter into the contract. Rupp may be liable to Troy because Troy may have entered into the contract only because of the confidence Troy had that Rupp would perform the contract. If Manger refuses to go through with the contract, Troy may hold either Rupp or Manger liable, but not both. If Troy elects to enforce the contract against Rupp, Rupp may then recover the amount of the liability from Manger.

The undisclosed principal, once discovered, may hold a third party to a contract made with the agent even though this third party did not realize that the agent was acting for an undisclosed principal.

> Pierson hired Wilshire to purchase an antique car from Rogers. Wilshire did not reveal that she was buying the car for Pierson but signed the contract in her own name. Rogers discovered that Wilshire was purchasing the car for Pierson and refused to go through with the deal because they were on unfriendly terms. Pierson, as the now-disclosed principal, may sue Rogers for breach of contract.

Agent Is Careless in Signing   If the agent is acting for a disclosed principal, the agent should be careful to sign the principal's name to a written contract first and then sign her or his name as agent. For example, an agent should sign the contract "Billie Holmes (principal) by Nancy Ling, Agent." By signing in this way, the agent makes clear that the contract is between the principal and the third party and that the agent is not a party to the contract. If the agent neglects to include the principal's name on the contract, only the agent is bound by the contract.

Agent Agrees to Personal Liability   Sometimes a third party, for one reason or another, is not willing to deal directly with the principal but will deal with the agent. For example, the principal may have an unknown or bad credit rating, but the agent has a strong credit rating. The principal may therefore ask the agent to sign the contract as a coprincipal. By doing so, the agent assumes equal liability with the principal on the contract. This situation frequently occurs when the agent and third party are well established locally but the principal is located out of town.

This same situation may also occur when an agent agrees to become personally liable on the contract to induce the third party to enter into the contract.

Person Pretends to Be an Agent A person who pretends to be an agent of another is personally liable for any contracts made with a third party.

> Beamer and several individuals decided to form a social club. Before the club could legally open its doors to members, it had to be officially registered with the state as a club. Before the club was officially registered, however, Beamer purchased some equipment for the clubhouse, claiming to be the club's treasurer. The state later refused to recognize the club. Beamer, who had claimed to be an agent for a club that legally did not exist, is personally liable on the contract for the equipment.

Tort Liability of Agent and Employee

An agent acting within the scope of the agency or an employee acting within the scope of employment is personally liable for torts committed against a third person even though the principal and employer are also liable. Actually, the third party may sue either the principal or the agent, the employer or the employee, or both jointly. The agent or employee is liable as the person who actually committed the tort. The principal or employer is liable because a benefit is derived from the agent's or employee's work and also because the principal or employer has the right of control over the agent or employee. In many cases, the third party sues the principal and the agent or the employer and the employee jointly.

If the third party elects to sue only one person (either the principal or the agent or the employer or the employee) and receives compensation for the tort in a court of law, that third party is then barred from suing the other party. Of course, if a successful legal action is brought against the principal or employer, the principal or the employer can then sue the agent or employee for the wrongful act.

> Flynn was a salesperson in the toy department at the Daw Department Store. During the Christmas rush, Flynn became angry and pushed a customer, causing the customer to fall to the floor and injure his back. The customer sued the store owner and received money damages for his injuries. Because the customer collected money damages from the store owner (the principal), he cannot also sue Flynn (the agent) for his injuries.

CRIMINAL LIABILITY OF PRINCIPAL, AGENT, EMPLOYER, AND EMPLOYEE

Generally, neither a principal nor an employer is liable for criminal acts committed by the agent or employee. The agent or employee is personally liable.

> Weir was a sales representative for Amco Manufacturing Company. While driving a company car to a company meeting in an intoxicated condition, Weir hit and killed Tydings, a pedestrian.

In this example, Weir would be criminally liable, but Amco would not. Amco would, however, have tort (civil) liability for damages (along with Weir) because Weir was acting within the scope of the agency.

A principal or employer may be held criminally liable (in addition to the agent and employee) if he or she authorizes the criminal act. Furthermore, a statute sometimes places criminal responsibility on a principal or employer such as a corporation. As an artificial person and a recognized separate legal entity, a corporation may commit crimes only through its human agents and employees.

Summary

A principal is liable to third parties for contracts that an agent makes if the agent is acting within the scope of the agent's express, implied, emergency, or apparent authority. An agent who makes an unauthorized contract with a third party does not bind the principal unless the principal chooses to ratify the contract.

The agent is liable for contracts made if (1) the agent acts without authority and the principal does not ratify the transaction, (2) the agent acts for an undisclosed principal, (3) the agent's name is placed on a contract in a way that binds the agent rather than the principal, (4) the agent agrees to be personally liable on a contract made on behalf of the principal, or (5) the person is not really an agent.

The principal is liable to an injured party for a tort that the agent commits while acting within the scope of

the agency and while carrying out the principal's business.

An employer is also liable to an injured party for a tort that the employee commits while acting within the scope of employment and while carrying out the employee's business.

An agent acting within the scope of the agency, or an employee acting within the scope of employment, is personally liable for torts committed against a third person even though the principal or employer is also liable.

A principal is not liable for the criminal acts of the agent unless he or she authorized the act. The agent is personally liable. The same holds true for an employer and an employee.

Important Legal terms

apparent authority	implied authority	scope of the agency
emergency authority	respondeat superior	undisclosed principal
express authority	scope of authority	vicarious liability

Questions and Problems for Discussion

1. Give examples of actual and implied authority.
2. What are the differences between the three types of authority that an agent has?
3. Compare the contract liability of the principal and the agent (a) when the agent acts within the scope of authority and (b) when the agent acts without authority or does not disclose the principal's identity to third parties.
4. When are a principal and an employer liable to a third party for a wrongful act committed by an agent or employee?
5. Why should an employer be responsible for the acts of an employee when the employer may have

no control over, or knowledge of, the acts of the employee?

6. Foster, owner of an art gallery, hired Garr to purchase a valuable painting from Wilson. Ten days later, Garr and Wilson entered into a contract for the purchase of the painting. Unbeknown to them, Foster had died the day before. Was the contract made by Garr valid?

7. Kerr knew that Jones was an agent for the Smith Company, seller of vacuum cleaners. He wanted to buy some vacuum cleaners, but while he trusted Johns, he knew nothing about the company, so he asked Johns to sign the purchase

contract as principal. If the Smith Company refuses to honor the contract, may Kerr hold Johns liable?

8. Bild owned a car rental agency and hired Bush as an agent to advertise his business in the newspapers. Bush was asked by a charitable organization to make a contribution on behalf of Bild and Bush promised the contribution. Is Bild responsible to make the gift?

9. Garcia purchased a valuable painting at an auction. The painting's owner had left the painting on consignment with the auction house, asking it to act as her agent in selling the painting. Garcia discovered that the painting was a forgery and sued the auction house for breach of warranty. The auction house owners claimed that the auction house was not responsible because it was acting as agent for the owner and any suit must be brought against the owner. Was it correct?

10. Lerner went to an auto repair shop to pick up her car that had been serviced. When she complained that the work had not been done properly, the employee who had done the work punched her and broke her arm. Lerner sued the shop's owner for damages. Was the shop liable?

11. Blaine was employed by the Acme Corporation to repair air conditioners. While working at an office one day, Blaine saw a secretary suffer a heart attack. He called for medical help. He could have called his employer for authorization but failed to do so. When the bill arrived for the medical services and the secretary could not pay for them, the medical service company billed Acme Corporation, which refused to pay on the grounds that Blaine was not authorized to obtain such services. Is the company correct?

12. Bixly worked for XYZ Corp., a public relations firm. He knew that a competitor, Direct Relations Corp., was trying to take business away from XYZ Corp., so he intentionally spread a rumor that Direct Relations was in financial distress and about to file for bankruptcy. The rumor was false but Direct Relations went out of business as a result. It sued XYZ Corp. for libel. Does it have a good case?

13. Baron agreed to buy a trailer from Alston, who failed to disclose that he was acting for Green, the real owner. Alston signed the contract in his own name. If Alston breaks the contract, can Baron sue him, or must he sue the undisclosed principal?

14. Munz, a paraplegic, was being flown from Houston, Texas, to a clinic in Rochester, Minnesota, for treatment. As Track Airlines personnel were carrying her hurriedly and roughly aboard in a special chair for people in wheelchairs, they dropped her on the plane's stairwell. As a result, she suffered bruises and muscle spasms and experienced a substantial period of pain and suffering. Munz sued Track Airlines, claiming negligence by its agents. Is Track Airlines liable?

15. Frost was hired by Universal Homes as an agent to sell new homes. During an argument with a customer, Frost struck him and was arrested and convicted of assault and battery. Can Universal be held criminally liable for Frost's action?

16. Grabin purchased a cruise from World Wide Travel. The cruise was interrupted because of a faulty generator. Grabin asked for a refund from World Wide, but World Wide refused, claiming that only the cruise line was liable. Is World Wide correct?

Cases for Review

1. Clark was driving a company-owned truck on the left side of the road instead of the right. He collided with Marchant's automobile, injuring him. When Marchant sued Clark, Clark's defense was that he had been instructed by his employer's supervisor to drive that way. Is that defense valid? (*Marchant* v. *Clark,* 273 P.2d 541)

2. Laccoaree employed his son part time in a grocery store he ran. He asked his son to pick up supplies for the store in a nearby town. While he was returning to the store with the supplies, he negligently struck Stanfield's vehicle, damaging it. Stanfield sued Laccoaree for damages to the car. Is Laccoaree liable? (*Stanfield* v. *Laccoaree,* 588 P.2d 1271)

3. Clarke and Manko, both agents of Reserve Insurance Company, attended a convention relating to their work, although their attendance was not required by the company. While at the convention, Clarke and Manko met Jones, a former agent of Reserve Insurance. Following one of the convention meetings attended by all three, a fight

developed between Clarke and Jones over a book, which Jones contended that Clarke had not returned to him. Jones, who was injured in the fight, sued the Reserve Insurance Company, claiming that the company was liable for the tort of assault and battery committed by one of its agents, Clarke, who was acting in the scope of the agency. Can the Reserve Insurance Company be held responsible for Clarke's behavior? (*Jones* v. *Reserve Insurance Co.,* Ariz. 253 N.E.2d 849)

4. Boudreaux was an employee of an oil well drilling company. He worked alternate weeks, and when his workweek ended, his pay stopped and he returned to his home. While driving home one day at the end of a workweek, his car struck another vehicle and its driver was killed. The driver's estate sued the oil well drilling company for damages for wrongful death. Is the employer liable in this situation? (*Boudreaux* v. *Yancey,* 319 So.2d 806)

5. Buckley, a New York City police officer, was shot in the leg when a gun being loaded by a fellow officer discharged in the stationhouse locker room. The city claimed that it was not responsible for Buckley's injuries because the injuries were caused by a fellow employee. Will the city succeed with this argument? (*Buckley* v. *City of New York,* 452 N.Y.S.2d 331)

6. Mr. and Mrs. Hart bought an auto insurance policy from an agent representing Farmers Insurance. The policy they bought did not include uninsured motorist coverage. They were injured and suffered losses when their car was hit by an uninsured motorist and were not covered under their policy. They sued the agent (and the insurance company), claiming that the agent had a duty to them as an agent. Are they correct? (*Harts* v. *Farmers Insurance Exchange,* 597 N.W. 2d 47)

7. Lanham and Clark, members of a limited liability company (LLC) contracted with Westec for engineering services for a restaurant the LLC was constructing. Westec did not know it was dealing with an LLC and this was not disclosed to it. When the work was completed, Westic submitted a bill, was not paid, and sued Lanham and Clark. Are they liable? (*Eater, Waste & Land, Inc., dba Westec* v. *Lanham,* 955 P. 2d 997).

8. Lewis, employed by Roselle Toyota, was driving a company car on a purely personal errand when he collided with another car owned by Taylor. The injured occupants of the Taylor car sued both Lewis and Roselle, claiming negligence. Roseville claimed it was not liable for the injuries because Lewis was not acting within the scope of his employment. Is Roseville correct? (*Taylor* v. *Roseville Toyota Inc.,* 138 Cal. App. 4th 994)

THE CASE OF THE FIRED EMPLOYEE

L inda Lewis, vice president of the Acme Trailer Company, enjoyed a wonderful reputation as a capable and trusted financial officer. She, her husband, and their two children lived in a beautiful suburb in a large, comfortable home. The president of a competitor firm, International Trailers Ltd., wanted to hire Lewis for a similar position and offered her an increased salary and many employee benefits. Lewis accepted the offer, sold her home, moved to the city in which her new employer was located, and purchased a home there. She did not have a written contract, but she was told she had a great future with the company and was given a salary of $150,000 per year.

Four months after Lewis joined the company, she was fired because of a downturn in the trailer production business, requiring a scaling back of expenses at International. She sued International for breach of contract.

The Trial

During the trial, Lewis testified about the reputation she had earned while at Acme Trailer and the wonderful life that she and her family had enjoyed. She told of the difficulties involved in moving, the expense of buying a new home, and the uprooting of her family. She described the difficulties involved in selling her new home and looking for a new position.

An officer of International testified about the recession in the trailer industry and how economic conditions were such that if International failed to cut expenses, it might be forced out of business.

The Arguments at Trial

Lewis's attorney argued that although she did not have a written contract, oral representations made to her had implied that her job would last a long time. That she was going to earn a yearly salary indicated that her employment would, at a minimum, last at least a year. The attorney stressed the difficulties involved in the move and the expenses occurred by the Lewis family, arguing that it would be unfair to terminate Lewis's employment except for cause relating to her activities. The argument was also made that the "employment-at-will" doctrine was an outmoded and unfair concept and should not be applied based on the facts in this case.

International's attorney argued that the lack of a written contact and the existence in the state in which International was located of the "termination at will" doctrine gave International the right to terminate Lewis's employment at any time for any reason, particularly when economic conditions required cutting of expenses, including termination of the employment of executives with high salaries.

Questions to Discussion

1. Based on the facts of this case, who do you think should prevail, Lewis or International? Why?
2. Are there other facts that would make it easier for the court to decide who should prevail?
3. What factors might a court consider in determining whether the employment at will doctrine should not be applied here?
4. Do you feel that the employment at will doctrine should no longer apply? If so, who should make the change, the legislatures or the courts?

A store specializing in expensive men's clothing decided to hire only employees who were female and under twenty-five years of age, believing that this policy would attract more male shoppers. Assuming that this policy is not illegal under any civil rights acts, consider the following ethical questions.

Questions for Discussion

1. Even though this policy may be legal, is it ethical?
2. Would your answer be different if the store only would hire both males and females under the age of twenty-five?
3. Do you feel the civil rights acts should cover this situation?

Other Ethical Questions for Discussion

1. Why shouldn't a business be able to hire whomever it wants if it feels this will help increase its sales?
2. To increase profits, should a business be able to hire only entry-level employees who could be paid less than older employees?
3. What do you think the rule should be regarding a store that sells religious items of one faith wanting to hire only employees of that same faith?
4. Do you think that the civil rights acts should adopt different standards regarding the various forms of prohibited discrimination?

PART 6

Business Organization and Regulation

After studying Part VI, you should be able to:

1. describe the three major forms of business organization.
2. list advantages and disadvantages of the sole proprietorship, the partnership, and the corporation.
3. describe the rights, duties, powers, and liabilities of partners to one another and to third parties.
4. describe the two types of stock issued by a corporation.
5. identify the two kinds of powers a corporation has and distinguish between them.
6. describe the rights, duties, powers, and liabilities of stockholders, directors, and officers of a corporation.
7. describe several ways in which government regulates business.

CHAPTER 26

Sole Proprietorships, Partnerships, and Limited Liability Organizations

CHAPTER PREVIEW

Forms of Business Ownership

The Sole Proprietorship

The Partnership
   Types of Partners and Partnerships
   Forming a Partnership
   Operation of a Partnership
   Termination of the Partnership
   Buy-Sell Agreements

Limited Partnership

Forming a Limited Partnership
Role, Rights, and Liability of the Partners
Dissolution

Limited Liability Company

Limited Liability Partnership

Other Forms of Business Organization
   Joint Venture
   Syndicate
   Cooperative

Chapter Highlights

This chapter discusses the two most common forms of business organization in the United States: the sole proprietorship and the partnership. It describes the advantages and disadvantages of each type of organization. It outlines the methods used to form each type and discusses the various types of partners a partnership may have. How a partnership is operated, what the rights and duties of partners are, and how a partnership may be terminated are all important matters examined here. The form of business organization selected will depend on the following factors: (1) ease of organization, (2) costs of organization, (3) legal implications, and (4) tax considerations. The limited partnership, another form of business organization being used with greater frequency, is discussed. Coverage of this topic includes its advantages and disadvantages, how one is formed, the liability of partners, and how it may be terminated. The chapter concludes with a discussion of other forms of business organization, including limited liability companies and limited liability partnerships.

FORMS OF BUSINESS OWNERSHIP

Many of you may decide to go into business. You may work for yourself or for others. You will need to select a business form that best fits your needs. Some of the factors you should consider in choosing a form are (1) the number of owners; (2) tax considerations; (3) the need for limited liability; (4) whether you plan to go public in the future; (5) how ownership of the business will be transferred; (6) whether you need to borrow a lot of money to operate the business; (7) the work and expense involved in setting up the business; (8) how management will be exercised; and (9) how continuity will be assured.

Whatever business you enter will have a distinctive type of ownership. Although there are a variety of ways in which businesses may legally organize, the three most common forms of ownership are the sole proprietorship, the partnership, and the corporation. Corporations are discussed in Chapter 27.

THE SOLE PROPRIETORSHIP

sole proprietorship
business owned and operated by one person

Most businesses in the United States are owned and operated by individuals. This form of business organization is known as the **sole proprietorship**.

There are no formalities required to establish a sole proprietorship. It is the most easily started of the three major types of business organization. Anyone who wants to start a business and has the money to do so may start a sole proprietorship. Any person starting a business must comply with all government rules and regulations that apply to businesses in general and to that person's business in particular. This compliance may include obtaining a license for a certain type of business or profession, such as operating a taxi or practicing medicine. It will also usually include registering as a collector of state and local sales taxes. In most states, a person using a business or trade name different from her or his own name must register that name in a public office, usually called a d/b/a form. The owner of the business must also be identified, thereby enabling consumers to know with whom they may be dealing.

> Alisa decided to open a dress shop under the name of Alisa's Sportswear. Alisa would not be required to register the name. If she used the name Upstate Sportswear instead, however, she would have to register the name and identify herself as the owner so that the public would know they were dealing with Alisa when buying clothes at her store.

In a sole proprietorship, the owner has the full responsibility for managing the business. Generally, the owner supplies all the capital (money and other property) needed to start and operate the business, although additional money may be borrowed. The income from a sole proprietorship goes entirely to the owner, but so do the losses. The owner of a sole proprietorship receives no special tax advantages. Income the owner receives from the business is added to whatever income the owner may have from other sources; all the owner's income is taxed at the same rate. A sole proprietor who has no employees is not considered to be an employee and need not withhold taxes from his or her own distributions from the business but may be liable for self-employment taxes.

As with any form of business organization, the sole proprietorship has both advantages and disadvantages. One advantage is that the sole proprietorship is a very flexible form of business organization, allowing the owner to manage the business as he or she likes. In addition, no special legal formalities are required to set up a sole proprietorship other than minor requirements such as purchasing a business permit or paying licensing fees.

The sole proprietorship also has disadvantages. Many small-business owners go out of business every year, some of them because they do not have enough capital to continue to operate the business. The risk of not being successful and losing all or most of the money invested in the business must be borne by the owner alone. The owner, and only the owner, is liable for all the debts of the business. Another disadvantage is that the sole proprietorship ceases to exist when the owner dies or retires. The business may continue, often under the same name, but the ownership changes.

THE PARTNERSHIP

partnership
association of two or more persons to carry on, as co-owners, a business for profit

partner co-owner of a business

The Uniform Partnership Act, Section 6, contains most of the laws relating to the formation, operation, and dissolution of partnerships. It has been adopted in all states except Louisiana and in the District of Columbia. The act defines a **partnership** as "an association of two or more persons to carry on as co-owners a business for profit." The persons who are associated in the business are known as **partners**. The essential elements of a partnership are (1) sharing profits and losses, (2) joint ownership of partnership assets, and (3) shared management.

People who join together for some activity are not always considered to be associated in a partnership. The Uniform Partnership Act specifically refers to people joining together in a *business,* which means the sharing of investment, management, profits and losses, joint ownership of the business, and work. The act would not include as a partnership the joint ownership of property in which no management would be involved. It would also not include joint efforts of nonprofit organizations or unincorporated associations that were formed for charitable or recreational purposes.

> Attorneys Juarez and Bolton formed a nonprofit law firm to provide legal services for needy persons. Their organization would not be considered a partnership because it was not formed to earn a profit.

Like a sole proprietorship, partners using a business or trade name different from their own names must register the partnership name and their own names in a public office. Identification of the partners is required so that the public may know with whom they are dealing.

Under the Uniform Partnership Act, a partnership is treated as a legal entity. It can buy, hold title to, and sell real estate in its own name. It can also make bank deposits and purchase securities. It is also treated as a legal entity for accounting purposes and in bankruptcy proceedings.

In some states, a partnership may sue or be sued in its own name. The title of a suit brought by a partnership, for example, would be "John Doe and Richard Roe, doing business as Doe and Roe, a partnership," and not "Doe and Roe." In other states, actions by or against a partnership must be brought in the names of the partners.

A partnership is not a legal entity for tax purposes. There is no such thing as an income tax on partnerships. The partnership acts like a funnel, pouring profits and losses into the hands of the partners. The partners must include on their personal income tax returns their individual shares of the partnership profits and losses. Partnerships are required, nevertheless, to file informational returns for federal and state tax purposes.

The advantages of operating a business as a partnership are the ease of organization and dissolution, informality in management, and lack of a partnership income tax. The disadvantages are the unlimited liability of partners for partnership debts and torts, the difficulty of settling disputes among the partners, the difficulty in transferring a partnership interest, the lack of continuity, and the danger of dissolution if a partner withdraws or dies. As seen in the next chapter, the advantages and disadvantages of a partnership are the opposite of the advantages and disadvantages of a corporation. Also, many banks and other lenders often require a corporate form for their business borrowers.

Types of Partners and Partnerships

trading partnership
partnership doing business for commercial purposes

Partnerships are often classified according to their purpose and the extent of the partners' liability. A **trading partnership** is an association for commercial purposes, such as

nontrading partnership
partnership doing business for professional purposes

general partner partner fully active and known to the public

silent partner partner known to the public but inactive in management

secret partner partner unknown to the public but active in management

dormant partner partner unknown to the public and inactive in management

limited partner partner whose liability is limited to amount of capital invested

a manufacturing, wholesale, or retail business. A **nontrading partnership** is an association for professional purposes, such as a law firm.

Partnerships may also be classified as general or limited partnerships. A *general partnership* is the customary partnership in which all partners share equal liability for the debts and torts of the partnership. A **general partner** is a fully active partner.

In addition to general partners, there are many other types of partners. A **silent partner** is inactive in a general partnership but is known to the public as a partner. A **secret partner** is active in the partnership but is not known to the public as a partner. A **dormant partner** is neither active in the partnership nor known to the public as a partner.

Another type of partnership recognized in most states is the limited partnership. A *limited partnership* has both general partners and limited partners. A **limited partner** contributes cash or property to the business but may not take part in its operation and thus has limited liability for partnership obligations. The limited partner is not bound by the obligations of the partnership and is not subject to any personal liability beyond the investment made in the business. A limited partner who does participate in the operation of the business will take on the same liability as the general partner. Often, however, limited partners have different roles in management and control of partnership operations.

Forming a Partnership

Like other commercial arrangements, a partnership arises from an express agreement or by implication from the acts of the parties.

As with other contracts, a partnership agreement, to be valid, must meet the usual tests of legal capacity of the parties and the absence of fraud and/or duress in the formation of the contract.

Express Agreement   An express agreement establishing a partnership may be either oral or written. If the term of the partnership will be greater than one year, however, the statute of frauds applies and the agreement must be in writing to be enforceable. In any instance, to avoid any disputes among the partners, a written contract is advisable.

partnership agreement
written agreement creating a partnership

The written agreement creating the partnership is usually called the **partnership agreement**, or the articles of copartnership. An example of a partnership agreement appears in Figure 26.1. It should include the name of the partnership, its main office, and the names and addresses of the partners. It should also state the term of the partnership, the initial investment of each partner, and a formula for sharing profits and losses. It is advisable to include provisions for settling disputes, for the death or retirement of a partner, and for the purchase of the interest of a withdrawing partner.

Implication   A partnership may also arise by implication from the acts of the partners. Two or more persons often join together in a business and conduct it as a partnership without formally agreeing that it is a partnership. It is treated as a partnership by the partners and by any third parties who deal with them.

A partnership will be implied only when the partners conduct their business in a manner typical of formal partnerships. That includes sharing profits and losses, sharing control over the business, sharing an interest in the partnership property, and showing the intention to have a partnership. If any of these factors is missing, the relationship is not a partnership.

Vanderver and Stern were partners operating a small department store. They brought in Lewis as a general manager and agreed to pay her 20 percent of the profits of the store for her services. Even though she shared in the profits, Lewis was not a partner because the other elements of a partnership were missing, such as sharing an interest in the partnership property and having an equal voice in controlling the business.

FIGURE 26.1
Partnership Agreement

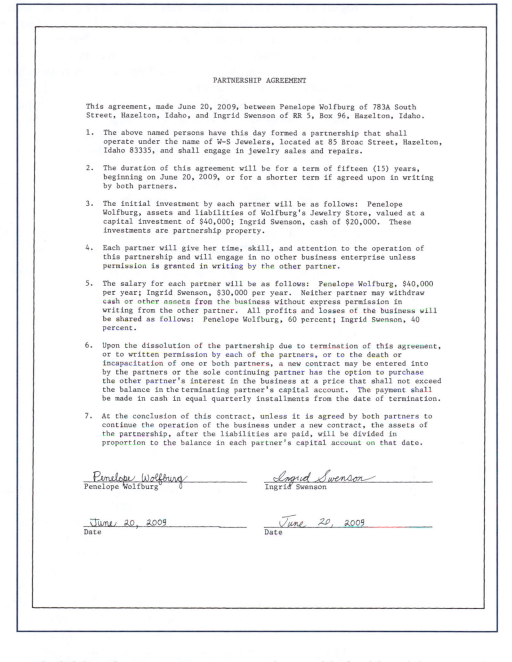

PARTNERSHIP AGREEMENT

This agreement, made June 20, 2009, between Penelope Wolfburg of 783A South Street, Hazelton, Idaho, and Ingrid Swenson of RR 5, Box 96, Hazelton, Idaho.

1. The above named persons have this day formed a partnership that shall operate under the name of W-S Jewelers, located at 85 Broac Street, Hazelton, Idaho 83335, and shall engage in jewelry sales and repairs.

2. The duration of this agreement will be for a term of fifteen (15) years, beginning on June 20, 2009, or for a shorter term if agreed upon in writing by both partners.

3. The initial investment by each partner will be as follows: Penelope Wolfburg, assets and liabilities of Wolfburg's Jewelry Store, valued at a capital investment of $40,000; Ingrid Swenson, cash of $20,000. These investments are partnership property.

4. Each partner will give her time, skill, and attention to the operation of this partnership and will engage in no other business enterprise unless permission is granted in writing by the other partner.

5. The salary for each partner will be as follows: Penelope Wolfburg, $40,000 per year; Ingrid Swenson, $30,000 per year. Neither partner may withdraw cash or other assets from the business without express permission in writing from the other partner. All profits and losses of the business will be shared as follows: Penelope Wolfburg, 60 percent; Ingrid Swenson, 40 percent.

6. Upon the dissolution of the partnership due to termination of this agreement, or to written permission by each of the partners, or to the death or incapacitation of one or both partners, a new contract may be entered into by the partners or the sole continuing partner has the option to purchase the other partner's interest in the business at a price that shall not exceed the balance in the terminating partner's capital account. The payment shall be made in cash in equal quarterly installments from the date of termination.

7. At the conclusion of this contract, unless it is agreed by both partners to continue the operation of the business under a new contract, the assets of the partnership, after the liabilities are paid, will be divided in proportion to the balance in each partner's capital account on that date.

Penelope Wolfburg
Penelope Wolfburg

Ingrid Swenson
Ingrid Swenson

June 20, 2009
Date

June 20, 2009
Date

The liability of a new partner in a partnership is solely for debts of the partnership incurred after entry, and not for prior debts.

Operation of a Partnership

A partnership operates according to the provisions of the partnership agreement and the Uniform Partnership Act. Principles of the law of contracts and agency also apply. To a great extent, a partnership operates according to custom, the nature of the business, and the relationship between the partners. All partnerships share one thing in common: The partners have rights, duties, powers, and liabilities to one another and to nonpartners.

Rights of Partners The first important right of partners is to participate in management. Unless the partnership agreement holds otherwise, all partners have a right to participate in management on an equal basis, regardless of how the profits and losses are shared. The partners may and usually do give certain partners more responsibility than others. Partners may also be given different types of responsibilities depending on their education, skills, and experience.

As in other business organizations, decisions in a partnership on most matters are decided by majority vote. If there are only two partners and they cannot agree, the dispute will be resolved according to the provisions included in the partnership agreement. If the agreement contains no provisions for settling disputes, the partners will have to go to court or dissolve the partnership.

Certain decisions are so important that they affect the existence of the partnership. In such a case, the decision must be unanimous. A unanimous vote is required, for example, when the partners wish to amend the partnership agreement so that there is a material change in the nature of the business. A unanimous vote is also required to change the contributions of the partners, start a new business, or admit other partners.

> Zivan had a 10 percent interest in a partnership that operated a computer store. If the partners decide to change the business to a bakery store, they cannot do so without Zivan's consent.

The second important right of a partner is to share in the profits (and losses) of the partnership. The partners may and usually do divide up the profits by agreement according to their individual investments in or contributions to the partnership. In actual practice, some partners are more active than others in the operation of a partnership. They may receive a salary in addition to a share of the profits.

> Lesser formed a partnership with two other persons to operate a pharmacy. The partnership agreement contained no provision about sharing profits. If Lesser does only 5 percent of the work involved in operating the pharmacy, she is still entitled to one-third of the profits.

A third important right is to share in the property of the partnership. Unless the partnership agreement provides otherwise, a partner has an equal interest in the property owned by the partnership and used for partnership purposes. The interest is not in a specific piece of property but only in all partnership property in general, including real property, accounts receivable, and goodwill. A partner cannot use specific partnership property for personal purposes and cannot transfer an interest in specific property.

A fourth important right is that of inspecting the books and records of the partnership. Any partner has the right to know how the business is being conducted. To accomplish that, a partner may examine any and all records kept by the partnership. The partner may also make copies of them. The records must be kept in a stated place and must be available for inspection at reasonable hours.

A fifth important right is that of an accounting. Under the Uniform Partnership Act, a partner has a right to an accounting of partnership assets and liabilities to determine the value of each partner's shares when

1. the partnership agreement provides for it.
2. the other partners wrongfully exclude a partner from management and/or inspection of the partnership records.
3. another partner withholds profits or benefits that rightfully belong to the partnership.
4. it is just and reasonable under the circumstances.

A court can compel an accounting, usually upon a dissolution of a partnership by court order.

Other rights of partners include the right to transfer one's partnership interest and the right to a return of capital upon dissolution of the partnership.

Duties of Partners   A partnership is a relationship based on trust and confidence. Partners usually work closely together, and certain duties are imposed upon them because of the personal nature of the relationship. These duties include loyalty, use of reasonable care, and accounting for actions taken.

Loyalty in a partnership means acting in good faith and in the best interests of the partnership. Whether dealing with the other partners or with outsiders, a partner may not obtain a personal benefit or take any action that harms the partnership. In addition, a partner may not participate in any activity that either competes with the partnership or interferes with the expected performance of duties.

> McVee and Carter were partners operating a drugstore. McVee had an opportunity to buy an interest in another drugstore one block away. McVee is not entitled to buy the interest because it would mean competing with his own partner. If McVee does go ahead and purchase the interest, he must account to Carter for a share of the profits from the second store.

A partner must use reasonable skill and care in conducting partnership business. Regardless of other obligations or participation in other businesses, a partner must devote time and skill to the partnership, or the relationship is considered breached.

A partner is required to account to the other partners for actions taken and any benefits obtained, which means that a partner is liable to other partners for breach of the duties of loyalty and use of reasonable care. It also means accounting for and sharing any advantages obtained that arise from the partnership business.

> Albertson and Posniak were partners in a used-car business. Albertson learned that a valuable antique car was for sale at a reasonable price. She bought the car and resold it at a large profit. Posniak is entitled to a share of the profit because the transaction concerned partnership business.

Powers of Partners   Just as a partnership may be created by express agreement or by implication, the powers of a partner may be either express or implied. The source of express powers is the partnership agreement as well as the Uniform Partnership Act. The sources of implied powers are the oral agreement among the partners, the nature and customs of the business, and the general laws of agency. These powers include the power to make contracts, to buy and sell partnership property, to borrow money, and to hire employees and agents. The general rule is that a partner has the power to do all these things and bind the other partners as well, provided what is done is carried out in the ordinary course of partnership business.

One partner may enter into binding contracts for the business, provided the contract is made in the ordinary course of partnership business and the partner has the apparent authority to enter into the contract. Such authority is often determined by what is customary in the business in question and in the type of business in general.

A partner may buy and sell goods and services, including real property, in the ordinary course of business. A partnership is bound by purchases made by a partner and must pay for them. It is also bound by sales made by a partner in the ordinary course of business and must execute any documents required to transfer title.

A partner may receive or borrow money for the business. When a bank agrees to lend money to a partnership, or a creditor is willing to extend credit, it wants to make sure that the partnership is bound by the loan or credit agreement. The general rule is that a partner may borrow money and obtain credit for the partnership and bind it, as long as the borrowing is in the ordinary course of business.

> Morton was a partner in a company that manufactured fencing. She wanted to borrow money to finance the purchase of a new boat for her family. At the bank's request, she signed a promissory note on behalf of the partnership and received the money. The partnership is not bound by the note because the loan was not in the ordinary course of the partnership business.

A partner may hire and fire employees and agents. Hiring is often the responsibility of one of the partners. As long as the employees or agents are hired for the usual and ordinary work of the business, the partnership is bound by the contracts of employment.

Liability of Partners Partners have obligations to one another and to outsiders. A breach of those obligations may impose liability on all the partners. A partner is liable to other partners for a breach of duty, such as benefiting at the expense of the partnership or defrauding the other partners. Just as partners share profits, they also share losses. A partner is liable to the other partners for his or her share of the partnership's debts and obligations. A partner who pays a higher share of partnership debts has a right to be reimbursed by the other partners.

The relationship of partners to third parties is the same as the relationship of principals and agents to third parties, discussed in Chapter 25. Partners are liable to outsiders for contracts made by other partners and for torts and crimes committed by other partners, provided they occur within the apparent scope of the business of the partnership. The types of authority partners have to bind other partners is the same that agents have to bind their principals: actual, implied, and apparent.

If a partner enters into a verbal agreement on behalf of the partnership, all partners are jointly liable on the contract. If a partner commits a tort for which the partnership is liable, such as fraud or negligence, all the partners are jointly and severally liable. **Joint and several liability** means that the wronged party may sue all the partners in a single legal action or any one of the partners individually. If a partner commits a crime in the course of the partnership operations and a fine is imposed, the partners are jointly liable for payment of the fine.

joint and several liability liability of partners as a group or individually

> Ames and Barr were partners in a truck rental business. Ames rented a truck with faulty brakes to Jones, who was injured in an accident caused by brake failure. Jones may sue Ames or Barr or both together for his injuries.

A judgment obtained against a partnership is satisfied first out of partnership assets. If those assets are insufficient, a judgment creditor may then proceed against the personal assets of the individual partners. A creditor with a judgment against a partner (as distinct from a judgment against the *partnership*) may not attempt to collect the judgment from partnership assets, only from a partner's interest in the partnership. A partnership may also file in its own name for protection under the bankruptcy laws.

New partners and retiring partners may also be liable for certain partnership actions. Under the Uniform Partnership Act, a new partner is liable for the obligations of the partnership arising before he or she joined the partnership. The personal assets of the new partner, however, may not be used to satisfy any of those obligations. Retiring partners are also liable for obligations created while they were members of the partnership, until those debts are paid. Retiring partners are also liable for obligations of the partnership arising after their retirement until a certificate showing the change of partnership members is filed in the appropriate office.

Termination of the Partnership

dissolution termination of a partnership

The termination of a partnership is known as **dissolution**. Dissolution may occur for several reasons, such as expiration of the partnership term, agreement among the parties, a change in the members of the partnership, death of a partner, bankruptcy, or court order.

Many partnership agreements provide for a specific term for the life of the partnership. When that term ends, the partnership is dissolved. The partners may, if they wish, renew the partnership. If the agreement does not set a time for the partnership to end, the partnership continues until it is dissolved for other reasons. Partners may, by agreement, dissolve the partnership at any time. The vote to dissolve must be unanimous, and the rights of creditors of the partnership must be respected.

If a partner retires from a firm or a new partner is added, the relationship among the other partners is considered changed to such an extent that the partnership is dissolved. Most agreements provide that the partnership will continue despite the admission of a new partner or the retirement or withdrawal of an old one, provided the other partners agree to the change.

If a partner withdraws from a partnership in violation of the partnership agreement, that partner may be liable to the other partners for breach of contract. If the partnership agreement is silent about withdrawal, there will be no liability unless the suddenness of the withdrawal causes severe damage to the partnership.

Jones and Gray, a partnership formed to paint office buildings, had a contract to paint the state capitol. Jones withdrew from the partnership in the middle of the job without any advance warning. The state then canceled the contract, and the partnership was forced into bankruptcy. The partnership agreement was silent about withdrawals, but Jones may be liable to the partnership for damages caused by his actions.

The death of a partner usually results in the dissolution of the partnership. Most partnership agreements provide for the purchase of the deceased partner's interest in the partnership, allowing the partnership to continue. Many partnerships carry insurance on each partner's life to finance the purchase of a deceased partner's interest in the business.

Under the Uniform Partnership Act, the transfer by sale or gift of a partner's interest in a partnership, or the sale of a partner's interest to satisfy a judgment, does not automatically cause the dissolution of the partnership. The remaining partners may permit the partnership to continue or may ask for dissolution of the partnership because of changed circumstances.

For many reasons, a partner may wish to buy another partner's interest. Many partnership agreements include a "buy-sell" clause that outlines when a partner may sell an interest, to whom, and at what price. This event might occur because of a disagreement among the partners or the death of a partner. Such agreements are often funded by the purchase of insurance on a partner's life.

The bankruptcy of the partnership itself or of an individual partner will dissolve the partnership. A dissolution may also occur by court order, which happens when a partner asks the court to dissolve the partnership for one or more reasons, including inability to continue in business, insanity of a partner, or a deadlock that prevents agreement from being reached.

Frey and Talbot were partners in a laundry business. The laundry needed to borrow money to remain in business, but the partners could not agree on the best way to borrow the money. Either partner could seek a court order dissolving the partnership because of the inability to reach an agreement.

Dissolution does not mean the immediate termination of the partnership. Certain steps must be taken to wind up the partnership affairs, such as liquidating it and final termination. After those steps are taken, the partnership either ends or starts up again under a new agreement.

One step involved in winding up the partnership is to give notice of the dissolution to creditors, which protects creditors who have first claim on the partnership assets. Another step is to prepare an accounting of the partnership assets and liabilities. The final step is to distribute the partnership assets. Creditors are paid first and then partners who have lent money to the partnership. Any funds remaining are paid to the partners according to the partnership agreement. Until all these steps are completed, the partners continue to have authority to bind the partnership. The liability of partners for contracts and torts during the partnership existence does not end when the partnership is dissolved.

Several states have adopted the Revised Uniform Partnership Act (RUPA), which makes significant changes to the Uniform Partnership Act. Some of the most significant changes are the following:

1. A partnership may file a document with the secretary of state in the state of organization outlining the authority of the partners to bind the partnership.
2. The liability of the partners is joint and several for all debts of the partnership.
3. The death of a partner does not automatically result in the partnership's dissolution.
4. If a partner leaves the partnership, that partner's interest must be purchased by the other partners and the partnership continues.
5. A general partnership may be changed into a limited partnership, and vice versa.

Buy-Sell Agreements

When a partner dies, becomes disabled, retires, or wishes to sell his or her partnership interest, a question arises as to how to transfer the interest and how to ensure the continuity of the business. The best answer is a buy-sell agreement, a contract between the partners that binds them to buy the departing partner's interest at a set price within a fixed period of time. This guarantees a ready market for the partner's interest, cash for the seller, and an orderly transfer of the interest. Buy-sell agreements are often funded with life insurance on each partner's life, which provides funds for the buyout in the event of a partner's death.

LIMITED PARTNERSHIP

In recent years, the limited partnership has become a popular form of business organization. It is typically used for the syndication of real estate purchases, the formation of leasing companies, and the financing of movies and plays. Unknown at common law, limited partnerships are the creatures of state law; all states and the District of Columbia have enacted laws permitting limited partnerships.

A limited partnership is in effect a hybrid, a partnership form that contains many elements of a corporation. It was designed to enable investors to put capital into a venture in a form that would have the advantage of operating as a partnership but in which liability would be limited, as in a corporation. A limited partnership has both general and limited partners. The general partner invests in the partnership and is completely responsible for its management. The limited partner also invests but has no management role.

Some families establish limited partnerships to protect family assets and reduce estate taxes upon a parent's death. Usually, the parents are the general partners and their children are the limited partners. As general partners, the parents continue to exercise control over family assets. At death, their interest is taxed on a reduced basis because they owned only a portion of the assets rather than the entire amount.

The law that governed limited partnerships in all states (except Louisiana) and the District of Columbia was, until 1976, the Uniform Limited Partnership Act (ULPA). Since 1976, most states and the District of Columbia have adopted the Revised Uniform Limited Partnership Act (RULPA), which now governs the organization and operation of most limited partnerships in the United States. These acts cover the formation of limited partnerships, the rights and duties of general and limited partners, and the dissolution of the partnership.

Forming a Limited Partnership

The RULPA contains specific requirements for the formation of a limited partnership. There must be a minimum of two partners: one general and one limited. They must execute a certificate that states the partnership's name, purpose, duration, and location of its principal place of business; the name and address of each general and limited partner; and the amount of capital each invested. The certificate must be filed with the secretary of state of the state of organization. In many states, notice of filing and a summary of the provisions of the certificate must be published in an official newspaper, a newspaper designated by a government body to carry official notices.

Role, Rights, and Liability of the Partners

The general partners in a limited partnership are completely responsible for managing the partnership; they are also personally liable for the partnership's debts. The limited partner may not participate in management, must contribute cash or property and not services, and cannot have his or her name as part of the partnership name. In return for these concessions, a limited partner's liability for partnership debts is limited to the amount of capital he or she contributed.

As is the case with regular partnerships, a limited partner has the right to inspect the books and records of the partnership, the right to an accounting, and the right to participate in the dissolution of the partnership and the distribution of its assets.

Dissolution

A limited partnership may be dissolved for the same reasons and in the same manner as a regular partnership with a few exceptions. It will be dissolved when its term ends; it may be dissolved by agreement among the general and limited partners. The bankruptcy of a general partner dissolves a limited partnership, but the bankruptcy of a limited partner does not.

LIMITED LIABILITY COMPANY

Although the limited partnership enjoys the corporate advantage of limited shareholder liability and the partnership advantage of a single tax on income, it has one disadvantage: Limited partners may not participate in management of the partnership's affairs and still maintain their limited liability status. This disadvantage is especially serious for businesses owned and operated by a small number of persons.

limited liability company limited partnership that permits all partners to participate in management while enjoying limited liability

In response, since 1977, all states have enacted legislation authorizing a new type of business ownership, the **limited liability company** (LLC). Like the limited partnership, the LLC is a hybrid of the corporation and the partnership. It is taxed like a partnership, enabling investors to take advantage of losses and to avoid the double taxation of corporations. Like the corporation, investors have limited liability; only the business assets, not the personal assets of the investors, are subject to judgments resulting from business lawsuits.

The LLC is very similar to a limited partnership but with two added advantages. Recall that in a limited partnership, only the limited partners, not the general partners, have limited liability. In an LLC, all members have limited liability. In a limited partnership, limited partners are prohibited from any active management of the business. In an LLC, all members may participate in active management and still enjoy limited liability; they may also designate a group, including nonmembers, to manage the LLC.

The Internal Revenue Service in 1988 issued a ruling confirming that an LLC organized in Wyoming would be treated as a partnership for income tax purposes. For an LLC to obtain the tax benefits of a partnership under IRS regulations, the LLC must be set up in such a way that it lacks at least two of the following characteristics of a corporation: (1) limited liability, (2) centralized management, (3) continuity of life, and (4) free transferability of interests. An LLC that possesses three or more of those characteristics will be treated as a corporation for federal income tax purposes.

An LLC has very few disadvantages, which accounts for its popularity. The main disadvantage is that because state laws regarding LLCs vary, members of an LLC formed in one state may not enjoy limited liability if the LLC does business in another state. It is believed that eventually a uniform LLC law will be enacted in most states.

State laws vary regarding the creation and operation of LLCs, and an LLC must be formed according to each state's requirements. The basic steps in most states are (1) drafting articles of organization that outline the purpose of the LLC and include other information required by law, (2) filing the articles of organization with the department of state of the state in which the LLC is organized (and paying a filing fee), and (3) publishing in an official newspaper a notice of the formation of the LLC (see Figure 26.2).

In some states, LLCs must have at least two members. In other states, only one member is required. The business name must include "Limited Liability Company" or "LLC."

LIMITED LIABILITY PARTNERSHIP

Many small businesses and professional groups operate as partnerships, avoiding the disadvantage of the double taxation of corporate profits but having the disadvantage of unlimited liability. In many states, certain professionals, such as attorneys, accountants, and doctors, can form professional corporations and thus avoid personal liability, but they must still pay corporate-type taxes.

limited liability partnership limited partnership in which professionals avoid personal liability but pay corporate-type taxes

To provide professionals and others, including family partnerships, with the advantages of the LLC, since 1991, some states have enacted legislation permitting the formation of **limited liability partnerships** (LLPs). Similar to LLCs, with the same advantages and disadvantages, LLPs, however, have certain disadvantages that require attention. One is that because not all states have enacted LLP laws, an LLP formed in one state but doing business in states without such legislation may not be recognized as an LLP in those other states. The second is that in two states, New York and California, use of an LLP is limited to professionals. A third disadvantage is that state laws vary on the type and extent of liability protection available so that the actions of an LLP in one state might be protected there but not in another state.

FIGURE 26.2
Articles of Organization
for a Limited Liability
Company

ARTICLES OF ORGANIZATION OF JONES PRODUCTS, LLC

Under §203 of the Limited Liability Company Law

FIRST: The name of the limited liability company is: Jones Products, LLC.

SECOND: The county within this state in which the office of the limited liability company is to be located: Prince.

THIRD: The secretary of state is designated as agent of the limited liability company upon whom process against it may be served. The post office address within or without this state to which the secretary of state shall mail a copy of any process against the limited liability company served upon him or her is: 1000 Island Boulevard, Prince, New York, 14888.

FOURTH: If all or specified members are to be liable in their capacity as members for all or specified debts, obligations, or liabilities of the limited liability company as authorized pursuant to Section 609 of the Limited Liability Company Law, a statement that all or specified members are so liable.

IN WITNESS WHEREOF, this certificate has been subscribed this 10th day of August 2009 by the undersigned who affirms that the statements made herein are true under the penalties of perjury.

Samuel Prince
_____
(signature)

Samuel Prince, Attorney
_____

A family limited liability partnership (FLLP) is an LLP in which the partners are family members who manage a business. These are often set up for estate planning and tax purposes. The FLLP has the same advantages as the LLP.

OTHER FORMS OF BUSINESS ORGANIZATION

In addition to the more common forms of business organization, other less common forms are used for special purposes. These forms include the joint venture, the syndicate, and the cooperative.

Joint Venture

joint venture association of two or more companies or persons engaged in a common project

A **joint venture** is a business arrangement in which two or more separate persons or business organizations join together to work on a project that each would be unable to handle separately. The project may be too large, too expensive, or too complicated for one of them but manageable if they work together. A joint venture may be treated as a partnership or a corporation, depending on how it is formed and how closely the parties are tied together.

Syndicate

syndicate a less formal type of joint venture

A less formal type of joint venture is called a **syndicate**, which is often used by individuals to purchase assets such as real estate, franchises, and racehorses. Depending on how it is formed, it may be either a corporation or some form of partnership. If the arrangement only involves ownership of property jointly, it is neither a partnership nor a corporation.

Cooperative

cooperative nonprofit business arrangement for the benefit of members; also, ownership and occupancy of real property through the purchase of stock

A **cooperative** is a nonprofit (often called not-for-profit) arrangement set up to provide certain benefits to its members. The members wish to pool their resources and talents to accomplish what they could not do individually. Some cooperatives are formed just for purchasing, enabling members to buy goods and services at reduced prices because of group volume. Some, such as farm cooperatives, are organized to market products to get the benefit of controlling supply and prices and to qualify for reduced shipping rates.

Cooperatives may be treated as partnerships or corporations depending on how they are formed and on state laws. Their business operations, powers, and liabilities will be determined by their form of organization.

Summary

The sole proprietorship is the most common form of business organization. It is also the easiest type of business to form, operate, and dissolve. The owner has sole responsibility for managing the business, receives all profits, and is responsible for all losses.

The operation of a partnership is governed by the partnership agreement and the provisions of the Uniform Partnership Act. Partners can agree on their respective shares of management, profits, losses, and partnership property. Unless otherwise stated in the partnership agreement, they share equally.

A partnership is treated as a legal entity; it can hold title to real estate in its own name and, in some states, may sue or be sued in its own name. It is not a legal entity for tax purposes, however, and there is no such thing as an income tax on partnerships.

Partnerships come into existence either by agreement or by the acts of the partners. After a partnership is formed, partners have the right to participate in management, to share in the profits (and losses), to share in the property of the partnership, and to receive an accounting. A partner also has obligations to the other partners, including loyalty, use of reasonable care, and accounting for actions taken. A partnership may be bound by the contracts, torts, and crimes of a partner if they are done with apparent authority and in the ordinary scope of partnership business.

A partnership may be dissolved because of expiration of its term, agreement, change in membership, death of a partner, bankruptcy, or court order.

The advantages of operating a business as a partnership are the ease of organization and dissolution, informality in management, and the lack of a partnership income tax. The disadvantages are the unlimited liability of partners for partnership debts and torts, lack of continuity, and dissolution if a partner withdraws or dies.

A limited partnership is permitted by law in every state. This form of organization is a hybrid of a corporation and a partnership. The limited partnership is treated as a partnership for income tax purposes, avoiding the double taxation of corporations. At the same time, the limited partners enjoy the limited liability of stockholders; they are not personally liable for the partnership's debts. In return for these advantages, however, a limited partner may not participate in management. A limited partnership is formed and dissolved in much the same way as a regular partnership, except that with a limited partnership the formation and registration requirements are much more complicated.

Other forms of business organization are the limited liability company, the limited liability partnership, the joint venture, the syndicate, and the cooperative. The limited liability company, permitted in almost all states, is similar to a limited partnership, with the added advantage that all partners have limited liability and all may participate in management. The limited liability partnership, similar to a limited liability company but used mostly by professionals, is a recent form of business organization that has been gaining acceptance in many states.

Important Legal terms

cooperative	limited liability company	partnership agreement
dissolution	limited liability partnership	secret partner
dormant partner	limited partner	silent partner
general partner	nontrading partnership	sole proprietorship
joint and several liability	partner	syndicate
joint venture	partnership	trading partnership

Questions and Problems for Discussion

1. What factors should you examine to decide what type of business entity you should use in starting a new business?

2. Explain the differences among general, silent, secret, and dormant partners.

3. What are the advantages and disadvantages of the partnership form of business organization?

4. What are the most important provisions of a partnership agreement?

5. Describe the duties and rights of partners.

6. Explain the difference between a limited partnership and a limited liability company?

7. What steps must be taken to dissolve a partnership?

8. Morgan and Stanley formed a partnership to operate a car dealership and they hired Jones to manage it. Jones' compensation is to be one-third of the business's profits. Is Jones considered a partner?

9. Frey and Fuld, a partnership, borrowed $10,000 from Citizens National Bank. When the partnership failed to repay the loan, the bank sued Frey for the entire amount due. Is Frey liable for the full amount?

10. Describe the liability of a partnership and the partners for torts and crimes committed by another partner.

11. Finkel joined a partnership that operated a securities firm. An investor sued Finkel and the other partners for fraud that occurred two months before Frey became a partner. Is Finkel liable for damages?

12. Berry and Jones form a partnership to sell trucks. Their partnership agreement is silent about what happens to the assets should either partner die. Berry dies and his wife claims that she is entitled to one-half of the partnership assets. Is she correct?

13. Ford and Doyle formed a partnership to sell television sets. Doyle was a minor. A customer who had purchased a set tried to cancel the sale on the grounds that Doyle was a minor, and therefore, there was no partnership. Will the customer succeed?

14. Fix and White form a partnership to sell farm machinery. Fix contributes $100,000 to the partnership; White contributes $50,000 and his services as accountant and attorney. Their agreement is silent as to how profits are to be divided. How will they be divided?

Cases for Review

1. Berke was hired by Hamby's professional medical corporation as an employee. When his employment term ended, he continued to work for the corporation. He was ultimately fired and claimed that he was a partner of an oral partnership. Can this claim succeed? (*Berke* v. *Hamby,* 719 N.Y.S.2d 280)

2. McCoy and Gugelman formed a partnership to operate an antiques business. The partnership borrowed money from Security State Bank. One of the partners signed a promissory note to the bank on behalf of the partnership. When the partnership defaulted on the note, the bank sued the partners individually rather than suing the partnership. The partners argued that before they could be sued, the bank first had to sue the partnership and get a judgment against it. Was

this claim correct? (*Security State Bank* v. *McCoy & Gugelman,* 219 Neb. 132)

3. Paul Schwartz and others formed a partnership to own and operate an apartment house in New York City. Schwartz died in 1975 and his widow was appointed administratrix of his estate. A few years later, the partnership advised the estate that it intended to convert the property into a cooperative and offered to buy the estate's interest in the partnership, an offer that Mrs. Schwartz refused. In 1986, she sued the partnership in her individual name for a partnership accounting. The partnership refused, claiming that she was not a partner and that only the estate, which had succeeded to Mr. Schwartz's interest, could get an accounting. Was the partnership correct? (*Sylvia Schwartz* v. *Lois Associates,* 539 N.Y.S.2d 360)

4. Mr. and Mrs. Volkman entered into a contract with DP Associates for construction advice on building a house. They brought suit, claiming a breach of contract. The principals of DP Associates claimed they were not partners and that no partnership existed. The evidence was that the Volkmans met both individuals at the company office and discussed the construction with them, received correspondence from them on stationary marked "DP Associates," and were assured that both individuals would be working on the Volkman's job. Was the evidence sufficient to support a finding that an implied partnership existed? (*Volkman* v. *DP Associates,* 268 S.E.2d 265)

5. Flynn, a patient of Reeves, a doctor, sued Reeves for injuries allegedly caused by Reeves's malpractice. Reeves was a partner in a medical firm. After Flynn won and obtained a judgment against Reeves, Reeves tried to get contribution from his partners, claiming that the negligence occurred during the course of the firm's business. Is Reeves entitled to contribution from his partners? (*Flynn* v. *Reeves,* 218 S.E.2d 661)

6. A partner sued another partner for compensation for services rendered to the partnership that were unforseen at the time the partnership agreement was signed. Is the partner entitled to extra compensation under these circumstances? (*Posner* v. *Posner,* 720 N.Y.S.2d 465)

7. Rice and Campbell were doing business as partners. They entered into an agreement with Travelers to write money orders. The partnership sold some of the money orders but failed to send the money to Travelers. To secure the debt, the partnership gave a promissory note to Travelers, with a guaranty by Campbell. When the note wasn't paid, Travelers sued both partners. Rice claimed that he was liable only if Campbell didn't pay. Was Rice correct? (*Rice* v. *Travelers Express Company,* Tex. 407 S.W.2d 534)

8. Moser and Williams were partners in a land development business. By agreement, title to the land was placed in Williams's name. Williams had contracted to sell the land to another for a much higher price. When Williams sold the land, Moser brought suit to have Williams account to him for his share of the profit. Will he succeed? (*Moser* v. *Williams,* Mo. 443 S.W.2d 212)

9. Lerner and Holmes started a business to produce and market unique nail polishes with unusual names, with the idea of selling the business for a profit. They researched the market, obtained capital, hired employees, and advertised, but they never discussed or put in writing how they were to share profits. Due to disagreements, Lerner tried to get Holmes out of the company. Holmes sued, claiming a breach of the partnership agreement, but Lerner contended that there was no partnership agreement because an essential element—the division of profits—was missing. Who is correct, Lerner or Holmes? (*Holmes* v. *Lerner,* 74 Cal. App. 4th 442)

10. Barch and Mensch was an accounting firm. It formed some real estate investment groups, and Blaustein had an interest in two of them. There was no partnership agreement for the groups, and Blaustein was never named as a partner. When the accounting firm dissolved, Blaustein claimed that he was entitled to an accounting and a share of the proceeds. Is he correct? (*Blaustein* v. *Barch and Mensch,* 555 N.Y.S.2d 776)

11. Miller was injured while eating at a McDonald's restaurant. The restaurant was owned privately and operated under a license from McDonald's. The license agreement gave McDonald's almost complete control over how the restaurant was to be operated, including designs and color schemes, food preparation, equipment, and inventory controls. Miller sued McDonald's as well as the restaurant operator, claiming that the operator was in effect an agent of McDonald's. McDonald's claimed that the operator was an independent contractor. Who should prevail? (*Miller* v. *McDonald's Corporation,* 945 P.2d 1107)

CHAPTER 27

Corporations and Franchising

CHAPTER PREVIEW

Chapter Highlights

This chapter describes the nature, formation, financing, operation, and termination of corporations. It covers both profit and nonprofit types of corporations and the steps that must be taken to form such corporations. When a corporation is formed, financing must be obtained to carry out the organization's business operations; both equity and debt financing are discussed. A corporation is owned by its stockholders and managed by its directors and officers. The chapter describes the rights, liabilities, and powers of stockholders, directors, debtors, and officers. The corporation portion of the chapter concludes with a discussion of the ways in which a corporation may be terminated and the advantages and disadvantages of the corporate form of organization. Finally, the chapter discusses franchising, what it is, its advantages and disadvantages, and how it is regulated by government.

NATURE OF A CORPORATION

corporation legal entity created by permission of government

A **corporation** is an artificial legal entity created by permission of the state or federal government. It is an entity in itself, separate from its owners. It is an artificial person and does business in its own name. Among other things, it can buy and sell property, sue and be sued, and borrow money all in its own name.

Corporations are usually classified as either public or private corporations. Public corporations are chartered by the state or federal government to carry out governmental purposes. Among the most common public corporations are state hospitals, state universities, and public utility companies. There are two types of private corporations: profit and nonprofit.

Corporations may also be classified as domestic or foreign. A domestic corporation is one that is incorporated under the laws of one state. A foreign corporation is one that is incorporated in one state but is licensed to do business in another state.

Profit Corporations

profit corporation
corporation organized to earn a profit

A **profit corporation** is one organized to make money. It is the typical type of business enterprise used to operate manufacturing, financial, and service businesses. Most of the material in this chapter is concerned with profit corporations.

professional corporation corporation organized to operate a professional practice

Professional Corporations   There is a special type of profit corporation known as a **professional corporation**, or professional association, as it is called in some states. This type of corporation is organized to operate a professional practice, such as that of a physician, attorney, or accountant. It is similar to a typical business corporation except that its directors and stockholders must be licensed to practice the profession for which the corporation has been created. In addition, stockholders may be individually liable for torts relating to professional activities, such as malpractice, but not for torts unrelated to the professional activities.

Kasdin and Saiger, P.C., practices accounting as a professional corporation. If one of the stockholders assaults someone, the corporation and the stockholder who commits the assault may be held liable but the other stockholders will not.

close corporation
corporation owned by a few people

Close Corporations   Many private corporations operate as **close corporations**. A close corporation is one in which the stock is held by a few people, often members of the same family. Although a close corporation is formed in the same manner as all other private corporations, many states have simplified the way in which such corporations may be managed, in recognition of close corporations being managed as if they were partnerships rather than corporations. These laws restrict the number of stockholders and the transfer of stock. The articles of incorporation and the bylaws may also control the transfer of stock.

Chapter S corporation
corporation treated as a partnership for tax purposes

Chapter S Corporations   Just as a limited partnership is a hybrid business organization, so too is a Chapter S corporation. A **Chapter S corporation**, authorized by Congress in 1982, is a private corporation that elects what is called Chapter S status under the U.S. Internal Revenue Code. Provided certain requirements are met, a Chapter S corporation is treated as a partnership for tax purposes but as a corporation for all other purposes. One advantage is that corporate income taxes are avoided; only the stockholders are taxed and only on their distributions from the corporation. Another advantage is that losses are passed along to the stockholders, enabling them to deduct them from their income, a benefit usually available only to sole proprietors and members of a partnership.

The requirements for qualifying as a Chapter S corporation are many, but the most important ones are that there must be seventy-five or fewer stockholders, the corporation must be a domestic one, and the corporation cannot derive more than 5 percent of its gross income from investments in which no active management takes place (passive investment income).

Nonprofit Corporations

nonprofit corporation
corporation organized primarily for nonbusiness purposes

A **nonprofit corporation** is organized not to earn money but to provide educational, charitable, or social services. This type of corporation includes religious organizations, private colleges, hospitals, and veterans' organizations.

The Great Woods Corp. was formed to provide camping experiences for children with disabilities. Even though the corporation may receive more than it spends (may earn a profit), it is a nonprofit corporation because its primary purpose is a social one.

FORMING A CORPORATION

Although some corporations are chartered by the federal government, most are incorporated under state law. Each state (and the District of Columbia) has its own laws regulating the formation of corporations. These laws differ in certain respects, but the basic steps in all states are signing and filing the articles of incorporation and setting up the corporate structure.

Articles of Incorporation

articles of incorporation application for permission to incorporate a business

capitalization description of the investment makeup of a corporation

stock ownership interest in a corporation

par stock stock having a value printed on stock certificate

no-par stock stock having no value printed on stock certificate

Once a decision is made to conduct business under the corporate form of organization, the first step is to prepare the application for incorporation. In most states, this application is known as the **articles of incorporation**, or charter. The articles normally include the name of the corporation, its purpose, its term of existence (usually indefinite), the location of its principal business office, and the names and addresses of the incorporators. State laws regulate the number of incorporators needed—usually one to three. The articles must also include a description of the investment makeup of the corporation, known as **capitalization**. This description includes a statement of the number of shares of stock the corporation is authorized to issue. **Stock** is the ownership interest in a corporation. The articles of incorporation indicate whether the stock is to have a stated value or no stated value. Stock with a value printed on it is known as **par stock**; stock with no printed value is known as **no-par stock**.

An important part of the articles of incorporation is the corporate name. Most states have laws limiting the types of names that may be used. The name must usually indicate that the business organization is in fact a corporation so that the public knows with whom it is dealing. The word *Corporation* or some abbreviation such as *Corp., Inc.,* or *Ltd.* is often used. To avoid confusion, the name must not be similar to an existing name. In addition, the name cannot mislead the public by appearing to indicate that the organization has some official status.

> Craig and Gregg decided to form a corporation to sell military samples, using the name U.S. Government Surplus, Inc. They would not receive permission to use the name because it would mislead the public.

asset property that has value

The name of the corporation is also important because of its advertising value. It is often considered a valuable **asset** of the corporation. In most states, an examination is made of state records to determine the availability of a corporate name before the articles of incorporation are prepared.

After the articles of incorporation are signed, they are sent to the appropriate state office for filing. There is usually an incorporation fee plus a tax on the number and value of shares of stock that the corporation is authorized to issue. When the articles are approved, a notice of approval is sent to the applicants, the corporate charter, often called the certificate of incorporation, is issued, and the corporation begins its existence. Two additional steps are required: obtaining for the corporation a tax identification number from the Internal Revenue Service and preparing the bylaws.

bylaws rules adopted by a corporation or unincorporated association

Bylaws are rules for managing the internal affairs of a corporation. They cover such matters as the number of officers and directors, the duties and powers of corporate officers, and the time and place of corporate meetings.

FIGURE 27.1 Stock Certificate

First Organizational Meeting   After the corporate charter is issued, the next step is an organizational meeting. At the meeting, the incorporators elect the board of directors, pass bylaws, issue stock, and transact other corporate business.

OWNERSHIP OF A CORPORATION

stockholders persons who own a corporation

stock certificate document indicating ownership interest in a corporation

A corporation is owned by its **stockholders**. Each stockholder owns one or more shares of stock in the corporation. The document that indicates the ownership of a corporation's stock is called a **stock certificate** (Figure 27.1). The certificate lists the name of the stockholder and the number of shares of stock owned. Each certificate is registered in the corporate records. When a stockholder sells her or his shares of stock, the certificate is returned to the corporation and canceled, and a new certificate is issued to the new owner.

RIGHTS OF STOCKHOLDERS

Stockholders have specific rights granted by state statute and protected by court decisions. In practice, the extent to which these rights are claimed depends on the size of the corporation and the number of stockholders.

In larger corporations, the stockholders have a tendency to permit the officers and directors to exercise complete control over corporate affairs. A stockholder is entitled to vote on matters that require stockholder approval. Voting usually takes place at annual

proxy written permission by a stockholder for another to vote his or her shares of stock

meetings of stockholders. It is often difficult or impractical for a stockholder to attend a meeting. A stockholder who cannot or does not wish to attend a meeting may vote by proxy. A **proxy** is a written authorization by a stockholder allowing another person to cast her or his vote. Most large corporations have so many stockholders that many votes are cast by proxy. The stockholder who votes by proxy may vote on specific issues or may give certain officers or directors the right to vote on the issues as they choose. For a valid meeting, there must be a quorum, usually holders of over 50 percent of the outstanding stocks.

Most voting is done on a one-vote-per-share basis. In a few states, however, a stockholder may cast a number of votes equal to the number of shares owned multiplied by the number of directors to be elected at an annual meeting. This type of voting is known as *cumulative voting*. It enables stockholders holding large blocks of stock to split their votes among several directors or to cast all the votes for one director. As such, it is a means of exercising control.

Another right of stockholders is to share in profits. If profits are earned and paid out as dividends, a stockholder is entitled to a share of them based on the number of shares owned.

The right to obtain a stock certificate as evidence of ownership is another important right. The certificate not only proves ownership but is used to transfer the ownership interest to others.

A stockholder has a right to inspect the books and records of the corporation and to copy them. This right is subject to reasonable rules and regulations to prevent harassment of a corporation or improper use of its records. The inspection must be for a reasonable purpose related to the business of the corporation. It must be done at a reasonable time and must not involve release of corporate secrets or confidential information that might harm the business.

> Noble, a stockholder in a computer manufacturing company, demanded to see price lists showing the cost and profit made on each computer sold. Because this information could harm the corporation if competitors obtained it, Noble is not entitled to see such lists.

preemptive right right of stockholders to buy new stock before its sale to the public

Unless eliminated by the articles of incorporation or the bylaws, whenever a corporation issues new shares, current stockholders have a right to purchase these shares before they are offered to the public. This right, known as the **preemptive right**, enables stockholders to maintain their proportional interest in the corporation.

The right to share in the assets of the corporation upon dissolution is another important right. Creditors, however, have first claim against the assets, followed by bondholders and then preferred stockholders. The common stockholders receive the remainder. Stockholders elect and may remove directors, may amend the charter and bylaws, must approve the sale of all of the corporation's assets, may approve a merger or consolidation, and must approve the termination of the corporation.

LIABILITIES OF STOCKHOLDERS

limited liability liability of stockholder for debts of a corporation

State laws vary on the liability of stockholders. Unlike partners, stockholders have **limited liability**. Their liability for the debts of a corporation is limited to the amount they have invested in the corporation through the purchase of stock. In certain states, however, certain stockholders owning the largest number of shares are liable for wages due employees who are not paid by the corporation.

FINANCING A CORPORATION

A corporation needs capital for its operations, both at the time it commences business and later on when it wishes to expand. The two most common forms of financing are known as equity (consisting of stocks) and debt (consisting of borrowed funds such as loans and bonds). *Equity* represents ownership of the corporation; **debt** represents borrowing by the corporation. State regulations and the articles of incorporation set the type of shares that a corporation may issue and the amount to be paid for them.

debt obligation to repay

Equity: Common and Preferred Stock

The two types of stock issued by corporations are common stock and preferred stock. **Common stock** is the ordinary stock of a corporation. It gives the owner the right to vote at stockholders' meetings and to share in the profits of the corporation according to the number of shares owned. A common stockholder receives a share of the profits only if the company earns a profit and votes to return a portion of those profits to stockholders. This share of the profits is called a **dividend**. The amount of the dividend depends on the profits earned by the corporation. All states and many lenders to corporations regulate the payment of dividends. Most states prohibit the payment of dividends if the corporation is insolvent (defined as the inability of the company to pay its debts as they become due) or would become insolvent because of the payment of the dividend. A stockholder may sue a corporation if dividends are not paid, but such cases are rare, as are judgments in favor of such stockholders.

common stock corporation's ordinary stock

dividend portion of corporate profits paid to stockholders

Common stockholders have the lowest priority when it comes to a claim on earnings. Various taxing authorities, employees, lending institutions, bondholders, and preferred stockholders are all entitled to be paid before common stockholders receive anything. On the other hand, common stockholders have the greatest chance to see their investments appreciate in value.

Preferred stock has a preferred, or prior, claim to dividends over other categories of stock. A preferred stockholder is entitled to receive a specific dividend for each share owned. A corporation may pay dividends on the common stock only after all preferred dividends are paid. Preferred shareholders usually do not have the right to vote on corporate matters unless a dividend is not paid.

preferred stock stock having a prior right to receive a stated dividend

There are many types of preferred stock issued by corporations. **Convertible preferred** may be exchanged for common stock of the corporation at the option of the stockholder, usually within a given period of time. **Cumulative preferred** requires that any preferred stock dividends not paid when due be accumulated and paid before any common stock dividends may be paid. **Callable preferred** is stock that may be redeemed by the corporation and bought back at a certain price, usually at any time but sometimes during a given period of time. **Participating preferred** enables the holder to share in the profits of the corporation, in addition to the preferred dividend payable.

convertible preferred preferred stock that may be exchanged for common stock at the option of the stockholder

cumulative preferred preferred stock for which accumulated dividends are paid before any common stock dividends are payable

Stocks may also be classified as par or no-par stock. A par value stock is one which states a minimum value for which the stock may be sold, often $1.00. This has nothing to do with the value of the stock, which is set by supply and demand. No-par stock has no stated value.

callable preferred preferred stock that a corporation may buy at its option

Corporations also may offer stock options to its stockholder, officers, and employees, giving the holder the right to buy corporate stock for a stated price during a certain period of time. Stock options are often given to management as a bonus for good performance.

participating preferred preferred stock that shares in corporate profits as well as receiving preferred stock dividends

Debt: Bonds and Loans

Instead of selling interest in a corporation in the form of stock, many corporations borrow money. Sometimes the money is borrowed from private investors or even from the stockholders themselves. A promissory note is given as evidence of the debt, and the loan is repayable over a fixed period of time (or sometimes on demand) and at a fixed rate of interest. Many corporations borrow larger sums of money from banks or insurance companies. Such loans are usually secured by a pledge of some or all of the corporation's assets.

bond written promise to pay a debt or loan

The most common form of corporate debt financing is the bond. A **bond** is an obligation of a corporation to repay a loan to it over a fixed period of time at a fixed interest rate. Bonds are sold to the public or to institutions and are traded on the various stock exchanges.

mortgage bond bond secured by a specific piece of real property

equipment bond bond secured by a specific piece of personal property

debenture unsecured corporate obligation to pay money

convertible bond bond that may be converted into common stock of the corporation

As with preferred stock, there are many different types of bonds. **Mortgage bonds** and **equipment bonds** are secured by specific pieces of real or personal property. If the corporation defaults in making payments, the specific property may be seized and sold and the proceeds used to pay the debt. A **debenture** is a bond that is unsecured and protected only by the general assets of the corporation. There are also **convertible bonds**, which may be converted into common stock of the corporation, and **callable bonds**, which the corporation may redeem and pay off at a given price within a given period of time.

callable bond bond that the corporation may redeem and pay off at a given price within a given period of time

Bondholders are entitled to be paid before any dividends are paid to common and preferred stockholders. They also have first claim against the assets of a corporation in the event of dissolution or bankruptcy; they have no voting rights and cannot participate in management.

MANAGING A CORPORATION

Stockholders, directors, officers, and employees all play a role in the management of a corporation.

The stockholders, the owners of a corporation, have the following powers:

1. To elect and remove directors
2. To vote on basic changes such as amending the bylaws, terminating the corporation, merging or consolidating, and selling all or a major part of the corporation's assets

board of directors group responsible for setting corporate policy

Directors manage a corporation at the highest level and make policy decisions for the corporation. They set the basic policies, make major financial decisions, and appoint and remove corporate officers and other high-ranking employees. Their terms, powers, and duties are established by the articles of incorporation, the bylaws, and state law. The **board of directors** of most corporations delegates power to an executive committee and to corporate officers to handle day-to-day operations.

The officers actually run the corporation. They are employees who manage the corporation on a daily basis and are accountable to the directors and the stockholders. The officers in turn hire the other employees of the corporation, who handle the details involved in the corporate business. A corporation must have certain officers as required by state law, the articles of incorporation, and the bylaws.

While management protocol for large, publicly held corporations is set by state law and the bylaws of a corporation, management is much less formal when the corporation is one that is closely held and often involves few stockholders who may be related to each other.

Powers and Liabilities of a Corporation

A corporation's powers may be either express or implied. The express powers are those contained in the corporate charter, the bylaws, or state corporation statutes. The implied powers are those a corporation must have to be able to function properly and to carry out its express powers. If a corporation does anything that goes beyond its express or implied powers, its actions are said to be **ultra vires**. The stockholders can invalidate an ultra vires act unless the act has been completely performed by all parties. Such an act is fully enforceable, however, by the parties to the act.

ultra vires acts of a corporation not permitted under its express or implied powers

> The president of Hightop Corp. signed an agreement to lend money to another corporation, an ultra vires act. Before the loan was completed, the stockholders brought suit to cancel the loan. They would succeed in their suit. Neither the lender nor the borrower, however, would be able to cancel the transaction on their own.

Like a partnership or an agency relationship, a corportion may be held liable for torts committed by its employees and agents. It may also be held liable for crimes committed by its agents and employees and fined accordingly.

The most important powers of a corporation are to have a name and corporate seal, to enjoy perpetual existence, to sue and be sued in its own name, to acquire and dispose of real property needed for the proper conduct of the business, and to borrow money for any proper corporate purpose.

Powers, Duties, and Liabilities of Directors

Directors govern a corporation. They have the power to direct corporate policies and to appoint officers and agents. They may do whatever is reasonable to accomplish that, limited only by the bylaws or state statutes. They can and usually do delegate powers to the officers and an executive committee. The board of directors must act as a group; individual directors cannot bind the corporation. Directors conduct business at normal meetings, the dates being set in the bylaws or by resolution. Special meetings may be called upon notice to all directors.

Directors may be liable for contracts and for negligence and other torts. They owe the corporation and the stockholders a duty of care and loyalty. They must act in the best interest of the corporation and are liable if they do not act as reasonable directors should act, as well as for intentional acts of negligence that harm the corporation, such as committing ultra vires acts and using corporate funds in an improper manner. They may be held both criminally and civilly liable for improper conduct. Directors are usually liable only to the corporation and not to third parties. Directors who commit fraud or intentionally deceive third parties dealing with the corporation, however, are liable for their actions.

> Berry was a creditor of the Atlas Corporation. The directors of the corporation were negligent in borrowing money without the ability to repay the loan, and the corporation had to file for bankruptcy. Berry would not be able to hold the directors liable for negligence.

Powers, Duties, and Liabilities of Officers

Officers have the responsibility of managing the corporation on a day-to-day basis. Like the directors, their powers are derived from the bylaws and state statutes. Their liability is usually only to the corporation and then only for negligence or intentional torts. Officers, like directors, however, are liable to third parties for such intentional torts as deceit or fraud and may be both criminally and civilly liable. They owe the corporation and the stockholders a duty of care and of loyalty.

TERMINATING A CORPORATION

Unlike partnerships, corporations do not terminate when there is a change of ownership. Corporate existence ends only when the term of the corporate charter ends, when the corporate charter is revoked, or when there is a consolidation or merger.

The charters of most corporations provide for perpetual existence. Other charters provide for a specific term, such as fifty years. When the term ends, the corporate existence terminates. A corporation may also be dissolved when the stockholders agree to end the corporate existence.

The state may dissolve a corporation and revoke its charter under certain limited conditions. Examples of such conditions are failure to pay corporate taxes and continuous violation of state statutes regulating corporations.

consolidation joining of two or more corporations with one surviving

merger joining of two corporations to form a new one

Corporate existence often ends with consolidation or merger, usually because a corporation wants to expand its business. In a **consolidation**, two or more corporations join together to form a new corporation, with the old corporations disappearing. The obligations and liabilities of the old corporations are assumed by the new corporation.

In a **merger**, one corporation buys another corporation. The buying corporation stays in existence, obtaining all the assets and assuming all the obligations and liabilities of the selling corporation; the selling corporation then ceases to exist (Figure 27.2).

> The Brant Corporation made an offer to purchase all of the stock of the Deke Corporation. The stock was purchased, and the Deke Corporation ceased to exist. This situation is an example of a merger.

All states have laws regulating merger and consolidation procedures. They usually require approval by the directors and stockholders of all corporations involved, as well as the filing of a merger or consolidation plan with the department of state in each state involved.

Suppose a stockholder does not agree with the merger or consolidation plan. The law in most states permits a dissenting stockholder to have the value of his or her shares determined as of the date of the merger or consolidation and to receive payment for those shares. The basic procedures may vary among the states, but they basically provide for the giving of notice by the dissenting stockholder and for an appraisal process to determine the value of the shares.

FIGURE 27.2
Merger versus Consolidation

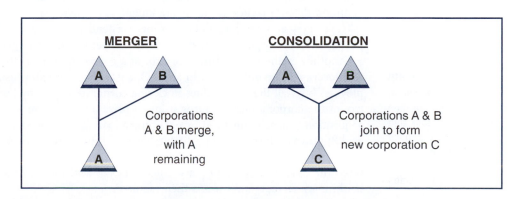

PURCHASE OF ASSETS AND STOCK

Corporations often expand by purchasing the assets or stock of another corporation. The method of acquisition depends on many factors, including tax consequences.

Purchase of Assets

Some corporations prefer to acquire the assets, rather than the stock, of another corporation. One advantage is that this step does not require approval by the stockholders of the acquiring corporation, although the corporation whose assets are being acquired must get the approval of its stockholders and directors. Another advantage is that, except in unusual circumstances, the acquiring corporation does not have to assume the obligations of the selling corporation. The "unusual circumstances" include (1) when the sale is fraudulent, (2) when the sale is in fact a merger or consolidation, and (3) when the buyer agrees to assume the seller's debts and liabilities. The disadvantage is that the assets must be valued, which is often an expensive and time-consuming process.

Purchase of Stock

A corporation can expand by buying a controlling interest in another corporation through the purchase of stock. The advantage is that only an overall purchase price for the stock, rather than the value of individual assets, has to be determined. The disadvantages are that the acquiring corporation must receive stockholder approval for such an acquisition and must also assume all the debts and liabilities of the selling corporation.

There are many different methods of purchasing stock to obtain a controlling interest in another corporation. One method is the use of a **tender offer**. A tender offer is a public offer to the stockholders of a corporation to purchase all or a portion of their shares at a stated price. The offering group may offer to pay for the shares so acquired by cash or its own stock. A tender offer may be seen as favorable by the directors as a means of getting a good price for the corporation. Or it may be viewed as an unfavorable attempt to take control of the corporation. It is for this reason that both federal and state securities laws regulate the terms and circumstances of tender offers.

To prevent unwarranted takeovers, many corporations have produced clever ways of resisting takeover attempts. One is known as the "poison pill," in which the corporation issues a large volume of shares to its stockholders at low prices, making it extremely expensive for an outside group to gain control. Another device is the "golden parachute," in which top executives are guaranteed huge bonuses if the corporation is purchased, making it also more expensive for the outside group to take control. One of the most common defense tactics is the "white knight," in which the corporation under threat of takeover gets another corporation to make a tender offer greater than that of the proposed takeover corporation, making it more expensive for it to get control.

Another method of obtaining control of a corporation by a stock purchaser is known as a **leveraged buyout (LBO)**. In an LBO, a group of investors (usually managers or employees) buys all the outstanding stock of a corporation held by the public, acquires control of the corporation, and turns it into a private rather than a public corporation. The acquisition is usually financed by obtaining a loan on the corporation's assets. Sometimes an LBO turns a formerly unprofitable business into a profitable one, and the private investors then sell stock in the corporation and turn it back into a public corporation. It is often the case that the LBO places such a heavy debt load on the business that it fails; bankruptcy or reorganization is then required.

tender offer public offer to stockholders to buy their stock

leveraged buyout (LBO) method of acquiring control of a corporation by buying stock and financing the purchase with a loan on the assets of the acquired corporation

ADVANTAGES AND DISADVANTAGES OF CORPORATIONS

Operating as a corporation has its advantages and disadvantages, and they are usually the exact opposite of those for a partnership. A comparison of the sole proprietorship, the partnership, and the corporate forms of business organization is shown in Table 27.1.

Unlike the partnership, a corporation continues its operations despite changes in ownership. The death of an owner (stockholder) rarely results in the termination of a corporation, unless it is a one-stockholder corporation.

Another advantage of the corporation is ease of transfer of ownership. To transfer stock, a stockholder need only sign the stock certificate and transfer it to the new owner. Transfer of a partnership interest usually requires a complicated contract and the approval of the other partners.

Centralized management is another advantage of corporations. In a partnership, all partners have a right to participate in management, and they usually take part. This participation can cause dissension and make management unwieldy. In a corporation, management functions are delegated to a small group of officers who can act on behalf of a large group of owners.

An important advantage of the corporate form is the availability of many fringe benefits, including tax-saving devices such as pension and profit-sharing plans. In addition, a corporation that provides its employees with disability insurance, term life insurance, medical and dental plans, and education benefits can deduct the cost from corporate income.

The most important advantage of the corporate form is limited liability. A stockholder is shielded from liability for corporate losses or judgments for any amounts in excess of the stockholder's investments in the corporation.

The exception to the benefit of limited liability may occur when a court finds out that the corporation (or its stockholders) is using the corporate form solely to avoid liability

TABLE 27.1   COMPARISON OF FORMS OF BUSINESS ORGANIZATION

	ADVANTAGES	DISADVANTAGES
Sole proprietorship	• Flexible method of business organization • Profits taxed as owner's personal income • No special legal formalities required to begin business • Opportunity for close personal contact between owner and customers	• Large initial capital requirements • Business risk is unlimited and must be borne by owner alone • Business ceases to exist when owner dies or retires
Partnership	• Simple to organize • Profits taxed as partners' personal income • Minimum government regulation • No restrictions of powers	• Unlimited liability • May have conflicts over management • Business may be dissolved by change or death of a partner • Ownership is difficult to transfer
Corporation	• Limited liability • Centralized management • Continuity of business (perpetual existence) • Ease of transferring ownership	• Expensive to organize • Double taxation • Extensive government regulation • Restrictions on powers

or to commit a fraud against potential creditors. If a court finds that to be the case, the court may do what is known as "pierce the corporate veil" and make stockholders fully liable for debts or losses of the corporation.

Courts may hold that a certain corporation is a sham if the business is run more like a partnership than a corporation. Failure to hold corporate meetings, keep minutes, and file corporate tax returns is evidence of an intent not to operate a business as a corporation. Mixing personal assets with corporate assets and using corporate funds to pay personal obligations constitute further evidence. Another indication of abusing the corporate form is "thin capitalization," or having too few or no assets in a corporation to pay creditors or judgments that may be imposed against it. If a court finds thin capitalization to be the case, it may ignore the corporate shield and hold the stockholders personally liable.

> Reynolds and Blaine were stockholders in Algin Corp. They each invested $100 in the corporation and then proceeded to buy $50,000 worth of inventory. If the corporation defaults in paying for the inventory, a court may hold Reynolds and Blaine personally liable on the grounds that they purposely failed to provide the corporation with sufficient assets to secure payment for purchases and were therefore operating the corporation as a sham.

One disadvantage of corporations is the expense and complication involved in incorporating and operating. A partnership is easy to form and requires little expense. Establishing a corporation takes time and involves the expense of incorporating, the issuance of stock to raise capital, recordkeeping for and payment of taxes, and so forth. Operating a partnership is relatively easy. The corporation must keep complicated records, take minutes of meetings, maintain employee records, and file different types of tax returns.

Another disadvantage of corporations is the double taxation that shareholders pay. Corporations, unlike partnerships, are considered legal entities, separate from their owners. As a result, they pay income taxes at the corporate level. In addition, the stockholders are taxed on the dividends they receive from the corporation.

State and federal regulation is another disadvantage of corporations. Partnerships are relatively free from government regulation and control. Corporations are subject to much control, including the filing of reports, issuance of stock, and payment of dividends.

Investor Protection

Investors in corporations, at the time of incorporation and during the corporation's existence, require extensive protection. This protection is provided by both law and regulations and is discussed in Chapter 28.

| FRANCHISING

One of the most common types of business arrangements in existence today is the franchise. The use of franchises began in the early part of the twentieth century. Some of the most well-known franchises include McDonald's, Burger King, and Holiday Inn. A **franchise** is an agreement in which

franchise business arrangement between a franchisor and a franchisee

- a franchisor (the person who grants the franchise) gives a franchisee (the operator of the franchise) the right to use the franchisor's name, trademark, and logo.
- the franchisor gives the franchisee know-how, assistance, and training and exercises a measure of control over the franchisee's operations.

• in return for these rights, the franchisee pays the franchisor an initial franchise fee and/or a fee based on gross sales and/or must purchase inventory and equipment from the franchisor.

> Owens entered into an arrangement with Ultra Vacuum Cleaner Co. to distribute its vacuum cleaners. The arrangement was that Owens would open a store called Ultra Vacuums and would sell cleaners sent to him on consignment. Owens was to be paid a commission based on a percentage of the sale price. This arrangement is not a franchise because Owens is not controlled by Ultra and pays no fee for the right to be a distributor. Owens is considered a consignee and an independent contractor.

A distributor may or may not be a product franchisee depending on the relationship between the distributor and the supplier of the merchandise.

The franchise relationship arises from a contract between the franchisor and the franchisee. Its important terms include the length of the term of the franchise, the responsibilities of the franchisor, the obligations of the franchisee, the down payment for the franchise, the monthly or annual franchise fee, the territory in which the franchisee will operate, and when a franchise may be terminated.

There are two basic types of franchising. One is *product franchising,* in which the franchisee sells a product manufactured or distributed by the franchisor. Gas stations, auto dealers, and soft-drink bottlers are examples of product franchising. The second type is *business plan franchising,* in which a service or business plan is the main element. Fast-food restaurants, equipment rentals, tax preparation companies, and motels are examples of business plan franchising.

There are many advantages of the franchise system for both franchisors and franchisees. The franchisor can expand, using the franchisee's capital instead of its own; can obtain a large network of distributors without having to set up its own network, thereby saving time and money; and can have a larger base of operations than it would normally have, enabling it to buy merchandise at lower cost and to borrow money on better terms.

The franchisee benefits as well. The franchisee can get into business with less capital and less experience than would normally be required. The franchisee also gets the advantage of using a well-known name, trademark, and logo that it ordinarily would not have access to. Finally, the franchisee gets training and supervision to enable it to conduct its business successfully. The franchisee can operate as an independent entity and enjoy the benefits of a national organization.

Franchising, however, has not been worry-free. As franchising has become so popular, many problems have emerged from this type of arrangement. Three major abuses have arisen.

Some franchisors fail to disclose to the franchisee all the risks involved in the franchise system and all the details of the proposed franchise relationship. As a result, many franchisees make poorly informed decisions to purchase a franchise.

In other cases, franchisors have not made proper provisions for a default by the franchisor or the improper termination of the franchise. In both cases, the franchisee may be left holding the bag, burdened by a large capital investment.

Some franchisee agreements are silent about the territory in which the franchisee has the exclusive right to operate, or they give the franchisor control over territorial rights. In such cases, a franchisee may discover a competing business involving the same franchise operating near his or her own business.

Extensive laws and regulations have been enacted on both federal and state levels to protect franchisees. Congress has passed laws to regulate franchises in certain industries. The Petroleum Marketing Practices Act and the Automobile Dealers' Franchise Act both protect franchisees from improper or arbitrary termination of franchises. Both acts enable franchisees to sue franchisors in federal court for improper termination of franchises. It is important to note that these laws apply only in the case of improper or arbitrary terminations. They do not affect the franchisor's right under most agreements to cancel or refuse to renew a franchise if the franchisee fails to purchase the required amount of inventory, to meet certain sales quotas, to meet certain health or safety standards, and so on. The Federal Trade Commission has also adopted regulations that regulate all franchise offerings in the United States. Most of these regulations are concerned with the need for making proper disclosure to potential franchisees. They make a franchisor subject to both civil and criminal penalties for failure to make proper disclosure or for making false representations.

In addition, many states have enacted laws and regulations that govern the sale of franchises and certain elements of the franchise such as financing, renewal of the franchise agreement, and termination of it. Some states even require the registration of franchises before they may be sold within the state.

LICENSING

license the right to sell products for a fee

There is a business arrangement similar to a franchise known as a license. A **license** gives the licensee rights to sell or use a particular product or service in a specified area in exchange for a fee. Unlike a franchise, there is generally no control over the business operations or how a product is sold.

Summary

A corporation is a legal entity created under state law. It can hold title to property in its own name and may sue or be sued in its own name. Corporations are classified as either public or private corporations. Public corporations, such as state hospitals and public utility companies, carry out public functions. Private corporations are either profit or nonprofit. Private corporations are organized to make money. Nonprofit corporations are organized to provide educational, religious, charitable, or social services.

A corporation begins to exist on filing articles of incorporation and with the issuance of a charter by the state. The articles of incorporation and the bylaws provide the corporate name, term, purpose, internal organization, and the financial makeup of the organization.

A corporation is owned by its stockholders. They have the right to vote for directors and on other major issues, to share in profits, and to inspect the books and records of the corporation, subject to reasonable rules and regulations.

They usually have the right to purchase new issues of stock before an offer is made to the public and the right to share in the assets of the corporation upon its dissolution. Stockholders enjoy limited liability: their liability for debts of the corporation is limited to their investments.

Corporations may be financed in many ways. Often, it is through debt, either bank loans or issuance of corporate bonds. Usually, it is through the issuance of stock, which may be either common or preferred.

Directors of a corporation establish general policies for corporate operations, hire officers, and declare dividends. The officers are responsible for day-to-day operations. Both directors and officers are liable to the corporation for negligence and intentional torts such as fraud. They are usually liable to third parties only for deceit and fraud.

Most corporations have perpetual existence; some have specific terms. Corporate existence ends when the term expires, by agreement of the stockholders, on revocation of the charter by the state, or on a consolidation or merger.

The advantages of the corporate form of doing business are continuity, ease of transfer of ownership, centralized management, availability of tax-deductible fringe benefits, and the limited liability of stockholders. Limited liability, however, may be unavailable if the corporate form is used solely to defraud potential creditors.

The disadvantages of corporations are the expense involved in incorporating and operating, double taxation, and extensive state and federal regulation.

Franchising is a common type of business arrangement in which a franchisee, for a fee, obtains products, management skills, and a logo (or trademark) from a franchisor. Both the state and federal governments have passed laws regulating the registration and sale of franchises and the disclosure of vital information to potential franchisees. Licensing is like a franchise, but with no control over business operations.

Important Legal terms

articles of incorporation
asset
board of directors
bond
bylaws
callable bonds
callable preferred
capitalization
Chapter S corporation
close corporations
common stock
consolidation
convertible bond
convertible preferred

corporation
cumulative preferred
debenture
debt
dividend
equipment bond
franchise
leveraged buyout (LBO)
license
limited liability
merger
mortgage bond
nonprofit corporation
no-par stock

par stock
participating preferred
preemptive right
preferred stock
professional corporation
profit corporation
proxy
stock
stock certificate
stockholders
tender offer
ultra vires

Questions and Problems for Discussion

1. Name six rights of stockholders.
2. What are the advantages and disadvantages of the corporate form of business organization?
3. Explain the double taxation of corporate earnings that shareholders pay.
4. What are the advantages and disadvantages of purchasing the assets of a corporation instead of its stock?
5. Explain the difference between the duties of a director and those of an officer.
6. What occurrences might result in the involuntary dissolution of a corporation?
7. Jackson owned one share of stock of the ABC Corp., a public corporation with 1 million stockholders. He sued the corporation for failure to supply him with a list of all stockholders so he could write them personally regarding his complaints against the corporation. Will he succeed?
8. Fairly, a director of the XYZ Corporation, issued a false report about the corporation's finances to a bank from which he was seeking a loan. Can the bank recover from the corporation for Fairly's fraud?
9. O & J, Inc., a public corporation, distributed a dividend to its stockholders at a time when the corporation was solvent. The distribution, however, would make the corporation insolvent. Was the dividend unlawful?
10. What are the restrictions on a corporation paying dividends to its stockholders?

11. Explain how close corporations and publicly held corporations are managed differently?

12. Loring and Jenkins were officers in Smithson, Inc., a publicly held corporation. They learned of a building for sale that would have benefited the corporation, but they instead bought it for themselves so they could rent it for a huge profit. Would a court invalidate this transaction? On what grounds?

13. Albertson, driving a truck owned by the Ajax Corporation, negligently drove the truck into a storefront. Can the store owner hold the corporation liable for Albertson's negligence?

14. Stetson owned 100 shares of the common stock of Blair Corp. For three years in a row, the corporation lost money and paid no dividends. Stetson sued to force the corporation to pay dividends on his stock. Will he succeed?

15. Morgan wanted to invest in and take control of Gemini Corporation but was concerned about its liabilities. Should Morgan purchase the corporation's stock or its assets?

Cases for Review

1. Miles and others, stockholders in the Heflin Bank, asked to inspect the books and records of the corporation to determine whether there had been misuse of corporate funds, abuse of corporate office, and other breaches of the directors' fiduciary duties. The bank refused to permit such an inspection. Was it correct in doing so? (*Bank of Heflin* v. *M. N. Miles,* 294 Ala. 462)

2. Free Baptist Church, a religious corporation, rented liquor-dispensing equipment from Southeastern. When Free Baptist defaulted on the lease, Southeastern sued the church for the rental due. Free Baptist claimed as a defense that the leasing of such equipment from Southeastern was an ultra vires act. Is the defense a good one? (*Free Baptist Church* v. *Southeastern Beverage Co.,* 218 S.E.2d 169)

3. Equitable Life Insurance Co. loaned money to Inland Printing, secured by a mortgage on Inland's property. When Inland failed to pay the mortgage debt, Equitable foreclosed on the mortgage and sold Inland's property. As the sale did not produce an amount sufficient to cover the debt completely, Equitable sued the corporation's officers and directors for negligence, claiming that they had mismanaged the corporation's business. Was Equitable entitled to a decision in its favor? (*Equitable Life and Casualty Co.* v. *Inland Printing Co.,* 454 P.2d 162)

4. Brandt and others, stockholders in Travelers Corporation, sued to prevent the merger of Travelers and Primerica Corporation, claiming that the merger offer was inadequate and that the directors of Travelers approved the merger offer only to advance their individual interests. The merger offer had been approved by over 95 percent of Travelers' shareholders. Should Brandt and others succeed in their desire to prevent the merger? (*Brandt* v. *The Travelers Corporation,* 665 A.2d 616)

5. Shaw was a farmer selling produce to Agri-Mark. She was not a stockholder of Agri-Mark but was considered a member of the company. She and others requested an inspection of the corporation's books to determine if its officers were being overpaid. Agri-Mark refused permission on the grounds that Shaw was not a stockholder. Was this correct? (*Shaw* v. *Agri-Mark, Inc.,* 663 A.2d 464)

6. Black and Graham were the sole stockholders of a corporation, each owning 50 percent of the shares. They were also the sole directors. A dispute arose between them about how the business should be run, and they could not resolve the issue. Because of this deadlock, Graham filed suit to dissolve the corporation. Should the court dissolve the corporation based on these facts? (*Black* v. *Graham,* 464 S.E.2d 814)

7. Babcock, an officer of Veco Corp., joined with another officer in an attempt to get fellow employees to leave Veco and join a competitor. Veco sued Babcock and the other officer, claiming that they had breached their fiduciary duties as officers of the corporation. Is this claim

correct? (*Veco Corp.* v. *Babcock*, 243 Ill. App. 3d 153)

8. Horton owned 112 shares of Compaq. He believed that Compaq was engaged in corporate wrongdoing that might affect the value of his stock. He asked to see a list of the corporation's stockholders so he could contact them about bringing a suit against the corporation. Compaq refused to provide the list, claiming the request was not for a proper purpose. Is Horton entitled to see the list? (*Compaq Computer Corporation* v. *Horton*, 631 A.2d.1)

9. Black and Graham each owned 50 percent of the stock of a corporation. When they disagreed about how the corporation should be managed and couldn't find a solution, Graham sued to have the state dissolve the corporation. Was a disagreement of this sort grounds for dissolution? (*Black* v. *Graham*, 464 S.E. 2d 814)

CHAPTER 28

Government Regulation of Business

CHAPTER PREVIEW

The Need for Government Regulation

The Authority of Government to Regulate Business

Areas of Government Regulation
Preventing Monopolies
Maintaining Fair Competition
Taxing Business
Regulating Crucial Industries

Regulating Securities
Regulating Corporate Conduct
Preserving the General Welfare and the Environment

How Government Regulations Are Enforced
Limitations on Agency Powers
Licensing and Liability of Professionals

Chapter Highlights

Government regulation of business has become a way of life in the United States. This chapter discusses why government regulation is needed and how such regulation protects the rights of business owners as well as consumers, employees, and stockholders. Under the constitutional form of government, the government must be supplied with the authority to regulate business. This authority comes from many sources, which are described in this chapter. There are many areas in which government seeks to regulate business, and these areas are described in detail, with particular emphasis on the area described as "Preserving the General Welfare and the Environment." Regulations are meaningless unless they can be enforced. The chapter concludes with a discussion of the ways in which government regulations are enforced and the agencies responsible for such enforcement.

THE NEED FOR GOVERNMENT REGULATION

Businesses in the United States operate on the private enterprise system, which means that private businesses compete in the marketplace and their success is determined by the quality and price of goods and services they offer. For this system to work, the rights of individual businesses must be protected and guaranteed.

Government regulation is designed to accomplish this protection. Regulation protects the rights of each business owner so that competition is maintained. It also protects the rights of consumers, employees, and in the case of corporations, stockholders.

THE AUTHORITY OF GOVERNMENT TO REGULATE BUSINESS

The authority of government to regulate business is found in Article 1, Section 8, of the U.S. Constitution, known as the commerce clause. It is also derived from statutes passed by Congress or state legislatures. It may come from court decisions that interpret the statutes passed. It may also arise from regulations or decisions of administrative agencies created to apply the statutes regulating business.

Because business affects the life of almost every person, both state and federal governments have exercised great powers to control and regulate it. Under the federal system, state and local governments have a basic power to provide for the general welfare of the public, known as the **police power**. From police power comes the power to regulate business activity to promote the public interest. There are only two limitations on this power. The regulation must be needed, and it must be reasonable. In addition, state and local governments may regulate only the business activity conducted solely within that government's boundaries. Such business activity is known as **intrastate commerce**. Moreover, state and local governments may not regulate areas of business already regulated by the federal government.

police power power of a state to protect the welfare of its citizens

intrastate commerce business activity solely within one state

> If Congress passed a law prohibiting the employment of persons under fourteen years of age, a state may not then pass a law prohibiting the employment of persons under sixteen years of age. The congressional act has priority.

interstate commerce business activity conducted in two or more states

The federal government regulates business activity conducted in more than one state, known as **interstate commerce**. The power to regulate interstate commerce comes from what is called the commerce clause of the U.S. Constitution: "Congress shall have the Power to regulate Commerce with foreign Nations, and *among the several States,* and with the Indian Tribes" (italics added). As a matter of practice and because of various court decisions, Congress has almost unlimited authority to control business. That control, however, must still be needed, must be reasonable, and must not violate anyone's constitutional rights.

AREAS OF GOVERNMENT REGULATION

Both the federal and state governments (including local governments) regulate almost every aspect of business activity. The regulation we discuss in this chapter affects business itself, and its ultimate goal is the protection of the public by maintaining competition and free trade. The most important areas of regulation are preventing monopolies, maintaining fair competition, taxing business, regulating crucial industries, regulating securities, and preserving the general welfare and environment.

Preventing Monopolies

monopoly limiting of competition by act or agreement

antitrust laws laws that prohibit monopolies

A **monopoly** is a condition in which competition is suppressed by act or agreement. If permitted to exist, a monopoly harms the public as well as individual businesses. Both the state and federal governments have enacted laws to prevent monopolies. These laws are known as **antitrust laws**.

Most of the antitrust activity is at the federal level and is based on the Sherman Act, passed by Congress in 1890. This law prohibits any monopolies or any acts that might lead to a monopoly. A violation of the acts is a criminal violation, the penalty being a fine, imprisonment, or both. Federal courts can enjoin violations of the act and can impose triple damages for violations of it. The Clayton Act, enacted in 1914, prohibits a merger of corporations in interstate commerce if it would tend to create a monopoly.

Not every monopoly is prohibited, only those that arise from unlawful or unreasonable acts.

> Richards Trucking Corp. operated in three states. Because it was efficient, had good customer relations, and was cost-conscious, it took over more than 90 percent of the business from its competitors. This business resulted in a monopoly, but not one that was prohibited.

Maintaining Fair Competition

Unfair competition hurts small businesses and results in higher prices for consumers. Many laws and regulations have been passed to prevent unfair competition or any activity that might prevent the private enterprise system from functioning.

The Sherman Act prohibits any contract, combination, or conspiracy in restraint of trade. Its purpose is to prevent businesses from combining their efforts to hurt competition and increase their share of the market. One of the most common practices that the act seeks to prevent is price fixing. Businesses often try to control the market by setting common prices for goods and services. Price fixing is a violation of the Sherman Act, regardless of whether the prices set are fair or unreasonable.

market allocation agreement by competitors not to compete in certain markets

The act also prohibits an indirect form of price fixing called **market allocation**. In this situation, competitors divide a market based on geography, population, product type, or potential customers and agree not to compete with each other in those markets.

> Ace Bicycle Co. and Zebra Bicycle Co. agree that Ace will have an exclusive right to sell bicycles in California, whereas Zebra will have similar exclusive rights to sell in Texas. This practice is illegal under the Sherman Act.

To show a violation of the Sherman Act, there must be proof of the involvement of multiple parties and an agreement, express or implied, to restrain trade. Not every restraint of trade is a violation, only an unreasonable one, depending on the purpose and the ability of competitors that challenge the restraint. There are some actions, called per se violations, that are such obvious violations that they are deemed automatic violations. They include three types of restraint: horizontal, vertical, and group boycott. A horizontal restraint involves collusion among competitors at the same level, for example, manufacturers. A vertical restraint involves collusion among firms at different levels, for example, manufacturers and distributors. A group boycott is an agreement among competitors not to buy from a particular seller or sell to a particular buyer.

The act only prohibits action by more than one concern. A single firm cannot be held to violate the act.

> Premium Jewelry Company's policy was to sell to certain retail stores only. This would not be a violation of the act because Premium acted alone.

There are certain exceptions to the coverage of the Sherman Act. They take the form of exempting certain businesses from application of the antitrust laws because of certain policy considerations. Labor unions, agricultural organizations, and professional baseball teams are all exempt. Professionals—such as doctors, lawyers, and accountants—used to be exempt from antitrust regulation, but these exemptions are being eroded by judicial decision and government regulations.

tying arrangement agreement between a buyer and a seller requiring the buyer, as a condition of sale, to buy other products by the seller

exclusive dealing arrangement agreement between a buyer and a seller requiring the buyer to refrain from buying a similar product from a competitor

The Clayton Act also prohibits certain practices that might reduce competition. Among these practices are price discrimination and mergers or acquisitions of another corporation's assets or stock that might create a monopoly or reduce competition. The act also seeks to prevent tying arrangements and exclusive dealing arrangements that might reduce competition. A **tying arrangement** is an agreement in which a seller of products requires the buyer to handle additional products of that company as a condition of the sale. An **exclusive dealing arrangement** is an agreement in which a seller of a particular product requires a buyer to agree not to purchase a similar product from a competitor.

The Robinson-Patman Act of 1936, an amendment to the Clayton Act, prohibits specific types of price discrimination, such as selling goods and services at prices designed to eliminate competition.

Adams owned a chain of department stores in several states. To attract customers and harm his competitors, he began to sell all furniture at cost. This practice is unlawful because it is an unreasonable act designed to eliminate competition. Smaller stores could not do the same thing and remain in business.

Other unfair methods of competition are prohibited by the Federal Trade Commission Act of 1914. The Act established the Federal Trade Commission and gave it the responsibility to prevent "unfair methods of competition in commerce, and unfair or deceptive acts or practices in commerce." One prohibited method is business defamation, such as spreading a damaging rumor about a competitor to reduce competition. Malicious competition, which involves acts done solely to eliminate a competitor, is also prohibited.

Government also maintains fair competition by making the public aware of prices of merchandise so that comparisons can be made among competing products or businesses. Local governments often require labels or signs that are clearly marked to indicate the total and unit costs of various products. As long as the regulations are reasonable, they will be upheld.

Taxing Business

Another important area of government regulation is taxation of businesses. Taxation involves every aspect of business and affects business decisions on every level.

One important tax is the income tax. Whether a business operates as a sole proprietorship, a partnership, or a corporation, a tax on income limits the amount the business may spend or may return in the form of profits. Many business decisions are based on tax consequences.

Government also regulates by means of the sales tax. Although this tax is passed on to the consumer, its presence affects sales and therefore also affects the profits of the business producing or selling the item that is taxed. Similarly, payroll taxes also reduce profits and have an important effect on spending and other business decisions.

Regulating Crucial Industries

Some industries are subject to unusual government regulation because their products and services are crucial to the public welfare. By necessity, these companies are allowed to operate as monopolies. Public utilities, such as electric and gas companies, are one such example; it would be impractical to have three electric companies operating in the same city. In return for their status as monopolies, public utilities are regulated very closely at the federal and state levels. Areas of regulation include rate charges, profits, advertising, and environmental effects.

Other industries, such as transportation and communication companies, are considered semimonopolies and are also subject to extensive governmental regulation. Their services are crucial for our well-being, and at the same time, only a limited number of them can operate in a given area at any one time. For economic and safety reasons, for example, only a certain number of flights can operate at the same time in the same area. The radio wave spectrum is limited and can accommodate only a limited number of radio and television stations. Some deregulation has taken place. Although the airline, motor carrier, and railroad industries—which operate interstate—have been deregulated with regard to rates and routes, they are still subject to regulation in the areas of passenger safety, advertising, and prevention of monopoly practices.

Regulating Securities

The securities industry is one of the most heavily regulated industries in the United States. The need to protect the public is so great that both the original issue of securities and their subsequent transfer are regulated at both state and federal levels of government. State laws do help to protect buyers, but they are not as effective as federal legislation. State laws are not uniform, and fraudulent promoters can move from state to state to avoid compliance. To prevent this sort of abuse and to achieve some degree of uniformity, many states have adopted the Uniform Securities Act. This act requires full disclosure to prospective purchasers of all relevant information regarding a security. It also requires securities salespersons to register and obtain a license, and it provides for injunctive relief and criminal penalties for those who engage in fraudulent sales of securities.

It is at the federal level, however, that the most effective regulation takes place. The stock market crash in 1929 and the resulting depression emphasized the need for uniform securities regulation on a national basis. In response, Congress enacted the Securities Act of 1933. The Securities Exchange Act of 1934 was passed to offer additional protection.

The 1933 act was designed to ensure that a prospective investor will receive the information she or he needs to make an informed decision on whether to buy a specific security. The act also prohibits fraud and misrepresentation in the sale of securities. It covers only initial issues of securities; it does not cover subsequent trading.

The main purpose of the 1934 act is to protect the buyer after the initial issue of a security. It requires registration of a security prior to an offer to sell. It also requires annual reports containing all relevant information about a company and its securities, including the sale of major assets, management changes, and litigation by and against a company. The 1934 act also established the Securities and Exchange Commission (SEC), the independent regulatory body charged with enforcing the provisions of both the 1933 and the 1934 acts. The SEC regulates the disclosure of facts regarding offerings of securities, investigates securities fraud, and regulates the trade of securities on stock exchanges. Because information about securities can be sent out so quickly to potential investor and investment personnel by e-mail, the Internet, and faxes, the SEC has issued guidelines for the dissemination of information by electronic means.

Investment companies, particularly mutual funds, are regulated by the Investment Company Act of 1940. This law provides for SEC oversight of investment company activities and requires registration of offerings.

Not all securities are regulated by these laws. It would be too cumbersome and expensive to have small-volume issues subject to this type of regulation. In addition, regulation is not necessary when the investors involved are extremely knowledgeable about the securities being issued. For this reason, there are a number of situations in which the sale of certain securities is exempt from the provisions of the 1933 and 1934 acts. Some securities are exempt from the act, based on who issues them, for example, securities issued by government organizations, banks, not-for-profit groups, and policies and annuities issued by insurance companies. Other securities are exempt because of their nature, including securities of corporations with limited assets, a limited number of stockholders, stockholders who all reside in the same state, and securities with a value below a certain amount.

The main purposes of government regulation are to provide full disclosure of information and to prevent fraud and misrepresentation. The SEC is responsible for setting standards for disclosure, investigating fraud, regulating the activities of brokers and dealers, and regulating the trading of securities. Regulation does not provide an evaluation of the securities themselves. It is up to the investor to decide whether it is worthwhile to buy a certain security.

insider trading trading in securities by someone having information not available to the public

In recent years, the SEC has been increasingly involved in regulating insider trading. **Insider trading** is trading in securities by those who, because of their position in a corporation, possess information not available to the public that may affect the value of the corporation's stock. The Securities Exchange Act of 1934, through Section 10B of the act and Rule 10b-5, makes liable those corporate officers, directors, stockholders, and others who use inside information for their own benefit when trading in the securities of their corporation. Under the act and subsequent legislation, those found to have traded using inside information may be assessed civil penalties, fined, and given jail terms. Rule 10b-5 applies to almost every type of security traded on any exchange, and it has even been extended to apply to outsiders (known as "tippees") who benefit from private information received from insiders, directly or indirectly. One theory for this rule states the outsider must know or be presumed to know that the person who gave him or her the information has breached some duty to the corporation, and therefore, the outsider has in effect participated in the breach. Another theory extending liability to outsiders is that they should not benefit from information they have in effect stolen from the corporation. Whether a tippee can be held liable depends on what the tippee heard, who told the tippee, and whether the tippee knew that the tipper should not have passed the information along. Also, the law prohibits trading in "material nonpublic information." News about a merger or a potential bankruptcy would be clear-cut examples of such information. There are many gray areas, however.

> At a restaurant, Jones told his friend that the stock of ABC Corp. would go up soon and his friend should buy it. This would be deemed mere rumor, and the friend's decision to buy stock would not be a violation of the law. The situation would be different if Jones was the president of ABC and the friend knew it.

Under the 1934 act, officers, directors, and stockholders owning 10 percent or more of a corporation's securities must file reports with the SEC showing how much stock they own and what and when they have traded in those securities. Failure to file such reports may result in the forfeiture of profits made from such trades.

Also, regardless of motivation or nonuse of insider information, any insider who purchases and sells, or sells and purchases, corporate stock within a six-month period may face the recapture by the corporation of any profits made by the insider on the transaction, regardless of whether or not the buying and selling were based on inside information.

In addition to the federal government, all states have laws regulating the sale of securities, known as blue sky laws. Like the federal laws, state laws also regulate the actions of brokers and dealers and are designed to prevent fraud. Unlike federal legislation, state laws apply only to securities sold or offered for sale solely within a single state.

Private organizations also exert control over the securities industry. The major exchanges, such as the New York Stock Exchange and the American Stock Exchange, as well as the National Association of Securities Dealers, have enacted regulations to protect investors.

Regulating Corporate Conduct

As a result of a series of corporate scandals involving some major U.S. corporations, Congress passed the Sarbanes-Oxley Act of 2002 to protect the public and stockholders from accounting errors and fraudulent practices. Three rules of the act deal with the destruction, alteration, or falsification of records; how long audit records must be kept; and what records need to be stored. The act covers issues such as auditor independence, corporate responsibility, enhanced public disclosure and the need to establish a public company oversight board. The act requires certification of financial reports by chief company officers, bans personal loans to any executive officer or director, and requires the disclosure of compensation of and profits for chief executive officers and chief financial officers. It provides for disclosure of transactions involving management and principal stockholders, stronger internal controls, disclosure of material changes in the financial condition of the company on a rapid and current basis, and requires the avoidance of a conflict of interest between officers and auditors including a provision prohibiting accounting firms from providing nonaudit services to companies. It imposes criminal and civil penalties for violations of securities laws and jail sentences and large fines for corporate executives who knowingly and willfully misstate financial statements. The Act established the Public Company Accounting Oversight Board to set standards for the audit of public companies.

Preserving the General Welfare and the Environment

Based on the constitutional power given to Congress to provide for the general welfare, government has become increasingly involved in regulating business. The courts have interpreted the term *general welfare* in such a broad manner that almost any type of regulation is considered permissible. Regulation is considered to be the price any business pays for the privilege of serving the public. It occurs at all levels of government, federal, state, and local.

One form of regulation is the licensing of certain businesses and professions. Most states require licensing of automobile repair persons, real estate brokers, attorneys, doctors, accountants, and so forth. The objective is to make sure that only qualified persons serve the public in areas in which qualifications and competence are important. Usually, a person must meet minimum educational standards, have a certain amount of experience, or a combination of both before she or he may obtain a license.

Another form of regulation controls the products a business may sell and the times it can sell them. Pharmacies, for example, may not sell certain products without a prescription. Other products, such as cigarettes and alcoholic beverages, may not be sold to minors. One of the most common regulations of this type is the prohibition against selling certain items on Sunday. These laws, known as Sunday laws, or blue laws, were passed to provide a day of rest in which business would be limited. Sunday laws vary from state to state but have been upheld by the courts as a proper exercise of a state's police powers. In actual practice, they are gradually being repealed or ignored.

The need to protect the environment has affected every aspect of the operations of many businesses. Regulations control where businesses may be located, how they may dispose of wastes, and what they may use for energy. A company may be prohibited from locating in an area if the noise from its machines will affect its neighbors or if disposing of its wastes will harm wildlife in the vicinity. Certain fuels may create a pollution nuisance as they are burned. All these factors have an effect on the environment and are subject to government review and regulation.

> Acme Music Company wanted to build a factory near an airport. Because the noise from the planes could seriously affect the hearing of Acme's employees, Acme could be denied permission to build in that area.

For centuries, common law provided many remedies to control harm to the environment. Suits for negligence or nuisance prevented pollution or provided damages payable by the offender. As the amount and types of pollution increased, however, statutes were needed to provide protection against all types of pollution.

Many states have enacted legislation dealing with zoning problems, noise and visual pollution, and waste disposal and recycling. On the federal level, Congress and the regulatory agencies have passed laws regulating air and water quality, toxic-waste disposal, and radiation control.

Some of the most significant federal legislation includes the Federal Water Pollution Control Act, later changed to the Clean Water Act (to control of the discharge of polluted matter into the nation's navigable waterways), the Atomic Energy Act (to regulate and control radiation from nuclear facilities), and the Clean Air Act (to regulate and limit air pollution). The National Environmental Policy Act of 1969 imposes environmental responsibilities on all federal agencies. It requires the preparation of an environmental impact statement that analyzes the impact on the environment of a governmental group's action.

Many federal agencies, such as the Nuclear Regulatory Agency and the Food and Drug Administration, are responsible for protecting special aspects of the environment. The Environmental Protection Agency, created in 1970, has the overall responsibility for protecting the environment and coordinating the environmental protection efforts of all federal agencies.

Visual pollution also affects the environment, and it is becoming a more important subject of government regulation. Federal, state, and local governments regulate the size and location of commercial signs, particularly signs near state and federal highways and residential districts. Such regulations have been upheld by the courts as long as they were reasonable and applied on a nondiscriminatory basis.

One of the major problems in this country is the large number of hazardous waste sites. These are expensive to study and clean up and many property owners are unable to cure such a problem. In 1980, Congress passed the Comprehensive Environmental Response, Compensation, and Liability Act, more commonly called the Superfund. Under the act, the federal government has established a plan to identify hazardous sites, determine which sites should be given priority for cleanup, and either get the property owner to undertake the cleanup or contract for it at the owner's expense. A trust fund, the Superfund, pays for the cleanup if the owner cannot. The fund is financed by taxes on businesses with incomes over $2 million per year and by a tax on petroleum.

Other areas of government regulation include health and safety, consumer protection (Chapter 40), and employment practices (Chapter 23).

HOW GOVERNMENT REGULATIONS ARE ENFORCED

Regulations are meaningless unless there is a way to enforce them. Business regulation is considered so important that three different groups—administrative agencies, courts, and the public—have the power to enforce compliance.

administrative agencies government bodies created to act in the public interest

Administrative agencies are government bodies created by Congress or a legislature to act in the public interest. They have legislative, executive, and judicial powers. In the legislative area, agencies make rules, set rates, and establish standards. Under their executive power, they enforce their own rules. In the judicial area, they determine whether their rules have been violated and impose penalties for any violations discovered. They have full power to have investigations and call witnesses.

Administrative agencies exist at all levels of government. Examples at the local level are zoning boards, tax assessment review boards, and bridge and tunnel authorities. At the state level are public utilities commissions, professional licensing boards, and transportation authorities. At the federal level, administrative agencies are part of larger government units. For example, the Occupational Safety and Health Administration is part of the Department of Labor.

The most active and powerful agencies are the independent regulatory agencies created by Congress. These agencies have unusual power because they are independent of Congress and do not have to account to anyone unless they exceed their powers. Their decisions affect almost every aspect of business, including rates, health and safety standards, right to merge, territory of operations, and business practices. Examples of such agencies are the Federal Communications Commission (FCC; television, radio, telephone), the Federal Reserve Board (banks and money supply), and the SEC.

Regulatory agencies can enforce compliance with their regulations in many ways. They may impose fines for violations of rules or get a court order to stop such violations. They may revoke a business's license or refuse to renew its license for failing to comply with the regulations.

> TV station WHMC was required by its license from the FCC to broadcast four hours of public-interest programming each week. If WHMC fails to provide this type of programming, the FCC could impose a fine or refuse to renew WHMC's license to broadcast.

The courts play an important role in enforcing compliance with regulations controlling business. Recall that the Sherman Act prohibits conspiracy in restraint of trade. A business that violated the act could be found guilty of committing a federal crime, which is punishable by fines and imprisonment. Government can go into court and seek to have a fine imposed or to obtain an order preventing such violations (an injunction).

Members of the public who have been harmed by a violation of government regulations may enforce those regulations by suing the business that is responsible. To make sure that the public is represented, the attorney general of a state may bring suit on behalf of its citizens for violation of regulations. In certain cases, the victim(s) may recover three times the amount of damages sustained. This amount is known as **treble damages**, a form of punitive damages.

treble damages
punitive damages awarded for violation of some government regulations

> A railroad was permitted to charge only $0.06 per mile for transportation on its lines. It violated the regulation and charged $0.13 per mile. The attorney general of the state in which the railroad does business could sue the railroad on behalf of its citizens and seek treble damages for the excessive and unlawful rate charged by the railroad.

Limitations on Agency Powers

Governmental agencies have extraordinary powers, but there are limits. Any person who believes that an agency has acted improperly or incorrectly in making a decision may sue in court for a review of that decision. In reviewing the action, the court will normally look at certain possible areas of agency error: (1) Did the agency violate due process? (2) Did the agency exceed its authority? and (3) Did the agency violate a state constitution or the U.S. Constitution?

Licensing and Liability of Professionals

Professionals, such as doctors, lawyers, accountants, and architects, occupy a distinct position in society. Limited in number because of examination and licensing requirements, they therefore enjoy something of a monopoly. To protect the public, all states require the licensing of professionals. In addition, most states require the licensing of other trade practitioners, including electricians, plumbers, real estate brokers, and stockbrokers. In some states, unlicensed persons or businesses may be fined. In other states, an unlicensed professional or businessperson may be unable to enforce an otherwise valid contract.

Most states, through statutes and judicial decisions, also protect the public by making professionals liable to their clients or customers for negligence and breach of contract.

Professionals may be held liable to clients for negligence in the performance of their services under the common law principles of negligence discussed in Chapter 4. These principles include the existence of a duty to act carefully, proof of a failure to act carefully, and proof that damage resulted from the negligence. A person damaged by improper or negligent services performed by a professional may sue for malpractice, the term for professional negligence.

Professionals may also be liable to clients for improper performance of services through breach of contract. Like parties to other types of contracts, professionals who fail to perform under the terms of the contract for services may be liable for damages for claims under that contract. Claims against professionals for breach of contract are subject to different standards of proof and time limitation periods than those in a negligence suit. In most cases, those who sue professionals claim both negligence and breach of contract in their suits.

In addition to being subject to common law, professional conduct is governed by state statutes, judicial decisions, and codes of professional conduct. Professional organizations, such as state bar associations, establish standards of conduct by which professional performance is evaluated. Violations of those standards may result in suspension or dismissal. Certain standards are also set by state and federal agencies. A violation of the standards is often proof of negligence on the part of professionals in malpractice cases.

Summary

Government regulation of business is needed to maintain competition, which protects the rights of business owners, their employees, and their customers. Regulation is also needed to protect the rights of consumers, employees, and stockholders.

Both the state and federal governments have the power to regulate business. A state's power is known as the police power and is concerned with intrastate (within one state) commerce. The federal government's power comes from the commerce clause of the U.S. Constitution.

There are certain industries, such as public utilities and transportation companies, whose services are so crucial to the public that they are subject to unusual government regulation. In return, such businesses enjoy monopoly status. Areas of regulation include passenger safety, advertising, and prevention of monopoly practices.

The securities industry is one of the most heavily regulated industries in the United States. Although regulation occurs at both the state and federal levels, the most effective regulation takes place at the federal level. The Securities Act of 1933 regulates the initial sale of securities; the Securities Exchange Act of 1934 regulates subsequent transfer of securities. Both acts are designed to prevent fraud and misrepresentation and to protect potential buyers of securities. Not all securities are subject to the provisions of the 1933 and 1934 acts.

Government has become increasingly involved in regulating business under the power given to Congress to provide for the general welfare. Such regulation occurs at all levels of government and includes the licensing of certain businesses and professions, controlling what products a business may sell and when it may sell them, and protecting the environment against pollution.

Government regulations may be enforced by administrative agencies, the courts, and the public. The means of enforcement include injunctions, fines, revocation of licenses to operate, and private lawsuits.

Important Legal terms

administrative agencies
antitrust laws
exclusive dealing arrangement
insider trading

interstate commerce
intrastate commerce
market allocation
monopoly

police power
treble damages
tying arrangement

Questions and Problems for Discussion

1. What are the six important areas of government regulation of business activity?

2. What are the limitations on the power of the federal and state governments to regulate the conduct of business?

3. Describe the ways in which compliance with government regulations may be enforced.

4. What is the difference between a tying arrangement and an exclusive dealing arrangement?

5. Explain which securities are exempt from regulation under the Securities and Exchange Acts.

6. Explain why the Sarbanes-Oxley Act was enacted and what does it provide?

7. The City of Chicago issued bonds to finance its general operations. Must these bonds be registered under the Securities and Exchange Acts?

8. The ABC Tool Corp. sold 10,000 shares of its stock to a private investor for $10 million. Must it register this stock with the SEC and provide the investor with information about the company and its stock?

9. Hokey and Company, an accounting firm, provided auditing services to Jones Pipe Company. One December, it provided every officer of the company with a free trip to Hawaii. Is this a violation of the Sarbanes-Oxley Act?

10. Copyrite Carbons sold carbon paper throughout the United States. To increase its sales in one part of the country, it offered to sell carbon paper to local dealers at a rate lower than the rate charged to dealers in other parts of the country. May it do so?

11. Four companies manufacturing paint were concerned about new government regulations affecting their industry. They decided to join forces and form an association for the purpose of keeping track of and affecting new legislation. Would this association be an unlawful combination in restraint of trade?

12. The state of New York passed a law prohibiting the importation of liquor by private individuals. Does it have the authority to do this?

13. Magnus Corporation produced chemicals for the defense industries. Waste from the production was dumped into a nearby stream, causing severe pollution. What agency or agencies are responsible for handling this problem?

14. The state of Missouri passed a law regulating the sale of securities anywhere in the United States to a Missouri citizen. Would such a law be upheld?

15. Herald Jewelry Company, a manufacturer of watches, agreed to sell its product solely to one store in a given area. Is such a policy legal?

16. Stanke, a first baseman for a professional baseball team, was traded to another team without his consent. He claimed that both teams had violated the antitrust laws. Is he correct?

17. The city of Briggs passed an ordinance prohibiting the sale of cigarettes within the city limits on the grounds that cigarettes are harmful to the health of its residents. Does the city have the power to pass such a law?

Cases for Review

1. Naugles gave a ten-year restaurant franchise to Vylene. During the franchise term, Naugles built a new and competing restaurant nearby. The new restaurant featured lower prices and discount coupons, damaging Vylene's business and causing Vylene to file for bankruptcy protection. During the bankruptcy proceedings, Vylene argued that Naugles had no right to franchise another restaurant so close to Vylene's, even though the franchise agreement was silent regarding exclusive territories. Was Vylene's argument sound? (*Vylene Enterprises, Inc.* v. *Naugles, Inc.*, 90 F.3d 1472)

2. Container Corporation and other container manufacturers agreed to exchange sales price information about certain products. The federal government brought an antitrust suit against the companies for violation of the Sherman Act based on evidence that exchanging this information had the effect of keeping prices stable. Would the exchange of this type of information be considered a violation of the antitrust laws? (*United States of America* v. *Container Corporation of America*, 89 S. Ct. 510)

3. Lockheed owned an airport serving carriers operating interstate. The city of Burbank passed a

law banning jet aircraft from taking off and landing between certain hours. Lockheed sought an injuction, claiming that the law was unconstitutional on the grounds that the federal government has sole jurisdiction over flights in interstate commerce. Should Lockheed succeed? (*City of Burbank* v. *Lockheed Air Terminal, Inc.,* 93 U.S. 1854)

4. Mary Carter Paint Co. advertised that a buyer purchasing a can of its paint would get a similar can free. Actually, the price paid for the first can was higher than its normal retail price so that the second can was in effect not free. The FTC claimed that this was a violation of the Federal Trade Commission Act. Was this claim valid? (*FTC* v. *Mary Carter Paint Co.,* 382 U.S. 46)

5. A Virginia county bar association established a schedule of minimum fees to be charged by lawyers within the county. The Goldfarbs interviewed several attorneys for legal services and were quoted the same fee. They sued the bar association, complaining that a minimum fee schedule was a violation of the Sherman Act. Is this claim correct? (*Goldfarb* v. *Virginia State Bar et al.,* 95 S.Ct.2004)

6. Datagate repaired Hewlett-Packard (HP) computers, a service that HP also offered its customers. However, HP would only provide software support to those who used its hardware components. Datagate sued HP, arguing that this practice was an illegal tying arrangement. Is this argument correct? (*Datagate Inc.* v. *Hewlett-Packard Co.,* 60 F.3d 1421)

7. David Findlay and Walstein Findlay were brothers who were in the art business together. They split up and David opened and operated a store in New York under the name Findlay Galleries for over twenty-five years. Walstein, who had been in business in a different state, opened up a gallery next to his brother's store under the name Wally Findlay Galleries. David sued to enjoin him from using the family name in the art gallery business. Should he succeed? (*David B. Findlay, Inc.* v. *Findlay,* 18 N.Y.2d 612)

8. Monroe County, New York, passed a local law requiring a sign on each fuel pump at a filling station showing the price, taxes, and octane rating. The law was passed to prevent fraudulent

practices in the sale of gas. It also allowed one additional sign, but the sign could not exceed 18 inches by 18 inches. A gas station owner claimed that the portion of the law controlling the size of the sign was unconstitutional because it exceeded the police power of the municipality. Is the owner correct? (*Stubbart* v. *County of Monroe,* 58 A.D.2d 25)

9. Two competing publishers of bar review courses for the Georgia bar exam entered into an agreement in which one agreed not to compete in Georgia, and the other agreed not to compete outside the state of Georgia. As a result, the price to take the course in Georgia increased from $150 to $400. Law students who had contracted to take the Georgia course sued, claiming that the price increase was due to an agreement in violation of the Sherman Act. Are they correct? (*Palmer* v. *BRG of Georgia, Inc.,* 498 U.S. 46)

10. Ford, Chrysler, and General Motors bought spark plugs for their cars from three or four independent spark plug manufacturers. To gain an advantage, Ford bought one of the manufacturers that had 15 percent of the market in the United States. The United States brought suit against Ford, claiming that this purchase would lessen competition among the independent manufacturers. Is the U.S. government right? (*Ford Motor Co.* v *United States,* 405 U.S. 562)

11. Continental had a franchise from GTE to sell its TV sets. The franchise agreement stated that Continental could sell GTE's products only from the specific location described in the franchise agreement and nowhere else. When GTE tried to enforce the agreement, Continental claimed it was an automatic (per se) violation of the Sherman Act. Is this claim correct? (*Continental T.V. Inc.* v. *GTE Sylvannia Inc.,* 433 U.S. 36)

12. Khan leased a gas station from State Oil; the lease agreement required Khan to buy gasoline from State Oil. The agreement in effect set the price at which Khan could sell gasoline to the public. In a lawsuit involving Khan's failure to make lease payments, Khan claimed that the price fixing arrangement was an automatic (per se) violation of the Sherman Act. Is Khan correct? (*State Oil* v. *Khan,* 118 S.Ct. 275)

THE CASE OF TOO MANY TELEVISIONS

Global Television was one of the country's largest manufacturers of television sets. It sold its sets to wholesalers who in turn sold them to retailers. One time, due to a production error, it found that it had an inventory surplus of 10,000 sets. It needed to sell them in a hurry so that it could raise some much-needed cash. Global placed an ad in newspapers throughout the country offering to sell the sets directly to the public at 10 percent below cost. The Federal Trade Commission brought an action against Global, claiming that Global's action was a violation of the Sherman Act and other acts.

The Trial

At trial, officers of Global described its outstanding performance as a producer of quality television sets and its state-of-the-art system of inventory control. They discussed how the error occurred and stressed what a serious effect having 10,000 surplus sets would have on the economic condition of the company. They emphasized that they had considered many other ways of dealing with the problem, but that the solution they chose was the only realistic one.

Competitors of Global testified that they had lost so much business because of Global's discount sale that they might have to go out of business. They stressed that as there was so little profit in the sale of television sets, having to compete against sales below cost was impossible.

The Arguments at Trial

Attorneys for the FTC and Global's competitors argued that Global's action was a violation of the Sherman Act and other trade regulations because it was unfair competition that would harm small businesses. Global's attorneys argued that Global's action was not intended to hurt competition but to solve a serious financial problem and that its action would not have the effect of raising prices to consumers.

Questions to Discussion

1. Who do you think has the stronger argument, Global or the FTC?
2. If you were the judge hearing this case, for whom would you decide? Why?
3. If the FTC is right, how would sales by discount stores be affected?
4. What do you believe should be the rule regarding promotional sales?

Automobile sales were down in a certain city because of economic problems. The owner of one of the leading car dealerships set up a meeting with the owners of all the other car dealerships to see what could be done about the problem. They decided to act as a group to promote the sales of cars by agreeing to set all car prices at a uniform level of 5 percent below the sticker price and advertised this in the local papers. Complaints were made that this was illegal price fixing and restraint of trade.

Questions to Discuss

1. Assuming that their action did not violate any laws, was this an ethical practice?
2. What is wrong with businesses trying to promote sales and help out potential car buyers using this type of sales pitch?
3. Would your answer be different if the dealerships had only decided to cooperate in marketing but had not set a price agreement?

Other Ethical Questions for Discussion

1. How far should government go to restrict trade when the public might benefit from certain actions that might be considered restraints of trade?
2. How do you feel about the need for government restrictions on monopoly power that results from great efficiencies and quality merchandise produced by a business?

PART 7

Real and Personal Property, Bailments, and Wills and Estate Planning

After studying Part VII, you should be able to:

1. distinguish between real and personal property and the ways in which each can be acquired.

2. list the characteristics of the various forms of property ownership.

3. describe the important terms generally found in a lease.

4. list the steps involved in buying a house.

5. define, characterize, and list the parties to a bailment.

6. differentiate among the types of bailments and state the standard of care of each type.

7. explain the rights and duties of the parties to a given bailment situation.

8. describe three types of special bailments.

9. state the requirements of a valid will.

10. describe how property is distributed upon a person's death according to the terms of the will and how it is distributed when a will does not exist.

11. point out the most important reasons for estate planning.

CHAPTER 29

Basic Legal Concepts of Property

CHAPTER PREVIEW

Chapter Highlights

This chapter discusses the nature of real and personal property. It describes the manner in which each type of property may be acquired. Both real and personal property are usually acquired by purchase, gift, or inheritance. In addition, the chapter describes how real property may be acquired by law through adverse possession, accretion, or condemnation by a public authority. Personal property may be acquired through taking control of abandoned or lost property. Valuable rights and personal property may also be acquired through one's intellectual efforts, including patents, trademarks, and copyrights. The chapter describes how these rights are acquired and for how long such rights exist. Title to property may be taken in many different ways, including various types of tenancies, community property, cooperative and condominium ownership, and time sharing. The chapter concludes with a discussion of the ways in which the use of real property may be restricted. These restrictions include private means, such as restrictive covenants, easements, and wills, and public means, such as zoning and building regulations.

THE NATURE OF PROPERTY

Property is defined by law as the right to possess, use, and dispose of something under the protection of the law. The term is commonly used to refer to the "something" that is subject to those rights. Property is generally classified as personal property or real property.

Personal Property

personal property
movable property

Personal property consists of movable property, such as motor vehicles, furniture, and books. It may be tangible—capable of being seen or touched—such as merchandise and livestock. Or it may be intangible and be a *right* to something of value, such as a patent, a promissory note, or a stock certificate.

Annuals—that is, plants and crops planted each year and producing vegetation for that year only—are considered personal property. Trees, shrubs, and perennials—other plantings that flower or produce crops year after year—are considered real property.

Real Property

real property
permanent property
pertaining to land

Real property consists of land, anything permanently attached to the land, and certain interests in land. Land includes the surface, what is below the surface, and the air space above the surface. Grass, trees, rocks, minerals, and liquids are all included within the definition of land.

If buildings are permanently attached to the land, they are considered real property. A temporary structure, such as a trailer or a mobile home, is personal property. A garage is permanent and is therefore real property, even if it can be removed easily.

fixture personal
property attached to
land or a building and
considered real
property

A **fixture** is any item of personal property that is attached to real property in such a way that it is treated as real property. It becomes a part of the real property to the extent that its removal would damage the real property. Elevators, built-in stoves, bathroom fixtures, and lighting fixtures are all considered fixtures.

Armand sold his home to Farber. Before the transfer of the home, Armand removed a built-in shower stall, claiming it was not part of the sale. Farber can insist that the shower stall be put back because it is a fixture.

Fixtures are a part of the real property and are included as part of the sale of real property. Items of personal property may or may not be included in a sale of real property depending on any agreements between the buyer and the seller.

The decision as to whether an item is a fixture or personal property is usually determined by the following rules:

1. An agreement between the parties concerning the items will govern the decision.
2. In the absence of an agreement, the law will make the decision based on the nature of the property, the intent of the parties, and the extent to which removal of the item would damage the real property.

The Hanover Company operated a department store in a building owned by Acorn. Hanover installed a central air-conditioning system and adjustable shelving throughout the store. The lease was silent regarding ownership of fixtures. At the end of the lease term, Hanover was entitled to remove and keep the shelving but not the air-conditioning system.

Landowners have rights in water that flows over, under, and alongside their land. The extent of these rights depends on the laws of the state in which the land is located and on the competing interests of the state and federal governments.

Easements, Licenses, and Profits

easement right,
granted in writing, to
use another's land for a
specific purpose

Rights to use the land of others are common and are often valuable. Such rights include easements, licenses, and profits.

An **easement** is a right to use the land or a portion of the land of another for a specific purpose and is either perpetual or for a specific period of time. For example, a public utility company may obtain an easement (sometimes called a right-of-way) across an owner's property for the purpose of installing a gas line. The owner of a land-locked parcel of land is entitled to an easement across the land of a neighbor to be able to get to the property, provided the two parcels of land were purchased from the same seller. Adjoining homeowners may give each other easements so they can build and share a common driveway. Easements may also be obtained by adverse possession and by condemnation by a governmental unit. Most easements are transferred to the purchaser when the land subject to the easement is sold. An easement must be in writing to be enforceable.

> Janeway gave Manley an easement across her property so that Manley could build a road from her property to the main highway. When Janeway sold her property, the buyer purchased it subject to the easement; the road would remain in existence.

license temporary right to use another's land

A **license** is similar to an easement except that it is usually temporary and binds only the person who gives it. Unlike an easement, a license does not bind successive owners of the property. An example of a license is permitting a neighbor to park a car on your property for a certain period of time.

profit right to remove water, natural gas, minerals, or wood from another's land

A **profit** is the right to remove water, natural gas, minerals, or wood from another person's land. An example of a profit is the right to cut down and take trees from someone's land.

ACQUIRING REAL AND PERSONAL PROPERTY

Real and personal property may be acquired in similar ways, such as by purchase, gift, or inheritance. Personal property may also be acquired when it is found after being abandoned or lost. Real property may also be acquired through adverse possession, accretion, or condemnation.

Purchase

Real and personal property may be purchased, or sold, under a contract of sale. (The contract of sale is discussed in Chapter 31.) Real property is always purchased or sold under a written contract of sale because the statute of frauds requires it. Personal property may be purchased or sold under a written or oral contract depending on the purchase price of the property involved. Under the Uniform Commercial Code (UCC), a contract for the sale of goods costing $500 or more must be in writing to be enforceable. A purchase of a vacuum cleaner from a friend probably would not be in writing.

deed formal document transferring title to real property

The formal document transferring title to real property is known as a **deed**. The various types of deeds are discussed in Chapter 31 in relation to buying real property.

Personal property may be transferred simply by delivery. If it is transferred by means of a formal document, the document is known as a bill of sale. A formal bill of sale is shown in Figure 29.1.

Gift or Inheritance

inheritance receiving property through the terms of a deceased's will or through laws of descent and distribution upon death of intestate

Real and personal property may be acquired and transferred by gift. A gift of real property is made by transferring title with a deed. A gift of personal property may be made by a document describing the gift or by delivery alone. Note that delivery of a check does not constitute a completed gift until the check is cashed.

A person may also acquire title to real and personal property through a will or, when there is no will, through **inheritance** (discussed in Chapter 34).

FIGURE 29.1
Formal Bill of Sale

Know all Men by these Presents,

That   JASON M. MILLER, 1721 Long Street, Brookville, Arkansas,

party of the first part, for and in consideration of the sum of FOUR THOUSAND AND 00/100--------------------
--- Dollars ($ 4,000.00   ) lawful money
of the United States, to the party of the first part in hand paid, at or before the ensealing and delivery of these presents, by
     LAVERNE E. NEWTON, 28 Mainland Avenue, Brookville, Arkansas

party of the second part, the receipt whereof is hereby acknowledged, has bargained and sold, and by these present does grant
and convey unto the said party of the second part, the heirs, executors, administrators, successors and assigns thereof.

     One (1) Martin Hi-Power Tractor, Model X-47, Serial Number XY4296H

To Have and to Hold the same unto the said party of the second part, the heirs, executors, administrators, successors and assigns thereof forever. And the party of the first part does covenant and agree to and with the said
party of the second part, to **Warrant and Defend** the sale of the said goods and chattels hereby sold unto the said
party of the second part, the heirs, executors, administrators, successors and assigns thereof, against all and every person and
persons whomsoever.

Whenever the text hereof requires, the singular number used herein shall include the plural and all genders.

In Witness Whereof: the party of the first part has duly executed this bill of sale on the

6th   day of   March   2009.

In Presence of

Jason M. Miller ....(L. S.)
Cornelia T. Ames ....(L. S.)
....(L. S.)

For a gift to be deemed effective, three requirements must be met: (1) the donor (the
one who makes the gift) intended to make the gift, (2) the gift was delivered to the donee
(the one to whom the gift is made), and (3) the donee accepted the gift. If any of these
requirements are not met, a valid gift has not been made.

John's uncle promised him a new motorcycle upon John's graduation from college.
Until John's uncle delivers the motorcycle to him or has it delivered, no gift has been
made.

Abandonment

abandoned property
property purposely
parted with by its
owner

Personal property may be acquired by taking control of lost or **abandoned property**. In many states, however, certain procedures must be followed before title may be obtained. Property that is found may have to be turned over to the police or other authorities. Often, a notice of lost or abandoned property must be published in a local newspaper. If the owner does not claim the property after a certain period of time, the finder may keep the property or sell it and keep the proceeds. If property is abandoned, there must be proof that the former owner intended to abandon it. A tresspasser cannot obtain title to an abandoned property.

> Hazelton was sitting on a bus next to Jordan. Hazelton had a camera with her. When the bus got to her stop, Hazelton got off the bus in a hurry and left the camera behind by mistake. Jordan could not claim title to the camera because Hazelton never intended to abandon it.

escheat state's right to
claim abandoned or
unclaimed property

Escheat is the process by which a state government obtains title to property that is abandoned or unclaimed. Many bank accounts, dividends, interest payments, and refunds are never claimed by their rightful owners. Most states have statutes providing that, after a public notice is published and a certain period of time passes, abandoned or unclaimed funds or property escheat to the state. The real property of a person who dies without a will or heirs also escheats to the state.

Lost Property

lost property property
whose owner has
involuntarily parted
with it

Abandoned property is property with which its owner parted purposely. **Lost property** is property with which its owner has parted involuntarily.

A person who finds lost property can claim good title to it against anyone else except its true owner. A finder of lost property who knows its true owner must return it to the owner or may be held liable for the tort of conversion. If the finder does not know who or where the true owner is, the finder must take certain steps to locate the owner, such as notifying the police or advertising in a local newspaper. In many states, a finder of lost property who takes the proper steps to locate its true owner may, after a certain period of time, obtain good title to the property if its true owner cannot be located.

Mislaid Property

mislaid property
property that has been
temporarily misplaced
by its owner

Mislaid property is property whose owner has temporarily placed it somewhere and forgotten its location. The finder becomes an involuntary bailee and cannot keep the property or obtain title to it.

> By mistake, Reynolds left her umbrella at the home of a friend. The property is considered mislaid, and Reynolds's friend must keep it until Reynolds returns to claim it.

Adverse Possession

adverse possession
obtaining title to real
property by occupying
it for a long period
without owner's
consent

prescription obtaining
an easement by
adverse possession or
use

Real property belonging to another may be acquired by occupying it without the owner's consent for a long period of time. Title obtained in this manner is known as title by **adverse possession**. Not only title to land but also rights in land such as easements may be obtained in this way. Rights in land obtained through adverse possession are obtained by **prescription**. Public property—property owned by a federal, state, or local government—may not be acquired by adverse possession.

Strict rules apply before title may be obtained by adverse possession. The first is that the possession must be actual. The person claiming possession must actually and physically occupy the property in question. The second rule is that the possession must be exclusive. The person claiming possession cannot occupy the land together with the owner, or a third party, and claim title. The third rule is that the property must be occupied under a claim of ownership that is hostile (opposed) to that of the owner. Mere possession is not enough. The claimant must actually occupy the land and claim ownership against all others, including the recorded owner. This rule applies even if the occupant is mistaken about the claim of title.

The fourth rule is that the possession must be continuous for a certain period of time. The period of time required to gain title by adverse possession varies from state to state; ten, fifteen, and twenty years are the most common time periods.

> Heller owned a home next door to Cromwell. A driveway he built between the homes was actually on Cromwell's land. He believed it was on his land and maintained and repaired the driveway. After the required period of time in his state had passed, Heller could claim ownership of the driveway land.

Possession sufficient to acquire title by adverse possession does not require that the occupation be by only one owner. As long as all the rules just outlined are met, periods of occupancy by various owners may be added together to reach the required time period. This practice is known as **tacking**.

tacking adding periods of occupancy by various owners to determine if title has been obtained by adverse possession

> Worthy occupied land for six years, meeting all the conditions required to obtain title by adverse possession. Worthy then sold the land to Blaine, who occupied it for fourteen years in a state in which a period of twenty years is required for adverse possession. At the end of fourteen years, Blaine could claim title to the land by adverse possession.

Accretion

accretion obtainment of title to property as a result of the movement of water

Land that borders water may increase in size by the flow of that water. When that occurs, the owner of the land acquires title to the additional land by **accretion**. Accretion may occur when waters recede, exposing land that was previously under water. Additional land may also be acquired when waters wash up soil or sand that remains in place and gradually builds up.

Condemnation

condemnation right of a government to take private property for public purposes

Federal, state, and local governments often require property for public use. They may need the property for a highway, school, airport, bridge, or urban renewal project. Government may take land for these purposes under the power of **condemnation**, or *eminent domain* as it is often called.

Although the power of condemnation is practically unlimited, there are two restrictions on its use. The first is that the condemnation must be for the public welfare. The second is that the owner of the land must receive fair compensation for the property taken.

ACQUIRING RIGHTS IN PERSONAL PROPERTY

Artists and inventors acquire interests in property as a result of their labors. The product of their work is often an exclusive and valuable right to property. This right is protected by Congress under the patent, trademark, and copyright laws.

Patents

patent exclusive right to manufacture, sell, or license others to make and sell an invention

A **patent** is the grant to an inventor of an exclusive right to manufacture, sell, and license others to make and sell an invention. The term of the patent is seventeen years for most patents, and it is not renewable. Without the patent, anyone can make, use, or sell a similar product without the permission of the inventor. A patent is therefore a valuable property right.

To obtain a patent, an inventor must prove that the invention or design is unique, useful, and not clearly obvious based upon existing technology. Obtaining a patent often involves considerable time and expense.

Trademarks

trademark exclusive, distinct mark by which a company identifies itself or its products

A **trademark**, as well as a service mark and a trade name, is a term used to identify a product, service, or business. It may be used to protect a name, such as Ford; letters, such as HBO; product packaging, such as a Coca-Cola bottle; or a slogan, such as "What Can Brown Do for You?" Because of the effect of advertising, a trademark can be a very valuable property right. The right to a trademark derives from proper identification and use of the mark. Additional protection is granted by registering the trademark with the U.S. Patent and Trademark Office. Registration, which gives the holder an exclusive right to use the trademark for a period of ten years plus unlimited renewal terms, given the mark is still in use, provides a relatively speedy way to enforce trademark rights and to prevent others from infringing on the trademark. Like a patent, a trademark must be unique and distinctive. Once a trademark is granted, its owner may sue anyone who uses it without permission. Without registration, the exclusive right to use a mark is limited to the market area within which the mark is used. With registration at the Patent Office, the right is extended throughout the United States.

Under the Trademark Revision Act of 1988, an applicant may apply for a trademark on the basis of (1) the existing use of the trademark or (2) an intent to use the trademark in the future. An applicant who intends to use a trademark in the future must put the trademark into use within six months after the application has been filed and must show that no one has opposed the application. The six-month period can be extended upon request and up to an additional two years for good cause.

Trademark rights are enforced in federal district courts or state courts by filing a lawsuit for trademark infringement. Remedies given to trademark owners may include a court order stopping further infringing use of the mark and an award of monetary damages. The courts can also order that all articles containing an infringing trademark be destroyed.

Basically, use of any reproduction, counterfeit, copy, or colorable imitation of a registered mark in connection with the sale, offering for sale, distribution or advertising of any goods or services that is likely to cause confusion, deception, or mistake will result in infringement liability.

Copyrights

copyright exclusive right to own, produce, sell, and license artistic and intellectual works

A **copyright** is a grant by Congress of an exclusive right to own, produce, sell, and license artistic and intellectual works. These include literary works, musical works, dramatic works, pantomimes and choreographic works, pictorial and sculptural works, motion pictures, sound recordings, and architectural works. A copyright may be obtained for such things as paintings, books, computer software, musical works, and plays. Like patents and trademarks, copyrights are granted only for original works and only for those that involve an expression of ideas rather than the ideas themselves.

For works copyrighted before January 1, 1978, the term of copyright is sixty-seven years. For works copyrighted after January 1, 1978, the term of copyright is for the author's lifetime, plus an additional seventy years after the author's death.

Darien had an idea for a motion picture. It involved a modern version of many Bible stories. Darien submitted the idea to the Copyright Office and applied for a copyright. A copyright was not granted because Darien's work involved an idea and not the actual expression of that idea.

Protection Against Infringement

A person who makes a product without the consent of the inventor may be charged with infringement of the patent. The same applies when a person uses the trademark of another or copies someone else's copyrighted material.

An injunction may be obtained to stop such infringement. In addition, penalties may be imposed, including fines, actual damages, and punitive damages.

There are exceptions, however, and not every use of another's invention or material is considered an infringement. Using some parts but not all of a patented process, for example, is not considered an infringement. Copying portions of a book for use in a literature class would also be permissible and not considered an infringement. What is or is not considered an infringement depends very often on who uses the material, to what end, and whether the use is for nonprofit or commercial purposes.

Computer Technology and Cyberlaw

With new computer technologies accessible to almost anyone, a conflict has arisen between creators of computer technology, who want their technology protected, and users, who want the ability to use that technology with as few restrictions as possible. The legal rules regarding protection of computer technology are those relating to patents, trademarks, and copyrights, discussed earlier, and trade secret protection.

One of the most important methods of protecting computer technology is through the use of copyright law. Congress passed the present copyright law in 1976 and extended the protection of that law to computer programs in 1980. Under the 1980 law, the developer of a copyrighted computer program has the exclusive right to reproduce and distribute it during the term of the copyright and may restrict all persons from copying it without consent and sue those who infringe it. There are certain exceptions to the exclusive use by the developer, namely, (1) a user can make a copy for backup purposes and (2) a user may make "fair use" of it, meaning that a user may use it for research, teaching, comment, or criticism.

Another important method of protecting computer technology is through the law of "trade secrets." A trade secret is information or a formula, including scientific and technical information, that is useful, even vital, to the success of a company's operations. An owner of a trade secret such as a computer process may permit certain people to know the information, provided they agree not to disclose it. To protect against unauthorized use, the owner of the trade secrets must take certain steps, such as confidentiality provisions contained in license agreements.

FORMS OF PROPERTY OWNERSHIP

There are many different forms of property ownership. These forms include tenancy, community property, cooperative, condominium, and time sharing.

Tenancy

Tenancy is the interest one has in the ownership of property. There are different types of tenancy, including sole tenancy, tenancy in common, joint tenancy, and tenancy by the entirety. The type of tenancy affects the rights of ownership and survivorship.

sole tenancy owner-
ship by one person

tenancy in common
ownership by two or
more persons that
passes at death to
heirs or beneficiaries

A **sole tenancy**, which is often called a tenancy in severalty, is ownership by one person.

A **tenancy in common** is a form of multiple ownership in which each co-owner's interest may be sold, given as a gift, inherited, or subject to sale by a judgment creditor. On the death of a tenant in common, the deceased tenant's interest passes to the person named in the tenant's will or to the tenant's heirs. It does not automatically pass to the surviving tenants. If a tenant in common sells her or his interest, the new owner becomes a tenant in common with the other tenants. This tenancy ends only when all interests are sold, when one tenant acquires the interest of the others, or when the property is physically divided among the tenants.

> Berger and Teele bought a home as tenants in common. Five years later, Teele bought Berger's interest in the house. This sale ended the tenancy in common; Teele became a sole tenant.

Today, these forms of ownership apply to both real and personal property, but it is rare to see multiple ownership of personal property referred to as a tenancy in common or as a tenancy by the entireties.

In most states, if property is transferred by deed or by will to two or more persons without any statement as to the type of tenancy, it is presumed that it is a tenancy in common.

joint tenancy owner-
ship by two or more
persons that passes at
death to surviving
tenants

right of survivorship
right ensuring owner-
ship interest passes to
surviving joint tenant

A **joint tenancy** also involves multiple ownership. It differs from a tenancy in common in that it has a feature known as the **right of survivorship**, which means that if a joint tenant dies, her or his interest passes directly to the surviving tenants. The deceased tenant's interest does not pass according to the deceased tenant's will or to the deceased tenant's heirs. The last remaining joint tenant becomes sole tenant of the property.

> Alvarez and Laredo had a joint bank account. When Alvarez died, she left her interest in the account to her children. This provision in her will would not be upheld. At her death, Alvarez's interest passed directly to Laredo as the surviving joint tenant.

Joint tenants own equal shares of the property; tenants in common may own unequal shares. If a joint tenant sells an interest, the joint tenancy ends and becomes a tenancy in common.

tenancy by the entirety
ownership of land
deeded to a husband
and wife

A **tenancy by the entirety** is a tenancy consisting of a wife and husband. It is similar to a joint tenancy, with one important exception: Neither the husband nor the wife may transfer her or his interest without the consent of the other. Such an attempted transfer would be void. Upon the death of one spouse, title passes to the survivor. If the husband and wife divorce, the tenancy changes to that of a tenancy in common. In some states, transfer of property to a wife and husband automatically creates a tenancy by the entirety. In other states, specific language must be used to set up this tenancy, or no such tenancy is created.

> The Halls bought a home and took title as tenants by the entirety. Mr. Hall sold the home and gave a deed to the buyer. The deed would be invalid unless Mrs. Hall consented to the sale.

community property
right of wife and
husband to share
equally in property
jointly acquired during
marriage

Community Property

In some states, co-ownership of property may arise by operation of law under a system known as community property. **Community property** is a system in which the wife and husband are considered to own equal and undivided interests in all property acquired by either spouse during marriage, excluding property received by gift or inheritance. Also excluded is any property owned prior to the marriage. Those states having community property laws are Arizona, California, Idaho, Louisiana, Nevada, New Mexico, Texas, Washington, and Wisconsin. Community property cannot be sold in those states without the consent of both spouses.

Cooperative Ownership

A special type of ownership, usually of an apartment house, is known as a cooperative. A *cooperative* exists when two or more persons form a corporation to purchase and manage the apartment house or building in which they live. Each person receives stock in that corporation. The individual stockholder does not own the apartment he or she resides in (real property) but owns only a share of stock in the corporation (personal property). The stock entitles its owner to occupy a specific unit in the apartment house for as long as the stock is owned. The stock may be sold, usually only with the consent of the other stockholders. All stockholders share the expense of repairing, maintaining, and operating the building. Major decisions are made by a majority vote of the stockholders. Management is usually handled by a board of directors elected by the stockholders and carried out by professional management personnel. If a stockholder fails to meet his or her financial obligations—payment of taxes, utilities, and so forth—the corporation is liable for payment.

> The Walters purchased a share of stock in a cooperative apartment building. A majority of the stockholders voted to construct a swimming pool and to charge each stockholder a proportionate share of the cost. The Walters are bound by a majority vote of the other stockholders and may not object that they do not swim and do not wish to share the cost.

Condominium Ownership

condominium ownership of a dwelling unit that is one of many

Another special type of ownership is the condominium, which is similar to a cooperative with one major difference. In a **condominium**, each person owns a specific unit or apartment in a building rather than a share of stock in a corporation. The owner receives a deed to the unit, which is recorded like a deed to any other type of real estate. Within limits, the owner has complete control over the unit she or he owns and can sell or mortgage it without the consent of the other unit owners. The owner is also responsible for the real estate taxes, the maintenance, and any repairs for his or her own unit.

A condominium owner also has an ownership interest in areas of the building shared by all owners, such as the sidewalks, grounds, and parking areas. Each owner pays a monthly maintenance fee for the upkeep of these areas. If an owner fails to pay this fee, the other owners may bring an action in court to collect the amount due. Any judgment entered becomes a lien on the unit and must be paid before the unit may be sold.

> Schultz bought a condominium unit as a summer home. She failed to pay the taxes on the unit for three years, and local officials sued to collect. The other unit owners would not be obligated to pay the taxes owed by Schultz.

Decisions involving the condominium as a whole are usually made by majority vote of all the owners. Generally, a condominium association is formed to meet periodically to decide matters of mutual interest. The owners may also elect a board of managers to make major management decisions.

time sharing right to use a certain property for a specific period of time each year

Time Sharing

In recent years, another form of ownership known as **time sharing** has developed. This form of ownership is similar to condominium ownership. The owner purchases the right to use a certain property, usually a resort condominium, for a specific period of time each year. In some cases, the time share is limited to a certain number of years. In other cases, the time share is perpetual, and the right to use the property may be sold or transferred by agreement or by will. Time-share owners can often trade with other owners for a different time of the year or trade for time in a different property or location.

State laws regulate the sale, financing, and operation of time-share investments, particularly investments that are purchased on credit.

INTERESTS AN OWNER MAY HAVE IN REAL PROPERTY

Anyone can have rights in real property. The most common rights are fee simple, a life estate, and a leasehold estate.

The highest form of ownership of real property is fee simple. One having a fee simple interest may do whatever he or she wishes with the property and everything above and below it, subject to certain restrictions described later in this chapter. An owner in fee simple may use the property, lease it, mortgage it, sell it, or dispose of it by gift or will.

A life estate is the right to possess real property during a person's lifetime. At death, the property reverts to the owner or someone else. The life tenant must keep the property in good order, subject to normal wear and tear.

A leasehold estate is the right of possession pursuant to a lease. This is discussed in greater detail in Chapter 30.

RESTRICTIONS ON THE USE OF REAL PROPERTY

Most property owners believe their right to use their property is unlimited. This belief arose from the early history of the United States, when people were free to use their land as they saw fit, provided they did not disturb their neighbors.

In recent years, however, an expanding population combined with an increase in environmental concerns have prompted a need for increased control over the way owners use their property. Property owners do have the right to the exclusive use of their property, and they have the right to dispose of it. Beyond these rights, however, their use is often limited by both private and public means.

Restrictive Covenants

restrictive covenant
restriction in a deed limiting the use of property

Use of property may be limited by a restriction, known as a **restrictive covenant**, in a deed. Restrictive covenants are used to maintain the appearance and value of a neighborhood, usually residential neighborhoods. They accomplish that by prohibiting owners from using their property for other than residential purposes and by regulating the size, cost, and location of dwellings. They may even prohibit such things as roof antennas and outdoor clotheslines. Some restrictive covenants require property owners to obtain approval before constructing dwellings or putting up fences. Other persons subject to the same restrictive covenants may sue in court to prevent a property owner from violating a restrictive covenant or to collect damages resulting from such a violation. A restrictive covenant becomes so much a part of a piece of property that it is referred to as being "attached" to or "running with" the land. A person who buys a piece of property subject to a restrictive covenant is held to be aware of the restriction at the time of purchase and is bound by it. When the property is transferred, succeeding owners are also bound by the restriction, regardless of whether the restriction is cited in the deed.

Hertz bought some land that had a restriction prohibiting its use for commercial purposes. Hertz sold the land to Ryan, but nothing was said in the contract of the sale about the restriction. Nevertheless, Ryan is bound by the restriction because it is attached to the land and cannot be changed by agreement.

Because restrictive covenants limit the use of the land and the rights of landowners, courts do not favor them. Often, courts will not enforce such covenants if they can find a public policy reason, such as change of circumstances, to support their decision.

Berger bought a piece of land that was subject to a seventy-five-year-old restrictive covenant preventing the use of the land for commercial purposes. If Berger decided to build a store on the property, and if all the surrounding properties are used for commercial purposes, a court would probably not enforce the covenant.

Courts have invalidated restrictive covenants that prohibit sale or lease to minority groups and that discriminate on the basis of race, color, religion, and ethnic origin.

Easements

The use of land may also be restricted by previously granted easements that "attach" to the land, such as access easements and public utility rights-of-way. Once an easement is granted and recorded, subsequent owners of the land are bound by the terms and conditions of the easement.

Barnes owned some land over which he gave a neighbor the right to cross to gain access to a street. This right was contained in a recorded easement. When Barnes sold the land to Lebow, Lebow became bound by the same easement.

Easements come in many forms: They may permit a utility company the right to lay pipe under property, a local government the right to build a highway through the property, or a neighbor the right to cross one's property.

Zoning Laws and Regulations

Government may restrict the use of land through zoning laws and regulations. Typically, a city or town establishes districts throughout the municipality for residential, commercial, and industrial purposes. In each district, only certain uses are permitted, and specific rules govern the uses of structures and their cost, design, and location. Zoning laws and regulations often set restrictions on the size, height, and set-backs of buildings and requirements for minimum parking space. In certain cases, a literal application of the zoning laws would produce economic hardship. In such cases, a property owner may apply for a **variance**, an exception to the strict requirements of the zoning ordinance, which may be granted if severe hardship can be shown.

variance exception to the requirements of a zoning ordinance

The use of land may also be restricted for health or environmental reasons. As our population increases, there is a greater awareness of health, safety, and environmental problems and the need to solve them. Most municipalities regulate methods of constructing structures and the materials, such as asbestos fibers or other potentially hazardous substances, that are used in them. Codes may regulate plumbing, heating, air conditioning, and electrical systems. Waste disposal, air and water purity, and noise pollution are also regulated by city and town ordinances.

Wills

Land use may also be restricted through a will. For example, an alumnus may donate his property to the college he graduated from and include a condition that it be used for a certain purpose, such as a science library. This restriction prevents the college from using that land for any other purpose, such as a new gym.

Taxes

The use of property may be conditioned on payment of real estate taxes. Failure to pay taxes on a piece of property may result in it being seized by a governmental body.

Eminent Domain

An owner of real property has exclusive use of it unless a governmental body needs it for a public purpose. It may seize the land by what is known as eminent domain, or condemnation. The owner is, of course, entitled to reasonable compensation for the property condemned.

Summary

There are two types of property, personal and real. Personal property consists of both tangible and intangible property, such as furniture, cash, stocks, and bonds. Real property consists of land, anything attached to the land, and certain interests in land, including easements, licenses, and profits.

Both real and personal property may be acquired by purchase, gift, and inheritance. Personal property may also be acquired through abandonment and escheat, by finding it, and by creative efforts, including patents, trademarks, and copyrights. When protecting computer technology, copyrights and trade secrets play important roles. Real property may also be acquired by adverse possession, accretion, and condemnation.

Title to real property is transferred by deed. Title to personal property may be transferred either by delivery or by delivery and bill of sale.

There are five common forms of ownership of real property: sole tenancy, tenancy in common, joint tenancy, tenancy by the entirety, and community property.

There are three special types of ownership: the condominium, the cooperative, and the time share. They involve either individual ownership of a property unit, ownership of stock in a corporation that owns the property, or ownership of a right to use a unit for a specific period of time. In all three cases, there is a right to use areas shared by all residents of the property in which the units are located.

Anyone can have rights in real property. The three most common rights are fee simple, a life estate, and a leasehold estate. However, the use of property is not unlimited; it is often restricted for value-maintenance reasons or for health and safety purposes. Restrictions may be imposed by property agreement, operation of law, or statutes and regulations. The most common examples of private restrictions are restrictive covenants, easements, and wills. The most common examples of public restrictions are zoning laws, health and safety regulations, environmental control laws, taxes, and eminent domain.

Important Legal terms

abandoned property	fixture	real property
accretion	inheritance	restrictive covenant
adverse possession	joint tenancy	right of survivorship
community property	license	sole tenancy
condemnation	lost property	tacking
condominium	mislaid property	tenancy by the entirety
copyright	patent	tenancy in common
deed	personal property	time sharing
easement	prescription	trademark
escheat	profit	variance

Questions and Problems for Discussion

1. What are the differences between real and personal property in how they may be acquired?

2. Jones owned a large tract of vacant land. To a construction company building homes on land adjacent to his, he gave permission to drive trucks along a path across his land. Five years later, Jones sold the land to Aborn, who refused to let the company cross his land. The company claimed it had an easement to do so. Was the company correct?

3. Describe the difference between a condominium and a cooperative apartment.

4. Albie built a home adjacent to a highway. One year later, the county condemned the land to add lanes to the highway. Albie claimed the county had no right to condemn his land because the county could have instead used the land on the other side of the highway for widening purposes. Will his claim prevail?

5. Pratt owned a cottage facing a lake. A developer, building a cottage behind Pratt's, without access to the lake, asked Pratt for permission to drive a bulldozer across Pratt's land and Pratt agreed. Six months later, Pratt sold the land to his cousin who refused to let the developer cross his property. The developer claimed he had an easement. Was he correct?

6. A county in Pennsylvania condemned Rohr's motel property for a new firehouse. Rohr claimed the condemnation was illegal because the county could have instead condemned vacant land across the highway and not ruined Rohr's property. Do you think Rohr's argument will prevail?

7. Thurgood was riding in a taxi and found a camera left there by a previous passenger. May she claim the camera as her own? On what grounds?

8. Owners of units in a cooperative received separate real estate tax bills for their units. Was this action permissible?

9. Foster's home extended 6 feet onto land owned by Hold. Hold sent a letter to Foster stating that Foster's home was partly on his land, but he never did anything to force Foster to remove the encroachment. When the time arrived to claim title by adverse possession, Foster made this claim. Is he correct?

10. Frank bought land in a residential area, subject to a restriction against fences. After building his house, Frank applied for a permit to build a swimming pool but was prevented from building the pool because the ordinance required a fence around the pool. Frank claims the restrictive covenant is illegal because of the ordinance. Will he prevail?

11. Mr. and Mrs. Fuller owned their home as tenants in common. Mr. Fuller's will left his share of the home to his son. When Fuller died, his wife claimed that as Fuller's wife, she was entitled to her husband's share of the home. Is she correct?

12. Explain the differences among the various types of tenancies of real property.

13. Describe the difference between a patent, a trademark, and a copyright.

14. Compare the rights of a finder of lost property with those of the finder of mislaid property and those of the finder of abandoned property.

15. Feller owned land in a residential area that was zoned to permit two-family homes. The deed for Feller's land contained a restrictive covenant prohibiting the construction of any buildings other than one-family residences. If Feller tries to build a two-family house, can his neighbors prevent him from doing so?

16. Polk owned a valuable piece of land that she planned to sell to a shopping center developer. The state condemned half the land for the construction of a highway. Can Polk prevent the state from taking this land on the grounds that she believes the highway should be built in a different location?

17. Berm bought from Lesser a lot fronting on a lake; Grainger bought from Lesser a lot adjacent to Berm's but landlocked and without access to the lake. Does Grainger have an easement to cross Berm's land to get to the lake? Explain.

Cases for Review

1. Bucella went to the recording office to register his title to a piece of land. Agrippino and others before him had used this land for more than twenty years for a passageway for access to and removal of ashes and garbage. Agrippino objected to Bucella's attempt to register the title, claiming that he had an easement by prescription. Is Agrippino correct? (*Bucella v. Agrippino,* 257 Mass. 483)

2. The Normans owned a condominium unit. The board of directors of the condominium association passed a rule prohibiting the use of alcoholic beverages in the clubhouse and adjacent areas. The Normans, believing that this violated their rights, tried to prevent the rule from being enforced. Will they succeed? (*Hidden Harbour Estates, Inc. v. Norman,* Fla. 309 S.2d 180)

3. Cottrell and others bought lots in a subdivision from Nurnberger. The seller told them, at the time they purchased their lots, that a certain piece of land in the subdivision was to be reserved for recreational and playground purposes. Later, Nurnberger sold the land to a developer for construction of a hotel. Cottrell sued to prevent construction of the hotel, claiming a violation of a restrictive covenant. Is Cottrell correct? (*Cottrell v. Nurnberger,* W. Va. 47 S.E.2d 454)

4. Mr. and Mrs. Conwell owned a lot next to Allen's property. They planted grass in an area that appeared to be between the two properties but actually belonged to Allen. After the statutory period had passed, the Conwells claimed that this was sufficient notice of their interest to obtain title by adverse possession. Allen brought suit to determine who has title to the land. Who is correct? (*Conwell v. Allen,* 21 Ariz. App. 383)

5. Yee gave Woo three checks for a total amount of $124,600. Yee died before Woo could cash them. Woo cashed two of the checks after Yee died and made a claim against Yee's estate for the amount represented by the third check, claiming that all the money was his because it was a gift from Yee. Is Woo correct? (*Smart v. Woo,* 20 U.C.C. Rep. Serv. 2d 1288 Va.)

6. New England Tel. filed suit against the city of Rochester, contesting tax assessments levied against its telephone poles and lines and the land upon which they were located, claiming that the items were personal property and not fixtures. The court hearing the case had held previously that the poles and lines were personal property and not subject to real estate property taxes. New England Tel., however, claimed that the land upon which the poles and wires were constructed was also personal property. Is this claim correct? (*New Eng. Tel. & Tel. Co. v. City of Rochester,* 740 A.2d 135 Conn.)

7. Mr. and Mrs. Charney bought a bank certificate of deposit in the name of "husband and wife." When Mr. Charney died, his wife claimed ownership of the certificate. A claim was made that she was not entitled to the certificate because of survivorship, as she was a tenant in common. Is this claim correct? (*Re Charney's Estate,* N.Y. 66 Misc.2d 963)

8. Redman and Kidwell bought adjoining parcels of land from the same seller. Redman was unable to build a house on his land because he had no access to a public road except over Kidwell's land. Is Redman automatically entitled to an easement for access over Kidwell's land? (*Redman v. Kidwell,* 180 So 2d 682)

9. Prior to Kitchum's death, Kitchum and Cundaro received title to a piece of property in the names of "Kitchum and his wife, as tenants by the entirety." Kitchum and Cundaro were not married when they received the deed. Place, who was administering Kitchum's estate, brought suit, claiming that Kitchum's interest passed to his estate and not to Cundaro. Was Place correct? (*Place v. Cundaro,* New York 34 AD2d 698)

10. Hill, in a letter, offered to buy Bell's property. He told her to mail him a warranty deed to the property and he would send her a check for the purchase price. She agreed to sell but wrote that she would send Hill only a quitclaim deed as that was the only deed she had ever received. Hill sued her to transfer the property to him by warranty deed. Will he succeed? (*Hill v. Bell,* 111 Vt. 131)

CHAPTER **30**

Renting Real Property

CHAPTER PREVIEW

Chapter Highlights

The landlord-tenant relationship is one of the most common business relationships. This chapter discusses the nature of that relationship and of many different types of tenancies, including tenancies that are for a specific period of time and tenancies that are open ended. The landlord-tenant relationship is based on a lease. This chapter describes the essential information each lease should contain. It also discusses the rights and duties of both landlord and tenant, and the rights and duties contained in the lease or imposed by law. The chapter also discusses the many ways in which a lease may be terminated. The landlord and the tenant have rights and duties between them, and they may also have obligations toward third parties, such as visitors on the premises. The chapter concludes with a discussion of the nature of those obligations.

THE LANDLORD-TENANT RELATIONSHIP

At some point in your life, you will probably rent real property—an apartment, an office, a summer cottage, and so on—from another person. The person who owns the property and rents or leases it to you is a **landlord**. When you occupy the property, you will be the **tenant**. You and your landlord will have some sort of agreement of rental, which will be your *lease*. The lease will exist for a length of time known as the **term** and will specify the amount of money, the **rent**, that you will pay for the use of the property.

A lease may be oral or written. Under the statute of frauds, a lease for a term of more than one year must be in writing or it will not be enforced by the courts. Oral leases are often used, but it is better to have a written lease that outlines the rights and duties of the landlord and the tenant.

> Dodge told Allen that she could rent Dodge's cottage for two years at a rent of $600 per month. A written lease was never signed. Just before Allen was to move in, Dodge changed his mind and canceled the lease. Allen cannot force Dodge to rent the property to her because the lease was not in writing.

landlord one who owns property and rents or leases it to others

tenant one who occupies rented property

term length of time a lease is in effect

rent sum of money paid by tenant for use of leased property

TYPES OF TENANCIES

A tenant acquires from the landlord an interest in the real property being leased. That interest is known as a *tenancy*. Note that a tenancy may be by ownership of specific property, as discussed in Chapter 29, or by lease of the property.

Tenancies by lease are classified by the length of the lease term: a tenancy for years, a periodic tenancy, a tenancy at will, and a tenancy at sufferance.

Tenancy for Years

tenancy for years tenancy for fixed period

The most common type of lease is a **tenancy for years**. You, as tenant, lease the property for a fixed period of time, such as one year. You may be given an option to renew the lease by giving the landlord notice of an intent to renew. At the end of the lease term, the lease terminates and possession of the property goes back to the landlord.

Periodic Tenancy

periodic tenancy lease that automatically continues for a time equal to original term until canceled by either landlord or tenant

A **periodic tenancy**, like a tenancy for years, is a tenancy for a specific period of time. Unlike a tenancy for years, a periodic tenancy automatically continues for periods of time equal to the original lease term until canceled by either the landlord or the tenant. State laws often determine when a notice of cancellation must be given. A periodic tenancy may be a tenancy from month to month or from year to year depending on the original term of the lease.

> You leased an apartment from Clarke for one year as a periodic tenant. Because the lease was renewable for its original term, the lease will continue for another year unless you or Clarke gives notice of cancellation.

Tenancy at Will

tenancy at will lease for indefinite period of time

A **tenancy at will** is a lease for an indefinite period of time. It may be canceled at any time by either the landlord or the tenant. Most tenancies at will are created by oral agreement.

Tenancy at Sufferance

tenancy at sufferance tenancy created when a lease ends and tenant is allowed to remain

A **tenancy at sufferance** comes into existence when a lease ends and the landlord allows the tenant to remain on the premises. Such tenancy usually lasts for as long as the original term of the lease. If the original lease was for one year, the landlord, by accepting additional rent payments, has agreed to continue the lease for another year. If the tenant does not vacate the premises on the last day of the lease term, the landlord has the right to hold the tenant to another year's lease.

NATURE AND ELEMENTS OF A LEASE

A lease is a form of contract, and to be valid, it must satisfy the usual requirements for a valid contract: offer and acceptance, consideration, competent parties, and lawful purpose.

There is no such thing as a required form for a lease or required language. All that is needed is language that expresses the agreement reached between the landlord and the tenant. It is important, however, that a lease be as complete as possible and contain all the elements agreed upon by the landlord and the tenant, which can avoid arguments and lawsuits arising out of the relationship. The essential elements of a lease are factual information (e.g., a description of the leased property, the term of the lease, and the rent) and a listing of the rights and duties of the landlord and the tenant. An example of a formal, written lease is shown in Figure 30.1.

FIGURE 30.1 Lease

This Agreement BETWEEN

UNITED PROPERTIES, INC., 180 14th Avenue, New York, New York

as Landlord

and   MINTON DRAPERY COMPANY, 429 Curtis Street, New York, New York

as Tenant

Witnesseth: *The Landlord hereby leases to the Tenant the following premises:*

The building at 1642 Draper Avenue, Brooklyn, New York

for the term of   one (1) year

to commence from the   1st   *day of*   June   2009 *and to end on the*

31st   *day of*   May   2112 *to be used and occupied only for*

the manufacture and sale of curtains and draperies

upon the conditions and covenants following:

1st. *That the Tenant shall pay the annual rent of* ONE HUNDRED FORTY FOUR THOUSAND DOLLARS ($144,000)

said rent to be paid in equal monthly payments in advance on the   1st   *day of each and every month during the term aforesaid, as follows:*
         TWELVE THOUSAND DOLLARS ($12,000) per month

2nd. *That the Tenant shall take good care of the premises and shall, at the Tenant's own cost and expense make all repairs* necessitated by tenant's use of premises

and at the end or other expiration of the term, shall deliver up the demised premises in good order or condition, damages by the elements excepted.

3rd. *That the Tenant shall promptly execute and comply with all statutes, ordinances, rules, orders, regulations and requirements of the Federal, State and Local Governments and of any and all their Departments and Bureaus applicable to said premises, for the correction, prevention, and abatement of nuisances or other grievances, in, upon, or connected with said premises during said term; and shall also promptly comply with and execute all rules, orders and regulations of the New York Board of Fire Underwriters, or any other similar body, at the Tenant's own cost and expense.*

4th. *That the Tenant, successors, heirs, executors or administrators shall not assign this agreement, or underlet or underlease the premises, or any part thereof, or make any alterations on the premises, without the Landlord's consent in writing; or occupy, or permit or suffer the same to be occupied for any business or purpose deemed disreputable or extra-hazardous on account of fire, under the penalty of damages and forfeiture, and in the event of a breach thereof, the term herein shall immediately cease and determine at the option of the Landlord as if it were the expiration of the original term.*

Unconscionability

The doctrine of unconscionability, discussed in Chapters 10 and 15, applies to leases as well as to other types of contracts. Courts can invalidate a lease or any of its provisions because of unconscionability when they determine that the provisions are unfair based on the circumstances involved and the difference in bargaining power between the landlord and the tenant.

Brower, a person with limited knowledge of English, signed a two-year lease containing a provision that allowed the landlord to terminate the lease at any time for any reason and keep Brower's security deposit. A court would declare such a provision unconscionable and invalid.

Factual Information

The important factual information of a lease includes the names and addresses of the landlord and tenant, a description of the property being leased, the term of the lease, the amount of the rent, the time and place for payment of the rent, and the signatures of the parties. Most of this factual information is so important that its absence from the lease may make the lease invalid. A lease missing the names of the landlord and tenant or the amount of rent, for example, would be considered incomplete and not enforceable.

Allbright leased a warehouse to James. A written lease was prepared but did not include the lease term. Neither party would be able to enforce the lease because the factual information was incomplete.

Rights and Duties

The most important part of a lease describes the rights and duties of the landlord and the tenant. These descriptions are known as the **covenants**, or conditions, of the landlord-tenant agreement. The number and type of covenants depend on the type of property leased. A lease for a large office building, for example, may contain extensive covenants and conditions, whereas a lease for a home may have few of them. The basic covenants cover utilities, taxes, repairs, security deposits, payment of rent, destruction of the property, condemnation, fixtures, enjoyment of the leased property, and assignment and subletting. Some covenants are controlled by state law.

covenant written promise or obligation; part of a lease listing rights and duties of landlord and tenant; promise made by a grantor in a warranty deed

Payment of Utilities   Payment of utilities, such as heat, air conditioning, water, gas, and electricity, is an important factor in a lease. The lease should state who is responsible for paying the utility charges. In some cases, the tenant's premises are separately metered, and the tenant pays the utility companies directly. In other cases, the landlord pays utility bills and charges the tenant for the tenant's share of the bills.

Payment of Taxes   If a lease is silent about who pays the real estate taxes assessed against the property, the landlord is responsible. In some cases, either the tenant pays the taxes or the taxes are added to and included in the rent. One practice, primarily for business leases, is to have the tenant pay any increase in real estate taxes over a base amount, usually the taxes existing when the tenant first occupied the premises. The tenant's obligation to pay the increased taxes is known as a **tax escalator clause**.

tax escalator clause condition in a lease requiring tenant to pay increases in real estate taxes

Coram rented a store that occupied 25 percent of a shopping center. Coram's lease contained a tax escalator clause. If the taxes for the shopping center increase by $10,000 a year, Coram will have to pay 25 percent of the increase, or $2,500.

Redecoration and Repairs   Another important item in a lease is the cost of redecoration and repairs, which can be very expensive. Most leases specify who is responsible for these items. In most cases, the tenant must keep the interior of the leased premises in good repair, and the landlord must make structural repairs, such as roof repairs. The landlord must also make repairs to common areas that all tenants share, such as stairs and hallways.

More and more states and municipalities are imposing repairs and other obligations on landlords regardless of what the leases state. In many states, a landlord owning residential property is deemed to have given the tenant a **warranty of habitability**, an implied warranty that the premises are fit for human habitation and that there are no defects or conditions that might be hazardous to the life, health, or safety of the tenant. If this warranty is broken, a court may permit the tenant to pay a decreased monthly rent or may order the landlord to use the rent to correct defects. This concept has even been applied to permit tenants to decrease their rent payments if essential services, such as heating and elevators, are interrupted.

Most leases state that the tenant must take reasonable care of the property. At the end of the lease term, the tenant must return the property, as most leases state, "in as good a condition as at the beginning of the term, wear and tear and damage by the elements excepted." This wording means that the tenant is not liable for ordinary wear and tear during the term but is liable for any unusual damage.

> Sunkis rented a lakeside cottage from Marple for a two-year term. The cottage was furnished with furniture and rugs. During the term of the lease, the rugs became discolored because of the sand and water coming in through the cottage door. Sunkis would not be liable for this wear and tear because this would be expected to occur.

Security Deposit Many landlords require a tenant to deposit a sum of money with the landlord to guarantee that the tenant will live up to the lease terms. This deposit, known as a **security deposit**, usually consists of one month's rent. The security deposit is often used to pay for any damages the tenant caused during the lease term. At the end of the term, if the tenant has fulfilled all obligations, the deposit is returned to the tenant. In some states, the landlord must deposit the money in a separate bank account, which earns interest for the tenant.

> Brandon rented an apartment and gave the landlord a security deposit of one month's rent. At the start of the last month of the term, Brandon told the landlord that he was not going to pay that month's rent because the security deposit could be used for that purpose. Brandon is not entitled to do so because the deposit is returnable only at the end of the lease.

Payment of Rent A lease generally specifies when and to whom the rent must be paid. In some cases, rent is payable in advance; in other cases, it is paid at the end of the rental period. Many leases allow the landlord to charge a penalty or interest if the tenant does not pay the rent on time.

Most leases also contain clauses outlining a landlord's remedies if the tenant does not pay the rent, usually after a certain amount of time. If a tenant fails to pay the rent, the landlord may sue her or him to collect the rent due. Another remedy is **eviction**, which is the legal action taken by a landlord to force a tenant to leave the premises. A landlord may bring a proceeding known as a summary (or dispossess) proceeding. After a hearing, the court may grant the landlord a warrant of eviction and/or a judgment for the rent due. If the tenant is required to pay taxes or other charges, failure to pay them may also result in eviction. An eviction hearing notice is shown in Figure 30.2.

---

warranty of habitability landlord's implied promise that property is fit for human habitation and free of hazardous conditions

security deposit money paid to landlord and applied to any damages caused by tenant

eviction legal action taken by a landlord to force a tenant to leave the premises

FIGURE 30.2 Eviction Hearing Notice

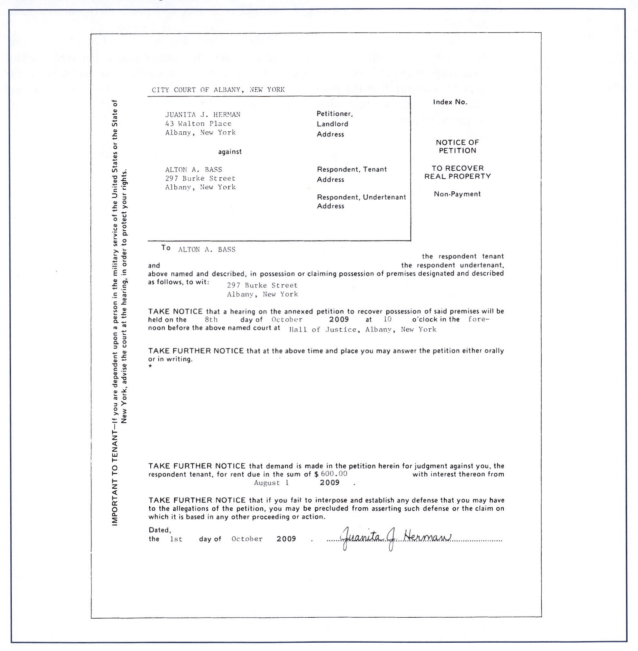

Destruction of the Property

Most leases provide that if the leased property is completely destroyed by fire or other means, the lease is terminated. The tenant is responsible only for the rent due up until the time of destruction. If the leased property is only partially destroyed, the landlord must repair the property as soon as possible. The tenant must continue to pay rent if he or she is able to stay in the premises while the repairs are made. If that is not possible, the tenant moves out and does not have to pay rent until the premises can be reoccupied.

Alden rented a barber shop owned by Noschang. When the shop was slightly damaged during a fire, Alden claimed that the lease was terminated due to the fire. The lease will continue because the property was only partially damaged by the fire.

Condemnation   Recall from Chapter 29 that condemnation, or eminent domain, is the right of a government unit, such as a city, to take private property for public use. After following certain legal procedures, the government takes the property and pays the owner the fair value. The tenant of condemned property, who may have invested a great deal in a store and its fixtures, may lose that investment. Whether the tenant will be compensated depends on the lease. Most leases provide that if only a portion of the property is taken and the major portion is still usable, the lease continues and the tenant pays less rent. If the entire property is taken, the lease ordinarily terminates and the tenant is entitled to compensation for the remaining portion of the lease. In some cases, the tenant may be reimbursed for moving expenses.

Fixtures   A tenant often makes improvements to property by adding valuable fixtures such as lights and shelves. Understandably, the tenant may want to take them when the term is over. The landlord, however, will want to make sure that removal of the fixtures will not damage the property. A lease usually provides that certain fixtures are considered temporary and belong to the tenant. Other fixtures are permanent and remain on the property when the lease term ends.

Permanent fixtures would include **trade fixtures** used in a business such as a restaurant soda fountain, a club's music system, or the pinsetters in a bowling center.

Use of Property   A tenant paying rent wants to make sure that he or she is able to use the property without being disturbed. In most leases, the landlord promises that the tenant will have undisturbed possession of the property. This promise is known as a **covenant of quiet enjoyment**. At the same time, the tenant is obligated to use the leased premises only for the purpose described in the lease. A tenant, for example, may be restricted by the lease or by a health law from having more than a certain number of people occupying the property. Some leases prohibit occupancy by pets.

A landlord usually has no right to enter the tenant's premises. Many leases, however, include a provision allowing the landlord to enter the premises to inspect the property, make necessary repairs, or show the property to prospective buyers or tenants. The landlord may enter the property for these purposes even if the tenant is not present.

Assignment and Sublease   Many tenants find it necessary to leave the premises before the end of the term. To avoid a loss, a tenant wants to be able to have a new tenant take over and pay the rent. A lease, the law, or both often give the tenant two different ways of doing this: assignment and subletting.

As with other types of contracts, a lease may be assigned. An assignment by a tenant is a transfer to another person of all the tenant's rights under the lease, including the entire unexpired term. The tenant is the *assignor;* the person who receives the assignment is the *assignee*. When the assignment takes place, the assignee becomes the new tenant and is bound by all the terms of the lease. Despite the assignment, however, the original tenant remains obligated under the lease and can be held responsible together with the assignee.

A **sublease** is a transfer of a portion of the lease term or a portion of the leased space. The original tenant remains as such and becomes the landlord of the new occupant of the property, known as the **subtenant**. The subtenant is not released from any obligations under the lease.

trade fixtures property considered permanent that remains with leased premises when lease ends

covenant of quiet enjoyment tenant's right to have undisturbed possession of leased property

sublease transfer of portion of lease term to another tenant

subtenant one to whom a portion of a lease term is transferred

In most states, a tenant may assign the lease or may sublease the premises unless the lease provides otherwise. Even where the right to assign or sublease is subject to the approval of the landlord, the law in many states is that this approval cannot be unreasonably withheld so as to prevent hardship on a tenant forced to vacate the premises before the end of the term.

Valor rented a store for a clothing business. Because of illness, Valor was forced to close the store six months before the end of the lease term. If the lease was silent on the matter, Valor could sublease the property and not be liable for the rent for the remainder of the term.

Nondiscrimination

The law imposes certain obligations on landlords in addition to those contained in a lease. One is the duty to keep leased residences in a safe and habitable condition. Another is a duty to refrain from discrimination in renting to anyone because of age, race, creed, color, gender, disability, or religion. Certain other forms of discrimination are permitted. For example, a landlord can refuse to rent to someone who has children or pets.

HOW A LEASE IS TERMINATED

In the unit on contracts, you learned that a contract may be terminated in many ways depending on the agreement between the parties or by operation of law. The same is true of leases, with some differences because of the nature of the lease agreement. A lease may be terminated by the passage of time, agreement between the parties, agreement in the lease, condemnation, destruction of the leased property, or operation of law.

A tenancy for years (a lease for a fixed period of time) expires when the fixed period is over and the notice of termination is given by either the landlord or the tenant. A periodic tenancy is terminated when either the landlord or tenant gives notice. The amount of notice required is determined by how often rent installments are paid. In a month-to-month tenancy, for example, notice must be given one month before the beginning of the last month of the lease term. If no notice is given, it is assumed that both parties wish to continue the tenancy for another month on the same terms and conditions. A tenancy at will continues indefinitely until notice of termination is sent by either the landlord or the tenant.

The death of the landlord or the tenant does not terminate the lease unless the lease provides otherwise. The estate of the deceased becomes bound by the lease.

If both landlord and tenant agree, the lease may be terminated before the end of the lease term. Early termination often occurs when the tenant is having financial problems or the landlord wants to raise the rent.

Most leases provide for termination upon the happening of certain events, usually nonperformance or breach of covenants by either the landlord or tenant. Examples of nonperformance include failure to provide heat, nonpayment of the rent, bankruptcy of the tenant, violation of the landlord's rules, or whatever makes the tenant's occupancy difficult or impossible.

Tanaka rented a store for one year from McGowen. The lease terms provided that the lease would terminate if Tanaka became unable to pay the rent. When Tanaka became insolvent three months after signing the lease, McGowen had the right to terminate the lease.

Upon failure of a tenant to move out at the end of the lease term or upon breach of a lease covenant such as failure to pay rent, a landlord has a number of options to remedy the situation. One is to sue for damages and/or unpaid rent. Another is to regain possession of the property, a process called in different states by different titles, such as summary proceedings or dispossess proceedings. To regain possession, a landlord must usually serve an eviction notice on a tenant; but if the tenant fails to move out voluntarily, a sheriff or other police officer may be called upon to forcibly remove the tenant from the premises.

A breach that would result in a termination of the lease must be substantial. Notice of the breach must be given to the landlord, who will then have reasonable time in which to cure the problem. A substantial breach, for example, would include failure to provide heat for two weeks during the winter months; failure to provide heat for two hours would not. In deciding whether a breach is substantial, a court would consider how long the breach existed, how it affected the tenant, and whether the tenant might be partially responsible for it. A substantial breach by the landlord might make the premises uninhabitable. In effect, the landlord has evicted the tenant by making it impossible for the tenant to occupy the leased premises. This kind of breach is known as **constructive eviction** of the tenant.

constructive eviction
action by landlord making it impossible for tenant to occupy leased premises

If the entire leased premises are condemned (taken) by a government body such as a city or state, it is impossible for the tenant to occupy the premises. The lease is therefore canceled.

Total destruction of the leased property also makes it impossible for the tenant to use the property for the purpose for which it was leased, and the lease is canceled.

Operation of law is a less dramatic, but equally effective way in which a lease ends. If property cannot be used for a certain purpose because the law prevents it, a lease will be considered terminated by operation of law. Examples are a change in the zoning laws that prevents use of property for a certain purpose and a new safety law that prevents the property from being used for its original purpose.

> Schwartz leased property from James so as to refine oil. A law was passed prohibiting the use of property in the area for any manufacturing that produced odors. Because Schwartz was prohibited from using the property by operation of law, the lease was terminated.

There are two situations in which a lease may be terminated prior to the end of the lease term regardless of what the lease provides. In many states, a residential lease may be terminated by a tenant over a certain age who enters certain health care facilities, adult care facilities, or housing projects. The tenant must give written notice of termination to the landlord and provide proof of admission to the facility. The second situation is when a servicemember, such as a reservist, is called to active duty. The Servicemembers Civil Relief Act of 2003 allows a tenant to break a lease under certain conditions. It provides that the tenant must have occupied the premises under a lease entered into prior to the call to active duty. Also, the tenant must give notice of termination of the lease and provide the landlord with proof of the call-up to active duty.

OBLIGATIONS TO THIRD PARTIES

Both the landlord and the tenant may be liable to guests who are injured on the leased premises. They may also be liable for damage to the personal property of a guest. To what extent each is liable depends on the covenants in the lease and on who has possession and control of the area where the property damage or injury occurred.

Between the landlord and tenant, the lease governs who will have to pay any claim for injury or damage. The guest who suffers injury or damage, however, is not bound by the lease and may recover depending on where the injury or damage took place. A tenant who has exclusive control of a rented area, such as the interior of an apartment, is liable to guests for injuries caused by a defective and dangerous condition of the property.

Gordon was a guest at Frost's apartment for dinner. While walking into the kitchen, Gordon was injured when he slipped on a loose rug. Frost would be liable to Gordon for this injury.

If the injury or damage takes place in an area in which the landlord has exclusive control, the landlord is liable for injuries or damage. Such areas include steps, elevators, halls, and stairs. A landlord might also be held liable for injuries incurred on a portion of the rented property upon which the landlord performed repairs negligently.

Cranshaw came to visit a friend at a boarding house owned by Owens. While climbing the stairs to the friend's apartment, Cranshaw fell down two flights of stairs and was severely injured. The cause of Cranshaw's fall was a faulty railing that collapsed when Cranshaw held on to it. Owens would be liable to Cranshaw for the dangerous condition.

Summary

A lease of real property is a contract between a landlord and a tenant for the rental of property for a specific time and for a specific price.

Tenancies of real property include a tenancy for years, a periodic tenancy, a tenancy at will, and a tenancy at sufferance. The most important differences among them are the length of the lease and the absence or presence of an option to renew the lease.

As with other contracts, a lease of real property must satisfy the usual requirements for a valid contract. It should contain every important element, including the names and addresses of the landlord and tenant, a description of the property being leased, the term of the lease, the amount of the rent, the time and place for payment of the rent, and the signatures of the parties. In addition, the lease should include all the terms outlining the rights and duties of the landlord and the tenant. These terms include the duty of repair, responsibility for payment of taxes and utility charges, the effect of destruction of the premises, and the effect of a condemnation of the property.

A tenant who wishes to leave before the end of the lease term may be able to either assign the lease or sublet the leased premises to another person. Assignment of a lease transfers the entire unexpired lease term. Subletting transfers a portion of the unexpired lease term or a portion of the tenant's rights and duties. Whether a tenant may assign the lease or sublease the premises depends on the terms of the lease and state law.

Most leases may be terminated by the lease terms, mutual agreement, breach of the lease covenants, condemnation or destruction of the leased premises, or operation of law.

Important Legal Terms

constructive eviction	rent	tenancy at will
covenant of quiet enjoyment	security deposit	tenancy for years
covenant	sublease	tenant
eviction	subtenant	term
landlord	tax escalator clause	trade fixtures
periodic tenancy	tenancy at sufferance	warranty of habitability

Questions and Problems for Discussion

1. Describe the important covenants that should be included in every lease.

2. Explain the difference between a tenant for years, a periodic tenant, a tenant at will, and a tenant at sufferance.

3. Describe the difference between an actual eviction of a tenant and a constructive eviction.

4. Haggard rented an apartment from Loomis for two years. At the end of the two years, Haggard continued to stay on, paying Loomis the monthly rental; no written lease was involved. After five months, Loomis asked Haggard to leave. Haggard claimed he had the right to stay for an additional thirteen months. Is he correct?

5. Borg rented a store from Lewis. The lease was silent about who paid the real estate taxes on the property. Borg claimed that Lewis, as a tenant, was responsible. Is Borg's claim valid?

6. James rented an apartment from Burns under a three-year lease. When the lease was up, Burns charged James for the repair of holes left in the walls by pictures that Burns had put up. Is Burns correct?

7. Jarvis rented an apartment in an apartment house. The lease prohibited any pets. Shortly after the lease was signed, Jarvis bought a gerbil, and the landlord sent him a notice to vacate the premises immediately. Jarvis claims that his rights are being violated and that he cannot be required to vacate the premises. Is he correct?

8. Harrison, a tenant, had steel cabinets installed in the house that she rented from Moss. She did not tell Moss of the installation, and the lease contained no mention of such improvements. Shortly before Harrison's lease expired, Moss learned of the cabinets and that they had been securely screwed into the walls of the kitchen. Moss sent Harrison a written notice that she could not remove the cabinets when she moved. Was Moss entitled to retain the fixtures?

9. Hynes rented a house from Jarvis under a two-year lease. The lease stated that it could be assigned only with the consent of the landlord. Six months after the lease was signed, Hynes decided to go to graduate school and asked Jarvis for permission to assign the lease to Mix, a friend of Hynes. Jarvis refused to permit the assignment under any circumstances, claiming that it was her right to do so under the lease. Is Jarvis correct?

10. Corwin rented an apartment on a month-to-month basis commencing March 1. On July 1, Corwin's landlord sent a letter to Corwin stating that the lease was being terminated and that Corwin must vacate the premises no later than July 15. Is Corwin obligated to vacate the premises by July 15?

11. Bowen, visiting Andrew's apartment, was injured when she tripped over a hole in the living room carpet. Will Bowen succeed if she sues the landlord for her injuries?

12. Faber and Smith signed a three-year lease for an apartment. The lease was silent as to the amount of the rent but stated "rent to be determined by mutual agreement." Is this lease valid?

13. Alison signed a two-year lease for a store, giving the landlord the right to terminate the lease at any time upon receiving an offer from another tenant at a higher rent. One month after signing the lease, the landlord told Alison she had to vacate the store because he had rented it to another tenant. May he do so?

14. Ferguson rented an apartment from Bill. A few months later, the city government, because of a water shortage, ordered that water be provided to homes and apartments only one hour a day. Ferguson claims that this is a violation of his lease and he can therefore consider the lease void. Is he correct?

15. Sam rented a store from Allen with parking in front for ten vehicles, as required by the zoning laws. The state took the entire parking area by eminent domain. Can Sam get out of his lease because of this taking of his parking spaces?

Cases for Review

1. IBM leased space from South Road Associates (SRA) in 1981 for certain manufacturing operations. The lease contained a typical provision that at the end of the lease term, the "premises" be returned in "good order and condition." Throughout the lease, the "premises" were

referred to separately from the land, parking lot, and the building itself. SRA sued IBM in January 2000, claiming that IBM had breached the lease and had not returned the property in good working order and condition because it had contaminated some of the property's soil by installing an underground storage tank that had leaked. IBM's defense was that the term "premises" would only include the interior of the building and not the grounds outside. Is this a good argument? (*South Road Associates, LLC* v. *International Business Machines Corporation*, 216 F.3d 251)

2. Shurgard Storage Center leased space to Lipton with an option for Lipton to purchase the property at a stated price. By mistake, the purchase price inserted was half what it should have been and half the value of the property. When Lipton attempted to exercise the option and buy the property at the contract price, Shurgard went to court, stating that the provision was unconscionable and that the lease be changed to reflect the true price. Is Shurgard entitled to the relief requested? (*Shurgard Storage Centers* v. *Lipton-U, City, LLC*, 394 F.3d 1041)

3. Ceridian Corporation built an office tower in Minnesota. Fourteen years later, to raise needed capital, it sold the building and leased it back, becoming the tenant instead of the owner. The buyer eventually sold the building to Fortune Funding. One month before the lease expired, Fortune requested that Ceridian repair the exterior wall of the building and replace the elevator system. Ceridian claimed that as the lease only required that the property be returned in the same condition it was in when the lease began, except for ordinary wear and tear, it was not responsible for major items like replacing an exterior wall and an elevator system. Is Ceridian's claim correct? (*Fortune Funding, LLC* v. *Ceridian Corporation*, 368 F.3d 985)

4. Colonial Court Apartments rented an apartment to Irene Kern. When she rented the apartment, she told her landlord that she required peace and quiet and was assured that this would be the case. Almost from the minute she moved in, however, Kern was subjected to noise from a neighbor's apartment, including parties twice a week, use of a dishwasher at late hours, and insulting and abusive language directed at her. After she lodged complaints, the landlord terminated the lease of the neighbors, but he did nothing about evicting them for more than three months. Unable to sleep and endure the noise, Kern moved out, claiming a constructive eviction. Was she correct? (*Colonial Apartments, Inc.* v. *Kern*, 163 N.W.2d 770)

5. The state of Massachusetts took, by eminent domain for highway purposes, land in Boston. Rite Media had a lease with the owners by which it maintained a three-and-one-half story high billboard on the property, supported by steel beams sunk into concrete footings. The lease provided that the billboard and structures were the property of the tenant and could be removed by the tenant at any time prior to the end of the lease. The owners of the land settled with the state, but the state refused to compensate Rite Media for its billboard and structures. Is it entitled to compensation? (*Rite Media, Inc.* v. *Secretary of the Massachusetts Highway Department*, 712 N.E.2d 60)

6. Lippman owned a cooperative apartment on 93rd Street in New York City. Dime Savings, which had loaned money to Lippman, declared the loan in default. Lippman tried to sublease his apartment, but the cooperative corporation refused to give him permission, claiming that it had a right to do so because the cooperative lease for each tenant provided that the cooperative board had an unlimited right to withhold its consent to a sublease. Lippman sued the bank and the cooperative corporation, claiming he should have the right to sublease. Is he correct? (*Roy Lippman* v. *Dime Savings Bank of New York, FSB, et al.*, 691 N.Y.S.2d 437)

7. Lewis rented space in the lobby of a Sheraton hotel. On the day the lease was to expire, Lewis gave a check for the next month's rent and stayed in possession. When the hotel cashed the check, Lewis claimed that the hotel's action had renewed his lease for another year. The hotel sued to evict Lewis. Is Lewis's claim valid? (*Sheraton-Chicago Corporation* v. *Lewis*, 290 N.E.2d 685)

8. Levine's young daughter lived with her family in a large apartment project owned by Miller. In the basement of one of the apartments, there was a large recreation room used by all the tenants. Levine's daughter was injured while playing in the room when a radiator fell on her. Is Miller liable for her injuries? (*Levine* v. *Miller*, 218 Md 74)

9. Genesee signed a lease with the Oatka Club for the use of Genesee's property for recreational purposes. The lease provided that the term was to be for "as long as the Club remained an active club." While Oatka was still in possession, Genesee sent a notice of cancellation of the lease, claiming the lease was a tenancy at will. Is Genesee correct? (*Genesee Conservation Foundation* v. *Oatka Fish and Game Club*, New York 63 AD2d 1115)

10. The state condemned land owned by Burk for a highway project. Included in the condemnation was a restaurant leased to Patzen and Winkenwerder. The lease was silent regarding who was entitled to any awards for property condemned by the state. Burk claimed that as the owner, he was entitled to the entire award. Is he correct? (*State By & Through Highway Commission* v. *Burk*, 265 P2d 783)

CHAPTER **31**

Buying and Selling Real Property

CHAPTER PREVIEW

The Buying and Selling Process	**Transfer of Title**
Contract of Sale	The Quitclaim Deed
Financing	The Bargain and Sale Deed
Title Examination	The Warranty Deed
The Closing	
Disclosure	

Chapter Highlights

The many important considerations in buying and selling real property, particularly a home, are discussed in this chapter. The chapter describes the formation of a contract of sale between seller and buyer. The topic of financing the purchase is also explored. The chapter then discusses the steps taken to ensure that the buyer gets good title to the property. The chapter concludes by describing the steps involved in the closing and transfer of title, including the various types of deeds that may be used to accomplish the transfer of title.

THE BUYING AND SELLING PROCESS

The largest investment most individuals make is the purchase of their home. A real estate purchase can be a very complex matter, and both the buyer and the seller should exercise great care. The material in this chapter, although concerned primarily with houses, is applicable to the purchase of any type of real property.

The specific steps and laws involved in buying and selling a home vary from state to state. The major steps in all cases, however, are signing the contract of sale, obtaining financing, completing a title examination, and closing.

Contract of Sale

Negotiations for the sale and purchase of a home may be handled directly by the buyer and seller or through a real estate agent or broker. Many owners try to sell their homes themselves by advertising or putting up FOR SALE signs. If they reach an agreement with the buyer, they enter into a contract of sale.

The statute of frauds requires that a contract for the sale and purchase of a home must be in writing to be enforceable. The buyer and seller often verbally agree on all the terms of the transaction. Their agreement is then incorporated into a written contract of sale, which they, a broker, or an attorney prepares.

listing contract
agreement between owner and broker listing broker's rights and obligations in selling the owner's real property

The Listing Contract   Sellers who work through a real estate agent or broker usually sign a **listing contract** giving the agent or broker the right to sell the house in return for an agreed commission. The commission may be a fixed amount, although a percentage of the sale price is more common. The listing contract also usually states the period of time the agent has in which to sell the property.

The broker brings the seller and the buyer together and negotiates the details of the transaction, including the purchase price, date of transfer, and method of financing.

Once this negotiation is done and a contract is signed, the broker's commission is considered earned. The seller is responsible for and usually pays the commission even if the seller decides not to go through with the sale.

> Willard signed a listing contract with Allen Realty for the sale of Willard's home. According to the terms stated in the listing contract, Allen produced a buyer willing to buy. Willard found another buyer willing to pay $2,000 more for the house and sold it to that person. Allen is entitled to a commission on the sale of Willard's house even though Allen was not responsible for the eventual buyer.

purchase offer offer submitted by buyer to seller for purchase of real property

Purchase Offer and Acceptance   Some buyers and sellers arrive at an agreement through a purchase offer and acceptance. A **purchase offer** is a written offer from a buyer to a seller to purchase the seller's house (Figure 31.1). It contains all the terms of the sale acceptable to the buyer. If the seller agrees to all the terms in the purchase offer, the seller signs an *acceptance*. The acceptance is usually at the bottom of the purchase offer. If the seller does not agree to all the terms, the seller may simply disregard the offer or may instead make a counteroffer with different terms. The buyer may agree to the new terms or may instead make a further counteroffer. When the buyer and seller finally agree on all the terms of the sale, the purchase offer and acceptance are considered a binding contract of sale.

A purchase offer and acceptance and a contract of sale are binding and enforceable agreements that may not be changed without the consent of both parties. They should contain all the terms and conditions of the sale, including the names of the parties, a description of the real property and any personal property included in the sale, the purchase price and method of payment, the date title to the property will pass, and adjustments (credits) for real estate taxes and other items paid by the seller. Fixtures, such as chandeliers and built-in appliances, are included in the sale unless specifically excluded in the contract. Trade fixtures, those used in business, would not be included unless the contract of sale provides otherwise.

contingencies conditions in a contract that may void the contract if not met

An important part of a contract of sale deals with certain conditions that, if not met, may void the agreement. These conditions are known as **contingencies**. They may be inserted to protect both the seller and the buyer and are essential in any agreement. For example, a buyer may be able to purchase a house only if a bank mortgage can be obtained. The buyer will therefore insert a clause in the contract making the obligation to purchase the house contingent upon obtaining financing. Without such a contingency, the buyer is obligated to purchase the house regardless of whether financing is available. A seller may be building a new home and may not be able to move out until the new home is completed. Without a clause in the contract making the date of transfer of the house contingent on completion of the new home, the seller may have to move out even if the new home is not finished.

> Bell decided to purchase a home owned by Abel. He knew that he had to sell his own home before he could purchase Abel's. When he submitted a purchase offer to Abel, he failed to make the purchase of Abel's house contingent on the sale of his own home. When Abel accepted the offer, Bell was obligated to buy Abel's home even if he had not sold his own home.

An important contingency is that the contract must be approved by both buyer's and seller's attorneys. Another important contingency provides for an inspection by a qualified person to determine any defects in the structure or in the heating, plumbing, water, sewer, and air-conditioning systems. If the results are not satisfactory, the buyer may void the contract.

FIGURE 31.1 Purchase Offer

Purchase and Sale Contract

WHEN SIGNED BY BUYER AND SELLER, THIS DOCUMENT BECOMES A BINDING AGREEMENT

COMMISSIONS OR FEES FOR REAL ESTATE SERVICES TO BE PROVIDED HEREUNDER
ARE NEGOTIABLE BETWEEN REALTOR AND SELLER

The undersigned offers to purchase the property situate in the
City or
Town of ___Homer_____, County of Monroe, State of New York,

known as Address ___42 Vestal Boulevard_____

Approx. Lot Dimensions __150' x 200'_____ Tax Acct. #___368942_____

Consisting of __a 2-story frame house with attached garage_____

OTHER ITEMS: Together with and including all appurtenances, all buildings and other improvements thereon and all rights of Seller in and to any and all streets, roads, highways, alleys, driveways, easements, and rights-of-way appurtenant thereto; the following items, if any, now in or on said premises, are included in this sale and shall become the property of Buyer at closing: all heating, plumbing, lighting fixtures, flowers, shrubs, trees, linoleum, window shades, venetian blinds, curtain and traverse rods, storm windows, storm doors, screens, awnings, TV antennas, water softeners if owned, tool sheds, sump pumps, bathroom fixtures, weather vanes, window boxes, fences, flag poles, wall to wall carpeting and runners, exhaust fans, hoods, and garbage disposers, electric garage door openers and remote control devices, intercom equipment, swimming pool and pool operating equipment; also (unless such items are free standing) all cabinets, mirrors, stoves, ovens, dishwashers, shelving, fireplace screens and equipment, air conditioning (except window) units, humidifier and dehumidifier; Buyer agrees to accept such items in their present condition.

PURCHASE PRICE AND TERMS: PURCHASE PRICE: ....($160,000.00) Payable as follows:

1. $3,000.00 deposit with this offer.
2. $7,000.00 by certified check at closing.
3. $150,000.00 by my obtaining a bank mortgage for that amount for a period of 30 years not to exceed 6% interest. I shall have 21 banking days in which to obtain mortgage approval. Otherwise, this offer shall be null and void and any deposit made by me shall be returned to me.

   OTHER TERMS:
1. Possession shall be given at closing.
2. Purchase price shall include draperies and stove.

ADJUSTMENTS AT TRANSFER OF TITLE: There shall be prorated and adjusted as of date of transfer of title, rentals, fuel, mortgage interest, F.H.A. mortgage insurance, water, pure water charges, sewer charges, current taxes computed on a fiscal year basis excluding embellishments in City tax bills, but including all items in the current county tax bill excepting delinquent school taxes. Buyer will accept title subject to and will pay all assessments for local improvements which are not payable as of date of delivery of deed. Seller represents that there is no additional assessment not appearing on the current tax roll. Buyer shall refund tax escrow balance to seller in the case of mortgage assumption.

SEARCH SURVEY AND COSTS: Seller shall furnish and pay the cost thereof and deliver to the attorney for the Buyer at least five (5) days prior to the date of closing, fully guaranteed tax, title and United States District Court Searches dated or redated subsequent hereto, and with a local tax certificate for village taxes, and a tape location map dated subsequent hereto. Seller shall pay for the continuation of said tax, title, United States District Court Search, local tax searches to and including day of transfer, and for the current tape location map and required tax stamp. Buyer shall pay for mortgage assumption charges, if any, recording deed, mortgage and mortgage tax.

TITLE DOCUMENTS: At the time of transfer, Seller shall tender to Buyer a Warranty Deed with lien covenant conveying good, marketable title in fee simple to said premises free and clear of all liens and encumbrances, except as provided herein; and Seller will furnish documents necessary to transfer title to other items above described, warranting same free and clear of all liens and encumbrances, except as provided herein; Buyer agrees to accept title to the premises subject to restrictive covenants of record common to the tract or subdivision provided the same have not been violated, and subject to public utility easements provided the same do not encroach on improvements.

REPRESENTATION: Seller represents that the premises and any improvements thereon are in full compliance with restrictive covenants and all statutes, ordinances, regulations, and/or other administrative enactments including but not limited to Building Codes

---

earnest money deposit made by buyer when purchase offer is submitted or contract of sale of real property is signed

At the time a purchase offer is submitted or a contract of sale is signed, it is customary for the buyer to give the seller a deposit. In some areas, this deposit is known as **earnest money**. The deposit is often held by the seller or the seller's attorney or broker until the transfer of title takes place. It is then applied toward the purchase price. If the buyer fails to go through with the transaction without a good reason, either the seller or the broker may keep the deposit depending on the terms of the listing contract.

Financing

A buyer may be able to purchase a home without obtaining any financing. Most people who buy homes, however, require financing for at least part of the purchase price. Financing is usually in the form of a mortgage; in some cases, it is in the form of a land contract. A **mortgage** is a lien against the property held by a bank or whoever is lending the money as security until the loan is repaid. The person borrowing money is called the **mortgagor**; the lender is called the **mortgagee**. Financing is usually obtained through a new mortgage or by assuming an existing mortgage.

mortgage lien against property held by a lender as security for repayment of a loan

mortgagor one who borrows money used to purchase real property

mortgagee one who lends money to purchase real property

purchase money mortgage new mortgage given for purchase of real property

mortgage commitment agreement on the part of lender to grant a mortgage

New Mortgage   When a new mortgage is obtained to finance all or part of the purchase price, it is known as a **purchase money mortgage**. The typical way to finance the purchase of a home is to obtain a mortgage from a bank, savings and loan association, or life insurance company. Some mortgages are insured by the Federal Housing Administration and are known as FHA insured loans; others are guaranteed by the Veterans Administration and are known as VA guaranteed loans.

After a purchase contract is signed, the buyer submits it to a lender and applies for a mortgage. The lender will evaluate the home and check the buyer's credit references. The lender will also examine the buyer's earnings, employment history, bill-paying record, and other assets. If the lender is satisfied that the buyer is a good credit risk, it will issue an offer to give a mortgage to the buyer. This offer is usually known as the **mortgage commitment**.

Sometimes the seller, rather than a bank or insurance company, will agree to finance a portion of the purchase price by giving the buyer a mortgage. Instead of paying all the purchase price to the seller in the form of cash, the buyer obtains a mortgage from the seller and pays the seller back over a period of years. This arrangement is often done when the buyer has had difficulty obtaining a bank mortgage. It is also done when a seller prefers to have an investment rather than receive a large sum of money at one time upon the sale of a house.

mortgage assumption right of a buyer to take over and be bound by an existing mortgage

Existing Mortgage   There is often an existing mortgage on a home that a buyer may take over and agree to pay. In a **mortgage assumption**, the buyer will pay the seller in cash the difference between the balance of the existing mortgage and the purchase price. The buyer becomes a substitute for the seller and assumes an obligation that was formerly the seller's. For example, if the purchase price of a home is $200,000 and there is a mortgage on the home with a balance of $150,000, the buyer may assume the mortgage and pay the seller $50,000 at the time of transfer.

The advantage of assuming a mortgage is that it is less expensive than securing a new mortgage. Also, if interest rates rise, the interest rate in an older, assumable mortgage may be lower than the interest rate on a new mortgage. In some cases, the consent of the holder of the mortgage (usually a bank or savings and loan) may be required before a mortgage can be assumed.

prepayment privilege right to pay balance of mortgage before the end of the mortgage term

Terms of the Mortgage   Regardless of the source of the mortgage, it is important that the terms and conditions of the mortgage be clear and understood by the mortgagor. The terms include the amount of the mortgage, the interest rate, the amount of the monthly payment, and the terms of the mortgage. The borrower should understand the rights that the lender has if the borrower defaults in making payment, including the right to foreclose.

Two important rights that a borrower should try to obtain in a mortgage are a prepayment privilege and assumption. The **prepayment privilege** is the right of the mortgagor to pay the balance due on the mortgage before the end of the mortgage term. By paying off the mortgage in advance, the borrower saves on interest costs. In addition, if interest rates drop, the borrower may wish to refinance by obtaining a new mortgage at a lower interest rate.

The assumption right, referred to earlier, allows an owner to sell the property and assist the buyer in financing the purchase by allowing the buyer to assume the owner's existing mortgage. Unless the mortgage contains language that permits prepayment and assumption privileges, they may not be available. FHA insured and VA guaranteed mortgages may be assumed with the consent of the lender.

> Byrd bought a home and financed it with a mortgage payable over a period of twenty years. The mortgage had no clause permitting prepayment. Six months after purchasing the home, Byrd inherited a large sum of money and wished to pay the mortgage in full. Byrd is not permitted to do so without the consent of the mortgage holder.

foreclosure action by a mortgagee to seize mortgaged property in payment of a debt

Foreclosure is a proceeding by a lender to force a sale of mortgaged property to satisfy a debt. Upon completion of the foreclosure, the owner loses ownership of the property.

Land Contract   A **land contract** is an agreement in which a buyer agrees to purchase property and pay for it over a period of time. When the final payment is made, the seller transfers title to the property to the buyer.

land contract agreement to purchase property and pay for it over a period of time

After a land contract is executed, the buyer takes possession of the property even though the seller retains title until the purchase price is paid in full. If the buyer defaults in making payments, the seller may retake possession of the property and evict the buyer. In many such cases, the buyer may forfeit all or part of the payments made to the seller.

The major difference between a mortgage and a land contract has to do with the transfer of title. When a buyer buys property and pays for it with mortgage proceeds, the buyer obtains title to the property immediately. In a land contract, the seller retains title to the property until the purchase price is paid in full.

Title Examination

title interest one has in real property

Title to real estate is the right of the owner to own it, use it, mortgage it, and sell it free from any claims of others. There are many types of claims that could affect the rights of the owner. For example, a former owner may still have a right to use the property. There may be restrictions on how the property may be used. State or local governments may have an interest in the property because of unpaid real estate taxes. A bank may hold an existing mortgage on the property.

Various methods are used to make sure that the buyer receives clear title (often called marketable title) to the property purchased. These methods vary from state to state and also by areas within the state. In many areas, the buyer's attorney examines the property records to determine whether there are any liens, mortgages, or other restrictions on the property. This process is called a **title search**. In some states, the title search is made by the attorney or a county clerk. In most states, it is made by a private title company that specializes in title searches.

title search examination of public records to determine if title to real property is clear

abstract of title summary of transactions affecting title to real property

The attorney, or whoever is doing the search, generally uses an abstract of title to assist in the search (Figure 31.2). An **abstract of title** is a copy or condensed summary of all transactions relating to a particular piece of property over a period of years. It will show deeds, mortgages, tax information, and other transactions that may affect the title to the property.

title insurance insurance that compensates owner of real property for damages if title is found to be flawed

Title insurance may be purchased by a buyer to ensure that the title is good. If it turns out that the title is not clear, the insurance protects against any resulting financial loss. Title insurance is valuable because the abstract examined by the attorney may be

FIGURE 31.2 Abstract of Title

10	Fletcher M. Hayes, Mary A., his wife	Warranty Deed

10   Fletcher M. Hayes, Mary A., his wife

              -To-

       Marcia Cole

Warranty Deed

Dated Nov. 1, 1945
Ack. Nov. 15, 1945
Rec. Nov. 25, 1945

Liber 69 of Deeds, page 354

       Conveys, with other property, all that tract or parcel of land situate in the Town of New Castle, New York, and described as follows: The southeast part of lot #3, in Township #14 in the 7th Range of Phelps and Gorham's Purchase; being the same land conveyed to Fletcher M. Hayes by John Frazer and others by deed, dated Sept. 30, 1935.

- -

11   Marcia Cole and Richard D. Cole

              -To-

       Joseph H. Cole

Warranty Deed

Dated June 4, 1961
Ack. same day
Rec. same day

Liber 164 of Deeds, page 165

       Conveys as follows: Town of New Castle, New York, the southeast part of lot #3 in Township #14 in the 7th Range of Phelps and Gorham's Purchase; being the same land conveyed to Fletcher M. Hayes by John Frazer and others by deed, Sept. 30, 1935, bounded north by the north half of said lot #3, now owned by Charles Statler; east by lot #6, now owned by said Marcia Cole; south by the highway; west by the southwest part of said lot #3; containing 57 acres, be the same, more or less.

- -

incomplete and not show every transaction affecting the title. Or the attorney making the title search may have given a faulty opinion as to whether the title was good. Title insurance does not ensure that the buyer may keep the property if there is another claim to the title, but it does guarantee that the buyer will be compensated for any loss.

Fifteen states have adopted a system known as the **Torrens system** of registration. With this system, the court examines the title and issues a certificate that is filed in a public office. Any time a deed or mortgage affecting the property is put on record, the documents are recorded at the public office and new certificates of title are issued. The registration fees are used to pay for any loss that results from errors made by the public officials involved.

Torrens system system of public registration of titles using title certificates

survey map showing location, boundaries, and size of a piece of real property

In addition to a title search, a survey is often made of the property. A **survey** is a map that shows the boundaries of a piece of land and the location of the structures on the land. If the survey is made by a surveyor and shows exact angles and distances, the survey is known as an *instrument survey* (Figure 31.3). If measurements are taken by using a steel or cloth measuring tape and are only approximate, the survey is known as a *tape location map*.

A survey is important for many reasons. Descriptions in deeds are often inaccurate or refer to landmarks, such as trees, that may no longer exist. A buyer should know how

FIGURE 31.3 Survey

much land is being purchased and its exact location. If the survey and the deed do not agree, the survey is accepted as correct because of its exactness. A survey is also important if an owner wishes to build structures and wants to make sure that they are built on his or her land. Without a survey, construction may take place on a neighbor's land.

> Melio bought a home from Corwin but did not have the property surveyed. Melio liked to swim and so built a large swimming pool in one corner of the property. After the pool was completed, Melio discovered that a portion of the pool had been built on land belonging to a neighbor. A survey would have prevented this error.

If flaws are found in the title after a title search is made, the flaws must be corrected to the satisfaction of the buyer. If the flaws cannot be corrected, the transaction is usually called off. If there are no flaws or if they are corrected, the next step in purchasing the home is the closing.

The Closing

After title is found to be good and all required documents are completed, the buyer and the seller and their attorneys meet for the transfer of title. Prior to such action, however, a buyer should take care of certain details, including obtaining insurance for the home and its contents, arranging with utility companies for service, and making a final inspection of the property. In most states, the transfer of title is known as the **closing**. The closing occurs at the place and time contained in the contract of sale, unless the parties make other arrangements. If a mortgage is involved, the closing may take place at the offices of the bank or the offices of the bank's attorneys. If no mortgage is involved, the closing is usually held at the office of the clerk of the county in which the property is located. If title insurance is involved, the closing may take place at the offices of the title insurance company.

closing meeting at which title to real property is transferred from seller to buyer

Adjustments are made at the closing for any charges paid by the seller from which the buyer will benefit. For example, the seller may have paid the annual real estate tax. If the closing takes place on July 1, the buyer will owe the seller one half of the total taxes paid. There may also be adjustments that benefit the buyer. For example, a water bill for the months of June, July, and August may not be received by the new owner until September. At the closing, the buyer is entitled to a credit for one month or one third of the total bill. A **closing statement** shows the purchase price, any adjustments made, and the expenses of the sale (Figure 31.4).

closing statement document showing financial details of the transfer of real property

After all adjustments have been agreed upon, the seller gives the buyer an executed deed to the property. The buyer pays the seller the purchase price plus adjustments, less any deposit given. If a mortgage is involved, the buyer signs the mortgage papers and receives a check for the amount borrowed. This amount is then turned over to the seller, and the buyer pays the seller any balance due. Payment of any balance due is usually made by certified check or cashier's check.

The buyer and seller must also pay their respective shares of the closing costs. These costs include transfer taxes, mortgage taxes, attorney's fees, survey costs, and other title expenses. In some cases, lenders will charge a processing fee, usually a percentage of the mortgage. Responsibility for payment of the closing expenses is determined by the terms of the contract of sale or by local custom.

A federal law, the Real Estate Settlement Procedures Act (RESPA), applies to all closings of residential properties. At closing, both buyer and seller must receive a detailed accounting of the price, costs involved, adjustments made for tax payments, and so forth involved in the sale. RESPA also provides that a lender financing the purchase of the real estate must respond within twenty days of a borrower's written request for information or for correction of an error in a mortgage account. The act (Section 8) also prohibits kickbacks between lenders and settlement service agents (e.g., title companies) in the real estate settlement process.

FIGURE 31.4 Closing Statement

```
               S T A T E M E N T    O F    T R A N S F E R

    PROPERTY:   28 Hermitage Lane, Cincinnati, Ohio
    SELLER(S):  Elizabeth A. Johnson and Elliot M. Johnson
    BUYER(S):   Marcia L. Jordan
    DATE OF CLOSING:  July 31, 2009
    ___ ___ ___ ___ ___ ___ ___ ___ ___ ___ ___ ___

    DUE SELLER:
          Purchase Price                              $ 60,000.00
          County Tax Adjusted -(___mos.____days)
          City/School Tax Adj.-( 3 mos.  0 days)          241.50
          Village Tax Adjusted
          Rents
          Escrow
          Fuel
                                                     _____
                  TOTAL:                               60,241.50
    CREDIT BUYER:
          Rents                      $
          Mortgage Assumed -Interest
          City/School Tax. Adj.
          Embellishments
          Water Adjusted
          Pure Waters Adjusted

          BALANCE DUE SELLER:                        $ 60,241.50
                                                     ===========
          PAID AS FOLLOWS:
              Deposit            $  3,000.00
              Mortgage Proceeds    50,000.00
              Mortgage Discharged
              Mortgage Assumed
              Balance               7,241.50        $  60,241.50
                                                    ============
    ___ ___ ___ ___ ___ ___ ___ ___ ___ ___ ___ ___

    CLOSING EXPENSES:
          Recording Fees           $   60.00
          Mortgage Tax -Broker's Fee 1,200.00
          Abstract Charge              25.00
          Bank Attorney's Fee         300.00
          Bank Processing Fee         150.00
          Legal Services
          Map
          Revenue Stamps                           $  1,735.00
    TAX ESCROW ACCT. ESTABLISHED AT CLOSING:
          County Tax   ____mos.    $
          City/School Tax  3 mos.      241.50
          School Tax   ____mos.
          Village Tax  ____mos.

                                                 $    241.50
```

Disclosure

At common law, *caveat emptor* (or "buyer beware") was the traditional rule regarding the sale of real estate. A seller of real property had no duty to tell a potential buyer of any defects the seller knew about, even though the buyer could not have learned of the defects after an inspection. This rule has changed in most states. A seller must now disclose to the buyer any defects that the seller knows about, that might materially affect the value of the property, and that a buyer could not reasonably discover. If a seller fails to disclose and the defects materially affect the value, the buyer may sue for fraud or rescind the contract of sale.

In most states, sellers must provide buyers with a comprehensive form disclosing the condition of the property, including the existence of lead, availability of utilities, and so forth. New York law, for example, applies only to sellers of one- to four-family homes. It does not apply to vacant land, new homes, condos, co-ops and dwellings containing five or more units. New home construction is covered in most states by certain warranties of habitability.

A federal law, the Interstate Land Sales Full Disclosure Act, protects buyers of homes in subdivisions. It requires developers who plan to sell or lease lots of one acre or more in a subdivision to file a statement with the Department of Housing and Urban Development (HUD) containing information about the subdivision and the developer. A buyer of a lot can revoke the contract within seven days after signing it.

TRANSFER OF TITLE

Title to real property passes to the buyer when the deed is delivered to the buyer and the purchase price is paid. The deed is a document by which real property is transferred from one owner to another. A person who transfers the title to real property is known as the **grantor**. The person who receives the title is known as the **grantee**. The deed must contain the names of the parties, words of transfer, a description of the property, and the parties' signatures, which are usually witnessed and/or notarized.

grantor one who transfers title to real property to another

grantee one who receives title to another's property

To protect the buyer, the deed must be recorded in the proper public office. Recording the deed notifies the public of the transfer of title. It also protects the buyer from an unscrupulous seller who might try to sell the same property to someone else. In actual practice, the deed and the payment of the purchase price are held in trust until a final title search is made and the deed is recorded. This is known as holding in **escrow**. The attorneys or title company representatives search the records right up until the point that the deed is to be recorded. If title is still clear, the deed is recorded and the purchase funds are released to the seller. If a mortgage is involved, it is usually recorded at the same time.

escrow holding closing documents and funds in trust until title to real property is clear

There are many different types of deeds. They vary according to the interests that are being transferred. The type of deed given depends on what the contract of sale calls for and often on local custom. The most common are the quitclaim deed, the bargain and sale deed, and the warranty deed.

The Quitclaim Deed

quitclaim deed deed that conveys whatever interest the seller has

The **quitclaim deed** passes to the buyer whatever title or interest the seller has and nothing more. The seller may have good title, faulty title, or no title at all. Whatever title the seller has is the title passed through a quitclaim deed. A quitclaim deed releases the seller from any further claims against the property.

> O'Connor sold her interest in a small apartment building to Rudd. A quitclaim deed was executed to transfer title to Rudd. If someone in the future questions Rudd's title to the property, Rudd cannot go back to O'Connor with any claims against the property.

The Bargain and Sale Deed

bargain and sale deed deed that conveys the interest the seller has, promising that seller has done nothing to disturb the title

The **bargain and sale deed** also passes to the buyer whatever title the seller has. In addition, the seller guarantees that she or he has possession of the property and has done nothing to disturb or harm the title to the property. It is a personal guarantee only, relating solely to any acts the seller may have committed. The bargain and sale deed is the most common deed when title insurance is involved.

The Warranty Deed

warranty deed deed
that guarantees
clear title

The **warranty deed** transfers the most complete interest in property. The seller not only transfers the seller's interest in the property but also promises and guarantees certain things known as *covenants*. One covenant is a guarantee that the title is good and that the grantor has the right to sell the property. Another covenant is a guarantee that the property is free from any interests or claims of others, such as claims for taxes owed, claims of a mortgagee, and so forth. These claims are known as **encumbrances**. A third covenant is a guarantee that if any claims are made by others, the grantor will do whatever is necessary to settle the claims. If a flaw in the title is eventually discovered, the grantor is personally responsible to the grantee. An example of a warranty deed is shown in Figure 31.5.

encumbrances
interests in property
that conflict with
owner's title

FIGURE 31.5 Warranty Deed

THIS INDENTURE, made the   7th   day of   May   2009
BETWEEN

SAMUEL SELLERS, 100 Title Way, Rochester, New York 14618

grantor

LISA BAUER, 300 East Avenue, Rochester, New York 14614

grantee

WITNESSETH, that the grantor, in consideration of
Three Thousand and-------------00/100--------------------($3,000.00) **Dollars,** paid by the grantee
hereby grants and releases unto the grantee, the heirs or successor and assigns of the grantee forever,

  ALL   THAT TRACT OR PARCEL OF LAND situated in the City of Rochester, Monroe County, New York, known and described as Lot #10, Genessee subdivision as shown on a map filed in the Monroe County Clerk's Office in Liber 800 of Maps, Page 20.

   Said Lot #10 is situated on the west side of Title Way and is of the dimensions as shown on said map.

   This deed is subject to all easements and restrictive covenants common to this tract or subdivision.

  TAX ACCT. NO. 24-7, 40-6

TOGETHER with the appurtenances and all the estate and rights of the grantor in and to said premises.
TO HAVE AND TO HOLD the premises here granted unto the grantee, the heirs or successors and assigns forever,
    AND the said grantor covenants as follows:
FIRST.—That the grantor is seized of the said premises in fee simple, and has good right to convey the same;
SECOND.—That the grantee shall quietly enjoy the said premises;
THIRD.—That the said premises are free from incumbrances;
FOURTH.—That the grantor will execute or procure any further necessary assurance of the title to said premises;
FIFTH.—That the grantor will forever warrant the title to said premises;
This deed is subject to the trust provisions of Section 13 of the Lien Law.
  The words "grantor" and "grantee" shall be construed to read in the plural whenever the sense of this deed so requires.
IN WITNESS WHEREOF, the grantor has executed this deed the day and year first above written.

In presence of:

....L. S.

....L. S.
SAMUEL SELLERS

STATE OF NEW YORK, COUNTY OF   ss.:
 On the   day of   2006 , before
me personally came   to me known,
who, being by me duly sworn, did depose and say that deponent resides
at No.
deponent is   of
       the corporation described in and which
executed, the foregoing instrument; deponent knows the seal of said
corporation; that the seal affixed to said instrument is such corporate
seal; that it was so affixed by order of the Board of Directors of said
corporation; deponent signed deponent's name thereto by like order.

STATE OF NEW YORK, COUNTY OF   MONROE   ss.:
  On the   7th   day of   May   2009 , **before**
me personally came
     SAMUEL SELLERS
to me known to be the individual   described in, and who executed
the foregoing instrument, and acknowledged that   he   executed
the same.

Burns transferred title to her home to Alwin with a warranty deed. Burns had purchased the home from three owners. When the property was sold, one of the three owners had failed to sign the deed of transfer and therefore legally still had an interest in the property. Because Burns guaranteed the title, Alwin has a claim against Burns even though the problem did not arise because of any action on Burns's part.

Summary

Buying real property usually involves four steps: signing a contract of sale, obtaining financing, title examination, and the closing. The contract of sale determines the rights and responsibilities of buyer and seller and should be examined carefully before it is signed. It should contain all the important terms of sale, including the names of both parties, a description of the property, the purchase price, the method of payment, any contingencies, and the closing date. Once signed, the contract of sale is binding and enforceable and may not be changed except on agreement between buyer and seller.

Some homes are purchased without any financing, but most purchases are financed by means of a mortgage. A mortgage may be either a new mortgage obtained from a bank or other lender or an existing mortgage that is assumed by the buyer. Two valuable rights a borrower should try to obtain in a mortgage are the prepayment privilege and the right to have the mortgage assumed upon sale of the property. When a buyer buys property and pays for it with mortgage proceeds, the buyer obtains title to the property immediately.

Another form of financing is the land contract, an agreement in which the seller retains title to the property until the purchase price is paid in full.

Before a closing can take place, the seller must be able to transfer clear title to the buyer. Proof of clear title may be accomplished by a title search, title insurance, or registration under the Torrens system.

Title to real property passes to the buyer at the closing, upon delivery of the deed and payment of the purchase price. To protect the buyer and the lender, the deed and mortgage should be recorded in a public office.

The three most common deeds used to transfer real property are the quitclaim deed, the bargain and sale deed, and the warranty deed.

Important Legal terms

abstract of title	grantor	purchase offer
bargain and sale deed	land contract	quitclaim deed
closing	listing contract	survey
closing statement	mortgage	title
contingencies	mortgage assumption	title insurance
earnest money	mortgage commitment	title search
encumbrances	mortgagee	Torrens system
escrow	mortgagor	warranty deed
foreclosure	prepayment privilege	
grantee	purchase money mortgage	

Questions and Problems for Discussion

1. What is the difference between a quitclaim deed and a warranty deed?
2. Is a deed valid if it is not recorded?
3. What important terms should a contract for the sale of real property contain?
4. Loeffler and White signed a contract for the sale of Loeffler's home to White. The contract stated that the purchase price included all furniture in the house. When it came time to transfer title, Loeffler realized that he had made a mistake and

refused to give White the furniture. May Loeffler do that?

5. Kern signed a contract to sell her home to Burns. There was a valuable chandelier in the dining room, but there was nothing in the contract excluding the fixture from the sale. At closing, Burns claimed she was entitled to the fixture. Is she correct?

6. Allen signed a contract to buy a home from Star and gave Star a $10,000 deposit. Two weeks later, Allen told Star he didn't want to go through with the purchase because he didn't like the trees in front of the house. He asked for the return of his deposit. Is he entitled to get his deposit back?

7. What guarantees, if any, are made by a seller of property who gives a bargain and sale deed?

8. Hurd signed a contract to purchase a home from Linz. Linz inspected the home but was unaware that there was asbestos in the walls, something that Hurd was aware of. When Linz found out, he canceled the contract and refused to go through with the purchase. Was he correct?

9. Frames signed a contract to purchase a condominium from Harley. The contract was silent about the date for closing and stated that "the purchase price shall be determined by the parties three days before closing." Frames decided to cancel the contract, claiming it was not valid. Is he correct?

10. Laube bought a parcel of land from Linze without examining the title. Before the contract of sale was signed, the city in which the property was located obtained a judgment against Linze for unpaid back taxes. The city sought to enforce its lien for unpaid taxes by selling the property. Can Laube stop that from happening?

11. Dalton sold his house to Little and gave him a deed to the property. Little put the deed in a desk drawer and failed to record it. Dalton then sold the house to someone else and gave that party a deed as well. If Little sues Dalton for damages, may Dalton claim as a defense that Little failed to record the deed?

12. After Byrd signed a contract to purchase a parcel of land from Devon, she learned that a railroad company had an easement for maintaining railroad tracks across the land. May Byrd refuse to go ahead with the purchase of the land?

13. Duke signed a contract of sale, agreeing to sell his home to Pembroke. Pembroke required a mortgage to purchase the home, but nothing was said about this in the contract. Pembroke applied for a mortgage but was turned down. Is Pembroke still obligated to purchase Duke's home?

14. Clark submitted a written purchase offer to O'Reilly, offering to buy O'Reilly's home for $150,000, subject to Clark's obtaining a mortgage of $100,000. O'Reilly accepted the offer but stated that the contract would not be subject to obtaining a mortgage. Do Clark and O'Reilly have a binding contract for the sale of O'Reilly's home?

15. Zena transferred title to her home to Carey with a quitclaim deed. Neither Zena nor Carey were aware that an electric utility had an option to purchase the home at any time for a set price. Does Carey have any recourse against Zena for the failure of title?

16. Thornton signed a contract with Grey to buy Grey's land. A title search showed that a prior owner had an interest in the land because he held a mortgage on it. Thornton refused to go through with the purchase because of the presence of the mortgage lien. Is he correct?

17. What are the different ways the purchase of property may be financed?

18. Sym signed a contract to sell his home to Perez. The contract was silent about adjustments for taxes paid, and so on. At the closing, which took place on June 1, Sym wanted Perez to reimburse her for the real estate taxes she had paid for the entire year. Is she entitled to this amount?

19. What type of deed gives the greatest protection to a buyer?

20. The mortgage on Flawn's home was foreclosed, and the bank sold the home to Smyth. Flawn claims that Smyth didn't get title to the home because Flawn never gave him a deed to it. Is Flawn's claim correct?

Cases for Review

1. The Smiths decided to sell their home, and a potential buyer had the house inspected. The inspection indicated that there was a defective foundation. The buyer told the Smiths about the report and decided not to buy the home. The Levines wanted to buy the house and asked about

its condition. The Smiths never mentioned the report. After they bought the house, the Levines learned of the condition and sued the Smiths for damages. Should they succeed? (*Smith* v. *Levine,* 911 S.W.2d 427 Tex.)

2. Safiol had a contract to purchase a lot from Sechrest. He wanted to build a house on the lot and gave Sechrest a deposit of $3,800. The contract was contingent on Safiol's obtaining all permits and other approvals necessary to build a residence. Safiol hired an architect to draw up plans and discussed the matter with the town but never submitted an application for a building permit. Safiol advised Sechrest that he was terminating the contract because he had never received the necessary permits and demanded the return of his deposit. Is he entitled to get his deposit back? (*Sechrest* v. *Safiol,* 419 N.E.2d 1384 Mass.)

3. Hill offered in a letter to buy Bell's property. He told her to mail him a warranty deed to the property and he would send her a check for the purchase price. She agreed to sell but wrote that she would only send Hill a quitclaim deed, as that was the only deed that she had ever received. Hill sued her to transfer the property to him. Will Hill succeed? (*Hill* v. *Bell,* 111 Vt. 131)

4. The Mitchells bought a tract of land from Brannen. They subsequently transferred it back to Brannen by a deed that was never delivered to Brannen. Brannen then conveyed the property by a deed that was delivered to Hardeman and then recorded. Mitchell sued Hardeman to determine who owned the property, claiming that the property was his. Is Mitchell correct? (*Hardeman* v. *Mitchell,* Tex. 444 S.W.2d 651)

5. Read wanted to buy property owned by the Henzels. He sent them a letter offering to buy the property for $220,000. He suggested two different down payments and two different mortgages to finance the transaction. At the end of the letter,

he stated, "This generally covers our agreement and should suffice until a more formal document can be drawn up." The Henzels returned the letter and suggested a number of changes, including a mortgage with a different term and different interest rate. When the Henzels refused to go through with the deal, Read brought suit, claiming that he had a valid contract to buy the property. Is he correct? (*Read* v. *Henzel,* N.Y. 67 A.D.2d 186)

6. In a letter Hill offered to buy Bell's property. He told her to mail him a warranty deed to the property and he would send her a check for the purchase price. She agreed to sell but wrote that she would only send Hill a quitclaim deed, as that was the only deed she had ever received. Hill sued her to transfer the property to him by warranty deed. Will he succeed? (*Hill* v. *Bell,* 111 Vt 131)

7. The Sayets agreed to buy property owned by the Cayres. They deposited $10,000 with Beekay Realty. Their contract to buy was subject to their obtaining a mortgage. The Sayets made few attempts to secure a mortgage. They were never turned down but their applications were rejected because the Sayets failed to provide the information requested. The Sayets sued to get their deposit back and to cancel the transaction. Are they entitled to do this? (*Beekay Realty Corp.* v. *Cayre,* Florida 256 So 2d 539)

8. Charter agreed to buy property at a sale in which a mortgage held by Jamaica was being foreclosed upon. Charter gave a deposit of 10 percent of the purchase price. Before closing, Charter discovered that the title was flawed because of an open judgement affecting the property. The problem could not be solved prior to closing so Charter refused to complete the transaction and asked for the return of his deposit. Jamaica sued to force Charter to complete the deal. Was Charter correct? (*Jamaica saving Bank* v. *Charter,* New York 22 Misc 2d 569)

CHAPTER 32

Nature and Types of Bailments

CHAPTER PREVIEW

Chapter Highlights

This chapter deals with one of the most common of transactions, the bailment. Initially, the chapter describes the requirements for a valid bailment. It then explains the ways in which a bailment may be created and ended. To help classify bailments, we also examine situations similar to bailments that are not treated in the same way. As we will see, people are involved in many types of bailments in their daily lives. This chapter classifies those bailments into categories so they can be more easily identified. It then discusses in detail the rights and responsibilities of the bailor and the bailee in each category. The chapter ends with a discussion of the ways in which bailees attempt to limit their liability.

WHAT A BAILMENT IS

bailment transfer of possession of personal property for a specific time and purpose

The word *bailment* comes from the French word *bailler,* meaning "to have in charge." Generally, a **bailment** exists when a person has possession or charge of personal property that belongs to someone else. Specifically, a bailment is a relationship that arises when a person takes charge of personal property that was in the possession of someone else, for a special purpose and for a limited period of time, with the understanding that the same or substantially the same property will be returned.

The following are some examples of bailments:

1. Your motorcycle doesn't work, and you borrow one from a friend for the day.
2. You enter a restaurant and leave your coat with the checkroom attendant.
3. You rent a minivan to go on a trip.

The importance of bailments cannot be too strongly emphasized. Other than sales, most of the transactions you engage in every day are bailments. When you borrow or lend something, rent an item, store a possession, or leave something to be repaired, you enter into a bailment. Thus, it is important to understand what a bailment is, how it is created, and how it ends.

bailor one who gives up possession of personal property to another

bailee one who accepts possession of another's personal property

The parties to a bailment are the bailor and the bailee. The **bailor** is the party who gives up possession of the bailed item. The **bailee** is the party who receives possession of it.

> You have a fine collection of record albums, some of which a friend wished to borrow for a party. You agreed to lend your friend the records provided that they were returned the day after the party. You are the bailor of the records and your friend is the bailee.

> Your floors needed refinishing and you rented a sander from a hardware store. You are the bailee of the sander and the hardware store is the bailor.

It is possible to be both a bailor and a bailee of the same property. If you rent a car from a rental agency, you are a bailee of the automobile. Upon leaving that car at a repair garage, you become a bailor of the car.

Each party in a bailment has certain rights and duties. In the next chapter, you will learn what these rights and duties are.

REQUIREMENTS FOR A VALID BAILMENT

The most important requirements of a valid bailment are personal property, retention of title by the bailor, possession of the property by the bailee, and return of the bailed property.

Personal Property

A bailment involves personal property only. You may recall that personal property is any property other than real property. Some examples of personal property are bicycles, clothing, calculators, books, and U.S. savings bonds. Land and buildings are examples of real property.

> You have just found a job and rented a furnished apartment. You are the bailee of the furniture because it is personal property. You are not a bailee of the apartment because it is real property.

Rental of real property, such as an apartment or a house, involves the landlord-tenant relationship, discussed in Chapter 30.

Retention of Title by the Bailor

A bailment transfers possession only. If *ownership* of property is transferred, the transaction is not a bailment; it is a sale or a gift.

Possession of Property by the Bailee

Generally, the bailor owns the property being bailed, but ownership is not required, only possession of the property. A bailor could be an employee, a person who finds an item, or even a thief.

Property must change hands before a bailment can be created. The property may be delivered by the bailor to the bailee, or a document (e.g., a car registration) may be delivered to the bailee or may be found by the bailee. In any case, the bailee must knowingly accept possession of the bailed property or no bailment is created.

You enter a restaurant to have dinner and leave your coat on a nearby chair. No bailment is created if the restaurant personnel are unaware that you left your coat there and therefore had not accepted delivery.

Acceptance can be shown in many ways. It can be something said or something written. Often, it occurs by some act or deed, such as picking up a lost item.

Brandon was riding his bicycle when he saw a camera on the ground. Realizing that the camera had been lost, Brandon picked it up. By doing so, Brandon had accepted possession and was therefore a bailee.

Return of Bailed Property

The very nature of a bailment assumes that the identical property bailed will be returned to the bailor, unless the agreement between the parties provides that the property will be returned to a third person or otherwise disposed of. The bailed property will usually be returned with little or no change.

You took your suit to the dry cleaners for pressing. You will get back the same suit that you took in, minus only the dirt and wrinkles.

Sometimes the bailed property is returned in a different condition because of alterations, repairs, or processing.

Ellis purchased some cloth to be made into a suit. Ellis gave the cloth to a tailor to have a suit made. The same cloth was returned to Ellis but in a different form.

Many bailments are contractual agreements, such as renting a car. As such, they must have all the characteristics of a valid contract: offer and acceptance, competent parties, consideration, and legal purpose.

HOW A BAILMENT IS CREATED

A bailment may be created by an express agreement or an implied agreement. Most bailments are created through an express agreement. As discussed in Chapter 6, an express agreement is one in which the agreement is stated in words, either oral or written. To be valid, such agreements must meet the test for contracts discussed in Chapter 6.

You rent a boat at a marina for the weekend. After reaching an agreement as to the rental cost, when the boat is to be returned, liability for damage, and so forth, you sign a rental contract and take the boat out. By doing so, you have entered into an express written contract of bailment.

Bailment Implied in Fact

bailment implied in fact bailment created by actions of bailor and bailee

A bailment can also come into existence by the actions of the parties. If a bailment arises because of the acts of the parties, without any oral or written agreement, it is known as a **bailment implied in fact**. The law holds that the parties intended to form a bailment because of their actions.

Fry went to a luggage store to have a suitcase repaired. He handed over the suitcase and received a receipt. Nothing was said about an agreement and nothing was signed. Because Fry expected to have his suitcase repaired and returned to him and because the storeowner expected to return it to him and be paid, however, Fry has an implied bailment.

Bailment Implied by Law

A **bailment implied by law** may also be created when a person obtains possession of another's property without any agreement at all. This bailment arises because the law requires it to promote justice and fair play.

> A stereo set purchased by Phelps was delivered to Brooks, a neighbor, by mistake. Brooks knew that the stereo belonged to Phelps and accepted delivery. By accepting delivery, Brooks agreed to hold the stereo as a bailee for the benefit of Phelps.

Brooks became a bailee even though there was no agreement between Phelps and Brooks. Bailments implied by law are often created when people find and take possession of lost, misplaced, or stolen property.

HOW A BAILMENT ENDS

A bailment exists only for a limited time and purpose; eventually, it will come to an end. A bailment may be ended by the completion of the terms of the bailment agreement, mutual agreement of the parties, the acts of the parties, the destruction of the bailed property, or operation of law.

Completion

The typical bailment, created by an agreement, ends according to the terms of the agreement. If the agreement provides that the bailment will last for a specific time or purpose, the bailment will end when the time period is over or the purpose is accomplished.

> Morton borrowed Allen's car for the weekend to visit his parents. When Morton returned the car to Allen, the bailment ended.

Mutual Agreement

Often, if there is no longer a need for the bailment, the bailor and the bailee agree to end it. It, in fact, then ends.

> You borrowed your friend's car for a week. Two days later, your friend told you that his plans had changed and he needed his car back. You agreed and returned the car to him. This act terminated the bailment.

Acts of the Parties

If nothing specific is said or written about when the bailment is to end, either the bailor or the bailee, without the consent of the other, can end it at any time. Either party can also end the bailment if the other party does not live up to its terms.

> Cruz took his car to a garage to have the transmission repaired. The garage promised to repair it within three days. If the garage does not complete the work at the end of the three days, Cruz can reclaim his car and end the bailment.

Destruction of the Bailed Property

A bailment also ends when the bailed property is lost, destroyed, or becomes worthless through damage. If the bailee's negligence causes the loss or damage, the bailee is liable to the bailor for the value of the property.

You bought your mother a present and asked your friend to keep it for you until your mother's birthday. Your friend negligently left the present in a store. When she returned for it, the present was gone. The bailment has ended, because your friend no longer has possession of the present. In addition, your friend is liable for the value of the present because of her negligence.

Operation of Law

A bailment implied by law ends when the need for the bailment ends.

A package belonging to your neighbor was delivered to your home because your neighbor was away on vacation. When your neighbor picks up the package, the bailment ends.

SITUATIONS SIMILAR TO BAILMENTS

There are other situations that resemble bailments but are quite different. Often, they have some of the same characteristics. Some of these situations—sales and trusts—are discussed in other chapters of this book. Other situations that resemble bailments are bank deposits, safe-deposit boxes, and public lockers.

Depositing money in a bank has many of the characteristics of a bailment. Personal property (money) is delivered to and accepted by the bank for a specific purpose (storage). The relationship between the bank and the depositor, however, is a debtor-creditor one. You are actually *lending* your money to the bank, which in turn promises to return the same *amount* of money to you. A bailment would occur only if the bank promises to return the identical currency that you deposited.

Many courts interpret the rental of a safe-deposit box to a customer by a bank as a bailment. The bank, however, does not actually receive and accept delivery of the articles in the box. Nor does the bank have complete possession of the articles in the box. *Two* keys are needed to open the safe-deposit box: one held by the customer and one held by the bank. For these reasons, some courts rule that the relationship is that of a landlord-tenant.

The same situation applies to the rental of a public locker. The owner of the locker never actually receives and accepts delivery of the articles in the locker. The renter retains possession of the articles by retaining the locker key.

CLASSIFICATION OF BAILMENTS

There are several ways to classify bailments. The most understandable way is based on whether the bailment arises from an agreement, which can be either express or implied, or without an agreement. In the first classification are *mutual benefit bailments* and *gratuitous bailments*. A **mutual benefit bailment** is a bailment in which both the bailor and the bailee benefit. It is the most common type of business bailment and is usually based on a contract.

mutual benefit bailment bailment in which both bailor and bailee benefit

Rhodes rented a snowmobile for $25 an hour. As bailee, Rhodes benefited by having the use of the snowmobile; the bailor, the rental agency, benefited by being paid for the use of the snowmobile.

gratuitous bailment bailment in which only one party benefits

The **gratuitous bailment** is a bailment in which only one of the parties to the bailment benefits; the other does not. An example of a bailment *for the sole benefit of the bailor* is when you ask a friend, as a favor, to watch your bicycle while you are out of town. Examples of bailments *for the sole benefit of a bailee* are letting your friend, as a favor, borrow a calculator or permitting a local library to exhibit your stamp collection free of charge.

A type of bailment in the second classification—one that does not arise from an agreement between parties—is known as a constructive bailment. A **constructive bailment** is a bailment implied by law. It occurs when a person comes into possession of another person's property without that person's knowledge or permission.

Bailments may also be classified according to the degree of care required, ordinary or special. Bailments in which an extraordinary standard of care is imposed on the bailee are known as special bailments. They are discussed in Chapter 33.

constructive bailment bailment implied by law created when one has possession of another's property without that person's knowledge

MUTUAL BENEFIT BAILMENTS

There are five types of mutual benefit bailments: renting, work and services, pledging, consigning, and storage and parking.

The standard of care required in a mutual benefit bailment is that of reasonable care. **Reasonable care** is the type of care a person would take in using her or his own property. For example, reasonable care of a rented lawn mower would include removing all the large rocks and branches from the path of the lawn mower.

reasonable care care taken by an average person under ordinary circumstances

Failure to use reasonable care may subject the bailee to liability for any damage that occurs to the property while it is in the possession of the bailee. The bailee may limit the responsibility to a certain amount or to certain events, provided the bailee brings the limitations to the attention of the bailor at the time the bailment is created.

Renting

The renting bailment, also known as leasing, is the most common type of mutual benefit bailment. It often involves a contract. Any time you rent or lease an item for a period of time, you are involved in a bailment.

Bailor's Rights and Responsibilities   The bailor, the person who rents an item to someone, has the right to be paid for the use of the property, to expect that the bailee will use reasonable care, and to have the same property returned when the rental period ends.

The bailor has a duty to provide goods or equipment that are fit for the purpose of the bailment. The bailor, of course, must be familiar with the equipment and know its uses.

Work and Services

A bailment for work and services occurs when you deliver property to someone (the bailee) for repairs or servicing for a fee. The bailed property is usually returned in a changed condition according to the agreement between bailor and bailee.

Bailor's Rights and Responsibilities   A bailee's acceptance of property for work or services is no assurance of skill. It is up to the bailor to choose a competent bailee. If the work is done poorly—if your clothes are returned from the dry cleaner's with wrinkles, for example—you have little claim against the bailee. If, however, the work is done so badly that the property cannot be used, you can insist that the work be redone, refuse to pay for the work, or demand your money back.

Johnson took some material to a tailor to have it made into a suit. The tailor mistakenly used someone else's measurements and made a suit that Johnson could not wear. The tailor was liable for the value of the material.

The bailor has a duty to pay for the work done and to warn the bailee of any hidden defects in the property that the bailee might not be aware of.

Your food processor turned on when the safety switch was in the "off" position. When you take it in for repair, you have a duty to tell the repairperson of this dangerous condition. If you do not, you are liable for any injuries to the bailee.

Bailee's Rights and Responsibilities   The bailee has the right to be paid. If the bailor does not pay, the bailee has the right to keep the property as security until paid. This right is known as the **bailee's lien**. In some states, the bailee may enforce this lien by selling the property. The bailee, however, must first notify the bailor that the property is going to be sold and may keep only the amount of money to which the bailee is entitled: the amount that covers the cost of the work or services plus any expenses. Any money left over must be returned to or held for the bailor.

> **bailee's lien** bailee's right to hold bailed property until paid for work or services

Bray's television was not working properly and he took it to a repair shop. If Bray failed to pick up the television and pay for it within a reasonable time after the repairs were completed, the shop owner, after notice to Bray, could sell the television to recover the cost of the repairs.

The bailee also has certain duties. One is the duty to take proper care of the bailed property. A bailee who uses reasonable care is not responsible if the property is damaged, destroyed, or stolen.

Lassen owned a valuable photograph that was fading. Lassen took it to a photography studio to have it restored. Despite the studio's alarm system, a burglar broke into the studio and stole many items, including Lassen's photograph. Lassen does not have a valid claim against the owner for the loss because the owner used reasonable care in protecting the photograph.

The bailee must also work on the property with the skill that a bailee of that type would normally have and must follow the terms of the bailment agreement. The bailee must not use the property without the owner's permission and must return it at the end of the bailment.

You contract with a driver to drive your car to a vacation home. On the way, the driver lets a friend use the car, and the car is damaged in an accident. The driver is liable for all damages because he loaned the car to someone without your permission.

Pledging

A bailment known as a *pledge* occurs when personal property is deposited as security for the repayment of a loan or debt or the performance of a duty. A pledge is a common transaction in the business world. Pledged property may be any type of personal property, including stocks or bonds. The bailor (or debtor) is called the **pledgor**. The bailee (or creditor) is known as the **pledgee**. A pledgee may be a bank, pawnbroker, credit union, or individual lender.

> **pledgor** one who transfers possession of personal property as security for a debt
>
> **pledgee** one who accepts delivery of personal property that is security for a debt

Bronson wanted a new digital camera but did not have enough money to buy it. Bronson owned a corporate bond that she didn't want to sell because of its value. If Bronson agreed to pledge the bond at a bank, she could receive a loan. When the loan is paid off, the bond will be returned to Bronson.

Pledgor's Rights and Responsibilities   The pledgor (bailor) has a right to get back the bailed property when the loan is repaid. If the pledgee (bailee) fails to return the bailed property after repayment, the pledgor may sue the bailee to get the property back or to recover its value.

> Price pledged a camera with a pawnbroker as security for a loan. On repaying the loan, Price learned that the pawnbroker had sold the camera by mistake. Price is entitled to get back a similar camera or an amount equal to the value of the pledged camera.

The pledgor has a duty to repay the loan with interest under the terms of the pledge. If the pledgor fails to repay the loan on time, the pledgee may keep the bailed property and sell it to recover the amount of the loan. The pledgor also has a duty to make sure that he or she has the right to pledge the property. Stolen goods cannot be legally pledged. If stolen goods are pledged, the pledgee must surrender the goods to the true owner. Such surrender does not, however, relieve the pledgor of repaying the debt. The pledgor also is not relieved of repaying the debt if the property is lost, stolen, or destroyed through no fault of the pledgee.

Pledgee's Rights and Responsibilities

The pledgee (bailee) has a right to have the loan repaid under the terms of the pledge. The pledgee also has a bailee's lien and may keep the pledged property until the loan has been repaid.

The pledgee has a duty to take reasonable care of the pledged property and to return it when the loan is repaid.

Consigning

consignment bailment for the purpose of purchase or sale by the bailee

consignor bailor in a consignment

consignee bailee in a consignment

A **consignment** is a mutual benefit bailment in which the bailor, called the **consignor**, delivers property to the bailee, called the **consignee**, for purchase or sale by the consignee. Ownership of the consigned property remains with the consignor until the goods are either purchased by the consignee or sold to another person. A consignment enables a person to examine goods without having to pay for them in advance.

> Geisler, an attorney, wanted to examine a set of law books before deciding to buy it. The publisher sent Geisler the set on consignment. Geisler may keep the set for a certain period of time and then must either return the set or keep and pay for it.

Another purpose of consignment is to enable a retailer to keep merchandise on hand without first having to buy it from the manufacturer. The retailer saves money and can carry more merchandise in the store.

> A manufacturer sent television sets to the Video Store on consignment. The manufacturer owns the sets until they are sold by the Video Store. The store owner must pay the manufacturer when the sets are sold or return the unsold sets to the manufacturer.

Consignor's Rights and Responsibilities

The consignor has a duty to provide property that is safe. The consignor must inspect the consigned property to make sure it is not dangerous and must tell the consignee if it requires special care.

The consignor has a right to have the consigned property stored under safe conditions. The consignor also has a right to have the property sold or returned within the agreed-upon period of time.

Consignee's Rights and Responsibilities

The consignee has a duty to take reasonable care of the consigned property. The consignee must either pay for the property or return it to the consignor within a reasonable time.

The consignee has a right to receive property that is safe. The consignee also has a right to keep the consigned property for the time agreed upon.

Another type of consignment involves shipments by common carrier. This type of consignment is discussed in Chapter 33.

Storage and Parking

Storing something for a fee is a common type of mutual benefit bailment. Leaving a pet at a kennel while you take a trip is a bailment of this type. Storing a boat at a marina during the winter is another example.

The most common type of bailment for storage occurs when a bailor delivers goods to a warehouse operated by the bailee, the **warehouse operator**. The warehouse operator gives the bailor a receipt for the goods, known as a **warehouse receipt**. To get the bailed goods back, the bailor must return the receipt to the warehouse operator and pay the storage charges.

warehouse operator
one who stores personal property for another for compensation

warehouse receipt
form issued by a bailee for the storage of personal property

Bailor's Rights and Responsibilities

The bailor has the right to have the bailed property stored with reasonable care. The care required depends on the nature of the goods stored. Perishable goods such as fruit would require cold storage, whereas furniture might require dry storage. After turning in the receipt and paying the storage charges, the bailor has the right to get back the bailed property.

> You moved into a partially completed house and needed to store some furniture at a warehouse until the house was completely finished. To obtain the furniture, you must produce the warehouse receipt and pay the storage charges.

The bailor must, of course, pay all storage charges. The bailor also has a duty to notify the bailee of any defects in the property or any special care required for its storage. Failure to notify the bailee of any problems or requirements may relieve the bailee of liability in the event of loss or damage.

> Braden owned a very valuable violin that required a high degree of humidity to prevent it from cracking. Before going on a trip, Braden arranged to store the violin but failed to tell the warehouse operator of the special care required. The warehouse operator would not be liable for any damage to the violin caused by low humidity because Braden did not warn the operator of the special requirements.

Warehouse Operator's Rights and Responsibilities

The warehouse operator has the right to be told of any special storage conditions. The operator also has the right to be paid for storing the property according to the terms of the agreement. The warehouse operator cannot use the property without the bailor's permission and must return the property at the end of the bailment period.

> The Vinson Company stored several crates of cabbage at the Granite Cold Storage Company. Granite placed the crates next to a container of fresh fish. When Vinson picked up the cabbage, it discovered that the cabbage had a fishy odor and could not be sold. Granite is liable for damages because it did not use reasonable care in storing the cabbage.

Some courts consider parking a car in a parking lot or garage a mutual benefit bailment. Others consider it a lease of space, which usually relieves the lot operator of liability in the event of loss or damage. What the relationship is depends on how much control the garage or lot operator has over the car. If you turn over your car to a parking lot attendant, who then parks it for you and retains the keys, you have lost control of the car and a bailment occurs. If you park the car yourself, lock it, and take the keys, a bailment does not occur. You are instead leasing space because you still have complete control over the car.

GRATUITOUS BAILMENTS

The most common type of nonbusiness bailment is the gratuitous bailment. In a gratuitous bailment, only one party benefits—either the bailor or the bailee—and there is no charge for the bailment. If the bailor delivers property to the bailee and does not pay for the bailee's services, it is a bailment for the sole benefit of the bailor.

> James received a motorcycle as a graduation present. He was going away on a trip and asked Alden to take care of it for two weeks. This arrangement is a bailment solely for James's benefit as a bailor.

If the bailor delivers property to the bailee for the bailee's use without charge, a bailment for the sole benefit of the bailee occurs.

> During the summer, Lewis earned extra money by mowing his neighbors' lawns. One day, the lawn mower broke. Abel, Lewis's friend, loaned Lewis a lawn mower free of charge while his was being repaired. This bailment is solely for the benefit of the bailee.

Bailments for the Sole Benefit of the Bailor

Even though only one party benefits from a gratuitous bailment, both the bailor and the bailee have rights and duties. Many of these rights and duties are similar to those in a mutual benefit bailment. There are some differences, however.

Bailor's Rights and Responsibilities   The bailor has a right to have the bailed property stored in the agreed manner and to have the property returned at the end of the bailment.

> Faber was going to a doctor for a physical exam and asked a friend to watch his car until he returned. His friend let another friend drive the car and it was damaged. His friend is liable for the damages because the bailment terms did not permit the use of the car by anyone but his friend.

As with other types of bailments, the bailor has a duty to inform the bailee of any defects or dangers connected with the bailed property.

> You asked a friend to repair your radio, as a favor, and you delivered it to the friend's home. The radio was overheating, but you did not mention that to your friend. The radio caused a fire in your friend's home. You are responsible for any loss that resulted.

The bailor must also reimburse the bailee for any expenses paid by the bailee while storing or taking care of the bailed property.

> Marx's neighbor agreed to store his car during the winter months. She put antifreeze in the radiator to protect the car. This expense was necessary to protect the vehicle, and Marx must reimburse his neighbor for the cost of the antifreeze.

Bailee's Rights and Responsibilities   The bailee has a right to be warned of any defects or dangers connected with the bailed property and to have the property picked up at the end of the bailment period.

The bailee's duties are to store the property in the agreed manner and to return the goods at the end of the bailment period.

In a bailment for the sole benefit of the bailor, the bailee is doing a favor for the bailor and does not receive any benefit or compensation. Therefore, the bailee is not held to the same standard of care as in a mutual benefit bailment. The standard of care imposed on the bailee is that of *slight care*, the minimum amount of care required under the circumstances. The bailee is liable for damages or loss only if there was gross negligence.

> Green went to visit a friend and asked Gorton to watch his stamp collection while he was gone. Gorton left it on the front seat of his car and failed to lock the doors. If the collection were to be stolen, Gorton would be liable because even slight care would involve locking the car doors.

Bailments for the Sole Benefit of the Bailee

In a bailment for the sole benefit of the bailee, the bailee may use the bailor's property free of charge.

Bailor's Rights and Responsibilities   The bailor has the right to have the bailed property returned at the end of the bailment period in good condition. The bailor also has the right to end the bailment at any time and demand the return of the bailed property.

The bailor has a duty to warn the bailee of any defects or dangers in the bailed property. If the bailor does not warn the bailee, the bailor may be liable for any injuries to the bailee.

Bailee's Rights and Responsibilities   The bailee has a right to use the bailed property as agreed and to be told of any defects or dangers. The bailee must use the property only as agreed, take proper care of the property, and return it in good condition at the end of the bailment period.

Because only the bailee benefits from this type of bailment, the bailee's standard of care is increased. The bailee in this type of bailment must use a *high degree of care*. Thus, the bailee must use the property only as agreed and is liable for damages even if there was only slight negligence.

> You borrowed your friend's camera for the day. It dropped from your hands because you were carrying too many things and was damaged. You are responsible for repairing the camera.

CONSTRUCTIVE BAILMENTS

The bailments discussed so far in this chapter come about through agreements between the bailor and the bailee. A person may, however, get possession of someone else's property without an agreement or without the consent of the owner. When that happens, the person who gains possession of the property is considered a bailee, and the bailment is known as a constructive bailment.

Bailments of Lost Property

bailment of lost property bailment occurring when one obtains possession of lost property

One type of constructive bailment is a **bailment of lost property**. This bailment occurs when someone finds lost property and takes possession of it. The finder is a bailee for the benefit of the bailor, the person who lost the property. The law makes the finder a constructive bailee to protect the owner's rights in the lost property.

Cohen was walking along the street and saw a purse on the ground. She took it home with her and notified the police. Cohen is a constructive bailee of the purse until the police or the owner takes possession of the lost purse.

Bailments by Necessity

bailment by necessity
bailment created when property comes into one's possession by mistake

Another type of constructive bailment is a **bailment by necessity**. This bailment occurs when property comes into someone's possession by mistake. The person who has possession is a constructive bailee for the benefit of the rightful owner until that owner is found.

Granger ordered a sofa, which was delivered to Byrd's house by mistake. Byrd placed the sofa in his living room until Granger picked it up. Byrd is a bailee for the benefit of Granger.

Constructive bailees have certain obligations toward the owners of property. They must take reasonable care of the property depending on the type of property and the circumstances of the bailment. In some states, the finder of the property must notify the authorities or must advertise that the property has been found.

If the true owner claims the property, the bailee must turn the property over to the owner. The bailee, however, is entitled to receive compensation for any expenses incurred in advertising or in taking reasonable care of the property. If a reward has been offered for the return of the property and the bailee knows of this reward, the bailee is entitled to collect it.

If the true owner does not appear to claim the property, the bailee is entitled to keep the property after a reasonable period of time has elapsed. The bailee may also sell the property and keep the proceeds of the sale.

LIMITING LIABILITIES: DISCLAIMERS

Many bailees attempt to avoid liability for damage to property while it is in their possession or at least to limit the amount of that liability. They do so by inserting certain language on a ticket or receipt or posting a notice on a sign on the premises where the bailment occurs. Language typically used to avoid liability includes the statement, "Not responsible for loss or theft of property while on these premises."

Courts are increasingly finding such disclaimers to be void on the grounds that they are against public policy, particularly when public or semipublic institutions are concerned. Attempts to completely avoid liability for loss or damage despite negligence by the bailee are almost certain to be held void. If attempts to limit liability are reasonable and are made known to the bailor in a clear and understandable way, however, they are usually upheld.

Summary

A bailment occurs when a person takes possession of property that was formerly in the possession of someone else, for a special purpose and for a limited period of time.

For a transaction to be a valid bailment, there must be a transfer of possession of personal property from one person to another and the eventual return of the property bailed. Title to property is not essential for a bailment, only possession.

Most bailments arise from an express agreement. They may also arise based on the actions of the parties, known as bailments implied in fact. They sometimes arise because justice and fair play require it; such bailments are known as bailments implied by law.

A bailment is a temporary transaction. It may end in many ways, such as through agreement of the parties, acts of the parties, destruction of the bailed property, and operation of law.

There are many situations that are similar to bailments but are treated differently. These situations include depositing money in a bank account, using a safe-deposit box, and renting a public locker. These situations are not considered bailments but either debtor-creditor or landlord-tenant relationships.

The degree of care required in a bailment depends on the type of bailment involved. It is therefore important to classify bailments to determine the standard of care that is required. The most common classification is based on whether the bailment arises from an agreement.

The most common bailment is a mutual benefit bailment, in which both parties benefit. There are five types of mutual benefit bailments: renting, work and services, pledging, consigning, and storage and parking.

In a mutual benefit bailment, the standard of care is that of reasonable care. Failure to use reasonable care may subject the bailee to liability for any damages that may occur, unless the bailee limits its liability. In a mutual benefit bailment, the bailor has certain rights and responsibilities. The bailor has the right to be paid for the services rendered and to have the bailed property returned in good condition when the bailment ends.

A gratuitous bailment is one in which only one party benefits and there is no charge for services rendered. In a bailment for the sole benefit of the bailor, the bailor has a right to have the bailed property stored properly and to have the property returned when the bailment ends. The bailee has the obligation to store the bailed property with a slight degree of care and to return the property when the bailment ends. The bailor is obliged to warn the bailee of any defects or dangers connected with the property bailed.

In a bailment for the sole benefit of the bailee, the bailee must use a high degree of care in taking care of the property bailed, must use the property only as agreed, and must return it when the bailment ends. The bailor has the right to have the property returned in a safe condition when the bailment ends. The bailor has a duty to warn the bailee of any defects or dangers in the property bailed.

Some bailments arise without agreement between the parties. These are known as constructive bailments. One type is a bailment of lost property. Another is a bailment by necessity, which arises when someone obtains possession of another's property by mistake. In both cases, the standard of care is that of reasonable care.

Important Legal terms

bailee	bailor	pledgee
bailee's lien	consignee	pledgor
bailment	consignment	reasonable care
bailment by necessity	consignor	warehouse operator
bailment implied by law	constructive bailment	warehouse receipt
bailment implied in fact	gratuitous bailment	
bailment of lost property	mutual benefit bailment	

Questions and Problems for Discussion

1. Explain the rights and duties of the bailor and the bailee in a mutual benefit bailment.
2. Describe the difference in the obligations of a person who finds lost property, abandond property, or mislaid property.
3. Rowan stole a camera from someone's home and took it to a pawn shop to get a loan. When Rowan returned to the pawnshop to get the camera back, the pawnshop owner refused to return it because he had learned the camera was stolen. Is the pawnshop owner correct?
4. While shopping in a department store, Lorna found a ring on the floor of a dressing room where she was trying on a dress. She took the ring with her and advertised in her local newspaper that she had found the ring. When no one

claimed it after a year, she considered it her property. Was she entitled to do this?

5. What are the characteristics of a bailment?

6. Describe the ways in which a bailment may end.

7. Explain the various ways in which a bailment may be created.

8. If you go to a car wash and a worker drives your car through the wash, has a bailment been created?

9. Blair drove a company car while on business. One day, he left the car at a garage for repairs. The car was stolen from the garage. When Blair sued the garage for the value of the car, the owners claimed that no bailment was created because Blair didn't own the car. Was the company correct?

10. What are the circumstances in which a constructive bailment might be created?

11. A delivery company tried to deliver a package to Barnes's home. Barnes was not at home, so the delivery company left the package on the front porch of the neighbor's home. The package was stolen from the neighbor's porch. Was the neighbor a bailee of the package? Would your answer be any different if the neighbor had previously told the delivery company that it could leave packages on his porch if Barnes were not at home?

12. Farber was leaving on a trip to Europe and asked his friend James to care for the deed to his home while he was away. James lost the deed, and when Farber returned home, he held James responsible, claiming James was a bailee of the deed. Is Farber correct?

13. Granger received a check for $100 and deposited it temporarily in his safe-deposit box at Lincoln Bank. Was the deposit a bailment?

14. Granby signed a contract with Arby effective January 2 to store Arby's car. On January 4, just before Arby was to deliver the car to Granby's garage, the car was stolen. Is Granby liable as a bailee for the loss of the car?

15. Explain the difference between a mutual benefit bailment and a constructive bailment.

Cases for Review

1. Kessman owned and operated a gold, silver, and coin exchange store. In accordance with a court order issued in a nuisance action against Kessman by the city and county of Denver, the sheriff closed the store and padlocked it. While the store was in the sheriff's control, the store was burglarized. Kessman sued for damages, claiming this was a bailment. Is he correct? (*Kessman* v. *City and County of Denver*, 709 P2d 975)

2. Marsh entered a railroad station and decided to store a package containing some jewelry. He found an open public locker, inserted a coin, put the package inside, and locked the door. He took the key with him and left. When he returned, the package was gone. Had a bailment been created? (*Marsh* v. *American Locker Company*, 7 N. J. Super. Ct. 81)

3. Pine Hill was in the concrete business and operated on its own land. Pine Hill sold its land and asked permission of the new owner to leave a cement mixer temporarily on the land until it could be picked up. The new owners agreed. Was a bailment created? (*Pine Hill Concrete Mix Corp.* v. *Alto Corp.*, N.Y. 25 A.D.2d 608)

4. Van Dyke Productions returned exposed color film to the manufacturer to be processed. The film was damaged during processing, and Van Dyke had to retake the pictures. Van Dyke sued for damages. Was a bailment created? Do you think it makes any difference whether the price of processing was included in the price of the film or was a separate charge? (*Van Dyke Productions, Inc.* v. *Eastman Kodak Co.,* N.Y. 16 A.D.2d 366)

5. Theobold entered a beauty shop operated by Satterwaite. She sat down in the waiting room until it was time for her appointment. When her turn came, she left her coat on a hook in the waiting room and went into a different room for her appointment. When she returned to the waiting room, her coat was missing. She claims that Satterwaite was a bailee of her coat. Is she correct? (*Theobold* v. *Satterwaite,* 30 Wash. 2d 92)

6. Quinto bought rough cedar lumber from Millwood and arranged for Millwood to mill the lumber into siding. When the job was done, Quinto asked Millwood to deliver a portion of

the wood to a third party and said that Quinto would send a truck to pick up the lumber. When a truck arrived, Millwood gave the lumber to the driver of the truck, but the truck had in fact been sent by someone other than Quinto. Quinto sued Millwood for the value of the lumber. Millwood claimed that it was a gratuitous bailee and was responsible for gross negligence only. Will Millwood succeed in this claim? (*Quinto* v. *Millwood Forest Products, Inc.,* 130 Idaho 162)

7. Gonzalez rented an 8-foot by 10-foot locker from A-1 Self Storage to store her personal belongings worth $5,000. When she returned to retrieve her belongings, she discovered that they had been either partially or completely damaged by the entry of water into the storage space from the top of the unit. No explanation was offered to show how the water entered. The rental contract limited A-1's liability to $50, disclaimed liability even for its own negligence, and stated that no bailment had been created by the storage arrangement. Can Gonzales recover the value of her personal items from A-1? (*Gonzales* v. *A-1 Self Storage,* 350 N.J. Super. 403)

8. Swarth parked her car in a parking lot maintained by Barney's Clothes for its customers. After she parked the car, she gave the keys to the attendant. By mistake, she left her wallet on the seat. When she returned to the car, the wallet was gone. She sued for the value of the lost wallet and its contents, claiming Barney's is liable as a bailee. Is she correct? (*Swarth* v. *Barney's Clothes, Inc.,* N.Y. 40 Misc.2d 423)

9. Kern delivered his pickup truck and camper to Harris's garage for repairs to a stove. He asked to keep the camper inside at night because of "all the stuff inside." Burglars ransacked the camper and stole camping equipment and fishing gear. Was the garage a bailee of what was stolen? (*Kern* v. *Harris,* 567 P.2d 1069)

10. Berglund, a student at Roosevelt University, was the photographer for the school newspaper. The university gave him an office and darkroom space. He stored his camera equipment there without telling anyone about it. One evening, he locked the door, but when he returned the next morning, his camera and equipment were missing. The university claimed it was not a bailee and therefore not responsible for the loss. Is the school correct? (*Berglund* v. *Roosevelt University,* 18 Ill. App.3d 842)

11. Three immigrants to the United States from Mexico learned that a friend, Alcaraz-Garcia, planned to travel to their hometown in Mexico. They asked him to take with him more than $25,000 in cash to deliver to their families. Because the amount he was carrying was more than what was permissible to bring into Mexico, he lied about the amount to the U.S. Customs officials at the border, was caught, and the money was confiscated. The three immigrants filed a petition for the return of their money, claiming that because Alcaraz-Garcia was a gratuitous bailee, they retained ownership of the money. Should they succeed? (*United States* v. *Alcaraz-Garcia,* 79 F.3d 769)

CHAPTER **33**

Special Bailments

CHAPTER PREVIEW

The Nature of Special Bailments

Exceptions to the Rule of Strict Liability
  Agreement to Limit Liability
  Act of God
  Act of a Public Enemy
  Act of Public Authorities
  Fault of the Bailor or Guest
  Nature of the Bailed Goods

Duties, Liabilities, and Rights of Hotelkeepers
  Duties of a Hotelkeeper
  Liabilities of a Hotelkeeper
  Rights of a Hotelkeeper

Duties, Liabilities, and Rights of Common Carriers
  Duties of a Common Carrier
  Liabilities of a Common Carrier
  Rights of a Common Carrier

Chapter Highlights

There are certain bailments in which an extraordinary standard of care is imposed. This chapter deals with such bailments, called special bailments. It begins with an explanation of why such a high standard of care is imposed. It then describes many exceptions to the general rule of strict liability. Finally, the chapter discusses the rights and liabilities of two groups upon whom extraordinary liability has been imposed: hotelkeepers and common carriers.

THE NATURE OF SPECIAL BAILMENTS

Chapter 32 emphasized that the type of bailment determines the standards of care imposed on the bailee. Mutual benefit and constructive bailments require reasonable care; gratuitous bailments require either slight care or a high degree of care depending on who benefits.

There are also benefits in which an *extraordinary* standard of care is placed on the bailee. These benefits are **special bailments**, often called extraordinary bailments. Examples of special bailees are hotelkeepers and common carriers, either of goods or of passengers.

The extraordinary standard of care required of special bailees arose out of necessity. In the days of stagecoach travel, travelers were often subject to hijacking and theft. The inns in which they stayed were quite vulnerable to robbery. Sometimes there was collusion or cooperation between the innkeepers and robbers. To promote travel and commerce and to protect travelers, special standards of care were placed on innkeepers and carriers.

Under common law, the liability of innkeepers and carriers of goods was absolute. They were considered insurers and, as such, were totally liable for the safety of goods left in their possession, unless loss was due to conditions beyond their control. It was thought that those who had total control over property should be completely responsible for it.

Today, these bailees may still be held absolutely liable for loss of or damage to property, but this liability may be limited by law and is subject to many exceptions. In most states, the rule of absolute liability has been limited by law. Unless they are negligent, hotelkeepers and common carriers are not liable for losses if the exceptions described in the following sections apply.

> **special bailment**
> bailment in which extraordinary standard of care is imposed on bailee

EXCEPTIONS TO THE RULE OF STRICT LIABILITY

Agreement to Limit Liability

Special bailees can limit their liability by agreement with bailors. Some limit the amount for which they can become liable; others limit the type of conduct for which they can be held liable.

The typical practice is to post a notice about the liability being limited or to include a statement on the receipt given to the bailor. Statements such as "liability limited to $100" and "stored at owner's risk" are examples of attempts to limit liability.

As long as the agreement is fair and the bailor is fully aware of the limitation, the limitation is effective.

Act of God

act of God natural occurrence that cannot be foreseen or avoided

A natural disaster that could not have been anticipated, such as a flash flood, a hurricane, or an earthquake, is considered an **act of God**. Even a special bailee is not liable for losses due to such natural forces because the bailee could not have avoided the disaster.

> A freight train carrying perishable fruit was stalled for three days when a flash flood washed out a railroad trestle. The fruit was ruined by the delay. The railroad was not liable for the loss because the loss was due to an act of God.

If the bailee can prevent or limit a loss by taking proper care and fails to do so, the bailee is held liable for losses even though a natural disaster is involved.

> A hotel stored its guests' baggage in a basement storeroom. An unusually severe snowstorm occurred. In the next few days, warm weather moved in and the snow melted. The hotel was flooded and the guests' baggage was damaged. The hotel was responsible for the destruction of the baggage because it did not move the baggage above the flood level.

Act of a Public Enemy

public enemy military-type force of a foreign country

A **public enemy** is a military or military-type force from another country. Pirates or saboteurs from a foreign country are good examples. Special bailees are not liable for losses due to the acts of a public enemy. Mobs, rioters, strikers, and robbers, however, are not considered public enemies.

> National Cars sent some cars by ship to a foreign country. Along the way, the ship was seized by a military force, and the cars were confiscated. The shipping line was not liable for the loss.

Act of Public Authorities

A special bailee is not liable for losses that occur when goods in its possession are seized by a government authority. The bailee is not liable if, for example, public officials seize stolen goods or contaminated foods during shipment.

> While on vacation in Europe, Ingram decided to ship a carton of oranges back to her family. When the fruit reached the United States, customs officials confiscated it because fruit cannot be imported into the country except by inspected, commercial means. The shipping company was not liable for the loss of the oranges because the fruit was seized by a government agency.

Fault of the Bailor or Guest

A special bailee is not liable for losses that occur because of the actions of the bailor. The bailee is not liable, for example, if the bailor does not pack the goods properly and the carton breaks during shipment. Of course, if the defect or fault is apparent and the bailee still accepts the goods, the bailee is liable for loss.

> Blaine shipped a valuable clock to a repair shop by a local delivery service. The package appeared to be wrapped and sealed properly, but there was nothing inside the package to keep the clock from moving around. The clock was damaged when the truck went over a bumpy road. The delivery service is not liable for this loss.

Nature of the Bailed Goods

A special bailee is not liable for losses arising from the basic nature of the bailed goods. Some goods are perishable or may evaporate or ferment. Special care, such as refrigeration, may be required to prevent damage. If perishable food is shipped, the bailee must take care to refrigerate the food properly and to ship it without delay. If these precautions are not taken, the bailee is liable for any spoilage during shipment. If these precautions were taken and the goods were damaged because of their perishability, however, the bailee would not be liable. If perishable items are delivered to a carrier in good condition but arrive in a damaged condition, it is up to the carrier to prove that the damage occurred because of the natural condition of the goods, such as normal deterioration of some fruits and vegetables.

DUTIES, LIABILITIES, AND RIGHTS OF HOTELKEEPERS

hotelkeeper one who provides accommodations to the public for a limited time

A **hotelkeeper** is one who, on a regular basis, offers to provide living accommodations to all transients. The essential elements of a hotel or motel business are (1) regular nature of business, (2) offer to the public, (3) living accommodations, and (4) guest relationship.

The renting of rooms must be continuous and the main business activity. A hotelkeeper may operate a hotel, motel, or tourist home.

> Your family had an extra bedroom at their vacation home that was not being used and rented it to some visitors for a week. The family members are not considered innkeepers because they did not regularly rent out the room to the public and because it was not their regular business.

Hotelkeepers must accept any person who arrives in a proper condition and who is willing to pay for the accommodations.

> Flower Hotel refused to accommodate a guest who was drunk. It has a perfect right to refuse to accept a guest who is not in a proper condition.

The main purpose of a hotelkeeper is to provide lodging for travelers. A hotelkeeper may also provide food and entertainment, but the main purpose is the renting of rooms.

> You entered a hotel to have dinner in the dining room. You were a patron of the restaurant, not a resident or guest of the hotel.

transient one who is not a permanent resident

For a hotelkeeper to be considered a special bailee, the hotelkeeper must provide lodgings for guests or **transients**, those who can stay as long as they wish and who may leave at any time.

Arvin registered at a hotel to attend a convention. While at the hotel, he was a guest or a transient because he could leave whenever he wished.

Many people enter hotels to use the facilities but not to stay there. Some people enter the hotel to attend a social function, visit a guest, or eat in the dining room. Some have business to transact with the hotelkeeper. These people are not transients but **business guests**. A hotelkeeper is only an ordinary bailee of the property of business guests.

business guest one who uses the facilities of a hotel but does not stay there

Berger entered the Valley Hotel to arrange for rooms for guests at a family wedding. Because Berger is a business guest, the hotel is responsible only for slight care with regard to Berger's possessions.

The relationship between a guest and a hotelkeeper begins when the hotelkeeper accepts a person as a guest, which usually occurs when that person checks into the hotel. A person may, however, become a guest by giving his or her luggage to a porter or a person operating the hotel's limousine service.

A person ceases to be a guest when he or she leaves the hotel or ceases to be a transient.

Anson checked into the Benning Hotel while on a business trip and enjoyed his stay. When the hotel owners decided to convert some suites into condominiums, Anson bought one and moved into the hotel. At that point, he ceased to be a guest of the hotel.

boardinghouse keeper one who offers living accommodations to permanent residents

A **boardinghouse keeper** is one who offers living accommodations to permanent residents. Unlike a hotelkeeper, a boardinghouse keeper does not have to accept everyone who applies for a room. A boarding house keeper is an ordinary bailee of the personal property of boarders and is not entitled to a hotelkeeper's special rights. A university dormitory is an example of a boardinghouse.

Bartos entered college and rented a room for the school year at a college-approved, off-campus house. The owner of the house is a boardinghouse keeper because Bartos's stay is considered permanent. Bartos is a roomer, not a transient.

Duties of a Hotelkeeper

A hotelkeeper, by definition and by law, must receive and accommodate all those who wish to stay and who are proper guests. The Civil Rights Act of 1964 prohibits a hotelkeeper from discriminating against any person on the basis of race, color, religion, or national origin. If a hotelkeeper does discriminate for any of these reasons, the hotelkeeper could be held liable for damages, criminal prosecution, or both. The Civil Rights Act, however, does not prevent a hotelkeeper from rejecting any person who is violent, drunk, or unable to pay.

A hotelkeeper has a duty to take all reasonable precautions for the safety and privacy of guests and their baggage. Such precautions include providing protection against danger from fires and providing safe elevators, rooms, hallways, and stairs. Hotelkeepers are also liable for any actions by their employees that might endanger guests.

Liabilities of a Hotelkeeper

As mentioned earlier, hotelkeepers are absolutely liable for the safety of their guests' property. They are considered insurers and, like common carriers, are responsible for all losses or damages except those caused by acts of God, acts of public enemies, acts of public authorities, or the actions of the guest.

In actual practice, hotelkeepers, like common carriers, may limit their liability in various ways. In many states, laws limit the liability of a hotelkeeper to a specific amount. In a few states, hotelkeepers are held liable for theft of or damage to a guest's property only if they are negligent. In other states, laws permit hotelkeepers to limit their liability by providing a safe for guests' valuables and posting a notice in rooms telling guests of this safe (Figure 33.1). If a guest fails to use the safe, the hotelkeeper is no longer a special bailee and is responsible only for providing reasonable care for the guest's property.

FIGURE 33.1 Hotelkeeper's Notice Limiting Liability

NOTICE TO GUESTS

State Laws

Chapter 140, Section 10 to 13 Inclusive, Laws of Massachusetts

Section 10. "An innholder shall not be liable for losses sustained by a guest except of wearing apparel, articles worn or carried on the person, personal baggage and money necessary for traveling expenses and personal use, nor shall such guest recover of an innholder more than three hundred dollars as damages for any such loss; but an innholder shall be liable in damages to an amount not exceeding one thousand dollars for the loss of money, jewels and ornaments of a guest specially deposited for safe keeping, or offered to be so deposited, with such innholder, person in charge at the office of the inn, or other agent of such innholder authorized to receive such deposit. This section shall not affect the innholder's liability under any special contract for other property deposited with him for safe keeping after being fully informed of its nature and value, nor increase his liability in case of loss by fire or overwhelming force beyond that specified in the following section."

Whenever an innholder provides a security box in the room of any guest, the innholder shall not be liable for the loss of any items deposited in the security box; provided, however, that the provisions of section thirteen have been complied with.

As used in this section, security box means a metal or alloy box used for the safekeeping of valuables or other property, which may be securely locked with a locking mechanism.

Section 11. "In case of loss by fire or overwhelming force, innholders shall be answerable to their guests only for ordinary and reasonable care in the custody of their baggage or other property."

Section 12. "Whoever puts up at a hotel, motel, inn, lodging house or boarding house and, without having an express agreement for credit, procures food, entertainment or accommodation without paying therefor, and with intent to cheat or defraud the owner or keeper therof; or, with such intent, obtains credit at a hotel, motel, inn, lodging house or boarding house for such food, entertainment or accommodation by means of any false show of baggage or effects brought thereto; or, with such intent, removes or causes to be removed any baggage or effects from a hotel, motel, inn, lodging house or boarding house while a lien exists thereon for the proper charges due from him for fare and board furnished therein, shall be punished by a fine of not more than one thousand dollars or by imprisonment for not more than one year; and whoever, without having an express agreement for credit, procures food or beverage from a common victualler without paying therefor and with intent to cheat or defraud shall be punished by a fine of not more than five hundred dollars or by imprisonment for not more than three months.

Proof that such food, entertainment, accommodation or beverage, or credit for the same, was obtained by a false show of baggage or effects, or that such baggage or effects were removed from any such place by any person while such a lien existed thereon without an express agreement permitting such removal, or if there was not an express agreement for credit, that payment for such food, entertainment, accommodation or beverage was refused upon demand, shall be presumptive evidence of the intent to cheat or defraud referred to herein."
Amended by St. 1965, c.490: St. 1972, c.513

Section 13. "Innholders shall post a printed copy of this and the three preceding sections in a conspicuous place in each room of their inns."

Kaye was a guest at the Cambridge Hotel, which posted notices in guests' rooms telling them to store their valuables overnight in the hotel safe. Kaye came back to the hotel very late one night and decided not to place her diamond earrings in the safe because of the late hour. During the night, several rooms were broken into, including Kaye's, and her earrings were stolen. The hotel was not liable for the loss of the earrings because Kaye had not deposited them in the safe. The hotel could be held liable only if Kaye could prove that the hotel was unusually negligent in allowing the thief to enter the hotel.

Rights of a Hotelkeeper

Hotelkeepers have a right to be paid for the rooms they rent. If not paid, they may keep baggage and other goods belonging to the guest until the bill has been paid. This right is known as a hotelkeeper's lien. After a reasonable period of time, the goods being held may be sold and the proceeds applied to the unpaid bill. Any money left over must be returned to the hotel guest.

Hotelkeepers also have the right to ask for payment in advance or for proof of ability to pay (usually by credit card).

Aldrich arrived at the Warren Hotel and asked for a room for one night. Aldrich had no luggage and had a disheveled appearance. The hotel desk clerk legally has the right to ask Aldrich to pay for the room in advance.

DUTIES, LIABILITIES, AND RIGHTS OF COMMON CARRIERS

carrier one who transports goods or people for pay

A **carrier** is one who transports goods or people for pay. There are three types of carriers: private carriers, contract carriers, and common carriers.

private carrier carrier that transports goods solely for the business owning it

A **private carrier** is owned and operated by a company for the sole purpose of transporting its own goods. The delivery trucks owned by a dairy or a department store are examples of private carriers. Private carriers are employers and are covered by the laws of employment discussed in Part V.

contract carrier carrier that transports goods or people under individual contracts for a limited number of customers

A **contract carrier** limits its customers and transports goods under individual contracts. A contract carrier, for example, may deliver goods only for department stores. A contract carrier is free to accept or reject customers as it chooses. Contract carriers are ordinary bailees and are covered by the laws of mutual benefit bailments and the law of contracts.

common carrier carrier that transports people and goods for the general public

A **common carrier** transports goods and people for anyone who wishes to hire it. A common carrier is a special bailee with special rights and duties. Railroads, shipping lines, bus lines, airlines, taxis, and trucking companies are examples of common carriers. Common carriers are different from other carriers because they must accept customers without discrimination, are considered insurers of their customers' property, and are subject to government regulations because they are often public monopolies.

bill of lading document issued to a consignor by a carrier; receipt for goods shipped, proof of title, and shipping agreement

One who delivers goods to a common carrier for shipment is called a *consignor*. The person to whom the goods are shipped is the *consignee*. When the consignor delivers goods to a common carrier for shipment to the consignee, the consignor receives a receipt for the goods. This receipt is called a **bill of lading**. The bill of lading is not only a receipt, but also a document of title and the shipping agreement between the consignor and the carrier.

Duties of a Common Carrier

A common carrier of people (passengers) has a duty to (1) accept anyone who applies for transportation, (2) provide reasonable accommodations, and (3) provide reasonable protection for its passengers.

A common carrier of goods has a duty to (1) accept and transport the lawful goods of all persons who request shipment, (2) provide adequate facilities for transporting goods and for storing goods awaiting shipment or delivery, (3) follow the consignor's shipping instructions, and (4) deliver goods to the consignee at the time and place agreed upon.

Liabilities of a Common Carrier

A common carrier is not, of course, an insurer of the safety of passengers, but it must exercise a high degree of care to protect them. A common carrier can, however, be held liable for injuries to passengers caused by the negligence of its employees. If the injuries were caused by the negligence of the passenger or by incidents beyond the carrier's control, the carrier is relieved of liability.

> You were a passenger on a bus. As you were getting off the bus, it began to move; you fell and were injured. You can collect damages for your injuries because the driver was negligent in moving the bus while a passenger was still getting off.

Unless one of the exceptions described earlier applies, a common carrier of goods is absolutely liable as a special bailee for any loss or damage to the goods after the goods are delivered to the carrier and during shipment. In most states, a common carrier may limit its absolute liability by contract with the consignor. Sometimes a carrier can limit its liability for damages caused by its own negligence, but the carrier cannot absolve itself from all liability.

A common carrier often limits its liability to a specific amount. To take advantage of this lowered liability, however, the carrier must give the consignor further consideration, usually in the form of lower shipping rates. The consignor must also have the option of shipping goods at the higher rate to receive higher limits of liability.

In some states, a common carrier can limit its liability for losses that arise from such hazards as fire, breakage, spoilage, or the actions of rioters, mobs, and thieves.

A common carrier is liable for losses or damages caused by its failure to deliver the goods within a reasonable time. The consignor, however, must bear the loss if the delay is one that would normally occur in shipping goods.

> Berry's Fruit Farm shipped 2,000 pounds of apples by ship rather than by truck or plane. The trip took two weeks because of delays due to rough seas, and the apples arrived in a spoiled condition. The farm has to bear the loss because the delay was one that could be expected when shipping fruit by sea.

A common carrier's liability begins when the goods are delivered by the shipper to the carrier. The carrier's liability ends when the goods reach their final destination and the consignee takes possession of the goods. In some states, the carrier's liability ends when the consignee fails to pick up the goods after receiving notice of their arrival and availability for examination. In other states, liability is held to end when the goods are removed from the railroad cars and delivered to a warehouse.

A common carrier's liability is often limited by law or treaty. Under the Warsaw Convention, for example, an airline's liability for loss of baggage carried on an international flight is limited to a specific amount. The notice shown in Figure 33.2 appears on most airline tickets.

FIGURE 33.2 Notice on Airline Ticket Limiting Liability

ADVICE TO INTERNATIONAL PASSENGERS ON LIMITATIONS OF LIABILITY

Passengers embarking on a journey involving an ultimate destination or a stop in a country other than the country of departure are advised that a treaty known as the Warsaw Convention may apply to the entire journey, including the portion thereof entirely within the countries of departure and destination. For such passengers, the Warsaw Convention, as amended, the Intercarrier Agreements, and special contracts of carriage embodied in applicable tariffs govern and may limit the liability of the carrier for death of or injury to passengers.

Additional protection can usually be obtained by purchasing insurance from a private company. Such insurance is not affected by any limitation of the carrier's liability under the Warsaw Convention. For further information, please consult your airline or insurance company representative.
The names of carriers party to such special contracts are available at all ticket offices of such carriers and may be examined upon request.

NOTICE: BAGGAGE LIABILITY LIMITATIONS

Liability for loss, delay or damage to checked baggage is limited as follows unless a higher value is declared in advance and additional charges are paid: (1) for travel wholly between U.S. points, to $2,500 per passenger (unless a higher amount is established by the Department of Transportation); (2) for most international travel (including domestic portions of international journeys), to $9.07 per pound ($20 per kilo) for checked baggage and $400 per passenger for unchecked baggage in the

custody/control of the carrier. For international travel, the weight of each piece of checked baggage will establish the carrier liability limit; maximum liability, unless excess weight is noted and additional charges paid, is limited to carrier free weight allowance. Excess valuation may not be declared on certain types of articles. Carrier assumes no liability for certain valuable, fragile, or perishable articles. Further information may be obtained from the carrier.

Rights of a Common Carrier

Common carriers are required to accept anyone who asks for service and can pay for that service. There are, however, exceptions to this requirement. A common carrier has the right to refuse service to passengers (1) if space is unavailable or (2) who might endanger other passengers (e.g., an intoxicated person or one with a contagious disease).

A common carrier of goods has the right to refuse service if it is not equipped or does not have adequate facilities for transporting the particular goods. For instance, if a carrier does not have refrigerated trucks, it may refuse to transport goods that require refrigeration.

A common carrier also has the right to make reasonable rules by which it conducts its business. It may charge reasonable rates for its services and may collect those rates in advance. Because many common carriers are monopolies, rates are often regulated by the Interstate Commerce Commission or by other state and local government agencies.

demurrage fee charged for unreasonably delaying equipment of a common carrier

If a common carrier's equipment is delayed for an unreasonable period of time by the consignee or the consignor, the carrier may make a special charge known as **demurrage**. For example, demurrage may be charged if a consignor is late in loading goods or if the consignee fails to remove goods within a reasonable time.

A common carrier has a right to be paid for its services. It therefore has a lien on goods it transports as security for payment of its charges. If the charges are not paid, the common carrier can enforce the lien by selling the goods after a specific period of time.

Summary

A special or extraordinary standard of care is imposed on certain bailees because of historical reasons. This special standard has been imposed primarily on hotel-keepers and common carriers. The standard of care is that of absolute liability for goods left in the possession of the bailee.

Today, the absolute liability of these bailees has been limited by law and by agreement. The exceptions to absolute liability of special bailees are (1) an agreement between the parties that is reasonable, (2) an act of God that causes the damage, (3) an act of a public enemy that causes the damage, (4) an act of a public authority that causes the damage, (5) fault on the part of the bailor, and (6) damage that occurs because of the basic nature of the goods bailed.

Hotelkeepers, defined as those who rent rooms to the public on a temporary basis, are special bailees upon whom an extraordinary degree of care is imposed. Today, however, the liability of hotelkeepers is limited by the exceptions described. In most states, hotelkeepers may also limit their liability by posting notices to this effect or providing safe-deposit boxes for their guests.

There are many types of carriers, including private and contract carriers. An extraordinary degree of care, however, is imposed only on a common carrier, a carrier that transports goods and people for anyone who wishes to hire it. This category includes airlines, railroads, trucking companies, and bus lines. Although a common carrier is not absolutely liable for injuries to passengers, it is absolutely liable for damage to goods being shipped with the carrier, unless one of the exceptions mentioned earlier applies. In most states, a common carrier may limit its liability to a certain amount unless the shipper pays a higher rate for the shipment.

A common carrier's liability begins when goods are delivered to it. Its liability ends either when the consignee takes possession or when the goods are removed from the carrier and delivered to a warehouse.

A common carrier has the right to refuse to service passengers who might present a special problem. It also has the right to refuse to transport goods if they are unsafe or if the carrier is not equipped to handle the goods involved.

Important Legal terms

act of God	common carrier	public enemy
bill of lading	contract carrier	special bailments
boardinghouse keeper	demurrage	transients
business guests	hotelkeeper	
carrier	private carrier	

Questions and Problems for Discussion

1. How is a bill of lading used?
2. Describe the difference in liability for losses of special bailees under common law and under modern statutes.
3. Why should a common carrier or hotel be held to a higher standard than an ordinary bailee?
4. Albert left his piano for repair at the Jones Piano Shop. A riot broke out on the street where Jones was located, and rioters broke into the shop and damaged the piano. Is Jones liable for the damage?
5. Adams rented a room in a university dormitory for the school year. His computer was stolen, and he sued the university for the loss. Is the university liable as a special bailee?
6. George, a guest in a motel, opened the window during the night because his room was very warm. A thief entered the room and stole his wallet, containing a lot of money. George sued the hotel, which raised the defense that the property was not in its possession and that the guest was primarily responsible for the loss. Can George recover his loss?
7. Frey shipped a valuable oil painting by rail to an exhibition. She did not disclose that the paint was very fragile and air conditioning was needed to protect the painting. Frey claimed that the railroad should be held responsible for the damage as a special bailee. Is she correct?
8. Grimm entered a train station to buy a ticket. On the way into the station, she tripped over a suitcase that had been left by a passenger and was injured severely. Grimm claimed that the railroad company was absolutely liable for her injuries. Is she correct?
9. The Amguard Company shipped two transformers by rail to an electric utility company. Along the way, hijackers stopped the train and stole the transformers. Is the railroad liable for the loss?
10. The Grand Moving Company was a common carrier engaged in the moving of household furniture. Alvarez asked the moving company to

transport two pianos to a neighboring city. Can the Grand Moving Company refuse to transport these pianos?

11. The Empire Ceramics Co. shipped a box of vases and dishes via the Sumoto Trucking Co. Some of the dishes were broken during transit. An examination of the box showed that the damage had been caused by improper packing. Is Sumoto Trucking Co. liable for the loss?

12. Rogers was notified by the hotel where she was a guest that valuables should be placed in the hotel safe. Rogers left a ring valued at $400 with the hotel clerk for safekeeping. That night, two robbers forced the clerk to open the safe, and the ring was stolen. Was the hotel liable to Rogers for the loss?

13. Cohen shipped merchandise on FXB Railroad. When Cohen didn't pay for the shipping charges after many requests to do so, FXB obtained a lien on Cohen's property and then sold it. May it do so?

14. Blake, a guest at the Sunshine Hotel, parked his car in the hotel's parking lot. The parking ticket he received stated, "This hotel is absolutely not liable for loss of, or damage to, any parked vehicle." The car was stolen and Blake claims the hotel must reimburse him for his loss. The hotel claims it is not liable regardless of who was at fault. Is this argument correct?

15. Blaine rented a room at a YMCA. His guitar was stolen from his room and Blaine claims the YMCA is liable as a special bailee. Is he correct?

Cases for Review

1. Nagashima was a guest at a Hyatt hotel and placed her jewelry in the hotel's safe-deposit box. Upon checking out of the hotel, she retrieved her jewelry from the box, and while at the checkout counter, her jewelry, valued at $72,000, was stolen. Hyatt claimed that its liability was limited to $500 based on notices posted in the hotel. Is Hyatt correct? (*Nagashima* v. *Hyatt Wilshire Corp.*, 228 Cal. App. 3d 1006)

2. Alteri, owner of a computer software business, shipped two packages containing computer equipment to a business in Illinois via Greyhound Lines. The equipment was valued at $8,000, but on the bills of lading, Alteri indicated the value at $1,100. Both packages were lost during shipment and were never recovered. What amount can Alteri recover from Greyhound? (*Alteri* v. *Greyhound Lines, Inc.*, 139 A.D.2d 878)

3. Mirski shipped thousands of boxes of cherries from Yakima, Washington, to Cincinnati, Ohio, over the Chesapeake and Ohio Railroad. The cherries were in good condition when they were delivered to the railroad, but they were spoiled when they arrived at their destination. There was no unusual delay while the cherries were being transported. Mirski sued the railroad for damages. Is the railroad liable? (*Mirski* v. *Chesapeake and Ohio Railroad Co.*, 31 Ill.2d 324, 202 N.E.2d 22)

4. A wholesale jewelry company employee registered at a hotel and entered his room. He was carrying $1 million worth of diamonds. Immediately upon entering, he was accosted by two men who assaulted him and robbed him of the diamonds. The hotel had a typical notice, which was posted on the inside of the bathroom door, limiting the hotel's liability unless valuables were placed in the hotel safe. The jewelry company sued the hotel for the loss of the diamonds and the injuries to its employee. The hotel's defense was its compliance with the law requiring the posting of a notice limiting liability. Who has the better argument? (*H.K. Mallak, Inc.* v. *Fairfield FMC Corp*, 209 F.2d 960)

5. Downstate Medical Center hired Purolator Courier to transport a computer valued at $4,509 from the hospital to a store in Manhattan. The bill of lading stated that the carrier was not liable for more than $250 for loss or nondelivery. There was proof that the carrier was grossly negligent, and the hospital claimed that the limitation of liability was invalid. Was this claim correct? (*Downstate Medical Center* v. *Purolator Courier Corp.*, N.Y. 138 Misc.2d 714)

6. While Mrs. Voorhis was buying a train ticket, her niece took Mrs. Voorhis's suitcase, containing $34,000 worth of jewelry, to the track from which the train was to depart. She asked a train usher if he would watch the suitcase while she helped her

aunt. The usher agreed and the niece left the suitcase with him. When she returned a few minutes later, the suitcase was gone. The usher claimed he did watch the suitcase but was called away, and when he returned, the suitcase was gone. Mrs. Voorhis sued the railroad, which defended the case on the grounds that the usher was a gratuitous bailee and the railroad could be held liable if there was gross negligence, of which there was no proof. Was this defense correct? (*Voorhis* v. *Consolidated Rail Corp.*, N.Y. 92 A.D.2d 501)

7. Mr. and Mrs. Penchas checked out of a hotel and were proceeding to enter a taxi parked in the hotel's U-shaped driveway in front of the hotel when a tote bag belonging to Mrs. Penchas that contained valuable jewelry was stolen from the backseat of the taxi. The hotel claimed that under no circumstances could it be held liable unless the theft had taken place within the confines of the hotel. Is this defense a good one? (*Penchas* v. *Hilton Hotels Corp.*, N.Y. 155 Misc.2d 867)

8. Marriott shipped canned goods from Kansas to Maryland on the Norfolk & Western Railroad. A severe rainstorm occurred and five inches of rain fell in four hours, something that had not happened in twenty years. The train derailed when a creek overflowed and washed out the road bed. Marriott sued for the loss of the canned goods. The railroad's defense was that the accident resulted from an act of God and thus the railroad was not responsible. Was the railroad correct? (*Marriott Corporation* v. *Norfolk & Western RR Co.*, 319 Fsupp 646)

9. The Ambassador Athletic Club was a nonprofit social club, organized to promote sports and recreational activities. It rented out a limited number of rooms to members and their guests for a fee. The state of Utah tried to collect sales tax from the club for the rental of hotel rooms. Would the club be considered a hotel? (*Ambassador Athletic Club* v. *Utah State Tax Commission*, 496 P2d 883, 27 Utah 2d 372)

10. Covington was injured when an ambulance in which she was a passenger collided with another car. The ambulance driver was speeding and had gone through a stop sign. Covington sued for damages. The ambulance's insurance company said that the ambulance was not a common carrier and was liable only for ordinary negligence. Was the insurance company correct? (*Home Insurance Co.* v. *Covington*, Arkansas 501 SW2d 219)

CHAPTER 34

Wills, Intestacy, and Estate Planning

CHAPTER PREVIEW

The Purpose of a Will

Requirements of a Valid Will
Testamentary Capacity
Freedom from Duress, Fraud, and Undue Influence
Written Form
Witnesses

Special Wills
Holographic Wills
Nuncupative Wills

Limitations on Disposing of Property by Will

Making a Will

Changing or Revoking a Will

Administering a Will
Probating the Will
Administering the Estate
Settling the Estate

Intestacy

Living Wills and Health Care Proxies

The Need for Estate Planning

Taxes and Estate Planning
Gifts
The Marital Deduction
Trusts

Developing an Estate Plan

Chapter Highlights

This chapter deals with the two ways in which property is distributed after death: by will or, if there is no will—a condition known as intestacy—by state law. A will provides for the distribution of property according to the wishes of the person making the will. Certain requirements must be met before a will may be declared valid. Certain limitations also apply to the disposition of property by will. The chapter discusses these requirements and limitations. Once executed, a will may be changed or revoked only if certain formalities are followed. The chapter discusses the steps involved in administering an estate when there is no will. In such a case, the law of the state in which the decedent resided determines how the estate will be distributed and who has the power to administer the estate. Hence, this chapter also discusses the need for estate planning and how to accomplish it. Estate planning has a threefold purpose: providing for the proper distribution of assets, providing for retirement, and minimizing estate taxes. The chapter discusses various means available to minimize estate taxes, including gifts, use of the marital deduction, and trusts. At the conclusion of the chapter, the various steps involved in achieving a successful estate plan are examined.

THE PURPOSE OF A WILL

will document disposing of one's property after death

testator/testatrix one who disposes of property by will

A **will** is a legal document directing how real and personal property should be distributed after the death of the person making the will, known as a **testator**. (Often, the term **testatrix** is used in the case of a woman.) There are many reasons it is important to have a will. A will enables a person to distribute his or her property as desired. The

551

manner in which a person's property is distributed depends on whether the decedent died with or without a will. A person who dies and leaves a valid will is said to have died **testate**. His or her property will be distributed according to the provisions of the will. If a person dies without a will, that person is said to have died **intestate**. In this case, the person's estate is distributed according to the laws of the state in which the person resided, regardless of that person's wishes.

Estate refers to the interest that a person has in property, both real and personal. A will may eliminate a struggle over the question of who is to benefit from your estate and

testate leaving a will upon one's death

intestate one who dies without a will

estate person's interest in property

FIGURE 34.1 A Simple Will

LAST WILL AND TESTAMENT
OF
SAMUEL WARREN

I, SAMUEL WARREN, of the City of Bridgeport, County of Fairfield, and State of Connecticut, declare this to be my Last Will and Testament, and I hereby revoke all prior wills and codicils.

First: I devise to my wife, SHARON, the residence at 2 Elm Street, Bridgeport, Connecticut.

Second: I bequeath $5000.00 to each of my children.

Third: I give all the rest of my estate to my wife, SHARON.

Fourth: I appoint my wife, SHARON, as Executrix of my Will and my son, JOHN, as successor executor, with full power and authority to sell and convey, and lease or mortgage, real estate.

IN WITNESS WHEREOF, I have subscribed my name this 8th day of January, 2009.

Samuel Warren
SAMUEL WARREN

The foregoing instrument was signed, published, and declared by SAMUEL WARREN to be his Last Will and Testament in our presence, and we at his request and in his presence and in the presence of each other, have subscribed our names as witnesses the day and year indicated above.

Sanford Byrnes   residing at   32 Maple Street
SANFORD BYRNES   Bridgeport, Connecticut

Sandra Kent   residing at   91 Mission Avenue
SANDRA KENT   Bridgeport, Connecticut

Robert Mason   residing at   1201 Ames Avenue
ROBERT MASON   Bridgeport, Connecticut

who is to administer it. A will may also save on estate taxes and legal costs. A will allows you to name a guardian for minor children. If you don't have a will, the court will appoint a guardian who may or may not be the person you would have chosen. An example of a simple will is shown in Figure 34.1.

residuary gift gift by will of one's entire estate to one or more persons

devise gift of real property in a will

legacy gift of personal property in a will

The most important part of a will is the section disposing of the property of the maker. There are many different ways of disposing of property by will. The maker's entire estate can be left outright to one or more persons. This gift is known as a **residuary gift**. "I give all my property to my children in equal shares" is an example of a residuary gift. A gift of specific real property is known as a **devise**. "I give my house at 243 Elm Street to my sister" is an example of a devise. A person who inherits property according to the terms of a will is called a *beneficiary*.

A gift of personal property is known as a **legacy**, or a bequest. A *specific legacy* is a gift of specific property that is easily identifiable. "I bequeath my piano to my brother" is an example of a specific legacy. A *general legacy* is a gift of any property of a general nature. "I bequeath $5,000 to my husband" is an example of a general legacy.

lapse gift to a beneficiary that is deemed ineffective because the beneficiary has died before the testator/testatrix

What happens if a beneficiary in a will dies before the testator/testatrix? The gift to that person will be deemed ineffective, known as a **lapse**, unless the beneficiary was a certain kind of relative of the testator/testatrix, such as a child, grandchild, sister, or brother, and provided that the beneficiary died leaving a descendant.

> Blass died, leaving a will naming his brother Adam and sister Alice as beneficiaries. Alice, however, died a month before Blass, leaving her husband and three children. Alice's children will share whatever amount Alice would have received had she survived Blass.

per stirpes distribution of an estate so that each beneficiary receives the share his or her ancestor would have received had that ancestor survived the testator/testatrix

per capita distribution of an estate so that each beneficiary receives an equal share

If a beneficiary or beneficiaries die before the testator/testatrix, the estate can be distributed among the surviving beneficiaries in either of two ways: through per stirpes distribution or through per capita distribution. **Per stirpes** means that the estate will be distributed to beneficiaries so that they take the share that their ancestor would have received had that ancestor survived the testator. In the example, Blass's brother Adam survived, and he is entitled to one-half of Blass's estate. Had Alice survived, she would have received the other half; instead, her children will share her one-half share, each receiving one-third of Alice's distribution.

In a **per capita** distribution, each beneficiary receives an equal share. In the example, Adam and each of Alice's children would receive one-fourth of Blass's estate. The manner of distribution applied in such cases depends on the language of the will and/or the court's determination of the intent of the person who executed the will and/or state law.

REQUIREMENTS OF A VALID WILL

Each state has its own laws describing the requirements of a valid will. In most states, these requirements refer to testamentary capacity; freedom from duress, fraud, and undue influence; writing; and witnesses.

Testamentary Capacity

testamentary capacity physical and mental condition and age of a person making a will

Testamentary capacity refers to the physical and mental condition and age of a person making a will. To make a valid will, a person must be of sound mind, of proper age (usually at least eighteen or twenty-one, with the exceptions of Georgia and Louisiana, where the age is lower), and in fair physical condition. At the time of making a will, a person must be capable of understanding the consequences of making the will—that is, what is being disposed of and to whom. Any evidence of mental incapacity or a physical condition that prevents the maker from understanding the effects of the will may invalidate it.

While in the hospital recovering from a serious operation, Blair decided to make a will. Blair was taking medication that caused drowsiness and made it difficult for her to concentrate. A court may not uphold the will because of Blair's physical and mental state at the time she made the will.

Freedom from Duress, Fraud, and Undue Influence

To make a valid will, a person must be free from outside influences, such as threats or pressure to leave property to a certain person. If a person is defrauded into making a will benefiting another person, the will may be invalidated.

Roderick pretended to be the son of Daniels, who had been separated from her real son when he was born. Roderick convinced Daniels that he was her real son and persuaded her to make a will leaving him all her property. The will may be declared invalid because of Roderick's fraud.

Written Form

A valid will must normally be in writing. An exception to this requirement is a nuncupative will, discussed later in the chapter. A will may be handwritten, typed, or printed, or any combination of the three. There are no special requirements regarding language, type, or size or type of paper. If handwritten, the will may be written with either pencil or pen.

The will must be signed by the maker. Most states require the maker's signature at the end of the document. It is also wise, but not required, for the maker to initial each page of the will. A person who is incapable of signing a will may "sign" it with an "X" and have the "X" witnessed, or the person may have someone sign the maker's name in the maker's presence and at the maker's direction and have that signature witnessed.

Calvin lost both her arms in an industrial accident. She made a will and asked her friend Farris to sign the will for her. Farris signed in Calvin's presence, and the signing was witnessed by others. This will is as valid as if Calvin had signed it.

Witnesses

In most states, a will must be signed in the presence of either two or three witnesses depending on the state. In some states, witnesses must sign their names to the will in the presence of the maker and in the presence of each other. Other states have different requirements. It is best for a person making a will to determine the requirements in her or his state.

Generally, a person making a will should execute it with the greatest degree of formality possible. This requirement means signing a will in the presence of the proper number of witnesses, telling them that the document is a will, and asking the witnesses to sign in the maker's presence and in each other's presence. The witnesses need not read the will or be familiar with its contents. A clause stating that the witnesses observed the signing of the will and were asked to witness it is usually included in the will. This clause is known as an **attestation**. An attestation is included in the will in Figure 34.1.

There are usually no specific requirements for witnesses. They need not be adults, but they should understand their role and what they are signing. Of greatest importance is that those who are beneficiaries under a will should not also act as witnesses. In most

attestation clause in a will stating the witnesses observed the signing of the will states, a witness who is also a beneficiary will not be allowed to share in the estate. Most states, however, allow a witness who would have received a portion of the deceased's estate if there had been no will to receive her or his share of the estate.

> Meade made a will in which he left $5,000 to his brother. The law in Meade's state required three witnesses, so he had two of his friends and his brother sign the will as witnesses. The will is valid, but Meade's brother would be disqualified from receiving the $5,000. He would, however, share in any part of Meade's estate that he would have been entitled to if Meade had not made a will.

SPECIAL WILLS

Special situations often arise that make it necessary to do away with the ordinary formalities involved in making a will. Many states recognize the validity of special wills, such as holographic wills, nuncupative wills, and wills of persons on active duty in the armed forces.

Holographic Wills

holographic will will handwritten and signed by the maker

A **holographic will** is a will written completely in the maker's handwriting and then signed and dated. It need not be witnessed because the handwriting is considered sufficient evidence of who signed the document. Although the majority of states do not recognize holographic wills, there are several states that will enforce them.

Nuncupative Wills

nuncupative will an oral will

A **nuncupative will** is an oral will. In those states in which it is permitted, it is valid only if made during the maker's final illness and in the presence of witnesses. It is usually valid only to dispose of personal property of a limited value. After the death of the maker, a nuncupative will must be put in writing and signed by the witnesses to whom it was orally made.

> Ryan became ill one day and, in the presence of her family, told them that she wanted a particular friend to have her house when she died. This act does not qualify as a nuncupative will because it disposes of real property and it was not made during a final illness.

One type of special will is that made by a person on active duty in the armed forces. It may be oral or written. If written, it need not be witnessed; if oral, it usually must be witnessed. It may be drawn and executed informally and is usually valid to dispose of personal property only. Once made, the will of a member of the armed forces is usually valid until it is revoked. The will is valid even when the tour of military service is finished.

LIMITATIONS ON DISPOSING OF PROPERTY BY WILL

Most people believe they have absolute freedom to dispose of their property by will. They do have broad powers, but most states limit these powers. A surviving wife or husband has a right to receive a certain portion of the estate of the deceased spouse. This right may not be defeated by will. If a surviving spouse does not receive by will at least as much as he or she would have received had there been no will, the surviving spouse may choose to disregard the will completely and take the portion he or she would be entitled to under state law. This limitation applies to the surviving spouse only. A person who disposes of property by will is not required to leave property, even a token amount, to any other family member.

> Clemens made a will and left his entire estate to his spouse. Clemens made no provisions for his children and did not even mention them in the will. Clemens's will is valid and his children are not entitled to receive anything from his estate.

A person may not dispose of property in a manner that is contrary to public policy. The state will not enforce a provision in a will that violates certain accepted policies and practices. For example, a provision requiring a beneficiary to remain single to qualify for a legacy would not be enforced. A legacy to an organization for the purpose of overthrowing the government would likewise be invalid. Most states also limit the amount that may be given in a will to charitable organizations.

> Baker executed a will leaving his entire estate to his daughter on the condition that she never marry. Such a provision would not be upheld because it is against public policy.

What happens if a person makes a bequest to a charitable or educational organization and the bequest cannot be carried out either because it is illegal or because the organization no longer exists? In such cases, the courts will often apply a doctrine known as *cy pres*, which means "as nearly as," and will choose another organization or purpose that comes close to what the donor wanted.

> Alden left a bequest in his will to the Siamese Cat Foundation. At his death, the foundation no longer existed. Applying the *cy pres* doctrine, a court would probably direct that the bequest go to an animal humane society or similar organization.

One of the most important limitations is that a will may dispose only of property that is solely in the name of the maker. For example, property held jointly cannot be disposed of by will. On the death of one party the property automatically belongs to the other. The same may be true of life insurance proceeds payable to a beneficiary. Pension benefits payable to a beneficiary are also unaffected by the provisions of a will.

Finally, certain obligations must be paid upon the death of a person. These obligations cannot be avoided through a will. Debts, estate taxes, funeral expenses, and certain costs relating to the administration of the estate must be paid before beneficiaries get anything under the terms of the will.

MAKING A WILL

The making of a will generally should not be a do-it-yourself project. A will does not have to be drawn by an attorney to be valid. The laws relating to wills are quite complex, however, and most people should consult an attorney to be sure they are executing a valid will.

The first step in making a will is to tell your attorney any information needed to draw up the will. The attorney will need information on your family (e.g., the names and ages of family members), Social Security information, a list of any assets and their value, and a list of any liabilities (debts, mortgages, loans, etc.). Information about your insurance and job benefits is also important.

The next step in making a will is to establish your goals. If you have children or other family members you want to take care of, what do you want them to receive and when? Will they be capable of handling money? Are there charities or schools to which you wish to make a gift? Whom do you wish to handle your assets? The answers to these questions should be reached after much thought and consultation with your attorney.

Once your goals have been established, your attorney will determine how they will affect your estate taxes. Often, a slight change in the way a will is drawn may produce great tax savings.

The next step in drawing a will is to name an executor (male) or executrix (female). An **executor/executrix** (called the personal representative in some states) is the person who will administer the estate after the death of the person making the will. The executor's function is to validate the will; gather and inventory the assets; pay all debts, expenses, and estate taxes; and distribute the balance among the beneficiaries.

An executor may be a spouse, child, parent, relative, friend, attorney, or a bank. The executor should be a person who knows the maker's family situation and is competent to handle finances. It is wise to appoint an alternate executor in case the person appointed cannot or will not serve as executor. It is also important to give an executor sufficient powers to be able to deal with the estate in a flexible manner. Such powers would include the power to sell property and the power to lease a home.

The final step in making a will is to sign the will and have it properly witnessed. The will should be kept in a safe place, such as an attorney's office or the office of the court. In addition, the maker should keep a copy of the will.

executor/executrix one who administers the estate of a testator/ testatrix

CHANGING OR REVOKING A WILL

A will doesn't become effective until the person making it dies. As a result, many people make new wills or make changes in their existing wills several times during their lives. It is a good idea to review your will periodically and change it when necessary. You may want to change your will because of a change in the tax laws, because of a change in your family situation, or because of a change in your assets or liabilities. There are five ways to change a will: by amendment, by destruction, by drawing a new one, by change of circumstances, and by operation of law.

An amendment to a will that changes one or more of its provisions is known as a **codicil**. A codicil may be either added to the will it changes or drawn on a separate piece of paper. A codicil is used when minor changes are needed. In almost all states, a codicil must be prepared with the same formalities as the will that it changes.

codicil addition or amendment to a will

> In his will, Alger named a brother as executor. Later he changed his mind and added a codicil that named his sister as executrix in place of his brother.

Destroying or mutilating a will revokes it, provided it is done by the maker of the will. This revocation is usually done when a new will is drawn so that there can be no doubt as to which will is effective. In most states, destroying a later will makes a prior will effective.

A new will ordinarily revokes a prior one and is preferred when many changes are being made. While not required, it is best to state in a new will that it revokes any prior wills and codicils.

A will may automatically be changed by a change in circumstances. If the maker disposes of property that is named in the will and that property does not exist at the maker's death, the will provision becomes ineffective.

> You provided in your will that your children were to have your boat upon your death. If you sell the boat, that provision becomes as void as if you had changed your will and omitted the provision.

A will may automatically be changed by state law as a result of children born after the will was executed or of marriage or divorce. A bequest to children includes all children born after the will was executed, it being presumed that the testator/testatrix would have intended to provide for such children but simply failed to do so. In general, marriage after a will is executed changes the will because under state law, a spouse is entitled to a certain share of the estate. A bequest to a spouse is usually unenforceable if a divorce occurs after the will is executed.

ADMINISTERING A WILL

There are three steps in handling a person's estate: probating the will, administering the estate, and settling the estate.

Probating the Will

probate process of validating a will

Probate is the process of proving or establishing a will's validity. The first step is to determine whether or not the deceased made a will and to locate it. The executor/executrix, usually with an attorney's guidance, then files a petition with a court to declare the will valid and operative. The court is usually called a surrogate's court, probate court, or orphan's court. The petition contains information about the will and the testator/testatrix. The petition is submitted with the will, together with affidavits of witnesses to the will stating that they witnessed it. In some states, the witnesses must appear in court and testify that they witnessed the signing. Probate procedures vary from state to state. Eleven states have adopted the Uniform Probate Code, a step toward uniformity throughout the United States in processing wills.

Notice of a hearing is sent to anyone who might have an interest in the will, such as persons who might have inherited property had there been no will. In some states, notice that a will has been offered for probate is published in an official newspaper. After a hearing, the court declares the will valid, and the executor/executrix named in the will receives official permission to act. The will is then said to have been probated. If a will is declared invalid, the state determines how the person's estate will be distributed. The rules governing distribution by a state are discussed later in the chapter.

Administering the Estate

After probate, the estate of the deceased is administered. The assets of the deceased must be located, identified, and then valued. If necessary, an expert may be hired to value the deceased's land, personal belongings, and so forth. Notice is given to insurance companies and the Social Security Administration that the person has died so that benefits may be determined. Debts of the deceased are also determined and paid.

After assets, debts, and estate expenses have been determined, estate tax returns are prepared and filed. If the assets of the estate exceed a certain value, a federal estate tax return must be filed. Some states also require a state estate tax return.

abated bequest bequest that is decreased according to formulas established by state law

Distribution pursuant to a will may at times involve problems even though the will provisions are clear and valid. For example, after estate debts and taxes are paid, there may be insufficient funds to pay all bequests in full. Such cases result in **abated bequests**; that is, the bequests are decreased according to formulas established by state law.

adeemed bequest bequest canceled because the specific item has been sold or given away prior to death

Suppose a will contains a bequest of a specific item, such as an automobile, but the item is sold or given away prior to death. In this event, the bequest is considered an **adeemed bequest**; that is, it is canceled.

antilapse laws laws providing for distribution of bequests when a beneficiary has predeceased the testator

Suppose a beneficiary named in a will predeceases the testator, and there is no provision in the will for an alternate gift. **Antilapse laws** in most states provide that the bequest to the deceased beneficiary does not lapse; the children or heirs of the deceased beneficiary take the bequest to which their deceased ancestor was entitled. State laws differ on how close a relationship must have existed between the deceased beneficiary and the heirs for the antilapse provisions to apply.

Settling the Estate

settlement distribution of estate after all debts, taxes, and expenses have been paid; also when parties to a lawsuit resolve their differences without having a trial

The final step in administering an estate is called **settlement**. After all assets have been collected, debts paid, and taxes determined and paid, the executor/executrix distributes the remaining assets according to the instructions in the will. In addition, the executor's commissions, expenses, and legal fees are paid by the estate. When these steps have been completed, the estate is considered settled.

Under some circumstances, an estate can be settled without court supervision. In such cases, the estate property is distributed and the beneficiaries file receipts for their gifts. In other cases, a court must approve of and direct the settlement.

INTESTACY

The property of a person who dies intestate (without a will) is distributed according to the laws of the state in which the person lived.

The estate of a person who dies intestate is handled in almost the same way as the estate of a person who dies with a will. One difference is that the person who manages the estate is called an **administrator** (male), or personal representative, or **administratrix** (female) rather than an executor/executrix. A second difference is that the administrator is appointed by the court rather than by will. Typically, the closest relative of the deceased petitions the court to be appointed as administrator. Notice of this appointment is sent to other persons who are entitled to share in the estate.

administrator/ administratrix one who manages the estate of an intestate

heir one who inherits property according to his or her relationship to deceased

Property of a person who dies intestate is distributed to the person's heirs according to state law. **Heirs** are persons related by blood or marriage to the deceased who share in the estate of a person who died intestate. The laws of each state differ as to who are heirs and what amount each is to receive. The closer the relationship of the heir to the deceased, the greater the share that the heir receives. In most states, if the intestate leaves a spouse and no children, the spouse receives everything. If the deceased leaves children and no spouse, the children receive everything. If the deceased leaves both a spouse and children, the spouse usually receives one-third of the estate and the children share the remaining two-thirds. The definition of *children* in intestacy laws usually includes adopted children. State laws vary considerably in cases in which an intestate dies without spouse or children. A typical pattern of distribution is shown in Figure 34.2.

If a person dies intestate and no living relatives (related by blood) can be found, the estate becomes the property of the state.

LIVING WILLS AND HEALTH CARE PROXIES

Until recently, health care decisions for a person unable to make such decisions for himself or herself were made by a physician or the patient's family. This situation raised many legal, medical, religious, and ethical issues.

To solve this problem, some states have enacted legislation (or some state courts have produced decisions) to ensure that a person's preferences regarding medical care would be followed in the event that the person lacked the capacity to make such decisions at the time required.

Many states now recognize two simple procedures to facilitate health care decisions: (1) the living will (Figure 34.3) and (2) the health care proxy (Figure 34.4).

FIGURE 34.2 Distribution of the Estate of an Intestate

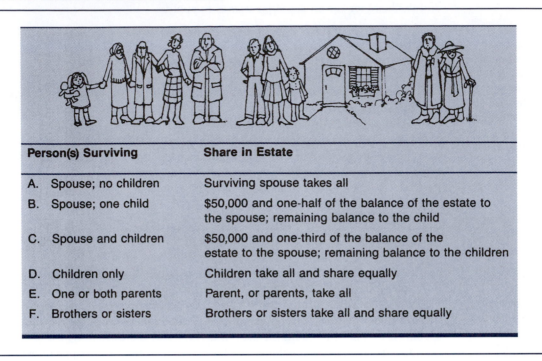

Person(s) Surviving	Share in Estate
A. Spouse; no children	Surviving spouse takes all
B. Spouse; one child	$50,000 and one-half of the balance of the estate to the spouse; remaining balance to the child
C. Spouse and children	$50,000 and one-third of the balance of the estate to the spouse; remaining balance to the children
D. Children only	Children take all and share equally
E. One or both parents	Parent, or parents, take all
F. Brothers or sisters	Brothers or sisters take all and share equally

living will document expressing one's health care preferences

A **living will** is a document that expresses a person's preferences regarding health care if the signer lacks the capacity to make such decisions when the need arises. Its terms may be very general or may describe specific treatments that the signer may or may not want. In those states that recognize such wills, the preferences expressed will be followed. In other states, the preferences may or may not be followed depending on many circumstances.

health care proxy power of attorney giving a designated person the authority to make health care decisions

A **health care proxy** is a durable power of attorney (i.e., it remains valid despite the incompetency of the signer) by which a principal appoints an agent (the proxy) to make health care decisions for the principal in the event that the principal lacks the capacity to make such decisions. The power of attorney may be very general or may give the agent specific instructions regarding the types of treatment to be given or withheld. A typical state law authorizing health care proxies is New York Public Health Law, Sections 2980–2994. Some of its important provisions are as follows.

1. Any competent adult may appoint a health care proxy. A competent adult includes a person over eighteen or a person who is married or has a child, regardless of age.
2. The document appointing the proxy must be signed in the presence of two witnesses; it need not be notarized.
3. There are certain limitations on who can act as an agent.
4. The proxy is activated only when the principal is deemed incapable of making health care decisions.
5. The principal's attending physician determines whether or not incapability exists. In certain circumstances, the attending physician must consult with another doctor before a decision to withhold or remove life-sustaining treatment is made, and both doctors must then agree on the final decision.

FIGURE 34.3 A Living Will

Living Will

INSTRUCTIONS:

This is an important legal document. It sets forth your directions regarding medical treatment. You have the right to refuse treatment you do not want, and you may request the care you do want. You may make changes in any of these directions, or add to them, to conform them to your personal wishes.

I, SARA ALLEN, being of sound mind, make this statement as a directive to be followed if I become permanently unable to participate in decisions regarding my medical care. These instructions reflect my firm and settled commitment to decline medical treatment under the circumstances indicated below:

I direct my attending physician to withhold or withdraw treatment that serves only to prolong the process of my dying, if I should be in an incurable or irreversible mental or physical condition with no reasonable expectation of recovery.

These instructions apply if I am a) in a terminal condition; b) permanently unconscious; or c) if I am conscious but have irreversible brain damage and will never regain the ability to make decisions and express my wishes.

I direct that treatment be limited to measures to keep me comfortable and to relieve pain, including any pain that might occur by withholding or withdrawing treatment.

While I understand that I am not legally required to be specific about future treatments, if I am in the condition(s) described above I feel especially strongly about the following forms of treatment:

I do not want cardiac resuscitation.
I do not want mechanical respiration.
I do not want tube feeding.
I do not want antibiotics.

I do want maximum pain relief.

Other directions (insert personal instructions): ______

______

______

These directions express my legal right to refuse treatment, under the law of New York. I intend my instructions to be carried out, unless I have rescinded them in a new writing or by clearly indicating that I have changed my mind.

Sign and date here in the presence of two adult witnesses, who should also sign.

Signed: Sara Allen Date: July 22, 2009

Witness: John Crowley

Address: 34 Market Street
Albany, New York

Witness: Kathleen Thompson

Address: 36 Market Street
Albany, New York

Keep the signed original with your personal papers at home. Give copies of the signed original to your doctor, family, lawyer, and others who might be involved in your care.

FIGURE 34.4 A Health Care Proxy

Health Care Proxy

(1) I, _____**JOHN GREEN**_____

hereby appoint _____**SALLY GREEN, 152 Adams Street, Adams, Oklahoma**_____
444-839-4223   (name, home address, and telephone number)

as my health care agent to make any and all health care decisions for me, except to the extent that I state otherwise. This proxy shall take effect when and if I become unable to make my own health care decisions.

(2) Optional instructions: I direct my proxy to make health care decisions in accord with my wishes and limitations as stated below, or as he or she otherwise knows. (Attach additional pages if necessary).

_____

_____

(Unless your agent knows your wishes about artificial nutrition and hydration [feeding tubes], your agent will not be allowed to make decisions about artificial nutrition and hydration. See the preceding instructions for samples of language you could use.)

(3) Name of substitute or fill-in proxy if the person I appoint above is unable, unwilling, or unavailable to act as my health care agent.

_____
(name, home address, and telephone number)

(4) Unless I revoke it, this proxy shall remain in effect indefinitely, or until the date or condition stated below. This proxy shall expire (specific date or conditions, if desired):

_____

(5) Signature *John Green*_____

Address _____**152 Adams Street, Adams, Oklahoma**_____

Date _____**July 19, 2009**_____

Statement by Witnesses (must be 18 or older)

I declare that the person who signed this document is personally known to me and appears to be of sound mind and acting of his or her own free will. He or she signed (or asked another to sign for him or her) this document in my presence.

Witness 1 *Tammy Beckett*_____

Address _____**154 Adams Street, Adams, Oklahoma**_____

Witness 2 *Felicia Navidad*_____

Address _____**156 Adams Street, Adams, Oklahoma**_____

6. The attending doctor must notify the principal, the principal's guardian (if one has been appointed), and the agent that the principal has been determined to be incapable of making health care decisions.

7. A health care proxy may be revoked orally, by written document, or by execution of another proxy.

The main difference between a living will and a health care proxy is the person designated to make health care decisions if the maker of the document is unable to do so. With a living will, it is essentially the doctor who makes those decisions. With a health care proxy, a designated person—usually a relative or friend—does so.

The Need for Estate Planning

estate plan plan to protect and dispose of one's assets

Almost every person acquires assets during her or his lifetime. Most people need a plan to dispose of these assets in the most advantageous way. An **estate plan** is a program designed to protect your assets and your family by properly disposing of those assets during your lifetime and after your death.

There is no set dollar amount to measure whether an estate plan is needed. In fact, small estates often present more problems than larger ones. It would be safe to say that almost everyone needs an estate plan.

Many people have no estate or a very small one. An estate may be created by the purchase of insurance or by setting up a business pension fund. With proper estate planning, a relatively large estate may be set up easily and at a modest cost.

> After working for a few years, Fazio purchased an insurance policy with a face value of $100,000. After the policy was issued and Fazio had paid the first premium, she immediately had an estate of $100,000.

It often takes a long time and a lot of hard work to acquire assets. It is important to make sure that your assets are distributed to the right people and in the way you choose. Proper estate planning will accomplish these things.

Estate planning involves many lifetime goals, one of which is providing for retirement. Whether a person is employed or self-employed, the need to plan for retirement is very important. As early retirement in corporations becomes more common and as the average life span increases, the need to plan becomes more significant, particularly because of the current trend to shift the responsibility for retirement planning from the employer to the employee.

The cost of disposing of the assets you have acquired can be high. Administrative expenses, court fees, and legal fees may reduce an estate considerably. With proper planning, those costs can be minimized.

> If you die intestate, the administrator/administratrix of your estate will be required to provide a bond to the court to ensure that the estate is administered properly. The amount of the bond is based on the value of the deceased's estate and can be very expensive. Preparing a will and naming an executor/executrix can eliminate the need for such a bond.

Having enough cash (or assets that can be easily converted into cash) to pay taxes and expenses is a major problem in many estates. If an estate does not have enough cash, property may have to be sold. It might be necessary to sell assets that should be kept or to sell them at less than their true worth. A proper estate plan using cash, marketable stocks and bonds, and insurance can solve this problem.

As you can see, there are many reasons an estate plan is important. The major reason, however, is to reduce taxes.

TAXES AND ESTATE PLANNING

The primary purpose of estate planning is to minimize taxes. Depending on the value of your assets, a tax problem could shrink their value considerably. The amount you save by minimizing taxes can often make a significant difference to the people you choose to be your beneficiaries. The means by which you minimize taxes must, however, fit the other goals of your estate plan.

The first goal of estate planning is to reduce income taxes. The less income tax you pay during your lifetime, the more assets you can accumulate. Making gifts is a good way to reduce income taxes. Giving gifts of property to someone who is in a lower tax bracket than you are (e.g., a child) results in income being taxed at a much lower rate. Putting property in certain kinds of trusts for the benefit of others can also accomplish the same thing. Of course, it is also important not to give away assets that may be needed later.

Another important benefit of estate planning is to reduce estate taxes. Both federal and state estate taxes may be considerable; proper planning will minimize them.

estate tax tax on transfer of property at one's death

An **estate tax** is basically a tax on the transfer of an individual's property when she or he dies. The federal tax is assessed against the estate itself. The amount of the federal tax is a percentage of the estate, and the rates increase as the amount of the estate increases. Some, although not all, states also impose an estate tax. In any states that do impose an estate tax, the tax is similar to the federal estate tax. Other states impose a tax called an inheritance tax, which is assessed against the beneficiaries, not against the estate. The rate of inheritance tax depends on the relationship between the decedent and the beneficiary: the closer the relationship, the lower the tax. The nature and amount of tax vary from state to state.

net estate assets left by a person at death, less certain legal deductions

Regardless of the nature of the tax, it is a tax on the deceased's net estate. The **net estate** consists of the assets left by an individual at death, less certain deductions permitted by law, such as funeral and administrative expenses and debts of the deceased. They also include gifts to charitable and educational institutions, in effect making such gifts tax-free. In some cases, a deduction also is allowed for property transferred to a spouse. This deduction is discussed later in this chapter. In 2009, federal taxes were imposed on a net estate of $3.5 million or more. The federal estate tax is scheduled to be dropped for the year 2010. However, it is expected that Congress will reinstitute the tax for the year 2010 and thereafter.

The primary goal of estate planning is to have as low a net estate as possible. Doing so means removing as many of your assets as possible from your estate and claiming the various deductions available. Most people need the advice of a lawyer and a tax accountant to help them achieve this goal. The most important ways to minimize estate taxes are through the use of gifts, the marital deduction, and trusts.

Gifts

Giving property as gifts during one's lifetime removes property from an estate so that at death there is less to tax. Each year, you may give away $12,000 in cash or property, tax-free, to as many people as you desire. If a married couple makes a gift jointly, they may give $29,000 to each recipient, $12,000 each from the wife and from the husband. If you make gifts over a period of years, you can reduce your estate considerably. In addition to these tax-free gifts, you may make gifts that can result in a savings in estate taxes.

As with other types of tax-saving ideas, gifts should not be made unless thought is given to nontax considerations. One question you should ask is, "Can I afford to give the property away?" If you will need the property later, giving it away just to save on estate taxes is not a good idea.

You must also consider the *type* of property you are giving away. Many estates consist of **liquid assets**, which are assets that can be used immediately to pay debts, taxes, and so forth. Liquid assets include cash, bank accounts, marketable stocks and bonds, and insurance proceeds. Most estates also include **nonliquid assets**, which are assets that can't be used immediately. Assets such as real estate, stock in a family business, or a valuable painting are examples of nonliquid assets. Giving away a liquid asset that might be needed to pay estate debts or taxes might not be a very wise idea. A wiser idea might be to give nonliquid assets that might have to be sold in a hurry at less than their fair value if beneficiaries needed cash quickly to settle debts.

How is a gift made? Most people simply deliver the gift to the recipient or, for example, open a bank account for a person. For a gift to be valid, there must be an intention to make a gift, delivery of the gift, and acceptance and control of the gift by the person receiving it. It is best to document gifts with a letter or other written document stating the name of the **donor** (the person making the gift), the name of the **donee** (the recipient), the date of the gift, and a description of the gift. This documentation is particularly important when the gift consists of property that is not normally listed in any recording office or in any other way, such as cash, art objects, or appliances. Unless a donor can prove that a certain gift has been made, the gift may be held invalid and its value included as part of the estate.

The Marital Deduction

Since 1948, married persons have had an estate tax advantage known as the marital deduction. Currently, the **marital deduction** allows all property passing to a surviving spouse to pass tax-free.

The marital deduction actually defers the federal and state estate taxes rather than eliminating them. If the marital deduction is used, the estate of the surviving spouse is increased by this amount. Estate taxes will be paid when the surviving spouse dies. The estate taxes that were deferred from the first estate by the marital deduction will be paid on the value of the second estate.

There are other advantages to using the marital deduction. Delaying payment of the estate taxes means that the surviving spouse has the use of more money during her or his lifetime. Also, the surviving spouse may be able to decrease her or his estate (and thus the potential estate taxes) by using the assets or making gifts during her or his lifetime.

> Hill left a will in which he bequeathed all his property to his wife. As a result, there were no estate taxes on his estate. During her lifetime, Mrs. Hill spent most of her assets and gave the rest away. When she died, no estate taxes were payable. No estate taxes were paid on either estate.

The marital deduction can also have disadvantages. For example, if the surviving spouse already has a large estate, the use of the marital deduction will increase that estate and make its potential estate taxes even larger.

The use of the marital deduction is a quite complicated matter, but you have a choice of whether to use it. It does not apply automatically. Also, property must be given to the surviving spouse in certain required ways for that property to qualify for the marital deduction. For example, the surviving spouse must have fairly complete control over the property transferred. Otherwise, the marital deduction will not be allowed.

---

liquid assets assets that can be used immediately to pay debts, taxes, and so on

nonliquid assets assets that cannot be used immediately to pay debts, taxes, expenses, and so on

donor one making a gift

donee recipient of a gift

marital deduction estate tax deduction for tax-free transfers of property to a spouse

Kirk left a will bequeathing a home to her husband. The will stated that he could use the home "for a period of ten years only, after which it is to become the property of our children." As her husband did not receive complete ownership or control of the home, its value did not qualify for the marital deduction. Its value would be included in the net estate and would be subject to estate taxes.

The third and most important thing to remember about the marital deduction is that it is available for all types of transfers of property. It is not limited only to those that take place by will. The passing of an interest in property held jointly by a husband and wife qualifies for the marital deduction. For example, a joint bank account passes to one joint tenant on the death of the other, regardless of the existence or nonexistence of a will. Other types of property that qualify for the marital deduction are real estate held jointly, stocks and bonds held in joint names, insurance proceeds payable to a spouse on death, and interests created by trusts.

Trusts

trust plan for transferring and holding property for the benefit of another

trustor one who establishes a trust

trustee one who manages a trust

A trust is a valuable estate planning device for many people. A **trust** is a plan by which you turn over property to someone to hold and manage for the benefit of yourself or another person. Although the titles vary in different states, the person who turns over the property is often known as the **trustor**. This person may also be known as the *settlor* or the *grantor*. One who holds and manages property in trust is known as the **trustee**. Those for whom the trust is set up are the beneficiaries.

Baxter wanted to set up a trust to assist her mother. She turned over $200,000 to Union National Bank with instructions to invest the money and use the interest and principal to provide for her mother's health needs and living expenses. Baxter is the trustor, the bank is the trustee, and Baxter's mother is the beneficiary.

living (inter vivos) trust trust set up during trustor's lifetime

Trusts may be set up either during the lifetime of the trustor or through a provision in a will. A trust created during the trustor's lifetime is known as a **living trust** or an **inter vivos trust**. To establish a living trust, a trust agreement is drawn up between the trustor and the trustee. The property to be placed in trust is then turned over to the trustee. The trustee is usually a professional experienced in financial matters and able to invest and manage the property in a competent way. Living trusts may be either revocable or irrevocable. In a revocable trust, the creator of the trust can change its terms or cancel it at any time. In an irrevocable trust, the creator cannot change any of its terms or revoke it once it has been established. An irrevocable trust offers a variety of tax advantages.

testamentary trust trust established according to the terms of a will

A trust set up after death through a will is called a **testamentary trust**. A testamentary trust is established during the lifetime of the trustor, but the property is placed in trust only at the trustor's death.

The main advantage of the trust is the flexibility it offers in providing income at the time it is needed. Another advantage is privacy. A living trust, for example, never becomes public knowledge, unlike a will after it has been probated. A trust also allows the trustor to determine who will get certain assets and when and how those assets will be distributed. The trustor can control how property is invested and used long after the trust is established.

There are other advantages to using trusts. Considerable income and estate tax savings are possible. In addition, a trust may help keep property in the family and prevent beneficiaries from wasting assets.

Henry wanted to provide for his family after his death. His children were attending college, and he could not be sure what their needs would be after they graduated. If he left them an equal amount of money or property, it might not meet their individual needs. By establishing a trust, Henry could give the trustee the flexibility to distribute money and property among his children according to their respective needs.

There are many different types of trusts that may be used for specific needs. For example, a **standby trust** becomes effective only when one or more predetermined events occur, such as the incapacity of the trustor. The proceeds of an insurance policy may be used to set up a **life insurance trust** at the trustor's death. A trustee invests the proceeds and distributes funds according to a trust agreement that is set up during the trustor's lifetime.

A **Totten trust** is a very common arrangement in which one person opens a bank account in trust for another. It is revocable until the depositor dies; at the depositor's death, the account belongs to the beneficiary. If the depositor gives the bankbook to the beneficiary or provides some other proof of a gift during the depositor's lifetime, a completed gift will have taken place, and the trust ends. A **charitable trust** is one established to benefit charitable, scientific, educational, or humanitarian agencies.

A **special needs trust** (sometimes called "supplementary needs" trust) is set up to enable a trust beneficiary who is disabled to receive income and principal from the trust without losing eligibility for certain public benefits. Such trusts are usually used to provide for comforts and luxuries, such as recreation, education and medical expenses, rather than basic support. This trust may be set up during a grantor's lifetime or in a will.

standby trust trust that comes into being when a certain event occurs

life insurance trust trust set up with proceeds of life insurance policy

Totten trust bank account in the name of a person, in trust for another person

charitable trust trust established to benefit charitable, scientific, humanitarian, or educational agencies

special needs trust a trust enabling a beneficiary to retain certain public benefits.

DEVELOPING AN ESTATE PLAN

The steps involved in developing an estate plan are seeking professional help, gathering information, deciding on the plan, and executing the plan.

The first step is to seek professional help from a lawyer or an accountant. He or she can advise you as to what information is required, both financial and personal. If insurance is involved, he or she may suggest that an insurance agent be consulted. If a bank is to be an executor or trustee, a bank's trust officer should also be involved.

After the initial consultation, the next step is to gather the information needed for proper planning. A complete list of your assets and liabilities is required. The list should contain information about the nature of the assets, their value, their liquidity, and who owns them. Personal data, such as Social Security information, family history, and insurance policy information, should also be provided.

After all the required information is collected, the next and most important step is to develop the plan itself. This team effort involves legal and tax professionals and the person making the plan. A frank discussion of needs, goals, and family situation is vital. The professionals involved can offer many suggestions but only if they have all the information they need.

After a plan is agreed upon, the final step is to implement it, which may involve making a will or changing an existing will. It may also involve setting up one or more trusts. Changes in the ownership of assets or in beneficiaries of an insurance policy might be suggested. With proper planning, an estate plan can be developed to meet any needs and any family situation.

Summary

After a person dies, his or her property is distributed to beneficiaries according to the provisions of a will. If a person dies without leaving a will, property is distributed to heirs according to the laws of the state in which the deceased resided.

To be valid, a will must be executed by someone with testamentary capacity, who is free from fraud or duress, and who observes the proper formalities. These formalities vary from state to state but usually require that a will be in writing, signed by the maker of the will, and properly witnessed. Some states permit special types of wills, such as handwritten wills, oral wills, and wills made by members of the armed forces on active duty.

There are restrictions on the manner in which a maker of a will may dispose of property. The maker of a will may not dispose of property in such a way as to be against public policy, defeat a spouse's rights, or defeat the rights of creditors.

The steps in making a will are gathering the necessary information, establishing goals, determining tax problems, naming an executor/executrix, and drafting and executing the will.

An executor/executrix is the person named in a will to administer the estate of the deceased. An administrator/administratrix is the person appointed by the court to administer the estate of a person who dies without a will.

To ensure that a person's preferences regarding medical care are followed upon the incapacity of the person to make such decisions, many states now recognize the validity of living wills and health care proxies.

Estate planning provides for the proper disposition of assets during one's lifetime and after one's death. The most important reasons for estate planning are to minimize taxes, dispose of property according to one's wishes, and provide for retirement.

The most important ways to minimize estate taxes are through the use of gifts, the marital deduction, and trusts. Factors to consider in the use of gifts and trusts include the need for the property later on, the need for liquidity, the type of property to be given, and to whom the disposition is to be made.

The marital deduction is a device for reducing estate taxes by transferring property to a spouse. It may be available for many types of transfers, including transfers by will, jointly held property, and insurance proceeds payable to a surviving spouse.

A trust is an estate planning tool that allows property to be transferred to a trustee and held for the benefit of either the grantor or another. A trust can be set up during one's lifetime (a living or inter vivos trust) or by a provision in a will (testamentary trust). Trusts can be set up to serve specific needs.

Developing an estate plan is a group effort. It involves the person who wants it and an attorney and often an accountant, insurance agent, and bank trust officer. The basic steps in developing an estate plan are consulting with professionals, gathering information, developing a plan, and implementing the plan.

Important Legal terms

abated bequest
adeemed bequest
administrator/administratrix
antilapse laws
attestation
charitable trust
codicil
devise
donee
donor
estate
estate plan
estate tax
executor/executrix
health care proxy

heir
holographic will
intestate
lapse
legacy
life insurance trust
liquid assets
living (inter vivos) trust
living will
marital deduction
net estate
nonliquid assets
nuncupative will
per capita
per stirpes

probate
residuary gift
settlement
special needs trust
standby trust
testamentary capacity
testamentary trust
testate
testator/testatrix
Totten trust
trust
trustee
trustor
will

Questions and Problems for Discussion

1. What are the four requirements of a valid will?
2. What is the difference between a holographic will and a nuncupative will?
3. What is the difference between a living will and a health care proxy?
4. What is the difference between an executor and an administrator?
5. Chase made a will leaving everything to his daughter on the condition that she never marry. Will such a provision be upheld?
6. In her will, Loomis provided that all of her grandchildren were to receive an equal share of her estate. Is this a per stirpes or a per capita distribution?
7. Curtis, who was blind, signed a will with an "x" in the presence of two witnesses. Is the will valid?
8. Farber made a will leaving his estate to his wife and three children. After making the will, he and his wife adopted two children. Are they entitled to a take under the will upon Farber's death?
9. Seward, age fifteen, made a will leaving all her property to her brother. She died ten years later. Will the will be upheld?
10. When Blue died, his executor found two wills in Blue's safe-deposit box. One will, executed in January 2002, left everything to Blue's children. The second will, executed in June 2002, left everything to Blue's nephew but did not specifically revoke the earlier will. Which will should be admitted to probate? Why?
11. Name three major reasons for developing an estate plan.
12. What are the steps involved in developing an estate plan?
13. Whom should a person consult to set up an estate plan?
14. Elder told his brother that he wanted to give him his car for a birthday gift but that he wanted to use the car for six months before handing it over. Was that a valid gift?
15. Curran's will contained a provision leaving the income from a $50,000 trust fund to her husband for ten years, after which the fund proceeds were to be distributed to her brother. Does this bequest qualify for the marital deduction?
16. Fox's will contained a provision leaving half his estate to his wife and half to the Salvation Army. Is there any estate tax on Fox's estate?
17. What is the difference between a living trust and a testamentary trust?
18. Morse opened a bank account in his name in trust for his sister. Prior to his death, Morse closed the account. His sister claims she is entitled to what was in the account because it was in trust for her. Is she correct?
19. Edwards wanted to make sure that no estate taxes would be payable upon his death. His will provided that one-third of his estate went to his wife and the balance to the college from which he graduated. Will any federal estate tax be payable on his death?
20. Frank owned a home that was in joint names with his wife and insurance payable to his children. Upon Frank's death, what assets will be subject to distribution pursuant to his will?

Cases for Review

1. Morris Scott executed a will in 1980. When he died in 1995, the will was found and all references to a certain beneficiary were cut from the will and some portions were marked through with the word *void* written nearby. Powers and Banks, sisters of Mr. Scott, objected to the probate of the will, claiming that the mutilations of the will effectively revoked it. Are they correct? (*Powers and Banks* v. *Lacgny et al.*, 671 N.E. 2d 1215)

2. Katheryn Brooks executed a will witnessed by a family friend. At a later time, a notary public signed the attestation page but had never actually witnessed the signing of the will, and Mrs. Brooks had never acknowledged to the notary that the document was her will. Should the will be admitted to probate? (In *The Matter of the Estate of Katheryn May Brooks, Deceased*, 279 Mont. 516)

3. Mr. Flohl and Mrs. Greenwood met when Flohl, a mechanic, helped Mrs. Greenwood with some car problems. A relationship developed between them, and subsequently, Mr. Flohl executed a will naming Mrs. Greenwood as his sole beneficiary and personal representative of his estate. He left nothing to his son, George. There was proof that Mr. Flohl told his attorney exactly what he wanted and that the will was executed in the presence of the attorney and two of his employees. After Mr. Flohl died, his son contested the probate, claiming that Mrs. Greenwood had exercised undue influence on his father. Was this a valid contention under the facts of this case? (In re *Estate of Walter William Flohl, Deceased*, 764 So. 2d 802)

4. A will contained a charitable bequest to a private nonprofit hospital known as the "Home for Incurables of Baltimore City." The purpose of the bequest was to construct a new building for "white patients who need physical rehabilitation." If the bequest was not acceptable, the bequest would instead go to the University of Maryland Hospital. Is such a bequest valid? If not, should the bequest go to the home to be used for all patients, or should it go to the university instead? (*Home for Incurables of Baltimore City* v. *University of Md.*, Court of Appeals of Maryland, No. 132, September Term)

5. Golden executed a will on March 22, 1967, and died on April 21, 1967. Prior to signing her will, she crossed out a paragraph that disposed of her home and wrote above it "omit and cancel." The notation was initialed by Golden and by two witnesses. The person who was to receive the home, the devisee, brought suit, claiming the notation was not valid. Is the devisee correct? (In re *Estate of Golden*, 211 So.2d 234)

6. Thompson wrote a will in her handwriting on an envelope and sheet of paper. She never signed the will, but five lines from the end, she wrote "I, Clara Thompson, do hereby swear that I am in very good health and sound mind." Certain heirs claimed the will was invalid. Are they correct? (*Wilson* v. *Polite*, 218 So.2d 843)

7. Casserie owned some land in Michigan. He executed a quitclaim deed to the property to Bishop, creating a joint tenancy but reserving to himself a life estate in the property. When Casserie died, the value of the property was included in computing his gross estate for estate purposes. Casserie's executrix claimed that a full tax should not have been imposed. She claimed that Casserie had given up substantial rights to the property during his lifetime by gifting half the property to Bishop. Is she correct? (In re *Casserie Estate*, 142 Mich. App.814)

8. Bouchard had an account with a stock brokerage firm. Worried about his health, he set up a joint account with his wife, with the survivor to own the account upon the death of either of them. He gave his wife the power to deal on his behalf as if she were the sole owner. When Bouchard died, she did not include the value of the account in his estate for estate tax purposes, claiming that he had made a gift of the account to her during his lifetime. Is she correct? (*Bouchard* v. *Commissioner of Internal Revenue*, 34 T.C. 646)

9. LeDuc bought a government bond that was payable on his death to Darcy LeDuc, a relative. LeDuc kept the bond in his safe-deposit box. After LeDuc's death, the state of Michigan held that the bond was taxable as part of his estate because title had not passed to Darcy LeDuc. Was that decision correct? (In re *LeDuc's Estate*, 5 Mich. App. 390)

10. Pohndorf could understand but not read English. Her attorney prepared a will for her, read it to her in English, and explained it to her. She then signed it and her signature was witnessed. Pohndorf died shortly after signing the will. Certain relatives contested the will, claiming it was invalid because Pohndorf could not read it. Is the will valid? (*In re Estate of Pohndorf*, 11 Arizona App 29)

11. Krause executed a will and left it with his attorney. Later, during a phone conversation, he told his attorney to destroy the will. The attorney did destroy the will but certain heirs claimed that the revocation was not effective. Are they correct? (*Matter of Krause*, New York 87 Misc 2d 492)

12. Dreyfus typed his own will and then signed and dated it in his own handwriting. Was it a valid holographic will? (*In re Dreyfus Estate*, 175 Cal 417, 165 P 941)

THE CASE OF THE UNFULFILLED PROMISE

Jason, age ninety, had a very valuable violin collection. He was helped by a nephew, Alden, who was an excellent violinist. Just prior to making a new will, Jason told his nephew that he was going to give him the collection. "It's yours," he said, adding that he would hold on to the collection for safekeeping. He also sent Alden a letter in which he said, "I give you my violin collection, and when I die, it will be yours."

Jason died four weeks later. In his will, which did not refer to the violins, he left his entire estate to his two children. Alden brought suit against the estate to have the violin collection declared his property.

The Trial

Alden testified at the trial about the help he had given his uncle over a period of fifteen years. He produced the letter his uncle had sent him and recalled their many conversations during which his uncle had promised to give him the violins. There was additional testimony that Jason's children had never even picked up a violin and had been estranged from their father for years.

The Arguments at Trial

Alden's attorney argued that the collection belonged to Alden because Jason had gifted the violins to Alden during Jason's lifetime and that there was symbolic delivery. He further argued that Jason's keeping possession of the violins was solely to protect them and in no way invalidated the gift. He also argued that to deprive Alden of the collection that his uncle obviously wanted to give him would be unfair.

The children's attorneys argued that the will was validly executed and promises made orally or in writing do not constitute valid gifts. They further argued that actual and not symbolic delivery is an essential requirement for a gift to be deemed valid.

Questions for Discussion

1. Who has the stronger argument, Alden or Jason's children? Why?
2. If you were the judge or jury hearing this case, for whom would you decide? Why?
3. Should considerations of fairness and the intentions of the person making the will take precedence over a validly executed will?
4. What problems do you think could arise if oral or written promises were considered under the circumstances of this case?

Mr. and Mrs. Jones went to a hotel for a conference. When they began to register at the hotel desk, the clerk told them that they could not leave their luggage at the foot of the registration desk while they registered but had to place the bags temporarily in a room next door. They complied, but when they went back to retrieve their luggage, it was gone, presumably stolen. The hotel refused to compensate the couple for the loss, claiming that none of its employees had exercised any control over the luggage, and thus, it was not responsible for the loss.

Questions for Discussion

1. Regardless of any question of whether a bailment existed, was the hotel's decision unethical under the circumstances?
2. What should a hotel's responsibility be for a guest's luggage when a guest checks in?
3. If either Mr. or Mrs. Jones could have watched the luggage while the other registered but failed to do so, why should the hotel be responsible for any loss?

PART 8

Consumer and Creditor Protection

After studying Part VIII, you should be able to

1. describe the laws passed by the federal and state governments to protect consumers.
2. explain the plain English law.
3. identify steps that consumers may take against sellers who violate consumer protection laws.
4. describe the laws that govern the rights of people who borrow money or who buy goods or services on credit.
5. explain the function of the Truth in Lending Act.
6. identify the methods creditors may use to collect payment from debtors.
7. state the main purpose of a security agreement.
8. list a creditor's remedies if a debtor cannot or will not make payments.

CHAPTER 35

Protecting the Consumer and the Taxpayer

CHAPTER PREVIEW

The Need for Consumer Protection

Regulation of Business Practices
The Right to Fair Advertising
The Right to Fair Pricing
The Right to Refuse Unordered Goods
The Right to Cancel Certain Contracts
The Right to Understandable Written Contracts
Truth in Savings Accounts

Product Standards
The Right to Safe Merchandise
The Right to Proper Labeling and Packaging

The Right to Purchase Quality Vehicles

Remedies for Violations of Consumer Protection Laws

Rights of the Air Traveler
Overbooking of Flights
Flight Delays
Liability for Lost, Delayed, or Damaged Baggage
Liability on International Flights

Rights of the Taxpayer

Chapter Highlights

This chapter describes the rules and regulations that federal, state, and local governments have enacted to protect consumers. This protection enables consumers to choose among competing brands and to purchase merchandise that is safe. These rules and regulations—and their enforcement—provide the consumer with many rights. Two of these are the rights to fair advertising and fair prices. Others enable the consumer to refuse to accept or return goods that were not ordered or to cancel contracts that were made in haste. One of the most recently developed consumer rights is the right to receive a contract written in language that is understandable by the average person. Consumers also need product standards to ensure that the merchandise they purchase is safe. Various government agencies are responsible for making sure that products meet set safety standards and that the packaging and labeling are safe and clear. Of particular importance to consumers are regulations relating to the age and quality of motor vehicles they purchase. Without enforcement, consumer laws and regulations are meaningless. The chapter, therefore, describes the various available methods for enforcing consumer rights. Finally, the chapter discusses the rights of two types of persons: the air traveler and the taxpayer.

THE NEED FOR CONSUMER PROTECTION

consumer one who purchases goods, products, and services for personal use

Every person is a consumer at one time or another. A **consumer** is one who purchases goods, products, and services for personal rather than business use. In the past, government had a "hands-off" attitude when it came to protecting the consumer. This attitude, discussed in Chapter 18, was known as caveat emptor, or "buyer beware." Government believed that a buyer knew what to buy and what price to pay and needed no protection from government. The law of supply and demand was expected to keep inferior and overpriced goods off the market.

This attitude has changed completely during recent years. Products have become more complicated, requiring greater knowledge on the part of consumers. Consumers must choose from among many different brands of goods today, requiring them to compare competing brands to buy the most suitable product. Modern packaging often makes it impossible to make such comparisons because consumers cannot examine a product before buying it.

To protect the consumer, many laws and regulations have been passed by state, local, and federal governments. These laws and regulations prohibit unfair business practices. They also set minimum standards of quality, weight and measurement, packaging, and labeling, and they provide procedures for correcting wrongs suffered by consumers. The group of laws and regulations that protect the consumer can be called a "Bill of Rights for the Consumer."

Enforcement of this bill of rights is the responsibility of the courts and administrative agencies. Consumers also have access to private, nonprofit organizations that can help settle complaints or grievances.

REGULATION OF BUSINESS PRACTICES

In the United States, consumers have the right to expect that businesses will deal with them fairly and honestly. One of the functions of government is to protect the interests of society, which includes the interests of consumers. Thus, a number of government agencies protect consumers. Figure 35.1 outlines some of the responsibilities of three federal agencies

FIGURE 35.1 Functions of Federal Consumer Agencies

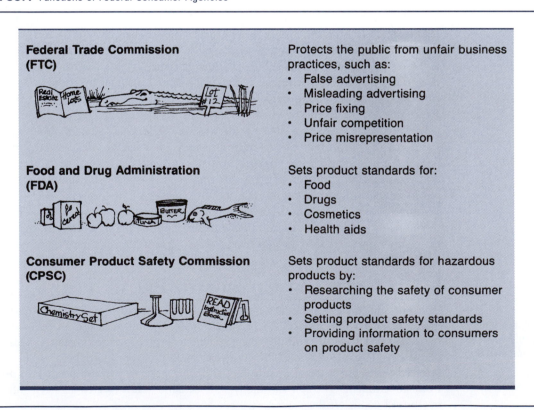

Federal Trade Commission (FTC)

Protects the public from unfair business practices, such as:
• False advertising
• Misleading advertising
• Price fixing
• Unfair competition
• Price misrepresentation

Food and Drug Administration (FDA)

Sets product standards for:
• Food
• Drugs
• Cosmetics
• Health aids

Consumer Product Safety Commission (CPSC)

Sets product standards for hazardous products by:
• Researching the safety of consumer products
• Setting product safety standards
• Providing information to consumers on product safety

charged with protecting consumers' interests. Among the business activities regulated by these agencies are advertising, pricing, and consumer rights in buying goods.

The Right to Fair Advertising

Manufacturers and sellers spend billions of dollars each year advertising their goods and services. Consumers may be influenced by such advertising without knowing whether the advertising is completely true. To protect the consumer, Congress and state legislatures have passed laws prohibiting false and misleading advertising. The agency primarily responsible for enforcing these laws is the Federal Trade Commission (FTC), which has established rules for companies doing business in interstate commerce. It is authorized to determine whether certain trade practices are unfair or misleading and might be harmful to sellers and to consumers.

The FTC has the power to accept complaints from the public and to determine whether acts or practices of businesses are unfair or deceptive. If the FTC decides that a company is guilty of an unfair business practice, it can order the company to stop the practice. It can also sue for damages and request refunds for consumers.

Another way the FTC protects the consumer is by requiring certain products, and the advertisements for those products, to carry warnings to the public. For example, cigarette ads must indicate that smoking is dangerous to your health. Also, if a company makes specific claims about its products, it must make available to consumers the data that support its claims.

false advertising
advertising containing lies or omitting important information

False Advertising   One business practice the FTC tries to eliminate is false advertising. **False advertising** contains untruths or fails to include information that a consumer needs to know. The FTC can prohibit such advertising—regardless of whether or not the advertiser knows its statements are false—if the advertising has the tendency to deceive consumers. In 2009, for example, the FTC prohibited a cereal manufacturing company from continuing to advertise certain health benefits from eating its products when there was no proof of such benefits.

> Optic Medicines Company advertised that using one of its new medicines would cure nearsightedness. Because Optic Medicines cannot prove this claim, the FTC can require it to remove the claim from its advertising.

Advertising that a product has been endorsed by a well-known person when that person has not actually endorsed the product is another example of false advertising. The FTC can force a company using such a tactic to stop doing so. In addition, the company may be liable for damages to the person whose name was used without permission.

In some cases, the FTC may require a company to run corrective advertising to inform the public that the claims made about a product in the past were untrue. Obviously, this requirement is a serious measure to be taken against a company. The majority of advertisers today do not make claims that they cannot prove.

bait-and-switch advertising advertising a product for sale, but then trying to sell the consumer another, more expensive product

Misleading Advertising   The FTC also prohibits misleading advertising. One misleading practice is **bait-and-switch advertising**. Such advertising offers a particular product or model for sale (the "bait"), but when the consumer tries to buy the advertised item, the salesperson tries to sell the consumer another, more costly item (the "switch").

> Davis saw an ad on television advertising a complete camera outfit for $39.95. She went to the store and was told that the camera was a good one but that it could not take flash pictures. For only $69.95, however, she could buy a camera that would take flash pictures and was of better quality. This tactic is bait-and-switch advertising.

Advertising for sale items that are not in stock or that are not available in sufficient quantities to meet consumer demand is also misleading advertising. Many states have passed laws requiring sellers to state in their advertising that quantities are limited. Such statements may be made by using such phrases as "only six per store" or "while supplies last." If a store runs out of a sale item, the customer must be given a rain check. A **rain check** is a coupon or certificate that allows the customer to buy the sale item at the sale price when the item is again in stock.

rain check coupon allowing one to buy out-of-stock sale item at sale price in the future

puffing salespersons' statements expressing opinions about goods they sell; type of advertising exaggerating the quality of merchandise

Puffing   One type of ad, known as **puffing**, borders on the illegal but is perfectly legal. In this type of ad, the quality of the merchandise is exaggerated or "puffed." Because advertising something as "nature's finest" or "world's best" is merely an opinion, not a statement of fact, the ad is legal. The theory is that any person reading such an ad would know better than to rely on it and therefore will not be deceived by it.

> Superior Used Car Sales advertised a used car for sale claiming it to be "in as good condition as a new car." This wording is puffing because it is an opinion and because no one would believe such a statement.

The Right to Fair Pricing

Most consumers have no way of knowing whether the price charged for an item is fair. Although consumers can (and should) compare prices of similar products, they often rely on their faith in the seller from whom they buy a product. Most sellers and manufacturers do price their products fairly, but some dishonest merchants use unfair practices, such as price fixing, loss leaders, and price misrepresentation.

price fixing agreement among sellers to set price of goods at a certain level

Price Fixing   When competing manufacturers, distributors, or sellers agree to set the prices of goods at a certain level, **price fixing** occurs. Such an action eliminates competition, which generally means that the consumer pays more for the goods. Price fixing is a violation of state regulations and the federal antitrust laws.

> Forest Drug Co. and Ross Pharmacy were the only drug stores in a small town. Their owners agreed to sell certain items at the same prices so they would not be competing with each other. This action is unlawful price fixing.

loss leader item sold at or below cost to attract customers

Loss Leaders   An item sold below cost or at little profit to entice a consumer into a store is called a **loss leader**. Once the consumer is in the store, the merchant tries to sell the consumer other goods at inflated prices. A loss leader may also be used as a tactic against competitors. For example, a large, successful store may be able to offer a number of loss leaders, decreasing its profits for a short time without too much damage to its financial health. A smaller, less successful competitor may not be able to match such price cuts and may lose customers to the larger store. If the smaller store loses enough customers, it may be driven out of business, eliminating competition for the larger store, which would then be free to raise prices on all its goods to make up for the losses it suffered while its prices were so low. Most states have laws against this practice because it harms competition.

> Midwest Supermarket wanted to eliminate competition from smaller food stores in its area. Because it could buy in large quantities, Midwest bought thousands of loaves of bread and offered them for sale at 50¢ a loaf, 90¢ less than the normal price. This loss-leader action is unlawful because it purposely prevents competition.

Price Misrepresentation   Some merchants put a "regular retail price" or "suggested list price" on an item and then offer the item at a so-called discount. In many cases, the item either does not have a suggested price, or the discount price is higher than the regular price charged by other stores. Such a practice is called **price misrepresentation**. Most states have laws prohibiting price misrepresentation.

price misrepresentation
offering of an item at discount price higher than regular price

The Automobile Information Disclosure Act is intended to prevent price misrepresentation in the sale of automobiles. Some dealers confuse the public with references to "sticker prices," "below cost," and so forth and then misrepresent the trade-in allowances being offered. The law requires disclosure of the true list price of automobiles and what that price includes.

> Downstate Auto Sales removed the price information stickers from a group of new cars and advertised them as selling for $200 below the invoice price. This action violates the Automobile Information Disclosure Act.

The Right to Refuse Unordered Goods

unordered goods
merchandise received even though not requested

Another unfair business practice is sending a consumer unordered goods. **Unordered goods** are goods not requested by the consumer. The goods usually arrive by mail with a notice that tells the consumer either to send them back or to keep and pay for them. Many people who receive such goods are confused and believe that they must keep the goods. Others pay for the goods because they don't want to bother returning them to the sender.

In most states, a person who receives unordered goods and has no agreement with the sender may keep the goods as a gift or may throw them away without paying the sender.

> You were sent a copy of a new book through the mail. You did not order the book and do not belong to a book club. You may either keep the book or throw it away. You have no obligation to return it to the sender or to pay for it.

A consumer who has an agreement with a sender, such as a book or record club, may not keep the goods as a gift or refuse to pay the sender. These agreements usually state that the monthly notice of shipment must be returned by a specific date. Failure to do so makes the consumer liable for the price of the merchandise sent. Some clubs no longer automatically ship goods but ship only on request.

The Right to Cancel Certain Contracts

Sometimes a consumer signs a contract in haste without giving the matter proper thought, such as when the consumer needs to act quickly or is faced with pressure from a salesperson. To protect consumers in such situations, both federal and state governments have passed laws allowing the consumer to cancel certain contracts after a change of mind, regardless of the reason, in two situations.

First, the federal Truth in Lending Act (discussed in Chapter 36) and Federal Trade Commission regulations permit cancellation of a contract to borrow money only when it involves a credit purchase in which the consumer's principal residence is taken as a security interest. A common example would be a home equity loan. Cancellation of the mortgage typically obtained upon the purchase of a home is not permitted.

> You bought a piano and agreed to pay for it in twelve monthly installments (payments). Two days later, you changed your mind and decided to return the piano. The Truth in Lending Act does not apply because your principal residence was not taken as a security interest and you must fulfill your obligations under the contract.

The Truth in Lending Act and federal regulations require that the creditor give the buyer a notice of rescission. This notice states that the buyer may cancel the contract for any reason within three business days after the contract is signed. The buyer has only to mail the notice back to the seller within the three-day period. The contract is then canceled, and any deposit must be refunded.

Second, FTC regulations also apply to door-to-door sales or sales away from the seller's place of business, regardless of whether an item is paid for in a lump-sum payment or on credit. In such a sale, a buyer must make an on-the-spot decision after hearing a fast, effective sales talk. The regulations require the salesperson to give the buyer a notice of cancellation form. The buyer may cancel the sale within three days for any reason by notifying the seller of the cancellation. Within ten days after the cancellation, the seller must either pick up the goods or make arrangements for the buyer to return the goods to the seller at the seller's expense. If the seller fails to comply with the law, the buyer may keep the merchandise (as well as the refund) and may also sue for any damages and attorney's fees. Many states have enacted laws similar to the federal regulations.

> You bought a typewriter from a salesperson, selling from a table at a school fair, who failed to give you the proper notice of cancellation. You gave the salesperson a deposit of $50 and agreed to pay the remainder in three monthly payments of $50 each. One week later, you decided to return the typewriter. Although more than three days have passed since you purchased the typewriter, the seller failed to give you the proper notice of cancellation and cannot refuse to take back the typewriter. If a seller fails to give the proper notice of cancellation for an installment sale, the merchandise may be returned for a full refund of any deposit or down payment.

Federal law provides that consumers who buy merchandise by mail have a right to have merchandise shipped on time. If an ad promises delivery by a certain date, the shipper must comply. If an ad contains no shipping date, the merchandise must be shipped within thirty days. A consumer has a right to cancel any order not shipped within the time stated or, if no time is stated, within thirty days.

The Right to Understandable Written Contracts

Many consumers complain that they do not understand the language in the documents they sign. The language is often complicated and understandable only by attorneys. As a result, consumers may sign contracts without really understanding what they are agreeing to. To protect the consumer, legislation has been introduced in several states and in Congress requiring that certain contracts be written so that they are understandable to the average person. This legislation is known as "plain English" legislation. It is based on the common law concept that if a person signs a contract without understanding its terms, that person could not have agreed to the terms and therefore cannot be bound by them. It is also based on the practical idea that a person who understands a contract is more likely to live up to its terms.

A typical, comprehensive plain English law applies to any consumer contract involving money, goods, or services valued at less than a set amount. It requires contracts to be written in clear language using words with common and everyday meanings. It also requires that contracts covered under the law be divided into meaningful sections and that each section have a heading or caption. These headings alert the consumer to the important terms of each contract.

Consider the difference in wording in the provisions of the following two promissory notes (signed statements agreeing to repay a certain sum of money with interest at a future time).

Before the plain English law

> For good and valuable consideration, the receipt whereof is hereby acknowledged, the obligor hereby acknowledges indebtedness to the obligee in the sum of $200.00, which the obligor hereby agrees to pay the obligee, together with interest on the unpaid principal balance from the day or date hereof, on such terms and under such conditions as hereinafter provided.

After the plain English law

> 1. BORROWER'S PROMISE TO PAY. In return for a loan that I have received, I promise to pay $200 to the Lender. The Lender is Friendly National Bank.
>
> 2. INTEREST. I will pay interest at a rate of 10% per year. Interest will be charged on that part of the loan that has not been paid. Interest will be charged starting on the date of this Note and continuing until the loan has been paid in full.

Failure to use plain English in a contract does not make a contract void or voidable. Instead, a creditor or seller who does not comply with a plain English law may be liable to the consumer for any actual damages plus $50.

Truth in Savings Accounts

Consumers often find it difficult to know exactly how much interest a bank is paying on savings accounts. Different banks compute interest in different ways, and because there is little uniformity on how this information is disclosed, it is difficult for consumers to make meaningful comparisons between competing claims of banks and other institutions in regard to deposit accounts.

To help consumers make informed decisions about deposit accounts, Congress passed the Truth in Savings Act in 1991. This law requires clear and uniform disclosure by banks and other institutions of the rates of interest paid on deposit accounts and the fees that may be charged against such accounts. Penalties may be assessed for failure to make such disclosure or for improper disclosure. The purpose of the law is to enable consumers who are about to open savings accounts to make meaningful comparisons between competing and often confusing claims of banks about interest payable. The law also requires financial institutions to pay interest on interest-bearing accounts based on the balance in the account each day rather than on the balance at the end of the month.

> Hall had an interest-bearing checking account at Trade Bank with a usual balance of $1,000. On January 25, he withdrew $900 from the account, leaving a balance on January 31 of $100. Hall is entitled to the interest on $900 for twenty-four days and on $100 for seven days.

PRODUCT STANDARDS

Consumers have a right to expect that the products they buy are of good quality and are safe when used properly and as intended. To make wise buying decisions, consumers also need to know what is in a product, such as the ingredients in a food product. Today, many products are packaged in such a way that consumers cannot examine them before making a purchase. In such cases, consumers need packaging that accurately describes the product inside the package.

The Right to Safe Merchandise

Many products either are basically dangerous or become dangerous because of the way in which they are used. Items such as poisons and insecticides are dangerous because of their ingredients. Others, such as rifles and power lawn mowers, are dangerous if not used properly. Some products, such as certain cosmetics and drugs that affect allergies, are dangerous only to some consumers and not to others.

Although the government cannot fully protect consumers from the improper use of a product, government agencies can set and enforce safety standards for most products. The Food and Drug Administration (FDA) sets standards for the preparation, manufacture, labeling, and sale of foods, drugs, and cosmetics. It regulates the conditions under which these products are prepared. The FDA requires testing of new drugs before they may be sold to the public. In addition, the FDA examines advertising and labeling to ensure that the public is properly informed about hazardous products and substances, such as cigarettes and insecticides.

The Consumer Product Safety Commission (CPSC) is the federal agency mainly responsible for product safety. It sets standards for most hazardous products, including poisons and flammable fabrics. The CPSC was established by Congress in 1972 with the passage of the Consumer Product Safety Act. The act gave broad responsibilities and powers to the CPSC to conduct research into the safety of consumer products, to set standards of product safety, and to provide information to consumers on product safety. The CPSC may ban from the market those products that present risks of death and personal injury to consumers. It can also require manufacturers to follow strict labeling procedures to warn consumers of dangers related to their products.

> Angus Manufacturing Company produced an electric blanket that could ignite when the temperature exceeded 100 degrees. The CPSC can require the company to warn the public of this danger. This warning would generally be placed in a conspicuous place on the product.

The CPSC also has the right to force manufacturers to recall hazardous items and to take corrective steps, such as replacing the item with something safer or refunding the purchase price to consumers. In 2009, for example, the CPSC fined a toy manufacturing company for not providing information about the dangers to children using its toys. It also requires firms to report to it within twenty-four hours after obtaining information that a product contains a defect which could create a substantial product hazard.

> Safemore Cream Company produced a suntan lotion that could burn the skin if applied too heavily. The CPSC discovered through research that 200 users of this cream had suffered burns in the past three years. The CPSC has the power to require Safemore to recall the cream from the market and either replace it with a safer product or refund the purchase price to all consumers who had bought the cream.

The act is very comprehensive. It covers "any article, or component part thereof produced or distributed for sale to a consumer for use in or around a permanent or temporary household or residence, a school, in recreation or otherwise, or for the personal use, consumption or enjoyment of a consumer."

To compile data on unsafe products, the CPSC has set up a toll-free hotline for consumers to call to report dangerous items. Each day, hundreds of calls come in from the public notifying the CPSC of such things as faulty toys or poorly constructed power tools.

The Right to Proper Labeling and Packaging

The labeling and packaging on products provide important information to consumers. Many consumers buy products solely on the basis of the information on a label. The federal Food, Drug, and Cosmetic Act and the Fair Packaging and Labeling Act (both administered by the FDA) are laws that were passed by Congress requiring manufacturers to give consumers correct information about their products.

The purpose of these acts is to inform the consumer about the nature, quality, quantity, price, and manufacturer of a product. Labels on foods, drugs, and cosmetics must show the name and address of the manufacturer or distributor so that the consumer will know who is responsible for the quality of the product. The quantity must be shown so that the consumer may compare prices of competitive products. Labels on food products must show the ingredients for health reasons and to help the consumer compare the quality of similar products. In addition, many packaged food products must be stamped with a date to indicate the product's freshness.

Congress has often required specific labeling and packaging to protect public safety. Since 1969, manufacturers of cigarettes and small cigars have been required to put statements on the packages that smoking is dangerous to one's health. Since 1970, manufacturers of products that might harm young children have been required to provide "childproof" caps and other opening devices. The Wool Products Labeling Act requires labels on wool products to indicate the country in which the product was processed. The Fur Products Labeling Act requires that labels on fur products indicate whether the fur is dyed or used and the English name of the animal from which the fur was taken. The Textile Fiber Products Identification Act deals with mandatory content disclosure in the labeling, invoicing, and advertising of products.

The Right to Purchase Quality Vehicles

A car with a serious defect that can't be repaired, or can't be repaired properly, has come to be known as a "lemon." In the past, consumers who found themselves with lemons either had to replace the cars themselves or had to pay for repairs after the warranty period had expired. Because an automobile is a necessity for so many people and because it is so expensive, thirty-nine states and the District of Columbia have passed laws to protect purchasers. These laws are known as **lemon laws**.

lemon laws laws that protect purchasers of new and used cars

The Magnuson-Moss Warranty Act, discussed in Chapter 18, set certain minimum standards for warranties on consumer products, including automobiles. The provisions of a warranty must be clearly listed and must state whether it is a full or limited warranty. In case of a defect, the seller must remedy it within a reasonable time. If the automobile, for example, can't be fixed after a reasonable number of attempts, the buyer has the option of getting a refund or a replacement.

Lemon laws vary from state to state, but in general, they provide that the purchaser must inform the dealer of the defects in the car within a certain period of time or before a certain mileage figure is reached. The dealer must be given a reasonable opportunity to fix them. If the car cannot be repaired after a certain number of attempts or after it has been in the repair shop a certain number of days, the owner is entitled to a refund or a new car. In most states, a consumer must first submit the case to arbitration. The consumer is not usually bound by the arbitration process and, if dissatisfied, can still sue in court to get relief.

It is important to understand that lemon laws do not cover all defects. They generally apply only to defects covered by the manufacturer's warranty and those that substantially reduce the use, safety, or value of the automobile.

The FTC and some states have passed lemon laws and rules that apply to the purchase of used cars. The rights and responsibilities are similar to those for the purchase of new cars but are limited in coverage. These lemon laws apply only to sales by used-car dealers and not private individuals. The FTC has a used-car rule that requires the placing of a window sticker in each used car offered for sale. The sticker gives warranty information and lists some of the major defects the car's system may have.

Tampering with an odometer makes a vehicle seem less used than it really is. To prevent such tampering, Congress enacted the Odometer Act, which prohibits the resetting or altering of the mileage on a motor vehicle's odometer. Anyone who sells or otherwise transfers a vehicle must give the new owner a written certification of the vehicle's mileage on the date it is transferred.

Warranties A consumer is protected in the purchase of merchandise by warranties covering the product. These warranties may be expressed in writing or may be implied from the transaction itself. Warranties are covered in detail earlier in the text.

REMEDIES FOR VIOLATIONS OF CONSUMER PROTECTION LAWS

A consumer's rights are of little value unless they can be enforced. Government agencies are primarily responsible for enforcing consumer protection laws. In addition, some laws, such as the Consumer Product Safety Act, permit a consumer to sue for violations and to recover a penalty from a manufacturer. A consumer may sue on her or his own behalf or on behalf of a group of consumers. A suit on behalf of a group of consumers is called a **class-action suit**.

class-action suit suit brought on behalf of a group of consumers

> You bought an iron that turned out to be a serious safety hazard. When you learned that other consumers had purchased the same defective iron, you brought suit against the manufacturer on your behalf and on behalf of the other purchasers. This lawsuit was a class-action suit.

The purpose of a class-action suit is to enable an individual with a complaint to obtain legal relief when the claim might otherwise be too small to warrant a separate lawsuit. A class-action suit also makes it possible to settle the claims of many individuals at the same time, eliminating the need for many separate lawsuits. One or more members of a group may sue as representatives of the entire group if

1. The group consists of so many people that having all the members of the group join in the lawsuit would be impractical.
2. There are questions of law or fact that are common to all members of the group, even though the individual claims may differ.
3. Parties bringing the class-action suit will fairly protect the interests of the rest of the group.

There are certain specific requirements for a class-action suit. A court order must be obtained permitting the filing of the class action. The other members of the group must be notified about the suit, unless the court finds that this step is unnecessary or that the cost would be prohibitive. A judgment issued in a class-action suit is binding on all members of the class, thus allowing the class action to be an effective means of helping consumers and other groups.

In many states, the attorney general can sue to prevent violations of consumer laws and to protect consumer rights. The attorney general may also bring a class-action suit on behalf of a group of consumers.

The seller who violates consumer protection laws may be subject to both civil and criminal penalties. Civil penalties include payment of damages and seizure of products. Criminal penalties include fines, imprisonment, or both.

RIGHTS OF THE AIR TRAVELER

Prior to 1978, many aspects of air travel were regulated by the Federal Aviation Administration and the Civil Aeronautics Board. In 1978, the airline industry was deregulated, and many aspects of air travel have now become contractual between the carrier and the traveler. Each passenger who purchases a ticket has in fact entered into a contract of transportation with a particular air carrier. Each ticket contains a statement, known as "Conditions of Contract" or "Terms of Transportation," which is printed on either the reverse side of the ticket or on the airline folder in which the ticket is contained. These conditions are brief and incorporate a whole variety of terms and conditions that are on file at the airport or airline city ticket office. In effect, each carrier sets its own terms and conditions, and the passenger becomes subject to these terms and conditions upon purchasing a ticket.

There are two important things to know about this system. The first is that liability of the airlines for injury to a person or death is not subject to federal law but is governed by ordinary rules of negligence. The second is that these terms and conditions represent the minimum that airlines are required to do for passengers. Airlines maintain all sorts of policies relating to travelers not specifically stated in the contract of carriage. These policies vary from airline to airline and often depend on the feelings of the passenger or those of the agent or supervisor in charge at any given time. These policies include compensation if you volunteer to be bumped from a flight, discounts for senior citizens, discounts for travel if there is a death in the family, and so on. A typical statement by an airline of its terms and conditions is shown in Figure 35.2.

The three most important aspects of the terms and conditions relate to overbooking of flights, flight delays, and liability for loss of, or damage to, baggage.

Overbooking of Flights

Because airline flights are sometimes overbooked, there is a chance that a person who has a confirmed reservation will not have a seat available. When this situation arises, airlines usually ask for volunteers willing to give up their reserved seats in exchange for some type of compensation. If no one volunteers, some people may not be able to board. A person denied boarding will be entitled to either compensation or free air travel; there are federal standards covering this situation as well as policies that vary from airline to airline. In general, an airline will provide either compensation or free air travel to a person denied boarding unless a substitute flight is provided that will get the traveler to her or his destination within one hour of the original arrival time or if the flight is cancelled for weather, safety, or "operational" reasons. The compensation is usually the face value of a passenger's tickets to the destination if the airline can get him or her there within two hours after the originally scheduled arrival time. If the delay is longer than two hours, the compensation is usually doubled.

FIGURE 35.2 Airline's Terms and Conditions

JETBLUE AIRLINE'S TERMS & CONDITIONS

ADVICE TO INTERNATIONAL PASSENGERS ON LIMITATION OF LIABILITY:

Where a passenger's journey involves an ultimate destination or a stop in a country other than the country of departure, either the Warsaw Convention and the Hague Protocol, their amendments, and any special contracts of carriage embodied in applicable tariffs that waive Warsaw/Hague limits, or the Montreal Convention may apply to the entire journey including the portion within the countries of departure or destination and, in some cases, may limit the liability of the carrier for death or personal injury, delay, and for loss of or damage to baggage. The Montreal Convention, where applicable, does not impose, and special contracts voluntarily entered into by many carriers, including JetBlue, waive, the Warsaw/Hague limitations for compensatory damages arising out of personal injury or wrongful death caused by an accident, as defined by the applicable treaty. The names of carriers party to the special contracts are available at all ticket offices of such carriers and may be examined upon request.

NOTICE OF BAGGAGE LIABILITY LIMITS

For international transportation (including domestic portions) governed by the Montreal Convention, JetBlue's liability for baggage is limited to 1,000 SDRs (see, www.imf.org for current value) per passenger unless a higher value is declared and an extra charge is paid. For international transportation governed by the Warsaw Convention and the Hague Protocol and their amendments, JetBlue's liability for baggage is limited to $9.07 per pound for checked baggage and $400 per passenger for unchecked baggage unless a higher value is declared and an extra charge is paid. Special rules may apply to valuable articles. For domestic transportation, JetBlue's liability for baggage is limited to $2,800 per passenger. General baggage rules: As set forth more fully in its Contract of Carriage and international passenger rules tariffs, JetBlue will not be responsible for fragile or perishable goods. JetBlue assumes no liability for oversized, overweight or overpacked baggage, or for loss of or damage to baggage parts such as wheels, straps, pockets, pull handles, zippers, hanger hooks or other items attached to baggage. JetBlue will not be responsible for the following items in checked or unchecked baggage: money, jewelry including watches, cameras, camcorders, any type of electronic equipment, including computers, valuable papers or documents and other similar items as described in more detail in the Contract of Carriage.

NOTICE OF OVERBOOKING OF FLIGHTS

While JetBlue Airways does not intentionally overbook its flights, there is still a slight chance that a seat will not be available on a flight for which a person has a confirmed reservation. If the flight is overbooked, no one will be denied a seat until airline personnel first ask for volunteers willing to give up their reservation in exchange for a payment of the airline's choosing. If there are not enough volunteers JetBlue will deny boarding to other persons in accordance with its particular boarding priority. With few exceptions persons denied boarding involuntarily are entitled to compensation. The complete rules for the payment of compensation and JetBlue's boarding priorities are available at all airport ticket counters and boarding locations. Some airlines do not apply these consumer protections to travel from some foreign countries, although other consumer protections may be available. Check with your airline or your travel agent.

NOTICE OF INCORPORATED TERMS

All travel on JetBlue, whether it is domestic or international travel, is subject to JetBlue's Contract of Carriage, the terms of which are incorporated herein by reference. International travel may also be subject to JetBlue's international passenger rules tariffs on file with the U.S. and other governments, and, where applicable, the Montreal Convention or the Warsaw Convention and its amendments and special contracts. Incorporated terms include, but are not restricted to:

1. Liability limitations for baggage, including special rules for fragile and perishable goods and the availability of excess valuation.
2. Liability limitations for personal injury or death.
3. Claims restrictions, including time periods within which passengers must file a claim or bring an action against JetBlue.
4. Rights of JetBlue to change the terms of contract.
5. Rules on reservations, check-in, and refusal to carry.
6. JetBlue's rights and limits on its liability for delay or failure to perform service, including schedule changes, substitution of aircraft or alternate air carriers, and rerouting.
7. Non-refundability of reservations.
8. The Contract of Carriage and tariffs may be inspected at all JetBlue airport customer service counters, and upon request you have the right to receive by mail a copy of the full text of the Contract of Carriage or tariffs.

Additional information on items one through seven can be obtained on JetBlue's website at www.JetBlue.com or at any U.S. location where JetBlue transportation is sold.

Reprinted by permission of JetBlue Airlines.

Flight Delays

More than half the contracts of carriage of the major U.S. airlines provide no specific benefits if a flight is delayed, regardless of the reason. The typical language is that the airline is not responsible for delays or for failure to make connections or to operate any flight according to schedule. Some airlines provide a meal and a free phone call if a flight is delayed for more than four hours and the delay was not caused by weather or air traffic.

If a flight is canceled or delayed for more than four hours, some airlines, as a matter of policy, offer a free meal, free transportation to a hotel, and free hotel accommodations. Whether an airline provides these benefits depends on the airline's policies, the reason for the delay, and the number of people affected by the delay.

Liability for Lost, Delayed, or Damaged Baggage

Each airline carrier establishes its own liability for lost or damaged baggage, but a typical plan provides that liability for loss or for damage to checked baggage is limited to $2,500 per passenger for travel wholly between points in the United States, with no liability for loss of baggage that is not checked. If a higher value is declared in advance and additional charges are paid, many airlines will be held liable for any loss, delay, or damage if higher amounts are involved. In most cases, unless specific insurance protection is purchased, an airline assumes no liability for items such as money, securities, manuscripts, jewelry, furs, and works of art.

If a piece of baggage is lost or delayed, many airlines will give the traveler funds to purchase necessaries, such as clothing or toiletries. Again, the amount depends on the airline, the reason for the delay, and other similar factors.

Liability on International Flights

Passengers on international flights are subject to provisions of one of two treaties, depending on which country has signed which treaty. These treaties apply to many aspects of the flight that are not subject to an individual carrier's terms and conditions, mainly liability for international carriage of persons, baggage, or goods. Liability of an airline is calculated in Special Drawing Rights (SDR), based upon an exchange rate established by the International Monetary Fund. On November 20, 2008, the exchange rate was 1.00 SDR = 1.176 Euro or 1.472 U.S. Dollar.

Warsaw Convention international treaty regulating liability of airlines on international flights

Montreal Convention A new international agreement limiting liability of international carriers for injuries or loss of baggage.

Under one of the conventions, the **Warsaw Convention**, a carrier's liability is limited to 16,600 SDR for personal injury, 17 SDR per kilogram for checked baggage and cargo, and 332 SDR for hand luggage. The **Montreal Convention**, signed in 1999, limits liability for personal injuries to 100,000 SDR and for lost baggage to 1000 SDR. An air carrier may be held to greater liability if negligence is proved.

The Montreal Convention will replace the Warsaw Convention when it is signed by all countries involved in international air transportation.

RIGHTS OF THE TAXPAYER

The Internal Revenue Service has stated that a taxpayer has the right to be treated fairly, professionally, promptly, and courteously. To make sure each taxpayer is treated fairly, the IRS has issued its Publication 1, which outlines the rights of a taxpayer. A copy of Publication 1 appears in Figure 35.3.

FIGURE 35.3 Your Rights as a Taxpayer

Your Rights as a Taxpayer

DECLARATION OF TAXPAYER RIGHTS

The first part of this publication explains some of your most important rights as a taxpayer.

The second part explains the examination, appeal, collection, and refund processes.

I. Protection of Your Rights

IRS employees will explain and protect your rights as a taxpayer throughout your contact with us.

II. Privacy and Confidentiality

The IRS will not disclose to anyone the information you give us, except as authorized by law. You have the right to know why we are asking you for information, how we will use it, and what happens if you do not provide requested information.

III. Professional and Courteous Service

If you believe that an IRS employee has not treated you in a professional manner, you should tell that employee's supervisor. If the supervisor's response is not satisfactory, you should write to your IRS District Director or Service Center Director.

IV. Representation

You may either represent yourself, or with proper written authorization, have someone else represent you in your place. You can have someone accompany you at an interview. You may make sound recordings of any meetings with our examination or collection personnel, provided you tell us in writing 10 days before the meeting.

V. Payment of Only The Correct Amount of Tax

You are responsible for paying only the correct amount of tax due under the law—no more, no less.

VI. Help From The Problem Resolution Office

Problem Resolution Officers can help you with unresolved tax problems and can offer you special help if you have a significant hardship as a result of a tax problem. For more information, write to the Problem Resolution Office at the District Office or Service Center where you have the problem, or call 1-800-829-1040 (1-800-829-4059 for TDD users).

VII. Appeals and Judicial Review

If you disagree with us about the amount of your tax liability or certain collection actions, you have the right to ask the IRS Appeals Office to review your case. You may also ask a court to review your case.

VIII. Relief From Certain Penalties

The IRS will waive penalties when allowed by law if you can show you acted reasonably and in good faith or relied on the incorrect advice of an IRS employee.

FIGURE 35.3 (Continued)

EXAMINATIONS, APPEALS, COLLECTIONS, AND REFUNDS

Examinations (Audits)

We accept most taxpayer's returns as filed. If we inquire about your return or select it for examination, it does not suggest that you are dishonest. The inquiry or examination may or may not result in more tax. We may close your case without change; or, you may receive a refund.

By Mail

We handle many examinations and inquiries by mail. We will send you a letter with either a request for more information or a reason why we believe a change to your return may be needed. If you give us the requested information or provide an explanation, we may or may not agree with you, and we will explain the reasons for any changes. Please do not hesitate to write to us about anything you do not understand. If you cannot resolve a question through the mail, you can request a personal interview with an examiner.

By Interview

If we notify you that we will conduct your examination through a personal interview, or you request such an interview, you have the right to ask that the examination take place at a reasonable time and place that is convenient for both you and the IRS. At the end of your examination, the examiner will give you a report if there are any proposed changes to your tax return. If you do not agree with the report, you may meet with the examiner's supervisor.

Repeat Examinations

If we examined your tax return for the same items in either of the 2 previous years and proposed no change to your tax liability, please contact us as soon as possible so we can determine if we should discontinue the repeat examination. Publication 556, *Examination of Returns, Appeal Rights, and Claims*

for Refund, will give you more information about the rules and procedures of an IRS examination.

Appeals

If you do not agree with the examiner's findings, you can appeal them to our Appeals Office. Most differences can be settled without expensive and time-consuming court trials. Your appeal rights are explained in detail in Publication 5, *Appeal Rights and Preparation of Protests for Unagreed Cases.*

If you do not wish to use our Appeals Office or disagree with its findings, you can take your case to the U.S. Tax Court, U.S. Court of Federal Claims, or the U.S. District Court where you live. If the court agrees with you on most issues in your case, and finds that our position was largely unjustified, you may be able to recover some of your administrative and litigation costs. You will not be eligible to recover these costs unless you tried to resolve your case administratively, including going through our appeals system, and you gave us all the information necessary to resolve the case.

Collections

Publication 594, *Understanding The Collection Process,* explains your rights and responsibilities regarding payment of federal taxes. It is divided into several sections that explain the procedures in plain language. The sections include:

1. *When you have not paid enough tax.* This section describes tax bills and explains what to do if you think your bill is wrong.

2. *Making arrangements to pay your bill.* This covers making installment payments, delaying collection action, and submitting an offer in compromise.

3. *What happens when you take no action to pay.* This covers liens, releasing a lien, levies, releasing a levy, seizures and sales, and release of property. Publication 1660, *Collection Appeal Rights (for Liens, Levies and Seizures),* explains your rights to appeal liens, levies and seizures and how to request these appeals.

Refunds

You may file a claim for refund if you think you paid too much tax. You must generally file the claim within 3 years from the date you filed your return or 2 years from the date you paid the tax, whichever is later. The law generally provides for interest on your refund if it is not paid within 45 days of the date you filed your return or claim for refund. Publication 556, *Examination of Returns, Appeal Rights, and Claims for Refund,* has more information on refunds.

Tax Information

The IRS provides a great deal of free information. The following are sources for forms, publications and additional information:

- **Tax Information:**
  1-800-829-1040

- **Forms and Publications:**
  1-800-829-3676
  (1-800-829-4059 for TDD users)

- **IRS FAX Forms:** From your FAX machine dial **703-487-4160**

- **Internet:** World Wide Web - http://www.irs.ustreas.gov
  FTP - ftp.irs.ustreas.gov
  Telnet - iris.irs.ustreas.gov

*U.S. Government Printing Office: 1996 - 411-952

Department of the Treasury
Internal Revenue Service
Publication 1 (Rev. 5-96)
Catalog Number 64731W

Summary

As more and more products reach the market, consumers require greater knowledge to make proper choices among competing brands. Complicated products often present many safety problems. All levels of government have enacted laws and regulations to assist and protect the consumer.

A number of government agencies, such as the Federal Trade Commission, are responsible for regulating certain business practices that affect consumers. The purpose of regulation is to make sure that the products are advertised and priced fairly. Other regulations cover the right of a consumer to return unordered goods, to cancel certain contracts, and to have understandable contracts.

Other government agencies, such as the Food and Drug Administration and the Consumer Product Safety Commission, have the responsibility of making sure that certain products are safe and packaged in a safe manner. Both the federal government and many states have enacted laws regulating the sale of new and used vehicles.

Laws must be enforceable if they are to mean anything. Consumer protection laws may be enforced by government agencies or by the courts through individual or class-action lawsuits against manufacturers and suppliers.

Certain individual rights are receiving more attention each year. Various laws and industry rules have been passed to offer greater protection to air travelers. The taxpayer also has certain rights, which are protected by Internal Revenue Service rules and regulations.

Important Legal terms

bait-and-switch advertising
class-action suit
consumer
false advertising
lemon laws

loss leader
Montreal Convention
price fixing
price misrepresentation
puffing

rain check
unordered goods
Warsaw Convention

Questions and Problems for Discussion

1. What protection is provided to buyers by the Magnuson-Moss Warranty Act?
2. What powers are provided to administrative agencies to enforce consumer protection legislation?
3. Should elimination of competition be allowed if it results in lower prices for the consumer?
4. Adams joined a record club that sent monthly notices to its members. If members did not want the monthly selection, they had to return the notice within two weeks. The club sent Adams two records she had not ordered. Must she pay for them?
5. Acme Auto Sales advertised a certain model at "10 percent below the manufacturer's retail price." The manufacturer had never set a retail price. Was this advertising misleading?
6. Atlantic advertised digital cameras for sale at $150 each. When customers arrived to buy the cameras, only two were available at the sale price. Was the advertising false and misleading?
7. Barnes owned a clothing store selling name-brand dresses at discount prices. Barnes did not want customers to know the name of the manufacturer so she removed that part of the clothing labels. Did she violate the law?
8. Tuthill wanted to increase his computer store's business and began to sell all his computers at cost. Has Tuthill violated the law?
9. Argus manufactured a toaster that could ignite if turned on for more than ten minutes. Must Argus warn potential customers of this problem?
10. Jones went to an appliance store to buy a new TV advertised for sale at $600. The salesperson told Jones that the store was out of that particular TV but that it had an even better set for $700. Was this bait-and-switch advertising?

11. Upon arrival at an airport, Brush was told that his flight would be delayed for four hours because of poor weather conditions. As a result, Brush missed his connecting flight. Does he have any recourse against the airline?

12. Egon Company advertised that its new diet pill could reduce one's weight by 10 percent. When a potential customer asked to see the data supporting this claim, Egon refused, claiming that the information was a trade secret. May Egon lawfully withold the data?

13. The Krill Corporation manufactured skis and ski equipment. It published an ad stating that the world's finest table tennis player used its skis exclusively. In reality, the table tennis player lived near the equator and had never even been on skis. Can the FTC prohibit Krill Corporation from using this advertisement?

14. A-1 Supermarket learned that a manufacturer of light bulbs was going out of business. A-1 bought the entire stock of bulbs and then offered them for sale in its store at fifty cents less than the normal price. Would this practice be considered an unlawful loss-leader action?

15. An automobile manufacturer introduced an SUV that tended to tip over at high speeds. What actions can the Consumer Product Safety Commission take to protect buyers of this vehicle?

Cases for Review

1. Charles of the Ritz sold a cream that the company claimed would restore youth to the skin, regardless of skin condition or the age of the user. The FTC ordered the company to stop the advertising, claiming it was misleading. The company argued that it wasn't misleading because "no straight-thinking person could believe that the cream would actually rejuvenate skin. "Is the company correct? (*Charles of the Ritz Distributors Corp.* v. *FTC,* 143 F.2d 676)

2. Miller was offered a free airline ticket for a companion if he signed up for an EAB Bank credit card. The offer contained no restrictions. Miller received and used the card but when he wanted to buy an air ticket for a companion, there were so many restrictions that he couldn't use the ticket. He sued EAB, claiming a violation of the Truth in Lending Act. Will he succeed? (*David Miller* v. *European American Bank*, 921 F. Supp. 1162)

3. Hiland Dairy sued Kroger to enjoin it from building a dairy processing plant in the St. Louis area that would supply 20 percent of consumers' demands. Hiland claimed that this plant would enable Kroger to sell milk as a loss leader and give it a monopoly in violation of the Sherman Act. Is this claim correct? (*Hiland Dairy Inc.* v. *Kroger Co.*, 402 F.2d 968)

4. Montgomery Ward, a nationwide store chain, advertised certain products as unconditionally guaranteed. When customers bought these products, however, the packages contained printed guarantees that had conditions attached. The FTC brought suit to enjoin this practice as being an unfair method of competition and deceptive advertising. Ward's defense was that no one was harmed by this practice because it honored all guarantees as if they were as advertised. Is this defense a good one? (*Montgomery Ward & Co.* v. *FTC*, 379 F.2d 666)

5. Resort Co. used the trade name Dollar-A-Day for its auto rental company. When people who wished to rent cars inquired, they were told that the rental was obviously more than $1 per day. The rental company claimed that this trade name was not deceptive advertising because the public was informed of the actual rental cost before any rental contracts were signed. Was the company correct? (*Resort Car Rental System*, Inc. v. *FTC*, 518 F.2d 962)

6. A supermarket owned by Abe Giles Supermarket, Inc., was cited as being in violation of the Connecticut Food, Drug, and Cosmetic Act after many inspections revealed violations and failure to remedy them. The state of Connecticut asked the court to order that the market be closed until it complied with the provisions of the act. Giles argued that the court should not close the market because fifteen employees would be out of work. Is Giles's argument a valid one? (*State* v. *Abe Giles Supermarket, Inc.*, 31 Conn. Supp. 242)

7. Kennir operated and controlled a private hospital. He was charged by the Internal Revenue Service with deducting certain expenditures that the IRS claimed were personal and not business expenses. At trial, Kennir tried to give testimony

regarding the expenditures, but he was denied permission on the grounds that only the checks themselves could be introduced in evidence. Should Kennir have been allowed to give testimony with regard to the expenditures? (*Kennir* v. *Commissioner of Internal Revenue*, 445 F2d 19)

8. Tashoff sold eyeglasses at his store. He advertised eyeglasses "from $7.50 complete, including lenses, frames, and case." The facts showed that of 144 pairs of glasses sold during each year, fewer than 10 were sold for $7.50. The FTC argued that this was a clear example of bait-and-switch advertising. Do you agree? (*Tashoff* v. *FTC*, 437 F2d 707)

9. Parker advertised pens using the words "guaranteed for life," It did not advertise the fact that each time a pen was brought or sent in for repairs, a 35¢ charge was made. The FTC brought suit, saying that failure to advertise the charge was deceptive advertising. Was the FTC correct? (*Parker Pen Co.* v. *FTC*, 159 F2d 509)

CHAPTER 36

Protecting the Borrower

CHAPTER PREVIEW

Chapter Highlights

Buying goods on credit and borrowing money have become increasingly prevalent. Both federal and state governments have enacted laws and regulations to protect the consumer in these areas. Under these laws, a consumer is entitled to obtain credit without regard to age, sex, and marital status and to know what that credit will cost. The consumer also has the right to pay only those interest charges permitted by law. Once credit has been obtained, a borrower is entitled to receive accurate bills indicating what is due and when. If bills are not paid on time and a creditor seeks to collect the amount due, the borrower is entitled to be free from harassment by the creditor. Sometimes a person is unable to pay debts as they come due. This chapter discusses the measures available to a person who is insolvent and who needs to be relieved from debt. These measures include protection under the bankruptcy laws and private arrangements with creditors.

THE USE OF CREDIT

Today, more and more people are borrowing money to purchase homes and cars and to pay for vacations and college educations. The use of credit cards has also grown dramatically. **Credit** is the right granted to a consumer to pay for goods and services after they have been received. A person who lends money or sells goods on credit is a **creditor**. A person who borrows money for any purpose or who buys goods or services on credit is a **debtor**, or borrower.

A number of laws and regulations are aimed at protecting the debtor. These laws govern the availability of credit, credit information, unfair credit practices, the collection process, and remedies for debtors. The most important of these laws is the Consumer Credit Protection Act, popularly known as the Truth in Lending Act, passed by Congress in 1968. All these laws and regulations may be termed a "Bill of Rights for the Borrower."

credit right to pay for goods and services "on time"

creditor one who loans money or sells goods on credit

debtor one who borrows money or buys on credit

TYPES OF CREDIT

Credit may be obtained in a number of forms, from charge accounts to long-term bank loans. Sources of credit include banks, savings and loans, finance companies, and retail businesses. The type of credit you obtain varies depending on what you are buying and how you want to finance (pay for) it.

There are two basic types of credit available to a consumer: unsecured and secured. **Unsecured credit** is credit that is based solely on a promise to repay. Charge accounts and credit cards represent unsecured credit. **Secured credit** is credit based not only on a promise to repay, but also on security: the borrower's pledge of property, which may be sold by the lender if the loan is not repaid. A home mortgage and an auto loan are examples of secured credit. (See Chapter 37, pages 609 and 610–611, for additional discussions.)

Three of the most-used types of credit are charge accounts, installment loans, and bank loans.

Charge Accounts

A **charge account** is an agreement between a consumer and a retail business allowing the consumer to purchase items or services now and pay for them later. Large department stores set up charge accounts and issue credit cards to their customers who qualify for credit. A **credit card** is a small card or other device that enables its holder to obtain goods and services on credit. A credit card generally may be used only in the store that issued it. Credit cards are also issued by oil and gasoline companies, airlines, and car rental agencies. Department stores and businesses usually issue their credit cards free of charge.

Banks also issue credit cards, such as MasterCard and Visa. These multipurpose bank cards may be used at many different types of businesses. You receive one bill from the bank for all your charges on the card. The bank in turn sends the proper amount to each of the businesses from which you have purchased something on credit. Banks sometimes charge an annual fee for the use of their credit cards. There are also companies that issue credit cards, such as American Express, Diner's Club, or Discover. These companies may charge an annual fee for the use of their cards.

There are two types of charge accounts: regular and revolving. With a **regular charge account**, you are expected to pay each bill in full when you receive it. With a **revolving charge account**, you may pay a portion of your bill. Your payment is deducted from the total bill and interest is charged on the unpaid balance. This interest charge, and the unpaid balance of your bill, will appear on the next month's statement. Usually, there is a maximum amount that you may owe on a particular credit card at any one time, which is your **line of credit**.

> Shelby had a charge account at Mountain Ski Shop. He bought a pair of skis and some winter clothing for $380 and charged them to his account. Shelby's line of credit is $500. Because he already owed the store $120 for previous credit purchases he had made, Shelby cannot charge any other items until he has paid a portion of his now $500 bill.

The ease of using credit, especially with revolving charge accounts, has led to much credit abuse and has created financial difficulties for people who keep buying and suddenly find that they cannot pay for what they have bought. It's quite easy to get into the habit of paying only the minimum amount on your credit bill, until one day you find

---

unsecured credit credit based solely on borrower's pledge to pay

secured credit credit based on borrower's pledge of property as well as his or her pledge to pay

charge account agreement between a consumer and a business allowing consumer to purchase items now and pay for them later

credit card card enabling its user to obtain goods or services on credit

regular charge account account on which each bill must be paid in full when received

revolving charge account account on which portion of bill may be paid each month

line of credit maximum amount that can be owed on a credit card at any one time

you owe several hundred dollars, a large part of which may be finance charges on your unpaid balance.

On May 19, 2009, Congress enacted a law giving credit card holders additional protection effective in February 2010. The law prevents credit card companies from retroactively raising interest rates on existing balances unless payments are sixty days overdue and requires credit card companies to send bills twenty-one days before the due date and provide at least forty-five days' notice before changing any significant terms on the card. In addition, anyone under twenty-one must either provide proof of financial ability to pay or have a co-signer on the card.

The Truth in Lending Act protects the owner of a credit card that is lost or stolen. If someone uses a credit card without consent, the cardholder is liable only for the first $50 of charges. When a credit card is issued, the issuer must tell the cardholder of this $50 limit and supply the cardholder with a form to use to notify the issuer if the card is lost or stolen. The cardholder must notify the issuer as soon as possible after the card has been lost or stolen. The law also protects a consumer from unauthorized credit card charges.

A credit card issuer who sends a card to a person who has not applied for the card is responsible for all unauthorized charges. The law prohibits sending a credit card to someone unless that person has requested it.

A system, known as the electronic fund transfer system, is rapidly becoming more popular and more widely used. Using a card known as a debit card, consumers can electronically pay for goods and services or withdraw cash from their bank accounts. Unlike a credit card, a **debit card** immediately transfers funds out of the user's bank account. Today, automated teller machines (ATMs), which allow consumers to do their banking twenty-four hours a day, are found in many stores and banks. Point-of-sale terminals used by businesses electronically and immediately deduct the amount of a purchase from the consumer's bank account and add it to the business's bank account.

debit card card that immediately transfers funds from user's bank account upon use

Because of the immediate transfer feature, the owner of a debit card is subject to greater liability for the unauthorized use of the card than the owner of a credit card is. Sometimes a debit card holder is not aware of unauthorized use until he or she receives a monthly statement. If the cardholder notifies the card issuer within two business days after learning of the loss, theft, or misuse of the debit card, the cardholder is liable only for the first $50 of losses. If the cardholder does not notify the card issuer within two days, however, the cardholder is liable for losses up to $500. If an unauthorized transfer on a statement is not reported within sixty days after the statement was mailed, the cardholder is liable for *all* losses.

Installment Loans

installment loan agreement to pay for an item in fixed, regular payments

When you buy expensive items and wish to pay for them over a number of months, you may obtain an installment loan from the store where you buy the items. An **installment loan** is an agreement to pay for an item in fixed, regular payments. An installment loan contract must be drawn up each time an item is purchased and paid for in this way. The terms of the contract apply only to that specific purchase. Usually, you must make a down payment on the purchase price. The lender holds an interest in the item and may repossess it (take it back) if you do not make your payments.

Bank Loans

A bank loan is similar to an installment loan. With a bank loan, however, you apply for a loan of a certain amount of cash. A bank loan may be repaid in full at the end of the loan period or in regular installments. Bank loans are often used to finance major purchases, such as a house or a car.

A bank will generally require you to have some sort of collateral before it will lend you the money. **Collateral** is any type of asset you own that may be pledged as security to the bank in case you fail to repay the loan. For example, if you finance the purchase of a car through a bank loan, the car will serve as collateral for the bank loan. You will not have clear title to the car until your bank loan has been repaid.

collateral asset that may be pledged as security for a loan

THE RIGHT TO OBTAIN CREDIT

In 1974, Congress passed the Equal Credit Opportunity Act to prevent creditors from discriminating against certain people when granting loans or credit. This law states that a creditor may not discriminate against anyone because of gender, marital status, age, race, color, religion, national origin, or receipt of public assistance. The law does not mean that everyone who applies is automatically entitled to receive credit or a loan. It simply means that a person cannot be denied credit or a loan *solely* because of age, gender, marital status, and so forth. It also limits the questions a creditor may ask of potential borrowers so that they will not be discouraged from applying for credit. The fact that an applicant for credit gave false information on the application form is not a defense under the act. An example of an application for credit is shown in Figure 36.1

A credit applicant's age may be considered only if the applicant is a minor, if the creditor favors applicants age sixty-two or over, or if age affects other factors (e.g., future income) that are used to determine whether the applicant is a good credit risk.

Samuels applied for a twenty-five-year mortgage loan with a 10 percent down payment. Samuels was sixty-eight when he applied for the loan and was due to retire at seventy. The bank denied the loan because Samuels's income would be reduced two years later. In these circumstances, the bank could consider Samuels's age in deciding whether to grant the loan.

In deciding whether or not to grant credit to an applicant, a creditor may consider such factors as the applicant's income; the amount the person wishes to borrow; the applicant's past credit history; and any other factors, such as other debts, that may relate to a person's ability to repay a loan.

When evaluating income, a creditor cannot consider an applicant's gender or marital status. It is illegal to deny credit to a woman in her own name if she has an income and otherwise qualifies for credit. The creditor may not consider the possibility that she may stop working to have a family. A creditor is also prohibited from discounting the importance of income just because it may come from part-time employment, alimony, or a pension.

Fuller applied for a credit card at Morgan's Department Store. She was employed full time and was earning $250 a week at the time. Store officials at Morgan's Department Store rejected her application for credit only because of the possibility that she could leave her job to raise her children. This rejection is a violation of the Equal Credit Opportunity Act.

A creditor must notify an applicant within thirty days about whether the credit application was accepted or rejected. If the application was rejected, the applicant is entitled to an explanation in writing. If the applicant was denied credit without just cause, the applicant may sue for damages.

FIGURE 36.1
Application for a Credit Card

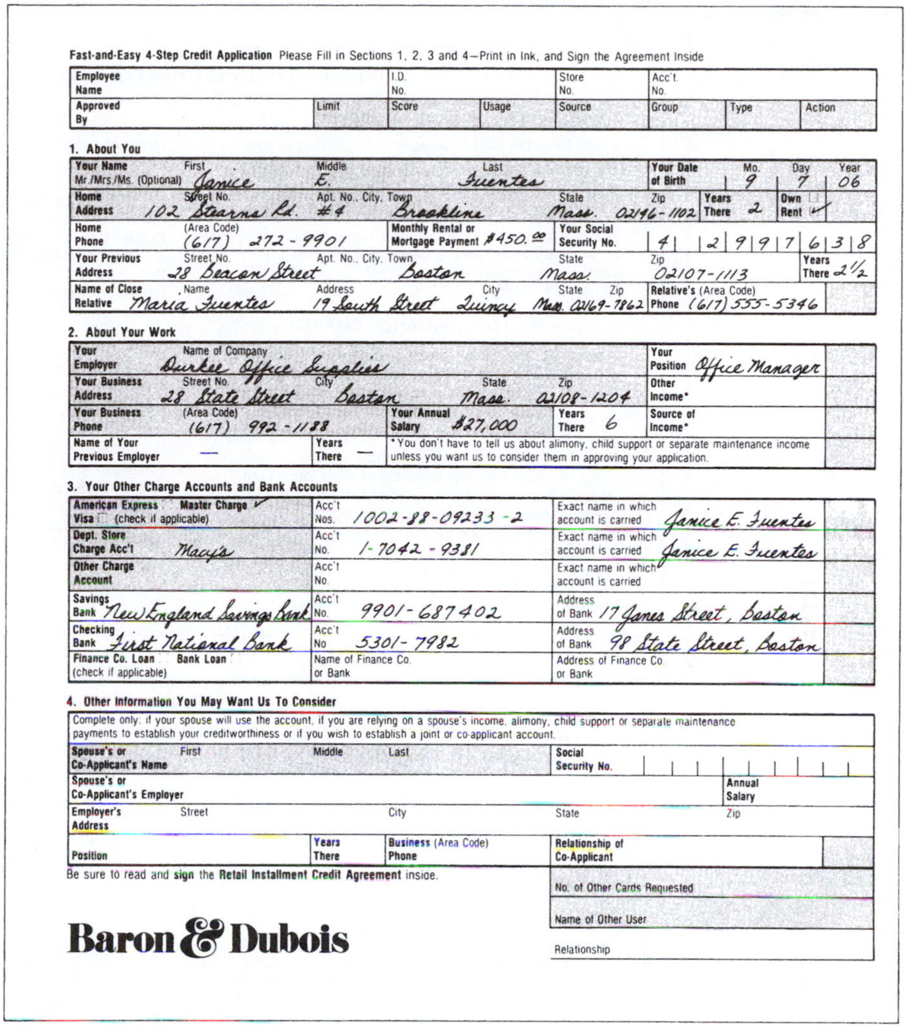

Fast-and-Easy 4-Step Credit Application Please Fill in Sections 1, 2, 3 and 4—Print in Ink, and Sign the Agreement Inside

Employee Name	I.D. No.		Store No.	Acc't. No.		
Approved By	Limit	Score	Usage	Source	Group	Type	Action

1. About You

Your Name Mr./Mrs./Ms. (Optional)	First: Janice; Middle: E.; Last: Fuentes
Your Date of Birth	Mo. 9; Day 7; Year 06
Home Address	Street No.: 102 Stearns Rd.; Apt. No., City, Town: #4 Brookline; State: Mass.; Zip: 02146-1102; Years There: 2; Own / Rent: ✓ Rent
Home Phone	(Area Code) (617) 272-9901
Monthly Rental or Mortgage Payment	$450.00
Your Social Security No.	4 1 2 9 9 7 6 3 8
Your Previous Address	Street No.: 28 Beacon Street; Apt. No., City, Town: Boston; State: Mass.; Zip: 02107-1113; Years There: 2½
Name of Close Relative	Name: Maria Fuentes; Address: 19 South Street; City: Quincy; State: Mass.; Zip: 02169-7862; Relative's (Area Code) Phone: (617) 555-5346

2. About Your Work

Your Employer	Name of Company: Durkee Office Supplies
Your Position	Office Manager
Your Business Address	Street No.: 28 State Street; City: Boston; State: Mass.; Zip: 02108-1204
Other Income*	
Your Business Phone	(Area Code) (617) 992-1188
Your Annual Salary	$27,000
Years There	6
Source of Income*	
Name of Your Previous Employer	—
Years There	—

*You don't have to tell us about alimony, child support or separate maintenance income unless you want us to consider them in approving your application.

3. Your Other Charge Accounts and Bank Accounts

	Acc't Nos.	Exact name in which account is carried / Address
American Express / Master Charge ✓ / Visa (check if applicable)	1002-88-09233-2	Janice E. Fuentes
Dept. Store Charge Acc't: Macy's	1-7042-9381	Janice E. Fuentes
Other Charge Account		
Savings Bank: New England Savings Bank	9901-687402	Address of Bank: 17 James Street, Boston
Checking Bank: First National Bank	5301-7982	Address of Bank: 98 State Street, Boston
Finance Co. Loan / Bank Loan (check if applicable)	Name of Finance Co. or Bank	Address of Finance Co. or Bank

4. Other Information You May Want Us To Consider

Complete only: if your spouse will use the account, if you are relying on a spouse's income, alimony, child support or separate maintenance payments to establish your creditworthiness or if you wish to establish a joint or co-applicant account.

Spouse's or Co-Applicant's Name	First / Middle / Last
Social Security No.	
Spouse's or Co-Applicant's Employer	
Annual Salary	
Employer's Address	Street / City / State / Zip
Position	
Years There	
Business (Area Code) Phone	
Relationship of Co-Applicant	

Be sure to read and sign the Retail Installment Credit Agreement inside.

No. of Other Cards Requested

Name of Other User

Relationship

Baron & Dubois

The Right to Know What Credit Costs

finance charge cost of borrowing money or buying on credit stated in dollars and cents

annual percentage rate cost of credit stated as a percentage of amount borrowed

Using credit almost always costs something. The amount of money paid for the use of borrowed money or for credit, stated in dollars and cents, is known as the **finance charge**. This charge must be clearly disclosed to the debtor. The finance charge must also be stated as a percentage of the total amount borrowed, which is known as the **annual percentage rate**. Some lenders and creditors add other charges, such as service or carrying charges, to the actual cost of borrowing the money. The law requires that these additional charges be disclosed as such.

One aim of the Truth in Lending Act is to help consumers and debtors know what they are being charged for the use of credit. Such knowledge helps consumers compare the cost of credit from various sources and make intelligent financing decisions. An example of information that must be given to the consumer is shown in Figure 36.2.

The Truth in Lending Act applies only to certain transactions and certain lenders or creditors. It does not apply to loans made for commercial purposes, such as buying items

FIGURE 36.2
Information Required by
the Truth in Lending Act

Disclosures Required Under Federal Law

1. The **FINANCE CHARGE** on a cash advance is imposed from the date such advance is posted to your cash advance account. A merchant advance becomes subject to **FINANCE CHARGE** on the first day of the billing cycle following the cycle in which the advance is first posted to your merchant advance account and will be imposed as of such date on so much, if any, of the balance of your merchant advance account as is subject to **FINANCE CHARGE.**

2. The balance subject to **FINANCE CHARGE** is the sum of (a) the total of the daily closing balances in your cash advance account during the billing cycle divided by the number of days in the cycle and (b) the total of the daily closing balances (excluding merchant advances posted to the account during the cycle) in your merchant advance account during the billing cycle divided by the number of days in the cycle, except that the balance of your merchant advance account shall be deemed to be zero for any billing cycle at the beginning of which no cash advances are outstanding and during which the total balance owed on the closing date of the previous cycle is paid in full prior to the debiting of any new cash advance. You will, therefore, incur no **FINANCE CHARGE** on a merchant advance, as

distinguished from a cash advance, if it is paid in full by the end of the billing cycle following that in which it is posted to your account.

3. The amount of the **FINANCE CHARGE** is determined by applying to the balance subject to **FINANCE CHARGE** a Periodic Rate of 1½% per month (**ANNUAL PERCENTAGE RATE 18%**) to the first **$500** thereof and a Periodic Rate of 1% per month (**ANNUAL PERCENTAGE RATE 12%**) to the excess over **$500.**

4. The minimum monthly payment required will be specified in your monthly statement and will equal the total of all minimum payments previously billed and unpaid plus the greater of **$10** or that amount which equals **3%** of your total balance outstanding on the closing date of the cycle covered by the statement. Payments are applied first to **FINANCE CHARGES,** then proportionately to the closing balance in your merchant advance account as of your last previous statement date and to the current balance in your cash advance account, and then to the current balance in your merchant advance account.

for a business, or to purchases of property for personal, family, or household use if the amount of credit is $25,000 or more. It also does not apply to assignees of consumer installment contracts unless they know of any fraud or misrepresentation. It only protects persons, not corporations, and applies only to persons who lend money or sell on credit in the ordinary course of business.

THE RIGHT TO FAIR CREDIT INFORMATION

In 1970, Congress passed the Fair Credit Reporting Act administered by the Federal Trade Commission. The purpose of this law is to enable consumers to determine whether the information in their credit records is accurate and to ensure their privacy. A credit record contains the history of your use of credit. It includes information on whether you made payments on time and whether you repaid your loans in full. Credit records are kept by credit bureaus in major cities. A credit bureau functions as a sort of clearinghouse of credit information for those who need access to a person's credit history. Credit bureaus obtain their information from banks, department stores, and finance companies.

Your credit record is very important because it is the basis upon which sellers or lenders decide whether to give or to deny you credit. Under the Fair Credit Reporting Act, if you are denied credit because of information filed with a credit bureau, you must be notified of the rejection and must be given the name and address of the credit bureau supplying the information on which the rejection was based. You have the right to contact the credit bureau and see the information in your credit record. The law provides that if any item in your record is found to be incorrect, or cannot be proven, the credit bureau must remove the item. The credit bureau must also give you the names of any persons who have received a credit report on you within the past six months.

A credit bureau must make a reasonable effort to verify the information it receives, particularly if the information is unfavorable. Failure to do so may subject the credit bureau to liability for noncompliance with the Fair Credit Reporting Act.

West applied to a bank for a student loan. The bank refused to grant the loan, claiming that West had a poor credit record. West may contact the credit bureau that supplied the information to the bank and get a copy of his credit record file.

Congress amended the Fair Credit Reporting Act in 1994 to provide added protection for consumers. Among the changes in the amended act are (1) lower-cost copies of one's credit report (in certain cases, the copies will be free), (2) toll-free phone numbers for credit bureaus, (3) mandatory resolution of disputes within thirty days, and (4) liability for creditors who neglect to correct errors in one's credit report.

Congress further amended the Fair Credit Reporting Act in 2003, the amendments being referred to as the Fair and Accurate Credit Transactions Act (FACTA). FACTA was enacted to help prevent identity theft and reduce the losses incurred by identity theft victims. A national fraud alert system was established which enables identity theft victims to place an alert on their credit history. These alerts prevent new credit accounts from being opened and prevent the ordering of additional cards on existing accounts. The law entitles consumers to a free annual credit report. A new provision enables those with a credit report dispute to take up the matter with the company that reported it so that a dispute need no longer be taken up only with the credit reporting agency.

THE RIGHT TO ACCURATE BILLING

The Truth in Lending Act requires that users of revolving charge accounts be sent monthly statements that contain the following information:

1. The unpaid balance at the beginning of the billing period
2. The amount of additional charges during the billing period
3. Payments made by the customer during the billing period
4. The amount of the finance charge in dollars and cents
5. The annual percentage rate used to compute the finance charge
6. The unpaid balance on which the finance charge is based
7. The new balance owed and the closing date of the billing period

As buying on credit has become more frequent, so have errors in billing become more frequent. Billing errors include arithmetic errors; failure to record payments made; a charge made to the wrong account; or charges made for the wrong merchandise, an incorrect amount, or merchandise that was never delivered.

In 1974, Congress passed the Fair Credit Billing Act to enable a consumer to resolve billing errors and disputes at little cost. Under this law, a person who receives a bill and thinks that it is wrong must notify the creditor in writing within sixty days after the bill was mailed. The creditor must acknowledge this letter within thirty days of receiving it. Within ninety days, the creditor must either correct the bill or state why it believes that the bill is correct as it is. The notice to the creditor must contain the name and account number of the person complaining, the nature of the complaint, and the amount believed to be in error. While waiting to have a bill corrected, the consumer does not have to pay any disputed amounts. The consumer must, however, pay all charges not being disputed. The creditor may not try to collect the disputed amount of a bill or damage the consumer's credit rating during the time the dispute is being investigated.

The law also provides that if a consumer receives defective merchandise or poor services bought on credit, the consumer may withhold payment, provided he or she has attempted to return the defective merchandise or resolve the problem with the seller. The consumer will not have to pay a penalty for withholding payment until the matter is solved.

THE RIGHT TO FAIR DEBT COLLECTION

Most people pay their bills and debts on time. When they don't, creditors may take steps to collect amounts owed. Some creditors have their own collection departments; others use attorneys or collection agencies. To protect consumers against unfair collection practices, Congress passed the Fair Debt Collection Practices Act in 1977. This law covers the collection of personal, family, and household debts but does not cover business debts. One of the major purposes of this law is to control the conduct of a debt collector. A **debt collector** is a person or company whose business it is to collect the debts owed to its clients; this includes attorneys engaged in collection practices. The act specifies what methods the debt collector may use in trying to collect a debt. The law, however, does not apply to the creditors themselves or to those who are not professional debt collectors.

The debt collector has a right to contact the debtor about the debt. The debt collector may not, however, contact the debtor at an inconvenient time (usually before 8 A.M. or after 9 P.M.), at an inconvenient place (e.g., a restaurant), or at the debtor's place of employment if the employer does not permit such contacts.

> Casey stopped making payments on a VCR because of financial problems. A debt collector called Casey at work every day, even though Casey's employer objected and told the debt collector so. The debt collector violated the Fair Debt Collection Practices Act.

The act requires a debt collector to send the debtor written notice (within five days after initially contacting the debtor) describing the amount due, the name of the creditor, and the debtor's rights. If the debtor informs the collector in writing within thirty days that the debt is not owed, further collection efforts must be stopped until the debt collector can supply the debtor with proof of the debt.

The act also prohibits specific abusive collection tactics, such as the use of obscene language, threats of violence, and annoying or anonymous telephone calls. Misrepresentation of the collector's identity or any indication that the debtor has committed a crime by failing to pay the debt is also prohibited.

> Bender failed to make several payments on a car loan. A debt collector advised her that failure to make payments would result in a jail sentence. This advice was false and was a violation of the Fair Debt Collection Practices Act.

Debt collectors also may not issue any official-looking documents to the debtor that have any resemblance to those used by public officials or regulatory agencies.

> Egan was late in paying a car loan installment. The account was turned over to Eagle Collection Company. Eagle sent Egan a letter that stated in part (in large, bold type): **"BY NOT PAYING YOUR DEBT, YOU HAVE VIOLATED THE LAWS OF THE UNITED STATES. IF YOU ARE SUED, YOU WILL NOT ESCAPE FEDERAL JUDGMENT."** At the top of this statement was the U.S. insignia of the bald eagle. The letter to Egan was a violation of the Fair Debt Collection Practices Act.

Various state laws and court decisions also protect the debtor from unfair collection practices. Most states require certain procedures to be followed before a judgment may be taken against a debtor. In some states, a debtor must be notified before a default judgment may be taken. A default judgment is a judgment entered against a debtor who fails to respond to a lawsuit brought to collect the debt. Once a judgment has been entered against a debtor, a creditor is limited in the actions it can take to collect the judgment. A creditor may ask a debtor to state, under oath, her or his assets. Certain assets may be taken to pay a debt, but some assets are exempt property under state law. **Exempt property** refers to

debt collector a person or company whose business is to collect debts owed to clients

exempt property property that cannot be taken to satisfy a debt

those assets that may not be taken to pay a judgment; they include clothes, household furniture, dishes, and other personal items.

Garnishment, which is a legal means of taking part of a debtor's earnings to pay a judgment, is also limited in most states.

THE RIGHT TO FAIR LEASING INFORMATION

Many people are now leasing products, particularly motor vehicles, instead of purchasing them. It is often difficult for consumers to know (1) whether they should lease or purchase, (2) what the lease costs will be, and (3) how to compare leases offered by competing companies.

To assist potential lessees, Congress passed the Consumer Leasing Act in 1976. The act requires a lessor to provide a lessee with a written statement describing what is being leased, the term, the lease payments, the interest rate being charged, who is obligated to maintain the product, and the price at which the lessor can purchase the item when the lease term ends. The act also regulates what lease advertising must disclose. A lessor who violates the act may be subject to the same penalties imposed by the Truth in Lending Act.

The act does not apply to all leases. It applies only to leases of consumer (non-business) products with terms exceeding four months and where the total consideration does not exceed $25,000.

THE RIGHT TO LEGAL INTEREST CHARGES

contract rate maximum interest rate that may be charged in a credit agreement

legal rate maximum interest rate that may be charged when no rate has been agreed to

Most states have laws that protect a debtor by setting a maximum rate of interest that may be charged. Most states set two rates. The **contract rate** is the maximum rate of interest agreed to by the parties and included in a credit agreement. If no interest rate is stated in a loan or credit agreement, the maximum that may be charged is the **legal rate**. In a few states, the contract rate and the legal rate are the same.

An agreement requiring payment of an interest rate higher than the contract rate is illegal and is known as *usury*. (Usury is discussed in Chapter 10.) In most states, the penalty for usury is the forfeiture of interest by the creditor. In many states, it is also a crime to charge usurious interest.

There are several situations in which usury laws do not apply. In most states, usury laws do not apply to loans to businesses or to loans under a certain dollar amount. Usury laws often do not apply to loans given by credit unions, pawnshops, and small-loan companies. The most common exception to the usury laws concerns installment loans and credit card charges. Usury laws generally do not apply to the sale of goods on credit because these transactions often involve long-term credit with a high degree of risk to the creditor. Because of this risk, the creditor is permitted to charge a rate of interest that exceeds the contract rate.

> Frank bought a new color television set and agreed to pay for it on an installment loan basis. The interest Frank will be charged is not subject to the laws governing usury. The creditor takes a risk that Frank will not pay off the loan.

THE RIGHT TO BE RELIEVED FROM DEBT

Most people in the United States do pay their debts, but some people are unable to handle their debts. To help consumers in this situation, Congress, persuant to article 1, section 8(4) of the U.S. constitution, passed the Federal Bankruptcy Act in 1898. This act, which has been amended several times, primarily by the Bankruptcy Reform Acts of 1978 and 2005, helps relieve a debtor of debt, allowing the debtor to start a new economic life. It also allows unpaid creditors to receive the maximum amount from the debtor's assets.

A person or corporation may be declared **bankrupt** under the act by committing one or more "acts of bankruptcy." The most common act of **bankruptcy** is admitting in writing an inability to pay debts as they become due, a condition known as **insolvency**. There are two types of bankrupts: voluntary and involuntary. A **voluntary bankrupt** is a person or corporation that voluntarily files a petition to become a bankrupt. An **involuntary bankrupt** is a person or corporation forced into bankruptcy when a creditor files a petition to have the person or corporation declared bankrupt. Farmers, low-income persons, and nonprofit corporations cannot be forced into involuntary bankruptcy.

The Bankruptcy Code covers five types of bankruptcy proceedings. Chapter 7 of the act covers the best-known type of bankruptcy proceeding, usually known as ordinary or straight bankruptcy. Chapter 9 covers insolvency of a municipality. Chapter 11 of the act governs reorganization, which permits a debtor to continue in business after working out a payment arrangement with creditors. Chapter 12 affords relief for farmers. Chapter 13 permits an individual debtor to work out a payment plan with creditors, thereby avoiding the necessity of going into bankruptcy.

Chapter 7 of the act applies to individuals, partnerships, and corporations. To begin voluntary bankruptcy proceedings, a debtor files a petition in the nearest U.S. Bankruptcy Court, each of which is under the jurisdiction of a specific U.S. District Court. (A creditor files the petition for an involuntary bankrupt.) The petition contains information about the bankrupt, a list of creditors, the type and amount of each debt, and a list of the debtor's assets. The debtor must swear to the truth of the information supplied; knowingly giving false information is a crime.

Immediately upon filing a voluntary bankruptcy petition, the debtor is declared a bankrupt. The petition acts as a restraint (stay) against creditors suing for amounts owed or attempting to enforce a lien against a debtor's property. Under certain circumstances, a secured creditor may ask the court to lift the stay regarding secured property. The court notifies all creditors of the filing of the petition and sets a date for a hearing. The court also notifies creditors to file their claims against the bankrupt by a certain date. At the hearing, the court and the creditors may ask the bankrupt about the truth and accuracy of the petition. They will want to know whether any assets have been concealed or given away to try to defraud creditors or whether payments have been made to favor one creditor over another (called a preference).

Certain transfers of property by a debtor within ninety days prior to filing a petition are voidable—that is, the person receiving the property or payment may be forced to return it. Also, a trustee may void a fraudulent transfer made within two years before the date of filing. A fraudulent transfer is one made to defraud creditors, or transferring property below its true value when the debtor is insolvent (unable to pay bills as they come due).

If the bankrupt has no assets, the bankruptcy proceeding is concluded after the hearing, and the bankrupt is released from his or her debts. If the bankrupt has assets, they are turned over to a trustee (an official appointed by the courts who performs administrative duties) who sells them to pay the creditors. Creditors are paid in proportion to the amounts they are owed, although some claims, such as taxes owed, have priority.

David owed $200 to the Internal Revenue Service for income taxes, $1,000 to Jones, and $500 to Smith. David filed a petition for bankruptcy. David's assets were sold for $800. The Internal Revenue Service would receive the full $200, Jones would receive $400, and Smith would receive $200.

---

bankrupt person declared to be entitled to the protection of the bankruptcy laws

bankruptcy federal procedure relieving a debtor from his or her debts once the debtor is found to be insolvent (liabilities greater than assets)

insolvency admission in writing of an inability to pay debts as they become due

voluntary bankrupt one who files a petition for bankruptcy

involuntary bankrupt one forced into bankruptcy by a creditor

The trustee represents the debtor's property, known as the debtor's estate, and may sue on behalf of the debtor. The trustee's duties include collecting the debtor's property and selling or leasing it. Trustees are selected by the creditors in Chapter 7 and Chapter 11 proceedings, and appointed in Chapter 13 proceedings.

To avoid leaving a bankrupt with absolutely nothing, certain assets may not be taken in a bankruptcy proceeding. These assets are exemptions granted under the federal law or under the laws of the state in which the bankruptcy proceeding is held. Under federal law, a bankrupt may keep Social Security benefits, IRA assets, unemployment compensation, and insurance policies. In addition, a bankrupt may keep interest in a home or other real property up to $17,450, equity in a motor vehicle up to $2,775, up to $1,150 worth of jewelry, up to $9,300 in aggregate value of personal items and household furnishings, and $925 worth of anything else. State exemptions vary, but in most states, they include personal property and a portion of the investment in a home. Exemptions may be claimed under either federal or state law, but many states have enacted legislation requiring debtors to accept exemptions under state law. Federal exemption amounts are adjusted every three years for inflation.

discharge in bankruptcy judgment relieving a bankrupt from liability for most debts

After all debts, taxes, and administrative expenses have been paid, the bankrupt receives a judgment called a discharge in bankruptcy. A **discharge in bankruptcy** frees the bankrupt from all debts except for certain ones not dischargeable, including certain taxes, alimony, child support, and education loans unless payment of such loans would place an undue hardship on the borrower or the borrower's dependents. A discharge will also not be granted to a debtor whose conduct has included obtaining money or property under false pretenses, failing to notify a creditor of the bankruptcy proceeding, or fraudulently transferring or concealing property.

A reorganization under Chapter 11 of the Bankruptcy Code enables a debtor to continue in business by making an arrangement with creditors to pay a portion of the outstanding debts over a period of time. Although Chapter 11 is used primarily by corporations, it is available to individuals as well.

A proceeding under Chapter 11 is brought in the same manner as a Chapter 7 proceeding. A petition is filed, listing all debts and creditors. During the proceedings, the debtor may continue to operate its business but is often supervised by a court-appointed trustee. A committee of unsecured creditors is usually appointed to work with the debtor and trustee to assist in the reorganization.

Ultimately, the debtor proposes a plan of reorganization to the bankruptcy court and the creditors. The plan must indicate the different classes of creditors (based on the presence or lack of security, the amount of the claims, etc.), how much will be paid to each class of creditor, and when payment will be made. The plan must also indicate how its goals can be achieved. If the creditors accept the plan and the bankruptcy court finds that the plan is in the best interests of the creditors, the court confirms it and the debtor continues in business and is known as the "debtor-in-possession." When the goals of the plan have been achieved, the debtor is discharged.

Any debtor, individual or corporate, who is eligible for Chapter 7 relief is also eligible for Chapter 11 relief.

Chapter 13 of the Bankruptcy Act enables an individual debtor to pay off debts under a court-approved plan. It is similar to a Chapter 11 reorganization (which is also available to individual debtors), except that it is available only to individuals, not to partnerships or corporations, and there are debt ceilings, as described earlier. The advantage of Chapter 13 over Chapter 11 is that using it involves less cost, less time, and fewer complications.

A debtor files a petition listing assets and debts. A trustee is appointed to develop with the debtor a reasonable payment plan. The plan provides for payment over a period of time of either all or a portion of the debts. Payment must be made within three years, although an extension of two additional years is available with court approval. Part of the plan must be that the debtor will turn over to the trustee sufficient earnings to ensure the success of the plan.

After the debtor files a plan, the court holds a confirmation hearing. If the plan appears feasible and the secured creditors accept the plan, the court will confirm it, and all debts provided for under the plan will be discharged. As is the case under Chapters 7 and 11 of the act, certain debts, such as alimony, child support, and education loans, are not dischargeable.

After completing the plan, the debtor is fully discharged from the Chapter 13 proceeding. Unlike Chapters 7 and 11 proceedings, a debtor may ask for the bankruptcy court's assistance under Chapter 13 any number of times.

Filing for bankruptcy and for assistance under Chapter 13 of the Federal Bankruptcy Act are considered proper solutions for financial distress. They are serious matters, however, and they should not be undertaken unless no other remedies are available. Under federal law, bankruptcy information remains part of a person's credit history for ten years. If a person files for assistance under Chapter 13, the time period is seven years. It becomes difficult for an individual or business to obtain credit during these periods so as to prevent individuals and businesses from going into bankruptcy solely to avoid paying their debts.

In recent years, Congress felt that the bankruptcy laws were being abused by persons who amassed large debts and then immediately filed for bankruptcy. To limit the right of persons to file for bankruptcy, Congress in 2005 enacted the Bankruptcy Abuse Prevention and Consumer Protection Act. The most significant provisions of the act are:

1. All debtors must receive credit counseling at least six months before they can file for bankruptcy.
2. All debtors must take a financial means test to determine whether they may file a liquidation plan under Chapter 7 or a repayment plan under Chapter 13. Basically, the bankruptcy court will determine a debtor's income after deducting certain expenses based on standards established by the IRS. The income figure is then compared to the median income of the residents of the state in which the debtor resides. If the debtor's income is below the state's median income figure, the debtor may file under Chapter 7; otherwise, the debtor must file under Chapter 13 and enter into a repayment plan.
3. All debtors must take a credit management course before receiving a final discharge in bankruptcy.
4. The bankruptcy court on its own initiative may convert a Chapter 7 case into a Chapter 13 case. Under prior laws, only a debtor could ask for and receive the right to proceed under Chapter 13. If the court does convert a Chapter 7 case into a Chapter 13 case or dismisses the petition altogether (something not allowed under prior law), the court may require the debtor and the debtor's attorney to pay court costs and other fees.

Other remedies available to persons with financial problems are not as drastic as the bankruptcy courts. A person in debt may be able to work out an informal arrangement with creditors to pay debts over a period of time. There are also debt-counseling services, which may be able to work out informal arrangements with creditors. Many of the counseling services are available without charge; others charge for their services.

Summary

Federal and state governments have enacted many laws to protect consumers who buy on credit and to protect borrowers of money. The areas of protection include the right to obtain credit, the right to be charged only those interest charges permitted by law, the right to receive accurate bills, the right to be free from harassing collection methods, and the right to relief from debt.

The two basic types of credit available to a consumer are unsecured credit, which is based solely on the consumer's promise to repay, and secured credit, which is also based on a pledge of the borrower's property. The three types of credit used most often are charge accounts, installment loans, and bank loans.

The right to obtain credit is controlled by the Equal Credit Opportunity Act. This law prevents creditors from discriminating against certain people and seeks to make sure that credit is based almost solely on the ability to pay. Age, gender, or marital status cannot legally be considered in determining whether to grant credit.

A borrower often does not know what credit is actually going to cost. The Truth in Lending Act helps consumers and borrowers know what they are being charged for the use of credit. This information enables them to make intelligent choices when deciding about borrowing money.

Billing errors and disputes can seriously damage a person's credit record. The Fair Credit Reporting Act provides consumers with a way to determine whether their credit records are accurate and with a method for recording any errors in such reports.

When a consumer has purchased goods on credit or borrowed money, it is important that any bills sent are accurate. The Fair Credit Billing Act enables a consumer or borrower to resolve billing errors or disputes in a simplified, inexpensive way.

The Fair Debt Collection Practices Act regulates the collection of all debts except business obligations. The purpose of this law is to control the acts of debt collectors and to prohibit abusive collection tactics.

Debtors are often faced with higher than normal interest charges that they feel powerless to contest. To assist them, most states have enacted usury laws. These laws regulate the interest rate that may be charged and provide penalties for those who charge interest rates higher than those permitted by law. There are some exceptions to usury laws.

Some people are unable to handle their debts and face suits from creditors. The Federal Bankruptcy Act helps debtors to seek relief from debt and get a new start on life. The act covers three types of proceedings. One involves straight bankruptcy, another governs reorganization for individuals and businesses, and the third permits an individual debtor to work out a payment plan with creditors. In addition to the plans permitted under the Bankruptcy Act, many voluntary plans are available, including voluntary arrangements with creditors. The latter may provide less drastic relief than that provided by the Bankruptcy Act, which affects a person's credit history for seven to ten years.

Important Legal terms

annual percentage rate	debit card	legal rate
bankrupt	debt collector	line of credit
bankruptcy	debtor	regular charge account
charge account	discharge in bankruptcy	revolving charge account
collateral	exempt property	secured credit
contract rate	finance charge	unsecured credit
credit	insolvency	voluntary bankrupt
credit card	installment loan	
creditor	involuntary bankrupt	

Questions and Problems for Discussion

1. What factors may a creditor consider in deciding whether or not to grant credit?

2. What is the difference between a credit card and a debit card?

3. Explain the difference between secured credit and unsecured credit.

4. A credit card company sent a card to Edwards, who hadn't asked for it. Edwards threw the card out but someone found it, signed Edwards's name to it, and used it to buy a digital camera. Is Edwards liable for the credit card charge?

5. Lawlor bought a computer for his business from Ace Computers. He fell behind in making payments on the computer. An Ace employee called Lawlor every day at work and at home to try to collect the debt. May Ace try to collect the debt in this manner?

6. Braun asked the Genesee Bank for a loan of $100,000 to expand her business. Must the bank disclose to Braun the finance charge and annual percentage rate?

7. Barnes bought a television set from Janeway on credit. The price tag indicated a price of $400. Barnes signed a contract agreeing to pay for the set in 12 monthly payments of $40 each. The contract contained no other terms. Did the contract violate the Truth in Lending Act?

8. Creary tried to open a charge account at Payless Stores. When the store checked Creary's credit rating with a credit bureau, it learned that Creary was a slow payer and refused to open an account for him. The store refused to tell Creary why the request for an account was denied, claiming that the information was confidential. Is Creary entitled to the information?

9. Marshall borrowed $1,000 from a bank, payable at the end of one year at the highest legal interest rate permitted in that state. The bank gave Marshall only $750, however, keeping the other $250 as part of the "cost" of the loan. Is this loan usurious?

10. Green borrowed money from a bank to finance her education; the loan was guaranteed by the federal government. Green then suffered financial problems and was forced to file a petition in bankruptcy. Is she still obligated to repay the loan?

11. Greer failed to make three payments on a music store installment purchase. A debt collector advised Greer that the store would sue her if the payments were not made up. Is this statement a violation of the Fair Debt Collection Practices Act?

12. Davis owed $200 to the IRS for income taxes, $300 to Olympia Bank for a student loan, $1,000 to Jones, and $500 to Smith. Davis filed a petition for bankruptcy. At the time of filing, Davis's assets were worth $800 and sold for that amount. How much money would each of Davis's creditors receive?

13. Ferris bought a new car and agreed to pay for it on an installment loan basis. A week after Ferris bought the car, he looked over the installment loan contract and discovered that the interest rate was 28 percent, although the laws in his state made it unlawful to charge any rate of interest in excess of 10 percent. Was the interest charged by the automobile dealer a violation of the state usury laws?

14. Because of financial problems, Casey stopped making payments on a VCR he purchased on an installment basis. Each night for two weeks, a debt collector called Casey at his home at 7:30 P.M. and requested payment of the amount due. Were these calls a violation of the Fair Debt Collection Practices Act?

15. If you find errors in your credit report, what can you do to correct them?

16. Allen burrowed $10,000 for his business from a friend and agreed to pay interest at the rate of 25 percent per year, but this was not disclosed in the promissory note he gave to his friend. Does this violate the Truth-in-Lending Act?

Cases for Review

1. Mr. and Mrs. Orlosky signed a contract for a security system for their home. There were Truth in Lending Act (TILA) violations in the retail sales agreement. The seller assigned the contract to a finance company that was unaware of the violations. The Orloskys brought suit against the seller and the assignee. The assignee claimed it was not responsible for the violations. Is this claim correct? (*Orlosky* v. *Empire Sec. Systems, Inc.* 657 N.Y.S.2d 300, 91 A.D.2d 401, 1997)

2. Miller took out a credit card from the European American Bank, induced by the bank's offer of a certificate for a free airline ticket. When the offer was made, the bank failed to disclose restrictions placed on the use of the free ticket. Miller sued, claiming the failure to disclose was a violation of the TILA. Will Miller succeed? (*Miller* v. *Empire American Bank*, 1996, 921 F.Supp. 1162)

3. Roarke borrowed money from the State Bank of Albany and signed four notes to evidence the loan. The notes were not accompanied by a Truth in Lending Act disclosure statement, but the loan forms stated that the loans were for business purposes. Roarke defaulted and the bank sued. Does Roarke have a defense against the suit because of alleged TILA violations? (*State Bank of Albany* v. *Roarke*, 458 N.Y.S.2d 300, 91 A.D.2d 1093, 1983)

4. WEB, Inc., had a corporate credit account with American Express. Cards were issued to four individuals, including a real estate broker who had a relationship with one of the company officers. When the relationship ended, the broker went on a spending spree for personal items and charged over $27,000 on the credit card. WEB claimed that under the Truth in Lending Act, it was not responsible for the broker's charges. Is the claim correct? (*American Express* v. *WEB, Inc.*, 261 Ga. 480)

5. Steele, while a patient in a hospital, let a friend use her credit card to buy one tank of gasoline for a trip to Cleveland. The friend not only used the card to buy many other things but also let friends use the card. Steele notified the credit card company of the problem. She claimed that her liability for the unauthorized charges was limited to $50 for purchases between the time she loaned the card and the time she notified the card company. Is her claim correct? (*Standard Oil Co.* v. *Steele*, 22 Ohio Misc.2d 27)

6. Jackson bought a car from South Holland Dodge (SHD). She also agreed to buy a service contract and extended warranty. The car was purchased using a retail sales installment contract that included, in addition to the purchase price, a separate charge for the service contract and warranty that was to be paid to the car manufacturer, the Chrysler Corporation. In fact, the amount listed was divided between SHD and Chrysler, and no one ever told Jackson or others that the charge was negotiable. SHD later assigned the contract to Chrysler Finance Corporation (CFC). Jackson and others brought a class-action suit against both SHD and CFC, claiming deceptive practices and misrepresentation under Illinois's consumer fraud acts. CFC asked to have the case against it dismissed on the grounds that it was an assignee of the contract and therefore should not be responsible for the dealer's acts. Should this defense prevail? (*Jackson* v. *South Holland Dodge, Inc.*, 312 Ill. App.3d 158)

7. Guimond discovered that information in her credit file was inaccurate. She notified the company, but it did not correct the mistakes until a year later. She sued the credit company under the Fair Credit Reporting Act. The credit company claimed that there was no violation of the act because she hadn't been denied credit during the year. Is this a good defense? (*Guimond* v. *Trans Union Credit Information Co.*, 45 F.3d 1329)

8. Rutyna failed to pay an outstanding medical bill because she believed that Medicare would pay it. After denying that she owed the amount claimed, she received a letter from a collection agency threatening to tell her neighbors and her employer about the debt if she didn't pay it immediately. Was this a violation of the Fair Debt Collection Act? (*Rutyna* v. *Collection Accounts Terminal, Inc.*, 478 F.Supp.980)

9. Allen took out a loan from Landmark in his own name but used the proceeds to buy a frozen yogurt machine for use in his business. Landmark failed to disclose the information required by the Truth in Lending Act, claiming this was a commercial transaction. Allen claimed the loan was covered by the law because the loan was taken out in his name. Who is correct? (*Allen* v. *Landmark Finance Corporation of Georgia*, USDC, ND of Ga 1979 CCH Consumer Credit Guide, Sec 1007.02)

10. Miller applied for an oil company credit card. He was refused the card because of a poor credit report that was based on incorrect information. Miller sued the credit bureau for violating the Fair Credit Reporting Act by failing to verify the truth of the credit report. The credit bureau claimed that its only duty was to collect information, not to decide whether it was accurate. Will Miller win? (*Miller* v. *Credit Bureau, Inc.*, DC Super, Ct, 1972 CCH Consumer Credit Guide, Sec 680.04, 680.79, 680.61)

CHAPTER **37**

Protecting the Creditor

CHAPTER PREVIEW

Protecting Creditors' Rights	Remedies for Debtor's Default
The Right to Be Paid	**Security Interests Created by Law**
Unsecured Debts	Mechanic's Lien
Secured Debts	Tax Lien
Other Methods of Protecting Creditors' Rights	Judgment Lien
Suretyship	Artisan's Lien
Guaranty	Hotelkeeper's Lien

Chapter Highlights

Just as consumers and borrowers have certain rights that need protection, so too do those who sell goods on credit and those who lend money. This chapter describes the methods by which creditors can protect themselves to ensure payment. It discusses the different types of debtor-creditor transactions. The chapter also discusses protection for creditors in the form of liens that are provided by statutes. Finally, the chapter describes remedies available to creditors if debtors default in making payments and discusses other devices that may be used to protect creditors.

PROTECTING CREDITORS' RIGHTS

In recent years, the consumer movement has stressed the need to protect the debtor. Creditors also have rights that need protection if creditors are to remain in business, however. Both statute and case law provide the creditor with methods to ensure payment. These methods may well be called a "Bill of Rights for the Creditor."

THE RIGHT TO BE PAID

A creditor has an absolute right to be paid unless the debtor has certain defenses against the creditor, such as fraud or misrepresentation. How and in what manner a creditor may enforce this right depend on whether the credit transaction is unsecured or secured.

Unsecured Debts

unsecured debt debt based solely on the debtor's promise to pay

An **unsecured debt** is one based solely on the debtor's promise to pay. This promise may be made orally or in writing. Much of consumer debt today is of the unsecured type. Examples of unsecured debts are purchases made on a charge account or a personal loan from a friend, family member, or bank.

> You borrowed money from Dane, a friend, and promised to repay the loan in two weeks. The only security Dane has for her loan to you is your promise to repay it.

A creditor holding an unsecured debt is limited in the methods that can be used to collect the debt. If a debtor goes beyond the time for repayment of the debt, a creditor will normally start the collection process by contacting the debtor and asking for payment. If this step fails, the creditor may ask a collection agency to collect the debt. If this step also fails, the creditor may sue the debtor for payment. If the creditor wins, the creditor will get a judgment against the debtor. A judgment, in this case, is a court order directing the debtor to pay the debt owed to the creditor. Once the creditor has obtained the judgment, the creditor may attempt to collect the amount owed out of the debtor's assets. If the debtor has sufficient assets with which to pay the debt, the creditor will be paid.

writ formal court command requiring the performance of an act

execution the seizure of a debtor's property to satisfy a judgment

If the judgment is not paid, the creditor can obtain an order, or **writ** as it is sometimes called, of execution. The **execution** directs the appropriate enforcement officer, usually a sheriff, to seize the debtor's personal property and sell enough of that property to pay the judgment, plus any costs or expenses. If the execution does not produce enough funds to pay the judgment, the judgment then becomes a lien on any real property owned by the debtor. The debtor's real property may then be sold to satisfy the judgment.

garnishment seizure of a portion of a debtor's wages to satisfy a judgment

Another method used by a creditor to collect a judgment is garnishment. **Garnishment** is a court-ordered process authorizing an employer to seize (deduct a portion of) the wages of a debtor. A bank account or any amounts owed to the debtor by a third party may also be garnished. The amounts seized are paid to either the court or a sheriff and are then applied against the debt. State laws limit the amount of wages that may be seized so that the debtor is not left penniless. Occasionally, a debtor will voluntarily consent to have a portion of her or his wages turned over to a creditor to repay a debt. This process is known as **wage assignment**.

wage assignment debtor's voluntary transfer of wages to a debtor to repay a debt

attachment seizure of a debtor's property prior to a judgment

Sometimes a creditor believes that a debtor may dispose of or transfer assets before a judgment can be obtained. If that is the case, the creditor may ask the court to issue an attachment. An **attachment** is an order to seize (attach) and hold property of the debtor before a judgment is obtained. If the creditor later obtains a judgment, the attached property may be sold to satisfy it.

Secured Debts

secured debt debt in which the creditor has a claim against specific property of the debtor

An unsecured creditor is not only limited in the methods that can be used to collect a debt but also may face competition from other creditors. Recall from Chapter 36 that some of a debtor's property may even be exempt from execution. To get an extra measure of protection, a creditor may insist on a secured debt. A **secured debt**, created by an agreement between the debtor and the creditor, is one in which the creditor has a claim against specific property of the debtor. The creditor's claim in the property is called a *security interest*. Secured debts occur at all levels of commerce, including the purchase of motor vehicles and the financing of inventory purchases.

security agreement agreement giving a creditor a security interest in a debtor's property

A secured debt, or *secured transaction* as it is often called, is created by a **security agreement**. This agreement must be in writing and signed by both the debtor and the creditor. The agreement includes the names and addresses of the debtor and the creditor, the amount of the debt, the terms of payment, and a description of the property in which the creditor gets a security interest. The property pledged by the debtor as security for the debt is the *collateral*.

Collateral may be either tangible or intangible property. Tangible property consists of such things as consumer goods, farm products, equipment, or the inventory of a business. Intangible property refers to the rights (claims) to property, such as money. Stocks and accounts receivable are examples of intangible property.

Blue borrowed $6,000 from Midtown National Bank to buy a car and gave the bank a security interest in the car. The contract that Blue signed is a security agreement. The car, a consumer good, is the collateral for the loan.

Property pledged as collateral may be in the possession of either the debtor or the creditor. In most cases, the debtor has possession of the property. For example, if you buy a boat on a secured installment loan, you have possession of the boat, but you must sign a security agreement giving the creditor a security interest in the boat. Occasionally, the creditor has possession of the collateral. For example, a pawnshop owner who lends you money on a piece of property (e.g., a ring or watch) holds the property until you repay the loan.

financing statement public notice of the existence of a security interest in certain property of the debtor

For certain transactions, a **financing statement** must be filed to give public notice that a creditor holds a security interest in specific property of the debtor. A security agreement is valid regardless of whether or not a financing statement is filed. The financing statement is filed only to give notice to third parties. The financing statement identifies the parties to the security agreement (i.e., the debtor and the creditor) and describes the property serving as collateral. This public notice warns others who may be interested in buying the collateral or lending money based on its value that a security interest already exists and has first claim on the property. The financing statement is usually filed in a county clerk's office or in the office of a state's motor vehicle bureau. When the debt is paid in full, a notice is filed in the same office indicating that the security interest is no longer claimed. This notice is called a **termination statement**.

termination statement public notice indicating that a security interest is no longer claimed in certain property

A financing statement is effective for five years from the date of filing and may be extended for an additional five years.

Article 9 of the UCC, now revised and effective in all states as of July 1, 2001, covers transactions involving security interests in personal property. The security must be to secure payment of a debt that has been agreed to between debtor and creditor; that is, it would not apply to liens, discussed later in this chapter. Obtaining a secured interest is usually involved when a person buys personal property, or needs credit to make the purchase and the seller wants to be assured of payment.

Not all security agreements require the filing of a financing statement to protect the creditor. The Uniform Commercial Code distinguishes between a sale of equipment or inventory goods on credit and a sale of consumer goods on credit. A financing statement must be filed for a credit sale of equipment or inventory but is not necessary for most consumer credit sales. The exceptions to this rule involve security interests in automobiles, farm equipment costing over $2,500, and goods such as elevators that are to be attached to buildings or land.

OTHER METHODS OF PROTECTING CREDITORS' RIGHTS

suretyship promise by a third party to be primarily responsible for another person's debt

There are many other ways creditors can protect their rights with the consent of the debtor. The two most common means are the use of a suretyship and the use of a guaranty. Both involve getting a third party to assume some form of obligation for repayment of the debt.

Suretyship

surety third party who agrees to be primarily responsible for another person's debt if the debtor defaults

A **suretyship** is a promise by a third party, the **surety**, to pay a creditor the amount of the debt if the debtor defaults. A surety agrees to be primarily responsible for the amount of the debt if the debtor defaults. That is, the creditor may look to the surety for payment without first having to sue the debtor. If the surety has to pay the creditor, the surety may then sue the debtor for payment. A surety's promise to pay may be oral or written.

> Campo borrowed money from First Trade Bank to start a lawn mower repair business. The bank would not lend the money unless Campo's father agreed to act as surety and be liable for the debt along with Campo. If Campo does not repay the loan, the bank may go directly to Campo's father to collect the amount due.

Defenses to a suit against a surety include the existence of fraud or duress against the debtor, a material alteration of the agreement between debtor and creditor, and release of the debtor by the creditor.

Guaranty

guaranty promise by a third party to be secondarily liable for the debt of another person

guarantor third party who agrees to repay another person's debt if the debtor defaults

A **guaranty** is similar to a suretyship except that the **guarantor**, the person who gives the guaranty, is not primarily liable for the debt. That is, if the debtor defaults, the creditor must first attempt to collect the debt from the debtor. If that fails, only then may the creditor look to the guarantor for payment. A guaranty must be in writing to be enforceable.

> Drumm agreed to act as guarantor for his sister's loan. If the sister fails to repay the loan, the lender must first sue the sister. If the lender obtains a judgment and still is unable to collect payment from the sister, the lender may proceed to Drumm for payment.

Both suretyship and guaranty agreements terminate when the debtor pays the debt in full. They also terminate if the debtor and the creditor make a significant change in the terms of the agreement without the consent of the surety or the guarantor. Such termination protects the surety and guarantor against an increase or change in their liability without their knowledge or agreement.

> Grodin agreed to act as guarantor for a loan of $10,000 made by Benevolent Loan Company to her brother. Benevolent later loaned her brother an additional $5,000, increasing the loan to $15,000, without notifying Grodin. The additional loan releases Grodin from her obligations under the guaranty.

Both a contract of guaranty and a contract of suretyship require consideration to be enforceable. When either contract is made at the same time as the original transaction, the consideration for the original promise is also consideration for the promise of the guarantor or surety. When the contract of guaranty or suretyship is entered into after the original transaction, however, there must be new consideration for the promise of the guarantor or surety.

> Sanders bought a new car and wanted to finance the purchase with a bank loan. Because she was unemployed, the bank would not give Sanders the loan unless her father acted as guarantor. The consideration for his promise as guarantor is the promise made by the bank to grant the loan.

Remedies for Debtor's Default

If a debtor cannot or will not make payments, the debtor is said to be "in default." A secured creditor has two options if a debtor defaults. One option is to sell the collateral and use the proceeds to pay the debt. If the creditor has possession of the collateral, such as stocks put up as security for a loan, the creditor may sell the property, keep an amount equal to the unpaid debt and any expenses of the sale, and return any amount left over to the debtor.

If the debtor has possession of the collateral, the creditor may take steps to gain possession of the property. This process is known as **repossession**. In some states, the creditor may repossess the collateral without court proceedings if it can be done peacefully. If that is impossible, or if state law requires, the creditor must get a court order authorizing the repossession.

The creditor who has repossessed the collateral does not have to sell it if the debtor agrees. The creditor may lease the collateral or keep it as payment for the debt. The creditor must notify the debtor of this intention. If the debtor objects to the creditor holding the collateral, the creditor must sell the collateral and use the proceeds to pay off the debt. A debtor who has made some payments on the debt may want to force the sale of the collateral to recover any money left over after payment of the debt. Otherwise, the debtor would forfeit any amount already paid.

If the creditor does decide to sell the collateral, it may be sold at a public or a private sale and on the creditor's own terms. The sale must be conducted in good faith, and the debtor must get advance notice of the sale. After the collateral is sold, the proceeds are used to pay the expenses of repossessing the collateral, the expenses of the sale, and the debt itself. If any money is left, it goes to the debtor. If the proceeds are not enough to pay the debt, the creditor may sue the debtor for the balance of the debt.

> Ewell defaulted on a car installment loan and the bank repossessed the car. The loan balance was $4,000. If the car was sold for $4,500 and the expenses amounted to $800, the bank could sue Ewell for the balance of $300.

The second option a creditor has for a debtor's default is to sue the debtor and try to obtain a judgment. If the judgment is granted, the debtor must pay the debt, or assets of the debtor may be taken and sold to pay the debt. After obtaining a judgment, a secured creditor has the same options as an unsecured creditor who obtains a judgment: execution and garnishment.

SECURITY INTERESTS CREATED BY LAW

Some creditors are given a security interest by law to protect them in the event of non-payment by debtors. This type of security interest, which can be enforced against property, is called a **lien**. The person who has the lien (the creditor) is called the **lienholder**. Liens give a creditor an extra measure of protection over and above the normal rights of an unsecured creditor. There may be many types of liens, including mechanic's liens, tax liens, judgment liens, artisan's liens, and hotelkeeper's liens.

Mechanic's Lien

A **mechanic's lien** is a lien given to those who supply labor, materials, or services in the construction of buildings and other structures. A lien may be placed against the building to ensure that the owner pays for all the materials and services provided in its construction. The lienholder files a notice of the lien in a public office. While the notice is on file, the owner cannot sell or mortgage the property against which the lien has been filed. If a debt is not paid, the lienholder may sue to have the property sold and apply the proceeds to pay the debt.

Tax Lien

A **tax lien** is a lien given to an agency or unit of the government to ensure the payment of property taxes. Most local governments rely on property taxes to supply a large part of their operating funds. They could not continue to operate if they could not collect

repossession steps taken by a creditor to gain possession of the collateral for a debt

lien security interest created by law

lienholder person holding a lien

mechanic's lien lien given to those who supply labor, materials, or services in construction projects

tax lien lien given to a government agency to ensure the payment of property taxes

property taxes. If taxes remain unpaid for a certain period of time, the taxing authority may sell the property and pay the taxes due out of the proceeds. This procedure is a last resort, and the property owner has several opportunities to pay the taxes before the property is sold.

Judgment Lien

judgment lien lien granted to a creditor who has sued a debtor and obtained a judgment against the debtor

A **judgment lien** is a lien granted to a creditor who has sued a debtor and obtained a judgment. As discussed earlier in the chapter, the creditor may sell the property of the debtor and pay the judgment out of the proceeds.

Artisan's Lien

artisan's lien lien a service provider has against personal property for unpaid bills

An **artisan's lien** is a lien given to someone who has performed labor on or added value to personal property. As long as the property is in the possession of the lienholder and payment is not made, the lienholder may sell the property to satisfy the debt, after giving notice to the owner of the property. Typical lienholders of this type are jewelers, auto repair shops, and dry cleaners.

Hotelkeeper's Lien

hotelkeeper's lien lien a hotel owner has against property of a guest for unpaid bills

A **hotelkeeper's lien** is one placed on a guest's baggage to ensure payment of hotel charges. If the charges are unpaid, the hotelkeeper may satisfy the debt by selling the baggage at a public sale.

Summary

If creditors are going to continue to sell goods on credit and lend money, their right to be paid must be protected. Statutes and case law both provide creditors with methods to ensure payment.

Debts are either unsecured or secured. The typical debt is unsecured; it is based solely on the debtor's promise to pay. A creditor who is unpaid has only one recourse: to go into court and sue the debtor. Once a creditor obtains a judgment, a number of devices are available to assist in collecting the amount due, including seizing and attaching the debtor's property, garnishment of wages, and a voluntary wage assignment from the debtor to the creditor.

A secured debt is one in which a creditor has a claim against specific property of the debtor. The debtor and creditor enter into a security agreement that establishes the secured transaction. The agreement, or a memorandum of the agreement, is filed in a public office, giving notice to the public of the existence of the security agreement. If the debtor fails to pay the debt, the creditor can seize the property involved, sell it, and satisfy the debt out of the proceeds. A mortgage and an automobile loan are examples of security interests in specific property.

Creditors may also protect their interests by getting a third party to guarantee repayment of a loan. The two methods most often used are suretyship and guaranty. In both cases, a third party guarantees repayment of the debt. The difference between them is that a surety may be held as liable for the debt as the debtor. A guarantor may be held liable only after the debtor is unable or unwilling to pay the debt.

The law gives certain creditors extra protection in the form of a security interest known as a lien. A lien is similar to a security interest in specific property. In the event of nonpayment, the creditor may seize the property covered by the security interest, force a sale, and apply the proceeds to pay the debt.

Important Legal terms

artisan's lien	judgment lien	suretyship
attachment	lien	tax lien
execution	lienholder	termination statement
financing statement	mechanic's lien	unsecured debt
garnishment	repossession	wage assignment
guarantor	secured debt	writ
guaranty	security agreement	
hotelkeeper's lien	surety	

Questions and Problems for Discussion

1. What is the difference between a secured debt and an unsecured debt?

2. Describe the methods available to an unsecured creditor to collect a debt.

3. Why do you think that certain liens, such as tax liens, were created by law?

4. Harper bought a TV set from a department store and charged it on his charge account. When he failed to pay for the set, the store tried to repossess it. Can the store legally do so?

5. Berke bought a car from Apex Autos and financed the purchase with an installment loan. Apex failed to file the financing statement. Is Apex protected if Berke sells the car to someone else without paying off the installment loan?

6. Rogers borrowed $10,000 from Upstate Bank, with Rogers's sister agreeing to act as guarantor of the loan. The loan agreement provided that loan payments were to be made in person. A month after the loan was made, Rogers and the bank agreed that the payments were to be made by mail but did not notify Rogers's sister of the change. Is Rogers's sister released from her guaranty?

7. Friendly agreed to act as surety on a loan given by Ace Finance Company to James. When James could not repay the loan, Ace came directly to Friendly for payment without attempting to get the money from James. Friendly refused to pay, claiming that Ace should first try to collect from James. Is Friendly correct?

8. Ramirez bought a used hay spreader from Hurdle for $3,000, paying $1,000 in cash and the balance in a promissory note secured by a security agreement. Before Hurdle filed the financing statement, Ramirez used the spreader as collateral to obtain a loan from Allen, who did file a financing statement. If Ramirez does not repay the loans, who has a prior right to repossess the spreader, Hurdle or Allen?

9. Stone, a home designer, designed a house for Berry. When Berry failed to pay Stone for her design services, Stone filed a mechanic's lien against the house. Berry claimed that the lien was invalid because it was not filed for materials used in building the house. Is Berry correct?

10. Drew sold Maple a car and agreed to take a security interest in the car in return for letting Maple make twelve monthly payments on the balance of the purchase price. When Maple defaulted on the payments, Drew sued Maple. Must Drew repossess the car before bringing a suit against Maple?

11. Blaine agreed to act as guarantor for a loan made to her brother. The guaranty was made orally at the bank. Is Blaine bound by the guaranty?

12. Rey owed Imperial Bank $400. When he couldn't pay, the bank took a judgment against Rey and filed a garnishment against his wages. Rey's employer agreed to turn all Rey's salary over to the bank until the debt was paid in full. May the employer do so?

13. Jordan bought a boat from Act Marine on credit and signed a security agreement. Act failed to file the agreement or a financing statement. May Jordan refuse to pay the balance due on the grounds that the security agreement is invalid?

14. Burger borrowed $10,000 on a three-year term from Valley National Bank. Burger's uncle signed as guarantor of the loan. At the end of the three years, Burger requested that the bank extend the

loan for an additional three years and the bank agreed. Burger's uncle was never notified of the loan extension. Is Burger's uncle relieved from liability as guarantor of the loan?

15. Young agreed to act as guarantor for a loan made to his sister. The guaranty was made orally over the telephone. Is Young bound by the guaranty?

16. Liang, an architect, designed a house for Sommers. When Sommers failed to pay Liang for the services rendered, Liang filed a mechanic's lien against the house. Sommers claimed that the lien was invalid because it was not filed for materials used in building the house. Is Sommers correct?

Cases for Review

1. Security Bank loaned money to Mr. and Mrs. Russell to buy a 50-foot cabin cruiser. The Russells signed a note and a security agreement. Under the terms of the agreement, an unauthorized sale of the boat constituted a default under the security agreement. The agreement was never filed in any public office. The Russells sold the boat without the bank's consent, and the bank declared the entire balance of the loan due and payable. The Russells claim that the bank does not have a valid security interest in the boat because the security agreement was never filed. Is the claim correct? (*Security Bank of Oregon* v. *Levens*, 257 Or. 630)

2. The Bank of Babylon had a security agreement in connection with a loan to Cherno that authorized the bank, in the event of default, to enter Cherno's home and retake the collateral. Using a key, employees of the bank entered Cherno's home and seized the collateral. Is the bank permitted to do so? (*Cherno* v. *Bank of Babylon*, N.Y. 54 Misc. 2d 277)

3. Koontz financed the purchase of a car with a loan from Chrysler Credit Corp. When Koontz defaulted in payment, Chrysler sent a collection agency to repossess the car. The agency found the car in Koontz's yard and began to tow it away, despite protests from Koontz. Chrysler resold the car and sued Koontz for the difference between the debt and the sale price. Koontz objected on the grounds that Chrysler had breached the peace in repossessing the car by taking it over his protests. Is Koontz correct? (*Chrysler Credit Corp.* v. *Koontz*, 661 N.E.2d 1171)

4. Anderson and For-Med, Inc. borrowed about $80,000 from First Westside Bank, using Anderson's mobile home as collateral for the loan. When a default in payment occurred, the bank repossessed the motor home. Before finally selling it, the bank obtained bids from other dealers, customers, and banks. It then sold the motor home for $60,000 and sued Anderson and For-Med for the difference between the debt and the sale price. Anderson and For-Med claimed that the sale was not reasonable because the bank had not advertised the sale sufficiently. Was this a good defense to the suit? (*First Westside Bank* v. *For-Med, Inc.*, 529 N.W.2d 66)

5. Daniels bought a car from Lindsay Cadillac Co. Because his credit rating was poor, he had his brother act as surety for the loan to purchase the car. His brother signed the purchase contract on the line marked "buyer" and he signed on the line marked "co-buyer." The contract was assigned to GMAC. When a default occurred, GMAC repossessed the car, found it was a total loss and sued both brothers. However, they couldn't find Daniels, so they sued the brother who was the surety. The brother argued that he was a guarantor only, and thus, the bank first would have to proceed against his brother before it could proceed against him. GMAC argued that as the brother had signed the contract as a buyer, he was not a guarantor but a surety, and thus, the bank could proceed against him directly. Who is correct? (*General Motors Acceptance Corp.* v . *Daniels*, 492 A.2d 1306)

6. Auer and others executed a promissory note to a bank in the amount of $87,000, secured by a lien on the inventory and equipment of Auer's business. When Auer and others defaulted on the loan, the bank took control of the assets and proceeded to sell them in bulk at a public auction. The assets were sold for $8,000. Prior to the sale, debtors were notified of the auction, advertisements were placed in the local newspaper, and announcements were sent to seventy-seven potential buyers. Auer complained that had the inventory and equipment been sold piece by piece rather than in bulk, a higher price might

have been obtained. Is that a valid reason to overturn the sale? (*In re Auer*, 103 Bankruptcy Reports 700)

7. Madden, a logger, bought timber-cutting equipment from MidSouth Machinery on credit. The loan agreement gave Deere Credit Services a security interest in the equipment. Madden defaulted in making payments. An area collection manager for Deere came on Madden's property at night, without Madden's knowledge or consent, and repossessed the equipment. No physical entry or violence was involved. Madden charges that Deere's action was a breach of the peace. Is this claim correct? (*Madden* v. *Deere Credit Services, Inc.*, 598 So.2d 860)

8. Ghosh was the guarantor for a promissory note given to the bank. The original note was renewed by the bank and the maker of the note but Ghosh never consented to the renewal. When the maker defaulted, the bank sued Ghosh. Is Ghosh liable? (*Bank of Waynesboro* v. *Ghosh*, 576 SW 2d 759, Tenn)

9. Penrose borrowed money from Old Colony and to secure the loan, Penrose pledged stock in a corporation that operates a radio station. When Penrose defaulted, Old Colony sold the stock at a private sale instead of at a public sale on the grounds that a radio station was unique and that a private sale might bring in more money than a public sale. Should Old Colony be permitted to do this? (*Old Colony Trust Company* v. *Penrose Industries Corporation*, 280 F Supp 698 aff'd 398 F2d [3d Cir])

10. Butler borrowed money from Ford Motor Credit to purchase a truck. When Butler defaulted on the loan that was secured by the truck, Ford Motor Credit arranged to have the truck repossessed at 2:00 A.M. while the car was parked in an open driveway in front of Butler's house. Butler contends that the repossession was illegal. Is Butler correct? (*Butler* v. *Ford Motor Credit Co.* 829 F2d 568 [5th Cir])

THE CASE OF THE OVERZEALOUS DEBT COLLECTOR

Greyson bought a boat from Arc Marine for the sum of $50,000. At purchase, Greyson paid $10,000 in cash and gave Arc a note for the balance, which was payable in sixty monthly installments.

After making several payments, Greyson had financial problems and fell behind in making payments. Arc's attorneys began calling Greyson every day at his place of work and at night at his home. The calls continued despite Greyson's demand that they cease. When they did not, Greyson brought an action against Arc pursuant to the Fair Debt Collection Practices Act.

The Trial

There was testimony at trial about the number of times that the law firm's employee called Greyson and that both Greyson and his employer were very upset. Greyson's attorneys questioned partners of the law firm regarding how many such suits they handled and their normal collection practices. A lawyer for Arc testified that it was very difficult to contact Greyson except during the daytime at work or in the evening at home.

The Arguments at Trial

Arc's attorneys argued that the suit should be dismissed because the Fair Debt Collection Practices Act did not include attorneys under the category of debt collectors, and therefore, the act did not apply to the facts of this case. Greyson's attorneys argued that a law firm that did extensive collection work should be considered a debt collector under the act. They also argued that when a collector misused the collection process in an unreasonable way, the act should apply regardless of the status of the collector.

Questions to Discussion

1. Who do you believe has the stronger argument, Greyson or Arc? Why?
2. If you were the judge hearing this case, how would you decide? Why?
3. Based on your reading of the text and ordinary common sense, do you believe that the Fair Debt Collection Practices Act should apply to all attorneys or just to those attorneys who specialize in collection work?

To entice buyers to its store, Ace Drug Store advertised a product for sale as being "at our cost." In fact, it had no such product in its store on the sale dates. When a customer asked for the product, he or she was told that there was such a demand that the store ran out of it and gave the customer a rain check instead.

Questions for Discussion

1. Assuming that the store's tactic didn't violate any consumer protection laws, was it ethical for the store to advertise as it did?
2. Does it make any difference that the store gave the customers rain checks?
3. To be ethical, how many of a product advertised as being on sale do you think a store should be required to carry?

Other Ethics Questions to Discuss

1. How much control do you feel a governmental unit should exercise over the advertising used by businesses?
2. Many pharmaceutical companies put a small number of pills into a large opaque bottle to convince buyers that the bottle is really full. Do you feel this is an unethical practice that should be prohibited by law?

PART 9

Insurance

After studying Part IX, you should be able to:

1. explain the need for insurance.

2. name the six most common types of property and casualty insurance and the risks covered by each type.

3. describe the standard clauses found in most property and casualty insurance policies.

4. distinguish among the various types of automobile insurance coverage.

5. explain and compare the basic types of life insurance available.

6. describe the standard clauses found in most life insurance policies.

7. define the five basic types of health insurance.

CHAPTER 38

Property, Casualty, and Automobile Insurance

CHAPTER PREVIEW

Chapter Highlights

This chapter describes the nature of insurance, with emphasis on loss of or damage to property. It discusses the ways in which insurance may be purchased and from whom. This chapter also outlines certain conditions that are peculiar to insurance policies in general, such as when protection begins, how claims must be made, and what deductibles are. The chapter continues with a discussion of the various types of property risks for which insurance may be obtained, including fire, theft, and liability for damage to others. It addresses standard clauses found in all policies that insure property, including what property the policy covers, how the policy may be canceled, and how the right to assign the policy to a third person is handled. The chapter offers an in-depth exploration of mandatory insurance coverage. We look at the need for such responsibility, explain why minimum amounts of coverage are required in each state, discuss the most common forms of automobile insurance, and look at the various types of insurance coverage available. The concept of no-fault insurance is explored, together with the administration of the no-fault system. We conclude this discussion by offering a detailed description of the steps to be taken in the event of an automobile accident.

THE NATURE OF INSURANCE

Risk and uncertainty are always with us. We are constantly exposed to the risk of accident, illness, theft, injury, and death. If we had to bear all these risks alone, we would have to keep large sums of money on hand to cover them or face financial disaster.

Insurance is a means of sharing risks with other people to limit economic loss. An insurance company sets up a fund to reimburse or repay those who suffer similar losses. This reimbursement is called **indemnification**. To join the fund, a person, the **insured**, submits an application to an insurance company, the **insurer**, sometimes called an underwriter. If the applicant is accepted, the insurance company issues a **policy**, a written contract of insurance, to the insured. The policy describes such things as the types of risks covered, the amount of coverage (called the **face value** of the policy), and the time period of the policy. The insured pays a set amount of money, called a **premium**, for the coverage.

The amount of the premium varies depending on the amount and type of loss covered, the number of people in the fund, and the risk involved. For example, the risk of loss by fire for a wooden home is much greater than for a brick home. A fire insurance premium for a wooden home will thus cost more than for a brick home.

The basis for insurance is that not everyone who participates will suffer a loss at the same time. As a result, there will always be money in the fund to pay for the losses that do occur. This practice helps keep premiums at a minimum.

PURCHASING INSURANCE

Insurance may be issued by insurance companies, savings banks, and government agencies. In many states, savings banks are permitted to sell life insurance, although the type and amounts of coverage are limited. The federal government provides flood insurance, crop insurance, bank deposit insurance, and health and disability insurance. In addition, it provides life insurance for members of the armed forces.

Most insurance is purchased from insurance agents or brokers. An **insurance agent** is an employee of a specific insurance company who sells insurance policies only for that company. An **insurance broker** is an independent businessperson who represents the insured. The broker determines the type and amount of insurance needed and secures it from one of several different companies. In most states, both agents and brokers must be licensed by the state.

A person wishing to buy insurance submits a written application to a broker or agent. Because insurance may provide a large return for a small investment, the possibility of fraud is always present. Insurance companies try to prevent fraud by learning as much as possible about the risks involved and the applicant. An application for insurance is a primary source of information. An applicant for auto insurance will be asked about age, health, occupation, address, driver training, and type of automobile. An applicant for health or life insurance will be asked about age, occupation, prior medical treatment, family history, and so forth.

Based on the information on the application and from its own investigation, the insurance company decides whether to issue the policy. The decision is usually based on the nature and extent of the risk. Any false information, concealment, or misrepresentation

insurance system of sharing risk of loss among a group of people

indemnification reimbursement for a loss

insured one who buys an insurance policy

insurer company that issues insurance

policy written contract of insurance between insurer and insured

face value amount of coverage on an insurance policy

premium cost of insurance coverage

insurance agent insurance company employee who sells insurance only for that company

insurance broker independent businessperson who buys insurance for insured from one of many companies

of information that misleads the insurance company permits the company to cancel the policy or to refuse to pay any claims, *provided* the company relied on the false information in issuing the policy and the false information was important in the decision to issue the policy.

> You applied for a life insurance policy and gave your height as 5′10″ in the application. Your actual height is 5′11″. Although this information is false, it would have little effect on the company's decision to issue a policy to you. The company cannot cancel this policy because you gave false information about your height.

False information provided by an applicant may make a policy voidable, regardless of whether the misrepresentation was accidental or deliberate. In addition, an applicant's failure to disclose important facts may make the policy voidable. The test is whether the insurance company would have issued the policy had it known of the withheld information.

> Grace applied for accident insurance and was asked if her occupation was hazardous. She answered this and other questions properly but did not disclose her hobby of racing cars. Even though she was not asked about her hobby, failure to disclose it may allow the company to cancel the policy or refuse to pay any claims. The company probably would not have issued the policy had it known of Grace's hobby.

The Insurance Policy

An insurance policy is similar to other types of contracts and is subject to the same rules regarding offer and acceptance, competent parties, and consideration. In addition, certain conditions are peculiar to insurance policies.

When Protection Begins

When a policy becomes effective depends on the type of policy, its terms, and from whom it is purchased.

A policy obtained from an insurance broker does not become effective until it is accepted by a company. A broker is not an agent of an insurance company and thus cannot bind any company. In contrast, an insurance agent is an employee of an insurance company and may bind the company when an application is made. The agent may orally agree to provide insurance protection until the policy is issued.

> You bought a home, paying for it with a bank mortgage. To protect its interest, the bank wanted you to buy property insurance. You called your insurance agent and requested immediate coverage. If the agent orally agreed to provide that coverage, the insurance company is legally bound on the policy when its agent accepts.

binder temporary insurance policy

The agent may also issue a **binder**, a temporary insurance policy. The binder is a written memorandum of the oral agreement reached. The binder is effective until the company either accepts or rejects the application. Any loss occurring during this time is covered. If a binder is not given, a policy becomes effective when it is delivered or mailed to the insured. Some policies, such as those for life insurance, become effective only when the first premium is paid. Very often, a policy becomes effective according to the terms stated in the application, such as approval of the application or payment of the premium.

Many people buy insurance through the mail or from vending machines in air, train, and bus terminals. Insurance purchased by mail is not effective until the policy is signed and mailed to the buyer. Insurance purchased through a vending machine becomes effective when the insured inserts a properly completed application and a premium in the machine and receives a receipt.

Insurable Interest

A person who wishes to buy insurance must have a beneficial interest in the item being insured, either the life of another person or property. The policyholder must suffer financially or in a personal way (e.g., the loss of a parent) if a loss occurs. This interest is known as **insurable interest**. For example, a person who has possession of stolen property does not have valid title to the property and would not suffer financially if a loss occurred. Therefore, that person would have no insurable interest and would not be able to obtain a valid insurance policy on the stolen property.

Without an insurable interest, a person who buys insurance is simply gambling that a loss will occur. This person may even cause the destruction of the insured property or the death of the insured person simply to collect the proceeds of the insurance policy. If there is no insurable interest, the policy is void. If a loss does occur, the policyholder may recover only the premiums paid, not the proceeds.

> Bargy owned a home that was insured against fire. She sold the house but failed to tell the insurance company that she no longer owned it. Bargy continued to pay the premiums on her policy. If the house burns, the insurance company will not be liable on the policy because Bargy no longer has an insurable interest in the house. The insurance company will, however, have to return to Bargy any premiums paid after she sold the house.

Exclusions

Insurance policies are very specific about the risks covered and any exceptions. An exception, or risk that is not covered, is known as an **exclusion**. An accident policy, for example, might exclude injuries suffered in a hazardous sport. An insurance company may often be very liberal in paying claims, but its responsibilities are limited by the terms of the policy.

> The insurance policy on your home covered damage to the roof caused by ice but excluded any additional damage. If ice on the roof caused water to leak into your home, damaging your carpets, your insurance company might indemnify you for the damage to your carpets, but it is not obligated to do so under the policy.

Amount of Coverage

The amount of coverage stated in the policy may be valued coverage or open coverage. **Valued coverage**, also called "actual cash value coverage," means that the insurance company will pay the original cost, less depreciation, when a loss occurs. **Open coverage**, also known as "replacement cost coverage," means that when a loss occurs, the insurance company will pay the cost of repairing or replacing the item damaged or destroyed up to the face amount of the policy, without subtracting anything for depreciation and regardless of the original cost of the item. Most property damage policies have valued coverage. For an additional premium, the coverage is changed to open coverage.

> Blake's car was insured for $25,000 under a policy with open coverage. If it is damaged in an accident and would cost $2,500 to repair, the insurance company would pay Blake only the sum of $2,500, not the full $25,000 amount.

Deductible Clause

deductible part of a loss that must be paid for by the insured

To reduce the premium amount, many insurance policies (other than life insurance) contain a deductible clause. The **deductible** is the agreed-upon amount of the loss that the insured pays. The insurance company pays all or a percentage of the loss over and above the deductible. Because most claims are small ones, the higher the deductible, the less risk for the insurance company and the lower the premiums for the insured. In effect, the insured becomes a partner with the insurance company in sharing the risk of loss.

> Corey insured his boat for $25,000, with a $250 deductible. The boat hit a submerged log and would cost $1,000 to repair. Corey will receive $750 from the insurance company ($1,000 minus the $250 deductible amount).

Claims

All insurance policies list specific procedures for filing a claim. The insured must notify the insurer of the loss, usually in writing, within a reasonable time after the loss. The insured must also provide the insurer with a sworn statement showing proof of the loss and a list of the property lost or damaged. If property is stolen, the insured must notify the police as well as the insurer. The police can then investigate the theft and perhaps recover the stolen property. If the insured does not follow these procedures, the insurer may not pay the claim.

> Bergin insured her camera against theft. While on a skiing trip, the camera was stolen from her locked car. She reported the theft to the insurance company but failed to notify the police. Because Bergin did not notify the police as required, the insurance company would not have to cover the loss of her camera, although it may.

adjuster one who settles claims for an insurer

After a claim is submitted, the insurance company will investigate and try to settle the claim. The insurance company representative who handles this settlement is called an **adjuster**. The insured should give the adjuster all the details of the claim: date and time of loss, circumstances, witnesses, damage, and any other helpful information. After investigating the loss, the company may repair the damaged property, replace it with similar property, or pay the agreed-upon value to the insured. The company, not the insured, chooses the method of settling the claim. If the insured and the company cannot agree on the value of the damaged or lost property, they may have to go to court or arbitration to determine the value.

subrogation right of insurance company to recover from person causing a loss

An insurance company often pays for a loss caused by someone other than the insured. If this kind of loss happens, the company has the right to try to recover what it paid out from the person responsible for the loss. This right is known as **subrogation**.

> Cable's boat was accidentally rammed by Ford's boat. After paying for the damage to Cable's boat, Cable's insurance company can sue Ford for the amount of damages paid out.

release document that is proof of the settlement of a claim

After a settlement is reached, the insured will be asked to sign a release before the claim is paid. A **release** is a formal document stating that the insured has been paid for the claim and that the insurer has no further responsibility. If the claim is a small one, the release is usually on the back of the settlement check. Often, however, it is a separate document. The insured should not sign a release without being fully satisfied with the settlement and its terms.

Property and Casualty Insurance

Property and casualty insurance protects the insured against loss or damage to real or personal property. The loss may affect the insured's property or someone else's property for which the insured is responsible. Most policies cover loss by fire, theft, windstorm, and water, but almost any peril can be insured against. Any risk or peril that is not covered is an exclusion, such as damage caused by a military invasion.

The most common types of property and casualty insurance are fire insurance, burglary and theft insurance, liability insurance, marine insurance, all-risk insurance, and multiperil insurance.

Fire

Fire insurance protects against loss caused by fire or lightning. The loss, however, must be the result of an actual fire—that is, by a burning or flaming fire. Scorching due to heat would not be covered.

> You dropped a hot iron onto a plastic tabletop, melting the tabletop. Because no flame or burning occurred, this damage is not covered by fire insurance.

The damage must also be caused by a hostile fire. A **hostile fire** is one that is accidental and uncontrollable or that escapes from its usual place. A **friendly fire** is one that is not out of control and remains in its intended place, such as a fireplace.

> Rupert started a fire in his fireplace one evening. He added too much wood and the fire became too hot. Sparks escaped from the fireplace and burned the nearby carpeting. Because the fire did not remain in its intended place, the damage to the carpeting was caused by a hostile fire.

In recent years, the hostile/friendly fire distinction has been rejected by more and more courts. Instead, "hostile" fires have been defined as those that are not related to a normal household use of fire. "Friendly" fires have been defined as those due to an intentionally lit flame, such as the pilot light in the furnace.

The fire must also be the proximate cause of the damage. **Proximate cause** means that the fire must be the direct or natural cause of the damage or loss.

> A fire started in the basement of a restaurant when a short circuit occurred. Smoke from the fire seeped into the kitchen above, spoiling large quantities of food. The loss of the food would be covered because it was due to smoke, a natural result of the fire.

Every state in the United States has adopted a similar form for basic fire insurance coverage. This form, known as the **standard fire insurance policy**, insures against loss or damage from fire or lightning. For an additional premium, extra insurance coverage may be obtained and added to the standard policy. These additions are commonly referred to as riders, forms, or endorsements.

The most common rider added to the standard fire policy is an **extended coverage rider**. It insures against loss or damage from windstorm, hail, aircraft, riot, vehicles, explosion, and smoke. A burglary and theft rider is often added to insure against loss of property owned by the insured or a member of the family. This rider covers property stolen or seized after a forcible entry.

Burglary and Theft

Burglary and theft insurance covers loss of property stolen from a residence or business. It also covers property that a person has placed in a bank or warehouse for safekeeping. This insurance covers only personal belongings. It does not cover automobiles and motorcycles, which are covered under other types of policies.

Personal and Public Liability

personal liability insurance insurance against claims by persons injured by actions of insured

public liability insurance insurance against claims for injuries caused by insured's or guest's negligence

Personal liability insurance protects against loss from claims made by persons injured as a result of the actions of the insured. Malpractice insurance is an example of personal liability insurance. **Public liability insurance** protects property owners against claims for injuries caused by the negligence or other acts of the insured, or others, on the insured's property.

Marine

marine insurance insurance covering ships, their crew, and cargo

Marine insurance protects against loss or damage to ships, cargo, crew, and passengers for such "perils of the sea" as sinking, bad weather, and capsizing. It is the oldest form of insurance and is often called ocean marine insurance.

All-Risk

floater policy all-risk insurance for loss or damage to personal property from almost any cause

An all-risk policy, called a **floater policy** (or inland marine policy), insures personal property against loss from all causes except those specifically excluded. How the loss occurred, where or when it occurred, and who caused it are not important. Such policies are often carried on jewelry, furs, cameras, musical instruments, and the baggage carried by travelers.

> You purchased an all-risk policy for your bicycle. One day, you left it outside a store while you went shopping. When you returned, the bicycle was gone. It was never found, although there was no proof of theft. You are insured for this loss.

Multiperil

multiperil policy insurance combining various types of coverage with emphasis on who is insured rather than perils insured against

homeowners policy multiperil policy insuring homeowners against many risks

Since 1947, there has been a growing tendency to combine various types of coverage in a single insurance policy, called a **multiperil policy**. The emphasis of the policy is on who is insured rather than what perils are insured against. The most common type of multiperil policy is a homeowners policy.

The **homeowners policy** is available to those who own a one- or two-family home. It combines fire and liability insurance, provides the convenience of having one policy and paying one premium and usually costs less than separate coverage for each peril.

A homeowners policy covers loss or damage to a house and other structures, such as garages and toolsheds. It also covers the contents of the house and personal property whether on or off the premises. A homeowners policy provides protection against claims made for damage to the personal property of guests or for injuries to them while they are on the property. An important part of a homeowners policy is the coverage for living expenses, including hotel expenses and meals at restaurants, because the insured cannot occupy his or her home due to the damage.

Special forms of homeowners policies are available for owners of mobile homes and condominiums and for renters. Special riders can even be added to cover losses due to floods and earthquakes.

FIGURE 38.1 Perils Insured Against in a Homeowners Policy

COMPREHENSIVE

BROAD

BASIC

1. Fire or lightning
2. Loss of property removed from premises endangered by fire or other perils
3. Windstorm or hail
4. Explosion
5. Riot or civil commotion
6. Aircraft
7. Vehicles
8. Smoke
9. Vandalism and malicious mischief
10. Theft
11. Breakage of glass constituting a part of the building

12. Falling objects
13. Weight of ice, snow, sleet
14. Collapse of building(s) or any part thereof
15. Sudden and accidental tearing asunder, cracking, burning, or bulging of a steam or hot water heating system or of appliances for heating water
16. Accidental discharge, leakage, or overflow of water or steam from within a plumbing, heating,
or air-conditioning system or domestic appliance
17. Freezing of plumbing, heating, and air-conditioning systems and domestic appliances
18. Sudden and accidental injury from artificially generated currents to electrical appliances, devices, fixtures, and wiring (TV and radio tubes not included)

All perils EXCEPT: Flood, earthquake, war, nuclear accidents, and others specified in your policy. Check your policy for a complete listing of perils excluded.

There are three types of homeowners policies. The *basic form* (also known as *HO-1*) insures against the first eleven perils in Figure 38.1. The *broad form* (also known as *HO-2*) covers eighteen listed perils. The *comprehensive form* (also known as *HO-3*) is practically an all-risk policy.

STANDARD CLAUSES IN POLICIES

Almost all the property and casualty insurance policies described in this chapter contain provisions or clauses that are standard throughout the United States.

Coverage

Each insurance policy contains a clause describing what risks are covered. Although some insurance companies are liberal when paying claims for losses, they are actually liable only for those risks mentioned in the policy. The standard fire insurance policy, for example, insures against losses caused directly or indirectly by a hostile fire. If your house catches fire, you could recover the value of the furniture destroyed in the fire, which is a direct loss. You could recover for damage to your furniture from smoke or the water used to put out the fire, an indirect loss. You could not, however, recover for furniture stolen during the fire. That loss is *too* indirect.

An insurance policy is issued for a specific amount, the face value. Generally, the insured cannot recover more than the face value of the policy for loss or damage to property. If a home is worth $150,000 and is insured for that amount, the owner will recover $150,000 if the home is destroyed. If the home is valued at $180,000 but is insured for only $150,000, the owner can recover only $150,000 if it is destroyed.

One problem with specific coverage is that because of inflation, the same amount of protection is worth less and less. In many states, you can add an inflation rider. As costs and the value of your property go up, coverage increases.

> Fraum insured her stamp collection for $5,000. Three years later, the collection, then worth $6,500, was destroyed in a fire. If Fraum had an inflation rider, the insurance company would pay her $6,500 for the loss.

Personal property often depreciates with age and use. Under most policies, the insurance company is liable only for the actual cash value of property if a loss occurs. Actual cash value is the cost of an item less depreciation because of age, condition, and so on. In many states, you can add a replacement value rider to your policy. The insurance company will then pay you the replacement value or the amount needed to replace the item in new condition.

> Lesser purchased a camera for $200. One year later, he lost the camera. At the time of the loss, the camera was worth only $150 but would cost $250 to replace. With a replacement value rider, the insurance company would pay Lesser $250.

Removal of Property

Premiums for property insurance are based on the insured property being located in a specific place. Moving the property to a different place usually increases the risk of loss. Most policies state that coverage stops if property is moved from its normal location, unless the insurance company has consented to the move.

> Carter purchased a standard fire insurance policy. A week later, she had to leave for six months on a work assignment. She stored her furniture at a friend's home. In case of damage, Carter could not collect for the loss because she did not notify her insurance company about the transfer.

Vacancy

Premiums are also based on the assumption that the insured property is occupied and is therefore secure. An unoccupied property is one from which the owner or tenant is temporarily absent, leaving furniture and clothing behind. A vacant property is one that the owner or tenant has abandoned with no intention of returning.

Most policies provide that coverage stops if the residence becomes vacant for more than sixty days. When the residence is reoccupied, coverage starts again. Coverage of property that becomes unoccupied continues, but it is often reduced to cover losses only for such occurrences as vandalism or frozen water pipes.

> Sanger had a standard fire insurance policy on a summer cottage he owned on Cape Cod. At the end of August, he closed up the cottage and removed all his possessions. In December, a fire destroyed the cottage. Because the cottage had been vacant for more than sixty days, he could not recover for the loss.

Pro-Rata Liability

Some people overinsure property, believing that they can collect more than the value of the property if it is destroyed. To prevent overinsuring, policies usually provide that if the same property is insured with more than one company, each company is liable only for its proportionate share of the loss. This provision is known as **pro-rata liability**. The insured cannot collect the full amount from both companies.

pro-rata liability insurance company's liability for loss when there is more than one policy on the same property

> Abbott owned a boat worth $5,000. She insured it for $5,000 with Ace Insurance Company and for $5,000 with Acme Insurance Company. If the boat is destroyed, Abbott could collect only $5,000, one half (or $2,500) from each company.

Increase in Risk

Insurance policies cover specific risks. Any increase in those risks increases the possibility of loss. Most policies provide that any increased risk caused by the insured will result in a loss of coverage. If the insurance company consents to the increased risk, however, the coverage continues.

> Lerner was planning to remove several tree stumps from his property. He bought some dynamite and stored it in the basement of his home. If the dynamite explodes, the insurance company is not liable for the damage.

Coinsurance

coinsurance insurance policy clause requiring insured to maintain a certain minimum amount of insurance

Most fire insurance and homeowners policies include a **coinsurance** clause. This clause requires that the insured carry a minimum amount of insurance on the insured property. This minimum is usually stated as a percentage of the current value of the property, normally 80 percent. If the insured carries the required amount of insurance, the insurer will pay any loss in full up to the limit or face value of the policy.

> Amino owned a home worth $200,000. Because her insurance policy contained an 80 percent coinsurance clause, Amino insured her home for $160,000, the required amount. A fire caused $35,000 damage to the home. Because she carried the required amount of insurance, the insurance company will pay the full loss of $35,000.

If the required amount is not carried, the insurer is liable only for a percentage of the loss.

> Assume that Amino carried only $80,000 worth of insurance, one half of the required amount. If a fire caused a $25,000 loss, Amino would collect only $12,500, one half of the actual loss.

Insurable Interest

As with other types of insurance, the insured must have an insurable interest in the property. The insured must suffer a financial loss if there is damage to the property. Property owners or renters have an insurable interest. A person who has a contract to buy property has an insurable interest in that property. Bailees and pledgees have an insurable interest in the property for which they are responsible.

The insurable interest must exist both at the time insurance is purchased and at the time of the loss.

> Farrel signed a contract to purchase Allen's house. He took out an insurance policy on the house. Two months later, the house burned down in a fire. Farrel can collect from the insurance company for the damage to the house because he had an insurable interest in the property when he took out the insurance and when the loss occurred.

Cancellation and Termination

Most property and casualty insurance policies terminate either when their terms expire or when they are canceled. They do not end just because a claim is paid. Property and casualty policies are written for specific periods of time, usually one year or three years. When the time period ends, the policy terminates.

Most property and casualty policies may be canceled by either the insured or the insurer at any time. Each party must notify the other of the cancellation. If the insured cancels the policy, the cancellation is effective when the insurance company receives the notice. If the insurer cancels the policy, the insurance company must notify the insured in writing that coverage will stop within a certain number of days. The number of days' notice required varies with each policy and with state law. The most common reason for cancellation of a policy by an insurance company is nonpayment of premiums.

Insurance premiums are always paid in advance. If the policy is canceled before the end of the term, the insured is entitled to a refund. The amount of the refund depends on who has canceled the policy. If the insurance company cancels, the refund is the full amount of the unused premium. This practice is known as the **prorated premium**. If the insured cancels, the refund is a smaller amount and is known as the **short rate**.

> On January 1, Meadows took out a fire insurance policy on his home and paid a one-year premium of $120. The insurance company canceled the policy as of August 31. The insurance policy was in effect for eight months, two-thirds of the original term. Meadows will receive a refund of one-third of the premium, or $40.

The insurance company is liable for any damage or injury that took place while the policy was in effect, even if the claim is filed after the policy has expired.

> Curtis fell on a rug in your home and injured himself. Two weeks after the accident, your policy expired. One month later, Curtis developed a limp because of the fall and made a claim against you. The insurance company that insured you when Curtis fell is liable for his injuries.

Assignment

Insurance is a personal contract between the insured and the insurer. An insurance company relies to a great extent on the character of the insured. It issues a policy only to someone it has investigated and found acceptable. If the insured could transfer rights in the policy to someone else, an insurance company could be in a difficult position. To prevent this situation, property and casualty policies cannot be assigned or transferred before a loss occurs without the consent of the insurance company. After a loss, the insured may assign the rights to the proceeds without the consent of the insurance company. In practice, most companies freely permit assignments when insured property is sold and the buyer wishes to take over an existing policy.

THE NEED FOR AUTOMOBILE INSURANCE

Buying a car is an exciting experience, especially when it's your first car. Accidents do happen, however, and you must be prepared for them.

Persons who own or drive cars need protection in case of injury to themselves or damage to their property. They also need to protect themselves against loss for injuries to others or damage to the property of others.

All states have **financial responsibility laws** that set minimum liability limits that registered vehicles must meet. The purpose of these laws is to ensure that the owner or

---

prorated premium amount of premium returned to insured when insurer cancels the policy

short rate amount of premium refunded when insured cancels a policy

financial responsibility laws laws requiring owners or drivers of cars to prove they can pay for any damage caused by an accident

driver of a vehicle involved in an accident is financially able to pay for any damage. A driver or owner must have proof of such responsibility at all times. In some states, a driver or vehicle owner must provide proof of such responsibility before a vehicle can be registered. In other states, proof must be provided at the time of an accident or within a certain period of time after one takes place. Failure to have such protection may result in a fine or the suspension or revocation of a driver's license.

Proof of financial responsibility may be a bond or a deposit to cover any damages, but the most common way of providing such proof is to carry vehicle insurance. In some states, vehicle liability insurance is compulsory. The minimum requirements vary from state to state.

In Florida, for example, an automobile owner must have insurance in the amount of $10,000 to cover injuries to each person injured and $10,000 to cover damage to property.

TYPES OF AUTOMOBILE INSURANCE COVERAGE

A vehicle owner may satisfy financial responsibility laws by obtaining insurance with basic bodily injury and property damage liability coverage. Other types of coverage are available and are often included in a package policy. The most common types of coverage purchased are bodily injury, property damage, medical payments, and uninsured motorist. If the vehicle is new or expensive to repair or replace, collision coverage and comprehensive physical damage coverage are often obtained. A portion of a page from a typical auto policy is shown in Figure 38.2.

Bodily Injury Liability

bodily injury liability insurance insurance for one whose car injures or kills another person

Bodily injury liability insurance protects the insured against claims for injuries to or the death of a guest in the insured's car, a pedestrian, or an occupant of another vehicle. Bodily injury insurance protects not only the insured but also members of the insured's family and anyone else who has permission to drive the insured's car. It also protects the insured and family members who drive a rented car or someone else's car with the owner's permission. If the insured is found legally liable for the injuries that occurred, the insurance company will pay for the damages awarded, up to the limits of the policy. This insurance will also pay for the legal and court costs involved in defending any lawsuits brought against the insured.

The insurance company is responsible *only up to the limits of the policy;* the insured is responsible for any amount beyond the policy limits. Therefore, it is important for an owner of a motor vehicle to carry bodily injury liability insurance far in excess of the minimum coverage required by law.

> Your car collided with another car, injuring that vehicle's occupants. They brought a lawsuit against you for $250,000 to recover for their injuries. Your bodily injury liability policy had a maximum coverage amount of $10,000. The insurance company will pay any damages awarded, plus your legal expenses, up to the $10,000 limit. You are responsible for any damages and legal expenses over that amount.

Property Damage Liability

property damage liability insurance insurance against claims for damage to another's property

Property damage liability insurance protects the insured whose car damages the property of others. It also protects members of the insured's family and anyone who drives with the insured's permission. The property damaged is usually another car but may also be buildings, utility poles, or fences. In addition to covering damages, it will also

FIGURE 38.2 Page Outlining Coverage from a Typical Automobile Insurance Policy

physical damage coverages (damage to your auto)

COVERAGES

COMPREHENSIVE COVERAGE   **We** will pay for **loss** to **your auto** not caused by collision or upset. **We** will pay for the **loss** less your declared **deductible. Loss** from contact with animals or falling or flying objects is covered. Broken glass is covered—even if caused by collision or upset—if **you** do not have Collision coverage. If **your** Comprehensive and Collision coverages have different **deductibles**, the smaller **deductible** will apply to broken glass.

Also, if **your auto** has a **loss** under this coverage **we** will:

1. pay for resulting **loss** of your clothing and luggage or that of any **relatives.** Maximum payment is $200. **We** will pay for stolen clothing or luggage only if **your auto** is stolen.

2. repay **your** travel costs after **your auto** is stolen. Maximum payment is $10 per day—not to exceed $300. These costs must be incurred within a certain time. It begins 48 hours after **you** report the theft to **us** and the police. It ends when **your auto** is returned to **you** or **we** pay for its **loss.**

3. repay **you** for the cost of travel from where **your auto** was disabled to where **you** were going. Maximum payment is $10.

COLLISION COVERAGE   **We** will pay for **loss** to **your auto** caused by collision or upset. This includes broken glass. **We** will pay for the **loss** less your declared **deductible.** However, **we** will not subtract the **deductible** amount:

1. if **your** auto collides with another **motor vehicle** insured by **us,** or

2. for broken glass if **you** have full (no **deductible**) comprehensive coverage in force.

Also if **your auto** has a **loss** under this coverage, **we** will:

1. pay for a resulting loss of **your** clothing and luggage or that of any **relatives.** Maximum payment is $200.

2. repay **you** for the travel cost to where **you** were going. Maximum payment is $10.

pay for court costs and legal fees. It can be purchased in amounts beginning at $5,000. Most states require minimum property damage liability coverage under their financial responsibility laws.

> While driving, Hetzke swerved to avoid hitting a child and sideswiped a parked car. Hetzke's property damage liability policy would cover the cost of repairing the damage to the parked car. Hetzke's property damage liability insurance would not, however, pay for the damage to his own car.

Medical Payments

medical payments insurance insurance for medical expenses for injuries suffered in a car accident

Medical payments insurance pays the medical expenses, up to the limits of the policy, for injuries suffered by anyone in the insured's car when an accident occurs. It also provides protection for the insured or members of the insured's family who are injured while riding in someone else's car or who are struck by a car while walking. Coverage is provided regardless of who was at fault. Coverage includes such expenses as x-rays, surgical expenses, ambulance charges, and hospital care. The expenses must have arisen within a certain time period after the accident, usually one year.

> While driving to a movie one night with some friends, Carly was forced off the road and into a ditch by another car. Carly and her friends required emergency medical treatment for their injuries. All their expenses are covered by Carly's medical payments insurance in spite of the fact that another driver caused the accident.

Uninsured Motorists

uninsured motorist insurance insurance for injuries caused by a driver who has no insurance or by a hit-and-run driver

Uninsured motorist insurance pays for injuries caused by an uninsured or a hit-and-run driver. It does not cover property damage. This insurance protects anyone in the insured's car who is injured when the accident occurred. It also protects the insured and members of the insured's family who are injured while in another person's car or while walking.

The insurance company will pay damages to those injured up to the amount of coverage required by the state's financial responsibility laws. In most areas of the United States, higher coverage can be purchased. To prevent false claims, most policies require that every effort be made to locate a hit-and-run driver.

> Your car was struck by a hit-and-run driver one night and was badly damaged. Your loss is not covered by uninsured motorist insurance because it does not cover property damage.

Collision

collision insurance insurance against damage to insured's car if it collides with something or turns over

Collision insurance covers damage to the insured's car when it collides with another car or object (e.g., a telephone pole or fire hydrant) or when it turns over. This insurance covers the damage regardless of who was at fault. If someone else is at fault, the insured can collect from his or her insurance company immediately and need not wait to receive payment from the other driver's insurance company. Regardless of the amount of insurance carried, the insured can collect only for the actual damage to the car or for its fair market value if it is considered a total wreck.

> Ritzmann lost control of his car and crashed into a tree. Damage to the car was $2,500. Ritzmann's collision insurance will cover the loss because he collided with another object (the tree). That is, even though the collision was not with another vehicle, the collision insurance will cover the damages.

Collision insurance usually has a deductible clause. The deductible is that amount of the damage the insured must pay. Some common deductible amounts are $250, $500, and $1,000. In any one accident, the insured must pay the first $250, $500, and $1,000 worth of damages. The insurance company pays the balance. In the example, if Ritzmann had a $500 deductible, he would pay $500 and the insurance company would pay $2,000.

The insured can reduce the premium for collision insurance by choosing a higher deductible. The higher the deductible, the lower the premium for this coverage.

Comprehensive Physical Damage

comprehensive insurance insurance protecting insured's car against damage from such perils as theft, vandalism, or falling objects

Comprehensive insurance covers damage to the insured's car from a variety of sources other than collisions. It includes damage from theft, vandalism, falling objects, fire, flood, windstorm, earthquake, riot, and breakage of windows. Comprehensive coverage also pays for the cost of renting a car if the insured's car has been stolen. It does not pay for damage caused by mechanical difficulties or ordinary wear and tear or for the loss of the insured's personal property. It also does not cover damage to the property of others or bodily injuries.

> Thieves stole your car from your garage. They had an accident and demolished your car. Comprehensive insurance protects you against the loss because the car was stolen. You can recover only the actual cash value of the car, however, not the amount you paid for it.

WHO IS COVERED BY AUTOMOBILE INSURANCE

Automobile insurance protects the owner of an automobile. If another person operates the car with the owner's permission, that person is also protected. This coverage is known as the **omnibus clause**.

omnibus clause insurance for members of insured's family and those who drive insured's car with permission

Coverage under the omnibus clause is often a question of fact. Generally, members of an insured's family and those who drive with the insured's permission are covered under this clause. Like most other insurance policy clauses, the omnibus clause is interpreted in such a way as to protect the owner as much as possible. "Permission to drive" is often implied if the owner does not object to the operation of the car by someone else.

> Chin asked for and received permission to drive Lyle's automobile. On many occasions after that, Chin drove Lyle's car and Lyle did not object. Lyle's permission to drive was implied because she did not object when Chin used her car.

guest laws laws defining the liability of a motor vehicle owner or operator for injury to passengers

Most states have passed automobile **guest laws**. A guest is a passenger who rides free of charge. A passenger who shares expenses, even if a friend or relative, is not considered a guest. The guest laws relieve drivers of private vehicles of all liability to guests for injuries from an accident unless gross negligence is proven. "Gross negligence" is extreme recklessness or driving an unsafe car but failing to tell the guest that it is unsafe.

In states that have not passed guest laws, a driver may be liable for a guest's injuries if the driver is found negligent. In states with no-fault laws, the driver's insurance will protect the guest whether the driver is negligent or not. A guest who contributes to or knows of the negligence, however, cannot recover for injuries even if the driver is negligent.

> Crane, a passenger in Cook's car, was injured when a worn tire blew out while the car was traveling at a high speed. Crane knew about the worn tire but still went along for the ride. She cannot hold Cook responsible for her injuries.

NO-FAULT INSURANCE

Until the end of 1970, an automobile accident victim could collect damages for injuries only after proving that the other driver caused the accident. This system was time consuming, often unfair, and expensive. The courts became clogged with lawsuits involving the question of fault. Delays were frequent, and accident victims often had to wait years before being compensated. Lawsuits often resulted in inconsistent decisions, with victims of similar types of accidents receiving different amounts of compensation. The cost of this system, including legal fees and court costs, resulted in a continuous rise in insurance premiums.

To solve this problem, no-fault insurance was developed. Massachusetts was the first state to enact no-fault auto insurance legislation. Many states have followed Massachusetts's lead.

no-fault insurance
insurance for bodily injuries regardless of who caused the accident

The principle of **no-fault insurance** is that a person who was injured in an automobile accident should be compensated fully and quickly, regardless of who was at fault. In operation, an accident victim is compensated for financial loss by her or his own insurance company without having to bring a lawsuit to determine fault.

No-fault insurance laws vary from state to state, but the basic elements are as follows:

1. If an accident occurs, the injured person collects from his or her own insurance company for medical expenses and loss of income, regardless of who was at fault. An occupant of a car or a pedestrian injured by a car is paid by the insurance company that issued the policy covering the car.

threshold figure
amount of medical expenses required before injured person may sue under no-fault laws

2. Except in a few states, property damage is not covered.
3. The right to sue the other parties to the accident is limited to cases involving death or serious or permanent injuries. In some states, the injured person cannot sue unless medical expenses exceed a certain amount, known as the **threshold figure**.

HOW PREMIUMS ARE DETERMINED

As with other types of insurance, auto insurance premiums are based on the risk involved. The risk varies according to certain factors, such as the type of car and its use. Experience has shown that the newer the car, the safer it is. A car with low horsepower can't go as fast as a car with high horsepower, and it is considered safer. Premiums are therefore higher for older and faster cars. Cars that are used only for occasional family trips have fewer accidents than those that are used for business. Consequently, the premiums for business-use cars are higher than for family-use cars. Premiums for more expensive cars, such as sports cars, are higher than for less expensive cars because of the higher cost of repairs and the difficulty of obtaining replacement parts.

The status of the driver affects premiums considerably. Experience has shown that younger drivers have more accidents than older ones, that men have more accidents than women, and that single drivers have more accidents than married drivers. Age is one of the most important considerations. Rates for drivers under twenty-five years of age are often extremely high, but a discount is often given if the young driver successfully completes a driver education course. In many states, a full-time student in high school or college with a good scholastic record is eligible for a "good student" discount on automobile insurance rates. Drivers who have had accidents or incurred traffic violations are usually charged additional premiums for a certain period of time.

CANCELLATION OF AUTOMOBILE INSURANCE

The insured may cancel an insurance policy at any time. The insurance company has the right to cancel a policy for any reason within a certain number of days (usually thirty or sixty) after issuing it. After that time, the insurance company may cancel a policy only after giving advance notice to the insured and only for one or more of the following reasons:

1. Fraudulent statements in the insurance policy application
2. Failure to pay the premium
3. Suspension or revocation of the driver's license or revocation of the automobile registration

At the end of the policy period, both the insured and the insurance company have the right not to renew an automobile insurance policy. The insurance company is usually required, however, to notify the insured that it does not plan to renew the policy.

Because of the financial responsibility laws, cancellation or nonrenewal of an automobile insurance policy is a serious matter. If it becomes difficult to buy insurance from any company, a person may be placed in an **assigned risk pool**. Under this plan, several insurance companies combine, or pool, funds to set up a special automobile insurance fund. A person needing insurance is assigned to this plan and receives a policy for public liability only (bodily injury and property damage). Such a policy is usually limited to the minimum required by the financial responsibility laws and is very expensive.

assigned risk pool
insurance plan for those who cannot get insurance from normal sources

WHAT TO DO IF YOU'RE INVOLVED IN AN ACCIDENT

An automobile accident may cause serious damage to persons and property. It is important to know what to do after an accident to minimize injuries and damage and to protect yourself if a claim is made. Certain steps should be taken at the time of the accident and after the accident.

At the Time of the Accident

If you are involved in an accident, stop at once and help anyone who is injured. Call the police and a doctor or an ambulance and make the injured person as comfortable as possible. Give first aid if you are capable of doing so. It is also important to prevent additional accidents by warning other motorists that an accident has occurred.

While these steps are being done, trade information with the other driver or drivers involved in the accident. Exchange names, addresses, phone numbers, license and registration numbers, and insurance information. Get the names and addresses of any passengers. It is a good idea to write down the details of the accident while they are still fresh in your mind. Note the time, weather and road conditions, and other data. If you can, draw a diagram of what took place.

If there are witnesses to the accident, it is very important to get their names, addresses, phone numbers, and the license numbers of their cars. These witnesses may be of great help if there is a question of who was at fault.

After the Accident

Report the accident to your insurance company as soon as possible after the accident. All reports should be in writing and should contain all the details of the accident: date and time, location, vehicle information, parties involved, and circumstances. The insurance company may refuse to cover your claim if you do not notify them within a reasonable period of time after the accident.

State laws vary on when a report must be filed, with whom, and in what circumstances. All states require the filing of an accident report in the event of injury or death. If only property damage is involved, accident reports must be filed if the damage exceeds a certain amount. The time limit for filing may be anywhere from five to thirty days after the accident. In most states, the report must be filed with the state's department of motor vehicles.

Filing an accident report is extremely important, and it may be used later if a claim is made. In many states, failure to file the accident report is grounds for suspension or revocation of a driver's license. If necessary, your insurance company representative will help you fill out this report. You can obtain a report form at a police station, the department of motor vehicles, or the office of your insurance company or agent.

When to Consult an Attorney

If an accident produces no injuries and only minor property damage, let your insurance company handle all the details. Your company will provide and pay for legal assistance.

If you are involved in a serious accident causing injuries or severe property damage to yourself or others, consult an attorney at once. Your insurance company is responsible only to the limit of your policy; you are liable for any damages beyond that limit. Your attorney can work with your insurance company to defend you in any lawsuits brought against you or in bringing any lawsuit you may wish to file. If in doubt, consult an attorney.

Summary

Insurance is a means of sharing risks of financial loss among a group of people. An insurance policy is a written contract between the insurance company and the insured, the costs of which (the premium) are based on the risk involved, the amount of coverage, and the number of people insured. All insurance policies, which may be purchased from a company agent or a broker who deals with many companies, contain similar provisions, including the term of the policy, the need for an insurable interest, what is excluded from coverage, the deductible that is paid by the insured, and the procedures for filing a claim.

Property and casualty insurance protects against loss from fire, burglary, and theft. It also covers injuries to the person insured and injuries to others. There are also special policies that insure against a variety of risks and others that cover loss from any cause whatsoever.

Property and casualty insurance policies contain standard clauses that define the legal relationship between the insurance company and the insured. These clauses state what the policy covers, what happens if property is removed from its home, and what happens if insured real property becomes vacant. Such clauses also cover what occurs if there is an increase in risk, how a policy may be canceled, and whether a policy may be assigned.

All states have financial responsibility laws to ensure that owners and drivers of motor vehicles involved in accidents can pay for any damage for which they are legally liable. The most common way for car owners and drivers to meet these obligations is by purchasing automobile insurance.

Automobile insurance policies protect against injuries to others (bodily injury liability), damage to the property of others (property damage liability), medical expenses for injuries (medical payments), injuries caused by uninsured drivers or hit-and-run drivers (uninsured motorist), and damage to the insured's vehicle (collision and comprehensive).

Automobile insurance policies contain many standard clauses. These clauses include who is covered by the policy, any deductible involved, and when a policy may be canceled.

No-fault insurance, which has been adopted in many states, eliminates the need to prove negligence in accidents involving nonserious injuries. The injured person's insurance company pays medical expenses regardless of who was at fault.

A person involved in an automobile accident should notify the proper public authorities and the insurance company immediately after an accident occurs. Failure to do so may result in the insurance company's refusal to honor any claim filed. Any person who has been involved in a serious accident that causes injury or serious property damage should consult an attorney.

Important Legal terms

adjuster
assigned risk pool
binder
bodily injury liability insurance
coinsurance
collision insurance
comprehensive insurance
deductible
exclusion
extended coverage rider
face value
financial responsibility laws
floater policy
friendly fire
guest laws
homeowners policy

hostile fire
indemnification
insurable interest
insurance
insurance agent
insurance broker
insured
insurer
marine insurance
medical payments insurance
multiperil policy
no-fault insurance
omnibus clause
open coverage
personal liability insurance
policy

premium
property and casualty insurance
property damage liability insurance
pro-rata liability
prorated premium
proximate cause
public liability insurance
release
short rate
standard fire insurance policy
subrogation
threshold figure
uninsured motorist insurance
valued coverage

Questions and Problems for Discussion

1. What are the six types of coverage available in an automobile insurance policy?
2. Why were no-fault insurance laws passed?
3. Johnson applied for fire insurance on his boat. He paid a premium and received a binder that stated: "This policy not effective until the property insured is inspected and the policy is approved by the company." Before the policy was issued, the boat was destroyed in a fire. Can Johnson recover for the loss?
4. Blake purchased a policy from Atlas Insurance to insure his car in the amount of $30,000. He purchased a similar policy from National Insurance. If his car is destroyed in a fire, how much can he collect?
5. Sanders owned a stamp collection on which she had a valued insurance policy for $1,500. The entire collection was stolen. The insurance company offered to pay Sanders $1,000, claiming that was the value of the collection at the time it was stolen. Must Sanders settle for $1,000?
6. Marshall purchased a standard fire insurance policy on his home. Marshall's policy contained a 90 percent coinsurance clause. The home was worth $150,000, and Marshall carried $120,000 worth of insurance on it. A fire broke out in the

home, causing $10,000 damage. How much can Marshall collect for the loss?
7. Why is having an insurable interest so important?
8. Gergen bought a house and wanted to get fire, theft, and liability insurance combined in one policy. What type of policy should he buy?
9. Brad's home was insured with The Acme Company for a two-year period. After three months, Acme advised Brad that it was no longer going to do business in Brad's state and terminated his policy. May it do so?
10. Describe the difference between valued coverage and open coverage.
11. Davis owned a fruit and vegetable warehouse. Smoke from a fire at a nearby building ruined his fruits and vegetables. Can he collect from the insurance company under his fire policy?
12. What are the two ways that a driver in most states can prove financial responsibility for accidents?
13. Blake backed his car through his garage door, damaging the vehicle severely. The company that insured the car refused to pay for the damage, claiming that the accident was due to Blake's negligence and it did not have to cover negligence. Is the company correct?

14. Tree had a collision insurance policy on her car. One day Tree fell asleep at the wheel and ran into a telephone pole. The car was badly damaged and Tree filed a claim with her insurance company for the damage. Would Tree's insurance cover the damage to her car?

15. Sturges was involved in an accident with another driver in which he sustained cuts and bruises on his arm. He had no-fault insurance. Can he sue the other driver for his injuries?

16. When should you consult an attorney after a serious accident?

17. Edie and Florence went on a trip in Edie's car, with Florence sharing the trip expenses. Florence was injured when Edie hit a tree after being blinded by sunlight. Is Edie liable for Florence's injuries?

18. Finkel told Harter that she could borrow Finkel's car to drive to work, but only on Mondays. One Tuesday, Harter's car wouldn't start, and she borrowed Finkel's car without telling her about it. On the way to work, Harter injured another person in an accident caused by Harter's negligence. Is Finkel's insurance company obligated to pay for the injuries Harter caused?

19. Valdez's car hit another car at an intersection, damaging both cars. When the police arrived, Valdez told them that the accident was her fault and that her insurance company would pay for all damages. She then reported the accident to her insurance company, but the company refused to pay because of Valdez's admission. Was the company correct?

20. Scott was involved in an automobile accident. The other driver told Scott that she would report the accident to the police. Relying on this statement, Scott did not file an accident report with the police. If Scott files a claim, can his insurance company refuse to cover it?

Cases for Review

1. Mr. and Mrs. Crowell owned a farmhouse in Minnesota. They took out a mortgage on the property and insured the house with Delafield Insurance. When they defaulted on the mortgage, the bank commenced foreclosure proceedings. When the proceedings had been completed, the bank permitted the Crowells to remain on the property until it could be sold. Under Minnesota law, the Crowells had a right to meet any proposal that came in to buy the property and reclaim their interest. A fire destroyed the farmhouse while the insurance policy was still in effect. The Crowells submitted a claim to Delafield, which denied the claim on the grounds that the Crowells had no insurable interest in the property. Is the bank correct? (*Crowell* v. *Delafield Farmers Mut.*, 463 N.W.2d 737)

2. Bowes and others, trustees of a church, sued the company that had insured the church when a fire damaged the building. The insurance company refused to pay for the loss, claiming that the fire was not a "hostile fire" and was therefore not covered under the policy. There was testimony that some heating units overheated and the resulting flames were so great that they caused a waffle unit to burn, resulting in smoke and soot damage. Was the insurance company correct in refusing to pay for the loss? (*Bowes* v. *Insurance Co.*, 26 N.C. App. 234)

3. Speth owned a home insured with State Farm Insurance Co. Vandals caused damage to the home. The insurance policy contained an exclusion for vandalism losses that occurred when a house remained vacant for more than thirty consecutive days. State Farm refused to cover the loss because Speth, the sole occupant, was in a hospital for over five months. During that time, the home had been empty of all contents but had an operable alarm system and was serviced by water, gas, and electric utilities. Was State Farm's position correct? (*Speth* v. *State Farm Fire & Casualty Co.*, 35 P.3d 860)

4. Quam owned a duplex apartment in Minneapolis that contained rental units. The property was condemned by the Minneapolis Department of Health for unsanitary living conditions. The house was destroyed by fire one day after it had been condemned. The two-story house was insured for fire loss with General Accident Insurance, which denied Quam's claim under the policy because of what it considered an increase in hazard by the insured based on the unsanitary conditions. Is this position correct? (*Quam* v. *Gen. Acc. Ins. Co., of North Amer.*, 411 N.W.2d 270)

5. Mitchell's family trust insured a commercial building it owned. The building was destroyed by fire, and during the investigation of the causes, the insurance company discovered certain misrepresentations in the application for the policy, including the age of the building, the use made of the building, and the existence of building code violations. It rescinded the policy and refused to pay for the damage. Was it correct in doing this? (*Mitchell* v. *United National Insurance Co.*, 127 Cal. App. 4th 457)

6. Beatty bought a Toyota Celica and gave it to his daughter as a gift. He retained title to the car but had it delivered to her for her use. The daughter was in an accident in which the car was totaled. The insurance company refused to pay any insurance proceeds to the daughter, claiming that as the father had an insurable interest in the car, the daughter could not have had an insurable interest. Is the insurance company right? (*Beatty* v. *USAA Car Ins. Co.*, 954 S.W.2d 250)

7. Vandergriff's dog bit Grisham's leg after escaping from Vandergriff's parked pickup truck. To avoid a lawsuit, State Farm sued to obtain a court order declaring that it had no duty to defend or indemnify its insured, Vandergriff, for injuries sustained by Grisham, under the automobile liability policy issued by State Farm. Should State Farm succeed? (*State Farm Mutual Insurance Co.* v. *Grisham*, 122 Cal. App.4th 563)

8. On January 17, the Arleys purchased insurance on some property they owned in Nevada. At the request of their broker, the insurance company backdated the policy five days, making it effective January 12. The insurance company then learned that the property had been severely damaged on January 15 and refused to cover the loss. Is the company bound by the action of the broker? (*Arley* v. *United Pacific Insurance Company*, 379 F.2d 183)

9. Coons and Lawlor began a trip in Coons's car. Shortly after leaving Coons's home, Coons felt tired and asked Lawlor to take the wheel. While Lawlor was driving, he fell asleep, the car hit a utility pole, and Coons was injured. Coons sued Lawlor. Lawlor's automobile insurance company claimed that Coons was not covered because he was a guest in his own car, and under the applicable guest statute, he could not recover without proving willful misconduct on Lawlor's part. Is this defense valid? (*Coons* v. *Lawlor*, 804 F.2d 28)

10. Zaffuto, a part-time student typist, was injured in an auto accident. She complained of headaches and pain, but there was no medical documentation to indicate any orthopedic damage. She was able to return to work two weeks after the accident. Is she entitled to no-fault benefits under her insurance policy? (*Zaffuto* v. *Mortorano*, N.Y. 161 A.D.2d 639)

11. Stumpf, an infant, was killed when a driver of an automobile ran up on the sidewalk into Stumpf, killing him. There was proof that the driver had suffered an epileptic seizure that caused the accident. When the driver had applied for his automobile insurance policy, the application asked, "Has applicant (or anyone who usually drives the applicant's motor vehicle) any mental or physical disability?" The driver had responded "No," even though he had suffered epileptic seizures in the past. The insurance company refused to cover the loss, claiming misrepresentation in the application. Will the insurance company succeed? (*Stumpf* v. *State Farm Mut. Auto Ins.*, 252 Md. 696)

12. While bicycling, Gray was injured as he was leaving a park. A driver, insured by Allstate, was driving into the park on the same road as Gray, in the opposite direction. There was no collision. The driver had veered toward the center of the road to avoid hitting a pedestrian and Gray, whose attention had been distracted, looked up and saw the driver heading in his direction. Gray lost control of his bicycle and crashed. Gray sued the driver, claiming no-fault benefits. The driver's insurance company refused to pay, claiming that the injuries were not due to an automobile accident. Was the insurance company correct? (*Gray* v. *Allstate Ins. Co.*, 668 A.2d 778)

13. Richmond and her husband had two minor children and owned a home jointly. They were divorced and Richmond moved out of the house with the children. Her husband died, leaving the children as his only heirs. Richmond moved back into the house with the children and insured it with Motorists Mutual. She maintained the house, paid the mortgage, and took care of her children. When the house burned down and was completely destroyed, Motorists refused to honour Richmond's claim for compensation on the

grounds that as Richmond didn't own the house, she had no insurable interest in the property. Is this argument correct? (*Motorists Mutual Insurance Co.* v. *Richmond*, 676 S.W. 2d 478.)

14. Haines Manufacturing Co. made farm equipment. A farmer was severely injured using one of the company's machines. Haines was notified of the accident. Because Haines did not believe it was responsible for the accident, Haines did not notify its insurance company even though the policy required it. When the farmer sued eleven months after the accident, Haines notified the insurance company. The insurance company claimed it was not liable. Must the insurance company cover the loss? (Utica Mutual Ins. Co. v. C. L. Haines Manufacturing Co., Inc., New York 55 Ad2d 834)

CHAPTER 39

Personal Insurance

CHAPTER PREVIEW

Chapter Highlights

Life insurance and medical insurance, the two most common forms of personal insurance, are presented in this chapter. After a discussion of the need for personal insurance, the chapter describes and explains the various types of life insurance available, including whole life, term, and endowment. It explains typical clauses found in most life insurance policies, as well as rules regarding when a policy may be assigned and how premiums may be paid. The chapter concludes with a discussion of health insurance, both private and government sponsored. This type of insurance protects against the cost of medical, surgical, and hospital care, as well as loss of income if a person is disabled.

THE NEED FOR PERSONAL INSURANCE

Personal insurance protects the insured and the insured's family against a loss of income because of death, illness, or accident. Personal insurance may be bought either individually or as part of a group. An individual insurance policy is issued to one person and can be written to cover that person's needs. A person who buys an individual policy must satisfactorily answer a series of health-related questions and may be asked to pass a medical examination. Individual policies usually may not be canceled and must be renewed by the insurer as long as the premiums are paid.

A group insurance policy is one that insures all the members of a specific group. The group may be people who have the same employer, who are in the same profession, or who are members of the same organization. A medical examination is usually not required. Group insurance is temporary; it expires when the member leaves the group. The member, however, generally has the option to convert to an individual policy after leaving the group. Group insurance is less expensive because the employer often pays for all or part of the premium. Also, because of the number of people in the group, risks are spread out and premiums are lower.

The two major types of personal insurance are life and health insurance.

LIFE INSURANCE

Life insurance is a contract between the insured and an insurance company. In return for the payment of premiums, the insurance company agrees to pay a certain sum of money (the face value of the policy) to a designated person, the **beneficiary**, when the insured dies. Although there are many reasons for buying life insurance, the main one is protection by providing money after the insured's death.

If the insured does not have an insurable interest in the life that is insured, the policy is void. A person obviously has an insurable interest in her or his own life and may take out insurance naming another as beneficiary. The policy is valid regardless of whether or not the beneficiary knows of the insurance. A person also has an insurable interest in the life of someone whose relationship is such that death or accident would cause a severe financial loss. A person therefore has an insurable interest in the life of a spouse, a child, a parent, a business partner, and so on. For a policy to be valid, the insurable interest must exist when the insurance is purchased but need not exist when the insured dies.

There are three basic types of life insurance policies, each performing a different function: whole life insurance, endowment insurance, and term insurance.

Whole Life Insurance

Whole life insurance (often called ordinary or straight life) offers lifetime protection for the insured. The insurance remains in effect as long as the insured pays the premiums. Premiums for whole life insurance remain the same, or level, during the insured's lifetime. The premiums are based on the gender of the insured, as well as on the insured's age, health, and occupation at the time the policy is taken out.

> You purchased a whole life insurance policy when you were twenty-two years of age. The annual premium, based on the face value of the policy and your age, was $127. Your annual premium will remain at $127 for as long as you keep the policy.

An important feature of whole life insurance is its **cash value**. With whole life insurance, a portion of the premium pays for the cost of the insurance protection. The other portion of the premium is placed in a savings fund. The amount in this savings fund is the cash value. This amount increases with each premium payment.

There are many variations on the basic whole life insurance policy. Many people who want lifetime protection prefer to limit their premium payments. They may not wish to pay premiums after a certain number of years (e.g., ten or twenty) or after reaching a certain age (e.g., sixty-five). A form of whole life insurance known as **limited payment life insurance** provides protection for an insured's entire life, even though premiums are paid only for a certain time. This insurance is more expensive than a whole life policy with the same face value because the number of payments is limited. At the same time, the cash value for a limited payment policy increases more quickly than for a whole life policy.

> Sparks, age thirty-two, wanted life insurance but did not want to pay premiums after she retired. She purchased a thirty-year limited payment life policy. After age sixty-two, she will not pay premiums, although the insurance will still be in effect.

Modified life is another variation. Many people who need insurance find it difficult to pay the premiums when they first start working. The premiums for a **modified life insurance** policy start out low and increase over a period of years as the insured's income increases. After a number of years, the premium becomes fixed.

life insurance contract in which insurance company agrees to pay a sum of money to a beneficiary upon insured's death

beneficiary recipient of the proceeds of a life insurance policy; one who inherits property as specified in a will

whole life insurance life insurance on which premiums are paid for as long as insured holds policy

cash value portion of an insurance premium placed in a savings fund; amount an insured receives if a whole life policy is given up

limited payment life insurance life insurance paid for after a set number of payments

modified life insurance life insurance with gradually increasing premiums

universal life insurance life insurance allowing insured to change premium payments, face value, and period of coverage

survivorship life insurance insurance covering the lives of two people with benefits payable on the death of the survivor

endowment insurance life insurance that accumulates a sum of money to be repaid to insured or beneficiary at a later time

term insurance life insurance purchased for a specific period of time

Universal life insurance permits an insured to change the policy based on changing needs. The amount of coverage may be increased or decreased by changing either the amount or frequency of premium payments, the period of coverage, or the amount of insurance. It combines term insurance (protection for a certain period of time) with an investment feature. Some versions of universal life insurance permit the insured to determine how the cash-value portion of the premium will be invested.

Survivorship life insurance, also know as "second-to-die" insurance, covers the life of two persons but pays only one death benefit upon the death of the second person insured. Its advantage is that it costs less than a single policy on either insured, because the insurance risk is spread over two lives, rather than one.

Endowment Insurance

Endowment insurance provides protection for a certain number of years or until the insured reaches a certain age. With an endowment policy, the insured accumulates a sum of money that will be repaid at a later date. If the insured dies during the term of the policy, the beneficiary receives the face value immediately. If the insured lives beyond the maturity date, the face value is paid to the insured.

Premiums are much higher for endowment insurance than for any other type of insurance because the entire face value must be accumulated before the maturity date. Endowment insurance is often used to accumulate money for a specific purpose, such as for retirement or the college education of a child.

Council wanted to make sure he had enough money when he retired at sixty-five and still wanted to protect his family should he die before that time. Council purchased an endowment policy that will mature when he reaches sixty-five.

Term Insurance

Term insurance provides protection for a certain period of time. The term may be one year, five years, ten years, or until the insured reaches sixty-five. If the insured dies during that term, the beneficiary receives the face value of the policy. At the end of the term, the policy expires and coverage ends.

Term insurance can be renewed at the end of the term but at a higher premium. The premium rate for each renewal is higher because the insured is older and the risk of death is greater. Most term insurance is not available or renewable when the insured reaches sixty-five or seventy. Term insurance may also be convertible. That is, the insured may exchange, or convert, the term policy for a whole life insurance policy.

Term insurance is much less expensive than whole life or endowment insurance because it offers only temporary protection and does not build up a cash value. Because the premiums are relatively low, term insurance offers young people the most protection for the lowest premium. It provides the maximum amount of protection when the insured's financial responsibilities are the greatest. Term insurance is often purchased to guarantee payment of a mortgage if the insured dies.

Lake bought a home, using a twenty-year mortgage loan. Should Lake die before paying off the mortgage, his family might find it difficult to make the mortgage payments. To protect them, Lake took out a twenty-year term policy. If Lake should die during the term of the policy, the proceeds can be used to pay off the mortgage.

Insurance for Special Purposes

Many people have needs that cannot be met by standard life insurance policies. Special policies and options have therefore been developed to provide the flexibility to meet those needs. The most common of these are the family income policy, the key-person policy, the guaranteed insurability option, and the annuity policy.

Family Income Policy A family with young children has special needs. The head of the family needs to provide permanent protection for a spouse and to pay off debts and expenses at death. At the same time, short-term protection is needed to provide for the children until they become self-sufficient. One answer is a **family income policy**, insurance that combines whole life and term insurance. In a typical policy, the term insurance portion provides an income for the spouse and children until the children become adults. The whole life insurance portion also provides income, which continues for the spouse after the children have become adults.

family income policy
insurance that
combines whole life
and term insurance

Key-Person Insurance The retirement or death of a business partner or large corporate stockholder may be disastrous for a business. The retired partner or the deceased stockholder's estate will want the business to purchase the retiree's or deceased's interest in the business, but the business may not have enough funds to do so. One answer to this problem is *key-person insurance,* a type of life insurance used to fund business buyouts. Such insurance may be purchased by partners or stockholders to insure the lives of the other partners or stockholders. In some cases, the business itself may purchase the insurance. Businesses can also purchase insurance to insure the lives of officers and other employees.

Guaranteed Insurability Option For health reasons, some persons cannot obtain insurance as they grow older. One insurance feature available to protect against this problem is the **guaranteed insurability option**. This plan is offered to those under a certain age who buy whole life insurance. It allows them to buy additional insurance coverage in limited amounts during their lives, even though they may be uninsurable for health reasons at the time they buy the additional insurance.

**guaranteed
insurability option**
allows people under a
certain age who buy
life insurance to buy
additional insurance in
limited amounts
despite poor health

Annuity Policy An annuity, which is also sold by insurance companies, provides an income for a specific period of time or for the life of the annuity owner (the *annuitant*). It is similar to whole life insurance because both accumulate cash that can be used as income later. An annuity, however, does not provide insurance protection. The entire premium goes into a savings fund, which earns interest.

An annuity differs from a life insurance policy in its purpose. Life insurance primarily provides protection for dependents if the insured dies. An annuity provides a guaranteed income to the annuity holder. Annuities are usually purchased by persons interested in providing retirement income for themselves. As a result, annuities are becoming more popular as a supplement to Social Security payments. You can purchase an annuity by making regular payments to the insurance company over a period of years or by paying one lump sum. In many cases, the proceeds of an insurance policy are used to buy an annuity and provide an income for a beneficiary.

Berg wanted to protect her family after her death by providing the maximum income. She purchased a whole life policy and specified that the proceeds of the policy be converted to an annuity to provide a lifetime income for her family.

Standard Policy Clauses

Most life insurance policies have standard clauses that outline the rights of the insured, the company, and the beneficiary. Some typical clauses are shown in Figure 39.1.

FIGURE 39.1 Clauses from a Typical Life Insurance Policy

PREMIUMS

WHERE AND HOW PAYABLE Premiums are payable in advance at the Home Office or to an authorized representative in exchange for a receipt signed by the President or Treasurer and countersigned by the person receiving payment. A premium is due and payable on the policy date and on the day following the expiration of each premium payment period thereafter during the lifetime of the Insured until premiums for the number of full years shown in the Schedule of Premiums have been paid. Premiums may be paid for any period shown in the Schedule.

GRACE PERIOD A grace period of 30 days will be allowed for the payment of each premium after the first. The policy will continue in full force during the grace period. If the Insured dies during the grace period, the premium for the policy month in which death occurs will be deducted from the policy proceeds.

SUICIDE If the Insured commits suicide, while sane or insane, within two years from the policy date, the amount payable by the Company shall be limited to the premiums paid less any indebtedness.

INCONTESTABILITY The policy will be incontestable after it has been in force during the lifetime of the Insured for a period of two years from the policy date except for non-payment of premiums and any agreement providing waiver of premium, accidental death or loss of sight or limbs benefits.

INCORRECT AGE OR SEX If the age or sex of the Insured is incorrectly stated, the policy proceeds and all other benefits will be adjusted to the amount which the premium would have purchased at the correct age and sex.

Beneficiary The proceeds of a life insurance policy are payable to the beneficiary. The beneficiary could be the insured, the insured's estate, or someone else. It could be a person or a company. It could also be more than one person, called *joint beneficiaries*. The insured has the right to change the beneficiary at any time, unless this right has been given up.

Misstatement of Age Premiums are based on the age of the insured at the time the policy is taken out. Some people misstate their age because of vanity. More often, people misstate their age so as to pay lower premiums. A misstatement about age does not void an insurance policy. Instead, the insurance company will adjust the face value of the policy to that amount of insurance the premium would have purchased if the insured's true age had been given.

> Denton bought a $25,000 life insurance policy and mistakenly gave her age as twenty-eight. She was actually twenty-nine. Because Denton was paying a lower premium at age twenty-eight than she would have at age twenty-nine, when she dies the proceeds of the policy will be adjusted to reflect the amount of insurance her premium would have bought at age twenty-nine. For example, if the premium she was paying would have bought only $23,000 of insurance, that amount will be paid to her beneficiary.

Incontestability Occasionally, an insured may misrepresent something on the insurance application or conceal important facts. The insurance company must have the right to cancel the policy or refuse to pay the proceeds because of these misrepresentations. At the same time, the insured should not have to worry that the policy will be challenged after his or her death, when no one may know the truth.

incontestable clause clause preventing insurer from canceling a policy after a set time for any reason except nonpayment of premiums

The **incontestable clause** provides that after a policy has been in effect for a period of time (usually two years), the insurance company cannot cancel the policy for any reason other than nonpayment of the premium.

Brady took out a life insurance policy. In the application, he forgot to state that his family had a history of heart disease. Brady died of a heart attack four years after the policy was issued. Because more than two years had passed, the insurance company cannot refuse to pay the proceeds if it learns of his misrepresentation.

Even if there is impostor fraud, that is, when someone other than the insured appears for the required physical exam, most states prohibit an insurance company from disallowing claims because of fraud under the incontestability clause.

Grace Period Premiums on all policies are payable by a certain date, but it would be unfair to the insured if a policy could expire, or lapse, because a payment was not received exactly on time. Therefore, most policies provide for a **grace period** of thirty days. The policy remains in force for thirty days after a missed premium payment.

grace period period of time a policy remains in effect after a premium is missed

Fleming forgot to pay her insurance premium, which was due on January 1. She died on January 15. Because of the grace period, Fleming's beneficiary can collect the proceeds of the policy, minus the amount of the missed premium.

Reinstatement Once the grace period ends, the policy lapses. Most policies, however, include a **reinstatement clause** that gives the insured the right to put the policy back into effect. The insured must pay the overdue premiums, plus interest, and prove that he or she is in good health, often by passing a physical exam.

reinstatement clause insurance clause allowing insured to put policy back into effect after it has lapsed

Double Indemnity Most deaths are due to natural causes. For a small extra premium, most insurance companies will pay double the face value of the policy if the insured dies because of an accident. This additional benefit is known as the **double indemnity clause**. Deaths from war, suicide, surgery, illegal use of drugs, or the commission of a crime are excluded. In those cases, the beneficiary would receive only the face value.

double indemnity clause life insurance clause doubling proceeds if insured dies accidentally

Hamm's insurance policy had a double indemnity clause. She slipped on some ice, struck her head, and died. Because her death was a result of an accident, Hamm's beneficiary will collect double the face value of the policy.

Suicide A person under great emotional strain might take out an insurance policy, pay a few premiums, and then commit suicide so that the beneficiary would collect the insurance proceeds. To protect against this occurrence, most policies contain a suicide clause. If the insured commits suicide within a certain period of time after the policy is taken out (usually two years), the insurance company only has to return the premiums actually paid. It does not have to pay the face value of the policy.

waiver of premium clause insurance policy clause relieving insured from paying premiums if disabled

Waiver of Premium An insured may become disabled and unable to pay the premiums. If the premiums are not paid, the policy will lapse. For a small additional premium, the insured can include a **waiver of premium clause**. If the insured is disabled and unable to work, the insurance company will waive, or do away with, the premiums either for a stated period or for life. The life insurance will still be in effect, even though the insured does not pay the premiums.

> You purchased a life insurance policy with a waiver-of-premium clause. You were involved in an accident that left you paralyzed and unable to work. You do not have to make premium payments for as long as your disability lasts.

Assignment   The right to the proceeds of a life insurance policy may be transferred, or assigned, by the insured. If the insured should die before the debt is repaid, the assignee has first claim on the proceeds. The beneficiary would receive any amount remaining. To be valid, an assignment must be submitted in writing to the insurance company, signed by the insured and usually the beneficiary.

After the insured's death, the beneficiary may assign the rights to the proceeds to anyone or any group without the consent of the insurance company.

> Dunn had a $25,000 life insurance policy, which named her husband as beneficiary. She borrowed $15,000 from a bank, assigning the proceeds of the policy to the bank as security for the repayment of the loan. Dunn died before the loan was repaid. The bank has first claim on the proceeds to recover the $15,000 loaned to her. The balance ($10,000) is paid to her husband.

Nonforfeiture Rights   People who have insurance policies often pay premiums for many years and suddenly find that they can no longer afford to pay them. To prevent the policies from lapsing, all states require whole life insurance policies to have **nonforfeiture rights**, which are ways of using the accumulated cash value to prevent a policy from lapsing. One of these rights is the *automatic premium loan*. If a premium is not paid, the insurance company lends the premium to the insured, using the cash value as security. The insured may repay the loan at any time. If the loan is not repaid, the amount is deducted from the proceeds paid to the beneficiary.

nonforfeiture rights ways of using cash value to prevent an insurance policy from lapsing

> Fine forgot to pay a premium one month. If the cash value of Fine's policy is more than the premium due, the insurance company will automatically lend Fine the amount of the premium. The policy will stay in effect and will not lapse.

Another nonforfeiture right is *reduced paid-up life insurance*. If a premium is not paid, the insurance company computes the amount of insurance the current cash value of the policy would buy. This amount, always lower than the face value of the old policy, is the face value of a new, completely paid-up policy.

> Foster had a ten-year-old, $10,000 whole life policy on which he could no longer afford to make payments. The policy had a cash value of $990. Foster exchanged it for a paid-up whole life policy with a face value of $2,750. When Foster dies, the insurance company will pay his beneficiary the proceeds of $2,750.

A third nonforfeiture right is *extended term insurance*, which is similar to reduced paid-up life insurance. Instead of exchanging the old policy for one with a lower face value, it is exchanged for a completely paid-up term policy with the *same* face value. The current cash value determines the length of time the term policy is in effect.

> Foster's $10,000 whole life policy in the previous example could be exchanged for extended term insurance. The $990 current cash value will purchase a $10,000 term policy that will be in effect for 15 years, 215 days. Foster does not have to pay any more premiums, but at the end of the term, the policy expires.

A fourth nonforfeiture right is that of cash surrender value. The insured can "cash the policy in," or surrender it to the insurance company and receive the total accumulated cash value. Of course, he or she then no longer has any insurance.

Foster's $10,000 whole life policy can be surrendered for the cash value. Foster would receive $990 from the insurance company.

Effective Date Most life insurance policies become effective on the date of issue. Some insurance companies provide that their policies become effective for brief, trial periods upon receipt of an application and an initial premium.

How Life Insurance Proceeds Are Paid

When the insured dies, the beneficiary must notify the insurance company of the death, usually by submitting a copy of the death certificate. The insurance company will then pay the beneficiary the face value, or proceeds, of the policy.

settlement options
ways in which life insurance proceeds may be paid to beneficiaries

There are several ways, called **settlement options**, in which the proceeds of the policy may be paid to the beneficiary. The insured may select the settlement option. Usually, however, the beneficiary has the right to select an option within sixty days of the insured's death. The settlement options are the following:

1. The *lump sum option,* in which the beneficiary receives the proceeds in one lump sum.
2. The *income for life option,* in which the beneficiary receives a fixed amount at regular intervals for life.
3. The *income for a fixed period option,* in which the beneficiary receives monthly payments for a specific number of years.
4. The *fixed income option,* in which the beneficiary receives a fixed amount until the proceeds have been paid in full.
5. The *interest only option,* in which the insurance company holds the proceeds and pays the beneficiary the interest at regular intervals. The beneficiary can withdraw any amount of the proceeds at any time.

HEALTH INSURANCE

Providing for the rapidly rising cost of health care should be an important part of any personal or family financial plan. Most people believe that they can handle the ordinary medical expenses. An accident or unexpected serious illness, however, not only deprives the family of the wage earner's income but may result in enormous medical or hospital bills. The best protection is some form of **health insurance**, which protects against the costs of medical expenses and the loss of income from illness. Today, the majority of Americans have some type of health insurance.

health insurance
insurance for medical expenses and loss of income due to illness

There are seven basic types of health insurance policies, which may all be issued under either individual or group plans. They are medical insurance, surgical insurance, hospital insurance, major medical insurance, disability income insurance, dental expense insurance, and long-term care insurance. The first three—medical, surgical, and hospital—are often combined into one basic health insurance policy.

Medical, Surgical, and Hospital Insurance

medical insurance
insurance covering emergency room costs and doctors' fees for non-surgical services

Medical insurance provides coverage for emergency room costs and doctor's fees for nonsurgical services. Visits to the doctor's office are covered. Some medical insurance policies also pay for annual physicals, x-rays, prescriptions, and dental services.

surgical insurance
insurance for surgical fees for specific operations

Surgical insurance pays for the cost of a surgeon's operating fee, whether the operation takes place in a hospital or in a doctor's office. Only specific operations are covered, and a maximum benefit amount is set for each type of operation. In some cases, the insured must pay the portion of the surgical fee that is over the amount stated in the policy.

hospital insurance
insurance covering fees for hospital care

Hospital insurance provides coverage for the expenses of a stay in the hospital, including room, board, nursing care, and charges for such things as drugs, lab tests, and x-rays. Most policies limit coverage to a maximum amount per day for a maximum number of days, such as 90 or 180.

Grady entered a hospital to have her appendix removed. After the surgery, she received nursing care, as well as medication to prevent infection. The cost of all these services would be covered by a basic health insurance policy.

Major Medical Insurance

major medical insurance insurance for extraordinary costs of illnesses or accidents

Major medical insurance protects against the very high expenses of a catastrophic illness or accident. It is used to pay those costs that exceed the coverage of the basic health insurance policy. It usually covers all types of medical expenses arising from an illness or accident. Depending on the policy, this insurance may cover expenses up to as much as $250,000. Some policies have no maximum limits.

All major medical policies have two distinguishing features: a deductible feature and a coinsurance clause. With the deductible feature, the insured must pay the initial costs in full, up to the amount specified in the policy. The deductible amount varies but may range from $250 to $500. The deductible reduces the premium by having the insured pay for smaller medical expenses. The higher the deductible, the lower the premium.

After the deductible has been paid, the coinsurance feature provides for the insurance company and the insured to share the medical costs. The insurance company usually pays 75 or 80 percent of the costs beyond the deductible amount; the insured pays the balance. This clause also reduces the amount of the premiums by discouraging unnecessary expenses and claims.

Flynn had a major medical insurance policy that paid 80 percent of any medical expenses resulting from an illness. His deductible was $100. Flynn suffered a heart attack and required medical attention. The total medical expenses were $30,000. Under the policy, Flynn would pay the first $100 plus 20 percent of the balance, or a total of $6,080. The insurance company would pay $23,920.

Medicare and Medicaid

Medical, surgical, and hospital insurance may be obtained from either private or public sources. Some insurance companies sell policies that cover basic needs. In most areas of the country, there are health maintenance organizations, semipublic groups that provide health services. In addition, there are government-sponsored health insurance programs known as Medicare and Medicaid.

Medicare federal program that pays for health insurance for persons sixty-five and older or for those with certain disabilities

Medicare is a federal health insurance program for people sixty-five and older or for those of any age who have certain disabilities. The program is administered by the Health Care Financing Administration of the U.S. Department of Health and Human Services.

Medicare has two parts: Part A, hospital insurance, and Part B, medical insurance. Part A helps pay for medically necessary services furnished by approved hospitals, nursing facilities, and some home health care. These services include hospital room and board, general nursing, home health care, and blood transfusions.

Part B helps pay for physician's services, including diagnostic tests, therapy, home health care, and laboratory services.

Although Medicare pays a large portion of health care costs, there are gaps in its coverage. First, it does not cover custodial (nonmedical) care, outpatient prescription drugs, dental care, routine physical checkups, and medical care received outside the United States. In addition, it provides coverage only for a limited time and usually for only 80 percent of an amount approved for services provided. The patient must pay the remaining 20 percent, known as coinsurance.

Those who want to supplement Medicare coverage to fill the gaps usually obtain private insurance known as Medigap insurance. Most states have adopted minimum standards for this type of insurance. It may be purchased on either an individual or group basis.

Part D is a prescription drug benefit plan for the elderly and the disabled. Benefits started on January 1, 2006. The drug benefit is offered through private insurance plans to those who apply for it. The private plans are reimbursed by the Centers for Medicare & Medicaid Services (CMS). Enrollment for most beneficiaries is voluntary. Some costs must be borne by the beneficiaries of the plans.

A federal-state program fills the gaps in Medicare coverage for low-income persons. This program, known as **Medicaid**, is administered by each state. A person whose annual income is limited and who has limited access to financial resources may qualify for Medicaid assistance in paying Medicare premiums and some of the Medicare deductible and coinsurance amounts.

Medicaid state-administered program that pays for health care for economically disadvantaged persons

Disability Income Insurance

Disability income insurance provides income to an insured person who cannot work because of illness or accident. The amount of benefits paid is either a specific amount or a certain percentage of the insured's income. The length of time benefits are paid depends on whether the policy is short term (up to one year) or long term (more than one year). Most policies also provide for an *elimination period,* which is a specific period of time before benefits are paid. The longer the elimination period, the less the insurer has to pay and the lower the premium.

disability income insurance insurance providing income to insured who cannot work because of illness or accident

> Hiro had a disability income insurance policy that paid a monthly benefit of $1,000 after a fifteen-day elimination period. He was out of work for one month due to illness. Under his policy, Hiro would receive $500, or one half of one month's benefits.

Dental Expense Insurance

Dental expense insurance is now available on a limited basis for individuals and groups. It provides coverage for routine dental care as well as for x-rays, dental surgery, and orthodontia (straightening teeth). Many policies either have a deductible amount or require the insured to pay an amount over the policy limit.

Long-Term Care Insurance

long-term care insurance insurance that covers custodial expenses for extended stays in a nursing home or in a patient's home

Long-term care insurance is available to cover expenses for extended stays in nursing homes and in a patient's home. It is intended to cover the cost of custodial care, as distinguished from medical care. Plans differ in various states. Factors affecting the cost of such insurance include the age of the insured when the policy is taken out, the amount covered, the term, and the deductible amount.

Summary

Personal insurance protects the insured and the insured's family against a loss of income because of death, illness, or accident. The most common type of personal insurance is life insurance, which pays a certain sum of money to a beneficiary when the insured dies.

There are three basic types of life insurance: whole life, endowment, and term. Other policies and options are available for special purposes. Whole life and endowment offer lifetime protection, whereas term insurance provides protection for a specific period of time. Whole life and endowment insurance build up a cash value in addition to providing insurance protection; term insurance does not. The cash value allows the insured to surrender the policy for cash, purchase additional insurance, or use it as a source for a loan.

A life insurance policy may not be honored if the insured has made a material misrepresentation in the insurance application. After a policy has been in effect for two years, however, the insurance company cannot cancel it except in the case of nonpayment of premiums.

Most insurance policies contain standard clauses dealing with changing a beneficiary, a grace period in the event of late payment of premiums, assignment of the policy, and waiver of premiums for disability.

Beneficiaries may usually choose among five settlement options, ways in which the proceeds of a life insurance policy are paid.

Health insurance provides protection against high medical costs that could result from an illness or an accident. It may be purchased to cover medical expenses, surgical costs, hospital expenses, major medical expenses, loss of income, dental expenses, and long-term care insurance. Many health policies are purchased from private companies. In addition, the federal government, through its Medicare program, and the federal and state governments, through their Medicaid programs, provide protection for health-related expenses.

Important Legal terms

beneficiary
cash value
disability income insurance
double indemnity clause
endowment insurance
family income policy
grace period
guaranteed insurability option
health insurance
hospital insurance

incontestable clause
life insurance
limited payment life insurance
long-term care insurance
major medical insurance
Medicaid
medical insurance
Medicare
modified life insurance
nonforfeiture rights

reinstatement clause
settlement options
surgical insurance
survivorship life insurance
term insurance
universal life insurance
waiver of premium clause
whole life insurance

Questions and Problems for Discussion

1. Describe and explain the differences among the three basic types of life insurance policies.
2. Which life insurance policies are more expensive than others? Why?
3. Justin asked an insurance broker to get him a life insurance policy. The broker had Justin fill out an application and then told him that everything was okay and that Justin was insured. None of the insurance companies that the broker used would issue a policy to Justin. Was Justin insured based on what his broker had told him?
4. Susan and Ann, close friends, took out insurance policies on each other's life, each being the beneficiary of the other's policy. When Susan died, the insurance company refused to pay the proceeds to Ann, claiming that she did not have an insurable interest in Susan's life. Was the insurance company correct?
5. Garth applied for a life insurance policy. On the application, he stated "none" in response to a question asking whether he had any hobbies, even though he was a famous stamp collector.

When he died, the insurance company refused to pay the policy proceeds on the grounds that Garth had lied on the application for insurance. Was the insurance company correct?

6. Gerber applied for a life insurance policy, and the insurance company agent gave him a binder. On the way home from the agent's office, Gerber was killed in an automobile accident. Was Gerber insured because the binder had been issued?

7. Denton applied for a life insurance policy. On the application, Denton stated that she had not received medical treatment within five years prior to the date of the application. Denton had, in fact, been treated for pneumonia eight months earlier. At Denton's death, five years later, may the insurance company refuse to pay the beneficiary?

8. Smith and Dale were business partners. Smith bought an insurance policy on Dale's life, naming herself as beneficiary. The partnership broke up two years later, but Smith continued to pay the premiums. When Dale died, Smith asked for the proceeds of the policy. Must the insurance company pay her?

9. Ryan insured his life for $100,000, naming his wife as beneficiary. One year later, Ryan was killed while attempting to rob a bank. Ryan's wife filed a claim for the proceeds. The insurance company offered to return the premiums paid but refused to pay the proceeds. Is the insurance company correct?

10. Taylor had a life insurance policy with a double indemnity clause, naming her daughter as the beneficiary. During a rainstorm, Taylor drove too fast and was killed when her car skidded off the road. The insurance company refused to pay the double indemnity amount, claiming that the accident was due to Taylor's negligence. Can Taylor's daughter collect under the double indemnity clause?

11. In applying for life insurance, Wells stated by mistake that he was twenty-three years old when he was actually twenty-four. After paying the premiums for thirty years, he died. The insurance company learned what his correct age was and agreed to return the premiums paid but refused to pay the full proceeds, claiming misrepresentation by Wells. May the insurance company refuse to pay the full proceeds?

12. Farrow, a man with leukemia, applied for life insurance. Knowing that he would probably not pass the required physical exam, he had a friend take the exam in his place. Three years later, Farrow died and his insurance company refused to pay the proceeds to his beneficiary, claiming fraud in the application process. Will the company succeed?

13. Gerber had a life insurance policy with his wife as beneficiary. Because he owed money to a friend, he assigned the proceeds of the policy to the friend to guarantee payment upon his death. He never notified either the insurance company or his wife of the assignment. Upon Gerber's death, would his friend be entitled to the policy proceeds to the extent of the loan balance?

14. Solon purchased a life insurance policy with a guaranteed insurability option. Ten years later, when very sick, he tried to buy additional coverage, but his insurance company refused, claiming Solon was uninsurable. Was this correct?

Cases for Review

1. Garcia and his mother applied for a $2 million insurance policy on her life from Old Line. She already had a similar policy from another company. On the application for the new policy, she indicated "yes" to the question whether the new policy "may" be used to replace the existing policy. In fact, Mrs. Garcia never replaced the old policy with the new one, and when she died, the insurance company refused to pay the proceeds, claiming a misrepresentation in the application. Was the insurance company correct? (*Old Line* *Life Insurance Co.* v. *Garcia*, 411 Fed.3d 605, amended 418 Fed.3d 546)

2. Bean signed an agreement to borrow $120,000 from Hazel. To protect Hazel, Bean was to insure his life with Hazel as beneficiary in an amount not less than the unpaid balance of the loan. Bean already had a life insurance policy for $200,000 and changed the beneficiary to Hazel to the extent of $120,000. At the time Bean died, the balance on the loan was $79,000. Hazel claimed the full proceeds of $120,000, while Bean's estate

claimed that Hazel had an insurable interest only in $79,000. Who is correct? (*Estate of Bean* v. *Hazel,* 972 S.W.2d 290)

3. Paul Revere Insurance Company solicited members of a county bar association to buy disability income insurance. The policy waived all age and health requirements and was open to all members. Blumberg, a new member, sent in his application with a check for the premium. His application was rejected because of prior health problems, and he sued the company to accept his application. Blumberg claimed that the solicitation was an offer and that he had accepted the offer. Is his claim correct? (*Blumberg* v. *Paul Revere Life Ins. Co.,* 677 N.Y.S.2d 412)

4. Callahan applied for health insurance on April 15. The application asked for the effective date requested, and Callahan selected "date of underwriting approval." He sent in a check for the premium, which was deposited by the insurance company on April 30. On April 30, Callahan was injured in a farm accident. The insurance company rejected his application because of his accident. The insurance company claimed that an application is not effective until approved by the company and that it had a right to reject the application because of Callahan's injuries. Is this claim valid? (*Callahan* v. *Washington Nat. Ins. Co.,* 608 N.W.2d 592)

5. Baker was insured under a policy with a double indemnity provision for death by accidental means. Baker was killed when he voluntarily agreed to take part in a shooting contest in which a can was placed on his head and a friend fired at it, killing Baker instantly. Baker's wife brought suit to collect the double indemnity amount after the insurance company refused to pay. Must the insurance company pay? (*Baker* v. *Nat. Life & Accident Ins. Co.,* 201 Tenn. 247)

6. Great Neck Saw applied to Manhattan Life Insurance Co. for a life insurance policy in the amount of $1 million for coverage of one of its corporate officers. It submitted the application and was told by one of Manhattan's agents that the coverage was in effect. It never received a receipt or policy, however. The application stated that no insurance would take effect until a policy had been issued and delivered. The proposed insured died two days after the application was delivered to Manhattan. Manhattan refused to pay the policy proceeds, claiming that no coverage ever existed. Is Manhattan correct? (*Great Neck Saw Mfr.* v. *Manhattan Life Ins.,* 163 A.D.2d 273)

7. Weinberg was a creditor of Dominic Cosentino, and he took out a $500,000 insurance policy on Cosentino's life to protect his interest in being repaid. When Cosentino died and the policy proceeds were paid to Weinberg, Cosentino's widow brought suit to recover the policy proceeds, claiming that Weinberg did not have an insurable interest in Cosentino's life. Should she prevail in the suit? (*Cosentino* v. *William Penn Life Insurance Co.,* 224 A.D.2d 777)

8. Cichowlas applied to Life Insurance Co. for a policy of life insurance, naming his wife as beneficiary of the policy. When he applied, his health was good and he answered all questions truthfully. Between the time of the application and the issuance of the policy, he developed a lung disease but never told Life Insurance about it. When he died, the insurance company refused to pay his widow the proceeds of the policy, claiming her husband was not insurable when the policy was issued. Is this position correct? (*Life Insurance Co. of North America* v. *Cichowlas,* 659 So, 2d 1333)

9. When Fima applied to Paul Revere Life Insurance Co. for a disability policy, he overstated his income by a large amount. Three years after the policy was issued, Fima became disabled and filed a claim for policy benefits. Paul Revere refused to pay because of the misstatement on the application. Is Paul Revere correct? (*Paul Revere Life Insurance Co.* v. *Fima,* 105 F. 3d 490)

10. Callicott bought a life insurance policy insuring her brother's life. She never told her brother about the policy. When the brother died, Callicott applied for payment of the proceeds. The insurance company refused to pay, claiming she had no insurable interest. Was the company correct? (*Callicott* v. *Dixie Life & Accident Insurance Co.,* 198 Ark 69, 127 SW2d 620)

THE CASE OF THE DRIVER WHO HAD ONE TOO MANY

Fred was insured under a life insurance policy with double indemnity coverage. The policy had a face amount of $1 million. Two weeks after taking out the policy, Fred was driving home from a party while intoxicated. He lost control of his car and was killed when the car hit a utility pole. His insurance company refused to pay the double indemnity amount, and Fred's wife sued the company to force payment.

The Trial

Testimony at the trial proved conclusively that Fred was very intoxicated when he left the party. There was also proof that there was nothing in the policy about no coverage in the event of an accident due to intoxication.

The Arguments at Trial

The insurance company's attorneys argued that double indemnity provisions apply only to death due to accidents and that although Fred was in an accident, his death was due to his being intoxicated and not the accident. They further argued that this concept was so logical that it did not need spelling out in the insurance policy. The estate's attorneys argued that because the policy was silent about accidents due to intoxication, the double indemnity provision should apply regardless of the cause of the accident.

Questions to Discussion

1. Who do you think has the stronger argument, the insurance company or Fred's estate?
2. If you were the judge hearing this case, how would you decide? Why?
3. Based on your reading of the text, do you think that the double indemnity provision of the policy would apply?
4. What do you think the rule regarding coverage of accidents due to use of drugs or excessive alcohol should be?

B rady, a successful engineer, wanted to retire and obtain a large monthly income to support his lifestyle. He purchased an annuity for a single payment of $250,000. He was given the option of receiving payments during his lifetime or receiving payments for a certain number of years, the payments to be made to his heirs if he died before all payments were made. Brady selected the lifetime payment option as it provided for a larger monthly payment.

Brady died after receiving two monthly payments. The annuity company, citing the terms of Brady's annuity, refused to make any further payments to Brady's family and kept the $250,000.

Questions to Discuss

1. Is it ethical for an insurance company to keep such a large premium after making so few payments to an annuitant?
2. Assuming that the law is on the annuity company's side, is the law correct?
3. From an ethical standpoint, what should the law be?

APPENDIX **A**

Understanding Statutes
and Court Decisions

As Chapter 1 of the text indicated, there are many different sources of the law, the most important being *statutes* and *court decisions*. Let's turn first to statutes. You can learn what the law is on a certain subject by researching a particular state's statutes or federal statutes enacted by Congress. Indexes in the statute books will guide you to the laws involving any subject that interests you. Indexes can help you find cases by subject matter, key words (e.g., *whistle-blower*) and case titles. Statute books can be found in a public law library, an attorney's office, and often in a general public library.

Reading and analyzing actual court cases are other ways to study law and learn what the law is on a particular subject. Each year, state and federal courts across the United States hear and decide thousands of cases. The court decisions are published in legal books called *Reports*. The cases presented in the section "Cases for Review," at the end of each chapter of this text, are shortened versions of actual court cases.

Reports of state and lower court decisions are printed for each U.S. state. In many states, reports are published both by official state agencies and by private law reporting companies. Regional reports are also published by private companies, and they include decisions from the courts of many states within a geographic region. To make it easier to find court decisions, each reported case decision is assigned a citation, which indicates the volume and the page number where the decision can be found. For example, in *Webster* v. *Blue Ship Tea Room,* 347 Mass. 421—a decision of the Massachusetts Supreme Court in which Webster and Blue Ship Tea Room are the parties to the case—the decision can be found in volume 347 of the *Massachusetts Reports,* on page 421. An example of a regional report is *Champaign* v. *Hanks,* Ill. 353 N.E.2d 405. Note that N.E. means Northeast and refers to a case tried in one of certain states located in the northeastern part of the United States.

Decisions of the federal courts are also printed in book form. Decisions of the federal courts are found in the *Federal Supplement,* which is abbreviated as "F. Supp." Opinions of the Federal Courts of Appeal are found in the *Federal Reporter,* abbreviated as "F.U.S." Supreme Court Reports are also published by official reporters and by private law reporting companies.

It is important to know how a court case develops. When judges and juries are called upon to determine the issues in a legal case and to decide who should win the case, they follow several steps.

1. The judge and jury hear testimony that is presented by both parties to the case to support their individual claims.
2. When all testimony has been given, the jury evaluates the testimony and decides the facts that it will believe.
3. The jury members discuss the facts and the issues of the case and reach a decision.
4. Once the jury has reached a decision, that decision is communicated to the court.

In studying the cases in this text, the first task is to "brief" each case. The purpose of the case brief is to organize and summarize the essential elements of a case to understand what the case is about. This briefing can best be done using the following method:

1. *State* the parties to the case, where the case can be located, and if desired, the date it was decided. This information is called the *citation*.
2. *Read* the case carefully and determine the relevant facts (circumstances that brought the parties into court). Summarize these facts.
3. *Determine* the legal issue—a one-sentence description in the form of a question— that describes the point that the parties are trying to get a decision on in court.
4. *State* your decision in the case, either "yes" or "no."
5. *Give* a reason or reasons for the decision. Summarize briefly the reason or reasons stated by the court for its decision and the law referred to by the court to arrive at its decision.

Study the following court case and then read the briefed version that follows. It will give you an idea of how to brief a case.

County of Champaign v. *Hanks*, 41 Ill. App. 3d 679. Defendant Hanks, charged with burglary, stated in an affidavit that he was indigent (had no money) and had no assets. Therefore, the County of Champaign appointed a public defender to represent him at no charge to Hanks. Actually, Hanks was not entitled to free representation by the public defender's office because he had legal interests in real property, but he had secretly transferred his interest in the property to some other members of his family to avoid legal fees. The County of Champaign now seeks to recover its costs. Hanks claims that the county has no right to collect for the services of the attorneys because he did not agree to pay for these services and couldn't because he was indigent during the criminal proceedings. It was determined by the court that Hanks did have to pay based on a legal principle called *quasi contract,* or contract implied in law. The court stated that "a contract implied in law does not depend on the intention of the parties, but exists where there is a duty to perform . . . based on the receipt of a benefit . . . under circumstances where it would be inequitable (not fair, unjust) to retain benefit without compensation." The court went on to say that the facts in this case "reveal that defendant received free legal representation when he clearly was not entitled to such representation and that defendant failed to disclose his assets. Under these circumstances the law will imply a promise by defendant to compensate the county."

COUNTY OF CHAMPAIGN V. HANKS 41 ILL. APP. 3D 679

FACTS:	Defendant Hanks, charged with burglary, swore that he was indigent and had no assets. Consequently, a public defender was appointed to represent him. Actually, Hanks lied about his finances. The County of Champaign is now claiming the right to recover its legal costs.
ISSUE:	Is the County of Champaign entitled to collect its legal costs?
DECISION:	Yes
REASON(S):	Hanks had to pay based on a contract implied in law (quasi contract). A contract implied in law is imposed upon parties when one of these parties receives a benefit at the expense of the other party. The court in this case therefore implied a contract between Hanks and the county for payment of legal fees because he was able to pay for such services. The court said that it would be unfair (unjust) for Hanks to retain a benefit to which he was not entitled without paying the required compensation.

Assume that you now read another case involving similar facts. If the judge in this case follows the decision in the *Champaign* case, the decision in the *Champaign* case is considered a precedent. If, however, the judge does not follow the decision in the *Champaign* case, to know what the law is you would have to determine how the facts differed and how that difference contributed to a different result. For example, another case might involve a situation in which the defendant possessed assets, but the public defender never asked the defendant if he had assets. In such a case, the court might well conclude that, because the defendant did not obtain free legal service through false means, there was no implied contract.

It is only by reading and analyzing many cases that a student of the law can determine what the law actually is on a certain subject.

In addition to books of statute laws and reports of court decisions, many texts summarize and explain what the law is on various subjects, such as torts, contracts, sales, and corporations. All these sources can help you understand state and federal statutes and decisions in a particular area of law.

APPENDIX **B**

Doing Legal Research on the Internet

Legal research is the process of searching for material to determine how a legal issue is resolved. Traditionally, legal research meant going to a law library, but today, there is another choice: You can undertake legal research on the Internet. There are two types of research available on the Internet: fee-based and free. Fee-based research is expensive; there is either a monthly or hourly charge or item charge. The advantages of this type of research are that the material is often better organized and easier to find than that found on free Web sites and there is some material that is not available on free Web sites. Some of the well-known fee-based Web sites are Westlaw (**http://www.westlaw.com**), Lexis-Nexis (**http://www.lexis.com**), Loislaw (**http://www.loislaw.com**), and VersusLaw (**http://www.versuslaw.com**). Excellent free websites such as FindLaw (**http://www.find-law.com**) are also available. On a free site, you will always be able to find something related to the topic you are researching, but the trick is knowing where to find it and how to use it.

How to Conduct Online Research

Before beginning your research, ask yourself some questions that will make your search easier. For example, ask yourself: What am I looking for? Am I looking for a federal or state statute, a Supreme Court case, a topic governed by the Uniform Commercial Code, or some information on illegal contracts or cyberbanking? You may also want to ask yourself: Which Web sites will best help me locate the information? Be cautious once you find what you are looking for, however, because some of the information you discover may not be credible if it is outdated. For example, because it takes time to place recently enacted legislation into the existing organizational framework and then place it on the Web, a federal statute is often a year behind.

Searching for Available Resources

Searching the Internet for information is similar to looking through the stacks at a library for this same information. There are different ways to go about this task. Excellent guides and directories describe what is available, how to use it, and specific useful websites. One guide is *Legal Research* published by Nolo Press (**http://www.nolo.com**), which includes a legal encyclopedia, a law dictionary, and information on access to federal and state statutes. *FindLaw* (**http://www.findlaw.com**) has information on an enormous array of legal subjects for legal professionals, students, businesses, and the general public. The Cornell University Law School site (**http://www.law.cornell.edu**) directs you to legal information that relates to federal and state court opinions, the federal and state constitutions, the most recent U.S. Supreme Court decisions, and codes such as the Uniform Commercial Code. Yahoo (**http://www.yahoo.com**) is a popular search engine used to locate specific topics on the Internet. To find legal information, for example, you would direct the search by typing words related to the legal topic in which you are interested. If what appears on the screen is not what you are looking for, you can redirect the search by keyboarding other words that finally lead you to the information you are seeking.

As you can see from this discussion, the Internet can provide a wealth of legal information to help you with your class assignments and to keep you updated on your rights as a consumer. The Internet can also produce information that can enrich your personal life and help you increase your knowledge base. Keep in mind, however, that the information found on Web sites changes quickly, so you always need to be aware of the timeliness of the information you are seeking.

Comparison Between Contract Law Under the Common Law and Sales Law Under the UCC

The following two columns are the laws relating to important areas of contracts. The left column summarizes contract law principles under the common law and applicable to all transactions other than contracts for the sale of goods. The right column summarizes the special rules of law, under Article 2 of the UCC that have changed or modified contract law under the common law relating to the sale of goods. These changes and modifications under the Code conform to the ways that modern business is conducted. Article 2 of the UCC has already been discussed in Part III: Sales and Lease Contracts under the UCC. Article 2 was amended in 2003, especially to accommodate electronic commerce; however, individual states must now decide whether or not to implement the new provisions. This may take some time. When a majority of states adopt the amendments they will officially become the law.

Common Law Contract

OFFER

1. The offer must be sufficiently definite to be enforceable.

2. Offers generally can be revoked at any time before acceptance, unless the parties have agreed to an "option" contract to keep the offer open.

ACCEPTANCE

3. If the offeror does not specify expressly that the offeree is to accept by a certain means or that the acceptance will be effective only when received, acceptance of an offer may be made by any reasonable means with this acceptance becoming effective when it is properly transmitted (sent).

UCC

1. A sales contract will not fail for indefiniteness even if one or more essential terms (e.g., price, quantity, place and time of delivery, terms of payment) are missing or the time of its making is undetermined as long as (a) the parties intended to make a contract and (b) there is a reasonably certain basis for the court to make an appropriate award for damages if the contract is breached (UCC 2-204). Rules for filling in the gaps left in the contract are found in Sections 2-305 through 2-311 of the Code.

2. If a merchant buyer or seller states in a signed writing that an offer to sell or buy shall remain open for a stated period of time, the offer is "*firm*"—that is, guaranteed (irrevocable) for the time stated—even if the offeree gives no consideration. If no time is stated, the offer remains open for a reasonable time, but no longer than three months. (UCC 2-205)

3. If the offeror does not specify the method of communication to be used, the UCC permits acceptance by any reasonable means, with this acceptance becoming effective when it is properly sent. (UCC 2-206)

4. When an offer is unilateral, only actual performance of the requested act constitutes acceptance by the offeree. When an offer is bilateral, acceptance occurs when the offeree promises to perform in the manner required by the offer. If the offeree attempts to accept with a response other than that prescribed in the offer, there is no contract. (Note: When there is doubt as to whether an offer is unilateral or bilateral, the courts tend to construe the offer as bilateral.)

5. No existing rule.

6. An offeree who is required to accept by doing the act requested (unilateral request) is not required to give notice to the offeror that he or she has started the performance. Such an offeree, however, generally has an implied obligation to give notice to the offeror that he or she (offeree) has completed the performance.

7. An attempted acceptance must match, term by term, the provisions in the offer. Any deviation from these terms, whether by addition, alteration, or omission, makes the communication a counteroffer (mirror-image rule).

4. An offer to buy goods (buyer initiates the offer) can be treated as though a unilateral contract offer has been made and can be accepted by the seller by shipping either conforming or nonconforming (substitute) goods to the buyer, or the offer may be treated as a bilateral contract offer (exchange of promises) and accepted by the seller by a prompt communication (notification) to the offeror promising to ship the goods. (UCC 2-206)

5. A shipment of nonconforming (substitute) goods (where the buyer initiates the offer) is simultaneously regarded as an acceptance of an offer which results in a contract and also as a breach of contract for which the buyer may pursue appropriate remedies. If the seller notifies the buyer that the shipment is nonconforming and is offered only as an accommodation to the buyer, however, this shipment would not constitute an acceptance and the seller would therefore not be in breach of contract. (UCC 2-206) (*Note:* Shipment by the seller in this case is a counteroffer, and the buyer would have the option to accept or reject the goods; rejected goods may be returned to the seller at the seller's expense.)

6. Where the beginning of a requested performance (e.g., beginning to manufacture and/or ship the goods amounting to a part performance) is a reasonable method of acceptance, the offeror (buyer) must be notified of such beginning within a reasonable time. An offeror who is not reasonably notified of acceptance may treat the offer as having lapsed before acceptance. (UCC 2-206)

7. A definite expression of acceptance of an offer by the offeree amounts to an acceptance, and a contract is formed even if the acceptance adds new terms or proposes terms different from those in the original offer unless the offeree expressly makes his or her acceptance conditional upon the offeror's assent to these additional or different terms. Between merchants, additional (new) terms (terms added by the offeree and not found in the original offer) will automatically become part of the contract (without the offeror's consent) unless (1) the new terms materially alter the offer (i.e., they would unfairly surprise or would cause hardship to the offeror), (2) the offeror objects to the terms within a reasonable time after receiving the offeree's acceptance, or (3) the original offer expressly limits acceptance to the exact terms of the offer. If either the seller or the buyer is a non-merchant, additional terms will not prevent acceptance by the offeree, but these terms will not

automatically become part of the contract. They become mere proposals that would have to be agreed to by the offeror. Different terms (terms that change or contradict a term of the offer) that involve minor changes will simply be ignored, but different terms that change the offer in any material way do not constitute an acceptance. Instead, they convert the response into a counteroffer and do not become part of the original contract unless specifically accepted by the original offeror. (What the Code is saying here is that the written contract will consist of the terms on which the parties agree as well as the terms included by one party without any objection by the other party.) (UCC 2-207)

CONSIDERATION

8. A modification of an existing contract must be based on consideration.

8. An agreement modifying a contract for the sale of goods needs no consideration to be binding. The Code treats a modification as a matter of good faith (honesty and fair dealing in the trade) rather than as a matter of consideration. A modification may be made orally. If, however, the original agreement is required to be in writing under the statute of frauds, the modification must also be in writing. (UCC 2-209)

9. If no price is agreed upon but is to be set in the future, the courts generally will not enforce the contract.

9. The parties can make a contract providing for a determination of the price at a later time. If there is a failure to agree on a definite price, a reasonable price at the time and place of delivery will be allowed. If the parties do not intend to be bound unless a price is agreed upon and an agreed price is never reached, there will be no contract. (UCC 2-305)

10. A written contract in which it is provided that there may be no oral modification can nevertheless be so modified, but only if this modification is supported by consideration.

10. A signed written agreement in which it is provided that there may be no oral modification can be modified only in writing, and only those changes agreed to in the signed writing are enforceable. (*Note:* In a sales contract entered into between a merchant and a nonmerchant [consumer], if the nonmerchant is to be held to such a clause written into a form supplied by the merchant, the non-merchant must sign a separate acknowledgment of such a requirement.) (UCC 2-209)

ILLEGALITY

11. Unconscionability of contract terms (that is, terms that unreasonably favor the other party) as a defense is available only in courts of equity.

11. Courts of law may now refuse to enforce a contract found to contain terms that are unconscionable. (UCC 2-302)

STATUTE OF LIMITATIONS

12. An action for a breach of ordinary contract must be brought within the time fixed by state statute. This time varies from state to state, but the range is from two to fifteen years, depending on whether the contract is oral or written.

12. An action for breach of a sales contract (oral or written) must be brought within four years from the time of the breach. (The 2003 amendments to UCC 2-725 extend the limitation period for up to one additional year to allow for a discovery of a breach beyond the four year period.) In their original

agreement, the parties may reduce the time period to one year (but not less), but they cannot extend it beyond the four-year limitation period. (UCC 2-725)

STATUTE OF FRAUDS

13. Every state has a statute of frauds that requires certain contracts be in writing to be enforceable. The five types of contracts frequently required to be in writing in the various states are a contract to pay the debt of another person, a contract by an executor or administrator to pay the debts of a deceased person from his or her own pocket, a contract for the sale of real property or an interest in real property, a contract in consideration of marriage, and a contract that cannot be performed within one year.

13. The UCC provision of the statute of frauds requires a writing for a contract involving a sale of goods when the price of the goods is $500 or more. (UCC 2-201) Under the 2003 amendment to UCC 2-201, a contract for the sale of goods in order to be subject to a writing under the Statute of Frauds, must be valued at $5,000.

14. The writing must include the subject matter of the contract, the names of the parties, the essential terms of the contract, and (in some states) the consideration.

14. There is only the requirement of "some writing," but this writing must indicate that the parties have entered into a contract for the sale of goods. The one essential term of the sale that must be in the writing is the quantity. Other essential terms in dispute (price, time and place of payment or delivery, the general quality of the goods, and so on) can be proved by oral testimony. (UCC 2-201)

15. The writing must be signed by the party against whom enforcement is sought (normally the buyer). (Note: Prior to a dispute, no one can determine which party's signing of the writing may be necessary to prove a case; from the time of contracting, each party should be aware that to him or her, it is signing by the other that is important.)

15. The UCC also requires the writing to be signed by the party against whom enforcement is sought. (UCC 2-201)

16 a. No existing rule.

16. The statute of frauds involving the sale of goods may be satisfied with other than a written memorandum under the following circumstances:
    a. Contracts for specially manufactured goods for a particular buyer (goods that cannot generally be resold to others in the ordinary course of the seller's business) where the seller, before notice of repudiation is received, has substantially started to manufacture the goods for the buyer or has made commitments for the manufacture of the goods, do not require a writing. (UCC 2-201)

16b. No existing rule.

b. An oral contract is enforceable if the person against whom enforcement is attempted makes a statement in his or her lawsuit admitting that he or she has a sale-of-goods contract with the other party. (Enforceability is limited to the quantity of goods admitted.) (UCC 2-201)

16c. No existing rule.

c. A partial performance rule applies. An oral contract will be enforced if the buyer receives (physically takes possession) and accepts (indicates an intention to become the owner) part of the goods, but only for the portion of the goods that were actually received and accepted by the buyer. Also, an oral contract is binding if the buyer makes a partial payment on the goods. The contract is enforceable, however, only for those goods covered by the partial payment. (UCC 2-201) (*Note:* The courts have ruled [*Lockwood* v. *Smigel,* 96 Cal. Rptr. 289] that an oral contract for the sale of goods consisting of a single item is binding when the buyer makes a down payment.)

16d. No existing rule.

d. If the contract is between merchants, and one of the merchants within a reasonable time sends a written confirmation of the oral agreement to the other merchant, and that merchant fails to object in writing to the confirmation within ten days, the contract is enforceable against the merchant who receives the confirmation even though he or she has not signed anything. (UCC 2-201)

17. The parol evidence rule states that once a contract has been put in writing as the final and complete expression of agreement between the parties, parol evidence—evidence of an oral agreement made prior to or at the time of signing the written agreement—cannot be presented in court to change or add to the terms of the written contract. (In other words, the court presumes that the written contract contained all the terms and provisions intended by the parties.) Parol evidence, however, may be introduced in court to (a) make changes and modifications after the original contract is entered into; (b) give meaning to unclear language; (c) show that the contract was void or voidable; (d) fill in gaps when essential terms are missing; or (e) correct obvious and gross clerical or typographical errors that would change the meaning of what the parties intended.

17. The UCC reaffirms the parol evidence rule and its exceptions as stated under basic contract law, but it goes a step further. The UCC allows oral evidence to explain or supplement the written contract by showing a prior course of dealing, usage of the trade, or course of performance. Evidence from these sources may be introduced even though the court finds the writing to be complete and free from ambiguities. (UCC 2-202)

RIGHTS OF PARTIES

18. An assignment of rights does not impliedly carry with it the delegation of duties; an express assumption of duties is necessary.

18. An assignment of a contract is impliedly a delegation of duties, and an express assumption is not required. (UCC 2-210)

The Constitution of the United States

Preamble

We the People of the United States, in Order to form a more perfect Union, establish Justice, insure domestic Tranquility, provide for the common defence, promote the general Welfare, and secure the Blessings of Liberty to ourselves and our Posterity, do ordain and establish this Constitution for the United States of America.

Article I

Section 1.   All legislative Powers herein granted shall be vested in a Congress of the United States, which shall consist of a Senate and a House of Representatives.

Section 2.   [1] The House of Representatives shall be composed of Members chosen every second Year by the People of the several States, and the Electors in each State shall have the Qualifications requisite for Electors of the most numerous Branch of the State Legislature.

[2] No Person shall be a Representative who shall not have attained to the Age of twenty five Years, and been seven Years a Citizen of the United States, and who shall, when elected, be an Inhabitant of that State in which he shall be chosen.

[3] Representatives and direct Taxes shall be apportioned among the several States which may be included within this Union, according to their respective Numbers, which shall be determined by adding to the whole Number of free Persons, including those bound to Service for a Term of Years, and excluding Indians not taxed, three-fifths of all other Persons. The actual Enumeration shall be made within three Years after the first Meeting of the Congress of the United States, and within every subsequent Term of ten Years, in such Manner as they shall by Law direct. The Number of Representatives shall not exceed one for every thirty Thousand, but each State shall have at Least one Representative; and until such enumeration shall be made, the State of New Hampshire shall be entitled to chuse three, Massachusetts eight, Rhode Island and Providence Plantations one, Connecticut five, New York six, New Jersey four, Pennsylvania eight, Delaware one, Maryland six, Virginia ten, North Carolina five, South Carolina five, and Georgia three.

[4] When vacancies happen in the Representation from any State, the Executive Authority thereof shall issue Writs of Election to fill such Vacancies.

[5] The House of Representatives shall chuse their Speaker and other Officers; and shall have the sole Power of Impeachment.

Section 3.   [1] The Senate of the United States shall be composed of two Senators from each State, chosen by the Legislature thereof, for six Years; and each Senator shall have one Vote.

[2] Immediately after they shall be assembled in Consequence of the first Election, they shall be divided as equally as may be into three Classes. The Seats of the Senators of the first Class shall be vacated at the Expiration of the Second Year, of the second Class at the Expiration of the fourth Year, and of the third Class at the Expiration of the sixth Year, so that one third may be chosen every second Year; and if Vacancies happen by Resignation or otherwise, during the Recess of the Legislature of any State, the Executive thereof may make temporary Appointments until the next Meeting of the Legislature, which shall then fill such Vacancies.

[3] No Person shall be a Senator who shall not have attained to the Age of thirty Years, and been nine Years a Citizen of the United States, and who shall, when elected, be an Inhabitant of that State for which he shall be chosen.

[4] The Vice President of the United States shall be President of the Senate, but shall have no Vote, unless they be equally divided.

[5] The Senate shall chuse their other Officers, and also a President pro tempore, in the Absence of the Vice President, or when he shall exercise the Office of President of the United States.

[6] The Senate shall have the sole Power to try all Impeachments. When sitting for that Purpose, they shall be on Oath or Affirmation. When the President of the United States is tried, the Chief Justice shall preside: and no Person shall be convicted without the Concurrence of two thirds of the Members present.

[7] Judgment in Cases of Impeachment shall not extend further than to removal from Office, and

disqualification to hold and enjoy any Office of Honor, Trust, or Profit under the United States: but the Party convicted shall nevertheless be liable and subject to Indictment, Trial, Judgment, and Punishment, according to law.

Section 4. [1] The Times, Places and Manner of holding elections for Senators and Representatives, shall be prescribed in each State by the Legislature thereof; but the Congress may at any time by Law make or alter such Regulations, except as to the Places of chusing Senators.

[2] The Congress shall assemble at least once in every Year, and such Meeting shall be on the first Monday in December, unless they shall by Law appoint a different Day.

Section 5. [1] Each House shall be the Judge of the Elections, Returns, and Qualifications of its own Members, and a Majority of each shall constitute a Quorum to do Business; but a smaller Number may adjourn from day to day, and may be authorized to compel the Attendance of absent Members, in such Manner, and under such Penalties as each House may provide.

[2] Each House may determine the Rules of its Proceedings, punish its Members for disorderly Behavior, and, with the Concurrence of two thirds, expel a Member.

[3] Each House shall keep a Journal of its Proceedings, and from time to time publish the same, excepting such Parts as may in their Judgment require Secrecy; and the Yeas and Nays of the Members of either house on any question shall, at the Desire of one fifth of those Present, be entered on the Journal.

[4] Neither House, during the Session of Congress, shall, without the Consent of the other, adjourn for more than three days, nor to any other Place than that in which the two Houses shall be sitting.

Section 6. [1] The Senators and Representatives shall receive a Compensation for their Services, to be ascertained by Law, and paid out of the Treasury of the United States. They shall in all Cases, except Treason, Felony and Breach of the Peace, be privileged from Arrest during their Attendance at the Session of their respective Houses, and in going to and returning from the same; and for any Speech or Debate in either House, they shall not be questioned in any other Place.

[2] No Senator or Representative shall, during the Time for which he was elected, be appointed to any civil Office under the Authority of the United States, which shall have been created, or the Emoluments whereof shall have been increased during such time;

and no Person holding any Office under the United States shall be a Member of either House during his Continuance in Office.

Section 7. [1] All Bills for raising Revenue shall originate in the House of Representatives; but the Senate may propose or concur with Amendments as on other Bills.

[2] Every Bill which shall have passed the House of Representatives and the Senate, shall, before it becomes a Law, be presented to the President of the United States; If he approve he shall sign it, but if not he shall return it, with his Objections to the House in which it shall have originated, who shall enter the Objections at large on their Journal, and proceed to reconsider it. If after such Reconsideration two thirds of that House shall agree to pass the Bill, it shall be sent together with the Objections, to the other House, by which it shall likewise be reconsidered, and if approved by two thirds of that House, it shall become a Law. But in all such Cases the Votes of both Houses shall be determined by Yeas and Nays, and the Names of the Persons voting for and against the Bill shall be entered on the Journal of each House respectively. If any Bill shall not be returned by the President within ten Days (Sundays excepted) after it shall have been presented to him, the Same shall be a Law, in like Manner as if he had signed it, unless the Congress by their Adjournment prevent its Return in which Case it shall not be a Law.

[3] Every Order, Resolution, or Vote, to Which the Concurrence of the Senate and House of Representatives may be necessary (except on a question of Adjournment) shall be presented to the President of the United States; and before the Same shall take Effect, shall be approved by him, or being disapproved by him, shall be repassed by two thirds of the Senate and House of Representatives, according to the Rules and Limitations prescribed in the Case of a Bill.

Section 8. [1] The Congress shall have Power To lay and collect Taxes, Duties, Imposts and Excises, to pay the Debts and provide for the common Defence and general Welfare of the United States; but all Duties, Imposts and Excises shall be uniform throughout the United States;

[2] To borrow money on the credit of the United States;

[3] To regulate Commerce with foreign Nations, and among the several States, and with the Indian Tribes;

[4] To establish an uniform Rule of Naturalization, and uniform Laws on the subject of Bankruptcies throughout the United States;

[5] To coin Money, regulate the Value thereof, and of foreign Coin, and fix the Standard of Weights and Measures;

[6] To provide for the Punishment of counterfeiting the Securities and current Coin of the United States;

[7] To Establish Post Offices and Post Roads;

[8] To promote the Progress of Science and useful Arts, by securing for limited Times to Authors and Inventors the exclusive Right to their respective Writings and Discoveries;

[9] To constitute Tribunals inferior to the supreme Court;

[10] To define and punish Piracies and Felonies committed on the high Seas, and Offenses against the Law of Nations;

[11] To declare War, grant Letters of Marque and Reprisal, and make Rules concerning Captures on Land and Water;

[12] To raise and support Armies, but no Appropriation of Money to that Use shall be for a longer Term than two Years;

[13] To provide and maintain a Navy;

[14] To make Rules for the Government and Regulation of the land and naval Forces;

[15] To provide for calling forth the Militia to execute the Laws of the Union, suppress Insurrections and repel Invasions;

[16] To provide for organizing, arming, and disciplining, the Militia, and for governing such Part of them as may be employed in the Service of the United States, reserving to the States respectively, the Appointment of the Officers, and the Authority of training the Militia according to the discipline prescribed by Congress;

[17] To exercise exclusive Legislation in all Cases whatsoever, over such District (not exceeding ten Miles square) as may, by Cession of particular States, and the Acceptance of Congress, become the Seat of the Government of the United States, and to exercise like Authority over all Places purchased by the Consent of the Legislature of the State, in which the Same shall be, for the Erection of Forts, Magazines, Arsenals, dock-Yards and other needful Buildings;—And

[18] To make all Laws which shall be necessary and proper for carrying into Execution the foregoing Powers, and all other Powers vested by this Constitution in the Government of the United States, or in any Department or Officer thereof.

Section 9. [1] The Migration or Importation of Such Persons as any of the States now existing shall think proper to admit, shall not be prohibited by the Congress prior to the Year one thousand eight hundred and eight, but a Tax or duty may be imposed on such Importation, not exceeding ten dollars for each Person.

[2] The privilege of the Writ of Habeas Corpus shall not be suspended, unless when in Cases of Rebellion or Invasion the public Safety may require it.

[3] No Bill of Attainder or ex post facto Law shall be passed.

[4] No Capitation, or other direct, Tax shall be laid, unless in Proportion to the Census or Enumeration herein before directed to be taken.

[5] No Tax or Duty shall be laid on Articles exported from any State.

[6] No Preference shall be given by any Regulation of Commerce or Revenue to the Ports of one State over those of another: nor shall Vessels bound to, or from, one State be obliged to enter, clear, or pay Duties in another.

[7] No money shall be drawn from the Treasury, but in Consequence of Appropriations made by Law; and a regular Statement and Account of the Receipts and Expenditures of all public Money shall be published from time to time.

[8] No Title of Nobility shall be granted by the United States: and no Person holding any Office of Profit or Trust under them, shall, without the Consent of the Congress, accept of any present, Emolument, Office, or Title, of any kind whatever, from any King, Prince, or foreign State.

Section 10. [1] No State shall enter into any Treaty, Alliance, or Confederation; grant Letters of Marque and Reprisal; coin Money; emit Bills of Credit; make any Thing but gold and silver Coin a Tender in Payment of Debts; pass any Bill of Attainder, ex post facto Law, or Law impairing the Obligation of Contracts, or grant any Title of Nobility.

[2] No State shall, without the Consent of the Congress, lay any Imposts or Duties on Imports or Exports, except what may be absolutely necessary for executing its inspection Laws: and the net Produce of all Duties and Imposts, laid by any State on Imports or Exports, shall be for the Use of the Treasury of the United States; and all such Laws shall be subject to the Revision and Control of the Congress.

[3] No State shall, without the Consent of Congress, lay any Duty of Tonnage, keep Troops, or Ships of War in time of Peace, enter into any Agreement or Compact with another State, or with a foreign power, or engage in war, unless actually invaded, or in such imminent Danger as will not admit of delay.

Article II

Section 1.   [1] The executive Power shall be vested in a President of the United States of America. He shall hold his Office during the Term of four Years, and, together with the Vice President, chosen for the same Term, be elected, as follows:

[2] Each State shall appoint, in such Manner as the Legislature thereof may direct, a Number of Electors, equal to the whole Number of Senators and Representatives to which the State may be entitled in the Congress; but no Senator or Representative, or Person holding an Office of Trust or Profit under the United States, shall be appointed an Elector.

[3] The Electors shall meet in their respective States, and vote by Ballot for two Persons, of whom one at least shall not be an Inhabitant of the same State with themselves. And they shall make a List of all the Persons voted for, and of the Number of Votes for each; which List they shall sign and certify, and transmit sealed to the Seat of the Government of the United States, directed to the President of the Senate. The President of the Senate shall, in the Presence of the Senate and House of Representatives, open all the Certificates, and the Votes shall then be counted. The Person having the greatest Number of Votes shall be the President, if such Number be a Majority of the whole Number of Electors appointed; and if there be more than one who have such Majority, and have an equal Number of Votes, then the House of Representatives shall immediately chuse by Ballot one of them for President; and if no Person have a majority, then from the five highest on the List the said House shall in like Manner chuse the President. But in chusing the President, the Votes shall be taken by States the Representation from each State having one Vote; A quorum for this Purpose shall consist of a Member or Members from two thirds of the States, and a Majority of all the States shall be necessary to a Choice. In every Case, after the Choice of the President, the Person having the greatest Number of Votes of the Electors shall be the Vice President. But if there shall remain two or more who have equal Votes, the Senate shall chuse from them by Ballot the Vice President.

[4] The Congress may determine the Time of chusing the Electors, and the Day on which they shall give their Votes; which Day shall be the same throughout the United States.

[5] No person except a natural born Citizen, or a Citizen of the United States, at the time of the Adoption of this Constitution, shall be eligible to the Office of President; neither shall any Person be eligible to that Office who shall not have attained to the Age of thirty-five Years, and been fourteen Years a Resident within the United States.

[6] In case of the removal of the President from Office, or of his Death, Resignation or Inability to discharge the Powers and Duties of the said Office, the Same shall devolve on the Vice President, and the Congress may by Law provide for the Case of Removal, Death, Resignation or Inability, both of the President and Vice President, declaring what Officer shall then act as President, and such Officer shall act accordingly, until the Disability be removed, or a President shall be elected.

[7] The President shall, at stated Times, receive for his Services, a Compensation, which shall neither be increased nor diminished during the Period for which he shall have been elected, and he shall not receive within that Period any other Emolument from the United States, or any of them.

[8] Before he enter on the Execution of his Office, he shall take the following Oath or Affirmation: "I do solemnly swear (or affirm) that I will faithfully execute the Office of President of the United States, and will to the best of my Ability, preserve, protect and defend the Constitution of the United States."

Section 2.   [1] The President shall be Commander in Chief of the Army and Navy of the United States, and of the militia of the several States, when called into the actual Service of the United States; he may require the Opinion, in writing, of the principal Officer in each of the Executive Departments, upon any Subject relating to the Duties of their respective Offices, and he shall have Power to grant Reprieves and Pardons for Offenses against the United States, except in Cases of Impeachment.

[2] He shall have Power, by and with the Advice and Consent of the Senate to make Treaties, provided two thirds of the Senators present concur; and he shall nominate, and by and with the Advice and Consent of the Senate, shall appoint Ambassadors, other public Ministers and Consuls, Judges of the supreme Court, and all other Officers of the United States, whose Appointments are not herein otherwise provided for, and which shall be established by Law; but the Congress may by Law vest the Appointment of such inferior Officers, as they think proper, in the President alone, in the Courts of Law, or in the Heads of Departments.

[3] The President shall have Power to fill up all Vacancies that may happen during the Recess of the

Senate, by granting Commissions which shall expire at the End of their next Session.

Section 3.   He shall from time to time give to the Congress Information of the State of the Union, and recommend to their Consideration such Measures as he shall judge necessary and expedient; he may, on extraordinary Occasions, convene both Houses, or either of them, and in Case of Disagreement between them, with Respect to the Time of Adjournment, he may adjourn them to such Time as he shall think proper; he shall receive Ambassadors and other public Ministers; he shall take Care that the Laws be faithfully executed, and shall Commission all the Officers of the United States.

Section 4.   The President, Vice President and all civil Officers of the United States, shall be removed from Office on Impeachment for, and Conviction of, Treason, Bribery, or other high Crimes and Misdemeanors.

Article III

Section 1.   The judicial Power of the United States, shall be vested in one supreme Court, and in such inferior Courts as the Congress may from time to time ordain and establish. The Judges, both of the supreme and inferior Courts, shall hold their Offices during good Behaviour, and shall, at stated Times, receive for their Services a Compensation, which shall not be diminished during their Continuance in Office.

Section 2.   [1] The judicial Power shall extend to all Cases, in Law and Equity, arising under this Constitution, the Laws of the United States, and Treaties made, or which shall be made, under their Authority;—to all Cases affecting Ambassadors, other public Ministers and Consuls;—to all Cases of admiralty and maritime Jurisdiction;—to Controversies to which the United States shall be a Party;—to Controversies between two or more States;—between a State and Citizens of another State;—between Citizens of different States;—between Citizens of the same State claiming Lands under the Grants of different States, and between a State, or the Citizens thereof, and foreign States, Citizens or Subjects.

[2] In all Cases affecting Ambassadors, other public Ministers and Consuls, and those in which a State shall be a Party, the supreme Court shall have original Jurisdiction. In all the other Cases before mentioned, the supreme Court shall have appellate Jurisdiction, both as to Law and Fact, with such Exceptions, and under such Regulations as the Congress shall make.

[3] The trial of all Crimes, except in Cases of Impeachment, shall be by Jury; and such Trial shall be held in the State where the said Crimes shall have been committed; but when not committed within any State, the Trial shall be at such Place or Places as the Congress may by Law have directed.

Section 3.   [1] Treason against the United States, shall consist only in levying War against them, or, in adhering to their Enemies, giving them Aid and Comfort. No Person shall be convicted of Treason unless on the Testimony of two Witnesses to the same overt Act, or on Confession in open Court.

[2] The Congress shall have Power to declare the Punishment of Treason, but no Attainder of Treason shall work Corruption of Blood, or Forfeiture except during the Life of the Person attainted.

Article IV

Section 1.   Full Faith and Credit shall be given in each State to the public Acts, Records, and judicial Proceedings of every other State. And the Congress may by general Laws prescribe the Manner in which such Acts, Records and Proceedings shall be proved, and the Effect thereof.

Section 2.   [1] The Citizens of each State shall be entitled to all Privileges and Immunities of Citizens in the several States.

[2] A Person charged in any State with Treason, Felony, or other Crime, who shall flee from Justice, and be found in another State, shall on demand of the executive Authority of the State from which he fled, be delivered up, to be removed to the State having Jurisdiction of the Crime.

[3] No Person held to Service or Labour in one State, under the Laws thereof, escaping into another, shall, in Consequence of any Law or Regulation therein, be discharged from such Service or Labour, but shall be delivered up on Claim of the Party to whom such Service or Labour may be due.

Section 3.   [1] New States may be admitted by the Congress into this Union; but no new State shall be formed or erected within the Jurisdiction of any other State; nor any State be formed by the Junction of two or more States, or Parts of States, without the Consent of the Legislatures of the States concerned as well as of the Congress.

[2] The Congress shall have Power to dispose of and make all needful Rules and Regulations respecting the Territory or other Property belonging to the United States; and nothing in this Constitution shall be so construed as to Prejudice any Claims of the United States, or of any particular State.

Section 4. The United States shall guarantee to every State in this Union a Republican Form of Government, and shall protect each of them against Invasion; and on Application of the Legislature, or of the Executive (when the Legislature cannot be convened) against domestic Violence.

Article V

The Congress, whenever two thirds of both Houses shall deem it necessary, shall propose Amendments to this Constitution, or, on the Application of the Legislatures of two thirds of the several States, shall call a Convention for proposing Amendments, which, in either case, shall be valid to all Intents and Purposes, as part of this Constitution, when ratified by the Legislatures of three fourths of the several States, or by Conventions in three fourths thereof, as the one or the other Mode of Ratification may be proposed by the Congress; Provided that no Amendment which may be made prior to the Year One thousand eight hundred and eight shall in any Manner affect the first and fourth Clauses in the Ninth Section of the first Article; and that no State, without its Consent, shall be deprived of its equal Suffrage in the Senate.

Article VI

[1] All Debts contracted and Engagements entered into, before the Adoption of this Constitution shall be as valid against the United States under this Constitution, as under the Confederation.

[2] This Constitution, and the Laws of the United States which shall be made in Pursuance thereof; and all Treaties made, or which shall be made, under the Authority of the United States, shall be the supreme Law of the Land; and the Judges in every State shall be bound thereby, any Thing in the Constitution or Laws of any State to the Contrary notwithstanding.

[3] The Senators and Representatives before mentioned, and the Members of the several State Legislatures, and all executive and judicial Officers, both of the United States and of the several States, shall be bound by Oath or Affirmation, to support this Constitution; but no religious Test shall ever be required as a Qualification to any Office or public Trust under the United States.

Article VII

The Ratification of the Conventions of nine States shall be sufficient for the Establishment of this Constitution between the States so ratifying the Same.

Amendments

Articles in addition to, and in amendment of, the Constitution of the United States of America, proposed by Congress, and ratified by the Legislatures of the several States pursuant to the Fifth Article of the original Constitution.

Amendment 1 (1791)

Congress shall make no law respecting an establishment of religion, or prohibiting the free exercise thereof; or abridging the freedom of speech, or of the press; or the right of the people peaceably to assemble, and to petition the Government for a redress of grievances.

Amendment 2 (1791)

A well regulated Militia, being necessary to the security of a free State, the right of the people to keep and bear Arms, shall not be infringed.

Amendment 3 (1791)

No Soldier shall, in time of peace be quartered in any house, without the consent of the Owner, nor in time of war, but in a manner to be prescribed by law.

Amendment 4 (1791)

The right of the people to be secure in their persons, houses, papers, and effects, against unreasonable searches and seizures, shall not be violated, and no Warrants shall issue, but upon probable cause, supported by Oath or affirmation, and particularly describing the place to be searched, and the persons or things to be seized.

Amendment 5 (1791)

No person shall be held to answer for a capital, or otherwise infamous crime, unless on a presentment or indictment of a Grand Jury, except in cases arising in the land or naval forces, or in the Militia, when in actual service in time of War or public danger; nor shall any person be subject for the same offence to be twice put in jeopardy of life or limb; nor shall be compelled in any criminal case to be a witness against himself, nor be deprived of life, liberty, or property, without due process of law; nor shall private property be taken for public use without just compensation.

Amendment 6 (1791)

In all criminal prosecutions, the accused shall enjoy the right to a speedy and public trial, by an impartial jury of the State and district wherein the crime shall have been committed, which district shall have been previously ascertained by law, and to be informed of the nature and cause of the accusation; to be confronted with the witnesses against him; to have compulsory process for obtaining witnesses in his favor, and to have the Assistance of Counsel for his defence.

Amendment 7 (1791)

In Suits at common law, where the value in controversy shall exceed twenty dollars, the right of trial by jury shall be preserved, and no fact tried by jury, shall be otherwise re-examined in any Court of the United States, than according to the rules of common law.

Amendment 8 (1791)

Excessive bail shall not be required, nor excessive fines imposed, nor cruel and unusual punishments inflicted.

Amendment 9 (1791)

The enumeration in the Constitution, of certain rights, shall not be construed to deny or disparage others retained by the people.

Amendment 10 (1791)

The powers not delegated to the United States by the Constitution, nor prohibited by it to the States, are reserved to the States respectively, or to the people.

Amendment 11 (1798)

The Judicial power of the United States shall not be construed to extend to any suit in law or equity, commenced or prosecuted against one of the United States by Citizens of another State, or by Citizens or Subjects of any Foreign State.

Amendment 12 (1804)

The Electors shall meet in their respective states and vote by ballot for President and Vice-President, one of whom, at least, shall not be an inhabitant of the same state with themselves; they shall name in their ballots the person voted for as President, and in distinct ballots the person voted for as Vice-President, and they shall make distinct lists of all persons voted for as President, and of all persons voted for as Vice-President, and of the number of votes for each, which lists they shall sign and certify, and transmit sealed to the seat of the government of the United States, directed to the President of the Senate;—The President of the Senate shall, in the presence of the Senate and House of Representatives, open all the certificates and the votes shall then be counted;—The person having the greatest number of votes for President, shall be the President, if such number be a majority of the whole number of Electors appointed; and if no person have such majority, then from the persons having the highest numbers not exceeding three on the list of those voted for as President, the House of Representatives shall choose immediately, by ballot, the President. But in choosing the President, the votes shall be taken by states, the representation from each state having one vote; a quorum for this purpose shall consist of a member or members from two-thirds of the states, and a majority of all states shall be necessary to a choice. And if the House of Representatives shall not choose a President whenever the right of choice shall devolve upon them before the fourth day of March next following, then the Vice-President shall act as President, as in the case of the death or other constitutional disability of the President.—The person having the greatest number of votes as Vice-President, shall be the Vice-President, if such number be a majority of the whole number of Electors appointed, and if no person have a majority, then from the two highest numbers on the list, the Senate shall choose the Vice-President; a quorum for the purpose shall consist of two-thirds of the whole number of Senators, and a majority of the whole number shall be necessary to a choice. But no person constitutionally ineligible to the office of President shall be eligible to that of Vice-President of the United States.

Amendment 13 (1865)

Section 1.   Neither slavery nor involuntary servitude, except as a punishment for crime whereof the party shall have been duly convicted, shall exist within the United States, or any place subject to their jurisdiction.

Section 2.   Congress shall have power to enforce this article by appropriate legislation.

Amendment 14 (1868)

Section 1.   All persons born or naturalized in the United States, and subject to the jurisdiction thereof, are citizens of the United States and of the State wherein they reside. No State shall make or enforce any law which shall abridge the privileges or immunities of citizens of the United States; nor shall any State deprive any person of life, liberty, or property, without due process of law; nor deny to any person within its jurisdiction the equal protection of the laws.

Section 2. Representatives shall be apportioned among the several States according to their respective numbers, counting the whole number of persons in each State, excluding Indians not taxed. But when the right to vote at any election for the choice of electors for President and Vice President of the United States, Representatives in Congress,the Executive and Judicial officers of a State, or the members of the Legislature thereof, is denied to any of the male inhabitants of such State, being twenty-one years of age, and citizens of the United States, or in any way abridged, except for participation in rebellion, or other crime, the basis of representation therein shall be reduced in the proportion which the number of such male citizens shall bear to the whole number of male citizens twenty-one years of age in such State.

Section 3. No person shall be a Senator or Representative in Congress, or elector of President and Vice President, or hold any office, civil or military, under the United States, or under any State, who having previously taken an oath, as a member of Congress, or as an officer of the United States, or as a member of any State legislature, or as an executive or judicial officer of any State, to support the Constitution of the United States, shall have engaged in insurrection or rebellion against the same, or given aid or comfort to the enemies thereof. But Congress may by a vote of two-thirds of each House, remove such disability.

Section 4. The validity of the public debt of the United States, authorized by law, including debts incurred for payment of pensions and bounties for services in suppressing insurrection or rebellion, shall not be questioned. But neither the United States nor any State shall assume or pay any debt or obligation incurred in aid of insurrection or rebellion against the United States, or any claim for the loss of emancipation of any slave; but all such debts, obligations and claims shall be held illegal and void.

Section 5. The Congress shall have power to enforce, by appropriate legislation, the provisions of this article.

Amendment 15 (1870)

Section 1. The right of citizens of the United States to vote shall not be denied or abridged by the United States or by any State on account of race, color, or previous condition of servitude.

Section 2. The Congress shall have power to enforce this article by appropriate legislation.

Amendment 16 (1913)

The Congress shall have power to lay and collect taxes on incomes, from whatever source derived, without apportionment among the several States, and without regard to any census or enumeration.

Amendment 17 (1913)

Section 1. The Senate of the United States shall be composed of two Senators from each State, elected by the people thereof, for six years; and each Senator shall have one vote. The electors in each State shall have the qualifications requisite for electors of the most numerous branch of the State legislatures.

Section 2. When vacancies happen in the representation of any State in the Senate, the executive authority of such State shall issue writs of election to fill such vacancies: *Provided,* That the legislature of any State may empower the executive thereof to make temporary appointments until the people fill the vacancies by election as the legislature may direct.

Section 3. This amendment shall not be so construed as to affect the election or term of any Senator chosen before it becomes valid as part of the Constitution.

Amendment 18 (1919)

Section 1. After one year from the ratification of this article the manufacture, sale, or transportation of intoxicating liquors within, the importation thereof into,or the exportation thereof from the United States and all territory subject to the jurisdiction thereof for beverage purposes is hereby prohibited.

Section 2. The Congress and the several States shall have concurrent power to enforce this article by appropriate legislation.

Section 3. This article shall be inoperative unless it shall have been ratified as an amendment to the Constitution by the legislatures of the several States, as provided in the Constitution, within seven years from the date of the submission hereof to the States by the Congress.

Amendment 19 (1920)

Section 1. The right of citizens of the United States to vote shall not be denied or abridged by the United States or by any State on account of sex.

Section 2. The Congress shall have power to enforce this article by appropriate legislation.

Amendment 20 (1933)

Section 1.   The terms of the President and Vice President shall end at noon on the 20th day of January, and the terms of Senators and Representatives at noon on the 3d day of January, of the years in which such terms would have ended if this article had not been ratified; and the terms of their successors shall then begin.

Section 2.   The Congress shall assemble at least once in every year, and such meeting shall begin at noon on the 3d day of January, unless they shall by law appoint a different day.

Section 3.   If, at the time fixed for the beginning of the term of the President, the President elect shall have died, the Vice President elect shall become President. If the President shall not have been chosen before the time fixed for the beginning of his term, or if the President elect shall have failed to qualify, then the Vice President elect shall act as President until a President shall have qualified; and the Congress may by law provide for the case wherein neither a President elect nor a Vice President elect shall have qualified, declaring who shall then act as President, or the manner in which one who is to act shall be selected, and such person shall act accordingly until a President or Vice President shall have qualified.

Section 4.   The Congress may by law provide for the case of the death of any of the persons from whom the House of Representatives may choose a President whenever the right of choice shall have devolved upon them, and for the case of the death of any of the persons from whom the Senate may choose a Vice President whenever the right of choice shall have devolved upon them.

Section 5.   Sections 1 and 2 shall take effect on the 15th day of October following the ratification of this article.

Section 6.   This article shall be inoperative unless it shall have been ratified as an amendment to the Constitution by the legislatures of three-fourths of the several States within seven years from the date of its submission.

Amendment 21 (1933)

Section 1.   The eighteenth article of amendment to the Constitution of the United States is hereby repealed.

Section 2.   The transportation or importation into any State, Territory, or possession of the United States for delivery or use therein of intoxicating liquors, in violation of the laws thereof, is hereby prohibited.

Section 3.   This article shall be inoperative unless it shall have been ratified as an amendment to the Constitution by conventions in the several States, as provided in the Constitution, within seven years from the date of the submission hereof to the States by the Congress.

Amendment 22 (1951)

Section 1.   No person shall be elected to the office of the President more than twice, and no person who has held the office of President, or acted as President, for more than two years of a term to which some other person was elected President shall be elected to the office of President more than once. But this Article shall not apply to any person holding the office of President when this Article was proposed by the Congress, and shall not prevent any person who may be holding the office of President, or acting as President, during the term within which this Article becomes operative from holding the office of President or acting as President during the remainder of such term.

Section 2.   This article shall be inoperative unless it shall have been ratified as an amendment to the Constitution by the legislatures of three-fourths of the several States within seven years from the date of its submission to the States by the Congress.

Amendment 23 (1961)

Section 1.   The District constituting the seat of Government of the United States shall appoint in such manner as the Congress may direct:

A number of electors of President and Vice President equal to the whole number of Senators and Representatives in Congress to which the District would be entitled if it were a state,but in no event more than the least populous state; they shall be in addition to those appointed by the states, but they shall be considered, for the purposes of the election of President and Vice President, to be electors appointed by a state; and they shall meet in the District and perform such duties as provided by the twelfth article of amendment.

Section 2.   The Congress shall have power to enforce this article by appropriate legislation.

Amendment 24 (1964)

Section 1.   The right of citizens of the United States to vote in any primary or other election for President or Vice President, for electors for President or Vice President, or for Senator or Representative in Congress, shall not be denied or abridged by the United States, or any State by reason of failure to pay any poll tax or other tax.

Section 2.   The Congress shall have power to enforce this article by appropriate legislation.

Amendment 25 (1967)

Section 1.   In case of the removal of the President from office or of his death or resignation, the Vice President shall become President.

Section 2.   Whenever there is a vacancy in the office of the Vice President, the President shall nominate a Vice President who shall take office upon confirmation by a majority vote of both Houses of Congress.

Section 3.   Whenever the President transmits to the President pro tempore of the Senate and the Speaker of the House of Representatives his written declaration that he is unable to discharge the powers and duties of his office, and until he transmits to them a written declaration to the contrary, such powers and duties shall be discharged by the Vice President as Acting President.

Section 4.   Whenever the Vice President and a majority of either the principal officers of the executive departments or of such other body as Congress may by law provide, transmit to the President pro tempore of the Senate and the Speaker of the House of Representatives their written declaration that the President is unable to discharge the powers and duties of his office, the Vice President shall immediately assume the powers and duties of the office as Acting President.

Thereafter, when the President transmits to the President pro tempore of the Senate and the Speaker of the House of Representatives his written declaration that no inability exists, he shall resume the powers and

duties of his office unless the Vice President and a majority of either the principal officers of the executive department or of such other body as Congress may by law provide, transmit within four days to the President pro tempore of the Senate and the Speaker of the House of Representatives their written declaration that the President is unable to discharge the powers and duties of his office. Thereupon Congress shall decide the issue, assembling within forty-eight hours for that purpose if not in session. If the Congress, within twenty-one days after receipt of the latter written declaration, or, if Congress is not in session, within twenty-one days after Congress is required to assemble, determines by two-thirds vote of both Houses that the President is unable to discharge the powers and duties of his office, the Vice President shall continue to discharge the same as Acting President; otherwise, the President shall resume the powers and duties of his office.

Amendment 26 (1971)

Section 1.   The right of citizens of the United States, who are eighteen years of age or older, to vote shall not be denied or abridged by the United States or by any State on account of age.

Section 2.   The Congress shall have power to enforce this article by appropriate legislation.

Amendment 27 (1992)

No law varying the compensation for the services of the senators and representatives shall take effect until an election of representatives shall have intervened.

Glossary

A

abandoned property property purposely parted with by its owner

abated bequest bequest that is decreased according to formulas established by state law

abstract of title summary of transactions affecting title to real property

acceptance agreement by offeree to do what offeror requests in offer; agreement by seller of real property to buyer's purchase offer

acceptor drawee who agrees to pay a draft

accommodation of interests acknowledgment of the equitable consideration of parties involved in a dispute

accommodation parties third parties who lend their name (signatures) on an instrument as security against nonpayment by a person obligated to pay

accord agreement to accept performance different from that in original contract

accretion obtainment of title to property as a result of the movement of water

act of God natural occurrence that cannot be foreseen or avoided

acts laws passed by Congress

actual breach when one party fails to perform the obligations required by a contract

adeemed bequest bequest canceled because the specific item has been sold or given away prior to death

adjudicated judgment in a lawsuit

adjuster one who settles claims for an insurer

administrative agencies government bodies created to act in the public interest

administrative regulations rules made by administrative agencies that have the same force and effect as statutes and court decisions

administrator/ administratrix one who manages the estate of an intestate

adverse possession obtaining title to real property by occupying it for a long period without owner's consent

affirmative action duty of employers to recruit women and minorities for positions usually held by white men

agency by estoppel situation in which one party creates the appearance that another has the authority to act as an agent

agency coupled with an interest agency in which agent has a personal interest in subject matter of the agency

agent one who represents another in making business transactions

allonge attachment to a negotiable instrument on which indorsements are placed

alteration deliberate material change in a contract by one party without consent

annual percentage rate cost of credit stated as a percentage of amount borrowed

answer formal written statement by a defendant responding to a civil complaint and setting forth the grounds for defense

anticipatory breach breach of contract occurring before stated time of performance

antilapse laws laws providing for distribution of bequests when a beneficiary has predeceased the testator

antitrust laws laws that prohibit monopolies

apparent authority authority principal leads third parties to believe agent has because of principal's words or conduct

appellate courts courts that hear appeals of lower court decisions

arbitration nonjudicial determination of a dispute by a third party rather than by a judge or jury

arraignment charging a person with a crime and asking for that person's plea

arrest to take into police custody

arson intentional, illegal burning of a home, building, or personal property

articles of incorporation application for permission to incorporate a business

artisan's lien lien a service provider has against personal property for unpaid bills

assault crime of unlawfully causing physical injury to another; tort of threatening another with bodily harm

asset property that has value

assigned risk pool insurance plan for those who cannot get insurance from normal sources

assignee one to whom a contract right is transferred

assignment transfer of contract rights from one person to another

assignor one who transfers a contract right to another

assumption of risk defense against people who voluntarily expose themselves to a risk of harm, suffer an injury, and then sue

attachment seizure of a debtor's property prior to a judgment

attestation clause in a will stating the witnesses observed the signing of the will

authority power to act for someone else

award binding decision in an arbitration

B

bad check check written by a drawer when there is not enough money to cover the check

bail money or property given to a court to obtain the release of a person from jail

bailee one who accepts possession of another's personal property

bailee's lien bailee's right to hold bailed property until paid for work or services

bailment transfer of possession of personal property for a specific time and purpose

bailment by necessity bailment created when property comes into one's possession by mistake

bailment implied by law bailment created when one acquires possession of another's personal property without that person's consent

bailment implied in fact bailment created by actions of bailor and bailee

bailment of lost property bailment occurring when one obtains possession of lost property

bailor one who gives up possession of personal property to another

bait-and-switch advertising advertising a product for sale, but then trying to sell the consumer another, more expensive product

bankrupt person declared to be entitled to the protection of the bankruptcy laws

bankruptcy federal procedure relieving a debtor from his or her debts once the debtor is found to be insolvent (liabilities greater than assets)

bargain and sale deed deed that conveys the interest the seller has, promising that seller has done nothing to disturb the title

battery unlawfully striking another person

beneficiary recipient of the proceeds of a life insurance policy; one who inherits property as specified in a will

bid offer made at an auction

bilateral contract contract in which one party makes a promise in return for a promise made by another party

bill of lading document issued to a consignor by a carrier; receipt for goods shipped, proof of title, and shipping agreement

Bill of Rights first ten amendments to the U.S. Constitution

bill of sale written proof of ownership of goods

binder temporary insurance policy

blackmail crime in which a person illegally obtains money or other property by making threats; also called extortion

blank indorsement indorsement consisting solely of indorser's signature

board of directors group responsible for setting corporate policy

boardinghouse keeper one who offers living accommodations to permanent residents

bodily injury liability insurance insurance for one whose car injures or kills another person

bond written promise to pay a debt or loan

breach of contract failure to perform the obligations required by a contract

bribery unlawful payment used to secure new business, obtain proprietary information, or manage some personal gain

broker type of special agent whose job is to bring a willing seller and a willing buyer together to form a contract

bulk sale sale of all or a major part of a merchant's stock of goods, fixtures, and equipment at one time

burglary unlawfully entering another's home or building with the intent to commit a crime

business ethics branch of ethics that relates to what is right or good in business settings

business guest one who uses the facilities of a hotel but does not stay there

buyer in the ordinary course of business one who purchases goods in good faith from a seller who normally deals in the goods

bylaws rules adopted by a corporation or unincorporated association

C

callable bond bond that the corporation may redeem and pay off at a given price within a given period of time

callable preferred preferred stock that a corporation may buy at its option

capacity to contract legal and mental ability to understand the nature of an enforceable agreement

capitalization description of the investment makeup of a corporation

carrier one who transports goods or people for pay

case law law arrived at through court decisions

cash value portion of an insurance premium placed in a savings fund; amount an insured receives if a whole life policy is given up

cashier's check check drawn by a bank on its own funds

casual gambler one who gambles for pleasure

caveat emptor "let the buyer beware"

caveat venditor "let the seller beware"

certificate of deposit bank's promise to repay an amount left on deposit for a certain time

certified check personal check whose payment is guaranteed by a bank

Chapter S corporation corporation treated as a partnership for tax purposes

charge account agreement between a consumer and a business allowing consumer to purchase items now and pay for them later

charitable trust trust established to benefit charitable, scientific, humanitarian, or educational agencies

check type of draft in which the drawee is always a bank

civil law law dealing with the relationships between individuals

class-action suit suit brought on behalf of a group of consumers

close corporation corporation owned by a few people

closed shop company requiring union membership as a condition of employment

closing meeting at which title to real property is transferred from seller to buyer

closing statement document showing financial details of the transfer of real property

code of ethics   document outlining the type of ethical behavior expected of an employee on the job

codicil   addition or amendment to a will

coinsurance   insurance policy clause requiring insured to maintain a certain minimum amount of insurance

collateral   asset that may be pledged as security for a loan

collecting bank   collects checks for other banks; usually a Federal Reserve Bank

collective bargaining   discussions between union leaders and employer representatives

collective bargaining agreement   contract negotiated between union leaders and company representatives

collision insurance   insurance against damage to insured's car if it collides with something or turns over

commercial claims court   special lower court, similar to small claims court, that allows businesses to sue debtors up to a certain limit.

commercial impracticability   doctrine recognizing those unanticipated events in which performance, while still possible, creates a hardship for the party obligated to perform and as a result discharges the contract

common carrier   carrier that transports people and goods for the general public

common law   unwritten law based on local English customs

common stock   corporation's ordinary stock

community property   right of wife and husband to share equally in property jointly acquired during marriage

comparative negligence   comparing the negligence of the injured party and the one being sued

compensatory damages   actual measurable damages

complaint   document listing the details of a lawsuit being filed and the relief sought

composition of creditors   agreement among creditors to accept a percentage of total owed by debtor in full settlement of debt

comprehensive insurance   insurance protecting insured's car against damage from such perils as theft, vandalism, or falling objects

computer crime   using a computer for fraudulent purposes

condemnation   right of a government to take private property for public purposes

condominium   ownership of a dwelling unit that is one of many

conforming goods   goods that meet requirements of a contract

Consequential damages   indirect damages awarded for breach of contract because they were or should have been forseeable by the breaching party

consideration   something of value given by each party to bind an agreement

consignee   bailee in a consignment

consignment   bailment for the purpose of purchase or sale by the bailee

consignor   bailor in a consignment

consolidation   joining of two or more corporations with one surviving

constitutional law   law derived from the U.S. Constitution and the constitution of the individual states

constructive bailment   bailment implied by law; created when one has possession of another's property without that person's knowledge

constructive eviction   action by landlord making it impossible for tenant to occupy leased premises

consumer   one who purchases goods, products, and services for personal use

contingencies   conditions in a contract that may void the contract if not met

contract   legally binding agreement between two or more competent persons

contract carrier   carrier that transports goods or people under individual contracts for a limited number of customers

contract of adhesion   contract containing clauses with unfavorable terms supporting a party seen as holding a superior bargaining position

contract rate   maximum interest rate that may be charged in a credit agreement

contract to sell   sale in which title to goods passes from seller to buyer at a future time

contributory negligence   defense that injured party's negligence led to injury

conversion   wrongfully exercising control or ownership over another's personal property

convertible bond   bond that may be converted into common stock of the corporation

convertible preferred   preferred stock that may be exchanged for common stock at the option of the stockholder

cooperative   nonprofit business arrangement for the benefit of members; also, ownership and occupancy of real property through the purchase of stock

copyright   exclusive right to own, produce, sell, and license artistic and intellectual works

corporation   legal entity created by permission of government

counteroffer   offer made by offeree to offeror, changing the terms of the original offer

course of dealing   conduct between parties that took place prior to a specific dispute

course of performance   way in which a particular transaction has been carried out

covenant   part of a lease listing rights and duties of landlord and tenant; promise made by a grantor in a warranty deed; a promise not to compete for a specific time in a certain geographic area

covenant of quiet enjoyment   tenant's right to have undisturbed possession of leased property

cover   buyer's right to purchase substitute goods if seller does not deliver the goods required or sends nonconforming goods

credit   right to pay for goods and services "on time"

credit card   card enabling its user to obtain goods or services on credit

creditor   one who loans money or sells goods on credit

crime   wrongful act against society defined by law and made punishable by law

criminal law   laws that deal with the relationships between individuals and society and that maintain order

cross-examination   questioning a witness by the attorney who did not produce the witness

cumulative preferred   preferred stock for which accumulated dividends are paid before any common stock dividends are payable

cure   seller's right to correct a defect in nonconforming goods

cyber crimes   crimes committed with or through the use of computers or computer technology

cyber torts   wrongful acts causing personal injury or damage committed on the Internet

D

damages   money paid by a defendant to a successful plaintiff in civil cases to compensate the plaintiff for his or her injuries

debenture   unsecured corporate obligation to pay money

debit card   card that immediately transfers funds from user's bank account upon use

debt   obligation to repay

debt collector   a person or company whose business is to collect debts owed to clients

debtor   one who borrows money or buys on credit

deductible   part of a loss that must be paid for by the insured

deed   formal document transferring title to real property

defamation   oral or written false statements that injure a person's reputation

defendant   party against whom criminal charges or a lawsuit is brought

defense   reason an accused offers to excuse his or her guilt in a criminal action; also, reason offered by defendant in a lawsuit for being relieved of responsibility

delegation   transfer of performance of one's duty under a contract to another

demurrage fee charged for unreasonably delaying equipment of a common carrier

deposition a witness's sworn statement in writing containing out-of-court testimony

depository bank the first bank to receive a check for payment

destination contract indicates that seller has risk until goods are actually delivered to buyer's location

devise gift of real property in a will

direct examination questioning a witness by the attorney who called the witness

disability income insurance insurance providing income to insured who cannot work because of illness or accident

disaffirmance refusal of incompetent party to carry out the terms of an agreement

discharge in bankruptcy judgment relieving a bankrupt from liability for most debts

disclaimer of warranty statement in a contract that excludes a warranty

discovery pretrial steps taken to learn the details of the case

dishonor refusal of a party to pay or accept an instrument

dissolution termination of a partnership

dividend portion of corporate profits paid to stockholders

donee recipient of a gift

donor one making a gift

dormant partner partner unknown to the public and inactive in management

double indemnity clause life insurance clause doubling proceeds if insured dies accidentally

draft instrument in which drawer orders drawee to pay a certain sum to payee

dram shop act law imposing liability on bars and taverns selling alcoholic beverages to intoxicated persons

drawee party to a check or draft who is ordered to pay the payee

drawer one who signs a check or draft ordering drawee to pay the payee

driving while intoxicated (DWI) having consumed sufficient alcohol that the ability to properly operate a motor vehicle is affected

drug courts courts that handle drug-related crimes

duress threat to do harm to a person for failure to perform an unlawful act against his or her will

E

earnest money deposit made by buyer when purchase offer is submitted or contract of sale of real property is signed

easement right, granted in writing, to use another's land for a specific purpose

electronic fund transfer (EFT) system allowing depositors to transfer money from their accounts to accounts of creditors and stores

emancipated minor minor who is no longer under the control and authority of his or her parents

embezzlement unlawful use or stealing of property by one who has been legally entrusted with the property

emergency authority authority an agent has to act in event agent cannot consult principal for express authority to act

employee one hired to work

employer one who hires another to work for him or her

employment at will employment that either the employee or employer may terminate at any time for any reason

encumbrances interests in property that conflict with owner's title

endowment insurance life insurance that accumulates a sum of money to be repaid to insured or beneficiary at a later time

entrapment a law enforcement officer persuading or forcing a person to commit a crime

equipment bond bond secured by a specific piece of personal property

equity   nonmonetary relief granted by courts when money damages are inadequate

escheat   state's right to claim abandoned or unclaimed property

escrow   holding closing documents and funds in trust until title to real property is clear

estate   person's interest in property

estate plan   plan to protect and dispose of one's assets

estate tax   tax on transfer of property at one's death

ethics   inquiry into the moral judgments people make in deciding what is right or wrong

eviction   legal action taken by a landlord to force a tenant to leave the premises

evidence   information submitted in testimony that is used to persuade a judge and/or jury to decide the case for one side or the other

exclusion   risk not covered by an insurance policy

exclusive dealing arrangement   agreement between a buyer and a seller requiring the buyer to refrain from buying a similar product from a competitor

exculpatory clause   contract clause excusing a party from liability for negligence

executed contract   contract that has been completely carried out

execution   the seizure of a debtor's property to satisfy a judgment

executor/executrix   one who administers the estate of a testator/testatrix

executory contract   contract that has not been fully performed by one or all parties

exempt property   property that cannot be taken to satisfy a debt

express authority   authority specifically given to agent by principal

express contract   contract in which the agreement is specifically stated

express warranty   seller's statement of fact, promise, description, or model that buyer relies upon when purchasing goods

extended coverage rider   additional insurance coverage for loss from windstorms, hail, and so forth

F

face value   amount of coverage on an insurance policy

factor   type of special agent who gets possession of the principal's property for the purpose of selling it

false advertising   advertising containing lies or omitting important information

false arrest   unauthorized detainment by an officer of the law

false imprisonment   unlawfully restricting a person's freedom of movement

false pretense   unlawfully obtaining, through deception or trickery, possession of another individual's lawful property

family income policy   insurance that combines whole life and term insurance

felony   serious crime punishable by death or imprisonment for more than one year

fiduciary   one who acts for another in a position of trust

finance charge   cost of borrowing money or buying on credit stated in dollars and cents

financial responsibility laws   laws requiring owners or drivers of cars to prove they can pay for any damage caused by an accident

financing statement   public notice of the existence of a security interest in certain property of the debtor

fixture   personal property attached to land or a building and considered real property

floater policy   all-risk insurance for loss or damage to personal property from almost any cause

forbearance   refraining from doing something one has a legal right to do

foreclosure   action by a mortgagee to seize mortgaged property in payment of a debt

forged check   check on which drawer's signature is made without authorization

forgery   making a false written instrument or the material alteration of an existing genuine written instrument with the intent to deceive

formal contract   written contract prepared with certain formalities, including a seal

franchise   business arrangement between a franchisor and a franchisee

fraud   deliberate false statement or concealment of a material fact.

friendly fire   fire that is not out of control and that stays in its intended place

fringe benefits   nonwage advantages received by an employee from an employer

full performance   when both parties do all they agreed to do under a contract

fungible goods   a unit is the equivalent of any other unit

future goods   goods not yet in existence and not yet identified

G

gambling   illegal agreement in which one party wins and another loses purely by chance

gaming   legal form of playing for stakes, such as in a lottery

garnishment   seizure of a portion of a debtor's wages to satisfy a judgment

general agent   agent with authority to perform acts relating to all business matters of principal.

general jurisdiction   power of a court to hear almost any case brought before it

general partner   partner fully active and known to the public

gift   voluntary transfer of property without consideration

goods   tangible personal property

grace period   period of time a policy remains in effect after a premium is missed

grantee   one who receives title to another's property

grantor   one who transfers title to real property to another

gratuitous agent   agent who acts for another in business transactions without receiving any compensation

gratuitous bailment   bailment in which only one party benefits

guaranteed insurability option   allows people under a certain age who buy life insurance to buy additional insurance in limited amounts despite poor health

guarantor   third party who agrees to repay another person's debt if the debtor defaults

guaranty   promise by a third party to be secondarily liable for the debt of another person

guardian   court-appointed adult who has custody and care of an incompetent party

guest laws   laws defining the liability of a motor vehicle owner or operator for injury to passengers

H

health care proxy   power of attorney giving a designated person the authority to make health care decisions

health insurance   insurance for medical expenses and loss of income due to illness

heir   one who inherits property according to his or her relationship to deceased

holder   one in possession of commercial paper

holder in due course   one who holds an instrument subject only to real defenses.

holographic will   will handwritten and signed by the maker

homeowners policy   multiperil policy insuring homeowners against many risks

hospital insurance   insurance covering fees for hospital care

hostile fire   uncontrollable fire that escapes from its usual place

hotelkeeper   one who provides accommodations to the public for a limited time

hotelkeeper's lien   lien a hotel owner has against property of a guest for unpaid bills

I

identified goods   exact goods being sold that have been decided on by seller and buyer

identity theft   unlawfully obtaining and using personal identifying information of another person

implied authority authority agent is understood to have to carry out purpose of the agency

implied contract contract formed from actions of the parties

implied warranty obligation imposed upon seller by law

in pari delicto persons equally at fault or equally guilty

incontestable clause clause preventing insurer from canceling a policy after a set time for any reason except nonpayment of premiums

indemnification reimbursement for a loss

independent contractor one hired to perform a task but not under hirer's direction or control

indictment formal, written accusation by a grand jury that one has committed a crime

indorsee the person to whom an order instrument is negotiated.

indorsement writing one's name on the back of a negotiable instrument to transfer ownership

indorser one who negotiates an order instrument by indorsement and delivery

infliction of emotional distress when one person's extreme conduct causes severe mental suffering in another; also called outrage

informal contract contract prepared without formalities

inheritance receiving property through the terms of a deceased's will or through laws of descent and distribution upon death of intestate

initial appearance person's first appearance before a judge after being arrested

injunction court order forbidding a person from doing a certain act

insider trading receiving and profiting from advance inside information about the stock of a publicly held corporation

insider trading trading in securities by someone having information not available to the public

insolvency admission in writing of an inability to pay debts as they become due

insolvent unable to pay debts as they fall due

installment loan agreement to pay for an item in fixed, regular payments

insurable interest financial interest in the property or life being insured

insurance system of sharing risk of loss among a group of people

insurance agent insurance company employee who sells insurance only for that company

insurance broker independent businessperson who buys insurance for insured from one of many companies

insured one who buys an insurance policy

insurer company that issues insurance

intentional tort when one person deliberately inflicts injury to another person or damages that person's property

interest fee paid by borrower to lender for the use of money; also, legal right to use of or claim on real property

interference with contractual relations intentional procuring of breach of a valid contract

interrogatories series of written questions directed to the adversary in a civil trial who must answer by written replies made under oath

interstate commerce business activity conducted in two or more states

intestate one who dies without a will

intrastate commerce business activity solely within one state

invasion of privacy violating one's right to be left alone

involuntary bankrupt one forced into bankruptcy by a creditor

issue original transfer of commercial paper by maker or drawer to payee

J

joint and several liability liability of partners as a group or individually

joint tenancy ownership by two or more persons that passes at death to surviving tenants

joint venture association of two or more companies or persons engaged in a common project

judgment official decision by a judge in a lawsuit tried without a jury

judgment lien lien granted to a creditor who has sued a debtor and obtained a judgment against the debtor

judicial review power of a court to review the decisions of a lower court

jurisdiction power to hear and decide a case

L

labor union organization of employees formed to promote welfare of members in relation to their working conditions

land contract agreement to purchase property and pay for it over a period of time

landlord one who owns property and rents or leases it to others

lapse gift to a beneficiary that is deemed ineffective because the beneficiary has died before the testator/testatrix

larceny intentional theft of the money or personal property of another

law enforceable set of rules of conduct

lease rental agreement for real or personal property

legacy gift of personal property in a will

legal detriment consideration that is a sacrifice by the offeree

legal rate maximum interest rate that may be charged when no rate has been agreed to

legality the point that a contract must not be against the law

lemon laws laws that protect purchasers of new and used cars

lessee tenant; renter of goods

lessor landlord; owner of goods

leveraged buyout (LBO) method of acquiring control of a corporation by buying stock and financing the purchase with a loan on the assets of the acquired corporation

libel written false statements that injure a person's reputation

license the right to sell products for a fee; temporary right to use another's land

licensing statutes laws requiring persons to be licensed to practice their occupation

lien security interest created by law

lienholder person holding a lien

life insurance trust trust set up with proceeds of life insurance policy

life insurance contract in which insurance company agrees to pay a sum of money to a beneficiary upon insured's death

limited jurisdiction power of a court to hear only certain kinds of cases

limited liability liability of stockholder for debts of a corporation

limited liability company limited partnership that permits all partners to participate in management while enjoying limited liability

limited liability partnership limited partnership in which professionals avoid personal liability but pay corporate-type taxes

limited partner partner whose liability is limited to amount of capital invested

limited payment life insurance life insurance paid for after a set number of payments

line of credit maximum amount that can be owed on a credit card at any one time

liquid assets assets that can be used immediately to pay debts, taxes, and so on

liquidated claim debt, amount of which is not in dispute

liquidated damages damages set in advance by the parties and stated in the contract

listing contract agreement between owner and broker listing broker's rights and obligations in selling the owner's real property

litigation lawsuit or legal action

living (inter vivos) trust trust set up during trustor's lifetime

living will   document expressing one's health care preferences

lobbying   trying to influence lawmakers to vote for or against legislation

long-term care insurance   insurance that covers custodial expenses for extended stays in a nursing home or in a patient's home

loss leader   item sold at or below cost to attract customers

lost property   property whose owner has involuntarily parted with it

M

Magnuson-Moss Warranty Act   law preventing deceptive warranties and requiring terms and conditions to be clear and understandable

mailbox rule   a common law rule used in contracts stating that an acceptance made in response to an offer is binding when placed in the mailbox, properly addressed

major medical insurance   insurance for extraordinary costs of illnesses or accidents

maker   one who makes out and signs a promissory note

malicious prosecution   wrongfully initiating a lawsuit against one who has done no wrong

malpractice   professional's improper or immoral conduct in performing duties done intentionally or through carelessness or ignorance

marine insurance   insurance covering ships, their crew, and cargo

marital deduction   estate tax deduction for tax-free transfers of property to a spouse

market allocation   agreement by competitors not to compete in certain markets

market price   price at which goods are currently bought and sold

material breach   violation of contract so substantial that it destroys the value of the contract and therefore excuses further performance by the injured party

mechanic's lien   lien given to those who supply labor, materials, or services in construction projects

mediation   intervention by a third person to settle a dispute between two parties

Medicaid   state-administered program that pays for health care for economically disadvantaged persons

medical insurance   insurance covering emergency room costs and doctors' fees for non-surgical services

medical payments insurance   insurance for medical expenses for injuries suffered in a car accident

Medicare   federal program that pays for health insurance for persons sixty-five and older or for those with certain disabilities

memorandum   informal written evidence of an agreement required by the statute of frauds

merchant   one dealing regularly in the sale of goods or having specialized knowledge of goods

merchantable goods   goods fit for the purposes for which they would ordinarily be used

merger   joining of two corporations to form a new one

Miranda warnings   rights read to a suspect upon arrest

misdemeanor   less serious crime punishable by a jail sentence of less than one year

mislaid property   property that has been temporarily misplaced by its owner

mitigate the damages   to try to hold damages down once a breach of contract occurs

modified life insurance   life insurance with gradually increasing premiums

monopoly   limiting of competition by act or agreement

Montreal Convention   A new international agreement limiting liability of international carriers for injuries or loss of baggage.

mortgage   lien against property held by a lender as security for repayment of a loan

mortgage assumption   right of a buyer to take over and be bound by an existing mortgage

mortgage bond   bond secured by a specific piece of real property

mortgage commitment agreement on the part of lender to grant a mortgage

mortgagee one who lends money to purchase real property

mortgagor one who borrows money used to purchase real property

motion request to a judge for a ruling on a point of law

multiperil policy insurance combining various types of coverage with emphasis on who is insured rather than perils insured against

mutual benefit bailment bailment in which both bailor and bailee benefit

mutual mistake error about certain facts made by both parties to a contract

N

necessaries things a person needs to live, such as food, clothing, and shelter

negligence breach of a legal duty to act carefully, resulting in injury to another or damage to another's property

negotiable legally transferable from one person to another

negotiable instrument written document that can be used as a substitute for money or as a credit device

negotiation transfer of commercial paper in such a way that transferee becomes a holder

net estate assets left by a person at death, less certain legal deductions

no-fault insurance insurance for bodily injuries regardless of who caused the accident

no-par stock stock having no value printed on stock certificate

nominal consideration dollar or other small sum of money used to bind a contract

nominal damages damages awarded for breach of contract when no real loss or injury occurs

nonforfeiture rights ways of using cash value to prevent an insurance policy from lapsing

nonliquid assets assets that cannot be used immediately to pay debts, taxes, expenses, and so on

nonmerchant casual or occasional seller

nonprofit corporation corporation organized primarily for nonbusiness purposes

nontrading partnership partnership doing business for professional purposes

notice of dishonor notice given to the secondary party orally or in writing that the primary party has refused to pay instrument

novation substitution of a new party for one of the original parties to a contract

nuisance use of one's property to annoy or disturb others

nuncupative will an oral will

O

objective impossibility performance becomes absolutely impossible and therefore unavoidable because of some extreme difficulty

obligee person to whom a contractual duty is owed

obligor one obligated to pay money or complete an act for another under a contract

offer promise made by one person to do something if another person either performs an act or promises to do or not do something

offer and acceptance process by which parties to a contract agree to its terms

offeree one to whom an offer is made

offeror one who makes an offer

omnibus clause insurance for members of insured's family and those who drive insured's car with permission

open coverage amount of insurance proceeds payable for loss or damage based on actual cost of repairs

open shop business where employees are not required to join a union

option agreement to keep an offer open and irrevocable for a certain time

ordinances laws passed by local governments such as cities, towns, and villages

ordinary holder one who does not qualify as holder in due course and is subject to both real and personal defenses

overdraft check written without sufficient funds that will be paid by the bank

P

par stock stock having a value printed on stock certificate

parole conditional release from prison allowing a person to serve the rest of a prison sentence outside prison

parol evidence rule rule stating that terms of a written contract cannot be changed by prior oral or written agreements

participating preferred preferred stock that shares in corporate profits as well as receiving preferred stock dividends

partner co-owner of a business

partnership association of two or more persons to carry on, as co-owners, a business for profit

partnership agreement written agreement creating a partnership

past consideration promise made for an act that has already taken place

patent exclusive right to manufacture, sell, or license others to make and sell an invention

payable to bearer words directing an instrument to be paid to person holding it

payable to order words directing an instrument to be paid to named payee or to whomever payee orders the paper to be paid

payee one who receives payment on a check, draft, or promissory note

payor bank the bank on which a checks is drawn

per capita distribution of an estate so that each beneficiary receives an equal share

per stirpes distribution of an estate so that each beneficiary receives the share his or her ancestor would have received had that ancestor survived the testator/testatrix

peremptory challenge right of each attorney in a court case to dismiss a prospective juror arbitrarily

perfect tender rule obligates the seller to tender goods that exactly match the terms of the contract

periodic tenancy lease that automatically continues for a time equal to original term until canceled by either landlord or tenant

personal (limited) defenses defenses arising after an instrument is executed that cannot be used against holder in due course

personal liability insurance insurance against claims by persons injured by actions of insured

personal property movable property

petit jurors jurors for civil or criminal trial

plaintiff one who begins a legal action

pleadings complaint and answers taken together

pledge promise to make a gift to a charitable, religious, educational, or scientific institution; bailment created when personal property is deposited as security for repayment of a debt

pledgee one who accepts delivery of personal property that is security for a debt

pledgor one who transfers possession of personal property as security for a debt

police power power of a state to protect the welfare of its citizens

policy written contract of insurance between insurer and insured

postdated check check dated after its actual date of issue

power of attorney formal written document giving agent authority to act

precedent example or standard for deciding subsequent cases involving the same or similar facts

preemptive right right of stockholders to buy new stock before its sale to the public

preferred stock stock having a prior right to receive a stated dividend

preliminary hearing hearing immediately following an arrest to determine if probable cause for the arrest existed and whether continued restraint of the accused was warranted

preliminary negotiations   in contract law, discussions between parties that usually lead one party to make an offer

premium   cost of insurance coverage

prenuptial agreement   agreement by a couple planning to marry regarding the rights and obligations of each person

prepayment privilege   right to pay balance of mortgage before the end of the mortgage term

prescription   obtaining an easement by adverse possession or use

present sale   sale in which title to goods passes from seller to buyer at the time parties make the contract

presentment   demand for payment of commercial paper made by holder; also, indictment

pretrial conference   hearing before a trial in which parties discuss the facts; may lead to settlement of the case

price fixing   agreement among sellers to set price of goods at a certain level

price misrepresentation   offering of an item at discount price higher than regular price

primary parties   parties who are first responsible for paying a negotiable instrument

principal   one who authorizes another to act for him or her in business transactions

private carrier   carrier that transports goods solely for the business owning it

privity of contract   contractual relationship

pro-rata liability   insurance company's liability for loss when there is more than one policy on the same property

probable cause   reasonable belief that a crime has been committed or certain facts exist

probate   process of validating a will

probation   allowing a person convicted of an offense to avoid prison and be free on good behavior, usually under the supervision of a probation officer

product liability   liability of manufacturers and sellers of products to persons harmed by defects in the products

professional corporation   corporation organized to operate a professional practice

professional gambler   one who gambles as a profession or business

profit   right to remove water, natural gas, minerals, or wood from another's land

profit corporation   corporation organized to earn a profit

promisee   person to whom a promise is made

promisor   one who makes a promise

promissory estoppel   equitable doctrine applied by the courts to enforce a promise unsupported by consideration

promissory note   instrument by which one person promises to pay a sum of money to another

property and casualty insurance   insurance against loss or damage to property

property damage liability insurance   insurance against claims for damage to another's property

prorated premium   amount of premium returned to insured when insurer cancels the policy

proximate cause   direct or natural cause of loss or damage

proxy   written permission by a stockholder for another to vote his or her shares of stock

public enemy   military-type force of a foreign country

public liability insurance   insurance against claims for injuries caused by insured's or guest's negligence

puffing   salespersons' statements expressing opinions about goods they sell; type of advertising exaggerating the quality of merchandise

punitive damages   damages imposed upon a wrongdoer as punishment for intentionally committing a wrongful act

purchase money mortgage   new mortgage given for purchase of real property

purchase offer   offer submitted by buyer to seller for purchase of real property

Q

qualified indorsement indorsement limiting indorser's liability

quasi contract contract implied in law to prevent one from benefiting at another's expense

quitclaim deed deed that conveys whatever interest the seller has

R

rain check coupon allowing one to buy out-of-stock sale item at sale price in the future

ratify to approve something

real property land, rights to land, and anything permanently attached to the land

reasonable care care taken by an average person under ordinary circumstances

receiving stolen property possession of property acquired as the result of some wrongful or dishonest act of taking

regular charge account account on which each bill must be paid in full when received

reinstatement clause insurance clause allowing insured to put policy back into effect after it has lapsed

rejection refusal of offer by offeree

release document that is proof of the settlement of a claim

remedy course of action an injured party may take to get satisfaction for breach of contract

removal for cause dismissal of a prospective juror during the selection process because of the juror's inability to be impartial

rent sum of money paid by tenant for use of leased property

replevin action by the buyer to recover through court order goods originally ordered but wrongfully detained by the seller

repossession steps taken by a creditor to gain possession of the collateral for a debt

rescind to cancel a contract and return parties to the position that existed prior to the making of the contract

rescission voluntary mutual surrender and discharge of each party's contractual rights under a contract

residuary gift gift by will of one's entire estate to one or more persons

restrictive covenant restriction in a deed limiting the use of property

respondeat superior doctrine that a principal is liable in certain cases for the wrongful acts of an agent

restrictive indorsement indorsement limiting what transferee may do with instrument

revocation withdrawal of an offer

revolving charge account account on which portion of bill may be paid each month

RICO Racketeer Influenced and Corrupt Organizations Act

right of survivorship right ensuring ownership interest passes to surviving joint tenant

robbery forcible taking of money or personal property from another

S

sale contract that transfers title in goods from seller to buyer for a price

sale on approval transaction in which goods are delivered to buyer for trial purposes

sale or return present sale under which buyer may return goods after a set or reasonable time

satisfaction performance of the terms of a new agreement resulting from an accord

scope of authority extent of agent's authority to carry out principal's business

scope of the agency extent of agent's duties to carry out principal's business

secondary parties parties responsible for payment of a negotiable instrument only if the primary party fails to pay

secret partner partner unknown to the public but active in management

secured credit credit based on borrower's pledge of property as well as his or her pledge to pay

secured debt debt in which the creditor has a claim against specific property of the debtor

security agreement agreement giving a creditor a security interest in a debtor's property

security deposit money paid to landlord and applied to any damages caused by tenant

separation of powers concept of independent branches of government

settlement distribution of estate after all debts, taxes, and expenses have been paid; also when parties to a lawsuit resolve their differences without having a trial

settlement options ways in which life insurance proceeds may be paid to beneficiaries

shelter principle transferees of negotiable instruments get all the rights of the transferor

shipment contract terms indicate that seller has risk until goods are given to the carrier for shipment to buyer

shoplifting taking merchandise from a store without paying for it

short rate amount of premium refunded when insured cancels a policy

silent partner partner known to the public but inactive in management

slander oral false statements that injure a person's reputation

small claims court court that hears minor civil cases involving small amounts of money

sole proprietorship business owned and operated by one person

sole tenancy ownership by one person

special agent agent who has authority to perform one type of act or a limited number of acts relating to principal's business

special bailment bailment in which extraordinary standard of care is imposed on bailee

special indorsement indorsement directing payment to a specified person

special needs trust a trust enabling a beneficiary to retain certain public benefits.

specific performance court order requiring a party to carry out a contract according to its original terms

stale check uncertified check more than six months old

standard fire insurance policy basic insurance policy covering loss from fire and lightning

standby trust trust that comes into being when a certain event occurs

standing to sue a person has legitimate issues giving him or her the legal right to bring a lawsuit

stare decisis practice by which judges follow precedents in previously decided cases

station in life person's economic and social status in a community

statute of frauds law requiring that certain types of contracts be in writing

statute of limitations law fixing a time limit within which lawsuits must be started

statutes laws passed by legislative bodies rather than by the courts

stock ownership interest in a corporation

stock certificate document indicating ownership interest in a corporation

stockholders persons who own a corporation

stop-payment order order to a bank to refuse payment of a check

stoppage in transit right of unpaid seller to notify carrier or warehouse operator not to deliver goods to insolvent buyer

strict liability legal responsibility for harm done to another even when there is no proof of fault on the part of the party that caused the harm

sublease transfer of portion of lease term to another tenant

subpoena court order requiring testimony in a case

subrogation right of insurance company to recover from person causing a loss

substantial performance performance in good faith of all but the minor details of a contract

substitute check   legal copy of an original check

substitute contract   new contract entered into to replace a contract before a breach occurs

subtenant   one to whom a portion of a lease term is transferred

summary judgment   motion for immediate judgment filed by either plaintiff or defendant, based on the information in the complaint and the answer

summons   written notification to the defendant that a lawsuit has been filed

Sunday laws   laws governing types of transactions that can be performed on Sunday

surety   third party who agrees to be primarily responsible for another person's debt if the debtor defaults

suretyship   promise by a third party to be primarily responsible for another person's debt

surgical insurance   insurance for surgical fees for specific operations

survey   map showing location, boundaries, and size of a piece of real property

survivorship life insurance   insurance covering the lives of two people with benefits payable on the death of the survivor

syndicate   a less formal type of joint venture

T

tacking   adding periods of occupancy by various owners to determine if title has been obtained by adverse possession

tax escalator clause   condition in a lease requiring tenant to pay increases in real estate taxes

tax lien   lien given to a government agency to ensure the payment of property taxes

tenancy at sufferance   tenancy created when a lease ends and tenant is allowed to remain

tenancy at will   lease for indefinite period of time

tenancy by the entirety   ownership of land deeded to a husband and wife

tenancy for years   tenancy for fixed period

tenancy in common   ownership by two or more persons that passes at death to heirs or beneficiaries

tenant   one who occupies rented property

tender of performance   offer to perform obligations of a contract

tender offer   public offer to stockholders to buy their stock

term   length of time a lease is in effect

term insurance   life insurance purchased for a specific period of time

termination statement   public notice indicating that a security interest is no longer claimed in certain property

testamentary capacity   physical and mental condition and age of a person making a will

testamentary trust   trust established according to the terms of a will

testate   leaving a will upon one's death

testator/testatrix   one who disposes of property by will

theft   unlawful taking of a person's property without the use of force and with the intent of permanently depriving the person of the property

theft of trade secrets   unlawfully acquiring information vital to a business

threshold figure   amount of medical expenses required before injured person may sue under no-fault laws

time sharing   right to use a certain property for a specific period of time each year

title   interest one has in real property

title insurance   insurance that compensates owner of real property for damages if title is found to be flawed

title search   examination of public records to determine if title to real property is clear

Torrens system   system of public registration of titles using title certificates

tort   wrongful act causing injury to another person or damage to another's property

tort law   law dealing with private wrongs and affecting individuals rather than society as a whole

Totten trust   bank account in the name of a person, in trust for another person

trade acceptance form of draft used by seller as a credit device

trade fixtures property considered permanent that remains with leased premises when lease ends

trademark exclusive, distinct mark by which a company identifies itself or its products

trading partnership partnership doing business for commercial purposes

transient one who is not a permanent resident

traveler's check check used primarily by travelers in which main feature is security against loss or theft

treble damages punitive damages awarded for violation of some government regulations

trespass illegally entering or remaining on the property of another

trust plan for transferring and holding property for the benefit of another

trustee one who manages a trust

trustor one who establishes a trust

tying arrangement agreement between a buyer and a seller requiring the buyer, as a condition of sale, to buy other products by the seller

U

ultra vires acts of a corporation not permitted under its express or implied powers

unconscionable agreement contract so unfair or one-sided that it will not be enforced

undisclosed principal principal whose identity is not known to third parties with whom agent makes contracts

undue influence power or dominance used to make persons enter into a contract against their will

unenforceable contract contract that is legal but fails to meet some requirement of the law

Uniform Commercial Code (UCC) uniform laws governing commercial transactions

unilateral contract contract in which one party makes a promise in return for the performance of an act by another party

unilateral mistake error about certain facts made by only one party to a contract

uninsured motorist insurance insurance for injuries caused by a driver who has no insurance or by a hit-and-run driver

union shop arrangement whereby new employees must join a union within a certain period of time after being hired

universal (real) defenses defenses valid against all holders of negotiable instruments

universal life insurance life insurance allowing insured to change premium payments, face value, and period of coverage

unliquidated claim debt, amount of which is subject to an honest dispute

unordered goods merchandise received even though not requested

unpaid seller's lien right of unpaid seller to retain goods sold to insolvent buyer until goods are paid for in cash

unsecured credit credit based solely on borrower's pledge to pay

unsecured debt debt based solely on the debtor's promise to pay

usage of trade standard custom or widely accepted practice in a particular occupation that can be applied to a dispute

usury charging a higher rate of interest than allowed by law

V

valid contract contract containing all the essential elements

valued coverage agreed-upon amount of insurance proceeds payable for loss or damage

variance exception to the requirements of a zoning ordinance

verdict decision of a jury

vested when an employee becomes entitled to pension benefits

vicarious liability person's liability for someone else's acts

void contract contract that has no legal effect and cannot be enforced

voidable contract contract enforceable against all parties until the party legally entitled to avoid the contract decides to do so

voir dire (meaning "to speak the truth") questioning of potential jurors by the judge and opposing attorneys to determine prior knowledge of the facts of the case and a willingness to decide the case only on the evidence presented in court

voluntary bankrupt one who files a petition for bankruptcy

W

wage assignment debtor's voluntary transfer of wages to a debtor to repay a debt

waiver voluntary surrender of a given right

waiver of premium clause insurance policy clause relieving insured from paying premiums if disabled

warehouse operator one who stores personal property for another for compensation

warehouse receipt form issued by a bailee for the storage of personal property

warranty guarantee by seller that goods are not defective and that they are suitable for intended use

warranty deed deed that guarantees clear title

warranty of habitability landlord's implied promise that property is fit for human habitation and free of hazardous conditions

Warsaw Convention international treaty regulating liability of airlines on international flights

whistle-blower laws legislation prohibiting an employer from firing an employee because the employee reports that the employer had violated certain laws

whole life insurance life insurance on which premiums are paid for as long as insured holds policy

will document disposing of one's property after death

workers' compensation state laws providing benefits to employees who are injured or become seriously ill on the job

writ formal court command requiring the performance of an act

writ of certiorari grants permission for a case to be heard by the U.S. Supreme Court

wrongful death wrongful act that causes the death of another

Index

"t" refers to a table on the page
"f" refers to a figure on the page

Disparate impact, 390
Disparate treatment, 389
Disputes, law and settlement of, 5, 5f
Dissolution
   of limited partnership, 439
   of partnership, 437–438
Diversity-of-citizenship cases, 34
Dividend, 450
DNA evidence, errors in, as criminal defense, 56f, 58
Donee, 565
Donor, 565
Dormant partner, 432
Double indemnity clause, life insurance, 650
Draft, 315–316, 316f, 317t
Dram shop act, 53
Drawee, of draft, 315–316, 316f, 322
Drawer, of draft, 315–316, 316f
Drawer's signature, forgery of, 363–364
Driving while intoxicated (DWI), 52–53
Drug courts, 32
Drugs, persons under influence of, 167–168
Due process, right to, 41
Durable power of attorney, 560–563
Duress
   in breach of contract, 231–232
   as criminal defense, 56f, 57
   freedom from, in wills, 554
   negotiable instruments and, 346, 348
   remedies, 234
Duty
   delegation or transfer of, 203–204
   nontransferable rights and duties, 204–205

E

Earnest money, in purchase offer, 511
Easements, 480–481, 490
Effective date, life insurance, 652
Electronic Communications Privacy Act (ECPA), 54–55
Electronic data interchange (EDI), 255
Electronic filing, in litigation, 111–112
Electronic funds transfer (EFT), 369–371
Electronic Fund Transfer Act (EFTA), 370–371
Electronic signatures, 195
Elimination period, disability insurance, 654
E-mail, privacy, 78–79
Emancipated minors, 165–166
Embezzlement, 49
Emergency authority, 418
Eminent domain, 491
E-money, 371
Emotional distress, infliction of, 74
Employee Retirement Income Security
   Act (ERISA), 395
Employees
   aliens as, 397
   criminal liability of, 421–422
   defined, 382
   discharge of, 387
   ethical behavior towards, 16–17
   family and medical leave, 396
   fringe benefits, 384

health and safety legislation, 392–393
health insurance protection, 395–396
hours, 396
independent contractor *vs.*, 382–383
minors as, 396
pension protection, 395
personnel records, 384–385
privacy legislation, 393
protection of, 393–396
rights of, 383–385
seniority, 392
sexual harassment of, 17, 390–391
Social Security insurance, 394–395
third party liability, 412–413
tort liability of, 421
unions, 385, 388
wages, 396
workers' compensation laws, 394
Employer-employee relationship
   creation of, 382–383
   legislation affecting, 388–392
   as principal-agent relationship, 404
   termination of, 385–388
Employers, rights of, 383
Employer(s)
   criminal liability of, 421–422
   defined, 382
   labor/management relations, 385
   tort liability of, 387
Employment, scope of, 418
Employment at will, 385–386
Employment contracts
   ethics and, 17
   termination of, 385–388
Employment discrimination
   affirmative action, 388
   age-based discrimination, 388–390
   Civil Rights Act provisions concerning, 382, 388–389
   disparate treatment/disparate
      impact, 388–390
   perpetuation of, 390
Employment process, 382
Encumbrances, 519
Endorsements
   forgery of, 364–365
   missing endorsement, 365
   products, 577–578
Endowment insurance, 647
Enforceable oral contracts, 250–252
Enforcement, of government
   regulation, 470–472
English law, 7
   understandable contracts, 580–581
English rule, of assignments, 206
Entrapment, as criminal defense, 56f, 57–58
Environment, government regulation of, 469–470
Environmental Protection Agency, 470
Equal Credit Opportunity Act, 596
Equal Pay Act of 1963, 391
Equipment bond, 451
Equitable remedies, breach of contract, 228–229